THE WORLD OF
CHILDREN'S
LITERATURE

THE WORLD OF CHILDREN'S LITERATURE

by Anne Pellowski

R. R. BOWKER COMPANY New York & London 1968

ENDPAPERS: FRONT UNICEF PHOTOS BY:
TOP (left to right) Jack Ling, M. & E. Bernheim,
Jack Ling, Jack Ling
BACK (left to right) Edward Miller, Prathana Konsupto,
Jack Ling, Phillipfe Billere

Illustrations by Vladimir Konashevich. From *Vgosti*
(Moscow, Izdatelstvo Detskoĭ Literatury, 1939.)

Contents

List of Abbreviations

Ag.	Årgång, Aargang
AIGA	American Institute of Graphic Arts
ALA	American Library Association
an.	anno, année
col.	column
dm.	Deutsche mark
ENSLA	Eastern Nigeria School Library Association
f	franc
Gos.	Gos. izd-vo detskoĭ lit-ry Gosudarstvennoe izdatel'stvo detskoĭ literatury
IBBY	International Board on Books for Young People
IFLA	International Federation of Library Associations
IYL	International Youth Library
Jg.	Jaargang, Jahrgang
kčs	Czech crowns
LA	Library Association (London)
mimeo.	mimeographed
NEA	National Education Association
NDEA	National Defense Education Act (United States)
no.	number, numéro, número, nummer
p. pp.	page, pages
Rio	Rio de Janeiro
s	schilling
sf	Swiss franc
SNDK	Státní Nakladatelství Detské Knihy
UNESCO	United Nations Economic, Social and Cultural Organization
UAR	United Arab Republic
USSR	Union of Soviet Socialist Republics
US	United States
Vol.	volume, volumen
YLG	Youth Libraries Group (Library Association, London)

List of Code Names of Libraries

APL   Amsterdam Public Library, Netherlands
APP   Author's personal possession
BBJ   Bureau Boek en Jeugd, Hague, Netherlands
BTJ   Bibliotekstjänst, Lund, Sweden
CJL   La Joie par les Livres, Clamart (Seine), France
CYU   Yale University, New Haven, Connecticut
DEW   Department of Health, Education and Welfare, Washington, D.C.
DLC   Library of Congress, Washington, D.C.
DPL   District of Columbia Public Library, Washington, D.C.
DPU   Pan American Union, Washington, D.C.
ICU   University of Chicago, Chicago, Illinois
IIU   Illinois University, Urbana, Illinois
IYL   International Youth Library, Munich, Germany
MBN   Biblioteca Nacional, Madrid, Spain
MHU   Harvard University, Cambridge, Massachusetts
NNC   Columbia University, New York, N.Y.
NNY   The New York Public Library, New York, N.Y.
PIP   Institut Pedagogique, Paris, France
PHJ   L'Heure Joyeuse, Paris, France
SPS   Statens Paedagogiske Studiesamling, Copenhagen, Denmark
WUW   University of Wisconsin, Madison, Wisconsin

International Youth Library

This library of 100,000 volumes has large collections of children's literature in each of the Western languages and smaller collections in languages using non-Latin alphabets. Not all of the latter are catalogued. In addition, there is an archive of reference books on children's literature and related subjects. The library lends books on inter-library loan, providing certain conditions are met. They have limited facilities for photo-duplication. Mr. Walter Scherf is the director.

Library of Congress

The collections of the Library of Congress were consulted in the course of collecting material for this book. Except for fiction, folklore, poetry and all foreign-language books, children's books are not maintained as separate collections, but are to be found in all subject areas of nonfiction. The Head of the Children's Book Section of the General Reference and Bibliography Division is Miss Virginia Haviland. Users of this book are advised to address reference inquiries about this field to her. Some of the pamphlets, manuscripts, current book lists and such, which are listed in this bibliography, are not catalogued and can only be found in the pamphlet files in the Children's Book Section. Under certain circumstances, the Library of Congress grants interlibrary loan privileges. It also has a complete range of photographic services for those wishing to purchase copies of an item, subject to copyright or other restrictions.

The New York Public Library

This library is both a reference library and a public lending library. The facilities of both the Research Libraries and the Branch Libraries were used in compiling this bibliography, but unfortunately it was not possible to list the particular collection in which each item was located. The main catalog, the division catalogs, and the catalog of the Central Children's Room provided 95% of the entries coded NNY. The remainder were found in the Office of Children's Services and in the Lincoln Center Library & Museum of the Performing Arts. The Research Libraries do not lend books to individuals or to other libraries, but photocopies are made available. A borrower's card for the Branch Libraries is issued to anyone who lives, works or goes to school in New York State.

Other Libraries

All of the remaining libraries were consulted during brief visits, or provided volumes on interlibrary loan. It was not possible to check into these collections thoroughly. Assuredly, each has many more of the items than those for which it is coded.

In 1955 the International Board on Books for Young People (IBBY) and the International Youth Library (IYL) in Munich, under the direction of Mrs. Jella Lepman, sent out a questionnaire to more than 30 countries, requesting information about children's books. The returns from 24 countries were analyzed and compiled into booklet form by Dr. Annaliese Hölder and Dr. Ursula Grunert (*Jugendbuch In Aller Welt*, München, Juventa Verlag; Wien, Verlag für Jugend und Volk, 1956, 176p. o.p.). This present study is a direct outgrowth of that work, which I observed as a Fulbright scholar working in the IYL during 1955–1956.

There have been other attempts at international cooperation in the study of children's literature. The International Bureau of Education in Geneva successfully completed two major surveys with the information culled from questionnaires. In spite of their limitations, these are milestones in the field, and their significance is explored further in the international section. More recently, entire organizations have sprung up, with the express purpose of promoting international good will through children's books; or already existing organizations, such as the International Federation of Library Associations (IFLA) and the United Nations Economic Social and Cultural Organization (UNESCO), have become active in publishing works of international scope.

Newly independent countries and nations with cultural patterns inherited from ancient times are discovering that, in order to achieve universal education, they must encourage and stimulate the growth of a native literature which gives a sense of personal and national identity and at the same time does not ignore the social and political realities of the world. Those countries with a longer history of children's literature and with firmly established methods of bringing child and book together, are often called upon for advice. Emulation can be salutary, it can also be discouraging. Much depends on the knowledge and understanding each country has of the other country. There is as much for the sophisticated, highly developed nation to learn, as there is for the fledgling state.

It seemed important, then to bring together into one volume the information (or the means to it) which would lead to an accurate picture of the development of children's literature in every country where it presently exists, even in the most formative stages. Only then should one turn to a comparative study of the literature itself. It is this task which the present work hopes to accomplish, in the form of an annotated bibliography, with introductory commentaries.

The bibliography hopes to encompass, as completely as is feasible, all monographs, series and multi-volume works relating to:

1. the history and criticism of children's literature;
2. public and school library work with children and books;
3. national book clubs, reading circles and similar programs which make books available to children;
4. subjects aligned to children's literature, such as storytelling, periodicals for children, folklore, etc., but only when they are discussed in the light of children's literature, or as a means of bringing literature to children;
5. the reading interests of children;
6. the criteria for and techniques of writing or illustrating children's books;
7. national bibliographies of children's books;
8. special exhibitions of children's books; and selected monographs and series which are:
9. lists of recommended books for children, especially those on special subjects and those considered critically selective for each decade;
10. anthologies, designed not for use with children, but for comprehensive study of large national or international areas of children's literature;
11. comprehensive studies or biographical dictionaries of children's authors and illustrators, but not those concerned with a single person;
12. indexes which assist in locating children's literature by author, type or theme.

In addition, significant chapters or sections of monographs, and articles in reliable periodicals relating to the points listed above are included. Arbitrarily, articles under three pages in length were excluded, except for:

1. those of outstanding importance or
2. those which represented all that was to be found in print about a given point (from the above) in a given country or
3. those which were concerned with children's books and libraries in countries other than the country of publication.

Articles from periodicals devoted entirely to the subject of children's books and libraries were excluded, unless they could fulfill any condition of the above three exceptions. Such periodicals are given a title entry in the appropriate bibliography, with an annotation indicating their years of publication, purpose, scope, and present availability. For most of the countries of Eastern and Western Europe, Scandinavia, the U.S.S.R., China, Japan, Great Britain, Canada, Australia and the U.S., only a very small selection of periodical articles is included, with emphasis placed on the uniqueness or completeness of subject coverage, significance of the author or subject, and on commentaries or impressions of literature and library work foreign to the writer. A cursory search through the periodical indices of these countries points to the obvious conclusion: one would need an entire volume to list all of the entries. A representative choice was difficult. It is recommended that, for a truly intensive study of the background literature from these areas, the researcher consult such already existing bibliographies as 1069, 1535, 2862, 2863, 3023, 3501, 3600, 3665 and 4463, as well as the following: *Library Literature, Reader's Guide to Periodical Literature, Essay and General Literature Index.*

It is not intended to include is this survey works which consider or relate to the purely pedagogical aspects of children's books. However, some entries written from an educational viewpoint are listed because they express the current trend of criticism of children's literature in certain countries, or because they also include material relevant to the literary and artistic merits of children's books. A few entries on less closely related subjects, such as children's films, theater, television and comic strips, are listed because they consider at some length the direct influence of these media on children's recreational reading.

Inclusion is not to be taken as a sign of approval or agreement. Often, differing points of view are included precisely for the purpose of indicating historical or current opposition to trends.

Each entry is given the following bibliographical description, when applicable and when known: author(s) or editor(s), title, title of periodical, publisher (not for periodicals), place of publication, edition volume, number, date, pagination, series. Children's literature has not been the most carefully researched field, and this bibliography suffers from incompleteness due partly to references cited in vague terms or numbers, in other bibliographies. Since this work is intended for use on an international level, it seemed vital to establish a form of entry which would result in the speediest and most accurate location of each item. The aim was not strict uniformity, but practicality.

There are four general types of entries:

1. Monographs (including individual volumes of series, governmental or organizational reports, catalogs of exhibitions, conference or seminar papers)

If an author or editor was given on the title page or the verso, the entry is under that author. In the case of dual authors or editors, the author appearing first on the title page is correspondingly listed first in this bibliography. In the case of three or more authors or editors, the entry is under the first only, and *et al* indicates there are others. Whenever possible, the names of the others are given in the annotations. Each of the three libraries most frequently consulted (Library of Congress, Washington, D.C., International Youth Library, Munich, Germany, The New York Public Library, New York, N.Y.) uses different rules for entering corporate authors. In general, if an item in this work is coded for only one library, the form of corporate author entry is given as found in that library. If an item is coded for more than one library, the form used is the one which seemed most easily traced in each of the libraries, either through a main entry, a secondary entry, or a cross reference.

N.B. A corporate author entry is *not* used when individual author(s) or editor(s) are listed on the title page or overleaf. In such cases the corporate author is given in curves after the pagination, the same as for a series.

Variations in title, place, publisher, date and pagination were not as frequent. When they occurred, and the book could be examined, the Library of Congress style of bibliographic description was used.

The transliterations into romanized characters are made according to the Library of Congress rules, except in the following cases: 1. When the original publication contained a printed title page in romanized letters, that title page was used. 2. If only IYL or NNY owned the item, their form of romanization was copied.

2. Chapters, sections or parts of the above types of monographs

The entry in these cases is under the author or editor of the individual chapter, section or part. When anonymous, it is under the title. The remaining information, concerning the monograph as a whole, is given according to the rules listed above.

3. Articles in periodicals

Each article is entered under its author or editor, or when anonymous, under the title. Phrases such as "Entire issue of:" or "Special issue of:" indicate the contents of a whole issue. The foreign terms (or abbreviations thereof) are given for volume and year, except in the case of periodicals in languages using non-Latin alphabets. When periodicals in these languages gave titles in English in the table of contents, those English titles are used. When the title of a periodical article appears in brackets, it indicates my own translation from the original title. Since such periodical articles are rarely located by title, it seemed sufficient to give the English translation.

4. Complete or continuing sets of periodicals

When a periodical was or is concerned entirely with children's literature and, or libraries, it is entered under its title. The publisher and place (and address for current periodicals) are followed by the frequency of appearance, date of first issue (and last issue date for discontinued titles), and the price of a subscription. Since comparatively few of these titles appear in the *Union List of Serials,* in *Ulrich's International Directory of Periodicals,* or in other directories of periodicals, accurate and up-to-date information was not always available. A question mark indicates doubt as to the correctness of the data given.

Prices are given for those items in *Books in Print* and for a few other current items. These amounts are always subject to change; they are listed here only as a general guide to availability. Inquiries concerning availability of other items should be addressed to the individual publisher concerned.

The code initials of a library where the material is to be found are given at the end of each entry. This does not claim to be a complete union list, since not all libraries coded were checked for all entries. Some items which were not located or seen are included, but only if a fairly complete bibliographical description could be found in a reliable source. These are not annotated, and are included in the hope that a copy may eventually be located. A few items are coded as being in one or another of the libraries, but are not annotated. This means that the item was temporarily not available, missing, or in the bindery.

The arrangement of the entries into eight large geographical areas, sub-divided by countries, was planned so as to have the linguistically or culturally related countries near to each other. Certain countries such as Germany, China and Korea which are now politically divided into two countries, were treated as single units insofar as the bibliographies are concerned. This is not to be construed as an expression of ideological or wishful thinking; it was necessary as a matter of expediency, because of the difficulty in separating the items from previous eras. Most of the English-speaking countries were grouped together into the ninth area, in spite of being far apart geographically. Within each country or region, the entries are alphabetically arranged by author or editor, or by title when no author was established. Diacritical marks were disregarded in the alphabetization of most languages. The author asks tolerance of those readers using languages which are normally alphabetized in other patterns in their native countries. Since this work will have its greatest use among those who read English it seemed wiser to stay with the form of alphabetization common to the English language.

In some instances it was difficult to decide where best to place an entry. Generally, it was placed in the country in which it first appeared. If it was distinctly about another area, it was placed in that bibliography, rather than under the country of origin. Important or influential works which were printed in several countries are listed in each country, but annotated only in the original. There are cross-references given for such items, e. g. see Hazard, Paul.

Each entry is numbered as it appears in alphabetical order within the bibliography of a given country or region. These numbers are placed in the upper left-hand corner of the entry. The numbering continues for the next country at the point where it has left off in the previous country.

The introductory essays at the beginning of each section and each country do not pretend to be definitive. Rather, they are meant to be general, brief surveys of the development of children's literature and libraries, as indicated by the items in the bibliographies. The conclusions are those which seemed common to the majority of available items. Specific statements are identified as to source. Whenever generalizations occur, inadvertently or purposefully, the reader must understand that they are made only on the basis of evidence presented in the materials listed in the bibliography. The translations into English are mine, with the few exceptions which are so indicated. An attempt was made to keep the length of each essay in direct proportion to the length and breadth of development of that country's work with children and books. This proved nearly impossible, due to the fact that the least is known about those countries which are only now beginning to develop a literature for children. It was necessary to explain in greater detail the movements in these countries, whereas in countries with a more developed literature, there is much that is already widely known, or at least accessible. Also, it would be folly to suggest that one could cover in ten or 20 pages the total picture of developments in such countries as the U.S., England, the U.S.S.R., etc. The introductions to these countries try to point out those developments of widest interest and those which are least known.

The longer annotations are also not necessarily for those items considered most important, but are meant to indicate scope, completeness of coverage, unique aspects treated, the reputation of the writer and the influence which the work has had.

It is not intended to give personal, subjective emphasis to one country's work as opposed to another's. Yet it is difficult, if not impossible, to assume indifference in the face of ideas one has enthusiastically embraced since coming upon them. It is usually one's native language which provides the best opportunity for perceptivity, so there are sure to be some sections of this book which strike the reader as somehow more complete, more expressive. If this is true, it can only be restated here that the intent was to be objective in the appraisal of the past and present trends of each country, and any favoritism is unintentional.

For most countries, the bibliographies were checked for accuracy and completeness by some person or persons recognized as knowledgeable in the field of children's books. In some cases no individual could be found to do this checking. In any case, there are certain to be inadvertent omissions or errors, due to the nature of such a multilingual work and the lack of communications with certain countries. The full responsibility for the information as it is given is mine, and I would appreciate hearing from persons who can point out entries in error, or omitted.

In acknowledgement for the assistance already received I wish to thank: The Fulbright Commission and the Council on Library Resources for grants to begin and complete this project; Mrs. Jella Lepman, founder and former Director of the International Youth Library (IYL); Mr. Walter Scherf, present Director of the IYL, and the entire staff of the library in the years 1955–1966; Mrs. Jean Godfrey, Chief of the Circulation Department, Mrs. Augusta Baker, Coordinator of Children's Services, and the many colleagues I worked with in the branches and in the Office of Children's Services of the New York Public Library; also Miss Maria Cimino, former Head of the Central Children's Room and Miss Mary Strang, Children's Librarian in the Lincoln Center Library of the Performing Arts; Mr. Edward DiRoma, Special Assistant to the Director, Mr. Joseph Rosenthal, Chief of Acquisitions, Miss Catherine A. Lundell and Mr. Joseph C. Mask both of the Stack Supervisors Section, Miss Irene Itina and Miss Eugenia Patterson of the Current Periodicals Division, and the other numerous staff members of the Reference Department of The New York Public Library; in the Library of

Congress, Miss Virginia Haviland and the staff of the Children's Book Section, Mr. Herbert Davis, Mr. Wiley Boyd and Mrs. Elizabeth Angell of the Stack and Reader Division, Mr. John H. Thaxter of the Government Publications Section, Miss Anna Horn of the Descriptive Cataloging Division, Dr. Edwin Beal, Dr. Lawrence Marwick, Mr. Cecil Hobbs, Mr. Young Hyun Yoo, Mr. Liang Hsü, Mr. Pe-kuang Tseng, Mr. Khalil Helou, Mr. Ranjan Borra and Mr. Myron Weinstein, all of the Orientalia Division, Mrs. Sharon Lockwood of the African Section; Mrs. Marietta Daniels Shepard and Mr. Arthur E. Gropp, Associate Librarians of the Pan American Union Library; Dr. Richard Bamberger, Former President of IBBY, and Mrs. Bamberger, Vienna, Austria; the following persons were of assistance when I visited their countries, or through their correspondence: Señora Carmen Bravo-Villasante and Srta. Concha Fernandez-Luna of Madrid, Spain, together with the staff in various departments of the Ministeria de Educación, the Instituto Nacional del Libro Español and the Biblioteca Nacional, all in Madrid; Signora Carla Poesio of the Centro Didattico Nazionale in Florence, Italy; Mlle. Lise Lebel, Institut National du Livre Français a l'Ètranger, Mlle. Marguerite Gruny, Bibliothèque L'Heure Joyeuse, Mlle. Geneviève Patte and Mlle. Lise Encrevé, La Joie par les Livres, all of Paris, France; Miss Annie Moerkercken van der Meulen, Miss Paula de Haas and the staff of Bureau Boek en Jeugd, The Hague, Netherlands; Miss Jannie Daane, Amsterdam Public Library, Netherlands; Mrs. Bettina Hürlimann, Zurich, Switzerland; Mrs. Aase Bredsdorff, Statens Bibliotektilsyn, Mrs. Vibeke Stybe, Statens Paedagogiske Studiesamling, and Miss Brita Olsson, Public Library, all of Copenhagen, Denmark; Mrs. Jo Tenfjörd, Oslo, Norway; Mrs. Lisa-Christina Persson, Bibliotekstjanst, Lund, Sweden and Mrs. Mary Ørvig, Stadsbibliotek, Stockholm, Sweden; Miss Kaija Salonen, Public Library, Helsinki, Finland; Mme. Wanda Dabrowska and the staff of the bibliographic section of the Biblioteka Narodowa, Warsaw, Poland; Mr. Bohumil Riha and the staff of Státní Nakladatelstrí Detské Knihy, Prague, Czechoslovakia and Mr. Dusan Roll, Mrs. Elena Duzurillová and Mrs. Hana Ferková, Mladé letá, Bratislava, Czechoslovakia, Miss Branka Furlan, Public Library, Zagreb, Yugoslavia and Mrs. Martina Sircelj, Children's Library, Ljubljana, Yugoslavia; the staff of the House of Children's Books, Sofia, Bulgaria; the staff of the House of Children's books, Moscow, U.S.S.R.; Mrs. Stella Peppa-Xeflouda, Athens, Greece; Mrs. L. Ayman, Children's Book Council, Tehran, Iran; Dr. Uriel Ofek, Nof Yam, Israel; Miss Mary Blocksma, Eastern Nigeria School Library Association (ENSLA), Enugu, Nigeria; Mr. Geoffrey Dellar, Library Association of Central Africa and Mr. R. Young, National Archives, both of Salisbury, Rhodesia; Miss Lydia Pienaar, Cape Town Provincial Library, South Africa; Miss Vanee Suekcharoen, Bangkok, Thailand; Mr. Sant Ram Bhatia, Jullundur City, India; Mr. D. R. Kalia, Delhi Public Library, India; Mr. Ibne Insha, National Book Centre, Karachi, Pakistan; Mrs. Cynthia B.

Geiser, University of Hawaii, Honolulu; Mr. V. O. de Alwis Gunawardane, Colombo, Ceylon; Mrs. Vilasini Perumbulavil, National Library, Singapore, Mrs. Ruth H. K. Wong, University of Malaya, Kuala Lumpur, Mr. Abdul Aziz bin Shaik Mydin, and Mr. Tuan Syed Ahmad, also of Kuala Lumpur, Malaysia; Miss Marguerite Bagshaw, Boys and Girls House, Toronto, Canada and Miss Blanche Faucher, Montreal, Canada; Mrs. Ruth Hill Viguers, Horn Book, Inc., Boston, Massachusetts and Mrs. Mary Childs, Children's Book Council, New York, New York. I would also like to thank Mrs. Kathleen Roedder, Mrs. Aileen O'Brien Murphy, Mrs. Metka Simoncic, Miss Mary Sun and Mr. Young Hyun Yoo for their assistance in writing annotations and translating items from languages not familiar to me. Mrs. Roedder was also of great help in tracking down many of the English-language items. I am grateful to Mrs. Grace Evans for the patience and accuracy with which she typed the thousands of entries in many languages, and for her care in handling my correspondence. Finally, I would like to put in writing my warmest thanks to my good friends Jindřich and Milada Zezula, New York, for the gracious hospitality they showed me during 1965–1966, when I commuted regularly between Washington and New York; without their constant readiness to put up with me and my bibliographical baggage, this work would not have progressed at the rate it did. Last, but certainly not least, I wish to thank the R. R. Bowker Company for its interest and support, especially that shown by my editors, Mr. John N. Berry III and Miss Carole Collins.

Internationalism in children's literature has at least three aspects. One is concerned with the development of children's books in countries which heretofore have had few printed materials of interest to the young. The efforts of other nations, organizations or individuals toward assistance in this development are also a part of this aspect. A second involves the commercial exchange of children's books from one country to another, either in translation or in the original. A third evolves around the depiction of different cultures in children's books.

One of the first agencies to accept the international challenge in the field of children's books was the International Bureau of Education in Geneva. In the years following the First World War the Bureau took advantage of the general longing for peace and cooperation and, under the direction of Blanche Weber, produced the first surveys of children's literature which were international in scope and intent (27, 28, 29, 51). With the coming of the later war years, the Bureau was forced to limit its work in the field. In the postwar era it shifted its research emphasis to the more general problems of education. The *International Yearbook of Education* is an excellent example of the useful documentations which are published by the Bureau.

Interest in international library work with children was an early concern of both the British and American Library Associations, stimulated principally by such leading figures as Gwendolen Rees (54) and Anne Carroll Moore (50). Their contributions had the greatest effect in the countries of Western and Northern Europe. Representatives of work with children had their voice at most of the international congresses of the library world, but not much in the way of concrete results appeared until the 1960's, when the sub-section on library work with children, of the International Federation of Library Associations, began its series of publications (31, 32, 33, 34).

The end of the Second World War brought about an even more widespread desire for international sharing, and children's books began to be translated in unprecedented numbers, once the first terrible years of aftermath had passed. It was in this climate that Mrs. Jella Lepman conceived of the idea of an International Youth Library (44). This Library has developed into the largest individual collection of children's books from many countries. It served as the prototype of similar collections in a number of other countries. Its chief use is as a study center for librarians, publishers and teachers, as well as writers and illustrators of children's books. It offers short-term grants for a number of foreign applicants each year. The exhibits of children's books which it has organized have gone around the world.

Out of the interest generated by the International Youth Library, the International Board on Books for Young People was formulated. Its membership of national sections has now grown to more than 30. Through its international congresses, its presentation of Hans Christian Andersen Medals, and through various publications it has brought about a dialogue among many nations and individuals, which might otherwise have remained unspoken (20, 21, 22, 23, 24, 25, 26.)

The international organization which has the widest scope in projects related to the international development of children's literature is most certainly the United Nations Educational, Scientific and Cultural Organization. Through school and public library development, seminars and conferences on the production and distribution of books, literacy campaigns, textbook improvement and countless advisory programs, it is working toward the goals of equal human rights for all. Another related agency, the United Nations Children's Fund, has also begun to attack the problems of education for the young child, working chiefly in conjunction with UNESCO on its projects.

Added to all of these are numerous private and religious organizations, foreign aid programs of governments and the grants of some of the larger foundations which have worked for the development of reading materials for children all over the world. While these have often been limited in their effectiveness because of the dual interests they must serve, they have nevertheless contributed greatly.

In spite of the efforts of these agencies, organizations and libraries, children's books are not exactly well-served, from an international point of view. The development of a written indigenous literature is moving along well enough in many of the countries which had only an oral literature for children up to a few decades ago. But the economics of publishing and distributing it still present serious difficulties. Much of what has real value is not available on the market except for brief periods and then only to a limited public. Many works from recent decades are lost forever, because the national libraries (when they exist) do not have deposit collections comprehensive enough to include children's books. When a new surge of publishing occurs, it must rely on the old world classics and the few works submitted currently. More often than not the books are written to order, and are completely devoid of any imaginative spirit. Reprinting rights are complicated to arrange because the publisher of the original is often defunct. The legal tangle of sorting them out appears out of all proportion to the amount of benefit gained. The study of children's literature is also hampered by the unavailability of the materials.

There has been a tremendous increase in the number of translations and exchanges, but the greatest proportion has involved the dozen or so countries which produce three-fourths of the world's books. Exchanges among these countries are not to be disparaged, because there is as much need for understanding among them as there is anywhere else. Yet might it not be true that the commercial and governmental channels are so taken up with the volume of materials to be contended with from these dozen countries, that they have no time, patience or resources left to explore sufficiently the possibilities of exchange with their neighboring nations and with others passing through the same phases of development? Are the private and governmental publishers too concerned with the profits (both monetary and ideological) of exchange, to the detriment of quality? Is there sufficient exchange between the economically advanced and the developing countries, or is this pretty much a one-way passage? What can possibly be the results of world education which relies on so few countries for its textbooks and other materials? Will it work for the common good and for mutual understanding or will it rather stifle the creative impulse to search for new and better forms? The massive programs of international aid in the production of reading and teaching materials would do well to consider these questions more carefully.

With respect to the depiction of other cultures, it is almost certain that there are as many children's books which are destroying or hindering the spirit of international understanding, as there are those creating and nurturing it. The reasons for this are chiefly political, ideological and pedagogical, but ignorance also plays a role. All too often a writer, illustrator or publisher has an overabundance of goodwill but a lack of appreciation for the sensitivities of other races and peoples. The stereotype is still so prevalent in all the printed and the audio-visual media that it is no wonder so little progress can be made in easing the tensions brought about by discrimination and ignorance.

It would be appalling if all the conclusions to be drawn from a work of this scope were as negative as the preceding paragraphs seem to indicate. Fortunately, this is not the case. In surveying this vast amount of material it was possible to compare the successes and shortcomings of a wide variety of situations. Recommendations and solutions were suggested in many instances. In others, they were only hoped for. The following proposals represent an attempt to define the areas and means of most fruitful action at the national and international level:

1. One of the first rights of children is the right to an identity—personal and national. Because educational and recreational media play so important a role in shaping this identity, and in defining it, they should meaningfully reflect the environments of the children using them. It seems logical that at least a portion of these materials be indigenous to the country or region in which the child grows up. There are a number of steps which have proven successful in improving children's literature in many countries.

   a. The existing oral literature should be translated into written and pictured forms. In particular, the literature stemming from the games and play of children themselves should be utilized in the child's first encounters with his written language.

b. The study of the history of children's literature should be encouraged. Sufficient support should be given to a limited number of researchers and over an extended period of time, in order that the recovery of "lost" children's books might be assured. Sufficient copies of these materials should be located (or reproduced) so that they are easily available in the major study centers of the country.

c. Simple course outlines should be developed for use in teacher training institutions. They should be designed for easy use in conjunction with anthologies already available, or they should be accompanied by newly compiled anthologies. Ideally, these should contain examples of all types of indigenous literature, as well as some of the best of the world's literature for children. These courses should also include information on the audio-visual material available, and they should give training in the methods of presentation of all types of media.

d. Courses in the writing of children's literature should be initiated to stimulate interest. If outside experts are engaged to conduct such courses, they should be thoroughly familiar with the language and literature of the country. They should be given sufficient time and resources to assemble a basic collection of suitable materials to be used as examples in teaching.

e. In smaller countries where no commercial publishing exists, and where state publishing is limited to textbooks, governments should be urged to seek the advice and assistance of the best literary and artistic talent available. Such texts might be the only exposure to his national culture that the child is likely to experience. Much more than those who have outside reading available, these children need lively texts and illustrations in good taste. This is not necessarily more costly, but it does involve a better arrangement than the customary system of mediocre writers and illustrators churning out material in a daily grind. Whenever possible, nations having similar cultures should attempt to cooperate in the production of such materials, but not at the expense of individuality and imaginativeness of approach.

f. The distribution of materials should be planned and facilitated at the national, regional and local level, and according to the system best suited to a country's needs and priorities. This might be through public or school libraries (or a combination of both), through other cultural or social institutions, book clubs, private purchase at state subsidized prices, or even through free gifts. Again, if experts are brought in to assist in the development of such distribution systems, they should be familiar with more than one type. An equitable distribution should be made of public funds set aside for the purchase of materials. The experiences of other nations in mass centralized purchasing, in granting of matching funds to localities, etc., should be carefully studied. Any international aid should be coordinated with the final plan selected.

g. An established central organization or agency should be designated to serve as a center of information on the availability of current materials. It could also serve as the channel for international inquiries and aid. This might be a professional organization, a private or governmental agency, or a commercial publisher. Provision should be made for the compiling of frequent, up-to-date lists, and for their free distribution to all educational and cultural institutions. Any existing journals should be encouraged to begin periodic reviewing of children's books and materials.

2. Simultaneously with the development of an indigenous literature, the introduction of the best and most suitable materials from other countries should begin. Logically, those in the same (or a similar) language would be among the first to be introduced. Translations should be made of some of the best of current production in other countries, as well as from the more recognized classics. Whenever possible, children should have the opportunity to see and use a few books of other nations in their original editions. Some of them can be useful for language study as well as to add vitality to the social studies curriculum. But no matter in what language or on what subject, the chief aim of exchange should be to provide a bond through a common experience of shared enjoyment or information.

3. It is unlikely that children's books will ever be completely free of nationalistic bias (as distinct from national identity), but it is not too impossible to hope for the elimination of exaggerated stereotypes, especially those derogatory to race, color or creed. The international organizations should sponsor studies with the specific purpose of defining and describing those stereotypes which are most offensive to a given race or people. These should be contrasted with examples of the successful characterization of national and racial traits. Such qualities are extremely difficult to pin down in textual form, but they are far more obvious in graphic illustrations which could serve as the starting point.

Publishers in the countries with a high percentage of children's books in production should examine more closely their stories and nonfiction books about other lands and peoples. Too many of these are written from the romantic point of view which can only see the extremes of the wretchedly poor, the exotic, the savage or the picturesque. In far too many there appears a tone of condescension or paternalism. In short, it should be recommended that these publishers spend more effort in locating and encouraging talent among the peoples of other nations. If they were to draw more on such talent, they could not help but advance the goals of international understanding. Written literature is at a crucial stage in its development. There are some experts who predict the decline of the printed forms of communication, to be replaced by the audio-visual. Since the greater majority of the world's population has yet to learn to read and write, it may well be that mass education efforts will have to by-pass the usual techniques of teaching reading and writing. It is more likely, however, that communication of all types will become more essential than ever before. Publishers, writers and users of children's literature should not be afraid of the challenge of new media, but should rather study its methods with the hope of finding new impetus for the total involvement in communication so necessary for today. Even with all of the media available, there is a great gap between the capacity for knowledge and understanding inherent in the human spirit, and the means whereby this knowledge and understanding can be acquired.

1. American Association of University Women. *Children's books around the world; catalog of an exhibition from 52 countries.* Washington, 1952. 46p. DLC, IYL, NNY.

Some 265 books were selected by the children's section of ALA. They are arranged by country, and briefly annotated. Illustrations from a few are reproduced.

2. Bamberger, Richard. "Young people and reading," *International journal of adult and youth education,* Paris, Vol. 16, Nos. 3–4, 1964, pp. 205–208. DLC, NNY.

In this issue devoted to cultural activities of youth around the world, the past president of IBBY commented upon the importance of reading as one of the most meaningful of cultural experiences.

3. Bauchard, Philippe. *The child audience, a report on press, film and radio for children.* Paris, UNESCO, 1952. 198p. DLC, IYL, NNY.

The first part of this study undertaken by UNESCO, "The Press for Children," has some bearing on the subject of children's literature, even though it treats precisely of those papers, comics and magazines not considered literature. An appendix gives the legislation and the nonofficial action taken in various countries to control this press.

4. Berlin. Deutsche Staatsbibliothek. *Internationale Kinderbuchausstellung, 1956/1957.* Berlin, 1957. 164p. DLC, IYL.

The catalog of an international exhibit of children's books, largely contemporary, but some historical items as well. Each of the 836 titles is described and a few have illustrations reproduced in color. They are arranged by subject or type, and then by country. There is an author-title index, and an illustrator index. The introduction is by Horst Kunze and Wilma Kunze who prepared the catalog. Most of the items came from the State Library, which in 1956, officially began a children's section for reference use.

5. Besterman, Theodore. "Children's book lists," *A world bibliography of bibliographies.* 4th ed. Vol. 1. Lausanne, Societas Bibliographica, 1966. DLC, NNY.

A bibliography which includes numerous book lists prepared by state and local agencies, organizations, and individuals. They are arranged by country.

6. *Bookbird.* International Institute for Children's, Juvenile and Popular Literature, Fuhrmannsgasse 18a, Vienna, Austria. Quarterly (Irregular). Vol. 1+, 1957+. Subscription: $3.00 per year in Europe; $3.80 for other countries. DLC, IYL, NNY.

This began as the official organ of IBBY, but due to production difficulties, the editorship has been assumed by the Institute. It contains articles of interest to anyone working in the field of children's books. Lists of recommended books for translation, which first appeared in separate pamphlets issued by IBBY under the title "International understanding through children's books" now appear regularly in almost each issue. There is also a very helpful review of recent publications about children's books and libraries, with entries submitted by the member countries of IBBY. Awards, congresses, special meetings, exhibits, seminars and many other types of activities throughout the world are reported on in brief news items. Occasional longer articles cover the various aspects of children's books in depth.

7. "Children's literature . . ." Shaw, Marian *et. al. Library literature 1933 ff.* New York, H. W. Wilson, monthly, annual, and bi-annual compilations. DLC, NNY.

This work took over the bibliographies begun by Cannons and Morsch (2862 and 2863). However, beginning with the 1933–1935 volumes, the entries are annotated, and include periodicals in many languages. They are entered under such categories as Book week, Book illustration, Children's readings, Children's libraries, School libraries, Young adult literature, etc.

8. Colwell, Eileen H. "Children's libraries," *Year's work in librarianship,* London, Vol. 9, 1936—Vol. 23, 1950. Annual. DLC, NNY.

For each of these 15 years, Miss Colwell provided a succinct resumé of the progress in children's librarianship, in the United Kingdom, the U.S. and other countries. She also prepared the report for the first *Five years' work in librarianship, 1951–1955,* but the subsequent issue 1956–1960 has a report prepared by F. Phyllis Parrott. Prior to 1936, the only years which contained special reports on children's libraries were 1929, written by M. M. Hummerston, and 1928, written by Gwendolyn Rees (see 55). School libraries were covered separately in almost each year, first by Monica Cant and subsequently by C. H. Osborne. In the *Five years'* . . . *1956–1960,* both school and public library work is reviewed by Miss Parrott. All together these articles afford a complete, cumulative view of the patterns of service to children over a long span of years. They are invaluable in the study of the history and development of these patterns.

9. *Documentation on methods and techniques of youth work in education for international understanding and for social responsibility.* Paris, UNESCO, 1954. 10p. (Mimeographed) IYL.

10. Douglas, Mary Peacock. *The primary school library and its services.* Paris, UNESCO, 1961. (UNESCO manuals for libraries, 12). DLC, IYL, NNY.

This has chapters on personnel, reading guidance, instruction in the use of libraries, materials for service, organization of materials, administration of the program, attracting readers, and the material facilities of the school library. Appendix 1 is a condensed Dewey decimal classification system, appendix 2 is a checklist of library standards, and appendix 3 contains a bibliography.

11. Fédération Internationale P.E.N. *Le jeune génération et la littérature.* Nice, Centre Universitaire Méditerranéen, 1952. 48p. IYL.

"The young generation and literature." This theme was chosen for the 24th international congress of the P.E.N. club and the discussions centered around the writers' concerns to "reach" the young reader, to be heard by him and to be understood. Taking part were such well-known persons as André Maurois, James T. Farrell, Jean Schlumberger, Peter Ustinov and others.

12. Geist, Hans Friedrich. "Illustrations for children's books," "Kinderbuch-Illustrationen." "Illustrations de livres d'enfants." *Graphis,* Zürich, Vol. 11, Oct. 1955, pp. 408–427. DLC, NNY.

The work of Czech, English, French, Polish, Swiss and U.S. illustrators is discussed, and some 60 pictures are reproduced from their illustrations for children's books. The task of the picture book illustrator is commented on, as being different from that of the illustrator of children's books.

13. Gollmitz, Renate. *Das Kinderbuch in den sozialistischen Ländern.* Berlin, Deutsche Staatsbibliothek, and Arbeitsgemeinschaft für das Kinder- und Jugendbuch, 1960. 119p. IYL.

Catalog of an exhibit arranged by the East German State Library and shown in Leipzig at the International Exhibit of Book Arts. The countries represented are Bulgaria, China, East Germany, North Korea, Poland, Rumania, Soviet Union, Czechoslovakia, Hungary, and North Viet Nam. The authors are listed in their original language, but in romanized letters. Titles are given in the original or in German, or both. There are no annotations but each country is given a short introduction. All of the books come from the state library. The last 20 pages contain reproductions.

14. Halbey, Hans Adolf. "Artistic quality in the children's book." "Künstlerische qualität im Bilderbuch." "La qualité artistique du livre d'images," *Graphis,* Zürich, Vol. 20, No. 3, 1964, pp. 30–51. DLC, NNY.

Before presenting some 80 reproductions from current children's book illustrations from around the world, the author sums up the qualities one should look for in an artistic children's book.

15. *Handbook for the improvement of textbooks and teaching materials as aids to international understanding.* Paris, UNESCO, 1949. 172p.

16. Haviland, Virginia. *Children's literature: a guide to reference sources.* Washington, Library of Congress, 1966. 341p. $2.50; Foreign countries, $3.13.

An annotated guide to about 1,000 books, pamphlets, catalogs, lists, and periodical articles concerning children's literature and its closely related subjects. The majority of items are in the English language, and deal with countries using English as the mother tongue. Annotations are sometimes critical, but most often simply explanatory, giving precise details as to chapter headings, subject coverage, etc. The entries are arranged under a broad outline, subdivided into narrower contexts. This is a useful arrangement, allowing the student a quick view of what is available on a given point. In some cases individual chapters are given separate entries, if they are about a subject or area covered in another part of the outline. Studies on individual writers and illustrators account for some entries. Foreign works are limited to major historical or critical studies, or national bibliographes and selective lists.

17. Hürlimann, Bettina. *Die welt im Bilderbuch.* Zürich, Atlantis Verlag, 1966. 213 p. IYL.

"Modern children's picture books from 24 countries," together with biographies and bibliographies of the artists, written by Elisabeth Woldman. This is a personal selection, made from the author's private collection of picture books. The pictures are arranged into general subject categories to show the varying interpretations of the same theme or object.

18. Hunt, Clara Whitehill. *International friendship through children's books.* New York, League of Nations Non-Partisan Association, 1924. 8p. Also in: *Publishers' weekly,* New York, Vol. 106, No. 26, Dec. 27, 1924, pp. 1967–1970. DLC, NNY.

A very fine essay, written in the spirit of true internationalism, but with a regard for the realities which cannot be changed over-night. If the titles were brought up to date, this could remain intact and be read with the same profit by present-day librarians. The book-list is not in *Publishers' Weekly,* only in the reprint.

19. ———. "Internasjonalt vennskap gjennem barnebøker," *For folkeoplysning,* Oslo, Bind 11, No. 4–5, Nov. 1926, pp. 100–104. NNY.

"International aspects of work with children's books." The author makes a plea for teaching peace and world understanding through children's books, and indicates a few cases in which this is being done in English language books.

20. International Board on Books for Young People. *Children's literature and international understanding; report on the 8th Congress of IBBY.* Vienna, 1963. Various pagings. (Mimeographed) IYL.

The official business report, together with the papers delivered at the plenary meetings of the congress.

21. ———. *Developing countries in books for young people.* Vienna, The Board, 1963. 20p. DLC, IYL.

A list of books from 12 countries (mostly European) but on subjects related to the developing countries. Annotated and arranged in the 3 categories of Africa, Asia and Latin America.

22. ———. *IX Congreso de la Organización Internacional para el Libro Juvenil.* Madrid, 1965. 449p. DLC, IYL.

The official texts and reports of the 9th Congress, given here in entirety in Spanish and English. Countries reporting were: Argentina, Austria, Brazil, Chile, Czechoslovakia, Denmark, Finland, France, Germany, Great Britain, Italy, Mexico, Norway, Paraguay, Peru, Portugal, Spain, Sweden, Switzerland, United States, Uruguay, and Venezuela. The acceptance speech of René Guillot, recipient of the Hans Christian Andersen medal, is also reprinted here.

23. ———. *International Board on Books for Young People* (IBBY). Vienna, The Board, 1962. 16p. DLC, IYL, NNY.

A pamphlet describing the establishment and development, object and aims, of the Board. There is also a set of the statutes (since changed), a list of the national sections (now incomplete), an explanation of the terms of the Hans Christian Andersen Award, some of the publications of the Board, and the presidents and members of the executive board at that time.

24. ———. *International understanding through books for children and young people.* Vienna, The Board, 1965. 24p. (Published by agreement with UNESCO). IYL, DLC.

A list of several hundred titles in five languages (English, French, German, Russian, Spanish) of books "which are particularly suitable to promote international understanding." Translations from other languages were not excluded. The categories were: folk and fairy tales, nonfiction books about other countries, fiction, world affairs, biographies of internationally recognized leaders, educational materials, literary classics.

25. ———. *International understanding through children's books.* Vienna, The Board, 1962–1963. DLC.

These lists were issued periodically during the period mentioned, and were later incorporated into the periodical *Bookbird.* Each dealt with the books of one member country, which were recommended for translation in other languages. The fourth issue dealt with books from a number of countries.

26. ———. *Jugendbuch in aller welt.* München, Juventa Verlag; Wien, Verlag für Jugend und Volk, 1956. 176p. DLC, IYL, NNY.

The results of a questionnaire on the status of children's books answered by 24 countries. Not all countries answered all questions, but information generally included: the organizations (official and private) having to do with children's books; literature about children's books, and book lists; the classics of each country, prize books, exhibits, and libraries for children.

27.   International Bureau of Education. *La coordination dans le domaine de la littérature enfantine.* Geneva, Bureau International d'Éducation, 1933. 46p. (Publications, No. 28) DLC, IYL, NNY.

"Coordination in the domain of children's literature." An admirable attempt to define the best ways and means whereby the Bureau could coordinate two particular aspects of the international study of children's literature: Critical, historical research and lists of books recommended for translation. Experts from several countries give their opinions here as to just how they believed this could best be achieved.

28.   ———. *Littérature enfantine et collaboration internationale. Children's books and international goodwill.* 2nd ed. Genève, Bureau International d'Éducation, 1932. 238p. (Publications, No. 11) DLC, IYL, NNY. (DLC and NNY also have 1st ed., 80p.)

Because of their indubitable spirit of objectivity, these two reports can be called the first truly international studies of children's literature. They were both edited by Blanche Weber. The first contained information on 26 countries; the second on 37 countries. The purpose was to collect information on children's books (and the children's books themselves) from as many countries as possible. These collections were then placed in the library of the Bureau. Working through the means of a questionnaire, personal interviews and correspondence, the editor achieved remarkable results for the time. The forward and introduction indicate the amount of cooperation which went into the study, and the persons who were responsible for the material from each country. The main portion of the reports are the lists of books from each country, alphabetically arranged by author and annotated. The categories of books included were: Books which are favorites with children and which give a true picture of child life; Children's classics; Books written by children. Also included are shorter lists of translations which had appeared in each country, and of books and articles on children's reading. There are author and title indexes.

29.   ———. *Some methods employed in the choice of books for children's libraries.* Geneva, 1930. 14p. DLC, NNY. (French edition title: *Quelques méthodes pour le choix des livres des bibliotheques scolaires*).

Report of an inquiry undertaken to determine how individual countries approached book selection in children's libraries. Selective booklists from the individual countries are listed.

30.   International Congress on Press, Cinema and Radio for the Young, Milan 1952. *Papers.* Verona, Mondadori, 1952, DLC.

A congress sponsored by UNESCO which dealt in part with books and magazines for children.

31.   International Federation of Library Associations. Committee on Library Work with Children. *Library service to children.* Lund, Bibliotekstjänst, 1963. 125p. DLC, IYL, NNY.

Reports by representatives of the following countries: Brazil, Canada, Czechoslovakia, Denmark, Finland, France, German Federal Republic, Netherlands, New Zealand, Northern Nigeria, Poland, Soviet Union, Spain, Sweden, United Kingdom, U.S. A six-point memorandum states the goals which the committee sets forth as indicative of good library service to children. The editing was done by Eileen Colwell.

32.   ———. Sub-section on Library Work with Children. *Library service to children, II.* Lund, Bibliotekstjänst, 1966. 92p. DLC, IYL, NNY.

This contains chapters on Australia, Belgium, Bulgaria, East Germany, Hong Kong, Israel, South Africa, Switzerland, Trinidad and Tobago, and Yugoslavia. There is also a paper on hospital library service to children, by Joy Lewis.

33.   ———. Sub-section on Library Work with Children. *Professional literature on library work with children.* The Hague, Bureau Boek en Jeugd, 1966. 48p. DLC, IYL.

A selective bibliography, collected and edited by A. J. Moerkercken van der Meulen. The entries are arranged into many categories under five general headings: History and Organization of Libraries, Literature, Creating of Books, Children's Reading, Book Reviewing. There are no annotations and bibliographical information is not always complete. The introduction and table of contents appear in English, French, German and Russian. This bibliography is most helpful because it is extremely selective, including only the important, basic works. Information on the following countries is included: Belgium, Denmark, Finland, France, Germany (DDR and BRD), Great Britain, Japan, Netherlands, New Zealand, Norway, Poland, Sweden, Switzerland, USA and USSR.

34.   ———. Committee on Library Work with Children. *Translation of children's books.* Lund, Bibliotekstjänst, 1962. 114p. DLC, IYL, NNY.

A reprint of three papers read at the IFLA conference in Edinburgh, 1961, together with a list of books recommended for translation (from suggestions sent in by 16 countries), and supplementary papers on the translation of children's books. The three major papers are by Aase Bredsdorff of Denmark, Virginia Haviland of the U.S., and Margareta Schildt of Sweden. The supplementary papers are the same as those in "The flow of children's books from country to country," (3754), with an additional paper by Monica Burns of England.

35. International Youth Library. *Die Bibel der Kinder*. Munich, The Library, 1960. 40p. DLC, IYL, NNY.

"The children's Bible." A catalog of Bibles for children from 20 countries, illustrated and indexed.

36. ———. *Catalogue. Children's and youth books from the western world*. Munich, The Library, 1961. 52p. DLC, IYL, NNY.

A list of 150 books arranged into two age groups and five subject areas. It was prepared for UNESCO, and serves as the catalog of a travelling exhibit of the books.

37. ———. *History and theory of youth literature*. München, International Youth Library, 1964. 59p. DLC, IYL.

An exhibit of some 479 books from 22 countries was held at the library in 1964. All were concerned with general history or theory, or with some specific author or group of authors. The introduction by Metka Simončič is in English, German, French and Russian.

38. ———. *Illustration*. München, IYL, 1963. 30p. (Mimeographed). IYL.

The catalog of an exhibition showing the work of illustrations from 25 countries, in 260 children's books.

39. ———. *Preisgekrönte Kinderbücher*. München, IYL, 1959. 48p. DLC, IYL, NNY. 1st Supplement: München, 1964, 49p. (Mimeographed). DLC, IYL, NNY.

The first, which served also as a catalog for the exhibition which opened at IYL and later toured many countries, contains information on the prize books of Belgium, Germany, England, Finland, France, Italy, Canada, Netherlands, Norway, Austria, Sweden, Switzerland, Spain and the USA. The first supplement brings these countries up to date, and adds information on the prizes given in Australia, Denmark, Yugoslavia, and Hungary. The second supplement (in preparation) is to add those of Bulgaria, Japan, Luxembourg, Poland, Rumania, the USSR, South Africa and Czechoslovakia. The first catalog is also available in English.

40. Internationale Tagung für das Jugendbuch. *Berichte und Vorträge*. Aarau, Sauerländer, 1954. 213p. IYL.

The report of the first meeting of IBBY, in Zürich, 1–4 October, 1953, at which time more formal steps were taken to develop the organization. Representatives of Denmark, Germany, England, France, Italy, the Netherlands, Norway, Austria, Sweden, Switzerland, Spain, the USA, UNESCO and the International Bureau of Education were present. Mrs. Jella Lepman, director of the IYL at the time, presented the aims of IBBY and a short report on the first answers to the questionnaire (see 26) was given. The problem of comics was discussed by J. K. Schiele, Marcus Morris and Heinrich Lades; Alois Carigiet and Hans Fischer discussed the role of the artist and the picture book. Finally, a resolution was passed to begin the Hans Christian Andersen Award for a children's author who had made a distinguished contribution to the world of children's literature. The texts of the reports and speeches are in German, French or English, and in all cases there are summaries in the two languages other than the one used by the writer or speaker.

41. "Kinder- und Schülerbibliotheken," *Internationale bibliographie des Buch und Bibliothekswesens*, Leipzig, Jahrgang 5, 1926–Jahrgang 15, 1940. NNY.

An annual bibliography of periodical articles, pamphlets, dissertations and studies on children's and school libraries. The items are arranged alphabetically by author, without regard to language. There is a preponderence of English-language periodical articles, but items in French, German, Italian, Japanese, Scandinavian and Slavic languages are also represented. Juvenile book lists are under *pädagogik*.

42. *Die Kunst durch Kunst zu erziehen*. Prag, Státní Nakladatelství Dětské Knihy, 1965. 460p. IYL, DLC.

"Teaching art through art." Papers given at an international seminar of children's writers, publishers and other interested persons working with children's books. There were 13 countries represented, mostly from Eastern and Western Europe. This is also available in Czech under the title *Umění Vychovávat Uměnním,* same publisher.

43. Kup, Karl. "An international exhibition of juvenile books in Germany," *Publishers' weekly*, New York, Vol. 120, No. 9, Aug. 29, 1931, pp. 827–830. DLC, NNY.

A description of an exhibition of children's books from all over the world, which toured many cities in Germany in that year. Reproductions from some of the books are included.

44. Lepman, Jella. *Die Kinderbuchbrücke*. Frankfurt-Main, S. Fischer Verlag, 1964. 211p. DLC, IYL, NNY.

A moving, personal account of this author's attempts to build a "bridge of understanding through children's books," in the International Youth Library at Munich and later through the founding of the International Board on Books for Young People.

45. ———. "Utopia or reality? International understanding through children's books," *Top of the news,* Chicago, Vol. 21, No. 4, June, 1965, pp. 323–325. DLC, IYL, NNY.

"Children's books worthy to create international understanding should never carry a missionary note. They should be free of nationalism and racialism and carry the message of true tolerance. They should be completely sincere, showing life in its deeper and broader aspects, portraying landscapes and customs of the most diverse countries. Children's books should never be made the instruments of political propaganda. They should dwell on the human side of life, especially in this age of atomic weapons and robots. They should be written with art and imagination and with hope. They should show the good and the bad sides of life quite realistically but also the wonders that courage and faith can create."

46. McColvin, Lionel R. *Public library services for children*. Paris, UNESCO, 1957. 103p. (UNESCO manuals for libraries, 9). DLC, IYL, NNY.

An elementary manual for the development of public library services to children, written from an international viewpoint, and aimed primarily at those countries and areas which are in the early stages of public library planning.

47. Martin, Helen. "International aspects of children's reading," *ALA bulletin,* Chicago, Vol. 28, No. 2, Feb. 1934, pp. 67–74. DLC, IYL, NNY.

In this report to the children's librarians meeting at the ALA conference, this librarian and teacher of children's literature surveys swiftly the work being done to bring children and books together in many countries.

48. Mistral, Gabriela. "Niño y libro." International Congress of Libraries and Bibliography, 2nd; *Actas y trabajos,* Vol. 3. Madrid, Librería Julián Barbazán, 1936; pp. 254–261; DLC.

A Nobel prize-winning poet summarizes her feelings on "the child and the book." She reiterates her belief in the public and school libraries, and in the necessity of a trained person to select and manage them.

The article is printed first in French, then in Spanish.

49. *Moderne Kinderbuch-Illustration. Contemporary children's books illustrations. L'illustration contemporaine dans les livres de l'enfance.* Berlin, Robert Fricke, 1966. 56p. IYL.

The catalogue of an exhibition first shown in Munich in 1963, and arranged by the International Youth Library. Books from 24 countries are included. The entries include only illustrator author and title information. Some illustrations are reproduced. Text in three languages.

50. Moore, Anne Carroll. *Children's books of yesterday: an exhibition from many countries.* New York, The New York Public Library, 1933, 21p. DLC, NNY.

Some 500 books were included in this exhibition, jointly arranged by the Metropolitan Museum and the New York Public Library. This is not a catalog, but a general review of the trends and styles of many eras and countries, as represented by the books in each category.

51. *Les périodiques pour la jeunesse.* Genève, Bureau International d'Éducation, 1936. 106p. (Publications du Bureau, No. 46). DLC.

Questionnaires sent out requesting information on the better children's magazines were returned by 24 countries. The lists of names are given by country. Valuable bibliographies *about* children's magazines are included for each country.

52. Poste, L. I. "Juveniles are nations' bond of friendship," *Library journal,* New York, Vol. 73, Sept. 1, 1948, pp. 1157–1159. DLC, NNY.

This was one of the first articles to appear in print on the efforts of Mrs. Jella Lepman to found an International Youth Library in Munich.

53. Puech, M. L. "Le rôle social des bibliothèques pour la jeunesse." International Institute of Intellectual Cooperation. *Mission sociale et intellectuelle des bibliothèques populaires;* Paris, Institut International de . . . , 1937; pp. 296–300. DLC.

A preliminary report by the president of the International Federation of University Women, on the questionnaire sent out by that organization to its 37 national sections, requesting information on the status of libraries for youth in their countries. The general conclusions, based on the responses of 22 nations, indicated that the social role of the children's library was uniquely important in those countries where libraries existed; in others, even books for children, not to speak of libraries, were nonexistent.

54. Rees, Gwendolen. "International library service for children abroad," *ALA children's library year-*

book, Chicago, No. 1, 1929, pp. 44–58. DLC, NNY.

The author expands the information she has received since the publication of her book *Libraries for Children* (55). India, South Africa, Australia, New Zealand, the Scandinavian lands, Germany, Holland, Belgium, Czechoslovakia, Russia and Italy are touched upon.

55. ———. *Libraries for children; a history and a bibliography.* London, Grafton, 1924. 260p. DLC, NNY.

The first major survey of children's libraries, covering their history and development in the British Isles, the British Empire, U.S., France, Belgium, Holland, Norway, Sweden, Denmark, Germany, Austria, Switzerland, Italy, and Russia. The extensive bibliography, pp. 195–254, is an invaluable source of books and articles on the early years of this specialized kind of service. Although distinctly from the British point of view, this is a commendable effort at using the international approach. Index.

56. ———. "Libraries for the young: school and public libraries," *Year's work in librarianship,* London, Vol. 1, 1928, pp. 93–114. DLC, NNY.

This extended the survey begun in 1924 (see 55).

57. "Storytelling around the world—a symposium," *Library journal,* New York, Vol. 65, No. 7, Apr., 1940, pp. 285–289; No. 9, May, 1940, pp. 379–381; No. 11, June, 1940, pp. 484–487; No. 13, July, 1940, pp. 574–577; No. 14, Aug., 1940, pp. 624–627. DLC, NNY.

Part 1 is on the U.S.; part 2 on Europe; part 3 on Canada; part 4 on Hawaii, and part 5 on South America.

58. Ullrich, Hermann. *Robinson und Robinsonaden. Bibliographie, Geschichte, Kritik; ein Beitrag zur vergleichenden Literaturgeschichte, im besonderen zur Geschichte des Romans und zur Geschichte der Jugendliteratur.* Weimar, Emil Felber, 1898, 247p. (Literarhistorische Forschungen, 7). IYL has Xerograph copy. DLC.

A fascinating study of the influence of Defoe's book on the development of the novel in general, and the novel of adventure for children in particular. The bibliography lists all of the first editions, in English and in many translations, and then it enumerates the books which were directly or indirectly modelled on the original. Most of these are children's books, and they are in many languages.

59. Valeri, Mario and Enrichetta Monaci-Guidotti. *Storia della letteratura per i fanciulli.* Bologna, G. Malipiero, 1961. 575p. IYL.

This is the only history of children's literature in Italian which can be called international. Although the short surveys are little more than listings of the names of important works and figures, the range of countries covered is by far the widest of any European history. More than 40 are included, from the oriental and Eastern European countries, to Europe and North and South America. There is a name index. It is not particularly deep in its critical values, but it is helpful in locating the names of major writers. Spellings are, naturally, given in the Italian form.

60. Weaver, Warren. *Alice in many tongues.* Madison, University of Wisconsin Press, 1964. 147p. NNY, DLC.

Strictly speaking, this should not qualify for inclusion, since it deals with a single author. However, the very lucid discussion of the problem of translation, and the checklist of editions, and translations (in 47 languages), point out that in fact, *Alice* is many books by many authors. See also the similar work on *Robinson Crusoe* (58).

61. Weber, Blanche. "La littérature enfantine du point de vue international." International Congress of Libraries and Bibliography, 2nd; *Actas y trabajos,* Vol. 3; Madrid, Librería Julián Barbazán, pp. 283–289. DLC.

The head of the children's literature section of the International Bureau of Education in Geneva explains the work of her office, and asks cooperation of all countries in furthering international studies of children's literature. This address was the major one presented at the children's section of the Congress. Those concerning individual countries are annotated in entries under the countries concerned.

62. ———. "Le rôle social et intellectuel des bibliothèques enfantines." International Institute of Intellectual Cooperation. *Mission sociale et intellectuelle des bibliothèques populaires;* Paris, Institut International de . . . , 1937; pp. 301–306. DLC.

Miss Weber, librarian at the International Bureau of Education in Geneva, writes of her work there, and describes the possibilities such a center has in developing an international movement in children's literature.

63. Whitenack, Carolyn I. "Around the world summary of school library services," *School libraries,* Chicago, Vol. 7, No. 3, Mar. 1958, pp. 8–15. DLC, NNY.

Brief summaries of the state of school libraries in Puerto Rico, England, France, USSR, Hungary, Libya, Egypt, Lebanon, India, Ceylon, Thailand, Malaya, Indonesia, Australia, Philippines, Hong Kong, Taiwan, and Korea. The summaries were written by visiting library school students in the U.S., from those countries, or by U.S. school librarians who had worked abroad.

No survey of the development of children's books and libraries in Latin America can be undertaken without first studying the theories of the educator who most influenced them: Domingo Faustino Sarmiento. Although Argentinian by birth, he spent a number of fruitful years in political exile in Chile as well as several years in travel to Europe and the United States. The important fact is that his enthusiastic manner and persuasive personality left their mark on the educators, librarians and writers of most of the republics. It was in 1846–1847 that Sarmiento visited Europe and the United States, observing the school systems, libraries, social and other agencies. In short, he occupied himself with any and all aspects of education, defining that term as those processes and institutions which elevate the human spirit and enlighten its intelligence. He returned to Chile and for about a year remained in self-imposed seclusion to ponder over these experiences and eventually to write about them with great urgency and passion.

Mr. King's essay on "Horace Mann's Influence on South American Libraries" (89) is indirectly a fine introduction to Sarmiento, his life, his educational theories and his writings; because it was through Sarmiento's acquaintance with Mann that Spanish-speaking America came to know of Mann's theories. More concerned with the education of children than with their entertainment, Sarmiento nevertheless showed in his writings a deep concern for all the feelings and needs of the child. There are numerous editions of his works and commentaries on them. One volume in the collection made on the 50th anniversary of his death contains those speeches and essays most relevant to the subject of children's literature and libraries (167).

Since public and school libraries for children both developed, for the most part, as a direct responsibility of the national departments of education, it is understandable that their educational values assumed precedence over the recreational. It is also understandable that this same precedence applied to the books being used in those libraries. Whereas in other parts of the world the didactic writers were beginning to be assailed and overcome by authors and critics who championed the right to existence of a children's literature that was primarily for pleasure, in the Latin American nations the last quarter of the 19th century marked the *beginning* of a native children's literature whose first and main objective was that it be "morally esthetic." The roots of this belief in the priority of the didactic established themselves so deeply that they have not been pulled out completely to this day.

Most of the books and articles which discussed the criteria of children's literature placed more emphasis on this ethical-esthetic aspect than they did on the pure pleasure and enjoyment to be found in such reading. True, many agreed that it would be a fine thing for all of these qualities to exist in all children's books so that delight, entertainment, moral inspiration and information could be part of one glorious experience. The fact of the matter is that in most cases this simply did not happen. Instead, the didacticists chose as their subjects some patriotic hero or event, or the glories of their native land, and contrived to add still another "moral" to the already message-laden books for children. Yet it was this patriotism, this "Americanization" of the literature, which turned out to be its saving grace.

Fifteen years ago, Helen Rand Parish wrote: ". . . Latin American didacticism might well have developed into modern realistic writing for children. But the transformation never took place. Didacticism still thrives—moralistic, deadly serious, ponderously instructive, though (oddly) still retaining its distinctive "Americanist" flavor. Today's productions are chiefly aimed at older children, and consist for the most part of tons and tons of biography—with a generous sprinkling of 'historia patria,' geography, natural history, and religious pamphlets trailing. No attempt is made to write historical *stories,* or stories of Latin American life, or anything resembling the 'artistic' biography; just 'exemplary lives' done in unabashed textbook fashion with few adornments of literary style or bookmaking; of course there are some exceptions . . ." It is of these exceptions that she writes at greater length: Rafael Pombo, Olavo Bilac, Jose Marti, J. B. Monteiro Lobato, Constancio Vigil, Antonio Robles, Horacio Quiroga, Gabriela Mistral, Juana de Ibarbourou and many others.

Until the appearance of the two volume study by Carmen Bravo-Villasante (70), Miss Parish's three-part article (98) provided the best and most complete critical survey of Latin American children's literature. The articles in *Americas* (85), *Panorama* (88), and *La Educación* (92), as well as the book by Morales (96), were also good surveys, in a more limited scope.

Señora Bravo-Villasante has done a great service to all educators, librarians and students in Latin America. One of the major difficulties to be faced when learning about the important writers of each of these countries has been the inaccessibility of their works. Admittedly, it is better for the student to work with the complete, original book, but this is virtually impossible under present conditions, and such an anthology as the *Historia y Antologia de la Literatura Infantil Ibero-Americana* is the next best thing. Perhaps it was just as well that the author restricted her critical comments and aimed at inclusivity rather than exclusivity. It leaves the reader free to compare a number of writers, and to come to his own critical conclusions.

Within the various countries, the criticism of literature for children was not an overlooked subject. But most often it was so fine in its abstract ideals and so poor in its cited examples that one can only

conclude it was because of a dearth of quality. This is especially true in the case of the Walt Disney books, so influential because of their sheer numbers in relation to the total output of books for children. More often than not, those librarians respected for their knowledge of children's literature gave way to popular demand in the case of Disney, and substituted this popularity for the true criteria to be used in judging literature. In all fairness, one must point out that the study of children's literature in these countries is hampered by the lack of meaningful communication and exchange of books from one country to the other. By combining the best native efforts from each of the countries, and adding to them the better translations and versions of the world's classics available in Spanish, one could come up with a rich and varied literature of excellent quality. But export-import laws, high book production costs, slow transportation, confusing monetary exchange regulations, and other petty difficulties prevent the librarian, teacher or individual collector from ever examining copies of a high proportion of the best books, if they hear of them at all. Comparative criticism can hardly be valid under such circumstances, so it is in the studies limited to native literatures that the Latin American critics are at their best, e.g., 170, 270, 287, 392, 419. The manuals and aids for establishing standards and patterns of organization for children's and school library service have fared little better in promulgation. Each country has had to develop its own body of professional tools, and if there were no librarians capable of writing them, a local edition of another country's work was printed. In the end, this probably proved less effort and expense than trying to import the original, but it caused needless duplication. The situation is somewhat remedied by the publications of the Pan American Union and UNESCO, which can be exchanged and imported with greater ease. Many of these are translations of U.S. works, because of the comparatively few qualified professional librarians in Latin America, and their general lack of opportunity to work in stimulating and productive circumstances. While it is commendable that a country, successful in practicing children's work in libraries, share its experiences with other interested countries, it seems essential that it be left to a native to explore the patterns by which good standards can be meaningfully and effectively adapted. This is an initiative which Latin American children's librarians have yet to take, with the possible exception of Lenyra Fraccaroli in Brazil.

Too often (and not only in the Latin American countries) much of the professional literature is so vaguely general, so repetitious, that one wishes one could condense a hundred articles into a few lucid sentences. Repetition does serve a purpose, of course, and there is always the possibility that such information is reaching an audience for the first time. But the few existing articles and books containing efficient, clear outlines of standards and policies as applied to the specific situations of each Latin American country are not enough. Since the school library movement began first, since popular and public libraries serve more as extensions of the school library, and since the literature developed largely as an adjunct to the educational curriculum, one question comes to mind: Why have there been so few constructive plans based on the premise that in Latin America school library systems should be the originators, the engineers of standards? It seems obvious that sufficient material and intellectual means to establish both public and school library movements firmly are lacking at the present time. Is it outrageous to suggest that government and private agencies concentrate on school libraries, rather than fragmenting their efforts? Some critics might feel that precisely because of the pedagogical orientation of so much of children's literature, it would be wiser to emphasize public library service with its tradition of wider, more liberal selection and service. This tradition is most common to the countries with highly developed systems. The mistake is to assume that such ideas will automatically be understood and take effect in every country. There are probably several solutions to the problem of the lack of children's libraries in Latin America; needed are inventive librarians to perceive the best trajectory and to blueprint every step of the way.

Before even the most basic plan is to take effect, however, the Latin American countries must have more and better children's books at reasonable prices. The complications of importing and exporting have been briefly pointed out above. These, and other problems such as high production costs, are further analyzed in the outlines of two constructive programs aimed at increasing book production and distribution in Latin America (68, 69). The first is a projection of the assistance which the Franklin Book Programs hopes to carry out as intermediary between U.S. publishers and their other American counterparts, in the selection of texts and illustrations to be used on a low-cost basis. It is similar to their programs in operation in the African and Asian countries, with modifications to suit the needs of this locale. This work has already begun, and the annual reports of the Franklin Book Programs document yearly progress. The second, Books for the People Fund, Inc., has aims analogous to Franklin, but they are broader: "To provide on a mass production basis low-cost editions of the best modern books for children and young people in the languages of Latin America and to encourage the development of library service to these groups" (69). Specifically, the Fund hopes to carry out these aims by suggesting titles for new or repeat publication, by arranging for rights and permissions, assisting in low-cost marketing as well as free distribution, encouraging authors and artists to write and illustrate for children by means of prizes and other inducements, and by educating interested and qualified persons in the field of library service.

64.   Adrianzén Trece, Blanca. "Servicios para los niños en la biblioteca pública," *Desarollo de las bibliotecas públicas en América Latina,* Paris, UNESCO, 1953; (*Manuales de la UNESCO para las bibliotecas públicas,* 5), pp. 97–104. DPU.

One of two papers on children's libraries presented at the São Paulo Conference on Latin American Public Libraries, 1951, sponsored by UNESCO. This is on services to children in the public library; the other is on services in school libraries, 315.

65. Bayer, Edna E. "Our co-workers south of the equator," *Library journal,* New York, Vol. 75, No. 20, Nov. 15, 1950, pp. 1962–1965. DLC, DPU, NNY.

A description of children's and school libraries in Argentina, Chile, Peru and Uruguay, visited by this American librarian.

66. Beust, Nora Ernestine. . . . *Libros para niños.* Washington, Library Service Division, Federal Security Agency, U.S. Office of Education, [1942], 13p. DPU.

U.S. books recommended at the time for translation into Spanish. About 100 titles are listed, with annotations in Spanish and English.

67. Boggs, Ralph Steele. *Bibliography of Latin American folklore.* New York, H. W. Wilson Co., 1940. 109p. (Inter-American Bibliographical and Library Association, Series 1, Vol. 5). DPU.

Approximately 600 entries on folklore, divided by type and then by country.

68. *Books for the children of Latin America: A plan from Franklin Book Programs, Inc.* New York, Franklin Book Programs, Inc., 1965. 4p. (Mimeographed). DPU.

An analysis of the problems of children's book production and distribution in Latin America, with a plan to aid children's book publishers and dealers in alleviating the situation. This plan has actually gone into the first stages of operation.

69. *Books for the children, young people and new adult literates of Latin America: A summary prospectus of the Books for the People Fund, Inc.* Washington, Pan American Union, 1963. 7p. (Cuadernos Bibliotecologicos, no. 12). (Mimeographed). DPU.

A summary of the purposes, objectives and operational organization of the Books For the People Fund, Inc., a nonprofit organization established with the approval and encouragement of the Pan American Union.

70. Bravo Villasante, Carmen. *Historia y antología de la literatura infantil iberoamericana.* 2 vols. Madrid, Doncel, 1966. Vol. 1, 636p. Vol. 2, 604p. IYL.

A monumental work consisting of brief histories and selections from the children's literature of Argentina, Chile, Colombia, Cuba, Costa Rica, Ecuador, Guatemala, Mexico, Nicaragua, Panama, Paraguay (all Vol. 1); and Peru, Puerto Rico, Santo Domingo, Uruguay, Venezuela, Brazil, Portugal, and the Philippines (all Vol. 2). Each volume has separate author and title indexes. For each country there is a bibliography of sources used. There are 16 plates in each volume, with photographs and color reproductions. In addition the text is enlivened by numerous drawings in black and white by Pepi Sánchez. This is an invaluable aid to the study of Latin American children's literature.

71. Buenaventura, Emma. *Bibliografía de literatura infantil.* Washington, Pan American Union, 1959. 70p. (Columbus Memorial Library, Bibliographic Series, No. 47). DLC, DPU.

Actually, only pp. 1–40 are concerned with the bibliography of some 575 children's books. They are arranged by age groups, and indexed by author and title. The second part, pp. 41–70, is a reprint of Emma Linares' work on the school library. For a note on it, see 91.

72. ———. *Introducción a las bibliotecas infantiles y escolares.* Washington, Pan American Union, 1955. 38p. (Organization of American States, Programa de Cooperación Técnica, Escuela Normal Rural, Rubio, Venezuela). DPU.

The outline of a course in children's and school libraries, first given in 1954 in Cuba, and later expanded for a course at the Normal School in Rubio, Venezuela. For a later edition, see below.

73. ———. *Manual para la organización de bibliotecas infantiles y escolares.* Rev. ed. Washington, Pan American Union, 1963, 57p. (Columbus Memorial Library, Bibliographic Series, No. 48). DPU.

For earlier edition see above. This course outline has been up-dated to include the more recent books on selection and processing. Also, it is now organized in such a way that it can serve as a beginning manual of library organization.

74. "Children and young people," *Development of public libraries in Latin America.* Paris, UNESCO, 1952, pp. 87–112. DLC, IYL, NNY.

For this hemispheral conference at São Paulo, Blanca Adrianzén Trece prepared a paper on public library services for children, Mercedes Meneses Rodríguez prepared one on school library services and Miguel Angel Piñeiro contributed one on secondary school libraries.

75. Cimino, Maria L. "South America in children's books," *Publishers' weekly,* New York, Vol. 138, Aug. 31, 1940, pp. 671–676. DLC, NNY.

A discussion of some of the classics of South American children's literature, which are also available in the U.S., together with some U.S. books which are set in one or another of the Latin American republics.

76. Daniels, Marietta. *Bibliotecas infantiles y escolares: Una bibliografia.* Washington, Pan American Union, 1955. 20p. (Columbus Memorial Library, Bibliographic Series, No. 45). DPU.

A bibliography of more than 300 entries of works concerning children's and school libraries, and children's literature. Complete bibliographical information is given, but no annotations. This is the most inclusive bibliography in Spanish on libraries for children. It contains many entries on the purely educational aspects which could not be included in this bibliography.

77. ———. "Children's library services in Latin America." *Library trends,* Urbana, Illinois, Vol. 12, No. 1, July, 1963, pp. 106–118, DLC, DPU, NNY.

A wide-ranging survey of public and school libraries which serve children in Latin America. The author precedes her description of existing libraries with a concise picture of the problems of book production, the effects of the exploding population on education in general and other significant factors which affect the child and his books in Latin America. Her conclusions are that although the libraries she describes are worthy examples, they are obscured by the dimensions of the needs for services for all the children and young people in Latin America.

78. ———. *Public and school libraries in Latin America.* Washington, Pan American Union, 1963. 155p. (Estudios Bibliotecarios, 5). DLC, DPU.

This is an expanded study, more inclusive than 77. It does not describe any specific examples of the libraries, but rather concerns itself with general conditions. Many charts and statistical tables are included.

A shorter version of this work appeared as No. 13 in the "Cuadernos Bibliotecologicos" series of the Pan American Union.

79. Delgado Nieto, G. "La literatura infantil de América Latina." *El tiempo,* Bogotá, Jan. 17, 1943. DLC.

A short, critical article on the status of children's literature in Latin America at that time.

80. Douglas, Mary Teresa Peacock. *La biblioteca de la escuela primaria y sus servicios.* Paris, UNESCO, 1961. 108p. (Manuales de la UNESCO para las bibliotecas, 12). DPU.

A translation of *The Primary School Library and Its Services.* For note see 10.

81. ———. *Normas para las bibliotecas escolares.* Washington, Pan American Union, 1963. 132p. (Publicaciones del Centro Interamericano de Educa-ción Rural. Proyecto No. 26 del Programa de Cooperación Técnica de la OEA). DPU.

A translation of *School Libraries for Today and Tomorrow.* For note to contents see 3674. (Translated by Cecilia Jiménez Saravia).

82. Ehlinger, Emily M. "Children's libraries in South America." *Wilson library bulletin,* New York, Vol. 25, No. 5, Jan. 1955, pp. 370–372, 374. DLC, NNY.

While on a trip through South America, this American librarian visited children's rooms in Peru, Chile, Uruguay, and Brazil. This is a brief account of her impressions.

83. "Encuesta sobre la literatura infantil en América Latina," *Educar,* Lima, No. 6, Dec. 1940, pp. 120–121.

84. "Estado de la encuesta sobre la enseñanza de la literatura infantil," *Boletín informativo, Centro de Documentación Pedagógica,* La Habana, Año 2, No. 7, Jan.–Mar. 1964, pp. 3–6. DPU.

A report on the questionnaire sent out by the UNESCO regional center, concerning courses in children's literature taught in the Americas, in normal schools, universities and libraries. Countries replying were: Argentina, Bolivia, Brazil, Cuba, Guatemala, Peru, El Salvador, and Uruguay. Abstracts of the descriptions of courses in these countries are given in the article.

85. Figueira, Gaston. "Wandering tadpoles and speckled roosters; Spanish-American poetry for children," *Américas,* Washington, Vol. 11, Jan. 1959, pp. 11–14. DLC, DPU, NNY.

A discussion and criticism of the major poets writing for children in the Latin American countries, covering the period from the 19th century when the Colombian Rafael Pombo first wrote for children, up to the present time.

86. Goetz, Delia. *Bibliography of Spanish books for children.* Washington, U.S. Department of Health, Education and Welfare, Office of Education, 1953. 11p. (Typewritten). DPU.

A list of several hundred recommended Spanish and Latin American books, with annotations in English.

87. Havana. Biblioteca Escolar Piloto. Proyecto Principal de la UNESCO para América Latina. *Bibliografía infantil selectiva.* La Habana, Centro Regional por UNESCO, 1960. 2 parts. 13p. and 10p. (Mimeographed). DPU.

A list of titles (approximately 500) recommended for the school library. Most are books published in Spain, rather than the Latin American countries. The list is not annotated.

88. "Juvenile literature in Latin America," *Panorama*, Washington, No. 19, May, 1942, pp. 1–10. DLC, DPU.

A brief history of children's literature in Latin America in general, followed by articles on the specific developments of eight of the American republics: Brazil, Argentina, Chile, Colombia, Mexico, Peru, Uruguay and Venezuela.

89. King, Clyde S. "Horace Mann's influence on South American libraries," *History of education quarterly*, Pittsburgh, Vol. 1, No. 4, Dec. 1961, pp. 16–26. DLC, NNY.

This is actually a discussion of Sarmiento of Argentina and Varela of Uruguay, Horace Mann's influence on them, and their influence, in turn, on the library movement in South America. There are innumerable books and articles on Sarmiento and Varela, but this seemed one of the more recent, and is one of the few which stresses their specific influence on the world of libraries and books.

90. "Libraries for children and young people." Assembly of Librarians of the Americas, May 12–June 6, 1947, Washington. *Proceedings*. Washington, Library of Congress, 1948, pp. 231–233. DLC.

Children's librarians from several of the American republics discuss libraries for children and their responsibilities.

91. Linares, Emma and Marietta Daniels. "La biblioteca como auxiliar de la educación." Seminario Interamericano Sobre Planeamiento Integral de la Educación, Washington, 17–24 June, 1958. (*Documento de Base, 12*).

See also the following entries: 71, 142, 273. "The library as an aid to education." A presentation of philosophy, standards and goals of library service to children, first presented at the Inter-American Seminar on Integral Planning for Education, Washington, 1958.

92. "La literatura para niños," *La educación,* Washington, Año 4, No. 14, April–June, 1959, pp. 3–65. DLC, DPU.

Includes: "La literatura para niños. Su idioma y su estética," by Ermilo Abreu-Gómez; "El caso de la literatura para niños," by Lillian H. Smith (translated from 3383); "Los niños se defienden de los hombres," by Paul Hazard (trans. from 814); "El poder de la juventud," by Cornelia Meigs; "Literatura para niños: historia y crítica," by Emma Buena-

ventura; "El cuento infantil al día," by Antonio Robles; "La literatura infantil en Francia," by Nicole Grandin; "La literatura infantil en el Brasil," by M. B. Lourenço Filho; "Literatura para la juventud en Italia," by Enzo Petrini; "Lectura y literatura para niños," by Guido Villa-Gómez; "Literatura infantil," by Agustín Nieto Caballero; the list of Newbery and Caldecott award winners to 1958.

93. Masten, Helen. *Thirty children's books from Latin America.* [Chicago], American Library Association, Section for Work with Children, 1941. 9p. DLC, NNY.

An annotated list of books in Spanish and Portuguese published in Latin America, and outstanding for their pictorial quality as well as for their content. Poetry dominates the list in number of entries.

94. Montevideo. Instituto Interamericano del Niño. *Bibliografía sobre literatura infantil y juvenil.* Mimeographed list on the occasion of the 38th Reunión del Consejo Directivo del Instituto . . . Lima, 29 July–3 Aug. 1957. 13p. DPU. Also appears in expanded form in: *Boletín del Instituto Interamericano del Niño,* Montevideo, Tomo 31, No. 3, 122, Sept., 1957, pp. 344–379. DLC, DPU.

In the mimeographed form, this is a straight alphabetical listing of some 300 items about children's literature and libraries; in the *Boletín,* there are more than 380 entries, and arrangement is according to the specific aspect of children's literature (e.g. history, study and teaching, etc.). There is an author index to the second one. Neither of them is annotated, but bibliographical information is fairly complete. This is one of the most important bibliographies concerning the Latin American area, and it proved extremely useful in compiling this present work. In addition, the *Noticiarias,* which is a supplement to the *Boletín,* contains many short informational notes on libraries and children's literature in Latin America. These can be traced through the indexes found yearly in the *Boletín.* (Both DLC.)

95. ———. *Literatura infantil y bibliotecas infantiles.* Survey on the occasion of the 38th Reunión del Consejo Directivo del Instituto . . . Lima, 29 July–3 Aug. 1957. 12p. (Mimeographed). DPU.

96. Morales, Ernesto. *Los niños y la poesía en América.* Santiago de Chile Editorial Ercilla, 1936. 152p. DLC.

A critical survey of Spanish-American poetry for children, including a chapter on Inca poetry. The author cites many examples. As a basis for his discussion, he states: "For the child, art is a manifestation of physical exuberance often confounded with the playing of games. Rhythm is an intrinsic part of this —therefore poetry should be of first importance in the literary life of the child."

97. Ogden, Rachel C. *Children's literature produced in Spanish America.* Typewritten, thesis, Master's Degree, Columbia University, 1929 [1930]. 54p. NNC.

This was written for the degree in Romance Languages. It is a critical study of the works of the following authors: José Joaquín Fernández de Lizardi, Manuel Gutiérrez Nájera, José Martí, Amado Nervo, José Ascunción Silva, Rubén Dario, Gabriela Mistral, Horacio Quiroga and Carmen Lira. The criticism is comparative, and based on general literary standards. Since it is rare, in Latin America, to find serious study accorded to children's books as literature, this is an important contribution to the field. The bibliography on pp. 45–54 is helpful in tracing the children's works of the authors mentioned above.

98. Parish, Helen Rand. "Children's books in Latin America," *The Horn book,* Boston, Vol. 24, No. 3, May–June 1948; pp. 214–223; No. 4, July–Aug. 1948, pp. 257–262; No. 5, Sept.–Oct. 1948, pp. 363–366. DLC, DPU, IYL, NNY.

The first part covers the 19th century and those aspects of the 20th which remained close to the didactic tradition of children's literature. The second and third parts cover modern trends, but the author explains that by modern she means more those trends away from the didactic, rather than modern in theme. She discusses fantasy at great length, pointing out examples which have appeared in many of the countries, and stating that she feels this is the area in which the finest writing is done in Latin America. She also briefly criticizes periodicals and theater for children.

99. Pidgeon, Marie Kiersted. "The discovery of Hispanic American junior books for reading in the United States of America." Inter-American Bibliographical and Library Association, *Proceedings of the Second Convention, Washington, 1939;* New York, H. W. Wilson Co., 1939; Publications of the Association, Series 2, Vol. 2); pp. 88–96. DPU.

Although the author's purpose was to tell of those Latin American children's books which had become known and used in the U.S., this has more meaning when placed here as an introduction to some Latin American authors and their books for children.

100. *Primer curso sobre bibliotecas escolares para escuelas secundarias, Medellín, 9 Aug.–6 Nov. 1965. La biblioteca escolar. Catalogación y clasificación simplificada para bibliotecas escolares y pequeñas.* Medellín, Universidad de Antioquia, Escuela Interamericana de Bibliotecología, 1965. 20p. and 41p. DPU.

The outline of a course on school libraries given this year at the Interamerican Library School. The first part is on organization and theory, and the second on cataloging and classification.

101. Rivera, Rodolfo O. "La biblioteca en la escuela," *Unidad,* San José, Año 1, No. 1, July 1943, pp. 25–26. DPU.

This delineates a proposal presented at the preliminary conference on school libraries held in Managua, Nicaragua and sponsored by the Oficina Inter-Americana de Educación. It was presented by the director of the Biblioteca Americana de Nicaragua and concerns the general standards for the organization of school libraries and the training of librarians.

102. Shepard, Marietta Daniels. *Selection aids on Latin America for primary and secondary school libraries.* Washington, Pan American Union, 1966. 8p. (Cuadernos Bibliotecologicos, No. 32) DLC, NNY.

A bibliography of lists, selection aids, sources of purchase and translation programs.

Argentina

Libraries for children, particularly in schools, have an older history in Argentina than a native children's literature. This is not surprising when one learns of the educational theories championed by Sarmiento. As Minister of Education he was able to formulate a system of school and popular libraries, and then later as President of the Argentine Republic he translated much of this sytem into law. The Sarmiento Law of 1870, had an enormous influence on all libraries, but particularly on school libraries. It provided for a national library commission, as well as for public funds for books and supplies, and persons to be in charge of them. Many of the small local libraries established at this time were destined to remain small and insignificant, when contrasted to the need. Others expanded and have continued to serve their communities well to this day. By decree, all of the libraries established in teacher-training and normal schools were opened to the general public, and in many cases this included children (114 and 134). The periodical founded by Sarmiento, *El Monitor de la Educación Comun,* referred frequently to the importance of children's reading, and gave instruction in organization of the school library and selection of materials (127, 145, 150, 152).

By the early 1930's, there was sufficient interest and enough professional background to warrant the appearance of a survey based on an inquiry into the school library (151), as well as a manual of practical methods of organization, administration and service (105). The latter grew out of Manuel Barroso's efforts to form school libraries. Treating reading as an art, it considered the successful library as a place where this art was allowed and encouraged to flourish. The ideas expressed and the standards set forth in this manual remained for a long time the basic authority. They were quoted in most articles and books on the subject, not only in Argentina, but many other Latin American countries as well.

Although the national library opened a children's reading room in 1931 (146), there does not seem to have been any arrangement for circulation. This, in spite of the fact that many authorities were writing of the importance of the public library in stimulating free reading. *El Monitor de la Educación Comun* and *Boletín de Educación* frequently printed pleas to teachers and educators to press for better children's libraries. Angelica Rojas de Alvarez defined the social and humanistic mission of children's books and libraries as so important that her predictions for the future were dire forecasts of more and more juvenile delinquency unless more books and libraries were accessible (163). Whether this strong militancy was the right approach or not, it had as meager an effect as most of the other pleas. Some authors wrote with equal despair of the situation, but from a different point of view. The Chilean poet, Gabriela Mistral, wrote of the lowering of standards in popular taste, and stated that the apostolate of the librarian was to fight this mass entertainment with its poverty of imagination; she maintained that good libraries were still considered a luxury, and the "young" or "ageless" librarians who knew that a book's purpose was to "circulate, ambulate, even trot" were even more rare.

It would seem likely that with such an impetus as Sarmiento gave in the third quarter of the 19th century, a native literature for children might have sprung into being. It was not to be so. The classics of other countries continued to be translated and adapted. A few native works written for the general public, but with themes of interest to children (such as Ricardo Güiraldes' *Don Segunda Sombra*) began to appear in juvenile editions. In 1937, Fryda Schultz de

Mantovani wrote: "For 50 years children's books have been appearing in Argentina and with few exceptions . . . all seem derived from one common model, inspired, doubtless without meaning to be, in the most atrocious designs against the child's spirit" (174). In a later book she defined more specifically what she felt children's literature should be, stating that the language of poetry and the language of childhood were one and the same (172).

There was, however, at least one Argentinian author who was developing a body of literature for children, and by 1939 he was already writing *on* the art of writing for children (106). Germán Berdiales obviously felt that much of the credit for the advances children's books had made was due to the editorials, articles and interest exhibited by *La Prensa,* of Buenos Aires. He pointed out that in 1936 it organized a contest with prizes for the best piece of writing for children, stimulating a number of authors to turn to that field (109). Certainly this newspaper must have had its influence in the criticism of children's books, for in some of the columns of the Sunday literary supplement, one can follow lively discussions on the subject. In one of these lead articles, Ernesto Montenegro went on at some length as to the reasons for a lack of an outstanding Spanish-language classic (written) for children. He felt it was the result of the culture and temperament of the Spaniard, and especially the *criollo* (descendants of the original settlers of the new world), who "showed a predilection for the austere, the sentimental and the sorrowful" (149).

Elena Fortun would have at least part of the blame fall on the parents, teachers and librarians who have failed to keep up the oral tradition, which she felt was vital to the formation of creative, imaginative minds, such as might in turn create from the old, a new literature for children (129). Her practical handbook on storytelling was very traditional in approach, insisting on simplicity, poetry of language, and a respect for the folk idiom (130).

The number of native writers for children increased during this period of discussion in the 1930's and 1940's. Whereas Berdiales, in 1944, discussed seriously the works of four major and an equal number of minor authors for children (109), in 1951, Martha Scala de Interguglielmo criticized at length some dozen writers and listed the works of many more; and in 1962, Dora Pastoriza de Etchebarne covered more than 50 authors in her study (156). Nevertheless, one must always come back to the point of what these authors were writing, and how. At least one critic felt constrained to chastise them for writing too many of the same adaptations of the same works on the same themes, creating for Argentine children too much *lectura* (reading matter) and not enough *literatura.*

Buenos Aires is still one of the major publishing centers of Latin America and Helen Rand Parish briefly sketches the role Constancio Vigil had in the development of children's book publishing and editing (98). This philosopher-educator is best remembered in this field as the editor of the school reader series used in Argentina and other countries, but he also adapted and edited innumerable legends and classics and wrote a series of nature fantasies.

In the present era, the most constructive work is being done by the Instituto "Summa" which organizes courses in children's literature for teachers, by the Spes Mundi (Información y Esparcimento Infantil y Juvenil), an organization which comprises the Argentine section of IBBY, by the Campaña por una Buena Literatura para Niños, and by the publishing house Kapelusz which has organized conferences on children's literature and publishes a large percentage of children's books in Argentina.

103.   Aramburu, Julio. *El folklore de los niños.* 2nd ed. Buenos Aires, El Ateneo, 1944. 203p. NNY.

A study centered on nursery rhymes, game songs, rounds, legends and tales which children pass on orally from one generation to the next.

104.   Azcoaga, Fernando. "Bibliotecas escolares," *Boletín de educación,* Santa Fe, Vol. 5, No. 59, Oct. 1949. pp. 19–28. DLC.

Brief article with suggestions for the organization of good school libraries.

105.   Barroso, Manuel. *La biblioteca en la escuela.* 2nd ed. Buenos Aires, Kapelusz, 1938. 182p. DLC, DPU, NNY.

The art of reading, its history, and what it has meant to man, as well as the history of libraries in Argentina are discussed in general. The author then specifically points out the history and importance of the school library, and goes into some detail about its program, organization, book selection policy and rules. An appendix contains eight short articles by well-known writers, poets, educators, etc. about books, reading, libraries and aspects of children's literature.

106.   Berdiales, Germán. *Del arte de escribir para los niños.* Buenos Aires, Librería Argentina, 1939.

107.   ———. *El cuento infantil rioplatense.* Santa Fe, Castellví, 1958. 59p. NNY.

The first part is a reprint of the author's article from the *Revista de Educación* (108) and the second is an expanded version of the article in *El Monitor de la Educación Común* (109). He considers both Argentinian and Uruguayan authors for children as part of the same literary heritage described by the adjective *rioplatense.*

108.   ———. "El cuento como auxiliar de la enseñanza," *Revista de educación,* La Plata, Año 1, No. 1 (new series), Jan. 1956. pp. 180–183. DLC, NNY.

A reminiscence by a well-known writer for children, concerning a teacher who helped him in his search for self-expression, through the use of folk tales and stories. The author suggests that present-day teachers might well make more frequent use of this technique.

109.   ———. "Literatura infantil rioplatense," *El monitor de la educación común,* Buenos Aires, Vol. 63, No. 857, May, 1944, pp. 54–61. DLC, DPU, NNY.

A brief history of Argentinian and Uruguayan children's literature, with a discussion of the works of Ada Maria Elflein, Horacio Quiroga, Selva, Francisco Espínola, Álvaro Yunque, Pedro Inchauspe and Ricardo E. Pose. The author points out that children's literature in this area did not really begin until the 20th century, and it was given an assist through the efforts of the newspaper, *La Prensa,* which consistently carried articles on the subject, and in 1936, originated a prize for the best writer of children's literature.

110.   Bertran, Jaime. "Aprenda a contar los cuentos," *Viva cien años,* Buenos Aires, Vol. 11, No. 6, June 18, 1941, pp. 376–377. DLC.

One of numerous short articles on children's literature and related areas which appeared in this popular magazine. This particular one is on storytelling, its importance in the home, and the value in learning to do it well, even as parents. This magazine also had a column devoted to the reviewing of children's books.

111.   *La biblioteca del Colegio Nacional No. 7 "Juan Martín de Pueyrredon," Proyecto experimental.* Buenos Aires, Fundación Interamericana de Bibliotecología Franklin, 1965. unp. DPU.

A pamphlet describing a school library which was designated a pilot project. Its purpose is to demonstrate what the most effective school library service can accomplish. Illustrated with photographs.

112. "Una biblioteca infantil modelo," *Transportes Argentinos,* Buenos Aires, Vol. 3, No. 20. Jan.–Feb. 1955. pp. 34–35. DPU.

Describes a children's library which was the first model of 20 to be installed in the federal capital. The program is covered briefly. Illustrated with photographs.

113. "Biblioteca y escuela," *Vida bibliotecaria,* Córdoba, Año 1, No. 1, Mar.–Apr. 1949, pp. 32–34.

114. "Bodas de plata de la Biblioteca Pedagógica Popular e Infantil 'D. F. Sarmiento,'" *Boletín de educación,* Santa Fe, Vol. 5, No. 22, Apr.–May, 1940. pp. 127–135. DLC.

Describes the opening of a new library for teachers and children, in a teacher training school. The library had been formed many years before, and had become important as a model for many other children's libraries. Illustrated with photographs.

115. Brambilla, Alberto Blasi. "El niño, el mito, y el cuento," *Revista de educación,* La Plata, Año 2, No. 6, (new series), June, 1957. pp. 577–581. DLC.

Brief article on the history of myths, folk and fairy tales, and a critical estimation of them, which maintains that they have their own logic, but logic they must indeed have to be effective.

116. Buenos Aires. Comité Cultural Argentino. *Guía del maestro; los libros para los niños.* Buenos Aires, The Committee, n.d. 8p. DPU.

Pamphlet which gives a brief history and criticism of children's literature, with special emphasis on Argentine writers.

117. Calderon, Lilia. "Bibliotecas infantiles," *Revista de educación,* La Plata, Año 86, No. 4, Jul.–Aug. 1944. pp. 53–55. DLC, NNY.

Very brief article stressing importance of having children's libraries in every school and community.

118. Caló, Giovanni. "Literatura infantil," *El monitor de la educación común,* Buenos Aires, Año 52, No. 720, Dec. 1932. pp. 3–14. DPU.

A general history and criticism of children's literature, translated from the Italian.

119. Castagnino, Raúl H. *La poesía épica y el alma infantil.* Buenos Aires, J. Lajouane y Cia., 1937. 126p. DLC.

This study of epic poetry and its effect on children is rather educational in approach, but it has some good sections on characteristics of the epic which appeal to children.

120. Civiny, Gabriela de. "Observaciones sobre literatura infantil," *Revista de educación,* La Plata, Año 4, No. 8, (new series), Aug. 1959. pp. 373–378. DLC.

The author observes that the popular oral tradition of Argentina, often affected by Indian (or other) myth, must undergo a "purification" just as similar tales did in Europe. Therefore, she feels that the best possible literature for children today are books of travel, biography, history, and adaptations of the classics.

121. Consejo Nacional de Educación. *Antología folklorica argentina para las escuelas primarias.* Buenos Aires, G. Kraft, 1940. 250p. NNY.

An anthology of Argentine folklore for children in primary schools. This was compiled and published to satisfy a resolution of the National Council of Education, concerning the importance of all children in Argentina learning their national folklore heritage. The resolution is reprinted here, as is a prologue commenting on it.

122. Cortina, Augusto. "Literatura infantil," *Revista de educación,* La Plata, Año 2, No. 4, (new series), April 1957. pp. 120–123. DLC.

A short critical essay on children's literature and its qualities.

123. "El cultivo de la poesía y el cuento en el jardín de infantes," *Revista de educación,* La Plata, Año 89, No. 4, Mar. 1948. pp. 32–49. DLC, NNY.

An article on the importance of use of poetry, nonsense rhymes, game songs, etc. with very young children, with examples of the kinds to use from Nervo, Mistral, Berdiales, Ibarbarou, etc. The author also insists that the narration of tales is vital to the linguistic development of children, and goes into the various techniques of reading, reciting, narrating, pointing out how this differs from the parent-child relationship, when only two share the experience. The point of view is aimed at work with kindergarten children, but is general enough in approach that it could be useful to other situations.

124. "Al cumplir medio siglo de existencia, la Biblioteca Pedagógica e Infantil de Rosario toma el nombre de su fundador," *Boletín de educación,* Santa Fe, Epoca 5, No. 29, Aug.–Sept. 1941, pp. 115–117. DLC.

After 50 years of operation, the children's and teacher's library of Rosario is given the name of its founder, Eudoro Díaz. This article also describes some of the work of this library.

125. "Curso de folklore argentino. Síntesis de la labor realizada por el Consejo Nacional de Educación

a partir de 1921 hasta 1960," *El monitor de la educación común,* Buenos Aires. Año 71, No. 936, Mar. 1961. pp. 49–75. DLC, DPU.

This is an outline of all aspects of folklore in Argentina and is included here because one large section has to do with folklore as it affects children, or as they produce it (counting-out games, rhymes, songs, etc.). A brief bibliography is included.

126.   Di Ció, Norma and Alicia E. Salvioli. "La biblioteca infantil," *Revista de educación,* La Plata, Año 89, Nov. 1947, pp. 103–110. DLC.

What the philosophy of service in a good children's library should be, and how it should differentiate among the various age groups.

127.   Dominguez, María Alicia. "El cultivo de la imaginación infantil," *El monitor de la educación común,* Buenos Aires, Año 52, No. 718, Oct. 1932. pp. 49–57. DLC, DPU.

The importance of using poetry and nursery rhymes, particularly with young children, in order to stimulate the imagination. The author also stresses the importance of oral storytelling.

128.   "¿Existe el gusto literario en los niños?," *El monitor de la educación común,* Buenos Aires, Año 66, Nos. 905–908, May–Aug. 1948. pp. 28–30. DLC, DPU.

A brief article which maintains that there exists a natural literary taste in most children.

129.   Fortun, Elena. "Hemos olvidado el arte de contar cuentos," *Boletín de educación,* Santa Fe, Vol. 5, No. 27, Apr.–May, 1941. pp. 33–35. DLC.

In connection with a review of her book on storytelling, *Pues, Señor,* the author writes an apology as to her reasons for writing the book. Basically, these were: the recognition that so little storytelling was done; the quality of the oral tradition seemed on the decline; radio, movies, theater and social life seemed to have overshadowed this important activity in the home and school.

130.   ———. *Pues, Señor . . . Cómo debe contarse el cuento y cuentos para ser contados.* Buenos Aires, Elefort, 1941. 170p. DLC, IYL.

The traditional approach to storytelling, including the universal tale through the centuries, the tale suited to the various stages of childhood, and the criteria for choosing, learning and actual telling of tales. Numerous examples of tales are given in entirety.

131.   Fournié, Emilio. "Bibliotecas infantiles," *Hijo mío,* Buenos Aires, Mar. 1937. pp. 775–777, 821. DLC.

Brief article describing a children's library in a park in Montevideo, as well as children's libraries in Argentina. Illustrated with photographs. *Hijo Mío* had, for many years, a monthly column about children's books and authors, as well as frequent short articles about storytelling, reading and choosing books for children. These were aimed at the general public, rather than teachers and librarians.

132.   Fuentes, Aldo. "Bibliotecas infantiles y escolares," *Universidad,* Santa Fe, No. 12, Oct. 1942, pp. 271–274. DLC.

The introduction to a course in children's librarianship, given over the radio in 1942. It is a statement of the basic goals of library work with children.

133.   García, Germán. "Las bibliotecas escolares en Estados Unidos," *Universidad,* Santa Fe, No. 58, Oct.–Dec. 1963, pp. 373–380. DLC, DPU.

Ostensibly a review of the Spanish translation of M. P. Douglas' *Normas . . .* (81), this is more a review of what particular significance this work can have on Argentine libraries.

134.   Giménez, Eudocio S. "Biblioteca popular pedagógica e infantil de Santa Fe," *Boletín de educación,* Santa Fe, Vol. 5, No. 42, Jul.–Aug. 1944. pp. 101–109. DLC.

The early history of this model library, for children and teachers, as it was founded on the concepts of Sarmiento and later merged with other collections. The library is connected with a teacher-training school.

135.   Huertas, José Guillermo. *El cuento y su hora.* Buenos Aires, Ediciones, "La Obra," 1962, 116p. DLC.

"The tale and its telling." In the first section the author explains the theory that the story hour is children's literature come to life. He analyzes the views on storytelling which were held by such educators as Montessori, Decroly, Dewey, Cousinet and Dalton, and selects from them certain ideas useful in the practice of storytelling. The remainder of the book is an outline of the course in storytelling which he had developed since 1941 for use in the department of education of Buenos Aires Province.

136.   "Instituto de orientación de la lectura infantil. Argentina," *Boletín del Instituto Internacional Americano de Protección a la Infancia,* Montevideo, Uruguay, Tomo 20, No. 1, 76, Mar., 1946, pp. 114–117. DLC.

A description of an institute which was created in Argentina to investigate the problems of children's literature. The formal statement of purpose and plan of action are given.

137. Jornadas Bibliotecarias Argentinas, 2nd. *Trabajos y resoluciones.* Buenos Aires, Escuela de Bibliotecología del Museo Social Argentino, 1951. (Mimeographed). DPU.

In these papers presented at the 2nd national library conference are included the following: "Bibliotecas infantines" and "Bibliotecas estudiantiles y escolares," by L. C. Pessacq, pp. 8–16; "Libros para niños en la República Argentina" by Martha Scala de Interguglielmo (see 170).

138. Jornadas Bibliotecarias Argentinas, 3rd. *Trabajos y ponencias a discutirse.* Buenos Aires, Escuela de Bibliotecología del Museo Social Argentino, 1952. (Mimeographed) DPU.

The working and discussion papers of the 3rd national library conference, which included: "Condiciones intelectuales y morales del bibliotecario para niños y jovenes" by María C. Marzano de Pérez Baratçabal, pp. 76–81; "Biblioteca Infantil No. 1 . . ." by Alicia Porro Freire de Maciel, pp. 82–87; "Las bibliotecas escolares de Mendoza" by F. Fernández Sagaz, 93–94.

139. Jornadas Bibliotecarias Argentinas, 4th. *Documentos de base.* Buenos Aires, Biblioteca Lincoln, 1956. (Mimeographed). DPU.

One of the papers presented at this 4th national library conference was "Bibliotecas infantiles, escolares y estudiantiles" by María C. Marzano de Pérez Baratçabal, pp. 53–37.

140. Lasso de la Vega y Jiménez-Placer, Javier. "La selección del libro para el niño," *La selección de libros;* Santa Fe, Universidad Nacional del Litoral, 1956, pp. 8–18, (Temas Bibliotecológicos, 6). DLC, DPU.

The principles of selection and evaluation to be used when choosing children's books.

141. Leguizamón, María Luisa Cresta de. "La educación y la literatura infantil," *Revista de educación,* La Plata, Año 5, Nos. 9–10, (new series), Sept.–Oct. 1960. pp. 17–31. DLC.

The author contends that no field has as much written about it and as little done to carry out the ideas, as the theory of children's literature. She feels that precocity is mistaken for intelligence in today's children, and they are given too much "reading" but too little "literature." She writes also of the few authors who have combined esthetics with ethics, of the adapters and the possible harm they can do, and of the unreasonable fear many educators have toward

the fairy tale. She concludes with the point that the looks of children's books are not carefully enough considered from an artistic viewpoint. Too many children in South America get their reading solely from magazines and comic books.

142. Linares, Emma. *La biblioteca como auxiliar de la educación.* Santa Fe, Universidad Nacional del Litoral, Departamento de Extensión Universitaria, 1959. 32p. (Temas Bibliotecológicos, No. 10).

For note see 91.

143. Lombroso, Paula. "¿Por qué gustan los cuentos a los niños," *El monitor de la educación común,* Buenos Aires, Tomo 32, Vol. 29, No. 445, Jan. 1910, pp. 26–38. DLC, DPU.

For note see 456.

144. Marasso, Arturo. "La lectura," *Revista de educación,* La Plata, Año 1, No. 1 (new series), Jan., 1956. pp. 156–179. DLC.

A general essay on reading, and more specifically on children's reading: What the child looks for and what his reading evokes. The author makes a plea for good school libraries.

145. Matassi, Laura María. "Literatura infantil," *El monitor de la educación común,* Buenos Aires, Año 50, No. 703, Jul. 1931, pp. 17–22. DPU.

A very general discussion of the influence of reading on children, and what children like to read.

146. Melo, Carlos F. . . . *Palabras del doctor don Carlos F. Melo, director de la biblioteca nacional, en el acto inaugural de la sala de lectura para niños, 30 Junio 1931.* Buenos Aires, Talleres Gráficos de la Biblioteca Nacional, 1931. 9p. DLC.

The speech of the director of the national library of Argentina, upon the occasion of opening a children's room in the library.

147. Mendióroz, Hugo Enrique. "Por una literatura infantil digna del niño," *Revista de educación,* La Plata, Año 90, No. 3, Mar. 1949. pp. 56–61. DLC.

The author pleads for a more modern approach to children's literature. It is all right, he says, to have the classics, but why only them, told and retold. In addition, his plea is for more purity and sensitivity, and less violence and truculence.

148. Mistral, Gabriela. "Biblioteca y escuela," *Revista de educación,* La Plata, Año 90, No. 2, Feb. 1949. pp. 72–80. DLC.

A well-known writer for children gives her personal views on the library situation in Argentina and Latin America. She despairs of the situation, pointing out that the children's room in the public or school library is too often considered a luxury. The books to be found in such libraries as exist are often mediocre or downright bad. She feels the apostolate of the librarian is to fight mass or popular taste, and that in teaching children to love good literature they can have more success than the pedagogue.

149. Montenegro, Ernesto. "Lecturas para chicos y grandes," *La prensa*, Buenos Aires, Feb. 1, 1948. (p. 1 of Sunday Literary Supplement) DLC.

The philosophy of children's literature and how it came to be is the beginning of this discussion which then ranges to the ultimate question as to why there exist in Spanish children's literature no truly immortal works of the calibre of *Alice in Wonderland* or Perrault's tales, for example. While Don Quixote can be appreciated in part by children, it is not truly part of their own literature. The author feels this is explainable in large part to the inflexibility of the Spanish culture. He states that too often the Spanish writer of children's literature shows a predilection for the austere, the sentimental and the sorrowful.

150. Moragues, Jerónimo. "Condiciones psicológicas de la literatura para los niños," *El monitor de la educación común,* Buenos Aires, Año 55, No. 762, June, 1936. pp. 3–13. DLC.

Although somewhat psychological in viewpoint, the basis of this article on criticism of children's literature is the creative, the imaginative impulse which makes a work successful or not. The author's formula would be "to create a literature on the base of imagination which would make one accept any deed, possible or impossible."

151. Morello, Antonio. "Encuesta sobre la biblioteca escolar infantil." Entire issue of *Revista de instrucción primaria,* La Plata, 1932. 80p. DPU.

The results of an inquiry symposium on the school and children's library. The articles are by many persons well-known in the field in Argentina, and cover all aspects of these libraries, children's literature and storytelling.

152. Moses, M. J. "Bibliotecas y salas de lectura para niños." *El monitor de la educación común,* Buenos Aires, Año 31, No. 481, Tomo 44, Mar. 1913. pp. 221–230. DLC, DPU.

In describing the services to children in public libraries of the US, the implications of this article are that such work could be equally effective in Argentina.

153. "Organización de las bibliotecas escolares," *El monitor de la educación común,* Buenos Aires, Año 60, No. 820, April 1941, pp. 3–34. DLC.

A résumé of the work noted in entry 10.

154. Ossola de Horas, Elena M. "Importancia de las revistas como lectura infantil," *Anales del Instituto de Investigaciones Pedagógicas,* San Luis, Vol. 3, 1954, pp. 194 ff.

155. Pastoriza de Etchebarne, Dora. *Bibliografía de literatura infantil (de 6 a 16 años).* Buenos Aires, Instituto "Félix Fernando Bernasconi."

156. ———. *El cuento en la literatura infantil; ensayo crítico.* Buenos Aires, Kapelusz, [1962], 232p. (Biblioteca de Cultura Pedagógica, 76). DLC.

The first part contains material on children's literature in general. Particularly good is a definition of the term *cuento* as opposed to the English terms *fairy tale, tale, short story, story.*

The second part contains short pieces of history and criticism on more than 50 authors, largely native, but also those who had worked and lived in Argentina. They are covered in alphabetical order. The concluding sections of part two are concerned with other aspects of children's literature in Argentina.

157. ———. "Necesidad de crear centros de investigación y estudio de la literatura infantil y juvenil." International Board on Books for Young People. *IX Congreso de la Organización Internacional para el Libro Juvenil.* Madrid, 1965, pp. 67–72. DLC, IYL.

This resolution, and another on storytelling clubs, were presented by the author at the IBBY Congress. Preceding them is an article by Martha A. Salotti Porta on the general role of IBBY in Argentina, and what is being done here in the field of children's literature. Following the resolutions are articles by Eleonora Pacheco, on reading guidance, and by Mane Bernardo and Sarah Bianchi on the puppet theater in Argentina. There are texts in Spanish and English, except for the article last mentioned which is only in Spanish.

158. Penchansky de Bosch, Lydia. "Una encuesta sobre literatura infantil," *Universidad,* Santa Fe, No. 55, Jan.–Mar. 1963. pp. 259–295. DLC, DPU.

Part of an inquiry, undertaken in collaboration with F. Schultz de Mantovani, on the reading interests of children. The five hypotheses which the author set out to prove were: The city child reads more newspapers and periodicals than children's books;

the child spends more time on other mass media than on reading in any form; teachers consider children's books more as an auxiliary means of instruction than as means to a pleasurable experience; teachers spend only a limited time in stimulating in the child a desire to read for pleasure; the value of recreational reading has never been clarified in teacher-training courses. The answers to the questionnaire seemed to bear out these hypotheses.

159. Perez, Erminda. "Bibliotecas infantiles." *Boletín de educación,* Santa Fe, Vol. 5, No. 58, Jul.–Aug. 1949. pp. 13–18. DLC.

The author stresses the importance of children's books and reading, and suggests that a new look be taken at all aspects, at the same time that a reorganization of libraries for children takes place.

160. Pérez Baratçabal, Maria C. Marzano de. "Organización de bibliotecas estudiantiles," *Bibliotecología,* Buenos Aires, Tomo 1, No. 1, Nov. 1946, pp. 15–33. DPU.

The work of the school library, and its proper organization for fruitful use.

161. Pizzurno, Pablo A. "Las bibliotecas infantiles como medio de la cultura y base de las bibliotecas populares," *El educador Pablo A. Pizzurno; recopilación de trabajos . . . Publicación resuelta como homenaje . . .* Buenos Aires, [Establecimiento Gráfico Argentino], 1934, pp. 304–309.

There are succinct suggestions on evaluating children's books and library work in this volume of the writings of an educator who carried out Sarmiento's principles.

162. Rojas de Alvarez, Angélica. *Bibliotecas preventorios; el niño del pueblo.* Buenos Aires, El Ateneo, 1943, 125p. DPU.

The lack of good reading material has a direct influence on juvenile delinquency, according to the author. She further goes on to define the social and humanistic mission of the public library and its children's rooms. The second part, which was a speech delivered to the Superior Tribunal of Justice, is entitled "Spiritual liberation through good reading." In it, she defines her idea of good children's literature.

163. ———. *El niño y sus libros.* Buenos Aires, Kapelusz, 1940. 153p. DPU.

Although the first part of this book had to do more with the psychology of the child's personality, the last part treats of children's literature in a critical and philosophical manner. Included are a list of Argentine authors, with about 75 titles given in all. There is also a short bibliography.

164. Ruiz, Leonor. "Panorama bibliotecológica argentino . . . Bibliotecas infantiles y escolares," *Biblioteconomía,* Barcelona, Año 12, No. 42, July–Dec. 1955, pp. 129–134. DLC, NNY.

A description of several public and school libraries for children, and the services they offer.

165. Salotti, Martha A. *Informe presentado al Consejo Nacional de Educación.* Sumario: Bibliotecas infantiles, Historia del cuento, El narrador, Cultivo de la imaginación . . . Buenos Aires, 1947.

(No copy of this was located. The bibliography of 156 indicated that it was the report of a trip made to the United States, with Gabriela Mistral, for the purposes of studying children's literature and libraries.)

166. Sánchez Trincado, J. Luis. "El cuento literario y el cuento folklórico en la escuela," *El monitor de la educación común,* Buenos Aires, Año 60, No. 820, Apr. 1941, pp. 35–39. DLC.

This author tries to differentiate between the literary tale and the folk tale, pointing out all along that both have their place in the child's literary experience.

167. Sarmiento, Domingo Faustino. *Páginas selectas de Sarmiento sobre bibliotecas populares, recopiladas por la Comisión Protectora de Bibliotecas Populares.* Vol. 4 of: *Argentine Republic.* Comisión Nacional de Homenaje a Sarmiento. . . . *Sarmiento, cincuentenario de su muerte . . .* Buenos Aires, [Imprenta Mercatali, 1939]. 243p. DLC.

This fourth of five volumes of the collected writings of Sarmiento concerns specifically what he wrote and said about libraries, with emphasis on school libraries.

168. Sbuelz, Maria Adriana. "Algunos aspectos de la literatura infantil," *Revista de educación,* La Plata, Año 1, No. 6, (new series) June, 1956. pp. 665–673. DLC, NNY.

A translation from the Italian, not located in the original (see 711). This is a very good article on general criticism of children's literature.

169. Scala de Interguglielmo, Martha. "Bibliografía de la literatura infantil-juvenil. Argentina," *El libro y el pueblo.* Mexico, D.F., Año 20, No. 33, Jan.–Feb. 1958. pp. 91–98. DPU.

Although it appears in this Mexican periodical, this is an annotated list of Argentine children's books, and those printed in Argentina. It includes 116 titles arranged by general subject and then by author.

170. ———. *Libros para niños en La República Argentina.* Contribución a las segundas jornadas bib-

liotecarias argentinas. Buenos Aires, no pub., September, 1951. 31p. DLC, DPU.

After defining children's literature the author goes on to describe the literature which has developed in Argentina by native writers. She mentions the lack of good critical reviews of books for children, as well as the lack of librarians working with them. A list of books mentioned in her text is included at the end. Also included are the six resolutions which the children's librarians at the conference passed, in regard to the improvement of children's literature and libraries in Argentina.

171.   Schultz Cazeneuve de Mantovani, Fryda. *Fábula del niño en el hombre.* Buenos Aires, Editora Sudamericana, [1951]. 195p. (Colección Ensayos Breves). DLC.

Six essays on Goethe, W. H. Hudson, H. C. Andersen, the *Pentamerone,* Unamuno, and José Martí. These writers and their works are discussed in general, but much of what the author discusses is applicable to the philosophy of children's literature.

172.   ———. *El mundo poético infantil.* Buenos Aires, El Ateneo, 1944. 157 p. DPU.

A stirring defense of the importance of poetry during childhood. The author maintains that most educational systems underestimate the value, necessity and wide range of use of poetry for children. She contends that all children's books, including textbooks, should bridge more naturally the world of the child's oral tradition of games, songs, tales, fantasies, and the world of written literature he must contend with in school and as an adult. Although written partly from the viewpoint of the psychology of the child's personality, this transcends the pedagogical. The study of the works of Alfonsina Storni and Gabriela Mistral, which appears at the end, puts the author's views into perspective with concrete examples.

173.   ———. *Sobre las hadas.* Buenos Aires, Editorial Nova, 1959. 130p. (Compendios Nova de Iniciación Cultural. 29). NNY.

Hadas or fairies is here interpreted very loosely, for the author includes a critical evaluation of the works of Verne, Martí, Lagerlöf, Carroll, Swift, Defoe, Barrie and Collodi, as well as the traditional collectors such as Grimm, Perrault and Andersen. She also selects a list of "100 and more good books for children."

174.   ———. *Sobre teatro y poesía para niños.* 2nd ed. Santa Fe, Universidad Nacional del Litoral, 1956. 54p. (Publicación de "Extensión Universitaria," No. 35). DLC.

Originally written in 1937, this essay treats of writing for children, particularly poetry and plays, and shows the influence of the Montessori philosophy of education. The author deplores the overt morality of most tales, and states that in spite of having a 50 year history behind it, children's literature in Argentina still appears to be derivative, and for the most part, contrary to what the spirit of children needs and likes. Included are examples of poetry and scenes from plays.

175.   Sosa, Jesualdo. *La literatura infantil.* Buenos Aires, Editorial Losada, 1959. 283p. DPU has the first edition, 1944.

This is the same as entry 465, but in book form and under a new title. For note see that entry.

176.   Torrente de Calvo, Angélica. "Función de la biblioteca en la escuela," *Revista de educación,* La Plata, Año 85, No. 2, Mar.–Apr. 1944. pp. 66–71. DLC.

Practical suggestions in setting up a school library, with samples of forms and a suggested list of basic reference works.

177.   Veronelli, Atilio A. "La literatura infantil," *Revista de educación,* La Plata, Año 1, No. 9 (new series) Sept. 1956. pp. 565–581. DLC.

(Probably a translation of the Italian, although no source is given.)

A definition of children's literature, criticism of several of its aspects, and an explanation of the difficulty of being a good children's writer.

Brazil

Children growing up in Brazil before 1894 had only textbooks and adult books from which to read (along with a few so-called "children's books" which made their way from Portugal), but in that year appeared *Contos da Carochinha,* the first book published in Brazil with the intention of pleasing and entertaining children. It was a collection of folk and fairy tales from several countries, translated and edited by Alberto Figueiredo Pimentel. By 1920, publishers had expanded the market by printing Brazilian editions of series taken over from European houses. Then, in 1921, native literature got its second start, with the appearance of *Narizinho Arrebitado* by José Bento Monteiro Lobato. He followed this with a stream of work, mostly informational or educational, but cleverly disguised as fantasy or accounts of voyages. These books remain in print and are still popular today. If one is to accept as generally true the feelings expressed by one group of children (212), he is probably read and admired because of what he represents in the world of Brazilian children's books, rather than for the general appeal of his work.

The above account is taken from the brief history of children's literature in Brazil written by Manuel Bergstrom Lourenço Filho. As in the other Latin American countries, educators here have had a strong influence on the development of children's literature and libraries, and his is the outstanding name in this area. He was long associated with the Instituto Nacional de Estudos Pedagógicos, and much of his work could not be included here because it falls into psychology and pedagogy.

As the largest of the Latin American republics, Brazil has also been the most successful in developing an extensive native literature for children, and publishing houses to give it an audience. The 2,400 titles listed in the most complete bibliography available (197) are perhaps more than the other countries could claim even if they combined their total output. A fair percentage of these are not translations or adaptations, but genuinely fresh and "modern" stories for children, with fantasy being the most popular form as well as the most successful. The best critical evaluations of these authors and their works appear in the articles by Gaston Figueira (85) and Helen Rand Parish (98).

In 1936, a national Commission for Children's Literature was conceived within the framework of the Ministry of Education. Later, this was incorporated into a section of the Instituto Nacional do Livro. This Institute has encouraged and stimulated the publication of more and better books for children, and through various exhibitions has brought to public notice the books already available. They have also awarded prizes for the best children's book of certain periods.

Where there are more books available, there can be better libraries, and better libraries are often known to create a demand for still more books. This circular interaction is partly responsible for the network of children's libraries in Brazil, the most extensive in Latin America. More credit, however, can be given to Lenyra Fraccaroli, who put forth a forceful, sustained and successful campaign to organize library service to children with local and state support. Early in the 1930's she began to work toward the goal of a special library for children. In 1936 her dreams were realized upon the completion of the Biblioteca Infantil Municipal of São Paulo. It had a good collection for reference and circulation, and space for activities such as story hours, book clubs, painting classes, puppet theater, and many more. Her conception of what the children's library should offer as services might find critics in certain countries, because it seems so inclusive of social and educational goals. Yet the patterns she established obviously suit the needs of her country for they have been duplicated with success, and the countless reports of visitors, native or foreign, to her library, all indicate a genuine respect for the imaginative work being done with children and books. On the national, state and local levels, library service now bears her personal stamp as much as the literature it employs bears the mark of Monteiro Lobato's style.

178.   Almeida, Lúcia Machado de. "Literatura para crianças," *Revista do ensino,* Belo Horizonte, Ano 17, No. 193, July–Dec. 1949, pp. 185–198. DPU.

A general criticism of children's literature, which the author feels ideally to be that which is educational, informational and recreational at the same time.

179.   Arroyo, Leonardo. *O tempo e o modo; literatura infantil e outras notas.* São Paulo, Conselho Estadual de Cultura, Comissão de Literatura, 1963. 170p. (Coleção Ensaio, 25). DLC.

The first essay is entitled "Literatura Infantil Brasileira" and at least half of the remaining essays are on aspects of children's literature, its history and criticism. The author feels that those who have written about children's literature from the universal aspects have overlooked the contribution of Brazil.

180.   Arruda, Helio de Quadros. "A influência da má literatura infantil," *Boletim do serviço social,* São Paulo, Vol. 9, Dec. 1950, pp. 27–38. DLC.

The author criticizes present-day literature for children pointing out its many defects, and contending that its bad influence can only be stopped by preventive legislation which will prohibit its production.

181.   Associação Brasileira de Educação. *Bibliotheca (sic) para crianças e adolescentes; organizada pela secção de cooperação da família.* Rio, Escuela Professional de Artes Graficas, 1930. 31p. DPU.

A booklist divided into two parts: books published in 1928, and those published in 1929. Each part has three sections, separating age groups. Author and title only are given, with no publishers or other bibliographical data.

182.   Avila, Antônio d'. "Leituras para crianças e adolescentes," *Revista de Educação,* São Paulo, Vol. 37, No. 59, June, 1951. pp. 10–16. DLC. NNY.

A study of what children like to read, from ABC's to detective stories. Specific Brazilian works are mentioned, as well as translated works.

183.   Biblioteca Infantil "Carlos Alberto." *Album documentario comemorativo.* Rio, Meier, 17 Dec. 1950. unp. IYL.

A commemorative album, illustrated with photographs, issued to celebrate an anniversary of this well-known children's library. Includes speeches, a brief history of the library, its program and something about the children it serves.

184.   Brazil. Secretaria General de Educação e Cultura. Comissão de Livros. "Seleção de livros recreativos para bibliotecas infantis," *Revista de educação pública,* Rio, Vol. 1, No. 1, Jan.–Mar. 1943, pp. 73–77. DLC, DPU.

An annotated list of 28 titles particularly suited to recreational reading.

185.   Campanha de Aperfeiçoamento e Difusão do Ensino Secundário (CADES). *Biblioteca escolar.* Rio, CADES, 1958. 77p. (Ministerio de Educação e Cultura). DPU.

A manual on the organization of school libraries. Later edition, edited by Ruth Villela de Souza, not located.

186.   Campos, C. Edissa Zulmires de. "Precisamos de melhores revistas para as crianças," *Revista do ensino,* Rio Grande do Sul, Ano 6, No. 41, Oct.–Nov. 1956, pp. 48–50. DLC.

A brief article on the better magazines for children and the type of literature they contain.

187.   Carvalho, Barbara Vasconcelos de. *Compendio de literatura infantil.* São Paulo, Editora Nacional, 1959.

188.   Carvalho, Manoel Marques de. "O que as crianças devem ler," *Criança,* Rio, Oct., 1941, pp. 16 ff.

189. Christiano, Oscar Guilherme. "'Bibliotecas escolares," *Educação,* São Paulo, Vol. 6, Nos. 1, 2, 3, Jan.–Mar. 1932. pp. 103.–104. DLC, NNY.

The importance of the school library, and a description of the program and organization of a specific school library, "Fernando Albuquerque." Includes a list of 42 basic titles.

190. Congreso de Escritores Infanto-Juvenis, 6th, São Paulo, 1952. *Estatutos.* São Paulo, [1952]. 32p. APP.

The statutes and proceedings resulting from the 6th Congress of Youth Authors. This group originated out of the work of the children's library in São Paulo, which encouraged young people to write for themselves.

191. Costa, Fermino. "Literatura juvenil," *Leitores e livros,* Rio, Vol. 3, No. 10, Oct. 1952. pp. 113–122. DPU.

A brief criticism of young adult literature, followed by an annotated list of 50 titles of the 1952 production. This periodical reviews children's books regularly, and has frequent articles on children's literature, reading, authors, libraries, storytelling, etc.

192. Druck, Elida de Freitas e Castro. "Biblioteca escolar infantil," *Revista do ensino,* Porto Alegre, Año 3, No. 17, Sept. 1953, pp. 19–20; No. 18, Oct. 1953, pp. 20–21; No. 19, Nov. 1953, pp. 24–25. DLC.

Only three of a long series on the school library and its activities, which appeared in this periodical from 1951 to 1954.

193. *Exposição internacional do livro infantil no Rio de Janeiro. Catálogo.* Rio, Biblioteca Infantil "Carlos Alberto," 1957. 2 vols. unp. IYL.

The catalog of an international exhibition of children's books, containing 2,543 entries listed by country, and then by author.

194. Ferraz, Wanda. "A biblioteca escolar e suas funções," *A Biblioteca.* 3rd ed., rev. and augmented. 2nd part. São Paulo, Edição Saraiva, 1949. pp. 99–204. DLC.

The history, objectives and organization of the school library. Includes a short bibliography.

195. Figueiredo, Adelpha S. R. de. "A literatura para crianças no Brasil," *Inter-American Bibliographical and Library Association, Proceedings of the Second Convention, Washington, Feb. 23 and 24, 1939.* New York, H. W. Wilson Co., 1939. (Series 2, Vol. 2 of the Publications of the Association). pp. 105–122. DPU. NNY.

A history of children's literature in Brazil, from its oral beginnings to the more recent work of Monteiro Lobato and Thales Castanho de Andrade. Included is a list of approximately 180 titles, with fairly complete bibliographic information, and with titles translated into English.

196. Fonseca, Elena. *Clubes de leitura. Instituições escolares. Seus objetivos. Seus valores.* Belo Horizonte, Imprensa Oficial, 1950. 69p. (Publicação de Secretaria de Educação do Estado de Minas Gerais).

197. Fraccaroli, Lenyra C. *Bibliografía de literatura infantil em língua portuguêsa.* 2nd ed. São Paulo, Editôra Jornal dos Livros, 1955. 280p. (Publicada sob os auspícios do Instituto Nacional do Livro). DLC, DPU, IYL. Supplement in: *Revista do ensino,* Rio Grande do Sul, Ano 12, No. 87, Sept. 1962. p. 73. DLC.

An annotated list of 2,388 titles divided into four age groups, and then listed by author, with complete bibliographical information. The list hoped to be inclusive rather than selective. Subject, author and title indexes are included. List of publishers of children's books, and children's periodicals are given at the end. The supplement contains 35 titles.

198. ———. *Miscellaneous papers on children's libraries.* Washington, Pan American Union, n.d. DPU.

Typewritten manuscripts of varying length, in English and Portuguese. Some of the titles are: "Children's literature—Origen," "The Municipal Library for Children in São Paulo," "The Children's Library—Organization and Functioning," "Study Plan for Creating Children's Libraries in Cities of São Paulo." Some are untitled.

199. Franco, João Evangelista. "Literatura infantil e delinquência dos menores," *Boletim do serviço social dos menores,* São Paulo, Vol. 2, No. 3, Dec. 1942. pp. 5–14. DLC, DPU.

The author blames the poor quality and violent content of children's literature for causing the rise in juvenile delinquency. He concludes with statement of what children's literature should be, in quality and content.

200. Gomes, Giselda G. "A literatura infantil e sua influência na estruturação de personalidade infantil," *Revista do ensino,* Rio Grande do Sul, Ano 10, No. 77, Aug. 1961, pp. 17–18, 67. DLC.

An article on the psychological effects of reading on the child's personality.

201.   "Inquérito de leituras infantis," *Boletim de associação brasileira de educação,* Rio, Ano 3, No. 11, May–June, 1927, pp. 8–23.

202.   "Uma investigação sôbre jornais e revistas infantis e juvenis," *Revista brasileira de estudos pedagógicos,* Rio, Vol. 2, No. 5, Nov. 1944, pp. 255–275; Vol. 2, No. 6, Dec. 1944, pp. 401–421; Vol. 3, No. 7, Jan. 1945, pp. 82–101; Vol. 3, No. 8, Feb. 1945, pp. 223–241. DLC.
    The results of an inquiry made by the Instituto Nacional de Estudos Pedagógicos, whose director was at that time Manuel Marques de Carvalho. No indication is given that Lourenço Filho directed the inquiry, but it is evident from his later articles that he did. The stated objectives were to learn of the periodicals published in Rio which had any influence on children and young people, and to analyze them from the points of content, language, literature, illustration. This was all transcribed into graphs and tabulated. Many illustrations from the magazines are given. The conclusions are based upon the attitude that children's books should be literature, and some of the special characteristics of this literature are critically evaluated. A brief bibliography is included.

203.   Katzenstein, Betti and Beatriz de Freitas. "Algo do que crianças gostam de ler," *Revisto do arquivo municipal,* São Paulo, June–July, 1941, pp. 5–95. DLC, DPU, NNY.
    A study of the reading interests and habits of children, undertaken in the municipal children's library. Only two children's books were used as a control basis. Includes graphs and charts, of results by age group, sex group, type of book, etc.

204.   ———."O cinema e o mundo infantil," *Boletim bibliografico,* São Paulo, Vol. 12, 1949. pp. 13–54. DLC, DPU.
    An inquiry into the influence of films on children's reading, undertaken at the municipal children's library. A control group of 22 books and 13 films were used. Includes graphs and charts.

205.   Leão, Pepita de. "O canto dos contos," *Revista do ensino,* Porto Alegre, Ano 2, No. 14, Vol. 4, Oct. 1940, pp. 136–138. DPU.
    A teacher-storyteller writes of her experiences, and her belief in the importance of storytelling in the life of every child.

206.   Lima, Alceu Amoroso. "Literatura infantil," *Estudos,* 1ª serie, Rio, Ed. "Terra de Sol," 1927. pp. 212–228. DLC.
    A critical essay about children's literature, as well as literature written by children—how they differ in approach, philosophy, content.

207.   ———. "Literatura infantil," *Leitores e livros,* Rio, Ano 3, No. 10, Oct.–Dec. 1952, pp. 103–111. DPU.
    A brief criticism of children's literature, stressing the religious aspects of children's books. Includes a short list of Brazilian children's books for 1952.

208.   Losa, Ilse. *A linguagem na literatura infantil.* Rio de Janeiro, 195?

209.   Lourenço Filho, Manuel Bergstrom. "Como aperfeiçoar a literatura infantil." Cruz, Marques da, *Historia da litteratura,* São Paulo, Melhoramentos, 1957. Also in: *Revista Brasileira,* Rio, Ano 3, No. 7, Sept., 1943. pp. 146–169. DLC.
    A history of children's literature, with special emphasis on that of Brazil. The author divides the Brazilian developments into three periods: before 1900, from 1900 to 1920, from 1921 to the 1940's. He concludes with a section on the characteristics and functions of children's literature, its forms and how to recognize them.

210.   ———. "Um inquérito sôbre o que os moços leem," *Educação,* São Paulo, Vol. 1, No. 1, Oct. 1927. pp. 30–39. DLC.
    The results of a reading interest inquiry made in a school. Graphs indicate answers to such questions as how many books were read, what kinds, and by which authors.

211.   ———. "Literatura infantil," *Revista do ensino,* Rio Grande do Sul, Ano 11, No. 85, July 1962. pp. 16–18. DLC.
    In an interview, the author answers questions about the criticism of children's literature, and explains his opinions on the characteristics, themes, and subjects appropriate to children's literature.

212.   ———. "La literatura infantil en el Brasil," *Educación,* Washington, Año 4, No. 14, Apr.–June, 1959, pp. 25–29. DLC, DPU, NNY.
    The history of children's books in Brazil, from 1894 to the present time. Not only are individual authors and their works discussed, but a survey of the organizations interested in children's books is included in the account.

213.   ———. *O ensino e a biblioteca.* Rio, Imprensa Nacional, 1946. 24p. (Departamento Administrativo do Serviço Público). DPU.
    The importance of the library in the school, and something about its organization and program.

214.   ———. *Publicaciones infantiles y juveniles. Una encuesta brasileña.* Washington, Pan American

Union, 1947. 16p. (Publicaciones de la Unión Panamericana, Serie Educación, No. 131). DPU.

A résumé, in Spanish, of the results of the reading interest inquiry described in 210.

215.   Louzada, Alfonso. *O cinema e a literatura na educação da criança*. Rio, Imprensa Nacional, 1939. 42p.

216.   Lunnon, Betty Sheehan. "Brazil's children ask better books," *Horn book,* Boston, Vol. 24, No. 4, July–Aug. 1948, pp. 285–289. DLC, IYL, NNY.

In November, 1945, the first Congress of Young Writers took place in São Paulo, sponsored by the municipal children's library. Directed by the children themselves, it had as its aims the establishing of new and better goals for Brazilian children's literature, and the instilling of responsibility in the young writer. In cooperation with the congress, the main library offered the first "Exposição do Livro Infantil e Didáctico."

217.   Luzuriaga, Lorenzo. "Finalidade e organização das bibliotecas escolares," *Educação,* São Paulo, Vol. 6, Nos. 1, 2, 3, Jan.–Mar. 1932, pp. 181–188. DLC.

The purpose and organization of the school library.

218.   Macedo, Maria Perciliana H. de. "A biblioteca escolar; como organizá-la," *Revista do ensino,* Porto Alegre, Ano 3, No. 24, Aug. 1954. pp. 10–15, 9. DLC.

The importance of the school library, and how to organize it, are discussed and diagrammed.

219.   Malin, Fany. *Biblioteca escolar*. Rio, CBAI, 1948. 17p. (Ministerio da Educação e Saúde, Comissão Brasileiro-Americana de Educação Industrial). DLC.

The importance of school libraries and a plan of organization. Includes illustrations of technical equipment, forms, furniture, etc.

220.   Meireles, Cecilia. Inquérito realizado nas escolas do Distrito Federal sôbre literatura infantil. Belo Horizonte, Departamento de Educação, 1934.

221.   ————. *Problemas de literatura infantil*. Belo Horizonte, Secretaria de Educação, 1951.

222.   Minssen, Lucília. "Aprendendo a selecionar," *Revista do ensino,* Rio Grande do Sul, Ano 6, No. 46, Aug. 1957. p. 11. DLC.

Twelve important points to look for in selecting children's books for personal or library use. The author is children's librarian in the Porto Alegre children's library.

223.   Montesanti, María de Lourdes M. "Uma visita á Biblioteca Pública Municipal Infantil," *Boletim do serviço social dos menores,* São Paulo, Vol. 4, Dec. 1944, pp. 58–67. DLC.

A visit to the municipal children's library of São Paulo, during which the author learns its rules and regulations. She describes its technical services, and reproduces sample cards and forms.

224.   Nizinska, Elvira, et al. "Problemas de literatura infantil," *O Jornal,* Rio, May 4, 1936.

225.   Nobrega, Nisia. "Aprendamos con los niños a darnos las manos," International Board of Books for Young People. *IX Congreso de la Organización Internacional para el Libro Juvenil*. Madrid, 1965, pp. 87–90. DLC, IYL.

A brief statement on the status of children's books and reading, preceded by an article on the creation of the Brazilian section of IBBY, by María Luiza Barbosa.

226.   Osório Mársico, Lygia. "A criança e o mundo encantado dos livros," *Revista do ensino,* Rio Grande do Sul, Ano 12, No. 93, June, 1963, pp. 16–19. DLC.

A report of a visit to the children's library "Monteiro Lobato" in São Paulo, and a description of its activities, illustrated with photographs.

227.   Pécora, Francisco. "Biblioteca escolar," *Revista de educação,* São Paulo, Vol. 31, Nos. 42–43, Jan.–June, 1944, pp. 87–92. DPU, NNY.

The organization and management of the school library, and the philosophy of service behind it.

228.   Pereira, Maria de Lourdes de Sousa. "Literatura juvenil," *Leitores e livros,* Rio, Vol. 7, No. 25, July–Sept. 1956, pp. 32–38. DPU.

What young people like to read and what they read, written from a psychological point of view.

229.   Pontet, C. S. de. "Que dá a seu filho para lér?," *Revista do ensino,* Belo Horizonte, Ano 11, Nos. 140–142, July, 1937, pp. 23–28. DPU.

A teacher recommends that all parents and teachers know well what they are giving their children to read, and suggests they give only that literature which "elevates the spirit and inspires noble and valid sentiments."

230.   Porto Alegre. Biblioteca Pública Infantil. *Nossa bibliotequinha*. Porto Alegre, Secretaria de

Educação e Cultura, Divisão de Cultura, 1955. Unp. (Boletim bibliográfico anual da biblioteca . . .). DPU.

A catalog of the library, in four parts: Reference Works, Classified Works (Nonfiction), Fiction (for three age levels), Biography. About 600 titles are listed, with an author and title index.

231. Queiróz, Zaide Alves de. "Uma biblioteca infantil," *Revista do ensino,* Belo Horizonte, Ano 12, Nos. 155–157, Oct.–Dec. 1938, pp. 206–209. DPU.

A teacher describes how she formed a library in her school, and details some of the activities she used to stimulate reading.

232. Quiros S., Carmen. "Breve historia de la biblioteca infantil 'Carlos Alberto,'" *Boletín de la asociación costarricense de bibliotecarios,* San José, Costa Rica, Año 1, No. 6, Oct. 1956, pp. 18–20. DPU.

A short history of the children's library "Carlos Alberto" in Rio.

233. Reis Campos, Maria dos. "Bibliotecas escolares," *Infância e juventude,* Rio, Ano 1, No. 4, Sept. 1936, pp. 288–292. DLC.

"The school library should not be an *annex,* or an *auxiliary,* but rather an *organ* of the school." This author further goes on to distinguish between the true school library and the classroom collection.

234. ———. "Literatura infantil," *Revista de educação pública,* Rio, Vol. 4, No. 15, July–Sept. 1946. pp. 333–341 DLC, DPU. Also in: *Revista Brasileira de estudos pedagógicos,* Rio, Vol. 10, No. 27, Mar.–Apr. 1947, pp. 178–186.

A history and criticism of children's literature, in particular that of Brazil.

235. ———. "Literatura infantil," *Infância e juventude,* Rio, Ano 1, No. 1, June, 1936, pp. 17–20; No. 3, Aug. 1936, pp. 177–181; No. 5, Oct. 1936, pp. 307–310. DLC.

Mentioning no specific books, the author treats of the more abstract qualities of children's literature.

236. Rivas, Margarita Mieres de. "O trabalho cultural da biblioteca infantil do Chile," *Revista do ensino,* Belo Horizonte, Ano 12, No. 148, Mar. 1938, pp. 157–167. DPU.

A translation into Portuguese of her article noted in 264.

237. Ruiz, Corina Maria Peixoto. "Literatura infantil," *Revista do ensino,* Rio Grande do Sul, Ano 11, No. 79, Oct. 1961, pp. 53–57; No. 80, Nov. 1961, pp. 33–35. DLC.

The first part is a succinct outline of the characteristics, basis, function, requisites and general principles of children's literature and its criticism. The second part is a criticism of children's poetry, with numerous examples. The third and fourth parts (in subsequent issues) are translations of sections of the book *How to Tell Stories to Children,* by Sara Cone Bryant.

238. Russo, Laura Garcia Moreno and Ricci, Zilah Mattos. *A divisão de bibliotecas infanto-juvenis, municipal de São Paulo.* São Paulo, Biblioteca Municipal, 1959. Unp. (Mimeographed). DPU.

A history of the children's library of São Paulo, its work, and the statistics of circulation, use of the collection, attendance at activities, etc.

239. Sa, Correa de. "Ainda sôbre literatura infantil," *Criança,* Rio, Dec. 1942, pp. 10 ff.

240. São Paulo. Biblioteca Infantil. *Lista de livros infantis organizada e recomendada pela Biblioteca Infantil Municipal da Cidade de São Paulo.* 1942. 41p.

241. Salem, Nazira. *Literatura infantil.* São Paulo, Editorial Mestre Jo, 1959.

242. Scavone, Rubens Teixeira. "For children only; unique library in São Paulo," *Américas,* Washington, Vol. 9, No. 11, Nov. 1957, pp. 30–33. DLC, DPU, NNY.

A description of the municipal children's library and its activities, illustrated with photographs.

243. Silveira, Ida. "Bibliotecas infantís," *Revista do ensino,* Porto Alegre, Ano 1, No. 2–Vol. 1, Oct. 1939, pp. 104–106. DPU.

The significance of the library in the life of the child.

244. Souza, Julio Cezar de Mello e. *A arte de ler e de contar histórias, por Malba Tahan* (pseud.). Rio, Conquista, 1957.

245. Starling, Nair. "Biblioteca infantil," *Revista do ensino,* Belo Horizonte, Ano 14, No. 176, Jan. 1946, pp. 26–30. DPU.

The author stresses the importance of the school library, calling it the heart of the school, and points out that it should always be organized by someone with professional training.

246. ———. "Na biblioteca infantil," *Revista do ensino,* Belo Horizonte, Ano 12, Nos. 146–147, Jan.–Feb. 1938, pp. 18–23. DPU.

A description of the activities in a particular school library, including a reading club which the author had directed.

247. Tavares, Denise Fernandes. *Sugestões para organização duma pequena biblioteca infantil.* 2nd ed., rev. and enlarged. Bahia, Biblioteca Infantil Monteiro Lobato, 1960. 146p. DLC, IYL.

The differences between public and school libraries for children, their objectives, organization, technical services, programs, and book selection policies. This is written from the point of view of the author's experience as head of the children's library in Bahia. A short bibliography is included.

248. Veras, Zelia Ladeira and others. "Introdução a um estudo da literatura infantil," *Revista de pedagogia,* São Paulo, Vol. 3, No. 6, July–Dec. 1957, pp. 77–86. DPU.

An introduction to the general history of children's literature and its criticism.

249. Villela, Ruth. "A hora de conto na biblioteca infantil," *Formação,* Rio, Ano 11, No. 12, Aug. 1948, pp. 23–27. DPU.

250. ———. "O serviço de empréstimo na Secção Juvenil da Biblioteca Central de Educação," *Revista de educacão pública,* Rio, Vol. 1, No. 4, Oct.–Dec. 1943, pp. 512–520. DLC, DPU.

While on a grant from the Institute of International Education, the author helped in the establishment of a circulating library for children in the central library of education.

251. Vissoky, Paulina. "As dimensões da fantasia, do sonho e do maravilhoso na literatura," *Revista do ensino,* Rio Grande do Sul, Ano 12, No. 95, Aug. 1963, pp. 33–38, 45. DLC.

This entire issue is devoted to a discussion of Brazilian folklore and its use with children. This particular article discusses the language children prefer in the folk tale or legend, and the care that must be taken in adapting.

Bolivia

252. Caballero, Geraldine Byrne de. "El cuento en la educación," *Revista de la biblioteca y archivo nacionales,* Sucre, Nos. 16–23, Aug. 1941, pp. 76–90. DLC.

Beginning with the origins of the folk tale, the author then goes on to describe the qualities which children look for in it, and how best to tell such tales to children. She deplores the poor quality of Bolivian tales presently in existence, and feels it is due partly to indifference on the part of parents who no longer do storytelling.

253. Gehain, Adhemar. "Reforma de las bibliotecas escolares y publicas," *Educación nueva,* La Paz, Año 2, Nos. 14–15, June–July, 1929, pp. 465–469; Nos. 17–18, Sept.–Oct. 1929, pp. 521–522. DPU.

254. Quezada, A. Humberto. "Didáctica del cuento," *Nuevos rumbos,* Sucre, Dec. 1943, pp. 83 ff.

255. Quiroz, Roberto. "Bibliotecas escolares," *Educación boliviana,* La Paz, Vol. 6, No. 2, 1958, pp. 48–53. DLC.

Chile

The number of writers of children's literature in Chile is considerably fewer than in Argentina, Colombia, Mexico, Uruguay and possibly even some of the other Spanish-speaking republics. Yet these statistics have only relative meaning, when confronted with the work of one poet—Gabriela Mistral. In her, Chile can lay claim to a unique voice: that of the true children's poet who writes with simplicity and is yet profound and universal in appeal. Individual critics might extol the native author particularly beloved in their country, but will point out her work as best exemplifying the qualities which good children's literature should have (85, 96). Gaston Figueira finds her work similar to the English traditional poetry for children and compares her to Robert Louis Stevenson; but he points out that she is not imitative, for she did not know the English works before writing her own.

Marta Brunet, perhaps the second most widely read native author for children, wrote fantasy and tales in the folk tradition. Both she and Gabriela Mistral defended the right of children to an imaginative and lively literature, available in libraries designed to stimulate their desire to explore the world of books (257, 148). It is disheartening to note that apparently they were the only strong voices expressing these opinions in Chile. Interest in the publishing of good children's books and the development of children's libraries seems less organized and less vocal here than in the neighboring republics. There has been a children's room in the national library for some time (264) but a 1955 visitor there reported it understaffed and lacking a good book collection (82). In a more recent survey, no Chilean library was signalled out as giving model service to children (77).

256. Barros, Berta Falconi de. "Importancia de las bibliotecas en la escuela secundaria," *Revista de educación*, Santiago, Año 7, No. 46, Nov. 1947, pp. 325–328. DLC.

In urging strong support for school libraries, the author compares those of Chile to the U.S.; she suggests standards which are similar to those of ALA.

257. Brunet, Marta. "El mundo màgico del niño," *Atenea*, Concepción, Tomo 131, Año 35, Nos. 380–381, 1958, pp. 265–276. DLC.

A well-known writer for children discusses the world of the child in relation to his reading. She defends the extremes of good and evil in the fairy tale. She contends that the works of Disney, although appealing outwardly to children, stifle the imagination of the child by their very perfection of plasticity and exaggerated style.

258. "Chilean commission for school libraries," *UNESCO bulletin for libraries*, Paris, Vol. 17, No. 5, Sept.–Oct. 1963, p. 301. DLC, NNY.

The announcement of the founding of a school library commission which will be responsible for the creation of all new libraries, as well as for the guidance of the existing ones.

259. Cuitiño C., Carlos and Inés Zabaleta G. "Motivación bibliotecaria y encuesta sobre literatura infantil en las escuelas primarias No. 17 y No. 56, de Santiago. (Primera communicación)," *Boletín bibliotecario*, Santiago, Vol. 2, Nos. 1–4, Dec. 1954, pp. 12–17.

260. Federación Asociaciones Padres de Familia. *Lista de libros clasificados por edades para niños*. Santiago, The Federation, n.d. 27p. (Typewritten manuscript). DPU.

261. Moreno Lagos, Aida. "Función cultural de las bibliotecas escolares," *Revista de educación*, Santiago, Año 1, No. 8, July, 1929, pp. 537–542.

262. Obregón de Pacheco, Clara. "Organización de la biblioteca en la escuela primaria," *Boletín bibliotecario*, Santiago, Vol. 2, Nos. 1–4, Dec. 1954, pp. 10–12.

263. Plath, Oreste. *Folklore chileno; aspectos populares infantiles*. Santiago, Universidad de Chile, 1946. 119p. NNY.

A study of folklore created orally by Chilean children, in their rhymes, songs, tales, counting games, etc. Many examples are given in the text.

264. Rivas, Margarita Miéres de. *Labor cultural de la biblioteca infantil de Chile*. Washington, U.S. Government Printing Office, 1935. 9p. (Unión Panamericana, Serie sobre Educación, No. 98). DLC, DPU.

A history of the children's section of the national library, in Chile, which dates to 1925. The author describes its activities at that time, the extent of the collection, and circulation statistics.

Colombia

Colombia is one of the few countries in Latin America which can boast of a full-length critical study of its literature for children (270). Olga Castilla Barrios' survey was certainly made easier because of the limited number of native works, a fact which she herself admits. It is a critical study based on sound literary values and extensive reading of both children's books and the secondary literature about them. Although she includes the work of more than 50 writers, in her final conclusions she states that, on the whole, their country has produced books which are poor in quality and few in quantity.

The first significant Latin American poetry for children was written by the Colombian, Rafael Pombo, who was directly inspired by the Mother Goose rhymes he had heard while living in England. These are not real translations but rather "rewritings" in Spanish. The central characters take on an entirely Latin American look; Old Mother Hubbard has a cat instead of a dog, and when Frog goes courting he wears a necktie in the latest Latin American style and a beribboned sombrero (85, 270).

As in Chile, the leading 20th-century Colombian author for children was also a pungent critic. Oswaldo Díaz Díaz defined children's literature in a very personal style (271) and was aware that all too often the person writing for children had no respect or feeling for their tastes.

Library work with children has been stimulated both by governmental and private agencies. The Pilot Library of Medellín, with its separate children's room and bookmobile, serves that community and the surrounding territory. An even more impressive children's room is to be found in the Luis Angel Arango Library, maintained for the public by the Banco de la República in Bogotá. This bank also maintains smaller collections in the outlying districts (78). The school library situation has also received attention. With the aid of UNESCO, the Ministry of Education planned a seminar which was to help Colombia determine the ways and means to better national support for libraries in all schools (276).

265. Arroyave, Julio César. "Biblioteca Pública Piloto de Medellín. Los servicios de la biblioteca a los niños," *Boletín de la Asociación Costarricense de Bibliotecarios,* San José, Costa Rica, Año 1, No. 4, May 1956, pp. 18–22. DPU.
This treats of the special services which the Pilot Library gives to the children of Medellín and other parts of Colombia.

266. ". . . Bibliotecas escolares," *Boletín de la Asociación Colombiana de Bibliotecarios,* Bogotá, Vol. 8, Nos. 1–2, Jan.–June 1964. pp. 27–33. DPU.

Four brief articles on aspects of the school library and its work.

267. Bohórquez Casallas, Luis Antonio. *Bibliografía infantil selectiva; lista provisional . . .* Bogotá, Ministerio de Educación Nacional, Sección de Servicios Bibliotecarios, 1962.

268. Botero Restrepo, Camila. *Catálogo de libros para una biblioteca escolar.* Medellín, Escuela Interamericana de Bibliotecología, 1962. 264p. (Thesis, typewritten copy). DPU.

An annotated list, in Dewey order, of suggested books for the high school library.

269. Caballero Calderon, Eduardo. "Ausencia de literatura infantil," *El tiempo,* Bogotá, Aug. 16, 1953. DLC.
      A short article in the Sunday supplement which bemoans the lack of good children's books in Colombia.

270. Castilla Barrios, Olga. *Breve bosquejo de la literatura infantil colombiana.* Bogotá, Aedita, 1954. 371p. (Thesis for Pontificia Universidad Católica Javeriana). DLC, DPU.
      A history and criticism of Colombian children's literature. In defining it the author states that it is that which has a content and form in accord with the psychology of the child. Limpidity of spirit is its greatest characteristic. The discussion covers 56 native authors and treats of five forms of children's literature: tales, fables, fantasy, history, drama and poetry. Examples from the major writers are included. The treatment of Rafael Pombo and Oswaldo Díaz Díaz is most extensive, since these authors are considered most important. Brief biographical sketches of all authors are given. The author's conclusions are that in spite of this number of native writers, there is really very little of originality and special interest, strong enough to combat the lack of taste in popular reading. She felt that the best work had been done in the genre of poetry.

271. Díaz Díaz, Oswaldo. "Aspectos de la literatura infantil," *Revista de las Indias,* Bogotá, Epoca 2, No. 26, Feb. 1941, pp. 427–433. DLC, DPU. Also in: *Revista Cervantes,* Bogotá, Aug. 1941.
      Children's literature "begins with the lullaby and reaches its conclusion with the end of innocence." Thus begins the personal definition of a man who himself wrote for children. Following a description of some of the qualities which make it good, is an impassioned plea to Colombian and other writers in the Americas to use the same care in writing for children as they would for adults.

272. Jaramillo Arango, Rafael. *Los maestros de la literatura infantil.* 2nd ed. Bogotá, 1958.

273. Linares, Emma. *La biblioteca como auxiliar de la educación.* Bogotá, Ministerio de Educación Nacional, Sección de Servicios Bibliotecarios, 1962.
      For note see entry 91.

274. ———. "Bibliotecas escolares," *Boletín de la Asociación Colombiana de Bibliotecarios,* Bogotá, Vol. 4, No. 1, Jan.–Feb. 1960, pp. 9–11. DPU, NNY.
      A chapter from her book published by the Pan American Union, entry 91.

275. Morales Pradilla, Prospero. "Sin literatura infantil," *El tiempo,* Bogotá, Mar. 29, 1953. DLC.
      In this article, on the third page of the Sunday literary supplement, the author deplores the status of children's books and states that nothing is as depressing as reading at length those books which are given to children as "literature."

276. Pardo V., Aristóbulo, comp. *Seminario sobre planeamiento de un servicio nacional de bibliotecas escolares.* Informe final. La Habana, Centro Regional de la UNESCO, 1962. 150p. DLC.
      The final report of a seminar on school libraries which took place in Bogotá, Nov. 9–11, 1961. It was sponsored by the Colombian Ministry of Education and organized by the national commissions of UNESCO from Colombia and Ecuador. The conclusions drawn are based largely on the school library situation in Colombia. A good bibliography is included.

277. Perez Zapata, A. "Bibliotecas escolares," *Boletín de la Asociación de Bibliotecarios de Antioquia,* Medellín, Vol. 2, No. 4, Mar. 1956, pp. 10–13.

278. Rodríguez, José María. "La biblioteca escolar," *Revista de educación,* Medellín, 2 epoca, No. 3, Jan. 1944, pp. 41–44. DPU.
      In pointing out the importance of the library as the heart of the school, this author quotes the educator Vasconcelos of Mexico.

279. Rodríguez de Rodríguez, Nelly. "Función de la biblioteca escolar," *Boletín de la Asociación Colombiana de Bibliotecarios,* Bogotá, Año 8, No. 4, Oct.–Dec. 1964, pp. 19–21. DPU.
      The author lists the functions of the school library, and briefly analyzes their importance.

280. Serer, Vicente. "El problema de las lecturas para la niñez," *Alborada,* Medellín, Aug.–Sept. 1955, pp. 228 ff.

281. Téllez, Hernando. "Libros para niños," *Revista de las Indias,* Bogotá, Epoca 2, Tomo 17, Nos. 50–51, Mar.–Apr. 1943, pp. 5–10.
      In discussing what distinguishes children's literature from adult, the author cites qualities of Jiménez and Kipling which appeal to children, even though much of the work of these two authors is adult in humor.

Costa Rica

One of the smaller Latin American republics, Costa Rica has not let its size deter it from self-development in the production of children's books, however small the scale. An entire issue of *Educación,* edited by Luis Ferrero Acosta, suffices to cite examples from the small body of literature which has developed in the past 80 years. This is an admirable survey, indicating a genuine interest in a good "national" literature, as well as the better works of other countries (287).

The Costa Rican Association of Librarians has also given ample space in its bulletin to discussions of the problems and joys of library work with children. Its first conference produced two useful aids in setting up a children's library and its collection (289).

282.   Alvarez, Miriam. "Una biblioteca escolar," *Boletín de la Asociación Costarricense de Bibliotecarios,* San José, Año 1, Nos. 2–3, Dec. 1955, pp. 18–20. DPU.

A description of the organization, functions and activities of a particular school library, opened in 1949.

283.   Asociación Costarricense de Bibliotecarios. *Plan orgánico para un servicio nacional de bibliotecas escolares.* San José, Universidad de Costa Rica, 1956. Unp. (Trabajo de base para el tema 1). (Departamento de Publicaciones, 1236). DLC.

Part of a plan presented at a UNESCO conference in Lima, concerning national service to school libraries. Presented in outline form, and including a bibliography.

284.   Bonilla, Abelardo. "Teatro y poesía infantiles," *Historia y antología de la literatura costarricense.* San José, Trejos Hermanos, 1957. (Editorial Universitaria, Sección de Literatura y Artes, No. 3). Tomo 1, pp. 249–254. DPU. A shorter version in: *Educación,* San José, Año 4, No. 6, Jan.–Feb., 1958, pp. 3–7. DPU.

A critical study of the poetry and drama written for children by Costa Rican authors. The author cites as the most important contribution to this literature the works of Carlos Luis Sáenz, poet.

285.   Buenaventura, Emma. "Bibliografía de literatura infantil: Trabajo de base," *Informe: primeras jornadas bibliotecológicas costarricenses, 14–16 June, 1956.* San José, Asociación Costarricense de Bibliotecarios, 1956. pp. 25–72.

For note see entry 71.

286.   Douglas, Mary Teresa Peocock. "Los objectivos y el programa de la biblioteca escolar." *Boletín de la Asociación Costarricense de Bibliotecarios,* Tomo 2, No. 17, Mar. 1965, pp. 13–21. DPU.

A chapter from the work noted in entry 81.

287.   Ferrero Acosta, Luis. "Literatura infantil costarricense." Entire issue of: *Educación,* San José, Año 4, No. 8, May–June 1958, pp. 2–84. DPU.

The introduction to this survey of Costa Rican children's literature was written by Carlos Luis Sáenz, a well-known poet who himself wrote for children. He evaluates the works of four writers, José María Alfaro Cooper, Anastasio Alfaro González, Carlos Gagini, and Aquileo J. Echeverría. He claims that in the 80 years during which children's books have appeared in Costa Rica, there have been only 16 native writers, and most of these were in the genre of poetry. The only good exception was the collection of tales written by Carmen Lira, *Cuentos de mi Tía Panchita.* Miss Lira is also remembered for the fine children's magazine which she edited, *San Selerín.* A list of 11 titles by Costa Rican authors is recommended to parents to buy for their children. Also included is a bibliography of Costa Rican children's literature, listed by type and then by author, with complete information as to editions including those translated into other languages. In all, there are some 67 titles. Following this is a list of works from other countries, published in Costa Rica. Short samples and extracts from the works of major Costa Rican writers for children are contained in the concluding portion of the study.

288.   Fraccaroli, Lenyra C. *A biblioteca infantil: Organização e funcionamento; sua influência na sociedade.* San José, Universidad de Costa Rica, 1956, 18p. (Asociación Costarricense de Bibliotecarios. Trabajo de Base Para el Tema 1). DPU.

A well-known children's librarian from Brazil writes an outline on the organization, functions and social meaning of the children's library, to be used by Costa Rican librarians in their professional study and preparation. This was part of the plan presented at the UNESCO conference in Lima, April–May, 1956.

289.   Jornadas Bibliotecológicas Costarricenses, 1st, San José, 1956. *Trabajos de base.* San José, Universidad de Costa Rica, 1956. 151p. (Departamento de Publicaciones, 1213). DPU.

Contains the working papers for the 1st Costa Rican library convention. For Tema 1: "Organización de la biblioteca infantil en Cuba" by Caridad Fernández Goicochea and "La biblioteca escolar en Costa Rica" by Miriam Alvarez Brenes. (Also, a list by E. Buenaventura, noted in 71). For Tema 2: "La clasificación y catalogación en los bibliotecas infantiles y escolares," two articles of same name by Fermín Peraza and Nelly Kopper Dodero. For Tema 3: "Preparación del maestro bibliotecario," two articles of same name by Julián Marchena and Miriam Alvarez Brenes. For Tema 4: "Servicios bibliotecarios para niños" by Ana María Paz, and the article by J. C. Arroyave annotated in entry 265.

290.   Lombroso, Paula. ¿Por qué gustan los cuentos a los niños?, *Boletín de educación pública,* San José, Vol. 1, No. 4, Sept. 15, 1912, pp. 53–61. DLC.

For note see entry 456.

291.   Maurois, André. "Como escoger las lecturas para los niños." *Boletín de la Asociación Costarricense de Bibliotecarios,* San José, Año 1, No. 4, May, 1956, pp. 22–25. DPU.

This is a strong plea to parents, teachers, librarians to give only the best books to children. Maurois lists the first five types which are important: 1) the classics, because even though they might be too difficult to read by today's children, they can stimulate precisely because of their difficulty and mystery; 2) the great myths; 3) the folk and fairy tales; 4) the better novels; 5) biographies of great men and women.

292.   Urioste, Antero. *Algunos libros que pueden servir para establecer una biblioteca infantil.* San José, Imprenta Maria vda. de Lines, 1924. 46p. DPU.

For note see entry 467.

Cuba

"Children should be given nothing less than the truth and no person should tell them that which he does not know to be true; for children believe implicitly what their teachers and their books say, and they work and think on the assumption it is all true, to the extent that if they discover a falsehood, there enters into their life an equivocal feeling, confronting them with a way of thinking which cannot please them; neither are they able to distinguish truth with certainty any longer, nor can they become again the young child trying to learn everything anew."

José Martí, *La Edad de Oro,* Oct. 1889.

Thus did Martí explain his goal for an ideal literary magazine for children, and at the same time he was inadvertantly explaining the reason for its imminent demise: such an idealistic, honest venture was sure to have difficulty finding financial sponsors. *La Edad de Oro* was published in New York, while Martí lived there in exile. Each of its four issues was the size of a book, and they were without question one of the high points in Spanish American children's literature. Herminio Almendros' book (294) is not so much a critical study as a tribute to Martí, an assessment of his influence. It is also a provocative questioning of the basic values of all children's literature.

During his lifetime Martí's resolve did not bring about a noticeable raising of quality or increase of interest in children's literature in his native country. Even later there is no evidence that it encouraged

Cuban authors in significant numbers to turn to such writing. What is more likely is that it did inspire those working with children, particularly in libraries, for Cuba moved ahead in this field more swiftly than many of her sister republics. By the 1950's there were any number of professionally trained and well-informed children's librarians, writing of all aspects of their work. Miss Daniels' survey indicated that "children's library services in municipal public libraries as well as excellent school libraries were prevalent in pre-Castro Cuba" and the statistics quoted in the tables bore this out (78). Unfortunately, little is available in print about the continuation of this work after 1960. The regional center for UNESCO, and the pilot primary school library, established in Havana in 1958 with UNESCO assistance, occasionally issue reports. The most recent one found (84) indicated that the children's department of the national library continued to give courses in children's literature and storytelling.

293. Aguayo, Jorge. "Algunas consideraciones sobre las bibliotecas y la educación," *Revista lyceum,* La Habana, Vol. 8, No. 31, Aug. 1952, pp. 9–17. DLC, DPU.

De Amicis wrote: "The destiny of man can depend on whether he has had books available in his childhood, and which ones." This quote serves as a springboard for the author to launch into a discussion of the importance of books and libraries for children.

294. Almendros, Herminio. *A propósito de "La Edad de Oro" de José Martí; notas sobre literatura infantil.* Santiago de Cuba, Universidad de Oriente, Departamento de Extensión y Relaciones Culturales, 1956. 268p. DLC, DPU.

José Martí founded and edited a magazine for Latin American children, *La Edad de Oro,* which, in spite of its short span of existence (4 issues), exercised a vast influence on educators and writers in much of Latin America. This is a well-documented study of the ideals of Martí, the substance of his writing, and that of the few other authors who wrote for his magazine. A sampling of stories and articles is given. Much of what the author has to say applies to children's literature in general.

295. ———. "La imaginación infantil y las lecturas para niños." *Casa de las Américas,* La Habana, Año 3, Nos. 20–21, Sept.–Dec. 1963, pp. 38–49. DPU.

Almendros defines imagination in children as those images which the child, with his limited experience, constructs when learning a new idea from some plane of the adult world. Therefore, he continues, most children will reach out for that literature with dwarfs, princesses, fairies, and other "unreal" crea- tures because he wants to find out more in order to create a more distinct image that is "real." While agreeing that fantasy is important, he feels it should match the epoch, and he agrees with Martí in that nothing written for children should be false, or create a false impression.

296. Alonso Sánchez, Andrés. "Las bibliotecas infantiles y la escuela nueva," *Revista bibliotecaria cubana,* La Habana, Año 1, Nos. 4–5–6, July, 1936–Dec. 1937, pp. 295–299. DLC.

A brief essay on the necessity of children's libraries, conditions ideal for their establishment in schools, and a short list of recommended titles to put in any children's room.

297. Becerra, Berta. "La biblioteca y la escuela," *Boletín de la Asociación Cubana de Bibliotecarios,* La Habana, Vol. 7, No. 3, Sept. 1955, pp. 85–90. DLC.

In illustrating the importance of school libraries, the author cites examples of U.S., Russian and German libraries. She mentions specifically the publications of the ALA which are so helpful in planning and operating the school library.

298. "La biblioteca en la escuela," *Boletín bibliotécnico,* La Habana, Vol. 1, No. 3, May, 1938, pp. 1–2. DLC.

The author stresses the importance of the library in the school, and describes some of the varied services it can offer.

299. Borrero Pierra, Dolores. "La lectura como medio esencial de cultura." Congreso Panamericano del Niño, 5th, La Habana, 1927. *Actos y trabajos,*

La Habana, Montalvo y Cardenas, 1928. Vol. 3, pp. 329 ff. DPU.

300. Buenaventura, Emma. "La bibliotecaria juvenil," *Boletín de la Asociación Cubana de Bibliotecarios,* La Habana, Vol. 7, No. 3, Sept. 1955, pp. 96–98. DLC.

The qualifications and study required to make a good children's librarian.

301. Cartaya, Berta and M. T. Freyre de Andrade. *Dos ensayos sobre bibliotecas escolares.* La Habana, Asociación Bibliotecaria Cubana, 1941. 20p. DLC, DPU.

Two essays on the school library. The Cartaya essay appears also in 444. In writing of the importance of the library in the primary school, she lists seven objectives which any such library should aim for. She also discusses the selection of reading materials for children. In her essay, Miss Freyre de Andrade suggests that the two most important objectives among the seven given by Cartaya are the emphasis of love of books and reading and the teaching of the use of books and libraries. She contends that the quality of education in the school is in direct proportion to the activities of the library, and she examines the shortcomings of the Cuban school system in meeting that criteria.

302. Chacon Nardi, Rafaela. "Bibliotecas para los miembros jovenes de la communidad," *Boletín de la Comisión Cubana de la UNESCO,* La Habana, Año 7, No. 4, April 1958, pp. 4–7. DPU.

A history and description of the children's library maintained by the Lyceum Club for the community. At that time it had a collection of 5,000 volumes, and had been functioning for 14 years.

303. Fernández Goicochea, Caridad. "La educación en el desarollo de las bibliotecas escolares y juveniles," *Boletín de la Asociación Cubana de Bibliotecarios,* La Habana, Vol. 7, No. 1, Mar. 1955, pp. 12–15. DLC, DPU.

The author contends that Cuban children have too few books available to them in school and public libraries and she includes statistics to prove her point.

304. ———. "El laminario en las bibliotecas infantiles, juveniles y escolares," *Boletín de la Asociación Cubana de Bibliotecarios,* La Habana, Vol. 8, No. 3, Sept. 1956, pp. 96–105. DLC, DPU.

This work stresses the importance of a picture collection in a children's library, as well as some practical advice on setting it up.

305. Francovich, Guillermo. "La Biblioteca Escolar Primaria Piloto de La Habana," *Boletín de la Comisión Cubana de la UNESCO,* La Habana, Año 7, No. 4, April, 1958, pp. 1–3. DPU.

The speech made by the director of the Regional Center for UNESCO, on the occasion of the opening of a model school library, which was to serve not only Cuba, but all of Latin America, as a training center for school librarians.

306. Freyre de Andrade, Maria Teresa. "El arte de contar cuentos," *Revista lyceum,* La Habana, Vol. 8, No. 31, Aug. 1952, pp. 18–26. DPU.

The author feels that there is a renaissance in the art of storytelling, particularly in the U.S., where, she points out, Marie Shedlock and Ruth Sawyer have done much to further this work. She regrets that they are not able to pursue such an activity in the Lyceum Library.

307. Godinez, Ada. *El arte de contar cuentos.* Habana, Carasa.

308. Gómez Vilá, María de los Angeles. "Ensayo sobre el desarollo de la literatura infantil universal," *Boletín de la Asociación Cubana de Bibliotecarios,* La Habana, Vol. 7, No. 4, Dec. 1955, pp. 136–140. DLC.

An extremely brief history of the major works of children's literature which have proven universal.

309. "Inauguración de la Biblioteca Juvenil de la Sociedad Económica de Amigos del País," *Boletín de la Asociación Cubana de Bibliotecarios,* La Habana, Vol. 3, No. 1, Mar. 1951, pp. 26–27. DLC.

A description of the opening of a children's library on a site provided by a private society.

310. Jornadas Bibliotecológicas Cubanas, 2nd. *Informe final; Recomendaciones y trabajos.* La Habana, Comisión Nacional Cubana de la UNESCO, 1954. pp. 1–41. DPU.

The working papers for the first theme of the conference were on the library in the primary school. They included: "Función de la biblioteca . . ." by Olinta Ariosa; "Organización y administración de la biblioteca . . ." by Guillermina de Galisteo; "Equipo y materiales de la biblioteca . . ." by Olga V. Capestany; "Servicio y actividades de la biblioteca . . ." by Audry Mancebo.

311. Jornadas Bibliotecológicas Cubanas, 3rd. *Informe final. Recomendaciones y trabajos.* Santiago, Universidad de Oriente, 1956. (Mimeographed). DPU.

As two of its major themes, the 3rd Cuban national library conference discussed a plan for national service to school libraries, and the training of the teacher-librarian. The working papers were: "Plan orgánico para un servicio nacional de bibliotecas escolares," 13p.; and "La preparación del maestro bibliotecario" by Mercedes Meneses Rodríguez, 12p.

312. Mancebo Melendez, Audry. "El trabajo de referencia en la biblioteca juvenil: su importancia," *Cuba bibliotecológica*, La Habana, Vol. 5, Nos. 1–2, Jan.–June, 1960, pp. 103–105. DPU, NNY.

How to approach reference work with children; their different ways of asking for help; the necessity of making certain that they have understood the answers to their questions.

313. Meneses Rodríguez, Mercedes. "Bibliotecas escolares en Cuba," *Boletín de la Asociación Cubana de Bibliotecarios*, La Habana, Vol. 1, No. 2, Sept. 1949, pp. 52–54. DLC.

The importance of the school library, and a survey of those Cuban schools which have one.

314. ———. *El laminario en las bibliotecas juveniles*. La Habana, Biblioteca Nacional José Martí, 1960. 146p. (Colección Manuales Técnicos, No. 1). DLC, DPU.

The organization of a picture collection in the children's library, its uses, and a suggested list of subject headings. An annotated bibliography of books and articles on the subject is included.

315. ———. "Los servicios de bibliotecas en las escuelas," *Boletín de la Asociación Cubana de Bibliotecarios*, La Habana, Vol. 3, No. 3, Sept., 1951, pp. 110–116. DLC.

The author, who was a professor working with children and young adults in the Cuban library school, outlines here the minimum preparation needed for children's librarianship, and the standards of school libraries. The plan was for presentation to UNESCO, at its São Paulo Conference (see 64).

316. Morales, Olinta Ariosa. "Peripecias en la organización de una biblioteca escolar," *Cuba bibliotecológica*, La Habana, Vol. 2, No. 1, Jan.–Mar. 1954, pp. 5–8. DLC.

The setting up of a school library of some 400 volumes as described by its librarian.

317. Rio, Narciso del. "Creación por el estado de bibliotecas infantiles." Congreso Panamericano del Niño, 5th, La Habana, 1927. *Actas y trabajos*, La Habana, Montalvo y Cardenas, 1928. Vol. 3, pp. 49–53. DPU.

A recommendation that each state take on the responsibility of organizing children's libraries, for they are as important to the child as the many other considerations of the congress, i.e., health and welfare.

318. Robés Masses, Raquel. "'Album de los niños,' el primer periódico de los niños cubanos," *Boletín de la Asociación Cubana de Bibliotecarios*, La Habana, Vol. 1, No. 1, Mar., 1949, pp. 5–7. DLC.

After an introductory statement about children's magazines in Cuba, the author begins an individual study of each of the major ones. This series is continued in subsequent issues of the *Boletín*.

319. ———. "La biblioteca en las escuelas de formación del magisterio y su influencia en el desarollo de las bibliotecas escolares," *Cuba bibliotecológica*, La Habana, Vol. 5, Nos. 1–2, Jan.–June, 1960, pp. 109–113. DLC, NNY.

The importance of having a good children's library in teacher-training schools, and to give courses to all teachers in the literature available for children.

320. ———. "Bibliotecas juveniles," *Revista lyceum*, La Habana, Vol. 8, No. 31, Aug. 1952, pp. 27–38. DLC.

The children's librarian of the Lyceum Club writes in glowing terms of the satisfaction and delight she has had in her work. She describes the activities of her library and gives a little of its history. Then she continues by giving the history of other children's libraries in Cuba and expresses the hope that soon every public library will have its children's room. She also discusses some favorite Cuban children's books of that time.

321. ———. "Los intereses de lectura en la selección de libros para niños y adolescentes," *Cuba bibliotecológica*, La Habana, Vol. 1, No. 3, July–Sept., 1956, pp. 5–11. DLC.

The principles of juvenile book selection, aimed at satisfying the interests of all kinds of children.

322. Robles, Antonio. *El maestro y el cuento infantil*. La Habana, Culturel S. A.

323. Roldán, María Antonia. "Las formas de literatura infantil," *Boletín de la Asociación Cubana de Bibliotecarios*, La Habana, Vol. 10, No. 2, June, 1958, pp. 49–54. DLC.

A definition of the various forms of children's literature: legends, tales, fables, fiction, songs, rhymes chants, heroic and lyric poetry. Examples of each form are given.

324. Sánchez Arrieta, María Teresa. "El Club de Lectura: que es y como se organiza," *Boletín de la*

Asociación Cubana de Bibliotecarios, La Habana, Vol. 10, No. 2, June, 1958, pp. 55–58. DLC.

Suggestions for organizing reading clubs for children.

325. "La semana de la lectura: lea más y mejor,"

Boletín de la Asociación Cubana de Bibliotecarios, La Habana, Vol. 10, No. 2, June, 1958, pp. 61–66. DLC.

To encourage more and better reading by children, this book week article gives a selection of the better books available, divided by subject.

Dominican Republic

326. Monsanto, Luis Humberto. *El cuento y su valor educativo.* Ciudad Trujillo, Servicio Cooperativo Interamericano de Educación, April, 1958. 10p. (Mimeographed). DPU.

327. Muñoz García, José Rafael. "Apuntes sobre las actividades de la biblioteca escolar," *Boletín del Instituto de Investigaciones Psicopedagógicas,* Ciudad

Trujillo, Año 2, No. 5, Jan.–Mar., 1951, pp. 21–28. DPU.

328. Sosa, Jesualdo. "¿Existe una literatura infantil propiamente dicha?," *Boletín del Instituto de Investigaciones Psicopedagógicas,* Ciudad Trujillo, Aug.–Sept., 1946, pp. 14–20. DLC.

The first chapter of 465.

Ecuador

The most eminent spokesman for children's literature in Ecuador is the educator Darío Guevara. In one of his first articles, he indicates his psychological orientation (337), and this is expanded even further in his later book (338). The schematic outline he has made of Ecuadorian folklore is particularly interesting for its section on the ways in which children parody and alter oral and written literature to suit their own needs, and the games and rhymes which often evolve from some story they have heard.

In 1938, the Ministry of Education made an effort to improve the status of library service to children. The result of their inquiry was evident in the spurt of articles which appeared at that time. From the general lack of recent articles, however, and the comments of the few who have written on the subject, one can only assume that not much progress has been made.

329. Andino Gallegos, Luis. "Apuntes de literatura infantil; la poesía al servicio de la educación," *Educación,* Quito, No. 118, Mar., 1943, pp. 105–110. DLC, DPU, NNY.

The importance of good poetry in the life of the child, especially in his literary education.

330. Barrera B., Jaime. "Libros para niños," *Nueva era,* Quito, Vol. 11, 1942, pp. 281–285. DLC.

Children's books should be, in a sense, more difficult than adult books, for children demand more because of their sensibilities.

331. ———. "¿Se comió el lobo a Caperucita?," *Nueva era,* Quito, Vol. 13, 1944, pp. 233–236. DLC.

Not a review, but comments on the themes of Antonio Robles' book (384) with which the author is usually in agreement.

332. "Bibliotecas escolares," *Educación,* Quito, Epoca 6, Año 14, No. 111, June, 1938, pp. 86–100. DLC.

A report on a questionnaire submitted to all schools by the Ministry of Education in order to determine the extent and quality of library service already existing, as well as means of developing more effective service.

333. Chaves, Fernando. "Libros y bibliotecas para niños," *Revista de la biblioteca municipal de quito,* Epoca 1, Tomo 1, No. 2, Mar., 1960, pp. 87–96. DLC, DPU.

A very general history of children's books and libraries, with no special emphasis on Ecuador.

334. Cornejo, Justino. "Bibliotecas infantiles," *Pedagogía y antipedagogía,* Quito, Talleres Gráficas del Ministerio de Educación, 1938, pp. 144–147. DLC.

A vigorous objection to the poor status of children's libraries in Ecuador, and to the fact that the National Library has no children's division.

335. Guevara, Dario C. "Biogenia de la literatura infantil," *Horizontes,* Quito, Epoca 3, No. 18, Dec., 1941, pp. 81–94. DLC.

An approach to children's literature from a "biogenetic" point of view, based on the law of Haeckel as applied to the intellectual growth of the child. The reasons for the child's early fascination with rhythm and poetic language are explained within this framework, as are fairy tales and stories.

336. ———. *Esquema didáctico del folklore equatoriano.* Quito, Editorial Ecuador, 1951. 80p. DLC, NNY.

A synopsis of the various types of folklore to be found in Ecuador. Especially interesting is the section devoted to folklore as children compose it or alter it, in the forms of tales, songs, chants, games, etc.

337. ———. "La fábula y la escuela," *Nueva era,* Quito, Epoca 2, Vol. 3, Nos. 10–11–12, 1938, pp. 64–93. DLC.

A critical study of the fables of Aesop and La Fontaine and their Spanish translators and adap-

tors, as well as original Spanish fables. The second part gives suggestions for using them with children.

338. ———. *Psicopatología y psicopedagogía del cuento infantil.* Quito, Casa de la Cultura Ecuatoriana, 1955. 200p. DLC.

In spite of the rather forbidding title, this is a very readable study of the fairy tale. Andersen, Grimm, Perrault, and the Arabian Nights are some of the authors covered. The point of view is definitely that of the psychologist, and the conclusion drawn is that we should not give up fairy tales, but rather use only those which have a minimum of violence.

339. Jacomé, G. Alfredo. "La literatura en la escuela primaria," *Revista ecuatoriana de educación,* Quito, Año 6, No. 20, Mar.–April, 1952, pp. 114–118. DLC.

Suggestions for using good literature with young children, and especially some Ecuadorian literature. The author mentions a good radio program for children using such literature.

340. Moreno Mora, Vicente. *Literatura infantil.* Cuenca, 1946.

341. Terán, Enrique. "La biblioteca escolar," *Nueva era,* Quito, Epoca 2, Vol. 3, Nos. 10–11–12, 1938, pp. 163–167. DLC.

The director of the national library writes of the efforts of teachers to introduce libraries into the schools of Ecuador.

342. Uzcategui, Emilio. *Compulsory education in Ecuador.* Paris, UNESCO, 1951, 60p. (Compulsory Education Studies, 7). DLC, NNY.

One of a series which documents the history of education in many countries and areas of the world. These are valuable as background studies, since they contain information not easily found in the usual histories of education. Frequently, mention is made of the availability (or lack of it) of children's reading materials.

Guatemala

One of the most unfortunate aspects of Guatemalan children's literature is that it has always lacked good, contemporary versions of its greatest treasure; the *Popol-Vuh,* or "Book of Counsel," of the Maya-Quiché Indians. This complaint is common to most of the books and articles listed below, and yet, as far as can be determined from the current *Libros en Venta,* there is still no edition designed for children. In his book (348), Villagran Paúl is especially cognizant of the regrettable result this situation has on children in Guatemala, for he feels that the native legends, as they are presented, fall short of the narrative and literary heights they could well attain.

Standards for library service to children are set by the National Library, which not only maintains a children's section, but is responsible for the creation and management of public school library collections throughout the country. A brief but impressive description of this work can be found in Marietta Daniels' *Public and School Libraries in Latin America* (78).

343. Barrientos, Alfonso Enrique. "La poesía y los niños," *Revista del maestro*, Guatemala, Año 2, No. 6, July–Aug.–Sept., 1947, pp. 13–16. DLC.

This work discusses the importance of using poetry with children, and some poets whose work is particularly liked by young children.

344. González Ramírez, Mario Gilberto. *Manual para la organización de bibliotecas escolares.* Guatemala, Editorial del Ministerio de Educación Pública "José de Pineda Ibarra," 1960. 168p. DLC.

After a brief history of books and printing in the Americas, and particularly in Guatemala, the author describes library development up to then. The larger portion of the book is a manual of organization for the school library, with many charts, diagrams and photographs. A short bibliography is given.

345. ———. "Organización de bibliotecas escolares," *Revista del maestro*, Guatemala, Epoca 2, No. 1, July, 1956, pp. 18–28.

An earlier, shorter version of the preceding entry.

346. Ramírez, Angel. "Hacia la conquista del valor de la literatura infantil," *Revista del maestro*, Guatemala, Año 2, No. 4, Jan.–Feb.–Mar., 1947, pp. 15–17. DLC.

A statement of the reasons why it is necessary to struggle for good literature for children.

347. Ramírez Flores, Adrián. "Ensayo sobre literatura infantil," *Revista del maestro*, Guatemala, Año 7, No. 22, Mar.–Apr., 1952, pp. 56–64. DLC.

In defining children's literature, the author points out that one should not consider writing by children, or adult reminiscences about childhood, as being necessarily literature for children. He approves of that literature which satisfies the esthetic and moral needs of the child. The *Popol-Vuh*, or *Book of Counsel* from the Maya Quiché culture, is the richest inheritance any literature for children could have, yet he claims it is better known outside Guatemala than by their own children.

348. Villagrán Paúl, Rubén. *Literatura infantil; condiciones y posibilidades.* Guatemala, Popol-Vuh, 1954. 163p. DLC, DPU, NNY.

The author defines children's literature as that which "evokes emotional response in the child, which speaks to his sensibilities, and which makes his world come alive—a world that oscillates between the real and the fantastic." He speaks of how indifferent children can be to even the greatest writers, if they do not possess these qualities. He gives numerous examples of the child as artist and author, but questions the validity of this work as truly art, however fresh and interesting it might be. The last section discusses Guatemalan literature as a source for children's books. Although there is a rich tradition of folklore, particularly from the Maya Quiché, very little has been put into attractive and suitable form for present-day Guatemalan children.

Honduras

349. "La biblioteca en la escuela moderna," *Boletín de la Secretaría de Educación Pública.* Tegucigalpa, Año 1, No. 3, Jan.–Mar., 1950, pp. 27–32. DPU.

The library in the modern school.

350. Gómez, Beatriz Parra de. "La biblioteca infantil de San Luis Tlaxiatemalco," *Tegucigalpa,* Tegucigalpa, Año 34, May 28, 1950, pp. 11–12. DPU.

In the city once famous for the gardens of Xochimilco, a children's library was founded, with the help of the Benjamin Franklin Library in Mexico City. This is a description of how the books were acquired, and how the library was organized.

351.   Honduras. Ministerio de Instrucción Pública. *Programas para la enseñanza primaria y reglamento para las bibliotecas escolares.* Tegucigalpa, Tipografía Nacional, 1906. 115p. DLC, NNY.

It is heartening to see that in this early document on the importance of school libraries, the first objective is listed as being "to stimulate free, leisure reading," while the usual educational objectives are also not forgotten.

352.   Prieto Figueroa, Luis Beltrán. *La magia de los libros; obras estimulantes para la juventud.* Tegucigalpa, Publicaciones del Ministerio de Educación Pública, 1955. (Colección Ramón Rosa, 2).

For note see 480.

Mexico

Of all the Latin American countries Mexico has the most stimulating variety of critical studies on children's literature, although by no means the most numerous. The reasons for this are too complicated to discuss here. Suffice it to say that they hinge on such things as political movements, general ferment and experimenting in the arts, proximity to the United States, and early development as a printing center for Spanish America. However, it must be made immediately clear that the interest has not yet produced a native literature of equal variety and extent.

Many points of view are evident in the studies: Diaz Cardenas recommended a "revolutionary literature" in keeping with the political upheaval (361) ; Florentino Torner felt that literature should not be presented to children with any specific teaching or indoctrinating in mind (389) ; Antonio Robles, although generally sympathetic to the revolution, advocated a more humanistic attitude toward children's literature, and urged a re-examination of the classics (384) ; Blanca Lydia Trejo believed that broader definitions of children's literature were needed, to include the media of radio, film and theater (392) ; Juana Manrique de Lara, after many years of service as a librarian, summed up her faith in children's books by defining them as the opportunities to experience the ennobling, useful and pleasureable moments of one's life (377). The single writer of children's books among these five is Antonio Robles. Perhaps it is for this reason that he is also the most frequently quoted, even outside Mexico. His first books were published in Spain, before he fled for political reasons, and took exile and then citizenship in Mexico. "His special creation is the lighthearted modern fantasy: tales in which props from real life . . . are endowed with magical properties . . . told with vivid staccato details, overflowing wit and invention, and often much tenderness," writes Helen Rand Parish (98).

In addition to the five general works mentioned above, there are a number of good articles on storytelling and the folk tale which did not merely repeat the same platitudes, but offered fresh insight and values (357, 359, 360, 368). Not too many entries are concerned with library work with children, but those which are available tend to be written by persons of obvious experience.

In the development of libraries, the first name worthy of mention is that of José Vasconcelos, creator and first minister of the Secretaría de Educación Pública. In 1922, he instituted a department of libraries under the jurisdiction of the Secretaría, which functions to this day as the source of planning and maintaining public and school library service throughout the country. It was during Vasconcelos' term of service that Gabriela Mistral was asked to come to Mexico to serve as an advisor on various educational tasks. One of them was choosing books for the Secretaría to publish and distribute to the newly created schools and libraries. Since that time they have assumed most of the duties of textbook publication, as well as issuing general works. The volumes of the Biblioteca de Chapulín, appearing in the 1904's and written and illustrated by Mexican artists, are considered by many to be the finest single publishing effort for children in the Americas. There are now more than 150 "popular" libraries supported by the Secretaría throughout Mexico, but Miss Daniels mentions in her survey that most of the present efforts are directed to the improvement of the 50 which are in the Federal District, and these include public as well as school libraries, and libraries in the parks (98).

An important library which does not come under the same jurisdiction is the Biblioteca Benjamin Franklin, founded in 1942 by the American Library Association under a grant from the U.S. Office of Coordinator of Inter-American Affairs. Later this was converted into an information library under the USIS program. The children's room has been a flourishing section from the very beginning, under the guidance of a series of gifted and creative librarians (355).

353.   Agnew, E. and D. Weatherby. "What do children read in Mexico?" *Horn book*, Boston, Mass., Vol. 14, No. 1, Jan.–Feb., 1938, pp. 46–50. DLC, IYL, NNY.

In effect, the authors answered "nothing" to their query. There were so few books for them to read—those imported from Spain were too expensive and what was produced in Mexico was not worth the effort. Only textbooks were getting attention.

354.   Anttonen, Eva J. "Children and books—A happy fusion," *Wilson library bulletin,* New York, Vol. 23, No. 2, Oct., 1948, pp. 165–169. DLC, DPU, NNY.

The children's librarian of the Benjamin Franklin Library writes of her experiences there, particularly the storytelling and group activities.

355.   ———. "México," *Top of the news,* Chicago, Vol. 7, Oct., 1950, pp. 21–23. DLC.

In this special issue devoted to children's library work in many countries, this librarian presented a brief review of the work being done in Mexico, particularly in the Biblioteca Benjamin Franklin.

356.   "Bibliotecas infantiles y escolares," *Civitas,* Monterrey, Oct., 1948, pp. 2 ff.

357.   Cardona Peña, Alfredo. "El arte de contar un cuento infantil," *El libro y el pueblo,* Tomo 17, Nos. 16–17, Apr.–May, 1955, pp. 43–56. DLC, DPU.

A poet writes about storytelling: It is no more than the art of love and understanding, and cannot be learned. The storyteller should not become preoccupied with ethical or esthetic education, but should have only a soul disposed to fantasy and a spirit which can accept the mysterious as a natural ideal.

358.   Cerna, Manuel M. *La lectura selecta en la escuela.* Mexico City, Luis Fernández, 1955.

359.   Congreso Nacional de Bibliotecarios, 1st, México, D.F., 1927. *Memoria.* México, Talleres Gráficas de la Nación, 1928. (unp.). (Publicaciones de la Secretaría de Educación Pública, Tomo 17, No. 11.)

The papers presented at the first Mexican library conference. Those related to children's books and libraries are: "Importancia de las bibliotecas infantiles" by Elodía Tornel Olvera; "Bibliotecas infantiles" by Ana María Pastor; "Bibliotecas infantiles" by Amado B. de Lefranc; "El mejoramiento y conservación de las bibliotecas públicas y escolares de México" by Ana María Peña; "La hora del cuento en las bibliotecas infantiles" by Enrique Sarro.

360. "Convocatoria para la primera mesa redonda sobre periodismo para la niñez y la juventud," *Educación,* México, D.F., Vol. 2, No. 7, Feb., 1962, pp. 93–237. DPU.

A selection of papers on children's periodicals, comics, etc. which were presented at a conference on the subject. Most of them discuss and criticize at length the literature, or non-literature, these periodicals contain.

361. Díaz Cardenas, Leon. *Literatura revolucionaria para niños.* Primera parte. México, D.A.P.P., 1937. 137p. DLC, DU.

The six chapters cover the school library and its functions, folklore, biography, the story hour, the selection of folk tales and other materials for the story hour. In his criticism of children's literature, the author points out that he advocates "changing or altering such words and phrases as *alma reza* and *mal aguero* because they express religious connotations or social prejudices. The teacher cannot always explain them conveniently."

Each section contains examples of children's literature.

362. Douglas, Mary Teresa Peacock. *Manual del profesor-bibliotecario;* trans. by María T. Chávez, México, Reverté, 1960. 189p. DPU.

A translation of 3676.

363. Ferrer de Mendiolea, Gabriel. "Organización de la biblioteca escolar," *El libro y el pueblo,* México, Tomo 15, No. 2, Jan., 1951, pp. 1–13. DPU.

The organization of the school library, with special attention to the cataloging of its contents.

364. Flores, Dinorah. *Bibliotecas infantiles y escolares.* México, Impreso en maquinas reproductivas del B. de M. A. A., 1952. 111p.

365. Gardiner, Jewel. *Servicio bibliotecario en la escuela elemental.* México, Centro Regional de Ayuda Técnica (AID), 1963. 198p. DPU.

A translation of 3782.

366. Guardia, Angel. *Divagaciones sobre el cuento infantil.* Pátzcuaro, Centro Regional de Educación Fondamental para la América Latina, 1955. 61p. DPU.

The history and criticism of stories and story-telling for children. How to use folk tales in the story hour and how to tell a story are also discussed. Numerous examples are cited.

367. Ibarra, Alfredo. "El cuento en México," *Revista hispanica moderna,* New York/Buenos Aires, Año 8, Nos. 1–2, Jan.–Apr., 1942, pp. 109–114. DLC.

An article on the origins, forms, and characteristics of the folk tale in Mexico, both native and translated tales.

368. Leguizamón, María Luisa Cresta de. "De la literatura infantil," *Cuadernos americanos,* México, Año 13, Vol. 73, Jan.–Feb., 1954, pp. 120–131. DLC.

The difficulty of selecting good literature for children, and the necessity for every child to have a personal library, however small. The author recommends that one begin with the best classics, even though they might be difficult for the child to read by himself.

369. List Arzubide, Germán. *Apuntes sobre literatura infantil.* México, Ediapsa, 1940. 166p.

370. Magaña, Gloria Lara. *Periodismo infantil en México.* México, Universidad Nacional Autónoma, 1962. 88p. (Escuela Nacional de Ciencias Políticas y Sociales). DLC.

A history of children's magazines in Mexico, and an analysis of their contents with regard to literary value.

371. Manrique de Lara, Juana. "La biblioteca escolar y la biblioteca pública infantil," *Boletín bibliográfico mexicano,* México, Año 1, No. 4, Apr., 1940, pp. 5–7. DLC.

A portion of her work, *Elementos de Organización y Administración de Bibliotecas Escolares,* (see 373), which is essentially an earlier version of the following entry.

372. ———. *Bibliotecas escolares y literatura infantil.* México, Secretaría de Educación Pública, Dirección General de Enseñanza Superior e Investigación Científica, Departamento de Bibliotecas, 1947. 132p. DLC, DPU, NNY.

After citing the differences between public and school libraries for children, the author expands more fully on those aspects which they have in common. She includes a manual of suggested organization and a list of basic books, in general categories, of about 225 titles, annotated and cited with complete bibliographic information.

373. ———. *Elementos de organización y administración de bibliotecas escolares.* México, Secretaría de Educación Pública, 1929. 107p. DPU.

374. ———. "Library service to Mexican children," *ALA children's library yearbook,* Chicago, No. 1, 1929, pp. 65–66. DLC.

In an official report on the status of children's libraries, the author indicated that such work was still in its infancy in Mexico at that time. She mentions also that in rural areas, public library work was assumed by the teachers of the local school, since this had more effect. The greatest hindrance to further development was lack of books.

375. ———. "Libros para niños," *Volantes de el libro y el pueblo,* México, D.F., No. 3, May, 1932, pp. 9–16. DLC, DPU.

A recommended list of 100 books for children from 6–10 years of age. Some are annotated, but complete information is not given in most of the entries.

376. ———. *Lista de libros para niños de escuelas primarias. Lista de libros para jóvenes de escuelas de segunda enseñanza.* México, D.F., Benjamin Franklin Library, 1948. (Microfilm reproduced from typewritten manuscript). DPU.

Lists of books suitable for use with primary school children, and young people in secondary education, made from the holdings of the Benjamin Franklin Library. Included are books in Spanish, published in many countries, and books published in English and Spanish from the U.S.

377. ———. "Literatura infantil y juvenil," *El libro y el pueblo,* México, Tomo 19, No. 28, Mar.–Apr. 1957, pp. 53–64. DPU.

Children's literature, like that destined for adults, "should aid the reader in lifting himself spiritually and intellectually. It should provoke emotion which ennobles, give one useful knowledge, . . . and delightful amusement and recreation."

378. Maurois, André. "Como escoger las lecturas para los niños," *Boletín de la Biblioteca Nacional,* México, D.F., Tomo 7, No. 4, Oct.–Dec., 1956.
For note see 291.

379. Mayol, Josefina. *La biblioteca en la escuela.*

Pátzcuaro, Centro Regional de Educación Fundamental para la América Latina, 1960. 21p. DPU.

A lecture, given by the librarian of the Centro, to students in a course there. It is concerned with the purpose, organization and basic principles of the school library.

380. México (City). Biblioteca Benjamin Franklin. *Annual report, 1946.* México, The Library, 1947. 27p. DLC, DPU.

Pages 15–27 of this report cover a retrospective view of the children's room and the services it had offered since its opening five years previously.

381. Nolen, Barbara y Delia Goetz. "Métodos para escritos de ficción," *Prontuario del escritor de materias educativas.* México, Centro Regional de Ayuda Técnica, 1961. pp. 154–169. DPU.

In this practical handbook on writing textbooks and other materials for children, the authors have also included one chapter on the writing of fiction. The qualities which they delineate as appealing to children are those generally accepted as good.

382. Palacios, Adela. "El cuento, la fábula y el niño," *El libro y el pueblo,* Tomo 19, No. 23, May–June, 1956, pp. 93–97. DPU.

How fables, folk and fairy tales can stimulate the imagination of the child when nothing else can.

383. Robles Soler, Antonio Joaquín. *De literatura infantil.* 2 conferencias. "Ensayos de teatro infantil." "La infantilización de las leyendas aborígenes." México, Secretaría de Educación Pública, 1942. 52p. DLC, DPU, NNY.

Two lectures which this author delivered at a government institute in July, 1942. The first is on writing for children's theater and the second is on adapting the primitive legends of Mexico and South America for children.

384. ———. *¿Se comió el lobo a Caperucita? Seis conferencias para mayores con temas de literatura infantil.* México, Editorial América, 1942. 145p. DLC, DPU, NNY.

Six lectures delivered under the patronage of the Secretaría de Educación Pública, in October, 1941. They are titled: "Was Andersen thinking of children (when he wrote)?" "Was Aesop thinking of animals?" "What is the moral of Ali Baba?" "Did the wolf eat Little Red Riding Hood?" "Are primitive legends children's stories?" "Where is the sweetness of de Amicis?" Basically, they all support his belief that too many children's stories have double meanings and are really not meant for children. There is too much violence and cruelty. He pleads his case with a picturesque analogy: "That the fairy tale be always like a Sunday! That it be like a Sunday, for example, in its proportion of one to six . . . with the stories of studious themes; but on arriving at that seventh day that it be a true respite, without any pretense of learning while playing, for enough is learned if the tale is clear and has a Sunday sky . . ."

385. Roldán, María Antonia. "Las formas de la literatura infantil," *El libro y el pueblo,* México, Tomo 21, No. 39, Jan.–Feb., 1959, pp. 26–40. DPU.
For note see 323.

386. Sánchez Arrieta, María Teresa. "El club de lectura," *El libro y el pueblo,* México, Tomo 21, No. 39, Jan.–Feb., 1959, pp. 41–49. DPU.
For note see 324.

387. Shepperd, Eugenia. "Bibliotecas infantiles," *Boletín de la Biblioteca Nacional,* México, Tomo 1, No. 3, July–Sept., 1950, pp. 42–48. DLC.
A brief history of children's libraries in the U.S., Latin America and Mexico, with emphasis on the latter.

388. Tirado Benedí, Domingo. *Bibliotecas escolares.* México, Publicaciones del Centro de Investigaciones Agológicas, 1945. 159p. DLC.
A well-known educator writes of the importance of the school library, mostly from the pedagogical point of view. Certain chapters on books and reading contain general criticism and are not wholly didactic in approach. Cataloging and classification are also discussed.

389. Torner, Florentino M. *La literatura en la escuela primaria.* México, EDIAPSA, 1940, 156p. (Ediciones Pedagógicas y Escolares, Técnica de la Enseñanza). DLC.
A handbook designed for the teacher to aid in selecting and using literature with children. The author states that the most important thing in awakening the sensibilities of the child and bringing him to distinguish the valid in literature, is to teach literature as such, not making it an excuse for a grammar lesson. He gives concrete examples on integrating literature into the curriculum, and lists 100 titles which he has found particularly good.

390. Torres Montalvo, Herculano Angel. "Las tendencias literarias en los adolescentes mexicanos,"

Revista del instituto nacional de pedagogía, México, Años 9–10, Nos. 35–36, Oct., 1955–Jan. 1956, 95p. (Entire issue). DPU.
The results of an inquiry into the reading interests of adolescents. The 1,600 students who participated answered questions about the classics, magazines, comics, etc., and the tabulated results are given in chart or graph form.

391. Trejo, Blanca Lydia. "La literatura infantil," *El libro y el pueblo,* México, Tomo 16, No. 2, Feb., 1954, pp. 5–22. DLC, DPU.
The purpose of children's literature is linked to that of education, according to Miss Trejo. Therefore, the school has the primary responsibility in forming aesthetic or literary taste. This they can best do through use of folk tales, drama, and poetry, the three kinds of literature preferred by children.

392. ———. *La literatura infantil en México; desde los Aztecas hasta nuestros dias.* Información-Crítica-Orientación. México, [Gráfica Moderna], 1950. 262p. DLC, DPU.
A wide-ranging survey of all that might be considered children's literature in Mexico: Aztec legends, colonial literature, folklore, narratives, poetry, radio, film and theater for children, and libraries for children. Miss Trejo attempts to include examples of each type of literature. At the end are two shorter articles by Juana Manrique de Lara and Vicente Magdaleno, both on children's books. This lacks a good index and bibliography; nevertheless, it is the most complete coverage of the subject in a single volume.

393. ———. "La narración del cuento infantil," *El libro y el pueblo,* México, Tomo 17, No. 19, Sept.–Oct., 1955, pp. 76–80. DPU.
Although in agreement on most counts, the author takes exception to one point in Cardona Peña's article (357)—that one cannot train for the work of storytelling. Just as a musician must practice his natural talent, so, too, the storyteller can observe other styles and practice and perfect his art.

394. Velásquez Bringas, Esperanza. "Las bibliotecas infantiles y escolares en Mexico." Congreso Panamericano del Niño, 5th, La Habana, Cuba. *Actas y trabajos,* La Habana, Montalvo y Cardenas, 1928. Vol. 3, pp. 95–104. DPU.
A statement on school and children's libraries of the time in Mexico, with emphasis on two which gave model service: the Biblioteca Fija of the Secretary of Education, and the Biblioteca Cervantes. Illustrated with photographs.

Panama

395.   Jornadas Bibliotecológicas Panameñas, 1st. *Informe general. Trabajos y recomendaciones finales.* Panamá, Universidad de Panamá, 1957. (Mimeographed). DPU.

During the 1st Panamanian library conference, several papers concerning children's work were presented: "Bibliotecas de las escuelas primarias" by Benigna Domínguez, 9p; "Bibliotecas infantiles" by Ligia H. de Castro, 10p; "Repercusión de la falta de bibliotecas escolares en los estudios universitarios" by Carmen D. de Herrera, 8p; "Consideraciones y conclusiones acerca de la posibilidad de adoptar en Panamá el plan orgánico para un servicio nacional de bibliotecas escolares," 4p.

396.   Panamá. Biblioteca Nacional. *Bibliotecas juveniles; una bibliografía selecta con motivo de la inauguración de la sección juvenil de la biblioteca nacional.* Panamá, Imprimeria Nacional, 1952. 34p. (Publicaciones, Vol. 2, No. 10). DPU.

A brief introduction by Galileo Patiño, director of the national library, indicating his pleasure at the opening of a children's section in the library. This is followed by a list of approximately 500 titles of children's books, not annotated, but with fairly complete bibliographic information.

397.   ———. *Secciones infantiles de nuestras bibliotecas publicas.* Panamá, Biblioteca Nacional, 1948. 20p. (Circular no. 23, Mimeographed). DPU.

A quick survey of children's rooms in the public libraries of Panama, followed by a list of about 375 titles, by subject, not annotated, but with complete bibliographic information.

398.   "Pilot school library in Panama," *UNESCO bulletin for libraries,* Paris, Vol. 14, No. 1, Jan.–Feb., 1960, pp. 36–37. DLC, NNY.

The Centro Manuel Amador Guerrero will serve five schools as well as the general public in the Chorillo district of Panama. UNESCO will provide funds to enable the collection and services to come as close to a model library as possible.

Paraguay

399.   Artecona de Thompson, María Luisa. "Literatura infantil y juvenil en el Paraguay," International Board on Books for Young People. *IX Congreso de la Organización Internacional para el Libro Juvenil.* Madrid, 1965, pp. 157–164. DLC, IYL.

The text of a speech on Paraguayan children's literature, presented at the IBBY conference. This gives a fine, brief historical survey. There is a short bibliography.

Peru

A perceptive article by Rimaneth Almonte Velásquez explains this educator's fears that books were not keeping up with the changing values in social and intellectual life (401). Agreeing that a child should know of his heritage through a national literature, he could not see that such a trend was possible in Peru. What is to be thought, then, of the books mentioned by Olivas Caldas (419), Izquierdo Ríos (413), Helen Rand Parish (98), and in *Panorama* (88)? Are these well-reviewed collections of poetry, folk tales and stories to be considered not so worth-while after all? The answer (and not only for Peru) lies in the observation that such books are not enough, and in fact do harm when their historical point of view is not balanced by a picture of present reality. Over and over again, when the Latin American critics write of the better contributions to children's literature, they are referring to folk tales, fantasy, poetry, history, biography. No mention of a realistic, "here-and-now" story, one which mirrors the present day life of the ordinary child with honesty and candor. An occasional school story, yes, but usually the result of some reminiscence so that it is already one generation past the experience of its current readers.

Peru has been fortunate in having such frank assessors as Almonte Velásquez, and the journalist who felt free to remonstrate a national library which assigned more value to "reference study" than to "reading stories" (401). A recent guide to library work dispels any fear that such service might have been accepted as standard (415). Indeed, if the approbation of UNESCO is any sign, library work with children has vastly improved, for the municipal library of Callao received a bookmobile to extend its excellent service to even more children (78).

In 1944 an American librarian was invited to give a course in children's literature at the national library (405). This was considered their natural responsibility, as it was in many countries, and the course was later repeated. However, in the survey made by the UNESCO regional center (84) Peru reported that children's literature was now most frequently taught in the normal schools and other teacher-training institutions.

400.   Adrianzén Trece, Blanca. *Bibliotecas infantiles y escolares*. Lima, Librería D. Miranda, 1949. 147p. DPU, NNY. Short sections also in: *Fénix*, Lima, No. 4, 1946, pp. 785–812. DLC; *La crónica*, Lima, Feb. 15, Mar. 7, 21, Apr. 4, 1948.

The history, significance and qualities of children's libraries, and their organization. Emphasis is on Peruvian and Latin American systems. The author gives a suggested classification system, as well as many practical suggestions on operation of the library. This is illustrated with many photographs, and has an 11 page bibliography.

401.   Almonte Velásquez, Rimaneth. "Literatura infantil y la educación," *Nueva educación*, Lima, Año 6, No. 35, Nov., 1950, pp. 21–27. DLC.

Only in the last few years has anyone expressed grave interest in an authentic present-day literature for children, one which is in accord with social reality. Whereas previously the child was expected to read only for education, now he was encouraged to read for diversion. It is important for children to have their own national literature, as well as the universal classics; unfortunately, in Peru the author sees no such trend developing.

402.   Angles, Cipriano. *La escuela y el cuento*. Lima, Imprenta Minerva, 1931. 39p. DLC, DPU.

A brief history of storytelling, its philosophy and purpose. The means of using storytelling in the school are also presented, and a short list of stories to tell ends the piece.

403.   Balarezo Pinillos, Ezequiel. "Los niños en la biblioteca nacional," *La prensa*, Lima, Mar. 4, 1945. DLC.

In a special Sunday supplement on the National Library, the author writes of the children's room: "There is a sign . . . which says children reading stories are obliged to give up their place to those who wish to consult reference works." He deplores the fact that such a sign need exist and asks when the country will become conscious of the need to have libraries for children who wish to read or browse as well as study.

404.   Basadre, Jorge. "Literatura infantil," *Boletín bibliográfico*, Lima, Año 11, Nos. 3–4, Oct.–Dec., 1938, pp. 243–244. DLC.

Although its brevity might exclude it, this discusses authors not mentioned in other sources.

405.   Bates, Margaret J. "Las bibliotecas infantiles," *Fénix*, Lima, No. 1, 1944, pp. 19–27. DLC, DPU.

The author wrote this while she was in Peru to teach a course on the organization of the school library. It is a warm assessment of the role of children's libraries. Citing countless examples from history, Miss Bates points out the proven effect which books can have on the mind and spirit of the child. She feels strongly that children should be given a free and wide range in their choice of reading matter, always provided it is the best in quality.

406. *Bibliografía para bibliotecas escolares.* Lima, Secpane, 1957.

407. Carpio de Márquez, María Esther del. "Bibliotecas escolares," *Revista de educación,* Lima, Tomo 16, No. 1, Jan.–Apr., 1942, pp. 93–101. DLC.
A discussion of a recent law which passed, initiating more school libraries in Peru. The author points out the difference between school and public libraries for children, and stresses the importance of both.

408. Carvallo Wallstein de Nuñez, Carlota. "La sección peruana de la organización internacional del libro juvenil," International Board on Books for Young People. *IX Congreso de la Organización Internacional para el Libro Juevnil.* Madrid, 1965, pp. 165–171. DLC, IYL.
Information about the Peruvian section of IBBY, and a brief summary on the general characteristics of children's literature.

409. Chiriboga Sotomayor, Beatriz. "Las bibliotecas escolares en educación secundaria," *Fénix,* Lima, No. 5, 1947, pp. 177–199. DLC.
A plan presented in 1946 to the national school for librarians, on the organization, special problems and activities of the school library.

410. Fernández Perez, Jorge Octavio. "Importancia y organización de una biblioteca escolar," *Nueva educación,* Lima, Año 7, No. 46, Dec., 1951, pp. 17–19. DLC.
A brief essay on the importance and organization of the school library.

411. *La fiesta del libro y las bibliotecas escolares en el Peru.* Lima, P. Scheuch, 1925.

412. Indacochea, Matilde. *Literatura infantil.* Lima, Editorial San Antonio, 1963. 118p.
Probably a revision and expansion of 415, but not located.

413. Izquierdo Ríos, Francisco. "Apuntes sobre literatura infantil en el Peru," *Correo de educación,* Lima, Año 3, No. 31, Sept., 1951, pp. 13–16; No. 32, Oct., 1951, pp. 9–11. DPU.

Children's literature should be pleasurable and educative at the same time. However, teachers think children must have everything explained and too often impress methodology on reading, insisting that the child be able to explain what he has read. Although he is able to mention a number of authors and anthologies, Izquierdo Ríos feels that no really Peruvian literature has developed for children. He ends by listing all known children's authors and books in Peru, from the late 19th century to 1950.

414. ———. "Literatura infantil en el Peru," *Trocha,* Lima, Vol. 1, No. 4, Dec., 1941, pp. 1–3.

415. Ministerio de Educación Pública. Servicio Cooperativo Peruano-Norteamericano de Educación. *Literatura infantil.* Lima, Secpane, 1958. 66p. IYL.
In her introduction, Matilde Indacochea indicates that this was the basic material which she used in a course on children's literature, given at the library school. It is divided into children's reading interests, a brief history of children's literature and its types, children's periodicals, library work with children, book selection, etc.

416. Minter, M. "Para una antología de la poesía infantil peruana," *El nuevo educador,* Lima, June, 1945, pp. 19–23. DPU.
The author mentions Olivas Caldas' bibliography (419) and stated that he hoped to make an anthology of Peruvian children's literature from these works, but had not been able to do so. This work was a short step toward that end, and the resulting collection from the poetry of Peruvian writers for children is what makes up most of the article.

417. Morote Best, Efrain. "Algunas de nuestras rimas infantiles," *Revista universitaria,* Cuzco, Año 38, No. 96, 1949, pp. 163–232. DPU, DLC.
How children's rhymes are formed, and their validity as literature. More than 150 examples of rhymes are given.

418. "A new Peruvian public library," *UNESCO bulletin for libraries,* Paris, Vol. 13, No. 1, Jan., 1959, pp. 22–23. DLC, NNY.
Despite its brevity, this is included for its description of a new library in Callao, which has an outstanding children's room, and a bookmobile provided by UNESCO.

419. Olivas Caldas, Antonio. "Hacia la formación de una bibliografía sobre literatura infantil peruana," *Boletín bibliográfico,* Lima, Año 13, No. 3, Oct., 1940, pp. 255–274; No. 4, Dec., 1940, pp. 389–396. DPU.

The beginnings of a nationalistic tone in children's literature can be found in the play, *El pabellón peruano* of Luis B. Cisneros (1855), but this tendency did not really become noticeable until the 20th century, when a number of writers achieved success in tales with Peruvian themes. Although poetry had always been popular, it was not until 1938 that a native poet turned to writing children's verse: Abraham Arias Larreta, author of *Rayuelo*. Theater and magazines for children contained some of the better work, and the ever-popular verse fables and nursery rhymes had their advocates as well.

420.   Ortiz de Zevallos, Carmen and Antonieta Ballon. "Servicio para niños y adolescentes," *La biblioteca pública en acción*. Lima, Biblioteca Nacional, Fondo San Martín, 1964, pp. 71–74. DPU.

Suggested standards of public library service to children and young adults, and ways in which to implement them.

421.   *Reglamento de bibliotecas escolares, autorizada por el Supremo Gobierno para los colegios y escuelas de la República*. Lima, El Progreso Editorial, 1923. 46p.

422.   Rodríguez Arce, Ciro. "¿Cual es el cuento que más gusta a los niños?," *Temas y experiencias pedagógicas*. Huancayo, Imprenta Unidas, 1947. Also in: *Boletín del instituto de experimentación educacional*, Lima, No. 4, 1946, pp. 48–53. DPU.

"What kind of story do children like best?" The results of this author's reading inquiry indicate it is the traditional fairy tale.

423.   Romero Peralta, Guillermo. *Las bibliotecas escolares*. Tesis para optar el grado de profesor en educación secundaria. Lima, 1947.

Puerto Rico

The scarcity of materials on the subject of children's and school libraries in Puerto Rico is an enigma in the light of the phenomenal developments there during the past two decades. One pauses to wonder if this is exactly the situation M. L. Cresta de Leguizamon was wishing for, in another context: less writing about, but more doing (141). The bibliographer might agree that this is a refreshing change if it were not for the exasperation and frustration encountered in trying to document this country's achievements.

Miss Gaver's recent survey (425) is the most helpful, and while her major concern is with school libraries, the introduction and certain chapters touch on the public library services, as she observed them in limited situations. Not mentioned in her bibliography are such efforts as the Rodriguez Bou and Ramirez de Arellano anthologies (434, 432), both published by governmental agencies and aimed at giving teachers and librarians literature sources of immeasurable value. They are included in the bibliography because no indication of their existence is given in any book or article, whereas similar ventures in other countries (Mexico, Switzerland, etc.) are described in several places. They would both certainly vindicate Miss Handelman's much earlier statement that Puerto Rican children could only learn of their native literature from oral narration of teachers or parents (824).

In certain cities and regions of the United States where Puerto Rican immigration is heavy, public and school libraries attempt to make the children more at ease with the sudden and sometimes drastic changes in their cultural life. Some aspects of this work are described in an article by Pura Belpré White (4457).

424. "Bibliotecas escolares," Puerto Rico. Universidad. Consejo Superior de Enseñanza. *Problemas de educación en Puerto Rico.* Río Piedras, Universidad de Puerto Rico, 1947, pp. 61–66. (*Publicaciones pedagógicas,* Serie 2, No. 4). DLC.

A brief text plus numerous charts, tables and diagrams indicate the growth of school libraries in Puerto Rico.

425. Culbert, Mother Mary Anthony. "An annotated reading list for Puerto Rican children," *Catholic library world,* Boston, Vol. 25, No. 6, Mar. 1954, pp. 184–186. DLC.

A list of U.S. books with themes which might be of interest to Puerto Rican children.

426. Gaver, Mary Virginia and Gonzalo Velásquez. *School libraries of Puerto Rico: A survey and plan for development.* (No place given), Pub. by the authors, 1963. 116p. DPU, NNY.

On a grant from the Council on Library Resources, the author spent some time in Puerto Rico analyzing the school library situation, in conjunction with Señor Velásquez, who was making his own independent analysis. Both reports are published here, with their recommendations for the improvement of existing libraries, and the creation of new ones. Included are numerous statistical tables and short bibliographies.

427. Gerena, Carmen. *Manual para la organización y administración de la biblioteca escolar en el nivel secundario.* San Juan, Departamento de Instrucción Pública, 1962. 99p. DPU.

The revised manual for the organization and administration of secondary school libraries, as printed and recommended by the governmental department responsible for library development and service.

428. Handelman, Pearl. "Children's literature in Puerto Rico," *Library journal,* New York, Vol. 64, No. 19, Nov. 1, 1939, pp. 859–861. DLC, DPU, NNY.

The pioneer in the local effort to provide suitable reading matter for children was Manuel Fernández Juncos. The greatest hindrance to native authors in Puerto Rico is a lack of publishers—most publish their work privately. The first book written, illustrated and published in Puerto Rico for children was Carmelina Vizcarrondo's *Poemas para mi niño,* 1938. Children come to know and love a native folk literature, but mostly through parents and gifted teachers.

429. Miller, Paul G. and Jose Padin. "Official library guide for the public school system," *Department of education bulletin,* San Juan, No. 7, 1916, pp. 1–144. (Entire issue). DLC.

A list of books recommended for school libraries, by grade and by subject. Included are more than 1,000 Spanish, Latin American, British and U.S. publications. They are not annotated or indexed.

430. Puerto Rico. Departamento de Instrucción Pública. *Bibliografía para las bibliotecas de las escuelas elementales.* San Juan, Departamento de Instrucción Pública. 17p. (Mimeographed.)

431. ———. División de Producción y Compra de Libros y Revistas Educativas. *Indice de publicaciones para uso en las escuelas públicas.* San Juan, Departamento de Instrucción Pública, Servicios de Imprenta, 1960. 266p.

An official list of books recommended for purchase, arranged by very general subjects, and then subdivided into three levels corresponding to the elementary, junior and senior high schools. Trade and text books are included, with no annotations and scant bibliographic information.

432. Ramírez de Arellano, Rafael W. *Cuentos folklóricos.* San Juan, Departamento de Instrucción Pública, 1957. 115p. (Serie 4, No. 93). DLC.

A collection of folklore, in verse and in prose, meant to be used by teachers. The versions are those found extant in Puerto Rico.

433. Rodríguez Bou, Ismael. *Bibliografía selecta para la escuela primaria.* Río Piedras, Universidad de Puerto Rico, Consejo Superior de Ensenanza, August, 1962. 10p.

Prepared as a working paper for the OAS Educational Task Force, Alliance for Progress Meeting, Aug. 1962.

434. ———. *Niños y alas. Antología de poemas para niños.* 2 parts. Río Piedras, Universidad de Puerto Rico, 1958. 567p. (Consejo Superior de Enseñanza). DLC.

The introduction by David Cruz López and "Criterio de Selección" by Dalila Díaz Alfaro de Sosa indicate that this extensive 2-volume collection of poetry was made for use by teachers and librarians and others working with children. It includes Spanish poetry for children, from all of the republics, with a slight emphasis on Puerto Rico. Indexes by authors and themes and very extensive bibliographies of poetry collections in books and magazines combine to make it a helpful source book.

435. Sullivan, M. D. "Children's libraries in Puerto Rico," *News notes of the Texas Library Association,* Dallas, Vol. 9, Jan., 1933, p. 4, DLC.

436. Toro, Josefina del. "El niño y el libro," Congreso del Niño, 1st, Puerto Rico, 1943. *Memoria.* San Juan, 1943, pp. 458 ff.

El Salvador

437.   Bruin, José and Francantonio Porta. "Influencia del cine, la radio y el periódico en la formación de la niñez," Congreso Nacional del Niño, 2nd. *Trabajos presentados; legajos completos*. San Salvador, pp. 122 ff.; 255 ff.

438.   "La hora del cuento," *Nueva escuela salvadoreña*, San Salvador, Año 1, No. 1, Tomo 1, Mar.–Apr.–May, 1931, pp. 80–84. DLC.

Suggestions for telling stories, gleaned from Sara Cone Bryant's *How to Tell Stories to Children*, and some tales to tell.

439.   Sosa, Jesualdo. "Confesiones sobre el difícil arte de escribir para los niños," *Revista del Ministerio de Instrucción Pública*, San Salvador, Vol. 3, No. 10, Oct.–Nov.–Dec., 1944, pp. 54–56. DPU.
The second chapter of his book, 465.

Uruguay

In 1942, the government council on education sponsored its annual competition for the best study related to pedagogy. It was a starring year for children's literature, because first prize went to Jesualdo Sosa (465) and second to Ana Amalia Clulow (445). The Sosa work stands out as the one most often quoted from and cited in the bibliographies of all the books and articles on the subject in Latin America. It was later published in book form in Argentina, thus giving it even wider circulation. Some persons, such as Germán Berdiales, do not separate the literature of these two countries, but consider them as one, under the descriptive term *rioplatense*, meaning those regions traversed by La Plata River (109).

An expansive influence was quite common for both Uruguay and Argentina, in the area of education. A 1909 translation from the Italian book by Paula Lombroso (456) was reprinted in so many journals that it had repercussions beyond those it created in its native language. A similar fate took hold of one of the earliest published lists of children's books in Latin America, compiled by Antero Urioste (467). In turn, the *Anales de Instrucción Primaria* carried a number of articles which had appeared first in other countries. There must have been a tremendous desire and need for intelligent appraisal of children's literature, and one can only bemoan the fact that a first-rate critic or two did not appear on the scene in those formative years.

Not much publishing of any kind was done in Uruguay, but authors there had good chances of appearing in print because of the cultural ties with Argentina. Two Uruguayan "classics"—collections of tales by Juana de Ibarbouru and Horacio Quiroga—were more often in print in editions from Buenos Aires than from Montevideo. The latter is also one of the few Spanish writers to be translated into English. His *South American Jungle Tales* have been likened to the works of Kipling.

The establishment of the Instituto Interamericano del Niño (first called Instituto Internacional Americano de Protección a la Infancia) in Montevideo gave that city the advantage of a research center evolving around the child. The interests of this Institute decidedly toward social and educational welfare, but the library reference materials have been acquired in greater depth and breadth than would customarily be found in Latin America, with the consequence that their bibliographic efforts are better than average (94).

The encounter of educator José Pedro Varela with Sarmiento led to resolute action on his part in formulating library laws. "Popular" libraries were initiated in many schools during his term of office, but their number has not been maintained or increased correspondingly to the population in the course of the years. In the statistical tables of Miss Daniels' study, this country is far behind Argentina in number of school and public libraries, and number of volumes per capita.

440. Abreu Gómez, Ermilo. "Aprovechamiento de las horas libres. La literatura," *Boletín del Instituto Internacional Americano de Protección a la Infancia,* Montevideo, Tomo 24, No. 4, Dec., 1950, pp. 342–346. DLC, DPU.

Suggestions for the parent and teacher in building up a library of literature for the child. The first choices should be the classics, and not in their adapted forms.

441. Aguilar Paz, Jesús. "Criterios para la organización y funcionamiento de bibliotecas escolares," *Seminario interamericano de educación primaria,* Montevideo, 1950. [Documento]? Tema 5, No. 6, pp. 20 ff.

442. Anzola Gómez, Gabriel. "Teatro escolar," *Boletín del Instituto Internacional Americano de Protección a la Infancia,* Montevideo, Tomo 24, No. 4, Dec., 1950, pp. 326–333. DLC.

Why children like drama, how it can serve as a vital means of introducing literature to them, and to the community through the school.

443. Areco, Palmira Vásquez de. "Literatura infantil," *Boletín de la Biblioteca Artigas-Washington,* Montevideo, Vol. 3, No. 2, June, 1947, pp. 49–54. DPU.

Highlights in the history of children's literature around the world.

444. Cartaya, Berta, "La biblioteca en la escuela primaria," *Anales de instrucción primaria,* Montevideo, Epoca 2, Tomo 5, No. 1, Mar., 1942, pp. 81–98. DLC.

For note see entry 301.

445. Clulow, Ana Amalia. "Literatura infantil," *Anales de instrucción primaria,* Montevideo, Epoca 2, Tomo 7, Nos. 3–4, Dec., 1944, pp. 10–98. DLC.

In her introduction, the author states that she wishes to approach children's literature in a fresh, new fashion, and she projects it to include children's theater, storytelling, and the use of song and ballet which has story interest. The first part deals with the philosophy and trends of present-day literature, the second with the various forms under which it exists, and the third with recommendations for a revitalizing of this literature with impetus from the government and private individuals. The literature which she discusses ranges over all the Latin American and Spanish writers, with slight emphasis on the Uruguayan. Her conclusions: that Latin America has the potential to produce a wealth of new literature, which will come about if enough use of present riches is made "to seed the voices, the pulses and the colors which America is growing in her midst"; that if enough persons take an interest, libraries for children will become the active places they should be, instead of "ponderous, showy places, sleeping through an unjust dream in the office of the school principal."

446. Colomba Petit, Ana T. "Los cuentos," *Anales de instrucción primaria,* Montevideo, Tomo 21, No. 1, Jan., 1927, pp. 117–121. DLC.

Storytelling, the author believes, is a much more effective method to teach love of books and reading than the methods currently in use by teachers. She mentions the programs of the New York Public Library and passes on some of the suggestions given her by the Shedlock book (see 4308).

447. Corbiere, Emilio P. "El padre, el niño y el libro." Congreso Americano del Niño, 2nd, Montevideo, 1919. *Report,* Carpeta 5, Tomo 9, pp. 46 ff.

448. Gallinares, Joaquín. "Cuentos para niños," *Boletín de la Asociación de Profesores de Enseñanza Secundaria y Preparatoria,* Montevideo, No. 13, Sept., 1944, pp. 22–27. DPU.

The author disagrees with educators such as José Enrique Rodó and feels that fairy tales with violence and bloodshed have no place in children's literature.

449. Garibaldi, Carlos Alberto. *Boletín bibliográfico; libros indicados para la formación de bibliotecas escolares.* Montevideo, Departamento Editorial del Consejo Nacional de Enseñanza Primaria y Normal, 1946. 181p. (Colección Ceibo, 5). DLC, DPU. Also in: *Anales de instrucción primaria,* Montevideo, Epoca 2, Tomo 9, No. 2, June, 1946, pp. 4*-134* (numbered separately at end of issue).

In his introduction, the compiler states that this list was not meant to be comprehensive, but rather an introductory guide to the selection of materials for the school library. The criteria used were that the work must have certain artistic, aesthetic and moral qualities, and that it must present the subject in an accurate and true fashion. The 400 titles are divided by age and grade levels, with only author and title information, and annotations for half of the entries. Included are Spanish and Latin American publications, either original or translated. There is no index. The list is expanded and brought up to date in *Anales . . . ,* Montevideo, Epoca 2, Tomo 11, No. 7, Sept., 1948, pp. 3–19; No. 9, Nov. 1948, pp. 70–84; Tomo 12, No. 7, July 1949, pp. 1–32.

450. Guadalupe, Delia E. Rietv de. "Poemas y cuentos para niños," *Anales de instrucción primaria,* Montevideo, Epoca 2, Tomo 19, Nos. 1–3, Jan.–Mar., 1956, pp. 195–204. DLC.

The qualities which children like in poetry, illustrated with examples from Spanish and Latin American poetry.

451. Julier, Auguste. "Bibliotecas escolares," *Anales de instrucción primaria,* Montevideo, Epoca 2, Tomo 7, No. 1, Mar., 1944, pp. 206–217. DLC.

A translation of an article originally appearing in Switzerland (not located), on the importance of school libraries.

452. Larrinaga, Albana. "Conveniencia y justificación de una sección infantil en la biblioteca nacional," *Boletín de la biblioteca nacional,* Montevideo, Año 1, No. 1, July, 1944, pp. 22–29. DLC.

A strong argument justifying the need for inauguration of a children's section in the national library.

453. ———. "Es una necesidad social la creación de bibliotecas infantiles," *Boletín de la biblioteca nacional,* Montevideo, Año 1, No. 2, May, 1945, pp. 9–13. DLC.

The role of the book in molding the life of the child, and the role of the library in getting the book to the child.

454. Lerena Martínez, Elvira. "150 libros para una biblioteca de niños," *Asociación,* Montevideo, Aug., 1942, pp. 14 ff.

455. *El libro en la enseñanza primaria.* Montevideo, Departamento Editorial del Consejo Nacional de Enseñanza Primaria y Normal, 1946. 214p. (Colección Ceibo, 6) DLC. Also in: *Anales de instrucción primaria,* Montevideo, Epoca 2, Tomo 10, No. 1, Mar., 1947, pp. 357–501. DLC.

Some of the pertinent articles contained in this study are: "La lectura libre como uno de los fundamentos de la acción escolar" by María Abbate; "Exploración de la infancia de los grandes hombres— sus lecturas" by Carlos Alberto Garibaldi; "Perrault, el cuento popular y el alma de los niños" by María A. Carbonell de Grompone; "La biblioteca personal del niño" by Alfredo Ravera; "Leer" by Carlos Sabat Ercasty; "El libro en la vida del niño" by Gerardo Vidal. All were lectures delivered on a radio program aimed at parents, teachers and librarians.

456. Lombroso, Paula. "¿Por qué gustan los cuentos a los niños?," *Anales de instrucción primaria,* Montevideo, Año 7, Tomo 6, Nos. 1–6, Jan.–June, 1909, pp. 266–277. DLC.

A chapter from the author's *La Vita dei Bambini* (674) which was not located in the original. This portion contains interesting comments on why children like fairy tales.

457. Méndez, Elsa. "El libro y las bibliotecas escolares," *Anales de instrucción primaria,* Montevideo, Epoca 2, Tomo 9, No. 2, June, 1946, pp. 205–236. DLC.

A discussion of children's books in relation to the educational goals of Uruguay, in which the author's main point is that the imaginative development of the child is equally important to the growth of his character as are the study of history, science, etc. She differentiates in the use of books with the "universal" child (one who develops naturally, without adult corrections and restrictions) and with the "circumstantial" child (who has been influenced by environment of adults).

458. Nosnitzer, Sofía. *Biblioteca popular infantil de Rocha.* 1947, 8p. (Typewritten). DPU.

A description and history of a public children's library in Rocha.

459. Paz, José G. "La escuela y la biblioteca." Congreso Americano del Niño, 2nd, Montevideo, 1919. *Report,* Carpeta 5, Tomo 9, pp. 49 ff.

460. Porro Freire de Maciel, Alicia. "Actividades de la biblioteca infantil No. 1 y el Centro Orientador del Periodismo Escolar del Uruguay," *Revista del maestro,* Guatemala, Año 3, No. 10, July–Aug.–Sept., 1948, pp. 52–54. DLC.

A librarian writes of her experience in a model library, and in particular of her work with children on a magazine which was distributed by the government to all of the schools.

461. ———. *Libros que pueden servir de base para formar una biblioteca infantil.* Montevideo, 1950.

462. Power, Effie L. *El trabajo con niños en las bibliotecas públicas.* Montevideo, Biblioteca Nacional, 1945. 217p. (Mimeographed). DPU.

A translation of 4226 made especially for the national library by E. Fournié.

463. Salati, Angelica Suárez de. "Bibliotecas infantiles." Congreso Americano de Enseñanza Especial, 1st, Montevideo, 1942. *Memoria. La enseñanza especial en America.* Montevideo, Urta y Curbelo, 1942, pp. 489–493. DPU.

Recommendations for the establishment of children's libraries, and some of the standards to be set up for them.

464. Save, Francisca. "Bibliotecas estudiantiles circulantes." Congreso Americano del Niño, 2nd, Montevideo, 1919. *Report,* Carpeta 5, Tomo 9, pp. 51 ff., and pp. 54 ff.

465. Sosa, Jesualdo. "Del mito primitivo a la sinfonía tonta," *Anales de instrucción primaria,* Montevideo, Epoca 2, Tomo 6, No. 4, Dec. 1943, pp. 3–238. DLC, DPU.

"From primitive myth to the silly symphony." Sub-titled "An essay on the ethical, aesthetic and psychopedagogical aspects of children's literature." In its four major parts the author considers: 1. The functions, principal characteristics, and general difficulty of writing for children; 2. The character and intelligence of the child, his language and psychology. 3. The myth and the child; 4. Principal forms of children's literature: Fable, tale, poetry, drama.

466. Urioste, Antero. *Bibliotecas escolares populares.* Montevideo, Barreiro y Ramos, 1923. 15p. NNY.

The functions of the school library which also serves the community as a public library.

467. Uruguay. Consejo Nacional de Enseñanza Primaria y Normal. Biblioteca de los Maestros. *Algunos libros que pueden servir para establecer una biblioteca infantil.* Montevideo, A. Barreiro y Ramos, 1923. 74p. DLC.

A note indicates that this list of recommended books was compiled by Antero Urioste, Librarian in the teachers' library of the Consejo. It consists of approximately 1,200 titles of children's books published in Spain and Latin America, as well as a few French and English titles. This is a reprint of an article which appeared in *Anales de Instrucción Primaria,* Año 19–20, Tomo 19, Nos. 9–10, Sept.–Oct., 1922, pp. 897–937. Included with this reprint is a chapter from the Spanish translation of Marcel Braunschvig's book *L'Art et l'Enfant* (759).

468. ———. Biblioteca Infantil No. 1. *Club infantil "Companeros."* 2nd ed. Montevideo, The Consejo, n.d. 11p.

469. Zarrilli, Humberto. "Teatro escolar," *Enciclopedia de educación,* Montevideo, Epoca 3, Año 8–12, No. 1, July, 1948–Jan., 1952, pp. 3–500. DLC.

An entire issue devoted to the use of drama in school to introduce children to literature.

Venezuela

In search of an explanation for the paucity of good Venezuelan literature for children the writer Oscar Rojas Jiminez observed: ". . . we must fix our attention on the old school of education with its limited criteria of child psychology. The desperate monotony and absurd methods resulted in a psychosis which impedes us from comprehending humanly and amply the imaginative world of our children . . ." (482). He indicted the literary world for not taking seriously the efforts of those who endeavored to write for a youthful audience. Others echoed these feelings, and objected to the lassitude of parents and teachers who were accepting the invasion of cheap comics and the poorly produced book versions of the Disney films, merely because "there was nothing else." More than their neighbors, Venezuelan educators and writers heaped criticism on these publications, for their denigration of public taste (475, 482, 485).

Good intention may govern the moral value of action, but it is no guarantee of artistic merit. The work of the Consejo Venezolano del Niño (National Child Council) and the Banco del Libro (Book Bank) has forced much public attention on the lack of good reading materials for children. The climate has been calm enough for even the faintest flowering of good literature to survive. Yet at this point the production trails far behind the interest, and high quality, locally produced books are as difficult to find as ever.

Ten years ago, in an attempt to provide a guide to national literature of which the Venezuelan child could be proud, Olga Mazzei de Giorgi compiled a bibliography (474). It is very small, and some of the most significant works, such as the poetry anthologies of Rafael Olivares Figueroa and Rafael Angel Insausti, are published outside the country; or the entries come from the pages of *Onza, Tigre y Leon* and *Tricolor,* two outstanding periodicals for children published by the ministry of education. That these are far and away the best children's magazines produced in Latin America in this century, is small compensation for the rarity of books.

Public libraries with children's rooms are springing up in this country as they are in many. Several have been opened in the housing developments of Caracas, according to Miss Daniels (78). Perhaps of greater import is the work of the rural teachers' training center "El Mácaro." Large proportions of the world's population live in rural areas, and this center, with the collaboration of the ministry of education, the Institute of International Education and the Alliance for Progress, is seeking to form a prototype of cultural service to rural communities, including production of children's books.

470.   "La biblioteca en la escuela moderna," *Educación,* Caracas, Año 6, No. 42, Apr.–May, 1946, pp. 61–77. DLC.

An outline guide to the organization of the school library.

471.   Egui, Luis Eduardo. "El cuento en la escuela primaria," *Educación,* Caracas, Año 6, No. 43, June–July, 1946, pp. 62–78. DLC.

A discussion of fairy tales, their characteristics, adaptations, and suitability for use with young children.

472.   Junyent, Alberto. "La nueva literatura para la infancia," *Educación,* Caracas, Año 6, No. 36, Apr.–May, 1945, pp. 9–13. DLC.

The general trends of children's literature, not only in Venezuela and Latin America, but throughout the world. The author feels that the prevalent theme of nationalism is good in each country's literature, as long as this is balanced by the universal classics.

473.   *Libros de texto en primaria.* Caracas, Banco del Libro, 1964, 24p. DPU.

This is a list of primary textbooks and supplementary reading materials published by the Banco del Libro. There are some books in each section which can be considered as general recreational reading matter.

474.   Mazzei de Giorgi, Olga. *Bibliografía infantil venezolana.* Caracas, Editorial Sucre, 1956. 39p. (Editado por la Division de Divulgación y Publica-

ciones, Consejo Venezolano del Niño). DLC, DPU. Also appears in: *Infancia y adolescencia,* Epoca 3, Vol. 11, No. 19, 1956, pp. 147–180. DLC.

A bibliography of some 275 titles, arranged by Dewey system, not annotated, but indexed by author and title. Included are children's books published in Venezuela, plus a few major works by Venezuelan authors published elsewhere. The earliest is dated 1841, but most are from the 20th century. Some stories and poems which appeared in magazines are also listed.

475.   Ocanto, J. Clemente. "La lectura infantil y la educación," *Educación,* Caracas, Año 16, No. 79, Etapa 2, Oct., 1955, pp. 26–29. DLC.

The mass production of comic books and cheap picture books has almost taken over control of children's literature, and the sad fact is that most of this material comes from one publishing house, which controls the market. The author cites legislation which might eventually help the situation.

476.   Olivares Figueroa, Rafael. "El folklore en la escuela," *Educación,* Caracas, Año 6, No. 39, Oct.–Nov., 1945, pp. 22–24; No. 40, Dec., 1945–Jan., 1946, pp. 76–85; No. 41, Feb.–Mar., 1946, pp. 46–51. DLC.

Only three in a major series of articles on folklore, its use with children (particularly in the school) and its qualities as literature. Each of the articles cites numerous examples, as well as a bibliography.

477.   ———. "El problema de las bibliotecas escolares," *Educación,* Caracas, Año 1, No. 5, May–June, 1940, pp. 1–3. DLC.

The author believes that the school library supported only by public funds has less chance of invoking interest and suggests private support be sought, either in funds or volunteer help. The important fact to remember is to set up standards and maintain them. He suggests that possibly in Venezuela, the national library should have a children's division which would be responsible for setting the standard.

478.   Perea Romero, Martin. "Departamento para niños," *Biblioteca Nacional, Boletín,* Caracas, Epoca 3, Vols. 4–5, July–Oct., 1959, pp. 12–14, 25. DLC, DPU.

The philosophy of service in the children's division of the national library. This is mainly to serve school needs, and secondarily for free reading.

479.   Prieto Figueroa, Luis Beltrán. "Las bibliotecas infantiles," *Ahora,* Caracas, Aug. 25, 1938.

480.   ———. *La magia de los libros; obras estimulantes para la juventud.* Caracas, Ministerio de Educación, 1961. 74p. (Colección Vigilia No. 1). DLC, DPU.

A lecture delivered in Costa Rica and first printed there, but unavailable in that edition. It is an evocation of the "magic" which books and reading wrought in his young life, and in the lives of others. He strives to present the most convincing means by which one can get young people to read, and concludes with a list of about 275 works he has found stimulating to youth.

481.   Rojas, Nelly. "El cuento en el kindergarten," *Infancia y adolescencia,* Caracas, Año 1, No. 1, Jan.–Feb., 1949, pp. 36–38. DLC.

A short guide on how to tell stories to kindergarten children. The author does not believe in using sad or gruesome stories with children of this age.

482.   Rojas Jiménez, Oscar. "Literatura infantil venezolana," *Infancia y adolescencia,* Caracas, Año 2, Nos. 7–8, Jan.–Feb., 1950, p. 30. DLC.

This one-page article is included because it gives revealing reasons which the author feels are responsible for the lack of children's literature in Venezuela.

483.   Salas, Rafael. *Las lecturas para menores.* Caracas, Ediciones de la Dirección de Divulgación y Publicaciones del C.V.N., 1955. An outline of the contents appears in: *Infancia y adolescencia,* Caracas, Epoca 3, Vol. 10, No. 18, 1956, pp. 81–89. DLC.

The pervasive influence of comic and cheap picture books has all but destroyed the taste of children for real books in Venezuela. The author points out that this was the reason for the founding of the Consejo Venezolano del Niño, and she mentions some of its work.

484.   Subero, Efrain. *Bibliografía de la poesía infantil venezolana.* Caracas, Banco del Libro, 1966. 118p. DPU.

A bibliography of Venezuelan children's poetry and folk rhymes, which appeared in books and periodicals published in that country and in other Latin American countries. The compiler is himself a children's poet. Author and title indexes.

485.   "El uso y abuso del grafico en la literatura infantil," *Infancia y adolescencia,* Caracas, Año 2, Nos. 7–8, Jan.–Feb., 1950, p. 19. DLC.

This brief article on the use and abuse of illustrations in children's books is included because it is the only reference made to this particular aspect of children's literature. The author contends that most illustration in Latin American children's books infringes on the literary quality of the material and is there only to distract, causing the child to rely too much on a graphic image printed in virulent colors.

486.   Yarza, Palmenes. "La poesía infantilista," *Educación*, Caracas, Año 6, No. 41, Feb.–Mar., 1946, pp. 40–45. DLC.

An article on some of the Venezuelan poets who write for children, and poetry written by the children.

Western Europe

The countries in this section have more in common with each other than have the nations of most of the other geographical groupings. Under the combined influence of England in the 18th and 19th centuries, the U.S. and Scandinavia in the late 19th and 20th, and the Western European countries in all three centuries, a specifically children's literature emerged from the didactic and educative materials which had been given to children in most of the civilizations of past history. Rightly or wrongly, this literature developed a style, recurrent themes and several forms different from "adult" or general literature. At its best it was refreshingly simple and child-like in tone, highly imaginative, and likely to be read with appreciation at any age level. At its worst it was condescending, cute, boring, or exaggeratedly adventurous.

There has been and continues to be much discussion about the definition of children's literature. The average person can recognize it, but can rarely define it. Authors whose works are read by children have explained their craft in different ways. At one extreme are those who have written specifically for children, sometimes for a certain child or a distinct group of children. At the other extreme are those who claimed they wrote not for children nor for adults, but for some undefined public or for their own pleasure. In the middle are those with gradations and varieties of these reasons, including some with no explainable reasons at all. Written specifically for them or not, children's literature nevertheless does seem to have some definable boundaries or characteristics. All basic issues, but especially those of good and evil, right and wrong, tend to be more clearly defined in children's books. There is more exterior than interior action. Fantasy and the adventure novel are favored forms, both by writers and readers, and a majority of the "classics" fall into one of the two categories.

These are only a few of the general characteristics which can clearly be traced to the general literary trends which took place in Western Europe. There is no question but that much of the theory of a separate literature for children is due to the influence of the countries in this section.

This is not to deny the often concurrent movements in other countries and areas of the world. Current children's books are so international that one can hardly guess where one influence begins and another leaves off. It is also true to say that Western European countries have been receptive to new approaches in the publishing and distribution of children's books. On the whole, however, traditional patterns hold sway. It is possible to say that this area is the most predictable and each era has gone by with a little progress so that the overall picture is comfortably positive.

487. "Bibliothèques pour enfants. Children's libraries." International Congress of Libraries and Documentation Centres. Brussels, 1955. *Proceedings,* Vol. 3. La Haye, M. Nijhoff, 1958. pp. 140–144. DLC, NNY.

This is a résumé of the discussions which took place among the librarians from Belgium, France, Germany, Italy, the Netherlands, Spain, Denmark and England. In Vol. 1 of the *Proceedings* is an article on children's libraries in general, by H. Rivier (pp. 139–140). There is also an article by M. Gruny in Vol. 2, reported on in France (801).

488. Cappe, Jeanne. *La littérature de jeunesse en Europe.* Bruxelles, Bureau Européen de la Jeunesse et de l'Enfance, 1951. 23p. (Mimeographed). IYL.

The report of a European conference on children's literature, held in Brussels in July 1951. It was concerned with the general postwar trends in children's literature, and what could be done to turn these trends toward higher goals.

489. Centro Didattico Nazionale di Studi e Documentazione. *Problemi della letteratura per l'infanzia in Europa.* Firenze, Centro Didattico . . . , 1955. 227p. (Atti delle Giornate Europee . . . May 27–30, 1954). IYL.

At this conference on children's literature general papers were presented by: Giovanni Calò, Jeanne Cappe, Enzo Petrini, Bianca Bianchi, Luigi Santucci, Giuseppe Flores d'Arcais, Pierina Boranza, Dino Origlia, P. Schmitt, Caterina Gasparotto Jacobelli and Elizabeth Clerc. Reports on the children's literature of specific countries were prepared by Jeanne Cappe (Belgium), Arthur Sleigh (England), Madaleine Bugge (Norway), Helena W. F. Stellwag (Netherlands), Felicina Colombo (Switzerland), and Armando Michielli (Italy). There are also reports on the press for children, by Raoul Dubois; on theater, by Italiano Marchetti; on children's libraries, by Fernand Stevart. All papers have French and English summaries, and in a few cases they are written in French. The majority are in Italian.

490. Davidson, Elisabeth W. *Orbis pictus: Comenius' contribution to children's literature.* Washington, Catholic University of America, 1958, 122p. Thesis. DLC has on microfilm.

A study of the historical background of the *Orbis Sensualiam Pictus* by Jan Amos Comenius, its influence on children's books, its numerous editions and translations, and its imitators.

491. *Enquête sur les livres scolaires d'après guerre.* Paris, Centre Européen de la Dotation Carnegie, 1923. 452p. PIP.

The results of an inquiry into the textbooks and other children's books in use in European schools after the First World War, and how they reflected the political changes, the past enmities, etc. Since general reading materials available to children are considered in the study, this proves interesting to the student of politics and national identity as reflected in children's books.

492. Hürlimann, Bettina. *Europäische kinderbücher in drei Jahrhunderten.* 2nd. ed. Zürich, Atlantis Verlag, 1963. 288p. DLC, IYL, NNY.

A lively, personal history of the highlights of children's literature in Europe during the past three centuries. Written in narrative style and illustrated with numerous reproductions from the books mentioned, it is more helpful as a background study than as a source book. An English edition was published by Oxford University Press in 1967.

493. Kalken, H. N. van, *Quelques pages sur la littérature enfantine allemande, française et anglaise.* Bruxelles, A De Boeck, 1913. 109p. DEW.

A selection of books from the French and German speaking countries of Europe, and from England. Critical comments are limited but in his "general considerations" at the end (pp. 102–109), the author lists his criteria of selection.

494. Lüthi, Max. *Das Europäische Volks-märchen; Form und Wesen.* 2nd ed. Bern, A. Francke, 1960. 132p. (Dalp Taschenbücher, 351). IYL.

A scholarly study of the European folktale, written by an eminent folklorist.

495. *Study and information meeting for editors of youth magazines.* Gauting (Munich), UNESCO Youth Institute, 1956. 65p. IYL.

The discussions, papers, talks and results stemming from a meeting held in May–June, 1956. Most of the participants were from European countries, but the U.S. and England were also represented.

496. Werring-Hansen, E. "Barnebibliotekarbeid—fra England til Genf," *Bok og bibliotek,* Oslo, Aug. 7, Mar., 1940, pp. 90–103. DLC.

Children's library work in England, Belgium, Holland and France, together with a few remarks about the work of the International Bureau of Education.

Portugal

While working on her history of children's literature in Latin America, Carmen Bravo-Villasante unearthed several "treasures" in Portuguese. In an article for the *Revista de Etnografia,* she bemoans the fact that this literature is so little known. There is even a lack of exchange between Portugal and Brazil. To help remedy this she includes in her book (70) a chapter of the children's literature of Portugal. This is the only recent study of the subject to be located. Earlier in the century Henrique Marques had attempted a comprehensive bibliography of Portuguese children's books, but it contained no critical or historical text.

Libraries for children are mentioned in several general reference works, but they do not seem to be widely developed in schools or in public institutions. Documentation on work with children's books is so scarce that it is not possible to make any observations and conclusions.

497.   Alvaro Alberto, Armanda. "Resultado do inquerito sobre leituras infantis, realisado em julho de 1926, pela secçao de cooperaçao da familia," *Jornal do comercio,* Lisboa, Mar. 18, 1928.

498.   Bravo-Villasante, Carmen. "Literatura infantil en Portugal," *Revista de etnografia,* Oporto, Vol. 5, Tomo 2, Oct., 1965, pp. 499–502. DLC.

In the course of reviewing the anthology, *15 Tales Never Heard,* this author relates of her encounter with a literature which is excellent, but almost unknown.

499.   Coelho, F. Adolpho. "Os jogos e as rimas infantis de Portugal," *Boletin da Sociedade de Geographia,* Lisboa, 4 ser, No. 12, 1883, pp. 567–595. NNY.

Nursery rhymes and game songs of Portugal, with many examples given in the text. This is only one part of a series on the subject, but the others could not be located.

500.   Correia da Silva, J. "Jornais para crianças," *A criança portuguesa,* Lisboa, Ano 9, 1949–1950, pp. 183–229. DLC.

The results of a study made on the contents of Portuguese magazines, comics and newspapers for children, and the implications to be made from the fact that they are much more widely read than books.

501.   Lisboa. Cámara Municipal. *Exposição de arte e bibliografía infantil.* Lisboa, Oficinas Gráficas de C. M. L., 1940. 24p. DLC.

The catalog of an exposition of children's books and art work by children. No actual titles are listed, only the exhibiting publishers.

502.   Machado, José Pedro. "Bibliotecas escolares," *Escolas técnicas,* Lisboa, Vol. 4, No. 16, 1954, pp. 176–200.

General thoughts on the school library, its purpose, and the position it should hold within the curriculum. Emphasis is on the high school library.

503.   Marques, Henrique (Junior). *Algumas achegas para uma bibliografia infantil.* Lisboa, Oficinas Gráficas da Biblioteca Nacional, 1928. 147p. DLC, NNY.

A bibliography of about 500 books produced for children in Portugal from 1603 to 1927. Each is annotated and described with minute bibliographic detail. Arrangement is by five general categories and then by date. Author and title indexes are included. An invaluable aid in the historical study of children's books in this country.

504.   Sá, Victor de. *As bibliotecas, o público e a cultura.* Braga, The Author, 1956. 310p. (Cultura e Acção). NNY.

This consists of many short articles which originally appeared in the *Correlo do Minho,* stemming from the journalist-author's inquiry into the various forces and agencies at work in the social and educational life of Braga. Many of these articles had to do with children's books, libraries and related matters. An index is given to help locate them in the book.

Spain

Before the 19th century, there were a number of outstanding works for children, copied or printed in Spain—among them *El Conde Lucanor o Libro de Patronio* by the Infante Juan Manuel, *La Vida del Lazarillo de Tormes, Fabulas* of Iriarte, and *Los Pastores de Belén* by Lope de Vega. Whether their original intent was exclusively for juvenile consumption is questionable, but speculation as to what children of those early centuries actually did read usually includes them. Both of the writers of histories of Spanish children's literature discuss these early works at some length (523, 604) and both seem to agree that the real germination of children's literature took place in the magazines of the 19th century.

The first periodical designated for children was *Gaceta de los Niños,* published from 1798 to 1800. It appears to have been directly influenced by the English publications of John Newbery and was followed by a number of attractive magazines with imitations and innovations. Within their pages appeared the stories and articles of a number of authors who were consciously striving for a style suitable and attractive to young readers. Most outstanding among these were Cecilia Böhl de Faber who, under the pseudonym of Fernán Caballero, dominated the pages of *La Educación Pintoresca.* These magazines were heavy with didacticism and even though they often had illustrations of great charm, their appeal was not as popular as that evoked by the *aleluyas,* or picture sheets. Forerunners of today's comic strips, they appeared in great quantities in Europe in the 19th century, and Spain took to them with particular delight.

And what of the tales of the Grimm Brothers, Ernst T. Hoffmann, Hans Christian Andersen, Jules Verne, the Contesse de Segur and other Europeans, whose works were spreading so quickly? Most of these were published in Spanish by the Editorial Calleja, established in Madrid in 1878; this firm achieved such a monopoly that the name was destined to become part of a proverb: "You have more tales than Calleja!"

Literature for children in Spanish reached its apex in the genre of poetry. This was true not only in Spain but in the Latin American countries as well. Writing prose for children was looked on with some disdain, or worse yet, was practiced with a great flourish of sentimentality. But many of the poets, even the great ones, chose to dedicate a few of their works to children, and their sincerity was matched with an unequalled delicacy of expression. Federico García Lorca, Rafael Alberti, Juan Ramon Jiménez and Miguel de Unamuno are only a few whose poetry achieved this special tenderness, so appealing to the young Spaniard. But they would be the first to admit that a poet aims at poetry, not at children. Thus, Paul Hazard was not forgetting them when he wrote: "There is no Spanish author who has written especially for his young brothers and who in doing so has expressed himself with genius" (814). Carmen Bravo-Villasante agrees with this judgement up to a certain point, but feels that both Elena Fortun and Salvador Bartolozzi qualify as good writers who produced work almost exclusively for children. The former is known for her *Celia* books, stories of everyday life centered around a girl's growing-up and school years. The latter was both an artist and writer, known for his *Pinocho* and *Chapete* adventure series. To say that he was inspired by Collodi's *Pinocchio* is not quite the correct approach to an assessment of his work. He certainly did use the central character as a beginning, but the story line and illustrations are distinctly his own invention. Many critics still find this a questionable technique, and there is always the doubt as to whether such stories would stand up on their own, if they had not the original character and his name to create the initial favorable impression. One might compare this situation with that of the *Oz* books in the United States. Suffice it to say here, the Bartolozzi *Pinocho* is widely read and liked in Spain, by children, parents and even teachers and librarians.

During the last ten years, production of children's books has burgeoned in Spain as it has in most countries. Public interest has been spurred by many book centered celebrations. The Feria Nacional del Libro, a commercial fair held in spring, had its 25th anniversary in 1966. The Fiesta del Libro, also in spring, is sponsored by the Instituto Nacional del Libro Español as is the Semana Nacional del Libro Infantil, held late in the year (584, 555). The last-named is similar to children's book week in other countries, while the former is the occasion for the announcements of the Lazarillo prizes, given for the best writing and illustration in children's books. These have been awarded since 1958, and are accompanied by a monetary reward as well as great honor (560). Other organizations broadcasting the word about the necessity of good children's books are the Spanish section of IBBY and the Gabinete de Lectura "Santa Teresa de Jesús." The Gabinete edits a selective children's catalog which they revise and update every few years (505).

There are indications, however, that children's books in Spain are not all the experts would wish them to be. Recent criticism is particularly strong among those who come in contact with what is being done in other parts of the world (525, 542, 544, 560). Most often, this criticism is directed at the lack of imaginative variety in stories and illustrations, at the small percentage of good nonfiction books, and at the relative expensiveness of better editions, which rarely reach the middle or lower class child.

Libraries, unfortunately, are still not developed to the point where they could assume the responsibility of getting books to children of all areas and social classes. Public libraries come under the jurisdiction of the Ministry of Culture; school library work is under the Ministry of Education. Control is exercised in varying degrees at the local, regional and national levels. In theory, and according to law, each locality and school should have free library service. As is so often the case in Spain the practice is well behind the proposed standard.

The Servicio Nacional de Lectura, an agency of the Ministry of

Culture, is working hard to bring books to the public, especially in rural areas. Their pre-selected boxes of books (there are separate children's sets) go out to any community which can guarantee a place to display and circulate them. They are completely catalogued and prepared for immediate use, and can provide the nucleus of a newly created small public library, or augment the collection of one which is already in existence. Additional copies and other titles may be ordered through the Servicio at reduced cost, but unfortunately there are no funds at present to catalog and prepare these.

More noticeable results are being achieved by the Comisaría de Extensión Cultural of the Ministry of Education, through the Biblioteca de Iniciación Cultural, known popularly as BIC. In much the same manner as at the Servicio, books are prepared in boxes. However, there are many more choices of different sets and the variety of materials is wider. In addition, there is a good assortment of audiovisual materials, as well as the equipment to use them. All of these services are offered free on extended loan to any teacher or adult individual requesting them. This results in a great number of small, temporary classroom collections, rather than central school libraries. Only at exceptional schools, such as the Antigua Escuela del Mar in Barcelona, has a first-rate school library been established and maintained. Nevertheless, it can be said that books and other cultural media are reaching Spanish children in numbers never reached before. And not only in Spain, but also in the many countries where industries employ Spanish laborers. These same services, and the literacy programs beamed via radio and television to the workers and their families, have merited the interest and assistance they are receiving from UNESCO. They are not described here in detail since the majority of them are aimed at adults and do not come within the scope of this work.

Also in Barcelona is the library school which includes in its courses the organization and administration of children's libraries. Their official publication, *Biblioteconomía,* repeatedly offers sound advice on work with children. What it and the other book and library organizations or establishments fail to produce is a means of regularly and speedily reviewing current children's books, from a consistent and critical point of view. Selective annual book lists will not suffice to supply information to the growing number of school and public libraries in Spain and Latin America. Thanks to the documentation produced by the Instituto Nacional del Libro (550, 551), checking and ordering can be done quickly and accurately. The Instituto is beginning an experiment with a column of regular reviews of children's books in its organ *El Libro Español.* It remains to be seen whether this will contribute a fresh, new, critical approach to the evaluation of children's books, and to the eventual triumph of *literatura* over *lectura.*

505. Acción Católica Española. Consejo Nacional de Mujeres. Gabinete de Lectura "Santa Teresa de Jesús." *Catálogo crítico de libros para niños.* Madrid, Servicio Nacional de Lectura, 1961. 314p. DLC, IYL.

A recommended list of 2,622 books for children, indicating age groups and interests. All entries are annotated and there are indexes by author, title and series.

506. ———. *Catálogo crítico de libros para niños.* Madrid, Dirección General de Archivos y Bibliotecas, 1954. 350p. DLC, IYL.

A booklist of 2,280 titles, arranged by age groups and types of reading matter, annotated for subject content, and indexed by author, title and series.

507. ———. *Catálogo crítico de libros para niños.* Madrid, Ibarra, 1945. 191p. IYL.

The first selected list published by the *"Gabinete . . ."* for parents. Arrangement is by age group and by subject.

508. ———. *Selección de lecturas para niños y adolescentes.* Madrid, Servicio Nacional de Lectura, 1963. 259p. DLC, IYL, NNY.

A recommended selection of 1,400 books arranged by general subject or category, with age levels indicated by symbols. All are annotated and indexed by author, title and series.

509. "Actuación de las secciones infantiles y juveniles de las bibliotecas populares," *Biblioteconomía,* Barcelona, Año 11, No. 39, Jan.–June, 1954, pp. 2–19. DLC.

The theme of the 30th reunion of school librarians of Barcelona was children's work in public libraries. Reported here are the comments of the various librarians attending, on their experiences, their cataloging problems, and their opinions as to what constitutes good service.

510. Altamira, Rafael. "Las primeras bibliotecas circulantes para maestros y alumnos de las escuelas públicas españolas, *Boletín de bibliotecas y bibliografía,* Madrid, Tomo 2, Nos. 1–2, Jan.–June, 1935, pp. 57–62. DLC.

The history of the first circulating libraries for teachers and students of Spanish public schools, begun in Madrid in 1912.

511. Amo, Montserrat del. *La hora del cuento.* Madrid, Servicio Nacional de Lectura, 1964. 104p. (Breviarios de la biblioteca pública municipal, 9). DPU.

Storytelling should be used as a means to in-

spire reading. Selection of materials and preparation should be thought of in terms of the age and interest levels of the children. The author, a storyteller, gives a sampling of stories for the beginner, with hints for telling them in particular situations. She concludes with a two page bibliography.

512. "Aniversario de la biblioteca juvenil de la Santa Cruz," *Biblioteconomía,* Barcelona, Año 8, Nos. 29–30, Jan.–June, 1951, pp. 97–99. DLC.

The Santa Cruz children's library celebrated its tenth anniversary, and in honor of this event one of the young readers wrote a discourse on what the library had meant to him, which is reproduced here.

513. Arias, Manuel Antonio. "Las lecturas de los niños," *Atenas,* Madrid, Año 26, Nos. 251–252, Jan.–Feb., 1955, pp. 10–12. DLC.

What good reading consists of, and what it can do for the child, particularly from the moral point of view.

514. Armiñan, Luis de. "Cien amigos de los niños . . . el libro infantil en la conciencia universal," *ABC,* Madrid, Oct. 17, 1964, 6p. (No paging given.) DLC.

On the work of the IBBY, and what the Spanish section is doing to further the cause of a world understanding of children's literature.

515. Barcelona. Antigua Escuela del Mar. *El alma del niño— el niño y su verdadero mundo poético—la literatura infantil . . . y otros estudios.* Barcelona, Ediciones "Garbi," 1950.

516. ———. *Biblioteca de los niños.* Barcelona, Ediciones "Garbi," 1954.

517. ———. *Los niños hablan de los libros.* Barcelona, Ediciones "Garbi," 1958.

518. Barcelona. Cámara Oficial del Libro. *Libros para niños y adolescentes.* Barcelona. Cámara Oficial del Libro, 1945. 79p.

519. "Biblioteca infantil del parque de la ciudadela Barcelona," *Anuario de la Biblioteca Central y de las populares y especiales 1961–1963.* Barcelona, Disputación Provincial de Barcelona, 1965. pp. 276–280 ff. 4p. insert. IYL.

This report contains information on the founding of this children's library in a park, on April 23, 1963. The librarian is Aurora Díaz-Plaja. A plan of the library is given, together with four photographs and a copy of the program, which includes short book lists. The work of the other juvenile library in

Barcelona is reported on (pp. 174–178) and each of the branch and bookmobile reports include mention of children's work.

520. Bonamich, Magdalena. "Trabajo sobre la hora del cuento," *Biblioteconomía,* Barcelona, Año 6, No. 21, Jan.–Mar., 1949, pp. 29–32. NNY.

At the 25th reunion of librarians from the Barcelona school, this storyteller recounted her experiences with a story hour program, begun the previous year in the Esparraguera library.

521. Braunschvig, Marcel. "La literatura infantil," *El arte y el niño;* Madrid, D. Jorro, 1914; pp. 298–321.

A translation from the French. For note see 759.

522. Bravo-Villasante, Carmen. *Antología de la literatura infantil en lengua española.* 2nd ed. 2 vols. Madrid, Doncel, 1963. DLC, IYL, NNY.

These volumes are designed as companions to the history (below). They are arranged so that the examples of each author coincide with the order in which they appear in the history. Short biographical sketches are given, and illustrations in black and white enliven the text. Many of the important artists have reproductions of their work in color.

523. ———. *Historia de la literatura infantil española.* 2nd ed. Madrid, Doncel, 1963. 280p. DLC, IYL, NNY.

The most outstanding history of children's literature in Spanish. More selective than the Toral y Peñaranda study (606), this gives longer critical evaluations of the more important writers. It is organized by period, with such general movements as "outside influences," "magazines," "folklore," "poetry," "press," and "theater" inserted when they made their strongest appearance. There are numerous illustrations in color of pages from historically important books, from the 12th century through the 20th. Literature from other countries is represented only when it appeared in Spanish translation or was the direct inspiration for some Spanish writer. The Hispanic American writers are covered, but only in limited numbers. Author and title indexes are quite complete.

524. Bryant, S. C. *El arte de contar cuentos.* Barcelona, Editorial Nova Terra, 1964.

A translation into Spanish of *How to Tell Stories to Children.*

525. Bustos Tóvar, Eugenio de. "El niño y sus lecturas," *El libro español,* Madrid, Tomo 1, No. 8, Aug., 1958, pp. 379–382. DLC.

A search for the definition of children's literature: is it what they *do* read, or what educators think they should read?

This periodical is the official organ of the Instituto Nacional del Libro Español, and it gives the current national bibliography of books published in Spain. Since children's books are listed separately, this is the most helpful index to books published since 1958.

526. Castañón, Julia G. F. "Los libros y los niños," *Bordón,* Madrid, Tomo 10, No. 73, Jan., 1958, pp. 3–6. DLC.

Under this same title, this author periodically writes a column for this magazine, usually discussing some special aspect or kind of children's books. Most of them are very short. This particular article deals with biography, and the problems of writing it truthfully, when aiming at the young reader.

527. "Club del libro infantil," *Familia española,* Madrid, Año 3, No. 29, Mar., 1962–Aug., 1963 (Each issue). DLC.

Starting with the above issue, this family magazine began to review four children's books each month. The reviews are critical, several paragraphs in length and signed. In later issues some children's books are reviewed in the regular family book review section.

528. Collado, Pedro. *La literatura infantil y los niños.* Madrid, Editorial Collado, 1955. 56p. NNY.

The text of a conference delivered at the Centro Gallego in Madrid. The speaker considered the following general questions: What is children's literature? What is poetry? What is the fairy tale? Why is Andersen so widely known and liked?

529. "Concesión de los Premios Lazarillo 1959 . . ." *El libro español,* Madrid, Tomo 2, Nos. 20–21, Aug.–Sept., 1959, pp. 483–504. DLC.

The report on the Lazarillo Prizes and their winners is followed by an article on the publishing house, Molino, which was celebrating 25 years of publishing for children.

530. Consejo Nacional de Prensa. Comisión de Información y Publicaciones Infantiles y Juveniles. *Selección de revistas y libros infantiles y juveniles.* Madrid, 1965. 70p. IYL.

A selected list of books and periodicals for children. Criteria for selection are not stated. Author and title indexes and an index by age groups are included.

531. Davis, Lavinia R. "A report on children's

books in Spain," *Horn book,* Boston, Vol. 33, Feb., 1957, pp. 76–77. DLC, NNY.

A brief report on the work of the Gabinete de Santa Teresa de Jesús, and on the other groups working with children's literature in Spain.

532. Díaz-Plaja, Aurora. "La biblioteca infantil," *Com es forma i com funciona una biblioteca.* Barcelona, Barcino, 1960. pp. 49–58. MBN.

The rationale of the children's library, and its organization. The text is in Catalan.

533. ———. "Las bibliotecas infantiles," *Biblioteconomía,* Barcelona, Año 5, No. 20, Oct.–Dec., 1948, pp. 226–227.

A reprint of an editorial first appearing in *Solaridad Nacional* on May 14, 1948, concerning the rise in public interest for children's libraries, and the need for even greater understanding of the social and educational roles they can play.

534. ———. "Ensayo de una clasificación para una biblioteca infantil," *Boletin de la dirección general de archivos y bibliotecas,* Madrid, Año 8, No. 49, Jan.–Mar., 1959, pp. 11–13. DLC, NNY.

Comments on existing systems of classification for the children's library, and recommendations for improvement.

535. Domenech Ybarra, L. "Prensa deficiente para el mundo infantil," *Gaceta de la prensa española,* Madrid, No. 112, Aug.–Sept., 1957, pp. 153–162.

536. "Donativo de libros norteamericanos a la biblioteca juvenil de la Santa Cruz," *Biblioteconomía,* Barcelona, Año 7, No. 25, Jan.–Mar., 1950, pp. 45–47. DLC.

In 1950 the American Library Association gave a group of 120 children's books to the Santa Cruz children's library.

537. Espinas, José María. *Los niños quieren leer libros.* Barcelona, Amigos de la Cultura y del Libro, 1961.

538. "Experiencias en las bibliotecas infantiles," *Biblioteconomía,* Barcelona, Año 3, Oct.–Dec., 1946, pp. 314–317. DLC.

"Experiences in children's libraries."

539. "La exposición del libro infantil, claro exponente de la labor educativa del pueblo Español," *Revista española de pedagogía,* Madrid, Año 3, Nos. 9–10, Jan.–June, 1945, pp. 137–140. DLC.

The recent exposition of children's books, described here, is a sure sign that at last the Spanish people are becoming more and more concerned with this important aspect of the education of their children. The catalog of the exhibition is noted in 549.

540. Fortun, Elena. "Libros de niños," *Almanaque literario;* Madrid, Editorial Plutarco, 1935; pp. 149–153. DLC.

Herself a writer of children's books, Miss Fortun here discusses the year's production of literature for children, which she found lacking in quality and amount.

541. Fromkes, Eva Maurice. "Spain, and the books her children read," *Horn book,* Boston, Vol. 10, No. 4, July, 1934, pp. 252–255. DLC, IYL, NNY.

Children in Spain were reading mostly adult literature, according to this observer. They also had available in Spain the universal children's classics. Educators and adults in general were of the opinion that it was better to plunge the child directly into the advanced literary world, rather than having a simplified set of standards for them. She mentions a unique exhibit which took place in the Fine Arts Club: children showed their private, home libraries.

542. Gefaell, María Luisa. "Literatura infantil," *Revista de educación,* Madrid, Año 3, Vol. 8, No. 23, July–Aug., 1954, pp. 163–165. DLC.

In spite of a tremendous rise in interest due to libraries, exhibitions, prizes, etc., the public has no true idea as to what children's literature should be. This author contends that most parents still give and allow their children to read material which is worthless.

543. Gonzalvo Mainar, Gonzalo. "El sentido profundo del cuento infantil." *Educadores,* Madrid, Año 1, Vol. 1, No. 2, Mar.–Apr., 1959, pp. 269–275. DLC.

A definition of the folk (or fairy) tale, theories on its origin, its value to children.

544. Grimalt, Manuel. *Los niños y sus libros.* Barcelona, Sayma, 1962. 163p. DLC.

The purpose of this book, writes the author in the introduction, is to impress upon parents, teachers, writers and publishers the importance of serious study of children's literature in Spain, for he feels they are far behind other countries in realizing the consequences of a lack of good children's books.

545. "Hay un nosotros que son los niños," *La estafeta literaria,* Madrid, No. 254, Dec. 1, 1962, pp. 1–7; 16–18.

Several articles on children's literature and some reviews of recent children's books.

546. Hazard, Paul. *Los libros, los niños y los hombres.* Barcelona, Juventud, 1950. 285p. DLC.

Translated into Spanish by M. Manent. For note see 814.

547. Illa, Faustino. "Un modelo de biblioteca escolar," *Antenas,* Madrid, Año 26, Nos. 258–259, Aug.–Sept., 1955, pp. 192–195. DLCC.

The author describes the library of the *Escuela del Mar* in Barcelona, which he says is a fine example of the theories of Lasso de la Vega, Selva, De Maqua, etc., put to practice. The library of 1,800 volumes serves 340 children.

548. Illa Munné, María Carmen. "Bibliografía sobre libros para niños," *Biblioteconomía,* Barcelona, Año 10, No. 38, July–Dec., 1953, pp. 142–189. DLC.

A bibliography of 1,553 children's books, listed by author, which appeared in Barcelona between 1900–1950. The entries are not annotated, and many titles (of the classics, for example) are repeated if they appeared in more than one edition.

549. Instituto Nacional del Libro Español. *Catálogo de la exposición del libro infantil.* Madrid, Instituto . . . , 1945. 135p. DLC, IYL.

The catalog of the first national exposition of children's books, arranged according to publisher, and then by author. Included are approximately 1,200 titles, published mostly in the 1930's and 1940's and still in print at that time.

550. ———. *Libros infantiles y juveniles.* Madrid, Instituto Nacional del Libro Español, 1965. 277p. DLC, IYL, NNY.

A list of 5,294 titles, by subject and age group, with author, title and series indexes. An alphabetical listing of publishers who produce children's books is given, with addresses. Bound with this are the catalogs of all publishers of trade books for children.

551. ———. Comision Asesora de Editores de Libros de Enseñanza. *Libros y material de enseñanza.* Madrid, Instituto Nacional del Libro Español, 1966/67. 273p.

"Books and materials for teaching." Although the major emphasis is on textbooks, this includes many general children's books, films and filmstrips, recordings, etc., because the trend is away from the single-textbook-style of teaching. The items are arranged by grade level, from pre-school on up. Bound with this are the catalogs of dealers and suppliers of all types of books and materials approved for use in Spanish schools. There are author and title indexes. Also, current laws governing the acquisition and funding of school materials are reprinted at the very beginning.

552. Lasso de la Vega y Jiménez-Placer, Javier. *La biblioteca y el niño.* Burgos, Hijos de Santiago Rodríguez, 1938. 102p. (Publicaciones del Ministerio de Educación Nacional). DLC.

The concept of the children's library, its organization, the duties of the librarian, the activities, and related types of libraries, such as in the school and bookmobiles. Illustrated with many photographs, and including a short bibliography.

553. ———. "Bibliotecas infantiles. Bibliotecas infantiles. Bibliotecas escolares," *Manual de biblioteconomía;* 2nd. ed.; Madrid, Editorial Mayfe, 1957; pp. 477–525. (DLC has 1952 ed., same pub.).

A manual of practical suggestions on organizing the school and public library for children, means of attracting the child reader, selection of materials, duties of the librarian working with children, etc.

554. Lázaro, María H. "La lectura en los colegios de niños," *Atenas,* Madrid, Año 26, No. 255, May, 1955, pp. 122–126; Nos. 256–257, June–July, 1955, pp. 163–168. DLC.

In error, the first part of this article was attributed to M. Digna Villabriga. It is a declaration of the aims of the *Gabinete de Lectura de Santa Teresa de Jesús,* and a discussion of selected titles from their recommended lists of books for children.

555. "El libro infantil," *El libro español,* Madrid, Tomo 4, No. 48, Dec., 1961, pp. 309–330. DLC.

Contains "La 1ª Semana Nacional del Libro Infantil" by José Miguel de Azaola; "Los niños también tienen su literatura," by Rafael Sánchez; and "El libro infantil: objeto de inquietud creciente," an unsigned article pointing out the problems and weaknesses of present day books for children.

556. "El libro infantil y juvenil." *El libro español,* Madrid, Tomo 5, No. 59, Nov., 1962, pp. 1–26. DLC.

This annual issue on the children's book in Spain has articles by Carmen Bravo-Villasante and Angeles Villarta on children's and adolescent literature, a report on the 7th IBBY Congress in Hamburg by Rafael Sánchez, the winners and runners-up for the Andersen Prize, 1962, and a chronology of national children's book week in Spain.

557. "El libro infantil y juvenil," *El libro español,* Madrid, Tomo 6, No. 71, Nov., 1963, pp. 1–18. DLC.

A report on the 8th IBBY Congress in Vienna by Carmen Bravo-Villasante, a description of a children's library in a Barcelona zoo by Concha Zendrera de Ferrés, articles on children's and young adult literature by José María Sánchez Silva and Francisco Pérez González, and a review of Carmen Bravo-Villasante's 3 volume work (522 and 523) by Rafael Sánchez.

558.   "Libros infantiles para Reyes," *Ecclesia,* Madrid, Año 4, No. 179, Dec. 16, 1944, pp. 1210–1212; No. 180, Dec. 23, 1944, pp. 1234–1237; No. 181, Dec. 30, 1944, pp. 1257–1261. DLC.

An annotated list of books recommended for gifts to children. Divided by age groups, the titles are all annotated, and designated as "highly recommended," "acceptable," and "tolerable."

559.   "Libros infantiles y juveniles," *Bibliografía española.* Madrid, Ministerio de Educación Nacional, Dirección General de Archivos y Bibliotecas, Servicio Nacional de Información Bibliografía, 1958. Annual. DLC, DPU, NNY.

A national bibliography which lists all books published in Spain during the year. Children's books are listed separately under the above heading. However, because these annual compilations are late in appearing, for more current information the monthly lists in *El Libro Español* are recommended.

560.   "Los libros juveniles en España," *El libro español,* Madrid, Tomo 1, No. 11, Nov., 1958, entire issue. DLC.

This issue carries various articles on children's literature, authors, libraries, publishing houses. One article explains the work of the "Gabinete de Santa Teresa de Jesús," and another the conditions and requirements for the annual prize for children's books, the "Premio Lazarillo.'

561.   . . . [Literatura infantil] . . . [Bibliotecas infantiles.] *Boletin de la dirección general de archivos y bibliotecas,* Madrid, Año 1, No. 6, Sept., 1952, entire number. DLC.

Includes "Instalación y ambiente de las bibliotecas infantiles" by Miguel Fisac; "La hora infantil en Soria" by José Antonio Pérez Rioja; "Tengamos en cuenta al niño" by Julia Figueira; "La biblioteca escolar" by María Luisa Poves Bárcenas; plus other shorter articles, and a catalog of the exhibition of children's books held the previous Christmas and arranged by the Gabinete de Santa Teresa de Jesús.

562.   Luzuriaga, Lorenzo. *Bibliotecas escolares.* 2nd ed. Madrid, Publicaciones de la Revista de Pedagogía, 1934. 46p. (Serie escolar, 10). DLC.

The importance of school libraries, and the means to properly organize them. Included are a list of books appropriate for the school library, and a plan of study to get an acquaintance with children's literature. The bibliography indicates that the author reviewed many U.S. publications before completing his work.

563.   Madrid. Asociación Nacional de Bibliotecarios, Archiveros y Arqueologos. *Catálogo crítico de libros infantiles.* Madrid, Publicaciones Españoles, 1951. 130p. DLC, IYL, NNY.

The catalog of an exhibition held in March, 1951 at the national library. Selection of books was made by the *Gabinete de Lectura "Santa Teresa de Jesús."* There are 572 titles, arranged by age and subject, briefly annotated, and indexed by author and title.

564.   Madrid. Museo Pedagógico Nacional. *Bibliotecas circulantes para niños.* Madrid, Tipografía Artística, 1931. 90p. (Ministerio de Instrucción Pública y Bellas Artes). DLC.

A book-list of approximately 500 titles, grouped by age and then by publisher. No annotations are given.

565.   Malo, Pascual. "Difusión de la prensa educativa," *Atenas,* Madrid, Año 26, No. 260, Oct., 1955, pp. 228–232. DLC.

The author points out the high circulation of the comics in relation to the much lower one of the better children's magazines. He feels that Spain should work toward improvement of those produced by governmental and other educational agencies so that there would be a natural swing away from the comics.

566.   Maqua, Alberto de. *Bibliotecas juveniles; su organización y funcionamiento.* Madrid, Ediciones Juventud de Acción Católica, 1942. 89p. MBN.

A manual of organization for children's libraries. There are also two chapters on general criticism of children's literature.

567.   Martínez y Nuria Ferrer, Dorotea. "Una guía de lectura en ocasión de Navidad," *Biblioteconomía,* Barcelona, Año 4, No. 16, Oct.–Dec., 1947, pp. 170–175. NNY.

These 250 books listed were recommended for Christmas giving, and were on display in the Calella children's room. No annotations.

568.   Medina de la Puente, Aurora. *Bibliografía infantil recreativa.* Madrid, Ministerio de Educación Nacional, Sección de Publicaciones de la Secretaría General Técnica, 1958. 72p. (Biblioteca de la Revista de Educación, 3).

An expansion of the list which first appeared in the *Revista de educación* (569). The introductory material has also been broadened.

569. ———. "Bibliografía selectíva sobre literatura infantil," *Revista de educación,* Madrid, Año 6, Vol. 22, No. 63, May, 1957, pp. 25–29; No. 64, June, 1957, pp. 49–60. DLC.

After considering the characteristics of children's literature, the author defines what she calls the six literary "cycles" of the child, and the ages at which they usually occur. She then lists about 200 books which children enjoy reading at each of these levels. Each is annotated, with some suggestions for use.

570. Medio, Dolores. "Psicología y técnica del cuento infantil," *Atenas,* Madrid, Año 21, No. 197, Mar., 1950, pp. 63–65; No. 198, Apr., 1950, pp. 95–97. DLC.

In her defense of fantasy and the fairy tale, the author cites Gorki and Ortega y Gasset, for she says they cannot be accused of romantic notions about children's literature. The second part is on the art of telling stories.

571. Mistral, Gabriela. "El folklore para los niños," *Revista de pedagogía,* Madrid, No. 160, Apr., 1935.

In this periodical, not located, were a number of articles contributed by Gabriela Mistral on the subject of children's literature and folklore. They are frequently mentioned as being important in the study of Spanish and Latin American children's literature.

572. Montilla, Francisca. *Organización de la biblioteca escolar.* Madrid, 1942. MBN.

573. ———. *Selección de libros escolares de lectura.* Madrid, C.S.I.C., Instituto "San José de Calasanz," 1954. 321p. DLC.

Although concerned mostly with general textbooks, there are also a number of trade books critically analyzed in this selective study.

574. Mora, Morichu de la. "Los niños tienen sus heroes," *Mundo hispanico,* Madrid, Año 9, No. 94, Jan., 1956, pp. 18–20. DLC.

Twelve famous characters from children's books, and why children take them as their heroes. On page 17 is an article of critical reviews of recent collections of children's books.

575. Moreno, Celestino. "Las revistas infantiles," *Atenas,* Madrid, Año 26, No. 261, Nov., 1955, pp. 274–281. DLC.

An evaluation of children's magazines, particularly from the moral and religious point of view.

576. Niño, María Isabel and María Africa Ibarra. *Bibliotecas infantiles.* Madred, Dirección General de Archivos y Bibliotecas, 1956. 49p. (Anejos del Boletín, No. 30). DPU.

A manual on the principles of organization behind the children's library and the philosophy of service which they entail.

577. "IX Congreso de la Organización Internacional para el Libro Juvenil," *El libro español,* Madrid, Tomo 7, No. 83, Nov., 1964, pp. 523–527. DLC.

A report on the ninth congress of IBBY, and a description of the exhibit of children's books sponsored by the *"Gabinete de Santa Teresa de Jesús,"* in conjunction with the congress. For full report of the meetings, see entry 22.

578. Pérez-Rioja, José Antonio. *La biblioteca en la escuela.* Madrid, Ministerio de Educación Nacional, Comisaría de Extensión Cultural, 1961, 83p. DLC.

This practical handbook on the primary school library gives suggestions for organization, elementary cataloging, a glossary of library terms, aids to use in selection of children's books, a suggested collection for teachers' use and a four page bibliography.

579. ———. *Catálogo-guía de cien obras infantiles de la Biblioteca Pública de Soria.* Madrid, 1950.

580. ———. "La colaboración de los maestros con la biblioteca," *Revista de educación,* Madrid, Año 6, Vol. 20, No. 57, Feb., 1957, pp. 6–9. DLC.

The cooperation of teachers with the school library, particularly in planning such activities as book talks and story hours, which do more than instruction in attracting children to the contents of the library.

581. ———. "La literatura y la lectura infantiljuvenil," *Revista de educación,* Madrid, Año 7, Vol. 29, No. 81, May, 1958, pp. 23–28; No. 82, June, 1958, pp. 51–56. DLC.

The first part is an attempt to define children's and young people's literature, and to illuminate some of its special problems. The second part is a bibliography of 310 books, periodical articles and pamphlets on the subject, in Spanish, English, French, Italian, German, and a few in other languages.

582. ———. "Literatura y publicaciones para niños y adolescentes," *Revista de educación,* Madrid,

Año 14, Vol. 58, No. 168, Jan., 1965, pp. 10–14. DLC.

The changing attitudes toward education mean a necessary change in attitude toward the books produced for children and young people. The influence of films and TV needs to be examined. The author calls for cooperation among the many centers springing up in Europe, all designed for the special study of children's literature.

583.   ——. *Mil obras para los jóvenes.* Madrid, Dirección General de Archivos y Bibliotecas, 1952. 141p. (Servicio de Publicaciones, Ministerio de Educación Nacional.) DLC, IYL.

This list of 1,000 books for young people is first divided into the two general categories of "informational" and "recreational" reading matter, and then by sub-divisions of type (e.g. poetry, novels, drama). Each entry is annotated and there is an author index.

584.   ——. "Una sugerencia para la fiesta del libro. Una sugerencia hecha realidad," *Boletín de la dirección general de archivos y bibliotecas,* Madrid, Año 3, No. 18, Mar., 1954, pp. 32–34; No. 21, July–Aug., 1954, pp. 45–48. DLC.

In the first article, this librarian suggests that Spain try out, for its annual "Festival of the Book," a scheme devised by some educators in Bremen, Germany: they opened a kiosk for the period of "Book Week," and let it be known that they would exchange good books for comics and cheap magazines. The suggestion was taken up by the Servicio Nacional de Lectura and the results are described here.

585.   ——. "En torno a la lectura infantil y juvenil," *Revista de educación,* Madrid, Año 10, Vol. 47, No. 137, June, 1961, pp. 59–62. DLC.

The actual preferences of young people in their books, and how to lead them on to more substantial reading and when censorship must be applied to children's books is also discussed.

586.   Petrini, Enzo. *Estudio crítico de la literatura infantil.* Madrid, Editorial Rialpa, 1962. (Biblioteca de educación y ciencias sociales.)

A translation from the Italian.

587.   Poves Bárcenas, María Luisa. "Bibliotecas infantiles," *Bibliotheca hispana,* Madrid, 1ª sección, Tomo 6, Nos. 1–2, 1948, pp. 303–328. DLC.

The school library merits attention equal to that accorded the public library. The author suggests selection and organizational aids to assist in the founding of better school libraries.

588.   *Los premios de literatura infantil y juvenil.* Barcelona, Diputación Provincial, Biblioteca Central, 1965. Unp. IYL.

"Prize-winning children's and youth books." This pamphlet gives the history, terms of award, and past winners for all prizes awarded in Spain and for the Hans Christian Andersen international prize.

589.   "Prensa juvenil," *Atenas,* Madrid, Año 27, No. 268, May, 1956, pp. 121–126. DLC.

The results and recommendations of a conference on the juvenile press in Spain, sponsored by the teachers in private, religious schools.

590.   Quílez, Juana. "Bibliotecas infantiles en España: su organización y porvenir." International Congress of Libraries and Bibliography, 2nd; *Actas y trabajos, Vol. 3;* Madrid, Librería Julián Barbazán, 1936; pp. 266–268. DLC.

"Children's libraries in Spain, their present organization and future," as reported to the Congress in 1935. Following this is a very short article on secondary school libraries in Spain, by Eduardo Juliá.

591.   ——. "Cooperación entre la biblioteca y la escuela," *Boletín de bibliotecas y bibliografía,* Madrid, Tomo 1, No. 1, July–Sept., 1934, pp. 33–39; No. 2, Oct.–Dec., 1934, pp. 170–175. DLC.

"Cooperation between the public library and the school." The author is specifically referring to the primary school, and bases her suggestions on criteria in effect in U.S. libraries.

592.   Ribas, Encarnación. "Biblioteca de la Caja de Ahorros de Sabadell. Bibliotecas escolares circulantes." *Biblioteconomía,* Barcelona, Año 3, No. 11, July–Sept., 1946, pp. 253–256. DLC.

A public librarian describes how she put at the disposal of the schools small circulating collections of children's books.

593.   Riera, María Rosa, et al. "Trabajo de la bibliotecaria en una sección juvenil," *Biblioteconomía,* Barcelona, Año 13, No. 44, July–Dec., 1956, pp. 133–140. DLC.

Three children's librarians report on their work in public libraries, the books children were reading, and the lists which they found helpful.

594.   Rivas, Luisa. "Experiencias en las bibliotecas infantiles," *Biblioteconomía,* Barcelona, Año 3, No. 12, Oct.–Dec., 1946, pp. 314–317. NNY.

At the 23rd reunion of librarians in Barcelona, Miss Rivas reported on her experiences in the Calella public library children's room.

595. Roca, María. "Una guía de lectura para las secciones juveniles de nuestras populares," *Biblioteconomía,* Barcelona, Año 4, No. 14, Apr.–June, 1947, pp. 72–85. NNY.

A basic book list for young adult sections in the public library. Arrangement is by subject, and the reference materials are stressed over the recreational.

596. Rovira, Teresa María. "Bibliothèques pour enfants," *Biblioteconomia,* Barcelona, Año 12, No. 42, July–Dec., 1955, pp. 117–119. DLC.

The official report on libraries for children in Spain, as given in French at the IFLA conference in Brussels.

597. ———. "Evolución del libro infantil," *Biblioteconomía,* Barcelona, Año 16, No. 50, July–Dec., 1959, pp. 88–92. DLC.

In commenting on the exhibition of children's books held in connection with the national library conference, the author points out how they have changed over the years.

598. ———. *La revista infantil en Barcelona.* Barcelona, Biblioteca Central, 1964. Unp. DLC.

This small pamphlet was printed on the occasion of the 4th Semana Nacional del Libro Infantil y Juvenil. It is a historical survey of children's periodicals from Barcelona, together with a chronological list, annotated and with fairly complete information.

599. Ruiz Crespo, C. J. *Bibliotecas escolares.* Madrid, 1932. 32p.

600. Semana Nacional del Libro Infantil, 1st. *Catálogo.* Madrid, Instituto Nacional del Libro Español, 1961. 28p.

601. Soldevila, Carlos. *Qué cal llegir.* Barcelona, Libreria Catalonia, 1928.

602. Spain. Dirección General de Primera Enseñanza. Bibliotecas Permanentes. *Catálogo de una pequeña biblioteca de cultura general para niños y maestros de las escuelas nacionales.* Madrid, Tipografía Yagües, 1929. 21p. DLC.

A list of 330 suggested books for the school library. No annotations or index, and no bibliographic information beyond author and title.

603. Tavares, Denise Fernandes. "La biblioteca escolar y la biblioteca infantil pública," *Boletin de la dirección general de archivos y bibliotecas,* Madrid,

Año 6, No. 43, July–Sept., 1957, pp. 15–17. DLC.

A translation of a portion of her work in Portuguese (247).

604. Toral y Peñaranda, Carolina. "Educación literaria del niño," *El libro español,* Madrid, Tomo 3, No. 36, Dec., 1960, pp. 388–394. DLC.

An address delivered in Luxembourg at the 6th International Congress on Children's Books. It is concerned with ways and means of awakening literary tastes and interests in the child.

605. ———. "Ensayo de selección de bibliotecas para niñas de once a dieciséis años," *Bibliografía hispanica,* Madrid, Año 5, No. 7, July, 1946, pp. 455–463. DLC.

Advice to parents and librarians on choosing books for children aged 11 to 16.

606. ———. *Literatura infantil española.* 2 vols. Madrid, Editorial Coculsa, 1957. 221p. and 367p. IYL.

A valuable study of children's literature with a unique approach. Taking the great classics from Spain and other countries, the author then lists all the adaptations which have appeared since the original and which were distinctly meant for children. Only Spanish adaptations are mentioned. Volume 1 includes the early epics and the prose of 19th and 20th centuries. Volume 2 treats of poetry, religion, drama, periodicals and translations, all largely from the 19th and 20th centuries. Although not particularly critical from the literary point of view, this is an invaluable aid in tracing the various editions of the great and lesser known works read by children. The indexes suffer from incompleteness, but the table of contents is of additional help. A few pages from historical works are reproduced in black and white.

607. Vázquez, Jesús María. *La prensa infantil en España.* Madrid, Doncel, 1963. 208p. MBN.

A survey on the juvenile press in Spain, sponsored by a private organization formed to further the cause of good children's magazines.

608. ———. "Sociología infantil. Encuesta sobre la lectura de los niños de un sector de Madrid," *Revista de educación,* Madrid, Año 6, Vol. 23, No. 67, Oct., 1957, pp. 41–48. DLC.

This sociologist completed an intensive study of one of the sectors of Madrid. One of the special aspects of the study was the reading of the children living there. Through observation, questionnaires, direct interview and work with parents and teachers, the author was able to make some definite conclusions on the reading patterns of the city's children.

609.   Vivanco, José Manuel. "Literatura juvenil," *Educadores,* Madrid, Año 3, Vol. 3, No. 13, May-June, 1961, pp. 529–548. DLC.

Seven types of books popular among young persons are: biography, adventure, westerns, detective stories, spy stories, science fiction, and war stories. The author examines each type and then suggests a list of stories and books which satisfy the needs of the young adult.

610.   Vives, María Dolores. "Literatura y libros de imaginación para la juventud," *Biblioteconomía,* Barcelona, Año 18, Nos. 53–54, Jan.–Dec., 1961, pp. 29–32. DLC.

The importance of introducing good novels to young people who have outgrown the easier children's books, and some comments on the authors which this librarian has used with success.

611.   Vives, María Dolores. "La producción actual de libros infantiles a través de los catálogos de editoriales," *Biblioteconomía,* Barcelona, Año 16, No. 50, July–Dec., 1959, pp. 95–99. DLC.

Choosing at random titles from the publisher's catalogs, a librarian reviews the current year's production, pointing out that there are still few original works being produced in Spain.

612.   Yerro Mainar, Mercedes del. "Revistas infantiles: las de ayer y las de hoy," *Bordón,* Madrid, Tomo 10, No. 76, April 1958, pp. 237–245. DLC.

Children's magazines of yesterday and today —a comparative study of their literary and artistic merits.

Italy

"It has been said, and may we reiterate, that Children's Literature should be interpreted as meaning, not literature for children, destined peculiarly for the young, with a different set of esthetic values placed upon it than upon that of adults, but rather a literature of children, written by men and women so gifted as still to possess the spirit that is youth's while they create such works of art as meet the exigent judgement of the world-old and the world-artists. It will be these works alone which can endure for children, and only these books should be included in the final reckoning of *what is Children's Literature."* The above was written by Louise Hawkes in the introduction to her history of Italian children's literature (665). This was by no means the first such history, but it was one of the first to assign a position to this literature within the framework of Italian literature as a whole. Paul Hazard had attempted much the same thing in a 1914 article in the *Revue des Deux Mondes* (667), which he later revised and included as a chapter in his book.

What is curious about the fact that two such early studies by non-Italians exist, is that both hinted at the inferiority of children's literature in Italian, apart from two or three classics. It is tantalizing to speculate whether the outpouring of writing *about* children's literature, which began in the 1920's and continues up to today, is the result of a desire to prove that there is, indeed, good Italian literature for children. That there are an unbelievable number of books about the subject is evident. The difficulty lies in tracking them down and then assessing them in relation to one another and to the amount of literature which they discuss. As far as could be determined, no one has yet come up with an answer (not even speculatively) as to why there are so many "critical histories" of children's literature in Italian, when the production of that literature has been comparatively low.

Like all of the European countries, Italy went through the didactic period. The names of Francesco Soave, Giuseppe Taverna, Gino Capponi, Luigi Alessandro Parravicini, Pietro Thouar and others are not likely to live on, except as vague contributors to the first feeble efforts at writing consciously for children. It is interesting to note that two of these authors Padre Soave and Parravicini, got their start by winning prizes offered for the best manuscript of a children's book, the former in 1775 and the latter in 1834. Both were named by default, because there were no manuscripts submitted which completely satisfied the judges and donors. Parravicini's work, *Giannetto,* became the center of controversy and "received consistently the most undeserved praise and the most bitter criticisms" (665, p. 39). It was an encyclopedic story in which the child reader was to acquire a knowledge of himself, the world around him, and the history of his country.

It was the decade of the 1880's which saw the creation of the two classics of Italian children's literature that have stayed alive and come to be known around the world. *Storia di un Burattino* (the original title of *Pinocchio*) appeared in the magazine for children *Il Giornale dei Bambini,* published in Rome in 1881–1882. It was written by Carlo Lorenzini under his journalistic pen name, Collodi. *Cuore dei Ragazzi,* by Emondo De Amicis, was first published as a book, by Treves of Milano, in 1886. So much has been written about these two books and their heroes, the one impudent and the other tender-hearted and sensitive to the extreme, that it would be foolish to attempt here even the briefest analysis of their styles, subject matter and relative popularity. Almost all of the histories cited in the bibliography have something interesting to say about both, and for those unable to read Italian, the chapters in Hawkes are quite satisfactory. One thing should be pointed out and that is the fact that Pinocchio had so many imitators, not only in Italy but around the world (see, for example, the Introduction to Spain). More than any other character from among the masterpieces of children's literature, Pinocchio has been adapted, put to music, filmed, changed to suit other national characteristics, and of course, used in theatre and puppet shows. One wonders if this is due to his show off nature, or if it is the natural fate of a puppet character!

With the appearance and success of these two works (and others as well) the floodgates were opened. Anyone and everyone, but most particularly women and teachers, thought he could try this new career of writing for the young. Of those whose works appeared in the last decade of the 19th and the first two decades of the 20th century, the five still read and remembered are Luigi Capuana, Renato Fucini, Giuseppe Ernesto Nuccio, Ida Baccini and Luigi Bertelli, better known as Vamba. The last named was the author most obviously influenced by Collodi, in style and themes. Fucini and Ida Baccini, on the other hand, wrote more in the spirit of De Amicis. Both were filled with a sense of the goodness and optimism in life. It was Capuana and Nuccio who brought to children's writing the movement toward realism which was a part of the general trend in European literature of the time. Capuana was especially concerned with remaining "objective" in his depictions of life and its trials. Both he and Nuccio are often criticized for introducing scenes and characters "not suitable" for the young reader, e.g. violent death, extreme suffering, murderers.

Another author from this period whose works continued to pour out in numerous editions was Emilio Salgari. His adventure stories have been most frequently called poor imitations of Jules Verne, but lacking a better writer, Italian children have continued to devour his books in much the same way their American counterparts still follow the adventures of Tom Swift and the Hardy boys. Giuseppe Fanciulli has suggested that the reason for Salgari's success lies in his use of "cinematographic technique." Jules Verne uses a slow, meticulous style to build up a sense of scientific veracity, but Salgari moves in flashes, building up an incredibly complicated background in a few scenes. In a word, his stories have action, and this is something which has always had a strong appeal for children, who do not stop to consider such things as literary merit.

The name of Fanciulli as critic brings out only one aspect of the life of this indefatigable worker for the cause of good children's literature. Fanciulli was active in writing, criticism, theater for children, and in generally keeping this field in the public eye. He on the literary side and Giovanni Calò on the educational were enough to generate a constant stream of words on the subject of children's literature.

As to the present state of children's books in Italy, there is much disagreement. There are critics who claim much improvement has been made, others who believe the quality of books to be worse than ever and still others who find fault not so much with the quality as with the relevance of subject matter. Perhaps it is significant that such an individualist as Pinocchio is the character who represents the best quality of children's books in Italy. In the research and teaching of children's books, in the development of children's libraries, in contemporary criticism, in current publishing—in all these no country in Europe shows its wont to go so many separate ways as does Italy. This is not meant to imply necessarily a sense of discord. The bursts of activity in all directions stem more from a lively sense of individuality and from convictions that no matter how the branches grow, as long as they grow vigourously, they are sure to enhance the tree.

The one force which can perhaps be considered unifying is the Italian section of IBBY. Its membership includes many of the leading figures from the three great "powers" behind work with children's books: the Centro Didattico Nazionale di Studi e Documentazione in Florence, the pedagogical institute connected with the University of Padua which has a chair in children's literature, and the Ente Nazionale per le Biblioteche Popolari e Scolastiche in Rome. The

Centro Didattico serves as the secretariat for the Italian IBBY, and their bulletin, *Schedario,* is also the official organ of the section.

There are numerous and varied activities centering around children's books going on throughout Italy, and the members of the section are usually involved in one way or another. However, this cooperation does not always extend to the activities within each of the three organizations. The standards of library service to children have been differently outlined by the Centro Didattico and the Ente Nazionale. Neither of them has come up with a plan for national service, acceptable on all sides. The few public and school libraries giving outstanding service are the exceptions rather than the rule.

To provide for a model study center, each of the three organizations has made admirable attempts to build up an international collection of children's books. Due to limited finances, these centers must rely largely on publishers' gifts, or exchanges, so that there cannot be much critical selection. Nevertheless, the exchange of more and better books does seem to be improving.

In spite of the fact that each of the organizations has a periodical or bulletin reviewing children's books, there is very little agreement as to what constitutes a critical review. By and large, the point of view is either pedagogical or socio-psychological. When it is literary it is often based on a popular standard. For all of the activity going on in the adult world of children's books, there still seem to be few persons who combine literary discrimination with the ability to observe and assess children's tastes without becoming pedantic. This is true in many countries, not only Italy.

Prizes for children's books receive perhaps the most publicity and this is understandable because there are several awarded in Italy which have received international attention. The third annual "Città di Caorle," sponsored by the city of Caorle and the Pedagogical Institute in Padua, was given in 1966. In connection with this prize the Institute always gathers a distinguished group of scholars who participate in a seminar on some aspect of children's literature. The prize itself is awarded to the book which in the opinion of the jury, expresses in the best manner the sense of Europe as a continental unity. There are numerous other prizes, usually offered by a city or an organization. Among these are the Castello Sanguinetto Award, Villa Taranto Award, Palma d'Oro Award, Uno-a-erre Award, Laura Orvieto Award and the Edmondo de Amicis Prize. There are also awards and prizes made in connection with the Bologna international children's book fair. The third of these was held in 1966.

There is still a long way to go before Italy can point to significant increases in the quality and quantity of books reaching children. There must be greater effort made to develop library service of one kind or another, since there are still a high percentage of families who cannot afford to buy books. There should be more and better translations made to augment the native literature. Publishers must learn to give the same care in editing and designing children's books, as they do adult books. When this begins to happen, there is no doubt that the children's book movement will progress by leaps and bounds, for there is a core of dedicated and spirited leaders to give it impetus and support.

613. Associazione per la Diffusione delle Bibliotechine pei Fanciulli. *Catalogo ordinato e dimostrativo dei migliori libri per fanciulli e giovinetti.* Bologna, Comitato Nazionale per le Biblioteche Scolastiche, 1914. 159p.

614. ———. *Catalogo sistematico.* Bologna, Libreria Treves, 1908. 71p. DLC.

Recommended books for children from 8–14 years of age, with an explanatory section at the end on the work of the Associazione . . . whose general aims were the furthering of public education.

615. Bargellini, Piero. *Canto alle rondini; panorama storico della letteratura infantile.* 4th ed. Firenze, Vallecchi, 1963. 231p. IYL. (DLC has 1961 edition, same publisher; NNY has 1953 edition, same publisher).

"A panoramic study of children's literature," which approaches it through the lives of individual authors whose work came to be loved and read by many children. Most of them here discussed are Italian (Salgari, Collodi, Capuana, De Amicis, Basile, Luigi Bertelli, Giuseppe Fanciulli, etc.), but some foreign authors are also included. The bio-bibliography on pp. 219–231 includes the important facts in the lives of the authors discussed.

616. Battistelli, Vincenzina. *Il libro del fanciullo. La letteratura per l'infanzia.* 2nd ed. rev. Firenze, La Nuova Italia, 1962. 469p. IYL. (1st ed. 1948, same pub.; DLC has 2nd ed., 1959, same pub., 429p.).

This is a complete revision, up-dating, and newly arranged version of the author's earlier work, *La Letteratura Infantile Moderna: Guida Bibliografica.* Firenze, Vallecchi, 1923, 180p. (This was later reissued as *La Moderna Letteratura per l'Infanzia e la Giovinezza.* Bologna, Capelli, 1925, 246p.) It is a history of children's literature from Greek and Roman classical times, to the present day, presented by eras, centuries, or periods of certain trends. The closing chapters give vignettes on the children's books of other countries, and some reviews of recent Italian books for children. There is a name index.

617. Bersani, Maria. *Libri per fanciulli e per giovinetti.* Torino, Paravia, 1930. 200p. IYL.

Brief plots and explanations of some 950 books for children, by 450 different authors, all printed in Italy. The purpose of this selection was not so much critical as inclusive.

618. Bertin, Giovanni Maria. *Stampa, spettacolo ed educazione.* Milano, Carlo Marzorati, 1956. 142p. DLC.

The first part, pp. 13–39 is on books and periodicals for children and the fourth section, pp. 85–112, is on theater and adolescence. Both have implications which affect children's literature, and to a lesser degree, so do the two middle sections, on films and TV for children.

619. Betta, Bruno. *Che cosa leggere dall'infanzia alla gioventú.* Brescia, Vita Scolastica, 1953. 200p.

620. *Bibliografia critica della moderna letteratura infantile.* Firenze, S.I.C.C.L.I., 1933.

621. "Biblioteche per i più giovani," *Bibliofilia,* Firenze, Anno 66, No. 1, 1964, pp. 88–90. DLC, NNY.

An editorial concerning the importance of library service to the very young, what other countries are doing in this type of work, and suggestions that Italy should do likewise.

622. Bitelli, Giovanni. *Scrittori e libri per i nostri ragazzi. Esposizione e critica.* Torino, Paravia, 1952. 142p. DLC.

An introduction and nine critical essays on the children's works of Luigi Alessandro Parravicini, Giovanni Battista Basile, Charles Perrault, Luigi Capuana, Giuseppe Ernesto Nuccio, Edmondo De Amicis, Enrico Novelli (Yambo), Emilio Salgari and Jules Verne.

623. ———. *Piccola guida all'conoscenza della letteratura infantile.* Torino, Paravia, 1947. 178p.

624. Bonafin, Ottavia. *La letteratura per l'infanzia.* 11th ed. Brescia, La Scuola, 1962. 214p. IYL.

This study of children's literature is divided into four parts: classical literature of Greece and Rome, the European classics of the 17th, 18th and 19th centuries which came to be regarded as children's books, the development of children's literature in Italy, libraries and periodicals for children. The appendix lists the books mentioned in the text and gives a short bibliography. Name index.

625. Calcagno, Guido. *Biblioteche scolastiche.* Milano, Mondadori, 1938. 148p. NNY.

A manual of school library organization, administration and operation, with suggested related readings. However, no specific standards are discussed (number of books per student, budget, location, space allotment, etc.).

626. Calò, Giovanni. "Letteratura infantile," *Educazione e scuola;* Firenze, Marzocco, 1957.

627. Calò, Giovanni. "Letteratura infantile," *Problemi vivi e orizzonti nuovi* . . . Firenze, Barbèra, 1935; pp. 61–85.
     A review of current thinking on children's literature, how it should be brought into the life of the child, its value in education, and what it really consists of, in language and illustration.

628. Campanile, Aristide. *Sommario di letteratura per l'infanzia.* Roma, Faita, 1946. 174p.

629. Canilli, A. C. "Letteratura infantile," *L'educatore italiano,* Milano, Dec. 20, 1955, pp. 29 ff.

630. "Caorle reenters history," *Times educational supplement,* London, Oct. 2, 1964, p. 515. DLC, NNY.
     A description as to how the Caorle Prize came into being, its terms and the methods whereby the jury decides on the winner.

631. Carollo, Francesco. *Letteratura infantile.* Palermo, Editrice Siciliana, 1942. 31p. (Problemi di Didattica, I). DLC.
     An essay on the importance of children's reading, aimed at teachers. Its terms are very general and the few specific Italian works mentioned are barely touched upon.

632. Casotti, Mario. "Ragazzo incontro alla poesia," *L'indice d'oro,* Roma, Anno 4, No. 5, May, 1953, pp. 115–118. DLC.
     "The child's encounter with poetry," what it can mean to him, and how the educators and parents of today's children abuse it by introducing little or mediocre poetry to their charges.
     This periodical is concerned with all of the arts as they relate to the education of the child (in the pure sense). It contains frequent short articles on children's literature, reviews of good books for children, and other related matters. Only the longer articles are listed in this bibliography.

633. Centro Didattico Nazionale di Studi e Documentazione. *Guida di letture giovanili per le biblioteche scholastiche e popolari.* Firenze, Centro Didat-

tico . . . , 1956. 173p. (Archivio didattico. Serie VI. Studi e documentazione). IYL.
     The first part contains general theory and criticism, and a revue of the history of children's books in Italy and other European countries, as well as in the other continents. There are also chapters on theater, periodicals, libraries and illustration of books for children. A recommended basic list of books is also given. The second part is a practical guide to cataloging and organizing a children's library.

634. Cerri, Giovanni. *Le predilezioni letterarie degli adolescenti e la letteratura scolastica elementare.* Firenze, Bemporad, 1911. 224p.

635. Ceselin, Ferruccio. "La letteratura per ragazzi, oggi," *Scuola libera,* Asolo, Anno 1, No. 5, Mar. 1947, pp. 20–24. DLC.
     Children's literature in Italy at this time was either overly didactic, or too much influenced by the mass popularity of Walt Disney and the comics.

636. "Che cosa leggono i nostri ragazzi? Le letture degli studenti delle scuole di Palermo," *Accademie e Biblioteche d'Italia,* Roma, Anno 11, No. 5, Oct. 1937, pp. 429–473; Anno 13, No. 1, Oct., 1938, pp. 12–25. DLC.
     In 1937 a reading interest survey was taken among the young people of seven schools in Brescia. The results are published in the first article, according to the type of school. This prompted an educator in Palermo to do the same, and his results are given in the second article, with comments as to how they contrast with the first survey.

637. Cibaldi, Aldo. *Criteri di scelta e valutazione del libro per l'infanzia.* 2nd ed. Brescia, La Scuola, 1961. 126p. IYL.
     The main chapters are concerned with: poetry and literature for children, aesthetics and pedagogy in the judging of children's books, other methods of integrating children's literature. There is a two page bibliography.

638. Cicogna Argentieri, O. *L'ordinamento educativo della letteratura infantile.* Cremona, Bignami, 1921.

639. "Com è nata la Biblioteca Internazionale del Fanciullo," *La parola e il libro,* Roma, Anno 48, No. 5, May, 1965, pp. 374–378. DLC, IYL, NNY.
     The history and aims of the international youth library which was established by the Ente Nazionale Biblioteche Popolari e Scholastiche in 1961. It is modeled on the library in Munich, and intended

mostly for the comparative study of children's literature, rather than for circulation to children.

640. Convegno Nazionale della Letteratura per l'Infanzia e la Giovinezza. *Atti.* Bologna, 1938.

641. Cottone, Carmelo. "Biblioteche scolastiche," *L'indice d'oro,* Roma, Anno 3, No. 11, Nov., 1952, pp. 327–331. DLC.

The laws which govern school libraries in Italy, how they are effected through agencies and the Ministry of Education, the allocation of funds, the lack of books and similar problems are discussed here with a view to pointing out why the school library situation is so far behind its proposed ideal.

642. Crocioni, Giovanni. "Le biblioteche per gli studenti delle scuole medie," *Revista di filosofia,* Modena, Anno 1, No. 3, May–June, 1909, pp. 84–94. NNY.

The library should be the central part of every school and its purpose should be dual—to furnish good reading to all students at no expense, and to habituate the student in the frequent use of books.

643. ———. *Prontuario per la biblioteca di studenti di scuole medie.* Varese, 1914.

644. Cuesta, Ugo. "Problemi attuali della letteratura infantile e giovanile." Congresso Sindacato Nazionale Fascista degli Autori e Scrittori; *Atti;* Roma, Sindacato Nazionale . . . , 1940.

645. *Cultura professionale del maestro. Serie B. Profili.* Firenze, Marzocco-Bemporad, 1952 ff. IYL.

A series of biographies of children's writers intended for the teacher and student of children's literature. Up to the present there are volumes on Andersen, Pierina Boranga, Luigi Capuana, Ida Baccini, De Amicis, Ignazio Drago, Renato Fucini, Paolo Reynaudo, Harriet Beecher Stowe, L. M. Alcott, Vamba, A. Daudet, R. Kipling, Collodi, Giuseppe Fanciulli, J. London, G. E. Nuccio, A. Cuman Pertile, and Mark Twain.

646. Draghi, Laura. "Questioni di letteratura infantile," *Il mulino,* Bologna, Anno 3, Fascicolo 34–35, Aug.–Sept., 1954, pp. 535–547. DLC.

The author questions whether the IBBY Congress, held in Florence in May, 1954, was truly an international exchange of ideas about children's literature, since many countries who have been leaders in the production of children's books were represented sparsely or not at all. She does not disparage their efforts, but wishes to raise the issue of proper and effective sequence in the development of libraries and good books, which she feels is lacking in Italy.

647. Fait, Beniamino. "La biblioteca," *L'indice d'oro,* Roma, Anno 6, No. 10, Oct., 1955, pp. 296–300. DLC.

The new educational program to be followed in Italy recommends classroom libraries of certain selected books for each level. The author believes that it is necessary to have great variety, and that teachers should be given a central collection from which to choose in order to suit the needs of their students. They should also be taught the means to a more advantageous use of children's literature.

648. Fanciulli, Giuseppe. "Delitti di lesa infanzia: I giornali pei ragazzi," *Nuova antologia,* Roma, Anno 73, Fascicolo 1594, Aug. 16, 1938, pp. 447–455. DLC.

Of late certain educators are condemning the children's magazines as being bad for children, but this author contends that they have brought much joy, adventure, and even literature into the lives of their young readers. He specifically defends some of them for instilling the qualities of fascist patriotism in youth.

649. ——— and Enrichetta Monaci-Guidotto. *La letteratura per l'infanzia.* 9th ed. Torino, Società Editrice Internazionale, 1940. 341p. NNY. (First published in 1926. IYL has 1934 ed., same pub.).

This work foreshadows the author's *Scrittori e libri . . .* (below). It treats of the history of children's literature from ancient times, to the more recent movements in Western and Northern Europe. The Italian sections are divided into Thouar and his influence, the period of Collodi, from Collodi to Vambra, and the contemporaries. There is an author index.

650. ——— and Mario Pucci. *Scrittori e libri per l'infanzia.* Rev. ed. Torino, Società Ed. Internazionale, 1960. 291p. IYL. (NNY has 1949 edition, same pub., 289p.).

Mr. Pucci has expanded G. Fanciulli's study of Italian children's literature, and deleted all but the most important names in covering the foreign influences. There is an appendix for a suggested home library for children, a short bibliography and a limited author index.

651. Fava, Onorato. *Il fanciullo nella letteratura.* Firenze, Nemi, 1932. 185p.

652. Flores d'Arcais, Giuseppe and Anna Maria Bernardinis. "The situation and problems of juvenile literature in Italy in the post-war period." *Bookbird,* Vienna, No. 2, 1965, pp. 8–13. DLC, IYL, NNY.

This is one of the few genuinely critical articles on contemporary Italian children's literature.

653. Fratini, A. *Note bibliografiche sulla letteratura per l'infanzia.* Torino, 1928.

654. Fuscà, F. *Storia della letteratura infantile.* Roma, Il Convivio, 1939. 85p.

655. Ganzaroli, Walter. *Breve storia della letteratura per l'infanzia.* 2nd ed. Rovigo, Instituto Padano di Arti Grafiche, 1952. 134p. NNY, IYL.

Brief biographical and critical sketches of many Italian authors for children, covered in chronological order. Following this are even shorter sketches of the major writers of foreign classics, mostly 19th century. There is an author index.

656. Garras, A. "Timori del misterioso e letteratura infantile," *Puer,* Siena, No. 3, 1954.

657. Giacobbe, Olindo. *Manuale di letteratura infantile.* 5th ed. Roma, Signorelli, 1947. 466p.

The first version is called *Note di Letteratura Infantile,* Roma, Berlutti, 1923; the later version is called *La Letteratura Infantile,* Torino, Paravia, 1925.

658. Giorgi, G. *La lettura e la recitazione; necessitá delle bibliotechine scolastiche.* Catanzaro, 1931. 27p.

659. Goretti, Maria. "Letteratura infantile," *Guida all'esame scritto . . . ,* Part 2; Firenze, Le Monnier, 1958.

660. Graziani-Camillucci, I. *La letteratura per l'infanzia.* Milano, Collana "La Fiore del Sapere."

661. Grossi, L. "Il problema della letteratura infantile," *Pedagogia e scuola;* Firenze, Casa Ed. Macrí, 1958.

662. Grotowska, Helena. [Literature for children and youth in Italy.] *Ruch pedagogiczny,* Warszawa, Vol. 31, No. 1, 1947/48.

Paper given at the Polish Congress on Children's Literature (see 2114). In Polish.

663. Guglielmelli, Amedeo. *Autori per l'infanzia.* Rovigo, Ster, 1954. 261p. IYL.

The author writes brief biographies and critical summaries on the work of the following: L. M. Alcott, H. C. Andersen, J. M. Barrie, G. Basile, H. B. Stowe, Luigi Capuana, Lewis Carroll, Collodi, E. De Amicis, D. Defoe, C. Dickens, Grimm Brothers, S. Lagerlöf, W. Hauff, R. Kipling H. Malot, Florence Montgomery, G. E. Nuccio, C. Perrault, A. Pushkin, Rudolf Raspe, G. Swift, Mark Twain, Vamba, Jules Verne, and Oscar Wilde.

664. Hassler, Harriot E. "Beginnings of children's libraries in Italy," *Pacific Northwest Library Association. Proceedings,* Walla Walla, Vol. 25, June, 1934, pp. 34–37. DLC, NNY.

An American librarian records the impressions of her visit to a children's library in Florence.

665. Hawkes, Louise Restieaux. *Before and after Pinocchio. A study of Italian children's books.* Paris, The Puppet Press, 1933. 207p. DLC, NNY.

A history and criticism of Italian children's literature from classical Roman civilization to 1930; a study undertaken for partial fulfilment of the doctoral degree in the Faculty of Romance Languages at Columbia University in New York. The works are treated as genuine literature, and assessed in that light. The final chapter is a summary of children's literature in Europe. The author and name index is helpfully complete.

666. Hazard, Paul. *Letteratura infantile.* Milano, Viola, 1954. 283p. IYL.

Translated into Italian by A. De Marchis. Preface by L. Volpicelli, with an appendix on Italian children's literature by Olindo Giacobbe, revised by Guglielmo Valle.

For note on original work, see 814.

667. ———. "La littérature enfantine en Italie," *Revue des deux mondes,* Paris, 84e année, 6 période, Tome 19, Feb. 15, 1914, pp. 842–870. DLC, NNY.

A penetrating commentary on Italian children's literature, from the *ninne-nanne* rhymes, to Salgari, to Collodi/Lorenzini, to de Amicis, to the rather second-rate children's magazines which can hardly be called literary, but which Italian children consume voraciously.

668. Jacucci, Giuseppe. *Letteratura per l'infanzia.* Forlì, Studio Editoriale O.D.C.U., 1947. 123p.

669. Jaquetti, Palmira. "La comptina." Congresso Internazionale di Studi Romanzi, 8th, Florence, 1956. *Atti,* Vol. 2. Firenze, 1960. pp. 567–599. NNY.

A study of children's counting rhymes and other nursery rhymes, with Italian versions compared to some in French, German and English.

670. Kyle, Anne Dempster. "Children's books in Italy," *Horn book,* Boston, Vol. 26, Jan.–Feb., 1950, pp. 56–62. DLC, NNY.

A general survey of postwar books for children in Italy, mentioning a few titles specifically, but in general bemoaning the poor quality and low number of children's books produced.

94

671. Leone, Giuseppe and Luigi Vecchione. *La letteratura per l'infanzia.* Salerno, Hermes, 1954. 212p. IYL.

This is subtitled "theoretical premises and critical notes" and includes a chapter on the history of Italian children's literature, sections on the Italian and foreign "classics" for children, and an appendix with short notes on the influence of film, radio, TV, and other mass media. There is a name index only.

672. *Libri per bambini; livres pour la jeunesse; children's books; Kinderbücher.* Firenze, Sansoni Antiquariato, 1949. 64p. IYL.

A dealer's catalog of old and new children's books in Italian, French, English and German. Each item is described fully and annotated, and there is an index.

673. "Libri per i giovani," *La parola e il libro,* Roma, 1918 ff. Monthly. DLC, NNY.

Since its beginning, this publication of the National Society of Popular and school libraries has had a column or section reviewing children's books. Other titles of the section have been: "Biblioteca dei giovani," "Per le biblioteche degli alunni," Letteratura giovanile," "Il libro del fanciullo," etc. In about one out of every two issues, there are articles on children's or school libraries, some aspect of children's literature, or reviews of professional aids.

674. Lombroso, Paula. [La letteratura infantile.] *La vita dei bambini.* Torino, Fratelli Bocca, 1904. 208p.

675. Lugli, Antonio. "Una mostra di illustratori," *L'indice d'oro,* Roma, Anno 6, No. 3, Mar., 1955, pp. 89–92. DLC.

Comments on an exhibition of the work of artists who illustrate children's books in Italy.

676. ———. "Processo alla fiaba," *L'indice d'oro,* Roma, Anno 7, No. 2, Mar., 1956, pp. 57–59. DLC.

A defense of the fairly tale in the face of modern educators who feel it has frightening or violent characteristics which damage the child's psyche.

677. ———. *Storia della letteratura per l'infanzia.* Firenze, Sansoni, 1960. 395p. DLC, NNY. (Le Piccole Storie Illustrate, 61)

A universal history of children's literature, with slight emphasis on the Italian. Arrangement is by type (fairy tales, fables, poetry), and then by period and by country. The universal classics are treated separately, as are modern writers around the world. A few reproductions from historically important works are included, and the name index is quite complete. There are six pages of bibliography.

678. Marchesini Gobetti Prospero, Ada. *Dai 4 ai 16; guida ai libri per ragazzi.* Torino, Ed. del Giornale dei Genitori, 1960. 147p. Supplement, 1961; 16p. IYL.

A recommended list, not too selective, arranged by age and subject categories, and not annotated. There is a short chapter on "children in the library." Author index.

679. Marchetti, Italiano. "Un antenato della letteratura per ragazzi," *"L'indice d'oro,* Rome, Anno 2, No. 1, Jan., 1951, pp. 23–26. DLC.

"A forefather of children's literature." The title refers to the *Panchatantra,* and the author points out some of the traces of its influence on Italian and French literature which eventually came to be known and read as children's literature.

680. ——— and Enzo Petrini. *Buonincontro; guida critico-storica e antologia della letteratura per ragazzi italiana e straniera.* 2nd ed. rev. Firenze, Le Monnier, 1963. 432p. DLC, IYL.

An introductory history of children's literature, followed by selections from the major classics, both Italian and foreign, but all in the Italian language.

681. Martinez, Eugenia. *Leggere; guida critico-bibliografica al libro per la gioventú.* Firenze, Le Monnier, 1966. 238p. IYL.

"A critical-bibliographical guide to books for young people." The author makes critical comments on some 800 works for children and youth. There are author and title indexes, but it is difficult to locate many of the English language authors, since they are listed under their middle names, rather than last names. There is a short bibliography.

682. Mastropaolo, Michele. *Panorama della letteratura infantile.* 2nd ed. Milano, A. Vallardi, 1955. 250p. IYL. (1st edition pub. by Marzocco, Firenze 1947.)

"Panorama of children's literature." Personal, critical evaluations of the work of about 200 writers for children, preceded by general comments on the nature of children's literature.

683. Mauro, Vincenzo. *Letteratura per l'infanzia.* 2nd ed. rev. and expanded. Napoli, Gioffi, 1959. 181p. IYL.

Essays on the genesis of children's literature, on Collodi, Andersen, and other authors, on realism in children's books, poetry for children, and a recommended list of books. Short bibliography and index.

684. Melegari, Vezio. "La biblioteca scolastica," *La didattica della lingua Italiana;* Roma, Ed. Richerche, 1956.

685. ———. "Children's books in Italy before Pinocchio," *Junior bookshelf,* Windermere, Vol. 18, No. 3, July, 1954, pp. 109–114. DLC, IYL, NNY.

A brief historical account in English of the period from 1775–1883. The writer continues the study with *"Pinocchio, Cuore* and the other Italian books," in Vol. 19, No. 2, Mar., 1955, pp. 71–77.

686. Michieli, Armando. *Della letteratura per l'infanzia e la fanciullezza.* 4th ed. rev. Padova, Cedam, 1948. 195p. IYL.

A rather superficial survey of the major works of western children's literature. There are also chapters on journalism, theater and radio for children. There is a name index.

687. ———. "I libri che non piacciono ai ragazzi," *Rassegna di pedagogia,* Padova, Sept.–Oct., 1949, pp. 225 ff.

688. ———. *Ragazzi e libri.* Rovigo, Instituto Padano di Arti Grafiche, 1952. 366p. DLC.

Part 1 is a commentary on the characteristics of children's literature, and a little of its history. Part 2 deals with specific types such as fables, legends, poetry, biography, etc. Parts 3, 4 and 5 are much shorter and deal with text-books, book illustration and periodicals for children. The author limits himself to Italian books, when examples are mentioned.

689. Mignosi, P. "Il pregiudizio della letteratura per l'infanzia," *L'Educazione nazionale,* Lugano, No. 2, Oct., 1924.

690. Nobili, Maria Nennella. "Le biblioteche specializzate per l'infanzia," *Accademie e biblioteche d'Italia,* Roma, Anno 8, No. 6, Nov.–Dec., 1934, pp. 609–618. DLC.

While there are numerous small collections of books in schools and adult rooms of public libraries, the true children's room, or individual library, is rare. The author here describes several, in Rome, Venice, and Reggio Calabria.

691. Nuccio, G. E. *Catalogo-guida per le formazione delle biblioteche scholastiche.* Roma, 1935.

692. Paolozzi, Giacomo Vittorio. *Letteratura per l'infanzia.* Napoli, Mezzogiorno, 1963. 120p.

693. Passarella, Lina (Sartorelli). *Biblioteche dei ragazzi e del popolo.* Brescia, La Scuola, 1945. 197p. DLC.

The functions and organization of the children's library; the difference between school and public libraries; suggestions for cataloging and book se-lection policies. Illustrated with photographs, mostly from the model children's libraries described in one chapter.

694. ———. *Breviario di letteratura infantile.* 2nd. ed. Brescia, La Scuola, 1948. 151p. IYL. (DLC and NNY have 1944 ed., 99p., same pub.).

A philosophical study of the general characteristics of children's literature, the principles of selection, and the beginnings of children's literature in Italy.

695. Petracchi, Giovacchino. "Incontro di scrittori sulla letteratura infantile," *L'Indice d'oro,* Roma, Anno 5, No. 4, Apr., 1954, pp. 110–112. DLC.

The outcome of a meeting of critics and editors of children's books, to determine some common values and boundaries which they should aim for. One of the conclusions was that children's books in Italy must reflect more accurately the social realities of the present, if they are to attract and have meaning for young readers.

696. Petrini, Enzo. *Avviamento critico alla letteratura giovanile.* Brescia, La Scuola, 1958. 227p. IYL.

"Critical opinions on juvenile literature." This is a complete revision and expansion of the author's earlier work *Idee sulla letteratura educativa* (below). A name index has been added.

697. ———. *Idee sulla letteratura educativa.* Firenze, Industria Tipografico Fiorentina, 1956. 127p. IYL

"Thoughts on educational literature." Some of the chapter headings are: Humanity and youth, Centrality of the fable, Adolescent literature, Adventure, Storytelling in education, Illustration, Libraries and reading rooms for children. The bibliography is arranged to match the chapters.

698. ———. "Literatura para la juventud en Italia," *Educación,* Washington, Año 4, No. 14, Apr.–June, 1959, pp. 30–34. DLC, DPU, NNY.

Literature for children began in Italy during the 19th century. Most was inspired by didacticism, but occasionally such authors as Lorenzini-Collodi and de Amicis rose above the mass. In 1912 appeared the first essay specifically on "children's literature" and in 1933 the first selective bibliography was printed in Florence. Giovanni Caló founded the Museo Didattico della Scuola in 1928, and later this was incorporated into the larger Centro Didattico Nazionale.

699. ———. "I ragazzi d'oggi aspettano una nuova letteratura," *L'Indice d'oro,* Roma, Anno 4, No. 6, June, 1953, pp. 155–158. DLC.

"The children of today are awaiting a new literature." In spite of the increasing amount of production, authors, illustrators and educators are not offering children enough choice in that which is truly new and meaningful.

700. ———. *Uomini e parole.* Firenze, Le Monnier, 1966. 151p. IYL.

Although this is a general study on the patterns of learning speech and the power of reading, it is included because of the implications it has on the use of books by children. There are reproductions from early Italian ABC and reading books and there is an extensive bibliography. Name index.

701. Raya, Gino. *Letteratura pedologica.* Catania, Studio Editoriale Moderno, 1932. IYL.

Critical study of life and works of Collodi, De Amicis, Capuana, Nuccio, Deledda, Ferretti, Sinatra.

702. Roma. Ente Nazionale per le Biblioteche Popolari e Scholastiche. *Catalogo della biblioteca internazionale del fanciullo.* Roma, Ente Nazionale . . . 1963–1964. 86p. 1st Supplement, 15p.; 2nd Supplement, 24p. DLC.

The catalog of an international library of children's books, from 34 countries, which was founded by the national organization of popular and school libraries. The two supplements give additions to the countries in the original collection, plus the books added from 6 other countries.

703. Romagnoli, Anna Maria. *Impariamo a recitare.* Roma, Palladium, 1956. 290p.

704. Rumi, Maria. *Il fanciullo e le biblioteche.* Bologna, Giuseppe Malipiero, 1959. 222p. DLC.

The four parts of this book are concerned with "the young person and literature," "books and libraries for young people," "the organization of a children's library," and "some children's libraries in Italy and other countries." From her text and bibliography, one notes that the author was influenced by the public library movements of the United States and France.

705. Ruta, S. *Letteratura per l'infanzia.* Milano, 1951.

706. Sachetti, Lina. *Storia della letteratura per ragazzi.* 3rd ed. Firenze, Le Monnier, 1966. 470p. IYL. (1st ed., 1955, same pub.; earlier work called *La letteratura per l'infanzia nello sviluppo degli ideali educativi e delle correnti litterarie,* 1954, same pub.)

A general history of children's literature in the Western countries, with the greatest emphasis on Italian and other Latin-language children's literature. France, England, North America, Russia and the German-speaking countries are treated in separate chapters. Of all the Italian histories, this is perhaps the most comprehensive. Bibliography and name index.

707. Sachetto, Aleardo. "Letteratura e stampa periodica per ragazzi," *Notiziario della scuola e della cultura,* Roma, Anno 5, Nos. 21–22, Nov. 30–Dec. 15, 1950, pp. 8–11. DLC.

A report on the discussions and conclusions of the international congress on literature and magazines for children, held in Milan.

708. *Saggi su gli scrittori per l'infanzia.* (Series) Firenze, Le Monnier, 1954 ff., IYL.

Perrault, Gina Vaj Pedotti, Angelo S. Novaro, L. M. Alcott, G. E. Nuccio, J. Verne, Ida Baccini, Collodi, H. C. Andersen, Luigi Parravicini, S. Lagerlöf, Antonio Stoppani, L. Capuana, G. Fanciulli, Vamba, the Grimm Bros., R. Kipling, Renzo Pezzani, De Amicis are the authors whose lives and works have been dealt with in this series. Each is in an individual volume.

709. Santucci, Luigi. *La letteratura infantile.* 3rd. ed. Milano, Fratelli Fabbri, 1961. 478p. IYL. (IYL and NNY have 1958 ed., same pub., 381p.).

The 1958 and 1961 printings of the 3rd edition are both the same up to page 381. The first part is concerned with methodology, i.e., the characteristics of children's literature and how best to address the child. The second part is a critical panorama of the history of children's literature, touching only on the important names. The third part is concerned with aspects and problems of present-day literature. An appendix covers theater, television and Walt Disney. There is a bibliography and index. In the 1961 edition there is a second appendix, prepared by Guglielmo Valle, which gives sketches of the life and works of 22 authors of children's classics, and a review of present trends in Italy, Spain, France, Switzerland, the U.S. and England, Germany and Austria, and the northern European countries. There are also lists of books recommended for home and school.

710. ———. *La letteratura infantile.* Rev. ed. Firenze, Barbèra, 1950. 177p. IYL.

This is a revised version of the author's earlier *Limiti e Ragioni della Letteratura Infantile* and is not to be confused with the longer book of the same title published by Fabbri (above). The main essay is concerned with the scope and content of children's literature.

711. Sbuelz, Maria Adriana. "Considerazioni su alcuni aspetti della letteratura infantile, *Scuola e città*, Firenze, An. 7, Jan., 31, 1956, pp. 23–29. DLC.

712. *Schedario*. Centro Didattico Nazionale di Studi e Documentazione, Via Michelangelo Buonarroti 10, Firenze. Bimonthly. Vol. 1 ff., 1953 ff. (Price: 500 L. per issue; 3000 L. yearly when ordered as part of *Il centro*. IYL, DLC has 1957 ff.

Co-editing this is the *Sezione Italiana dell' Unione Internazionale per le Letteratura Giovanile* (IBBY). Each issue generally contains one or two articles plus current reviews of children's books, printed on sheets of 3 x 5 cards which are perforated for easy removal for the purposes of keeping in file order or possibly even for catalog use.

713. *Scrittori per l'infanzia.* (Series.) Brescia, La Scuola, 1954 ff. IYL.

This series of biographies of writers for children includes volumes on the Grimm Brothers, Alcott, Capuana, Perrault, J. M. Barrie, Mark Twain, H. Malot, Vamba, Collodi, De Amicis and Swift. They are intended for teachers and librarians, rather than children. Each volume is by a different author and about 100 pages in length.

714. *Il segnalibro; manuale del bibliotecario per ragazzi.* Firenze, Centro Didattico Nazionale . . . , 1965.

The first official handbook for children's librarians to be written and published in Italian, this was prepared under the guidance of Maria Bartolozzi Guaspari and includes the work and ideas of many experts. It is divided into seven parts, covering such things as reading guidance, bibliography, library laws, story hours and other activities, the influence of comics, etc. There is a general bibliography and index.

715. *Il segnalibro; almanaco della letteratura giovanile; 1957–1958.* Firenze, Centro Didattico Nazionale . . . , 1958. 369p. IYL.

An almanac of juvenile literature. The first sections are very extensive bibliographies of periodical literature on the subject, and a brief textual survey of developments in the years concerned. The second part is a list of conventions, exhibits, prizes and similar events. The third section contains a list of recommended books, compiled by Maria Bartolozzi Guaspari. Part four is a "gallery of authors" (short biographical sketches) compiled by Enzo Petrini. In Part 5 Vezio Melegari does the same for illustrators. A short guide to storytelling and some stories to tell make up Part 6. Part 7 is a short handbook on organizing children's libraries and information on some of the types of materials which are more and more included in children's libraries (films, recordings, etc.).

716. Spadoni, Lidia. *La poesia per i fanciulli, con appendice storico-bibliografica su questa poesia in Italia.* Pavia, Artigianelli, 1922. 95p.

717. *Specchio del libro per ragazzi.* U.S.P.I. Via Orto Botanicos, Padova, Italy. Quarterly. No. 1, July–Sept., 1960. Annual subscription: L600.

This periodical is associated with the Pedagogical Institute of the University of Padua, and more indirectly with the association "Friends of the Children's Book" (*Amici del Libro per Ragazzi*). It regularly contains critical and historical articles on books and reading, and signed reviews of juvenile books.

718. Squassi, Alberico. "Le biblioteche speciali per i fanciulli e per i giovinetti," *La biblioteca popolare;* Milano, Mondadori, 1935. 153–166. DLC.

How the special children's library can operate within the framework of the public library, and some examples of these libraries in Italy.

719. *Stampa per ragazzi, scuola e famiglia.* Roma, Edizioni UISPER, 1961. 104p. IYL.

"Acts of the 2nd national congress of UISPER (Unione Italiana Stampa Periodica Educativa per Ragazzi)." IYL also has the *Atti* of the first congress, published in Rome by Sales, 128p. All of the discussions centered around journals for children and youth.

720. Tibaldi Chiesa, Maria. *Letteratura infantile.* 4th ed. rev. Milano, Garzanti, 1961. 342p. IYL, (IYL also has 4th. ed., 1959, same pub., 343p.)

The chapter titles are: myths and legends of early days and of Greece and Rome; the first books of the imperial Roman empire and the Renaissance; children's literature in the 18th century in Italy; Italian children's literature from the 19th century to today; German children's literature; children's literature in the Anglo-Saxon countries; children's literature in the north and other countries. Short bibliography.

721. Valeri Mario. *Antologia della letteratura infantile; panorama storico-critico.* Bologna, G. Malipiero, 1959. 346p. IYL.

"Anthology of children's literature; a critical-historical panorama." The selections are arranged according to type and content. The introduction gives the criteria for selection. Sources are given and there is a name index.

722. ——. *Il ragazzo e la letteratura*. 2nd ed. Bologna, G. Malipiero, 1960. 242p. IYL.

This is a study aimed more at educators who are concerned with the problem of reading. There are extensive bibliographies on reading interests and related areas, but unfortunately they are rather confusingly arranged and are not always cited correctly or in full. Name index.

723. Van Sickler, Florence. "Establishing a children's library in Italy," *Public libraries*. Chicago, Vol. 28, Feb., 1923, pp. 88–89. DLC, NNY.

A description of a library founded in Reggio, Calabria, through the efforts of the Junior Red Cross.

724. Venturi, Armando. *Nuovi orientamenti nella letteratura infantile*. Roma, Casa Editrice Gismondi, 1949. 14p. (Conversazioni di Maestri, 6). DLC.

A philosophical essay on the new orientation of children's literature to subjects and treatment more in line with child psychology.

725. Verdina, Renato. *I libri della verde età*. Milano, Vallardi, 1953. 122p.

726. Verusio, Vittorio. *Lineamenti di letteratura per l'infanzia*. 2nd. ed. Napoli, Instituto Editoriale del Mezzogiorno, 1960. 199p. DLC. (IYL has 1955 edition).

Short reviews of the lives and works of children's writers in Italy from the 18th, 19th and 20th centuries, as well as a few foreign authors. The reviews are not critical, but factual. There is no index, and since they are not arranged alphabetically, it is difficult to locate an individual writer.

727. Visentini, Olga. *Letteratura infantile dell'*

Italia nuova: conferenza. Milano, Cecchi Cecchini, 1934. 52p.

728. ——. *Libri e ragazzi*. Milano, Mondadori, 1940. 421p. NNY. (IYL has 1936 ed., same pub.).

"A historical survey of children's literature." Fables, legends, "the marvelous East;" the didactic period; journals; children's theater; other countries; young people's literature; an appendix of short summaries of the stories in Italian and foreign classics (50 of them in all).

729. ——. *Primo vere*. Milano, Mondadori, 1961. 439p. IYL.

An extensively revised version of the author's earlier history (see 728).

730. ——. *Scrittori per l'infanzia*. Milano, Mondadori, 1946. 283p.

731. Volpicelli, Luigi. *La verità su Pinocchio con saggio sul "Cuore" e altri scritti sulla letteratura infantile*. 3rd ed. Roma, Armando, 1963. 145p. IYL (DLC has 2nd ed., same publisher).

Essays on *Pinocchio* and *Cuore,* and their place in Italian children's literature. Includes a nine page bibliography on Collodi, his life and works.

732. Zannoni, Ugo. *La moderna letteratura per l'infanzia e la giovinezza*. 4th ed. Bologna, Cappelli, 1946. (NNY has 1st ed., same pub., 1925, 206p.).

After a general introduction the author gives biographical sketches of 23 Italian writers whose works are considered classics. Following this are paragraphs on some 100 contemporary authors, with general characteristics of their work. In addition, 23 foreign authors whose works are well-known in Italy are also discussed. A name index is helpful in locating each author. (Note describes 1st ed.)

France

"Children's literature is dying and it is a great pity. It is through books that the present is linked to the past, but it is also books which prepare for the future." Thus did Mme. Latzarus express her conviction concerning the deplorable state of French children's books around 1920 (824). She did not have to wait long for further affirmation of her belief. In 1927, Paul Hazard wrote an article on children's reading for the *Revue des Deux Mondes*. This he later revised and included as a portion of his book, *Les Livres, les Enfants et les Hommes*. While he was not willing to go as far as Mme. Latzarus, he did agree that France was not as richly productive as the Northern countries. At one point, he condenses into a few sentences the reasons why this literature has never received enough serious attention in France: ". . . our art turns away a little from the primitive, which it confuses with the puerile. I know many Frenchmen who cannot hear children's literature spoken of without shrugging their shoulders and this adjective alone, applied to literature, "enfantin," lowers its value in their minds. Books for children are no more interesting to them than dolls or puppets, and perhaps a little less" (813, p. 80).

If it is true that children need a literature of their own to fully satisfy their imaginative and emotional needs, how then have French children managed to grow up into creative thinkers and artists? Insofar as such things can be measured, France possesses one of the most sophisticated cultures of the world. Does this mean that children's books are not a decisive factor in the literary and artistic education of the child? Perhaps the best answer can be found in the pages of the great French writers, when they speak of their childhood, either in direct reminiscence or through the medium of a fictional character. Who can doubt that childhood reading has importance after coming upon (to give just one example) the evocative passage in *Remembrance of Things Past,* where Marcel Proust recalls how his mother read to him, or how his grandmother chose his birthday gift of the novels of George Sand. Here then, is part of the answer, and it is the same one Paul Hazard would give: children have simply accepted as their own the most exciting stories available to them, regardless of whether they are designated for adults or children. And few countries have more than France to offer in the way of historical and adventure novels, romances and stories of social manners. The works of Hugo, Dumas, George Sand, Jules Verne, Balzac, Daudet, Maupassant, Anatole France and many others have been read by generations of French children, without much protest that they were not exciting or interesting. In addition, there were the translations of foreign novels which children the world over have usurped as their reading. In England, the U.S. and parts of Europe, these were presented in editions especially appealing to the young. In France, they were more often than not only available in severe adult format, but it did not prevent them from being enjoyed by the children who discovered them.

The children who found them forbidding, the children of working classes whose families could not or would not buy even adult books— these were the ones who in large numbers did not get to develop a taste for the pleasure of reading, and it is this group which librarians, publishers, critics and organizations are concerned about at the present time. In their desire to provide a literature more in keeping with the experience of today's child, they are perhaps going too far in the direction of recommending the controlled-language book, the book with all difficult and incomprehensible ideas sifted out. This is true of a number of leading critics in the field, and recalls similar movements in the U.S. and the U.S.S.R. It is a trifle dismaying to see such a trend in France, but on the whole, it shows signs of a more healthy and deep-seated interest in children's books than was heretofore evident.

It is misleading to observe the state of children's books in France from the stocks of book stores and the few children's libraries which exist. It is a bit exaggerated to state, as does Herbert Lottman, that "the problem in France is that nothing worthwhile has been published for children in the past 50 years," or that "no author of importance, except André Maurois, writes expressly for children" (850). This would simply wipe off the slate such books as Charles Vildrac's *L'Isle Rose,* Marcel Aymé's *Contes du Chat Perché,* the series of Père Castor, *Le Petit Prince* by Saint-Exupéry (not the best work and not always understood by children but written for them by an "author of importance"), the Babar books of Jean de Brunhoff, the novels of Colette Vivier and more recently those of René Guillot. Admittedly the list is not long and perhaps not as distinguished as it might be, but there is a small core of good books available, particularly when one adds to this some of the recent excellent translations of foreign works.

To look at only the surface of children's library development in France is equally misleading. A recent survey (757) pointed out the existence of some 60 libraries in the provinces which give service to children. This of course does not include the two children's libraries which have the greatest influence on standards. These are L'Heure Joyeuse in Paris and La Joie par les Livres in Clamart, a suburb of Paris. So much has been written about the former that it is by now well-known throughout the Western World. Let it just be reiterated that this is a municipal library, operating as a branch of the Paris public library system. It still serves as the leading practical training center for children's library work in France.

La Joie par les Livres is much newer, having been opened in 1965 as a "public" library with private support. It is a model library in every sense of the word. Walking through its light-filled and spacious rooms, observing the children as they use the excellent collections and partake of numerous activities, one is immediately struck by the imaginative forces which went into the building and planning of this library. The professional staff are coordinating the first French reviewing service of children's books, aimed at libraries and schools as a selection aid. They are also kept busy showing the premises to admiring visitors, many of whom are educators and who are seeing for the first time the potential of the children's library. It may well be that this outstanding success will point the way to a new phase of French library development.

Publishing, promulgating and criticism of children's books are also showing signs of betterment. For the first time, there are joint attempts on the part of religious, secular and governmental offices to coordinate efforts toward a common goal, instead of duplicating work. This is due in large measure to the French section of IBBY, under the direction of Mlle. Lise Lebel. Such modest beginnings as recommended lists, agreed upon by all factions, are a definite start in the right direction. Also, the publicity resulting from such joint work tends to be more widely accepted.

Added promotion is given to the children's book movement by the awarding of a number of prizes. The report of the French section of IBBY at the 1966 conference listed nine different prizes given by various organizations and publishers. They are the Prix Fantasia, Prix Guy Hachette, Prix Jean Mace (given by the Ligue Francaise de l'Enseignement), Prix Jeunesse, Prix de la Joie par le Livre (chosen by young people and not by the library of the same name), Grand Prix de Litterature Enfantine (awarded by the Salon de l'Enfance), Grand Prix de la Litterature pour les Jeunes (given by the Fédération des Associations de Parents . . .), Grand Prix de l'O.R.T.F. pour la Jeunesse, and the Prix Sobrier-Arnould (given by the Académie Francaise).

It would not be just to leave out one of France's most important contributions to the world of children's literature—the work of Paul Hazard. One has only to look at the number of translations and editions to realize that his was indeed a philosophy which knew no national boundaries. There are some critics who feel his enthusiasm outweighed his sound judgement, and to a very limited extent this might be the case. Still, there is no one who has stated the "case for children's literature" so well.

Hazard acknowledged his debt to the two earlier critical histories which had appeared in France: the one already mentioned above, by Mme. Latzarus, and the later work by Marie Lahy Hollebecque. Both of these are excellent for their appraisal of the 19th-century children's authors, but, of course, do not cover much from the 20th. Paul Hazard is rather hard on his compatriots and does not find much in their children's literature (except for Perrault) which is worthy of praise. One must turn to the Latzarus and Lahy-Hollebecque histories to realize that in France, the didactic tone of the 19th century was not nearly as strong as in other countries. After Berguin and Madame de Genlis there was a definite tendency toward softening of the moral or better yet, making it a part of that much more palatable form—the fairy tale.

The French attitude of the 20th century—that it is childish even to discuss children's literature—seems to have its basis in much earlier times. Although respected as a philosopher, Rousseau did not have the same direct impact on children's books in France, as he did on those of England and Germany. In France, the ideal of *Émile* seemed to be more one for adults to think about and revel in, than one to actually practice on children. This is implied by Marie Lahy-Hollebecque in her long article on the origins of children's literature (823).

Contemporary histories are lacking, although there is a fine résumé by Isabelle Jan in the *Encyclopédie "Clartés"* (819). Marc Soriano also includes some history in his 1959 book (878), but his main purpose was a survey of contemporary thinking on the theory of children's literature. The Jean de Trigon history which appeared in

1950 must be used with judicious care, for it is somewhat colored by the author's long association with one of the leading publishers of children's books in France. There is room for expansion and improvement in the formal study of French children's literature.

733. Ahern, Mary E. "Books for the children of France," *Public libraries,* Chicago, Vol. 25, No. 4, April, 1920, pp. 259–261. DLC.

Chicago librarians collected funds to provide 30 sets of 25 picture books for kindergartens in devastated areas of France.

734. Alfani di Lella, Maria. "Le biblioteche scolastiche in Francia," *Accademie e biblioteche d'Italia,* Roma, Anno 29 (12th new ser.). No. 2, Mar.–Apr., 1961, pp. 133–146. DLC.

The history and present status of primary and secondary school libraries in France, as reported by an Italian observer.

735. Arnaud, Mme. Robert. "Bibliothèques d'enfants," *Femmes diplomées,* Paris, 6e année, No. 24, 4e trimestre, 1957, pp. 7–10. PIP.

A description of the ten libraries in Paris which served children and young people at that time.

736. Audic, Anne-Marie. "Littérature enfantine," *Pédagogie, Centre d'Études Pédagogiques,* Paris, each Feb., and Dec., since 1956. DLC.

An annual selection of best books for children, usually preceded by a short article on some trend or unique aspect of the year's output.

737. Aurillac. Bibliothèque Municipale. *Le livre pour enfants, l'èdition enfantine d'hier et d'aujourd'hui.* Aurillac, Bibliothèque Municipale, 1959. 28p. (Mimeograph.)

"An exhibition catalogue prepared by Anne Marie Royer."

738. Averill, Esther. "Political propaganda in children's books of the French Revolution," *The Colophon,* New York, Part 20, Mar., 1935. Unp. NNY.

A fascinating 8 page article on the extent to which the Revolution influenced children's books, particularly catechisms and alphabet books. In one alphabet book, A is for *Assemblée Nationale!* This is illustrated with 4 reproductions from some of the books discussed.

739. Balsen, André. *Les illustrés pour enfants.* Tourcoing, Duvivier, 1920.

740. Baucomont, J. *Catalogue de livres pour les enfants.* Albertville (Savoie), Pub. Rey Gorrez, 1929. 46p. IYL.

A list of children's books, selected mostly from other lists put out by l'Heure Joyeuse.

741. Bay, André. "La littérature enfantine." Queneau, Raymond; *Histoire des littératures, Vol. 3: Littératures françaises, connexes et marginales;* Paris, Gallimard, 1958; pp. 1604–1621. (Encyclopédie de la Pléiade, 7.) NNY.

A brief history of, and critical commentary on, the major writers whose works became popular with children in France. This includes some of the classics of other countries.

742. "La bibliothèque de L'Heure Joyeuse vue par ses lecteurs," *Revue du livre,* Paris, 2e année, Nos. 8–9, June–July, 1934, pp. 213–220. DLC.

Several patrons give their impressions of this well-known children's library in Paris.

743. Cohn, Louis. "La bibliothèque scolaire," *Hamoré,* Paris, 4e année, No. 14, Mar., 1961, pp. 13–29. NNY.

Includes articles on the role of the library in the Jewish school by Louis Cohn; on a special library in a Paris school for Jewish children by R. Schwob; the religious library for children by Colette Sirat; and an annotated list of 40 French and Hebrew books especially recommended for the Jewish child.

744. "Les bibliothèques pour les jeunes," *Association des bibliothécaires français. Bulletin d'informations,* Paris, No. 13 (new series), Mar., 1954, pp. 31–39. NNY.

Articles by Myriem Foncin, Jacques Lethève and Odile Altmayer on library work with young adults.

745. *Bibliothèques scolaires. Catalogue d'ouvrages de lecture.* Paris, Imprimerie Nationale, 1887. 120p. (Musée Pédagogique. Mémoires et Documents Scolaires. Fascicule No. 21.) DLC.

An early guide to the organization of the school library, together with a catalog of 2,600 books, arranged by subject, and especially recommended for library use. An author index appears at the end.

746. "Les bibliothèques scolaires," Special issue of: *L'éducation nationale,* Paris, Dec., 1950. PIP.

747. Binder, Jean. "Entente cordiale," *Library assistant,* London, Vol. 41, May–June, 1948, pp. 35–37. DLC, NNY.

This is the second in a two-part article on the public libraries of Paris. This treats of the children's library services available in that city.

748. Bishop, Claire Huchet. "Seven centuries of children's books in France," *Horn book,* Boston, Vol. 18, No. 3, May–June, 1942, pp. 183–187. DLC, IYL, NNY.

In 1942 the Wildenstein Gallery of New York held an exhibition of French children's books of the past seven centuries. Mrs. Bishop here describes some of the entries in detail. The catalog is noted in 771.

749. Blanchard, Gérard. "Les bestiaires de l'enfance," *Le courrier graphique,* Paris, 26e année, No. 114, May–July, 1961, pp. 19–30. DLC.

A study of the art in the medieval bestiaries, why they appealed to children, and some recent versions which indicate that the animal tale still has great appeal.

750. Blanchetière, A. "Quelques livres récents de lecture. Les lectures de nos enfants," *L'éducation,* Paris, An. 15, No. 3, Dec., 1923, pp. 136–153; An. 16, No. 3, Dec., 1924; An. 17, No. 3, Dec., 1925, pp. 132–162. DEW.

The first of these annotated booklists is arranged by publisher. The second and third are for children under 10 and children 10–15 years, respectively, and are arranged by type.

751. Blaze de Bury, Yetta. "Girls' novels in France," *North American review,* New York, Vol. 169, Aug., 1899, pp. 273–284. NNY.

The extent to which social attitudes and mores were reflected in 19th-century novels for girls is here explored in interesting, but Victorian, fashion.

752. Bley, Roger. "L'influence des contes sur les enfants," *L'école des parents,* Paris, No. 1, Nov., 1952, pp. 22–27. PIP.

One of many articles on children and juvenile literature appearing in this periodical. The author comments on the work of a storyteller in *écoles maternelles* and what results she had.

753. Bonnerot, Jean. "Bibliothèques. L'Heure Joyeuse," *Mercure de France,* Paris, No. 1135, Mar., 1958, pp. 526–530.

A journalist records a visit he made to *l'Heure Joyeuse* library in Paris, and how impressed he was with its program.

754. Bonnet, Dejaeger, R. "Organisation d'une bibliothèque enfantine," *L'information pédagogique,* Paris, No. 3, 1948.

755. Bourges, Maurice. *Activités de loisir pour les jeunes. La lecture.* Paris, Éditions du Scarabée, 1958. 168p. IYL.

How to organize a library for young people and a list of recommended books, annotated and arranged alphabetically by author.

756. Bouyssi, Marcelle. "Littérature enfantine: de quelques classiques anglais." *Bulletin des bibliothèques de France,* Paris, 4o Année, No. 5, May, 1959, pp. 213–227. DLC, NNY.

A French librarian questions why so few of their children's books are translated into English. There are a number of the better authors from England translated into French, but the masterpieces of nonsense have, for the most part, proven too difficult to translate. She discusses some of these works, and mentions the few translations which exist.

757. ———. "Les sections pour la jeunesse dans les bibliothèques municipales de province," *Bulletin des bibliothèques de France,* Paris, An 9, No. 7, July, 1964, pp. 283–294. DLC, NNY.

"Children's rooms in the municipal libraries of the provinces." This up-to-date review is accompanied by photographs. In all, some 60 libraries reported having children's corners, rooms or separate library buildings for the young.

758. Brauner, Alfred. *Nos livres d'enfants ont menti.* Paris, S.A.B.R.I., 1951. 179p. DLC, IYL.

M. Brauner questions the validity of most French evaluation and criticism of children's literature (including Hazard) and claims that none of it leaves the parent or relative (who does most of the purchasing in France) with a clear idea of judging good taste in books for children, as well as children's tastes in what they would choose to read. A tantalizing study, with thought-provoking comments on such things as nonsense rhymes, translations, books for the culturally impoverished, illustrations, and many other points.

759. Braunschvig, Marcel. "La littérature enfantine," *L'art et l'enfant;* Paris, Henri Didier, 1907; pp. 327–355. DLC.

Literature is only one of the expressions of art to be introduced to the child, but it is the one which, above all others, can cultivate the imagination, if it is introduced orally while the child is still young. The author, himself a teacher, rails against the pedagogues who would introduce only that which is factual, or teaches some lesson. He praises the forwardness of the English in providing the beautiful picture books of Caldecott, Greenaway, and Crane to children and claims that France has only Boutet de Monvel to come up to their quality in comparison. There are many well-written books which are "souvenirs" of childhood, but these are rarely of interest *to* the child, yet they are the books most frequently purchased by parents for children. The best books for children are those universal classics which may have been written for adults, but which have strong story-threads and adventurous heroes.

760. Breillat, Pierre. "Bibliothèques scolaires," *ABCD* (*Archives, bibliothèques collections, documents*), Paris. No. 1, May–June, 1951, pp. 15–20. DLC.

A review of some of the important dates in the development of the school library in France, and some comments on the types of reading materials selected for them in the past and present.

761. Bretschneider, H. "Zur französischen jugendliteratur," *Franco-Gallia*, Cassel, 7 Jahrgang, No. 10, Oct., 1890, pp. 145–150. DLC.

Because French children read more general, adult literature and have fewer editions of books specifically printed for them, one is tempted to state that books for children receive less attention in France than they do in England or Germany. The author then proceeds to discount this mis-conception by writing of numerous books which French children like.

762. Brunhes-Delamarre, Mariel-Jean. "Sur une littérature enfantine non tout à fait gratuite," *Entretiens sur les lettres et les arts*, Rodez, No. 12, Mar., 1958, pp. 13–16.

The writer deplored the present state of children's reading in France and found the few good books unknown to children.

763. *Bulletin d'analyses de livres pour enfants.* La Joie par les Livres, 29 boulevard Edgar Quinet, Paris 14. Quarterly. No. 1 ff., 1965 ff. Annual subscription: 18 f.

A reviewing service for French children's books, sponsored by the private agency La Joie par les Livres, but having the support of the Association of French Librarians. Reviewers are members of the Association. Each review is signed and gives a very complete description. Eventually, the editors hope to review not only all current books, but also those older ones still in print.

764. Calvet, Jean. *L'enfant dans la littérature française.* 2 vols. Paris, F. Lanore, 1930. Vol. 1, 213p.; Vol. 2, 231p. DLC.

Although the author's purpose was to discuss the child *in* French literature, in doing so he covers many authors and works which are now considered part of children's literature, sometimes perhaps incorrectly, since it is not always that a story of childhood is interesting to children.

765. Chassé, Charles. "Héros enfantins," *Bulletin du livre français*, Paris, Nov.–Dec., 1935, pp. 232–235. NNY.

The writer considers some of the book characters which have been the heroes and heroines of children past and present. On pp. 230–249 are annotated recommendations of books for holiday giving, divided by four age categories. This periodical extended this service in the annual *Etrennes* issue, usually November, from 1932 to 1940.

766. Clément, H. *Les livres qu'ils aiment; 5000 enfants de 9 à 14 ans révèlent leurs préférences.* Paris, Éditions de l'École, 1966. 215p. IYL.

Results of a reading interest survey undertaken by the libraries of the Catholic Action organization in France.

767. Coulet, Eugène. *Les bibliothèques pour enfants, nécessité sociale.* Toulon, Imprimerie Toulonnaise, 1938. 8p. PIP.

The philosophy of library service to children, its aims and its social significance. L'Heure Joyeuse is cited as an example of the new type of forward-looking libraries for children.

768. Cousinet, Roger. "Les lectures des enfants," *L'éducateur moderne*, Paris, An 6, Apr., 1911, pp. 145–159; July, 1911, pp. 304–309. DEW.

Children must not only be given educational and instructional material, they should also be given books to read for pure pleasure. This educator then discusses some of the books which, in his experience, have proven popular with children. In the second article he defends and explains his position further, answering attacks made against his ideas.

769. Davaine, P. "Un club d'enfants à Lille," *Vers l'éducation nouvelle*, Paris, No. 116, Sept., 1957, pp. 25–28. PIP.

The "Thursday reading club" in this library is modeled on that of the library l'Heure Joyeuse in Paris.

770. *Des livres, des disques; un choix pour les bibliothèques scolaires—pour vos enfants de 4 à 16 ans.* Paris, Institut Pédagogique National, 1964. 115p. IYL.

A list of recommended books and records suitable for school libraries and for home purchase. Arrangement is by four age groups. There are no annotations or indexes. The introduction states that the choices were subjective and many times arbitrary. This was first published in a 1958 edition.

771. Deschamps, J. G. *The history of French children's books, 1750–1900.* Boston, Bookshop for Boys and Girls, 1934. 39p. DLC.

The catalog of an exhibit of 200 books from the collection of Mr. Deschamps, with an introduction on their history by Esther Averill. Annotated.

772. Dubois, Raoul. "La littérature pour la jeunesse; essai de bibliographie des études en langue française sur ce sujet," *Vers l'éducation nouvelle,* Paris, No. 107, Oct.–Nov., 1956, pp. 25–29; No. 109, Jan.–Feb., 1957, pp. 23–26; No. 112, May, 1957, pp. 17–20. PIP.

773. ———. "Où en est la littérature pour la jeunesse?" Reprint from: *Europe,* Paris, Sept.–Oct., 1965. 21p. IYL.

In this thoughtful essay the author ranges over such questions as what is children's literature? How is it effected? What is its place in the life of contemporary children? And who are some of the persons writing in this genre?

774. Dubois, Jacqueline and Raoul. *La presse enfantine française.* Neuchatel, H. Messeiller, 1964. 79p. IYL. DLC has earlier ed. Paris, Éditions des Francs et Franches Camarades, 1957. 48p.

Following a brief historical survey of the development of French children's periodicals, there is a list of currently issued newspapers and periodicals. The laws governing printing for children are also reviewed.

775. Duproix. "Les bibliothèques enfantines en France," *Rapport de la Deuxième Assemblée de "La Nouvelle Éducation,"* Paris, 20–22 Mai 1923; Garches, M. Baucomont, [1923], pp. 83–88. NNC.

"Childrens libraries in France." Their history and present situation.

776. Dupuy, Aimé. *Un personnage nouveau du roman français: L'enfant.* (Paris), Hachette, 1931. 422p. NNY.

A study of more than 100 novels appearing in France from 1876–1926, with children or childhood as the central or important characters. In his preface, the author states that he chose *only* novels obviously intended for adults, but he aimed this study at educators and those working with children. His belief was that such literature could illumine the needs and feelings of childhood far better than more formal works.

777. Durry, Marie-Jeanne. "La bibliothèque de Paul Hazard," *Annales de l'université de Paris,* Paris, 27e année, No. 1, Jan.–Mar., 1957, 36p. DLC, NNY.

A former colleague of Paul Hazard writes that Mme. Hazard had decided to give his library to the Sorbonne instead of selling it to an interested U.S. institution. It is housed in the Salle Jules Ferry of the Institut de Français.

778. L'enfant et la lecture." Special issue of: *A livre ouvert,* No. 15–16, Aug., 1960.

779. "L'enfant et ses livres." Special issue of: *Revue familiale d'éducation,* Paris, Jan., 1930.

780. "Les enfants et les livres." Special issue of: *L'éducation nationale,* Paris, Nov., 1952. 31p. IYL.

Some of the longer articles are by J. P. Seguin, Simone Lacroix and J. Bleton. Two reading interest inquiries are reported on by René Zazzo and André Bourin; M. Gruny and Charles Schmidt wrote on libraries for children.

781. *Les enfants, leurs livres et leurs jeux sous le Second Empire.* Catalogue d'exposition 1956. Bibliothèque de la Rochelle, 1956. 30p.

782. "Les enfants veulent être pris au sérieux. 375 nouveaux livres pour les enfants," *Le bulletin du livre,* Paris. No. 44. Nov., 1, 1960, pp. 12–25. DLC.

Children wish to be taken seriously, and the changing format of their books reflects this. The list of books following the article is not selective, but rather an indication of what was available for the various age groups.

783. Evans, Jessie M. "Children's books in France," *Junior bookshelf,* Huddersfield, Vol. 12, Dec., 1948, pp. 172–176. DLC, NNY.

"A visit to a French bookshop or a publisher's offices today suggests that translations of English books are the chief literary diet throughout France." This was the observation of this critic, although she does note some exceptions of good French books for children.

784. Famin, M. M. "Children's libraries in France," *ALA children's library yearbook,* Chicago, No. 1, 1929, pp. 59–63. DLC, NNY.

An instructor in the Paris Library School writes of the major developments in school and public library service to children in France.

785. Faucher, Paul. "Comment adapter la littérature enfantine aux besoins des enfants à partir des premières lectures, *Bulletin des bibliothèques de France,* Paris, 3e année, No. 5, May, 1958, pp. 345–352. DLC.

The founder and director of the Père Castor picture book publications gave this address at the IBBY meeting in Florence, May, 1958. In it, he explains his methods of choosing the materials for picture books for very young children.

786. Fédération des Francs et Franches Camarades. *Une année de lecture.* Paris, Sept., 1965. 23p. Documentation Techniques, No. 1. IYL.

A booklist in three parts (nonfiction, fiction and not recommended) put out by a youth group. The introduction indicates selection was made by Jacqueline and Raoul Dubois. No annotations.

787. Félix-Faure-Goyau, L. *La vie et la mort des fées.* Paris, 1910.

788. Fillet, R. "The school bookmobile service, Tours," *UNESCO bulletin for libraries,* Paris, Vol. 12, Nos. 8–9, Aug.–Sept., 1958, pp. 184–187. DLC, NNY.

A French librarian describes how a bookmobile is used to service schools in the Tours area.

789. Fontaine, André. *Comment constituer une petite bibliothèque scolaire?* Paris, Ministère de L'Instruction Publique et des Beaux-Arts, 1919. 70p. PIP.

"How to construct a small school library." This educator was openly critical of the poor state of French school libraries. He claimed: "Administrators still make more of burning or getting rid of books than they do of acquiring new ones." He was for open circulation, against accepting gifts of books, and for a highly selective policy for all school materials. The concluding section is a table of the books suggested as "best" by the school inspectors, and the 20 titles eventually chosen for inclusion in all school libraries.

790. Fouilhé, Pierre. *Journaux d'enfants, journaux pour rire?* Paris, Centre D'Activités Pédagogiques, 1955. 160p. DLC.

An evaluation of children's magazines in France, as they express literary or non-literary values. The author was particularly concerned with "comic" magazines, and his conclusions are that they have no literary merit and many are not even "funny."

791. Gérin, Elisabeth. "L'enfant, cet inconnu. Une enquête sur les lectures," *Pédagogie, Centre d'Études Pédagogiques,* Paris, 11e année, No. 7, July, 1956, pp. 556–568. DLC.

The Centre de Recherches et d'Information Pédagogiques distributed a questionnaire on vacation reading to children of primary and secondary schools throughout France. About 900 replies were analyzed and the results are discussed here. Following the article is a list of recommended reading for the vacationing child, on nature subjects.

792. ———. "L'enfant devant son journal." Que peuvent-ils lire?" *L'Anneau d'or,* Paris, No. 86, Mar.–Apr., 1959, pp. 141–157. PIP.

This magazine contained frequent articles on the problems of children's reading, and reviews of children's books. This is on methods of bringing children to read more than comics or magazines. Each year at Christmas there are selected lists of books recommended as gifts. This is Roman Catholic in point of view.

793. ———. *Tout sur la presse enfantine.* Paris, Centre de Recherches de la Bonne Presse, 1958. 190p. DLC.

Research involving the magazines, comics and other serials which children read, as opposed to books and literature in more substantial form.

794. Godart, M. "Littérature enfantine," *Revue pédagogique,* Paris, Tome 45, No. 11, Nov. 15, 1904, pp. 464–474. DLC.

A teacher of foreign languages to children points out that one of the best methods to pique their interest is to use children's books from the various countries where these languages are spoken; they are far less dull, and the vocabulary, although difficult for the beginner, is still of more interest to the child than his textbook.

795. Grandin, Nicole. "La literatura infantil en Francia," *Educación,* Washington, Año 4, No. 14, Apr.–June, 1959, pp. 15–24. DLC, DPU, NNY.

More than in any country, literature for children in France can be described as truly literary. The author contends that this is true, in spite of the fact that books for children are not as numerous. She backs up her statement by citing the works of Perrault, Saint-Exupery, Marcel Aymé, Jules Verne, Victor Hugo, Alain Fournier, Théophile Gautier, Charles Vildrac, A. Dumas, Alfred de Musset, Michel Aimé Baudouy, Alphonse Daudet, René Guillot, and many others.

796. Grolier, G. and E. de. "Livres recents pour les enfants," *Revue du livre,* Paris, 2e année, No. 12, Nov.–Dec., 1934, pp. 281–292. DLC.

A selection of the better recent books for children, annotated and listed by age groups. These reviewers have periodic columns in this magazine, but this is the largest and longest.

797. Gruny, Marguerite. "Apprentissage de la documentation et bibliothèques pour enfants." International Congress of Libraries and Bibliography, 2nd; *Actas y trabajos, Vol. 3;* Madrid, Librería de Julián Barbazán, 1936; pp. 237–247. DLC.

The librarian of l'Heure Joyeuse writes of the importance of early library training in young people, and describes how such work is carried out in her library in Paris.

798. ——— and Mathilde Leriche. *Beaux livres, belles histoires.* 2nd ed. Paris, Bourrelier, 1947. 78p. IYL. Supplement: Paris, Bourrelier, 1952. IYL. (DLC has 1st ed., 1937).

A selective list of 2,000 books for children, based on literary, educational and moral values, as well as artistic merit. Bibliographic information is complete, but the entries are not annotated. They are arranged by subject and age levels. The supplement contain 687 titles. The first edition had slightly more than 500 entries.

799. ———. "La bibliothèque pour enfants," *Revue médico-sociale sur la protection de l'enfance,* Paris, An 6, No. 4, 1938. PIP.

800. ———. "L'enfant et la bibliothèque," *Techniques graphiques,* Paris, No. 30, Mar.–Apr., 1960, pp. 53–58.

801. ———. Expériences françaises dans le domaine des bibliothèques pour enfants," International Congress of Libraries and Documentation Centres, 4th, Brussels. *Reports and communications,* Vol. 2A. La Haye, Martinus Nijhoff, 1955; pp. 257–263. DLC, NNY.

At the time of this report, there were approximately 25 children's rooms in Paris and environs, 41 in provincial cities, and 33 bookmobiles serving children (as well as adults) in rural areas of France. The author-librarian mentions particularly the work of the Centre International de l'Enfance and the Ligue de l'Enseignement. She concludes with brief comments on the contemporary children's literature of France.

802. ———. "France," *Library service to children,* Lund, Bibliotekstjänst, 1963, pp. 46–56. DLC, IYL, NNY.

This chapter in the IFLA publication deals with the history and present status of children's library work in this country.

803. ———. "France; three examples of vocations," *Top of the news,* Chicago, Vol. 7, Oct., 1950, pp. 17–19. DLC.

In this special issue devoted to children's library work in many countries, this librarian of many years' experience recounts some of the aspects of this work in France.

804. ———. "L'heure de conte, quelques conseils sur l'art de raconter les histoires," *Education par la recreation,* Nancy, 1938, pp. 70–86.

805. ———. "La lecture à l'Heure Joyeuse," *La nouvelle éducation,* Paris, No. 98, Oct., 1931, pp. 145–154; No. 99, Nov., 1931, pp. 161–165. PIP.

Two of a series on the details of children's services, as practiced in this well-known children's library.

806. ———. et al. *Pour les jeunes—une centaine de livres français. For the young—a hundred French books.* New York, Services Culturels de l'Ambassade de France, 1963. 12p. (French ed.). 11p. (English ed.). DLC.

One hundred books in French appropriate for the young reader, selected by a committee of librarians. Book dealers throughout the U.S. where these books may be obtained are listed.

807. Guillien, G. "Une bibliothèque des jeunes à Villeurbanne," *Bulletin des bibliothèques de France,* Paris, 6° Année, No. 7, July, 1961, pp. 337–341. DLC, NNY.

In December, 1960, a library for children opened in a new building in Villeurbanne, separate from the main municipal library but dependent on it for administration.

808. Gumuchian, MM. et Cie. *Les livres d'enfance du XVe au XIXe siècle.* 2 vols. Paris, Gumuchian et Cie., [1931?]. Vol. 1, 446p. and Vol. 2, 336 plates. DLC, IYL, NNY.

Paul Gavault has written a preface to the catalogue, in which he points out the trends in children's books of Europe from the 15th to the 19th centuries, as far as they can be noted from the evidence of the books themselves. The introduction (in English) by the Messers Gumuchian explains why they assembled the collection and something of its extent. There are 6,251 items, which include books printed in most of the countries of Europe, as well as some 160 from the U.S. and about twice that number from England. The majority are from France, Germany and Italy. Arrangement is by type of book or subject, with one section devoted to games and toys closely related to the early bookshops for children. Bibliographical description is very complete, but unfortunately there are no author or title indexes. The second volume is composed entirely of reproductions from the books themselves.

809.   Hachette, Louis. *Les bibliothèques scolaires* . . . Paris, Hachette, 1862, 48p. PIP.

The author was a bookseller and publisher who feared that the new school libraries would take away all his trade. His pamphlet was answered anonymously by another, titled *Les Bibliothèques Scolaires et M. Hachette,* and he in turn then wrote *Rèponse à l'Auteur de la Brochure Intitulée "Les Bibliothèques . . ."*

810.   Halphen-Istel, Claire. "Le club-bibliothèque pour enfants." International Congress of Libraries and Bibliography, 2nd; *Actas y trabajos, Vol. 3;* Madrid, Librería Julián Barbarzán, 1936; pp. 275–277. DLC.

Because children do not learn to concentrate on reading as do adults, this librarian feels it is necessary to have more than a public library available to them: the ideal is a reading club connected to the library, for the purpose of stimulating them to choose and stay with the better books.

811.   ———. *Quelles histoires raconter vous à vos enfants?* Paris, Nathan, 1926. 272p.

812.   ———. *Quelles livres donnerez-vous à vos enfants?* Paris, Maison du Livre Français, 1934. 123p. PIP.

A booklist, not annotated, arranged into 4 age groups and with a final general section on theater, poetry and periodicals for children. There is a list of books for parents and educators. The preface and introductory remarks give the general criteria of selection.

813.   Hazard, Paul. "Comment lisent les enfants?" *Revue des deux mondes,* Paris, 97e année, 7e période, Vol. 42, Dec. 15, 1927, pp. 860–882. DLC, NNY.

Here are germinating the ideas which came to life in *Les Livres, les Enfants et les Hommes;* in fact, whole sections from this article have been kept intact in the book, e.g., the part beginning "Give us books, . . . Give us wings! . . ." plus the section on Perrault.

814.   ———. *Les livres, les enfants et les hommes.* 2nd ed. Paris, Boivin, 1949. 232p. DLC, NNY, IYL. (1st ed., 1932, pub. by Flammarion, 278p.

DLC, NNY). Quotation from the English translation *Books, children & men.* Boston, Horn Book, 1960.

A critical approach to the theory of children's literature as a part of all literature. No other critic has better answered the question "What are good books for children?" than has Paul Hazard: "I like books that remain faithful to the very essence of art; namely, those that offer to children an intuitive and direct way of knowledge, a simple beauty capable of being perceived immediately, arousing in their souls a vibration which will endure all their lives.

"And those that provide them with pictures, the kind that they like; pictures chosen from the riches of the whole world; enchanting pictures that bring release and joy, happiness gained before reality closes in upon them, insurance against the time, all too soon, when there will be nothing but realities.

"And books that awaken in them not maudlin sentimentality, but sensibility; that enable them to share in great human emotions; that give them respect for universal life—that of animals, of plants; that teach them not to despise everything that is mysterious in creation and in man.

"And books which respect the valor and eminent dignity of play; which understand that the training of intelligence and of reason cannot, and must not, always have the immediately useful and practical as its goal.

"I like books of knowledge; not those that want to encroach upon recreation, upon leisure, pretending to be able to teach anything without drudgery. There is no truth in that. There are things which cannot be learned without great pains; we must be resigned to it. I like books of knowledge when they are not just grammar or geometry poorly disguised; when they have tact and moderation; when, instead of pouring out so much material on a child's soul that it is crushed, they plant in it a seed that will develop from the inside. I like them when they do not deceive themselves about the quality of knowledge, and do not claim that knowledge can take the place of everything else. I like them especially when they distill from all the different kinds of knowledge the most difficult and the most necessary—that of the human heart . . .

"Finally, I like books that contain a profound morality. Not the kind of morality which consists in believing oneself a hero because one has given two cents to a poor man, or which names as characteristics the faults peculiar to one era, or one nation; here snivelling pity, there a pietism that knows nothing of charity; somewhere else a middle class hypocrisy. Not the kind of morality that asks for no deeply felt consent, for no personal effort, and which is nothing but a rule imposed willy-nilly by the strongest. I like books that set in action truths worthy of lasting forever, and of inspiring one's whole inner life; those demonstrating that an unselfish and faithful love always ends by finding its reward, be it only in oneself; how ugly and low are envy, jealousy and greed; how people who utter only slander and lies end by coughing up vipers and toads whenever they speak. In short, I like books that have the integrity to perpetuate their own faith in truth and justice."

One of the clearest indications of the influence of Hazard is the number of translations, in Eastern and Western languages. They are noted in: 546, 666, 1244, 1699, 2068, 2596, 3852.

815. Hormeau, Arthur. "Les enfants et les livres," *Savoir et beauté,* Paris?, An 3, No. 8, 1923, pp. 244–247.

816. Huchet, Claire. "Les bibliothèques enfantines," *La nouvelle éducation,* Paris, No. 26, June 1924, pp. 72–81. PIP.

A report on children's libraries, given at an annual convention of educators. Miss Huchet, (later Mrs. Bishop), deplored the lack of good books and libraries in France.

817. Huguet, Jean. *Les jeunes devant la littérature.* La Colombe, Editions du Vieux Colombier, 1958. 109p. PIP.

The author is founder and president of Jeunesses Littéraires de France, an organization for young persons (15–30) which aims at stimulating interest in reading and literature. This documents how it came to be founded, and the work it has done so far.

818. Jan, Isabelle. "Composition d'une bibliothèque pour enfants," *Encyclopédie "Clartés,"* Volume *Loisirs.* Paris, 1964, col. 9132. CJL.

"The composition of a children's library." This is aimed more at the home than at the school or public library.

819. ———. "La littérature enfantine," *Encyclopédie "Clartés,"* Volume *Littératures.* Paris, 1965, col. 14325–14327. CJL.

An excellent critical and historical survey of French children's literature.

820. Jordan, Muriel S. "Children's libraries in France," *Wilson library bulletin,* New York, Vol. 14, No. 7, Mar., 1940, pp. 506–510. DLC, NNY.

An American librarian gives her impression of the condition of children's libraries in France, and contrasts their standards with those of the U.S.

821. "Les journaux pour enfants," *Enfance,* Paris,

6ᵉ année, No. 5, Nov.–Dec., 1953, pp., 369–524. IYL.

After a preface by Henri Wallon, there are articles by G. Sadoul, R. Dubois, C. Vildrac, G. Monod, P. Fouilhé, H. Gratiot-Alphandéry, A. Brauner, A. Cantenys, P. Guilbaud, R. Rossi, M. Bellet, P. Charbonnel, J. Chazal, R. Labrusse, P. Ménard, R. Finkelstein, T. Klipffel, all on various aspects of the magazines, newspapers and comic book publications for children in France. All points of view are present; laws governing the regulation of this press are cited; and an extensive bibliography covers most monographs and articles appearing on this subject in France.

822. Lahy-Hollebecque, Marie. *Les charmeurs d'enfants.* Paris, Editions Baudinière, 1928. 286p. PHJ.

The first part of this study is a critical review of a dozen well-known writers for children, among them Perrault, d'Aulnoy, Andersen, George Sand, Jules Verne, Selma Lagerlöf, Kipling. The second part concerns the selection of books. The author writes here: "The aim of a library for children is that of grouping together works of great variety in order to explain and bring to life the marvels of nature, the history of the universe and its civilizations, the slow, difficult and splendid development of man —all that which fixes the quality of human effort and enlarges the limits of the real world." She selects a list of 100 books and critically annotates them. Paul Hazard was inspired by Mme. Lahy-Hollebecque, and frequently quotes from this study.

823. ———. "Les origines de la littérature enfantine," *Cahiers de l'étoile,* Paris, 3ᵉ année, No. 17, Sept.–Oct., 1930. pp. 725–748. NNY.

It is incorrect to begin the history of children's literature with the didactic and instructive materials of the distant past. The first true children's literature is an innovation of the 19th century. Some earlier works properly belong to the study because they have since become known and enjoyed by children. The author then traces the movement as it spread throughout Europe.

824. Latzarus, Marie Thérèse. *La littérature enfantine en France dans la seconde moitié du xix⁰ siècle.* Paris, Presses Universitaires de France, 1924. 309p. PLH.

This study of children's literature in France in the second half of the 19th century is preceded by a short survey of children's reading before 1860, which the author characterized as purely didactic. The following chapters treat of realistic and idealistic tendencies, progress in printing and illustrating techniques, the rise of science, socialist ideals and pity for the weak, all as reflected in children's literature. The author ends on a note of pessimism, expressing the belief that, however charming they might be, the late 19th-century works were not of interest to the 20th century child, and no other literature had come along to replace it.

825. Leblond-Zola, D. "La littérature enfantine," *La revue mondiale,* 33e année, Vol. 151, 7e série, No. 24, Dec. 15, 1922, pp. 457–462. DLC.

To children, reading represents an initiation into the realities of life. For this reason, too many of the favorites of another generation have no social meaning to the young people of today. They need more books which mirror the contemporary world.

826. "La lecture des adolescents," *Association des bibliothécaires français. Bulletin d'informations,* Paris, No. 33 (New series), Nov. 1960, pp. 169–179. NNY.

The preferences of young adults in reading, and ways in which to interest them in better reading, as observed by Marguerite Gruny, René Fillet, Odile Altmayer, R. de Pechebrun, R. Dalimier.

827. "La lecture et les bibliothèques." Special issue of: *Cahiers pédagogiques,* Paris, Oct., 1962.

828. "La lecture et les jeunes." Special issue of: *Loisirs jeunes,* Paris, Nov., 1960. 58p. DLC, PIP.

Advice to parents on the selection of books; a list of periodicals which review children's books regularly, together with a comment on the point of view; some recommended and selective lists of children's books; Paris libraries which have juvenile collections; other information related to books and reading for young people. "Loisirs Jeunes" is an organization which publishes a weekly review of the same name, in which books, recordings, theater and other entertainments are reviewed. It is partly subsidized by the government.

829. "Les lectures des enfants. Résumé des conclusions de l'enquête menée par l'U. N. A. F.," *Pour la vie,* Paris, No. 76, Mar., 1959, pp. 79–94. NNY.

The results of an inquiry into reading interests of children and young people, conducted by the Union Nationale des Associations Familiales.

830. "Lectures préférées de nos enfants," *Le livre français,* Paris, An 59, No. 63, Apr.–June, 1961, pp. 65–71. NNY.

831. Lefébure, Nadine. "Noël dans les livres," *La table ronde,* Paris, Dec. Yearly from 1956 through 1960. DLC.

A yearly review of children's books recommended as holiday gifts.

832. Lemaître, Henri. La bibliothèque enfantine de la rue Boutebrie "l'Heure Joyeuse," *Revue des bibliothèques,* Paris, 35e année, Nos. 1–6, Jan.–July, 1925, pp. 28–54. DLC.

The most complete contemporary account of the beginnings of the l'Heure Joyeuse children's library in Paris. This documents the efforts of the French and U.S. librarians to establish the library, the speech given by Eugène Morel on the occasion of its opening, the special organization and rules of the library, and its activities. Sketches of the interior are included, as well as reproductions of the printed forms used for cataloging, charging, registration, story hour announcements, etc.

833. ———. "Les bibliothèques pour enfants," *Mercure de France,* Paris, 49e année, No. 972, Tome 288, Dec. 15, 1938, pp. 590–600. DLC, NNY.

The phrase "children's library" hardly evokes an image in France, except possibly the faint remembrance of some glassed-in cases in the office of the school principal. However, thanks to the persistence of some foresighted librarians, the situation is slowly being remedied. The author cites examples of libraries giving good service to children.

834. Leriche, Mathilde. "Les albums et le journal Tintin," *Vers l'éducation nouvelle,* Paris, No. 138, Dec., 1959, pp. 33–35. PIP.

An effective and convincing argument *for* artistic children's books and *against* comics and cheap magazines. This is only one of many articles which this outstanding librarian contributed to this periodical.

835. ——— *with* Georges Prevot. *Bibliothèques scolaires – bibliothèques d'enfants.* Paris, Bourrelier, 1950. 123p. IYL.

A practical manual of organization, with the problems of school libraries considered separately from general children's libraries.

836. Leriche, Mathilde. "Les contes dans l'éducation des enfants de 6 à 11 ans," *Revue du livre et des bibliothèques,* Paris, 2e année, No. 12, Nov.–Dec., 1934, pp. 261–272. DLC.

The story hour, and its importance in the education of children from 6 to 11. The author speaks from her personal experience at *l'Heure Joyeuse* in Paris, and places special emphasis on the element of joy which stories can bring into the educative process.

837. ———. "Les enfants et la bibliothèque,"

Bulletin du livre français, Paris, No. 49, July–Aug., 1936, pp. 100–101. NNY.

Miss Leriche writes that the children of France do not get sufficient opportunity to enjoy free reading, and the books selected for home purchase are often the poorest in quality. Preceded by "La bibliothèque 'vivante' pour la jeunesse" by M. Lahy-Hollebecque, in which she writes that there is more to organizing a children's library than finding an attractive room, putting in rows of books, and painting the walls with color.

838. ———. "Essai sur l'état actuel des périodiques français pour enfants," *Revue du livre et des bibliothèques,* Paris, An 3, Dec., 1935, pp. 191–230. DLC.

A study which evaluated about 80 periodicals for children. Each is critically annotated. There is also a bibliography.

839. ———. *On raconte.* Paris, Bourrelier, 1956. 391p. PHJ.

A guide to storytelling, with a collection of stories to tell, classified by type and general age interest.

840. Leroy J. "Enquête sur les goûts en matière de lectures des enfants des écoles primaires d'Indre-et-Loire," *Binop,* Paris, 2ᵉ série, 12ᵉ année, No. 2, Mar.–Apr., 1956, pp. 87–100; No. 3, May–June, 1956, pp. 167–182. DLC.

The Centre d'Orientation Professionelle de Tours conducted an inquiry among students in the schools concerning their reading interests. The results are given in tables and accompanying explanations.

841. Levecq, E. "Les adolescents et les livres," *Livres et lectures,* Paris, No. 123, June, 1958, pp. 315–320.

842. Lévy-Bruhl, Odette. "Les adolescents et la lecture," *Enfance,* Paris, No. 5, Nov., 1957, pp. 561–567.

Observations on the reading interests and problems of adolescents. This is obviously the preliminary thinking behind the inquiry noted in the entry below.

843. ———. "Enquête sur les goûts de lecture des adolescents par le 'nouveau test du catalogue,'" *Bulletin des bibliothèques de France,* Paris, 5ᵉ année, Nos. 9–10, Sept.–Oct., 1960, pp. 321–366. DLC, NNY.

An inquiry into reading interests was made among some 1,200 young persons, aged 14–18, with the cooperation of the library in Boulogne-Billan-

court. The form was based on a test developed by the Swiss psychologist Tramer. The results are analyzed here, and the tables are explained with clarity.

844. "Littérature enfantine," *Cahiers de Neuilly,* Paris, July, 1959, pp. 172–177. PIP.

845. "Les livres," *Loisirs et formation culturelle de l'enfant rural.* Paris, Centre International de L'Enfance Travaux et Documents, 1956. pp. 95–155. CJL.

Results of an inquiry among many village school children in France. The conclusions are stated in very broad terms rather than being sweeping generalizations.

846. *Livres pour l'enfance et la jeunesse 1962–1964.* Paris, Association Nationale du Livre Français à l'Étranger, 1965; 62p. IYL.

A list of French books for children. (none are translations) compiled by Mme. J. Despinette, for the French section of IBBY. They are arranged into 11 general categories, with age levels and prices given. Some have one sentence annotations. There are title and author indexes. The text of the introduction is also in English and Spanish.

847. "Les livres pour enfants," *Enfance,* Paris, No. 3, 1956, pp. 1–214. IYL.

One of the most important studies in trends in modern children's literature. All points of view are aired. After the preface by Henri Wallon, 23 editors of firms which publish children's books answer such questions as "On what criteria do you select the books you publish?"; "Do you pay attention to the opinions of children? educators? critics?"; "What do you think of the criticism of children's books in the contemporary press?"; "What percentage of your books are translations and from what countries?"; "Do you adapt adult books for children?" etc. Following this, similar questions were asked 22 authors, chosen from those who write for children and adults, and from those whose work has been generally praised, or awarded prizes. Among those answering were Marcel Aymé, Aimé Baudouy, Paul Berna, Henri Bosco, Georges Duhamel, René Guillot, Jeanne Loisy, André Maurois and Charles Vildrac. Their answers are varied, not always in agreement, and often surprising. After this, the illustrators, critics, booksellers and editors of large journals and magazines all give opinions on the state of children's books in France, and what they are doing, would like to see done, or hope to do themselves.

The second part of the issue contains articles by Pierre Brochon, François Paul Delarue, Natha Caputo, J. Grandjeat, Françoise Guérard, René

Brandicourt, Raoul Dubois, Marie-Louise Darier, Marguerite Gruny, Hélène Gratiot-Alphendéry, and Andrée Clair; all are on aspects of children's books—the writing of them, use in home and library, criticism, their place in education, and the definition as to what makes a book a children's book. The articles on children's literature in China, USA, England, Poland and the USSR are noted in each of their respective countries.

848. "Livres pour les jeunes," *Biblio*, Paris, 30ᵉ année, No. 10, Dec., 1962, pp. 1–15. DLC.
Following short articles by Jean Cocteau, Paul Guth, Georges Bayard and Armand Rio, is a selected list of recent books for children, by subject, not annotated.

849. Loeffler-Delachaux, Marguerite. *Le symbolisme des contes de fées*. Paris, Arche, [1949]. 248p. (Action et Pensée). NNY.
The symbolism of fairy tales is discussed in a scholarly fashion, and in the light of the influence it has had on literature in general.

850. Lottman, Herbert. "No time for childhood," *School library journal*, New York, Vol. 13, No. 3, Nov., 1966, pp. 47–50. DLC, IYL, NNY.
This observer gives some of his personal reasons as to why there are so few good books for children in France.

851. Massaloux, Lucette, et al. *Bibliothèques de jeunes*. Paris, Èditions du Seuil, 1945. 107p. DLC.
Practical counsels on the organization of small libraries for young people. A list of basic reference works is included.

852. Maurois, André. "Lecture pour les enfants," *Figaro*, Paris, May 17, 1927, p. 1. NNY.
In recalling the effects of his childhood reading and comparing them to the effects of reading on present day children, this eminent author makes a graceful plea for adults not to be too concerned about the questionable morals and difficult situations implied in the classics and in many folk tales. Rather, he writes, it is "that which is poor in style and platitudinous which depresses the spirits."

853. Mayence, Serge and Marcel Gibon. *Lectures enfantines; les illustrés pour enfants*. 2nd ed. Charleroi, Centre d'études culturelles de l'Ecole Provinciale d'Educateurs et d'Educatrices de Châtelineau, 1965. 163p. IYL.
Results of a survey on comics outlined in text and with many statistical tables and lists.

854. Mazeydat, Pierre L. "Que liront nos enfants?" *Journal des instituteurs et des institutrices*, Paris, No. 38, June, 15, 1929.

855. Melin, Gabriel. *Les lectures de nos enfants*. Paris, Librairie Vuibert, 1911. 40p. DLC. Also appears in: *L'éducation*, Paris, An. 1, No. 4, Dec., 1909, p.600; An. 2, No. 2, June, 1910, pp. 290–302; No. 3, Sept., 1910, pp. 444–452. NNY.
Recommended reading for children, divided by three age groups and sub-divided by types. Bibliographical information is limited and there are no annotations or indexes.

856. Michelet, J. "Des lectures pour nos veillées," *Revue pédagogique*, Paris, Tome 9, Dec., 1886, pp. 489–495. DEW.
The author objects to a list of books for youth, selected by M. Buisson and published in the same journal the previous December. She felt it contained too many translations. Young people should have first the books which help them develop a love for their race and their country.

857. Migneaux, Marie. *Livres pour enfants et jeux éducatifs*. Paris, Confédération Nationale de la Famille Rural, 1957. 88p.

858. Montégut, Émile. "Des fées et de leur littérature en France," *Revue des deux mondes*, Paris, 2ᵉ période, 32ᵉ année, Tome 38, Apr. 1, 1862, pp. 648–675. DLC.
"There are fairies in every country, but the real fairies are Celtic and French, as in the ancient world the true nymphs were Greek." The author points out that France is decidedly not a country of "the marvelous" but there are corners (such as Brittany) which have been receptive to faerie. He then discusses the writers who spread fairy literature in France: Perrault, Mme. d'Aulnoy, Mme. Leprince-Beaumont, Mme. de La Fayette, and others.

859. Moore, Anne Carroll. "Report of sub-committee on children's work in other countries," *ALA bulletin*, Chicago, Vol. 15, No. 4, July, 1921, pp. 142–148. DLC, NNY.
After the war, the American Committee for Devastated France, together with the American Library Association worked toward the establishment of some model public libraries, with separate children's rooms. This is the report of Miss Moore's first trip to observe the results, in Soissons, Anizy, Blerancourt, Vic-sur-Aisne, and Paris.

860. Morin, Edgar. "Tintin, le héros d'une gén-

ération," *La nef,* Paris, 15e année, No. 13, Jan., 1958, pp. 56–61. DLC.

A more dispassionate account of the rise of the comics in France than is given in 872 and 793 and many other articles not included in this work. The author attempts to explain the reasons for the popularity of such magazines in France.

861. Pange, Pauline de. *Les clefs du paradis.* Paris, Editions Bloud & Gay, 1947. 134p. DLC.

The title translates as "The Keys to Paradise." These are essays on books, theater, cinema, radio and libraries for children. Aimed at parents, they give advice on selection and critical judgement. There is also a chapter on storytelling, and its importance in the life of the young child. It concludes with a one page bibliography.

862. Parvillez, Alphonse de. *Que liront nos jeunes?* Paris, Éditions du Temps Present, 1943. 62p.

Advice to parents and teachers on good reading for children and young people. This is written from the Roman Catholic point of view.

863. Pérez, Bernard. "La lecture," *L'Art et la poésie chez l'enfant;* Paris, Félix Alcan, 1888; pp. 240–266. DLC.

M. Pérez was an educator who early suggested a liberation of children's books from the purely didactic purpose. Citing numerous cases of children he had worked with or come to know he builds a picture of the effects reading can have on the sensibilities of the child. Although decidedly 19th-century in his thinking, he can probably be considered one of the forerunners of the more liberal pedagogists and educators.

864. Planque, Michel. *L'enfant et l'imaginaire.* Bar-le-Duc, Imprimerie Saint-Paul, 1959. 47p.

865. ———. "Pinocchio chez les Muses," *Pédagogie, centre d'études pédagogiques,* Paris, 13e Année, No. 1, Jan. 1958, pp. 68–76. DLC.

There are two types of admirers of the *conte:* those folklorists, mythologists, and psychologists who like to find precise definitions and applications for each tale; and those philosophers, poets, educators and critics who seek more the literary pleasure a tale can instil. Both types combined do not make a large number of persons, and this writer argues that it is time Pinocchio (and all his companions from children's literature) were allowed to take a rightful place among the Muses.

866. *Pour l'enfant lire c'est apprendre à vivre; 255 livres analysés ou cités pour garçons et filles de 4 à 14 ans.* Nogent-sur-Marne, Centre de Culture Ouvrière, 1966. Unp. (Supplement to IN-FOR-DOC, no. 180). CJL.

An annotated list, arranged by age groups. This was done in cooperation with "La Joie par les Livres." Each review is signed.

867. Pradel, Henri. *Les lectures des jeunes.* Paris, Téqui, 1938.

868. "Quelques livres français pour enfants intéressants à la fois par le texte et l'illustration choisis à l'intention des bibliothèques étrangères," *Association des Bibliothécaires Français. Bulletin d'informations,* Paris, No. 35 (New series), June, 1961, pp. 79–83. NNY.

Fifty-five children's books which a committee selected as most appropriate in representing France in the foreign book collections of libraries in other countries.

869. Ravier, André. "Livres d'étrennes pour les enfants et les adolescents," *Études,* Paris, Dec., Each year since 1948. DLC.

A yearly review of children's books, begun by Jean Rimaud and now continued by M. Ravier.

870. Richou, Gabriel. "Bibliothèques de l'enseignement secondaire; et . . . primaire," *Traité de l'administration des bibliothèques publiques;* Paris, P. Dupont, 1885; pp. 246–263. DLC.

The history, government, and legislation of primary and secondary school libraries in France, up to 1885.

871. Roger, Maurice. "Situation des bibliothèques scolaires," *Revue des bibliothèques,* Paris, Chronique, No. 1, Jan., 1930, pp. 1–20. DLC.

In this report to a special *Commission Ministérielle de la Lecture Publique,* the inspector general reviews the general history of school libraries in France, and the laws governing them, and then concludes with the results of an inquiry made into the current state of school libraries in 40 *cantons* of 19 *départements.*

872. Sadoul, Georges. *Ce que lisent vos enfants.* Paris, Bureau d'Éditions, 1938. 56p. DLC.

A plea for parents to look into the reading of their children, which consists almost entirely of comics and cheap magazines or paperbacks.

873. Scheid. "L'évolution du sens littéraire chez l'enfant," *Revue pédagogique,* Paris, Tome 56, No. 1 (New Series), Jan. 15, 1910, pp. 1–26. DLC.

In exploring the development of the literary

114

sense in the child, the author comes to the final conclusion that it is best to stop pretending that such a thing can be directed, and instead, just see to it that each child has enough imaginative fiction and other good literature available; the rest will come of itself.

874. Schmidt, Charles. "Bibliothèques pour enfants," *La revue de Paris,* Paris, 38e Année, No. 11, June 1, 1931, pp. 596–612. DLC, NNY.

New approaches to library work with children were brought to France after the war by American librarians. Here, a Frenchman records how these ideas were received by the public. It is interesting to compare this article with that of Anne Carroll Moore (859) since the same libraries are under scrutiny.

875. Seine (Dept.) Direction de L'Enseignement Primaire. *Liste des ouvrages adoptés pour les distributions de prix dans les établissements scolaires de la ville de Paris.* Paris, Imprimeries Réunies, 1885. 94p. DLC. Also: Paris, Société Anonyme de Publications Périodiques, 1898. 128p. DLC.

Two early lists of books approved for the distribution of prizes in Paris schools. They are divided into several general subject categories and then listed by author. Most are trade books.

876. Selz, Jean. "La renaissance des livres d'enfants en France," *Arts et métiers graphiques,* Paris, No. 56, Jan., 1937, pp. 31–41. DLC, NNY.

Exciting new artists and techniques have given new life to French children's books through use of attractive format and illustration. A number of pictures from recent books are reproduced here.

877. Semiontek, H. *L'enfant et la littérature enfantine contemporaine en France.* Toulouse, Imprimerie Régionale, 1932. 146p. Dissertation. NNY.

The five chapters deal with children's reading through the centuries, 19th-century children's literature, the novel of childhood and the novel for children, the new physiognomy of the child in postwar children's literature, and the new genres of children's literature which have evolved as a result of the new conception of the child.

878. Soriano, Marc. *Guide de la littérature enfantine.* Paris, Flammarion, 1959. 278p. DLC.

Although this begins with a short history of children's literature and biographical sketches of some of the universally known authors, the most interesting and valuable section is the third, a "lexicon of the problems posed by children's literature." A random sampling of the entries includes: "Adaptations," "Classics," "Cruelty," "Encyclopedias," "Fairies," "Parents," "Detective Stories," "The Rural Child,"

"Science Fiction," etc. No attempt is made to be comprehensive, but rather the author hoped to cover the variety of questions posed by parents, in order to reassure them that these "problems" are often exaggerated. The closing sections are trends in children's literature around the world, and a list of the author's personal recommendation, with comments.

879. ———. "Les livres pour enfants," *Enfance,* Paris, 1955–1961. DLC.

In this bi-monthly periodical, M. Soriano reviews children's books in almost every issue. Sometimes the articles deal with trends in children's literature rather than with individual books or authors.

880. Souché, Aimé. *Quels livres faut-il avoir lus?* Paris, F. Nathan, 1950. 313p. DLC.

"What books should one have read?" This is concerned with the young adult who has not yet read the books considered "classics" and necessary for a liberal background in general literature. It can also be used with the younger child in directing reading to the books of lasting value.

881. Soumille, G. "Les bibliothèques enfantines," *Éducateurs,* Paris, No. 31, Jan.–Feb., 1951, pp. 3549; No. 33, May–June, 1951, pp. 297–306; No. 34, July–Aug., 1951, pp. 389–398. PIP.

The first part is on municipal libraries for children in Paris, and a few other French cities. The second is concerned with the role of the Catholic Action movement in forming libraries. The third is a very brief account of children's work in Australia, Canada, Denmark, the U.S., Norway, Netherlands, Sweden, and Switzerland.

882. Storer, Mary Elisabeth. *La mode des contes de fées, 1685–1700.* Paris, Champion, 1928. 291p. IYL has xerograph copy.

883. Suran-Mabire, Claire. "Pour un nouvel aménagement des bibliothèques scolaires," *Revue universitaire,* 45e année, No. 3, Mar., 1936, pp. 245–249. DLC.

The situation in the so-called school libraries in France is intolerable, according to this educator. There is no real service offered to the young people, and instead of inspiring a love of books, the librarian usually succeeds in discouraging it, due to generally harassing conditions.

884. Tarsot, Louis and Albert Wissemans. *Catalogue des livres de lectures récréatives.* Paris, Imprimerie Nationale, 1888. 51p. (Musée Pédagogique, Mémoires et Documents Scolaires, Fascicule No. 23). DLC.

A list of recommended recreational reading, divided into the categories of: accounts of travels, poetry, novels, drama, and miscellaneous. The introduction is also of interest, for its forward-looking point of view.

885. Trigon, Jean de. *Histoire de la littérature enfantine de ma mère l'oye au roi Babar*. Paris, Librairie Hachette, 1950, 241p. DLC, IYL, NNY.

An effectionate history of French children's literature from Perrault to de Brunhoff. Many foreign works are touched on as well, particularly if they had been translated into French. Some of the outstanding works have reproductions taken from them and portraits of the best loved writers are frequently included. A synoptic table of the major developments in the literature around the world is a useful aid. There is little attempt made at criticism.

886. Valotaire, Marcel. "Children's books in France," *Creative art*, New York, Vol. 5, No. 6, Dec., 1929, pp. 845–854. DLC.

Some of the outstanding illustrators working in France at this time in the field of children's books were André Hellé, Joseph Hémard, Edy Legrand, Maggie Salzedo and Jean Bruller. Examples of their work are reproduced here.

887. Vaucaire, Michel. "Les livres d'enfants," *Art et décoration*, Paris, Vol. 58, Dec., 1930, pp. 161–176. NNY.

This critic's view is very much the same as the one expressed by Mme. Latzarus in her conclusion: The 19th-century books are not suited to the tastes of 20th-century children, and yet most publishers insist on reprinting them and shy away from the new and innovative. However, this critic is concerned more with the art in these books than with the texts. He shows examples of the few contemporary artists whose books are exceptions.

888. Venaissin, Gabriel. "Introduction a la littérature enfantine," *Critique*, Paris, Tome 10, No. 85, June, 1954, pp. 485–500. DLC.

An adult critic takes exception to several of the French critics of children's books (Brauner, Trigon, Hazard, Latzarus) and even questions whether there can be such a thing as criticism of children's books. Rather, he believes that it must be a criticism of literature which, by chance and by proof, has been children's literature by their own choice.

889. Vergnes, M. L. *"Les bibliothèques pour enfants."* Lyon, École Pratique de Psychologie et de Pédagogie, 1951.

890. Vérot, Marguerite M. C. *Les enfants et les livres*. Paris, S.A.B.R.I., 1954. 195p. DLC, IYL.

The results of a reading inquiry among the students of five French schools, and comments thereon. Although the statistics of the questionnaire were tabulated and put into tables, the author wisely states that they should not be considered as firm conclusions, because of the tendencies of children to answer questionnaires according to what the teacher thinks. She draws her conclusions in very general terms.

891. Weyergans, Franz. *La bibliothèque idéale des jeunes*. Paris, Editions Universitaires, 1960. 385p. IYL.

An annotated booklist of some 600 titles, arranged by age groups and subject categories, and indexed by author and title. The list is directed toward young people from 15 to 18 years of age, and includes many adult titles.

Belgium

Situated between France and the Netherlands, Belgium has naturally come under the influence of both, but there are also moments in her past and present when she is as much the generator of ideas as the receiver. Children's books have as long a history in Belgium as they do in the rest of Europe but there is no single author or work that stands out to the extent of being known on a world-wide basis. The one exception in the French-speaking world might be Madeleine Ley, but her child-like poetry has not been translated to any extent. Individual inspiration has come more from the three leading Belgian critics of children's literature, Hendrik van Tichelen, Gerard Schmook and Jeanne Cappe.

In view of present day politics, van Tichelen seems to have been born ahead of his time. The importance he ascribed to literature for children in their mother tongue struck sympathetic ears in the earlier decades of this century, but did not cause much discussion among the general public. It is possible that he might have stirred stronger emotions among a wider public had he come on the scene in this decade. The language question was only one of the concerns expressed in van Tichelen's criticism. His most frequent plea was for a better literature that could be more widely available. Because his viewpoint was often that of the teacher, he had his greatest effectiveness in reaching this group.

Gerard Schmook attempted a critical approach to children's books through the aid of the leading world critics. His study and bibliography only proved how difficult it was to exchange information and ideas on an international level.

Jeanne Cappe, on the other hand, aimed more at the audience of parents, booksellers and librarians. She founded the Conseil de Littérature de Jeunesse which still functions as a center for giving advice on the selection of children's books. Because the Conseil followed closely the principles of the Roman Catholic Church (the leading religion in Belgium) it did not have the wide support it might have attained with a more objective approach. On the other hand, the views were not so narrowly presented that they could not be of some use to French readers throughout Europe, no matter what their faith. Perhaps the greatest accomplishment which can be credited to the Conseil and Jeanne Cappe is that they succeeded in raising the quality of the religious book to an artistic level more in keeping with the subject. In the introduction to one of her selective lists (903) Mme. Cappe wrote of the deplorable taste exhibited in religious books, and stated that those with the imprimateur and other signs of official approval were often the worst. By appealing to parents and churchmen to look more carefully at what they gave to children under the guise of religious reading, she was instrumental in raising the standards in this type of book. At the present time Belgium is producing some of the best designed and illustrated religious books for children.

In the same introduction, Mme. Cappe described yet another unsatisfactory condition—the state of children's libraries in Belgium. She wrote: "It is lamentable that the public libraries are not developed to good advantage, particularly in the provinces, and that the bourgeoisie neglects sending their children to them and do not use them as a source of information when buying their gift books." This was some two decades ago, and the situation has improved, but not to the extent one could hope for. Only in the larger cities where the public library administrators are more than usually sympathetic to the cause of good children's libraries, has there been marked progression. The Antwerp Public Library is an example of this, as are the libraries in Liège and Mechelen. Belgium has a system of Roman Catholic and general public libraries similar to that of the Netherlands. However, they have not made as many significant steps toward unification.

There had been some early examples of children's library initiative in Belgium. In 1909, the Union of Ghent Women went so far as to send a young librarian to the U.S. for training in children's work. They set up a model library in the city, but it does not seem to have had a long standing effect, for not much was written about it after the initial years. After the First World War, a bibiothèque, L'Heure Joyeuse was opened in Brussels, but it, too, ran into difficulties and never got the solid grounding that was accorded its "twin" in Paris.

There has been no recent book length study on library work with children in Belgium, and even the number of articles in the professional journals are small in number, compared to similar countries. Consequently, librarians must turn to works in Dutch, or such translations as that of the McColvin work (924). The same is true of critical histories and studies of contemporary children's books. There are some from the Netherlands and France which can be used, but these are not entirely satisfactory. The whole approach to criticism differs too widely in each of these countries. The lack of these professional materials is a great drawback in the training of librarians and teachers.

892.   Adriaensens, H. "Samenwerking onder bibliotheken, school, jeugdbeweging, kindervacanties, werken voor volksopleiding," *Bibliotheekgids,* Antwerpen, Jg. 36, No. 6, Nov.–Dec., 1960, pp. 156–158. DLC, NNY.

"Cooperation among libraries, schools, youth movements, vacation camps, and public education work." The author refers to the Antwerp and Mechelen public library systems in particular.

893.   Antwerpen. Openbare Bibliotheken. *Centrale jeugdcatalogus.* Antwerpen, Openbare Bibliotheken, approximately every 2 years. IYL has 1956, 131p.; 1958, 180p.; 1958–1961, 70p.; 1961–1962, 47p.

The catalogue of holdings in the children's libraries of the Antwerp Public Library. The later catalogs supplement the earlier, rather than replacing them. Arrangement is by age and subject groups. No annotations.

894.   Belgium. Administration de l'Enseignement Primaire. *Première liste de livres destinés a être distribués en prix aux élèves des écoles gardiennes et primaires communales.* Bruxelles, Imprimerie de la Régie du Moniteur Belge, 1882. 28p. DLC.

A list of books approved for prizes in the primary schools. Information includes general subject category, author, title and price.

895.   Belleghem, E. Van. "Jeugdboekenselectie en bibliografische apparatuur," *Bibliotheekgids,* Ant-

werpen, Jg. 38, No. 4, July–Aug., 1962, pp. 83–90. DLC, NNY.

"Children's book selection and bibliographic tools." The author surveys the extent to which children's books are reviewed in periodicals and lists published in Belgium and the Netherlands. Comparisons are made of the points of view and the conclusion is that the overall coverage is not very good.

896.   Bernaerts, J. *Over kinderpoezie.* Mechelen, Rijckmans, 1913.

897.   "Les bibliothèques pour enfants à Anvers et à Liège." Congrès International Des Archivistes et Bibliothécaires; *Actes;* Bruxelles, 1910, pp. 759–760. DLC.

After hearing reports on library work with children in the United States and England, two Belgian librarians gave brief summaries of the beginnings of such work in Anvers and Liège.

898.   Boni, Armand. *Over kinderlektuur.* Antwerpen, Vlaamsche Boekcentrale 1942. 40p (Bibliotheekkundige Reeks, No. 5). DLC.

The five chapters of this booklet cover the psychological and pedagogical foundations of children's literature, boys' books and girls' books, old and new forms of children's books.

899.   Cappe, Jeanne. *Catalogue des bibliothèques enfantines.* Liège, 1956.

900. ———. *Contes bleus, livres roses. Essai sur la littérature enfantine, suivi d'un guide critique des livres destinés a la jeunesse.* Bruxelles, Éditions des Artistes, 1940. 228p. IYL.

The introductory essays deal with criticism and selection of books for children, illustration, and children's libraries. Following these are lists of books arranged by type and subject, with critical annotations. There are author and title indexes. This was one of the first truly selective lists in the area of French children's literature. Jeanne Cappe was the founder and late director of the Conseil de Littérature de Jeunesse.

901. ———. *Experiences dans l'art de raconter des histoires.* 2nd ed., Tournai, Casterman, 1953. 350p. IYL. (1st ed. called *L'art de raconter des histoires aux enfants et des histoires a leur raconter,* 1946, same publisher).

"Experiences in the art of storytelling." A personal account, aimed at inspiring teachers and parents to do more "educating by storytelling."

902. ———. *Lectures pour jeunes filles.* Bruxelles, Conseil de Littérature de Jeunesse, 1957. 61p. DLC, IYL.

An annotated list of some 250 books for girls, divided into 10 general subject categories. No specific bibliographic information is given, other than publisher, and there are no indexes. Many of the titles are translations.

903. ———. *Les livres destinés a la jeunesse.* 2nd ed., Tournai, Casterman, 1945. 101p. (Série clartés sur. . .). PIP.

Chapters on various types of children's and youth books, plus a selected list of each type, recommended by the author.

904. Christiaens, Fons. *De kinderlectuur en hare rol in den strijd om ontvoogding der gedachten.* Antwerpen, De Rechain, 1905. (Tijdschrift van het Komiteit voor Geestesontwikkeling, No. 9).

905. Custers, Math. *Welk boek geven we het kind?* Lier, J. Van In, 1939. 19p. (Pedagogische Trakten, No. 63).

906. Decaigny, T. *La presse enfantine.* 2nd ed. Bruxelles, Ministère de l'Instruction Publique, 1958. 56p. (Service National de la Jeunesse, Série, No. 1). IYL.

The role of "comics" and cheap magazines in the life of the child, and the dangers and problems this press can create.

907. Devos-Van Hoof, C. Belgium. *Library service to children, 2.* Lund, Bibliotekstjänst, 1966, pp. 16–21. DLC, NNY.

This publication was sponsored by IFLA, and in this chapter, the history and present status of library work with children in Belgium is discussed.

908. Dominique, Jean Marie Closset. *Les enfants et les livres.* Bruxelles, H. Lamartin, 1911. 54p.

909. Empain, Louis and Marcel Jadin. *Nos enfants lisent.* 9th ed. Namur, Editions du Soleil Levant, 1964. 222p. IYL.

A booklist divided into fiction and nonfiction, and sub-divided into smaller age and subject categories. There are one sentence annotations and the fiction is indexed by author and title.

910. Funck, Antoine. "Les lectures pour enfants," *Gymnastique scolaire,* Bruxelles, An 35, No. 1, Jan., 1912, pp. 1–5. DEW.

In the 1910 congress of the "Ligue de l'Enseignement" three resolutions concerning children's literature were passed. The first recommended good, artistic picture books for preschool children; the second recommended 7 steps toward providing school children with good reading; the third offered several suggestions for encouraging children to continue reading after their school years. This editor disagreed with several of the recommendations, particularly the one concerning the types of reading school children should have.

911. Gitée, Aug. "La rime d'enfant," *Revue de Belgique,* Bruxelles, An 19, Tome 57, 1887, pp. 301–324. NNY.

A brief history of children's rhymes, together with a number of examples, comparing them with Mother Goose.

912. Halsberghe, C. "Enquête sur la lecture enfantine," *Rencontres,* La Louvière, No. 1, 1958, pp. 83–111. IYL has reprint.

A resume of the results of a reading interest survey made among more than 900 children attending a vacation camp. The author was responsible for a well-known children's radio program in Belgium.

913. Heurck, Emile H. van and G. J. Boekenoogen. *Histoire de l'imagerie populaire flamande et de ses rapports avec les imageries étrangères.* Bruxelles, G. van Oest, 1910. NNY.

A history of "popular" or "folk" picture stories, in particular as they appeared in chapbooks, flysheets and the like. Many of these works are to be considered as the children's books of their day. The authors, recognized authorities in the field, produced several other studies on the same subject.

914. Hileghem, Andrea van. "De lievelingslectuur van het vlaamse meisje," *Vlaams opvoedkundig tijdschrift,* Antwerpen, Jaargang 29, Nos. 3–4, Dec., 1948–Jan., 1949, pp. 157–171. DLC.

"The favorite reading of Flemish girls." A report on a reading survey made in 46 classes in Flemish Belgian schools. The author based her questionnaire upon similar ones found in German, English and United States studies.

915. *Illustrés pour les jeunes.* Bruxelles, Confédération Nationale des Associations de Parents, 1960. 32p.

916. *Jeugdboekengids.* "Algemeen Secretariaat voor Katholieke Boekerijen," Raapstraat 4, Antwerpen. Monthly. Vol. 1 ff., 1959 ff. IYL has 1962.

Short reviews of books for children and young people, written from the Roman Catholic point of view.

917. Kalken, H. N. van. *Een en ander uit de geschiedenis der Nederlandsche literatuur voor de jeugd.* Brussel, Van der Linden, 1913. 96p.

918. ————. "Over leesboeken van vroeger eeuwen," *Vlaamsche gids,* Antwerpen, Jaargang 14, No. 4, Jan., 1926, pp. 167–175. DLC.

About early primers and other reading books for children, from earlier centuries.

919. *Lectures pour les jeunes.* Bruxelles, Confédération Nationale des Associations de Parents, 1960. 20p. (Note documentaire, 12).

920. Limbosch-Dangotte, R. C. Les bibliothèques pour enfants à Gand, *Revue des bibliothèques et archives de Belgique,* Bruxelles, Tome 7, Nos. 4–5, July–Oct., 1909, pp. 263–275. DLC.

Inspired by the work done in the United States and England, the Union des Femmes Gantoises determined to set up library service to children in Gand. To that end, they were collecting funds, and had sent a young woman to train in the library course for children's work in the Pittsburgh Public Library.

921. *Littérature de jeunesse.* Conseil de Littérature de Jeunesse, 19 Boulevard A. Reyers, Bruxelles. 10 nos. yearly. Vol. 1 ff., 1948 ff. (Price: 175 F Belgian, 20 F French, 200 F Belgian for foreign subscriptions, except Canada and U.S., $4.25 Canadian). DLC, IYL.

Articles on children's literature and reading problems and reviews of current books.

922. Loock, Marcel J. van. *Boekenweelde; een keur van werken voor ontwikkelde jongeren.* Antwerpen, Vlaamsche Boekcentrale, 1945. 126p.

923. ————. *Keurboeken voor een degelijke klas- en schoolbibliotheek.* Antwerpen, Vlaamsche Boekcentrale, 1945. 65p. DLC.

"A choice selection of books for a classroom or school library." More than 750 titles, not annotated, but listed in subject categories. There is no index. In the foreword, the author specifies the bases of selection he has used.

924. McColvin, Lionel R. *Jeugdbibliotheekwerk.* Antwerpen, Ontwikkeling, 1959. 147p. BBJ.

A translation of entry 46, made by L. Schevenhels.

925. Meel, Jan van. *Openbare boekerijen, vak-en kinderbibliotheken, leeszalen, reizende boekerijen.* Antwerpen, Veritas, 1923. 264p.

926. Mennekens, J. *Kinderpoezie in verband met de opvoeding en het onderwijs.* Brugge, Centrale Boekhandel, 1924. (Cultuur en Wetenschap.)

927. Mercelis, Johan. "Welke eischen stelt men van pedagogisch standpunt aan het kinderboek?," *"Vlaamsch opvoedkundig tijdschrift,"* Antwerpen, Jaargang 15, No. 9, June, 1934, pp. 551–561; No. 10, July, 1934, pp. 614–621. DLC.

"What requirements, from the educational point of view, should one place upon the children's book?" A discussion of the critical and selective works of Hendrik van Techelen, Saskia Lobo, and S. Rombouts, in which the author points out his agreement or disagreement with them.

928. Michel, A. "Les lectures des enfants," *L'éducation familiale,* Bruxelles, An 14, No. 2, Feb., 1907, pp. 57–63; No. 3, Mar., 1907, pp. 121–126. DEW.

"Read, and read much," was the advice this educator offered to his students. He also advocated much reading aloud to children, by parents and teachers.

929. Moore, Anne Carroll. "Report of sub-committee on children's work in other countries. Belgium," *ALA bulletin,* Chicago, Vol. 15, No. 4, July, 1921, pp. 148–152. DLC, NNY.

With the interest of Mlle. L. E. Carter to push, prod, plead and guide it into existence, l'Heure Joyeuse opened in Brussels on September 24, 1920. It was a reading room for children, staffed, stocked and and equipped with funds received from various U.S. committees. Visiting it a year after its opening, Miss Moore points out that it is still far from being the ideal children's room.

930.   Nyns LaGye, J. *Cinq cents bons livres pour enfants et adolescents de 6 à 16 ans.* Bruxelles, Ligue de L'Enseignement, 1925. 63p. (Document No. 56, Bulletin No. 3, May–June, 1925). Supplements in Document No. 59, 1926, 8p; Document No. 62, 1927, 8p.

931.   *Ons kinder-en damestoneel; verzameling van 1500 besprekingen van kinder- en damestoneelstukken.* 2 vols. Brussel, Algemeene Toneelboekerij, 1929. 362p. and 152p.

932.   "Organisation des bibliothèques enfantines," *Oeuvre nationale de l'enfance,* Bruxelles, 2e année, No. 3, Dec., 1920, pp. 370–376. DLC.

A translation based on a short section from Sophy Powell's *The Children's Library,* (4219).

933.   Pals, Jozef and A. Huysmans. *Kinderlectuur en kinderbibliotheken.* Brussel, Christelijk Onderwijzersverbond, 1953. 137p. DLC.

The qualities which children look for in their reading at different age levels, and some recommended books for them. Written from a Christian point of view.

934.   Pels, Alice. "Les bibliothèques enfantines en Amérique et en Angleterre et les premiers essais en Belgique," *Bulletin des bibliothèques publiques,* Bruxelles, Vol. 1, No. 2, Mar., 1922, pp. 70–76.

935.   Piérard, M. "Les bibliothèques enfantines en Belgique." International Congress of Libraries and Bibliography, 2nd; *Actas y trabajos, Vol. 3;* Madrid, Librería Julián Barbazán, 1936; pp. 278–179. DLC.

Library work with children in Belgium owes its existence to the influence of the United States, and in particular as it was manifested in Mlle. L. E. Carter, who began the first children's library in Brussels.

936.   "Les problemes de la lecture et le rôle de la bibliothèque de jeunesse." Entire issue of: *Rencontres,* La Louvière, No. 4, Oct.–Dec., 1965, pp. 5–131. CJL.

The papers and discussions resulting from a day of study organized by the Centre Culturel du Hainaut and the Service des Bibliothèques Publiques of the Ministry of Education. On pp. 74–91, is a bibliography of 239 books and articles on the problems of children's literature and libraries, mostly in the French language.

937.   Renault, J. "Bulletin des romans et livres de lecture capable d'interesser utilement la jeunesse," *L'éducation familiale,* Bruxelles, An 14, No. 7, July, 1907, pp. 345–350; No. 10, Dec., 1907, pp. 516–519. DEW.

Reviews of current books for youth. Similar columns by this and other authors appeared sporadically in this journal.

938.   *La ronde des livres.* Bruxelles, Édition Universelle, 1947. 148p.

939.   Schmook, Gerard and Victor van den Berghe. *Jeugdboekenlijst.* Antwerpen, De Sikkel, 1929. 96p. (Bibliotheekkunde, Vlugschriften voor den Bibliothecaris Aansluitend bij De Bibliotheekgids, 6). DLC.

The Flemish association of librarians had met in 1925 and suggested that a basic book list be compiled, to serve as a guide in establishing and maintaining small children's libraries. This list is the result. It has almost 2,000 titles, arranged by age and subject, but not annotated. There is an author index and a 7 page bibliography.

940.   Schmook, Gerard. *De klasse-bibliotheek.* Antwerpen, De Sikkel, 1929. 64p. (Brochurenreeks van de Vlaamse Opvoedkundige Vereniging).

941.   ———. "Literatuur voor de jeugd," *Inwijding in de Literatur Bronnenopgave;* Antwerpen, De Sikkel, 1937; pp. 115–125. (Bibliotheekkunde. Vlugschriften voor den Bibliothecaris Aansluitend bij De Bibliotheekgids, 14). DLC. Also in: *Bibliotheekgids,* Antwerpen, Vol. 16, No. 5, Oct., 1937, pp. 104–114. DLC.

A bibliography of some 400 books about children's literature, its theories, genres, history, illustration and critical selection. Most of the entries are from the U.S., Great Britain, Germany, France, Belgium and Holland. There are a number of inaccuracies, and the bibliographical information is not always complete. Nevertheless, this is important for its attempt at broad, international coverage and for its breakdown of materials by subject coverage.

942.   ———. *Het oude en het nieuwe kinderboek.* Antwerpen, De Sikkel, 1934. 106p. (Brochurenreeks van de Vlaamse Opvoedkundige Vereniging).

943. ———. "Het terrein en de grenzen van een bibliografie van het kinderboek," *Wetenschappelijk Vlaamsch Congres voor Boek- en Bibliotheekwezen,* 4th, Gent, 1936; *Handelingen;* Gent, Drukkerij Vyncke, 1937; pp. 91–118. DLC.

The summary in English, on p. 118, translates the title as "How to delimit the field of a bibliography of children's books." The author is describing here the manner in which he went about compiling his bibliography (note in 941), and he suggests an outline of study for the scholar interested in children's literature.

944. Stevart, Fernand and Reine Thone. *L'orientation nouvelle des bibliothèques pour la jeunesse. Une passionante expérience: Le Club ACB de la bibliothèque pour la jeunesse du Thier à Liège.* Liège, Echevinat de l'Instruction Publique, 1959. 19p. IYL.

"The new orientation of libraries for youth," followed by a report on the experiences of a library club for young people in one of the libraries near Liège.

945. Stevens, Jacques. *Antennes; les plus beaux livres du jeune homme.* 3rd ed. Bruxelles, Goemaere, 1947. 83p.

946. Tichelen, Hendrik van. [Articles on children's literature, libraries and related subjects.] Arents, Amédée; *Bibliografie van en over Hendrik van Tichelen;* Antwerpen, L. Opdebeek, 1943, 266p. DLC.

Mr. van Tichelen was for many years the curator of the Stedelijk Schoolmuzeum in Antwerp. Not only did he write for children, both poetry and prose; but he was also a voluminous critic on the subject of children's literature and libraries. All of his books on this subject are listed in this present bibliography, but it was felt to be needlessly repetitious in listing his numerous articles in periodicals, his reviews of specific children's books and the regular columns he contributed to several magazines. They can be traced easily through the Arents bibliography.

947. ———. *Het kinderuur; zijn ontstaan, zijn ontwikkeling en werking, zijn mogelijke toekomst.* Antwerpen, V. Resseler, 1923. 11p.

948. ———. *Leve de daad!* Brugge, De Kinkhoren, 1944. 157p. DLC.

Based on essays which first appeared in the periodical *Moderne school* in 1931, and later as the pamphlet *Voor het kinderboek in Vlaanderen* (950). Tichelen is particularly concerned here with the

rights of Flemish-speaking children to have their own literature in schools, in libraries, and at home. The ideas of the original essays have been revised and expanded.

949. ———. *Over boeken voor kindsheid en jeugd.* Antwerpen, Uitgeverij Ontwikkeling, 1952. 430p. IYL. (Earlier work, 1928, called *Over boeken voor kinderen;* pub. by De Nederlandsche Boekhandel, Antwerpen, 234p.).

"About books for children and youth; a study to aid teachers, parents and librarians, together with a select list of recommended books arranged according to the various genres and according to age groups." There is an index and an annotated bibliography.

950. ———. *Voor het kinderboek in Vlaanderen.* Antwerpen, De Sikkel, 1931. 49p. (Also appeared in *Moderne school,* Antwerpen, each month from March through October, 1931).

951. ———. *Wat onze kinderen lezen.* Antwerpen, De Sikkel, 1936. 106p. (Brochurenreeks van de Vlaamse Opvoedkundige Vereniging). DLC, IYL.

A questionnaire was sent to the teachers, principals, inspectors and like personnel of Flemish-speaking Belgian schools. The questions asked related to the official reading materials used, the extent of class, school and public libraries in their area, whether prize books were given and what kind, and what they observed to be the recreational reading of their school-children.

952. Tichelen, P. van. "Bibliotheekinwijding voor jongeren door school-bibliotheken ofwel door openbare bibliotheken?" *De bibliotheekgids,* Antwerpen, Jaargang 27, No. 3, May–June, 1951, pp. 49–55. DLC, NNY.

In pointing out the standards for school library service which exist in England and the United States, the author contrasts the situation which exists in Belgium and the Netherlands. He answers the title—"Introduction to the library for young people, through school or public library?"—with suggestions for using both.

953. ———. "Jeugdboeken als spiegel voor ons beroep," *Bibliotheekgids,* Antwerpen, Jg. 35, No. 6, Nov.–Dec., 1959, pp. 132–135. DLC, NNY.

"Children's books as a mirror of our profession." This librarian discusses some fictional books which have themes centered around the public library.

954. Vader, A. de. "Livres pour la jeunesse," *La*

revue nouvelle, Tournai, 13ᵉ année, Tome 25, No. 4, Apr. 15, 1957, pp. 472–475. NNY.

A review of recent good books for children and young people. This reviewer contributed articles on children's books to this periodical at irregular but frequent intervals.

955. Vandevelde, E. H. A. *Over kinderlezing.* Brugge, D. Walleyn, 1931. 26p. (Brochurenreeks Geloofsonderricht Canisiusblad).

956. Vanhaegendoren-Groffi, Y. M. *Wat vertellen? 52 thema's voor verhalen.* Leuven, S. V. de Pijl, 1942. 240p. DLC.

"What to tell? 52 exercises in telling." In her introduction, the author states that this is not for children to read aloud from, nor to be read aloud to them, but rather as a practical aid to selection and techniques for use by parents, teachers and librarians.

957. Vereniging Vlaamse Schrijvers voor de Jeugd. *Vlaamse boeken en herdrukken voor de jeugd.* Antwerpen, 1962?

958. Villermont, M. de "Les lectures pour jeunes filles," *L'éducation familiale,* Bruxelles, An 14, No. 10, Dec., 1913, pp. 593–600. DEW.

Suggested reading for young girls.

959. Walckiers, Anne-Marie. *Tes livres, jeune fille.* Bruxelles, Editions Famille et Jeunesse, 1947. 56p.

960. Wielenga, B. *Moderne letterkunde en christelijke opvoeding.* 1922.

961. *Zestig! Gedenkboek ter eere van Hendrik van Tichelen.* Hoogstraten, Moderne Uitgeverij, 1943. 423p.

A memorial collection of essays, presented to Mr. van Tichelen on the occasion of his 60th birthday. They are written by educators, writers, poets, musicians, artists and friends of his. Several are concerned with aspects of children's literature. The bibliography of Mr. van Tichelen's works is not as complete as that noted in 946.

Netherlands

To the small country hampered by further breakdown of its culture into traditional language, religious and political divisions, the Netherlands provides a praiseworthy example of steady progress in a unified effort to improve the status of children's books and libraries. This is due largely to the existence of a single agency, the Bureau Bock en Jeugel der C.V., or Bureau Book and Youth of the Central Association for Public Libraries. Behind it, however, lie the efforts of far more individuals than merely those connected with the library association.

When, in November 1951, a group of children's librarians suggested a conference on "the value of a good children's book as a factor in education," the organization of the program was undertaken by a committee composed of teachers, youth group leaders, booksellers, publishers and, of course, librarians. With typical Dutch thoroughness they not only carried out the congress with success, but resolved to cement the newly established professional relationships into a concrete form. Out of this resolution came the plans for the Bureau. When it finally came into being about a year later, it was wisely placed within a parent organization, i.e. the library association. Later it began to receive state subsidy as well.

Miss A. J. Moerkercken van der Meulen, director of the Bureau, has presented very clear accounts of the Bureau itself, and children's library work in general (1019, 1022). Since these are widely available in English, it seems unnecessary to relate here, second-hand, the points which she makes. What is not specifically stated are the difficulties which had to be overcome, and some which are still being faced. Perhaps the greatest obstacle to progress through unity is the public library situation.

In the publication *Libraries and Documentation Centres in the Netherlands* (The Hague, 1966), Margreet Wijnstroom gives an exceptionally lucid explanation of the complexities of Dutch public libraries. There are, in fact, no public libraries at all, if by that term is meant free service. All must pay, children and adults, albeit a negligible amount. If by the term public is meant support by municipal or state funds, then there are public libraries. Indeed, there are three kinds of public libraries: general, Roman Catholic and Protestant. All three types receive governmental support (provided they meet certain requirements), and all three types may exist in one locality, no matter what the population. One doesn't have to stretch the imagination too far to realize that the overlapping of work and expense could be monstrous. Fortunately, the situation is becoming better all the time, and the tendency is toward federation of the various types, or toward one general library supported entirely by the municipality. This is an extremely brief account of a complicated set of systems, but it will suffice to point out one of the problems with which the Bureau Bock en Jeugel must cope. To provide book lists, book reviews, catalog cards, information and inspiration on a national basis to all three types of libraries, and to satisfy them all, is no mean accomplishment.

The Netherlands has a long way to go before it will be providing acceptable library service to all of its children, but it has the kernels of such a goal at work in the Bureau. As in so many countries, now, the greatest lack is in human resources—there are not enough children's librarians to use the materials available. In 1960, for example, children's work was carried out by 81 professionally trained persons, scattered throughout 430 libraries for juvenile readers (1022 p. 68). There is now a new library school, operated by the Stichting Bibliotheek en Documentatiescholen, which provides for a specialty in children's work. Miss Jannetje Daane, head of children's work in the Amsterdam Public Library, is the lecturer. Of course, the Central Association continues to administer a program of training and education, as it has in the past, but even the combined efforts of these two associations are not producing sufficient trained personnel.

Ever since the development of printing, the Netherlands has been a leader in fine publishing. Books for children did not receive the attention to artistic detail which some of their "grown-up" counterparts did. Nevertheless, the early productions of the 18th and 19th century were far superior, in beauty of format and illustrations, to the books of the 1900's. Many of the best examples can be appreciated by paging through the volume which Leonard De Vries collected (1052). The flowering of English picture-book illustration (Walter Crane, Randolph Caldecott, Kate Greenaway) did not go unnoticed in the Netherlands, but it had its effect on general book illustration only, and did not bring about much change in the design of picture books for young children. It is a curiosity that these beautiful picture books from England, as well as others from Germany, Switzerland and France, were so widely purchased and admired, and yet did not essentially change the trends in children's book illustration and format. This has remained true to this day. It is very common to see, on the shelves of many libraries, the finest examples of picture books from Western countries, and the standards of Dutch counterparts do not stand up. Miss Moerkercken van der Meulen explains: "On the whole in the Netherlands, children's books are not taken seriously. A children's book must be cheap, and so it is . . . Not much care can be given to its production, and the fees for author and translator are very low" (1022).

Insofar as the text is concerned, the history of children's books follows another pattern. The didactic books of the previous century have been replaced by a growing number of native, realistic stories of today, and by an even greater number of translations. It is here that the pressure exerted by a united front of librarians has made publishers pay more attention to standards. To risk the non-approval of this group is to lose a high percentage of sales—more than one-third. In all fairness, it must be stated that some publishers are anxious to improve the quality of their children's books, and seek out the advice of the Bureau. Translations in particular are now often generated there, when a publisher first sees a copy of a book which has received high praise in foreign reviewing journals.

The first name of any note which appears consistently in all historical studies of Dutch children's literature is that of Hieronymus van Alphen, whose poetry for children appeared in the second half of the 18th century. "Whoever studies the dignified, somewhat self-sufficient countenance of this children's poet has a difficult time imagining that he had his moments of foolish and gay childhood pranks," wrote D. L. Daalder (974, p. 59). Yet that must have been the case, for he was known as "a child of Satan" in his student years. However, with maturity came a sense of religious conviction, and his poetry for children was of a purely didactic nature. This did not prevent it from having a tremendous influence all over the northern part of Europe. It was the Dutch contribution to the flood of such literature which seemed to spread without effort in these countries.

Some three-quarters of a century later, while didactic literature still held sway, the poet and critic De Genestet took van Alphen to task for his pietistic moralizing (982). One can say that at this moment the critical history of children's literature was born in the Netherlands. From then on, a few voices were always raised against pure didacticism in children's books, and the very essence of what constitutes a good children's literature was debated in each generation.

The last years of the Victorian age and the first of the 20th century witnessed perhaps the strongest voices of any given period, insofar as both children's literature and its criticism is concerned. N. van Hichtum, J. Stamperius, M. Wibaut-Berdenis van Berlekom, J. Bos-Meilink, Ida Heijermans, Nellie van Kol were all as much writers of children's books as they were critics and social commentators. Their comments seem a little high-flown at times, and show a distinct ignorance of many practical realities. But they stirred up interest to the point where books for children were very much in the public consciousness, and paved the way for children's libraries as well as more publishing.

The period between the two wars was dominated by translations, but the works of such authors as Top Naeff and N. van Hichtum continued to appear and new writers and illustrators, among them Cor Bruijn, Rie Cramer, Leonard Roggeveen and J. M. Selleger-Elout, augmented the list of natively produced works. Some of these works were translated into other languages, so that the flow of books was in both directions.

In the postwar years these trends continued. Translations are still providing a high percentage of the total of approximately 2,000 titles published each year. The best native productions are in fictional stories for the middle grades, e.g. those of An Rutgers van der Loeff-Basenau. The greatest deficiencies are in nonfiction and picture books for the younger children. This seems to be the one type of children's book which is either too expensive to produce in translation, or which publishers fear will not find an understanding public because the illustrations represent such foreign elements. In spite of much talk about international understanding through children's pictures, there is the least amount of exchanging done in the picture book field, and the Netherlands is only one of the many countries which would benefit greatly if this barrier were more easily broken down.

962. Amsterdam. Stedelijk Museum. *Kinderen lazen kinderen lezen.* 31 October 1958–7 January 1959. Catalog No. 195 of the Museum. 66p. DLC, IYL, NNY.

The catalog of an exhibit of old and new children's books, of which almost 600 were from the Netherlands and the remaining 600 from various other countries. The Dutch books are described in great detail, with illustrations reproduced from some. All types are represented: chapbooks, ABC's, magazines, editions of the classics, Bibles for children, and even some early school books.

963. Bergstra, A. "Bibliotheeklessen," *De openbare bibliotheek,* 's-Gravenhage, Jaargang 2, No. 3, May, 1959, pp. 134–137. NNY.

The librarian of the Haarlem city library children's room describes her work in teaching the use of the library to children.

964. *Boek en jeugd.* 's-Gravenhage, Bureau Boek en Jeugd der Centrale Vereniging voor Openbare Bibliotheken, 1965 ff. Annual. DLC, IYL, BBJ.

An attractive, selective booklist, begun as a substitute for the defunct *Kleine Vuurtoren* (1003). It is hoped that this can be issued each year, either in a completely new edition, or as a supplement. This main list consists of more than 1,000 titles, arranged by subject or age group. Each annotation is signed and there is an author index.

965. *Boek en jeugd.* Bureau Boek en Jeugd der C.V. 's-Gravenhage. Irregular. 1954–1958? BBJ, IYL.

This information bulletin contained news of the work of children's libraries in the Netherlands and other pertinent information. It was issued very irregularly.

966. Boerlage, Louise M. *Jeugdboeken lezen en kiezen.* Groningen, Wolters, 1964. 108p. DLC.

The five parts of this book deal with the reading and selection of children's books: why they need a special type of reviewing; means whereby the reviewer can come to know the imprint; how to judge the contents by their separate elements; and some points to touch on.

967. Bomhoff, J. G. "Overdenkingen over het kinder- en jeugdboek," *De openbare bibliotheek,* 's-Gravenhage, Jaargang 5, No. 1, Jan., 1962, pp. 1–5. NNY.

A speech given on the opening of children's book week, 1961. Thoughts on the true meaning of education, the place of the children's book as part of education, and the use of books by parents (with their children) an ideal beginning in the educative process are expressed.

968. Bos-Meilink, J. *Lektuur voor kinderen.* Amsterdam, Wereldbibliotheek, 1914. (Maatschappij tot Nut van't algemeen, 2ᵉ Reeks).

969. Bruggen, Jan Reinder Leonard van. *Lektuurvoorsiening vir kinders en jeugdige persone.* Amsterdam, Swets & Zeitlinger, 1922. 191p. DLC.

"Provisions for reading for children and young people." By this, the author means not only the literature which has developed, but libraries where it is readily available to all children. He contrasts the Dutch and South African libraries for children with those of other countries, particularly the U.S.

970. Bureau Boek en Jeugd. *Keesje Kruimel Krant.* 's-Gravenhage, Vereniging ter Bevordering van de Belangen des Boekhandels, 1962. DLC, BBJ.

A pamphlet and booklist printed on the occasion of children's book week and distributed nationally through schools and libraries.

971. Clercq, E. de. "De taak der vrouw in zake kinderlectuur en kinderbibliotheken," *De vrouw, de vrouwenbeweging en het vrouwenvraagstuk,* Deel 2; Amsterdam, Elsevier, 1918. pp. 106–121. APL.

The role of women in children's literature and libraries. This is a brief historical survey of events up to that time. The author's conclusion is that some of the most constructive work being done by women was in the field of children's libraries.

972. Corbett, Phyllis T. M. "Observer in Dutch children's libraries," *Junior bookshelf,* Kirkburton, Vol. 1, No. 2, Feb., 1937, pp. 21–23. DLC, IYL, NNY.

This British librarian found two obvious characteristics of library work with children in the Netherlands: it is paid for (in small amounts) by the children, and it works on the closed access system.

Reading rooms, separate from the lending departments, did have free access.

973. Daalder, Dirk Leonardus. *Het boek in de jeugdbeweging.* Amsterdam, Moderne Jeugdraad, 1952. 24p. BBJ.

A brochure on the role of the book in the youth movements of the contemporary period. It is written in a popular style.

974. ———. *Wormcruyt met suycker.* Amsterdam, De Arbeiderspers 1950. 298p. DLC, IYL, NNY.

This is subtitled "a critical-historical survey of children's literature in the Netherlands, with illustrations." Chapters from this well-documented study include the periods of the Middle Ages, the 16th, 17th and 18th centuries, 1800–1830, 1830–1880, 1880–1900, 1900–1920, 1920–1940, after 1940, religious children's books, Friesian and Flemish children's literature, foreign classics, and book illustration. A chronological table, portraits of leading writers, a six-page bibliography, and a very complete index make this an invaluable aid in the study of the world's children's literature.

975. Daane, Jannie. "Indians in Amsterdam; Dutch children enjoy American books in translation," *Top of the news,* Chicago, Vol. 13, Dec., 1956, pp. 24–25. DLC, NNY.

The head of the central public children's library in Amsterdam tells here of some of the books on American Indians which have become popular in Dutch translations.

976. Doodkorte, J. J. *Jeugd en lectuur.* Tilburg, R. K. Jongensweeshuis, 1922, 43p. (Opvoedkundige Brochurenreeks, 11). BBJ.

"Youth and reading." A critical essay, written from the Roman Catholic point of view.

977. Driel, A. A. E. van. *De kunst van het vertellen.* Leiden, Spruyt, Van Mantgem and De Does, 1955. 98p. DLC, BBJ.

"The art of storytelling." The history, influences and practice of storytelling, from the early days of language up to the present. Unfortunately this is arranged in a confusing manner and brings in the subject of films (with photographs reproduced from several), which fragments the information even further.

978. Forceville-van Rossum, J. *Kan mijn dochter dit boek lezen?* Lanoo, 1964. 212p. BBJ.

"Can my daughter read this book?" A guide for parents on the selection of good reading materials and the avoiding of bad. Th. de Laat contributed a chapter on girls' stories and K. Fens wrote on poetry for girls.

979. Gebhard, Annie C. *Kinderboeken als vitamines; een ABC over kinderen en lezen.* 2nd ed. Amsterdam, Ploegsma, 1963. 128p. BBJ.

"Children's books as vitamins; an ABC on children and reading." A very warm and sympathetic approach to reading guidance.

980. ———. *Over kinderen en hun boeken.* Amsterdam, Museum voor Ouders en Opvoeders, 1919. 77p. APL.

A yearly list in which a number of books for children were listed, with reviews from leading sources. There are also essays on the subject of choosing good books for children.

981. ———. "Tien jaar kinderleeszaal- en bibliotheekwezen in Nederland, 1912–1921," *Bibliotheekleven,* Utrecht, Jaargang 7, No. 3. March, 1922, pp. 83–89. DLC, NNY, BBJ.

"Ten years of children's library work in the Netherlands." An annotated bibliography of 30 items (mostly periodical articles) concerned with this work in the period 1912–1921. The citations are quite complete.

982. Génestet, Petrus Augustus de. *Over kinderpoëzie.* Amsterdam, Gebroeders Kraay, 1865. Unp. (Reprint from *Nederland, 1858?*). APL.

Comments on the children's poetry of Van Alphen, and on what characteristics children's literature should have. He blamed Van Alphen for the heavily didactic tone which had developed in writing for children.

983. Gerhard, J. W. *De kunst in het leesboek voor het eerste schooljaar.* 's-Gravenhage, Ontwikkeling, 1911. (Nederlandsche Vereeniging Schoonheid in Opvoeding en Onderwijs, 12).

984. ———. *Onze kinderliteratuur in de aesthetische opvoeding.* Haarlem, Bohn, 1905. (Studies in Volkskracht, 2ᵉ Serie, No. 4). APL.

"Our children's literature in aesthetic education." An early and influential work which discussed the qualities needed in good children's books. In his general book on aesthetics *De esthetische opvoeding der jeugd* he stressed the importance of good picture books. Gerhard was influenced by Wolgast and the earlier German theoreticians and educators.

985. ———. "Over 'schund-literatuur.' Hare oorzaken en hare bestrijding," *De boekzaal,* Zwolle, Jaargang 4, 1910, pp. 31–40, 59–72. NNY.

A study of the reasons for the rise and success of cheap, serial literature. The author suggests a list of good series, periodicals and "library sets" to counteract this influence.

986. Gerhardt, Mia I. *The art of story-telling.* Leiden, E. J. Brill, 1963. 500p. BBJ.

Although this is a scholarly study of the many forms of the thousand-and-one-nights theme, there are several parts of interest to all storytellers.

987. Giessen, H. W. van der. "De jeugdbockenauts van de provinciale plattelandsbibliotheek voor Drenthe," *De openbare bibliotheek,* 's-Gravenhage, Jaargang 3, No. 10, Dec., 1960, pp. 394–396. NNY.

"The children's bookmobile from the province library in Drenthe." This article tells how it serves the rural areas.

988. Haas, Paula de and L. J. de Vries. "Sprookjes . . . wat heb je daar nov an!" *De openbare bibliotheek,* 's-Gravenhage, Jaargang 4, No. 4, May, 1961, pp. 114–119. NNY.

On fairy tales, and telling fairy stories.

989. Heijermans, Ida. *Onze jongeren en de moderne literatuur.* Baarn, Hollandia Drukkerij, 1919. 43p. (Paedagogische Vlugschriften voor Ouders en Opvoeders). BBJ.

"Our young people and modern literature; a pedagogical critical overview." This essay of criticism mentioned specific authors and titles. The author was one of the leaders in the early development of libraries for children.

990. Hichtum, N. van. *Prikkeliteratuur.* Amsterdam, De Ploeg, 1909.

991. Hildebrandt, Marie. "Bibliografie van kindertijdschriften," *De boekzaal,* Zwolle, Jaargang 3, 1909, pp. 217–219. NNY.

An annotated list of 26 children's periodicals, with a brief introduction explaining the general characteristics.

992. Huet, Conrad Busken. "Kinderboeken," *Litterarische fantasien en kritieken;* Haarlem, H. D. Tjeenk Willink, 1882; Vol. 8. pp. 18–39. DLC.

Critical comments on some mid-19th-century children's books in the Netherlands, and in France.

993. Hulst, W. G. van de. *Het vertellen; inzonderheid van de bijbelse geschiedenissen.* 4th ed. Nijkerk, G. F. Callenbach, 1965. 140p. BBJ.

"Storytelling." The author writes of experiences gained largely in telling Bible stories, but the chapters on the art in general are quite good and are applicable to any type of storytelling work.

994. *150 jaar kinderboeken in Nederland; catalogus bij de tentoonstelling in de openbare bibliotheek.* . . 's-Gravenhage, Bureau Boek en Jeugd, 1963. 46p. DLC.

An exhibition of 300 books for children, produced in the Netherlands during the past 150 years, was held in the public library. This catalog lists them by subject and type. No annotations are given.

995. "Inrichting en werking der schoolbibliotheken," *Opvoeder,* Jg. 22, No. 5, Feb., 23, 1925, pp. 73–78.

996. "Jeugdbibliotheek," *De openbare bibliotheek,* 's-Gravenhage, Monthly, 1958 ff. (with some exceptions). NNY.

This column appears in almost every issue and includes a wide variety of articles on children's library work. Frequently they are translations from periodicals of other countries. Reports on national and international congresses are covered here, and professional literature is sometimes reviewed.

997. "Jeugdbibliotheeknummer," *De openbare bibliotheek,* 's-Gravenhage, Jaargang 3, No. 7, Sept., 1960, pp. 237–297. DLC, NNY.

This special number includes many articles on school and public library work with children and on children's literature written by A. J. Moerkercken van der Meulen, Paula M. de Haas, Annie C. Gebhard, A. M. Elsen, L. D. Woltjer and E. M. van der Poort, among others.

998. "Jeugdbibliotheken en -leeszalen." Greve, H. E. *Geschiedenis der leeszaalbeweging in Nederland.* 's-Gravenhage, Uitgeversfonds der Bibliotheekvereenigingen, 1933. pp. 64, 209, 230, 251–255, 353. BBJ.

A documentary of the development of children's library work as a part of general library work. This publication commemorated the 20th anniversary of the founding of the association of public libraries.

999. Katholiek Lectuur Centrum. *De lectuur van de middelbare schooljeugd.* 3 vols. Nijmegen, Hoogveld Institut, 1963. 74p., 115p., 89p. (Mimeographed). DLC.

"The reading of middle-grade school children." Vol. 1 explains the purpose, organization and methodology of this research project. Vol. 2 evaluates the reading situations and content of the reading of the children taking part in the project. Vol. 3 examines the psychological aspects of their reading. There are many statistical tables throughout the volumes.

1000. Kerstens, Piet. *Invloed van de lectuur in de jaren der karaktervorming.* Leiden, Kolff & Co.

1001. Keuls-Francis, Tiny. *Ouders, wat lezen uw kinderen?* Leiden, Nederlandsche Uitgeversmij, 1954. 64p. DLC.

"Parents, what are your children reading?" A pamphlet which has as its purpose a skimming of the old and new trends in children's books.

1002. *Kinderen en boeken, 1963. Een onderzoek naar koop-, lees- en studiegewoonten.* 2 vols., 's-Gravenhage, Nederlandse Stichting voor Statistiek, 1963. Vol. 1, 106p. Vol. 2, 82p. BBJ.

"Children and books, 1963. An inquiry into the buying, reading and studying habits of children." Vol. 1 contains the text and Vol. 2 the statistical tables.

1003. *De kleine vuurtoren.* Vereeniging ter Bevordering van de Belangen des Boekhandel's, 's-Gravenhage. Annual. 1927–1961 (with exception of war years). DLC and IYL have some years; BBJ has complete set.

A booklist sponsored by the booksellers association and selected in the earlier years by children's librarians from the association of public libraries; since the founding of Bureau Boek en Jeugd, that agency has coordinated the selection. The last year contained about 500 titles, arranged by subject and age groups and annotated. The booklet *Boek en Jeugd* (964) now replaces this list to some extent.

1004. Kleisen, J. "De lectuur voor de middelbare scholier," *De openbare bibliotheek,* 's-Gravenhage, Jaargang 5, No. 5, June, 1962, pp. 143–149. NNY.

A teacher writes of her observations of the reading which young people of the middle schools like or do not like.

1005. Kluit, H. J. "Jeugdbibliotheekwerk." Gerhard, Annie C. *Vit de leeszaalwereld.* Amsterdam, Swets en Zeilinger, 1949, pp. 34–55. BBJ.

Historical and contemporary aspects of children's library work in the Netherlands, by one of its enthusiastic pioneers.

1006. ———. "Lectuurproblemen voor teenagers," *KENO (Kinderverzorging en oudervoorlichting),* No. 3, Sept., 1961, pp. 76–85.

1007. Knuttel-Fabius, Elize. *Oude kinderboeken; paedagogie en moral in oude nederlandsche kinderboeken.* 's-Gravenhage, Martinus Nijhoff, 1906. 172p. BBJ.

"Old children's books; pedagogy and morals in old children's books of the Netherlands." A survey of some of the earliest didactic books printed for children.

1008. ———. "Over oude kinderboeken en prenten," *Boekzaal,* Zwolle, Jaargang 6, 1912, pp. 175–191. NNY.

Some early examples of picture books are discussed and illustrated with reproductions from their pages.

1009. Kol, Nellie van. "Wat zullen de kinderen lezen?," *De gids,* Amsterdam, Jg.70, Serie 4, Deel 4, Oct., 1899, pp. 288–330. NNY. (?Same as a reprint titled *Over kinderlectuur,* Rotterdam, Masereeuw en Bouten, 1901?)

"What should children read?" The author was a pioneer in campaigning for better children's books and libraries in which they could be read freely. In this long article she describes the qualities which good children's books should have.

1010. Koninklijk Institut voor de Tropen. *Raadgever voor koloniale jeugdlectuur.* Deel 1. Amsterdam, Druck de Bussy, 1935. 30p. DLC, NNY.

A list of 130 children's books in Dutch, suitable for use in the colonies. All are annotated, and symbols indicate those books recommended for Protestant and Catholic missionary schools.

1011. Kruyt, J. *De kunst van vertellen.* 's-Gravenhage, Boekhandel Zendingsstudieraad.

1012. Landwehr, John. *Fable-books printed in the Low Countries; a concise bibliography until 1800.* Nieuwkoop, B. de Graaf, 1963, 43p. IYL.

"A survey on fable-books printed in Holland and Belgium before 1800 . . . when fable-literature was published mainly for the use of children." It is interesting to compare this with the recent Library of Congress catalog (4230).

1013. *Lectuur voor de jeugd . . .* rev. ed. 's-Gravenhage, Centrum Jeugd en Lectuur, 1965. 24p. DLC, BBJ.

"Reading for youth," first prepared in 1960 in commemoration of liberation day, and recently revised. The Centrum is an organization of publishers, booksellers, teachers, youth leaders and librarians which works closely with the Bureau Boek en Jeugd in promoting children's literature. The selection of titles on this list was made by the staff of the Bureau. It is largely of books about the war, liberation, and friendships among nations.

1014. Lens, J. *Bibliotheekgids voor chr. school- en jeugdbibliotheken.* Goes, Van Oosterbaan & Le Cointre, 1930. 150p. DLC.

"A library guide for the Christian school or youth library." Reviews of some 500 books, pointing out the merits and uses of each for the teacher or librarian. They are arranged by author alphabetically, and each is signed.

1015. *De lectuur van onze middelbare schooljeugd.* 's-Hertogenbosch, 1958. 28p. (Publikaties van het Katholiek Paedagogisch Bureau ten behoeve van het V. H. M. O., No. 5). BBJ.

A preliminary report on the survey completed and described in 999.

1016. Lobo, Saskia. *Het kinderboek 1920–1924.* 's-Gravenhage, Centrale Vereniging voor Openbare Leeszalen en Bibliotheken, 1925.

A forerunner of *De Kleine Vuurtoren.*

1017. Maatschappij tot Nut van't Algemeen. *Lijst van boeken, geschikt of opgenomen te worden in de bibliotheken voor jongelieden.* Amsterdam, S. L. van Looy and H. Gerlings, 1895?, 40p. NNY.

"A list of books suitable for use in young people's libraries." The arrangement is alphabetical by author and there are no annotations. The Maatschappij was among the many private foundations supporting libraries for the public, upon payment of a fee.

1018. Mercelis, Johan. "Schets van een ontwikkelingsgang van het Nederlandsch Kinderboek 17ᵉ, 18ᵉ, 19ᵉ eeuw," *Vlaamsch opvoedkundig tijdschrift,* Antwerpen, Jaargang 15, No. 8, May, 1934, pp. 495–506. DLC.

"A sketch of the development of the children's book in the Netherlands in the 17th, 18th and 19th centuries." This actually covers Flemish-speaking Belgium as well.

1019. Moerkercken van der Meulen, A. J. *Bureau Boek en Jeugd der C.V. Bureau "Book and Youth."* The Hague, 1966. 4p. (Mimeographed). APP, BBJ, DLC.

Contents of a speech delivered by the director of the Bureau at the IFLA conference in The Hague in September, 1966. The text is in English, and explains very clearly the history, present status, and aims of the Bureau.

1020. ———. "Bureau Boek en Jeugd der C. V.," *De openbare bibliotheek,* 's-Gravenhage, Jaargang 4, No. 4, May, 1961, pp. 110–113. NNY.

The aims, work, and organization of the Bureau, described by its directress.

1021. ———. "Het Jeugdbibliotheekwerk; een eigen plaats?," *De openbare bibliotheek,* 's-Gravenhage, Jaargang 1, No. 2, Feb., 1958, pp. 78–83. DLC, NNY.

"Children's library work; a separate place?" A discussion of the special qualities of the work, which distinguish it from work with the adult public. This is followed by comments of some children's librarians on their work, and what it meant for them to have had the special course given by the library association, children's section.

1022. ———. "The Netherlands," *Library service to children.* Lund, Bibliotekstjänst, 1963, pp. 63–71. DLC, IYL, NNY.

This chapter in the IFLA publication deals with the history and present status of children's library work in that country.

1023. ———. "Het pretenboek, toen en nu," *De openbare bibliotheek,* 's-Gravenhage, Jaargang 2, No. 1, Jan., 1959, pp. 27–37. NNY.

After stating the qualifications of the good picture book, the author discusses a few old and some new picture books from several countries.

1024. ———. "De problematiek van ons school-bibliotheekwerk," *De openbare bibliotheek,* 's-Graven-hage, Jaargang 6, No. 6, Aug., 1963, pp. 27–36. NNY. (DLC has a separate reprint, 14p.).

After reviewing the history of the school library in the Netherlands, which officially began in 1806, the author comments on some present-day school libraries in her country. She states that as of 1963, most of these were essentially classroom libraries, and the three major cities in the Netherlands had no real central school libraries. She ends with specific recommendations for action to remedy the situation. This is followed by a report (pp. 37–38) on the discussion which took place after the delivery of this speech to the national congress of librarians.

1025. Mooij-Gaastra, L. "Den Haag bezit een moderne schoolbibliotheek," *Boek en vorming,* 's-Gravenhage, No. 2, Mar., 1961, pp. 25–32. BBJ.

A description of an unusual school library which also serves as a branch of the public library for the young adult readers in that area. This is the official periodical of the Protestant Foundation for the Advancement of Libraries and Reading in Netherlands, and it contains many articles on the general subject of children's books and libraries.

1026. Niemöller, W. H. J. *Een onderzoek naar de kwaliteit van het Nederlandse kindertijdschrift.* Groningen, Wolters, 1964. 76p. (Pedagogische monografiën). BBJ.

"An inquiry into the quality of children's periodicals in the Netherlands," which the author concludes is very poor indeed. The author describes the questionnaire and other methods used in arriving at this quantitative and qualitative analysis of the periodicals. Thirteen are described in great detail, and 28 pages from them are reproduced. Bibliography and statistical tables are included.

1027. Nijkamp, W. M. *Het boek en kleuterland.* 6th ed. Assen, Van Gorcum, 1966. 112p. IYL, BBJ.

"The book in the small child's world." A handbook on using books and stories with the preschool child, and the importance of early experience with books, stories and pictures.

1028. Oldersma, A. "Een pleidooi voor een ruimer plaats van het kinder- en jeugdboek in het klassegebeuren," *Vernieuwing van opvoeding en onderwijs,* 's-Gravenhage, Jg. 21, No. 200, Nov., 1962. DLC.

1029. Oorthuys-Backer, M. E. G. "Doel en mogelijkheden van een jeugdbibliotheek," *Bibliotheekleven,* Delft, Jg. 43, May, 1958, pp. 118–125. DLC.

"Goals and possibilities of a youth library."

1030. Otto, Anna. "Kinderen, boeken en ik," *Boek en vorming,* 's-Gravenhage, No. 4, Sept., 1961, pp. 54–57.

A teacher writes on her methods of working with children and books, and building literary taste in the early years.

1031. Pawlakówna, H. "Biblioteki dla dzieci w Holandii," *Bibliotekarz,* Warszawa, Rok 31, Nos. 2–3, 1964, pp. 67–72. DLC, NNY.

"Libraries for children in the Netherlands." A short history, and data on specific libraries and services in Amsterdam, the Hague and Rotterdam.

1032. Pieters, P. *De sprookjes van Moeder de Gans. Hun oorsprung en beteekenis.* Amsterdam, P. Pieters, 1913. 41p. APL.

"The folk tales of Mother Goose; their source and meaning."

1033. Peeters, Edward. *Letterkunde voor kinderen.* Rotterdam, Masereeuw & Bouten, 1916. 20p.

1034. Ramondt, Marie. *Sprookje-vertellers en hun wereld.* Groningen, Wolters, 1948. 190p. BBJ.

"Story-tellers and their world." On the art of folk storytelling, and how one person sees it.

1035.	*Recensiedienst jeugdlectuur. Bureau Boek en Jeugd der C. V.* 's-Gravenhage. Ten times yearly. 1965 ff. BBJ.

A reviewing service which goes out to most of the children's libraries in the Netherlands.

1036.	Reenin, C. J. H. van. "De rijdende jeugdbibliotheek," *Bibliotheekleven,* Rotterdam, Jg. 39, Jan., 1954, pp. 4–7. DLC.

The work of a travelling children's library in Rotterdam, serving children from 10 to 14 years of age.

1037.	Riemens-Reurslag, Johanna. *Het jeugdboek in de loop der eeuwen.* 's-Gravenhage, Van Stockum & Zoon, 1949. 255p. IYL, DLC, NNY.

"Children's books through the centuries." A general history, beginning with the 17th century, and touching upon the major events and trends in Europe, with emphasis on the Netherlands. The last chapter deals with modern trends. The author's point-of-view is sometimes psychological-sociological, rather than literary. There are three pages of bibliography, and 16 plates of reproductions.

1038.	Riemsdijk, G. A. van. "De centrale administratie ten behoeve van filialen en jeugdbibliotheken," *De openbare bibliotheek,* 's-Gravenhage, Jaargang 6, No. 3, Apr., 1963, pp. 92–94. NNY.

"A central administration for the benefit of branch children's libraries." A description of administration and organization of children's work in the public libraries of Amsterdam. Followed by a short article on school class visits to the Surinameplein children's library.

1039.	Rombouts, S. *Wat laat ik mijn kinderen lezen?* Tilburg, R. K. Jongensweeshuis, 1915.

1040.	Schenk, W. J. H. *et al. Jeugdboek en school.* 3rd ed. Groningen, J. B. Wolters, 1963. 128p. IYL, BBJ.

"The juvenile book in school." According to the forward, the aims of this handbook were to widen general knowledge about good children's books, to aid in the selection of books, to assist in planning and expanding school and classroom libraries and to point out means whereby schools and libraries might make more meaningful contacts. This is followed by a recommended book list and a bibliography.

1041.	Schmidt, Annie M. G. *Van schuitje varen tot van Schendel.* Vereeniging ter Bevordering van de Belangen des Boekhandels, 1954, 76p. BBJ.

In this essay, a well-known children's writer asks and answers the following question: Have children's books such an essential part to play in the education of the child that their choice cannot be left to chance?

1042.	Schuurman, Cornelis Johannes. *Er was eens . . . en er is nog.* Arnhem, Van Loghum Slaterus, 1946. 253p. NNY, DLC, BBJ.

"There was once . . . and there is still; an introduction to the folk tale world of symbol and reality." This work studies the folk tale from the psychological, sociological and anthroposophical points of view.

1043.	Sprey, K. *Middelbare school en bibliotheek.* 's-Gravenhage, Bond van Verenigingen voor Christelijk Middelbaar en Voorbereidend Hoger Onderwijs, 1953. 19p. (No. 18).

1044.	Stamperius, J. *Over kinderlectuur.* Baarn, Hollandia-Drukkerij, 1910. 32p. (Paedagogische Vlugschriften, Serie 1, No. 9). BBJ.

A review of the best children's books of the previous 30 years. Each is annotated.

1045.	Stoop-Snouck Hurgronje, J. *Brieven over kinderlectuur.* Amsterdam, Ontwikkeling, 1920. 63p. (Socialistische Vrouwen Bibliotheek). BBJ.

A short study of the qualities of good children's literature by one of the pioneers in the movement to make books available to all children. The writer was a staunch supporter of the Socialist Labor Party.

1046.	Tierie-Hogerzeil, E. *Hoe men het ABC begeerde en leerde.* Utrecht, Het Spectrum, 1946. 94p. BBJ.

"How the ABC's have been taught." An appealing glimpse into the history of the ABC picture book. Pages 48–94 are reproductions, in black and white and in color, of some of the early examples.

1047.	*Verslag van het congres "Boek en Jeugd."* 's-Gravenhage, November 2–3, 1951. 28p. BBJ.

This report of the first congress on "Book and Youth" includes articles by J. R. Wolff on children's libraries, and by C. van Breda de Vries on the publishing of children's books.

1048.	*Verslag van het kinder-en jeugdboekencongres . . .* Amsterdam, Commissie voor de Collectieve Propaganda van het Nederlandse Boek, 1961. 16p. BBJ.

"Report on the children's and youth book congress." This includes articles by J. G. Bomhoff and A. de Vries on criticism of children's books, and by N. C. A. Perquin on young people's reading.

1049. *Verslag van het kinder-en jeugdboekencongres op 25 en 26 oktober 1963 te Delft.* Amsterdam, Commissie voor de Collectieve Propaganda van het Nederlandse Boek, 1964. 30p. BBJ.

A report on the children's and youth book congress of 1963, in Delft. Includes: "The school and reading habits," by W. de Hey; and reports and comments on a reading interest survey by A. Rutgers van der Loeff-Basenau, and M. Zeldenrust-Noordanus.

1050. Veth, Cornelis. "Evolutie van het kinderboek," *Elsevier's Geïllustreerd Maandschrift,* Amsterdam, Jaargang 46, Deel 92, July–Dec., 1936, pp. 170–174. DLC.

"The evolution of the children's book," and more specifically, the book with a moral or cautionary lesson. Illustrated with plates from Boutet de Monvel, Belloc, Hugh Lofting, William Nicholson and Ellen Houghton, all of whom the author discusses, together with such writers as Wilhelm Busch and Heinrich Hoffmann.

1051. ———. "Kinder-prentenboeken. Jongensboeken," *De boekzaal,* Zwolle, Jaargang 4, No. 5, 1910, pp. 187–202; Jaargang 6, 1912, pp. 9–20, 70–76. NNY.

The first article covers some of the work of Caldecott, Greenaway, Crane, Cruikshank, Kreidolf, Busch, Boutet de Monvel and Doré. The second and third are concerned with the classics of Defoe, Swift, Scott, Cooper, Mayne Reid, Karl May, Dumas, Verne and others.

1052. Vries, Leonard de. *Bloempjes der vreugd' voor de lieve jeugd.* Amsterdam, De Bezige Bij, 1958. 236p. BBJ.

Selections from the most charming works of the 18th and 19th century published for Dutch children. The texts and illustrations are reproduced as a whole, so that one can get a feeling for the period. The compiler did a similar volume in English, culling his materials from the Osborne collection of the Toronto Public Library (see 3393).

1053. ———. *A short history of children's books in the Netherlands.* The Hague, 1964. 6p. (Mimeographed).

1054. Wagamaker, Wim. "About Dutch children's books, and fairy tales," *Junior bookshelf,* Huddersfield, Vol. 9, July, 1945, pp. 41–44. DLC, NNY.

A report of some of the Dutch books which were sent to the refugee children (Dutch) in England. Many of these books came from Indonesia.

1055. ———. "Dutch children's books," *Junior bookshelf,* Huddersfield, Vol. 7, July, 1943, pp. 48–54. DLC, NNY.

The favorite books of children in the Netherlands, both from the past and the present, from their own country and from others.

1056. Wibaut-Berdenis van Berlekom, M. *Het boek en het volkskind; geschreven voor de moeders der arbeiderskinderen.* Rotterdam, H. A. Wakker, 1906.

1057. ———. and Saskia Lobo. *Het boek en het kind. Leidraad bij de keuze van boeken voor de jeugd.* Amsterdam, Ontwikkeling, 1928.

1058. Wirth, Louise Jeanne Thérèse. *Een eeuw kinderpoëzie, 1778–1878.* Groningen, J. B. Wolters, 1928. 244p. IYL. (DLC has 1925 ed., same pub.).

"A century of children's poetry." A critical, historical study of poetry in the Netherlands from 1778–1878. Emphasis is on Hiëronymus van Alphen, but some thirty other minor poets and their work are included. Treatment is often according to the subject of the poetry. A list of the children's books used as sources, together with the libraries in the Netherlands where they were located, is given on pp. 219–241.

1059. Wolff, J. R. "Jeugdbibliotheekwerk," *Bijdragen tot een handboek voor de openbare bibliotheek in Nederland.* 's-Gravenhage, Centrale Vereeniging voor Openbare Bibliotheeken, 1965. pp. 79–91. BBJ.

The aims, functions, and equipment of the children's library. How to order books, administration, contact with readers and many types of activities are covered. The chapter on school libraries, pp. 91–100, was written by Miss. L. D. Woltjer.

1060. Wouters, D. *Letterkunde en lezen voor jonge en rijpere jeugd.* Groningen, Noordhoff, 1925.

1061. ———. *Over het illustreeren van leesboeken voor kinderen.* Bussum, van Dishoeck, 1913. 182p. BBJ.

"On the illustration of children's reading books." This is not restricted entirely to textbooks or school books. The author concluded that "the best is never good enough for children" and recommended more attention to the art in children's books. There are some 192 reproductions of illustrations from early children's books.

Luxembourg

Like the Republic of Costa Rica in Latin America, this European Grand Duchy has produced not only a native literature for children, but also one comprehensive history of the development of that literature (1062). Mr. Noesen's study indicates that before 1800, there was hardly a children's book published in Luxembourg. The 19th century brought some of the same didactic works as were to be found in the rest of Europe, and a number of children's journals. In the 20th century, children's books in French and German began appearing on a regular basis, although in small numbers. Theodore Zenner is considered to be the most successful writer of children's books.

1062.   Noesen, Paul. *Geschichte der Luxemburger Jugendliteratur*. Luxemburg, Verlag der L. K. A., 1951. 101p. IYL.
    "A history of children's literature in Luxembourg." This covers in detail all those authors born in Luxemburg, and all children's books printed there, both in French and German. There are also sections on school libraries, and on periodicals and theater for children. Important critics were Jos. Bernhard Krier, J. B. Ensch, Marie Speyer and Frantz Clement. The last chapter is on the future of children's books in Luxembourg.

Austria

Austria is the single European country to consciously direct its main children's book distribution through a program different from that of normal store sales or availability in school and public libraries. This came about in 1948 when the Ministry of Culture set out to investigate the best methods of counteracting the flood of cheap and sensational literature for children which was inundating postwar Austria. In order to evaluate the various means through which children and books are brought together, experts studied the library and book distribution systems of England, the U.S., and some of the European nations. It was decided that libraries were not sufficiently developed in Austria to assume the work quickly enough. Instead, a national book club was set up with state support. So as to protect commercial interests, a process was devised whereby children can join the club through their school, but purchase the books at a 25% discount through their local booksellers. Books of all Austrian publishers and some from Switzerland and Germany are considered and rated by a committee of librarians, parents and teachers. Those approved are published in bi-yearly lists which are then distributed to all members of the Book Club. Membership is arranged through the voluntary aid of classroom teachers, but all records are kept centrally in the Book Club offices in Vienna. For their assistance, the teachers receive complimentary copies of *Die Barke,* as well as other publications put out by the Club. Children who are members of the Club also receive a yearbook, which is an anthology of stories and selections from Club approved books.

Because this operation receives financial support from the Ministry of Culture, and because it is organized on a national level, the number of children reached by the program is impressive. In 1966, 750,000 children purchased approximately 3,000,000 books. This means that about 90% of Austria's school children buy their own books, without taking into account the number which buy books not found on the Book Club lists. Also, the figure includes only hardcover books published for normal trade purposes, and does not include the paperback or magazine type of publications which the Book Club recommends to a lesser degree.

The Book Club also supports many other programs related to children's books. Among them is a group of "reading rooms" which are used to experiment with Book Club projects and which serve also as a kind of local public children's library, having a wide variety of book-related activities such as story hours, puppet shows, etc. Book exhibitions are arranged through the Club, which has 60 complete sets of the books on the approved lists. They also assist teachers in selecting small classroom collections, which can also be ordered through the Club.

In spite of its great success, there is one minor, negative reaction possibly resulting from the size of the Book Club. Because such a high percentage of sales stems from Club approval, there has been a tendency toward sameness in Austrian children's books of recent years. Publishers seem loath to try experimental or unusual types of books, when they know from experience that the reviewing committee is more certain to approve a work with traditional values. This is more true of the design and illustration of the books than it is of the text. It might well be that there is a current lack of talent in Austria, so that the small number of illustrators and writers necessarily produces a limited amount of styles. This observer felt that it was more a result of the "collective" aspect of the Book Club. Without taking anything away from its accomplishments, it might be in order to suggest that the Book Club now begin to press for more artistic production of the children's books it approves. There is another agency which works on practically the same principles of selection and consequently adds more pressure on the publishers to conform. This is the Jugendschriftenkommission in the Ministry of Education, which reviews every single book published in Austria for children, as well as some from Germany and Switzerland. It is this agency which is informally responsible for school library development.

Because of the funds and personnel efforts infused into the Book Club, public and school libraries for children are very rare. This refers to genuine children's rooms, rather than "corners" or classroom collections. It is debatable whether the child benefits more from personal ownership of a select library, or the opportunity to browse freely among a large, diverse collection. As yet there has been no comprehensive study of the total effectiveness of the Book Club, as opposed to, for example, a widespread school and library program such as is in effect in Sweden, which has approximately the same population and some similarity in governmental policies. Such a study might well prove enlightening to both types of countries; those hoping to improve library service and those wishing to bring about more direct book purchases by children.

Many reasons for the success of this Austrian Children's Book Club lie in its energetic director, Dr. Richard Bamberger. His is certainly the leading position in the children's literature movement in Austria, and much of his writing in the field touches all of the German-speaking countries. The second edition of his *Jugendlektüre* contains more information on the subject than any other single volume work in German. During the years 1962–1966, Dr. Bamberger was President of the IBBY. Under his direction an International Institute for the Study of Children's Literature was set up within the framework of the Book Club, but having its own entity. They now publish *Book-bird,* the official journal of IBBY.

Austria has not always been as forthright and independent as she is today in the children's book field. There was a time in the 19th century when Vienna, as a publishing center, produced more children's books for Germany than she did for herself (1069 p. 455). In the last quarter of the century, a specifically Austrian book movement developed. This can be laid to two reasons, according to Koester (1295) : the first materialization of the public schools prescribed by law and the appearance of Engelbert Fischer's massive collection of reviews on children's and folk literature (1085). This was followed closely by the *Kritischen Führer* of J. Panholzer, the *Wegweiser* of J. Langthaler, and the works of Anton Peter and K. Huber. All of these were booklists purporting to be selective, but in actuality their only selectivity was in keeping off the list books offensive to, or not in agreement with, the Roman Catholic religion. It was not until the opening year of the next century that a list appeared which questioned the religious motive as the prime basis of selectivity. In getting away from this restrictive point of view, Moissl and Krautstengel substituted another. They felt they could only recommend those books which would not do damage to the German-Austrian consciousness, its customs and its way of life (1109).

Present day criticism is by no means completely free of both the religious and patriotic points of view. Since the end of the last war, nationalism has been of a very mild character. The religion, however, remains predominantly Roman Catholic, and while there is a good percentage who profess this faith but do not practice it formally, there is still much hesitancy about accepting children's books critical of the church, even in a historical context.

1063.   Ajdovic, K. "Aufgabe und Verantwortung der Kinder- und Jugendbücherei," *Neue volksbildung,* Wien, Jg. 6, No. 4, 1955, pp. 138–142. DLC.
"The tasks and responsibility of children's and youth libraries."

1064.   Auböck, Inge. *Die Literarischen Elemente des Sachbuches.* Wien, 1963. 322p. Dissertation.

1065.   Badstüber, H. *Die deutsche fabel von ihren Anfängen bis auf die Gegenwart.* Wien, Gerold, 1924. 48p.

1066.   Bamberger, Richard. *The Austrian Children's Book Club.* Wien, Österreichischer Buchklub der Jugend, 1964? 10p. (Mimeographed). APP.
A pamphlet in English, explaining the aims,

methods and results of the Austrian *Buchklub der Jugend*.

1067. ———. *Dein Kind und seine Bücher*. Wien, Verlag für Jugend und Volk, 1957. 134p. DLC, IYL, NNY.

Practical advice to parents and teachers in bringing books to children. In the first part, the author answers many objections and questions, and in the second part he lists 375 titles of recommended books for the various age levels. Brief annotations and an author index assist in selection.

1068. ———. *Erdkundeunterricht und Jugendlektüre*. Wien, Österreichischer Buchklub der Jugend, 1958. 64p. (Schriftenreihe des Buchklubs der Jugend, 3). IYL.

"Children's literature and the teaching of geography." Suggestions on how to introduce other countries through children's books.

1069. ———. *Jugendlektüre*. 2nd ed. Wien, Verlag für Jugend und Volk, 1965. 848p. DLC, IYL, NNY. (IYL also has 1st ed., same pub., 1955, 564p.).

The author writes in his preface: "I have tried to give an overall view of the complexity of problems concerning juvenile literature." This is indeed what the book achieves but that same complexity overwhelms the reader at times to the point of confusion, and the organization of materials to counteract this is lacking. The major sections are: the significance of reading for the young; the study of the reader as a prelude to the teaching of reading, principles of criticism of children's books; the types and forms of children's literature; juvenile literature and its authors; on the translation of books for the young; cheap and sensational literature; history; methods of introducing books; the teaching of reading and literary education. The most useful for the student of children's literature are the chapters on history, with their separate coverage of the movements in Austria, Germany and Switzerland, and the chapters on 11 German-language authors for children: Hans Baumann, Karl Bruckner, Vera Ferra-Mikura, Hertha von Gebhardt, Erich Kästner, Herbert Kaufmann, James Krüss, Hans Georg Prager, Eva Rechlin, K. v. Roeder-Gnadeberg and Erich Wustmann. One might disagree with the choice and the critical comments, but this information is difficult to come by in any form. Also, the bibliography of 1369 items is of great importance for anyone studying children's literature. There are subject and name indexes.

1070. ———. *Kinder- und Jugendliteratur*. Wien, 1965. 18p. (Mimeographed). IYL.

The outline of a seminar on children's literature, held in the Pedagogical Institute of Vienna. This provides an excellent résumé of all types of work with children's books in Austria.

1071. ———. *Die Klassenbücherei*. Wien, Leinmüller, 1961. 64p. (Schriftenreihe des Buchklubs der Jugend, 11).

"The classroom library."

1072. ———. *Leseunterricht und literarische Erziehung*. Wien, Leinmüller, 1960. 112p. (Schriftenreihe des Buchklubs der Jugend, 7).

1073. ———. and Hans Mayer. *Naturgeschichtsunterricht und Jugendlektüre*. Wien, Österreichischer Buchklub der Jugend, 1962. 64p. (Schriftenreihe des Buchklubs der Jugend, 4). IYL.

"Children's literature and the teaching of natural history." Suggested books to use in stimulating children's interests in this subject.

1074. ———. *Der österreichische Jugendschriftsteller und sein Werk*. Wien, Leinmüller, 1965. 152p. (Schriftenreihe des Buchklubs der Jugend, 18).

1075. ———. *Übersetzung von Jugendbüchern*. Wien, Österreichische Sektion des IBBY, 1963. 80p. DLC, IYL.

The problem of translating children's books; a list of some recommended books translated from German into other languages; a list of some recommended books of other countries translated into German.

1076. ———. *Wege zum Gedicht*. Wien, Leinmüller, 1959. 48p. (Schriftenreihe des Buchklubs der Jugend, 6).

1077. Bindel, Jakob. *Gestern, heute, morgen*. Wien, Verlag Jungbrunnen, 1958. 95p. DLC, IYL.

A report issued on the 50th anniversary of the founding of the Austrian Kinderfreunde für das gute Buch, an organization dedicated to the work of bringing good books to children. A year-by-year account of its work, an evaluation of present-day children's books, some statistics and facts on book production, prizes, etc., and a forecast of the work still ahead are the main points covered.

1078. Bornemann, Karl. *Die wichtigsten Verordnungen und Erlässe österreichischer Schulbehörden, welche auf Schülerbibliotheken Bezug haben*. 6th ed. Znaim, 1886.

1079. "Buch und Bild," *Oesterreichischer Jugend-informations dienst,* Wien, Jahrgang 9, Folge 2, Nov., 1955, pp. 1–19. DLC.

This year's special issue devoted to children's books dealt with their illustration. See also 1087 and 1095.

1080. "Bücher für Jugendliche," *Die Jugend,* Wien, Jahrgang 2, Folge 3, Dec., 1959, pp. 3–23. DLC.

Many short articles on reading interests and tendencies, the paperback book for young people, library work with the teen-age, recordings of literature of interest to the young adult.

1081. Cornioley, Hans. "Erziehung zum Buch: Ziele und Methoden," *Die jugend,* Wien, Jahrgang 3, Heft 8, May, 1961, pp. 5–10. DLC.

A lecture delivered in Luxembourg, Sept., 1960, on goals and means of educating children to the use of books.

1082. Drescher, Johann. *Auswahl geeigneter Jugendschriften für Schülerbibliotheken an Volks- und Bürgerschulen.* Graz, H. Wagner, 1900.

1083. Fadrus, Viktor. "Die Jugendliteratur im Wandel der Zeiten," *Beiträge zur Neugestaltung des Bildungswesens;* Wien, Verlag für Jugend und Volk, 1956, pp. 207–221. DLC. Also in: *Graphische Revue Österreichs,* Wien, Jahrgang 53, 1951, pp. 134 ff.

A rather superficial survey of children's literature through the ages. It is mostly a listing of names, titles and dates, with very little critical commentary.

1084. *Fenster in die Welt.* Wien, Österreichische Sektion des Internationalem Kuratoriums für das Jugendbuch, n.d. 64p. DLC.

An annotated list of the best children's books of many lands, available in German translation, and arranged by general subject and age groups. Subject and author indexes are provided.

1085. Fischer, Engelbert. "Die Grossmacht der Jugend- und Volksliteratur." Erste Abteilung: *Jugendliteratur, vom patriotischen, religiösen und pädagogisch-Didaktischen Standpunkt kritisch beleuchtet.* 4 Vols. Wien, Sallmayersche Buchhandlung, 1877. Zweite Abteilung: *Volksliteratur,* 1878.

1086. Goerlitz, Theo Ludwig. *Kinderbücher.* Wien, Ostmarken, 1936. 114p.

1087. "Das gute Jugendbuch," *Oesterreichischer Jugendinformationsdienst,* Wien, Jahrgang 7, Folge 3, Dec., 1953, pp. 1–31. DLC.

Each year this magazine devoted an entire issue to children's literature. At this time the year's production was reviewed, and pertinent articles on reading, on national and international developments in children's literature were brought to the fore. See also 1079 and 1095.

1088. *Gute Jugendbücher aus Deutschland, Österreich und der Schweiz.* Wien, Österreichischer Buchklub der Jugend, n.d. 49p. DLC.

A list of some 500 books, arranged by age and subject, but not annotated. Author index.

1089. Hafner, Gustav and Heinz Weber. *So fängt es an; Bildnerisches Gestalten im Kindergarten, im Vorschulalter und auf der Unterstufe der Volksschule.* Graz, Stiasny, 1965. 164p.

1090. Hayek, M. "A Viennese children's newspaper," *Junior bookshelf,* Huddersfield, Vol. 8, No. 2, July, 1944, pp. 55–58. DLC, NNY.

The editor of a weekly newspaper for children, which was inserted in one of the most popular of the adult papers, here reminisces of how he came to start this venture, and how it came to an abrupt stop under Hitler.

1091. Hofer, Josef. *Wegweiser durch die Jugendschriftenliteratur.* Wien, Kirsch, 1906. 359p. (Katholischen Lehrerbund für Österreich).

1092. Huber, K. *Über Jugendschriften und Schülerbibliotheken.* Wien, Manz, 1886.

1093. Hubinek, K. *Die Lektüreinteressen der männlichen Jugend.* Wien, 1952. 100p. Dissertation.

1094. Jalkotzy, Alois. *Märchen und Gegenwart.* 2nd ed. Wien, Jungbrunnen, 1952. 128p. IYL. (1st ed., same publisher, 1930. 110p. OCL).

"Fairy tales and the present." The author wishes to point out that fairy tales still have importance and meaning to today's children. He stresses their literary value and feels that they are best introduced through kindergartens. For this reason, he has made a complete listing of the Grimm tales, indicating those suitable for the very young, for older children, and those only for adults.

1095. "Jugend und Buch," *Oesterreichischer Jugendinformationsdienst,* Wien, Jahrgang 8, Folge 2, Nov., 1954, pp. 1–27; Jahrgang 10, Folge 2, Nov., 1956, pp. 1–23; Jahrgang 11, Folge 2, Nov., 1957, pp. 1–19. DLC.

Three special issues dealing with young people and books. In addition to these yearly issues, many shorter articles appeared throughout the year. See also 1079, and 1087.

1096. *Jugend and Buch.* Österreichischen Buchklub der Jugend, Fuhrmannsgasse 18a, Wien VIII. Quarterly. Vol. 1 ff., 1952 ff. (Price: 10 S Austrian, 1.80 M German, 1.80 F Swiss). DLC, IYL.

This contains articles on national and international problems of children's book production, dissemination and quality, occasional lists of books, and reviews of current children's books.

1097. *Die Jugendbibliothek.* Eine Auswahl der gediegensten Werke der deutschen Jugendschriften-Literatur. Ein Ratgeber bei Zusammenstellung von Schüler und Volksbibliotheken. Wien, Pichler's Witwe & Sohn.

1098. *Jugendbuchratgeber.* Bundesministerium für Unterricht. Wien 1, Minoritenplatz 5. Issued 10 times yearly as part of *Die Jugend,* 1958 ff. (Annual subscription: 32 S.). Originally issued as supplement to *Oesterreichischer Jugendinformationsdienst,* 1949–1958, with title variations: *Jugendbuchrater; Ratgeber für das gute Jugendbuch.*

The reviews are several paragraphs in length and indicate age suitability, contents, style, illustrations, price. Only recommended books are included. Names of reviewers appear in each issue, but individual reviews are not signed. Books from Austria, Germany and Switzerland are considered. Yearly index.

1099. Kahl, Virginia. "Children's books in Austria," *Horn book,* Boston, Vol. 30, Oct., 1954, pp. 307–314. DLC, NNY.

A librarian from the U.S. writes here of the poor quality of books available for children in Austria in the postwar period. She mentions the founding of the Children's Book Club as a sign of improvement in the situation.

1100. Katholisches Jugendwerk Österreichs. *Studien- und Beratungsstelle für Kinder- und Jugendschrifttum.* Katalog VII. Wien, 1962. 40 p. IYL, DLC.

One of a number of catalogs issued by this Roman Catholic organization. This lists recommended books for the various age groups.

1101. König, Karola. "Über den Zweck und die Bedeutung von Kinderlesehallen," *Die Quelle,* Wien, 1928.

1102. Kraft, Josef. *Über Schülerbibliotheken . . . in Oesterreich, Deutschland und der Schweiz.* 2nd ed. Wien, Karl Graeser, 1882, 55p. DEW.

The status of school libraries in Austria, Germany (by *länder*) and Switzerland (by canton). The types of organization and service, control of material, and many other aspects were discussed. It is interesting to note that the author questioned whether school libraries should also serve as public libraries, whether they should be open in the summer, etc. This is a useful and careful study, based on personal observation.

1103. Kropatsch, Otwald. *Leseerziehung der Zehn-bis-Vierzehnjährigen.* Wien, Leinmüller, 1962. 96p. (Schriftenreihe des Buchklubs der Jugend, 13). IYL.

"The reading education of 10-to-14-year-olds." Results of a study sponsored by the Buchklub der Jugend, and carried out in Austrian schools.

1104. Kunzfeld, Alois. *Vom Märchenerzählen und Märchenillustrierten.* Wien, Verlag für Jugend und Volk, 1926. 95p. (Lehrerbücherei, No. 50).

1105. Langthaler, Johann. *Wegweiser bei Anlegung oder Ergänzung von Kinder- Jugend- und Volksbibliotheken.* Wien, 1885?

1106. Linke, Karl. *Neue Wege der Jugendschriftenbewegung und der Klassenlektüre.* Wien, Verlag Jugend und Volk, 1929. 99p.

1107. Lussnigg, Willy and Hilda Laible. *Das religiöse Kinderbuch.* Wien, Leinmüller, 1962. 56p. (Schriftenreihe des Buchklubs der Jugend, 13).

"The religious children's book." The reasons for and the uses of good religious books for children, together with a short list of recommended books. Roman Catholic in point-of-view.

1108. Mayer, Andreas. "Zur Reorganisirung unserer Schülerbibliotheken," *Freie pädagogische blätter,* Wien, Jahrgang 18, No. 13, Mar. 29, 1884, pp. 193–197. DLC.

"On the reorganization of our school libraries." This teacher recommended fewer books of better quality, rather than a lot of second-rate reading matter. He considered it best for each child to read only one book every three weeks.

1109. Moissl, Konrad and Ferdinand Krautstengl. *Die deutsch-österreichische Jugendliteratur.* 2 parts. Aussig, Grohmann, 1900 and 1901. 176p. and 221p. IYL has Xerograph copy.

These critics took exception to the selections of earlier Austrian lists, stating that the religious criteria were not sufficient. They believed that one of the more important criteria was the patriotic tone of the book, and felt that all good children's books should enhance the child's national sense of identity.

1110.   Panholzer, Johann. *Kritischer Führer durch die Jugendliteratur.* 4 Vols. in 3. Wien, E. Schmid, 1886 ff. Vols. 1 and 2, 371p. Vol. 3, 120p. Vol. 4, 120p.

1111.   Peter, Anton. *Jugendlektüre und Volksbibliotheken.* Teschen, Prochaska, 1879.

1112.   ———. *Verzeichnis von geeigneten und nicht geeigneten Jugendschriften für Volks- und Bürgerschulbibliotheken.* 2nd ed. Troppau, 1886.

1113.   Pichler, Maria. *Bücher für jugendliche Leser.* Wien, The author, 1955. 132p. DLC.
    A booklist of 1,000 titles of recommended children's books, undertaken for the Bundesministerium für Unterricht, and meant for use by librarians. All titles are of books which appeared after 1945; they are annotated, arranged by author in alphabetical order, and were for the most part still in print.

1114.   *Preisgekrönte und wertvolle Kinder- und Jugendbücher Österreichs.* Wien, Verlag für Jugend und Volk, n.d. 55p. DLC.
    An annotated list of the Austrian children's books which have won national and/or international prizes, and their runners up. Unfortunately, no dates are given.

1115.   Ricek, L. G. *Der Kampf um die Schülerbüchereien.* Wien, Pichler's Witwe, 1923. 42p.

1116.   Rümann, Arthur. *Alte deutsche Kinderbücher.* Wien-Leipzig-Zürich, Herbert Reichner Verlag, 1937. 101p. plus 367 plates. DLC.
    While the introductory essay on the history of children's books is not as complete in this case as in Hobrecker (1256), the many plates of reproductions are unsurpassed in historical value. Most are in black and white. The books from which they are taken are given complete bibliographical description.

They include titles published in Austria, Germany and Switzerland.

1117.   Scheu-Riesz, Helene. *Open sesame!* New York, Island Press, 1942? 16p. NNY.
    A personal account of the author's part in the "Sesame Libraries" opened for children in Vienna after World War I. These libraries also distributed free booklets to the children. The author was strongly influenced by Wolgast.

1118.   Schmidt, Heiner. *Las lesende Mädchen. Eine Untersuchung der Mädchenlektüre.* Wien, Österreichischer Bundesverlag für Unterricht, Wissenschaft und Kunst, 1959. 105p. IYL.
    "The reading girl." An inquiry into the reading interests of girls from 10 to 15 years of age, together with a recommended list of books for girls. Extensive bibliography.

1119.   Schwab, Edith. *Beiträge zur Geschichte des Kinder- und Jugendschrifttums in Österreich.* Wien, 1949. 449p. (Dissertation). IYL.

1120.   Ulrych, M. *Die Schülerbibliothek im Lichte der neuen Jugendschriftenbewegung.* Wien, 1932. 101p. (Dissertation).

1121.   Vierlinger, Rupert. *Buchpädagogik in der reifen Kindheit.* München, Ernst Reinhardt, 1964. 96p. (Erziehung und Psychologie, Beihefte der Zeitschrift *Schule und Psychologie,* Heft 27). IYL.
    Results of reading interest studies carried out in Vienna, as part of the work preparatory to a doctoral dissertation.

1122.   *Die Volksbücherei; die Verwaltung der Klein- und Mittelbücherei.* Wien, Verband Österreichischer Volksbüchereien, 1949. 39p.

1123.   Wien, Volksbildungsverein. *Verzeichnis empfehlenswerter Jugendlektüre.* Wien, Volksbildungsverein, 1903–1914. Annual.

1124.   Zellweker, Elwin. *Was soll mein Kind lesen?* Wien, Saturn, 1935. 71p.

Germany

At the risk of being judged hyperbolic or facetious one could claim that there are probably more printed words about children's literature, than there are of children's literature. This is not as exaggerative as it might seem and the only reason anyone can give for writing still more about the subject is that, for all of the studies made concerning the child and his world, we are still far from understanding completely the processes through which the young mind acquires knowlege, discrimination, judgement, and all of the other abstract powers which fit into the category of education, depending upon how one defines that term. Nowhere is this more strikingly true than in the country of Germany, where children's literature is inextricably bound up with the idea of education, as well as with the more general term of culture. Comparatively speaking, there are more studies on the subject than in any of the other countries with equally developed children's literatures. Yet recently a critic, commenting in *Bücherei und Bildung* on the 2nd edition of Bamberger's *Jugendlektüre,* stated that Germany still lacks a comprehensive, contemporary evaluation of children's literature.

The researcher in this country soon becomes lost in a sea of materials and the distinction between books destined to give children a literary experience and those aimed at giving him an educative one, becomes less and less clear. One could point out that an aesthetic, literary experience is almost sure to be an educative one, in the best sense of the word. One might also conclude that educative is not the same thing as didactic, and that after the wane of the didactic period, Germany moved into a period of children's literature which might best be called "educational" and which extended up to about 1940. It is this aspect which makes the history of German children's literature different from that in other languages, although this difference is not always very distinct. It comes not so much from the contents, forms or style of the literature, as it does from the use to which it is put and the manner in which it us crtically evaluated. This is true in Austria, Germany and Switzerland, but is discussed at length only in this introduction, in order to avoid repetition.

Three of Germany's leading educators were Johann Basedow (1723–1790), Johann Friedrich Herbart (1776–1841) and Friedrich Froebel (1782–1852). Together with Rousseau and Pestalozzi, they elaborated most of the theories which were to shape modern teaching methods. Each of them had something special to say about children's books. Basedow, like Comenius, conceived of education as an appeal to the natural interests of children. Therefore, he believed children should have books with pictures to clarify abstract expressions, or to illustrate history and natural science. He himself composed the *Elementarwerk,* a set of elementary texts with accompanying pictures. Herbart was the most theoretical of all three and perhaps the most influential. He argued that education should be based upon psychology and ethics and placed great importance on apperception. In his *Allgemeinen Pädagogik* he stated that the child would take out of his reading exactly and only what he needed and wanted at that moment, so it was useless to attempt to educate him by purposefully writing with teaching in mind. Froebel, who was the founder of the kindergarten, was the most idealistic of the educators and the most mystical in his writing. Consequently he is often misinterpreted or misunderstood. It was his belief that pictures, story telling and books were all a part of the child's artistic environment and as such should be of the highest quality.

These three were only the leading names in a long list of educators and teachers who expressed their views on children's reading. Others who were important for what they had to say on the subject were B. Auerbach, A. Detmer, Friedrich Gedicke, Lorenz Kellner, C. Kühner, A. Luben, W. Menzel, A. Merget, O. Willmann and Wackernagel. Some were for a specific children's literature, some against; others advocated the use of folk literature, still others did not; only a few were sharply critical of the didactic tone which held children's books in thrall. The fact that they were all teachers, criticizing books written mostly by other teachers, was of the greatest significance, but it was overlooked or at any rate not much commented on. With the arrival of Heinrich Wolgast on the scene, the domination of the field by the teaching profession was complete. The word domination is used here in a positive, not derogatory, sense.

Wolgast was a teacher who early in his career set out to brush away the cobwebby sentimentalism which clouded the average teacher's approach to children's books. His poetic sensibilities were outraged at the reading material which was introduced to children under the guise of literature. He especially condemned as worthless what he called "specific" literature, by which he meant those books written with an exact didactic purpose in mind. They were the type of book which might well begin with an opening exhortation to the dear child reader, begging him to walk through the woods to observe and discover the secrets which Mother Nature had to share with him. They were written to cover a wide variety of teaching situations, and were used in many schools. In many ways they foreshadowed the nonfiction series book of contemporary U.S.

Probably in order to stir his colleagues into some lively and serious discussion, Wolgast exaggerated the sad state of children's books and their misuse in school and home. He stirred up a controversy which lasted until the outbreak of the Second World War. The echoes are still being heard. In his book and in numerous articles, Wolgast deplored poor selection policies as practised by most school book committees. He defended the criteria which the Hamburg Teacher's Association had formulated as the basis of their list, and he campaigned for more teachers to back the efforts of all the sections of the Vereinigte Jugendschriftenausschusse. Not all of the teachers were in favor of his "exclusivity" and the educational press was kept busy with heated exchanges between pro and anti-Wolgast factions. The end result was that it stimulated wide interest among the whole teaching profession, and we come back full circle to the lack of distinction between the literary and the educative, as discussed in critical context. Wolgast's plea, that reading material for children must be artistic in order to be called literature and that didacticism had no place in children's books, was somewhat self-defeating, by virtue of the fact that it was listened to almost exclusively by teachers. Didacticism had admittedly come about through the misguided theories of teachers and pseudo-teachers and in the late 19th century, a group of strong new critics came forward in England, Canada, the U.S., Scandinavia, the U.S.S.R. and parts of Eastern Europe, even in France. Many were public librarians or eventually went into that field or publishing. In the German-speaking countries criticism changed for the better but it also remained teacher oriented. There was no German-language critic before 1940 who combined literary judgement with long experience in observing children's reading tastes *outside of the school*. The only approach which differed slightly from that of the educators was the psychological-sociological, of which an outstanding example is the 1918 study by Charlotte Buehler (1171). It brought about another trend, which will not be discussed here because it belongs more in the field of educational psychology. The important point to be made here is that there is not really such a vast intrinsic difference between the criticism of children's literature in the German language and that in English and the rest of the European languages. Too many librarians are too quick to attach the stigma of didactic to something linked with teachers' associations, merely because of past history. On the other hand, it is partly true that the one-sidedness of views in Austria, Germany and Switzerland has prevented public children's librarians from having a decisive voice in criticism, and this in turn has probably hampered development of children's library services. There is no question, however, that the juvenile literature movement of the teachers' associations was responsible for much of the general improvement in children's book publishing in German, beginning with the 20th century.

To go back to the first literature for children is to begin with the period of Johann Heinrich Campe, J. K. A. Musaus, Clemens Brentano, Achim von Arnim, the Grimm Brothers, Christoph von Schmid and many less remembered figures. Campe's *Robinson der Jüngere* was not so much a translation of Defoe as it was a retelling to suit the Rousseau-influenced translator. Campe's Robinson lands on his island completely without reminders or tools of civilization. He has no wrecked ship to turn to for food and fuel and minutions. His story ends differently as well. Who could have guessed the success it would have! It was translated in all of the European languages, many of the oriental languages, and even back into English. Curiously it never "caught on" as well in English, so that the original Defoe, or a cut version of it, is the one English-reading children have been enjoying for generations. In Europe, chances are that it was Campe's version, or still another from the unbelievable number which kept appearing well on into the 19th century. Of these imitations of an imitation, only *Swiss Family Robinson* has survived to the present time. The *Robinson Crusoe* fad has been written about in a number of books; one of the most complete studies is described, in Herman Ullrich's *Robinson und Robinsonaden* (58).

Musaus was the collector of folk tales and legends; the fact that he changed and rewrote so much of the text probably accounts for their lesser popularity. Brentano and Von Arnim were the compilers of the truly innovative *Des Knaben Wunderhorn*. The rhymes and sayings, ballads and game songs which this collection contained were mostly of anonymous folk origin. Not as rhythmical or nonsensical as the English Mother Goose rhymes, they are nonetheless rich in poetic imagery and rhyme. They, too, were widely translated and copied. Christoph Von Schmid is hardly remembered or read today, but his voluminous works had a large corner of the market throughout the 19th century. Finally, there are the Grimm Brothers, Jakob and Wilhelm. The first volume of their *Kinder- und Hausmarchen* appeared in 1812. Its impact is impossible to describe, the effects were so far-reaching. But as Paul Hazard pointed out, it is not so much their scholarly influence which accords them immortality, it is the ineradicable quality of the stories which keeps the name of Grimm alive.

Up to 1900 translations into German were limited to the classics and the series, by well-known didactic writers, of the neighboring European countries. With the new interest generated by Wolgast a few modern works began to appear. However it was not until after the First World War that consistent numbers of them were made available. Germany has led Austria and Switzerland in the number and excellence of translations and continues to do so.

Among all of the unimaginative and preachy books of the 19th century, there are a few which light up the scene with their refreshing candor and humor. Some, such as *Struwwelpeter* by Heinrich Hoffman and *Max und Moritz* by Wilhelm Busch, relied on the grotesque for their humor. The very fact that these became so popular and influential was proof of the need children felt to find release in comic relief. Also, the artistry of Busch and his other colleagues of the *Munchener Bilderbogen* was of high quality and appealed as much to adults as well as to children.

The normal production of books for children was interrupted in Germany by both World Wars. Prior to and during the First World War, there was a marked increase in books with nationalistic and militaristic themes, but not to the extent that they overwhelmed the remainder. The rise of Hitler and Nazism brought quite different results. The consequences of subtle, convincing propaganda which can be conveyed to children through their books have never been fully explored, but there is now ample proof that they can be appallingly effective, either for the "good" or the "bad," if one can speak of this in such simple moral terms. The line between patriotism and super-nationalism is very thin indeed, and it is not only Germany and Japan which were guilty of stepping over too far on one side. There are many governments which pride themselves on having removed all comics and sensational literature. There are others trying to pass laws to control the production of such materials. Yet the most potentially "dangerous" books of all, i.e., those claiming or implying one system or government to be superior over another are never mentioned as being under suspicion although there is every reason to believe that our wars have stemmed from build-up of exactly such nationalistic feelings. This is not to be taken as a plea for censorship of overly patriotic books. It is merely to question whether those groups campaigning for a good children's literature are right in spending so much of their energy fighting comics and pornography. It is also meant to point out that there are many nations which preach about international understanding, but fail to practice it in their children's books. The struggle to win young minds over to the cause of democracy and humanity does not seem to apply, once it goes beyond national or political boundaries.

After the war, many children of Europe were left with no nourishment of any kind—parental, comestible, spiritual or intellectual. While the opportunity for parental and spiritual guidance was lost to some forever, the chance to get food became a tangible reality not too long after the end of the war. In their understandable desire to save lives and bring about civil order, the authorities established certain priorities, and provision for books and reading materials was not at the top of the list by far. Because the occupation powers were anxious to prevent a resurgence of Nazism, practically all of the existing books, periodicals and newspapers were confiscated and permission to print new materials was under strict control. It is hard for us today to understand what it means to be without books or other information media, but we have an extremely vivid and poignant recollection of the situation in postwar Germany, written by Mrs. Jella Lepman for the first chapters of her *Kinderbuchbrücke*. Mrs. Lepman had come as a public information officer attached to the occupation government, and soon decided that her special task should be to provide war-weary children with reading matter which could lift their spirits and provide them with hope for the future. She was not satisfied that this should be accomplished within the national boundaries, and conceived of the idea of an international children's library, where German children could begin to catch up on the years that had passed them by, where publishers could look to the new and old books of other countries for material to translate, where authors could be inspired by new trends and new thinking along international and universal lines. Although her overflowing enthusiasm was often stopped short by hard reality and practicality, Mrs. Lepman did succeed, with the aid of the Rockefeller Foundation, in establishing such a library. Its influence, while not always direct, has certainly been one of the major forces behind the swift and steady rise of a German children's literature which is more varied, more tolerant, more natural and free than that of the previous decades. It is said that modern German writers, in general, have yet to come to terms with their country's recent past. Perhaps it is to be the children's books that will be remembered for facing this issue with honesty and sensitivity.

According to *Buch und Buchhandel in Zahlen*, since 1960 there have been more than 1,000 children's books published each year, with about 25 percent of them translations. This is to serve a population of almost 60 million. In East Germany, the situation is a bit different. The majority of children's books are published by the state publishing house, the Kinderbuchverlag. There are a few private publishing houses in East Germany (the only country in the Communist-Socialist bloc to have such presses) but they do not publish more than a dozen or so titles for children each year. These are often quite distinctive and provide a little contrast to the publications of the Kinderbuchverlag. Although the population of East Germany is less than half of West Germany, and the number of children's books published is at about the same ratio, the number of volumes is often greater, because the editions are two to three times as large as those in West Germany. German-speaking children still share pretty nearly the same classics in Austria, Switzerland and both Germany's, but there is a vast difference in the books of present-day life. Quite naturally, they reflect the political and economic differences of the two sides. In a few instances, books are available in the East and West, but these exceptions cannot alter the fact that a new generation on each side has passed through childhood and youth without the common bond of the same heroes and heroines, the same jokes and slang, the same discoveries shared.

Because Eastern Germany has been so strongly influenced by the U.S.S.R. and the other Eastern European nations, a similar library service to children has developed. It is based on much practical and theoretical training, and on all levels receives the support and advice of state methodological institutes. As in the other countries, libraries are found in schools and Pioneer houses, as well as in city public libraries. The state library in East Berlin has built up a large children's collection, which has proven fruitful as a source of research and exhibitions (4, 1306).

In West Germany, although organization is not yet very centralized, libraries for children are growing in number year by year. They are usually supported by local authorities, although rural library service is funded on a national basis, through the bibliographical offices in various regions. There is much pressure on the federal government to provide a legal basis for a common form of organization for each type of library service. As in the Benelux countries, there are also church libraries in West Germany, but they are not as prevalent, and the fact that the Protestant and Roman Catholic populations live in fairly distinct areas means that there is not as much duplication of service as might be thought. While there are no firm rules for minimum standards, children's libraries do have some central guidance through the bibliographic centers, and they also have the opportunity to purchase centrally processed books and materials. The Einkaufszentrale in Reutlingen is modeled on similar outlets in Scandinavia.

Children's librarians take the usual professional course at one of the four approved institutes for training of librarians. There is some theoretical and practical preparation for work with children, but not as much as in Eastern Germany. Unfortunately, this has not prevented the children's librarian from being looked down upon as a kind of second-rate professional, and many leave the field as soon as they can. There has been no leader with critical acumen, forward-looking views, and an effective means of airing them. This often results in non-representation in top-level meetings, and decisions are made involving children's library service, with no specialist present. Yet half or more of library work is directly with children and youth in most libraries. The same lack of organization and leadership is present in the school library situation, which is even less developed.

Currently, the most active group in the children's literature movement is the Arbeitskreis fur Jugendschrifttum which publishes lists, administers the national youth literature prize, organizes seminars on the problems of juvenile literature, and coordinates the efforts of many organizations working to promote good children's books. They represent the German section of the IBBY. In addition, there are any number of religious and parents' groups, publishers' organizations and private agencies and individuals which are active in making selective book lists or supporting the cause of children's literature in some way.

1125.   Ackerknecht, Erwin. "Jugendlektüre und deutsche Bildungsideale." *Büchereifragen;* Berlin, Weidmann, 1914; pp. 54–70. NNY.

This librarian took exception to Wolgast's theory of the purely aesthetical approach to criticism of children's literature. He believed that even some unartistic works had great merit, because they could reach out to children through spiritual experience which they had in common.

1126.   ———. *Die kleine Eigenbücherei.* Stettin, Verlag "Bücherei und Bildungspflege," 1929.

1127.   ———. *Vorlesestunden.* 2nd ed. Berlin, Weidmannsche Buchhandlung, 1926. 116p.

A handbook of practical suggestions on giving reading aloud and story hour programs. Although meant for the librarian, teacher and parent to use with mixed groups or the entire family, a large number of the 123 suggested programs are aimed at children and young people.

1128.   Aichberger, Rose von. "Kinderurteile über Bücher," *Bücherei und Bildungspflege,* Stettin, Jahrgang 6, Heft 2–3, 1926, pp. 87–96. DLC, NNY.

"Children's opinions of children's books." This is one of many articles appearing in this periodical in the 1920's and early 1930's, on the subjects of children's books and libraries. This was superceded by *Bücherei.*

1129.   *Almanach für die Freunde des Kinderbuchs.* Berlin, Kinderbuchverlag, 1954. 88p. DLC.

In honor of its first five years of publishing, this East Berlin firm put out this collection of essays, letters, poems, and stories about children's books. A bibliography of further material about children's literature is on pp. 72–88.

1130.   Antz, Joseph. *Führung der Jugend zum Schrifttum.* 2nd. ed. Ratingen, Aloys Henn, 1950. 190p. DLC, IYL.

"Leading youth to literature." Guidelines for the teacher to use in stimulating a love of reading and literary taste. Bibliographies at the end of each chapter, and a recommended list of some 600 titles, listed by interest group but not annotated. Author and subject indexes.

1131.   *Die Arbeit der öffentlichen Bücherei für die Jugendlichen.* Bremen, Arbeitsstelle für das öffentliche Büchereiwesen im Verband Deutscher Bibliotheken, 1953. 40p. IYL.

"Work with youth in public libraries." Results of a conference of West German children's librarians, held in Munich, Oct., 1952; short bibliography.

1132.   "Arbeit mit dem Kinderbuch," *Der Bibliothekar,* Berlin (East), 1946 ff. DLC, IYL, NNY.

Since its beginning in 1946, this official library publication has included a regular column devoted to children's work under various titles of which the above is the latest. There are also regular reviews of children's books, longer articles on many aspects of children's literature and libraries, and book lists.

1133. "Die Arbeit mit dem Kinder- und Jugendbuch verbessern!" *Deutschunterricht,* Berlin (East), Jahrgang 15, Heft 1, 1962, pp. 10–19. DLC.

Before holding their 6th national congress, the Zentralstelle für Kinder- und Jugendliteratur in Dresden asked for teachers' opinions as to how children's books could be improved. Recorded here are the answers of some of them, as well as comments on how they use books in their teaching. An article by Hans Hübner on what children read follows on pp. 20–25. This periodical has many articles on children's literature, from the educational point of view.

1134. Arndt, Marga. *Das Bilderbuch als künstlerisches Mittel der sozialistischen Erziehung.* Berlin, (East), Volk und Wissen Volkseigener Verlag, 1963. 190p. (Diskussionsbeiträge zu Fragen der Pädagogik, 37). DLC.

"The picture book as an artistic means toward socialist education."

1135. ———. "Zur Beurteilung der Bilderbücher," *Neue Erziehung in Kindergarten und Heim,* Berlin [East], Jahrgang 15, Heft 10, May 1962, pp. 6–10. DLC.

Frequent articles on picture books for young children appeared in this periodical, and new picture books were reviewed regularly. This author expanded the ideas in many of her articles and they appear in book form (above).

1136. Association of German Public Librarians. German Federal Republic. *Library service to children.* Lund, Bibliotekstjänst, 1963, pp. 57–62. DLC, IYL, NNY.

This chapter in the IFLA publication deals with the history and present status of children's library work in this country.

1137. Auerbach, Berthold. [Jugendliteratur.], *Schrift und Volk,* Bd. 2. Leipzig, Brockhaus, 1866.

1138. Ballauff, L. "Über Kinder- und Jugendlektüre," *Pädagogisches Archiv,* Leipzig, Bund 1, 1859, pp. 37 ff, 122 ff.

1139. Bang, Ilse. *Die Entwicklung der deutschen Märchenillustration.* München, F. Bruckmann, 1944. 149p. ff. 72p. NNC.

"The development of German fairy tale illustration." A historical and critical approach to the work of illustrators of the *märchen* of Germany, and the fairy tales of other countries translated and well-known in German. The first chapter covers the period prior to the 19th century, and the influences which remained in force during the 1800's. Chapter 2 is on the first half of the 19th century and Chapter 3 is on the second half. Chapter 4 covers the period after 1900. Each of the major illustrators is discussed at length. There are 261 reproductions on the 72 plates following the text. The bibliography contains general items, as well as a section on individual artists. There is also a catalog list of all fairy tale collections consulted.

1140. Bartholomäus, Wilhelm. *Ratgeber für Eltern, Oheime, Basen, sowie für Kinderfreunde und Leiter von Volks- und Schulerbüchereien bei der Auswahl von Jugendschriften.* Bielefeld, 1892.

1141. Bass, J. *Wege zur künstlerischen Erziehung und literarischen Bildung der Jugend und des deutschen Volkes.* Stuttgart, 1905.

1142. Becker, Walter. *Wie schützen wir unsere Jugend vor Schmutz und Schund.* 2nd ed. Gütersloh, Gütersloher Verlagshaus, 1959. 64p.

1143. Beeg, Armin. *Leseinteressen der Berufsschüler.* München, Reinhardt, 1963. 134p. (Erziehung und Psychologie, 23). IYL.

"Reading interests of the trade school child." Results of an inquiry, undertaken as part of the work for a dissertation at Köln University. In the introduction, the author compares previous German reading interest studies. His bibliography is quite complete.

1144. Beer, Ulrich. *Umgang mit Massenmedien.* Düsseldorf, Rau, 1964. 99p.

1145. *Begegnung mit dem Buch.* Ratingen, Aloys Henn, 1950. 180p. (Fredeburger Schriftenreihe). IYL.

Articles by W. Fronemann, J. Peters, E. Schliebe-Lippert, E. Griesar, Th. Rutt, E. Schmücker, J. Antz, all on children's and young peoples' first experiences with books and reading; some are written from the psychological point-of-view, others the pedagogical, still others the purely literary.

1146. "Beim ersten Buch fängt die Erziehung an!" *Börsenblatt für den deutschen Buchhandel,* Leipzig, Jahrgang 121, No. 8, Feb. 20, 1954, pp. 159–162. DLC, NNY.

"Education begins with the first book." A review of some of the forthcoming books for children, with portraits of four leading authors.

1147. Beinlich, Alexander. *Das Lesen und die literarische Erziehung.* Vol. 2 of: *Handbuch des Deutschunterrichts.* Emsdetten (Westfalen), Lechte, 1961. 577p. IYL.

A teacher's handbook which includes many chapters on children's books and reading, often presented from the pedagogical point of view.

1148. *Beiträge zur Arbeit mit dem Kinder- und Jugendbuch.* Bonn, Borromäusverein, 1963. 95p. (Werkhefte zur Büchereiarbeit, 9). IYL.

The three essays contained in this volume are by Walter Scherf, Christa Maria Platz-Bielefeld (on picture books) and Jutta Nellen-Piské. Each has a separate bibliography. Included are six photographs of the children's libraries of Hamburg.

1149. *Beiträge zur Kinder- und Jugendliteratur.* Berlin (East), Kinderbuchverlag, 1963. Irregular. (Arbeitsgemeinschaft für das Kinder- und Jugendbuch). IYL.

These booklets appear approximately three times yearly and contain many critical and informational articles on children's literature, and related areas. There are sometimes reviews of individual children's books. Each issue contains a list of recent professional literature on children's books and libraries.

1150. Benfer, Heinrich. *Buch und Bild in Erziehung und Unterricht.* Bochum, Kamp, 1950. 103p.

1151. ———. *Schundkampf und literarische Jugendpflege.* Langensalza, Beltz, 1933. 213p.

1152. Bergner, Tilly. "Einige Betrachtungen über Kinder- und Jugendbücher," *Heute und Morgen,* Berlin (East), Heft 12, 1953, pp. 763–769. DLC.

Reviews and comments on the previous season's children's books. Such articles appear frequently in this periodical.

1153. Berlin. Deutsche Staatsbibliothek. *Kinderbuch und Sozialismus.* Berlin (East) 1958. 111p. IYL, DLC.

The catalog of an exhibition held in the library in 1958–1959, demonstrating the development of children's literature in socialist East Germany. More than 500 titles are annotated here. Author and title index.

1154. Berlin. Stadtbibliothek. *Auswahl von gern gelesenen Jugendbüchern.* Berlin, Volksbüchereizentrale, 1928. 32p. NNY.

A selected list, arranged by types, but not annotated or indexed.

1155. Bernhardi, Karl. *Erster Nachtrag zu dem Wegweiser durch die deutschen Volks- und Jugendschriften.* Leipzig, Gustav Mayer, 1856. 211p. DLC.

A revision of work first appearing in 1852 (not traced). It is a selective, annotated list of books recommended for reading aloud to children, and for children to read to themselves. Arrangement is by age and subject. Author and title indexes are complete.

1156. *Bibliographie zum Gesamtproblem der Jugendgefährdung.* Frankfurt/Main, Dipa Verlag, 1955. 68p. (Schriftenreihe zur Jugendnot, Band 2). IYL.

The first two parts of this bibliography on child welfare are concerned with children's reading materials. There are more than 200 entries in all; including books, pamphlets and periodical articles. They are not annotated and bibliographical information is not always very complete. About 50 of the entries are concerned with comics and their effects on children.

1157. Bierwagen, Marion. *Arbeit mit jugendlichen Lesern.* Berlin (East), Zentralinstitut für Bibliothekswesen, 1962.

1158. Blüthgen, Victor. "Über Jugendliteratur und das Jugendschriftenverzeichnis des Hamburger Lehrervereins," *Deutsche Monatschrift für das gesamte Leben der Gegenwart,* Berlin, Jahrgang 2, Heft 3, Dec. 1902, pp. 411–417. DLC.

"What does not interest youth, what they cannot take account of in their innermost wishes and feelings, is of worthless literary value to them, even though it be of the highest esthetic quality." This critic expressed some of his ideals in rather nationalistic terms.

1159. Bode, Helmut and Kurt Debus. *Bücher, Schlüssel zum Leben, Tore zur Welt.* Frankfurt/Main, Das Bücherschiff, n.d. 352p. (Lese- und Literaturführer, Vol. 1). IYL.

A collection of essays on books and readings, put out by a popular book club. This contains many articles on the subject of children's books and reading, including some by Erich Kastner, M. Hausmann, W. Michels, F. Schramm, H. Lades and S. Andres.

1160. Bodensohn, Anneliese. *Untersuchungen zur Jugendlektüre.* 4 Vols. in 3. Frankfurt/Main, Dipa Verlag, Vol. 1, 157p., 1960; Vol. 2–3, 264p., 1961; Vol. 4, 192p., 1963. DLC, IYL.

Volume 1 deals with adventure stories of the sea, islands, ships; volume 2–3 with adventure stories of the wilderness, desert, ancient lands; volume 4 with the works of J. F. Cooper and his imitators. In each case individual works are discussed at length.

Translated and original German works are included. Each volume lists the books discussed, but unfortunately no page numbers are given. Short bibliographies. No index.

1161. Böhme, Franz M. *Deutsches Kinderlied und Kinderspiel.* Leipzig, Breitkopf and Härtel, 1897. 756p. DLC, NNY.

"German children's songs and game rhymes." A classic in the field, this has as much to do with children's oral literature as it does with music, and can be compared with the more recent work of the Opies (3191). The introduction, pp. V–LXVI, contains excellent historical material, and a very extensive bibliography. There is a subject index and an index of first lines.

1162. Borstel, F. von. "Die Bedeutung des Kunstwerkes als dichterische Jugendschrift für Kind und Litteratur," *Versuche und Ergebnisse der Lehrervereinigung für die Pflege der künstlerischen Bildung in Hamburg.* 3rd ed. Hamburg, 1902. pp. 97–111.

1163. Brandt, Sabine. "Bewahrung oder Zerstörung des Volksmärchens?" *Sonntag,* Berlin (East), Jahrgang 7, No. 49, Dec. 7, 1952, p.4. DLC.

"Preservation or destruction of the folk tale?" The author contends that it is wrong to change the folk tale endings, to suit national-socialist ideals. She cites recent examples of the Grimm collections in which this was done, and states that although the motive was good, the result is tampering with a natural folk art.

1164. Braun, Eva. "Von der zweiten Literatur," *Neue deutsche Literatur,* Berlin (East), Jahrgang 2, Heft 11, Nov. 1954, pp. 82–94. DLC.

The author agrees with Gorki, when he stated that the "new" literature for children must be written by those who can write well for adults . . . only for children they must write better. She states that after 1945, writers in East Germany turned to the Russian children's books for inspiration, and to learn to write of the rational strength of man, rather than the fiction of fate.

1165. Breslau. Verein Katholischer Lehrer. *Verzeichnis von Jugend- und Volksschriften.* Breslau, G. P. Aderholz, 1904. Vol. 1, 2nd ed., 96p.; Vol. 2, 3rd ed., 96p.; Vol. 3, 2nd ed., 104p. (1901); Vol. 4, 2nd ed., 110p. (1903); Vol. 5, 100p. (1897); Vol. 6, 108p. (1900); Vol. 7, 100p. (1905); Verzeichnis, Vols. 1–7 (1907). DLC.

Book reviews arranged into four age-levels, and intended for family or school selection of good children's books, from the Roman Catholic point of view. Each volume is indexed separately, and all are indexed in the final *Verzeichnis.* Bibliographic information is complete.

1166. *Das Buch der Jugend.* München, Arbeitskreis für Jugendschrifttum, e.V., Yearly, 1953 ff. IYL.

An annotated list published by a federation of organizations concerned with children's books (teachers, librarians, publishers, booksellers, social workers, etc.). Each list is annotated and illustrated. See also *Bücher für die junge Generation.*

1167. *Bücher für die junge Generation.* München, Arbeitskreis für Jugendschrifttum, e.V., 1962. Annual. IYL.

An annotated list of books for young people. This replaces *Bücher für unsere Jugend.*

1168. *Bücher für unsere Jugend.* Hamburg, Vereinigten Jugendschriftenausschüssen, Arbeitsgemeinschaft deutscher Lehrerverbände, 1951–1961. Annual. IYL.

An annotated list of books for young adults, now superceded by *Bücher für die junge Generation.*

1169. *Bücher, Wegbegleiter fürs Leben.* Ratingen, Aloys Henn, 1956. 88p. DLC.

Subtitled "What should our children read? A serious question for parents," this paperback is aimed at stirring up interest in guiding children's reading, so as to counteract the influence of comics and other popular literature of questionable taste.

1170. *Büchereiarbeit mit Kindern und Jugendlichen in öffentlichen Büchereien.* Berlin, Deutscher Büchereiverband, 1964.

1171. Buehler, Charlotte and Josephine Bilz. *Das Märchen und die Phantasie des Kindes.* München, J. A. Barth, 1958. 111p. IYL, DLC, NNY.

This first appeared as *Beiheft 7* of the *Zeitschrift für angewandte Psychologie* in 1918. Although this famous study falls definitely in the realm of psychology, it had such an influence on the writing and use of fairy tales (and even children's literature in general) that it is included here. Charlotte Bühler noted that most children read only fairy tales at a given period in their lives. From intensive observation related to the imagination of children she gives the conclusions that she was able to draw.

1172. Burhenne, Heinrich. *Kinderherz; ein Beitrag zur Frage der Kinderzeitschrift.* Langensalza, H. Beyer and Söhne, 1921. 80p. (Pädagogisches Magazin, Heft 866.). NNY.

A study on an attempt to get children to write and illustrate their own literature. The introduction has much to say on the contemporary children's literature, and its failure to reach the heart of the child. The main portion is a selection of writing done by the children.

1173. Busse, Hans. "Die häusliche Lektüre der Volksschulkinder," *Vierteljahrsschrift für wissenschaftliche Pädagogik,* Münster, Heft 3, 1927, pp. 407–433. IYL has xerograph copy.
"The home reading of elementary school children." Results of a study made among 764 boys and girls (10–14 years) in Hanover.

1174. ———. *Das Literarische Verständnis der werktätigen Jugend zwischen 14 und 18.* Leipzig, Barth, 1923. 289p. (Zeitschrift für Angewandte Psychologie, Beiheft 32). NNY.
The results of a survey on the reading interests and literary capacities of working youth from 14 to 18. Presented more from the psychological approach, with many charts and graphs. The bibliography on pp. 273–278 includes many U.S. studies, and there are author, title and subject indexes.

1175. *Centralblatt für deutsche Volks- und Jugendliteratur.* Edited by H. Schwerdt. Gotha, Scheube Verlag. Band 1, Heft 1, 1857-Band 2, Heft 1, 1858. Quarterly.
This short-lived review contained articles on children's literature, authors, and reviews of current works. Some of the contributors were Ludwig Bechstein, A. W. Grube, O. Glaubsrecht, Biernatzki and Kriebitsch.

1176. Chadburn, Isabel. "Book-selection committees for juvenile literature in Germany," *Library association record,* London, Vol. 9, No. 2, Feb. 15, 1907, pp. 56–59. DLC, NNY.
A British librarian comments on the work of the Vereinigten deutschen Prüfungsausschüsse für Jugendschriften, the Union of German Committees for the Criticism and Selection of Children's Books. After recounting its history, she gives specific examples of the type of reviews and concludes with a brief comparison of British reviewing media and book lists.

1177. Cludius, Heimart and Karl. *Die evangelische Volks- und Schülerbibliothek.* 5th ed. Berlin, Cludius & Gaus, 1903.

1178. Detmer, A. *Musterung unserer deutschen Jugendliteratur.* 2nd ed. Hamburg, 1844.

1179. *Das deutsche Jugendbuch.* München, Deutscher Volksverlag, 1942. 87p. DLC.
Four addresses originally given at a government-sponsored conference on children's literature in Bayreuth, 1939.

1180. Diehl, *Die Bedeutung der Jugendliteratur.* Gütersloh, Bertelsmann.

1181. Diekmann, Jos. *Katalog der Schülerbibliothek nebst einer kurzen Einleitung über den Lesetrieb der Knaben und seine Befriedigung.* Viersen, 1882, 18p.

1182. Dierks, Margarete. *Vom Bilderbuch zum Arbeitsbuch.* Reutlingen, Ensslin & Laiblin, 1965, 72p. IYL.
A history of early works of the 17th, 18th and 19th centuries which could be called the forerunners of today's dictionaries, encyclopedias and similar lexicons for children and youth. Such authors as Johan Amos Comenius, Johan Bernhard Basedow, and Friedrich Bertuch are among the many who are mentioned.

1183. Dittrich, Günther. *Das deutsche Jugendbuch.* Rheinhausen, Verlagsanstalt Rheinhausen, 1952. 310p. DLC.
An attempt to create a national bibliography of children's books produced in Germany since the end of the war, including those which are translations and some published in Switzerland, East Germany and Austria. The entries are arranged by general age and subject categories, with keys to reviews of each title. Subject-title and author indexes are at the end. An inclusive list, rather than a selective one.

1184. Doderer, Klaus. *Jugendliteratur heute.* Frankfurt-Main, Institut für Jugendbuchforschung, 1965. 64p. IYL.
An attempt to analyze the total production of more than 1,000 titles from the previous year (1964). The editor is head of the Institute for the Study of Children's Books, attached to the University in Frankfurt. The books were divided into groups, which were then characterized and criticized as to themes, styles, etc. In each group the best books are pointed out and there are, in addition, comments about books which are needed, but do not exist. Translations are pointed out, with books from the English language being highest in total.

1185. ———. *Das Sachbuch als literatur-pädagogisches Problem.* Frankfort/Main, Verlag Moritz Diesterweg, 1961. 72p. (Schriften zur Literaturpädagogik . . . Pädagogischen Institut Darmstadt).

DLC. Also: Wien, Verlag für Jugend und Volk, 1961.

"The factual (or nonfiction) book as a literary-pedagogical problem." A broad definition of the factual book, its historical development, and its place as literature among the rest of the children's books. A two-page bibliography appears at the end.

1186. Doetsch, Marietheres. *Comics und ihre jugendlichen Leser.* Meisenheim/Glan, Verlag Anton Hain, 1958. 144p. DLC. (Schriftenreihe der Hochschule für Internationale Pädagogische Forschung).

A survey of the previous studies and questionnaires compiled on the question of comic books, together with a new research questionnaire and its results.

1187. Dost, Georg. *Jugend und Buch.* Leipzig, B. G. Teubner, 1929. 84p. IYL. (IYL also has earlier version, *Was und wie soll unsere Jugend lesen?*, same pub., 1920, 49p.).

Critical essays on the aesthetic of children's literature, as defined by Wolgast and here defended by Dost. The notes contain many bibliographical references.

1188. Dressler, Irmgard. "Gedanken zur Arbeit mit dem Kinder- und Jugendbuch in der Tageserziehung," *Der Bibliothekar,* Berlin (East), Jahrgang 17, Heft 8, Aug. 1963, pp. 821–831. DLC, IYL, NNY.

Bringing children and books together in the daily life of the school. The author recommends class visits to the library, cooperation of schools and libraries in setting of hours of opening suited to the needs of all children, vacation privileges, etc.

1189. ———."German Democratic Republic," *Library service to children, 2.* Lund, Bibliotekstjanst, 1966, pp. 27–35. DLC, NNY.

This publication was sponsored by IFLA (see 32). In this chapter library work with children in East Germany is discussed. West Germany is covered in the first volume of this series.

1190. ———. *Literarische Veranstaltungen in der Kinderbibliothek.* Berlin (East), Zentralinstitut für Bibliothekswesen, 1966.

1191. Dreyer, Georg. *Die Jugendliteratur.* Gotha, E. Behrend, 1889. 87p. (Pädagogische Zeit- und Streitfragen, Bund 2, No. 2). DLC.

The author opens on a note familiar to present-day ears: "Like a mighty torrent a flood of children's books has been tumbling over our land during the past century. Every year new rivers and brooks, some light and clear, others turbid and murky, add their mixtures to the surge. The experienced friend of children and books can only stand on the bank and look on with dismay." A note indicates that the "flood" was an increase of 464 new titles in 1887 as compared with 397 in 1886. This study contained no particularly new or advanced ideas, but it expressed in vigorous terms the theory that literature for children is not exempt from the principles which govern literature in general.

1192. Duboc, Julius. "Die moderne Jugendliteratur," *Gegen den Strom;* Hannover, C. Rümpler, 1877. pp. 227–251.

During the previous 35 years, wrote this critic, children's literature improved in two aspects: illustration, and the utilization of natural science information. He expands each of these ideas, explaining how he came to these conclusions.

1193. Dyhrenfurth-Graebsch, Irene. *Geschichte des deutschen Jugendbuches.* 2nd ed. Hamburg, Eberhard Stichnote, 1951. 324p. IYL, NNY. (DLC has 1st ed., Leipzig, O. Harassowitz, 1942, 274p.).

In her forward, the author mentions that the first edition had been censored. She based her history on the Hobrecker old book collection, which was dispersed during the war. The chapters are arranged chronologically, covering the period of the first printed books up to 1950. Swiss-German books are treated separately. Many black and white reproductions and 29 plates illustrate the items discussed.

1194. Eckardt, Eva von. *Kinderseele und Kinderbuch.* Worms, Verlag Ernst Wunderlich, 1949. 61p. DLC.

Advice to mothers on introducing literature to the children in the home, through rhymes, storytelling, and reading of the classics.

1195. *Das Elend der Hamburger Jugendschriftenkritik.* Berlin, Freie Lehrervereinigung für Kunstpflege, 1911? 32p. NNY.

One of the pamphlets objecting to Wolgast and his type of critical approach to children's books.

1196. Ellendt, Georg. *Katalog für die Schülerbibliotheken.* Halle/Saale, Buchhandlung des Waisenhauses, 1905. 166p. DLC.

A suggested basic collection for the school library, arranged by grades and subjects, with an introduction explaining its principles of selection and use. Pp. xv–xxi are a bibliography on children's books and libraries; pp. xxii–xxxxi are a list of books *not* recommended for the school library, even though they might be good for other uses.

1197.   *Empfehlenswerte Jugendschriften.* Leipzig, Ernst Wunderlich, 1904. 51p. DLC.

An annotated list of some 400 children's books, selected and recommended by the Vereinigten Deutschen Prüfungsausschüssen für Jugendschriften.

1198.   Engl, Hans. *Die Kinderlesehalle; ein pädagogisches Problem.* München, Ernst Reinhardt, 1932. 104p. NNY.

The history, necessity, aims and organization of the children's library and the various aspects of work with children and books, as observed and tested in the Munich city libraries and others. The author pays special tribute to the work of Hans Ludwig Held. Bibliography on pp. 102–104.

1199.   Ensch, J. B. *Gesichtspunkte und praktische Ratschläge für die Anlegung von Schülerbibliotheken.* Berlin, Kribe Verlag, 1916. 31p. (Die Jugendschriftenfrage, No. 2–3). IYL has xerograph copy.

"Viewpoints and practical advice for the establishing of school libraries, with a list of recommended books."

1200.   Enzensberger, Hans M. *Allerleirauh: viele schöne Kinderreime.* Frankfurt/Main, Suhrkamp, 1962. 384p. DLC, NNY.

A modern collection taken from *Des knaben Wunderhorn,* Böhme, and many other sources, illustrated with old woodcuts and arranged according to age and very general subject groups. There are also chapters on the origin and history of nursery rhymes, their various forms and the manner in which they are transmitted. Bibliography and index of first lines.

1201.   Epstein, C. *Die Bedeutung der Schülerbibliotheken und die Verwertung derselben zur Lösung der erziehlichen und unterrichtlichen Aufgabe der Volksschule.* Wiesbaden, Behrend, 1901. 90p. (Pädagogische Zeit- und Streitfragen, Heft 58).

The author disputes Lüben (1326) point for point, arguing that reading *is* good for children and the best way to stimulate and develop good reading habits is through the school library. However, he negates his own arguments in many cases, by placing restrictions on the kind and amount of reading children should have available. The reading list of 271 titles is not very critical, according to Koester (1295). The tone is in part heavily nationalistic.

1202.   Falkenberg, Heinrich. *Jugendlektüre und Kulturleben.* Kempten, Kösel, 1919. 70p.

1203.   Fick. *Zur Reform der Jugendliteratur.* Berlin, Zillessen.

1204.   Fikenscher, Friedrich and Josef Prestel. *Jugend und schönes Schrifttum.* Ansbach, Michael Prögel, 1925. 287p. IYL.

"Youth and literary writing." These eleven essays are by F. X. Schönhuber, H. Burhenne, J. Antz, S. Rüttgers, Fl. Seidl, W. Ledermann, J. Prestel, J. Beck, Emma Wismeyer, H. Loschky and Chr. Keller. They deal with general or special aspects of children's literature, e.g., girls' stories, animal stories, illustration, fairy tales, periodicals, the classics.

1205.   Förstemann, Ernst Günther. *Über Einrichtung und Verwaltung von Schulbibliotheken.* Nordhausen, Forstemann, 1865.

1206.   Frank, Rudolf. "Kinderliteratur," *Die Literatur,* Stuttgart, Jahrgang 30, Heft 3, Dec., 1927, pp. 146–149. DLC.

There is good literature being printed for children, but the parent or other buyer rarely finds it, since the reviewing media are so scarce and poor. The author then discusses some recent books which can qualify as literature, and which are available in an attractive format.

1207.   Frankfurt am Main. Hochschule für Internationale Pädagogische Forschung. *Jugendschriftenkunde und Jungeleserkunde. Bibliographie der von 1945 bis 30.12.1954 erschienenen Bücher und Zeitschriftenaufsätze.* Frankfurt, The Hochschule, 1955. 25p.

A bibliography of books and periodical articles on juvenile literature and the reading interests of young people, edited by Lotte Dolezalek.

1208.   Frick, Otto Paul Martin. *Kanon der Schülerbibliothek.* Potsdam, 1869.

1209.   Fricke, Wilhelm. *Grundriss der Geschichte deutscher Jugendlitteratur.* Minden/Westfalen, Bruns, 1886. 216p. IYL has xerograph copy.

The history of children's literature, in four periods: up to 1774; 1775–1800; 1800–1850; 1850 to 1885. He treats of the six tendencies of children's literature: didactic, Christian, realistic, novelistic, *märchen* and *sagen,* poetic. A book list of 500 titles is included. Koester referred to this as "a very superficial and uncritical stuffing-together of names and dates." (1295, Vol. 2, p. 156).

1210.   Friesicke, Konrad *et al.* "Jugendzeitschriften," *Handbuch der Jugendarbeit.* München, Juventa Verlag, 1961. pp. 171–269. DLC.

Complete information on 250 current periodicals for children and youth, including those published by private and religious organizations. All are

West German in origin. The first part of this handbook is a list of all local, state, national, private and religious organizations working with children and youth in West Germany. Since many of these publish book lists and other materials, this is an extremely useful source of information. Index to organization names.

1211.   Fronemann, Wilhelm. *Das erbe Wolgasts*. Langensalza, Julius Beltz, 1927. 246p. IYL, NNY.

The present state of children's literature has been greatly influenced by the ideas of Wolgast. During the war, the major task was to keep the cheap, sensational literature from flooding the market. To demonstrate the work involved, the author lists 496 titles of "bad" books which had to be censored. The section on contemporary children's books is divided by types, and one chapter discusses journals and periodicals. A bibliography, pp. 230–242, is very helpful since it is divided into such categories as the psychology of reading, children's literature and teaching, children's libraries, booklists, histories, studies of single authors, etc.

1212.   ———. "Die heutige deutsche Jugendliteratur, *Das deutsche Buch*, Leipzig, Jahrgang 1, Heft 8, Aug. 1921, pp. 3–9. DLC.

An evaluation of children's literature of the time, as it represented the ideal set forth by Wolgast, i.e., it must above all be literature. The article is followed by two shorter ones on "the artistic picture book" by Dr. Julius Zeitler, and on music literature for young people by Dr. Arnold Schering. From pp. 14–35 is a "Bibliographie der Jugendliteratur," a selected list of some 750 titles which Fronemann felt acceptable as literature. Arranged by subject, with complete information, but not annotated.

1213.   ———. *Lesende Jugend*. Langensalza, Julius Beltz, 1930. 344p. IYL.

The five major sections cover: Theory and history; On the teaching of literature and literary values to children; The basis and extension of children's literature; The struggle to stamp out "unhealthy" books for children. The bibliography on pp. 285–321 is very extensive and arranged into sections matching the above areas. There is a list of important organizations working with children's literature (of which the author states there were some 300 in all of Germany!). Name and subject index.

1214.   *Gebt uns Bücher gebt uns Flügel*. Hamburg, Friedrich Oetinger, yearly 1963 ff. IYL.

Although these almanacs are meant as commercial advertising for the books of this publisher, they contain information about many authors, essays

of general criticism, selections from their best children's books and similar material.

1215.   Gedike, Friedrich. "Einige Gedanken über Schulbücher und Kinderschriften," *Gesammlete Schulschriften*. Berlin, Johann Friedrich Unger, 1789. Vol. 1, pp. 422–466. IIU.

This educator was strongly in favor of the informational or moral type of children's book, and felt that imaginative works could be harmful when read too early. He wrote: "It is true, our former books for children were often unbearably dry and boring. But compared to them our current books are unbearably watery and facetious."

1216.   Gelderblom, Gertrud. "Germany; children's libraries of Frankfurt am Main," *Top of the news*, Chicago, Vol. 7, Oct., 1950, pp. 14–15. DLC.

In this special issue devoted to children's library work in many countries, this librarian tells of the paucity of this service in Germany, and gives specific examples of what kind of work is being done in one large city.

1217.   ———. "Vom neugegründeten deutschen Arbeitskreis für Jugendschrifttum," *Libri*, Copenhagen, Vol. 6, No. 4, 1956, pp. 380–386. DLC, NNY.

"Concerning the newly founded German Study Group for Youth Literature." This gives the background history and reasons for the establishment of this group, which is now one of the most active organizations working in the field in Germany.

1218.   Gesamteuropäisches Studienwerk. *Das kinder- und Jugendbuch im sowjetkommunistischen Einflussbereich*. Vlotho/Weser, May, 1958. 70p. (Auswahlverzeichnis, No. 11). DLC.

"Children's and youth literature in the Soviet-Communist range of influence." A bibliography of items about children's literature and a list of books published for children. Most of the items in both parts are from East Berlin, but there are a few in Russian. There is an author and title index. The Gesamteuropäisches Studienwerk is a West German agency which has established a library-institute to study "East-West" problems.

1219.   *Gespräche mit Lesern in der Kinderbibliothek*. Berlin (East), Zentralinstitut für Bibliothekswesen, 1963. 131p. DLC.

"Talks with readers in the children's library." Some recommended methods of approaching children, individually or in groups, when introducing books.

154

1220. *Das gestaltete Sachbuch und seine Probleme.* Reutlingen, Ensslin & Laiblin, 1955. 79p. (Jahresgabe). DLC.

Three essays on the factual book for children and young people. Hermann Bertlein writes on history in children's books, Heinrich Pleticha on geography and Otto Metzker on the animal book.

1221. Giehrl, Hans Eberhard. *Zur Entwicklung der Leseinteressen und der literarischen Erlebnisfähigkeit im Jugendalter.* München, 1952. 165p. Dissertation. IYL.

1222. Gierke. "Die Arbeit mit der Schülerbücherei im Unterricht," *Bücherei und Bildungspflege,* Leipzig, Jahrgang 9, Heft 6, 1929, pp. 392–398. DLC, NNY.

The author writes in favor of the class library as opposed to the central school library, for, she contends, only the teacher knows the real interest and reading level of each of her students, and furthermore, to be surrounded by books and constantly to turn to them is the best method of inculcating a love of books.

1223. Gieseler, Hanns. *Dichtung und Sachschrift in der Schule.* Lübeck and Hamburg, Matthiesen Verlag, 1961. 86p. IYL.

"Poetry (literature) and nonfiction in school. Published for the Vereinigte Jugendschriften-Ausschüsse." A booklist of recommended titles, annotated and arranged by grades. In the introduction various series of use to teachers are appraised.

1224. Glaser, Martha. *Jugend und Dichtung.* Lahr, Ernst Kaufmann, 1948. 71p. IYL.

"Youth and poetry; which books are best suited for the young?" The author's critical evaluations are made from a Christian point of view.

1225. Göbels, Hubert. *Bildergalerie für Gross und Klein; alte deutsche Kinderbuch-illustrationen.* Gütersloh, Sigbert Mohn, 1962. 48p. (Das kleine Buch, 154).

1226. Goehring, Ludwig. *Die Anfänge der deutschen Jugendliteratur im 18. Jahrhundert. Ein Beitrag zur Geschichte der deutschen Jugendliteratur.* Nürnberg, Verlag der Korn'schen Buchhandlung, 1904. 140p. IYL has xerograph copy.

"The beginnings of German children's literature in the 18th century." According to Koester (1295) this was one critic who combined a good style with aesthetic feeling and taste.

1227. Goerth, Albrecht. "Über Jugendlectüre für Mädchen," *Pädagogium,* Leipzig, Jahrgang 4, Heft 1, 1882, pp. 17–43. DLC.

Speaking from 18 years' experience in teaching in a girls' school, this author writes at length as to what he believes *is* read by girls, and what *should be* read by them. His conclusion is: "In managing the reading of young girls, extensive and purely recreational literature should be avoided; instead one must constantly exhort them to read with pen in hand [for taking notes] and to treat reading as a serious task."

1228. Götze, O. *Die Erziehung der Jugendlichen zu unserm deutschen Volksschrifttum.* Langensalza, Beyer and Söhne, 1920. 26p. NNY.

"Leading young people to their native German literature." An address delivered as part of a course given in Weimar. The author stresses the importance of introducing the best of literature to youth, rather than giving them only what strikes their fancy momentarily.

1229. ———. *Die psychologische Seite des Jugendschriftenproblems.* Langensalza, Beyer and Söhne, 1928. 38p.

1230. Gorki, Maxim. *Über Kinderliteratur.* Berlin (Ost), Verlag Neues Leben, 1953. 313p. IYL.

A translation of 1906.

1231. Gottschalk, Rudolf. *Vaterländische Erziehung und Jugendschriftenfrage.* Berlin, Kribe Verlag, 1917. 30p. (Die Jugendschriftenfrage, Nr. 5/6). IYL has xerograph copy.

"Patriotic education and the question of children's literature." An essay on the importance of native political identity as expressed in children's books.

1232. Graucob, Karl. *Das Lesen auf der Oberstufe der Volksschule.* Kiel, Hirt, 1958. 55p.

1233. Graebsch, Irene. "Aus der praktischen Arbeit der Jugendbücherei," *Bücherei,* Leipzig, Jahrgang 6, Apr., 1939, pp. 212–220. DLC, NNY.

This article, together with an earlier one by the same author (in Jahrgang 3, Jul.–Aug., 1936, pp. 357–366) provide a survey of the type of children's library work which was carried out in the late 1930's in Germany.

1234. Gross, Julius. *Über Jugendlektüre und Schülerbibliotheken.* Programm des Evang. Gymnasiums zu Kronstadt, 1888.

1235. Günnell, J. G. "Über Kinderlektüre," *Nach-*

richten über die allgemeine Bürgerschule zu Plauern. 1846.

1236.   Günther, Victor. "Unsere Jugendschriften," *Deutsche Blatter für erziehenden Unterricht,* Langensalza, Jahrgang 7, No. 1, 1880, pp. 3–4; No. 2, pp. 15–17; No. 3, pp. 23–25; No. 4, 31–34. DLC.

A teacher writes of the contemporary state of juvenile literature and states his plans to organize a reviewing service, which would point out the best books suitable for use in schools.

1237.   Günzel, Marianne and Harriet Schneider. *Buch und Erzeihung.* Leipzig, Klinkhardt, 1943. 164p.

The seven sections deal with all of the educational aspects of books, as used with children, and the aesthetic and spiritual implications books can have for the young. There is a chapter on the importance of political writing for children. Bibliography (pp. 159–164) and suggested book lists.

1238.   *Das gute Jugendbuch.* "Arbeitskreis 'Das Gute Jugendbuch, e.V,'" 403 Ratingen bei Düsseldorf, Düsseldorferstrasse 46. 3 issues yearly. Vol. 1 ff., 1951 ff. Annual subscription: 4.80 DM. IYL.

This periodical is sponsored and published by a private organization concerned with furthering the cause of good children's books. Each issue contains articles of general interest, historical and critical comments on authors and illustrators of the past and present, articles on library work with children and similar subjects. There are about 100 signed reviews in each issue. The point of view is Christian Protestant.

1239.   "Das gute Jugendbuch," *Pädagogische Welt,* Donauwörth, Jahrgang 8, Heft 4, April, 1954, pp. 169–222 (Entire issue). DLC.

Articles by Jos. Prestel, Anna Krüger, W. Treiber, Martin Ibler, Maria Barthel, and others, on the use of children's books in the school.

1240.   Haenel, Charlotte. *Für dich, für mich, für uns alle.* Berlin (East), Berliner Stadtbibliothek, 1964. 48p.

"For you, for me, for us all; a list of books for pupils in grades 1 to 4."

1241.   Hamann, Chr. *Was unsere Kinder lesen.* Bielefeld, A. Helmich, 1891. 13p. (Sammlung pädagogischer Vorträge, ed. by W. Meyer-Markau, Band 4, Heft 8). DLC.

Every teacher and parent should work toward urging the state to provide libraries in all schools, even the humblest villages. Until such provi-

sions are made they must choose personally the books their children read. The author then cites examples of the best choices. This is followed by a short article by F. Aberle, "Klassen- und Massenlektüre," in which the author recommends less reading for children, but of better quality.

1242.   Hartung, Hermann and Gottfried Paulsen. *Was liest die Jugend der Sowjetzone?* 2nd ed. Bonn, Berlin [West], Bundesministerium für Gesamtdeutsche Fragen, 1961. 107p. DLC.

A West German study of what East German children read, aimed at learning the amount of political significance existing in their literature.

1243.   Haupt, Heinz. "Der Weg zum guten Jugendbuch: Vom Leben zur Literatur," *Die neue schule,* Berlin (East), Jahrgang 7, No. 24, June 13, 1952, pp. 564–566. DLC.

A report on the 2nd congress on children's and young people's literature, which took place in May, 1952, with more than 200 writers, publishers, teachers, librarians, book dealers and Pioneer group leaders taking part.

1244.   Hazard, Paul. *Kinder, Bücher und grosse Leute.* Hamburg, Hoffmann und Campe, 1952. 213p. DLC, IYL.

For note see 814. Translated into German by Harriet Wegener, with a forward by Erich Kästner.

1245.   *Die Heimbibliothek; das Buch in der Jugendheimstätte der NSV.* Berlin, Nationalsozialistische Volkswohlfahrt, n.d. 26p. DLC.

A list of titles recommended for the children's home library, put out by the agency responsible for youth problems under the Nazi party.

1246.   Heintze, Albert. "Zur Einrichtung von Schülerbibliotheken," *Zeitschrift für das Gymnasialwesen,* Berlin, Jahrgang 40, June, 1886, pp. 321–331. DLC.

Suggestions for the building of a (secondary) school library. The author pays particular attention to the editions and translations of the various universal classics, pointing out the poor literary qualities of some of them.

1247.   Held, Hans Ludwig. *Die Kinderlesestube; eine Auswahl guter Kinderliteratur.* München, 1928. 68p.

1248.   ———. "Die Münchener städtischen Kinderlesehallen," *Volk und Heimat,* München, Jg. 2,

Nos. 17–18, 1926, pp. 14–15; No. 21, 1926, pp. 6–7; Jg. 3, No. 1, 1927, p. 6. APP.

Very detailed statistics and data on the early work of the Munich city libraries for children.

1249. Herbart, Johann Friedrich. *Allgemeinen Pädagogik*. Göttingen, Johann Friedrich Röwer, 1806. 482p. DEW.

According to Koester (1295, p. 130), Herbart's was a fresh voice for his time, but it went unheard. In this treatise, he rails against the overly didactic and moral tones which were used with children, in books and in teaching. The introduction is especially significant to the study of children's literature, but there are numerous comments scattered throughout the book, all related to children and books.

1250. Hesse, Kurt Werner. *Schmutz und Schund unter der Lupe*. Frankfurt am Main, Deutsche Jugend-Presse-Agentur, 1955. 133p. DLC.

"Smut and trash under the magnifying glass." An exposé of the violence, poverty of language and illustration, and lack of morality evident in the magazines and books which provide much of young peoples' reading.

1251. Heyden, Franz. *Volksmärchen und Volksmärchenerzähler*. Hamburg, Hanseat. V., 1922. 86p.

1252. Heydner, Georg. *Das Lesebuch in der Volksschule*. Nürnberg, F. Korn, 1891. 72p. DEW.

This is concerned with the reading book in the elementary school, but it goes beyond the pedagogical. The author's central theme is that "only the poet can speak to children."

1253. ———. "Wie kinder lesen," *Beiträge zur Kenntnis des kindlichen Seelenlebens*. Leipzig, Friedrich Brandstetter, 1894, pp. 7–41. WUW.

"How children read." What children look for and understand in their reading, with emphasis on folk and fairy tales.

1254. Hild, Otto. *Die Jugendzeitschrift*. Leipzig, Ernst Wunderlich, 1905. 87p. IYL.

"The youth periodical in its historical development, educational harmfulness and artistic impossibility, with criticism of the current periodicals."

1255. Hirsch, Elizabeth. "Children's books for Germany," *Junior bookshelf*, Huddersfield, Vol. 7, Nov. 1943, pp. 89–94. DLC, NNY.

This attempts to answer the question: "What can we put in place of the books that must be taken out of the hands of Germany's children?" The author is referring to books with Nazi ideals which had almost completely replaced the standard classics.

1256. Hobrecker, Karl. *Alte vergessene Kinderbücher*. Berlin, Mauritius Verlag, 1924. 159p. DLC.

"Old, forgotten children's books," of the 15th through 19th centuries, described with care and affection, and illustrated with many reproductions of great detail and charm. Some 130 books are mentioned, and each is given complete bibliographic description.

1257. Hoegg, F. X. *Verzeichnis der von den höheren Bildungsanstalten Westfalens für Schülerbibliotheken empfohlenen Werke*. Paderborn, Schöningh, 1869.

1258. Hölder, Anneliese. *Die Entwicklung des literarischen Interesses in der männlichen Reifezeit im Rahmen des Abenteuerbuches*. Tübingen, 1947. 227p. Dissertation. IYL.

"The development of literary interest during the age of puberty in boys, in the framework of the adventure book."

1259. Hopf, G. W. *Mittheilungen über Jugendschriften an Eltern und Lehrer, nebst gelegentlichen Bemerkungen über Volksschriften*. 5th ed. Nürnberg, Friedr. Korn, 1875. 174p. IIU.

"Advice to parents and teachers, about children's literature, with some remarks on folk literature." The author's introduction indicates the criteria to be used in selection, together with something about the proper activities of children's libraries. He did not believe that the standard classics were suitable for children under 12. Such works as *Don Quixote*, *Munchhausen*, *Eulenspiegel* suggested too many mischievous pranks. There follows a list of 400 titles he did recommend, annotated and arranged by general age and subject groups. There is an author index. The 1st edition appeared about 1849.

1260. Hormann, Hanna. *Die sozialistische Kinder- und Jugendliteratur in der DDR*. Droyssig, Zentralschule der Pionier-organisation "Ernst Thälmann," 1965. 96p.

1261. Hülsmann, J. *Über die Einrichtung der Schülerbibliotheken*. Duisberg, 1855.

1262. Hugk, Margarete. "Das Foto als Illustrationsmittel des Kinderbuches," *Der bibliothekar*, Berlin (East), Jahrgang 8, Heft 23–24, Dec. 1954, pp. 694–700. DLC, IYL, NNY.

"Photographs as means of illustrating children's books." This librarian was a frequent contributor on the subject of the picture book.

1263. Izhevskaia, M. A. *Aus der Arbeit der sowjetischen Kinderbibliotheken.* Leipzig, Verlag für Buch- und Bibliothekswesen, 1954. 124p. DLC.

A translation into German of the Russian work. For note, see entry 1920.

1264. Johannesson, Fritz. *Was sollen unsere Jungen lesen.* Berlin, Weidmannsche Buchhandlung, 1911. 279p. IYL.

Twelve essays on the worth and meaning of juvenile literature together with a recommended list of books, annotated and arranged according to age and type. Author index.

1265. Jordan, Alice M. "German principles for the selection of children's books," *Public libraries,* Chicago, Vol. 13, Jan., 1908, pp. 1–3. DLC, NNY.

Concerning the work and theories of Wolgast, and the *Jugendschriftenwarte.*

1266. *Jugend liest.* Verband der Katholischen Lehrerschaft Deutschlands, Jugendschriftenzentrale, Theodor-Heuss-Ring 36, Köln. Issued as a supplement to: *Der katholische Erzieher.* Vol. 1 ff., 1956 ff. (Title variations: *Das Jugendbuch, das christliche Jugendbuch*). IYL has 1956–1963.

This supplement usually contains a leading critical article followed by reviews of current children's books. Written from the Roman Catholic point of view.

1267. *Jugend und Buch. Bericht über die IV. Mainau-Jugendbuchtagung 1958.* Konstanz, Bahn, 1959. 159p. (Schriftenreihe des Internationalen Instituts Schloss Mainau, 2). IYL.

A report on the 4th children's book conference at the International Centre, Schloss Mainau. Initial articles are by J. Chr. Hampe, Th. Rutt, H. Vonhoff, A. de Vries, V. Böhm, R. Bamberger. This is followed by group reports on the four major themes of: the nonfiction book, rebellion in books for young people, the meeting of the sexes in children's books, and the adventure book from the Christian viewpoint.

1268. "Jugend und Buch." Special issue of: *Deutsche Jugend,* München, Dec. 1953, 58p. DLC, IYL.

This issue contains articles by Hanns Ott, Fritz Westphal, Fritz Pfeffer, Helmut Weber, Erich Kästner and a selection from Paul Hazard. On pp. 55–56 are some good booklists of children's books, followed by a short bibliography.

1269. *Das Jugendbuch als Bildungsmacht.* Mainau, Internationales Institut Schloss Mainau, 1961. 35p. IYL.

A report on the 7th Mainau Conference, which was concerned with juvenile literature as a cultural-educational force.

1270. *Jugendbuch und Bücherei als Wege der Selbstbildung.* Bonn, Borromäusverein, 1960. 47p. (Werkhefte zur Büchereiarbeit, 5). IYL.

"Youth books and libraries as means to self-education. Addresses delivered at the 9th working seminar for children's and youth librarians." The four speeches were by Walter Scherf, Theo Rombach, Klaus Malangré and Maria Bollig.

1271. [Jugendbuch und Jugendbüchereien.] Entire issue of: *Bucherei und Bildung,* Reutlingen, Jahrgang 13, Heft 6, June, 1961, pp. 225–265. DLC, IYL, NNY.

All of the articles in this issue are concerned with youth, their literature or their libraries. Public and school library cooperation is also discussed.

1272. *Das Jugendbuch und die Massenmedien. Berichte über die VIII. Mainau-Jugendbuchtagung.* Konstanz, Bahn, 1963. 119p. (Schriftenreihe des Internationalen Instituts Schloss Mainau, 7). IYL.

The 8th conference on children's literature at the Schloss Mainau had to do with children's books and mass media. Lead articles by O. Hartmann, M. Keilhacker, R. Bamberger, W. Scherf and G. Simmerding, as well as the group reports, all deal with such things as radio, television and the press, and their influence on children's reading.

1273. *Jugendbücher bauen Brücken. Berichte über die VI. Mainau-Jugendbuchtagung 1960.* Konstanz, Bahn, 1961. 131p. (Schriftenreihe des Internationalen Instituts Schloss Mainau, 5). IYL.

"Children's books build bridges" was the theme of the 6th conference on children's literature held at the Schloss Mainau. The articles by various authors are on such themes as the problems of translation, the "world" speech of children, building an accurate picture of other countries through children's books, and the work of the International Youth Library in Munich.

1274. *Jugendbücher der Weltliteratur.* Stuttgart, Ensslin & Laiblin, 1952. 88p. (Jahresgabe). IYL.

Some children's books which have become known around the world, such as *Heidi, Treasure Island, Tom Sawyer* and something about their authors.

1275. "Jugendbücher 64; Auswahlverzeichnis zum Gebrauch der Stadt- und Gemeindebüchereien für die Jugendarbeit." Special issue of: *Die Bücherei,* Koblenz, Jahrgang 10, 1964. 158p.

Sponsored by the state office for library affairs of Rheinland-Pfalz. This brought up-to-date an earlier list, published in 1962. It was arranged by age and subject groups, briefly annotated and has an author index. Illustrated with 8 photographs of children's libraries in Rheinland-Pfalz.

1276. *Die Jugendbücherei; ein Buchverzeichnis für die 10–16 jährigen.* Berlin, Volksbücherei Charlottenburg, 1935. 135p. DLC.

A catalog of the children's collections in the Berlin public libraries of the Charlottenburg sector. Arrangement is by subject, with an author index. Not annotated.

1277. *Jugendliteratur.* Issued jointly by several individuals in Austria, Germany and Switzerland; printed by Juventa Verlag, München. Monthly. Vol. 1, Jan., 1955–Vol. 9, Dec., 1963. IYL has complete set.

This now defunct periodical had lead articles on the history and criticism of juvenile literature, news items of general interest and signed book reviews.

1278. "Die Jugendliteratur," *Neue Bahnen,* Wiesbaden, Jahrgang 11, Heft 2, Feb., 1900, pp. 112–117; Heft 5, May, 1900, pp. 291–299. NNY.

An anonymous review of the theories of children's literature which had been newly expressed by Wolgast, Herbart, Gallmeyer and others. This critic disagreed with Wolgast. He felt that such high-minded idealism in children's books did not meet the everyday needs of children, particularly in regard to nationalistic and religious feelings.

1279. *Jugendschriftenwarte.* Vereinigte Jugendschriftenausschüsse, Rothenbaumchausee, 2 Hamburg 13. Monthly, as a supplement to the *Allgemeine Deutsche Lehrerzeitung.* Erste Folge: Jahrgang 1, Aug., 1893–1945?. Zweite Folge: Jahrgang 1 ff., 1947 ff. Annual subscription: 4.50 DM. IYL has 1947.

The organ of the United Juvenile Literature Committees of the National Teacher's Association. Each issue consists of 4 pages, and usually contains one lead article of criticism followed by general news and 5 to 10 reviews of current children's books.

1280. Kaiser, K. *Jugendlektüre und Schülerbibliotheken nebst einem nach Klassen geordneten Kataloge.* Barmen, Taddelsche Buchhandlung, 1878.

1281. *Der Kampf um die Jugendschrift.* Mainz, Scholz, 1913.

1282. Kaselitz, Fritz. *Gefahren moderner Jugendlektüre.* Berlin, Stubenrauchsche Buchhandlung, 1868. 20p. NNY.

A reprint of a lecture, in which the ideas expressed were taken largely from Kühner (1303).

1283. Keckeis, Gustav. "Gedanken zur Jugendliteratur," *Literarischer Handweiser,* Freiburg/Breisgau, Jahrgang 65, Heft 2, Nov., 1928, pp. 81–91. DLC.

"Thoughts on children's literature," brought up by the conference held in Marktbreit, on the theme of spiritual-biological bases for children's literature. See also the report by Leo Weismantel (1443).

1284. Kelchner, Mathilde and Ernst Lau. *Die Berliner Jugend und die Kriminalliteratur.* Leipzig, J. A. Barth, 1928. 110p. (Zeitschrift für angewandte Psychologie, Beiheft 42.). DLC, NNY.

"Berlin youth and crime literature." Although this is of more interest to the sociologist, because the study was based on essays written by young people, this is also of some value to the librarian or teacher working to bring books and youth together.

1285. Kellner, Lorenz. "Einiges über Jugendschriften." *Kurze Geschichte der Erziehung und des Unterrichts;* Freiburg/Breisgau, Herder, 1877, pp. 256–260. DLC.

A brief survey of the history of children's literature in Germany, and comments on some contemporary writers. The author believed that writing for children demanded the same care as writing for grown-ups; another of his theories was that children under nine or ten should not be taught to read, or given books to read, but should rather be told stories and shown artistic picture books.

1286. Kiesgen, Laurenz. *Randglossen zur Jugendschriftenfrage.* München, Kösel & Pustet, 1925. 69p. (Pädagogische Vorträge und Abhandlung, Heft 36). IYL.

"Marginal notes on the question of children's literature." Still another study following in the steps of Wolgast.

1287. "Kinder- und Jugendbücher," *Bücherei und Bildung,* Reutlingen, 1949, monthly. DLC, IYL, NNY.

Since 1949, this library periodical (the official organ of the German Public Librarian's Association) has carried signed reviews of children's and youth books. They are easily traced through the monthly and annual indexes. There are also many articles on children's books and libraries.

1288. *Kinder- und Jugendbücher aus aller Welt.* Stuttgart, Kulturamt-Stadbücherei, 1958. 96p. IYL.

"Children's and young people's books from around the world, a selection of the best . . . for 10 to 15-year-olds." Arranged into general subject categories and geographic areas. Annotated and indexed. Illustrated with drawings and art work by young people.

1289. Klaiber, Julius. *Das Märchen und die Kindliche Phantasie.* Stuttgart, S. G. Liesching, 1866. 44p.

1290. Kleinschmidt, Albert. *Über Jugendschriften.* Ohrdruff, Stadermann, 1869.

1291. Kloepper, K. "Jugendliteratur," *Grundriss der Pädagogik.* Rostock, Wilh. Werther, 1878. pp. 157–183. DEW.

A rather superficial survey of the history of juvenile literature, followed by a list of recommended books for children and youth.

1292. Knudsen, Hans and Willy Pieth. *Die Schulbibliothek.* Berlin, Weidmann, 1920. 40p.

1293. Kocialek, Anneliese. "Die Verbreitung unserer Kinderbücher ist die beste Waffe im Kampf gegen Schund- und Schmutzliteratur," *Pädagogik,* Berlin (East), Jahrgang 8, Heft 1, 1953, pp. 63–67. DLC.

"The wider increase of our children's books is the best weapon in the fight against smut and trashy literature." The report of a special conference called to deal with this problem in September, 1952.

1294. König, Carola. *Wegweiser durch die Jugendlektüre und die Möglichkeiten ihrer unterrichtlichen Verwertung.* Leipzig, A. Haase, 1904. 276p. (Schulreformbücherei, 13).

1295. Köster, Herman L. *Geschichte der deutschen Jugendliteratur.* 4th ed. Braunschweig, Verlag Georg Westermann, 1927. 478p. IYL. (DLC has Vol. 2 of 1st ed., Hamburg, Alfred Janssen, 1908; NNY has 2nd ed., 1915).

A critical history of German literature for children. Volume 1 is concerned with the content and illustration of picture books, folk songs and rhymes, poetry, *märchen,* the literary fairy tale, folk *Sagen* and other folk literature. Volume 2 treats of the *Sagen* of gods and heroes, and the novel or "story"

literature. A very useful chapter on the criticism of children's literature is most helpful in the study of developments up to the 20th century. There is no separate bibliography of the items discussed (histories, critical studies, book lists, etc.), but many can be traced through the name and author index.

1296. ———. *Das Geschlechtliche im Unterricht und in der Jugendlektüre.* Leipzig, Ernst Wunderlich, 1903. 69p. DEW.

On the treatment of sex in education and in juvenile literature. This critic believed there was a false and dishonest approach to the problem, especially in the so-called "girls' stories."

1297. Korff, W. *Das Kind und das Märchen.* 2nd ed. Kreuztal, Jung-Stilling, 1948. 26p.

1298. Korn, Ilse. *Märchenstunden; eine Anleitung für Lehrer, Erzieher und Pionierleiter.* Berlin (East), Verlag Volk und Wissen, 1955. 111p.

1299. Krack, Hans-Günther. "Wie steht es um die abenteuerliche Jugendliteratur?" *Börsenblatt für den deutschen Buchhandel,* Leipzig, Jahrgang 121, No. 6, Feb. 6, 1954, p.127; No. 7, Feb. 13, 1954, p.147; No. 8, Feb. 20, 1954, p. 167; No. 9, Feb. 27, 1954, pp. 187–88. DLC, NNY.

A review of past and present adventure books with good literary quality. The author regrets the lack of present day writers in this genre.

1300. Krüger, Anna. *Das Buch—Gefährte eurer Kinder.* Stuttgart, Ernst Klett Verlag, 1952. 56p. DLC.

The recently passed law controlling the production of *schund und schmutz* in reading material for children will not automatically assure them of getting the best. This booklet is to help parents choose reading material for their children as they grow up.—Summary from the forward.

1301. ———. *Kinder- und Jugendbücher als Klassenlektüre.* Berlin-Spandau, Luchterhand, 1963. 274p. IYL.

1302. Kuder, Manfred. *Problemas dos livros para a juventude.* Lisboa, Barreiro, 1958. 15p. (Publicacões do Instituto Alemão, No. 3). IYL.

A speech delivered on the occasion of an exhibition of children's books, held in Lisbon.

1303. Kühner, C. "Jugendlectüre, Jugendliteratur." Schmid, Karl Adolf, *Encyklopädie des gesammten Erziehungs- und Unterrichtswesens;* Gotha, Rudolf Besser, 1862; Band 3, pp. 802–840. DLC.

One of the best early studies in history and criticism of children's literature in Germany. The author, director of a model school in Frankfurt, had modified his early stand against all "children's" books, and here points out that it was only because of their poor literary and artistic qualities that he had denounced their use in home and school. He particularly berates the writers of religious books for their unrealistic, pietistic efforts which he says do more harm than good in promoting true (Christian) ideals. He advocates the use of the classics, folk tales, mythology and poetry.

1304. Künneman, Horst. "Twenty years later," *School library journal,* New York; Vol. 13, No. 3, Nov., 1966, pp. 37–41. DLC, IYL, NNY.

The situation in contemporary West German children's books.

1305. ———. "Zur situation der Jugendliteratur in zweigeteilten Deutschland. Das Kinderbuch in der DDR," *Jugend und Buch,* Wien, Jg.14, Heft 1, 1965, pp. 9–14; Heft 2, 1965, pp. 9–12. IYL.

A West German critic looks at the trends in East German children's books and comments on the themes, the ideology, the similarities and differences to West German publications, and many other aspects.

1306. Kunze, Horst. *Schatzbehalter; vom besten aus der älteren deutschen Kinderliteratur.* Berlin (East), Kinderbuchverlag, 1964. 437p. DLC, IYL.

"A treasury from the best of the old German children's books." In the first chapter, the author gives his reasons for writing this book and collecting the "best" selections from German children's books. Each of the previous histories, he claims, has by-passed important works: these are the ones he will emphasize. This is the only recent study to compare and evaluate the critical histories of children's literature, similar to the fashion in which Köster reviewed the earlier works (1295). Bamberger also does this, to a lesser extent (1069). However, the greater value in this book lies in its superb reproductions from the 18th century up to about 1920. The quality of the plates surpasses all of the previously illustrated histories in German. Samples of text are given as well. Sources for each selection and illustration are cited in full. There is a bibliography and an index.

1307. Lang, Paul. *Jugendschrift und Tendenz.* Leipzig, Ernst Wunderlich, 1907. 164p. IYL.

"Youth literature and tendency." The writer was against literature for children which had as a prime reason for existence an obvious purpose, whether moral, political or social.

1308. Lange, K. "Bilderbücher." Rein, W. *Encyclopädisches Handbuch der Pädagogik,* Band 1; Langensalza, H. Beyer and Söhne, 1903; pp. 647–654. DLC. (1st ed., 1894).

The nature of artistic taste, and how important the picture book is in bringing it out in children. The author characterizes the styles and types of illustration most pleasing to children.

1309. Lange, Marianne. "Die Bildungs- und Erziehungsarbeit der Arbeiterklasse mit Hilfe des Kinder- und Jugendbuches," *Der Bibliothekar,* Berlin (East), Jahrgang 17, Heft 9, Sept., 1963, pp. 922–932; Heft 10, Oct., 1963, pp. 1049–1054. DLC, IYL, NNY.

Cultural and educational work among the working class, using children's and young people's books. The author contends that the new socialistic approach to writing for children has brought this literature much closer to them, particularly in the working classes. The author is a frequent contributor to this periodical.

1310. Langfeldt, Johannes. "Children's books in Germany," *Junior bookshelf,* Huddersfield, Vol. 12, July, 1948, pp. 66–74. DLC, NNY.

A history, beginning in the 18th century, and continuing through the 19th, with emphasis on the theories of Wolgast. Some of the works of the 20th century are also mentioned, but more current literature is discussed in a later article, in Vol. 14, Mar., 1950, pp. 46–49.

1311. ———. "The children's library in Germany," *Junior bookshelf,* Huddersfield. Vol. 16, No. 5, Dec., 1952, pp. 257–264. DLC, IYL, NNY.

The postwar status of children's libraries and some of the things being done to relieve the situation. Dr. Langfeldt contributed an earlier article on postwar children's literature in Vol. 14, No. 2, Mar., 1950, pp. 46 ff.

1312. ———. "Gehört die Kinderbüchereiarbeit zum Aufgabenkreis der Schule oder der Bücherei?," *Bücherei,* Leipzig, Jahrgang 5, Sept.–Oct., 1938, pp. 530–541. DLC, NNY.

An eminent and well-known public librarian here discusses at some length the question as to whether children's work is best suited to the public library or school library.

1313. ———. "Kind und Buch," *Bücherei und Bildung,* Reutlingen, Jg 5, Sept., 1953, pp. 831–843. DLC, NNY.

A thoughtful article on the ethical content of children's books as opposed to their aesthetic quality. The author believed the former to be more important. He also advocated taking out the violence in fairy tales, and indeed, from all literature given to children.

1314. Ledermann, W. *Das Märchen in Schule und Haus.* 2nd ed. Langensalza, Beltz, 1926. 164p.

1315. Lehmann-Haupt, Hellmut. "What the Nazis did to children's books," *Horn book,* Boston, Vol. 25, No. 3, May–June, 1949, pp. 220–230. DLC, IYL, NNY.

Subtle propaganda is much more effective than exaggerated claims, and in the opinion of this writer the children's books of Germany were a powerful means of changing the ways of thinking to ideas in line with Nazi policies.

1316. Lehmensick, E. "Die Rolle der Jugendschriftenfrage in der neuen Lehrerbildung," *Bücherei,* Leipzig, Jahrgang 5, May, 1938, pp. 257–267. DLC, NNY.

"The role of children's literature in the new education of teachers." In many articles in this periodical it is possible to trace the emphasis placed upon using children's books as subtle propaganda for the Nationalist-Socialist party ideals. There were opinions expressed for and against this emphasis, except during the war years, when the tone of the articles became entirely a propagandistic one.

1317. Leipzig. Fortbildungsschule No. 4. *Katalog von Bibliotheken . . .* Wittenberg, R. Herrosé, 1904. 70p. (Schriften des deutschen Vereins für das Fortbildungsschulwesen, 16). DLC.

An annotated catalog of some 500 children's books, arranged by subject, and with three age levels indicated. Selection was made by teachers.

1318. Levi, Hermann. *Lehrbuch und Jugendbuch im jüdischen Erziehungswesen des 19. Jahrhunderts in Deutschland.* Köln, Dissertation for Universität Köln, 1933. 93p. IYL.

"Textbooks and children's books in Jewish education in Germany during the 19th century." There is a very extensive list of sources and bibliography.

1319. Lichtenberger, Franz, *et al. Beiträge zur Jugendschriftenfrage.* Leipzig, Scheffer, 1905 ff.

1320. ———. *Der neue Weg der deutschen Jugendschrift.* Halle, Marhold, 1930. 55p. IYL.

"The new way to German children's literature." This essay is an explanation and extolling of the work of Berthold Otto, specialist in the study of the language and pronunciation of children. The author, himself a writer for children, was opposed to the puristic ideas of Wolgast. He clearly explains his position and points out the areas of agreement and disagreement.

1321. Liebeskind. *Über Jugendlektüre.* . . . Breslau, Woywod., 1895.

1322. Linnig, Franz. *Die deutsche Jugendliteratur und Methodik des deutschen Unterrichts in Katechetischer Form.* Leipzig, 1876.

1323. Lippert, Elisabeth. *Der Lesetoff der Mädchen in der Vorpubertät.* Erfurt, K. Stenger, 1931. 132p. (Preussische Akademie Gemeinnütziger Wissenschaften und Jugendkunde, Veröffentlichungen, No. 30). NNY.

"The reading matter of girls in the years before puberty." Considered from the psychological, pedagogical, and aesthetic points of view. Bibliography on pp. 131–32.

1324. Lohrer, T. *Vom modernen Elend in der Jugendliteratur.* Müchen, 1905.

1325. Lorenz, Karl. *Verzeichnis der Schülerbücherei.* Hamburg, Oberrealschule vor dem Holstentore, 1911. 56p. DLC.

The catalog of a Hamburg school library, with an introduction on the importance of reading, at home and in the classroom. Author and title index only.

1326. Lüben, August and K. Nacke. "Jugend- und Volksschriften," *Pädagogischer Jahresbericht,* Leipzig, Fr. Brandstetter, 1851–1913. (Yearly Volume). DLC.

This yearly collection of pedagogical studies began to include reviews of children's books in 1851, written by K. Nacke. Upon his death in 1873, the reviewing was taken up by August Lüben, then successively by B. Lüben, Albert Richter, Georg Hendner, and W. Opitz. Their criticism emphasized the value of the classics, the literature of the Romantic period, and above all, folk literature. A. Lüben, in fact, went so far as to suggest that specifically "children's" literature was not good, for it gave children "unusable knowledge," led them to the superficial, and developed their imagination at the cost of other powers.

1327. Lüders, I. "Warum hören Kinder so gerne Märchen?, *Neue erziehung in Kindergarten und Heim,* Berlin (East), Jahrgang 15, Heft 1, Jan., 1962, pp. 5–8. DLC.

"Why do children like to listen to fairy tales so willingly?" This is only one of many articles on fairy tales which have appeared in this periodical since 1948, by this author and by others. They can be traced through the annual index.

1328. Lüthi, Max. *Es war einmal; vom Wesen des Volksmärchens*. 2nd ed. Göttingen, Vandenhoeck and Ruprecht, 1964. 128p. DLC.

Ten essays, originally given as radio talks to parents and teachers, on the nature of fairy tales.

1329. "Märchenbuchdiskussion," *Börsenblatt für den deutschen Buchhandel*, Leipzig, Jahrgang 119, No. 31, Aug. 2, 1952, pp. 541–544. DLC, NNY.

What value the fairy tale book has in today's society, and how it should be presented to children. The author recommends realistic illustrations in keeping with folk origins.

1330. Maier, Karl Ernst. *Jugendschrifttum*. Bad Heilbrunn, Julius Klinkhardt, 1965. 183p. IYL.

An introduction to the types of juvenile literature, its history and the general trends in the field. There are also sections on the use of children's literature in teaching, and children's books from the viewpoint of the child. The author refers to specific books in his discussions. There is a long list of references and an index.

1331. Maurer, H. *Das Jugendbuch im neuen Reich*. Leipzig, 1934.

1332. Menzel, Wolfgang. "Die Literatur, welche für die Kinder bestimmt ist . . . ," *Die deutsche Literatur*. 2nd ed. Stuttgart, Hallberger, 1836; Vol. 1, Part 2, pp. 76–94. DLC. DLC also has in translation: *German literature;* Boston, Hilliard, Gray and Co., 1840; Vol. 1, pp. 337–352. (Specimens of Foreign Standard Literature, Vol. 7).

An outspoken critic of the didactic, Menzel and his theories were far ahead of the majority of teachers and librarians, whom he berated for writing largely for personal gain. His appraisal here of the market in recreational children's literature is worth quoting (from the English translation): "The entertaining literature for children, properly so called, is still more abundant than the religious. Germany is flooded with it. Here the pedagogues do not labor alone; the matter has been used for book speculations by the publishers. Entire magazines of children's books, as of other children's toys, are established, and a real rivalry in trade is carried on. The book-makers are able to do this, because there is no union among the teachers, and because the love of fashion goes so far, that people will give only new

things to children. About Christmas time the booksellers' shops are overrun with parents and friends of children, who buy up all the brilliant little trifles that the last fair has supplied. The old folks snatch most eagerly at the tinsel, just like the children themselves. But the pedagogues, too, cooperate with the booksellers, and are always writing new things, not to improve what is old, but to get money and a name by them. Against this deluge of children's books the genuine children's friend struggles in vain."

1333. Merget, A. *Geschichte der deutschen Jugendliteratur*. 3rd ed. Berlin, Verlag der Plahn' schen Buchhandlung, 1882. 272p. IYL has Xerograph copy.

"A history of German children's literature." This first appeared in 1867. It covered three periods —the so-called philanthropic (from the school founded by Basedow), the Christian-didactic period which was also the era of the Grimms and the other collectors of *sagen* and *märchen,* and the contemporary period, meaning the 1860's and 1870's, when the children's novel, women writers, poets, and advocates of the realistic school all began to appear. Koester (1295) feels this was a step backwards, from the point of view of criticism, since Merget overstressed the moral and religious aspects of children's literature. There is a name index only.

1334. Metzger, Juliane. "Gute Bücher, frohe Kinder." Special issue of: *Das Seminar,* Witten-Ruhr, Heft 4, 1956? 64p. IYL.

"Good books, happy children." A mother writes of her experience in choosing and sharing books with children. There is an author index to the books referred to in the text. Charmingly illustrated with reproductions from some of the books.

1335. Meyer, Hans Georg. *Pionierleben im Kinderbuch—Gedanken zur deutschen Kinderliteratur der Gegenwart*. Berlin (East), Kinderbuchverlag, 1962.

1336. Meyer-Markau, Wilhelm. *Sozialdemokratische Jugendschriften*. Minden/Westfalen, C. Marowsky, 1898. 36p. (Sammlung pädagogischer Vorträge, Band 11, Heft 12). DLC.

Politics are well and good in their place, but when they usurp the place of literature given to children, it is time for conscientious teachers to speak up, wrote this educator. He gives some examples of Social Democratic party theories which he felt had come to pervade even the simplest ABC and counting books.

1337. Ministerium für Volksbildung and Zentralinstitut für Bibliothekswesen. *Das Kinderbuch in der Feriengestaltung.* Berlin (East), Verlag Volk und Wissen, 1962. 95p.

1338. Minke, Fromut. *Kleinkind und Bilderbuch. Empirische und theoretische Untersuchung des Bilderbuches aus psychologischem und pädagogischem Aspekt.* München, Uni-Druck, 1958. 127p. (Dissertation) IYL.

"The small child and the picture book." Results of a survey made among 3–6 year old children in kindergartens and private homes. Portions of this study also appeared in *Jugendliteratur.*

1339. Mühlenfeld, Johanna. "Aus der deutschen jugendbüchereiarbeit." International Congress of Libraries and Bibliography, 2nd; *Actas y trabajos,* Vol. 3; Madrid, Librería Julián Barbazán, 1936; pp. 262–265. DLC.

Children's libraries are too new and too varying in form and size in Germany to be able to have overall standards, writes the author. However, she continues, with more and more interest on the part of the government, there is certain to be an increase in the work done with youth.

1340. ———. "Aus der ersten städtischen Kinderlesehalle in Berlin," *Blätter für Volksbibliotheken und Lesehallen,* Leipzig, Jahrgang 16, Hefte 3–4, 1915. pp. 37–40. NNY.

A report on the first municipal children's library in Berlin, opened in 1913. Many statistics are included.

1341. ———. *Kinderlesehallen; ihre Einrichtung und ihre Verwaltung.* Stettin, Verlag "Bücherei und Bildungspflege," 1928. 24p. (Volksbibliothekarische Berufskunde, 1).

"Children's libraries; their organization and management." The author writes from experience gained in the Berlin library children's rooms. Bibliography.

1342. Müllermeister, Johann. *Die Jugend- und Volksliteratur.* Aachen, 1886.

1343. Münter, H. A. *Jugend und Zeitung,* 1932.

1344. Muth, Ludwig. *Der Buchhandel und die jungen Leser.* Freiburg/Bresgau, Herder, 1964. 49p. (Jahresgabe für Freunde des Hauses Herder). IYL.

An attempt to analyze the book buying habits of young adults. There are numerous statistical tables, carefully interpreted.

1345. Naumann, Franz. *Jugendfürsorge in den Volksbibliotheken.* Berlin, Weidmannsche Buchhandlung, 1912. 142p. DLC.

The results of an inquiry and questionnaire sent to more than 700 libraries in Germany, with the aim of discovering how many gave service to children, and what kind. A list of the libraries answering is given, together with indications as to whether they maintained children's collections. The last part of the book is an attempt to suggest a basic book collection, for the small library (500 volumes), the medium-sized (2,000 vols.) and the larger (5,000 vols.).

1346. Niegl, Agnes. "Kind und Bilderbuch," *Fortbildungstagung für Kindergärtnerinnen.* Bregenz-Mehrerau, 1956.

1347. Nieland, Wilhelm. *Der Kampf um die Jugendschriften.* Minden/Westfalen, C. Marowsky, [1904]. 32p. (Sammlung pädagogischer vorträge, W. Meyer-Markau. Band 13, Heft 6). DLC.

A defense of Wolgast, his ideas, and the book-list formulated under his direction (1470).

1348. Nürnberg. Stadtbibliothek. *Bibliographie der Nürnberger Kinder- und Jugendbücher 1522–1914.* Bamberg, Meisenbach, 1961. 181p. DLC.

A catalog of the exhibit of Nürnberg children's books 1522–1914, which was arranged in honor of the 300th anniversary of the publication of *Orbis sensualium pictus* by Johann Amos Comenius, often considered the first picture book for children. This exhibit contained 1,667 items, each bibliographically described in the catalog. Reproductions of illustrations from about 20 books are also included. Indexes are very complete.

1349. Oehler, H. J. "Jugend und Buch," *Handbuch der Jugendpflege in Hessen;* Wiesbaden, Landesjugend-Ausschuss Hessen, 1951, pp. 124–129. DLC.

Ways and means of bringing young people and books together. Pp. 181–184 describes the work of the Arbeitsgemeinschaft für Jugendschrifttum, an organization in the state of Hesse which works for the expansion of the children's literature movement.

1350. Palmgren, K. E. "Über Jugendlektüre," *Erziehungsfragen; gesammelte Aufsatze.* Altenburg, Oskar Bonde, 1904, pp. 231–248. DLC.

The author's view was that too few parents knew what their children were reading and that they were especially careless in giving them *märchen* of the wrong kinds at the wrong ages.

1351. Panthen, Herbert. "Lehrerbildung und Jugendbuch; ein Bericht über die Kinderlesestube an der Pädagogischen Hochschule Göttingen," *Bücherei und Bildung,* Reutlinger, Jg. 6, Mar., 1954, pp. 198–203. DLC, NNY.

"The education of teachers and the children's book; a report on the children's library connected with the pedagogical university at Göttingen."

1352.   Pauli, Gustav. "Das Bilderbuch," *Dekorative Kunst,* München, Jahrgang 5, No. 8, May, 1902, pp. 273–299. NNY.

Too often parents think only of the expense (instead of the artistic value) when buying picture books, writes the author. He stresses how important these first books are in building taste, and reviews the artists and styles which best combine child-like quality and fine artistic expression. Four colored plates and 40 black and white reproductions illustrate the examples he describes.

1353.   Pfeiffer, Johannes. *Wege zur Erzählkunst.* 4th ed. Hamburg, Wittig, 1965. 139p. IYL.

"Ways to the art of narration."

1354.   Pleticha, Heinrich. *Begegnungen mit dem Buch in der Jugend.* Reutlingen, Ensslin, 1963. (Ensslin Jahresgabe, 1963).

1355.   ———. *Was soll mein Kind lesen?* München, Manz Verlag, 1959. 64p. (Wir und die Schule, 6). IYL.

Advice to parents on introducing books to children and learning to select them critically.

1356.   Plischke, Hans. *Von Cooper bis Karl May.* Düsseldorf, Droste Verlag, 1951. 208p. DLC.

The adventure novel from Cooper to Karl May, and the reasons for its appeal to young people. The major emphasis is on the "Wild West" novel as it appeared in Germany.

1357.   Popelka, Friedrich. "Jugendschriften bewegung," *Pädagogischer Jahresbericht/Pädagogischer Jahresschau,* Leipzig, Fr. Brandstetter & B. G. Teubner, 1914–1915, pp. 137–145; 1916–1917, pp. 124–129. DLC.

A two-part résumé of the children's literature movement and its activities during the war years. Both have extensive notes on periodical articles, book lists and other material which would be helpful in tracing what books were recommended at the time, and for what reasons.

1358.   Prestel, Josef. *Geschichte des deutschen Jugendschrifttums.* Freiburg/Breisgau, Herder & Co., 1933. 163p. (Handbuch der Jugendliteratur, Part 3). DLC.

This history of German children's literature treats the material in three categories: reading matter of a moral or didactic purpose, folk literature, and reading matter written especially for children, but without specific didactic intent. There are separate chapters on illustration and on contemporary literature. No bibliography, but there is an index.

1359.   ———. *Lesende Jugend.* München, Bayerischer Schulbuchverlag, 1950. 95p. IYL.

1360.   Probst, Hans. *Über den deutschen Märchenstil.* Bamberg, 1901. 28p. (Programm des K. alten Gymnasiums, 1900–1901). IYL.

"On the German folk tale style."

1361.   Prüwer, A. and R. Kanter. "Erzählen von Geschichten nach Bildern - eine Methode der Spracherziehung," *Neue Erziehung in Kindergarten und Heim,* Berlin (East), Jahrgang 15, Heft 24, Dec., 1962, pp. 10–13. DLC.

One of a number of articles on the methods of story-telling effective with very young children. The purposes are usually described as educational, but the recreational factor is not overlooked. Collections of fairy tales and books suitable for reading aloud are reviewed at intervals.

1362.   Raskop, Heinz. *Die Verwaltung der Schülerbücherei.* Langensalza, Beltz, 1929. 28p.

1363.   Rebele, Kasimir. *Die Entwicklung der deutschen Jugendliteratur.* 1894.

1364.   Roderburg, Andreas. "Aufgaben und Ziele der Kinderlesehallen," *Neue Bahnen,* Leipzig, Jg. 30, Heft 11, Nov., 1919, pp. 328–332. NNY.

"The work and aims of the children's library."

1365.   ———. *Jugendlektüre; Geschichte, Wesen und Wert der Jugendschrift.* 1917.

1366.   Rolfus, Hermann. *Verzeichnis ausgewählter Jugendschriften, welche katholische Eltern und Lehrern empfohlen werden können.* 2nd ed. Freiburg im Bresgau, Herder, 1876.

1367.   Rombach, Hans. "Wege und Umwege in der Jugendschriftenfrage," *Literarischer Handweiser,* Freiburg/Breisgau, Jahrgang 63, Heft 9, June 1927, pp. 641–647; Jahrgang 64, Heft 2, Nov. 1927, pp. 97–99. DLC.

In spite of many valuable and practical studies on children's reading interests and needs, there are those who ask the same interminable, abstract questions, far removed from the real world of children. While they are ruminating, a flood of poor quality books is almost engulfing the few excellent works which exist. This critic analyzes such works as Bühler (1171), Busse (1174), Fronemann (1211), and others.

1368. Rougemont, Charlotte. . . . *dann leben sie noch heute. Erlebnisse und Erfahrungen beim Märchenerzählen.* Münster, Aschendorff, 1962. 177p. IYL.

A storyteller writes of how she came to practice this profession, and then gives selections from her journals of the past 15 years, in which she shares some of her wide experience.

1369. Rüttgers, Severin. *Die Blumen des Bösen.* Leipzig, Ernst Wunderlich, 1911.

1370. ———. *Lesebuch und Klassenlektüre.* Bielefeld and Leipzig, Velhagen & Klasing, 1922. 60p. IYL.

"Reading books and class-room reading." Although pedagogical in outlook, this is important as one of a number of writings by this influential educator, who strove to bring art to the methods of teaching reading.

1371. ———. *Literarische Erziehung. Ein Versuch über die Jugendschriftenfrage auf soziologischer Grundlage.* Lagensalza, Verlag von Julius Beltz, 1931. 152p. DLC.

The first part of this study is mostly on child psychology, but the second part is on introducing literature to the child in school. It is theoretical rather than specifically practical.

1372. ———. *Über die literarische Erziehung als ein Problem der Arbeitsschule.* Leipziz, Teubner, 1910. 156p.

1373. Rumpf, Albert. *Kind und Buch.* 2nd ed. Berlin, Bonn. F. Dümmler, 1928. 164p. ICU.

Sub-titled, "The favorite books of German youth from 9 to 16." A survey of the reading interests of children, conducted in various libraries and schools, at different periods. Numerous tables and graphs indicate the results in statistics and percentages, and the text expands on these. A bibliography on pp. 143–154 is very complete in its listing of reading interest studies made in Germany and other countries up to 1928. Subject and name indexes.

1374. Runkel, Christa. *Kennst du schon? Weisst du schon?* Berlin (East), Berliner Stadtbibliothek, 1963. 56p.

A book list for pupils in grades five to seven.

1375. Rutt, Theodor. *Buch und Jugend.* 2nd ed. Konstanz, Friedrich Bahn, 1960. 150p. IYL.

Some of the chapter titles indicate the scope of this work. Youth and language, characteristics of the book, objections to books, methods of reading, motives to read, *ersatz* literature, the nonfiction book, the adventure book, rules for the book critic, etc. There is a name and subject index.

1376. Sallmon, Heinz. *Aufgaben der Schülerbüchereien an den zehnklassigen Oberschulen.* Berlin (East), Verlag Volk und Wissen, 1962. 140p. (Schriftenreihe Ausserunterrichtliche Erziehung und Bildung, 1). DLC.

The tasks of the school library, its organization and functioning. There are also chapters on the meaning of literature to the young, and the means of equipping the student to read good literature. There is also a basic list of books recommended for the school library.

1377. Scheiner, Peter. "Activities in the field of juvenile literature in Germany today," *Bookbird,* Vienna, No. 3, 1965, pp. 9–13. DLC, IYL, NNY.

This issue had several articles on the history and present status of children's books in Germany. Other contributors are Klaus Doderer, Jella Lepman, Walter Scherf and Dieter Gerber. The last named has prepared a useful summary of the history and work of the *Vereinigten Jugendschriften-Ausschüsse* and their reviewing organ, the *Jugendschriftenwarte.* There is also a biography and critical review of the work of Hans Baumann, a leading writer of German children's books.

1378. Scherf, Walter. *Kindermärchen in dieser Zeit? Die psychologischen Seiten der Volksmärchen und ihr erzieherischer Wert.* München, Don Bosco Verlag, 1961. 38p. IYL.

"Fairy tales for children in this era? The psychological view of the folk tale, and its educational value." The author defends the reasons for keeping folk tales true to their original form, in which the stronger emotions (fear, hate, love, etc.) play an important role.

1379. ———. Politische Bildung durch das Jugendbuch? Bestandsaufnahme zu einem actuellen Thema. München, List Verlag, 1963. 94p. (Harms Pädagogische Reihe. Schriften zur Politischen Bildung, 51). IYL.

"Political education through children's books? Taking stock of a given theme." Using specific German children's books as examples, the author attempts to point out how the young person's political ideas (in regard to other places and other times as well as the present) are formed. Almost 250 titles are cited. Author index.

1380. Schierer, Herbert. *Das Zeitschriftenwesen der Jugendbewegung.* Berlin, Adolf Lorentz Verlag, 1938. 114p. (Beiträge zur Erforschung der deutschen Zeitschrift, Band 3). DLC.

A review of children's and young peoples' magazines and newspapers, and the effects this reading has on its subscribers. This is written entirely from the viewpoint of one who has observed the Hitler Youth.

1381. Schmidt, Heiner. *Bilder, Kinder, Jugendbuch; ein kritisches Auswahlverzeichnis: 1948–1958.* Bonn, Köllen, 1959. 150p.

A critical selection of German children's books of the ten year period 1948–1958. Arrangement is by age and subject groups and many are annotated. Each entry is coded for critical reviews in leading periodicals and for appearance in other selective lists of Germany, Austria and Switzerland. The introduction defines the principles of selection.

1382. ———. *Jugendbuch im Unterricht.* Weinheim, Beltz, 1966. 560p. (Earlier edition called *Schulpraktische Jugendlektüre.* Duisberg, Alfons Eidens Verlag, 1960. 374p. DLC, IYL).

A practical handbook intended as a guide to all Austrian, German and Swiss books for children (in German). The more than 3,000 titles are arranged into 9 subjects, with subdivisions in each. Age levels are indicated, and cross-indexing is extensive. Since this is not a selective list, it could prove useful as a general finding list of books from these countries. It does indicate two degrees of superiority for titles which are especially recommended. Prizes won by individual titles are also cited. There is an author and title index. (This note for 1960 edition; 1966 edition not seen.)

1383. Schmidt, Heiner. *Die Lektüre der Flegeljahre.* Duisberg-Beeck, Junge Lesefreunde, 1954. 130p. IYL.

"Reading in the adolescent years." This was prepared for a private book club as a guide to be used by parents, teachers and group leaders in directing the reading of youth.

1384. Schneider, Harriet. *Münchner Bilderbogen in ihrer Wirkung auf Kinder.* Leipzig, Diss., 1947. 141p. IYL has xerograph copy.

1385. Schneider, Julius. *Das Bilderbuch; eine psychologische pädagogische Studie.* Munchen, 1922. Dissertation. IYL has xerograph copy.

1386. Schöne, Annemarie. "Das 'Grausame' im deutschen und englischen literarischen Kinderhumor," *Psychologische Beiträge,* Meisenheim, Band 3, Heft 1, 1957, pp. 108–125. NNY.

The author compares the work of W. Busch, Heinrich Hoffmann's *Struwwelpeter* and the Grimm *Märchen,* with the Mother Goose rhymes, and the poetry of Edward Lear, Lewis Carroll, and Hilaire Belloc. She attempts to analyze some of the reasons children find humor in these works.

1387. *Schöne Kinderbücher aus der DDR.* Berlin (Ost), Kinderbuchverlag, 1965. 152p. IYL.

The fifty titles here chosen from the previous ten years' production, were selected for their attractive illustrations and format. For each one there is a reproduction of the cover and one or two pages of illustrations. The bibliographic descriptions are quite complete. The introduction, by Bruno Kaiser, gives further general information about some of the authors, illustrators and books.

1388. Scholz, Josef and W. Kotzde. *Der Vaterländische Gedanke in der Jugendliteratur.* Mainz, 1912.

1389. Scholz, Karl Christian. *Das deutsche Bilderbuch und sein Verlag.* Mainz, Scholz, 1932. 12p. (Institut für Völkerpädagogik).

1390. Schriewer, Franz. *Das Schülerbüchereiwesen der Volksschulen in Leitungszahlen.* Leipzig, Einkaufshaus für Büchereien, 1938. 44p. DLC.

An analysis of school library work as evidenced by statistics of pupil enrollment, extent of collections, per cent of student use, etc.

1391. ——— and Johannes Langfeldt. *Zur Schülerbüchereifrage.* Stettin, Verlag "Bücherei und Bildungspflege." 1929.

1392. Schröcke, Kurt. *Märchen und Kind.* Leipzig, Wunderlich, 1911. 96p.

1393. *Schüler- und Jugendbücherei.* Bonn, Borromäus Verein, 1960?. 100p.

1394. *Die Schülerbücherei.* Landesanstalt für Erziehung und Unterricht, Hegelplatz 1, Stuttgart. 6 issues yearly. Issued as a supplement to *Schulwarte.* Vol. 1 ff. 1951? ff. Subscription: 1.00 DM per issue.

Reviews of children's books mostly by teachers. Written from the pedagogical point of view.

1395. Schultze, Ernst. *Die Schundliteratur; ihr Wesen, ihre Folge, ihre Bekämpfung.* Halle, Buchhandlung des Waisenhauses, 1909. 114p.

1396.	Schulz, Kurd and Erich Sielaff. *Die Schüler-bücherei in der Volksschule.* Stettin, Verlag "Bücherei und Bildungspflege," 1930. 80p. DLC.

The four parts treat of the purpose, scope of collection, technical organization and use of the school library.

1397.	Schwenke, Martha. "Die bibliothekarische Arbeit an Kindern und Jugendlichen in Deutschland," *Aus dem deutschen Büchereiwesen.* Stettin, Verlag "Bücherei und Bildungspflege," 1929; pp. 27–32. DLC.

A short history of the development of library work with children in Germany.

1398.	Seyfarth, Friedrich. *Führer durch die deutsche Jugendliteratur.* Bühl (Baden), Konkordia, 1928. 211p. IYL.

A booklist with critical comments at the head of each section making comparisons and general suggestions as to the qualities each type of children's literature should have.

1399.	Sielaff, Erich. *300 Bücher für die Schüler-bücherei.* Stettin, Verlag "Bücherei und Bildungspflege," 1930. 80p.

1400.	———. "Das Jugendbuch - eine literarische Lücke," *Heute und Morgen,* Berlin (East), Heft 11, 1949, pp. 683–687. DLC.

The first of many critical articles contributed to this periodical by Sielaff. Others appeared in Heft 8, 1950, pp. 498–503 (on fairy tales); Heft 6, 1952, pp. 376–383 (on the theme of rich and poor in fairy tales); Heft 2, 1953, pp. 121–127 (on picture books); Heft 4, 1953, pp. 250–255 (on novels and stories for children).

1401.	———. *Jungmädchenlektüre. Was lesen unsere Jungmädchen, und was sollen sie lesen?* Stettin, 1933. 23p.

1402.	Siemering, Hertha, *et al. Was liest unsere Jugend?* Berlin, R. von Decker, 1930; 118p. (Veröffentlichen des Preussischen Ministeriums für Volkswohlfahrt, 12). DLC.

"What do our young people read?" Two studies based on questionnaire inquiries, and another surveying the many inquiries on reading interests which already exist.

1403.	Siemsen, Anna. *Die Kunst des Erzählens.* 2nd ed. Bielefeld, Velhagen and Klasing, 1924. 108p. (Bücherei der Volkshochschule, Bund 13).

1404.	Simon, Ilse. *Die neue Kinderliteratur in der Unterstufe.* Berlin (East), Volk und Wissen Volkseigener Verlag, 1965. 104p. IYL.

The aims and meaning of today's children's literature, how to use it in the elementary school, and practical examples of work with children and books. Recommended booklist and bibliography.

1405.	Spohr, Wilhelm. "Künstlerische Bilderbücher." Droescher, Lili, *Die Kunst im Leben des Kindes.* Berlin, Reimer, 1902; pp. 105–154. NNY.

The first picture a child sees can mold his artistic taste for life. Therefore it is important that these books be of the best quality. The Germans have not developed the art of the picture book as extensively as the English and French, writes the author. He gives high praise to their illustrators and reproduces some pages of their work. The concluding pages are an annotated list of 132 recommended picture books in German.

1406.	Stapel, Wilhelm. *Gegen den Missbrauch des Vaterländischen in Jugendschriften.* München, G. D. W. Callwey, 1913. (Dürerbund-Flugschrift, 119).

1407.	Stimpfig, Ernst. *Vom Leseheft zum Taschenbuch; gutes Schrifttum für junge Menschen von 12 bis 18.* Bad Heilbrunn, J. Klinkhardt, 1964. 155p. IYL.

"From reading book to pocket book; good writing for the young adult from 12 to 18." Annotated booklist arranged by period and subject. Publishers specializing in books for youth are listed and described. Short bibliography. Author and subject index.

1408.	Stoy, C. V. *Schrift und Jugend, sonst und jetzt.* 1858.

1409.	*Studien zur Jugendliteratur.* Ratingen, Aloys Henn, Yearly since 1955 (with some exceptions). IYL.

Heft 1–6 were under the editorship of Karl Langosch. Since 1961 Klaus Doderer has carried out the editing of the series. They include:

1410.	Heft 1, 1955, 103p.: "Moderne christliche Jugendbücher" by S. Heuser; "Jugendliteratur über Musik und Musiker" by M. Becker; "Das moderne Backfischbuch" by H. Roos.

1411.	Heft 2, 1956, 108p.: "Das Bild der Frau in den Comics" by T. Brüggemann; "Die Jugendschriftstellerin Lise Gast" by I. Schönbein; "Zum Stil der 'Roten Zora' Kurt Helds" by K. Denk; "Kurt Held . . ." by H. Schönhorst.

1412. Heft 3, 1957, 123p.: "Moderne christliche Jugendbücher für die reifere Jugend" by A. Clotz; "Neuere ausländische Mädchenbücher" by B. Jehmlich; "Neue Indianerbücher" by W. Köhlmann.

1413. Heft 4, 1958, 117p.: "Alma de l'Aigle, ihre Jugendbücher und deren Sprache" by K. Doderer; "Die Jugendbücher Erich Kästners" by E. C. Breul; "Die Dichtung Jeanna Oterdahls" by K. Gehrling.

1414. Heft 5, 1959, 84p.: "Die Problematik der 'Lederstrumpf' Bearbeitung in den westdeutschen Ausgaben" by R. Pasewald; "Die Märchen Ernst Wiecherts" by A. Goeritz; "Phantastische Erzählung für Kinder" by R. Koch.

1415. Heft 6, 1960, 120p.: "Zum Wesen und zur Formung der Missionsliteratur" by G. Iben; "Die Problematik der Weihnachtserzählung in Heften und Anthologien" by E. Ditter; "Weitere Anthologien . . ." by H. Emrich; "Weihnachtsbücher für die Jugend" by G. Voss; "Bibliographie zur Missionsliteratur und Weihnachtserzählung" by C. Engel.

1416. Heft 7, 1961, 78p.: "Das Jugendbuch und die technische Welt" by M. Dierks; "Der junge Leser im Blickfeld der Forschung" by U. Wölfel; "Fabel und Parabel als literarisches Bildungsgut" by W. R. Lehmann; "Untersuchungen zum Wandel der Gedichtmethodik" by A. Baumgärtner; "Einbau der Privatlektüre in der Unterricht" by E. J. Bendl; "Ein Jugendbuch als Klassenlektüre" by E. Jungmann.

1417. Heft 8, 1962, 92p.: "Für eine literarische Verfrühung" by R. Geissler; "Zum Begriff des Nonsense in der englischen Kinderliteratur" by M. Boulby; "Ur- und Endfassung des Grimmschen Märchens 'Hänsel und Gretel' " by E. Winter; "Das politische Sachbuch im Erleben seiner Jugendlichen Leser" by S. Lichtenberger; "Trends im amerikanischen Jugendbuchwesen" by H. Künnemann; "Versuche mit dem zeitgeschichtlichen Jugendbuch in Schule und Jugendgruppe" by H. Schaller; "Zur Frage der Klassen- oder Schulbücherei" by R. Bamberger; "Über die Schulbücherei" by R. Schmidt.

1418. Stümmer, Erich. *Jugendschutz auf dem Gebiet des Schrifttums und der Abbildung*. Köln, Volkswartbund, 1957. 32p.

1419. *Systematik für Kinder- und Jugendbüchereien*. Reutlingen, Bücherei und Bildung, 1964. 18p. IYL.

A system for cataloguing children's books according to a code of letters and numbers, much simpler than the decimal classification system.

1420. Terrasa Mescha, Ruth. "A raíz de la inauguración de la biblioteca popular infantil-juvenil de Friburgo (Alemania)," *Biblioteconomía*, Barcelona, Año 16, No. 50, July–Dec., 1959, pp. 140–143. DLC.

A description of the newly opened library for youth and children in Freiburg/Bresgau.

1421. Tetzner, Lisa. *Vom Märchenerzählen im Volke*. Jena, Diederichs, 1925. 65p.

This is the first of three volumes in which a well-known writer and storyteller reminisces about the first time she went out into remote villages and farm areas of Thuringia, telling stories to the children (and the grown-ups). The 2nd and 3rd volumes describe later similar "wanderings."

1422. Thalhofer, Franz Xaver. *Die Jugendlektüre*. 2nd ed. Paderborn, Schöningh, 1925. 168p. (Handbücherei der Erziehungswissenschaft, Band 10). IYL has xerograph copy.

The three sections cover the history, fundamental principles, and practical use of children's reading matter. This brings up suggestions for use in the home, school, in the theater, and other cultural outlets. Booklists and periodicals for children are covered in separate chapters. Bibliography.

1423. ———. *Sind Jugendschriften von literarischen oder erzieherischen Gesichtspunkten zu beurteilen?* 2nd ed. Berlin, Kribe Verlag, 1916. 15p. (Die Jugendschriftenfrage, 1). IYL has xerograph copy.

"Should writing for children be judged from the literary or the educational point of view?" The author's conclusion is that both literary (aesthetic) and educational (ethical) are important, and the best children's books are those which combine the two purposes in a natural manner.

1424. Theden, Dietrich. *Die deutsche Jugendliteratur*. 2nd ed. Hamburg, Berendsohn, 1893. 144p. IYL has xerograph copy. (1st ed., 1883).

In Part A, a discussion of the criteria of judging children's literature, the author writes of its three main purposes: to amuse, to ennoble, to educate. He gives suggestions on using books with children and organizing and maintaining a children's library. Part B is an annotated book list divided into three age groups (6–9 yrs., 10–14 yrs., 15–18 yrs.) and sub-divided into types of literature. There is an author index only.

1425. ———. "Die Litteratur für unsere Jugend,"

Allgemeine deutsche Lehrerzeitung, Leipzig, Jahrgang 36, No. 8, 1884, pp. 61–66. DLC.

The author defends here his definition of good children's literature, as set forth in his book (above). His ideas had come under attack because of being misunderstood. He explains here in greater detail the characteristics mentioned in his book.

1426. Tholuck, A. "Über die Literatur unserer Jugend-schriften in christlicher Beziehung . . . ," *Litterarischer Anzeiger,* Halle, No. 21, Apr. 9, 1832, pp. 161–166; No. 22, Apr. 14, 1832, pp. 169–173. DLC.

"Children's literature consists of those reading books which youth turn to outside the school, to help them in their learning and to entertain themselves," writes this educator. He goes on to discuss specifically those books which used Christian moral values to instruct and inspire the young mind.

1427. Thormählen. *Jugend-Bibliothek-Prospekt.* 1869.

1428. Touaillon, Christine. "Literarische Strömungen im Spiegel der Kinderliteratur," *Zeitschrift für den deutschen Unterricht* (*Zeitschrift für Deutschkunde*), Leipzig, Jahrgang 26, 1912, pp. 90–97, 145–158. NNY.

There has always been a children's literature, but each age has known it under different forms. During the age of rationalism, educators tried to suppress it, but the succeeding age of romanticism only brought it out in greater amounts. This critic then compares some of the works of the two ages. Reviews of children's books appeared frequently in this periodical.

1429. "Über Jugendlektüre," *Allgemeine deutsche Lehrerzeitung,* Leipzig, Jahrgang 39, No. 38, 1887, pp. 361–364; No. 39, pp. 369–372. DLC.

An editorial advising teachers and parents to oversee if, what and how their children were reading. The author recommended at most one hour free reading per day. "Reading is entirely a matter of work, not play," he wrote.

1430. *Über Jugendschriften und Schüler-bibliotheken.* Witten, R. Gräfe.

1431. Ulshöfer, Robert. *Das gute Jugendbuch.* Stuttgart, Klett, 1957. 120p. IYL.

1432. Vaupel, Karl. *Die Jugendschrift im Auftrag der Erziehung.* Hamburg, 1950. (Westermann's Pädagogische Beiträge, 6).

1433. Vereinigung des Berliner Lehrervereins. *Kind und Kunst.* Braunschweig, Westermann, 1928. 300p. (Beiträge zur Jugendschriftenbewegung).

1434. Voigt, M. *Das deutsche Kinderbilderbuch.* Hamburg, 1950. Dissertation.

1435. *Volksgut im Jugendbuch. Märchen - Heldensage - Volksbuch.* Reutlingen, Ensslin & Laiblin, 1952. 80p. (Jahresgabe). IYL.

Essays by E. Mudrak, H. Kuhn and L. Mackensen on the *märchen, sagen,* and other folk literature of Germany.

1436. Wackernagel, K. E. Ph. [Jugendliteratur]. *Handbuch deutscher Prosa.* 1837.

1437. Wagner, Paul. *Die Schülerbücherei in der Volksschule.* Leipzig, Dürr, 1930. 141p.

1438. ———— and W. Hofmann. *Richtlinien zur Einrichtung und Ausgestaltung der Schülerbüchereien in den Volksschulen.* Leipzig, Deutsche Zentralstelle für Büchereiwesen, 1929.

1439. Weber, Helmut. *Das Jugendbuch im Urteil seiner Leser.* Reutlingen, Ensslin & Laiblin, 1954. 80p. (Jahresgabe). DLC.

For many years this publisher put postal cards in its children's books, on which were a few questions the children were asked to answer, e.g., "Did you like this book or not?" "What other books have you liked?" From the thousands returned, 5,000 cards were chosen for their completeness, and the results were analyzed in general terms.

1440. Wedding, Alex. "Der Schrei nach dem Mädchenbuch," *Neue deutsche Literatur,* Berlin (East), Jahrgang 2, No. 2, Feb. 1954, pp. 164–167. DLC.

It is useless to say that girls can read the same things as boys. Too many are turning to "Western" ideas because they are not given good girls' stories of literary quality showing what life really is like and what it can bring.

1441. *Wege zum guten Jugendbuch.* Nürnberg, Sebaldus Verlag, 1961. 47p. IYL.

In commemoration of 50 years of publishing, this house sponsored a prize for the best children's book manuscript which would help youth come to better realization of self and the surrounding world. The prize was shared by two authors, Hans Peter Richter and Thomas Zacharias, for their individual works. Reprinted here are the terms of the award, short biographies of the two winners; an article on political books for youth by Horst Schaller; one on the nonfiction book by Heinrich Pleticha; and a brief history of Nürnberg children's books by Carl-Günther Schmidt.

1442. Weihrauch, Gustav. "Über Bilderbücher," *Versuche und Ergebnisse,* 3rd ed., Hamburg, 1902.

1443. Weismantel, Leo. *Über die geistesbiologischen Grundlagen des Lesegutes der Kinder und Jugendlichen.* Augsburg, Benno Filser, 1931. 290p. ICU.

In August, 1928, a group of 80 teachers, etc., met to discuss this subject. It was then 30 years since the first work of Wolgast. However, the group came to the conclusion that the fight against poorly written, cheap books for children had to be carried out as vigilantly as before. What the country needed was a central place which could direct this work, rather than the fragmentary, if noble, ventures of the many organizations and individuals heretofore active in the field. This book aims at carrying out the ground work, and includes sections by leading critics and experts on the history, theory and practice of good writing for children. Also included are the answers officially stated in the return of the questionnaire sent out by the International Bureau of Education (see 28). The bibliography of materials on children's books and reading (pp. 237–249) is divided into such categories as the psychological, literary and aesthetic approaches, the school reader, book lists, school and children's libraries. The concluding list of recommended books for children up to 18 years is arranged by age and subject, and has at the end a list of source material on puppetry and theater for children. No indexes.

1444. *Weisse liste; gutes Jugendschrifttum 19—.* Frankfurt/Main, Deutsches Jugendschriftenwerk, 1960 ff. Annual. IYL.

A selective list made for use by children with annotations.

1445. Weissert, Elisabeth. *Vom abenteuer des Lesens.* Stuttgart, Verlag Freies Geistesleben, 1959. 80p. DLC.

Essays which appeared in the periodical *Erziehungskunst,* and which treat of "Fairy Tales," "Storytelling in the home," "Historical stories," "Picture books," and other themes of interest to parents.

1446. Wenk, Walter. *Das Volksmärchen als Bildungsgut.* Langensalza, H. Beyer & Söhne, 1929. 126p. (Erziehungswissenschaftliche Arbeiten, Heft 9; Mann's Pädagogisches Magazin, Heft 1254). ICU.

"The folk tale as educational material." Part one is on the basis and methods of criticism of juvenile literature in general. Part two considers the folk tale and its place in juvenile literature. The index is only to individual tales mentioned, and there is a one-page bibliography.

1447. Wentzel, C. A. *Die Entwicklungsgeschichte der deutschen Jugendschriftenliteratur.* Minden/Westfalen, Bruns Verlag, 1888.

1448. *Werke der Weltliteratur für die Jugend.* Reutlingen, Ensslin & Laiblin, 1951. 84p. (Jahresgabe). IYL.

Studies of some adult works which came to be almost universally used with young people, and some reasons why. Included in the discussions are *Robinson Crusoe,* the Leatherstocking tales of Cooper, *Moby Dick,* and *Simplizius Simplizissimus* by Grimmelshausen.

1449. Wewel, Meinolf. *Anregungen und Vorschläge zur Jugendbuchwoche und zu anderen Veranstaltungen.* Stuttgart, Arbeitskreis für Jugendschrifttum, 1961. 93p. IYL.

"Ideas and suggestions for a children's book week and other events." The author indicates the careful preparation necessary to make such events successful in the right way.

1450. Wiącek, H. "Bibliotekarskie dziesięciolecie NRD," *Bibliotekarz,* Warszawa, Rok 28, No. 4, 1961, pp. 119–124. DLC, NNY.

"Children's libraries in the German Democratic Republic." A review of public library work with children during the previous ten years.

1451. Wiegand, Ludwig. *Die deutsche Jugendliteratur.* Hilchenbach, Verlag von L. Wiegand, 1903. 128p. DLC.

A history of German children's literature followed by the principles of criticism used in judging books for children, and finally advice on the use of these books in the home and school.

1452. Wiegel, A. *Das Kinderbuch der guten alten Zeit.* Leipzig, 1905. Dissertation. IYL has xerograph copy.

1453. Wildner, Adolf. *Die Jugendliteratur.* Reichenberg, Paul Sollors, 1937. 72p. IYL.

A very general survey of the history and general qualities of children's literature followed by a recommended list of books.

1454. Wille, Hermann Heinz. "Für das Glück unserer Kinder!" *Börsenblatt für den deutschen Buchhandel,* Leipzig, Jahrgang 120, No. 22, May 30, 1953, pp. 429–430. DLC, NNY.

"For the happy future of our children!" Report on children's literature in connection with International Children's Day, June 1. Followed by reviews of new books for young people, pp. 431–434.

1455. Willmann, O. "Volksmärchen und Robinson als Bildungsstoffe," *Pädagogische Vorträge* 2nd ed. Leipzig, Gustav Gräbner, 1886, pp. 17–34. DEW.

Folk tales are ideal reading material for children because they are characterized by the five qualities appealing to the young. They are child-like, morally constructive, of lasting value, instructive, and have a coherent unity.

1456. Winker, Wilhelm. *Die Jugendbücherei; Grundsätzliches und Praktisches.* Düsseldorf, Verlag des Landesjugendamtes, 1928. 28p.

1457. Wolfersdorf, Peter. *Märchen und Sage in Forschung, Schule und Jugendpflege.* Braunschweig, Waisenhaus Buchdruckerei, 1958. 189p. (Schriftenreihe der Pädagogischen Hochschule Braunschweig, Heft 7). IYL.

"Folk tales and *Sagen* in research, school and youth care." Only portions of this study are of interest to the person working directly with children and books. The general approach is psychological-folkloristic. There is an extensive bibliography.

1458. Wolgast, Heinrich. *Das Elend unserer Jugendliteratur.* 7th ed. Worms, Ernst Wunderlich, 1950. 351p. IYL. NNY and DLC have 6th ed., 1921. (1st ed., 1896).

This is the most important and influential book on the theory of children's literature written in the German language. The author was an educator who shaped the trends in children's books through an organization of teachers (the Vereinigten Jugendschriften-Ausschüsse) united for the purpose of bringing about a better literature for children. This organization, through its organ *Jugendschriftenwarte,* became the most authoritative voice in the criticism of children's books, giving the teachers of Germany a position similar to that of children's librarians in other countries. Wolgast's prose was lively and he was not afraid of taking on controversial aspects. His opinion of the contemporary literature for children can be surmised from the title—"The misery of our children's literature." He was to campaign all his life for a more aesthetic, literary approach to children's books.

1459. ———. *Das religiöse und patriotische in der Jugendschrift.* Erlangen, E.Th. Jacob, 1900. 20p. IYL.

"Religious and patriotic elements in juvenile literature." A speech given at a meeting of Munich teachers in December 1899, and first printed in *Freie bayerische Schulzeitung.*

1460. ———. *Über Bilderbuch und Illustration.* Hamburg, Selbstverlag, 1894. 22p. DLC.

"On picture books and illustration," a reprint from the No. 1 and No. 2 issues of *Jugendschriftenwarte.* This is an anguished cry of outrage at the poor taste exhibited in the design and illustration of German picture books. Crane, Caldecott, Greenaway and other English illustrators were cited as examples of excellence in this art form.

1461. ———. "Ein verhängnisvoller Irrtum in der Beurteilung der Jugendliteratur," *Magazin für Literatur,* Berlin, Jahrgang 61, No. 23, June 4, 1892, pp. 365–367. DLC.

The first article to appear in print by Wolgast in which he formulated the ideas later expanded in his book (1458), namely, that the wretchedness of quality in children's literature was the cause of much that was lacking in the literary education of young people, and that the teachers and parents perpetrated the continuance of such literature by their lack of criticism when judging the children's book.

1462. ———. *Vom Kinderbuch.* 2nd ed. Leipzig, B. G. Teubner, 1906. 140p. DLC.

Selections from the author's writings on children's literature which first appeared in various periodicals, pamphlets or as speeches. They treat of such aspects as teen-age girls' stories, picture book illustration, children's songs, the meaning of the public library for children, the organization of the school library, religious and patriotic motives for children's literature, and several others.

1463. Wostrischew, J. "Die schöne Literatur und ihre Rolle in der Jugenderziehung," *Junge Generation,* Berlin (East), Jahrgang 6, Heft 4, Beilage. (Heft des Propagandisten, 11). DLC.

"Belles-lettres and their role in the education of youth."

1464. *Zehn Jahre deutscher Jugendbuchpreis: 1956–1965.* München, Arbeitskreis für Jugendschrifttum, 1966. 104p. IYL.

An introductory section gives the history, aims and accomplishments of the Arbeitskreis für Jugendschrifttum, a federation made up of 37 German organizations interested in furthering the cause of good children's books. One of the main tasks of the Arbeitskreis is to select the prize books to be honored by the national government, through the Ministry for Family and Juvenile affairs. The means and standards of selection are explained. The prize books in each category are then listed. This is one of the few countries which does not require that the book be a native work, and more than 50% of the prize books have been translations. Included in this catalog is a selective list of some 400 books of the same period. There is also a bibliography, pp. 22–28. Author and illustrator index.

1465. Zentralinstitut für Bibliothekswesen. *Die Arbeit mit dem Kinderbuch in der Aktion "Frohe Ferientage für alle Kinder 1955"; Anleitungen für Veranstaltungen*. Berlin (East), 1955. 71p. DLC.

Suggestions for storytelling, reading aloud, simple dramatic pieces, puppet shows, and other group work to be used in bringing children and books together during the special summer vacation programs in camps sponsored by the "Pioneer" groups or other agencies in East Germany.

1466. ———. *Bücher zeigen dir die Welt; Sachliteratur für Kinder*. Leipzig, VEB Bibliographisches Institut, 1965.

"Books show you the world; nonfiction for children."

1467. ———. *Illustrierte Kinderbuchbibliographie*. Berlin (East). 1953 ff. Annually.

1468. Zeynek, Gustav. *Über Errichtung und Einrichtung von Volkschulbibliotheken*. Teschen, Prochaska, 1875.

1469. Zimmermann, Josef. *Vorlesestunden und Volksbildungsabende*. 2nd ed. Bonn, Verlag des Borromäusvereins, 1931.

1470. *Zur Jugendschriftenfrage*. 2nd ed. Leipzig, E. Wunderlich, 1906. IYL. 1st ed., 1903.

Essays and a recommended booklist, compiled by the Vereinigte Jugendschriften-Ausschüsse.

Switzerland

Because it is a country with a history of political, economic and social stability for more than a century, Switzerland has distinct advantages over many other countries of similar size and population. In the realm of books, however, this size and number of peoples is a slight disadvantage, because books involve language and Switzerland uses four official tongues. This means that she must develop separate literatures for each, and the effort required to produce good work in each of the four cultural and linguistic sections is considerable. Because these peoples guard their heritage so carefully, they cannot be satisfied entirely with translations and rightly so. Although the number of children's books produced annually in Romansch and Italian is very small, these books are usually the products of local or regional talent, and as such reflect very intimately the daily lives of these folk.

This regionalism due to language and culture patterns is emphasized even more in the educational systems, which differ from canton to canton. It is the canton's responsibility to provide for cultural and educational services. Some are more advanced in their theories than others, but so far, there has been little discussion of centralization or sharing of technical details. Perhaps there are just too many individuals who do not wish to give up any control of their materials, at any level. It makes for a great deal of repetition to have 16 reviewing committees, for example, but seemingly it is what is wanted and needed. This does hamper school and public library development because a modest staff is not able to cope with book selection and processing and distribution. Central units where books could be reviewed, catalogued and prepared for use (as in Sweden and Denmark) might bring a marked improvement in service to Swiss children.

There are three major organizations working on a national level for the improvement of children's books. The newest of these is the Schweizerischer Bund für Jugendliteratur (Swiss League for Juvenile Literature). Founded in 1955, it also comprises the Swiss National Section of IBBY, and is made up of individual membership from all levels of society and embracing all aspects of work with children's books. Within the League are cantonal groups, but only in some five of the 25 cantons. The League is very active in the publication of selective book lists, in arranging for lectures and conferences on juvenile literature, and in general promotion of good children's reading.

The largest and oldest of the organizations is the Jugendschriftenkommission des Schweizerischen Lehrervereins (Juvenile Literature Committee of the Swiss Teacher's Union). The Teacher's Union has had a committee of this type since 1858, which published guidelines and recommended lists of books in the Union's official periodical (1521). They also co-sponsor touring exhibitions of children's books and award the Children's Book Prize of 1,000 francs to a living Swiss author for one outstanding book or for an entire oeuvre.

The third agency is the Schweizerische Jugendschriftenwerk, founded in 1932. This was established to initiate the production of pamphlets and booklets of the best quality, which could be sold for about the same amount as comics and mass magazines. Leading authors and illustrators were asked to contribute and by the end of 1965 there were some 923 titles which had been published: 548 in German, 210 in French, 126 in Italian and 39 in Romansch. The most popular ones are reprinted over and over. In all, more than 19 million copies have been sold.

There are many other smaller groups working in the field of children's literature. In Zürich, Dr. Franz Caspar is hoping to set up an Institut für Jugendbuchforschung similar to that in Frankfurt, Germany. Religious and women's organizations often have as part of their aims the spread of good books and reading materials to children.

As was noted above, school and public library service to children is far behind what it should be in such an advanced nation. Only the cantons of Zürich and Bern can be said to have adequate, in places outstanding, libraries. A concerted effort to train teacher-librarians and to open new libraries has resulted in Bern's taking the lead in this field. To serve the many English-speaking children of Zürich, the American Women's Club and other private agencies got together and formed a library out of donations, gifts and exchanges. Rural children in Switzerland are also beginning to get service through the central Schweizerischer Volksbibliothek. These are localized efforts, and they do not cover a large proportion of the children. Because cantons are responsible in this area as well, it is not possible to set up legislation on a national level, except in an advisory capacity.

As in Austria and Germany, the largest percentage of children's books is bought for the child in the home. There is a fair amount of exporting and importing by agreement among these three countries, so that the German-speaking child has a wide choice of current books from which to choose. In Switzerland alone some 289 titles were published in 1965. Almost one-half were translations. The French, Italian and Romansch titles numbered 30, eight and six respectively. Of course, French and Italian books are also imported to cater to the additional needs of these children. Only the Romansch child has a very limited choice, but often he reads in one of the other languages as well.

Mrs. Hürlimann discusses the history of children's books in Switzerland in one of the chapters of her book on European children's literature. Since this is also available in English there is not much point in including here a chronological outline. She points out the authors who have used their Swiss heritage to enrich their books and make them so typically local and yet so universal. There is also a chapter on the picture book, and certainly some Swiss children's books in this form have been outstanding models of taste and artistry. The work of the best illustrators has come to be known in many countries, so that Hans Fischer, Alois Carigiet and Felix Hoffman are interpreting both old and new tales for children who read them in their own languages and versions. It seems highly appropriate that this country of great natural beauty should also give the world's children picture books that are equally fresh and inviting.

It is not possible to discuss any phase of children's education or culture in Switzerland without mentioning the name of the influential educator, Johann Heinrich Pestalozzi. Hampered by an erratic temperament, he nevertheless conveyed such insight and understanding in his theories of educating children, that his indirect contribution to a natural, spontaneous children's literature cannot be overlooked. The Pestalozzianum in Zürich, his birthplace, maintains a library on education and related subjects. It also has a central children's library with many branches and reading rooms scattered throughout Zürich. There is also a Pestalozzi youth library in Neuchâtel.

1471.   Angst, Anny. *Die religions- und moralpäda-gogische Jugendschrift in der deutschen Schweiz von der Reformation bis zur Mitte des 19. Jahrhunderts.* Zürich, Fluntern, 1947. 148p. Dissertation. IYL, DLC.

A study on religious and moral literature for children in German-speaking Switzerland from the Reformation to the middle of the 19th century, undertaken as part of the author's doctoral work at Zürich University. Pp. 135–148 are a bibliography of the children's books and source materials consulted.

1472.   Beit, H. *Symbolik des Märchens.* Bern, Francke, 1952. 792p.

1473.   *Les bons livres français choisis pour nos enfants.* Vevey, Klausfelder, 19? 38p.

1474.   *Das Buch dein Freund.* Bern, Schweizerischer Bund für Jugendliteratur. Yearly, 1964 ff. IYL.

A very attractive pamphlet reproducing many illustrations and selections from recent children's books, as an invitiation to children to turn to the original.

1475.   *Bücher für die Jugend.* Zürich, Schweizerischer Lehrerverein, 1957 ff. Bi-annually. IYL has 1957, 1960, 1962, 1964, 1966.

This attractive booklist is published in cooperation with the juvenile literature commissions of German-speaking Switzerland. On the first two, the Swiss Booksellers and Publishers Union also co-operated. Forerunner of this list was *Das gute Jugendbuch* (see 1487). Each issue gives a complete list of prize-winning Swiss children's books. There are annotations and many reproductions.

1476.   Burkhalter, Gertrud. "Vorbereitung und Durchführung der Kinder Vorlesestunden," *Vereinigung schweizerischer Bibliothekare, Nachrichten,* Bern, Jahrgang 34, Jan., 1958, pp. 14–22. DLC.

"Preparation for and carrying out of the children's story hour." A detailed list of suggestions.

1477.   Colombo, Felicina. "De bons livres pour les enfants entre douze et quinze ans," *Études pédagogiques,* Lausanne, 1954, pp. 79–90. DLC, NNY.

It is most difficult to select books for children aged 12 to 15. In order to discover some of the broad reading interests of this age group, the author conducted a survey in the schools of Italian-speaking Switzerland. She summarizes the results in this article.

1478.   Cornioley, Hans. *Notwendigkeit, Aufgaben und Grenzen der Jugendbuchkritik.* Zürich, Conzett and Huber, 1959. 19p.

Reprinted from the *Schweizerischer Lehrerzeitung.*

1479.   Donzé, Fernand. "La bibliothèque et l'école," *Nouvelles de l'association des bibliothecaires suisses,* Berne, Jahrgang 42, No. 2, 1966, pp. 54–59. NNY.

A librarian reports on the way in which the public library cooperates with the schools in La Chaux-de-Fonds.

1480.   Ebersold, Walter. *Unsere Märchen.* Zürich, Roter Reiter, n.d. 63p. NNY.

"Our fairy tales; a short introduction to their allegorical metaphorical language and their folk meaning."

1481.   *Einrichtung der Jugendbibliotheken und die Auswahl zweckmässiger Schriften für dieselben.* Zürich, Schweizerischer Lehrerverein, 1858.

1482.   *Empfehlenswerte neue Jugendbücher.* Zürich, Schweizerischen Katholischen Arbeitsgemeinschaft für das Jugendschriftenwesen, Yearly, 1956 ff. IYL.

An annotated list of juvenile books recommended by the Swiss Catholic Organization for Juvenile Literature.

1483.   Epstein, Eugene V. "American books for American children in Switzerland." *Publishers' weekly,* New York, Vol. 189, No. 2, Jan. 10, 1966, pp. 64–65. DLC, NNY.

A description of a children's library in Zurich which is open to any children who wish to read in English.

1484.   Follen, August Adolf Ludw. *Bildersaal deutscher Dichtung.* Winterthur, Steinerischen Buchhandlung, 1828. 2 vols. 336p. and 426p. MHU.

This teacher was one of the first to recognize the importance of using poetic literature with youth. His foreword, Vol. 1, pp. ix–liv, contains convincing arguments on the necessity of awakening and building up of the imaginative powers in young people. He felt this could best be accomplished through reading aloud and reciting the great epics and oral masterpieces, and he gave suggestions on how to do so, using the material in these two volumes.

1485.   Gardy, Denise. "Les bibliothèques de jeunesse en Suisse," *Nouvelles de l'association des bibliothecaires suisses,* Berne, Jahrgang 42, No. 2, 1966, pp. 49–53. NNY.

A city by city and canton by canton review of library services to the young.

1486.   ———. "Switzerland," *Library service to children,* 2. Lund, Bibliotekstjänst, 1966, pp. 62–67. DLC, NNY.

This publication was sponsored by IFLA (see 32). In this chapter the general history and present status of library work with children in Switzerland is surveyed.

1487.   *Das gute Jugendbuch.* Zürich, Jugendschriftenkommission des Schweizerischen Lehrervereins, 1930–1953. Bi-annually. IYL has sample.

This important list appeared in a revised edition every two years. It has now been superseded by *Bücher für die Jugend.*

1488.   Hürlimann, Bettina. "Schweizerische Kinderbücher einst und jetzt," *Der schweizer Buchhandel,* Bern Jahrgang 21, No. 22, Nov. 15, 1963, pp. 795–799. DLC, NNY.

On the occasion of a children's book exhibition in Hanover, Mrs. Hürlimann delivered this address on some of the Swiss exhibit of old and new books, mostly picture books. This periodical is the official organ of the Swiss book trade, and lists the children's books published each month, in a separate section. This has been done since 1943.

1489.   "Die Jugend und ihre Lektüre." Entire issue of: *Pro juventute,* Zürich, Jahrgang 35, No. 2–3, Feb.–Mar., 1954, pp. 37–152. IYL.

This issue contains many short articles on work with children's books in Switzerland from the point of view of publisher, author or illustrator, librarian, teacher, parent. The articles are in German, French and Italian. There is a bibliography on pp. 108–112 which includes many periodical articles concerning Swiss children's books and libraries.

1490.   *Jugend und Lektüre. Vorträge gehalten am Jugendbuchkurs 1956 der Jugendschriftenkommission des Schweizerischen Lehrervereins.* Zürich, Bühler, 1957. 127p. (Schriften des Schweizerischen Lehrervereins, 31). IYL.

"Youth and reading. Lectures delivered during the course given in 1956 by the children's literature committee of the Swiss Teachers' Association." In addition to the general problems of children's literature, these speeches are concerned with comics, with theater for children and also public school and youth libraries.

1491.   "Die Jugendbibliothek," *Vereinigung schweizerischer Bibliothekare, Nachrichten,* Bern, Jahrgang 35, No. 2, Mar.–Apr., 1959, pp. 33–46. DLC.

A special issue devoted to children's libraries. Includes articles on the Pestalozzi library in Neuchâtel, children's library work in German-speaking Biel, and on the organization and statistics of work with children carried out in all the cantons through book boxes selected by the Library Association.

1492.   *Das Jugendbuch.* Jugendschriftenkommission des Schweizerischen Lehrervereins. Zürich. 6 times yearly. Vol. 1, 1935—? Defunct.

1493.   "Jugendliteratur." *Moderne Formen der Jugendbildung.* Zürich, Artemis Verlag, 1958. pp. 15–71. IYL.

Children's literature and libraries as modern forms of cultural education. Great emphasis is placed here on the necessity of curbing comics and cheap serial publications.

1494.   "Jugendliteratur und Jugendlektüre." Special issue of: *Schweizerische Lehrerzeitung,* Zürich, No. 19, May 8, 1964.

1495.   *Jugendschriften-Fragen.* Zürich, Fachschriften Verlag, 1947. 72p. IYL.

A collection of essays on the introduction to problems and questions of juvenile literature.

1496.   Kessi, Mary. "Children's library service,

European style, in Zürich," *Top of the news,* Chicago, Vol. 12, Dec., 1955, pp. 11–13. DLC, NNY.

A description of the children's libraries managed by the Pestalozzihaus.

1497.   *Kind und Buch.* Zürich, 1962. 68p. (Schriften des Schweizerischen Lehrervereins, Nr. 36). IYL.

The papers delivered at the youth literature course held by the juvenile literature committee of the Swiss Teachers' Association in 1962. Heinrich Altherr, Hans Zulliger, Walter Klauser and Hans Cornioley were the speakers.

1498.   Klausmeier, Ruth-Gisela. *Völkerpsychologische Probleme in Kinderbüchern.* Bonn, Bouvier, 1963. 111p. IYL, NNY, DLC. (Abhandlung zur Philosophie, Psychologie und Pädagogik, Band 25).

A comparison of English, French and Swiss German children's books as they reflect such social and psychological aspects as "the relationship of the child to his world," "the group," "I-and-you," etc. About 75 books from each country are used as examples with the majority being from current production.

1499.   Koch, Margrit. "Die Solothurner Jugendbibliothek," *Vereinigung schweizerischer Bibliothekare, Nachrichten,* Bern, Jahrgang 36, No. 2, 1960, pp. 49–53. DLC.

A description of the new children's library in Solothurn, which is housed in a former ballroom next to the central library. Two photographs of this attractive library follow p. 56.

1500.   Kraut, Dora. *Die Jugendbücher in der deutschen Schweiz bis 1850.* Bern, Schweizer Bibliophilen Gesellschaft, 1945. 89p. (Bibliothek des Schweizer Bibliophilen, Serie 2, Heft 17). IYL, NNY.

"A history of children's books in German-speaking Switzerland up to 1850," together with a chronological catalog of 316 books printed in Switzerland from the early 17th century to 1850. Descriptions are complete, but the books are not annotated.

1501.   Krebser, H. *Die erste Jugendbuchwoche im Kanton Zürich.* Zürich, 1958. 36p. IYL.

"The first children's book week in Canton Zürich. Experiences gained for further work with reading children." There are three articles by Fritz Brunner.

1502.   Larese, Dino. *Schweizer Jugendschriftsteller der Gegenwart.* St. Gallen?, Amriswiler Bücherei, 1963. 114p. DLC.

"Swiss children's authors of the present

day." Biographies of almost 70 writers with lists of their works, and a photograph portrait of each. The text is in German, but authors writing in Italian and French are also included.

1503. Lévy, Bernard. *Vers la création d'une bibliothèque enfantine*. Neuchâtel, Delachaux & Niestlé, 1952. 28p. DLC.

In her preface to this work, Elisabeth Clerc writes that there were at that time only five public libraries in French Switzerland which had children's rooms. These essays by M. Lévy were written for various papers, stressing the importance of public interest in the wider establishment of children's rooms.

1504. *Livres pour la jeunesse*. Genève, Librairie Ancienne F. Baumgartner, n.d. 21p. DLC.

A bookseller's catalog of early French and Swiss books for children. Mainly of historical interest. Author, title and price are the only information given.

1505. *Les livres suisses choisis pour les enfants*. Vevey-Montreux, Association "Morges," 1925. 10p.

1506. Maier, F. G. and E. Waldmann. "Was lesen die Kinder einer schweizer Stadt?" *Jugendliteratur*, München, Jahrgang 7, Heft 11, 1961, pp. 507–514. IYL.

A fairly extensive reading interest survey undertaken among the children of one Swiss city (Biel). Specific authors and titles are cited. There is also a list of children's book reviewing committees of various organizations in Switzerland.

1507. Maier, Franz Georg. "Was lesen unsere kinder?" *Vereinigung schweizerischer Bibliothekare, Nachrichten,* Bern, Jahrgang 37, No. 2, 1961, pp. 33–54. DLC.

"What do our children read?" The results of an inquiry and questionnaire answered by 1500 children of the city Biel, and some general comments on the "universal classics" as well as recent children's books.

1508. Matthey. *Das Kinder- und Jugendbuch, seine pädagogische und künstlerische Entwicklung.* Basel, Gewerbemuseum, 1943–1944.

1509. Meyer, Olga. *Die Bedeutung guter Jugendliteratur.* Zürich, Pro Juventute, 1951.

1510. Michaelis-Jena, Ruth. "Reflections on children's books," *Publishers' circular,* Kent, Vol. 165, Sept. 15, 1951, pp. 1225–1227. DLC, NNY.

Some comments about the first Swiss Children's Book Week, and the activities connected with it. Mention is also made of the national contest conducted in Germany, "The Book I Liked Best."

1511. Moor, Emmy. *Jugendgefährdung-Jugendschutz; zum Problem Schund und Kitsch.* Zürich, Kommissionsverlag der Genossenschaftsbuchhandlung, 1954. 56p. IYL.

A conference on the problem of comics, smutty and trashy literature for youth sponsored by the Swiss Union of Public Workers.

1512. *Nachrichten des schweizerischen Bundes für Jugendliteratur.* Herzogstrasse 5, Bern. Quarterly. Vol. 1 ff. Dec., 1955 ff. Subscription included in annual membership of 4 S. Fr.

"Newsletter of the Swiss League for Juvenile Literature." This does not contain regular reviews of children's books, but is rather intended as a kind of general source of information on children's books in Switzerland. The activities of the League and other organizations are reported on in detail.

1513. Poncini, Noemi. "Le biblioteche e la letteratura per l'infanzia," *Pro juventute,* Zürich, No. 9, Sept., 1931, pp. 338–342.

1514. Rahn, Magdalena. *Leitfaden für Volks- und Schulbibliotheken.* Bern, Vereinigung Schweizerischer Bibliothekare, 1951. 44p. (Publikationen, 21). IYL.

An organizational handbook for public and school libraries with emphasis on service to the young.

1515. "Répertoire alphabétique des auteurs des pièces écrites pour les enfants en Suisse Romande," *Mois theatral,* Genève, Sept., 1941, pp. 15–23. NNY.

1516. *Richtlinien für die Errichtung und Führung einer Schulbibliothek.* Bern, Lehrmittelverlag, 1955.

1517. Rochat, Elisabeth. "Le probleme des adolescents et de la lecture d'après les experiences faites à la bibliothèque municipale de Lausanne," *Vereinigung schweizerischer Bibliothekare, Nachrichten,* Bern, Jahrgang 36, No. 6, 1960, pp. 170–176. DLC.

Experiences in working with young adults in the municipal library of Lausanne.

1518. "Schweiz." Special issue of *Jugendliteratur,* München, No. 11, 1961, pp. 481–542. IYL.

This entire issue is devoted to contemporary trends and problems of children's literature in Switzerland.

1519.   Seebass, Adolf. *Alte Kinderbücher und Jugendschriften. Livres d'enfance. Children's books.* Basel, Haus der Bücher, n.d. 240p. ff. 24 plates. (Katalog 636). IYL.

   A rare-book-dealer's catalog containing more than 2000 entries, alphabetically arranged by author (or title) The books are from many countries and are carefully described in bibliographic detail. They are coded to indicate whether they are mentioned in the major catalogs of rare and old collections, e.g., Rümann (1116), Hobrecker (1256), Gumuchian (808), Muir (3180), etc. There is an illustrator index and the plates (not in color) reproduce selected illustrations.

1520.   Tschudi, H. P. *Gedanken zum Jugendbuch.* Amriswil, Armiswiler Bücherei, 1963. 13p.

   "On the opening of Schweizer Jugendbuchwoche 1963."

1521.   Uhler, Konrad. *Die Jugendschriftenkommission des Schweizerischen Lehrervereins in ihrer 50 jährigen Tätigkeit von 1858–1908.* Zürich, Orell Füssli, 1908.

1522.   Zehender, F. *Kurze Übersicht der Entwicklung der deutschen Jugendliteratur, begleitet von Ratschlägen zur Begründung von Jugendbibliotheken.* Zürich, Schulthess, 1880.

1523.   Zollinger, Max. *Das literarische Verständnis der Jugendlichen und der Bildungswert der Poesie.* Zürich, Orell Füssli, 1926.

1524.   Züricher, Gertrud. *Kinderlieder der deutschen Schweiz.* Basel, Helbing & Lichtenhahn, 1926. 599p. (Schriften der Schweizerischen Gesellschaft für Volkskunde, 17). LYL.

   Children's rhymes, songs and games collected from oral sources. This is similar to the work of the Opie (3184) and Böhme (1161).

1525.   *Zwanzig Jahre Jugendbuchpreis in der Schweiz: 1943–1963.* Zürich, 1963. 24p. (Schriften des Schweizerischen Lehrervereins, Nr. 37.) IYL.

   The winners of the Swiss national children's book prizes are presented here in photo and short textual portraits. The children's books of each are listed in chronological order.

Scandinavia and Finland

In actuality, one could take most of the entries in each of these bibliographies and place them together in this general one. There has been and still is so much cooperation and dialogue going on among these countries that they are very quickly aware of what new studies have been made and how they might benefit from them. There is ease in understanding because of close linguistic and cultural ties. Finnish is an exception to this, but there are enough individuals who can communicate in one or another of the Scandinavian tongues, or in English, so that it is not a serious obstacle.

Since the early decades of this century there have been meetings of librarians from the "northern" countries. There was a mutual sharing of experiences, of reports on study tours to other countries, and of proposals to meet future needs. This is certainly one of many reasons why these countries hold today a pre-eminent position in library work.

More recently there has been an attempt at cooperation directly involving all those who work with children and books in Scandinavia and Finland. The national sections of IBBY have sponsored, jointly or individually, annual meetings at which authors, illustrators, publishers, librarians, and many individuals working with children and books have discussed their mutual interests in furthering the cause of good children's books. A notable example of what results such cooperation can have is the *Barndomsland Anthology* of eight volumes, published by Gyldendal Norsk Forlag in Oslo, 1963–1965. It gives a cross section of the best in children's literature, internationally and chronologically.

While these countries do have much in common, there is a tendency for foreigners to lump together under the term "Scandinavian" many characteristics which are distinctly those of one country rather than of all. Each of these nations has a history all its own, and therefore it is better to let the works of each speak for themselves alone.

1526.   Andrews, Siri M. "Traditional Scandinavian literature for children," *Reading and the school library,* Chicago, Vol. 1, Oct., 1934, pp. 13–15. DLC.
A review of Scandinavian folklore, myths and modern stories which have become popular in the U.S. as well. Includes a graded list.

1527.   "Barnboksnummer." Entire issue of: *Ord och Bild,* Stockholm, Argang 73, No. 5, 1964, pp. 376–466. DLC, NNY.

Articles in Swedish, Danish and Norwegian on contemporary and historical aspects of children's literature. Some of the writers of longer articles are: Lennart Hellsing, Eva Von Zweigbergk, Kari Skjønsberg, Stina Hammar, Göte Klingberg. There are also articles on music, theater, film, graphic art, and poetry for children. Eight well-known writers (from Scandinavia and Finland) express their personal views (sometimes rather radical!) on writing for children.

180

1528. Deinboll, Rikka, *et al.* "Paa hvilke omraader kan nordens børne bibliotekarer samarbejde?" Nordiske Biblioteksmøde, 5th, København, 1947; [*Report*]; København, Dansk Bibliografisk Kontor, 1948; pp. 205–214.

A report on the session for work with children which was part of the 5th Library Convention for the Northern Countries. The librarians from the three countries exchanged views and discussed means of cooperation.

1529. *Förteckning över norsk litteratur lämplig för skol och folkbibliothek.* Stockholm, Föreningen Norden, 1962. 32p.

1530. Kunstman, J. L. *Selected annotated bibliography of Scandinavian children's literature appearing in English.* Washington, Catholic University of America, 1965. 53p. Thesis.

1531. Melhus, A. C. "Litteratur för barn-og ungdom," *For folkeoplysning,* Kristiania, Bind 6, Nos. 4–5, Dec., 1921, pp. 78–86. NNY.

"Children's and young people's literature." An address delivered at the 14th Northern library conference in Oct., 1921, concerning Scandinavian and foreign authors which this librarian had successfully used with children. Pp. 85–86 are the discussions among the librarians present following the speech.

1532. Mollerup, Helga, *et al.* "Bedömningsprinciper för barn- och ungdomsböcker," *Biblioteksbladet,* Stockholm, Ag. 35, No. 5, 1950, pp. 231–242. DLC, NNY.

"Principles of judging children's and youth books." This librarian summarizes all that she has learned from her years of experience in working with children and books.

1533. Pedersen, Jens. "Indtryk fra børnebiblioteker," *Bogens verden,* København, Aargang 18, No. 2, Mar., 1936, pp. 88–92. DLC, NNY.

A comparison of the work with children being done in the libraries of Göteborg, Stockholm and Oslo.

1534. Schaaning, Maja. "Samarbeide mellem skole og bibliotek," *For folkeoplysning,* Kristiania, Bind 3, No. 4, Dec., 1918, pp. 144–158. NNY.

"Cooperation between school and library." An address delivered at the 11th Northern library conference held in Oct., 1918. Although the author spoke mostly from her experience in Kristiania, the conclusions were meant for general situations in Scandinavia, and the discussion, pp. 153–158, bore this out.

1535. Skjønsberg, Kari. *Fortegnelse over litteratur på norsk, svensk og dansk over barns og unges fritidslesning.* Oslo, 1964, 24p. SPS.

An important bibliography, comprising some 500 items written about Norwegian, Swedish and Danish children's literature. The great majority are periodical articles, and there are no annotations, but bibliographical information is complete enough so that they are easily traced.

1536. Wiig, Hanna. "Om barnearbeidet." Nordiske Bibliotekmøte, 3rd, Oslo, 1933; *Foredrag og ordskrifte;* Oslo, Hellstrøm & Nordahls, 1933; pp. 52–65. DLC.

The children's librarian in Bergen, Norway, shared her experiences with colleagues from Denmark and Sweden, and reviewed the general trends in work with children.

1537. Banke, Jørgen and Aage Bredsted. *Biblioteket i undervisningens tjeneste.* København, H. Hagerups, 1941. 159p. NNY. (DLC has 1933 ed., pub. by Danske Bibliotekers Forretningsafdeling, 174p.).

This school library handbook gave general information on: the history of books and printing; specific information on the school library and its improvement; lists of local, regional and national school library organizations; public and community libraries serving schools and children; special libraries. Illustrated with photographs.

1538. Bengtsson, G. *Ungdommen og litteraturen.* Odense, A. C. Normann, 1944. 64p. SPS.

"Youth and literature." The five main chapters treat of what young people read, the comics, "unhealthy" reading, a recommended book list, and quotations on books and the importance of reading.

1539. *Bogen i undervisningen; katalog over fagbøger og en del skønlitteraere bøger, som hovedskolens og realafdelingens elever kan anvende i tilknyting til undervisningen.* 2nd ed. København, G. E. C. Gad, 1965. 112p. SPS.

This list was compiled by a group of school and public librarians, under the sponsorship of the Ministry of Education. It is annotated, arranged by subject and grade, and indexed.

1540. "Bøger for børn. Bøger for ungdommen," *Bogens verden,* København, 1919 ff. DLC, NNY.

A column of signed current book reviews, appearing frequently but not in every issue. It was originally called *Børne og Ungdomsbøger.* Most often it appears in the general section *Ungdommen* (see 1617).

Denmark

Denmark is by far the most advanced country in its application of standards to the legal apparatus of library development. Due to its size and population, and to the comparative success of the social welfare programs of the state, it is understandable that such steady progress could be made. The first library legislation appeared in 1920, and each decade since that time has seen significant changes in existing legislation, or completely new laws. According to the pamphlet put out by Bibliotekstilsynet and Bibliotekscentralen, (1555) the main features of the 1964 Act are the following:

1. The area served by a public library system shall be a commune or a joint library area comprising two or more communes.
2. All commune councils are required to provide by 1969 a public library service for both children and adults, either alone or jointly with other commune councils.
3. The majority of non-communal public libraries are taken over by the communes.
4. All libraries shall be available free of charge to all residents in Denmark.
5. Public libraries shall make available both books and audio-visual materials.
6. Libraries serving a population over 5,000 shall appoint a full-time professionally qualified librarian before 1969.
7. The expenses of public libraries are covered jointly by the state and the communes. The state grants have been improved.
8. The expenses of county libraries incurred in the provision of service to their districts are covered jointly by the state and the county councils concerned.
9. The Act provides for school libraries in primary schools co-operating with the local public library.

It will not be as difficult as it might seem to implement the orders of the new law. There has been good service within most communes for many years already. There is the central library supply agency, Bibliotekscentralen, which has coordinated much of the technical work and freed librarians from tedious duplication. Mrs. Aase Bredsdorff, a children's librarian of long experience and now on the State Inspection for Libraries (Bibliotekstilsynet), has written of the modes of service which were widely practiced before the 1964 Act (1549). She does point out that this service needed improvement in further development of school libraries, extension activities, and work with young adults. But most of all, the need was for more children's librarians.

Since schools must all have libraries by 1969, this need is likely to double or triple in the next few years. Denmark might well be facing a situation similar to that in the U.S., where school libraries are springing up much faster than the number of professional librarians to staff them. A well-planned library law cannot have its full effect

182

unless there are sufficient individuals capable of executing its orders. Training and pay for children's librarians are on a par with those in other specialties. Still, the shortage in the children's field is out of proportion to the others. Mrs. Bredsdorff writes: "It is often said that it is more exhausting to work with children than with adults and that reading children's books is in the long run tiring and unsatisfying." Perhaps this provides the clue to one reason for the current lack of interest in this work as a profession.

Children's book publishing in Denmark does not keep up with the current demand, either in quantity or quality. For all of the public monies available for purchase, there are still not enough publishers willing to risk producing a larger list of titles. More important, there is lacking a group of young, exciting writers who try out new themes and add freshness to old ones. No matter how fine and extensive the translations are, they do not substitute entirely for a native literature. The fact of the matter is that Danish children's books are, in large proportion, translations or adaptations. It might be important for newly developing countries to note well this fact. Schools and libraries with funds to purchase books in quantity are not enough to assure the evolution and growth of a healthy children's book trade. There must be, in addition, some underlying force of interest, some stimulation whereby author, publisher, librarian, parent and teacher all come to know and appreciate each other, and somehow generate the kind of creative atmosphere necessary for artistic productivity.

Denmark has not had the variety of book-related activities which are more common in Norway and Sweden. This might be in part the result of state support of so many other recreational activities. Nevertheless, the book world is beginning to expand on its promotional methods, notably in the National Book Week celebrations. These have been held three times: in 1956, 1961 and 1966. It is hoped they will be continued at five year intervals. The cooperation of teachers, librarians, booksellers and publishers was enlisted and the results have been noticeable increases in sales and, more importantly, in interest. Special, attractive lists were distributed to every child. Television and radio programs featured books and authors of interest to children and young people. There is also a prize given each year by the Ministry of Education (since 1954), for the best children's book. It carries both a financial and an honorary reward.

It is at this point when many foreigners might be tempted to ask: "Why isn't the country which produced Hans Christian Andersen able to produce a modern children's literature that lives up to his name?" The answer from a Dane is more than likely to be an exasperated sigh, and rightly so. It is almost impossible for the outsider to realize the position Andersen holds in his native country. One thing is sure: it is not likely to be the position most would have it be, i.e., one of adulation. Apart from the fact that many consider a good portion of his work overly emotional and bordering on the sentimental, there is the more obvious problem of language. Andersen's style was very modern for its time, and did have a tremendous influence on the language of his day. Nevertheless, for all its revolutionary use of everyday speech patterns, it was distinctly a literary style, as opposed to the folk idiom in the collection of *Danske Folkeeventyr* by Svend Grundtvig for example. Whereas in translation this quality may be rendered in modern-day equivalents, Andersen is not translated newly for each generation of Danish children! Consequently, many critics feel that only his best stories stand the test of being read with pleasure and appreciation by the present generation.

Whether the world-wide reputation of Andersen has been a stifling or an expansive influence on other Danish writers is hard to tell. In the minds of a number of persons, the name of Andersen and Danish children's literature are synonymous. It might well be that a modern writer pauses before he risks such comparison. The synonym is, of course, not at all valid. There are a number of other 19th-century writers whose works have stood up very well. The afore-mentioned collection by Svend Grundtvig is one of them. Johan Krohn's nursery rhymes and his Christmas picture book, *Peters Jul,* are still favorites. Curiously enough, old-fashioned illustrations have not kept the latter from remaining a favorite. The texts in these books are short rhymes, so that a comparison with Andersen's prose style is not possible. Louis Moe was another who collected the old nursery rhymes, and he also illustrated them with imagination and humor. Christian Winther and Christian Richardt both wrote original poetry for children, using simple rhythms and meter. They are still found in most reading text books.

What Denmark has not produced to any extent are novels for children. At least one critic (1588) feels this might be the direct result of the *Bornenes Bogsamling* or "Children's Book Collection" edited and published by Christian Erichsen, beginning in 1896. This was a series of translations and adaptations (many from popular adult novels), illustrated in appealing but not always artistic, styles. A few are still published and read today. This was the beginning of mass publication of children's books in Denmark, and the mediocre quality of much of the series has influenced many similar publishing ventures up to the present day.

1541. "Bogliste, 1–7 skoleår, ordnet efter klasse-trin og fag." Special issue of: *Unge paedagoger,* København, 1959. 44p. (Special number P). SPS.

A booklist of grades 1–7, arranged by grade and subject, not annotated or indexed. Illustrated.

1542. Børnebibliotekarernes Faggruppe. *117 gode børnebøger.* København, Bibliotekscentralen, 1964 [11p]. SPS, APP.

An annotated list of 117 good children's books, selected by a committee of librarians.

1543. Børnebibliotekarernes Kontaktgruppe. *Bør-nebøger; genrelister og serier.* København, Folkebibliotekernes Bibliografiske Kontor, 1960. 30p. SPS.

This is the last edition of this finding list of children's books in series, and by types.

1544. *Børnebøger.* 11th ed. København, Bibliotekscentralen, 1966. 114p. Annual supplements. SPS.

A list of children's books, not annotated, arranged by Dewey system, and with author and title index.

1545. "Børns laesning." Special issue of: *Unge paedagoger,* København, 1952. pp. 1–48. SPS.

Thirteen articles on children's reading, in

the home, school and library. They are by such well-known persons as C. C. Kragh-Müller, Helga Mollerup, Aase Bredsdorff and others. There are several short bibliographies and book lists.

1546. *Børns og unges laesning.* København, 1960. 89p. DLC. (Betaenkning afgivet af det Undervisningsministeriet . . ., 268).

The report of several conferences which took place in 1954, 1955, 1956, and 1957. The discussions were concerned with children's reading, libraries, and related subjects, and special emphasis was given to discussions of means to counteract the influx of cheap, mass media literature.

1547. Bredsdorff, Aase. "Børne- og skolebiblioteksarbejde." Dansk Bibliografisk Kontor. *Laerobog i biblioteksteknik,* Vol. 3. København, Dansk Bibliografisk Kontor, 1959, pp. 490–526.

1548. ———. "Børns forsyning med bøger under den nye bibliotekslov." *Bogens verden,* København, Årgang 46, No. 7, Nov., 1964, pp. 454–463. DLC, NNY.

The children's specialist in the State Inspection for Libraries explains how the new library law will affect children's access to books in school and public libraries.

1549. ———. "Denmark," *Library service to children.* Lund, Bibliotekstjänst, 1963, pp. 30–40. DLC, IYL, NNY.

This chapter in the IFLA publication deals with the history and present status of children's library work in this country. However, the new library law up-dated this in certain areas (1555).

1550. ———. "Det danske børnebogsmarkeds pleje," *Bogens verden,* København, Ag. 45, Dec., 1963, pp. 547–55. DLC, NNY.

The author comments sadly on the state of Danish children's books, and the poor variety available on the market. She gives numerous comparative statistics with those of other Scandinavian countries.

1551. ——— and Knud Hermansen. *Småbørns bøger; billedbøger, letlaeselige børnebøger, eventyr.* 2nd ed. København, Bibliotekscentralen, 1963. 20p. Annual supplements. DLC, IYL. (1st edition, pub. by Dansk Bibliografisk Kontor, 1960. 16p. Annual supplements 1961–1962. IYL).

A booklist of 260 titles, divided into five groups with grade indications. No annotations are given, but first-purchase books are starred. Author and title index. Designed as the list for schools to use on initial orders.

1552. Clausen, Chr. Krug. *Skolelaesestuen.* 2 Vols. in 1. København, L. A. Jørgensen, 1920 and 1923. 55p. ff. 56p. SPS.

"School libraries." A practical handbook giving advice on organizing the materials, a list of recommended books, and suggestions for developing collections. Illustrated with photographs.

1553. Dahlsgaard, Marius. "Vore børns fritidslaesning," *Bogens verden,* København, Årgang 4, No. 7–8, July–Aug., 1922, pp. 129–136; No. 9–10, Sept.–Oct., 1922, pp. 175–180. DLC, NNY.

An address delivered at the 1st Danish Library Association conference in June, 1922. This was a strongly-worded statement on the right of children to have free use of reading materials for pleasure.

1554. Dam, Axel "Ungdommen og bøgerne," *Vor ungdom,* København, 1923, pp. 417–428. SPS.

"Young people and books." A teacher writes of their interests as observed in his experiences.

1555. *The Danish Public Libraries Act 1964.* Copenhagen, Bibliotekstilsynet and Bibliotekscentralen, 1965. 19p. APP.

The English text of the law which is currently in effect in Denmark. It is also available in French and German. The original, of course, is in Danish and there are many accompanying orders. However, it is very helpful to have this important law available in the more widely used languages so that it can be studied as a model. Children's services are an intrinsic part of the whole.

1556. Dansk Bibliografisk Kontor. *Ungdomskatalog et udvalg af bøger for unge.* 4th ed. København, Dansk Bibliografisk Kontor, 1961. 51p. IYL.

A booklist for young people arranged by subject and indexed. Revised periodically.

1557. ———. *Børne- og ungdomsbøger.* København, Dansk Bibliografisk Kontor. 1954 ff? IYL has 1954, 1957, 1960, 1963.

A booklist which is revised approximately every three years. Its forerunners are listed under Helga Mollerup and E. Allerslev Jensen.

1558. *Den danske billedbog gennem 100 år.* København, Gyldendal, 1954. 6p. SPS. (SPS also has in French text.)

Not a catalog but general comments on an exhibition of "100 years of Danish picture books," held in the Kongelige Bibliotek. The exhibition was later shown in Paris at the Maison du Danemark.

1559. Denmark. Undervisningsministeriet. *Beretning og indstilling fra Undervisningsministeriets udvalg vedrørende underlødig litteratur.* København, typewritten manuscript, 1957. 29p. DLC.

"Report and recommendations from the Ministry of Education." This is the plan for the conferences described in 1546.

1560. Dueled, V. "Skole- og børnebiblioteket for Nordvestsjaelland og Samsø," *Bogens verden,* København, Ag. 30, Apr.–May, 1948, pp. 122–125. DLC, NNY.

"Children's and school libraries in northwest Seeland and the island of Samsø." A description of the libraries, and some of the special difficulties they face because of their inaccessability.

1561. Erichsen, Chr. *Ti aar. Et lille tilbageblik over "Børnenes Bogsamlings" virksomhed i tiaaret 1896–1905.* København, 1905.

"Ten years: a restrospective view of the *Bornenes Bogsamling* in the period 1896–1905." Mr. Erichsen was the editor of this popular, mass-produced series.

1562. Erslev, Anna. "Vore børns laesning; et lille oversyn for faedre og mødre," *Vor ungdom,* København, 1900, pp. 715–740. SPS.

"Your child's reading; a short review for fathers and mothers." This includes specific suggestions for each age level.

1563. *Flere børnebibliotekarer—hvordan? Betaenkning afgivet af det af Biblioteksrådet den 8 februar 1961 nedsatte udvalg vedrørende børnebibliotekarmangelen.* København, Dansk Bibliografisk Kontor, 1962. 28p. SPS.

"More children's librarians—how?" Results of a library conference devoted to this problem.

1564. Florander, Jesper. *Børns serielaesning. Et forsøg på en belysning af årsagsforholdene.* København, Munksgaard, 1955. 24p. Reprinted from: *Nordisk psykologi,* København, Årgang 7, 1955, pp. 188–211. SPS.

"Children's reading of comics. An attempt at an explanation of their causal circumstances." This pedagogue has also written on the same subject in the *Dansk Paedagogisk Tidskrift,* København Årgang 3, 1955, pp. 409–415.

1565. Franck, Gudrun and Helga Mollerup. "Børnebibliotekesarbejde," *Laerebog i biblioteksteknik og dansk biblioteksvaesen,* 2nd ed. København, Statens Bibliotekstilsyn, 1945, pp. 207–228. Also reprinted separately. SPS.

"Library work with children." Practical suggestions for organizing and administering the various services. Illustrated with photographs. Short bibliography.

1566. Frederiksberg. Kommunes Børnebibliotekar. *Faelles bogsamlingens klassesaet.* 3rd ed. Frederiksberg, 1958. 67p. IYL.

An annotated booklist arranged by subject and indexed.

1567. Gutry, Maria. "Biblioteki dla dzieci w Danii," *Bibliotekarz,* Warszawa, Rok 30, No. 5, 1963, pp. 104–110. DLC, NNY.

"Libraries for children in Denmark." Their present status, organization, and form of service.

1568. Hansen, Knud. "Ungdom, borgerlighed og digtning," *Dansk udsyn,* Askov, Årgang 44, No. 5, 1964, pp. 388–400. SPS.

"Youth, middle class values and poetry." A critical essay on the lack of poetic feeling among today's children and youth.

1569. Hansen, Rasmus, et al. *Undersøgelser af 186 frilaesningsbøger, med henblik på en vurdering af deres laesesvaerhed.* København, Skolepsykologiske Undersøgelser, 1950. 36p. SPS.

"Introduction to 186 books for recreational reading with a view to an evaluation of their value as reading material." Collaborators were Torben Gregersen and Frede G. Jensen. The first versions appeared in the *Paedagogisk-psykologisk tidskrift,* København, Bind 1, Heft 7, 1941, pp. 115 ff. and Bind 4, Hefte 3–4, 1944, pp. 76–97.

1570. Holm, Viggo. "Børndedigte," *Vor ungdom,* København, 1885, pp. 333–351. SPS.

"Children's poetry; a literary historical survey." This critical essay was one of the first on the subject in Denmark and covers the important poets and their works from the 18th and 19th centuries.

1571. Hørding, Tove. *Børnebøger.* Bejle, Udbye, 1922. 56p. DLC.

Catalog of the children's room collection in the Bejle library arranged by Dewey system, not annotated and not indexed.

1572. Hunø, L. M. *Børns fritidslaesning.* København, 1918. 41p. Reprint from: *Foreningen for eksperimental paedagigik, Aarbog.* SPS.

"Children's free-time reading." A survey of interests, with some statistical tables of results.

1573. "Hvorfor saelges der så få børnebøger? Samtale om børnebøger og børnebogssalg," *Bogormen,* København, Årgang 62, No. 3, 1965. 28p. SPS has reprint.

"Why do they sell so few children's books?" Articles by C. C. Kragh-Müller, Anine Rud, Ib Permin and Poul Christiansen on the subject of books in the private life of the child.

1574. Jensen, E. Allerslev. *Fortegnelse over børne- og ungdomsbøger.* 2nd ed. København, 1938. 92p. (Statens Bibliotekstilsyn, Publikationer, 12). DLC.

For 1st edition see Mollerup, Helga and Jens Pedersen. For subsequent editions see entries under Dansk Bibliografisk Kontor. This list of books for children from 9–16 is not annotated; the nonfiction is arranged by Dewey number, and there is an index.

1575. Jeppensen, Poul. "Børnebøgernes udformning," *Bovennen 1960; aarbog for bogkunst og boghistorie;* København, Gyldendal, 1960. pp. 35–50. NNY, SPS.

"The design of children's books." "Books for children used to be classified with toys; nowadays, most of them come under the category of pulp. Therefore, educationalists and librarians are now focusing their attention on the problem of children's sparetime reading. But the discussion has so far centered on the contents rather than the appearance of these books. However, if a book embodies an artistic experience, although expressed in a simple, unpretentious style, there is every reason why it should also be presented in an attractive form." (From the English summary.)

The author goes on to discuss the books (particularly picture books) which have achieved this artistic unity. Illustrated.

1576. Juel-Hansen, N. "Om ungdommens morskabslaesning," *Vor ungdom,* København, 1884, pp. 150–157. SPS.

The leisure reading of young people. This is one of the earliest articles on the subject in this periodical. Many others followed, among them one by Therese Brummer, in 1893, pp. 277–291 and another by Georg Bruun in 1899, pp. 735–740.

1577. Kastberg, K. *Hvorledes bør et skolebibliotek indrettes?* København, 1939, 43p. (Statens Bibliotekstilsyns. Publikationer, 15.)

1578. København. Kommunebiblioteker. *Katalog over bøger for børn og ungdom.* København, J. Jørgensen, 1930. 52p. DLC.

The catalog of the children's room in the Københaven library arranged by author in fiction and nonfiction parts, but not annotated or indexed.

1579. ————. *Katalog over Dansk og Norsk litteratur; ungdomslitteratur.* København, J. Jørgensen, 1939. 99p. NNY. DLC has 1st ed., same pub., 1931, 57p.

A booklist of Danish and Norwegian literature for young people. No annotations are given. The books are arranged by Dewey, and there is no index.

1580. ————. *Klassesaet i faellesborgsamlingen.* 5th ed. København, 1964. 69p. SPS. (Supplement: 1966, 16p. SPS.)

A list of books in the Copenhagen Public Library's special loan collection for schools. It is regularly revised by children's librarians in the central office.

1581. ————. *Nye bøger i skole- og børnebibliotekernes udlan.* København, yearly, 1954–1962. 8p. SPS.

A yearly list of new books for loan in the school and children's libraries of Copenhagen. From 1963 on, the library began to use the booklist *Børnebøger,* published by Bibliotekscentralen.

1582. Kragh-Müller, C. C. "Børns laesning—mentalhygiejnisk set," *Mentalhygiejne,* København, Årgang 9, 1956. pp. 59–69. SPS.

This well-known psychologist and pedagogist is the founder of the Bernadotte School in Copenhagen. His theory regarding children's literature is that there is danger in the concept of separate types of books for boys and girls. He feels that too few children's books treat of the differences in sex honestly, and furthermore, that they encourage an over-idealization of the masculine so that children have difficulty in living up to these ideals.

1583. Kristensen, Niels K. "Børnebøger," *Vor ungdom,* København, 1899, pp. 524–529. SPS.

What characteristics children's books should have in order to qualify as good literature.

1584. ————. "Laererne og børnelitteraturen." *Laererne og Samfundet; folkeskolen kendte maend og kvinder jubilaeumsskrift 1814–1914.* København, 1913. pp. 267–336. SPS.

"Teachers and children's books." After a survey of the development of children's periodicals, there are some general remarks on early children's books and authors. Following this are biographical-critical sketches of teachers who were important either as writers of children's books, or as translators, critics, etc. Mr. Christensen was himself one of the important early writers and critics of children's literature in Denmark.

1585.   Larsen, Joakim. *Børnelaesning.* København, 1906. 10p. SPS.
"Children's reading." An address given at the 9th conference of northern educators held in Copenhagen in 1905.

1586.   Mollerup, Helga. "Børn og bøger." Andersen, Oluf and Sofie Rifbjerg. *Alt om børn.* København, Jespersen og Pios Forlag, 1942. pp. 436–443. SPS.
A general article on children and books written for an encyclopedia on child study.

1587.   ———. *Børns yndlingsbøger; erfaringer fra et børnebibliotek.* København, Det Danske Forlag, 1947. 141p. DLC, IYL, NNY, SPS.
"Children's favorite books; experiences from a children's library." What children like at various stages, and some books to match these tastes. This is a warm and personal account by a librarian who not only was enthusiastic about work with children, but also was insistent on high standards in the field.

1588.   ———. "Danish children's books before 1900," *Junior bookshelf.* Huddersfield, Vol. 15, No. 2, Mar., 1951, pp. 50–56. DLC, IYL, NNY.
A short historical and critical review written in English.

1589.   ——— and Jens Pedersen. *Fortegnelse over børne- og ungdomsbøger.* 1st ed. København, Danske Bibliotekers Forretningsafdeling, 1932. 64p. DLC.
The first recommended list of children's books officially sponsored by the Danish Library Association. For later similar lists see the entries under E. Allerslev Jensen and Dansk Bibliografisk Kontor.

1590.   ———. "Juvenile and school libraries," *Danish foreign office journal,* Copenhagen, No. 204, Jan., 1938, pp. 8–12. DLC, NNY. Also in: *Librarian and book world,* Gravesend, Vol. 29, No. 3, Nov., 1939, pp. 53–55. DLC, NNY.
In 1931 a national Libraries Act was passed, stating that local authorities were to decide whether the public or school library (or both) was best suited to fulfilling the reading needs of Danish children. This resulted in a variety of organizational patterns, but all followed the same general standards. Illustrated with photographs.

1591.   Olsen, Anker. *Eventyr-index.* København, Dansk Bibliografisk Kontor, 1954. 42p. SPS.

This work was sponsored by the Børnebibliotekarernes Faggruppe (Children's Librarians' Study Group) and edited by Anker Olsen. It is an index to all important fairy tale collections in Danish.

1592.   Olsson, Brita, *et al. Biblioteksarbejde blandt unge.* København, Dansk Bibliografisk Kontor, 1961. 114p. NNY.
"Library work among youth." Chapters on book selection, programs, public relations, booklists and other services, as related to work among teenagers.

1593.   ———. *Ungdom og bøger.* København, Dansk Bibliografisk Kontor, 1956. 57p. (Biblioteker og Laesning, 1). DLC.
"Youth and books." Their reading interests, how to turn them from light reading to literature, special library training needed to work with them, and a suggested year's program to carry out.

1594.   Paaske, Gudrun. "Vejledning i valg af børnelitteratur," *Børnesagens tidende,* København, Årgang 45, 1950, pp. 134–140. SPS.
A very general article on work with children and books. This children's librarian is working on a major book on children's authors in Danish.

1595.   Paedagogiske Institut. *Børns lån og køb af bøger. En undersøgelse i forbindelse med børnebogsugen 1956.* København, 1965. 27p. (Mimeographed). SPS.
"Children's borrowing and purchasing of books; an inquiry in connection with Children's Book Week, 1956."

1596.   Paulli, Betti. *Laesning og oplaesning.* København, C. A. Reitzels Boghandel, 1922. 48p. (Reitzels Bogserie, "Det Danmark der Arbejder," 1). SPS.
Experiences in working with young and older children in the N. Zahle School. The author discusses their interests at different age levels, mentioning specific titles.

1597.   Rohde, H. P. *Peters Jul af Johan Krohn. Med tegninger af Otte Haslund og Pietro Krohn. Gengivet efter den første udgave 1866.* København. Rosenkilde og Bagger, 1962. 60p. SPS.
This reprint of the original *Peters Jul* by Johan Krohn (1866) is preceded by Mr. Rohde's remarks on its history, which is indirectly the history of the first books for children in Denmark. There are portraits of the author, artist and book dealer concerned with the first production.

1598.   Roos, Carl. "Den danske børnebog," *Homo sum.* København, Gyldendal, 1946. pp. 23–35. SPS.

A well-known essayist writes of his impressions of Danish children's books, largely from a reminiscent point of view.

1599. Schlüter, Mogens. Børnebøger fra hele verden. Reprint from: *Laesningens glaede,* København, Den Danske Antikvarboghandlerforening, 1960. 17p. SPS.

"Children's books from the whole world." The author is a private collector of children's books, and here describes some of the items in his collection. Seven illustrations from them are reproduced here. His particular interest is in ABC books in unusual editions and languages.

1600. Sigsgaard, Jens. "Billedbøger og moral." Reprint from: *Politikens kronik,* København. Feb. 16, 1966. 6p. SPS.

"The picture book and morality." A children's author writes of the influence which picture books can have on the very young.

1601. ————. "Moderne danske billedbøger," *Salmonsen leksikon tidskrift,* København, Ag 4, Heft 7, 1944, pp. 1091–1098. SPS.

"Modern Danish picture books." A survey with many illustrative examples.

1602. Simonsen, Inger. *Den Danske børnebog i det 19 aarhundrede.* København, Nyt Nordisk (Arnold Busck), 1942. 294p. NNY.

"The Danish children's book in the 19th century." A history and criticism arranged chronologically, with the first period actually covering 1760–1835. There are many black and white and some colored plates of reproductions. The bibliography is annotated, and there is an index. An important contribution to the history of children's books.

1603. Skolebiblioteksforeningen. *Bogfortegnelse for laesestuen.* København, 1917. SPS.

A list of 300 books for recreational reading. This was the first such list published by the school Library Association.

1604. Skolebiblioteksforening af 1917. *Bøger til fritidslaesning; et udvalg ordnet efter skoleaar.* København, Bibliotekscentralen, 1966.

This is a companion list to *Skolelaesestuen* (*see* 1606), and published approximately at concurrent times.

1605. ————. *Opgaver til 18 børne-og ungdomsbøger.* New edition. København, Bibliotekscentralen. 1965. 47p. SPS.

A handbook prepared by the school library association, giving help to the teacher or librarian on how to give books programs for young people, particularly in the classroom. The 18 specific examples are well-known Danish books (some translations) and for each there is a series of questions and a summary.

1606. ————. *Skolelaesestuen: handbøger, supplerende laesning.* København, Bibliotekscentralen, 1966.

This is the fifth edition of a list which appears every six years. It is compiled by the School Library Association, and published by Bibliotekscentralen, the successor to Dansk Bibliografisk Kontor.

1607. Sørensen, Eleanora. Børne-og skolebiblioteksarbejde. Kolding Centralbibliotek, *Festskrift til Th. Døssing.* Kolding, Danske Folkebiblioteker, 1937, pp. 94–104.

1608. Statens Paedagogiske Studiesamling. *Fortegnelse over litteratur om børns og unges fritidslaesning.* København, S. D. Møllers, 1959. 19p. DLC, IYL.

"A bibliography of literature about children's and young people's reading." The first 200 entries are on children's free reading interests and the remaining 75 are on the history of children's books. About one half are sources from the Scandinavian countries, and the others are in German, English, French and Russian. The entries which can be found in the library (SPS) are given their classification number. Bibliographical information is not always complete.

1609. Steenberg, Andr. Sch. "Barnet og det skrevne ord." Bang, Einar; *Foraeldrenes bog;* København, E. Jespersen, 1923; pp. 237–259. SPS.

"Children and the written word." Two chapters on the awakening of interest in books and reading in the life of the young child.

1610. ————. *Skolen og bøgerne.* København and Kristiania, Gyldendalske Boghandel and Nordisk Forlag, 1905. 44p. SPS.

"Schools and books." Brief summaries of public and school library work with children in the U.S., in Germany and in Denmark, followed by a few practical suggestions for beginning school collections.

1611. Stybe, Vibeke. "Børnebogen i kulturhistorisk perspektiv," *Dansk paedagogik tidskrift,* København, No. 2, 1961. pp. 48–56. SPS has reprint.

"Children's books in a cultural-historical perspective." This led to the author's book-length study (1613).

1612. ———. "Den første danske Bastian," *Bog-vennen*, København, 1963, pp. 100–109. SPS.

"The first Danish *Bastian* (cautionary tale)." Illustrated with reproductions from this early book for children. In this same yearly issue of this periodical (pp. 111–126) is an article by Ida Bachmann on *Rama Sama*, another important early Danish children's book, written by Conrad Staugaard in the late 19th century.

1613. ———. *Fra Askepot til Anders And; børne-bogen i kulturhistorisk perspektiv*. København, Munksgaard, 1962. 133p. DLC, IYL.

"From Cinderella to Donald Duck; children's books in a cultural-historical perspective." A general survey covering the highlights of Western children's literature, with special emphasis on Danish and Scandinavian works. The arrangement is chronological and the last section has chapters on the psychological-pedagogical and on the political influences which entered into children's books in this century. Illustrated with black and white reproductions. Name index.

1614. ———. *Survey of the history of books for children in Denmark*. [København, Statens Paedagogiske Studiesamling, 1963.] 6p. Mimeographed, APP.

A short summary in English of the author's book (*see* 1613) on the history of Danish children's literature.

1615. Teisen, H. "Skolebiblioteksforeningen af 1917—Danmarks skolebiblioteksforening," *Bogens verden*, København, Vol. 16, Apr.–May, 1934, pp. 119–120. DLC.

The history and accomplishments of the Danish School Library Association of 1917.

1616. Thording, Carl. *Skolelaesestuen og dens anvendelse*. København, C. C. Woel, 1926. 51p. NNY.

"The school reading room and its use." General information on organization and practical use.

1617. "Ungdommen; tidende for børne-og ung-domsbiblioteker." *Bogens verden*, København, Årgang 5, Nos. 9–10, Sept.–Oct., 1923 ff. DLC, NNY.

A column devoted to the affairs of children's and school libraries in Denmark in the official publication of the Danish Library Association. It includes many announcements of courses, congresses, book fairs, meetings, awards and prizes, etc., and occasional articles of varying length on aspects of children's literature and libraries.

1618. *Vi har det rart, vi laeser*. København, Dansk Bogtjeneste, 1966. 16p.

A booklist given out to all Danish school children, on the occasion of the 3rd national book week. There are actually two editions, one listing books for grades 1–3, and the other for grades 4–8. The 1961 book week list was titled *Gode Bornebøger er Vaerd et Fa Fat I*.

1619. Winther, Christian. *Børn og bøger*. København, Grønholt Pedersen, 1946. 159p. NNY.

"Children and books." Essays of criticism and history, with such titles as "The literary heritage all children have in common," "Danish writers for children," "The requirements of the good children's book," "Adventure books," "Picture books for small children," "The boundaries of children's literature," and others.

1620. ———. *Danske børnebogs-forfattere*. Århus, Søren Lund, 1955. 133p. DLC, IYL, NNY. (DLC also has 1934 ed., Kolding, K. Jørgensen, 64p.; NNY also has 1939 ed., same pub., 124p.).

Biographies and brief analyses of the work of 16 authors who wrote for children in Denmark or are still writing.

1621. ———. "Fortegnelse over bøger for børn og unge, der kan laeses i Tilknyting til Danmarkhistorien." Schjaerff, Poul, *Historisk digtning*. København, F. E. Pedersen, 1937, pp. 71–100. NNY.

A list of fictional books (for children and young people) which are connected with Danish history followed by those with some phase of world history as their background. Arranged by period with very brief annotations.

Norway

How is it that Norway, which used Danish as a literary language until almost the middle of the 19th century, could develop in that intervening century a lively and varied literature for children? This question is more intriguing in view of the fact that Denmark, with its larger population, has not produced as many writers for children and suffers a shortage of good children's books, in comparison with the demand. One answer might be that the models for putting into prose "modern" spoken Norwegian were the folk tales collected and published by Peter Christen Asbjørnsen and Jørgen Moe. No country could be more fortunate than Norway in having possessed such a felicitous combination of rich oral tradition, perceptive recorders of it, and the time ripe for its favorable reception as a written literature. The humorous and light-hearted stories contained in the *Norske Folkeeventyr,* first published in 1845, are part and parcel of the childhood of every Norwegian. The fact that they are still published in practically the original text is great tribute to the poetic and linguistic genius of the two collaborators. Jørgen Moe was also the author of an original work, *I Bronnen og i Tjernet,* a nature fantasy centered around a boy and girl, which is still read by today's children.

Asbjørnsen and Moe were by no means the first to write for children in Norwegian. Their most illustrious predecessor was the poet Henrik Wergeland. He not only wrote many original poems, but also adapted folk rhymes, translated freely from the German *Des Knaben Wunderhorn* and used themes from other sources. Some critics believe that these works are out-dated and are kept alive by sentimental aunts and mothers. Nevertheless Wergeland cannot have lost touch entirely with today's children, because, like Stevenson, he wrote verses which are still learned by heart and repeated by children almost as though they were folk rhymes.

Translations came first from Germany and only later, after 1870, from England, France and the United States. The first fine picture book did not appear until 1888. It was produced by the unusual combination of a scientist-turned-folklorist, Elling Holst, and an artist Eivend Nielsen. The material in this *Norsk Billedbok for Barn* proved to be just what tickles the imagination in children of very young years—jingles, rhymes, riddles, counting-out chants and the like. That the pictures are old-fashioned seems to bother present day children not at all.

According to Jo Tenfjord, "the last decade of the 19th and the first two decades of the 20th century might well be thought of as the golden age of children's literature in Norway" (1636). This was the period which brought forth such authors as Dikken Zwilgmeyer, Barbra Ring, Hans Aanrud, Gabriel Scott, Bernt Lie, Halvor Floden, Sven Moren. All of them wrote stories of everyday children and their fantasies, mischiefs, dreams and disappointments.

In the years between the wars, the most noticeable trend was in the wider publication of nonfiction, and in experimentation with various forms for its presentation. This was mostly confined to facts told through the device of a boy or girl (or twins) visiting some place or living through some experience. History and biography were also plentiful. Real nonfiction, where scientific facts were presented in a straight-forward style, did not appear in any significant amount until well after the Second World War. It was at that time that the critic

Sonja Hageman expressed the opinion that children's books in Norway were becoming entirely "school" books, and that more attention should be paid to fantasy and children's novels.

Actually, Norway seems to have less cause to worry about a lack of stimulating new books, than do her neighbors. The past generation of children have grown up on a diversified diet of Thorbjörn Egner, Alf Proysen, Zinken Hopp, Finn Havrevold, Leif Hamre, Aimée Sommerfelt, as well as numerous translations and most of the old favorites. No statistics were compiled to prove it, but it is probably accurate to state that of all these four countries Norway has the largest percentage of its postwar children's books translated into other languages. Most Norwegians feel that the translations do not do justice to the original works, but they are justifiably proud of their number and extent.

A major contribution to children's literature has been the work of the state radio programmes. In her article (1636) Astrid Feydt mentions that English fantasy and nonsense never really "caught on" in Norway until children got used to this type of material through skillful radio presentation. This appears to be one instance which has disproved the theory that there are certain works which just do not lend themselves to understanding and acceptance in all countries. Apparently, when introduced with care and with respect for the original it is possible to introduce children to a new type of humor, a new kind of imaginative release. The annual prizes given to children's books since 1948 are awarded by the Ministry of Education. Since 1957, there have been prizes for the best illustrations as well. These are not limited to one per year, but have been awarded to anywhere from two to six titles annually.

Children's libraries in Norway have a history which dates back to the 19th century. Libraries in schools, however pedantic they were, had been fairly well organized before public library work came on the scene. The articles in the periodical *For Folke-Og Barneboksamlinger* document these early beginnings quite well. It is quite amazing to read Nordahl Rolfsen's article (1647) and to discover how advanced in theory the Norwegians were, by the time this century opened. Actual application of the theory was another matter; very few schools could afford to put it into full practice.

Somewhere in the early 1900's, the emphasis on school libraries shifted to children's libraries in general, and for the first time public libraries became conscious of their duties to young readers. Like Denmark and Sweden, they were much influenced by British and U.S. reports on the extent and importance of children's work in those countries (England and the U.S.). However, Norway did not forge ahead at the same rate as Denmark and Sweden, due in part to the sparse population scattered over more remote areas. It was only natural that the school libraries should continue to be of greater importance in the role of getting books to the child. Outside of the large cities, this remains true today. The Deichmanske Bibliotek in Oslo (until 1925 called Kristiania) has always been an outstanding exception in its service to children.

1622. Amundsen, Sverre S. "Skolebiblioteket," *Bok og bibliotek*, Oslo, Ag. 5, Nov., 1938, pp. 382–400. NNY.

"School libraries." Their history in Norway, their aims and organization.

1623. Arnesen, Arne. "Vor folkeskoles aeldste barnebiblioteker," *For folke- og barneboksamlinger*, Kristiania, Bind 9, No. 1, Feb., 1915, pp. 1–6; No. 2, May, 1915, pp. 36–41. DLC, NNY.

"Our public schools' oldest children's libraries." The development of the first school collections in the period from 1830–1861, and something about the books which went into them.

1624. Arstal, Aksel. [Children's reading.] *Foraeldre og børn*. Kristiania, 1902, pp. 451–489.

1625. *Barn og bøker*. Oslo, 1938. 84p. (Ny opdragelse, 3). SPS.

Four articles on children's reading by Rikka Deinboll, Karsten Heli, Ase G. Skard and Marianne Rumohr.

1626. Bibliotekkontor. Kirke- og Undervisnings-Departementet. *Katalog over bøker skikket for skoleboksamlinger*. Oslo, O. F. Arnesens, 1929. 125p. DLC, NNY.

Based on an earlier list, *Centralstyre for de Norske Folkeskolers Barne- og Ungdomsbiblioteker*, published in 1915 by the Kirkedepartmentets Rådgivende Komité for Skoleboksamlingene. This is an annotated list arranged by Dewey classification, with an index. For later editions of this booklist, see entries under Statens Bibliotektilsyn.

1627. Bjølgerud, Rikka. "Årets barne og ungdomsbøker," *For folkeoplysning*, Kristiania, Bind 10, Nos. 1–2, Apr., 1925, pp. 9–12; Bind 11, Nos. 1–2, May, 1926, pp. 17–21; Bind 12, No. 2, May, 1927, pp. 74–77; etc. NNY.

A yearly review of the best children's books in Norway by a well-known children's librarian.

1628. ——— et al. *Håndbok i norsk barnebibliotekarbeide*. Oslo, O. F. Arnesen, 1927. 161p. (Norsk Bibliotekforenings Småskrifter, 7.) NNY.

"Handbook of Norwegian children's library work." A historical survey as well as an introduction to theory and practice. Both school and public library service are covered. This was one of the pioneering works in this area. Illustrated with photographs. Bibliography.

1629. *Bokbladet*. Statens Bibliotektilsyn, Munkedamsveien 62, Oslo. 1959 ff. Quarterly. Annual subscription, 5 kr. IYL. (DLC has sample issues only.)

"A periodical for school and children's librarians." Each issue is from ten to twenty pages in length, and contains articles on children's literature.

1630. Deinboll, Rikka. "Barn og bøker. Tillegg." Bergersen, Hans. *Morsmålsoplaeringen*. Oslo, 1935, pp. 293–318.

1631. ——— and Aud Risberg. *Boka i undervisningen; høyere skoler og framhaldsskoler*. Oslo, Deichmanske Bibliotek, Skoleavdelingen, 1950. 138p. DLC, IYL. (DLC also has 1936 edition.)

A booklist of some 2,000 titles arranged by Dewey, not annotated, but indexed.

1632. ———. *Bøker for barn og ungdom*. Oslo, Opplysningskontoret for den Norske Bokhandel, 1950. 69p. IYL.

An annotated booklist arranged by type and age groups. Title index.

1633. ———. *Bøker til fritid og undervisning; for barn i folkeskolen*. Oslo, Folkeskoler, 1954. 70p. IYL.

A booklist for children's and school libraries, arranged by age and subject groups, and illustrated with reproductions from some of the books listed.

1634. ———. "Samarbeide mellem skole og bibliotek." Norsk Biblioteksforening. *Jubileumskrift 1913–1938*. Oslo, pp. 73–82. DLC.

"Cooperation between schools and public libraries." Pp. 83–96 in this same volume contain an article by Hanna Giaever on school libraries.

1635. Eng, Helga. "Barn og bok," *Den nye barneskole*; Oslo, Steenske Forlag, 1937; pp. 141–154. NNY.

"Child and book." An essay on reading interests, written for this special collection in honor of Anna Sethne.

1636. Feydt, Astrid. "Norwegian books for children," *Junior bookshelf*, Windermere Vol. 18, No. 5, Nov., 1954, pp. 225–233; No. 6, Dec., 1954, pp. 277–283. DLC, IYL, NNY.

A general review of some of the best-known and loved books for children (old and new) illustrated with reproductions from some of them. A later article by Jo Tenfjord, in Vol. 26, No. 1, Jan., 1962, pp. 7–12 discusses many of the same works and some of the more recent children's books in Norway.

1637. Giaever, Hanna. "Noen tall og spredte trekk fra bibliotekarbeidet for barn i Norge," *For folkeoplysning*, Oslo, Bind 18, No. 4, Dec., 1933, pp. 118–123. NNY.

"Some statistics and features of library work with children in Norway."

1638.   Hagemann, Sonia. *Barnelitteraturen i Norge inntil 1850*. Oslo, H. Aschehoug and Co., 1965. 351p. DLC, IYL.

"Norwegian children's literature up to 1850." A well-known critic of children's books, Mrs. Hagemann has produced an excellent study on the beginnings of Norweigian children's literature, with the greatest emphasis on the three most important figures of the time: Peter Christen Asbjörnsen, Jörgen Moe, and Henrik Wergeland. She treats the early children's literature as only a part of the general cultural life of each period, judging it not by present day standards but by those contemporary to the appearance of the literature.

1639.   Hernes, Tore. *Barnebøker i serie*. Oslo, Biblioteksentralen, 1963. 18p. (Blant bøker, 14). IYL.

"Children's books in series." A list to help librarians in tracing the order of titles in well-known children's series, so that the stories follow one another logically.

1640.   Kontoret for Kunst og Kulturarbeid. *Barns og unges lesning*. Oslo, 1960. 36p.

1641.   Kvaløy, Anders. "Eventyra i oppsedinga," *Skole og samfunn*, Oslo, Ag. 4, 1955, pp. 56–59–88–90, 122–125, 153–56. DLC.

1642.   "Laesesaler for barn og ungdom," *For folke- og barneboksamlinger*, Kristiania, Bind 6, No. 1, Mar., 1912, pp. 10–20. DLC, NNY.

"Reading rooms for children and young people." Those described are the ones in the Deichmanske Bibliotek in Oslo, and in the Bergen and Trondjhem public libraries. Illustrated with photographs.

1643.   Magnussen, Edith. *Leseinteresser i realskolealderen*. Oslo, Cappelen, 1951. 94p. (Avhandlinger fra Universitets Pedagogiske Forskningsinstitut, 9).

1644.   Nergard, Sigurd. . . . *Eventyr, barnevers, spurningar og ordspraak* . . . Kristiania, Norsk Folkeminnelag, 1923. 145p. (Skrifter, No. 7). NNY.

A collection of children's game songs, sayings, counting-out rhymes and other oral folklore.

1645.   Olden, O. F. "Barnas altmuligbok," *For folkeoplysning*, Kristiania, Bind 4, No. 1, May, 1919, pp. 5–7. NNY.

"Children's reference books." A discussion of encyclopedias, handbooks and other nonfiction for children.

1646.   Rolfsen, Nordahl. *Centralstyret for de norske folkeskolders barne- og ungdomsbiblioteker*. Kristiania, 1910. 103p.

1647.   ———. "De norske barnebiblioteker," *For folke- og barneboksamlinger*, Kristiania, Bind 1, Mar., 1907, pp. 17–22; No. 2, May, 1907, pp. 41–44. DLC, NNY.

"Norwegian children's libraries; ten years' work, results and reforms." The improvements were mostly due to the organization of a *Centralstyret* (Central Committee) for developing public school libraries for children and young people. This work began in 1896. The author mentions the great forward strides of the previous ten years and outlines the steps still to be taken.

1648.   Schulstad, Olav. "Nyordning av barnebibliotekene ved Kristiania folkeskoler," *For folkeoplysning*, Kristiania, Bind 5, No. 3, Sept., 1920, pp. 79–86. NNY.

"New arrangement of the children's libraries in Kristiania schools." The title refers to the changing from classroom collections to a central library as well as other organizational and content improvements.

1649.   Sigmund, Einar. "Bibliotekerne ved våre gamle katedralskoler," *Bok og bibliotek*, Oslo, Vol. 1, Dec., 1934, pp. 318–323. DLC.

A history of libraries in the cathedral schools of Norway from the mid-18th century through the 19th.

1650.   ———. "Et forslag til omordning av barnebibliotekene ved Drammens folkeskoler," *For folke- og barneboksamlinger*, Kristiania, Bind 7, No. 4, Dec., 1913, pp. 131–135. DLC, NNY.

"A proposal for the reorganization of the children's libraries in Drammen's public schools." The proposal was concerned with the distinction between children's libraries and teaching collections, the areas of responsibility for librarian, teacher and principal, the budget and other related matters.

1651.   Skard, Åse Gruda. "Rapport om arbeid med barnebøker," *Bok og bibliotek*, Oslo, Ag. 12, Oct., 1945, pp. 89–102. DLC, NNY.

Observations on children's library work in Norway, the U.S., and the other Scandinavian countries together with reminiscences of the contact this work has brought with many of the creators of children's books.

1652.   Sletvold, Sverre. *Barna og litteraturen. En analyse av utviklingen av litteraer vurdering hos norske skolebarn.* Oslo, Universitetsforlaget, 1958. 456p. IYL, NNY.

"Children and literature. An analysis of the development of literary appreciation in Norwegian school children." A study made over a period of years among children from 9–14 years. Types of literature (e.g., adventure stories, poetry, folk tales) are analyzed separately for appeal and reader interest. Many statistical tables give results of various questionnaire answers. The bibliography on pp. 452–456 is quite complete in its coverage of reading interest studies up to 1956.

1653.   Statens Bibliotektilsyn. *Bøker for barn og ungdom. Et utvalg av bøker for skoleboksamlinger. Hovedkatalog.* Oslo, Statens Bibliotektilsyn, 1957. 245p. IYL. Supplements: 1958, 27p.; 1959, 32p.; 1960, 29p.; 1961, 29p.; 1962, 37p. IYL.

A list of books for children and youth put out by the central library inspection department. There are annual supplements. A new, revised basic catalog is available, but was not located.

1654.   ———. Kirge- og Undervisnings Departementet. *Bøker for skoleboksamlinger.* Hovedkatalog. Oslo, Statens. . . , 1963. 338p. DLC, IYL. Supplements: 1963, 48p.; 1964, 46p.; 1965, DLC, IYL.

1655.   Svensen, Sven. "Hvad barn leser," *For folkeoplysning,* Kristiania, Bind 3, Nos. 5–6, Feb., 1919, pp. 191–198. NNY.

"What children read." A report on a reading-interest survey made in the children's libraries of Trondjhem and Drammen.

1656.   Tenfjord, Jo. *Barn og lesning.* Oslo, Aschehoug, 1947. 159p. IYL.

An illustrated, selective booklist arranged by age groups and with some annotations. There are also short essays on children's reading.

1657.   Vigander. "Om barnelaesning og barnebøker," *For folke- og barneboksamlinger,* Kristiania, Bind 5, No. 2, June, 1911, pp. 33–38. DLC, NNY.

"About children's reading and children's books." Good books, writes this author, increase perception and knowledge, refresh the wells of fantasy, strengthen and support character, and supply important linguistic practice and increase in vocabulary. He reviews some of the books which qualify as good literature.

1658.   Wettre, Leiv H. *Leseinteresser i gymnasalderen.* Oslo, Cappelen, 1942. 122p.

1659.   Wiig, Hanna. "Barnearbeide i norske byer og ladesteder," *Bok og bibliotek,* Oslo, Ag. 5, No. 5, Sept., 1938, pp. 319–327. NNY.

"Children's work in Norwegian cities and towns." A report accompanied by extensive statistics.

1660.   ———. "Barneboksamlingen i folkebiblioteket eller ved skolen?" *For folkeoplysning,* Kristiania, Bind 9, Nos. 3–4, Dec., 1924, pp. 65–68. NNY.

"Children's book collections in the public library or the school?" The author concludes that children cannot have enough contact with good books, and both school and public library should have them available.

Sweden

If one were to conjure up an imaginary list of those countries doing most in the area of original research on children's literature, certainly Sweden would place high, if not at the top. Most countries feel themselves fortunate if they have one good critical history. In the last few years alone, Sweden has produced two of considerable length. It might be assumed that these volumes are repetitious, and contain much of the same material, for Sweden is not, after all, such a vast country. To a certain extent they do repeat material, but it is more a question of complementing each other, since the points of view are so different. Anyone paging through the beautifully printed reproductions in Mrs. von Zweigberg's survey (1786) cannot help but be drawn into the subject. On the other hand, to do the same with Göte Klingberg's study (1718) leaves one with a great respect for the scholarship which is possible in this type of literature, as in any other.

One can indirectly study much of Western children's literature by virtue of the fact that both include this literature as it came to be known to Swedish children through translation or adaptation.

There is a third recent critical-historical work, but on a very special type of children's book—the ABC. Ingeborg Willke's dissertation (1784) is a thorough study of this important kind of book—the very first to which most children are exposed.

There are only three among numerous studies published in recent years. Yet it cannot be said that Sweden is ready to sit back and rest on its laurels. Plans are well under way for the opening of an institute for the study of books for children and adolescents. Mary Ørvig, a leading children's librarian with the Stockholm City Library, was given a leave of absence to begin laying the groundwork for this institute. It is to be a joint venture of the Stockholm Library, the Swedish Association of Authors of Juvenile Books, the Association of Publishers and Stockholm University.

There is no doubt that the new institute will have an abundance of work. Its very existence, and such evidence as the newly published studies, are signs of the lively and growing interest which has been stimulated in Sweden during the past years, in the subject of children's books. Like the other three countries in this section, Sweden publishes a great many translations. Unlike them, she publishes an equal number of native works. The report of the Swedish Section to the Tenth Congress of IBBY states: "At present it is possible to say that the Swedish production of books for children and young people is plentiful, varied and qualitatively on a high level, which does not prevent a lot of books that are not so good being produced and the good books having to compete with poor quality comics and similar publications. If only the more valuable kind of work is considered, one can say that they cover a wider field, deal with social settings and problems that were not dealt with formerly and are more realistic also from a psychological point of view."

Both the Klingberg and von Zweigbergk histories document this gradual change from the didactic to the romantic to the modern style. Since these books are widely available and have English summaries, only the highlights will be pointed out here.

Some of the first literature for children was written by Carl Gustaf Tessin, a tutor, to his young charge, Crown Prince Gustavus III. These fables and fairy tales were in the form of instructive letters and were probably admired more by parents than by the children themselves. The first real books intended for children were written by Zakarias Topelius of Finland. He rightly belongs more to that country and is mentioned further in that section. A friend of Topelius, C. A. Wetterburgh, edited a magazine called *Linnea,* in which many of the best early stories for children appeared.

Late in the 19th century, the ideals of popular education took hold of the reading public and there was much discussion back and forth as to what this education consisted of and what its aims were. Almost all were willing to agree that good books were a part of it, but there were very different interpretations of the term "good." Women's groups were especially active in this movement, and for them "good" often meant "realism with a healthy and moral content." Imagination and playfulness were still considered rather disturbing (1786). Ellen Key was an exception to this in that she felt, like Humble and Wolgast, that children's books should be above the message or moral which might or might not be there.

Perhaps the single event of greatest importance was the commission Selma Lagerlöf received from the Ministry of Education, along with a number of other writers. The result went against all the laws of average. For the most part, when works have been commissioned by well-meaning patrons or governments, the outcome has been unsatisfactory. This was not the case with Selma Lagerlöf. She found obvious stimulation and enjoyment in her assignment and this imbues each of the episodes she narrates with an excitement that carries the reader right along on Nils Holgersson's wonderful journey.

Another venture which spans the first and last years of the two centuries was the *Barnbiblioteket Saga*. Similar to the Danish *Bornenes Bogsamling,* in that it also adapted classics, it nevertheless enjoyed a better reputation for quality compared to its counterpart. This was perhaps because it stayed more with recognized children's classics rather than ruthlessly cutting down adult adventure books.

The illustration of children's books in Sweden had its "golden age" from 1900 through the 1920's. Elsa Beskow, Ottilia Adelborg and Ivar Arosenius, are the names most familiar to this period, and still known to today's children through a select number of their works still in print. Their charm and artistry have great appeal.

Anglo-American influence was not limited to library development; it provided hundreds of titles for translation into Swedish as well. This high percentage of English language sources is only slightly diminished in the present decade, because of the addition of more German, Dutch and other language sources. Since the end of the Second World War it has been accompanied by a new crop of Swedish authors, writing in a fresh, new style. Humor and fantasy have an element of the absurd in them, as for example, in the works of Astrid Lindgren, Lennart Hellsing, Ake Holmberg, Hans Peterson, Britt Hallgvist, and Inger and Lasse Sandberg. A number of these have been widely translated, and contrary to many who believed they were too "Swedish" in humor, they have had success with children of many lands. The most audacious of all the new heroes and heroines is Pippi Longstocking, the creation of Astrid Lindgren. For her entire oeuvre, this author was awarded the Hans Christian Andersen Medal in 1958.

Book programs of all types are popular with children in Sweden. The annual Children's Book Week celebration is modeled on that of the U.S. Television and radio programs also stimulate reading for pleasure. Much publicity is given to the winners of the Nils Holgersson Medal, awarded annually since 1950 to an outstanding writer, and of the Elsa Beskow Medal, awarded each year since 1957 to an illustrator who has produced an excellent picture book. In addition, state grants to distinguished authors have occasionally gone to children's writers. Some publishing houses have their own prize competitions. All of these awards bring much esteem as well as monetary rewards, so that the author of children's books in Sweden has achieved a position of widely recognized importance.

Hand in hand with all of these activities go the efforts of public and school librarians. Although Sweden has not reached the pinnacle of library legislation in mandatory library service in every school and community (as has Denmark), she has nevertheless developed laws which provide for very extensive service on a highly professional level. Through Bibliotekstjänst, an agency of the National Association of Swedish Librarians, all children's librarians are provided with centralized services such as book reviewing, cataloging, binding, and professional advice in many categories. Bibliotekstjänst also publishes numerous book lists, handbooks, pamphlets and bibliographic aids on subjects related to children's books. These are always very attractively designed and could well be imitated by other countries. Since both this agency and Bibliotekcentralen in Denmark are modeled on the same lines and operate under similar conditions, it might be well to go into a few details behind their services.

The booksellers associations are very strong in both of these countries, and their influence is felt in the set-up through which books are sold to schools and libraries. In order to protect their rights, all orders must be placed through a local bookseller, even though Bibliotekstjänst catalogs, processes and binds a large percentage. In this way, small book dealers are not forced out of existence and they feel they can then give more personal service to the individual child buyer. This might well be true, for in the case of the U.S., where the highest percentage of children's books are bought by libraries, most sales go through book jobbers or are made directly by the publishers; consequently, it is rare to find a good bookseller who maintains a stock of the best books, and sales to individuals are small and seasonal. Although the Swedish process of book-ordering might seem complicated, it does not work out to be nearly as much work for the individual librarian, since much of the work of compiling order lists and sending them regularly is assumed by Bibliotekstjänst. They have also been extremely forward-thinking in their designs for library buildings and equipment, which can do so much to make the role of the children's librarian an efficient and attractive one.

All things considered, Sweden can be pointed out as one of the few countries where children's book publishing and distribution, and library service to children have achieved a rare standard of quality, if not excellence.

1661.   Ågren, Karl. "Bibliotekets plats i skolarbetet," *Biblioteksbladet,* Stockholm, Årgång 13, 1928. pp. 240–248. DLC, NNY, BTJ.
    "The library's place in school work." A paper read at the annual library association conference.

1662.   Ahlgren, Stig. "Socialism och barnböcker," *Orfeus i folkhemmet.* Stockholm, Albert Bonnier, 1938. pp. 156–162. IYL, BTJ.
    A well-known columnist and essayist comments here on socialism and children's books in a lively style and somewhat radical approach.

1663. Ahlström, Gunnar. *Den underbara resan.* Stockholm, Bonnier, 1958. 196p. DLC, IYL, NNY.

"The wonderful journey," referring to the book about Nils, written by Selma Lagerlöf. Strictly speaking, this should not be included here since it is about one author's work, but there is much in the text about other children's books, and the criticism is valid for all children's literature.

1664. *Alla tiders ungdomsböcker.* 6th ed. Stockholm, Svensk Boktjänst, 1963. 69p. IYL, BTJ.

A booklist arranged by age and subject groups, not annotated, but with author and title indexes. The general editor was Lisa-Christina Persson.

1665. Attorps, Gösta. *Ungdomsskeppen.* 2nd ed. Stockholm, Rabén & Sjögren, 1958. 152p. IYL.

Essays on classics for young people: *Huckleberry Finn, Lorna Doone, The Leatherstocking Tales; Jungle Books, Three Musketeers, Treasure Island; Uncle Tom's Cabin, Don Quixote* and others.

1666. Aulin, Lars Axel Alfred. "Ungdomslitteratur," *Pedagogisk tidskrift,* Stockholm, Vol. 1, 1865, pp. 43–48, 108–114, 280–287.

According to Klingberg (1718) this was the earliest article, specifically on the subject of juvenile literature, to appear in Sweden. Aulin was directly influenced by Kühner (1903) and took over and expanded many of his ideas.

1667. "Barn- och ungdomsbibliotek," *Biblioteksbladet,* Lund, Årgang 38, 1953 ff. DLC, NNY, BTJ.

A column on library work with children and young people which appears frequently, but not in every issue.

1668. "Barn- och ungdomsböcker," *Svensk litteraturlexicon.* Lund, C. W. K. Gleerup, 1964.

Besides this general article on children's literature compiled by Erik A. Ohlson, Eva von Zweigbergk and Elisabeth Olvång, there are several articles on individual writers of juvenile books, e.g., Edith Unnerstad, Astrid Lindgren, etc.

1669. "Barnböcken," Svensk tidskrift index, Lund, Årgang 1 ff., 1952 ff. DLC, BTJ.

Articles in Swedish periodicals on the subject of children's books and libraries can be traced through this current index.

1670. *Barnböcker.* Stockholm, Svensk Boktjänst, 1960. 77p. (Småskrifter för Bokhandeln, 6). DLC, BTJ.

These eight essays on children's books cover: reviewing and criticism; books for the very young, the middle graders, and teenagers; the influence of TV; publishing; selling; selecting for home purchase. The general editor was Lisa-Christina Persson.

1671. Barthel, Sven. *Äventyrens värld.* Stockholm, Bonnier, 1958. 172p. IYL, NNY.

"The world of adventure." The title essay is concerned with adventure novels for young people.

1672. Beckman, Brita and Lisa-Christina Persson. *Böcker för tonåringer; skönlitteratur i urval.* Lund, Bibliotekstjänst, 1953. 23p. (Sveriges Allmänna Biblioteksförening, Småskrifter, 42). IYL.

"Books for the teen-age." This included both fiction and nonfiction; it was the predecessor of two current lists, 1673 and 1740.

1673. Beckman, Brita and Inga Wärne. *Facklitteratur för ungdom.* Lund, Bibliotekstjänst, 1961. 52p. (Bokurval, 27), IYL, DLC. Supplement, 1965. 16p. DLC.

A list of nonfiction books for young people, arranged by subject. They are not annotated, but author and title indexes are included.

1674. Bejerot, Nils. *Barn—serier—samhälle.* Stockholm, Folket i Bilds Förlag, 1955. 224p. DLC, IYL, NNY.

"Children, comics and the state." A study of their rise to popularity, the changing values in content and illustration, the problem of control and censorship, and what some countries have done through legal action or social agencies in an attempt to control the influence of comics on children.

1675. Berg, Fridtjuv. "Våra barns nöjesläsning," *Svensk läraretidning,* Stockholm, No. 48, 1902, pp. 911 ff. Also in: *Pedagogiska skrifter,* Stockholm, No. 101, 1922, pp. 5–10.

1676. Bergstrand, Ulla. *Högläsning för hela familjen.* Lund, Bibliotekstjänst, 1965. 29p. (Bokurval, 49). DLC.

A basic reading list for the whole family arranged by general subjects and with short annotations.

1677. Böcker för barn och ungdom," *Biblioteksbladet,* Stockholm and Lund, Årgång 1, 1916 ff. DLC, NNY, BTJ.

Signed, annotated reviews of current children's books, indicating price, age level, original title if a translation, and other pertinent information. In the first volumes, these reviews appeared once a year, and were usually the work of one librarian, Gurli Linder. Later, they began to appear with more frequency and finally some reviews were included in each issue.

1678.   "Boken ock barnen," Special issue of: *Vi, husmödrar,* Stockholm, No. 10, 1956. 31p. BTJ.

This entire supplement of a popular consumers magazine was devoted to children and books. Astrid Lindgren, Eva von Zweigbergk, Elsa Olenius, Egon Mathiesen, Björn Wester and Märta de Laval assisted the editor, Birgitta Ek-von Hofsten. This was a rather new approach to mothers (for its time) and contains some very good basic articles.

1679.   Bolin, Greta and Eva von Zweigbergk. *Barn och böcker.* 6th ed. Stockholm, Rabén and Sjögren, 1966. 226p. IYL, BTJ. (1st ed., 1945).

"Children and books." This sixth edition has the addition of Mary Ørvig as one of the compilers. This has become the standard selection list for use by librarians, teachers, parents and others to learn the best means of bringing children and books together, and to discover some of the best literature available in children's books. There are chapters on picture books and other favorites of the very young, on nonfiction, on the classics and fiction for middlegrade children, on girls' stories and the teen-age novel, and on sources of information concerning children's books and libraries. Each chapter has book lists and a short bibliography. There is a name index.

1680.   Brandell, Georg. "Børn och ungdoms nöjesläsning," *Pedagogisk tidskrift,* Stockholm, Nos. 3–4, 1945, pp. 41–60.

1681.   ———. "Skolbarns bokliga intressen," *Skolbarns intressen.* Stockholm, Nya Tryckeri Aktiebolaget, 1913, pp. 215–225. BTJ.

An early study on the reading interests of Swedish school children. There are a number of statistical tables.

1682.   Bredelius, Margit and Gerd Schoultz. *Böcker för flickor och pojkar.* Lund, Bibliotekstjänst, 1962. 56p. (Bokurval, 29). IYL, DLC.

"Books for boys and girls," a list modeled on the earlier *Ett Urval Böcker för Ungdom* (1781). There are no annotations in this list, but the books in series have been kept, separately listed as in the previous editions.

1683.   Broström, Karin. "Folkskolornas biblioteks-lokaler," *Biblioteksbladet,* Stockholm, Årgång 16, 1931, pp. 269–271. DLC, NNY, BTJ.

"Library collections in public schools." This is preceded by an article on books in the schools by N. O. Bruce, pp. 266–268 and it is followed by a similar article by Karl Regfors, pp. 319–322.

1684.   Bruhn, Karl. *Från prinsessan Snövit till kavaljererna på Ekeby.* Helsingfors, Söderström, 1944. 206p. DLC, IYL.

"From princess Snow White to the cavaliers of Ekeby; a study on the reading interests of school children." Emphasis is as much on the literary as it is on the psychological. Some graphs are included, and there is a bibliography, but no index.

1685.   ———. "Den lille vilden," *Skolar och hem,* Stockholm?, Ag. 7, Heft 3, 1944, pp. 1–9.

1686.   Cederblad, C. "Ungdom och läsning," *Skola och samhälle,* Stockholm, Ag. 23, Heft 7, 1942, pp. 236–244. DLC.

"Youth and reading." This teacher's professional periodical had a number of such general articles at intervals.

1687.   Cutforth, J. A. and S. H. Battersby. *Böcker och barn.* Stockholm, Natur och Kultur, 1965. 110p. BTJ.

A translation from the English *Children and Books* (see 3044).

1688.   Dahlgren, Lotten. "Våra barns nöjesläsning." Några ord med anledning of Gurli Linders broschyr, *Dagny,* Stockholm, Vol. 17, 1902, pp. 411–419.

A commentary on the brochure and book list compiled by Gurli Linder (1738).

1689.   Enberg, Brita. "Bibliothèques d'enfants en Suède," *Biblioteconomía,* Madrid, Año 5, No. 18, Apr.–June, 1948, pp. 83–87. NNY.

A brief history in French of Swedish library work with children.

1690.   Engström, Lilly. "Något om våra nyare barnböcker," *Dagny,* Stockholm, Vol. 5, 1890. pp. 103–110.

"Something about the new children's books."

1691.   Feuk, Mathias. "Barnet i litteraturen," *Biblioteksbladet,* Stockholm, Årgång 10, 1925, pp. 1–9. DLC, NNY, BTJ.

A lecture on the changing position of the child in literature and on children as they experience literature.

1692.   "First Swedish book week is successful,"

Publishers' weekly, New York, Vol. 125, Apr. 14, 1934, pp. 1453–1454. DLC, NNY.

A report on the first children's book week, as it was celebrated in Stockholm and Malmö. The list by Landergren and Jacobson (1710) is described.

1693. Fransson, Evald. "Serielitteraturen- ett uppfostringsproblem," *Folkskolan,* Stockholm, Årgång 7, No. 9, 1953, pp. 198–208.

On the problem of comics and cheap series literature. This is one of a number of articles appearing in this periodical.

1694. Gunnemo, Bertil. *Ungdom och literatur.* Stockholm, Evangeliska Fosterlands-Stiftelsens, 1950. 84p. IYL, NNY. (IYL also has earlier version called *Ungdom och läsning,* same pub., 1941. 55p.)

"Youth and literature." Essays on the pleasures of reading with particular emphasis on Christian values.

1695. Gustafsson, Axel. *Serie magasinen – en samhällsfara.* Stockholm, Filadelfia, 1955. 23p.

1696. Hagemann, Sonja. "Barnebokkritikerens oppgave," *Bonnier's litterära magasin,* Stockholm, Årgång 27, No. 5, May–June, 1958, pp. 379–385. DLC, NNY.

"The task of the children's book critic." A discussion of the qualifications and experience necessary to review children's books. The author recommends a thorough knowledge of the literary history of children's books, and the ability to give objective as well as subjective judgement.

1697. Hallqvist, Britt G. "Askungen's önskedröm," *Bonnier's litterära magasin,* Stockholm, Årgång 20, No. 4, April, 1951, pp. 276–282.

"Cinderella's dream-wish; a retrospective look at some old girls' stories." The heroines of such authors as L. M. Alcott, L. M. Montgomery, Jean Webster and Susan Coolidge are examined, to determine why they were and have remained popular, and how extensively they influenced the girl's novel of today.

1698. Haste, Hans. *Läsning för barn?* Stockholm, Folket i Bilds Förlag, 1955. 24p. BTJ.

A strongly worded essay questioning the suitability of comics as children's reading material.

1699. Hazard, Paul. *Böcker, barn och vuxna.* Stockholm, Rabén & Sjögren, 1955. 194p.

Translated into Swedish by Eva von Zweigbergk. For note see 814.

1700. Hellman, Gunnar. *Några svenska sagokonstnärer.* Stockholm, Lindqvists, 1949. 78p. DLC.

"Our Swedish fairy tale illustrators." Following twelve pages of introductory text are more than fifty plates reproducing (in black and white) the illustrations of some forty artists.

1701. Hellsing, Lennart. *Tankar om barnlitteraturen.* Stockholm, Rabén & Sjögren, 1963. 143p. BTJ.

"Thoughts on children's literature." This writer of children's books considers here such questions as: "What is children's literature?" "What are its aims and methods?" "Are girls' books an anachronism?" "What are the real means of critically evaluating books for children?" etc. The author points out his debt to Lucy Sprague Mitchell, and her stories for very young children.

1702. Hofvendahl, Inga. "Children's books in Sweden," *Junior bookshelf,* Huddersfield, Vol. 17, No. 4, Oct., 1953, pp. 159–167. DLC, IYL, NNY.

An annotated list of 16 outstanding contemporary books.

1703. Humble, Julius. *Vår tids ungdomsläsning, hennes inflytande och riktiga ledning.* Stockholm, 1871. Also in: *Pedagogisk tidskrift,* Stockholm, Vol. 6, 1870, pp. 33–45, 93–110, 209–224, 359–382. IYL has xerograph.

"How to influence and direct young people's reading." In the same periodical, Vol. 21, 1885, pp. 373–385 and pp. 421–431, this author has a two-part article on "What folk tales are for children?" Mr. Humble was a teacher who questioned whether educators were the ones who should be writing and editing children's books.

1704. *Hur man hittar sagor.* Lund, Bibliotekstjänst, 1963. 488p. DLC.

"How to find fairy tales: a catalog of Swedish folk and fairy tales 1910–1960 compiled in the Stockholm *Stadsbibliotek.*" A title listing of 4,500 fairy tales with collections in which they can be found. Cross references on title variations are very complete. Separate listings of the collections, and the authors and collectors of the tales, appear at the end. The forward indicates that most of the work was done by Mary Ørvig, and she has written the introduction.

1705. Husén, Torsten. "Läsintressena under adolescensen," *Adolescensen.* Uppsala, Almgvist & Wiksells, 1944, pp. 387–499. BTJ.

This 9th and final chapter in a book on adolescents deals with their reading interests. It contains references to many other studies and reproduces many statistical tables. There is a six page bibliography.

1706.   Jacobson, Helja. "Barnavdelningar i folkbiblioteken," *Biblioteksbladet,* Stockholm, Årgång 20, Häfte 7, 1935, pp. 245–251. DLC, NNY.

An address given at the national library conference in June, 1935. It is a review of the history of children's library work in Sweden, the trends in other countries, and some recommendations for strengthening the quality of children's libraries.

1707.   ———. "En pionjär ser tillbaka; de första svenska barnbibliotekens historia," *Biblioteksbladet,* Stockholm, Ag. 38, No. 1, 1953, pp. 7–14. DLC.

"A pioneer looks back; the history of the first Swedish children's libraries."

1708.   ———. "Specialutbildning för ungdomsbibliotekarier," *Biblioteket och vi,* Örebro, 1950, pp. 95–101. DLC.

A survey of the training children's librarians undergo in Denmark, Norway, England, Holland, USA, and Sweden with special emphasis on the last.

1709.   ———. [Swedish literature for children and youth.] *Ruch pedagogiczny,* Warszawa, Vol. 31, No. 1, 1947/48.

Paper given at the Polish Congress on Children's Literature (see 2114). In Polish.

1710.   ——— and Anna Landergren. *1001 böcker för sveriges ungdom.* Stockholm, Svensk Boktjänst, 1933. 62p.

A book list published in connection with the first Swedish Children's Book Week. This also contained a story by Selma Lagerlöf.

1711.   Järnesjö, Eva and Mary Ørvig. *Sagor för sagostunden.* Lund, Bibliotekstjänst, 1965. 101p. (Bokurval, 44). DLC, IYL, NNY.

"Stories for storytelling." A brief introduction to the art, a bibliography of literature on storytelling and a list of stories to tell. There are also lists of collections from which the stories come, and general subject groups from which one can refer back to the main entry. Illustrated with reproductions from story collections.

1712.   Jonnergård, Margot. *Barn, serier och böcker; studieplan.* Västerås, Svenska Landsbygdens Studieförbund, 1955. 24p. BTJ.

"Children, comics and books." A study guide prepared for the Swedish Rural Study Circle.

1713.   Key, Ellen. "Böckerna mot läseböckerna," *Barnets århundrade,* Vol. 2. Stockholm, Albert Bonnier, 1900. pp. 173–189. Also in: *Tidskrift verdandi,* Stockholm, Vol. 2, 1884, pp. 56–66.

This foresighted woman was a pioneer in the drive for women's rights and other social justice movements. This article was a plea for better reading materials in the schools, and shows the influence of Humble (1703) and Wolgast (1458). There is a suggested list of good books for children and young people in the "Bilaga," pp. 245–256 of this volume.

1714.   ———. "Patriotism och läseböcker," *Ord och bild,* Stockholm, Årgång 7, 1898, pp. 136–144. NNY.

"Patriotism and [children's] reading books." A comparison of the books used commonly by Norwegian and Swedish school children, and how they do or do not effectively reflect the new patriotism.

1715.   Klingberg, Göte. *Barnboken genom tiderna.* Stockholm, Natur och Kultur, 1962. 123p. IYL, NNY, DLC.

"Children's books through the years; an overview." Treating the literature by types—folk, fables, drama, adventure novels, realistic stories, nonsense, science fiction—the author ranges through the major works of the Scandinavian countries, as well as France, England, the U.S. and Germany. One chapter is on 19th-century literature of the didactic type. A bibliography on pp. 115–116 is followed by author and title indexes.

1716.   ———. *Läsning för ungt folk; äldre europeisk barn- och ungdomslitteratur.* Stockholm, Natur och Kultur, 1966. 254p. BTJ.

"Reading for young folk; old European children's literature." The selections are mostly from French, German and English children's books of the 17th, 18th and 19th centuries, which were translated into Swedish. There are eight plates of reproductions. This can be used as a companion volume to the author's major historical work.

1717.   ———. *Sekelskiftets barnbokssyn och Barnbiblioteket Saga.* Stockholm, Svensk Läraretidnings förlag, 1966. 121p. (Pedagogiska skrifter, 239). BTJ.

"View of the turn-of-the-century children's books and the Saga Children's Library." Mr. Klingberg begins his study with a survey of the first critical essays to appear in print in Sweden. He points out the influence of the German critics. The major portion of the work deals with the series called "Saga," which appeared from 1899–1904 and contained some of the best literature for children. There is an excellent bibliography.

1718. ———. *Svensk barn- och ungdomslitteratur 1591–1839. En pedagogikhistorisk och bibliografisk översikt*. Stockholm, Natur och Kultur, 1964. 413p. DLC, IYL.

"This treatise is a contribution to the history of education. Therefore, literature for children is defined, not as the books that young people have read . . . but as the literature that has been published for or mainly for children and adolescents. The pedagogical point of view further implies that the interest is centered around the leading ideas that guided the authors and publishers. All literature that was published for children and adolescents in Sweden is treated whether or not the works are Swedish originals or translations." (From the English summary, p. 341.) The author indicates that a chronological list of the literature in question will be published separately as a *Bibliographical Catalogue of Swedish Literature for Children and Adolescents 1591–1839*. There are English summaries for each of the chapters treating with specific types of the literature: religious, courtesy literature, mythical and historical figures used as moral examples, fables, chimerical tales, books about natural history and geography, instructive and moral adventure stories, moral stories about ordinary children, animal stories, and children's literature without instructional intent. This is a masterful study, and combined with the recent work of Eva von Zweigbergk, provides a sweeping and penetrating view of Swedish literature for children. Bibliography and author and title indexes.

1719. Knudsen, Thora. "Stockholms barn - och ungdoms bibliotek," *Kvinden og samfundet*, København, Ag. 28, No. 1, Jan. 15, 1912, pp. 1–3.

1720. Kylberg, Anna Maria, *et al. Våra barn och deras böcker*. Stockholm, Sveriges Radio, 1963, 131p. IYL, BTJ.

"Your child and his books." Reprints of speeches given in a series of radio programs in 1963 by leading critics, authors, librarians and others working with children and books. Index.

1721. Langfeldt, J. "Die Organisation des Schulbüchereiwesens in Gotenburg," *Aus dem Volksbüchereiwesen der Gegenwart;* Stettin, Verlag "Bücherei und Bildungspflege," 1930; pp. 75–86. NNY.

A German librarian describes the organization of school libraries in Göteborg, which he had visited numerous times. He found them singularly well-organized and far ahead of school libraries in Germany.

1722. Larson, Lorentz. *Barn och serier*. Stockholm, Almqvist and Wiksell, 1954. 175p. NNY.

"Children and comics." Why they read them, what their effects are, and the analysis of their contents from the point of view of language and illustration.

1723. ——— and Mary Ørvig. *Barnböcker i sverige 1945–1965*. Stockholm, Svenska Sektionen av Internationella Ungdomsboksrådet, 1966. 40p. DLC, IYL, BTJ.

A catalog of the exhibition selected and shown first at the International Youth Library and now touring other countries. This may also be obtained in German and English versions. It includes brief textual introductions to the various categories, a chronological list of selected translations into Swedish, biographical sketches of the authors and illustrators who have been awarded the Nils Holgersson or Elsa Beskow Medals, a select list of authorities writing about children's literature in Swedish, and a short list of Swedish children's books which have appeared in other languages. This was jointly sponsored by the Swedish section of IBBY and the Swedish Institute for the Study of Children's Books.

1724. ———. *Bibliotek i klassrum och facksalar*. Lund, Bibliotekstjänst, 1960. 70p. (Bokurval, 20). IYL. (DLC has 1952 ed., 31p., issued by Sveriges Allmänna Biblioteksförening, Småskrifter, 36).

"The library in the classroom and professional areas." The first part suggests collections for each class, from one through eight, and the second recommends collections for the music, physics and chemistry, fine arts and handicrafts, physical education and other departments.

1725. ———. *Bild i bok*. Stockholm, Svenska Sektionen av Internationella Ungdomsboksrådet, 1965. 32p. IYL, BTJ.

Brief biographies of almost 50 illustrators whose work is well known in children's books. Each is accompanied by a sample or two of illustration. This was prepared for the Swedish section of IBBY.

1726. ———. *Böcker för bibliotek i folkskoler och deras överbyggnader*. Stockholm, på uppdrag av Kungl. Skolöverstyrelsen, 1941. 56p. DLC.

"Books for libraries in schools, and their overall structure." A list of basic reference and general books of use to the school library, arranged by subject. First purchase books are starred. Index.

1727. ———. *Böckernas lustgård*. 7th ed. Stockholm, Seriekommittén, 1965. 31p. DLC.

"Pleasure house of books." Short essays on the pleasures reading can bring, written by authors, librarians and others who work with children. At the same time books are suggested to parents to whom this is aimed.

1728. ———. *Enhetsskolans bibliotek.* Stockholm, Almqvist and Wiksell, 1952. 62p. DLC.

"The basic school library: organization and utilization." This librarian recommends both a central library, and classroom collections.

1729. ———. *Facklitteratur för skolbibliotek.* 2nd ed. På uppdrag av Kungl. Skolöverstyrelsen, Stockholm, 1958. 80p. (Kungl. Skolöverstyrelsen, Skriftserie, 1). DLC.

"Nonfiction books for the school library." Arranged by subject in two categories: books for loan and reference materials. Not annotated, but indexed. Actually, a revision and up-dating of *Böcker för Bibliotek i Folkskolor . . .* (1726).

1730. ———. *Ungdom läser.* Göteborg, Elanders Boktryckeri, 1947. 380p. (Sveriges Allmänna Folkskollärarförenings Litteratursällskap, Pedagogiska Skrifter, Häfte 195–198). BTJ, IYL.

"Young readers." A reading-interest survey conducted among children and youth from 7–20 years of age. The author, a teacher, is one of the leading figures in the Swedish children's literature study movement. There are many comments and criticisms accompanying the charts and graphs reproduced in this study, as well as general conclusions.

1731. ———. *Vanner världen runt.* 3rd ed. Stockholm, Serie-kommittén och Svenska Sektionen av IUR, 1965. 12p. BTJ.

A booklist intended to be used by children, to lead them to books about other lands and peoples, and to international understanding.

1732. *Låt oss läsa högt.* Lund, Bibliotekstjänst, 1963. 28p. (Bokurval, 34) DLC.

"Let's read aloud." An annotated list of books for reading to the very young, and to older children.

1733. Leijonhielm, Christer. *Ungdomens läsvanor.* Stockholm, Forum, 1954. 199p. IYL, NNY.

"The reading habits of youth; a survey among 19-year-old youth, with particular attention to the habits connected with schooling and intelligence." The author attempts to determine how and why these reading habits were formed. Bibliography, pp. 197–199.

1734. Lidén, Anita. *20 års bästa barnböcker: 1944–1964.* Lund, Bibliotekstjanst, 1965. 122p. (Bokurval, 52). DLC, IYL.

"The best children's books of the 20-year-period 1944–1964." Annotated and arranged according to general age and subject groups. Illustrated with black and white reproductions. Author and title indexes.

1735. Lilius, Albert. "Barn och böcker," *Tidskrift for folkskolan,* Stockholm, 1942, pp. 483–87, 503–506. DLC.

A series of radio addresses on various aspects of children and books.

1736. Linder, Gurli. "Den första europeiska lärokursen i biblioteksteknik för läroverksbibliotekarier," *Folkbiblioteksbladet,* Stockholm, Ag. 6, No. 3, 1908, pp. 98–100.

"The first European study course in library techniques for school librarians." Valfrid Palmgren was the organizer and chief lecturer.

1737. ———. *Våre barns fria läsning.* Stockholm, Norstedt & Söners, 1916. 237p. IYL.

An up-dating and expansion of the author's earlier work (*see* 1738). In this study, he considered groups of children's books by type and then concluded with essays on: the trends which were becoming important in "modern" children's books; free reading in the home and school; the manner in which childhood reading affected the great Swedish writers. There is also a chapter on journals for children.

1738. ———. *Våre barns nöjesläsning.* Stockholm, Bonnier, 1902. 103p. IYL.

Critical comments on some of the leading writers of the day, as well as general comments on the status of children's literature. This was one of the first Swedish books of serious criticism of children's books as literature.

1739. Linderberg, Kerstin and Olle Wingborg. *Läsa lätt; ett urval böcker för läsretarderade.* Lund, Bibliotekstjänst, 1966. 37p. (Bokurval, 53). DLC.

A book list for poor readers which is divided into fiction and nonfiction and includes some 300 titles, not annotated, but indexed. A bibliography of books about reading problems includes items in English as well as Swedish.

1740. Linderberg, Kerstin. *Skönlitteratur för ungdom.* Lund, Bibliotekstjänst, 1966. 111p. (Bokurval, 55.) IYL, BTJ. (DLC has 1st. ed., 1960, 93p.)

An annotated list of current fiction and classic literature for young people. Its attractive format is typical of the appealing style of Swedish lists. There are author and title indexes. Mary Ørvig was the compiler of the first edition.

1741. Lundberg, Hildur. "Några nyare metoder för bokpropaganda inom bibliotekens ungdomsavdelningar," *Biblioteksbladet,* Stockholm, Ag. 17, 1932, pp. 261–268. DLC, NNY, BTJ.

"Some new methods of book propaganda within the juvenile departments of libraries."

1742. ———. "Några synpunkter vid val och utstyrsel av ungdomsböcker," *Biblioteksbladet,* Stockholm, Årg. 8, 1923, pp. 126–133. DLC, NNY, BTJ.

"Some views on the choice and looks of juvenile books." This librarian points out what children look for in choosing books, and he emphasizes the idea that books should have format and design matching their content.

1743. Lundewall, Elin. "Barn- och ungdomsläsning," *Biblioteksbladet,* Stockholm, Ag. 6, 1921, pp. 117–125. DLC, NNY, BTJ.

A lecture given at one of the first library courses on children's work. It is concerned with the reading interests of children and youth, and the importance of selecting good literature for them.

1744. ———. *Om skolbiblioteket i folkskolan och dess samband med skolarbetet.* Några praktiska erfarenheter. 1933. (Pedagogiska Skrifter, 144).

1745. Maak, Ivan. "Vad läser 12–15 åringar? *Modersmålsläranas Förening. Årsskrift.* Lund, 1944, pp. 77–84.

"What do 12–15 year olds read?"

1746. Möhlenbrock, Sigurd. "Biblioteken och ungdomen," *Biblioteksbladet,* Stockholm, Ag. 43, No. 7, 1958, pp. 490–496. DLC.

"Libraries and youth." The special problems of service to young people.

1747. Moll, Lizzie. "Några erfarenheter från arbetet vid Stockholms barn- och ungdomsbibliotek," *Biblioteksbladet,* Stockholm, Årgång 1, 1916, pp. 65–70. DLC, NNY. BTJ.

"Some experiences in working with children in the Stockholm children's and youth library." The author was a leading children's librarian in the early years of children's library work.

1748. Munck, Kerstin. "Barn- och ungdomsbibliotekariekursen 1948," *Biblioteksbladet,* Stockholm, Ag. 34, No. 1, 1949, pp. 4–8. DLC, NNY.

"Children's and youth libraries courses in 1948." A description of some of the different courses sponsored by the library association and by some libraries.

1749. Norbeck, Axel. *Skolbiblioteket och undervisningen.* Stockholm, H. Gerber, 1935. 251p. DLC.

"The school library and education." This was the standard handbook for many years, covering all aspects of school library work. A basic list of recommended books appears on pp. 161–251 divided into those suitable for class libraries and those recommended for the central library according to subject. Pp. 157–161 contain a bibliography on school library work.

1750. Nordlander, Johan. *Svenska barnvisor ock barnrim. . .* Stockholm, R. A. Norstedt, 1886. 285p. (Nyare bidrag till kännedom om de svenska landsmålen ock svenskst folklif, Bd. 5, No. 6). NNY.

A collection of Swedish nursery rhymes, divided by types. The forward discusses the distinctions of each type, and some of the patterns of formation. There are sources listed at the end.

1751. Norling, Hans. *Indianer och Robinsöner.* Stockholm, Oskar Eklunds, 1955. 30p. BTJ.

Two essays, one on adventure stories concerning American Indians and the other on Robinsonades.

1752. Nyström, Bruno. *Om läsning och bibliotek.* Stockholm, Svenska Missionsförbundets Ungdoms, 1915. 40p. (Småskrifter, 10).

1753. Ohlson, Erik A. "Det var en gång. . ." Johansson, J. Viktor. *Bokvandringar.* Stockholm, Wahlstrom & Widstrand, 1945, pp. 77–184. BTJ.

"Once upon a time . . . a history of children's and young people's reading." This begins with a review of some of the first translations of the classics to appear in Swedish, and the early attempts at ABC books for children. The authors of the 18th and 19th century who contributed major works are discussed. There are some 20 pages of reproductions which are mostly covers or title pages of early Swedish children's books.

1754. Olenius, Elsa. "Barn och böcker," *Föräldraboken.* Malmö, Bernces Förlag, 1963. pp. 559–572.

"Children and books." A children's librarian gives advice to parents on how and when to introduce good literature. Mrs. Olenius has a similar article in the encyclopedia *Familjens Hjälpreda,* Stockholm, Svenskt familjebibliotek, 1960, pp. 193–204.

1755. Ørvig, Mary. *Barnen, böckerna, barnbibliotekarien.* Lund, Bibliotekstjänst, 1963. 32p. DLC, IYL.

"Children, books, children's librarians." A bibliography of books and periodical literature on each of these areas, not annotated, and not always bibliographically complete. The last parts are: a chronological list of famous children's books, with a side list as to their appearance in translation in Swedish; lists of prizes for children's books; children's book weeks and other propaganda; a list of Swedish publishers of children's books.

1756. ———. "Bör barn- och ungdomsavdelingarna skiljas at?" *Biblioteksbladet*, Stockholm, Ag. 41, No. 8, 1956, pp. 534–536. DLC.

"Should there be separate departments for children and youth?" The answer is in the affirmative, and reasons are given. There is an English summary.

1757. ———. På resa för Svenska "Barnbokinstitutet," *REOL*, København, Årgång 4, No. 4, 1965, pp. 194–205. BTJ.

This well-known Swedish children's librarian tells of her work (while on leave of absence from Stockholm Public Library) to establish a children's book institute in Sweden. She describes the European centers she visited and some of the conclusions she has come to believe are good reasons for the founding of such an institute.

1758. ———. "The Stockholm cooperative program," *Wilson library bulletin*, New York, Vol. 25, No. 8, April, 1951, pp. 620–621. DLC, NNY.

An early report on the cooperation between schools and the public library in Stockholm, which is still in existence but operating in a different manner than is described here.

1759. Osborne, Kerstin and Lisa-Christina Persson. "Sweden." *Library service to children*. Lund, Bibliotekstjänst, 1963, pp. 98–108. DLC, IYL, NNY.

This chapter deals with the history and present status of library work with children in this country. The publication was produced under the auspices of IFLA.

1760. Palme, Sven Ubric. *Några anteckningar ur de svenska barntidningarnas historia*. Stockholm, Ahlén & Akerlund, 1963. 31p. BTJ, IYL.

"Some notes on the history of Swedish children's periodicals." This history covers the period from 1777, when *Magazin för Svenska Ungdomen* (the first magazine for Swedish youth) began to appear, until 1923 when the scouting magazine *Sveriges pojkar* first appeared. Illustrated with reproductions of many title pages from the periodicals.

1761. Palmgren Munch-Petersen, Valfrid. "Stockholms barn och ungdomsbibliotek," *Biblioteksbladet*, Lund, Årgång 46, No. 10, Dec., 1961, pp. 750–759. DLC, NNY.

The author tells of her visit to the U.S. in 1907, her meeting with Anne Carroll Moore, and the subsequent founding of the children's library in Stockholm in 1911, the first in Sweden for public use. Illustrated with early photographs of children in the library.

1762. Persson, Lisa-Christina. "Bibliotekstjänst's work for children and young people," *Bookbird*, Vienna, No. 2, 1966, pp. 3–9. DLC, IYL, NNY.

A review of the work of this service organization of the Swedish Library Association as it is related to children's books and libraries. This is followed by a complete list of their publications concerning children's books, a list of Swedish prize-winning children's books and a selected list of contemporary children's books in Sweden.

1763. Petersens, Hedwig. *Ett barns litterära memoarer*. Stockholm, Bokvännerna, 1960. 92p. NNY, DLC.

"A child's literary memoirs." In recalling her own early acquaintance with a varied literature, the author champions the child's right to broad and deep literary experience outside of his school requirements.

1764. Rehn, Walborg. *Den Kristna ungdomen och litteraturen*. Stockholm, Svenska Missionsförbundets Ungdoms, 1933. 16p. (Småskrifter, 33).

1765. Renborg, G. "Barnebibliotekariers drömmar —och mal," *Biblioteksbladet*, Stockholm, Ag. 40, No. 7, 1955, pp. 379–381. DLC.

"Children's librarians' dreams—and goal." A speech delivered at a workshop for children's librarians sponsored by the Stockholm Department of Education.

1766. Roth, Nils. *Urval av senare års svensk skönlitteratur ordnad i ämnesgruppen*. Lund, Bibliotekstjänst, 1954. 28p. (Sveriges Allmänna Biblioteksforening. Småskrifter, 46). NNY.

"A selection of recent Swedish fictional literature arranged according to subject." A catalog aimed largely at young people.

1767. *Sagas stora katalog 1899–1956*. Stockholm, Svensk Läraretidnings Förlag, 1957. 147p. IYL.

A retrospective catalog of 320 works which appeared in the "Saga" series. Since this included most of the early classics in Swedish this is a valuable bibliographical tool. There are title, author, editor, and illustrator indexes and the bibliographical information is quite complete. Illustrated with reproductions from some of the editions.

1768. Sandberg, Alvida and Helja Jacobson. "Förhållandet mellan skolornas boksamlingar och de allmänna bibliotekens ungdomsavdelningar," *Biblioteksbladet*, Stockholm, Årgång 2, 1917, pp. 162–172. DLC, NNY, BTJ.

"Relations between the school libraries and the public library juvenile departments." An early description of cooperative work.

1769. Sandberg, Alvida. "Några sidor av svenskt biblioteksarbete," *For folkeoplysning*, Kristiania, Bind 5, No. 4, Dec., 1920, pp. 134–140; Nos. 5–6, Feb., 1921, pp. 164–168. NNY.

"Some aspects of Swedish library work." The article actually refers to school library work, and cites the specific advances made in some schools, particularly Göteborg.

1770. ———. "Skolbiblioteket åt alla sveriges barn!" *Biblioteksbladet*, Stockholm, Årgång 5, 1920, pp. 122–127. DLC, NNY, BTJ.

School libraries for all Swedish children was the standard this librarian would have liked to see fulfilled.

1771. Sigurd, Gustav. *Skolbibliotekens framtida organisation*. Lund, Bibliotekstjänst, 1960. 124p. BTJ.

The future of school library organization. This official report was made at the request of the Royal Board of Education.

1772. "Skol och barnbibliotek," *Biblioteksbladet*, Stockholm, Ag. 9, 1924–Ag. 20, 1935. DLC, NNY, BTJ.

This column appeared irregularly during the period mentioned. Sometimes it included the book review section "Böcker för barn och ungdom" and other times it only contained articles. Some of the longer ones were: A history of work in Stockholm's children's library from 1911–1927 by Anna Landergren and Eva Ringenson (Årgång 12, 1927, pp. 181–186); Children's libraries in England by Elisabeth Berggren (Årgång 11, 1926, pp. 91–93; On school library work by Hjalmar Berg (Årgång 17, 1932, pp. 93–96); and Aids in selection of children's books by Karl Regfors (Årgång 17, 1932, pp. 176–182).

1773. *Skolbiblioteket*. Bibliotekstjänst, in coopera-

tion with Sveriges Lärarförbund, Sveriges Småskolläraförbund (samt Läroverksbibliotekariernas Rijksförbund). Lund, Bibliotekstjänst. 1955 ff. Quarterly, 1955–1960; six times yearly, 1961 ff. (Annual subscription: 22 kr). DLC, IYL.

The official publication of the Swedish Library Association and the Swedish Teachers' Associations. Each issue has articles on library work, reading, children's literature or related subjects. Reviews of children's books are signed, as are reviews of professional literature. Illustrated with many attractive photographs and reproductions from books.

1774. Söderhjelm, K. "Barnböcker längs Torne Träsk," *Biblioteksbladet*, Stockholm, Ag. 40, No. 2, 1955, pp. 104–105. DLC, NNY.

A description of an unusual children's library in Lapland which is operated on a train. Serving as a school during the week, and a public library on the weekends, the train makes a dozen stops up and down Torne Lake. Some children ride up and down all day reading and looking at books.

1775. Stockholm. Stadsbibliotek. *Katalog för Stockholms grundskolors elevbibliotek och Stockholms stadsbiblioteks barn- och ungdomsavdelninger*. Stockholm, Stadsbibliotek, 1946 ff. IYL has 1950 ff.

An annotated buying list of children's books selected by a joint committee of public and school librarians and published twice a year by the Stockholm City Library. This is one of the results of the cooperative program carried out by the City Library and the Stockholm city school system.

1776. Strömstedt, Bo. *Min väg till barnboken*. Stockholm, Rabén and Sjögren, 1964. 168p. IYL.

Twenty-one eminent writers of juvenile books tell how they came to write, what they themselves read as children, and what this reading meant to them.

1777. Svenska Sektionen av Internationella Ungdomsboksradet. *Barnböcker bygger broar*. Stockholm, Arbetarnas Bildningsförbund, 1960. 8p. IYL, BTJ.

"Children's books build bridges." A selection of Swedish books about other countries and areas of the world.

1778. Tynell, Knut Olaf Laurentius. *Skolbiblioteket; dess skötsel och dess plats i skolarbetet*. Stockholm, Norstedt, 1927. 110p. (Sveriges Allmänna Biblioteksförenings Handböcker, 4).

"The school library; its care and its place in the school." A handbook of organization, together with suggestions on the selection and use of the collection. The final chapter is an essay by Hildur Lundberg on the qualities which distinguish children's literature.

1779. "Ungdomens bokvecka," *Biblioteksbladet,* Stockholm, Ag. 18, No. 6, 1933, pp. 218–219. DLC, NNY.

An outline of the programs held in connection with the first children's book week, which included lectures, radio programs, parents' meetings, story hours and readings, discussions, etc. The catalog compiled by Landergren and Jacobson is described (1710).

1780. "Ungdomsavdelningar och skolbibliotek." *Biblioteket och vi,* Örebro, 1954, 111p. DLC.

This eighth yearbook of the Swedish Public Library Association is devoted to children's and school libraries. The articles include: "Det var en gång," by Valfrid Palmgren Munch-Petersen on her visit to U.S. libraries and her early struggles to start library work with children in Sweden; a summary on public and school libraries for children in Sweden today by Karen Persson and Emmy Reventberg; the cultural foundations of library work with young people, by Eva von Zweigbergk; teen-agers in the public library by Brita Olsson; the school library as a place for study or leisure time by Sven Lagerstedt; the training of children's librarians by Folke Löfgren; experiences in the Lidingo public and school libraries by Sigrid Maslov; cooperation between school and public libraries by Gudrun Franck, Barbro Bolt, Rikka Deinboll and Sten Hagliden; and another on the same cooperation, but in rural areas, by Bengt Helmqvist. There are English summaries for each article.

1781. *Ett urval böcker för ungdom.* Örebro, Bibliotekens Försäljningscentral, 1948. 15p. (Sveriges Allmänna Biblioteksförening. Småskrifter, 27). DLC.

"A selection of books for young people." Brief annotations are given for this list which is mostly fiction. Novels in series are listed separately.

1782. *Vad vet vi om barn? Böcker om barn i förskoleåldern.* Lund, Bibliotekstjänst, 1959. 10p. (Bokurval, 17). IYL.

A booklist containing titles of interest to preschool children. There is a companion list for the elementary grades (Bokurval, 25) published in 1960. Both are presently being revised.

1783. *Vi läser på fritid. Bästa böcker 19- för barn och ungdom.* Lund, Bibliotekstjänst, 1962 ff. Annual. 8p. IYL, DLC, BTJ.

"Your reading for the holidays." From

1952–1961 this was issued under the title *Läsning under Lovet* and from 1944–1951 it was issued by the Swedish Library Association as *Böcker för Jullovet.* It comprises some 150 titles arranged by age groups and briefly annotated.

1784. Willke, Ingeborg. *ABC-Bücher in Schweden. Ihre Entwicklung bis Ende des 19. Jahrhunderts und ihre Beziehungen zu Deutschland.* Stockholm, Scandinavian University Books, 1965. 411p. IYL, BTJ.

This was a dissertation for the doctoral degrees at Mainz University and Stockholm University. It is a scholarly presentation of the pedagogical elements in the development of the ABC book in Sweden up to the end of the 19th century. The text is concerned mainly with early reading methods, the effects of catechetical, religious teaching on the development of first reading books, and finally with an exhaustive description of the characteristics of early ABC books. Of major interest to the general student of children's books are the 32 plates of reproductions from early ABC books. The sources listed number more than 700 and there is a name index.

1785. Wranér, Signe H. *Sagan om SAGA.* Stockholm, Svensk Läraretidnings Förlag, 1955. 20p. BTJ.

"The saga of SAGA." This essay on the history of the famous Swedish children's series was printed as a kind of Christmas greeting from the SAGA publishers.

1786. Zweigbergk, Eva von. *Barnboken i sverige 1750–1950.* Stockholm, Rabén & Sjögren, 1965. 520p. kr. DLC, IYL, NNY.

An illustrated history of Swedish children's literature from 1750–1950. The text is clear and well-organized by historical periods, and is interspersed with many black and white reproductions and 24 colored plates which do much to further enliven and explain the history. Included among these are examples of every leading illustrator of children's books in Sweden, and portraits of most of the authors, illustrators, and editors mentioned. Foreign books are discussed only as they influenced, or were translated into, Swedish children's books. Children's magazines are treated in detail, as are picture books. An English summary on pp. 475–481, is followed by a biographical sketch of the author, who is neither a teacher nor a librarian, but an art historian and a reviewer of children's books (for some twenty years). Name and title indexes are separate, and the bibliography on pp. 515–520 provided many additional entries for this survey, and is a good source for further literature on individual Swedish authors.

Finland

According to Kaija Salonen, the Sunday School Library founded in Turku in 1869 can lay claim to being the first especially for children in Finland. Later, in 1890, the Finnish Ladies' Society, Suomalainen Naishydistys, began its work of compiling book lists, writing articles on children's literature and giving lectures. From 1893–1925, they maintained a youth library in Helsinki, named after the beloved writer Topelius. It had high standards of selection and was very actively used by young adults from 12 to 18 years old.

Public libraries began including children's rooms right from the turn of the century, but the two periods of most active growth were the years succeeding each of the World Wars. At present, the more than 4,000 libraries all have children's sections, at least to the extent of having a separate corner. School libraries got a much slower start, but as of 1957, the elementary school law demands a library in each school. In many rural areas the public library is in (or close to) a school and it can serve both purposes.

In the survey written by Soile Kaukovalta for the IFLA publication, *Library Service to Children,* there is a good general description of the activities and services of a typical children's library. That same article, by the way, specified an unusual reason for the widespread literacy which has been prevalent for about 300 years. It is explained that this is largely due to the church because "it refused to perform the marriage ceremony, unless the bride and groom gave proof of being able to read."

Over the years, certain children's books have become classics in Finnish, and although there appear annually from 200 to 250 new or reissued titles, there are on the market some 1600 children's books. This trend toward keeping established favorites in print is remarked on in the 1966 report of the Finnish national section of IBBY, which states: "Though the number of books published in recent years has diminished, the content and literary value of the books have improved."

The history of children's books in Finnish began in 1847, when the first three children's books were published (all translations). In 1848, the first Finnish translation of a work by Zakarias Topelius appeared. Although he wrote in Swedish, Topelius was and is considered very much a part of Finnish culture, since his works reflect the folklore, customs and environment of Finland. His situation typified the general pattern of educated families who spoke Swedish. Because the universities taught in Swedish, and because the leading families from the era of Swedish domination remained pretty much in positions of honor and power, it was not uncommon for a young poet, no matter how nationalistic his feelings, to have to express himself in a language not understood by the folk.

This was dramatically changed by the appearance in 1835 of the first edition of the *Kalevala,* as collected by Elias Lönnrot. In fact, it was the senior Zakarias Topelius, father of the children's writer, who had published a few fragments of the epic, which inspired Lönnrot to search for more. This publication stirred the hearts of many nationalities, but it especially gave to the Finns a sense of pride in their national past.

Although a grand duchy under the protection of Russia, Finland had almost complete autonomy and freedom throughout the 19th century, except for part of the 1850's when the Finnish language was forbidden. The 1860's brought a more liberal attitude, and the first original works for children appeared then in Finnish. The most comprehensive collection of Finnish folk tales, *Suomen Kansan Satuja ja Tarinoita,* collected by Eero Salmelainen, also appeared around this time. It was works such as this, as well as the many volumes of proverbs, riddles and tune songs collected by Lönnrot, in addition to his *Kalevala,* that helped to give Finland a reputation for scholarly work in folklore. This has been enhanced in the 20th century by the establishment of the Folklore Fellows' archives in Helsinki. Their communications are erudite studies which have little meaning for the average student of children's literature, but which do have some bearing on its sources.

By the second decade of this century, children's books had come into their own as a type of Finnish children's literature. Such authors as Helmi Krohn and Arvid Lydecken began to assume places of the first rank. Nevertheless, Finnish writers in Swedish also continued to be important and their books were often issued simultaneously in both languages. Important among this group is Anni Swan. The significance of her work can be partly noted in the fact that the prize for the best book for young people, to be awarded every three years from 1961 on, has been named after her. The most recent winner of this prize is Tove Jansson, who also has the distinction of being a recipient of the Hans Christian Andersen Medal, in 1966. Her imaginative books, peopled by "Moomin" creatures, are pervaded by what one can best call a sense of security and secret intimacy, as opposed to fear and exposure.

There are two other national prizes, both awarded annually. Since 1946, the Topelius Prize has been given for the best children's or youth book published in Finland during the preceding year. The Rudolf Koivu Medal has been conferred to an illustrator each year since 1949.

In glancing through the list of the prize winners, and the list of Finnish children's authors who have been translated, one finds a few names recurring: Tove Jansson, Anniki Setläala, Aili Konttiness, Arvid Lydecken, Aili Palmén. It is unfortunate that there is no translation or English summary of Jorma Mäenpaa's history of Finnish children's literature (1802). It is quite likely that there might be more translation, if the Finnish language were more accessible to other cultures. Considering the liveliness of the *Kalevala* and the folklore, which is about all that is known among other Western readers, modern Finnish children's literature should also find its response in foreign translation. How to select it is the problem. The extensive work done by Arvo Lehtovaara and Pirkko Saarinen in their *School-Age Reading Interests* (1800) gives some idea of the variety of reading enjoyed by Finnish children. Some authors are specifically mentioned more frequently than others, but it is impossible to draw any critical conclusions from such statistical data.

1787.   Ellilä, E. J. *Nuorisoseurojen käsikirjastot.* Lahti, 1934. 48p.

1788.   *Kansakoulujen kirjastoihin lapsille ja nuorisolle suositeltavia kirjoja.* 1948. 32p.
"Books for children and young people in the libraries of the public schools."

1789.   Karahka, Helvi. *Lastemme kirjat; valikoima lasten ja nuorten kirjoja.* Helsingissä, Kansanvalistusseura, 1943. 128p. DLC.
"The books of our children; a selection of children's and young people's books."

1790.   *Kasvatus ja koulu.* Jyväskylän Kasvatusopillinen Korkeakoulu and Jyväskylän Yliopistoyhdistys. Bi-monthly. Vol. 1, 1914 ff. DLC.
This professional journal is similar in scope to *Elementary English* in the U.S. It contains frequent articles related to children's reading, and has regular reviews of schildren's and youth books. There are English summaries.

1791.   Kaukovalta, Soile. "Finland," *Library service to children.* Lund, Bibliotekstjänst, 1963, pp. 41–45. DLC, IYL, NNY.
This chapter in the IFLA publication deals with the history and present status of children's library work in this country.

1792.   *Kirjavalikoima.* Helsinki, Kouluhallitus, 1940 ff. Annual. DLC.
An annual list of books recommended by the School Ministry of Finland. From this approved list, school libraries choose their books, although they are not entirely limited to this selection.

1793.   "Lapset, kirjat ja kirjastot," *Kirjastolehti,* Helsingissä, Vuosikerta 56, No. 9, Nov., 1963, pp. 269–294. DLC, IYL.
An issue devoted to children, books and libraries. Longer articles are by: I. von Weissenberg (on young adult reading); Kaija Salomen (on the decrease in number of Finnish children's books); Ulla Lehtonen (on children's reading in the 19th century); Kerttu Varjo (on cooperation between libraries and youth work committees); and Annikki Aro (on developing successful children's libraries).

1794.   "Lasten ja nuorison kertomakirjallisuus," *Kirjastolehti,* Helsingissä, 1908 ff. DLC has 1916 ff; NNY has 1952 ff.
A section devoted to signed reviews of current fiction for children. Nonfiction for children appears under the respective decimal classification number and is not separated from general adult books.

1795.   "Lasten ja nuorten kertomakirjallisuus." *Suomessa ilmestyneed Kirjallisuuden vuosiluettelo. Arskatalog over i Finland utkommen litteratur. Catalog of books published in Finland.* Helsinki, 1946–1951. Quarterly and annual DLC, NNY.
Finnish, Swedish and other language books published in Finland are listed here with children's books included under the above heading. This bibliography is continued in *Kirjastolehti.*

1796.   "Lasten ja nuorten kirjoja." Helsingissä, Wsoy, 1965. 80p. DLC, IYL. IYL also has 1953 ed., 144p. and 1959 ed., 180p. (Both published by Suomen Kirjastoseura).
"Books for children and young people." An annotated list arranged according to the decimal system. Author and title index.

1797.   *Lasten ja nuorten kirjojen valioluettelo.* 1926. 96p.
"Selective list of books for children and young people."

1798.   "Lastenkirjastokurssit," *Kirjastolehti,* Helsingissä, Vuosikerta 47, No. 1, Jan., 1954, pp. 13–16. DLC, NNY.
"Course for children's librarians." Helsinki Library School and the State Library Bureau sponsored the first course for Finnish children's librarians in December, 1953. Preceding this account of the points of study is a résumé of the lecture given by Arvo Lehtovaara on children's reading; following the account is a comment on the course, written by a children's librarian, Sirkka E. Salovius.

1799.   Lehtovaara, A. and P. Saarinen. *Mitä nuoret*

lukevat. Helsingissä, Kustannusosakeyhtiö Otava, 1965. 143p. (Kansalaiskasvatuksen Keskuksen, Julkaisvja No. 2). IYL.

"What young people read." A supplement, in Finnish, to the earlier reading interest study by the same authors. This is concerned specifically with the young adult.

1800. ——. *School-age reading interests; a methodological approach.* Helsinki, Suomalainen Tiedeakatemia, 1964. 216p. (Annales Academiae Scientiarum Fennicae, Sarja-Ser. Bride-Tom. 131.2). DLC.

Based on study done from 1945–1952 and in 1960 and 1961, among a large, representative group of school children, using questionnaires, book lists, tests, interviews and observation. The results are clearly explained in text and graphs, and rate separately boys from girls, elementary from high school students. Questionnaire and test samples are given in the appendix. A bibliography of published and unpublished sources is on pp. 194–195. Within the limitations set by the authors in their stated objectives, this is one of the clearest, best documented studies on the reading interests of children. The text is in English, translated by Jaakko Railo and Herbert Lomas.

1801. "Lue enemmän—lue parempaa." Special issue of: *Kirja airut,* Helsingissä, Mar., 1962, 23p. IYL.

"Read more—read better" is a special issue of the *Book Herald* which is put out on occasions such as book "week" or "day" or similar book-related celebrations. It is not issued regularly. This issue contains an annotated booklist, arranged by age group and subject, and illustrated with reproductions from the books.

1802. Mäenpää, Jorma. *Sata vuotta sadun ja seikkailun mailla.* Helsingissä, Osakeyhtiö Valistus, 1958. 199p. IYL.

"One hundred years in the land of fairy tales and adventure." A history of Finnish children's literature with a chapter devoted to each of the three most important figures: Anni Swan, Helmi Krohn and Arvid Lydecken. Illustrated with numerous photographs and reproductions. Name index.

1803. Manninen, Kerttu. *Nuorille aikuisille.* Helsingissä, suomen Kirjastoseura, 1964, 30p.
A booklist for young adults.

1804. Lapset Kirjastoissa. *Kirjastolehti,* Helsingissä, Vuosikerta 51, No. 3, Mar., 1958, pp. 58–64. DLC, NNY.

"Children in libraries." Thirteen libraries report on the favorite titles of children using the collections and on aspects of their work with these children.

1805. Saukkonen, M. A. *Finnish folk tales for children.* Kent, Ohio, Kent State University, 1962. 60p. Thesis.

1806. Salonen, Kaija. *Finnish children's libraries.* Typewritten manuscript. DLC.

A more specific historical account of children's work than is given by Soile Kaukovalta in *Library Service to Children* (31). There is also a brief survey of important events in the development of children's literature.

1807. [School library issue], *Kirjastolehti,* Helsingissä, Vuosikerta 55, No. 8, Oct., 1962, pp. 217–235. DLC, NNY.

Longer articles are by: R. H. Oittinen (on secondary school libraries); Inkeri Airola (on standards); Anniki Aro (on school library experiences); Aulikki Vainio (on the influence and success of the school library); and Elma Nallinmaa (on reading guidance).

1808. Tikkanen, Raija-Leena. "Kirjojen valinta lastenkirjastoihin," *Kirjastolehti,* Helsingissä, Vuosikerta 48, No. 1, Jan., 1955, pp. 9–14. DLC, NNY.

"Book selection in children's libraries. Not only books written specially for children should be counted as children's books but also the books for adults which children choose by instinct. Suitable books for different ages and stages of development are discussed . . . Thanks to competent press reviews and other encouragement the standard of children's books in Finland is improving steadily. A great number of Finnish . . . translations are discussed." Quoted from the English summary, p. 70.

Eastern Europe, Turkey and Greece

With the exception of the last two countries named, all of the nations in this section are governed according to Communist-Socialist principles. Turkey and Greece were placed at the end, due to their geographical location. Both are in the developing stages of children's literature, and the influence of both western and eastern ideas has been limited. Therefore, what is discussed here is not applicable to either of them nor is their proximity meant to imply anything.

Because the child and his education are considered to be of prime importance in the socialist countries, there has been in these countries a tremendous surge in the study of children's literature as well as a staggering increase in the number of books produced. Communications between these countries and the West are still not very satisfactory, so that the bibliographies in this section are not entirely representative of all the activity which is going on.

Apart from the fact that each nation has developed a literature with its own national characteristics, most of the other qualities are common to all.

1. Publishing houses are state owned, although in some cases they have more autonomy than others.
2. First editions tend to be very large, and go out of print very quickly; only select titles are reprinted, as there is a scarcity of paper and shortage of other materials.
3. Translations from among this group of nations are extensive. Translations of the classics of world literature are also widely known. Translations from other modern, Western literature are growing year by year, and one could even go so far as to say they outnumber the translations in the other direction.
4. Because publishing houses are large, state-owned and designed to produce for a whole nation, there is a tendency for children's books to have a sameness of appearance and writing style. Although there are very few which are poor or even mediocre in quality, by the same token there are few which rise above the others to shine out with unquestionable superiority.
5. State control of publishing has literally wiped out the production of comics, and obscene or pornographic publications for youth are almost totally absent.
6. A variety of magazines for children cater more to popular taste, and are printed in enormous editions in all of these countries. They are even less expensive than the paper-covered books, and although printed on poor paper, are attractive in design and illustrations.

7. The highest percentage of books and magazines is sold to individuals, mostly from the corner kiosks which dot the towns and cities. Rural children have less choice and access to books and this problem is of great concern to the cultural and educational authorities.

Library service to children is widely developed and also has characteristics common to most of these countries.

1. There are usually three types of children's libraries: public, school, and "Pioneer."
2. They are heavily used and have fairly selective and representative book collections.
3. Most serve children in two or three separate age groups, with individual collections for each. Sometimes these are housed on different floors or even in separate buildings. Very few serve the preschool child.
4. There is usually open access to the shelves.
5. Staff size is generous by the usual Western standards and therefore programs and activities are extensive.
6. There is extensive professional literature on organizing, maintaining and running a children's library.
7. Training and methodology are taken very seriously.

Hungary

The same enthusiasm in the new field of children's literature which burst forth in Czechoslovakia in the period from 1913 to 1940, appeared in more subdued form in the neighboring country of Hungary. The first history of Hungarian children's literature, by Istvan Szemak, was published in 1928. It was followed by another in 1934, by Pál Drescher. This latter covered the period from 1538 to 1875, and therefore is restricted mostly to the early didactic works. It is interesting to note the first translations, however, of Campe's *Robinson* (1787) and Defoe's *Robinson Crusoe* (1844), as well as that of a number of the other classics. It is amazing that Drescher could locate the number of works he did, when one realizes that until the 19th century, the official and literary language was Latin.

A vernacular literature did exist, but it was not a particularly rich one, except in the area of folklore. This is only today being carefully recorded in some rural areas, notably by the folklorist Gyula Ortutay. Contemporary literature is not exactly plentiful, but there are a number of writers who have turned successfully to the juvenile reader. Perhaps the single work which can be considered as reaching wide international acceptance is Ferenc Molnar's *A Pál-utczai Fiúk* ("The Paul Street Boys"). At the present time, the state publishing house for children is working hard to build up a wider variety of children's books, with a larger number of translations from other Western countries.

A brief but pointed survey of the history of library service to children can be found in Aranka Racz's pamphlet (1825). She indicates that public library work was more firmly established than school library work. The Ervin Szabo Library in Budapest was particularly outstanding, and a large number of the children's librarians working in Hungary have been trained there.

1809. *Az ifjúsági irodalom; néhány kérdéséröl.* Budapest, Szikra, 1950. 75p. (A Szociálista kultura idöszerü Kérdései, 4). DLC.
"Juvenile literature; some questions." Translated from the Russian; articles which appeared in *Literaturnaja Gazeta,* Jan.–Feb., 1950, and two essays, by K. Szimonov and A. Kornyejcsuk.

1810. Bikácsi, Lászlóné. "A gyermekkönyvallomány vizsgálata a Fövárosi Szabó Ervin könyvtár kerületi könyvtáraiban," *Magyar könyvszemle,* Budapest, Evf. 77, Aug.–Oct., 1961, pp. 264–278.
"Survey of the stocks of children's books of the branches of the Szabó Ervin Municipal Library of Budapest." Includes many statistical tables.

1811. ———. *Kézikönyvtár a gyermekkönyvtárakban.* 2nd ed. Budapest, Oszk, Könyvtártudományi és Módszertani Közpiont, 1965. 54p. IYL.
"Model reference library for children." Arranged by subject and then by author. The last part is a recommended reading list and reference library for children's librarians. Published by the national library.

1812. Budapest. Szent István-Társulat. *V-ik számu összesitett hivatalos Katholikus iskola ifjusági tanitó, tanári, levente és cserkész könyvtárjegyzék.* Budapest, Kiegészitö Füzet, 1931.

1813. Donáth, G. *et al. Olvasó gyermekeink.* Budapest, Tankönyvkiadó, 1957. 302p.
"Reading children; the study and basic needs that concern literary education."

1814. Drescher, Pál. *Régi magyar gyermekkönyvek 1538–1875.* Budapest, Magyar Bibliophil Társaság, 1934. 133p. DLC, IYL, NNY.
"Old-time Hungarian children's books, 1538–1875." A general survey and history of the books of that period, together with a list of 985 titles, arranged by author, and a union list of the copies in

leading libraries of Hungary. More than 80 illustrations are reproduced (some in color). This is a handsome and important introduction to this country's literature for children.

1815. Fekete, P. *Az iskolai könyvtárak szervezése és kezelése.* Debrecen, 1939. 16p. (From: A hajdúböszörményi ref. Baltazár D. polg. leányisk. 1938/1939 évkönyve).

1816. "Ifjúsági és gyermekirodalmi kiadványok," *A szép magyar könyv.* Budapest, Közzéteszi a Müvelödésügyi Minisztérium, 1958 ff. IYL has some years.
Each year the best books are chosen for their design, illustration and content. This section includes the children's and youth books.

1817. Kolta, Ferenc. *Az ifjúsági irodalom tankönyve.* Budapest, Tanitóképzö Föiskolák Számára, 1964.
"Study book of juvenile literature for the teachers' college.

1818. ———, *et al. Ifjusági irodalom; a tanitóképzök számára kiegészitö tankönyv.* 2nd. ed. Budapest, Tankönyvkiadó, 1955, 75p.
"Children's literature for the pedagogical normal school."

1819. *Köznevelés.* Müvelödésügyi Minisztérium, Budapest. Semi-monthly. Vol. 1 ff., 1945 ff. DLC.
A journal which has essentially the same purpose in Hungary as *Elementary English* does in the U.S. There are many articles on children's reading, as well as regular reviews of children's and youth books.

1820. Lakits, Pál. *Középiskolásaink és irodalom.* Budapest, Tankönyvkiadó, 1962. 149p. IYL.
"Our middle-school children and their literature." Results of a reading interest survey with many tables and graphs.

1821. "Literature for young people and children," *Books from Hungary,* Budapest, 1959 ff. Quarterly. DLC.

An illustrated selection published in English, French and German editions.

1822. Neményi, Imre. *Ifjúsági könyvtárak és ifjúsági olvasmányok a nevelés szolgálatában.* Budapest, Wodianer F. és Fiai, 1902.

1823. Nógrády, László. "A gyermekmese." Vol. 1 of his: *A mese.* Budapest, Magyar Gyermektanulmányi Társ, 1917, 232p. (Gyermektanulmányi Könyvtár 7).
"The children's tale."

1824. Rácz, Aranka, *et al. Gyermek és ifjúsági könyvtárak.* Budapest, Müvelt Nép, 1955. 103p.
"Children's and young people's libraries."

1825. ———. *Gyermekkönyvtáraink helyzete.* Budapest, Magyar Nemzeti Muzeum, 1959. 17p. (Országos Széchényi Könyvtár Kiadványai, No. 46). NNY.
"The state of children's libraries in Hungary." Although there were some libraries with service to children in prewar Hungary (before 1940–45) their formal organization did not take place until the state established a central bureau for public library development. As of 1959, there were 81 public libraries which served children, 47 of them in separate facilities. The first formal training of children's librarians took place in the Ervin Szabó library in 1957–58. Although there are 2.21 books per child in public libraries this is not enough to serve present needs. Summary of pamphlet in German.

1826. Szemák, István. *A magyar ifjusági irodalom története.* Budapest, Neuwald, 1924. 108p.

1827. Szász, Eta and Ágnes Kepes. *Beszélö könyvtár.* Budapest, Móra Könyvkiadó, 1958. 299p. DLC.
"A model library." Advice to those working in Pioneer libraries and a suggested basic collection.

1828. Szondy, György. *A magyar ifjusági irodalom gyermekkora.* (1669–1848). Kecskemét, Elsö Kecskeméti, 1932. 20p.

1829. Tiszay, Andor. *A könyv, a mi barátunk.* Budapest, Gondolat, 1962. 167p. (Gondolattár 15).

1830. Tóth, Béla. *A gyermek és az irodalom.* Budapest, Tankönyvkiadó Vállalat, 1955. 161p. (Szociálista Nevelés Könyvtára, 103).
"The child and literature."

1831. ———. *Irodalmi érdeklödés a gyermekkorban.* Budapest, Tankönyvkiadó, 1961. 176p. DLC.
"Literary interests of children; study and teaching."

1832. Ujváry, Lajos. *A mai gyermek és a könyv.* Budapest, Egyet, 1936. 72p. (A tanitás problémai, 14).

1833. Vargha, Balázs. *Gyermekirodalom.* OSZK, Könyvtártudományi és Módszertani Központ, 1964. 61p. IYL.
"Children's literature." A critical history with illustrations reproduced from some of the more important works. There is a four page bibliography.

1834. Waldapfel, Eszter. "Az I. országos gyermekkönyvtárügyi konferencia munkájáról," *Magyar könyvszemle,* Budapest, Évf. 77, Apr., 1961, pp. 207–208.
"The first national conference of children's librarians" which took place in Dec., 1960, is reported on by the director of the state pedagogical library.

Rumania

Each of the Eastern European nations seems to have had one individual deeply committed to the cause of children's literature during the 1920's, just after the First World War. In Rumania this person was Apostol Culea and like his counterparts, he wrote a book about the subject which was amazingly well-informed considering the era. Curiously, he shows more the influence of Ellen Key and the Scandinavian socialists, than that of Wolgast and the other German critics. The public library movement in the U.S. and Great Britain had also impressed him, and one wonders how far and how long his schemes to put such library service in effect in Rumania lasted.

Culea's place in the present time has been assumed by Ilie Stanciu, who has written the only contemporary book on theory of children's literature in Rumanian (1849). Much of the other professional literature consists of translations from the Russian.

This heavy reliance on the Slavic is perhaps a bit irritating to the Rumanian writer and reader, for this country has prided itself on the much closer ties it has with the Latin countries, at least as far as language and literature are concerned. Modern Rumanian dates only to the 19th century, when the conscious movement to remove all non-Latin elements in the language resulted in a new literature. Two important figures of this period, Ion Creanga and Mihail Sadoveanu, belong also to the study of children's literature, for many of their short stories and novels have a great appeal to youth. Coming from the folk as they did, they are honored today all the more for their ideals.

1835. *Biblioteca de copii.* Bucureşti, Ministerul Culturii, 1953. 178p.
    "Children's library."

1836. Bologa, Lucian. *Lectura tineretului.* Cluj, 1933.

1837. *Concurs de ghicitori literare pentru copii.* Bucureşti, Biblioteca Centrală de Stat a R.P.R., 1957. 16p.
    "A literary quiz for children's libraries."

1838. *Concursul pentru citirea literaturii "Iubiţi Cartea."* Bucureşti, Comisia Centrală de Organizare a Concursului, 1955. 82p.
    "Children's Reading Contest—'Love the book.'"

1839. Constantinescu, Al. C. "Literature for the young," *Rumanian review,* Bucharest, Vol. 7, No. 1, 1953, pp. 83–91. DLC. (Also available in French and German editions of the same periodical).
    After a brief review of the "classic" writers for children in Rumania, the author delineates the characteristics of modern day literature and concludes with the statement: "Our literature for children has the noble task to contribute to the education of our children in the spirit of the lofty ideals which inspire our people in the building of Socialism and in their participation in the all-out fight for peace."

1840. *Copii povestesc copilor . . . Concursul de basme al bibliotecii de copii din Arad.* Bucureşti, Ministerul Culturii, 1956. 75p.

1841. Culea, Apostol D. *Literatura copiilor şi şezătorile cu copii.* Bucureşti, Fundatia Culturala Principele Carol, 1923. 296p. (Din Publicatiile Casei Şcoalelor, Biblioteca Pedagogică). OCL.
    "Children's literature and group work with children." Some of the theories inherent in the writing of good literature for children and how to introduce children to it. There is also a chapter on the organization of children's libraries with photographs of some mobile libraries in use. The concluding section is a list of approximately 300 titles of recommended books in Rumanian, a few of which were translations.

1842. Gorki, Maxim. *Despre literatura pentru copii.* Bucureşti, Editura Tineretului, 1955. 295p.
    A translation of 1906 into Rumanian, made by N. Lupaşcu.

1843. Krupskaia, N. K. *Despre literatura pentru copii şi indrumarea lecturii micilor cititori.* Bucureşti, Editura Ministerului Culturii, Direcţia Generală a Aşezămintelor Culturale, 1955. 76p.
    A translation from the Russian of 1941.

1844. Makarenko, A. S. *Cartea pentru părinti.* Bucureşti, Editura de Stat, Pedagogie şi Psihologie, 1950. 351p.
    A translation of 1956 made by R. Donici.

1845. Popp, Elvira. *Organizarea fondurilor de cărţi şi a cataloagelor în bibliotecile pentru copii.* Bucureşti, Editura de Stat Didactică şi Pedagogică, 1959. 125p.
    "The organization of the collection and catalog in the children's library."

1846.   Simonescu, Dan and D. Murărașu. *Lectura particulară și biblioteca scolară*. București, Biblioteca Liceului Romînesc, 1939.

1847.   Stanciu, Ilie. *Cele mai frumoase cărți de aventuri*. București, Editura de Stat pentru Imprimate si Publicații, 1955. 35p. (Ministerul Culturii. Direcția Generală a Așezămintelor Culturale.)

1848.   ———. *Cele mai frumoase cărți de vitejie și eroism*. București. Editura de Stat pentru Imprimate și Publicații, 1956. 71p. (Ministerul Culturii. Direcția Generală a Așezămintelor Culturale).

1849.   ———. *Copilul și cartea*. București, Editura de Stat Didactica și Pedagogică, 1958. 235p. DLC. (DLC also has earlier edition with title: *Literatura pentru copii și îndrumarea lecturii copiilor;* published by Biblioteca Centrală de Stat a R. P. R., 1957; 214p.).

"Children and books." The seven sections in addition to the title chapter are: Fairy tales; adventure stories; realistic stories; poetry; technical and scientific nonfiction; the role of parents in guiding children's reading; the public library, a precious aide in the guidance of children's reading. Lists of children's books match the 2nd through 6th sections. Bibliography.

1850.   ———. "Unele aspecte ale problemei conflictului in literatura noastră pentru copii," *Analele universității "C. I. Parhon,"* (Seria Stiințelor Sociale-Filologie), București, No. 4, 1956.

1851.   Zara, Ileana. "Biblioteci pentru copii," *Școală și viață,* București, 1937. (Also available as a reprint, series Biblioteca Asoc. generale a învățătorilor, 2. 52p.).

U.S.S.R.

This introduction to the Soviet Union must begin with an explanation and apology for the small number of entries in the bibliography covering 15 republics and almost as many literatures. Although communications have improved in the last decade, there is still a paucity of research materials from the U.S.S.R. in Western libraries. Of a certainty the books and articles described here represent only a small fraction of the outpouring of writing on the subject of children's literature.

Russia is the most populous of the republics, comprising more than one-half of the inhabitants of the Soviet Union. It is also the most influential, in all spheres of life. This brief survey will refer mostly to Russia, because it is from her that the other republics get much of their literature, either in translation or through direct emulation. There are, however, substantial bodies of literature in Armenian, Estonian, Georgian, Latvian, Lithuanian and Ukrainian. This is especially true in the area of folklore, in which each region has distinct types and styles. Actually, there are books printed in over 100 languages and dialects for the numerous minorities which exist.

In the 18th and 19th centuries, education was the privilege of the nobility and the wealthy landowning classes. It imitated Western European methods, but in a rather superficial way. French and German literature was as likely to be read as Russian. Of course, the early classics were all translated; but the most powerful Russian literature, for all classes, were the folk tales which were narrated orally. In the peasant and serf families, this was as much entertainment for the adults as it was for children. In the wealthy classes, it was the nursemaid (often illiterate) who recounted these tales for her charges.

Russian folklore has many of the same themes to be found in the rest of Europe. Whether its versions are in any way stronger or more effective is a moot point. Its potency as literary substance can hardly be questioned in view of the number of great Russian writers (and musicians) who used its themes for some of their major compositions. Folk literature was and probably will continue to be a source of inspiration to writers and composers in many countries and languages. It would be interesting to compare and see if any of them used it to the extent which the Russians did, in the period from about 1830 to 1930.

The best-known of all the collections of Russian folk tales is that made by Aleksandr Nikolaevich Afanas'ev. He was an ethnographer, and did not actually do most of the recording of the tales, but rather searched them out from the holdings of the Russian Geographical Society. He published them in a series, from 1855 to 1864. Since that time many complete editions have appeared in print, and in a number of other languages as well. The editions for children which came out usually selected only some of the favorites. One of the most handsome of these was illustrated by Ivan Bilibin, and appeared in English as well as a number of the European languages.

It is precisely these works based on folklore, and other stories centering on the heroism of the common man which form the bulk of the "classics" for Soviet children today. Pushkin's folk tales in verse, Krylov's fables, the incomparable short stories of Tolstoy, the poetry of Zhukovsky and Nekrasov, some of the short stories of Chekhov, and of course the tale in verse written by P. P. Ershov, *Konek-Gorunok* ("The Little Hump-Backed Horse").

Ershov deserves a special place in Russian children's literature although he, no more than the other writers above, did not specifically write his masterpiece for children. It was at least 30 years after its first publication (in 1834) before it appeared in a children's edition. It was only natural that with the emancipation of the serfs and the establishment of more primary schools for the common folk, this type of literature would have wider and wider appeal. For Ershov had written it in the colloquial language of the peasants, yet with a sense of poetry that was in the best Russian tradition. He himself was unhappy at his choice of this idiom and he never went back to the use of it, so that his other writing suffers by comparison. Samuel Johnson is supposed to have said: "Poetry cannot be translated; and therefore, it is the poets that preserve the languages." Perhaps this will be part of Ershov's contribution, and will make up for his lesser popularity in translation.

Some years before the emancipation of the serfs, Lev Nikolayevich Tolstoy tried to set up a school for them at his country estate. He soon abandoned this because he believed himself ill-prepared. Ten years later, in 1859, he began again on the same project and again failed, although he sensed he was nearer to the heart of the problem. Almost two decades then passed before his soul-searching culminated in a spiritual conversion, not to any formal religion but to a kind of Christian anarchism in which the power of love as exemplified by Christ was at the center of all life. While Tolstoy had no intention of spreading his beliefs as a set way of life, by virtue of his renown, they were read and discussed around the world, and profoundly affected many educators and writers. It is for this reason, and because of his tales centered on folk themes, that Tolstoy must be considered as a leading figure in children's literature.

In the same years during which Tolstoy was formulating the written account of his beliefs, Aleksey Maksimovich Pyeshkov was growing up in Nizhni Novgorod. Today, that city is called by the pen name this young man chose when he began to write—Gorki. Maxim Gorki (to call him by the most widely used name) did not take a special interest in children's literature until in his later years. As a young boy and man, he was too involved in absorbing the experiences of life to write. His first works were stories and plays of social and political protest, with the heroes chosen from the lower classes.

It was the recollections of his grandmother, so vividly portrayed in the first book of his autobiography, which brought Gorki to a full realization of the impact stories had had on him as a child. He became concerned about the role children's books were to play in the new Russia. Some years after the revolution, he went so far as to write to leading Western literary figures sympathetic to the Russian cause, begging them to write the grand and noble stories which were the child's due. These could be translated into all languages, he felt, wherever the revolutionary spirit was in force. Gorki also wrote several essays on the subject of children's literature and its characteristics, and was certainly instrumental in seeing to it that sufficient attention and funds were given to the state publishing houses which began to produce books for children on a mass basis. His collected writings on the subject form only one small volume, and much of it seems disjointed from the rest. However, one must recall the circumstances under which these articles were written and also take into account the general tone and spirit of any political writing. There is no doubt at all that Gorki's few essays were powerful enough to sway all post-revolutionary Russian children's literature over to trends that were in keeping with Marxist ideology. His speech at the First Congress of Soviet Writers, in 1934, made the style of Socialist realism almost a commandment.

It was the strong weeding out of "imperialist" tendencies, particularly from folk and fairy tales, which brought about the conflict between Gorki and Kornei Chukovsky, the man who was destined to take Gorki's place as the chief critic of children's literature. In actuality, there was not that much difference in the views of the two men. Gorki did not entirely renounce the fairy tale, as Chukovsky sometimes has claimed. Chukovsky, with his nonsense verse, was not guilty of betraying the new dictum, but was rather giving children something which they needed as part of their linguistic education.

Unfortunately, the diagreement which resulted from the misunderstanding of aims caused Chukovsky's critical work to fall into official disgrace for a time. This did not prevent it from being printed, nor did it prevent the author's children's books from having tremendous success. Gradually, more and more teachers, librarians and parents have come to see the value of Chukovsky's research, and at present there is more acceptance of his theories, without a decline in Gorki's importance.

The crux of Chukovsky's ideas are to be found in his book, *Ot Dvukh do Piati,* available now in numerous languages, and in English as *From Two to Five* (1877). Basically, what the author tries to point out again and again, is that fairy tales, fantasy, poetry and nonsense are as important to the child's mental development as food is to his physical growth. Socialist realism has its place in children's literature, but should not usurp the place of the imaginative, and above all, should not be given as a sole diet to the very young child.

Had Chukovsky been fighting against books which were poorly designed, badly written and with mediocre illustrations, he would perhaps not have had such a difficult time proving his point. But one must admit that the new children's books were quite attractive and obviously appealing to the young Russian who had not had much available on a mass basis, prior to 1920. A steady diet of Socialist realism was not so unpalatable, when there was not much to compare it with from previous times! The fact that the books were so inexpensive was also quite important. One can find any number of glowing contemporary reports on the status of Soviet children's books, made by visiting publishers, librarians and other individuals from Western countries.

Another reason for the great success of many of these children's books of the 1910–1940 period is that there were a number of authors who were able to turn the techniques of socialist realism to their advantage, using themes of nature, the new evolution of science, the advance of technology, etc., and making these very much an exciting part of the modern life of the child. Such authors as S. Marshak, A. P. Gaidar, M. Ilyin, V. Bianki, E. Charushin, and M. M. Prishvin used one or another of these subjects to good advantage.

It is only in the last decade or two that this emphasis on the realistic began to pall. With the great number of children now finding no novelty in the very fact of owning or being able to borrow a book freely, there began a search for materials of greater variety. More translations were sought out from other countries, and a resurgence in folk and fairy tales took place. Although there are more than 3,000 titles published for children each year in the Soviet Union (in all languages) there is still not the variety in types and subjects which one finds in some other countries publishing an equivalent number of titles.

The documentation of the history of children's literature in the U.S.S.R. is a formidable task, but if the examples to be found in libraries in the U.S. and Western Europe are any indication, the bibliographic and theoretical work already accomplished is tremendous. Prior to 1920, there had been only a few studies on the subject. There were, however, a number of comprehensive and/or selective lists of children's books, so that one can trace fairly well the books of the last decades of the 19th century (see 1860, 1903, 1913, 1979, 1980, 1981, 1989, 1997, 1998, 1999). Now, the results of research are flowing out of the House of Children's Books, the National Library, the methodology centers, and the Leningrad and Moscow Public Libraries.

There is even more secondary literature on the subject of children's library work, and the methods to be used in bringing children and books together. Many of these are the results of conferences, seminars and symposiums held regularly for children's librarians, both experienced and neophyte.

Children's libraries are organized as separate institutions, as departments of public libraries or Pioneer Houses, and as central and classroom libraries in schools. In all cases, they are heavily used. It is the distinct division of children's services from those to adults which, to offer one comparison, makes the Soviet children's library most different from libraries in the U.S. or Scandinavia. Mrs. Spain, in commenting on this, points out how much this can change the whole philosophy and purpose of library service. She wrote: "The separation of book and library service to children from that for adults tends to make the transfer from one level to the other a deliberate break instead of a smooth flow from one unit of book service to the other which is possible if all readers use the same building . . . On the other hand, it gives children a special feeling of identity with a library that is exclusively theirs. This sense of belonging was noticeable among the children who were using the libraries of the U.S.S.R."

1852. Abel'skaiā, R. S. and Olga Khuze. *Domashnee chtenie detei.* Moskva, Molodaiā Gvardiiā, 1940, 60p. DLC.

"Children's home reading." A guide for parents to use in directing their children's reading. Many specific titles are suggested.

1853. Aizerman, L. S. "Contemporary literature through the eyes of uppergrade pupils," *Soviet review,* New York, Vol. 6, Spring, 1965, pp. 32–45. NNY.

A translation from *Literatura v Shkole,* Moskva, No. 5, 1964. This includes a number of lengthy and perceptive comments by young adult readers, on novels by Soviet and foreign writers.

1854. Akademiiā pedagogicheskikh nauk RSFSR. *Kniga-uchitel' i drug.* Moskva, 1962. 175p. DLC.

A history of children's literature approached through critical essays by a number of writers, each treating of some important period or author.

1855. ———. *O vospitatel'nom znachenii sovetskoĭ detskoĭ literatury.* Materialy nauchnoĭ sessii Akademii pedagog. Nauk i Ministerstva prosveshcheniiā RSFSR, posviashchennoĭ obsuzhdeniiū pedagog. Trebovanii k sovetskoĭ detskoĭ lit-re 4–6 fevr. 1952 g. Moskva, 1952. 61p. DLC.

"The educational significance of Soviet children's literature." Papers presented at the conference on children's literature, Feb., 1952, sponsored by the Pedagogical Academy and the Ministry of Education.

1856. Alekseeva, O. V. et. al. *Detskaiā literatura; posobie dliā pedagogicheskikh uchilishch.* Moskva, Gos. uchebno-pedagog. izd-vo, 1957. 333p. DLC. NNY has 1960 ed., same pub., 422p.

"Children's literature; a textbook for pedagogical schools." A history of children's literature described chronologically through the biographies and works of its chief writers from Pushkin to Gorki to Chukovsky.

1857.   Alksnis, Gertrude. *Objectives and functions of the Soviet Russian children's libraries presented from recent Russian sources.* Chicago, University of Chicago Library School, 1961. 56p. (Thesis)

1858.   ———. "Soviet Russian children's libraries: a survey of recent Russian sources," *Library quarterly,* Chicago, Vol. 32, No. 4, Oct., 1962, pp. 287–301. DLC, NNY.
    A summary of the author's Master's thesis in 1857. This seems to be one of the most objective presentations of all those undertaken by U.S. librarians.

1859.   Annenskaia, Alexandra N. *O dietskikh knigakh; kritiko-bibliograficheskii ukazatel' knig, vyshedshikh do 1. Ianv. 1907 g., rekomenduemykh dlia chteniia dietiam v vozrastie ot 7 do 16 liet.* [Moskva, 1908] 831p. DLC.
    A critical-bibliographical list of books in memory of the first anniversary of the 1907 revolution. There are some 2,000 titles, each annotated and indexed.

1860.   Antipova, P. D. *Chetyrekh-shkol'naia biblioteka. Tipa knizhnago sklada "Kostromich."* Moskva, T-stvo "Pechatnia S. P. Iakovleva," 1893. 16p. DLC.
    A classified catalog of books suitable for school and public libraries. The Kostromich firm was one specializing in bookselling to schools.

1861.   Babushkina, Antonina Petrovna. *Istoriia russkoi detskoi literatury.* Moskva, Gos.ucheb.-pedagog.izd-vo, 1948. 479p. DLC.
    "History of Russian children's literature," from the 15th to the 20th centuries. Bibliographies.

1862.   Barbanov, G. "Nedelia detskoi knigi," *Bibliotekar',* Moskva, Aug., 1949, pp. 23–27. DLC.
    "Children's Book Week." The first such week was celebrated in Moscow in 1944, but in 1949 (March) it was promulgated on a national basis. Described here are the types of reading and other programs which took place, and a number of statistics as to the libraries and individuals taking part.

1863.   Baumstein-Heissler, Nina, "Que lisent les enfants soviétiques?" *Enfance,* Paris, No. 3, 1956, pp. 208–214. IYL.
    "What do Soviet children read?" Children's literature is treated as a branch of all literature in the Soviet Union today; therefore, they are given works by the great writers, and present-day authors do not consider it degrading or embarrassing to write for children.

1864.   Belinskii, Vissarion Grigor'evich *et al. O detskoi literature.* [Sostavitel'sbornika i primechanii S. Shillegodskii. Tekst podgotovlen E. Kniko. Sbornik soderzhit stat'i i retsenzii, spetsial'no posviashchennye detskim knigam.] Moskva, Gos. izd-vo detskoi lit-ry, 1954. 430p. DLC.
    A collection of articles and reviews concerned with historical or critical aspects of children's books. There are bibliographical notes for each chapter.

1865.   Berdnikova, K. and R. Kraček. "Catalogues for children and young people in the Lenin State Library of the USSR," *UNESCO bulletin for libraries,* Paris, Vol. 17, No. 2, Mar.–Apr., 1963, pp. 65–69. DLC, NNY.
    Very detailed descriptions of the types of catalogues and their use.

1866.   Berestneva, Aleksandra Iakovlevna. *Chas vneklassnogo chteniia v pervom klasse; iz opyta raboty.* Moskva, Izd-vo Akademii pedagog. nauk RSFSR, 1958. 62p. DLC.
    A manual containing a lesson plan for the study and teaching of children's literature. There are graded booklists as well as short excerpts from the works of the major authors mentioned in the text. Bibliographies.

1867.   Berkhin, Naum Borisovich. *Kniga- drug i pomoshchnik pionera.* Moskva, Akademii pedagogicheskikh nauk RSFSR, 1958. 82p. DLC.
    The methodology of work with Pioneer groups and books.

1868.   Bilets'kyi, Dmytro Petrovych. *Ukrains'ka dytiacha literatura.* Kiev, Radians'ka Shkola, 1963. 234p. DLC.
    A history of Ukrainian children's literature beginning with the late 18th century.

1869.   Binder, Pearl. "Books for children in modern Russia," *The studio,* London, Vol. 107, No. 495, June, 1934, pp. 309–313. DLC, NNY.
    "Some characteristic productions in which the direct appeal of pictures plays a large part." Illustrated.

1870.   Bobinska, Helena. [Children's literature in the USSR.] *Ruch pedagogiczny,* Warszawa, Vol. 31, No. 1, 1947–1948.
    Paper given at the Polish Congress on Children's Literature (see 2114). In Polish.

1871.   Borshchevskaia, A. I. *et al. Detskaia literatura (vtoraia polovina XIX i nachalo XX vv.);*

khrestomatiía dlía pedagogicheskikh institutov.
Moskva, Gos. uchebno-pedagog. izd-vo, 1954. 517p.
DLC.

"Children's literature (from the second half of the 19th and the beginning of the 20th century); an anthology for pedagogical institutes." The actual period covered is 1850–1917.

1872. Brandis, Evgenii Pavlovich. *Ot Ezopa do Gianni Rodari.* Moskva, Prosvechenie, 1965. 311p. DLC.

"From Aesop to Gianni Rodari; translated children's books of the 18th, 19th and 20th centuries." A survey of some of the children's books which have been translated into Russian.

1873. Budnitskaya, P. Miller. "Children's books in wartime Russia," *Horn book,* Boston, Vol. 19, Mar.–Apr., 1943, pp. 85–89. DLC, NNY.

A review of current writing and publishing trends, mostly as represented in the publications of Detgiz, the state publishing house for children's books. Chukovsky, Marshak, Pasternak and other authors are mentioned.

1874. Bzhozovskaía, M. "Izuchenie rodnogo kraía," *Bibliotekar',* Moskva, Jan., 1953, pp. 25–28. DLC.

"The study of one's native land." An interesting project in which the children's libraries in the region of Gorki centered their programs around the study of nature, historical developments and the culture of the area.

1875. Chekhov, Nikolăi Vladimirovich. *Dïetskaía literatura.* Moskva, Pol'za, 1909. 256p. DLC.

An interesting critical history of children's literature replete with information on many writers whose works were considered suitable for children, as well as those who specifically wrote for children. For each there is a portrait, and in some cases black and white reproductions from some of their books. There is a very extensive bibliography.

1876. Chernysheva, Y. "Soviet school libraries," *School libraries,* Chicago, Vol. 8, Oct., 1958, pp. 13–14. DLC, NNY.

A brief article outlining the types of Soviet school libraries which exist and the kinds of service they give. This is preceded by a one-page article by Boris I. Gorokhoff, "School libraries in the USSR."

1877. Chukovskii, Kornei Ivanovich. *Ot dvukh do piati.* 14th ed. Moskva, Svetskaía Pisatel', 1960. 373p. DLC. DLC also has numerous other editions.

This important work was first published in

1925 under the title *Malen'kie Deti.* While it appeared steadily in new editions in Russian, it has only recently been recognized in other countries and translated into other languages. To describe it as a study of the development of language in the young child is not to give it its full due. It is also a strong defense of the imaginative needs of the young child, particularly as regards the fairy tale and poetry. The author, who is a noted poet, translator and writer of children's books, has based his conclusions on intensive observation of children, on the recorded observations of others (parents, teachers, scholars) and to a lesser degree on previous research in the field. The result is a very personal work, but one of great conviction and a delight to read.

1878. Cohen, L. O. *Reading guidance of the young in the Soviet Union as reflected in Soviet library literature, 1953–1957.* Los Angeles, Immaculate Heart College, 1961. 148p. Thesis.

1879. *Detskaía literatura.* Dobroslovodskii per. d. 14, Moskva B-66, USSR. Monthly, Jan., 1966. (Subscription: 30 kop. per copy). IYL.

A periodical containing articles of criticism and history, techniques of writing for children, reviews, and other pertinent news.

1880. Dom detskoĭ knigi. *Chto chitat' detíam; rekomendatel'nyĭ ukazatel' literatury dlía uchashchikhsía V–VII klassov.* [Moskva] Detgiz, 1957. 173p. (Shkol'naía biblioteka). DLC. DLC also has editions of: 1948, 220p.; 1949, 47p.; 1953, 126p.

"What children read." An annotated list of books for children in grades 5–7 arranged by subject areas. There is a matching list for grades 1–4, revised at the same intervals.

1881. ———. *Detskaía literatura i viprosy masterstva; sbornik stateĭ.* Moskva, Gos. izd-vo detskoĭ lit-ry, 1956. 229p. DLC.

"Children's literature and literary mastery." A series of articles and papers on many types of children's literature compiled by the House of Children's Books.

1882. ———. *Étikh dneĭ ne smolknet slava.* Moskva, Gos. izd-vo detskoĭ lit-ry, 1957. 29p. DLC.

"The glory of those days will never die." An annotated list of books for children, chosen to suit the theme of the Revolution.

1883. ———. *Knigi—detíam; sbornik metodicheskikh stateĭ o rabote s knigoĭ.* Moskva, Gos. izd-vo detskoĭ lit-ry, 1956. 157p. DLC.

"Books—children; articles on the methodology of work with children." Using specific types of available literature as examples, this explains to teachers how they can introduce books to children. Bibliography.

1884. *Knigi o shkole i detiakh; kratkiĭ rekomendatel'nyĭ ukazatel' khudozhestvennoĭ literatury dlia uchashchikhsia 1–7–kh klassov.* Moskva, Gos. izd-vo detskoĭ lit-ry, 1953. 61p. DLC.

A recommended booklist for grades one through seven, alphabetically arranged by author, and annotated.

1885. ———. *Kommunisticheskoe vospitanie i sovremennaia literatura dlia deteĭ i iunoshestva.* Moskva, Gos. izd-vo detskoĭ lit-ry, 1961. 338p. DLC.

"Communist education and contemporary literature for children and youth, edited under the direction of B. A. D'iakov." Papers and reports given at a conference of the Union of Writers, Moscow, Dec., 1960.

1886. ———. *Literaturno-kriticheskie chteniia.* Moskva, Gos. izd-vo detskoĭ lit-ry, 1951. 127p. DLC.

Each of these four essays is concerned with some critical aspects of children's literature. One is on Gorki.

1887. ———. *Nedelia detskoĭ knigi.* Moskva, Gos. izd-vo detskoĭ lit-ry, 1950. 157p. DLC.

Children's Book Week was the occasion for the publication of these essays of history and criticism.

1888. ———. *Ob izdaniiakh skazok dlia deteĭ.* Moskva, Gos. izd-vo detskoĭ lit-ry, 1955. 421 p. DLC.

"On the publishing of folk tales for children." Articles concerning problems of authenticity and selection, together with a list of Soviet folk tales for children, published in the 19th and 20th centuries. There are indexes for authors, illustrators, editors and translators.

1889. ———. *Propaganda knig sredi shkol'nikov; sbornik metodicheskikh materialov k nedele detskoĭ knigi.* Moskva, Gos. izd-vo detskoĭ lit-ry, 1951. 113p. DLC.

"Propaganda for the book among school children." This handbook was especially designed for use in connection with Children's Book Week. There is a recommended booklist at the end.

1890. ———. "Sovetskaia detskaia literatura." [Moskva] Detgiz, 1955. Unp. DLC.

This pamphlet is useful for its numerous photos and portraits of Soviet writers for children (since the Revolution), as well as for its reproductions of the covers of several hundred children's books. There is very little text.

1891. ———. *Sovetskie detskie pisateli; bibliograficheskiĭ slovar' 1917–1957.* Moskva, Gos. izd-vo detskoĭ lit-ry, 1961. 429p. DLC.

"Soviet writers for children; bibliographic dictionary 1917–1957; compiled by A. M. Vitman and L. G. Os'kina." This is actually bio-bibliographic covering several hundred writers whose works appeared in the Soviet Union during the period 1917–1957.

1892. ———. *Voprosy detskoi literatury.* Moskva, Gos. izd-vo detskoĭ lit-ry, 1952–1957, annual. DLC.

"Questions related to children's literature." This annual compilation of articles and reviews is essentially concerned with the theory of children's literature, its criticism, and the methodology of bringing children and books together.

1893. ———. Leningradskii Filial. *Latyshskaia detskaia literatura.* Leningrad, Gos. izd-vo detskoĭ lit-ry, 195 .7204p. DLC.

An annotated bibliography of Latvian children's books, covering the period 1940–1955. They are arranged by type, and there is an author index.

1894. ———. Leningradskii Filial. *Litovskaia detskaia literatura, 1940–1955.* Leningrad, Detgiz, 1957. 150p. DLC.

A history of Lithuanian children's literature, divided into the pre-Soviet period and the Soviet period, and treated in two major categories: Folk tales, and books for school children. There is a matching bibliography of books in these categories, as well as lists of children's books translated into Lithuanian and Polish.

1895. Doniger, Simon. "Children's literature in the Soviet Union," *American quarterly on the Soviet Union,* New York, Vol. 1, No. 3, Oct., 1938, pp. 3–18. DLC, NNY.

A glowing review of the new Soviet literature, particularly the works of Marshak, Chukovsky and Ilin.

1896. "25 let na bibliotechnom fronte," *Krasnyĭ bibliotekar',* Moskva, No. 9, 1938, pp. 32–36. DLC.

A review of 25 years' work of the pioneer children's librarian, L. M. Sosnikhina.

1897. Efros, M. "Rabota s khudozhestvennoĭ literaturoĭ v detskoĭ biblioteke," *Bibliotekar',* Moskva, Feb., 1954, pp. 32–37. DLC.

"Work with fictional literature in the children's library." This describes the programs of the Krupskaia library in Moscow, named after the wife of Lenin who was a leading figure in education.

1898. Evans, Ernestine. "Russian children and their books," *Asia,* New York, Vol. 31, No. 11, Nov., 1931, pp. 686–691, 736. DLC.

This American editor had warm praise for the colorful, well-designed, mass-produced children's books of Soviet Russia. She believed that their propagandistic qualities did not detract from their genuine appeal and literary quality, and felt that the elevating of mass taste far outweighed any objections as to political implications of some of the contents.

1899. Fediaevskaia, Vera Mikhaĭlovna. *Chto i kak rasskazyvat' i chitat' doshkol'nikam.* Izd. 2. Moskva, Gos. uchebno-pedagog. izd-vo, 1955. 204p. DLC.

A manual of storytelling for use with young children. A number of illustrations from books mentioned in the text are reproduced in black and white. Bibliography.

1900. ———. " 'Here and Now' stories in Russia —an experiment," *Elementary school journal,* Chicago, Vol. 26, No. 4, Dec., 1925, pp. 278–289. DLC.

The writer, who was a teacher and storyteller, describes her efforts at using the stories and techniques of Lucy Sprague Mitchell in Russian adaptations.

1901. Feoktisov, Ivan Ivanovich. *K voprosu o dietskom chtenii.* S.-Peterburg, Izd. M. M. Lederle, 1891. 271p. DLC.

"On the question of children's reading." This early critical study contained essays on talented children and their reading, on fairy tales, books for very young children (picture books), and the role of reading in education.

1902. Gankina, E. *Russkie knudozhniki detskoĭ knigi.* Moskva, Sovetskiĭ Khudozhnik, 1963. 276p. DLC.

A history of children's book illustration in Russia, from the early days of printing up to the present day. Profusely illustrated in black and white and color reproductions. There are extensive bibliographies on individual artists, as well as general book illustration. This is a major contribution to the history of children's books.

1903. Garshin, V. M. and A. IA. Gerd. *Obzor dietskoĭ literatury za 1883–1888,* g.g. 3 vols. St.-Peterburg. DLC.

Selected, annotated lists of children's books

arranged by author and indexed by title. Because the information is quite complete, this is a very helpful list in locating Russian children's books of the late 19th century.

1904. Gil'man, M. "Voprosy stroitel'stva detskikh i skol'nykh bibliotek," *Krasnyĭ bibliotekar',* Moskva, No. 4, 1938, pp. 59–64.

The needs of the school library in terms of physical space and furnishings.

1905. Gobetti, A. Marchesini. "La letteratura infantile nell' URSS," *Scuola e pedagogia nell' URSS.* Siena, 1951.

Also contains: "Stampa e letteratura infantile nell' URSS" by Gianni Rodari.

1906. Gor'kiĭ, Maksim. *O detskoĭ literature; stat'i i vyskazvaniia.* Moskva Gos. izd-vo detskoĭ lit-ry, 1958. 431p. DLC. (DLC also has 1952 ed., 254p).

This edition of Gorki's essays on children's literature contains also a number of his reviews of the works of Soviet writers for children. There are also some closing essays on the influence which Gorki has had on the writing of children's books in the Soviet Union. The articles which Gorki wrote were not intended for a single volume; thus, they must be read individually, rather than as part of an intrinsic whole. The one note which is common to all is that of urgency—Gorki felt convinced that the only hope for Russia's future lay in her children, and their education. Books were an important part of that education, and he pleaded with the best writers in the country (as well as in other lands) to turn to writing seriously for children, for he knew that the task was not easy. "Simple and clear style is achieved not by lowering the level of literary standards but through consummate craftsmanship," he wrote. Above all, however, he stressed the revolutionary aspects of children's books. They were to help the new generation understand the new Soviet Union, and the Communist ideology which nurtured it.

1907. Gorkina, A. "The new children's bookshop," *Horn book,* Boston, Vol. 13, No. 1, Jan.-Feb., 1937, pp. 41–44. DLC, IYL, NNY.

A Moscow mother describes the books and services of the model children's bookshop on Gorki street.

1908. Gorodkina, L. "Pisateli v detskoĭ biblioteke," *Bibliotekar',* Moskva, June, 1951, pp. 27–29. DLC, NNY.

"Writers in the children's library." A description of a series of evening programs in which leading authors of children's books came to discuss their work with the young readers.

1909. Graham, Gladys Murphy. "Picture of Russia for Russia's children." *N.Y. times magazine,* New York, Feb. 8, 1948, pp. 16, 42–43. DLC, NNY.

The themes of nationalism, Stalinism and military preparedness were very prevalent in the postwar books for children according to this observer. She quotes numerous examples from the texts of Russian children's books.

1910. Grechishnikova, A. D. *Sovetskaia detskaia literatura; uchebnoe posobie dlia uchitel'skikh institutov.* Moskva, Gos. uchebno-pedagog. izd-vo, 1953. 249p.

A critical survey of Soviet children's literature, with a few illustrative examples in text and pictures. This deals entirely with the 20th century.

1911. ———. *Velikie revoliusionery-demokraty o detskoi literature; stenogramma lektsii, prochitannoi v Dome detskoi knigi.* Moskva, Gos. izd-vo detskoi lit-ry, 1952. 23p. DLC.

A critical essay on the revolutionary-democratic children's literature. This was given as a lecture at the House of Children's Books.

1912. Grossman, S. "Zadachi detskikh bibliotek letom," *Krasnyi bibliotekar',* Moskva, No. 5, 1937, pp. 59–61.

A description of the children's libraries opened in the parks of Moscow in summer.

1913. Gul'binskii, Ignatii Vladislavovich. *Chto chitat'? Ukazatel' sistematicheskago domashniago chteniia dlia uchashchikhsia.* Moskva, Nauka, 1911.

An annotated list arranged systematically and alphabetically.

1914. Hurvych, Fenia Khaimivna. *Ukraïns'ka dytiacha literatura; khrestomatiia kritichnikh materialiv.* Posibnik dlia pedagog. in-tiv. Uporiadkuvali F. KH. Gurvich, V. S. Savenko. Kiïv, Radians'ka shkola, 1962. 311p.

An anthology of Ukrainian children's literature, together with biographies and bibliographies on the leading writers. There is also an extensive general bibliography on the history of Ukrainian children's literature.

1915. ÎAmpol'skaia, Marianna Leont'evna. Kratkii ocherk istorii iakutskoi detskoi literatury. ÎAkutsk, ÎAkutskoe knizhnoe izd-vo, 1959. 114p.

A critical history of Yakut children's literature. There is no bibliography or index, but there are a few sources traced in the notes.

1916. Ibbotson, Peter. "Soviet children's books,"

New statesman, London, Vol. 44, Sept. 27, 1952, pp. 350–351. DLC, NNY.

In this reply to an article by Naomi Mitchison (in the Sept. 6, 1952 issue), this observer writes of what impressions he gained on children's books and reading, while on a trip through the Soviet Union. There is further discussion of these articles in the October, 1952 issues.

1917. Inozemtsev, Ivan Vladimirovitch, *et al. Sovetskaia detskaia literatura; programma kursa dlia bibliotechnykh institutov.* Moskva, Sovetskaia Rossiia. 1957. 31p. DLC.

An outline and bibliography on Soviet children's literature intended for use by students in the library school.

1918. Ipolitov, S. "Literatura infantil," *Cultura soviética,* México, Año 2, No. 11, Sept., 1948, pp. 38 ff.

1919. Ivich, Aleksandr, pseud. *Vospitanie pokolenii; o sovetskoi literature dlia detei:* [Gor'kii, Maiakovskii, Marshak 1 dr.] Moskva, Sovetskii pisatel', 1960. 390p.

Essays on Gorkii, Maiakovskii, Marshak, Chukovskii, Panteleev, Zhitkov, Gaidar, Il'in and other Soviet writers for children.

1920. Izhevskaia, M. A. *Detskaia biblioteka; prakticheskoe posobie dlia detskogo bibliotekaria.* Pod red. A. A. Khrenkovoi. Moskva, 1958. 229p. DLC. DLC also has earlier editions.

A handbook and manual of organization and management of children's libraries which has come to be the standard reference work in the field in the Soviet Union as well as in many of the other Socialist countries.

1921. Jamieson, Nigel J. "Soviet books for children," *Comment,* Wellington, Vol. 5, No. 3, Apr.–May, 1964, pp. 25–27. NNY.

A general statement on the types of books available in the Soviet Union.

1922. Kal'nev, Ivan. *Sistematicheskii katalog knigam.* Odessa, Stereotipnoe P. Fantsova, 1876. 181p. DLC.

A systematic catalog of 1,352 children's books published from 1864 to 1875 in Russia. Each is annotated and has complete bibliographic information. This includes some types of textbooks.

1923. Jurevičiūtė, I. *Vaiku literatūra; bibliografija, 1940–1964.* Vilnius, Vaga, 1965. 398p. DLC.

"Children's literature; a bibliography, 1940–

1964." After a brief historical and contemporary survey of Lithuanian children's literature, there are lists of books for four age levels. Each is subdivided into native works, translations from the other Soviet republics, and translations from other foreign languages. Science literature is listed in a separate section. There are some 1700 entries in all. A most important part is the list of critical and historical material on children's literature in Lithuanian, pp. 319–346. Works on individual authors are listed separately. In all, there are some 300 items, mostly periodical articles. Index.

1924. "Juvenile literature." Entire issue of: *Soviet literature*, Moscow, No. 4, 1964, pp. 1–192. DLC, NNY, IYL. (Also available in German language edition).

In addition to numerous recent selections of literature for children, there are articles of criticism; biographies of two children's writers, Boris Zhitkov and Valentin Katayev; a survey of Russian translations of English and U.S. and other countries' children's books; and short items of general interest to persons working with children. Each year there is an issue of this periodical devoted to children's literature, and there are other articles in intervening issues as well.

1925. Kaspina, E. "Rabota s det'mi," *Krasnyǐ bibliotekar'*, Moskva, No. 3, Mar., 1941, pp. 32–36. DLC.
Work with children in Moscow public libraries giving statistics and details of many activities.

1926. Khrenkova, A. "Povysit' uroven' raboty oblastnykh detskikh bibliotek," *Bibliotekar'*, Moskva, Sept., 1957, pp. 25–32. DLC, NNY.
"Let us raise the level of work in *oblast* (region) children's libraries." The author contended that these libraries were not up to the standards of the large city libraries, and that there was much room for improvement.

1927. King, Beatrice. "Children's books in Soviet Russia," *Junior bookshelf*, Huddersfield, Vol. 6, No. 3, Nov., 1942, pp. 87–91. DLC, NNY.
Some characteristics and statistics concerning the books published for children.

1928. ——. "Children's libraries in the USSR," *Library assistant*, London, Vol. 35, No. 5, May, 1942, pp. 85–78. DLC.
A brief review of services and ideals by a British observer.

1929. Kittredge, William A. "Juvenile books from the Russia of today," *Publishers' weekly*, New York,

Vol. 146, No. 18, Oct. 28, 1944, pp. 1734–1737. DLC, NNY.
A U.S. collector of Russian books for children describes some of his acquisitions. Illustrated.

1930. Klenov, A. V. *Technika škol'noj biblioteke.* Moskva, 1938. 168p.

1931. Kon, Lidiǐa Feliksovna. *Detskaǐa literatura v gody grazhdanskoǐ voǐny.* Moskva, Gos. izd-vo detskoǐ lit-ry, 1953. 39p.
"Children's literature in the years of civil peace." A critical essay.

1932. ——. *O detskoǐ literature.* Moskva, Gos. izd-vo detskoǐ lit-ry, 1950. 415p. DLC.
An earlier edition of the work noted below.

1933. ——. *Sovetskaǐa detskaǐa literatura, 1917–1929; ocherk istorii russkoǐ detskoǐ literatury.* Moskva, Gos. izd-vo detskoǐ lit-ry, 1960. 318p. DLC.
"Soviet children's literature, 1917–1929." A critical history with many illustrations.

1934. "Konferenz über kinderliteratur," *Sowjetliteratur*, Moskau, Heft 9, 1952, pp. 131–157. DLC.
A report on the second children's writer's conference followed by articles by A. Surkov, S. Marschak and O. Pissarshevski on various types of Russian children's literature. A report of the 1st conference was in Heft 5, 1950, pp. 143–152, of this same periodical.

1935. Kopeckij, Platon V. *Očerki po istorii russkoj i sovětskoj dětskoj literatury, s obrazcami iz proizvědenij avtorov.* [Vyd. 1] Praha, Státní pedagogické nakl., 1957. 271p. (Učební texty vysokých škol). DLC.
Although printed in Czechoslovakia, this history of children's literature (Russian and Soviet) is in Russian.

1936. Korovenko, A. "Rukovodstvo chteniem deteǐ mladshego vozrasta," *Bibliotekar'*, Moskva, May, 1955, pp. 24–27. DLC.
"Reading guidance with small children." The author describes her experiences with first and second graders in children's libraries in Moscow.

1937. Krasovskaǐa, N. "Kak rabotaet nasha chital'nǐa," *Krasnyǐ bibliotekar'*, Moskva, No. 7, 1937, pp. 53–57.
An account of work in the L. N. Tolstoy children's library in Moscow.

1938. Krivoshapkin, Il'ǐa Grigor'evich. *Besedy o*

proizvedenaiiakh sovetskoĭ detskoĭ literatury; vneklass-noe chtenie v V-VII klassakh. Moskva, Izd-vo Akademii pedagog. nauk RSFSR, 1956. 71p. DLC.

A manual for the study and teaching of children's literature. This is limited to works for the fifth through seventh classes.

1939.   Kruglov, Aleksandr Vasil'evich. *Literatura "malen'kago naroda"; kritiko-pedagogicheskiia besiedy po voprosam dietskoĭ literatury.* Moskva, Izd. M.D. Naumova, 1897. DLC.

The author considers the definition of children's literature, its history, and some of the persons who have chosen to write for children, or whose works have come to be accepted by children. An interesting study from the 19th-century point of view.

1940.   Krupskaiā, Nadezhda Konstantinovna. *Bibliotekoe delo.* Moskva and Leningrad, Gosudarstvennoe . . . Sotsial'no-ekonomicheskoe Izdatel'stvo, 1933. 157p.

Mme. Krupskaiā was the wife of Lenin, and an important figure in the development of popular education after the revolution. In this book on libraries, Part 2 deals with children's work.

1941.   ———. N. K. *Krupskaiā o detskoĭ literature i detskom chtenii; stat'i i vyskazyvaniiā.* [Sostavitel' A. Kravchenko] Moskva, Gos. izd-vo detskoĭ lit-ry, 1954. 76p. DLC.

A collection of selected passages from the speeches and articles of Mme. Krupskaiā having to do with children's literature and reading.

1942.   ———. *O bibliotechnom dele; sbornik.* [Sostavitel' A. G. Kravchenko] Moskva, 1959. 714p. DLC.

A revised and greatly expanded edition of the work noted in 1940 (above). In this edition, Part 7 is concerned with children's work, and there are several protographs of Mme. Krupskaiā with groups of children. This is more theoretical than the later work by Izhevskaiā (1920), but it had and still has great influence on the methodology of work with children in the libraries of the Soviet Union.

1943.   Kupriianova, Kseniia N., *et al. Vneklassnoe chtenie.* Moskva, 1965. 148p. DLC. DLC also has 1962 ed., 93p.

An annotated booklist arranged according to grade levels and intended for use by students and teachers.

1944.   Latvia. Izglitibas Ministrija. *Bērnu un jaunatnes grāmatu saraksts, līdvz ar īsu satura at-* *stāstījumu un atsauksmēm.* Riga, Izglitibas Ministrijas Izdevums, 1930. 174p. DLC.

"Children's and youth books in Latvian." An annotated booklist of 953 items arranged alphabetically by author. There is also a short list of books in old Latvian and in the Latgalean dialect.

1945.   Lehmbruck, G. W. "Die Moskauer Kinderbuchkonferenz," *Die neue Schule,* Berlin (East), Jahrgang 7, No. 24, June 13, 1952. pp. 566–568. DLC.

Report on the activities and speeches presented during one of the national conferences on children's literature.

1946.   Leningrad. Gosudarstvennyĭ pedagogicheskiĭ institut imeni A. I. Gerfsena. Pokazatel'naiā biblioteka detskoĭ literatury. *Ukazatel' detskoĭ literatury dliā shkol i detskikh bibliotek.* Leningrad, Rabotnik prosveshcheniiā, 1928. 85p. DLC.

A booklist arranged under broad subject categories. Part 1 is for the lower grades and Part 2 for the intermediate and higher grades. The first-choice titles are so marked, and second choice and passable titles are also thus indicated.

1947.   Leningrad. Publichnaiā biblioteka. *Chto chitat' moim detiam: Besedy dliā roditeleĭ o detskom chtenii.* Leningrad, 1959. 141p. DLC, IYL.

An annotated booklist arranged by types with an introduction for each section. Many illustrations from the books are included. This was intended for use by the children as well as by librarians and teachers.

1948.   ———. *Druzhba, editnstvo, mir; rekomendatel'ny ukazatel' literatury dliā iūoshestva.* Leningrad, 1957. 51p. DLC.

"Friendship, unity, peace: recommended guide to literature for young people, compiled by Mariiā Leonovna Arkina." This list was issued in connection with the 6th World Youth Festival. The entries are annotated.

1949.   ———. *Saliūt Il'ichu; o trudovykh pionerskikh delakh. Rekomendatel'nyĭ spisok literatury dliā uchashchikhsiā 5–7 klassov.* [Sostavitel' Nina Filippovna Belokon'] Leningrad, 1957. 19p. DLC.

An annotated reading list for Pioneer children in honor of Lenin. This is for classes 5 through 7. It has a number of illustrations from the books.

1950.   ———. *Skazki narodov mira; rekomendatel'nyĭ ukazatel' dliā mladshikh shkol'nikov.* Leningrad, 1957. 83p. DLC.

"Folk tales of the world's people; compiled

by I. N. Timofeeva." An annotated guide for use by primary school children with many attractive illustrations. The works described were all published in the Soviet Union.

1951.   Levonevskiĭ, Dm. A. *Leningradskie pisateli—detĭam.* Leningrad, Gos. izd-vo detskoĭ lit-ry, 1954. 461p. DLC.

A bio-bibliographical dictionary of Leningrad authors who wrote for children. Most are from the 20th century.

1952.   Lietuvos TSR Knygu Rūmai. "Vaiku literatura." *Knygu metraštis; valstybinė bibliografija.* Kaunas, Valstybinė Enciklopediju Zodynu ir Mokslo Literatūros Leidykla, 1947 ff. Quarterly and annual. DLC.

Literature for children published in Lithuanian is listed separately in this national bibliography.

1953.   Lietuvos TSR Mokslu Akademija. "Literatūra vaikams," *Tarybine lietuviu literatūra ir kritika. 1945–1955. 1956–1960.* Vilnius, 1957, 1961. 2 Vols. DLC.

In this index to periodical literature, articles on children's literature are listed under the above title. They are quite extensive.

1954.   Lövgren, Oliver. "Skolbibliotek i Sovjetunionen," *Skolbiblioteket,* Stockholm, Årgång 8, No. 3, 1962, pp. 97–105. DLC.

"School libraries in the Soviet Union," written by a Swedish observer.

1955.   Lyubimova, S. "200 million books for Soviet children," *Indian librarian,* Jullundur City, Vol. 15, No. 2, Sept., 1960, pp. 68–70. DLC.

A description of some of the types of books available to children in Russia. The author mentions especially those about India or those with an Indian setting.

1956.   Makarenko, Anton Semenovich. *A. S. Makarenko o detskoĭ literature i detskom chtenii; stat'i, retsenzii, pis'ma.* Moskva, Gos. izd-vo detskoĭ lit-ry, 1955. 182p. DLC.

"A. S. Makarenko on children's literature and children's reading; articles, reviews, letters." This includes almost everything which this educator had to say on the subject of children's books and reading. Many translations of Makarenko's work have appeared in the eastern European countries, as well as in China and Japan. Basically, he emphasized the didactic role of children's literature, and its place in Communist education.

1957.   Marschak, Samuil. "Vom Kinderbuch mit Erkenntniswert," *Sowjetliteratur,* Moskau, Heft 4, 1958, pp. 189–193. DLC.

How the children's books of the USSR reflect the theories of Gorki. This is followed by biographical sketches of Kornei Chukovsky and S. Marschak.

1958.   Medvedeva, Nadezhda. "Esteticheskoe vospitanie ĭunykh chitateleĭ," *Bibliotekar',* Moskva, Dec., 1958, pp. 45–53. DLC, NNY.

"The aesthetic education of young readers." The author believed that this type of education was very important and necessary to achieve the Communist ideal.

1959.   ———. "The Soviet Union," *Library service to children.* Lund, Bibliotekstjänst, 1963, pp. 93–95. DLC, IYL, NNY.

This chapter deals with the history and present status of library work with children in this country. The publication was produced under the auspices of IFLA.

1960.   Mezhdunarodnaĭa kniga, Moscow. *Detskaĭa literatura; katalog knig. Children's literature; catalogue.* Moskva, 1938. 48p. DLC.

A catalog of children's books put out by this state publishing house. Only the title is in English as well as Russian. No annotations.

1961.   *Moi upechtlĭeniĭa.* Ekaterinoslav, Kommercheskoe uchilishche, 1903. 80p. DLC.

A reading-record book for children, preceded by a booklist of the classics, not annotated and not very complete in description.

1962.   Moscow. Institut Metodov Vneshkol'noĭ Raboty. Otdel-detskogo Chtenĭia. Komissĭia po Istorii Russkoĭ Detskoĭ Literatury. *Materialy po istorii russkoĭ detskoĭ literatury. 1750–1855.* Moskva, 1927 304p. DLC.

"Materials for a history of Russian children's literature." A very detailed study containing an extensive bibliography, numerous portraits and photographs of authors, reproductions of illustrations from children's books, a list of books published during the period, and a chapter on magazines for children. A 16-page supplement was issued in 1929.

1963.   Moscow. Publichnaĭa biblioteka. *Deti-patrioty sovetskoĭ rodiny; ukazatel' povesteĭ, rasskazov i stikhotvoreniĭ dlĭa deteĭ.* Moskva, 1948. 59p. DLC.

"Children—patriots of the Soviet motherland." An annotated list of children's books with patriotic themes selected by K. P. Kiparisova.

1964. ———. *Katalog detskoĭ biblioteki; knigi dlia uchashchikhsia I–VIII klassov.* Moskva, Sovetskaia Rossiia, 1958–59. 4 Vols.

This catalog of the children's department of the Moscow Public Library is arranged as follows: Vol. 1, systematically arranged by the decimal system with the exception of the 400's and 800's which are in Vol. 2; Vol. 3, popular works of fiction; Vol. 4, books for the guidance of children's reading. Each volume is well indexed by author, title, subject and each entry is numbered. Bibliographical information is quite complete. Chief editor was F. S. Abrikosova.

1965. Moskovskoe obshchestvo sel'skogo khoziaistva. Komitet gramotnosti. *Katalog knig dlia shkol'nykh bibliotek i chitalen na summy do 350 r.* Moskva, Tvo. tipografii A. I. Mamontova, 1896. 24p. DLC.

A basic booklist of approximately 900 titles which the school could purchase for 350 rubles. The descriptions are not very complete.

1966. National Council of American Soviet Friendship. *Children's books in the U.S.S.R.; facts about children's books in Soviet Russia and a bibliography of books for children about the U.S.S.R.* New York, Committee on Education of the National Council of American Soviet Friendship, 1946. 13p. NNY.

What the new regime had done for the cause of better children's books, and a list of U.S. children's books which present a favorable picture of life in the Soviet Union. This was prepared by an organization sympathetic to the Communist ideology.

1967. Oslo. Deichmanske Bibliothek. *SSSR utstilling av barnebøker, tidskrifter og plakater fra Sovjetunionen.* Oslo, Forening for Norsk Bokkunst, May–June, 1936. 27p. (Meddelelse No. 16). NNY.

A catalog of an exhibition of children's books and magazines from the Soviet Union held in Oslo in 1936.

1968. Perfilova, A. "Sviaz' biblioteka so shkoloĭ," *Bibliotekar',* Moskva, Mar., 1952, pp. 13–17. DLC.

"Cooperation between libraries and schools." The author describes the techniques of book lists and meetings for teachers, class visits to the library, etc.

1969. Połeciowa, D. "Biblioteki dziecięce w ZSRR," *Bibliotekarz,* Warszawa, Rok 27, No. 10, 1960, pp. 291–295; Rok 28, No. 1, 1961, pp. 15–19. DLC, NNY.

"Children's libraries in the USSR." Their history, organization and form of practical work.

1970. Prushitskaia, Rakhil'Isaakovna, *et al. Zhivoe slovo i knizhka v doshkol'noĭ rabote.* Moskva, Lenin-grad, Narkompros-RSFSR-Glavsotsvos, Gosudarstvennoe izdatel'stvo, 1928. 160p. DLC.

A manual on the use of books and storytelling techniques for kindergarten children. Each of the 14 chapters is by a different author. Some have bibliographies at the end.

1971. Ragozina, S. *Navaja detskaia literatura.* Leningrad, 1924. 142p.

1972. Rapp, Helen. "What Russian children read," *The listener,* London, Vol. 50, Nov. 26, 1953, pp. 903–905. NNY.

This radio discussion was centered on the themes and styles of contemporary Russian children's literature.

1973. Razanaŭ, I. I. *Kazka ŭ belaruskaĭ dzitsiachia literatury.* Minsk, Vydva Ministerstva vysheĭshaĭ, siaredniaĭ spetsyial'naĭ i prafesiianal'naĭ adukats'll BSSR, 1962. 130p. DLC.

A critical history of Byelo-Russian children's literature with particular emphasis on the folk and fairy tale. There are three pages of bibliography.

1974. Razin, Izrail' Mikhaŭlovich. *Bibliografiia pionerskoĭ i detskoĭ knigi. (1919–1925).* Moskva-Leningrad, "Molodaia gvardiia," 1926. 222p. DLC.

A list of books for children and Pioneers. The 861 titles are arranged by general subject areas and there is an author index.

1975. Rebesiówna, Józefa. "Formy pracy z czasopism w pałacu młodzieży w Stalingrodzie," *Bibliotekarz,* Warszawa, Rok 33, No. 3, 1956, pp. 65–70. DLC. NNY.

"Methods of work with periodical literature in the Youth Palace of Stalingrad." Translated from the Russian into Polish.

1976. Reese, Elsa de. "Sowjetische Kinder- und Jugendliteratur," *Russischunterricht,* Berlin (East), Jahrgang 5, Heft 12, 1952, pp. 533–540. DLC.

"Soviet children's and youth literature." A short study on its qualities and a list of the most important recent works, with the translations which have appeared in East Germany so far.

1977. Rubinshtein, Moiseĭ Matveevich. *Vospitanie chitatel'skikh interesov u shkol'nikov.* Moskva, Gos. uchebno-pedagog. izd-vo, 1950. 212p. DLC.

The reading interests of school children as explored through various surveys. There are some statistical tables and graphs, but no bibliography or index.

1978.   Rudolph, Marguerita. "Children's literature in the Soviet Union," *Horn book,* Boston, Vol. 40, No. 6, Dec., 1964, pp. 646–650. DLC, IYL, NNY.
   A writer from the U.S. comments on the children's book situation as she observed it while visiting in the Soviet Union. She makes specific references to certain modern books which are popular, as well as to the classics.

1979.   Russia. Ministerstvo Narodnogo Prosveshcheniĭa. *Katalog knig dlĭa upotreblenĭ v nizshikh uchilishchakh vĭedomstva ministerstva narodnago prosvĭeshchenĭa i dlĭa publichnykh narodynykh chtenĭĭ. Izdan po rasporĭazhenĭa ministerstva narodnago prosvĭeshchenĭa.* S.-Peterburg, Tipografĭa M. Akinfieva i I. Leont'eva, 1899. 204p. DLC.
   A list of books selected by the Ministry of Public Instruction for use in their reading rooms. It is arranged by general subjects, not annotated, and has rather incomplete citations.

1980.   ———. Kievskĭa Uchebnyĭ Okrug. *Ukazatel'knigam, odobrennym . . .* Kiev, 1887. 407p. DLC.
   A list of books published in the years 1856–1885, not annotated, and not always complete in information.

1981.   ———. Uchenyĭ Komitet. *Opyt kataloga . . .* St. Petersbourg, Tipografia V. S. Balasheva, 1896. DLC.
   A catalog of almost 1500 children's books arranged according to subjects, but not annotated. There is an author index.

1982.   Russia. Upravlenie Optovoi Knizhnoĭ Torgovli. *Katalog knig dlĭa uchiteleĭ nachal'noĭ . . . shkoly.* Moskva, Gos. Ucheb-pedagog. Izd-vo, 1949. DLC.

1983.   Schierová, Alexandra. *Sovĕtská dĕtská literatura.* Praha, Státni Pedagogicke Nakladatelstvi, 1952. 77p. DLC.
   A critical history of Soviet children's literature, written in Czech. There is a short bibliography. This is in mimeographed form.

1984.   Shishareva, Elisaveta. "Children's books in Russia," *Horn book,* Boston, Vol. 21, Sept.–Oct., 1945, pp. 333–336. DLC, NNY.
   An account of some of the authors and titles which were popular with children in postwar Russia.

1985.   Simonova, M. "K itogan konkursa na luchshuĭ khudozhestvennuĭ knigu dlĭa deteĭ," *Bibliotekar',* Moskva, Nov., 1950, pp. 20–25. DLC.
"Some results of a contest for the best fiction books for children."

1986.   ———. "Rabota detskoĭ biblioteki letom," *Bibliotekar',* Moskva, May, 1951, pp. 36–40. DLC.
   "Work with children in the libraries in summer." The programs generally stressed some aspect of nature or the outdoors.

1987.   Sinikina, S. "Propaganda poznavatel'hoĭ knigi," *Bibliotekar',* Moskva, Jan., 1957, pp. 34–40. DLC, NNY.
   "Propaganda for books of information." Some of the methods to use in introducing this type of nonfiction book to children.

1988.   Smirnova, Vera Vasil'evna. *O detĭakh i dlĭa deteĭ.* Moskva, Gos. izd-vo detskoĭ lit-ry, 1963. 380p. DLC.
   Critical essays on the works of Chukovskii, Gaidar, Zhitkov, Marshak, Gorkii, and other writers of children's books. Some illustrations from the books are reproduced.

1989.   Sobolev, Mikhail Viktorovich. *Spravochnaĭa knizhka po chtenĭa dĭeteĭ vsĭekh vozrastov. Izdano pri sodĭeĭstvii glavnago upravlenĭa voenno-uchebnykh zavedenĭĭ.* S.-Peterburg, Tipografĭa kn. V. P. Meshcherskago, 1903. 468p. DLC.
   A catalog of 3,608 children's books arranged into four age groups, with very complete bibliographical description. Index.

1990.   Soldatova, A. "Proizvedenĭa klassikov-detĭam," *Bibliotekar',* Moskva, Aug., 1958, pp. 49–53. DLC, NNY.
   "The great classics and children." The author recommends that the great Soviet and foreign writers should be given to children to read in the purest form possible for this will do more than any teaching about the past.

1991.   *Die sowjetische Kinder- und Jugendliteratur der Gegenwart.* Dresden, Zentralstelle für Kinder und Jugendliteratur, 1964. 64p.

1992.   Spain, Frances Lander. "Books and library service for children in the USSR," *Top of the news,* Chicago, Vol. 22, No. 2, Jan., 1966, pp. 176–185. DLC, NNY.
   This is a report on Mrs. Spain's observations made during a visit to libraries in the USSR. At the time, Mrs. Spain was president of ALA and Coordinator of Children's Services in the New York Public Library.

1993. Startsev, Ivan Ivanovich. *Detskaia literatura; bibliografiia, 1918–1931.* Moskva, Gos. izd-vo detskoĭ lit-ry, annual?

1994. ———. *Detskaia literatura za gody Velikoĭ Otechestvennoĭ Voĭny, 1941–1945; ukazatel' knig.* Moskva, Gos. izd-vo detskoĭ lit-ry, 1947. 109p. DLC. 1946–1948, Moskva, 1950, 242p. DLC. 1949–1950, Moskva, 1952, 254p. DLC. 1953–1954, Moskva, 1958, 359p. DLC.

These cumulative national bibliographies of children's books are arranged according to type (folklore, classics, etc.) and are indexed according to author and title. They are quite complete for the entire period from 1918 to the present.

1995. Tallinna eesti kirjastus-ühisus. *Kirjandus koolikogudele ja noorsoole.* Tallinna, Tallinna eesti kirjastus-ühisuse raamatukauplus, 1922. 47p. NNY on microfilm.

A list of Estonian children's books arranged by age level and subject, and with occasional annotations. Many translations are included.

1996. Tamarchenko, Anna Vladimirovna. *Rozhdenie kharaktera.* Leningrad, Gos. izd-vo detskoi lit-ry, 1962. 85p. DLC.

"The birth of character." Four essays which have to do in large measure with the criticism of literature for children and young people.

1997. Toll, Feliks Gustavovich. *Nasha detskaia literatura.* St. Petersburg, 1862. 332p. DLC.

An extensively annotated booklist arranged into three age groups, and subdivided by type or subject. There are approximately 250 items in all. Title index.

1998. Tovarishchestvo M. O. Vol'f. *Chto chitat' dietiam; katalog luchshikh russkikh knig dlia dieteĭ i iunoshestva.* Novoe, vnov' prosmotrennoe izd. S.-Peterburg [1897]. 70p. DLC. DLC also has 1889 catalog, 148p.

A bookseller's catalog, well-illustrated with black and white reproductions from many of the books. Indexed.

1999. ———. *Polnyĭ katalog izdaniĭ, 1853–1905.* S.-Peterburg, 1905. 244 col. DLC.

A bookseller's catalog giving very complete information for the books both published and distributed by this company in the period 1853–1905. This is an important bibliographical tool for the identification of 19th-century Russian children's books.

2000. Trease, Geoffrey. "A children's library in the Ukraine," *Library association record*, London, Vol. 39, No. 9, Sept., 1937, p. 485. DLC, NNY.

A description of the central children's library in Kharkov. Housed in the Pioneer's palace, it included some 50,000 volumes.

2001. *V pomoshch' detskim i shkol'nym bibliotekam; sbornik metodicheskikh i bibliograficheskikh materialov.* Moskva, Nauchno-metodicheskii otdel bibliotekovedeniia i bibliografii, Gosudarstvennaia biblioteka SSSR imeni V. I. Lenina. 1962. 141p. DLC. DLC also has 1958 and 1961 editions.

A yearly review of work with children in public and school libraries. Methodological and bibliographical approaches are used.

2002. Vechnovskij, I. Rabota s knigoj sredi molodeži. Moskva, 1932. 155p. (V pomošč' knigorasprostranitelju, 13).

2003. Woody, Thomas. "Children's literature in Soviet Russia," *School and society*, New York, Vol. 30, No. 763, Aug. 10, 1929, pp. 181–189. DLC.

Views on the new kind of children's literature which began developing in the USSR after the Revolution. This US educator found the books to be attractive, "more human, more modern, more intimately identified with child life," than the literature under the old régime.

2004. Zelobovkaia, I. and P. Rubcova. *Detskaia literatura.* Moskva, 1927. 134p.

2005. Zhavoronkova, A. "Osobennosti letneĭ raboty v detskoĭ biblioteke." *Krasnyĭ bibliotekar',* Moskva, No. 7, 1938, pp. 40–45. DLC.

Work with children and books which can be carried out in the summer in camps, playgrounds, parks, etc.

2006. Zhitomirova, Nataliia Nikolaevna, *et al. Rukovodstvo chteniem deteĭ v biblioteke.* Moskva, Gos. izd-vo detskoi lit-ry, 1964. 264p. DLC.

Essays on work with children in libraries.

2007. Zhivova, Z. S. *Rabota s bibliograficheskimi posobiiami v detskoĭ biblioteke.* Moskva, 1961. 46p. DLC.

"Work with bibliographic tools in children's libraries;" compiled by the Lenin State Library and Moscow Library Institute staffs and issued jointly by them. This contains articles of discussion on the use of lists with children. There is a bibliography of book lists, divided into those for use by adults and those for use by children.

2008.   Zhukovskaĭa, R. I. *Chtenie knigi v detskom sadu.* Izd. 2. Moskva, Gos. uchebno-pedagog. izd-vo, 1955. 102p. DLC.
     A handbook on the use of books and reading materials with the very young child. The emphasis is on poetry and nursery rhymes. A few illustrations from some picture books are reproduced.

2009.   Zolotova, S. "Kak ĭa rukovozhu vneklassnym chteniem deteĭ," *Bibliotekar',* Moskva, Oct., 1953, pp. 21–24. DLC.
     "How I guide children's home reading." The author refers specifically to the girls in the elementary school where she is librarian.

Bulgaria

Each of the Eastern European countries had its political difficulties in the past and Bulgaria was no exception. It remained under Ottoman domination for five centuries, and this hampered cultural and educational development to a great extent. The Bulgarian revival, in political as well as literary spheres, did not begin until around 1850, but it was already in 1824 that the first book specifically for children was published: *Primer with a Fish* by Peter Beron. Throughout the remaining decades of the century, children's books suffered the same didactic ups and downs as occurred in other countries. The translations which appeared were the same ones sweeping across the rest of Europe: *Robinson Crusoe, Uncle Tom's Cabin, Gulliver's Travels,* the tales of Andersen and the Grimm Brothers, etc.

In the decades of this century, two main trends took shape, described by Ivanov as follows: "The progressive-realistic on one hand, and the anti-realistic, decadent, anti-democratic on the other . . . In the struggle between these two trends the realistic tendency got the upper hand. This achievement was one of the chief reasons for the subsequent rapid growth of our juvenile literature, following the establishment of the people's democratic rule in 1944" (2027). Admittedly, this resulted in a kind of uniformity of style and subject, but the methodologists are confident that this is slowly being overcome by the introduction of new types (popular science and science fiction), by the use of translations, and by the appearance of humorous books and books with more current interest.

Libraries follow the patterns set up in the Soviet Union, but they are not quite as extensive nor as well-equipped. "Owing to the greatly increased need in classrooms, working rooms, etc., in many schools there is a shortage of adequate premises for the school libraries, no separate halls for reading rooms are available, whereas modern and beautiful library furniture is hardly to be seen. The main efforts so far have been directed to the steady enrichment of the holdings, and to the extensive book-circulation" (2027).

Book promotion takes the usual form of library and extension programs. There is a Children's Books and Songs Week in spring, during which time many of the new books are released and special activities take place. The House of Children's Books acts as a kind of information and methodology center on all activities related to children's books, but does not actually carry out programs, leaving that to the public and Pioneer libraries and other organizations.

2010.   Aleksandrov, Vasil. *Chuzhdestranni pisatelitvortsi na literatura a detsa i iunoshi.* Sofia, Narodna Mladezh, 1962. 182p. DLC.

An outline of children's and youth literature. There are chapters on Perrault, Swift, the Grimm brothers, Cooper, Hauff, Andersen, H. Beecher Stowe, Dickens, T. Mayne Reid, B. Nemcova, Verne, H. Malot, Sienkiewicz, E. Seton Thompson, R. L. Stevenson, de Amicis and Kipling.

2011.   ———. *Detska literatura 1962.* Sofia, Narodna Prosveta, 1964. 98p. DLC, IYL.

An annual bibliography of children's books published in Bulgaria. The year involved here contains 368 titles.

2012.   ———. *Detska literatura 1963.* Sofia, Narodna Prosveta, 1965. 111p. DLC.

For note, see above.

2013.   ——— and Dimit'r Urgrin. *Voprosi na detskata literatura.* 2 vols. Sofia, Narodna Prosveta. Vol. 1, 1964, 169p. Vol. 2, 1965, 144p. DLC.

"Questions on children's literature." Essays and studies for teachers, librarians and Pioneer leaders.

2014.   Atanasov, Zhecho. *Detska literatura i vozpitanie.* Sofia, Nauka i Izkustvo, 1960. 152p.

"Children's literature and education."

2015.   ———. *Knigata i deteto.* Sofia, Narodna Prosveta, 1963. 130p.

"The book and the child."

2016.   Bozhinovitz, L. *O bugarskoi dechioi knjizevnosti.* Beograd, 1938. 19p. (Biblio. Iogoslovenskobugarske lige, 5).

"On Bulgarian children's books." Text in Serbo-Croatian.

2017.   Demchevsky, M. "Introducing the principles of cooperation in children's libraries." International Congress of Libraries and Bibliography, 2nd; *Actas y trabajos, Vol. 3;* Madrid, Librería Julián Barbazán, 1936; pp. 280–282. DLC.

There are as yet no special libraries for children in Bulgaria, but the president of a bank in Sofia organized a popular, cooperative library system in some of the schools. Sums which he gave had to be matched by the schools, and were used to purchase books. Any child could join, but there was a small fee.

2018.   *Detska literatura; uchebnik za instituta za detski uchitelki.* Sofia, Narodna Prosveta, 1963. 240p.

"Children's literature; a manual for teacher-training institutes."

2019.   Dimitrov-Rudar, Pet'r. *Namata detska literatura.* Sofia, Khemus, 1927. 72p.

2020.   ———, et al. *Detska literatura.* Sofia, Narodna Prosveta, 1964. 368p. DLC.

A history of Bulgarian children's literature, with final chapters on Russian, Soviet and foreign authors. Illustrated with a number of portraits of Bulgarian writers.

2021.   ———. *Kakvo da chetat detsata.* Sofia, Narodna Mladezh, 1956. 272p.

"What should children read?"

2022.   Diogmedzhieva, Petinka, *et al. Prikliocheniia, puteshestviia, fantastika.* Sofia, Durzhavna Biblioteka Vasil Kolarov, 1959. 62p.

"Adventures, voyages, fantastic tales."

2023.   Furnadzhiev, Nikola. *Doklad za systoianieto na detskata literatura.* Sofia, Bulgarskite pisateli, 1952. 37p.

2024.   ———. "Die Kinderliteratur in Bulgarien," *Die länder der volksdemokratie,* Berlin (East), No. 208, 1952, p. 1196. DLC. Also in: *Informationsbulletin der Volksrepublik Bulgarien,* No. 36.

Two of the best-known early writers for children were Petko R. Slaveĭkov and Ivan Vasov. The present day trend is toward nationalistic realism in children's stories. Many translations are made from the Russian.

2025.   Iankov, Nikolai. *Knigi, avtori vreme literaturni statni.* Sofia, Bulgarski Pisatel, 1961. 296p.

"Books, authors and the period of state literature."

2026.   Ivanoff, Stephan. "Bulgaria," *Library service to children,* 2. Lund, Bibliotekstjänst, 1966, pp. 22–26. DLC, NNY.

This publication was sponsored by IFLA

(see 32). In this chapter the history and present status of library work with children in Bulgaria is outlined.

2027. Ivanov, St. *et al. Juvenile literature and library work with children in Bulgaria.* Sofia, 1963. 14p. (Mimeographed). DLC.

A report, in English, delivered at the IFLA conference held in Sofia in September, 1963. N. Todorova and N. Kharalampieva of the House of Children's Books in Sofia, were also contributors to the paper, which deals more with present conditions than with history.

2028. *Khrestomatiía po detska literatura; uchebnik za uchitelskite instituti i pedagogicheski uchilisha za nachalni uchiteli.* Sofia, Narodna Prosveta, 1957. 403p.

An anthology of children's literature for the use of teacher-training institutes and pedagogical schools.

2029. Konstantinov, Georgi. *Bulgarski pisateli.* Sofia, Narodna Mladezh, 1958. 471p.

"Writers of Bulgarian children's and youth literature."

2030. Koralov, Emil and Mara Penkova. *Geroi na stsenata; teatralen sbornik za detza, iunoshi i mladezhi.* [Sofia] Narodna Mladezh, [1948]. 448p. DLC.

"The hero on the stage." An anthology of drama for the young, intended for the use of the teacher.

2031. Mikhailova, Ganka. *Bulgarska detska literatura.* Sofia, Nauka i Izkustvo, 1964. 312p.

2032. Nikitov, Nicolas. "La littérature enfantine en Bulgarie," *La Bulgarie,* Sofia, Apr., 1932, pp. 2606–2610.

2033. *Sedmitsa na detskata kniga; sbornik ot materiali.* Sofia, Ministerstvo na Narodnata Prosveta, 1956. 52p.

2034. Sergienko, Vladimir. *Masova rabota s detskata kniga.* Sofia, Narodna Prosveta, 1964. 71p. DLC.

"Mass work with the children's and youth book." An exploration of the theory and aims behind this work.

2035. Sofia. Dŭrzhavna Biblioteka "Vasil Kolarov." *Tipov katalog za detski biblioteki.* Sofia, 1958. 173p. DLC.

"Model catalog for children's libraries," compiled by Lora Daskalova-Ribarska, Nadežda Todorova and Violeta Stoilova. The list comprises almost 900 titles, arranged by subject areas and annotated. Index.

2036. Tsvetanov, Tsenko. *Detski biblioteki.* Sofia, Nauka i izkustvo, 1960. 130p.

"Children's libraries."

2037. ———. "K'm nova poesiía za detsa," *Uchilishen pregled,* Sofia, God. 43, Nos. 5–10, 1944, pp. 359–366.

2038. Umlenski, Ivan. *Tezisi po detska literatura.* 2nd ed. Sofia, Narodna Prosveta, 1951. 314p.

"Theses on children's literature."

2039. Veselinov, Georgi. *Bulgarska detska literatura.* Sofia, Nauka i izkustvo, 1964. 282p.

2040. ———. *Detska literatura; uchebnik za institutite za detski uchitelki.* Sofia, Narodna Prosveta, 1963. 240p. DLC.

A history of Bulgarian children's literature, arranged chronologically and treating of each major author in a separate chapter. This was originally intended as a course outline for teacher-training institutes.

2041. ——— *et al. Khrestomatiía po detska literatura; za instituta za detski uchitelki.* Sofia, Narodna Prosveta, 1963. 291p.

2042. Veseva, Malina and Elka Petrova. *Khrestomatiía po detska literatura.* Sofia, Narodna Prosveta, 1954. 304p.

Poland

In a penetrating article on Polish children's literature, Krystyna Kuliczkowska quotes Wanda Grodzienska as saying in 1951, that the children's book was the "Cinderella" of literature (2086). This was a particularly apt description of postwar Polish children's books, which did not get into new themes, a variety of formats and a distinctly modern prose style until the late 1950's and 1960's. As Mme. Kuliczkowska wrote, the majority consisted "of bad poems, by second-rate authors, with moralistic themes incapable of stirring profound sentiments in the child reader." About the only point on the credit side, as compared with the prewar situation, was the ready accessibility of books to all levels of society.

If children's literature can be improved by a careful study of its past history, all of the Eastern European nations are on the right track. All of them have established methodological and bibliographical centers of information, which are now beginning to publish the fruits of long years of study. Poland is no exception to this. On the contrary, her bibliographies and histories are models of the best type of documentation.

One needs more than a compilation of dry facts to stimulate a healthy interest in literature and in this respect, too, Poland has forged ahead. There is a broader acceptance of Western ideas, as shown by the translations of Hazard (2043) and Douglas (2054). In fact, the tendency is to accept any theories and techniques which work to bring child and book closer, and the origin is not of importance.

In the 19th century, the literature was first dominated by the Romantic movement of the writers in exile, and then by realistic positivism following the unsuccessful uprising against Russia in 1863. In most of the country the Polish language was banned in schools, but this only increased the desire of parents to teach their children of their cultural heritage, so that books in Polish became part of every educated home. One which every girl at least was sure to read was the "journal" which Klementyna Tanska Hofmanowa recreated out of the life of Countess Françoise Krasinska. It provided a detailed picture of life in Poland during the second half of the 18th century and was just the sort of literature which appealed to the nationalistic spirit of the oppressed Poles. It was also written in an excellent style suited to 18th-century manners, and became an immediate success in most of Europe. However, it was often mistaken as an actual diary, rather than as the work of Mme. Hofmanowa.

Children's magazines were also popular in the period from 1860–1880. They imitated the French periodicals and were rather sweetly didactic, although occasionally one comes upon good material.

In the last quarter of the century, a powerful voice was added to the realm of children's books—that of Adolf Dygasiński. He was a novelist who had chosen the field of natural history as a background. A number of them had animals as central characters. These were read by young people, but Dygasiński's real contribution lies in the publication of his "critical catalog of books for children" (2057) and in its critical introduction. This was the first serious work of criticism of Polish children's literature.

The fact that so many contemporary writers for children choose the medium of poetry is no accident. They are invariably imitative of one or another of the better poets who wrote successfully for children.

The best-known are Maria Konopnicka and Julian Tuwim, both lyricists of great imagination. It is their greatness which makes so much of current writing seem poor in comparison.

The longer fictional story for children has never had many practitioners in Polish, but the number of translations of this type indicate that the form is as well-liked there as anywhere. The first translations were the usual *Robinson Crusoe* and *Gulliver's Travels,* but the 20th century brought a much wider variety, from all of Europe, Scandinavia, England and the U.S. At the present time, the largest publisher is the state-owned Nasza Ksiesgarnia, but some titles are published by *Iskry, Czytelnik, Ruch* and other smaller houses.

Libraries for children have been widely developed since the end of the Second World War. Warsaw had an extensive branch system with children's rooms, but most of these were destroyed and had to be completely rebuilt and replaced. The central library inWarsaw did manage to save much of the collection in its "Museum of Children's Books," and this has been added to extensively in the last decades.

2043.   Białkowska, Emilia and Stefan Bzdęga. *Organizacja i metody pracy bibliotek szkolnych*. Warszawa, Centralny Zarząd Bibliotek, 1957. 40p. (Kurs dla Pracowników Bibliotek Powszechnych, No. 16).

2044.   *Bibliografia literatury dla dzieci 1945–1960*. Warszawa, Stowarzyszenie Bibliotekarzy Polskich, 1963. 296p. (Prace Biblioteki Publicznej M. St. Warszawy, No. 5). IYL.

A bibliography of children's books published in Poland in the years 1945–1960. The almost 2000 titles are arranged into types. There are author, illustrator, title and subject indexes. This work is overlapped by the series annotated in 2045. Ferlicja Neubert, Alina Łasiewicka, Maria Gutry and Barbara Groniowska collaborated on the work.

2045.   Biblioteka Narodowa. Instytut Bibliograficzny. *Literatura piękna dla dzieci i młodzieży*. Warszawa, Stowarzyszenie Bibliotekarzy Polskich, Annual. 1956 ff. IYL. DLC has 1956–1962.

A reprint of the children's book section from the national bibliography prepared by the national library. This work keeps up-to-date the earlier bibliographies 2044 and 2052, and makes Poland one of the few countries to have a fairly complete national bibliography of children's literature.

2046.   *Biblioteki dla dzieci w Polsce*. Warszawa, Nakładem Szkoły Bibljotekarskiej, 1934. 19p. (Bibljoteka Publiczna. Wydawnictwa, No. 59). NNY.

A reprint from the Bulletin of the Warsaw Public Library, Rocznik 6, Nos. 3–4–5, 1934–1935. The history of the first children's libraries in Łódż and Warsaw, including some of the private ones. Includes statistical tables on size and use of collections. Illustrated with photographs. Annotated bibliography, pp. 17–19.

2047.   Budzyk, K. *Książka i literatura na poziomie szkoły podstawowej*. Warszawa, Panstwowe Zakłady Wydawnictw Szkolnych, 1949.

2048.   Bykowski, Leon. *Zakres i zadania dyskusyjny*. Warszawa, J. Swietonski, 1938. 11p. (Fundacja popierania bibliotekoznawstwa imienia Maurycji Goczałkowskiej, Wydawnictwa No. 3). NNY.

"The scope and problems of discussion," referring to the children's library.

2049.   [Children's and young people's reading]. Krajowa Konferencja Bibliotekarska, Warszawa, 1958; *Problemy czytelnictwa w wielkich miastach;* Warszawa, Stowarzyszenie Bibliotekarzy Polskich, 1960; pp. 96–180. DLC.

In a library conference on "the problems of reading in the large city" one section was devoted to children and young people. Here are reprinted the papers presented and the discussions which ensued. The subjects of the papers were: "The role of the book in the life of the city child," by Tadeusz Parnowski and Anna Przecławska; "Cultural reading of graduates of public elementary schools" by Maria Walentynowicz; "Contests as a means of furthering reading among children" by Jadwiga Wernerowa; "The popularity of Jules Verne" by Maria Szubertowa; and "Practical experience in working with children and books" by Janina Leśniczak.

2050. Chmielowski, Piotr. "Czasopisma polskie dla młodego wieku," *Encyklopedia wychowawcza*, 1885, Tom 6, pp. 134–141.

2051. Čukovskij, Kornej. *Od dwóch do pieciu*. Warszawa, Nasza Księgarnia, 1962. 310p.

A translation of 1877, made by Wiktor Woroszylski and illustrated by children from Warsaw Public School No. 50.

2052. Dąbrowska, Wanda. *Wybor ksiązek dla dzieci i młodziezy; powiesci, opowiadania, poezje*. Warszawa, Skłod Głowny: Poradnia Bibljoteczna, 1936. 63p. DLC.

2053. Dmochowska, Maria. "Moja praca w bibliotece dziecięcej," *Bibliotekarz*, Warszawa, Rok 28, No. 7–8, 1961, pp. 229–232. DLC, NNY.

"My work in a children's library." A fragment of a study which won the 1960 contest for a descriptive essay on library experience. This librarian wrote of work in the Warsaw central children's library.

2054. Douglas, Mary Peacock. *Biblioteka w szkole podstawowej i jej dzielalność*. Warszawa, Pánstwowe Zaklady Wydawnictw Szkolnych, 1964. 130p.

A translation of *The Primary School Library and Its Services* made by Wanda Koszutska.

2055. Durajowa, Barbara. "Młodociani czytelnicy korespondują z autorem," *Bibliotekarz*, Warszawa, Rocznik 18, Nos. 3–4, Mar.–Apr., 1951, pp. 56–58. DLC, NNY.

"Young readers correspond with authors." The librarian in Łódź describes a special reading club and program for young adults.

2056. ———. "O współpracę powszechnych bibliotek dziecięcych z rodzicami młodocianych czytelników," *Bibliotekarz*, Warszawa, Rok 33, Nos. 11–12, 1956, pp. 335–338. DLC, NNY.

"The need for cooperation between the children's public libraries and parents." The author-librarian stresses the fact that winning over parents to the use of the library is as important and effective as working directly with the children.

2057. Dygasiński, Adolf. *Krytyczny katalog ksąžek dla dzieci i młodzieży*. Warszawa, Leśman i Świszczowski, 80p.

2058. Filipkowska-Szemplińska, Jadwiga. *Organizacja bibliotek szkolnych*. Warszawa, Polskie Towarzystwo Wydawców Książek, 1940. 115p.

2059. Goriszowski, Włodzimierz. "O współpracy bibliotek szkolnich z publicznymi bibliotekami powszechnymi," *Bibliotekarz*, Warszawa, Rok 27, No. 2, 1960, pp. 34–39. DLC, NNY.

"On the cooperation between school and public libraries." A survey of what has been done in some of the major cities in Poland.

2060. Groniowska, Barbara and Maria Gutry. *Organizacja i metody pracy bibliotek dziecięcych*. Warszawa, Pánstwowy Ośrodek Kształcenia Korespondencyjnego Bibliotekarzy, 1957. 54p. (Kurs dla Prazowników Bibliotek Powszechnych, 17.) DLC.

"The organization and methods of work in the children's library." Specific examples for each type of problem are given.

2061. Grosglikowa, B. "Przyczynki do badań czytelnictwa dzieci i młodzieży," *Polskie archiwum psychologji*, Warszawa, Tom 6, No. 1, 1933, pp. 38–60; No. 2, pp. 116–155. DLC.

"Contribution to the investigation into the reading of children and young people." The first part is an assessment of the techniques of three previous reading interest surveys by Terman and Lima (4378), C. Washburne (4429) and Potworowska-Dmochowska (2105). The second is an account of the author's own methods and results in an extensive questionnaire survey among Polish children.

2062. Gutry, Maria. "Børnebibliotekerne i Polen," *Bogens verden*, København, Årgång 43, No. 6, Oct., 1961, pp. 333–337. DLC, NNY. Also appeared in German in: *Der Bibliothekar*, Berlin (East), Jahrgang 14, Heft 11, Nov. 1960, pp. 1127–1131. DLC, NNY.

"Children's libraries in Poland." The author mentions that the first children's libraries were in Łódź (1922) and Warsaw (1928) but that by 1939 there were only 27 such libraries in Poland. She concentrates on the development and structure of children's libraries since 1945.

2063. ——— and Barbara Grosglikowa. *Dwadzieścia poczytnych książek*. Reprint from: *Ruch pedagogiczny*, Warszawa, 1933. 7p.

2064. ——— and A. Łasiewicka. *Dział literatury dla dzieci i młodzieży*. Warszawa, Bibljoteka Wzorowa dla Dzieci.

2065. ———. "Muzeum książki dziecięcej biblioteki publicznej m. st. Warszawy," *Bibliotekarz*, Warszawa, Rocznik 13, Nos. 8–9, Sept.–Oct., 1946, pp. 190–191. DLC, NNY.

"The museum of children's books in the central public library of Warsaw." An explanation of the aims and the organization of this museum, which hoped to be a kind of national library of children's books. On p. 192, Miss Gutry outlines the course for children's librarians given at the library.

2066. ———. "Poland," *Library service to children*. Lund, Bibliotekstjänst, 1963, pp. 87–92. DLC, IYL, NNY.

This chapter deals with the history and present status of library work with children in this country. The publication was produced under the auspices of IFLA.

2067. ———. "Sekcja bibliotek dla dzieci biblioteki publicznej m. st. Warszawy," *Bibliotekarz*, Warszawa, Rocznik 10, No. 9, Dec., 1938, pp. 120–124. DLC. Also available in expanded version in Wydawnictwa 86 of the Bibljoteka Publiczna. NNY.

"The children's department of the Warsaw Public Library." The development of the department from its beginning in 1928, to the end of 1938, when it had 16 branch children's rooms throughout the city. The programs and policies are outlined here. The periodical article is followed by an exposition in outline form of the forms and methods of public library work with children, pp. 125–131. On pp. 133–134 is a brief description of the library's work with young adults. The reprint contains the first two articles, plus 16 photographs of children's rooms of the Warsaw Public Library and its branches.

2068. Hazard, Paul. *Książki, dzieci i dorośli*. Warszawa, Nasza Księgarnia, 1963. 151p.

A translation into Polish, by Irena Słońska, of 814.

2069. Joost, Siegfried. "Die polnischen Schulbüchereien nach dem Krieg," *Zentrallblatt für Bibliothekswesen*, Berlin (Ost) Jg. 65, May–June, 1951, pp. 213–215. DLC.

"Polish school libraries after the war." This is a very extensive statistical report, covering all aspects and types of school libraries.

2070. Jurewicz, Ignacy. *Technika udostępniania księgozbioru w bibliotece szkolnej*. Warszawa, Ministerstwo Kultury i Sztuki, 1958. 30p. (Kurs dla Pracowników Bibliotek Szkolnych).

2071. Kaniowska-Lewanska, Izabella. *Literatura dla dzieci i młodzieży od początków do roku 1864. Zarys rozwoju. Materiały*. Warszawa, Panstwowe Zakłady Wydawnictw Szkolnych, 1960. 190p. IYL.

"Literature for children and youth from the beginnings to 1864." A history and anthology of early Polish literature for children.

2072. ———. "Żmudna droga do bibliografii literatury dla dzieci," *Bibliotekarz*, Warszawa, Rok 31, No. 6, pp. 185–189. DLC.

"A hard way to the bibliography of books for children." The author is referring to the national bibliography of children's books, noted in 2045. She refers also to earlier efforts at collecting the bibliographic information of Polish children's literature.

2073. Karłowicz, Jan. *Paradnik dla osób wybierających książki dla dzieci i młodzieży*. 1881.

2074. Karpowicz, Stanisław and Aniela Szycówna. *Nasza literatura dla młodzieży*. Warszawa, Księgarnia Naukowa, 1904. 107p. Also in: *Encyklopedia wychowawcza*.

2075. *Katalog Biblioteki Wzorowej dla dzieci i młodzieży*. Warszawa, Związku Księgarzy Polskich, 1927. 127p.

Edited by J. Filipkowska-Szemplińska, Maria Gutry and H. Radlińska.

2076. *Katalog rozumowany książek dla dzieci i młodzieży*. Warszawa, J. Mianowski, 1895. 213p.

2077. Kozubowski, Feliks. *Przewodnik w wyborze ksążek dla młodzieży szkolnej*. 1879.

2078. Królinski, Kazimierz. *Polska literatura dla dzieci i młodzieży, zarys historyczny z wypisami*. Lwów, Wisniewski, 1927, 268p.

2079. ———. "Przygotowanie młodzieży szkolnej do korzystania z bibliotek publicznych," *Bibliotekarz*, Warszawa, Rocznik 10, No. 6, Sept. 1938, pp. 53–57. DLC.

"Instruction of school children in the use of public libraries." An outline of a recommended plan.

2080. Krzemińska, Wanda. *Literatura dla dzieci i młodzieży*. Warszawa, Stowarzyszenie Bibliotekarzy Polskich, 1963. 183p. IYL.

Chapters on writers of classics for children, both Polish and foreign. Illustrated with reproductions and photo-portraits. Bibliography.

2081. *Książka w szkole*. Warszawa, Panstwowe Zakłady Wydawnictw Szkolnych, Quarterly. 1957 ff. (Title variations 1957–1960: *Biuletyn informacyjny, Książki dla nauczycieli, Informator dla nauczycieli, Biuletyn informacyjny pracowników panstwowych zakładow szkolnych*).

240

"The book in the school." A periodical intended for the use of school librarians.

2082. Kuchta, Jan. *Ksiązka zakazana, jako przedmiot zainteresowania młodzieży w okresie dojrzewania*. Warszawa, Museum, 1933.

2083. Kułagowska, Zofia. "Praca bibliotek miejskich z dziećmi w okresie letnim," *Bibliotekarz*, Warszawa, Rok 33, No. 6, 1956, pp. 163–167. DLC, NNY.
"Summer activities in the municipal children's libraries." These included reading aloud, reading clubs, contests and other festivities.

2084. Kuliczkowska, Krystyna. *Literatura dla dzieci i młodzieży w latach 1864–1914; zarys rozwoju*. Warszawa, Panstwowe Zakłady Wydawnictw Szkolnych, 1965. 260p. DLC, IYL. DLC also has 1959 ed., same pub., 229p.
"Literature for children and young people in the years 1864–1914; a developmental outline." A critical study of the period, illustrated with portraits and reproductions from children's books and magazines. The second part of the book contains selections from the work of some 15 writers, and about 10 selections from critical works and reviews of the time.

2085. ———— and Irena Słońska. *Mały słownik literatury dla dzieci i młodzieży*. Warszawa, Wieda Powszechna, 1964. 436p. DLC.
"A short dictionary of literature for children and young people." An extremely useful handbook which gives biographical and bibliographical data on authors (native and foreign) and their children's books, and on editors, critics, illustrators and librarians who have distinguished themselves in some phase of work with children and books in Poland. This provides indirectly a very clear picture of the extent to which translations have been published. An annotated bibliography of the major critical works in Polish and a shorter bibliography of the foreign histories and critical studies consulted, are followed by a title index.

2086. ————. "Quelques remarques sur la littérature pour les enfants et la jeunesse en Pologne," *L'enfance*, Paris, No. 3, 1956, pp. 200–207. IYL.
Good books by fine writers are still a rarity in Poland. The majority consist of bad poetry by second-rate poets, with moralistic themes which are incapable of stirring profound sentiment in the reader. Some exceptions are Helena Bobinska, Igor Newerly, Janina Broniewska, Julian Tuwim, Jan Brzechwa, Janina Porazinska, and Hanna Januszewska. Book production has increased ten-fold since before the war and the best efforts have gone into producing inexpensive picture books with simple texts for the very young child.

2087. ————. *Rozprawy z historii literatury dla dzieci i młodzieży*. Wrocław, Ossolineum, 1958. (Studia Pedagogiczne, Tom 5).

2088. Kunczewska, Ludmiła. "Biblioteki szkolne," *Przegląd biblioteczny*, Warszawa, Rocznik 19, No. 1, Jan.–Mar., 1961, pp. 49–52. DLC, NNY.
A brief history of school libraries in Poland, with a discussion of present organization and standards. The greatest difficulty is the lack of space in schools.

2089. Lenica, J. "Polish posters and children's books," *Graphis*, Zürich, Jg. 5, No. 27, Nov., 1949, pp. 248–257. DLC, NNY.
An account of an exhibition of Polish children's books and posters, together with numerous reproductions in color and black and white. Text is in German and French as well as English.

2090. Leśniczak, J. "Adnotowane karty katalogowe książek dla dzieci," *Bibliotekarz*, Warszawa, Rok 33, No. 9, 1956, pp. 262–265. DLC, NNY.
"Annotated catalog cards for children's books." Recommendations for the national library on the annotations for children's books, which they only recently began to include.

2091. *Literatura dla dzieci i młodzieży*. Warszawa, Stowarzyszenie Bibliotekarzy Polskich, 1959. 379p. (Książki dla Bibliotek. Katalog. Tom 2). DLC.
A booklist divided into fiction (four age groups) and nonfiction (by decimal classification). The appendices are arranged to help locate books by type, by theme, by period, by country of original language, etc. There are author, title, illustrator and translator indexes. General editor was Wanda Dąbrowska.

2092. Łodyński, Marian. "Organizacja bibliotek szkolnych księstwa warszawskiego i królestwa polskiego w latach 1807–1831," *Przegląd biblioteczny*, Warszawa, Rocznik 28, No. 1, Jan.–Mar. 1961, pp. 1–31. DLC, NNY.
"The organization of school libraries in the Duchy of Warsaw and the kingdom of Poland from 1807–1831." A scholarly, well documented history of the libraries in elementary and secondary schools during the period.

2093. Michalska, W. "Ramowe wytyczne współpracy publicznych bibliotek dla dzieci z bibliotekami szkolnymi," *Bibliotekarz*, Warszawa, Rocznik 19, No. 3, May–June, 1952, pp. 77–78. DLC, NNY.

"The guiding principles for cooperation between public library children's rooms, and school libraries," followed by a report on the national conference on children's libraries, pp. 79–80.

2094. Mikucka, Aniela. "Zainteresowania czytelnicze młodzieży," *Bibliotekarz*, Warszawa, Rocznik 13, No. 4, Apr., 1946, pp. 79–83. DLC, NNY.

"Reading interests of young people." The results of a survey, made in schools in the larger cities of Poland. This is followed by "The best-loved books of school youth" by Z. Makowiecka and "Students' week in the high school library" by A. Korczewska.

2095. Ministerstwo Kultury i Sztuki. Centralny Zarząd Bibliotek. *Zagadnienia czytelnictwa dziecięcego*. Warszawa, Państwowe Wydawnictwo Popularno-Naukowe, 1953. 90p. (Wiedza Powszechna). DLC.

"Problems of children's reading." A report on a children's library conference, and essays on contemporary children's literature, and work with children and books in the public library. Illustrated with photographs.

2096. Narwoysz, A. "Formy pracy z czytelnikiem w bydgoskich bibliotekach dla dzieci i młodzieży," *Bibliotekarz*, Warszawa, Rocznik 22, No. 7, July, 1955, pp. 293–299. DLC, NNY.

"Work with the readers in the children's and young people's libraries of Bydgoszcz." A description of activities in the five children's libraries of the city.

2097. "Numer poświęcony sprawom bibliotek szkolnych," *Bibliotekarz*, Warszawa, Rocznik 17, Nos. 1–2, Jan.–Feb., 1950, pp. 1–26. DLC, NNY.

"Number devoted to discussions of the school library." Articles are by 14 librarians, on various school library problems, from organization to activities.

2098. Parnowski, Tadeusz. "Badanie czytelnictwa dzieci i młodzieży a zbliżenie szkoły do życia," *Nowa szkoła*, Warszawa, No. 11, Nov. 1960, pp. 8–12. DLC.

"Research into the reading of children and young people and the school's approach to life." A survey of current ideas on reading interests.

2099. ———. *Czytelnictwo dzieci i młodzieży w obliczu przemian*. Warszawa, Panstwowe Zakłady Wydawnictw Szkolnych, 1961. 106p.

2100. ———. "Dyskusje na temat literatury dla dzieci i młodzieży," *Kwartalnik pedagogiczny*, Warszawa, Rok 5, No. 1 (15), 1960, pp. 173–178. DLC.

"A discussion on the theme of literature for children and young people." A report on several discussions, on the theme of illustration of children's books, which took place during 1958–1959 in the Institute for Books and Reading at the National Library.

2101. ——— et al. *Dziecko i młodzież w świetle zainteresowań czytelniczych*. Warszawa, Nasza Księgarnia, 1960. 200p. DLC.

"Children's and young people's reading interests." A study of the role of children's and youth books in the development and achievement of the cultural process. Some specific reading interest surveys are discussed at length, and the notes lead to many books and articles on the subject of reading interests.

2102. Połeciowa, Danuta. "Seminarium poświęcone czasopismom dla dzieci," *Bibliotekarz*, Warszawa, Rok 29, Sept., 1962, pp. 278–281. DLC.

A report on the seminar on children's magazines, held by the Ministry of Culture.

2103. ———. "Seminarium pòświęcone literaturze dziecięcej XX-lecia," *Bibliotekarz*, Warszawa, Rok 31, No. 12, 1964, pp. 375–377. DLC, NNY.

A report on a seminar on children's literature, conducted in June, 1964 under the sponsorship of the Ministry of Culture. The theme was the criticism and appraisal of children's literature of the past 20 years.

2104. *Polskie książki dla dzieci i młodzieży—katalog historyczno-rozumowany*. Kraków, Wyd. Ks. Jesuitów, 1931. 185p.

2105. Potworowska-Dmochowska, Marja. "Upodobrania literackie dzieci szkolnych," *Szkoła powszechna*, Warszawa, 1926, pp. 49 ff.; 116 ff.; 199 ff.; 318 ff.

2106. Przecławska, Anna. *Książka w życiu młodzieży współczesnej*. Warszawa, Nasza Księgarnia 1962. 184p.

"Books in the life of contemporary youth." A study on reading interests of children and young adults, with sample questionnaires and a bibliography.

2107. ———. "Rola książki w kszłtowaniu perspektyw życiowych młodzieży," *Kwartalnik pedagogiczny*, Warszawa, No. 3, 1958.

2108. Radlińska, Helena. "Biblioteki dla dzieci i

młodzieży. Badanie czytelnictwa dzieci i młodzieży," *Zagadnienia bibliotekarstwa i czytelnictwa;* Wrocław-Warszawa-Kraków, Zakład Narodowy Imienia Ossolińskich, 1961; pp. 66–74, 184–195. (Zródła do Dziejów Myśli Pedagogicznej, Tom VI). DLC.

"Libraries for children and young people. A survey of the reading interests of children and young people." Two sections of this author's study on the problems of libraries and reading materials in Poland.

2109. ———, *et al. Czytelnictwo dzieci i młodzieży.* Referaty, wygłoszone na II Polskim Kongresie Pedagogicznym. Warszawa, Nasza Księgarnia, 1932. 39p.

2110. Rubakin, Mikołaj. "Czytelnictwo młodzieży i różnice zainteresowań pokoleń," *Ruch pedagogiczny,* Kraków, Rok 17, No. 9, Sept. 1930, pp. 405–415. NNC.

An address delivered in Geneva at the International Pedagogical Congress, Section for Libraries. It was the report on a reading interest survey among young people.

2111. ———. "Jak badać wpływ książki na cztelnika," *Praca szkolna,* Warszawa, 1929.

2112. Rusinek, Kazimierz. *Polska ilustracja książkowa. Polish book illustration* . . . Warszawa, Wydawnictwa Artystyczne i Filmowe, 1964. 164p. DLC.

Text in Polish, English, French, German. Although this covers book illustrators in general, the majority are children's book illustrators. A portrait and short biographical sketch is given for each one, and about four or five examples of their illustrations are reproduced in full color.

2113. Skowronkówna, Irena. *Antologia polskiej literatury dziecięcej.* Warszawa, Panstwowe Zakłady Wydawnictw Szkolnych, 1946. 263p. DLC.

"An anthology of Polish children's literature." The compiler indicates in her preface that this is meant for teachers and librarians. A 30-page introduction to the major writers and a brief historical survey precede the actual selections. The work of 42 writers is represented. There is an author index.

2114. ———, *et al.* "Materialy z I Ogodnoplskiego Zjazdu poswieconego literaturze dla dzieci w dn. 1–4 April, 1947," *Ruch pedagogiczny,* Warszawa, Vol. 30, No. 4, 1947; Vol. 31, No. 1, 1947–1948.

Papers presented at the Polish Congress devoted to children's literature. They include studies on literature for children of various age levels, by Maria Arnoldowa, Alina Łasiewicka and Maria Gutry; Pol-

ish poetry and fairy tales, by Hanna Januszewska; the social aspects of the role of children's books by Helena Radlinska; aesthetics of literature for children by Stefan Baley. The articles on children's literature in other countries are listed in their respective countries.

2115. Słońska, Irena. *Dzieci i książki.* rev. ed. Warszawa, Panstwowe Zakłady Wydawnictw Szkolnych, 1959. 335p. IYL.

"Children and books." A guide to the study and use of children's literature, by type and by age group interest. This is meant for parents, teachers and others working with children. There is a four-page bibliography of books and articles about children's literature.

2116. *Spis książek poleconych do bibljotek szkolnych przez Komisję oceny książek do czytania dla młodzieży szkolnej przy M. W. R.i.O.P. w latach od 1923–1928 włącznie.* Warszawa, Skł. Gł. Książnica Atlas, 1929. 357p.

2117. Szuman, Stefan. *Ilustracja w książkach dla dzieci i młodzieży.* Kraków, T. Zapiór, 1951. 129p.

"The illustration of books for children and young people; aesthetic and educational problems." Many reproductions are scattered throughout the text, in which the author writes of children's book illustration as an enhancement to the literature, and the importance of choosing the right style.

2118. Szyszowskiego, Władysława. "Lektura domowa," *Bibliografia metodyki nauczania języka polskiego (1918–1939).* Warszawa, Państwowe Zakłady Wydawnictw Szkolynch, 1963. p. 87. DLC.

A bibliography of 22 periodical articles in Polish publications from 1918 to 1939, on the subject of reading in the home. This section is only one of several which has articles related to children's recreational reading. The information is very complete, so that each item could be easily and accurately traced.

2119. Tłuczek, P. *Prowadzenie bibljoteki szkolnej.* Warszawa, Księgarnia polska, 1930. 102p.

2120. Towarzystwo Przyjacioł Bibliotek Dziecięcych. *Formy pracy w bibliotekach dziecięcych.* Warszawa, J. Swiętonski, 1939. (Towarzystwo . . . , Wydawnictwa, No. 1). NNY.

"Methods of work in children's libraries." The four parts are: "Albumy" by M. Stopczanska, on picture books; "Katalogi" by K. Gruzewska on catalogs and book lists; "Konkursy" by Maria Gutry, on contests; and "Szkolenie czytelnika" by B. Groniowska, on school readers.

2121. Warszawskie Towarzystwo Dobroczynności. Czytelni Bezpłatnych. *Poradnik dla czytających książki.* Warszawa, 1901.

2122. Wernerowa, J. "Jedna z prób propagandy czytelnictwa wśród młodzieży szkolnej," *Bibliotekarz,* Warszawa, Rok 24, No. 3, 1957, pp. 72–79. DLC, NNY.

"Another experience in propagandizing reading among school children." This deals with contests, reading clubs and other activities.

2123. Witz, Ignacy. *Grafica w książkach naszej księgarni.* Warszawa, Nasza Księgarnia, 1964. 87p. IYL.

Short biographical sketches and photograph portraits of 60 illustrators of children's books. Some examples of the work of each artist are reproduced in color. The preface is in Polish, Russian, English, French and German.

2124. Wojciechowski, Kazimierz. *Zainteresowania młodzieży pracującej.* Warszawa, Wiedza Powszechna, 1960. 206p.

2125. Wortman, Stefania. *Baśń w literaturze i w życiu dziecka. Co i jak opowiadać?* Warszawa, Stowarzyszenie Bibliotekarzy Polskich, 1958. 205p.

"Fairy tales in the literature and life of children." A comparative study of fantasy, folk and fairy tales, from the collections of the Grimms, Andersen, native Polish authors, and some of the better known English and other language writers, such as Kipling, A. A. Milne, Lagerlof, Collodi, etc. The last part of the book is on how to tell stories to children. Illustrated with photographs and reproductions. Bibliography and index.

2126. Wuttkowa, J. "Czytelnictwo dzieci w świetle nowych badań," *Polonista,* Warszawa, Rok 1, Nos. 5–6, 1931, pp. 177–199.

2127. "Z prac bibliotek dziecięcych," *Bibliotekarz,* Warszawa, Rocznik 17, Nos. 5–6, May–June, 1950, pp. 92–94. DLC, NNY.

"From work with children in public libraries." Three librarians discuss puppet shows, picture books and art shows. On pp. 83–84 of this issue is an article by L. Bandura on foreign research concerning children's and young people's reading.

Czechoslovakia

Czechoslovakia is comprised of two nations, the Czech and the Slovak, each of which has its own history, national character, and language. The Czechs are in the majority, numbering over 8 million as compared to about 4 million Slovaks. While the languages are quite similar and can usually be understood by either nationality, the characteristics of the two literatures are quite different. Most works are published simultaneously in both languages, but literature native to one nation is always more popular there than in the other.

The two leading publishers of children's books are Státní Nakladatelství Detské Knihy (SNDK) in Prague and Mladé letá in Bratislava. The first publishes in Czech and Slovak, the second almost entirely in Slovak. Both are, of course, state-owned. There is some competition between the two, and from the other state pedagogical and textbook publishing houses as well, but in most cases one publisher must supply all the book needs of the nation's children. Both SNDK and Mladé letá express pride in the high quality of design and illustration evident in their books. In 1958, SNDK won the Grand Prix for book illustration at the Brussels Exposition.

Critics and theorists are not always as pleased with the literature itself, as with its presentation. The classics are still beyond reproach, for the most part, and they are reprinted every few years in attractive new editions. As to the modern literature, there is some disagreement concerning the suitability of themes, the use of realistic style and the extent to which political idealism should permeate writing for children. There are many conferences held on the subject and the critical literature has increased by leaps and bounds over the past decade. There is also much interest in what other countries are doing, and seminars such as the one reported on in *Die Kunst durch Kunst zu Erziehen* (42) are not uncommon.

This interest in children's books from the literary-aesthetic point of view is by no means a new thing in Czechoslovakia. This small country can boast of having one of the earliest periodicals devoted exclusively to the critical review of children's literature, *Uhor,* meaning "fallow field." It began in 1913 as a very modest venture, and improved considerably over the years, especially after 1919 when the editors founded the Association of Friends for Children's Literature, and then again in 1927 when V. F. Suk assumed the editorship. What a pity that the public library movement was not more firmly established at the time, for the influence of *Uhor* seems to have been limited in that area, whereas its most similar contemporary, *The Horn Book* in the U.S., played a definite role in the development of library service to children.

Today there is a similar organization at work in Czechoslovakia, the Kruh Přátel Dětské Knihy (Circle of Friends of Children's Books), which is attempting to raise the standard of good children's books and stimulate more reading through its many activities and through the publication of *Zlaty Maj* (2206), a journal of comment and criticism. It is the Circle which awards the annual Marie Majerová prizes for children's books for high artistic value. Awards are usually made in several categories, such as poetry, prose, illustration, translation, etc. There is a sister organization with the same name in Bratislava, for the Slovak nation. Their prizes are named after Frano Král. The Kruh Přátel Dětské Knihy also serves as the Czechoslovak national section of the IBBY.

Most school children are members of the Young Readers' Club, which is a bit like the Austrian Children's Book Club in that membership is encouraged through teachers and Pioneer leaders. The children are allotted choices from about 40 titles per year, chosen from among the total production of books put out by the state publishing houses. They have their own conferences and meetings, sharing in book discussion groups and other book-related activities.

Books are also available to children through public libraries, through Pioneer organization libraries, and through school libraries. The latter tend to be almost entirely curriculum oriented. Public library service is perhaps the most advanced of the three, and usually offers the widest choice in book selection as well as activities. In Czechoslovakia, as in most of the Eastern European countries, there are difficulties created by the fact that the good books go out of print so quickly and are often not reprinted soon enough to replace worn-out copies. In some cases libraries don't act quickly enough and don't get copies of what turns out to be a favorite book. This makes book selection and reading guidance far more difficult than in countries where books tend to stay in print year after year. Libraries purchase about one quarter of the production while the remaining three-fourths is sold through book markets to individuals (2165).

Not only in criticism does Czechoslovakia have outstanding pioneers, but also in the production of books for children they can lay claim to the person many call the "father of the picture book," namely Jan Amos Komenský, better known as Comenius. This great educator firmly believed in universal education, and advocated teaching in such a manner as to relate knowledge to the things of everyday life. He believed this could best be carried out in the vernacular, and through the use of objects which could be perceived by the senses. To this end, he compiled the *Orbis Sensualium Pictus,* usually referred to by the shorter title of *Orbis Pictus.* It was published in Nürnberg in 1658 in Latin and high German and was almost immediately translated into the other European languages and into English in 1659. No serious student of children's literature should fail to read a little about this extraordinary and inspiring man. There exist any number of book-length studies about his life and work, in a variety of languages. Mrs. Hürlimann (492) includes a very appreciative section on Comenius and the *Orbis Pictus,* as does the *Critical History of Children's Literature* (2869).

Of course, the *Orbis Pictus* must in retrospect be classified as a part of didactic literature. The same is true of the later Czechoslovak classic *Broučci,* written in the early 1870's by Jan Karafiát, who was, like Comenius, a religious leader as well as an educator. *Broučci* ("Glowworms") is still widely read and reissued in attractive new editions every few years. As with so many 19th-century classics, it is difficult to tell whether it is kept alive by the recommendation from grown-ups who remember it with fondness, or whether modern children truly find pleasure in the delicate but old-fashioned prose.

The interest in folklore and language was as prevalent in Czechoslovakia as in the rest of Europe. In the mid-19th century, Karel Jaromír Erben began collecting Czech tales, thereby earning the distinction of comparison with the Grimm Brothers. Erben's works are still considered the leading source for Czech folk tales, songs, and rhymes. Another source are the books of Božena Němcová, who did not really collect folk tales systematically, but rather recorded them from the recollection of childhood listening. In the latter part of the century Alois Jirásek wrote his stories and novels about legendary and historical figures, many of which became popular for young people, and remain so today.

There were a large number of writers for children in the first decades of the 20th century, but the greatest and most lasting contribution was in the perfection of graphic arts as applied to children's books. The design, format and illustration of many books from this period far surpass the contributions of original writing. This same excellence of design was evident in a parallel field of entertainment—that of the children's puppet theater. The stages, sets and puppets were full of imaginative character and style, so that this medium became a favorite one through which children learned to love folk and fairy tales. This tradition has been carried on in the last three or four decades by Jiří Trnka, who also uses his puppet forms to illustrate children's books.

2128. *Anketa o umělecké výchově.* Praha, 1904.

2129. Bečka, J. V. *Sloh literatury pro mládež.* Praha Státní Nakladatelství, 1948. 40p. IYL.
"The style of children's literature." Six short chapters on various aspects of style important in the writing of children's books.

2130. Bulánek-Dlouhán, František. *"Novost" v písemnictví pro mládež.* Praha, Vladimír Zrubecký, 1941. 29p. IYL.
"The new ideas in writing for children."

2131. ———. *Osvícenství a romantismus v písemnictví pro mládež.* Praha Pokorného, 1943. 16p. IYL.
"Enlightenment and romanticism in writing for children." An essay of criticism.

2132. ———. *Rodiče četba mládeže.* Třebechovice, 1937.

2133. ———. *Úvod do literatury pro mládež.* Praha, Nákladem Ústředního Nakladatelství a Knihkupectví Učitelstva Českoslovanského, 1937. 70p. IYL.
The theory, forms and criticism of children's literature. Specific writers are used as examples. Name and title index.

2134. Čapek, Karel. "Towards a theory of fairytales," *In praise of newspapers and other essays on the margin of literature.* London, G. Allen, 1951, pp. 49–73. DLC, NNY.
A somewhat disjointed essay, but full of pithy remarks. This leading writer of sophisticated fairy tales defined that genre thus: "A fairy-tale is the usurping of all poetry; in it are manifested original folk imagination and the poetical urge; national myths and old heroic sagas survive to the present day in the unspoiled naïveté of children's fairy-tales. The very soul of a nation is expressed in them, with its wisdom, phantasy and simplicity, with its faith in supernatural forces and its national deities." This essay is followed by two others which are related, "A few fairy-tale motifs," and "Some fairy-tale personalities."

2135. Červenka, Jan, *et al. Literatura pro mládež. Pomocná kniha pro pedagogické školy.* Praha, Státní Pedagogické Nakladatelství, 1961. 283p. ff., 16 plates. IYL.
A textbook for the study of children's literature containing history, theory and criticism together with illustrative examples of text and pictures. The text is in Czech and the Slovakian book 2175 is quite similar.

2136. ———. *O pohádkách.* Praha, SNDK, 1960. (Knižnice Teorie Dětské Literatury, 9).

2137. Chlup, Otakar and Antonin Sychra. *O estetické výchové.* Praha, Státní Nakladatelství Dětské Knihy, 1956. 77p. (Knižnice Teorie Dětské Literatury, 5). IYL.
Two essays on the science of aesthetics and the aesthetics of education, particularly as related to children's literature.

2138. Cigánek, Jan. *Umění detektivky.* Praha, Státní Nakladatelství Dětské Knihy, 1962. 410p. (Knižnice Teorie Dětské Literatury, 13). IYL.
A study on the detective novel, particularly as it affects young persons.

2139. *Co vydalo Státní Nakladatelství Dětské Knihy v letech 1949–1954.* Praha, Státní Nakladatelství Dětské Knihy, 1955. 76p. DLC, IYL.
A survey of the previous five years of publishing by one of the leading state publishing houses of children's books.

2140. Čukovskij, Kornej. *Od dvou do pěti.* Praha, Státní Nakladatelství Dětské Knihy, 1960. 371p. (Knižnice Teorie Dětské Literatury 8). IYL.
A translation of 1877 into Czech. There is also a Slovakian translation published by Mladé leta, Bratislava, 1959.

2141. *Deset let péče o dětsko četbu.* Praha, 1930.

2142. Dolenský, Jan. *Pruvodce četby mládeže.* Brno, 1897.

2143.   Dubrovinová, L. V. *Dětská literatura s hlediska komunistické výchovy*. Praha, SNDK, 1953. (Knižnice Teorie Dětské Literatury, 2).

"Children's literature from the standpoint of the tasks of Communist education."

2144.   Frey, Jaroslav. *Boj o pohádku*. Praha, 1941.

2145.   ———. *Čtenářský výzkum pražského dítěte*. Praha, F. Landgráfa v Hodoníně, 1931.

2146.   Fučík, Bedřich. *O knihu pro mládež*. Praha, 1941.

2147.   Fučík, Julius. *O umění pro děti*. Praha, Státní Nakladatelství Dětské Knihy, 1960. 39p. IYL.

"The arts for children." The four essays are on children's toys, Soviet books for children, fantastic literature, children's literature.

2148.   Gorkij, Maxim. *O dětske literatuře*. Praha, SNDK, 1953. (Knižnice Teorie Dětské Literatury, 1.)

A translation of 1906.

2149.   Heřman, Zdenek. *Dobrodružné poznávání*. Praha, SNDK, 1962. (Knižnice Teorie Dětské Literatury, 13.)

2150.   Holešovská-Genčiová, M. *Provídka o škola v sovětské literatuře, poválečných let*. Praha, SNDK, 1953. (Knižnice Teorie Dětské Literatury, 3).

2151.   Holešovský, František. *Naše ilustrace pro děti a její výchovné působení*. Praha, Státní Nakladatelství Dětské Knihy, 1960. 75p. (Knižnice Teorie Dětské Literatury, 8). IYL.

"Our illustrations for children and their educational effect." A critical study using many specific reproductions as examples.

2152.   Hostáň, K. *Pro dětskou knihou*. Praha, 1939. 35p.

2153.   Hrnčíř, Fr. *O dětské literatuře*. 1887.

2154.   Hykeš, Pravoslav and Zdeňka Marčanová. *Bibliografie české a slovenské literatury pro mládež*. Praha, Státní Pedagogická Knihovna Komenského, yearly, 1951–1953; Státní Pedagogické Nakladatelství, yearly, 1954–1956; Státní Nakladatelství Dětské Knihy, yearly, 1957 to present. DLC, IYL.

An annual bibliography of all children's books published in Czechoslovakia. The entries are arranged by author, and bibliographic detail is very complete. Age levels are given, but there are no annotations. Books in both national languages are included. Beginning with the 1960 list, published in 1964, Anna Holubová worked as a third co-editor. The 1957 list, published in 1961, was issued as No. 12 in the series Knižnice Teorie Dětské Literatury.

2155.   Ivanová-Šalingová, Mária. *Hľadanie výrazu; o štýle súčasnej prózy pre mládež*. Bratislava, Mladé Letá, 1964. 179p. IYL.

"The search for expression; about style in prose for youth." This critic examines current and classic literature pointing out elements of style particularly suited to the needs of youth. Short bibliography and index. Text in Slovakian.

2156.   Klátik, Zlatko, *et al. Literatúra pre najmenších. Pomocná kniha pre 3. a 4. ročník pedagogických škôl*. Bratislava, Slovenské Pedagogické Nakladatelstvo, 1964. 301p. IYL.

A handbook and anthology designed for students in pedagogy, as a guide to the best in children's literature in Slovakia. Most of the text is selections from this literature.

2157.   ———. *Poetka detstva a bolesti*. Bratislava, Mladé Letá, 1957. 160p. IYL.

"Poetess of childhood and pain." This study of Mária Rázusová-Martáková is included for its general information on Slovak poetry and because this poetess was perhaps best-known for her collections of folk rhymes.

2158.   ———. *Veľký rozprávkár*. Bratislava, Mladé Letá, 1962. 129p. (Otázky Detzkej Literatúry, 1). IYL.

Essays on some of the major writers of children's classics: Carroll, Collodi, Čapek, Dickens, Defoe, Erben, Hrubín, Majerová, Němcová, etc. Emphasis is on Czech and Slovak writers.

2159.   Kováč, Bohuš. *Svet dieťaťa a umelecká fantázia*. Bratislava, Mladé Letá, 1964. 149p. IYL.

"The world of children and artistic fantasy." Perceptive essays on imaginative literature by a rising young critic. Text in Slovakian. Name index.

2160.   *Literatura pro mládež*. Brno, 1940.

2161.   *Literatura pro mládež*. Praha, 1956.

2162.   Lužík, Rudolf. *Pohádka a dětská duše*. Praha, 1944.

2163.   Majerová, Marie. *O dětské literatuře; výbor*

248

ze statí a projevů. Praha, Státní Nakladatelství Dětské Knihy, 1956. 138p. (Knižnice Teorie Dětské Literatury, 7). DLC. IYL.

"On children's literature; a collection of articles and speeches." After an introduction about the life and work of Marie Majerová, who achieved the status of national artist for her many books of children's literature, there appear some thirty selections from speeches or periodical articles in which she discussed her ideas on the subject.

2164. Malék, Rudolf. "Amongst young readers," *UNESCO bulletin for libraries,* Paris, Vol. 19, No. 4, July–Aug., 1965, pp. 195–198. DLC, IYL, NNY.

The director of the Prague Public Library describes its work with children and adolescents. Current statistics are given as is a brief history.

2165. ———. "Czechoslovakia," *Library service to children.* Lund, Bibliotekstjanst, 1963, pp. 17–29. DLC, IYL. NNY.

This chapter in the IFLA publication deals with the history and present status of children's library work in this country.

2166. ———. *Práce s knihou mezi dětmi a mládeži.* Leden, Ústřední Rada Odborů, 1954. 31p.

"Work with children and books."

2167. Nagiškin, Dm. *O pohádce.* Praha, SNDK, 1953. (Knižnice Teorie Dětské Literatury, 4).

"About fairy tales."

2168. Pazourek, Vladimír. *Divadlo pro mládež.* Praha, Komenium, 1947. (Knihovna Výzkumného Ústava Pedagogického J. A. Komenského. Drobné Spisy. Čis. 3 Řada C).

2169. ———. *Literatura pro mládež.* Praha, 1942.

2170. ———. *Přítomnost české literatury pro mládež.* Praha, V. Petr, 1946. 98p. (Výchova Mládež Uměním, 1). IYL, NNY.

"Contemporary Czech literature for children." Its new mission as seen in ideological perspective and in a profile of new theory. The first part concerns the historical developments, and the second treats of the trends of present-day literature. Name index.

2171. Petrus, J. *Přehled československé literatury pro mládež.* Brno, 1937.

2172. Pleva, Josef V. *Svět dítěte a kniha.* Praha, Státní Nakladatelství Dětské Knihy, 1962. 125p. (Knižnice Zlatého Máje, Blok 1). IYL.

Essays by a writer of children's books on the general aspects of children's literature.

2173. Polášek-Topol, Štěpán. *Česká literatura pro mládež.* Praha, Nákladem České Grafické Unie, 1937. 79p. IYL.

A critical review of the contemporary books for children. In many cases the recommendations are merely cited, rather than discussed. No index.

2174. Poliak, Ján. *Literatúra, mládež a súčasnosť.* Bratislava, Mladé Letá, 1963. 203p. (Otázky Detskej Literatúry, 5). IYL, DLC.

"Literature, children and the present." The various chapters treat of folklore, fairy tales and education; a return to the national past; the new interest in the child; the anti-fascist movement in children's books; books of nature and natural history; the future of children's literature. Author index. Text in Slovakian.

2175. ——— and Zlatko Klátik. *O literatúre pre mládež.* Bratislava, Slovenské Pedagogické Nakladatelstvo, 1963. 265p. IYL, DLC.

"Literature for children; a textbook for the pedagogical institute." A history and criticism of Czech children's literature with particular emphasis on Slovakian. There are also long chapters on Russian children's literature, and the universal classics. Shorter sections cover Poland, E. Germany, Bulgaria, Rumania, Hungary, Yugoslavia, China, North Korea, and "the capitalistic states." Illustrated with a few reproductions from current Czech children's books. Text is in Slovakian.

2176. Poppeová, M. *Anketa o dětské četbě.* Plzn, 1930.

2177. Pospíšil, Otakar and V. F. Suk. *Dětská literatura česká.* Praha, Státní Nakladatelství Dětské Knihy, 1924. 308p. IYL, NNY.

"Czech children's literature; a handbook of literary history for schools, libraries and the general public." This was sponsored by the Association of Friends of Children's Literature. The first chapter is on the early history and development, and the succeeding chapters cover specific books by type, which have appeared since around the turn of the century. The final two chapters are on Slovak literature and the illustration of children's books, respectively. The 17 colored plates and numerous black and white illustrations are reproduced from important Czech children's books. There is a name index only.

2178. *Poznáváme přírodu; výběrový seznam liter-*

atury pro starši děti. Praha, Městská Lidová Knihovna, 1965. 11p. Mimeographed. IYL.

"We learn about nature." An annotated booklist for children, prepared by the public library in Prague.

2179. Pražák, František. *Dětská četba. Pedagogický, psychologický a esthetický úvod do literatury pro mládež.* Turnov, Jiránek, 1939. 131p. IYL.

Short chapters on children's literature, public and school libraries, reading guidance, children's theater, storytelling and other related areas. For each chapter there is a bibliography of books and periodical articles.

2180. ———. *Výzkum českého dítěte.* Praha, Nakladatel Vaclav Petr, 1945. 33p. (Szazky. Úvah a studií. Čislo 92). IYL.

"Research concerning Czech children." A survey of previous studies made among or about Czech children. A number of them concern books and reading.

2181. Rambousek, Antonin. *O četbě děti.* Praha, Melantrich, 1922.

2182. ———. *Seznam knih pro mládež.* Praha, 1910.

2183. ———. *Snahy a směry naši lidové výchovy.* Praha, Svaz Osvětový, 1922. 175p. NNY.

"The struggles and tendencies of our folk culture." The editor has included many writings on children, and advocates school systems which give emphasis to the use of folk background, rather than imposing on them formalized art and literature.

2184. Sbornik Vyské Školy Pedagogické v Praze. *Studie o jazyce a literatuře národního obrozeni.* Praha, Státní Pedagogické Nakladatelství, 1959. 275p. (Jazyk-literatura I). IYL.

"Studies on the language and literature of our national enlightenment." A pedagogical study with some interest for those studying nationalism in children's literature.

2185. Siegl, Jaromír. "O lepši organisaci knihoven pro mládež," *Časopis čsl. knihovníků,* Praha, Roc. 15, No. 3, 1936, pp. 97–104. DLC, NNY.

"For better organization of libraries for children." A review of the contemporary situation in public and school libraries for children which the author found poor in quality and quantity. Only 2% of all books in public libraries were children's books.

2186. Slabý, Z. K. *O současné literatuře pro děti a mládež.* Praha, 1950.

2187. ———, et al. *Rozpory a vyhry dnešní dětské knihy.* Praha, Státní Nakladatelství Detské Knihy, 1962. 287p. (Knižnice Teorie Dětské Literatury, 15). DLC, IYL.

"The inconsistencies and gains of today's children's literature." The eight essays cover such topics as writing prose for very young children, past and present reading trends, poetry for children, the illustrations of Jiři Trnka, drama and the theater for children, etc. Index.

2188. Sliacky, Ondrej. *Bibliografia slovenskej literatúry pre mládež 1945–1964.* Bratislava, Mladé Letá, 1965, 333p. (Otázky detskej literatúry). IYL.

"Bibliography of Slovakian literature for youth." A national bibliography listing all Slovakian children's books published in the period. Bibliographic information is quite complete. There are author and illustrator indexes. This replaces two earlier mimeographed bibliographies covering the periods 1945–1952 and 1953–1955, both printed in Bratislava. Sources of reviews of each book are listed. A final chapter, by Ján Poliak, gives a survey of the major trends in this 20 year period of children's books. Text in Slovakian.

2189. Šmatlák, Stanislav. *Básnik a dieťa. Reflexie o detskej poézii.* Bratislava, Mladé Letá, 1963. 163p. (Otázky Detskej Literatúry, 4). IYL, DLC.

"Poetry and children." The author explores the relationship of the poet to the child; the movement from the poetry of childhood to poetry written for children, in the lives and works of Nezval and Halas; what children like in poetry and what makes them laugh. There is an author index. Text in Slovakian.

2190. Stanovský, Vladislav. *Gajdarovské marginálie.* Praha, Státní Nakladatelství Dětské Knihy, 1963. 96p. (Knižnice Teorie Dětské Literatury, 14). IYL.

2191. Štefanik, J. *Súpis slovenskej literatury pro mládež.* Praha, 1933.

2192. Stejskal, Václav. *Cesty současné literatury pro děti.* Praha, Státní Nakladatelství Dětské Knihy, 1960. 85p. (Knižnice Teorie Dětské Literatury, 10). IYL, DLC.

"The trends of contemporary literature for children." The author discusses current writers and the ways in which they depict the child's world of present-day Czechoslovakia. The chapter on poetry singles out Hrubín, and questions where poetry is headed with the new poets.

2193. ———. *Moderní česká literatura pro děti.*

Praha, Státní Nakladatelství Dětské Knihy, 1962. 347p. DLC, IYL.

"Modern Czech literature for children." The author treats of it in five periods: the classics (including Czech translations of foreign classics), the years prior to the first European war, the war years, after Munich, and the period after 1945. Numerous examples are cited, but there is no bibliography or index.

2194. ———. [Report on children's literature.] Prague, SNDK, 1959. 16p. (Typewritten manuscript). APP.

A survey of contemporary developments written in English especially for the author of this bibliography. There are book-lists of classics, professional literature, and prize-winning books.

2195. Stříž, Jaromír. *Práce s pohádkou.* Praha, Výzkumný Osvětový Ústav, 1954, 25p.

"Work with the fairy tale for the use of public libraries."

2196. Stromšiková, A., *et al. Práce s knihou se žáky osmileté školy; připrava a průběh "Týdne dětské knihy."* Praha, Státní Pedagogické Nakladatelství, 1954. 148p. (Za Socialistickou Výchovu, sv. 23). DLC.

"Work with books with pupils in the elementary schools; preparations and events for children's book week." Suggestions for reading clubs, programs, contests and many other activities which can be related to children and books. F. Tenčik and F. Vítek worked with the author on this book.

2197. Suk, V. F. "Czech literature for children," *Library journal.* New York, Vol. 54, No. 19, Nov. 1, 1929, pp. 898–900. DLC, NNY.

There has been a movement toward better literature for children since the beginning of the 20th century in Czechoslovakia. This was the result of teachers' organizations and a group called the Friends of Literature for Youth. The magazine, *Uhor* (see 2201), helped to mold better taste in children's books. Mr. Suk, its editor, mentions here some specific authors and illustrators who have achieved distinction.

2198. ———. *Dobré knihy dětem; výběr četby pro mládež.* Praha, Nákladem Masarykova Lidovýchovného Ústavu, 1929. 87p. NNY.

"Good books for children; selections of readings." This was intended as a supplement to the earlier work by Suk and Pospíšil (2177). It lists all children's books published from 1924–1929. The arrangement is by types: books for small children,

poetry, fairy tales, fiction, informational reading, selections, and magazines. Each entry is annotated.

2199. Tax, Zdeněk. *Výchovný vyznam knihoven v ústavech pro dorost.* Praha, Státní Pedagogické Nakladatelství, 1959. 115p. (Edice Národní Knihovny v Praze, Sv 9). DLC.

A manual of organization for school and children's libraries. There is an extensive bibliography.

2200. Tenčík, František. *Četba mládeže v počátcích obrození.* Praha, Státní Nakladatelství Dětské Knihy, 1962. 107p. IYL, DLC.

"Children's reading at the beginning of the revival." A history of Czech children's literature from its beginnings to the present. Bibliography and index.

2201. *Úhor; kritická revue literatury pro mládež.* Masarykův Lidovýchovný Ústav, Praha. Monthly. Roc 1–28, 1913–1940. NNY has 1927–1940 with 1930 and some issues of 1939 missing.

This critical revue of literature for children is one of the pioneers in the field. It was founded by the children's author Otakar Svoboda, and in 1919, when he joined with Otakar Pospišil to found the "Association of Friends for Children's Literature," it improved in scope and quality. Each issue contained reviews of recent children's books, and articles on authors, illustrators, criticism or other related subjects. The format was attractive, with reproductions from some of the books reviewed, or old classics. There was also a page to which children could contribute their literary attempts, similar to that in the *Horn Book* (3892). In fact, in format, content and approach, this resembles the *Horn Book* very much, and might easily be taken as a forerunner or a model, except that there is no indication on record that one influenced the other. The editorship was taken over by V. F. Suk in 1927.

2202. *O umelecko-náučnej literatúre.* Bratislava, Mladé Letá, 1963. 137p. (Otázky Detskej Literatúry, 3). IYL.

Essays by various theorists on artistic educational literature for children and youth, and on the illustration of such books. Text in Slovakian.

2203. *Vzorový katalóg pre ľudové knižnice na slovensku. Zväzok 2. Literatúra pre mládež.* Martine, Vydala Matica Slovenská, 1960. 380p. IYL.

A model catalog of children's books in Slovakian arranged by age groups and subject areas, and attractively illustrated with reproductions from some of them. Translations are listed separately. Author, title and subject indexes. Text and annotations in Slovakian.

2204. Witkowski, Witold. [Literature for children and youth in Czechoslovakia.] *Ruch pedagogiczny,* Warszawa, Vol. 31, No. 1, 1947–1948.
In Polish.

2205. *Za cieľavedomú prácu s knihou medzi mládežou.* Bratislava, Slovenské Pedagogické Nakladateľstvo, 1956. 111p. IYL.
"Toward successful work with books among young people." Materials from a conference on practical work with books. Text in Slovakian.

2206. *Zlatý máj.* Vydává Kruh Přátel Dětské Knihy, Ulibušiných Lázni 5, Praha 4. Monthly. Ročník 1 ff. Oct., 1956 ff. Subscription: 30 Kčs. yearly. IYL.
A critical revue of children's and young people's literature, sponsored and published by the Society of Friends of the Children's Book. Each issue contains articles of general interest and reviews of current books. The magazine is published simultaneously in both Czech and Slovak. There are résumés in Russian, English, French and German. The format is attractive, and frequently has illustrations or photographs related to the children's books and their authors.

Yugoslavia

As a united republic, Yugoslavia does not have a very lengthy history, but the six former republics or provinces which make up the present nation each have a long history full of national heroes celebrated in folk and epic ballads. It is this literature which furnishes an outlet for the patriotic spirit of the many minorities. Contemporary literature, while built up from these foundations, is more general in its expression of national feelings, so that one can say there is a genuine "Yugoslav" literature, whether it is written in Slovenian, Macedonian or Serbo-Croatian.

Before 1945, the South Slavic republics had been extremely poor, relying almost entirely on agriculture as a means of living. Educational systems were very poor and only the cities of Ljubljana, Zagreb and Novi Sad had publishing houses which produced books with regularity. The few books for children which existed (other than text books) were almost sure to have emanated from one of these places. There was not much translation of books from other languages, so that children usually read the classics in German.

After the war, with the establishment of the People's Republic, the state set up separate publishing houses for children's books, similar to those in the U.S.S.R. However, they were careful to utilize the already existing publishing centers, and it was not long before each of them had virtually complete autonomy. There is much exchanging and sharing of books, with each printing largely in the language of the region. Mladinska Kniga in Ljubljana is the largest, and often does the printing on joint editions. Since 1950 it is possible to trace all of the books published for children, through the national bibliography (2210).

Libraries for children before the war were also not as developed as in the other Slavic countries. There are the same three types of libraries: school, public and those in Pioneer Houses. However, they do not follow the strict methodology of those in the U.S.S.R., for example, nor is their organization as centralized or controlled. This has both advantages and disadvantages, but in general the librarians would prefer even wider freedom of selection and organization. Two cities with central children's libraries doing outstanding work are Zagreb and Ljubljana. The latter has its own building and maintains a small but well-chosen collection of foreign books, as well as large collections in Slovenian and Serbo-Croatian.

2207.   Beograd. Pedagoški Institut. *Šta treba da čitaju naša deca.* Beograd, Znanje, 1950. 75p. DLC.

An annotated list of children's books in Serbian concerned with national themes, either historical or current, and in all subject areas, such as music, dance, travel, etc. Some books about other countries are included as are a few translations.

2208.   Cucic, Sima. *Iz dečje književnosti.* Novi Sad, Matitsa Srpska, 1951. 211p. DLC.

"Retrospections on children's literature." A selection of articles from newspapers and periodicals.

2209.   Ćunković, Srećko, *et al. Šta i kako pričati i čitati deci pretškolskog uzrasta.* Radnički univerzitet. Podizanje i vaspitanje dece. II kolo. Beograd, Izdavačko preduzeće "Rad," 1957. 31p. IYL.

The methods and effects of storytelling and reading aloud, together with a list of stories to tell and special suggestions on their telling. Text in Serbo-Croatian.

2210.   "Dečja i omladinska književnost," Bibliografski Institut. *Bibliografija jugoslavije,* Beograd, 1950 ff. Monthly or semi-monthly.

Children's books are listed separately in this national bibliography under the decimal number 886 (024.7). The information given is very complete.

2211.   *Dečje literarno stvaralaštvo. Treće zmajeve dečje igre.* Novi Sad, 1960. 40p. IYL.

Papers and discussions on the subject of the literary interests of children. The leading paper was by Vlatko Milarić. In it he discusses the role of the educator in stimulating the spontaneous and imaginative expression of children. Text in Serbo-Croatian.

2212.   *Dječji pisci o sebi.* 2 vols. Sarajevo, Izdavačko preduzeće "Veselin Masleša," 1963. Vol. 1, Biblioteka Lastavica, 137p. Vol. 2, Romansirane biografije, 158p. IYL.

Reminiscences of 23 leading Yugoslavian writers for children concerning their own childhood, their reading, and how they came to write for children. Although the text is in Serbo-Croatian in this edition, the authors concerned come from all parts of Yugoslavia, and some write in the other languages. This edition is meant for use by children, as well as a source book for adults.

2213.   Falkowska, H. "Wrazenia z bibliotek szkolnych w Jugosławii, *Bibliotekarz,* Warszawa, Rok 28, Feb., 1961, pp. 45–50. DLC, NNY.

A detailed article on the organization and work of school libraries in Yugoslavia, but written in Polish.

2214.   Furlan, Branka. "Kurzer Abriss der serbo-kroatischen Kinder und Jugendliteratur," *Jugendliteratur,* München, Jahrgang 9, Heft 5, May, 1963, pp. 193–196. IYL.

This short survey of Serbo-Croation children's literature is followed by an article on Slovenian juvenile literature (pp. 197–200), by Martina Sircelj and by general remarks on Yugoslavian juvenile literature by Metka Simončić (pp. 201–203). All three papers were originally read at the opening of an exhibition of Yugoslavian children's books in the IYL in Munich.

2215.   ———. "Yugoslavia," *Library service to children,* 2. Lund, Bibliotekstjänst, 1966, pp. 77–81. DLC, NNY.

This publication was sponsored by IFLA (see 32). In this chapter the history and present status of children's library work in Yugoslavia is surveyed.

2216.   *Izbor knjiga za decu. Izdanje Saveta Drustava za Staranje o Deci i Omladini.* Beograd, 1955. 117p. IYL.

An annotated catalog of books for children and young people, selected by the Yugoslavian Union of Organizations for Children's and Youth Problems. It includes books published since 1945, arranged in subject and interest groups.

2217.   Jancovic, M. "Prilog, metodici rada sa decom u narodnim bibliotekama," *Bibliotekar,* Beograd, 12, Jan., 1960, pp. 39–47. DLC, NNY.

Some methods of work with children in public libraries.

2218.   Krsmanović, Marija and Olivera Zečević. *Zlatni fond knjiga za decu. Jugoslovenske pionirske igre.* Beograd, Mlado pokolenje, 1960. 34p. (Savet Društava za Staranje o Deci i Omladini Jugoslavije, No. 3). IYL.

In the form of an imaginary conversation among the great educators and writers for children, the authors convey the theory of children's literature as it might have been expressed by such persons as Locke, Rousseau, Goethe, the Grimm brothers, Andersen, Gorki, Hazard, V. G. Belinski, Nadezda Krupskaiʌ, Erich Kästner, and the Yugoslavian figures in the field, Dositej Obradović, Ivana Brlic-Mažuranić and Branko Čopić. The second part contains a list of the world's best children's books which have been translated into Serbo-Croatian.

2219. *Knjiga radosti.* Zagreb, Mladost, 1958. 154p. (Biblioteka "Vjeverica" sv 26). DLC.

2220. *Književnost za decu i rad u dečjim bibliotekama. Zbornik materijala sa seminara za rad u dečjim bibliotekama.* Beograd, Akademija, 1958. 247p. (Savet Društava za Staranje o Deci i Omladini Jugoslavije, No. 6). IYL.
Papers read at a seminar for children's and youth librarians held in 1957. They dealt with various aspects of the history and criticism of Serbo-Croatian, Slovenian and Macedonian children's literature. Some of those who wrote the papers were: Franček Bohanc, Tode Čolak, Slobadan Marković, Bogo Pregelj, Ivan Toličić, Branka Furlan and Alenka Gerlović. Text in Serbo-Croatian.

2221. Marjanović, Sanda. *Moje dete i knjiga. Mi i naša deca.* Beograd, Narodna knjiga, 1962. 118p. IYL.
The author attempts to answer the question as to why it is especially important in this day to stimulate the literary interests of children. She speaks of the book as the toy of the human spirit, as the fountain of sensibility and humanity. Since this is aimed chiefly at parents, she stresses the importance of the home library, of reading aloud, and of introducing the child to the public library. Text in Serbo-Croatian.

2222. ———. *Literarne družine pionira. Jugoslovenske pionirske igre.* Beograd, Mlado pokolenje, 1960. 39p. (Savet Društava za Staranje o Deci i Omladini Jugoslavije, No. 2). IYL.
Essays on the significance of reading in the life of today's children, on the selection of books to suit the reading interests of children, on the organization and direction of book clubs, and on other methods of bringing children and good books together. Text in Serbo-Croatian.

2223. Martinovic, M. "Rad sa citaocima u decjem odeljenju biblioteke grada Beograda decjoj biblioteci Neven i odeljenju u Zmaj," *Bibliotekar,* Beograd, Rok 13, Nov., 1961, pp. 722–726. DLC, NNY.

2224. Milasavljevic, S. "Skolske biblioteke," *Bibliotekar,* Beograd, 13, Jan., 1961, pp. 39–43.

2225. *Pišite za mladino!* Ljubljana, Mladinska knjiga, 1947. 53p. IYL.
A collection of essays by Gorki, A. Beljajev and V. Tauber. The two by Gorki are taken from the Russian collection, see 1906. That of Beljajev is also translated from the Russian, and concerns the writing of science fiction for children. The third is by a Yugoslavian critic, and is concerned with illustration of children's books. Text in Slovenian.

2226. Pula. Pedagoški Centar. *Teorija književnosti; odgojna vrijednost dječje literature.* Pula, 1951. 104p. DLC.
The study and teaching of children's literature with numerous examples cited within the text.

Albania

2227. Kunze, Horst. *Das Bibliothekswesen in Albanien seit 1945.* Munchen, 1960. 18p. (Hausdrucke der Südosteuropa-Gesellschaft, 1). DLC.
This general history of libraries in Albania since 1945 contains frequent references to children's work and work with young adults.

Greece

Children's books are only beginning to reach the rural areas of Greece, and in very limited numbers. The fact that they are getting at all to more than 1600 villages is due to the Mobile Library, operated under the Ministry of Education. There are actually four bookmobiles, the first donated by UNESCO in 1957. They visit given centers every three months, exchanging the previous collection for a new one. While 30 to 60 children's books does not seem a large amount, in a given year the number of titles ranges from 100 to 200, and there are some children who literally read every book in the library.

Translations do not seem to find a response in Greek children, but this might be due to the fact that books in themselves are considered rare and strange in the rural areas. Most popular (and most plentiful) are the stories of Greek heroes, the myths and legends. The two best-known writers of today are Mrs. Alki Goulimis and Antigone Metaxa. Both use themes involving Greek history and nationalism. Also widely read are the works of Penelope Delta, who wrote in the first decades of this century.

Publishing of children's books is still not a big operation. In all, some 50 to 70 new titles are published each year. One extremely popular movement in recent years has been the purchase of children's encyclopedias for the home. Parents and children alike seem to be more willing to save up for such a major expenditure, than they do for an individual title.

2228.   Camba, Neneta. *Children's books and the mobile library in Greece.* 4p. Mimeographed. IYL. DLC.

A report prepared for the 10th Congress of IBBY in Ljubljana, 1966. This tells of the work of the bookmobiles operated directly by the Ministry of Education, and their efforts to bring books to children in more than 1,680 villages.

2229.   Peppa-Xeflouda, Stella. *A note on the publication of children's books in Greece.* n.p., n.d. 2p. ff. 2p. Mimeographed. DLC.

A report and speech given at one of the meetings of the IBBY. This gives a résumé of the history of children's books in Greece, and lists the names of important contemporary writers and illustrators.

Turkey

Modern Turkey dates to the year 1923, when Mustafa Kemal Pasha was declared president of the new Republic. Mustafa Kemal is better known as Ataturk, the surname he chose in 1935 when all titles, such as *pasha* were abolished. Ataturk himself participated in the massive campaign toward literacy, begun in 1928 with the substitution of a modified Roman alphabet for the Arabic. This did spread education, but the war interrupted progress. It was not until after the war that primary education became widespread, leaving an adult population still 80% illiterate. To help in filling the needs for adult education "Cultural Houses," libraries and mobile schools were established. The Ministry of Education was anxious to keep children from reverting to illiteracy, and they, too, stepped up efforts to build more libraries.

This strong movement has been fairly well documented through the reports of the Turkish section to the IBBY congresses. The

Turkish section of IBBY sponsors a prize for the best children's books, and organizes various meetings and conferences on the subject. However, it has been difficult to get additional information in print so that the contemporary situation is not entirely clear.

Books specifically for children are comparatively recent in Turkey, and while there is not yet an extensive list of modern titles by native writers, there have been a number of editions of most of the classics and other translations from Western literature. Of course, the epic and folk literature of pre-republic days provides a rich storehouse for modern publishers to exploit. So far, children's books have not done justice to the quality of this literature. Most of the collections based on the Turkish classics have been in cheap, unattractive editions, as has much of the entire production of children's books.

2230.   Acaroğlu, M. Türker. "Fransa'da çocuk kütüphaneleri," *Türk kütüphaneciler derneği bülteni,* Ankara, Cilt 2, No. 2, 1953, pp. 165–184. DLC, NNY.
"French children's libraries." Their history and development, and their influence on Turkish children's libraries. There is a three-page bibliography.

2231.   Argon, Ikbal. "Çocuk kütüphaneleri," *Türk kütüphaneciler derneği bülteni,* Ankara, Cilt 1, No. 1, 1952, pp. 34–35. DLC.
"Children's libraries."

2232.   Drury, Gertrude C. "Library service in Turkey," *Library journal,* New York, Vol. 84, Nov., 15, 1959, pp. 3509–3513. DLC, NNY.
The author describes her work in a girls' school near Izmir. The library was used as the central point for a bookmobile service to villages surrounding Izmir as well.

2233.   Grieder, Elmer M. "Ankarada çocuk kitaplari haftasi. Children's Book Week in Ankara," *Top of the News,* Chicago, Vol. 12, No. 3, Mar., 1956, pp. 48–49. DLC, NNY.
A description of an early Children's Book Week program in Turkey organized by a U.S. librarian.

2234.   Kınalı Fahriye. "Çocuk kütüphaneleri ve çocuk kitapları," *Türk kütüphaneciler derneği bülteni,* Ankara, Cilt, 2, No. 1, 1953, pp. 36–39. DLC, NNY.
"Children's libraries and children's books."

2235.   Meservey, Sabra. "Children's books in Turkey," *Horn book,* Boston, Vol. 25, July–Aug., 1949, pp. 274–279. DLC, NNY.
Although there is a rich tradition of legendary and folk material in Turkey, there is a great poverty of books actually written or printed for children. This observer describes the excitement generated by the first children's Book Week in Turkey.

2236.   Nolen, Barbara. "How to write a reader in Turkish," *Library journal,* New York, Vol. 84, Apr. 15, 1959, pp. 1301–1303. DLC, NNY.
This American was sent as an expert in the writing of elementary children's materials. She describes here how she went about this task in Turkish.

2237.   Salgır, Abdülkadir. "Çocuk kütüphaneleri," *Türk kütüphaneciler. Derneği bulteni,* Ankara, Cilt 1, No. 2, 1952, pp. 140–142. DLC, NNY.
"Children's libraries."

2238.   Tibbetts, L. "Books for the children of Turkey," *Audiovisual instruction,* Washington, Vol. 8, Mar. 1963, pp. 144–145. DEW.

2239.   Tuncor, Ferit Rağıp and Rami Akman. *Seçme çocuk masal ve hikâyeleri kilavuzu.* Ankara, Arbas Matbaası, 1948. 96p. DLC.
An annotated list of some 160 books for children and young people. The bibliographical information is very complete. Many are translations from the European countries, England and the U.S.

2240.   Turkey. Maarif Vekâleti. *1953 denberi yayınlanan. Çocuk kitapları broşürü.* Ankara, Maarif Basımevi, 1955. 20p. DLC.
A list of 300 children's books in Turkish, not annotated, selected by the Ministry of Education.

2241.   Turkey. Millî Eğitim Vekâleti. *Çocuk kütü-*

phaneleri yonetmeliği. Istanbul, Millî Egitim Basımevi, 1953. 16p. (Millî Eğitim Şûrasi Dokümanları, No. 15).

2242. ———. *Çocuk kitipları kataloğu.* Istanbul, Millî Eğitim Basımevi, 1953. 73p. (Millî Eğitim Şûrasi Dokümanları, No. 24).

2243. Walker, Barbara K. and Ahmet Uysal. "Folk tales in Turkey," *Horn book,* Boston, Vol. 40, No. 1, Feb. 1964, pp. 42–46. DLC, IYL, NNY.
Some of their characteristics, and the qualities of their language. The authors believe that many more should be made available to English-speaking children.

2244. Yurttabir, Mediha. "Istanbul Ragib Paşa çocuk kütüphanesi," *Türk kütüphaneciler derneği bülteni,* Ankara, Cilt 5, No. 1, 1956, pp. 49–52. DLC, NNY.
The children's library Ragib Paşa in Istanbul. Something of its history and activities. Followed by three photographs of the library.

Arabic-Speaking North Africa, The Arab States and Israel

It has been impossible to trace significant source material on either children's literature or libraries, in most of these countries. While it is known that a few are on the way to first-rate library service, even this has been hard to document in reliable sources. The single exception is Israel, which is now beginning to provide adequate library service in school and public libraries, and has a professional literature expanding to meet the informational needs of parent, teacher and librarian.

2245. *Compulsory education in the Arab states.* Paris, UNESCO, 1956. 83p. (Studies on Compulsory Education, 16). DLC, NNY.

One of a series which documents the history of education in many countries and areas of the world. These are valuable as background studies since they contain information not easily found in the usual histories of education. Frequently, mention is made of the availability (or lack of it) of children's reading materials.

Israel

The history of Israeli children's literature begins in all those corners of the world which had been settled by the Jewish people, because it was from these diverse backgrounds that they brought not only themselves, but their literature, to Palestine and later to the State of Israel. Dr. Uriel Ofek, in his dissertation *The Beginning of Hebrew Children's Literature* (2253), traces these scattered sources very well. The first Hebrew children's books appeared in Central Europe, as part of the general period of literary enlightenment, or *Haskalah*. This movement affected all of Hebrew literature and reached its peak in Hayyim Nahman Bialik, whose poetry and stories for children are still read and translated.

In Palestine the first book printed in Hebrew was a translation of Goethe's *Sorrows of Young Werther,* published in 1912 (2252). Although not intended for children, it was the first of many translations of the classics which were to form the bulk of children's reading during the first years of settlement. The few native works were didactic stories "about brave children and their parents working daily in the wilderness and guarding their homes nightly from robbers" (2254). Eventually, writers such as Anda Pinkerfeld Amir, Lewin Kipnis, Nahum Gutman, Leah Goldberg and others, added a little more quality and substance to children's books. A still younger generation is producing even greater variety. Curiously, most of the present day critics observe that Israeli children prefer the translations of books from many countries. Perhaps it is a natural reaction in this nation made up of one people, but coming from many cultures.

There are more than 300 books for children published each year, with more than a half coming from other languages. A number of the publishing houses can boast of sizable lists of children's books, but some of the most attractive and striking books are being produced by the two kibbutz organizations, Halkibbutz Hameuchad and Sifriat Po'Alim, and by the trade union association, Histadruth. The number of good translations is somewhat outweighed by the extent of translations of comics, cheap series and poorly produced picture books modeled on the Golden Books. There are two prizes awarded annually for children's books, the Lamdan Prize and the Yatziv Prize. Only two children's authors, Miriam Shtekelis and Eliezer Smoli have received the State of Israel Prize for Literature.

Libraries for children, in the formal sense, got off to a much slower start than did the literature. That the pioneer efforts were influential is made touchingly evident, if one compares two articles which appeared almost 30 years apart (2247, 2255). In the first, a visitor gives a contemporary account of a children's library, and expresses the hope that this work can continue, expand and bear fruit. In the second, a noted children's author and critic writes of the dramatic impact this very library had on his thinking as a young child. Presently, there are small libraries in every school and municipality, as well as a number of private libraries for which a subscription fee must be paid. The school libraries are under the Ministry of Education and Culture and receive stronger subsidies. However, the choice of titles is limited to the approved lists published by the Ministry. The public libraries still use mainly the closed shelf system (except in the kibbutzim) so it is no wonder that Israeli children must buy a fair number of their own books if they want a little more breadth of choice.

After Palestine became the independent State of Israel, the immigration swelled to such an extent that almost a million children from 50 countries had to be somehow introduced to and absorbed into Israeli culture. Children's books played a major role in this mass-scale education. Mrs. Rachel Ben-Zvi, wife of the President of Israel, established a foundation called the "President's House Fund for Children's Libraries." Through this fund and through donations of books, thousands of newly arrived children were provided with books as gifts, to ease the period of integration.

Children's literature is now taught in most of the teacher-training institutions, as well as at Hebrew University. There is lively disagreement as to what constitutes literature for children (see, for example, 2249) but the dialogue has opened up avenues of discussion heretofore not possible.

2246.   Bergson, Gershon. *Shloshah dorot be-sifrut ha-yeladim ha-ivrit.* Tel Aviv, Yesod, 1966. 268p. $6.00 DLC.
   "Three generations of children's literature."

This history is divided into three parts, the first of which is concerned with the critical evaluation and content of children's literature in general. Part Two is a summary of the early development of children's literature in Hebrew and Part Three is a set of critical and biographical essays on the creators of Hebrew literature for children arranged into three chronological groups. There are separate bibliographies for Parts One and Two, and Part Three has sources of information and a short list of books for each author.

2247. Gottgetreu, Erich. "What children read in Palestine," *Publisher's circular*, London, Vol. 143, No. 3604, July 27, 1935, p. 173. DLC, NNY.

In 1935 a library for children was opened in Tel Aviv. This describes its program briefly. It was founded by a German woman who had emigrated to Palestine.

2248. Israel Library Association. *Bibliographical list of books in Hebrew sent to the International Youth Library Exhibition.* 1961. Mimeographed. 20p. IYL.

A list of some forty outstanding books, with annotations in English.

2249. Israel. Misrad ha-ḥinukh veha-tarbut. *Li-be' ayat ha sifrut li-yeladim.* Jerusalem, Ministry of Education, 1957. 23p. DLC.

The papers and discussions delivered at a national conference on children's literature. Most of them dealt with the question of the quality of children's literature, and whether this can remain high in standards and still carry a nationalistic spirit and be liked by children. The existing literature was characterized as negative in actuality but positive in potentiality. It was felt that the publishing market relied too much on translations and on the mediocre efforts of kindergarten and school teachers, rather than seeking out the works of poets. All in all, this was a lively confrontation of the ideas held by many different factions if the country. The participants were such well-known children's authors and educators as Emanuel Harussi, Eliezer Snalli, Zeev Anda Amir, Uriel Ofek, Herzliya Ray, Nahrem Gutman and others. This was also printed in *Ba-hinukh uva Tarbut* (*Education and Culture*), in February, 1957.

2250. ———. *Reshimat sifre-keri' ah li-yeladim.* Jerusalem, Ministry of Education, yearly? DLC has 1956–57, 47p., 1959, 107p.

A recommended list of children's books, approved by the Ministry of Education for use in schools and libraries. Arrangement is by grade and subject, and there are no annotations. Later editions were not available.

2251. Kraus, Hadassa. "Israel." *Library service to*

children, 2. Lund, Bibliotekstjänst, 1966, pp. 46–51. DLC, NNY.

This publication was sponsored by IFLA (see 32). In this chapter the history and present status of library work with children in Israel is discussed.

2252. Lebrecht, Hans. "The juvenile book in Israel," *Bookbird*, Vienna, No. 4, 1965, pp. 18–24. DLC, IYL, NNY.

A survey of the first early literature for children and what is being done at the present time to propagate good books. The results of a reading interest survey are also given. This is followed by a two-page recommendation of recent Hebrew books for young people in Israel.

2253. Ofek, Uriel. *The beginning of Hebrew children's literature.* Doctoral thesis submitted to the Senate of the Hebrew University, Jerusalem, October, 1959. 379p. ff. 43p. Mimeographed. NNY.

"The present thesis is a first experiment of investigation into the beginning of literature for Hebrew-reading youth from the end of the 18th century until the beginning of the 20th." The introduction outlines the general development of children's literature. Part 1 is concerned with the Haskalah Movement in Central Europe (1790–1840); Part 2 covers the same movement in Eastern Europe from 1840–1880 and Part 3 deals with the period of "Hibath-Zion" from 1881–1905. The bibliography includes a list of some 300 books for children, published in Hebrew from 1506–1905 (in many countries); there is also a short list of sources. A most important work in the history of children's literature. The text is in Hebrew but the title page and summary are given in English.

2254. ———. "Books of a pioneer culture," *School library journal*, New York, Vol. 13, No. 3, Nov., 1966, pp. 44–46. DLC, IYL, NNY.

A prominent historian and critic of Israeli children's literature surveys the major contemporary trends.

2255. ———. "Leaves along the road," *Horn book*, Boston, Vol. 37, Aug., 1961, pp. 363–366. DLC, IYL, NNY.

When the author was a young boy, a children's library was opened in Tel Aviv. He remembers the day he went to get his first book—a Hebrew translation of *Cuore,* and how, upon coming home, he began his own journal. Now, he is himself an author of children's books, and a historian of Hebrew children's literature.

2256. Reiter-Zedek, Miriam. *Bibliyografiyah le-nose' im be-hora' ah.* Tel Aviv, Federation of Teachers, 1951. 24 ff. 798 cl. (Otsar ha-moreh Series). DLC.

"Topics for teaching." A list of stories, poems, songs, idioms, jokes, and other types of material, arranged according to general subject or theme, and suitable for use with elementary school children. The author, title, publisher, date and paging are given for each book or part of a book. This has been brought up-to-date, but no exact information on the more recent edition could be located.

2257. Scharfstein, Zevi. *Yotsre sifrut ha-yeladim shelanu.* New York, 1947. 122p. NNY.

"Our creators of literature for children." The contributors were Zeev Yavetz, Yehuda Zwi Levin, Yehuda Steinberg, and others. Each author writes about his work in the field of children's literature.

2258. Shimoni, Samuel. *Mah ekra?* 2 vols. Jerusalem, Hebrew University and the Ministry of Education, 1958. Vol. 1, 240p. Vol. 2, 235p. DLC.

"What shall I read?" A recommended list of books for young people, with annotations. Translated and native works are included. Vol. 1 has books for Grades 7, 8, and 9, Vol. 2 for Grades 10, 11, and 12.

Kuwait

This small Arab state became independent in 1961. Because of its enormous national income from oil, the government has been able to expand educational and cultural activities so that they now reach virtually every citizen. Public and school libraries have one major difficulty—to find enough good Arabic books for children. Most of them come from the publishing houses of Cairo, but eventually Kuwait might well have to expand its own facilities, in order to keep up with the demand.

2259. [Library service in Kuwait], *'Alam al-maktabat, Library world,* Cairo, Vol. 4, No. 6, Nov.–Dec. 1962, pp. 27–30. DLC.

Children are given library service in schools, rather than in the adult public library. Each school library has an extensive collection of Arabic and foreign books and reading guidance is stressed.

2260. [Trends of reading in Kuwait school libraries], *'Alam al-maktabat, Library world,* Cairo, Vol. 7, No. 2, Mar.–Apr., 1965, p. 29. DLC.

Children get the highest share of the book budget in Kuwait. The schools contained a collection of some 550,000 books by 1963–1964, and of these 248,000 were children's story books. The remainder were reference and text books, and other nonfiction. Storytelling and other means are used to introduce the books to children and to encourage them in good reading habits.

Iraq

2261. Clark, Victor. *Compulsory education in Iraq.* Paris, UNESCO, 1951. 76p. (Studies on Compulsory Education, 4). DLC, NNY.

One of a series which documents the history of education in many countries and areas of the world.

These are valuable as background studies since they contain information not easily found in the usual histories of education. Frequently, mention is made of the availability (or lack of it) of children's reading materials.

Saudi Arabia

2262.   al-Shaykh, 'Abd al-'Azīz ibn Ḥasan. [The school and public libraries in Saudi Arabia], *'Alam al-maktabat, Library world,* Cairo, Vol. 3, No. 3, May–June, 1961, pp. 36–37. DLC.

The beginnings of library service to schools were established in 1961.

2263.   [The development of public and school libraries in Saudi Arabia], *'Alam al-maktabat, Library world,* Cairo, Vol. 4, No. 2, Mar.–Apr., 1962, pp. 25–27, 61. DLC.

The text of the decree made by the Ministry of Education, concerning means and methods of establishing library service in school and public libraries. Standards were specifically set by the Bureau of Libraries, which is directly responsible to the deputy minister of cultural affairs. A purely symbolic fee is charged each student, in the hope that it will impress upon the young the importance of books and libraries.

United Arab Republic

The United Arab Republic comprises only Egypt since the withdrawal of Syria from the union, in late 1961. However, the cultural center of Cairo has been the source of many of the books, films, and other materials for all Arabic-speaking countries since the late 19th century. Education is free and compulsory but this has been difficult to enforce, due to the nomadic character of much of the population. The greatest strides have been made in the large cities, but even in these there are numbers of children who do not get a basic education.

The number of juvenile books published yearly has averaged about 200 titles over the past five years. It is possible to trace them since 1961, through the *Arab Book Annual* (2266) which lists children's books separately. The largest and best-known publisher is Dar al-Ma'aref, which issues a number of "series" for each age level. These are known throughout the Arab world. Not unattractive in appearance, they have nevertheless a sameness which is not relieved by a variety of other good publications from different houses. As far as could be determined, there has as yet been no study on Arabic children's literature, and its classical and modern sources.

Since school libraries have opened in most of the newer schools, as well as in a few of the older, it will be necessary for intensive effort and time to be spent on producing more and better quality books for children. Already the librarians who work in this field are beginning to realize that the best equipment and staff can do little good if there are not enough books from which to select. Secondary school libraries fare better, since they can often turn to adult literature. According to recent statistics, there are libraries in most of the secondary schools, although only about half are staffed by professionals. Primary school libraries are now in the beginning stages, as is public library service to children.

2264.   al-Ansari, 'Abd al-Dā'im Abū al- 'Ata al-Baqarī al-Maktabah al-madrasiyah. *School library.* Cairo, Anglo-Egyptian Publishing Co., 1953, 1954, 1955. 116p. 54p. 134p. (Silsalat fann al-maktabāt. Librarianship series 1, 2, 4). DLC.

A set of manuals on the school library. The

first volume is concerned with the goals and organization of the library, the second is an Arabic and English index to the decimal classification, and the fourth is the classification scheme set out in Arabic.

2265. al-Dasūqī, Muḥammad Abdal-'Azīz. [The school library is a fundamental element in the educational program], 'Alam al-maktabat, Library world, Cairo, Vol. 2, No. 2, Mar.–Apr., 1960, pp. 39–42. DLC.

Written from the educational point of view stressing the relationship between the principal and the school librarian.

2266. [Arab book annual. Juveniles], 'Alam al-maktabat, Library world, Cairo, 1961 ff., Annual in the July–Aug. issue. DLC.

An annual listing of all books published in the UAR. Juvenile books are listed by type (picture books, fairy tales, history, science, stories, etc.) and include information on translations.

2267. Barakāt, M. Khalifah. [How can friendship be established between books and children?], 'Alam al-maktabat, Library world, Cairo, Vol. 1, No. 4, May–June, 1959, pp. 12, 20. DLC.

Reading is one of the most important educational factors, and the Arab countries still have much to learn in bringing a good selection of books to children. The author advocates an attitude of more freedom on the part of parents in allowing their children to read for pleasure rather than only for educational ends.

2268. [Children and junior books], 'Alam al-maktabat, Library world, Cairo, Vol. 1, No. 5, July–Aug., 1959, pp. 13–18; No. 6, Sept.–Oct., 1959, pp. 14–17.

What does the child read and how does he read at different age levels and in the different places of home, school, and library.

2269. Dawson, M. A. "Library in the land of the Nile," Wilson library bulletin, New York, Vol. 24, Apr., 1950, pp. 584–586. DLC, NNY.

The author helped to develop the library in the American College for Girls, a school serving kindergarten through high school.

2270. Fair, Ethel M. and Mohammed Kafafy. Fann al-maktabat fi-khidmat al-mash'. Cairo, Dar al-Ma'aref, 1955. 186p. NNC.

"Library techniques in service to youth." A handbook of organization with special reference to Arabic situations.

2271. Gambee, Budd L. "Library programs in the Middle East; American School library in Egypt," Library journal, New York, Vol. 80, Jan. 15, 1955, pp. 108–111. DLC, NNY.

This gives a more complete description of the library in the American College for Girls (see 2269). This librarian was sent to set up a complete audio-visual department in the library.

2272. Ḥāfiz, Muḥammad 'Alī. [The role of school libraries and librarians in the field of education], 'Alam al-maktabat, Library world, Cairo, Vol. 6, No. 1, Jan.–Feb. 1964, pp. 5–8. DLC.

An address delivered by the deputy minister of culture and education to the annual meeting of school librarians. He stressed the tremendous strides made in book production and library services. This issue also contains an article on the role of school libraries in the life of the adolescent.

2273. [Library services in UAR schools], 'Alam al-maktabat, Library world, Cairo, Vol. 5, No. 3, May–June, 1963, pp. 29–32. DLC.

The results of the questionnaire sent out to teachers and students in UAR schools asking them for opinions on the school library service they were receiving. The primary schools were almost totally without service, but 97 per cent of the secondary schools had libraries. Of these only 73 per cent were considered adeqate, and only 41 per cent had trained librarians. This lack of trained staff is the greatest block to developing better library service.

2274. Long, Harriet G. [Library service for children; origin, objectives and development], 'Alam al-maktabat, Library world, Cairo, Vol. 6, No. 5, Sept.–Oct., 1964, pp. 51–53; No. 6, Nov.–Dec., 1964, pp. 42–44. DLC.

A translation of the first chapter from Rich the Treasure (4029) made by Mr. Hassan A. Al-Shafi.

2275. Murray, M. A. "Rhymes and rain charms," Ancient Egypt and the East, London, Mar.–June, 1933, Parts I, II, pp. 45–48. NNY.

Comparatively few of Egyptian children's rhymes have been collected. The author here gives some sources and examples.

2276. Raḍwān, Abū al-Futūḥ. [School library as it should be], 'Alam al-maktabat, Library world, Cairo, Vol. 1, No. 3, Mar.–Apr., 1959, pp. 8–10. DLC.

The ideal school library should have its contents scrutinized as carefully as a doctor scrutinizes the drugs and medicines he uses on patients.

2277. Rashād, Ḥāsan. [School libraries in Egypt between 1954 and 1958], *'Alam al-maktabat, Library world,* Cairo, Vol. 1, No. 2, Jan.–Feb., 1959, pp. 45–46.

A statistical table indicates that from 1954–1958 the number of good (or model) school libraries jumped from none to 265, each with a trained librarian. The budget was increased from £19,000 to £92,000. Preceded by "Function of the library in the school curriculum" by A. F. Radwān.

2278. ———. [School libraries in Egypt; objectives, problems, development], *'Alam al-maktabat, Library world,* Cairo, Vol. 1, No. 4, May–June, 1959, pp. 38–42. DLC.

The school libraries of pre-1955 Egypt were little more than closed collections guarded by overprotective custodians whose only aim seemed to be to punish the loss or damaging of a book. The author describes the aims of the present, and recommends methods of counteracting the indifference of teachers and the shortage of funds.

2279. Sulaymān, Luṭf Allah. [What about the juvenile book trade in Egypt?], *'Alam al-maktabat, Library world,* Cairo, Vol. 3, No. 2, Mar.–Apr., 1961, pp. 41–42, 47. DLC.

The author writes that the Arab publishing world must change its attitudes on pricing in order to assure wide distribution. He describes the book trade as more than a business—it is a link between the author and the public. This is followed by an interview with Munro Leaf, US writer of children's books.

2280. [School libraries], *'Alam al-maktabat, Library world,* Cairo, Vol. 1, No. 6, Sept.–Oct., 1959, pp. 29–30.

A library class period is administered as part of the school curriculum. Described here is the government publication which shows teachers how to carry out this kind of work.

2281. [School and junior libraries], *'Alam al-maktabat, Library world,* Cairo, Vol. 2, No. 5, Sept.–Oct., 1960—present. DLC.

A section which appears frequently but not in every issue. It contains accounts of the annual meetings and short news items on school and children's library work.

2282. [School library], *'Alam al-maktabat, Library world,* Cairo, Vol. 4, No. 3, May–June, 1962, pp. 36–38. DLC.

Describes the library in a secondary school in Zaqāzīq Educational Zone, a lower Egyptian province. This library celebrates a book festival each year which excites great interest in the entire community.

Sudan

2283. Hodgkin, Robin. "The Sudan Publications Bureau: beginnings," *Oversea education,* London, Apr. 1948, pp. 694–698. NNY.

"Sudanese children have fairly normal literary tastes and appetites. . . . But though a healthy appetite exists, and grows daily with the spread of primary education, there is practically nothing with which to satisfy it." The author then goes on to describe the work of the Publications Bureau, and some of its materials, among them one of the better journals for boys in Arabic.

With great reluctance, it was finally decided to survey this great continent under two categories, separating the nations according to the two main languages of colonization. To do this is to admit the double effects, good and bad, which "Westernization" has had on each of the nations. At first glance, the evidence seems to indicate that the greatest progress in educational and economic affairs is taking place in those areas where colonial rule and missionary activities were most broadly expanded. Closer examination reveals that the benefits brought by the missionaries and colonists were greatly offset by a loss of dignity and self-respect on the part of the African population. Only the African of the future will be able to tell which was more fortunate: the nation that received little or no colonial and missionary guidance but remains today free and proud in spirit although educationally and materially poor—or the nation whose peoples got an educational head start at a high cost in terms of the denigration of their own culture.

Whether from purely commercial interests or otherwise, a few British publishing firms began to include sizable numbers of African books on their lists, starting about the 1930's. These were either written by Africans in English, or were written by an English-speaking settler or teacher. The earliest of these have a strong aura of paternalism but this has gone out of the later series. Most of them are inexpensively produced in similar formats, and were intended as supplementary reading materials, but are sometimes used in place of text books. Often there are a number of the classics in each series as well, but in extremely watered-down versions. While the African child often enjoys these simplified versions tremendously because he is reading them in his "second" language, he is nevertheless being cheated out of much of the best literature. On the one hand, librarians and teachers alike are pleased that they can find something which the children appreciate, but on the other they deplore the necessity of giving something that is second-rate (2298). This will continue to be the problem as long as children learn one language in the home and in primary school, and another in middle, secondary and higher education.

Literature in the vernacular is accumulating slowly. Many countries or regions have set up bureaus whose task it is to encourage the writing of books in the national languages, and in many cases to undertake the publication of it as well. Some of them have 20 years of experience behind them already.

Library service tends to follow the pattern established by Ghana (Gold Coast). A country or region sets up a Library Board which determines the rate and feasibility of expanding services. It coordinates local and state expenditures and sets standards and policies. In this way maximum use of funds, equipment and professional services is achieved. Children's services often account for more than 50% of the staff and book budgets. Emphasis is placed on training local personnel as soon as possible.

The overwhelming eagerness of the population for education, their ample capacity for enjoyment and new experiences, the establishment of satisfactory library systems and book marketing programs all predict a dynamic future for the indigenous literatures which are already emerging in significant quantities.

2284. Allen, Joan. *The organization of small libraries; a manual for educational institutions in tropical countries.* London, Oxford University Press, 1961. 80p. DLC, NNY.

Actually, most of the references are to Nigeria and other countries in English-speaking West Africa. Short bibliography and booklists.

2285. Davis, Russell and Brent Ashabranner. "The young reader in Africa," *Horn book,* Boston, Vol. 37, No. 2, Apr. 1961, pp. 142–146. DLC, IYL, NNY.

African children tend to prefer nonfiction, according to these observers. They relate some of the reasons why this is true, and comment on the facilities (or lack of them) for the distribution or circulation of children's reading materials.

2286. Gray, Patricia. [Reading and telling stories], *A tropical nursery school.* London, Evans Brothers, 1966. 190p.

The author writes of her experience in a school in West Africa.

2287. Henry, Marie C. "Books for young Africa," *Horn book,* Boston, Vol. 37, No. 5, Oct., 1961, pp. 419–423. DLC, IYL, NNY.

A description of the few libraries which serve children in several sections of Africa, together with an outline of a plan for U.S. schools to exchange gifts of books for information from their fellow pupils in Africa.

2288. Horrocks, S. H. "Public and school libraries and popular education in Africa," *UNESCO bulletin for libraries,* Paris, Vol. 15, Sept. 1961, pp. 259–262. DLC, NNY.

A short summary of the role libraries have played and are continuing to play in the new programs of mass education in African countries.

2289. Lewis, Charles. "Expatriate publishers in East Africa," *East Africa journal,* Nairobi, Apr., 1966, pp. 31–33. DLC, NNY.

"Since Independence, the massive increase in the number of schools and in the enrollment of students together with the urgent needs for new courses and textbooks suited to present and future needs, have placed a heavy burden on the resources of overseas publishing firms." With these and other similar statements, the author attempts to refute Mr. Nottingham's contention that expatriate publishers have "made a killing" in the market (see 2291).

2290. Mason, R. J. "What do they like to read?" *Corona,* London, Vol. 7, No. 7, July, 1955, pp. 255–258. NNY.

An education officer gives his impressions of the reading tastes of children and young people in East and Central African countries.

2291. Nottingham, John. "The book trade in East Africa," *East Africa journal,* Nairobi, Feb., 1966, pp. 25–29. NNY.

A paper given at a seminar on African Culture and new East African Writing. The author claims that "expatriate publishers have made a mammoth financial 'killing' (involving hundreds of thousands of pounds of business a year) over the last decade in the production of books prepared under the auspices of East African Ministries of Education. . . . The vital act of choice, the choosing of what books you and I can buy, is still not in the hands of East Africans. This is not to say that this control is exercised harshly or unreasonably." He then goes on to say that this control maintains a stranglehold on the publishing of texts and supplementary materials which local publishers have a hard time breaking; in addition, booksellers compete for a contract to supply local schools and disregard the needs of the individual buyer. He concludes: "If we are . . . to prevent a total take-over by Biggles, Yogi Bear and the Flint- stones every man, woman and child in East Africa who can write a story for East Africans should start straight away."

Ghana

The Ghana Library Board was established on January 1, 1950, due in large measure to the exhaustive efforts of a British Council librarian, E. J. A. Evans. Miss Evans' book, *A Tropical Library Service* outlines briefly the history of education and library service prior to the Library Board's inauguration, as well as the developments in library service which came about as a result of the Board's initiative. The chapter concerning work with children is of the greatest interest, but the entire volume must be read to get a full picture of the vitality and amazing speed with which library services have developed in this country.

All of the public libraries in the larger cities of Ghana now have children's rooms housed in attractive new buildings and with books in English and the vernacular languages. In addition, mobile library service is provided to most middle schools, at the rate of one book per child. These are books for out-of-school reading which are allowed to circulate. The stocks are kept fresh by twice yearly visits of the Library Board van.

Books for children in the vernacular are still pitifully few. There are some books in English which have Ghanaian or general West African backgrounds, but these are also not enough to fill the demand. So that a reasonably good quality of literature remains the standard, selections are made from British publishing lists or culled from the British reviewing media. The results of a reading-interest survey conducted by the Library Board indicated that the overwhelming majority of children preferred these English books. But as Miss Evans wisely points out: "There is very little doubt that if books of equal attractiveness were produced in the vernacular languages, their popularity would increase enormously." Now that the Library Board is well on its way to making Ghana a reading-conscious nation, there is much to be awaited from the development of a national literature and the publishers to make it available.

2292. Biney, E. F. "A library list for secondary schools," *Gold Coast education,* Edinburgh, No. 3, Sept., 1953, pp. 54–61. DLC.

A selected list of English books of interest to the Ghanaian child in the lower grades of secondary school.

2293. Evans, Evelyn J. A. "Work with children. The School library service," *A tropical library service; the story of Ghana's libraries.* London, Andre Deutsch, 1964, pp. 106–131. DLC.

These two sections deal with the progress made during the past 15 years. In the first, Miss Evans describes the results of a reading survey undertaken in Ghana in 1956, among some 16,000 children. The second tells of the service to schools which was begun by the Ghana Library Board in 1959 through a mobile unit and depository collections.

2294. Griffin, Ella. "Popular reading materials for Ghana," *International journal of adult and youth education,* Paris, Vol. 15, No. 3, 1963, pp. 125–132. DLC, NNY.

This describes the history and work of the Bureau of Ghana Languages (formerly Vernacular Literature Bureau) which published materials for children and adults and conducted reading interest surveys as well as other research.

2295. Insley, N. J. "Primary and middle school class libraries," *Gold Coast teachers' journal,* Edinburgh, No. 2, April, 1957, pp. 4–8. DLC.

The importance of the class library, and how to organize it.

2296. "International children's book fair," *UNESCO bulletin for libraries,* Paris, Vol. 18, No. 3, May–June, 1964, p.139. DLC, NNY.

This book fair was held in connection with Children's Book Week. The British writer, Pauline Clarke, conducted a writer's seminar in connection with the fair.

2297. Nylander, Doris. "A children's library 'correspondence club,'" *Wala news,* Ibadan, Vol. 1, No. 2, Sept., 1954, pp. 5–6. DLC, NNY.

The children's librarian in the Accra Public Library describes a kind of international pen-friend club which she organized in her library. This issue has some photos of the children's room.

2298. Ofori-Atta, Grace. "Notes on children's reading in Ghana," *Library world,* London, Vol. 64, No. 752, Feb., 1963, pp. 218–221. DLC, NNY.

A librarian reports on her years of observing the reading tastes of Ghanaian children. She points out the differences in background and experience which city and rural children bring to their reading which must of necessity be in English because of the lack of books for children in the vernacular.

2299. ———. "School libraries and children's libraries in Ghana," *Wala news,* Ibadan, Vol. 3, No. 1, July, 1958. DLC, NNY.

Since 1949, when Miss Evans opened up the first true children's room, library service to children in Ghana has expanded rapidly. There were fifteen separate children's libraries by 1958, all maintained and serviced by the Ghana Library Board. An annual subscription, although small, was necessary, in order to maintain a good collection. The author, who was librarian in the central Accra children's library, reviewed the philosophy and aims of this service and indicated the need for further expansion.

2300. Strickland, J. I. "Work in progress—Ghana," *Top of the news,* Chicago, Vol. 14, May, 1958, pp. 20–21. DLC, NNY.

The work of the Ghana Library Board as it related to children's services in its early history.

Nigeria

The Federation of Nigeria was composed of four regions with separate administrations (Northern, Western, Mid-Western and Eastern) and the Federal Territory of Lagos. With the recent political unrest, it is not yet clear what form of government will emerge. There are numerous tribal groups in the country, but the three largest are the Yorubas in the Western, the Hausas in the Northern and the Ibos in the Eastern regions.

Because there is no single native language which could be understood by all, English is used as the official language (except in the Northern region where Hausa is official) and practically all instruction is carried out in English. This has both advantages and disadvantages. It has been easier to develop texts and reading materials in English, to find qualified teachers and to build up school libraries; consequently literacy is moving forward at a good pace. On the other hand, village and rural children find the change in language drastic because they have not heard as much English spoken as the city child. Also, there is the danger of losing contact with one's indigenous culture, without gaining a real understanding of the new one.

Library services to children, particularly in the schools of the Eastern region and in the public libraries of the Western region and Lagos, are expanding at a surprising rate, considering the few resources with which the programs were begun. The Eastern Nigeria School Libraries Association began publishing a bulletin in 1965, with helpful articles on library problems and reviews of books in English, but having special interest for the African child. Such publications, as well as the handbooks written by Allen (2302) and Crookall (2305) have proven that the availability of guides suited to local patterns are more effective than those imported from other countries.

Another agency which has stimulated interest in children's books is Franklin Publications. Their offices in Lagos have been the center for training seminars for new writers of children's books. They also provide the central meeting place for the Juvenile Book Writers' Group, founded in 1964 by Mrs. Jean Dupont Miller and a number of Nigerian writers. The most important publisher of children's books is the African Universities Press, which has a fairly extensive series of children's stories, all written and illustrated locally.

2301.   Achebe, Chinua. "The role of the writer in a new nation," *Nigerian libraries,* Lagos, Vol. 1, No. 3, Sept. 1964, pp. 113–119. NNY.

What this author has written applies to all writing, including that for children. This article is "must" reading for anyone who wishes to understand better the needs of every nation to find appropriate means of self-expression. The author is a well-known African writer.

2302.   Allen, Joan. *Books for secondary and senior primary schools; a list of books suitable for schools in Northern Nigeria.* Kaduna, Northern Regional Library, Ministry of Education [1960], 38p. NNY.

Books in English, arranged according to general subject.

2303.   Atedoghu, S. "Development of primary school libraries in Ibadan province: 1953–1954," *Wala news,* Ibadan, Vol. 2, No. 3, Aug., 1956, pp. 85–87. DLC, NNY.

A review of the previous year's work in children's library development. There were in all 14 children's libraries in Oyo and Ibadan provinces. School libraries were provided with books from the Regional Library.

2304.   Bonny, H. V. "UNESCO's role in school library development," *UNESCO bulletin for libraries,* Paris, Vol. 20, No. 2, Mar.–Apr., 1966, pp. 71–77. DLC, IYL, NNY.

The school library pilot project in Lagos, as well as other projects, benefited from UNESCO aid and advice.

2305.   Crookall, Robert Egerton. *School libraries in West Africa.* London, University of London Press, 1961. 128p. DLC.

The special problems of organizing and servicing a school library in the West African countries, as observed by a teacher-librarian who worked many years in Nigeria.

2306.   *Eastern Nigeria School Libraries Association bulletin.* Nigerian Library Association, c/o Librarian, University of Nigeria, Enugu. 3 times a year. Vol. 1 ff. No. 1 ff. Mar., 1965 ff. Subscription: £1:1:0.

An official publication which contains articles on libraries and literature for children, and signed book reviews in each issue. The format is attractive and professional-looking. This will certainly be an invaluable tool for all of English-speaking Africa.

2307.   Knox, Margaret. "Story hour at Samaru,"

Northern Nigeria library notes, Zaria, Nos. 2–3, Oct., 1964–Jan., 1965, pp. 74–76. NNY.

A librarian writes of adapting English folk tales to the Nigerian culture and climate. The houses of the "Three Little Pigs," for example, are made of dried grass, mud, and breeze blocks in her version. An interesting experiment described with humor.

2308. "School libraries," *The library needs of Northern Nigeria,* Kaduna, Ministry of Information, 1963, pp. 55–98. DLC.

An excellent outline of the needs of school libraries based on visits to 30 schools. Recommendations are made very specific.

2309. Spiby, D. R. "Northern Nigeria," *Library service to children.* Lund, Bibliotekstjänst, 1963, pp. 85–86. DLC, IYL, NNY.

This chapter in the IFLA publication deals with school and public library services in Northern Nigeria, which were not very widespread according to the author.

2310. "UNESCO pilot school library service in Nigeria," *UNESCO bulletin for libraries,* Paris, Vol. 18, No. 6, Nov.–Dec., 1964, p. 420. DLC, NNY.

This pilot school library was set up as a training center for teacher librarians in Nigeria, as well as the central service point for the schools of the Lagos federal district.

Kenya, Tanzania and Uganda

Each of these three newly independent nations has a national library service plan, developed by the respective national Library Board. Original plans had called for a joint library service operating under the East African Common Services Organization, but this did not prove feasible. Tanzania is the only one which has its central headquarters built (and very handsome they are) while Kenya and Uganda are housed in temporary quarters.

In each country there had been a few city and provincial libraries developed by the colonial British administration. The largest library of this type in East Africa is the Macmillan Library in Nairobi, Kenya. Attempts are being made (not always successfully) to include these existing libraries into the national service plan, so as not to duplicate or fractionate service. Service to schools is also an intrinsic part of all three national plans.

In the libraries which do exist, a high percentage of the work is with children and young people. Most of the staff is expatriate but in a few years the graduates of the new Library School at Makerere University (Kampala, Uganda) can be expected to fill more and more of these positions. Most of the work is done in English with the books imported chiefly from the United Kingdom. The East African Literature Bureau does have quite a number of simple paper-back publications in the vernaculars, but they are by no means sufficient. Very few of them are of direct interest to children. The only significant local publisher of English-language children's books for the region is the East African Publishing House, which has its headquarters in Nairobi.

Sierra Leone

2311. "Junior Department. Primary Schools Service." Sierra Leone Library Board. *Annual Report.* Freetown, 1959 ff. NNY.

The annual reports include sections related to children's work and to work with schools. They provide a good picture of the development of this library service, begun in 1959 and now expanded to include libraries in all large cities and towns, and bookmobile service to some 600 primary schools and 37 secondary schools. The Library Board has also organized short courses for the training of children's librarians, and has compiled book lists. The 1963–1964 report includes photographs of the attractive new library in Freetown. Eventually, the Library Board will publish the national bibliography of Sierra Leone.

Zambia, Rhodesia and Malawi

No special bibliographies or studies exist for the children's literature of the Central African countries of Malawi, Rhodesia and Zambia, which were all once part of the Federation of Rhodesia and Nyasaland. The National Archives of Rhodesia publishes annually (since 1961) a list of publications deposited in the library of the Archives but the few children's books are hard to trace since they are not listed separately. The Literature Bureau of the former Federation was founded in 1948, and began publication in the vernacular soon after that. The Bureau was dissolved with the break up of the Federation, and its work has been assumed by the new Literature Bureaus of Zambia and Malawi (2313). There is virtually no publication in the vernacular in Rhodesia at the present time.

Schools and public libraries do exist, and use mainly English-language books imported from the U.K. The Bulawayo Public Library and Queen Victoria Memorial Library in Salisbury have large children's sections. The extent of their services is described in the annual reports of each of the libraries. As in the Republic of South Africa, service is carried out on a racially separate, or apartheid policy.

The Zambia Library Board is responsible for the development of school and public libraries in that country. It has established a library school for training in basic services.

2312. "The Zambia Library Service." Ministry of Education. *Annual report.* 1964. Lusaka, 1965, pp. 39–40. DLC, NNY.

An account of the founding of this Service, originally under a Ford Foundation grant in 1960. In 1964, the name changed to the Zambia Library Service. Two mobile libraries serve schools in outlying regions. The page following this report is concerned with the Publications Bureau, and a count of its more than 300 vernacular publications in print by language and by type of material.

2313. Zambia Publications Bureau. *A descriptive and classified list of books published by or in association with the Zambia Publications Bureau.* Lusaka, March, 1966. 47p. DLC.

An annotated list, arranged by language and type with children's books. Title index.

2314.	Mason, H. "Literacy and community development." East African Literature Bureau. *Occasional papers on community development,* 1. Dar es Salaam, Kampala, Nairobi, 1962. pp, 47–58. NNY.

A report on a literacy project conducted chiefly among the women and young people of the Turu tribe, Singida district. Many international agencies cooperated with local government. This provides a good picture of one of the ways in which such projects develop, although it is by no means typical, since each world area has its own special and individual differences and problems.

2315.	Mahood, M. M. "Need for supplementary readers; local themes essential," *East Africa journal,* Nairobi, Dec. 1966, pp. 38–39. NNY.

A report on a Writers' Workshop held at University College, Dar Es Salaam.

2316.	Richards, C. G. "The place of books in a developing region," *East Africa journal,* Nairobi, Aug., 1964, pp. 12–15. NNY.

The history and work of the East Africa Literature Bureau.

2317.	Varley, D. H. "School library work in the Rhodesias and Nyasaland," *South African libraries,* Cape Town, Vol. 20, No. 2, Oct., 1952, pp. 59–64; No. 4, Apr., 1953, pp. 108–116. DLC, NNY.

The author comments on the libraries he visited, most of which were in private schools, but some of which were in public schools, with book stocks supplied by the Beit Central Library in Bulawayo. In Nyasaland there were very few schools, and less libraries to observe. This first article concerned only European schools. The second dealt with service to Africans, which was almost non-existent.

2318.	Worsley, E. "What Rhodesian children read," *South African libraries,* Cape Town, Vol. 27, Oct., 1959, pp. 49–51. DLC.

A general discussion including some specific titles, mostly from England.

South Africa

In spite of widespread educational advancement, there are still many problems thwarting the further development of children's literature and libraries in South Africa. Schools have been and continue to be divided into those teaching in English and those teaching in Afrikaans; they are further divided into schools for whites and schools for non-whites. The English-speaking population has, for the most part, imported its books from other English-language countries, notably Great Britain. Afrikaans children's literature has limped along with a few native works, a number of translations, and the usual run of classics and folklore. Neither of the two languages has developed a solid native literature which reflects the cultural, social, political and geographical differences of the Republic of South Africa. What is available is often imitative or of extremely poor quality.

It is possible now to trace all books for children published in South Africa, because they are listed separately in the national bibliography published at Pretoria (2328). One notices immediately the translations into Afrikaans, which since 1958 have improved consistently in number and quality. However, one of the leading children's librarians in South Africa questions whether translations are the final answer and an entire substitute for a locally produced literature (2341).

Although library service to children has been going on for a number of decades, there have been no set standards for its development. Professional children's librarians are very few in number, and the work is spread very thin as a result. School libraries also exist, but have an equal lack of professional direction and selection. None of the universities provides regular courses in children's literature, although the Cape Town School of Librarianship did (at least in the past) include children's library work within the framework of the other courses (2347). Most library work is done by dedicated teachers who have taken special summer courses or courses organized by the South African Library Association.

2319.   Barry, R. "Once upon a time in Africa," *Junior bookshelf*, Vol. 18, Oct., 1954, pp. 181–184. DLC, NNY.

A review of some of the work of the best-known collectors of South African folklore, and the qualities this folk material possesses.

2320.   *Book guide*. Transvaal Education Department, Library Service, P.O. Box 1730, Pretoria. Half-yearly. 1952 ff. Cumulative volume 1952–1960.

This official publication has articles of interest to the school librarian, up-to-date lists of books, reviews of professional literature, etc. The text is given in Afrikaans and English. Vol. 9, No. 3, June, 1964 contains a very extensive bibliography of professional literature helpful to the children's and school librarian.

2321.   Bosman, Louisa. *Bibliografie van Afrikaanse kleuterboeke ontvang in die Suid-Afrikaanse Openbare Biblioteek, Kaapstad, tot in Junie, 1945*. [Kaapstad], The Library, 1945. 63p. (Mimeographed.) DLC.

A list of Afrikaans children's books in the South African Public Library, Cape Town. Some are annotated and there are series and author indexes, and a short bibliography.

2322.   Bruggen, Jan Reinder Leonard van. "Lektuurvoorsiening vir kinders en jeugdige persone in Suidafrika. Die erfgoed van stories in Suidafrika." *Lektuurvoorsiening vir kinders en jeugdige persone;* Amsterdam, Swets & Zeitlinger, 1922; pp. 48–63; pp. 85–98. DLC.

A review of libraries and books for children in South Africa, together with a chapter on the wealth of folklore available among the tribes of that country.

2323.   Cape Town. Cape Provincial Library Service. *Catalogue of children's books. Katalogus van kinderboeke*. Cape Town, Cape Provincial Library Service, 1961. 608p. 1st supplement: 1963, 264p. IYL. 2nd supplement: prepared but not published.

An annotated list of English and Afrikaans children's books in the Provincial Library. The intro-

duction and all annotations are in both languages. There are author, title and subject indexes.

2324.   Cape Town. South African Public Library. *Choosing children's books*. Cape Town, South African Public Library, 1941.

This pamphlet was distributed during the celebration of Children's Book Week, July 14–19, 1941 in the Library. It contains: "Some outstanding children's books" by Elizabeth Taylor; "Die Kinderverhaal" by I. D. Du Plessio, on children's stories; "Hints on choosing children's books" by Douglas Varley.

2325.   "For young people who read," *South African libraries*, Johannesburg, Vol. 6, No. 1, July, 1938, pp. 29–32. DLC, NNY.

A list of some 125 books, divided by age group, with brief phrase annotations. On p. 41 is a list of juvenile additions to the children's library in Johannesburg.

2326.   Hean, Jessie. "Kinderlektuur in Afrikaans vir kinders tot op die ouderdom van 12 jaar," *South African libraries*, Johannesburg, Vol. 6, No. 2, Oct., 1938, pp. 51–66; No. 3, Jan., 1939, pp. 99–114; No. 4, Apr., 1939, pp. 151–161. DLC, NNY. (Also published as a reprint by the South African Library Association.)

A thesis presented for the Master's Degree at the University of South Africa. This is the most extensive study ever written on children's literature in Afrikaans. Miss Hean divided it into periodical literature, prose, poetry, and drama. In each of these categories she further breaks down the material into age group. The bibliography appears only in the reprint, not in the periodical.

2327.   Immelman, René F. M. and D. H. Varley. *The school library, a handbook for teacher-librarians*. Cape Town, M. Miller, 1942. 116p. DLC.

The 8 sections are headed: "The library's function in the school," "Types of school libraries," "The teacher-librarian and his training," "The librarian's work," "Choosing books and other materials for the library," "The book as a tool and how to use it," "Teaching the use of books and libraries," and "Library extension and co-operation." The appendices contain a list of reference books for school libraries, a bibliography on school and children's libraries, and names and addresses of library associations and suppliers.

2328. "Juvenile fiction. Jeugdlektuur." *Sanb: Suid-Afrikaanse nasionale bibliografie*, Pretoria, 1959 ff. DLC, NNY.

Quarterly and annual compilations of the bibliography list the juvenile fiction separately. Nonfiction can be traced by careful search for the "J" preceding the decimal classification number. Literature in the African languages is also included in a separate section, and many of the titles would be considered juvenile.

2329. Kennedy, R. F. "Children's classics, old and new," *South African libraries*, Johannesburg, Vol. 2, No. 2, Oct., 1934, pp. 41–47. DLC, NNY.

A listing of 100 titles divided into four age groups. Most of the books are British publications, and all are in English.

2330. Levy, E. *Books for adolescents; a select list.* Cape Town, University of Cape Town, School of Librarianship, 1951. 250p. DLC.

2331. Lugtenburg, R. "Distribution of books to farm schools in the Transvaal," *South African libraries*, Johannesburg, Vol. 1, Apr., 1934, pp. 115–116. DLC.

A distribution of books (second-hand) to rural schools was carried out by the South African Association of University Women.

2332. Lyndhurst, Bessie. "Book selection in the juvenile department," *Cape librarian*, Cape Town, Sept., 1959, pp. 18–22, DLC, NNY.

The children's librarian in the Cape Town Public Library outlines their standards and policies of juvenile book selection.

2333. McArdell, A. M. "Towards excellence in school library programs," *South African libraries*, Pretoria, Vol. 32, No. 1, July, 1964, pp. 17–27. DLC, NNY.

The author is lecturer in school librarianship at the University of South Africa. She outlines here the objectives and standards of school library service in South Africa.

2334. Mandelbrote, J. C. "Work with children in the city libraries, Cape Town," *South African li-*

braries, Cape Town, Vol. 25, July, 1957, pp. 36–38. DLC.

A description of the types of work carried out in the Cape Town libraries.

2335. Nienaber, P. J. "Kinderboeke," *Bibliografie van Afrikaanse boeke 6 April 1861–6 April 1943*, 2nd ed., Vol. 1; Johannesburg, P. J. Nienaber, 1956; pp. 621–644. DLC.

An alphabetical listing, by author, of children's books in Afrikaans appearing between 1861 and 1943. Not annotated.

2336. Ogilvie, J. H. "Africana and some Africana books suitable for the school library," *South African libraries*, Pretoria, Vol. 19, No. 2, Oct., 1951, pp. 33–40. DLC, NNY.

A discussion of selected books about Africa, by people living in Africa, written in any of the African languages, or published in Africa, from the collection in the Johannesburg Public Library. A large proportion of them are folk tales or natural history books on the flora and fauna of Africa.

2337. Oppenheim, Gladys. "Why not have a children's free library?" *South African libraries*, Johannesburg, Vol. 1, No. 1, July, 1933, pp. 31–33. DLC, NNY.

An account of the founding of the Bloemfontein Children's Room, one of the first free libraries for children in South Africa.

2338. Pienaar, Lydia. "Die Afrikaanse kinderboek," *Cape librarian*, Cape Town, May, 1959, pp. 12–14. DLC, NNY.

The author comments on the sad state of the children's book in Afrikaans. She feels Afrikaans children will never have respect for their native literature when they see the much greater variety and attractiveness of books printed in English.

2339. ———. *Basic children's books. Basiese kinderboeke.* Cape Town, Cape Town City Libraries, 1966. 133p. IYL.

A selective list of children's books in English and Afrikaans, intended for use by librarians, parents and teachers. In her introduction, the author has stated her criteria for selection. Arrangement is by fiction (sub-divided into types) and nonfiction (under broad subject headings). There are no annotations.

2340. ———. "South Africa," *Library service to children*, 2. Lund, Bibliotekstjänst, 1966, pp. 52–61. DLC, NNY.

This publication was sponsored by IFLA (see 32). In this chapter is recounted the general history and present status of library work with children in South Africa.

2341.   ———. "Vertaalde kinderboeke—'n verdringende euwel?" *South African libraries,* Pretoria, Vol. 31, No. 4, Apr., 1964, pp. 120–123. DLC, NNY.

"Translated children's books—a supplanted evil?" Afrikaans has no real children's literature of its own, so that in recent years more and more translations have appeared. This librarian stressed the need for judging carefully before the translation was made, so that poor or mediocre books did not get a wider audience than they deserved.

2342.   "School and children's library number," *South African libraries,* Johannesburg, Vol. 5, No. 3, Jan., 1938, pp. 97–152. DLC, NNY.

Articles included are: "A singing, reading, and working nation" by E. A. Borland (on school libraries); "The children's room that suffers from growing pains" by M. W. Shilling; "The uses and arrangement of a picture collection" by H. M. Austin; "Suggestions for the organization of a primary school library" by Elizabeth Taylor; "The Sir John Adamson primary school library, Johannesburg" by E. J. Butler; "The children's free library, Bloemfontein" by Betty Levy; selected lists of new children's books, nonfiction for children, basic reference books, periodicals for the school and children's library; and a bibliography on the school and children's library. Some of the lists were concluded in the next issue.

2343.   "School and children's library section," *South African libraries,* Johannesburg, Vol. 8, No. 1, July, 1940—Vol. 21, No. 4, Apr., 1954. Quarterly. DLC, NNY.

This section was a regular feature during the period 1940–1954 and expressed the official point of view of the newly formed School and Children's Library Section of the South African Library Association, Transvaal Branch. In the first issue, the aims of the Section were delineated. In subsequent issues are articles describing school and children's library experiences, lists of books for children, book reviews, and news of interest to children's librarians. Some of the articles of special interest are: "School libraries in the Cape Province" by W. de Vos Malan, Vol. 10, Nos. 1 and 2, July and Oct., 1942, pp. 19–22, 45–47; "Criteria in children's literature" by A. Findlay, Vol. 14, Nos. 3 and 4, Jan.–Apr., 1947, pp. 109–111; "Reading interests of Durban children" by M. M. Barnes, Vol. 16, No. 1, July, 1948, pp. 35–40; "The development of school and children's libraries in South Africa" by D. M. Turner, Vol. 19, No. 4, Apr., 1952, pp. 134–139.

2344.   Smith, A. "Meeting of school principals and school librarians at the Johannesburg Public Library," *South African libraries,* Johannesburg, Vol. 7, No. 1, July, 1939, pp. 19–22. DLC, NNY.

An address which stressed the importance of good school libraries, and the great difficulties to be overcome in South Africa before adequate standards could be reached and maintained.

2345.   Speight, S. T. "The library in a high school," *South African libraries,* Vol. 3, No. 2, Oct., 1935, pp. 73–80; No. 3, Jan., 1936, pp. 81–90. DLC, NNY.

The organization, management and program of the school library. Short bibliography.

2346.   Taylor, L. Elizabeth. "The library and the child," *South African libraries,* Johannesburg, Vol. 7, No. 3, Jan., 1940, pp. 132–137; No. 4, April, 1940, pp. 182–192; Vol. 8, No. 1, July, 1940, pp. 21–31. DLC, NNY.

The children's librarian in the Johannesburg Public Library reports on a trip to England, Canada and the U.S., for the purposes of observing work with children in libraries. In commenting on what she has seen, Miss Taylor contrasts or compares the service given in South Africa and points to the ways and means of using some of the methods she observed, or she concludes that they would not be practical or effective in South Africa, and gives reasons.

2347.   ———. "School and children's libraries in South Africa," *Wilson library bulletin,* New York, Vol. 22, No. 2, Oct., 1947, pp. 137–140, 143. DLC, NNY.

The author writes about the children's libraries in Bloemfontein, Durban, and Johannesburg, some of the school libraries which have developed to a creditable degree, and the training of children's librarians.

2348.   Transvaal. Education Department. *Departmental circular 2,* No. 6, Dec., 1934.

Contains: "Children's classics old and new" by R. F. Kennedy; "Books for school libraries" by the Department Book Committee; "School libraries" by M. M. Stirling.

2349.   Turner, D. M. "Development of school and children's libraries in South Africa," *South African libraries,* Cape Town, Vol. 19, Apr., 1952, pp. 134–139. DLC, NNY.

A brief history and summary of modern status.

2350. ———"Wat skort aan die kinderboek?" *South African libraries,* Cape Town, Vol. 20, Apr., 1953, pp. 137–140. DLC, NNY.

What is wrong with children's books? asks this critic, and then proceeds to give some possible answers.

2351. Vleeschauwer, H. J. de. "Generalities in school-librarianship," *Mousaion,* Pretoria, No. 43, 1961, pp. 1–49; No. 44, 1961, pp. 50–120. DLC.

An attempt to analyze the theories of, the reason for, the aims of and the management of the school library. The author does not attempt to cover the practical application of the theories, but rather explores them to some depth. A provocative study, which can be seen in just this one statement, culled at random: "I find that I am rather at loggerheads with Anglo-Saxon technical literature and its so oft-declared 'ultimate' aim of the library, which is the deification and imposition of 'one's own way of life.' "

French-Speaking Africa

It is extremely difficult to document the work which is being done in children's literature and libraries in the many new nations of French-speaking Africa: Algeria, Cameroons, Central African Republic, Chad, Republic of the Congo, Democratic Republic of the Congo, Dahomey, Gabon, Guinea, Ivory Coast, Mali, Mauritania, Morocco, Niger, Senegal, Togo, Tunisia, Upper Volta, and the island republic of Malagasy. Before their independence, most of these countries had a limited number of public schools and educational facilities, in which the books used were obtained from France or Belgium. The missionary orders, which conducted the majority of schools, also imported their materials and limited their vernacular printing to Bible stories and the like. Some of these nations have declared an indigenous language as the official language of instruction, but in most cases even this cannot be implemented because of the time and expense involved in training masses of teachers, in building new schools and in producing new teaching materials. Other nations merely nationalized all of the existing schools, often keeping the staff intact. They were then able to build on to these a complete educational structure. A few of the countries can claim tremendous progress, to the extent of having schools in all villages. Of course, the larger coastal cities, especially on the north, have had extensive school systems for a number of decades. In Algeria there was a fair amount of local publishing of books.

Unlike the British publishers who began to develop an eager market for works with local African background, French publishers have practically no such books to offer at all. Whereas the English-reading African child can at least find a few stories and nonfiction books set in his own milieu, the French-reading African child has to be content with an alien literature in a foreign tongue. This situation is at last changing, and government as well as private agencies are attempting to bring about a more meaningful relationship between the child and his reading. In the Cameroons, for example, the Association des Poètes et Ecrivains Camerounais was founded in 1960 to arouse popular awareness in national folklore and to begin building up a record of national literature. At Yaoundé, a center for the development of textbooks has been established with the aid of UNESCO. Most of the French-speaking countries of West Africa are cooperating on this venture, which, it is hoped, will also stimulate more general publishing of children's materials.

Although there is not much to show proof, there are a great many projects in the making in these countries, and in another decade there are sure to be a number of additions to this list.

2352. Delrieu, Suzanne. "The Ivory Coast Central Library: a UNESCO project," *UNESCO bulletin for libraries,* Paris, Vol. 18, No. 5, Sept.–Oct., 1964, pp. 201–206. DLC, NNY.

Children's service are an intrinsic part of this library in Abidjan. The author describes the floor plan, program, hours of service, etc.

2353 "Mission to Malagasy," *Library journal,* New York, Vol. 89, Nov. 15, 1964, pp. 4476–4477. DLC, NNY.

A brief description of a bookmobile service offered in a rural area of Malagasy. Most of the work was with children and young people.

Contrary to what many persons believe, there is not so much a lack of literature for children in the Asian countries, as there is a lack of books. Immediately, the reader will think that only oral literature is implied, because of the admitted riches of folklore and mythology in the languages of Asia and the Pacific. This is not the entire picture. There are a fair number of good native "classics," in the same sense that this word is applied to 19th-century Western works. In addition, there are a goodly number of translations of the masterpieces of world literature for children. The great difficulty is to find these works in print, and when they are in print, to find them in an acceptable edition. Thus, where the Western countries have always had these books around, and where writers and children alike have been able to use them as touchstones for judging contemporary writing, in the Eastern countries such books have always reached an extremely limited audience, and they have rarely been available in large numbers over a long period of years.

This may be one of the chief reasons why writers of today are in such scarcity, and why the few who exist do not always command the respect of their colleagues from other fields of writing. Unless one has experienced personally the intense involvement which the child allows himself in his voluntary reading, it is difficult to imagine the importance and consequences of such reading, as contrasted with imposed reading.

Because many parents and educators also have been brought up without this literary experience, they too, find it hard to break the tradition in allowing the child to read more for pleasure than for moral or didactic guidance. They might agree in the abstract with theories which more or less prove that children are apt to remember longest what they read by choice (often clandestinely). But to put this into practice is another thing. Consequently there is a built-in resistance to the notion that children's books should exist in large measure for the delight of children, not for their edification. Critics from Western countries have deplored this didactic element in much of the oriental literature. It would perhaps be wiser to accept it as an inevitable characteristic and rather to attempt an evaluation based on that assumption.

Because some of these countries are materially among the poorest, much aid in educational and cultural projects is being extended by other nations, mostly Western. Along with this aid goes advice, much of which is totally at odds with the situation as it stands. There are also a number of promising young men and women sent to Western lands to study librarianship, writing, publishing and the like. Rarely is it admitted in public, but the greater proportion of these projects fail to live up to expectations. In some cases they are too tied up with political strings; in others, the political involvement is not great enough and the project ends up with no local government support; in still others, the problem is simply one of grave misunderstanding between representatives of two cultures. When studied with honest objectivity, one has to admit these situations develop due to mistakes made on both sides. Yet very few of the professional individuals involved question whether such exchanges should continue. Is it right, though, to train someone in advanced techniques which he will have little hope of employing? Is it not natural for him to be dissatisfied, so that he feels inadequate to work either in his native country or in the one he completed his professional studies?

The time seems to be ripe for much closer investigation of the ways and means to educational betterment which are acceptable to all sides. It is not correct to judge such projects in the same way one assesses agricultural or other economic assistance, although there are general problems common to all areas. It is imperative to realize that in education, one is touching primarily the inner development of the individual, and only secondarily the outer environment.

2354.   Bhatawdekar, Shakuntala. *Books for Asian children; a selective list of publications from world literature for use in Asia, in the original, in translation or in adaptation.* Paris, UNESCO, 1956. 77p. IYL.

The former children's librarian of the Delhi Public Library compiled this list of 500 titles in response to a recommendation made at the UNESCO Seminar on Public Library Development in Asia in October, 1955. Each entry is annotated.

2355.   Bonny, Harold V. "Libraries in the South Pacific," *UNESCO bulletin for libraries,* Paris, Vol. 17, No. 3, May–June, 1963, pp. 147–156. DLC, NNY.

Mr. Bonny was sent by UNESCO to survey the extent of all types of library service in existence in the islands of the South Pacific. His brief reports specifically note when children's or school libraries were active, and to what extent.

2356.   "The children's market . . ." Sankaranarayanan, N., *Book distribution and promotion problems in South Asia,* Madras, Higginbothams (by arrangement with UNESCO), 1964, pp. 62–63, 71, 270–271. DLC.

The reports cover each of the countries separately, and frequently children's books are mentioned only in passing. The pages indicated, however, contain revealing remarks on some of the problems facing children's book production and distribution in South Asia.

2357.   Conference of Ministers of Education and Ministers Responsible for Economic Planning of Member States in Asia, Bangkok, 22–29 Nov. 1965. *Final report.* Paris, UNESCO, 1966. 74p. APP. (Document no. UNESCO/ED/222).

This conference was convened to review progress in the implementation of the Karachi Plan, drafted at an earlier conference, and to discuss overall development of education in relation to economic and social development. Many of the working papers and the sections of the final report have direct bearing on the future of libraries and children's books in the 16 members states from Asia which were represented here.

2358.   Hurlimann, Bettina. "Children's books in the East," *Library association record,* London, Vol. 66, No. 3, Mar., 1964, pp. 95–97. DLC, NNY.

A Swiss publisher writes of her impressions of children's reading as observed on a trip to the Far East.

2359.   *Information bulletin on reading materials.* UNESCO Regional Centre for Reading Materials in South Asia, 26/A, P.E.C.H.H.S., Karachi 29, Pakistan. Quarterly. Vol. 1, No. 1, Apr., 1959 ff. DLC.

Although this publication is concerned with all of the problems of general book writing, publishing and distribution, a major emphasis is on materials for children and new literates. This provides an up-to-date picture of the developments in the South Asian countries, and includes information in such things as prizes, congresses, exhibits, seminars, studies, lists, and national bibliographies. This is an invaluable aid to the person interested in a study of the newly developing children's literature of these countries.

2360.   Insha, Ibne. "Reading habits and book publishing in Asia," *UNESCO courier,* Paris, Nov., 1966, pp. 12–16. DLC, NNY.

A survey of reading habits in general, with more emphasis placed on those of children.

2361.   Kamm, Antony. "Children's literature in South Asia," *Books,* London, No. 356, Nov.–Dec., 1964, pp. 217–223. DLC, IYL.

Before attending the UNESCO Regional Seminar in Teheran, this editor visited the countries of South Asia. Here he reports on what he observed in the way of developments toward a children's literature in these countries.

2362.   Meeting of Experts on Book Production and Distribution in Asia, Tokyo, 25–31 May, 1966. *Final report.* Paris, UNESCO, 1966. 35p. APP. (UNESCO/MC/55).

In addition to a general assessment of Asia's book needs, there are specific statements in regard to children's book needs. The problems of promotion and distribution are also discussed in detail.

2363.   Munger, Harold N. "Children's books in Asia," *Horn book,* Boston, Vol. 38, No. 1, Feb., 1962, pp. 79–81. DLC, NNY.

Concerning the role of Franklin Publications in production of children's books in some of the Asian countries.

2364.   Regional Conference on Compulsory Education, Bombay, Dec., 1952. *Compulsory education in South Asia and the Pacific.* Paris, UNESCO, 1954. 157p. (Studies on Compulsory Education, 13). DLC, NNY.

One of a series which documents the history of education in many countries and areas of the world. These are valuable as background studies since they contain information not easily found in the usual education histories. Frequently, mention is made of the availability (or lack of it) of children's reading materials.

2365.   Regional Seminar on Literature for Children and Juveniles, Teheran, 11–25 April, 1964. *Final report.* Karachi, UNESCO, 1964. 19p. (UNESCO Document PRM/1964/1). NNY.

Representatives from Afghanistan, Ceylon, India, Iran, Pakistan, Nepal, and Thailand met to consider the problems of preparation, production, promotion and distribution of children's books in these countries. Indonesia, Malaysia, Philippines and South Viet Nam were invited to participate as observers. This report presents only the outline of the material covered at the sessions, and a suggested outline for teaching children's literature to future teachers in these countries. The papers themselves can only be found in portions in the *Information Bulletin on Reading Materials,* or in some cases they may be obtained from the individuals who prepared them. These persons presented papers: U Tin Swe, for Burma; H. D. Sugathapala, for Ceylon; K. Seshadri, for South India; Ala Kiaie, for Iran; B. C. Sharma, for Nepal: Ibne Insha, for West Pakistan; Sardar Fazlul Karim and Syed Ali Ahsan, for East Pakistan; Mrs. Maenmas Chavalit for Thailand.

2366.   "Review of eductional progress in the Asian region," *Bulletin of the UNESCO regional office for education in Asia,* Bangkok, Vol. 1, No. 1, Sept., 1966. 150p. APP.

This is a recent compilation of trends and statistics, which brings up to date many of the facts brought out in the Compulsory Education series (see 2435, 2473, 2509, 2524, 2529).

2367.   "Serving children." *Public libraries for Asia.* Paris, UNESCO, 1956. pp. 109–147. DLC, IYL, NNY.

The children's section of the Delhi seminar gives here its final report and recommendations. The major papers delivered at the seminar are also reprinted. They are by Margaret Gardner (public library services), Marjorie Cotton (reading interests), Sohan Singh (cooperation between public and school libraries), Hector Macaskill (school library services) and by the Japanese Library Association (statistics on Japanese school libraries).

2368.   Smith, Datus. "Children's books in developing countries," *Horn book,* Boston, Vol. 39, Feb., 1963, pp. 36–49. DLC, NNY.

An address given at the IBBY Congress held in Hamburg in September, 1962. Mr. Smith describes the general problems faced by authors, publishers, booksellers, libraries and any individual interested in bringing good books to children in the developing countries of Asia and Africa. He describes also the role of Franklin Publications in meeting some of the problems and solving them.

2369.   UNESCO Regional Centre for Reading Materials in South Asia. *Exhibition of juvenile literature.* Karachi, 1960. 24p. APP.

A catalog of the exhibition organized by the Karachi Theosophical Society under the auspices of the Regional Centre in September, 1960.

Iran

Although it had a head start over most of its neighboring countries in the establishment of schools, a ministry of education and educational laws, Iran had progressed at a very slow rate toward the eradication of illiteracy. This was drastically changed by the establishment of the "knowledge corps" in 1963, whereby all military conscripts, who have completed their high school education, are required to spend their time in teaching basic reading and writing to the rural and village population which have had no opportunities for schooling.

This literacy campaign has naturally created an increased demand for simple reading materials. At the same time, the government felt it was important to provide children with sufficient books so that their interest in reading would not wane, causing them to revert back to illiteracy. The Children's Book Council was founded in 1960? to provide publishers with an outlet through which they could disseminate information about their books and also get information on likely needs of the future. The Council has been very active in its first years, sponsoring a national seminar on children's books (2376) publishing a list (and supplements) of currently available children's books (2572) and putting out a new circular on children's book events and promotion (2375). They have also sponsored short-term courses for the training of school librarians.

Another agency important in the field of children's books is the Institute for the Intellectual Development of Children and Young Adults. Under the able direction of Mrs. Lily Jahanara Arjomand, the Institute has established children's libraries in a number of locations in Teheran and other parts of the country.

In 1960, an intensive campaign was undertaken to improve school libraries on the secondary level. This has been the priority project, so that elementary school libraries have had to wait their turn and are restricted to small collections, for the most part. Public library development is also scattered, although mention should be made of the much publicized efforts of the town of Tabriz, to provide a library for its inhabitants.

2370. Ardalan, F. *Survey of the reading interests of juveniles who read in Persian.* Tehran, Rahnamay-e-Kitab, 1963. 40p.

2371. *Fehrest kitab baräye kudakan va naujawän 1963–1964.* Tehran, Shurā Kitab Kudak, 1964. 21p. APP.

A list of books in Persian for children from 3 to 15 years of age, divided by age and type. These are currently available.

2372. Kiaie, Ala. "Children's literature in Iran," *Information bulletin on reading materials,* Karachi, Vol. 6, No. 3, Oct., 1964, pp. 39–41. DLC.

Information on the Children's Book Council and its work, some statistics on children's books, and the general results of a reading interest survey conducted among some Iranian school children.

2373. "Libraries for children," *Texas library journal,* Vol. 34, Dec., 1958, pp. 131, 146. DLC, NNY.

A brief account of the efforts of Miss Flora Mansour to set up a children's library in Teheran. She came to the U.S. in order to study children's librarianship.

2374. "Library improvement of Iran," *Library*

journal, New York, Vol. 86, Feb. 15, 1961, p. 864. DLC, NNY.

A brief description of the plans of the Ministry of Education to set up libraries in 400 schools with the aid of the National Teachers College in Teheran and the Ford Foundation.

2375. [*Quarterly bulletin.*] Shura Kitab Kudak (Children's Book Council) P.O. Box 741, Teheran, Iran. 1964.

This bulletin lists activities in the field of children's book publishing in Iran, articles on children's literature in general, and related areas of interest.

2376. [Seminar on children's books.] Teheran, Children's Book Council, 1964. 16p. DLC. (DLC also has a typed summary in English).

More than 100 interested persons took part in this seminar, which was divided into seven study groups: appropriate subjects for different age groups; translations or originals, Persian folklore and traditional literature; style and method of writing; purpose of illustrations; the format, printing and pricing of children's books; how children's and school libraries can help in the progress of book production. The report itself is in Farsi.

India

The richest literature in India, as far as children's books are concerned, is in Bengali, although Hindustani, Tamil and Marathi come close behind. Urdu and Hindi are essentially the same languages as Hindustani. Urdu is written in a modified Arabic script; Hindi is written in the Davanagari script. This does not mean that there are large numbers of books available in each of these languages, but rather that they have a longer, more developed history of children's book production. Because Urdu and Bengali are also the major languages of Pakistan, these literatures are shared with India. To avoid repetition, the Urdu literature will be treated in the introduction to Pakistan, and the Bengali here under India. It must be kept in mind that most of the authors are known by both countries.

The princely state of Bengal was settled by the British East India company in 1642 and came under the rule of the British from the middle of the next century up to 1947. At that time it was divided into two parts, with West Bengal (mostly Hindu) becoming a state under the dominion of India, and East Bengal (mostly Mohammedan) becoming a province of Pakistan.

As the 19th century began, some enlightened missionaries realized that there was great value in producing works in the vernacular, and they consequently wrote the first Bengali textbooks as well as religious tracts. Many of these were published by the School Book Society, founded in 1817 in Calcutta. All of the histories of juvenile literature begin with the date of this society's first publication, 1818. Practically all of these first efforts were written by British colonials or missionaries. It was not until 30 years later, when Iswar-Chandra Vidyasagar began his work, that we find a native attempt at writing for children. Vidyasagar was an educator and social reformer. He sought to write in a pure, simple language, uncluttered by the Anglicisms of the missionaries or the formalities of traditional Bengali literature which stemmed from the Sanskrit. Vidyasagar's collections of tales and biographical sketches nevertheless turned out more as educational readers than as original works of art.

By 1850, there was a sufficient demand for literature in Bengali for publishers to turn to the world masterpieces for translations. The very first work to appear was *Robinson Crusoe*, in 1852?, and the second was a collection of stories from Shakespeare. More were added each decade, but for the most part the publishing was of a didactic sort which the missionaries could use in schools and churches.

Toward the end of the century, Bengali literature got a tremendous lift with the appearance of the first works of Rabindranath Tagore. His interest in folk songs and tales aroused the curiosity of several writers. Tagore himself collected a number of them and put them into his own inimitable style. These tales in poetry had moral lessons as most folk and fairy tales do, but they were implicitly rather than overtly stated. In 1901, Tagore founded a school at Bolpur which he named Santiniketan, the "Home of Peace." Although he continued to be interested in its educational principles for the rest of his life, his literary interests became further and further removed from those also of interest to children. All the same, there is much of his poetry which is read and appreciated by Indian youth today.

Almost a co-leader in this movement was Jogindranath Sarkar, whose best-known story is perhaps *Hashi Kushi* ("Happiness and Smiles") which appeared in 1897. He was especially fond of writing animal stories. Two other writers who became and remained great favorites were Dakshina Charan Mitra and Upendra Kishore Roy Chaudhuri. Later, when they were no longer living or, like Tagore, were devoting much time to other pursuits, children's literature seemed to suffer a decline. This was somewhat revived with the movement toward independence, when nationalism infused a new spirit in many writers. In 1947, the first children's encyclopedia was printed in India, in Bengali.

Throughout this entire period there was as much literature for children appearing in magazines as in books. Bani Basu lists the titles of about 150 published during 1818–1962 (2381). This is not to say that there are that many now in print. In fact, most have not survived and present-day children get such reading in weekly supplements to the adult paper which the family usually purchases. The Basu bibliography of Bengali juvenile literature is a very helpful aid in studying the trends of each period. In fact, in this respect Bengali is well served on all sides for there is more in print about this children's literature than there is about all of the others combined.

Of all the Dravidian languages, Tamil is the oldest and richest. It possesses a wealth of nursery rhymes, dance songs, ballads, folk tales and myths. Kamala Dongerkery gives a few good examples of this treasure (2395). There is lively interest in putting it into published form as well as encouraging writing of modern tales in Tamil. The Southern Languages Book Trust, which was founded in 1955 on a grant from the Ford Foundation, has conducted surveys and seminars on the subject of children's literature. The published reports make very interesting reading. They are concerned not only with Tamil, but also with Telugu, Malayalam and Kannada.

The Children's Writers Association in Madras has been responsible for about 40% of the books now available in Tamil. They arrange for exhibits, award prizes, conduct discussions and promote children's books in general. The Children's Book Council in Mysore, the Teachers College, Saidapet, Madras, the Children's Library in the Department of Education, Madras, the Educational Research Bureau, Bangalore, the Children's Library of the Indian Institute of World Culture, Bangalore, the All-Kannada Children's Association, Bangalore, the Makkala Mantapa, Bangalore and the Andhra Pradesh Library Association, Vijayawade, are some of the organizations working to improve the status of children's books in South India (2438).

Marathi is spoken in the state of Maharashtra (formerly Bombay state), by some 37 to 40 million persons. The "father" of children's literature in this language is Vasudev Govind Apte, who at the beginning of this century published a magazine for children. He himself wrote many of the stories which appeared in it, and he also later compiled a kind of encyclopedia. Since that time a number of important writers have turned to producing works for children. As in the case of Bengali, Marathi children's literature has been influenced by the translation of Western works, sometimes unfavorably so. It is unfortunate that the history written by M. N. Dandekar has no English or French summary, for it obviously contains much of interest to the Western reader.

In the remainder of the 14 official state languages there is much less literature for children available, as well as few sources for the outsider to turn to for information. Kannada, Telugu and Malayalam are all known to have rich lodes of folklore that have never been fully mined by the local writers. Gujarati has a limited number of children's books which date back to the beginning of the century, and a dozen or so modern writers. Assamese, Kashmiri, Iriya and Punjabi works are very sparse indeed, although each of the states where these languages are spoken are making efforts to improve both text and trade books.

Library service to children in India is sporadic in its development and progress. It was an intrinsic part of the Baroda library movement, begun in the first decades of the 20th century. In certain areas school libraries have received considerable attention and the great name of S. R. Ranganathan added to its prestige with his publication of a book and numerous articles on the subject. The standards he set were high, but could not be supported in most areas, due to lack of funds or interests. The few outstanding school libraries are in private, not public schools.

One of the first major library projects of UNESCO was the model public library established in Delhi in 1951 with the joint cooperation of the Indian government. It consists of a central library, a bookmobile and deposit stations, all having children's books. By 1961 there were some 10,000 registered juvenile borrowers using collections totaling 19,000 volumes (2442).

2377. Asadullah, Khan Bahadur, K. M. "School library," *Indian library journal,* Bezwada, Vol. 4, No. 5, June, 1936, pp. 131–134. DLC.

The aims and principles of management of the school library.

2378. Bagul, Devidas. *Bālavāṅmaya.* Poona, Joshi, 1961. 90p. DLC.

The nature of children's literature, the basic qualities of the child's way of thinking, and the forms of writing for children (prose, poetry, drama) are explored at some length. There is also a chapter on illustration of children's books. The author quotes frequently from Hazard (814), L. Smith (4328) and Arbuthnot (3436). Text in Marathi.

2379. Banerjea, P. K. "Problems of school libraries in India," *Indian librarian,* Jullundur City, Vol. 17, No. 2, Sept., 1962, pp. 100–103. DLC.

The greatest problem school libraries in India have is one created by the educational system itself: a phobia for examinations. It prevents young people and children from turning to reading for pleasure and personal information or inspiration.

2380. Bangalore. Indian Institute of World Culture. "A children's library," *Book news,* Madras, Vol. 2, No. 12, Dec., 1958, 12p. DLC.

A description of the children's library in this Institute illustrated with two photographs.

2381. Basu, Bani. *Bāṃlā śiśusāhitya: Granthapañjī.* Calcutta, Bangiya Granthagar Parishad, 1965. 38p. ff. 429p. DLC.

A bibliography of Bengali children's literature from 1818–1962, prepared by a technical assistant at the National Library, and published by the Bengal Library Council. The entries are arranged alphabetically by author and bibliographical information is quite complete. In the preface, the compiler indicates he has excluded all but a few text books, but included children's periodicals, of which there were some 150 (including children's supplements in adult periodicals). Capsule histories of the four major periods of development of Bengali children's literature are followed by a list of the Bengal State prize-winning books from 1954–1965. There are a number of portraits and reproductions from the pages of historically important works. This is a significant contribution to the history of children's literature. Text in Bengali.

2382. Benade, M. "Reading for children," *Modern librarian,* Lahore, Vol. 6, No. 2, Jan., 1936, pp. 77–83. DLC.

The qualities to look for in choosing books for home enjoyment.

2383. Bhargava, G. D. "Libraries and children welfare," *Indian librarian,* Jullundur City, Vol. 16, No. 3, Dec., 1961, pp. 133–137. DLC.

The author writes in general terms how a "children's library can play a definite and effective role in building up a nation."

2384. Bhatt, Mūlśankar. *Bālakone vārtā kevī rīte kahiṣuṭṭ?* Disa, Parichay Pustika Pravritti, 1958. 30p.

"On children's reading." In Gujarati.

2385. Boga, D. K. "School and children's libraries in India," *Journal of the Indian Library Association,* Calcutta, Vol. 1, No. 3, April, 1956, pp. 2–4. DLC.

The author points out that there are still very few children's libraries in India, but that school library service will hopefully be developed on a state-to-state basis following the examples of New Zealand. Although the Bal Bhavans do good work, she questions whether they are the best place for children's libraries.

2386. Bohanon, Eunice Blake. "American specialist abroad," *Horn book,* Boston, Vol. 40, Dec., 1964, pp. 642–645. DLC, NNY.

This former editor of children's books was sent abroad to India, Pakistan and Israel to consult with publishers and editors of children's books in those countries. She gives here her impresssions of some of the problems of publishing in those countries.

2387. "Children's Libraries," *Report of Advisory Committee for Libraries;* Delhi, Ministry of Education, 1961; pp. 42–43. (Publication No. 494.) NNY.

The Delhi, Ahmedabad and Baroda Public Libraries have children's rooms and Mysore City has a special children's library established by the Rotarians. However, all lack good collections due to shortage of books and funds. A central state children's library had been suggested by some experts, but this committee felt it would not have much value under present circumstances.

2388. "Children's library," *Library service in India today.* Calcutta, Bengal Library Association, 1963; pp. 88–120.

2389. Clark, Herbert A. "Some school libraries I have known in Bengal," *Modern librarian,* Lahore, Vol. 5, No. 3, Apr., 1935, pp. 100–102. DLC.

Comments on the sad condition of school libraries in the Bengal district.

2390. *Communist children's books in India.* 26p. ff. 37p. Typewritten manuscript. DLC.

A report on the extent to which the communist countries print books in the vernacular and distribute them throughout India.

2391. Dadachanji, B. M. "The child and the library," *Library miscellany,* Baroda, Vol. 1, No. 4, May, 1913, pp. 203–214.

2392. Dandekar, Malatibai Madhavrao. *Bālasāhityācī rūparekhā.* Bombay, Mumbai Marathi Granthasangrahalaya, 1964. 18p. ff. 276p. DLC.

The history and development of children's literature in Marathi. The writer is herself a novelist and folklorist, and has here provided an excellent survey of the subject in general, how Western ideas have influenced children's books in India, the importance of the children's magazine, and something about the major writers and translators in the children's literature movement. There are portrait sketches of eight persons in the last-named category. Index and bibliography. Text in Marathi.

2393. Dey, Prabhash Ranjan. *Śiśu-sāhitya o sāhityika.* Calcutta, Children's Publications, 1964. 12p. ff. 82p. DLC.

A history of children's literature in Bengali followed by biographical sketches of the major writers and educators connected with the movement, with photographs or portraits of each. Text in Bengali.

2394. Dey, Provash Ronjan. *Who's who of Indian children's literature.* Calcutta, Calcutta Publishers, 1962, 56p. IYL.

"Includes information about one hundred and fifty living writers of repute in all regional languages." Authors who have only written occasionally for children are not included. Each biographical sketch mentions one or two of the titles of children's books which the authors have written.

2395. Dongerkery, Kamala S. *Juvenile literature in India, a symposium.* Bombay, Thacker, 1946. 64p. (All-India Women's Conference, Cultural Series). DLC.

Contents: "Juvenile literature in Marathi" by Kamalabai Tilak. "Books for children in Urdu" by Sultana Asaf Fyee. "Juvenile literature in Tamil" by Ranganayaki Thatham. "Juvenile literature and eduaction in Kannada" by V. Sitaramiah. "Juvenile literature in Punjabi" by Jagadish Singh.

2396. Fāṭimah, Mashīr. *Baccon ke adab kī khuṣūṣiyyāt.* Aligarh, Anjaman Tarraqi Urdu, 1962. 79p. DLC.

The problems of children's literature as a part of children's culture. This has a critical introduction, and some examples of good stories, fairy tales and poetry for children. It was published by the Association for the Promotion of Urdu, and the text is entirely in Urdu.

2397. Gangopādhyāya, Āśa. *Bāmlā śiśu-sāhityera kramabikāśa, 1800–1900.* Calcutta, D. M. Library Publisher, 1961. 333p. DLC.

A history of children's literature in Bengal from 1800–1900. The author covers this in eight periods: the traditional literature, missionary period (1818–1850), era of Iswar Chandra Vidyasagar (1845–1870), the period of vernacular development, the age of the children's periodical (1878–1900), the golden age of Tagore, the movement toward independence, and the first years of the 20th century. The final chapter is a review of European and U.S. literature for children. Text in Bengali.

2398. Gardner, Margaret. "Libraries and children," *Indian librarian,* Jullundur City, Vol. 7, No. 3, Dec., 1952, pp. 74–77. DLC.

Although in its beginning stages, library service to children in India has begun to take shape. The greatest obstacle is the lack of literature in the vernacular and the author calls on mothers and teachers to lead the way in producing more books which represent the life and culture of their people.

2399. Gould, F. J. "The child and the book," *Library miscellany,* Baroda, Vol. 1, No. 3, Feb., 1913, pp. 89–90.

2400. Gupta, Rādhākrṣṇa. *Vihār kā bāl sāhitya.* Chapra, Gupta Sahitya Bhandar, 1961. 16p.

"History of children's reading." In Hindi.

2401. Harper, A. E. "Educational use of school libraries," *Modern librarian,* Lahore, Vol. 3, July, 1933, pp. 157–160. DLC.

A paper read at the third annual Punjab Library Conference. This discussed the use of the library in the teaching of reading.

2402. Hingorani, Rattan P. "Bombay's mobile library for children," *Indian librarian,* Jullundur City, Vol. 12, Dec., 1957, pp. 203–205. DLC, NNY.

The Bombay State Women's Council set up a mobile library service for the youth of Bombay. The work of this library is described here in brief.

2403. India. Information Services. *Books on India for children.* New York, 195?. 6p.

2404. India. Ministry of Education. *National prize competition for children's literature, 8th competition.* New Delhi, Ministry of Education, 1962. 24p.

2405. Jagannadhan, S. "Library service for elementary school children," *Modern librarian,* Lahore, Vol. 3, No. 1, Oct., 1932, pp. 25–27, NNY.

The importance of such service and its qualities.

2406. Job, M. M. "School libraries," *Indian librarian,* Jullundur City, Vol. 15, Mar., 1961, pp. 201–203. DLC, NNY.

The importance of the library in the life of the school.

2407. Joshi, P. M. "School library," *Modern librarian,* Lahore, Vol. 11, No. 3, Apr.–June, 1941, pp. 125–129. NNY.

A librarian outlines what he considers to be the aims and functions of the school library.

2408. Kaula, P. N. "All India seminar on school libraries," *Herald of library science,* Bangalore, Vol. 1, No. 3, July, 1962, pp. 141–143. DLC, NNY.

A report similar to the one by Ranganathan (2423).

2409. Kolhatkar, V. P. "The school library and its librarian," *Indian librarian,* Jullundur City, Vol. 15, No. 3, Dec., 1960, pp. 110–114. DLC.

The author recommends that schools give more concerted attention to their libraries rather than hastily attempting to collect any and all kind of materials to pass inspection with full shelves.

2410. Kudalkar, Janardan S. "Library work with children," *The Baroda library movement.* Baroda, Central Library, 1919; pp. 22–28. DLC.

The children's section was formed in 1913. Its collection consists of a "few hundred" books in the Gujarati and Marathi languages and about a dozen children's magazines. Storytelling and film programs were regularly scheduled. Books were not allowed to circulate, but annually some 20,000 children visited the library.

2411. "Libraries in schools." Entire issue of: *Teaching,* Bombay, Vol. 30, No. 3, Mar., 1958, pp. 73–108. DLC.

Articles include: "The use of books in a school library" by J. Smeaton; "The need for a children's public library in towns" by Janet Irwin; "Towards a functional school library" by Austin A. DeSouza; "General and class libraries" by G. Sundaram; "A children's library" by Joseph Vernon Furtado; and book lists for school libraries.

2412. Magna Nand. "School libraries in India," *Indian librarian,* Jullundur City, Vol. 9, No. 1, June, 1954, pp. 1–6. DLC.

In a recent directory of Indian libraries of 5,000 or more volumes, the school library entries were rare. The author discusses some of the reasons why.

2413. Malik, D. M. "The school library and reference materials," *Punjab educational journal,* Lahore, Vol. 52, Nos. 10–11, Jan.–Feb., 1958, pp. 682–694. NNC.

Why reference materials are important in the school library, and a list of basic tools which should be in every school library.

2414. Manchanda, Ratanchand. "The school library," *Modern librarian,* Lahore, Vol. 2, No. 1, Oct., 1931, pp. 17–25. NNY.

The philosophy and practical measures which this educator outlines are basically similar to those of S. R. Ranganathan.

2415. Mitra, Khagendranath. *Śatābdīra śiśu-sāhitya.* Calcutta, Vidyodayaya Library, Private, Ltd., 1958. 9p. ff. 248p. DLC.

A history of Bengali children's literature from 1818–1918. This author treats of the literature in two categories: periodicals and books. He traces the work of such organizations as the Calcutta School Book Society and the Christian School Book Society, both pioneers in the production of books for children in the vernacular. He particularly emphasizes the work of Vidyasagar and Tagore, but mentions as well many other persons who figured in the development of children's literature. There are some photographs and reproductions to illustrate the text which is in Bengali.

2416. Mohanraj, V. M. "School libraries, an educational problem," *Herald of library science,* Varanasi, Vol. 2, July, 1963, pp. 167–171. NNY.

2417. Mukherjee, Ajit Kumar. "Children's literature and its place to the library," *Library herald,* Delhi, Vol. 7, July–Oct., 1964, pp. 152–174. DLC, NNY.

A general survey as to the history and criticism of children's literature, and book lists in English and Hindi, recommended for basic purchase in the school library. The author is librarian of the Curriculum Department of the National Council of Educational Research and Training.

2418. ———. *School library: Some practical hints.* New Delhi, National Council of Educational Research and Training, 1965.

2419. Naik, Chitra. *The school library.* Bombay, Government Central Press, 1950. (Publication of the Education Section, No. 9).

2420. Pandia, M. N. "Some aspects of children's literature in Gujarati," *Aryan path,* Bombay, Vol. 20, No. 5, May, 1949, pp. 219–221. NNY.

Until the appearance of Gijubhai Badheka and others, the only children's books were the *Hitopadesa* and *Panchatantra* tales, and these were given to children more for their moral emulation than for entertainment. Other authors who have recently become successful in writing for children are Kavi Lalitji and Shrimati Hansaben Mehta, Avinash Vyas and Pinakin Trivedi.

2421. Prabhudesai, Anandibai. "The children's library," *Modern librarian,* Lahore, Vol. 1, No. 1, Nov., 1930, pp. 2–4. NNY.

The children's librarian of the Baroda Central Library writes of her work.

2422. ———. "Children's section in Central Library, Baroda." *Indian library journal,* Bezwada, Vol. 4, No. 5, June, 1936, pp. 134–135. DLC.

The librarian of the children's room writes of its history, from the opening date in 1913, to the mid-1930's. The library gave free, open service to all ages, but it was noted that due to a paucity of books for the younger children, table-games, puzzle boxes and picture cards were used to interest them and keep them occupied until books were available.

2423. Ranganathan, S. R. "All India seminar on school libraries," *Annals of library science,* New Delhi, Vol. 9, Sept., 1962, pp. 100–107. DLC, NNY.

The aims and objectives of this important seminar are here outlined according to the Ranganathan classification system, and the findings of the participants are likewise categorized.

2424. ———. "Books for the young," *Modern librarian,* Lahore, Vol. 11, No. 3, Apr.–June, 1941, pp. 140–142, NNY.

Portions of a radio broadcast in which this librarian exhorted teachers to become more interested in children's books.

2425. ———. "Children's books and mass distribution," *Book news,* Madras, Vol. 1, No. 7, Nov., 1957, pp. 8–9. DLC.

A recommendation for the development and expansion of existing school libraries rather than the establishment of children's rooms in public libraries. The author feels it would be more effective and less wasteful. This periodical contains frequent short articles on news related to the production, editing, illustration, and distribution of children's books.

2426. ———. "How to create reading habit," *Modern librarian,* Lahore, Vol. 6, Nos. 3–4, Apr.–July, 1936, pp. 136–147. DLC.

A lecture delivered to a teacher's meeting in which this librarian urged those attending to attempt writing children's books out of their experiences in working with and observing children. Only in mass effort will the famine of books be overcome.

2427. ———. "The physiology and anatomy of the heart of the school," *Modern librarian,* Lahore, Vol. 1, Nos. 3–4, Jan.–Feb., 1931, pp. 49–55. NNY.

This was part of the formulative stage of the author's ideas about the school library which later expanded into his book on the subject.

2428. ———. *School and college libraries.* Madras, Madras Library Association (London, Edward Goldston), 1942. 426p. DLC, NNY.

Certainly the book of theory which has most influenced the school library planning of India. The freshness of approach, the clear and convincing manner of presentation should have resulted in even wider influence, but due to a lack of communication, resistance to new ideas, and lack of funds, many of the ideas here expressed never took root. Many are still relevant today, and it is to be hoped that a new, revised edition can be brought out to give new impetus. The five parts are the "Why," "What," and "How" of school libraries, the present difficulties, and the elements of good school library practice. Part 6 is on college libraries, and does not come within the scope of this work.

2429. ———. "The school library and civic training," *Modern librarian,* Lahore, Vol. 7, No. 2, Jan., 1937, pp. 1–21. DLC.

How the well-run library can naturally inculcate in the young a respect for public property and the rights of others.

2430. ———. "The school library as a social centre," *Modern librarian,* Lahore, Vol. 5, No. 1, Oct., 1934, pp. 35–41. DLC.

"A collection of books, dissociated from users, has as little right to the appellation 'library,' as a mere group of children dissociated from books." This librarian recommends larger, open collections for free use by all pupils, and with a professional staff to guide them. A shorter article preceding this, by Radha Raman Manna, advocates the same up-dating for children's rooms in public libraries.

2431. Roy, Binay. "A children's library at Bansberia," *Modern librarian,* Lahore, Vol. 3, No. 1, Oct., 1932, pp. 47–49. NNY.

A description of a newly-opened children's public library.

2432. Sahasrabudhe, Prabha. *Writing for children today: Why, what and how?* New Delhi, Bal Bhavan and National Children's Museum, 1963. 52p. DLC.

A collection of papers presented at the seminar which took place at Bal Bhavan and the National Children's Museum in April–May 1963. The *Washington Post* Book Fair sent the collection of books used in its annual exhibition, and the USIS cooperated in arranging the fair in India. The eight papers are on the standards of writing and illustrating for children, reading interests and reading readiness, science books, books for the adolescent girl, and story books available in the Indian languages. The tone of the essays is set by B. B. Agarwal in his opening paper: "Nothing is more repugnant to a child than to be told that his present is merely a preparation for the future, that he is today somehow less than living. He is very much alive to everything that goes around him, but only in his own peculiar way. The writer has to set himself on that way and then see life—steady and whole. A child is never satisfied with a partial vision or a diluted or disinfected version of life. Whatever we give him must be complete and full-blooded."

2433. Sahaya, Shymnandan. "Books for the young," *Indian librarian,* Jullundur City, Vol. 1, No. 1, June, 1946, pp. 8–14. DLC.

The children's library movement in India is restricted almost entirely to Baroda. This is partly due to indifference, partly to lack of funds, but mostly to lack of reading materials and means of selecting them.

2434. ———. "Introducing the young to 'Never Failing Friend,'" *Indian librarian,* Jullundur City, Vol. 12, No. 4, Mar., 1958, pp. 254–266. DLC.

A paper read at an educational conference. The title refers to books, and the subject is the importance of reading aloud, storytelling, book discussions and like activities in school and library since so few Indian children have access to books.

2435. Saiyidain, K. G., *et al. Compulsory education in India.* Paris, UNESCO, 1952. 191p. (Studies on Compulsory Education, 11). DLC. NNY.

One of a series which documents the history of education in many countries and areas of the world. These are valuable as background studies since they contain information not easily found in the usual histories of education. Frequently, mention is made of the availability (or lack of it) of children's reading materials.

2436. Satyarthi, Devendra. "Indian children's rhymes and chants," *Modern review,* Calcutta, Oct., 1936, pp. 394–396; Nov. 1936, pp. 532–534. NNY.

"We are like a stray line of a poem, which ever feels that it rhymes with another line and must find it, or miss its own fulfillment. This quest of the unattained is the great impulse in man which brings all the best creations." Tagore.

The author cites this quote as the best reason for the success and power of literary feeling which are evident in children's rhymes. He gives a number of rhymes in English translated from Bengali and Punjabi.

2437. Sen, Anima. *Bangla śiśu ramya sahitya.* Calcutta ?, 1964?

"A history of Bengali children's literature."

2438. Seshadri, K. "Survey on problems of literature for children and juveniles in the South Indian languages," *Information bulletin on reading materials,* Karachi, Vol. 7, No. 1, Apr., 1965, pp. 10–14; No. 2, July, 1965, pp. 34–39. DLC.

An abridged form of the report prepared for the Regional Seminar in Teheran, April, 1964 (see 2365). The first part treats of the work being done in children's literature in South India, and lists a group of ten agencies and organizations specializing in providing suitable reading material in Tamil, Telugu, Malayalam, and Kannada. The few existing libraries for children are also pointed out. The second part is concerned with the technical details of producing and disseminating children's literature.

2439. Singh, Sohan. *Manual of library service for children for use in Indian libraries.* Lahore, S. Dyal Singh Library, 1941. Unp. APP.

The modes of service, materials and their selection, organization and management of staff and material, etc. The appendices include lists of best books for children in Urdu and Hindi, and a list of publishers in these languages. Short bibliography.

2440. Sinha, Kumari Uma. "The children's library; its services to the community," *Indian librar-*

ian, Jullundur City, Vol. 10, No. 3, Dec., 1955, pp. 115–118. DLC.

The general philosophy which is behind service to children in the library.

2441.   Tandon, M. M. L. "Library service in schools and development of reading habits," *Indian librarian,* Jullundur City, Vol. 13, No. 1, June, 1958, pp. 6–8. DLC.

The director of the Delhi Public Library comments on the poor status of school libraries in India, and urges extensive development and reform.

2442.   ——— and Frank M. Gardner. *Reading interests of the new reading public and juvenile readers in Hindi.* New Delhi, Ministry of Education, 1961. 60p. APP.

Results of studies made at the Delhi Public Library of which Mr. Tandon was director at the time. In the period in question the Library had some 10,000 registered borrowers below the age of 15, using a collection of 13,000 volumes in Hindi (6,000 titles). The general conclusions were: that the majority of children preferred fiction, but that nonfiction might well be equally popular if there were enough variety available; that children like books to be illustrated; that there is a dearth of children's periodicals; and that there must be more encouragement for writers, illustrators and publishers to produce books in each of the states, with regional flavor expressed in the language, design and illustrations.

2443.   Thomas, Gilfren. "Books and an Indian village," *Junior bookshelf,* Huddersfield, Vol. 6, No. 2, July, 1942, pp. 53–56. DLC, NNY.

How "Know books" (how-to-do-it books) collected by children into a book club enabled a village to improve its social and cultural life.

2444.   Trehan, G. L. *Administration and organization of school libraries in India.* Jullundur and Delhi, Sterling Publishers, 1965. 291p. DLC.

The most recent and most complete work on the school library in India. Areas discussed are the educational need, the concept, aims, functions, uses, standards, services, planning, organization and administration of the library. The chapter on reading interests of school children in India is of particular interest. Appendices include government recommenda-

tions, a report on a school library survey in Punjab, diagrams of lay-out, sample forms, a syllabus for training of teacher librarians, an annotated list of reference books for school libraries, and descriptions of the work done by the Delhi Public Library and the Chandigarh Central State Library, for their child users.

2445.   Vajpayee Bhimpure, S. B. "Orientation course for teaching of school libraries," *Herald of library science,* Bangalore, Vol. 4, Apr., 1965, pp. 164–167. DLC, NNY.

A report on a course held in Bangalore and Allahabad by the Ministry of Education.

2446.   Valliappa, Al. *A report on the survey of the reading interests of juveniles in Tamil.* Madras, The Southern Languages Book Trust, n.d. 25p. ff. 11p. of appendix. DLC, IYL.

A report prepared in 1960 under the auspices of UNESCO. The aim was to provide authors, publishers and librarians with information which which would be helpful in the production and dissemination of suitable literature for children. Some 4,000 questionnaires were sent out, and the results published here are based on 1,500 replies. The appendices include a sample of the questionnaire, the suggestions formulated on the basis of the replies, and a very interesting note on the present situation in Tamil language books for children.

2447.   Viswanathan, Caduveti G. *The high school library; its organization and administration.* 2nd ed. New York, Asia Publishing House, 1962. 170p. DLC. (DLC also has 1st ed., 1957).

This was written specifically for use in Indian libraries, as reflected in the list of "basic reference works."

2448.   Waknis, T. D. "Aims of school libraries," *Indian librarian,* Jullundur City, Vol. 12, No. 3, Dec., 1957, pp. 208–211. DLC.

A talk given at a teacher's college, in which the author stresses the enhancement the library can bring to any educational program.

2449.   Wasi, Murial. "Wanted—good books for children," *Educational quarterly,* Delhi, Dec., 1963. DLC.

Pakistan

The individual wishing to learn about children's literature in Pakistan can do no better than to begin by reading the paper which Mr. Ibne Insha prepared for the UNESCO Regional Seminar on Literature for Children and Juveniles, in Teheran, 1964 (2457). Since this study is not to be found in many libraries, it is perhaps best to digest here a few of the major events and trends which are described therein. It actually includes much of Indian children's literature in Urdu, but this is evened out by the coverage of all Bengali literature in the India section.

At about the same time that Lewis Carroll was writing *Through the Looking Glass,* Maulvi Nazir Ahmad was writing *Mirāt Ul 'Arus in Urdu,* which means *Looking Glass for the Bride.* It constitutes the first modern novel in this language, and because it was received with the greatest of enthusiasm by young girls, it can also be called the first landmark in Urdu children's literature. The author himself characterized it in these words: "I was in search of a book which should be absorbing in interest as well as instructive to young girls and should equip them to grapple the problems in adult and married life." A fellow student of Nazir Ahmad, Maulvi Muhammad Husain Azad, was composing at the same time, at the request of a British education officer, a series of elementary school books in Urdu. Mr. Insha quotes a very touching letter of Azad's, which is requoted here with permission: "A precious part of my life was spent in compiling elementary books for children. Elementary in name but most exacting in labour. Those who know would appreciate that a book for children cannot be conceived and written unless the author becomes a child himself. Amending, correcting, erasing, rewriting, I became a veritable child in my old age. Resting or on the move, awake or asleep, I was engrossed in child-like thoughts. Months, nay years passed by in this pursuit and only then could I devise these toys for children. Well, my countrymen, maybe I could not serve you, but I served your children." These readers, although written a century ago, are still prized as models of simplicity and charm. The illustrations, incidentally, were by John Lockwood Kipling, father of Rudyard.

Some 25 years later Maulvi Muhammad Ismail of Merath compiled another set of readers, and he wrote for them a number of poems, still popular with Urdu speaking children. Mr. Insha writes about them: "Their simplicity has a freshness and abandon in spite of the occasional moralization which is characteristic of pioneers everywhere." This was the beginning of a new interest among poets in Urdu, and after the turn of the century a number of them turned to writing for children.

Fiction and nonfiction books did not get a start until a little later, when three publishing houses appeared on the scene. The first of these was Darul Insha'at Punjab, which initiated among other things, the "Paisa Library." By saving a paisa a day and sending the money in at the end of a month children would receive one book. These were attractive books of about 100 pages, and the scheme became so popular that the "Paisa Library" became a household word. Unfortunately it ran into financial difficulties and was discontinued after a few years. In addition, Darul Insha'at Punjab published the leading children's periodical in Urdu, *Phool*. It appeared from 1909 to 1957, and was the training ground for any number of children's writers.

The second publisher was Ferozsons, which had started as an educational publisher at the end of the 19th century, but began in the 1930's to publish the classics, native and foreign, which were more suitable for the older children, e.g., Dickens, Jules Verne, etc. This publisher is still in existence today, and has extended its list to nonfiction, poetry, science and hobby books and series. They are considered to be among the best publishers in the Urdu language, and are among the few to use some hard-cover bindings and attractive illustrations in their children's books.

Jamia Millia at Delhi, was begun in the early 1920's as a national university, to satisfy the demands of some educators who felt the existing system was not sufficient. At the same time it founded associated elementary and secondary schools, so that it could provide model education at all levels. In order to provide texts and other reading materials for this educational system, Maktabai Jamia was created. It still exists and continues to publish many books for children which are well-written, but usually not well-produced. They have also published a children's encyclopedia. There is a similar establishment in Karachi, which carries on the same type of work. Admittedly, they publish more to satisfy curriculum needs, but they perform a valuable service in doing so, for there would be an even greater dearth of materials without their publications.

There were other publishing houses which brought out creditable, even outstanding, works. Some, like Gulab Singh and Utter Chand Kapoor, are no longer in existence and their fine books are impossible to locate on the market. Others published only a few titles for children, but of good quality. They are too numerous to mention here. Mention must be made, however, of the role of Franklin Publications, through which some 110 juvenile books have appeared on the market in the last decade. These have all been translations, most of them in the fields of science and general knowledge.

At the present time there are some 1,000 titles available for children in Urdu. But as Mr. Insha points out, these are all of comparatively recent date, and do not include the best of the literature which was once available. It is not always due to the demise of a publisher—some of the classics in the public domain are not even being kept in print. The better translations from foreign classics are often long out of print. This is in part due to the expense of keeping heavy stocks on hand and also to the fact that marketing procedures are so poorly developed. For all these years schools and libraries have had to rely on haphazard purchasing because often there were not even publisher's catalogs available, much less selective lists. Now they are able to use the lists published by the National Book Centre, which hopes to print frequent revisions (2462, 2463).

This Centre is performing other valuable services as well. It has on permanent display all of the children's books of quality currently available. It gives an annual prize for the best designed juvenile book. It sponsors conferences and programs at which the production of books is discussed, and it promotes in a hundred ways the idea that books are a vital part of the cultural life of any country and there is no better way to begin than with the children.

UNESCO is also very active in Pakistan, and maintains a Reading Materials Center for South Asia in Karachi. Through this program, awards and subsidies are offered every two years to authors of good juvenile manuscripts. It has even commissioned occasional series, and had them published at the center or through commercial publishers.

Library service to children is only beginning, but there is an expressed willingness to learn from the experience of other countries. Some schools have had small libraries in English from the decades of British rule. These are now being expanded and filled out with works in Bengali and Urdu. As soon as they are allotted more funds for the purchase of books, they are sure to improve consistently, because the tools and guidelines for selection are slowly making their way into print.

2450. Ahmad, Rashid Uddin. "Some thoughts on school libraries," *Jamia educational quarterly,* Karachi, Vol. 4, No. 2, Apr., 1963, pp. 60–64. DLC.

It is difficult to speak of the requirements for school libraries when in Pakistan many schools do not have room enough for all the children. Nevertheless, this librarian believes that a start must be made and suggests minimum standards.

2451. "Books for children," *Dawn,* Karachi, June, 21, 1958. Also in: *Kitabi dunya,* Karachi, Vol. 3, No. 7, July, 1958, pp. 1–2.

2452. Dey, Provash Ronjan. "Reading interests of juveniles in Bengali," *UNESCO information bulletin on reading materials,* Karachi, Vol. 2, No. 2, July, 1961, pp. 30–31. DLC.

2453. Gaver, Mary V. "The role of a professional association in developing services for children," *Pakistan library review,* Karachi, Vol. 3, No. 2, June, 1961, pp. 9–14. DLC.

Although Miss Gaver does stress the need of a strong professional sense, this is more a review of the lack of children's books in Pakistan which represent the contemporary world of the child at home or in other countries, and the similar lack in the U.S. of books which represent the true life of present-day children of India and Pakistan.

2454. ———. "School libraries and international development," *Pakistan library review,* Karachi, Vol. 4, Nos. 3–4, Sept.–Dec., 1962, pp. 53–56. DLC.

A comparison of some of the manuals and other publications which are proving useful in developing school library service around the world. Among those discussed are 10, 72, 427, 2447, 3782.

2455. Glaister, Geoffrey. "School libraries, their purpose and administration," *Pakistan observer,* Karachi, Jan. 15, 1959.

2456. Hanif, Akhtar. "Library in school education," *Clarion,* Karachi, 1961, pp. 66–68.

2457. Insha, Ibne. *Survey of preparation, production and distribution of literature for children and juveniles in West Pakistan.* Karachi, UNESCO Regional Center for Reading Materials in South Asia, 1964. 21p. (UNESCO Project on Reading Materials, Regional seminar on Literature for children and Juveniles, Teheran, 11–25 April, 1964, Working Paper No. 7). APP.

Some of the chapters are: "The contribution of the pioneers," "Twentieth century and some specialized agencies," "The role of Franklin publications," "Children's periodicals," "Problems of production," "Library services and bibliographical aids,"

"Incentives for better juveniles." This is certainly the most complete survey of the field in Pakistan.

2458.   Irshad Ali, Syed. "School libraries," *Jamia educational quarterly,* Vol. 3, No. 4, Oct. 1962, pp. 58–66. DLC.

2459.   Khan, Safia. "School libraries," *Pakistan library review,* Karachi, Vol. 3, No. 2, June, 1961, pp. 57–61. DLC.
     A paper read at the seminar on "The purpose and function of the library in national education" held in Karachi in 1961. It is an outline of the objectives of the school library, and the place of pupil, teacher and parent in implementing its use.

2460.   Mahmud, Satnam. *A century of children's literature in West Pakistan.* Honolulu, University of Hawaii, East-West Center, 1964. [82p.] Typewritten manuscript. APP.
     A paper which was the result of a study grant at the East-West Center. The author is a leading educator in Pakistan. Her study covers much of the same material as that of Mr. Ibne Insha, but it has been expanded. There are sections on the history and background of children's books, pioneers in the field, 20th century books for children in Pakistan, and general comments on the art of writing for children, the problems and possibilities.

2461.   Momen, Abdul. "Children's corner in public libraries: Let thousand flowers bloom." Pakistan Library Association. *Proceedings of the Fifth Annual Conference.* Dacca, Pakistan Library Association, 1964. pp. 88–91. NNY.
     The difficulties of building a children's collection in Pakistan, and some of the libraries and agencies which are doing this work there. This is followed by an article on "Book promotion in school libraries" by M. Siddig Khan.

2462.   National Book Centre of Pakistan. *Bachchōmkī kitābēm Urdu mēm.* Karachi, National Book Centre of Pakistan, 1965. 167p. $1.00.
     "Children's books in Urdu." A list of 1,282 titles arranged by subject and with good bibliographic description but no annotations. All are currently available. Text in Urdu.

2463.   ———. *Grantha panjee; śiśu sahitya.* Karachi, National Book Centre, 1965. 86p. $.40. APP.
     "Children's books in Bengali." A list of 450 titles arranged by subject and with good bibliographic description but no annotations. All are currently available. Text in Bengali.

2464.   Nur Elahi, Khwaja. [Importance of library for children] *Amozish,* Lahore, Vol. 3, No. 5, May, 1950, pp. 32–37.

2465.   Rustomji, Behram S. H. J. "Recommendations of Group C: school libraries," *Proceedings of the seminar on the "purpose and function of the library in national education."* Karachi, Society for the Promotion and Improvement of Libraries, 1961, pp. 53–56.

2466.   Rakib Hussin. "Children's services in the public library." Pakistan Library Association. *Proceedings of the Fourth Annual Conference.* Karachi, Pakistan Library Association, 1963, pp. 97–100.

2467.   Riazul Islam. "Juvenile reading interests in East Pakistan," *UNESCO information bulletin on reading materials,* Karachi, Vol. 3, No. 3, Oct., 1960, pp. 44–45. DLC.

2468.   Tamannai, Z. A. *Bibliography of reading materials for new literates in Urdu.* Karachi, East Publications, 1959. 49p.

Ceylon

After observing at first hand the status of children's books in Southeast Asia, Anthony Kamm wrote the following concerning Ceylon: "Of all the countries in the region, Ceylon is the greatest enigma in the field. The people of Ceylon are book readers and book buyers. The children themselves are encouraged to come, and [do] come, to the bookshops. In Colombo there are a number of first-class bookshops, at least four of which have extensive sections of children's books (mainly English and American)." Yet, he reports further, there are virtually no children's books in the national languages! (2361).

This is not difficult to understand, after reading the survey prepared by H. D. Sugathapala, for the Teheran seminar (2469). A writer, in order to express himself in pure literary Sinhalese must have studied and read the language many years. This was impossible under the past system of education, where the child had to switch to English as the language of education. It left the educated person with no thorough knowledge of either language because from his home he learned a spoken idiom quite different from the accepted norms of written, literary Sinhalese, and from his schooling he learned a functional English quite devoid of the imaginative power that language can have. It was not until some writers began to free themselves of the constraint of writing in formal Sinhalese style, that native children's books began to appear. Mr. Sugathapala concludes: "The use of an idiom close to that of the spoken language and free of the grammatical inflections of the written language has now become a standard practice in books for young children." Perhaps this book-eager country is on its way to a new type of literature for its children.

It is possible to track down some of the children's books which have been published, by using the *Catalogue of Books of the Office of the Registrar of Books and Newspapers.* Those published in Sinhalese, Tamil and English are included, not always in a separate section.

2469.   Sugathapala, H. D. "Reading for children and juveniles in Sinhalese," *Information bulletin on reading materials,* Karachi, Vol. 7, No. 1, Apr., 1965, pp. 5–10. DLC.

Although rich in oral tradition, there is almost no native literature in Ceylon, due mostly to the fact that English was the language of education and few writers are able to express themselves and use the Sinhalese language in an imaginative way.

Burma

As in many of the other Southeast Asian countries, it was the second or third decade of this century before writers, teachers and educators began to be concerned about children's books which were not textbooks. U Tin Swe's article describes some of these early efforts, among them the stories translated by U Thant, then a high school teacher and presently, the Secretary-General of the United Nations. There are in all, some four or five commercial Burmese publishers producing books for children in very small numbers.

2470.   U Tin Swe. "Survey of children's literature in Burma," *Information bulletin on reading materials,* Karachi, Vol. 6, No. 1, Apr., 1964, pp. 71–74. DLC.

An excerpt from the paper delivered at the seminar in Teheran (see 2365). This is an excellent survey of the developments and present status of children's books in Burma. There are publication statistics and an account of distribution, library, and other problems facing this country before it can achieve widespread use of books among children.

Indonesia

Indonesia is the archipelago formerly known as the Netherlands East Indies. Until her complete independence in 1949, the official language was Dutch. This and English were the main languages of instruction in the schools, which had begun in the 19th century through missionary efforts. Practically all schools are now managed by the government or controlled through subsidies. Primary education is free, but not yet available to all, due to a shortage of teachers and schools. Nevertheless, the republic made great strides in education, and it is the young student group which has shown itself to be a powerful force in the ever-changing political scene.

The official language is Bahasa Indonesia, a form of Malay. Classical literature for the entire Malay archipelago was influenced by Sanskrit, Arabic and Persian literatures. Therefore, folk literature picked up many of the stories of the *Ramayana,* the *Mahabharata,* the *Ocean of Story,* etc. The shadow play was a popular form of story presentation, after it was introduced by India centuries ago. In Java and Bali it acquired artistic distinctions in keeping with local traditions. Only recently have these stories been put down in written forms suitable for children.

2471.   Dewall, H. von. "Eenige te Batavia inheemsche speel- en kinderliedjes," *Tijdschrift voor indische taal-, land- en volkenkunde,* Batavia and 's Hage, 1901, Deel 43, pp. 182–194. NNY.

A discussion of children's rhymes and game songs of Batavia, Indonesia. Text is in Dutch, but the rhymes and songs are in the original Malay dialects.

2472.   Gana, Oejeng S. *Literature for children in Indonesia during the Dutch independence and after her independence.* Bandung, N. V. Ganaco, n.d., 16p. IYL.

Some of the popular authors with children were Nj. Hafai Abu Hanifah, Nj. Limbak Tjahaja, Mrs. Hamidah, Arti Purbani, S. Djojopoespto, Madio Soetilarso, and L. Pringgoadisurjo.

2473.   Hutasoit, M. *Compulsory education in Indonesia.* Paris, UNESCO, 1954. 111p. (Studies on Compulsory Education, 15). DLC, NNY.

One of a series which documents the history of education in many countries and areas of the world. These are valuable as background studies since they contain information not easily found in the usual histories of education. Frequently, mention is made of the availability (or lack of it) of children's reading materials.

2474.   McVickar, Polly B. "Storytelling in Java," *Horn book,* Boston, Vol. 40, No. 6, Dec., 1964, pp. 596–601. DLC, IYL, NNY.

An American tells of her experiences in observing storytelling in Surabaja, Java.

2475.   Rud, Anine. "School library services in Indonesia," *UNESCO bulletin for libraries,* Paris, Vol. 14, No. 6, Nov.–Dec., 1960, pp. 274–275. DLC, NNY.

This Danish librarian was sent to Indonesia as a UNESCO school library expert. She reports here on the status of school libraries in Indonesia, and makes recommendations for further development.

Malaysia and Singapore

The Federation of Malaysia is a constitutional monarchy comprised of 13 states. It was formed in September, 1963, and for two years, Singapore was also a member state. Political tensions resulted from the fact that Singapore, with its majority of ethnic Chinese population, was being governed largely by Malays. By mutual agreement, Singapore, separated from the Federation on August 9, 1965, became an independent state. Both remain members of the Commonwealth.

Since instruction in schools is in English as well as in Malay, many of the books are imported from the U.K. There is a strong movement to use more Malay in the elementary schools and a growing number of children's books in Malay has reflected this concern. The Chinese and Tamil speaking minorities also use their languages in school together with English or Malay. The Borneo Literature Bureau provides inexpensive and attractive children's books in quite a number of the lesser known languages, as well as in Malay and Chinese. It is through the schools and their libraries that children have access to books, although in the larger cities, public libraries are also developing strength.

The National Library in Singapore has a very active children's program. Thir attractive lists show that most of the collection is in the English language (2481). In 1957, UNESCO had arranged for a bookmobile gift to the Singapore government. It began a series of visits to schools in 1960, circulating books in Malay, Chinese, English and Tamil.

2476. Anuar, Hedwig. "Organizing the school library," *Journal kementerian pelajaran,* Kuala Lumpur, Vol. 3, No. 3, Sept., 1960, pp. 203–208. (Also appears in Malay in Vol. 6, No. 3, Dec., 1963, pp. 180–185.)

2477. Aroozoo, Eleanor. *Books for Malayan children: A list of fiction with a Far Eastern background.* Singapore, Teachers' Training College Library, 1959. 12p. Supplement in: *Singapore library journal,* Singapore, Vol. 1, No. 2, Oct., 1961, pp. 79–85. DLC.
Books in English with suitable characters and background arranged by area covered and annotated briefly. The main list contains some 120 titles and the supplement more than 100.

2478. Arulanandam, Mrs. P. "Opening of the library at Methodist English school, Parit Buntar," *Malayan library journal,* Kuala Lumpur, Vol. 3, Jan., 1963, pp. 49–50. DLC, NNY.
A description of this school library which was a model one for the region.

2479. Baldwin, C. F. "Every child needs a school library," *Malayan library journal,* Kuala Lumpur, Vol. 3, Nov., 1963, pp. 65–67.

2480. Bhupalan, Mrs. R. R. "The need for history books in a school library: An introduction to the bibliography of writings in English on Southeast Asian history for use in Form VI," *Malayan library jour-*nal, Kuala Lumpur, Vol. 3, Jan., 1963, p. 40. DLC, NNY.
Followed by: "Bibliography of writings in English on Southeast Asian history for use Form VI," pp. 41–44 by D. F. Sutter.

2481. "Books for children," *Books about Malaysia.* Singapore, National Library, 1964. pp. 23–25.
A general list of books in English available in the library. This library also publishes attractive four-page pamphlets containing booklists for children on various subjects, e.g., Hobbies and sports, Picture books, Art, music and poetry, Fairy Tales, Stories, etc. All are in English and are revised periodically.

2482. Chin, Liew Yew and John R. Gurusamy. "Survey of reading interests of children between 10 to 14 years using the British Council Library," *Malayan library journal,* Kuala Lumpur, Vol. 3, Part 2, Jan., 1963, pp. 45–48. DLC.
Results of a questionnaire survey among 200 children using the library of the British Council.

2483. Daroesman, Ruth. "Books in Malay suitable for school libraries," *Malayan library journal,* Kuala Lumpur, Vol. 3, Part 1, Oct., 1962, pp. 11–15; Vol. 3, Part 2, Jan., 1963, pp. 51–52; Vol. 3, Part 3, Nov., 1963, pp. 77–78. DLC.
A list compiled under the auspices of UNESCO. It is divided into: classical Malay tales; folk tales, historical and adventure stories; translations, textbooks and reference books.

2484.   Federal Inspectorate of School. "The remove form library [and] A suggested list of books for the remove form library," *Journal kementerian pelajaran,* Kuala Lumpur, Vol. 4, No. 4, Dec., 1961, pp. 331–333.

2485.   Lim Wong Pui Huen. "Some reflections on the classifications of school libraries," *Singapore library journal,* Singapore, Vol. 1, No. 1, Apr., 1961, pp. 26–27; No. 2, Oct., 1961, pp. 86–89. DLC.
A survey of systems in use by school libraries and some recommended points of each system.

2486.   McCalla, Nelle. "The importance of the teacher in the school library programme," *Journal kementerian pelajaran,* Kuala Lumpur, Vol. 5, No. 2, Aug., 1962, pp. 72–76.

2487.   Martin, W. M. and Ghanzali Yunus. "Publishing books for children: Two views," *Malayan library journal,* Kuala Lumpur, Vol. 3, Part 4, Apr., 1964, pp. 152–159. DLC.
The first author was a librarian for many years in the Penang library, and is now with Oxford University Press. The second is with Franklin Book Programs. Mr. Martin stresses the importance of quality in content and illustration. Mr. Yunus points out how difficult it is to achieve any kind of quality in publishing either translations or original works due to expense and other complications.

2488.   Ministry of Education. School Libraries Advisory Committee. *A basic booklist for school libraries.* Current.

2489.   Muhammad Salleh Khir. [Classroom libraries.] *Journal kementerian pelajaran,* Kuala Lumpur, Vol. 3, No. 3, Sept., 1960, pp. 209–213.

2490.   "Neglect—with consent," *Singapore library journal,* Singapore, Vol. 3, Apr., 1963, pp. 35–38.

2491.   Plank, L. Caroline. "Care and repair of books in Malayan school libraries," *Malayan library journal,* Kuala Lumpur, Vol. 1, Part 3, Apr., 1961, pp. 10–16. DLC.
A librarian in a girls' school tells of her work with pupil assistants in caring for books.

2492.   ———. "Organizing libraries in Methodist schools in Malaya," *Malayan library journal,* Kuala Lumpur, Vol. 2, Part 4, July, 1962, pp. 136–139. DLC.
A librarian tells of experience in setting up school libraries. In this issue is also a list of sources of where to buy supplies and equipment.

2493.   "School libraries." Special issue of: *Malayan library journal,* Kuala Lumpur, Vol. 2, Part 1, Oct., 1961, pp. 1–40. DLC.
This special issue contains articles on the function and activities of the school library, training student assistants, operation and equipment of the library, books in English for Malayan primary and post-primary schools, and a list of Malayan children's books. There is also one article in Malay on children and books.

2494.   *Senarai pertama buku² Melayu yang sesuai untok perpustakaan sekobah rendah dan menengah.* Di-susun oleh Enche Abdul Rashid bin Ismail, Pensharah dan Pegawai Pustaka, Maktab Perguruan Bahasa dengan kerjasama Pelajar² Kursus Al, 1960.

2495.   Tee, E. L. H. "Classification scheme for Malayan school libraries," *Malayan library journal,* New York, Vol. 1, Apr., 1961, pp. 2–9. DLC, NNY.
Based on the Dewey decimal system.

2496.   Walker, Margaret L. *School library development in perspective; based on a study made of national type English medium secondary schools in the States of Malaya; final report.* Kuala Lumpur, 1964. Various pagings.

2497.   ———. *School library manual.* Kuala Lumpur, Ministry of Education, 1964. 76p.

2498.   Waller, Jean M. "Within their reach . . . the blind, the teacher and the library," *Malaysian journal of education,* Kuala Lumpur, Vol. 2, No. 2, Dec., 1965, pp. 217–223.

2499.   Wiese, Marion Bernice. "School libraries as an aid to comprehensive education," *Journal kementerian pelajaran,* Kuala Lumpur, Vol. 7, No. 3, Dec., 1964, pp. 186–192. (Also appears in Malay in Vol. 8, Dec., 1965, pp. 22–28.)

2500.   Yunus, G. "Publishing books for children," *Malayan library journal,* Kuala Lumpur, Vol. 3, Apr., 1964, pp. 155–156.

Philippines

This republic is composed of more than 7,000 islands, scattered over a wide area of the Western Pacific. Conquered by Spain in 1565, the Philippines were ceded to the U.S. in 1898, after the Spanish-American War. Their independence was agreed upon in an Act of Congress, signed March 24, 1934, but the ten year transitional period as a commonwealth was extended slightly by the war, and full independence came on July 4, 1946. Because of this history of Spanish and U.S. rule, the languages used most in commerce, education and government are Spanish and English. However, the official language is Filipino, which is a hybrid of Tagalog and other Malayan dialects, with some traces of Spanish. Primary education is given more and more in Filipino, but the other two languages are necessary for university studies, so that most children learn them as well.

This has created a kind of vacuum in literature. The cultural heritage can be appreciated only by one who reads Spanish. The new writer may have grown up speaking Tagalog-Filipino, but he has only models in Spanish to inspire him. The need for a literature in the vernacular is pressing. Books for children are printed in all three languages, and in addition, English language books are imported from other countries producing them.

Señora Bravo Villasante has devoted a chapter in the 2nd Volume of her work (70), to the Philippine children's literature in the Spanish language. Unfortunately, no equivalent study for Tagalog-Filipino could be located.

2501. Balayo, J. C. "For our children—the best," *Philippines today,* Manila, Vol. 9, No. 2, 1962, pp. 1–3. NNY.

A report on the Children's Museum and Library, Inc., an organization which sponsors cultural activities for children. This describes the project of a large children's library which was to be built in Quezon Memorial Park.

2502. Batalla, B. C. "The importance of storytelling to growing children," *Philippine educator,* Quezon City, Vol. 12, No. 7, Dec., 1957, pp. 58–59.

2503. Coquia, R. T. "Mother's guide to children's literature," *Philippine journal of home economics,* Manila, Vol. 10, No. 2, Oct.–Dec., 1958, pp. 15–16.

2504. Costes, R. G. "School libraries: let's make them functional," *Philippine educator,* Quezon City, Vol. 12, No. 8, Jan. 1958, pp. 8–14.

2505. Department of Education. Bureau of Public Schools. *A guide for school librarians.* Manila, Bureau of Printing, 1949. 48p. DLC.

A revised edition of Part 1 of the Bulletin No. 44 of the old Bureau of Education, 1928. This was a practical handbook demonstrating basic techniques of organization and maintenance of the school library.

2506. Dimaculangan, G. S. "School libraries in the United States through the eyes of a Philippine librarian," *School libraries,* Chicago, Vol. 3, Dec. 1953, pp. 2–8. DLC, NNY.

Although these comments were stimulated through a period of study in U.S. school libraries, they are actually concerned more with Philippine school libraries, and how they measure up to standards.

2507. Galloway, L. "I went, I saw, I learned," *Library journal,* New York, Vol. 79, Feb. 15, 1954, pp. 279–281. DLC, NNY.

"School library problems in the Philippines are not very different from ours in the States," concluded this observer.

2508. Guerrero, Lilia A. "Maternity and children's hospital library," *Association of Special Li-*

braries of the Philippines, Manila, Vol. 10, Sept. 1964, pp. 7–9.

2509. Isidro, Antonio. et al., Compulsory education in the Philippines. Paris, UNESCO, 1952. 84p. (Studies in Compulsory Education, 9.) DLC, NNY.

One of a series which documents the history of education in many countries and areas of the world. These are valuable as background studies since they contain information not easily found in the usual histories of education. Frequent mention is made of the availability (or lack of it) of children's reading materials.

2510. Montemayor, Teodoro. Handbook for elementary school librarians. Manila, Progressive Schoolbooks, 1937. NNY.

A manual giving practical advice on the organization, selection and management of the school library. Appendix A is a list of 200 children's books selected from the nonfiction collection of the Philippine Normal School, Manila. Appendix B is a basic list of 500 titles, in English, for the elementary school library. Most are now out-of-print or out-of-date. No index.

2511. Olaguer, V. O. "Let's write our own children's books," Weekly women's magazine, Manila, Vol. 7, No. 36, Jan. 16, 1959, pp. 14–17.

2512. Osborn, Lois Stewart. "An adventure in dreams," Library journal, New York, Vol. 52, Nov. 15, 1927, pp. 1068–1072. DLC, NNY.

A pioneer in Philippine school library development writes of the history of this work which began around 1910.

2513. Pastrana, C. C. "Wanted: Filipino books for Filipino children," Sunday times magazine, Manila, Vol. 16, No. 43, June 4, 1961, pp. 12–13.

2514. Polo, Elena. "Puppetry in children's literature," Philippine educational forum, Manila, Vol. 10, No. 1, Mar., 1960, pp. 41–45. DLC.

How puppetry can be used to introduce children to literature.

2515. Rodriguez, Ernesto R. "Our youth and their decadent culture," Education quarterly, Diliman, Rizal, Vol. 6, No. 3, Jan., 1959, pp. 277–280. DLC.

The officer in charge of the bureau of public libraries gave this speech on the occasion of National Book Week. In it he berates the public library for not providing enough good literature for the young. This is preceded by an article by Amor C. Guerrero on the ways in which administrators and teachers can help to develop good libraries.

2516. Sison, P. S. Book festival handbook; a collection of materials and suggestive ideas in celebrating book week. Manila, Philippine Library Association, 1938.

2517. "10,000 books for Mabini schools," Philippines free press, Manila, Vol. 52, No. 38, Sept. 19, 1959, 65p. NNY.

How a small town received gifts of 10,000 books, through the initiative of a school teacher. A special library was to be constructed to house the collection.

2518. Townes, Mary Ella. "Philippines," Top of the news, Chicago, Vol. 7, Oct., 1950, pp. 13–14. DLC.

In this issue devoted to children's library work in many countries, this librarian describes some of the libraries serving children in the Philippines.

2519. Watterson, Hannah J. "Librarian in the Philippines," Wilson library bulletin, New York, Vol. 23, Apr., 1949, pp. 620–622. DLC, NNY.

This librarian set up a school library in a girls' school in Batangas, Luzon. She writes of the problem of books which the Japanese had censored during the war, and the difficulties of getting suitable materials.

Thailand

Native children's literature in Thailand is still closely associated with the pedagogical aspects of such writing. It was the Ministry of Education which published the first books designed and written for Thai children. This was in the second decade of the 20th century, and until the outbreak of the revolution in 1932, the ministry continued to publish a few titles on a regular basis. Finally, in 1945, the Ministry authorized the Teacher's Institute (Kurusapa) to take over this work, and from 1945 to 1961 they published some 30 titles, mostly fairy tales and other stories, collected or written by members of the staff of the Institute. The sale of some of these books inspired commercial publishers to begin producing children's books, but on a minimal level, and of the poorest quality. Many of them are put on sale only on special occasions—children's day, school fairs, library conventions, etc.,—because the channels of bookselling are so poorly developed, and because the average Thai family (even the educated one) seems resistant to the reading habit. Illiteracy is not as prevalent as might be imagined but oral tradition is still the most powerful didactic force, and teaching methods have not been sufficiently altered to make the transition from oral to spoken word a natural and spontaneous one. Consequently, there is little to inspire the parent or child to buy books on his own.

The few public and school libraries which exist are the best purchasers, and would be better ones, were they supplied with an adequate budget for books. Most do not circulate their books but have been able to stimulate an interest in the books they possess so that there is constant demand by children to read them on the premises. The Thai Library Association is doing much to stress training of the staff in special methods of work with children. They have also begun an experiment in the publication of books for children.

2520. Anglemyer, Mary. "Village book room," *Library journal*, New York, Vol. 83, Nov. 15, 1958, pp. 3272–3273. DLC, NNY.

A reading room in a village in Ubol was set up on the instigation of a student from the rural teacher training school. He began a program of reading aloud each evening to the children and adults which proved to be popular with the entire village.

2521. Ansari, A. Rahnema. "Suggestions in a research on the children's reading," *T.L.A. bulletin*, Bangkok, Vol. 10, No. 1, Jan.–Feb., 1966, pp. 42–46. APP.

The author makes suggestions for standards to follow in observing and testing the reading tastes of children. There is also an editorial, "Children's reading problems," pp. 57–59 in this issue devoted almost entirely to children and books. Text in Thai.

2522. Chavalit, Maenmas. "Some observations about books for children and juveniles," *T.L.A. bulletin*, Bangkok, Vol. 10, No. 1, Jan.–Feb., 1966, pp. 29–33. APP.

The author took part in the UNESCO regional seminar on children's literature in Teheran (see 2365). These are some comments on statements made at the seminar, and on children and books in general. The author quotes from May Hill Arbuthnot and Dorothy Neal White (2946). Text in Thai.

2523. ———. *Survey of preparation, production and distribution of literature for children and juveniles in Thailand*. Bangkok, Ministry of Education, Department of Educational Techniques, 1966. 16p. APP.

In addition to the points mentioned in the title, this also covers a brief history of the development of children's books in Thai, statistics on school libraries, and a list of agencies and organizations engaged in publishing children's books. This is an invaluable source of current information, in spite of the inaccuracies in some of the statistics, which the Ministry is now revising.

2524. Manich Jumsai, M. L. *Compulsory education in Thailand*. Paris, UNESCO, 1951. 110p. (Studies in Compulsory Education, 8). DLC, NNY.

One of a series which documents the history of education in many countries and areas of the world. These are valuable as background studies since they contain information not easily found in the usual histories of education. Frequent mention is made of the availability (or lack of it) of children's reading materials.

2525. *Reading materials situation and programme in Thailand.* n.p., n.d. 19p. Mimeographed. APP.

This document was prepared in the Ministry of Education offices as a preliminary appraisal of the status of children's books (including text books). It includes specific titles and series, which have appeared in Thai, through official, semi-official and private publishing houses.

2526. Spain, Frances Lander. "Library development in Thailand, 1951–65," *UNESCO bulletin for libraries,* Paris, Vol. 20, No. 3, May–June, 1966, pp. 117–125. DLC, NNY.

Dr. Spain was twice in Thailand as a special lecturer in library service at Chulalongkorn University. This gives a very general survey of development in the period mentioned with occasional references to school and public library work with children. The most outstanding of the latter is accomplished at the Sala Wan Dek in Bangkok. It is a children's library under the Ministry of Education with trained staff and a regular program designed for children.

2527. Sunthara, Maria Lou. "A survey of Thai children's interests," *T.L.A. bulletin,* Bangkok, Vol. 10, No. 1, Jan.–Feb., 1966, pp. 24–28. APP.

An article based on tests made in the International Institute for Child Study. This is actually concerned most with the teaching of reading. Text in Thai.

2528. Thai Library Association. *Rai chue nang sue sam-rab dek phu yao phrom duao bhanithas.* Bangkok, Thai Library Association, 1965. 104p. APP.

A booklist prepared by the Thai Library Association in cooperation with the Asia Foundation. More than 500 Thai children's books are annotated. Translations are easy to locate because they are given in the original title as well as in Thai.

Cambodia, Laos and Viet Nam

2529. Bilodeau, Charles. *et al. Compulsory education in Cambodia, Laos and Viet Nam.* Paris, UNESCO, 1955. 157p. (Studies on Compulsory Education, 14.) DLC, NNY.

One of a series which documents the history of education in many countries and areas of the world. These are valuable as background studies, since they contain information not easily found in the usual histories of education. Frequently, mention is made of the availability (or lack of it) of children's reading materials.

China

Because of present political tensions it is virtually impossible for an accurate exchange of information to take place between China and the West. This section can only survey a pitifully small proportion of the materials which describe the history and development of children's books in this vast country.

Since there were no public schools until after the revolution of 1911, the few children who got to read anything at all were either of the privileged ruling families or were among those fortunate enough to have found a place in one of the private or missionary schools. Sometimes groups of families banded together to form a "school," to which each family could send its most gifted son. Under the old system of education, this "school" was very different from present-day institutions. Children began at seven or eight years of age, and their progress depended largely on their ability to memorize. Beginning with the "three-word classic," and then going on to the "hundred family names," the "thousand word classic," the "filial piety classic," etc., the young student continued until he was ready to take the civil examinations. Not until after the Boxer Rebellion was educational reform begun, and then the few existing schools were thrust into chaos because teachers were not equipped to shift to Western style education. The exceptions were the schools run by the missionaries and a few other private institutions. When the republic was founded in 1911, one of the greatest tasks to be faced was the establishment of schools for the 60 to 70 million children and young people who had previously had no chance at education.

These children and their predecessors had not gone entirely without a literature. Oral narration was practised in many forms, as was popular theater. The stories which children were thus exposed to were largely based on the exploits of legendary or folk heroes. Some of these were: Hsu Wen Chang, a trickster judge who had failed his civil examinations but usually won out by his cunning (he resembles closely the Hodja character in Turkish folklore), Lu Tung Ping, a young man who met a Taoist priest and then shared his adventurous wanderings; Chao Kwang Yin and Chu Hing Wu, heroes from the lower classes who saved the country from barbarians; Hsuan Tsang, a priest who traveled to India and brought back many Buddhist stories, among them the monkey tales which later got mixed up with other motifs of Chinese folklore; the brigands, outlaws and rebels of the 12th century whose adventures were recorded in the *Shui Hu Chuan;* Pao Chen, and 11th-century judge of great wisdom who is one of the central figures in the folk cycle known as the *Adventures of the Eight Knights.* All of these stories and many more were popular with the general reading public, and were constantly remodeled into new styles and forms in succeeding centuries. They became standard repertoire in the shadow plays and the professional storyteller was judged by how well he could remember and tell a beloved version. In later years there were added to these legendary tales the stories of filial piety (two parts of 24 stories each), the recounting of the creation of the gods of Taoism and Buddhism, and the *Wonderful Voyages of Li yu Chin,* a kind of Chinese *Gulliver's Travels.* By the late 19th century, all stories such as these were usually written and told in the vernacular, or *pai hua,* and as such they were not recognized as literature by the educated Chinese, who might speak in *pai hua,* but who wrote and read only in *wen yen,* the literary form of the Chinese language. In 1917, Hu Shih announced a movement to substitute *pai hua,* the living language, for the outmoded and artificial literary *wen yen.* This is the beginning of what is usually called the "literary renaissance." It established *pai hua* as a respectable, even preferred, form of creative expression, and profoundly affected all writing from then on.

The first considerations of literature as being specifically written for children, or selected from the classics with only their interests in mind, did not appear until the 20th century. The most influential figure to emerge as a critic was Lu Hsün. He was born in 1881, and died in 1936, and was thus almost an exact contemporary of Maxim Gorki, whose works and life are very similar. Lu Hsün first was known for his translations of Jules Verne, which he undertook while studying in Japan. Upon his return to China, he became involved in the political party of Sun Yat-Sen and with the revolution of 1911 definitely began to identify himself with the Communist-Socialist movement. In 1912, he was named a member of the Nanking Department of Education and then began writing about the failures of the old methods of teaching, prescribing new ways to replace them. He also wrote his first stories for children and continued his translations. His last years were filled with a deep interest in fairy tales, both Chinese and foreign. He gathered several collections from the old sources (particularly those of the T'ang and Sung dynasties, 600 to 1004 A.D.) and translated many from Russian and other foreign languages.

Although his theories of children's literature were not widely known while he was still alive, he became more and more important to the leaders of the Communist movement, and by 1950, he was accepted as the chief theorist in regard to children's literature and language education.

Because of his importance, it might be well to review here the basic ideas expressed in his writings. In his essay "How Are We Educating Our Children?" he pointed out that the most important books in children's lives are their school textbooks, yet these are given scant attention by educators and writers alike. He criticized the illustrations as being of poor quality and stereotyped, and stated that the ideas, content and format of children's books should express a totality of artistry and style. The ideological education of the child must also be served by good books. "We have only to observe foreign children's literature and foreign toys, which often teach the importance of weapons, to know the origins of war," he wrote. He believed that the traditional tales and stories were good and had a necessary place in the life of every child, but that a total diet of them was like giving food which had been stored a long time. There had to be as well a modern literature to satisfy the needs of the new classless society. The great classics of foreign literature should also be made available to Chinese children, so that they could have a common ground of understanding, but the more modern works (except those of Russia) were not always in keeping with the spirit of the new era. The greatest emphasis in Lu Hsün's writings on children's literature is given to folk and fairy tales. Some showed the imperialistic influence and were to be deleted from children's collections, but the majority caught the spirit of the revolutionary struggle of the common man and showed the breadth of his imaginative spirit. Fairy tales reflect the craving of every man for a happy life, they show the good qualities and wisdom of the folk and use poetic expressions to recount the beauty of human hopes and progress (2541).

Another educator who was deeply concerned with the problem of reading was Yen Yang-chu, best known by his Western name, James Yen. He had devised a system of teaching reading through the use of 1,000 basic characters. Initially tried out among the Chinese laborers sent to Europe during the First World War, this gradually spread into a literacy campaign of vast proportions in China. It involved the writing and printing of books and periodicals using the 1,000 basic characters (later expanded to 1,300) since ordinary reading materials were not suited to the new literate. Although most of this work was accomplished with adults, the implications of the program stretched into the teaching of reading to children as well. Unfortunately, this movement came to an abrupt halt with the Japanese invasion of 1937, and the gradual disintegration of China's internal politics prevented a later resumption of the literacy campaign modeled on the Yen system.

Still another movement which gained some impetus in the 1920's and 1930's was that concerned with children's libraries. Word of Western progress in this area began to spread, and many educational and cultural journals contained articles on the importance of children having access to good books. There was even a recognition of the need to provide children with interesting and lively reading materials in the home, although the idea that they must also teach respect was still inherent. In 1920, the Boone Library School was founded in connection with Boone University, a Christian school. It included some teaching on children's services in its curriculum.

According to Ruth Hsü, there was a strong interest in nursery rhymes among folklore and literature scholars at National University in Peking, in the late 1920's and early 1930's. They gathered and published some collections, from which she eventually made her translations (2548). These rhymes are characterized by humor and an "inability to take anything seriously." Their similarities to the Mother Goose rhymes are often quite striking.

The contemporary scene must be looked at from three angles: the situation on the mainland, in Hong Kong and on Taiwan. The People's Republic of China controls virtually all of mainland China. Latest figures in most source books indicate a population well over 700,000,000. Education is given high priority and is based on Marxist principles. Books are an intrinsic part of that education, and those for the young are given special attention.

Children's literature is modeled on that of the U.S.S.R. and published in huge amounts. This serves the dual purpose of satisfying the public hunger for reading materials and guiding the new generation into patterns of thinking along Marxist lines. Libraries and reading rooms have been opened in great numbers, and book stalls have mushroomed on street corners in all the cities and towns. Because children are taught to read by using simplified characters and romanized letters (according to the Pin Yin system), they have been able to learn to read much more quickly than previous generations. Some traditional scholars regard this as an emasculation of the Chinese language; nevertheless, it has helped to bring the written word to an unprecedented number of persons who would otherwise not be literate.

Since the Foreign Languages Publishing House prints works in all the major languages of the world, it is possible to judge some of the contemporary children's books. They are usually attractively illustrated, printed on cheaper quality paper, and range over broad subject areas. The language is often didactic in tone, although light-hearted humor is also evident. There are many translations from the Russian, and from the other countries of the communist group.

Hong Kong is a Crown Colony of the United Kingdom, comprising numerous islands and a small portion of adjacent mainlaind area. It has a population estimated at close to 4,000,000, of which more than 1,000,000 are refugees from communist China. This has created grave problems, and education is one of the means being used to help solve them. Children are served by public and school libraries, which try their best to reach the refugee areas as well. There is some publishing done in Hong Kong, and the books from the mainland as well as from Taiwan are also widely available.

Curiously enough, it is almost as difficult to obtain information on children's books from Taiwan as it is from the mainland. While a number of educational journals have mentioned in general the progress being made in developing not only books, but libraries for children as well, few sources specifically describing these programs could be located. UNICEF and UNESCO have cooperated on a project to produce sets of children's books to be used as supplementary reading in the schools. It is possible to trace other children's books through one of the national bibliographies (2540).

2530. [Articles on children's libraries], *Wen hua t'u shu kuan chuan k'o hsüeh hsiao chi k'an, Boone library school quarterly*, Wu-chang, Vol. 9, Mar., 1937. DLC, NNY.

Articles include: "Survey of the school libraries in Kwangsi province" by Chung Chia Li, pp. 17–28; "Training of children's librarians," pp. 60–91; "Library service for children in China" by Ruth A. Hill, pp. 155–163. The first two are in Chinese, the last is in English.

2531. Bishop, Claire Huchet. "What Chinese children read," *Commonweal*, Philadelphia, Vol. 82, No. 10, May 28, 1965, pp. 323–325. DLC, NNY.

A French-American librarian and children's book writer comments on the wide variety of Chinese children's books she has seen in France, but not in the U.S. In spite of their inexpensive format she praises these books for the excellent quality of illustration and good text. For the most part, they fell into the categories of folk tales, modern didactic tales, and Communist stories.

2532. Brunhes-Delamarre, Mariel-Jean. "Lectures pour jeunes en Chine nouvelle," *Enfance*, Paris, No. 3, 1956, pp. 187–190. IYL.

The author reports on impressions gained by a recent visit to China. There were many libraries for children and young people; three special ones are in the national library, in the Shanghai Pioneers' Palace, and in a park in Peking. The literature for children is "exultant, optimistic, and having themes which glorify the fatherland and the heroes of the people."

2533. Ch'en, H. "On the improvement of middle school libraries in Chekiang province," *Chekiang kuan-k'an*, Hangchow, Vol. 2, Feb., 1933, pp. 29–38. NNY.

The writer describes the sad state of school libraries in this area. Most of the funds for books had been withdrawn, and very little professional attention was given to the existing collections. Text in Chinese.

2534. Chen, Kuang-Yao. "An attempt at compiling a bibliography of Chinese folk literature," *Boone library school quarterly*, Wuchang, Vol. 3, No. 4, Dec., 1931, pp. 433–443. NNY.

A bibliography of some 100 items all in Chinese.

2535. Chen, P. T. H. "China's tricycle libraries," *Library journal*, New York, Vol. 67, Feb. 15, 1942, 138p. DLC, NNY.

A librarian describes a plan for small travelling libraries which would reach all the children in Shanghai.

2536.　Ch'ên, Po-ch'ui. *Êrh t'ung wên hsüeh chien lun*. Wu-han, Ch'ang-chiang wên yi, 1959. 302p. DLC.

"A brief discussion of children's literature." There are chapters on the history and theory of children's literature in China, on foreign translations available in Chinese, and on folk-lore and its interpretation. There are examples of stories given, with this critic's opinions of them, and their value in the education of children.

2537.　——. *Tso chia yü êrh t'ung wên hsüeh*. Tien-Tsin, People's Publisher, 1957. 104p. DLC.

"The author and children's literature." Essays based on the works of Lu Hsün, Andersen, Gorki, Gaidar, and others, concerning children's literature and its significance. The majority of the essays are from Lu Hsün, who is considered the leading Chinese theorist on this subject, as well as being a writer of many children's books. His theories are based on Marxist-Leninist principles.

2538.　[Children and the home library.] *Fu nü tsa chih, The ladies' journal*, Shanghai, Vol. 13, No. 7, July 1, 1927, pp. 65–68. DLC.

The importance of having good books in the home, how to choose and organize a home library and the value of reading aloud and storytelling. The article recommends giving children more freedom of choice, and not insisting only on books which will help him in school or teach him something.

2539.　"Children's Library Number." Special issue of: *T'u shu kuan hsüeh chi k'an, Library science quarterly*, Peiping, Vol. 10, No. 1, Mar., 1936, pp. 1–162. DLC, NNY.

Articles include: "Experience in running children's libraries" by Ven-ch'i Lee, pp. 1–29; "Planning and equipment of children's libraries" by Chia-pi Hsü, pp. 69–82; "Training of children's library workers" by Shu-yuan Leng, pp. 83–89; "Book selection for children's libraries" by Tze-ch'iang Sun, pp. 147–152; "Periodical articles on children's libraries" by Chün Ting, pp. 153–162; "Proposal to install children's libraries in public elementary schools" by Pe-nien Wang, pp. 31–60; "The place of children's libraries in elementary schools" by Te-lin Lu, pp. 61–68; "A general survey of ancient children's literature" by Yen-cheng Wung, pp. 91–146. Text is entirely in Chinese.

2540.　"Children's literature," *The monthly list of Chinese books*, Taipei, Vol. 5, No. 11–12, Nov.–Dec., 1964 ff. DLC.

This list, published by the Bibliography Center of the National Central Library, began, with this issue, to include selected titles of children's literature. Text is in Chinese and English, and bibliographical information is quite complete. Not every monthly issue has this section, but it does appear in at least half of the issues for each year.

2541.　Chou, Shu-jên. *Lu Hsün lun êrh t'ung chiao yü ho êrh t'ung wên hsüeh*. Shanghai, Youth Press, 1961. 86p. DLC.

"Children's literature and education from Lu Hsün's point of view." A selection and editing of the major ideas which this theorist expressed. Lu Hsün's first work in children's literature was a translation of Jules Verne into Chinese. However, he soon became more concerned with the broader issues, and although he wrote many short stories for children, his importance is largely due to his critical and theoretical works. Most of these were in essay form, and selections from them are included here. He felt that the literature given to children in China was not adequate—neither in quantity nor quality. He criticized both text and illustrations for their banal and stereotyped expressions. He expressed indignation at the misuse of parental power, and the instilling of blind obedience to out-moded and ultra-conservative patterns of thinking.

2542.　Chueh, Be-Tsung. "The influence of reading on children," *Boone library school quarterly*, Wuchang, Vol. 9, No. 2, June 15, 1937, pp. 169–172. NNY.

Text in Chinese.

2543.　Douglas, Mary Peacock. *Hsiao-hsioh t'u-shu-kuan*. Taipei, Cheng Chung Book Co., 1964. 118p.

A translation of 3676, made by Chen-ku Wang.

2544.　[The educational value of the children's library.] *Chiao yü tsa chih, The educational review*, Shanghai, Vol. 18, No. 3, Mar., 1926, pp. 1–2, DLC.

There are too few schools in China which stress the importance of books and libraries. Many primary school children see only text-books throughout their entire school life, and have no notion of the pleasure reading can bring. The article then outlines the educational reasons why each school should have a library.

2545.　Fang, Chi-shêng. *Êrh t'ung wên hsüeh shih lun*. Pao-ting, People's Press of Ho-pei Province, 1957. 97p. DLC.

"An elementary discussion of children's literature." The present situation of children's literature, its responsibility to the child, the main themes, kinds of fairy tales needed in China today, the special features of children's poetry and a brief history are covered in this book.

2546. Gleave, Betty M. "Hong Kong," *Library service to children, 2.* Lund, Bibliotekstjänst, 1966, pp. 36–45. DLC, NNY.

This publication was sponsored by IFLA (see 32). In this chapter, the history and present status of library service to children in the crown colony of Hong Kong are discussed.

2547. Headland, Isaac Taylor. *Chinese rhymes for children, with a few from India, Japan and Korea.* New York, Fleming H. Revell Co., 1933. 156p. DLC.

This extensive collection in translation was meant for children, but it contains a preface which has good source information.

2548. Hsü, Ruth. *Chinese children's rhymes.* Shanghai, Commercial Press, 1935. 98p. NNY.

A collection of traditional rhymes and game songs, translated into English. There is an 11 page introduction by the compiler which gives some of the history and background of children's rhymes in Chinese.

2549. [The importance of children's literature.] *Chiao yü tsa chih, The educational review,* Shanghai, Vol. 18, No. 3, Mar., 1926, pp. 4–6. DLC.

Children's needs are different from those of adults, and their literature should reflect this. Some of the qualities it should have are: liveliness of language, ethical in tone but not openly didactic, realism in its portrayal of present-day children.

2550. Lin, S. [Children's books: how to select them.] Shanghai, China Library Service, 1935.

A list of 76 titles.

2551. Lindeman, Norma C. "The kindergarden and the library," *Boone library school quarterly,* Wuchang, Vol. 4, No. 1, Mar., 1932, pp. 67–74. NNY.

Translated into Chinese by Huang, Lian-Tsin.

2552. Mei-lan, Sun. "Illustrations for children's books," *Chinese literature,* Peking, No. 6, June, 1959, pp. 149–152. NNY, DLC.

The characteristics of some of the artists' styles in contemporary children's books in China.

2553. Shang, Chung I. *A method of selecting foreign stories for the American elementary schools: Applied to the evaluation of stories translated by the author from the Chinese folk literature.* New York, Columbia University Teachers' College, 1929. 46p. (Contributions to Education, No. 398.) DLC.

For note, see 4304.

2554. Shang-hai shih nien wên hsüeh hsuan chi pien chi wei yüan hui. . . . *Êrh t'ung wên hsüeh hsüan.* Shanghai, Shao nien erh t'ung ch'u pan shê, 1959. 607p. DLC.

A comprehensive selection of children's literature from 1949–1959, preceded by an essay on the importance which children's literature has in the new China, its purpose of educating youth in Communist ideals, and its revolutionary spirit. The selections are arranged into short stories, essays, poetry and song, drama, and folk and fairy tales.

2555. Shaw, E. T. "School administrator's experiences in developing a library for primary and junior middle school students in China," *Educational review,* Shanghai, Vol. 22, 1930, pp. 166–175.

2556. Tseng, Hsien-Wen. "Children's library classification and cataloging," *Boone library school quarterly,* Wuchang, Vol. 1, No. 4, Dec., 1929, pp. 371–380. NNY.

A scheme for classification in Chinese.

2557. ———. "A study of the children's library," *Boone library school quarterly,* Wuchang, Vol. 1, No. 1, Jan., 1929, pp. 23–34—No. 3, Sept., 1929, pp. 251–258. NNY.

Text in Chinese.

2558. Wingate, R. O. "Children's stories from Chinese Turkestan," *London University, School of Oriental Studies, Bulletin,* Vol. 5, Part 4, 1930, pp. 809–822. NNY.

Three stories are given in the original Turki and in English, and the compiler then comments on the themes and their development. The Chinese influence is paramount.

2559. "Writing for the children," *Chinese literature,* Peking, No. 1, 1955, pp. 195–196. DLC, NNY.

In reviewing briefly the development of Chinese children's literature, the author states that there were almost no books for children prior to the revolution, because only children of the rich and upper classes were educated, and they were given mostly certain types of adult literature thought to be suitable also for children. In present-day China, there is an abundance of books. Between 1950–1952 more than 2,300 children's books in 41,600,000 copies were printed. Some of the most favored are those awarded prizes by the state.

2560. Wu-han. Ch'ang-chiang wên i ch'u pan shê.

Êrh t'ung wên hsüeh lun wên hsüan. Wu-han, Ch'ang-chiang . . . , 1956. 112p. DLC.

"A collection of articles on the new children's literature" edited and published by the Wuhan Literary Society Press. The 11 articles are concerned with such aspects as writing verse for the very young, the problems of children's drama, the realistic as opposed to the imaginative, the special problems of the fairy tale, etc. These articles all appeared in magazines and were selected as being among the most representative.

2561. Wylie, Margaret. "Children's reading,"

Children of China. Hong Kong, Dragonfly Books, 1962. pp. 49–64. DLC.

A general review of publishing, the "One Hundred Flowers" period and its effect on reading, and the systems of mass distribution in use throughout mainland China. Although the author's general tone is pro-Western and anti-Communist, she is objective in her citation of quotes, facts and statistics from many newspapers, periodicals and government publications of the mainland. This is an important and revealing chapter in the study of present-day Chinese children's literature.

Japan

Children's literature in Japan is approximately 100 years old. The earliest stages appeared in the first years of the Meiji era, from 1868–1876. Folding picture books, didactic tales and biographical stories began to appear in formats more distinctly designed for the young. In 1872, the promulgation of a new educational law spurred further interest. Translations from other literatures began to appear, notably *Aesop's Fables* (translated from the English text in 1872), *Robinson Crusoe,* and the *Arabian Nights* (1875). The first periodical for children, *Gakutei Shuhōroku* ("Fragrant Collection from the Learning Ground"), made its appearance in 1874. These were merely the forerunners, the first signs. The period of real birth was from 1877–1886, when the influence of Western civilization came storming along to blow away, as it were, the stilled air of traditionalism in Japan. Much of what these Western winds of change brought was mediocre, badly translated, or not suited to Japanese character or tastes. Nevertheless, translations abounded and their publishers became prosperous. There was at least one major effort to imitate, rather than translate. Impressed by the importance and number of nursery rhymes in Western languages, the Ministry of Education, collected and edited a study on Japanese nursery rhymes and songs. From 1887 to 1894 came a period of formation. Translations were continued, and a few native writers were feeling their way toward a new form and style. The educational system was still centered around royal, imperialistic ideals, but women and children were accorded a new dignity. In adult writing there was a momentous turning to realism. For the first time a conversational style was employed, using everyday terms. It took 10 years for this style to filter into and permeate children's literature. Meanwhile, children's books remained the privilege of the upper and middle classes, and thus reflected the typical taste of the bourgeoisie.

Among the first to break away even slightly from this tradition was Sazanami Iwaya. His initial work was a 32 volume collection of children's literature (1891–1894). Only the first volume, *Kogane-*

maru, was his original conception. The remainder were translations or adaptations. All emphasized patriotism, loyalty to royal ideals and filial piety. In 1896, he published a 24 volume collection of Japanese fairy tales which were more independent in spirit. From then on he continued to edit and translate tremendous numbers of folk and fairy tales and novels, in which the story was the primary thing, and the language was patterned on the new conversational style. The moral found its place in many as well. These were chiefly published by Hakobunkan, which dominated the field of publishing for children. Through its multi-volume sets and its numerous periodicals it reached nearly all of the reading youth of Japan. At the same time it provided employment and a voice for the younger writers coming on the scene. In general, one can say that mass production of Japanese books for juveniles dates to this period, just at the turn of the century. Prototypes of a children's encyclopedia were developed. Daily and weekly newspapers for children had very high circulation figures. Still more translations came out, often "based on" a Western classic, rather than adhering to the original text. In 1907, the Ministry of Education began a system of prizes for the best pieces of juvenile literature.

In the period from 1914–1926, children's literature reached a climactic point in Japan. Interest in this new field waxed on all sides. Teachers and school administrators began calling for a new kind of reading material for children and accordingly Jido Bungaku was conceived by Tokyo Shuppansha ("publishing house") and issued in six different grade levels. The Japanese Nursery Rhyme Society was organized and initiated its studies of folk and nursery rhymes. A collection of Mother Goose rhymes was translated for the first time. Children's drama prospered, and the first modern, free verse for children was written. The publisher Fuzanbo brought out the *Shin-yaku Eiri Mohan Katei Bunko* ("Standard Illustrated Family Library"), the first deluxe editions of children's books in Japan. But most important, *Akai Tori* began publication in 1918. This periodical had much the same effect in Japan (on a smaller scale) as the *St. Nicholas Magazine* had had in the United States. *Akai Tori* ("Red Bird") was published monthly for children from 1818 to 1936, with a two year lapse from March 1929 to January 1931 when publication was interrupted. Its editor was Miekichi Suzuki and one of its chief contributors was Mimei Ogawa. Before long every writer of note was represented in its pages. Many of the stories which first appeared there are still being read by Japanese children, and are on the way to becoming "classics."

Both Suzuki and Ogawa had been strongly influenced by reading the translations of tales by Sazanami Iwaya. Suzuki turned to writing as a kind of joyful reaction to the birth of his first child. He did not write much after that, but rather edited, translated and adapted. Ogawa, on the other hand, was a tireless writer. He composed more than 100 tales in his lifetime and not one is recognizable as a translation or adaptation, either from a foreign or Japanese work. Koji Uno has characterized him as "headstrong, nervous and passionate in temperament" (2723).

While *Akai Tori* was at the peak of success, children's literature began a period of subtle, and then pronounced, transformation. During and after Japan's wars with China (1894–1895) and Russia (1904–1905) there had been a noticeable increase in patriotic and heroic stories, but they had not persisted to any great extent. From 1927 to 1937, however, one can trace a slow and then a swift rise in the appearance of militaristic and political themes. A new materialism began showing itself in children's books, and not only in their contents, but also in their physical make-up. Suddenly the publishers began competing for the largest markets, resorting to cheap, mass-produced books with no literary or artistic value. Several groups tried to counter this trend. A few outstanding picture-book series managed to survive longer than most. The chief resistance to governmental pressure for emphasis on militaristic, nationalistic themes came from Yuzo Yamamoto. He edited a 16 volume collection of children's stories for *Shinchosha* which had high literary standards and pacifist ideals. But the effort to maintain them in the fact of so much opposition eventually broke his spirit. Among the young writers who worked for Yamamoto was Momoko Ishii, who, after the war, was to become Japan's strongest and most outspoken champion in the struggle for good children's books.

During the war years children's books had to conform to standards set up by the Bureau of Social Education of the Ministry of Interior. They consolidated all magazines into 26 approved titles. Since many children were recruited to work in factories while still very young, there was little time or incentive to read. The books printed in these years can hardly be considered literature, although here and there one sees a story which appears to be devoid of any imposed message. There is an extensive collection of this literature in the Library of Congress. It was part of the masses of material confiscated at the end of the war by the occupation forces, and later released for study.

The postwar period brought with it an attempt at reconstructing the whole of children's education and culture. There was a humanistic trend in much of the writing for and about children. Many felt that at long last the chance had come to cast aside the restrictive impedimenta which had characterized traditional teaching methods in the imperialistic eras. A number of societies of writers and educators were formed, with aims to promote artistic value within the framework of a democratic ideal.

Because publishers were under strict observance of the occupation forces, they had to choose materials which would be quickly approved. The logical materials were existing translations of the world's masterpieces, so these were brought back in heavy doses, and still more were added. Many were translated so hastily that the original story can scarcely be recognized, but others were newly translated in very good style. Unfortunately these full-length books were soon overwhelmed by another type of import—the comic book and cheap illustrated magazine. The few other books and publications of literary merit simply disappeared under the weight of the millions of comics. The United States has been blamed for the comic strip and its dangers (real or supposed) in practically every country where such publications exist. No conclusive evidence could be located in print proving that the comics did or did not have their start in behind-the-scenes agreements between unscrupulous publishers, in the U.S., or elsewhere. To get involved in the most basic of inquiries would take more space than is possible here. The one question which does not seem out of order is: No matter what their origins, why were comics of the worst quality allowed to be published while at the same time many established Japanese classics were delayed or not published at all? Whether U.S. education officers, Japanese publishers or postwar circumstances get the blame, it is certain that the high hopes for artistic, democratic education were not always given a chance to mature.

It is this situation which Momoko Ishii deplores in so much of her writing on the subject of children's literature. She writes:

. . . few libraries were opened to children until after World War II, and the damage had been done meanwhile. We had almost lost touch with children's special way of thinking and their reactions to fun and artistic values. Several writers appeared who were considered to be of high literary standard, and parents and aunts bought their books for children. In fact adults thought so highly of these authors that they are still "big names" in the history of Japanese children's literature. But do children read their stories? Not very much today. Almost all these stories are short ones, full of sentiment, but with no plot or action (2603).

Good or bad, there is much discussion and writing done on the subject of children's literature. Many of the so-called histories are mere citations of names, dates and events. The critical works are not so much that, as explanatory. The repetitious titles cited in every bibliography often serve no other purpose than to get the name of a teacher or writer into print. This is unfortunate because it tends to lump the few good critics in with the rest, and the result is that no one seems to pay serious attention to any of them. If one perceptive scholar could be persuaded to spend several years in comparative study of the various eras of Japanese children's literature, and if he in turn could persuade a publisher to do justice to his study by careful reproductions of many illustrations, perhaps Japan would begin to assume her rightful place in the international picture.

Such a work might also provide the guidance needed by school and public librarians and by teachers. There are countless books on reading guidance available to them, but most are filled with high-minded theory expressed in the vaguest terms. Few of them offer really practical advice in approaching the right child with the right book at the right moment. This is in contrast to the number of fine, practical handbooks which are available for help in the technical side of setting up a library.

Critical studies aside, nothing would help further progress so much as more definite government support of the library laws already enacted, and more decisive leadership on the part of a few public and school librarians. This is very easy for an outsider to observe and comment on, but seemingly difficult for the insider to act upon. There exists a potential for excellent library service to Japanese children, especially in school libraries. There is even evidence of some highly innovative spirit at work among this group, which is more vociferous in its demands for better work situations than the present prevalent teacher-librarian system allows. Certainly the school librarians are better organized than public children's librarians, who also bemoan their lot, but in a less specific manner. It is very difficult to assess the precise points around which the problems evolve. Perhaps it is somewhat due to fear of reprisal, in a system whereby much public library administration is linked with political power. The one fact agreed upon is that library service to children is shamefully behind the times in Japan.

This is all the more crucial at this time, when children's books of good quality are beginning to appear in significant numbers. Publishers such as Kodansha, Kaiseisha and Fukuinkan Shoten are coming out with attractive series illustrated in many styles, yet with distinct Japanese flavor. The texts are printed in horizontal lines, which modern Japanese children seem to prefer to the vertical style. Translations of some of the best literature, Eastern and Western, are appearing regularly, and in full editions, rather than in badly adapted versions as was often the case in previous eras. All of this places Japan in a leading position among the Far Eastern nations, as far as children's literature is concerned. It is to be hoped that children's libraries will soon be able to assume a like position, for the emulation of both East and West.

2562.   Aoyagi, Kōichi, *et al. Shōgaksei no dokushu shidō kōza.* 6 vols. Tokyo, Iwazaki Shoten, 1957–1958.

"Reading guidance for elementary school children."

2563.   Chiba, Shōzō, *et al. Shinsen nihon jidō bungaku.* 2 vols. New ed. Tokyo, Komine shoten, 1959.

"Japanese juvenile literature." Shin Torigoe has written the section on the Wat period, Tadamichi Suga on the Showa period, and Ichitaro Kokubun on proletarian children's literature.

2564.   Chiba-Ken. Ichikawa-shi Dokushokai Renraku Kyōgikai. *Kodomo to okāsan no dokushokai kiroku.* Ichikawa City Library, 1962. 3 vols.

"Records of the mother-children reading club" of Ichikawa city library in Chiba prefecture.

2565.   ["Children and reading."] Special issue of: *Toshōkan zasshi, Library journal,* Tokyo, Vol. 52, No. 7, July, 1958, pp. 203–220. DLC.

The title article was done by Setsuko Hani, "A children's library and a public library" was written by Kōko Kanamori; "Miss Caroline M. Hewins" by Momoko Ishii; "The present situation of children's libraries in Japan" by Iishi Shōbun; "The course of school libraries in Japan for these ten years" by Matsuo Yataro, "Children's library and school library," a discussion by several leading librarians.

2566.   [Children's books and reading guidance.]

Kyōiku kagaku, Tokyo, No. 12, June, 1948, pp. 15–19. DLC.

One of a number of articles appearing on this subject in this educational periodical.

2567. [Children's literature and reading.] *Kyōiko fukkō,* Tokyo, Vol. 3, No. 3, Apr., 1950, pp. 2–37. DLC.

Subjects of some of the articles in this issue are book selection, a demand to publishers to produce better children's books, illustration, the direction of children's magazines, school library practice, reading guidance and book reviews.

2568. [Children's reading.] *Kyōiku daijesuto,* Tokyo, Vol. 1, No. 2, July, 1948, pp. 1–10, 28–32, 48. DLC.

The four articles include a study of the *Akai Tori* movement, list of recommended children's books, children's literature and culture and reading guidance.

2569. [Collection of storytelling materials for the classroom.] *Kyōiku techō,* Tokyo, Vol. 1 ff. No. 1 ff. Feb., 1950 ff. DLC.

A regular feature of this educational periodical was a selection from folklore or modern children's stories, with notes on how to use this material in storytelling. There were also reviews of children's books, and articles of general interest, on children and books, in almost every issue.

2570. Dokusho Shido Kenkyūkai. Yoi Hon o Susumeru Iinkai. *Yoi hon no risto.* 19? ff. Annual. DLC has sample.

A selective list of good books made annually by a committee of the Reading Guidance Circle.

2571. Douglas, Mary Peacock. *Gakkō toshōkan handobuk.* Tokyo, Maki Shoten, 1952. 177p.

A translation of 3676, made by Masai Watanabe.

2572. *Dōwa.* Tokyo, Nihon Dōwakai. Monthly. Vol. 1, No. 1, May, 1946—?

"Fairy tales," published by the Japanese Fairy Tale Society. This contained critical articles in each issue as well as examples of stories.

2573. *Dōwa kyōshitsu.* Tokyo, Kiri Shobō. Monthly. Vol. 1, No. 1, July, 1947—? DLC has sample issues.

"Classroom of children's stories," edited by Joji Tsubota. This included critical articles, as well as children's stories themselves.

2574. *Dōwakai.* Tokyo, Ie no Kyōikusha and Nihon Dōwa Kyōkai. Irregular. Vol. 1, No. 1, Nov. 1946—?

"The world of children's stories," devoted more to essays on children's literature than to actual publication of the stories.

2575. Ezuka, Yukio. *Gakkō toshōkan no techō.* Shizuoka, Shizuoka Kyōiku Kenkyūjo, 1950. 99p. DLC.

"A memo-book on the school library." How to begin establishing a school library: the plan, budget, furniture and equipment, selection and processing of the collection, staff, transformation of an old library into a new, standards, and setting up library activities. There is an extensive bibliography on the school library, and a price list of library furniture and equipment.

2576. Flory, Esther V. and Eiko Takahashi. "The Grimm and Andersen of Japan and other authors of children's books," *Horn book,* Boston, Vol. 37, No. 6, Dec. 1961, pp. 529–538, DLC, IYL, NNY.

Sazanami Iwaya is considered the Grimm of Japan, and Mimei Ogawa the Andersen. This reviews their contributions and comments on their different style. Whereas Iwaya was the translator and adapter of existing tales, all of Ogawa's stories were highly original, and there were more than a hundred of them, some book length. The work of Miekichi Suzuki is also important. Some of the recent authors whose works are briefly mentioned are: Hachirō Satō, Momoko Ishii, Hanako Muraoka, Hirosuke Hamada, Joji Tsubota, Sakae Tsuboi.

2577. [For the new culture of children.] *Kyōiku Kōron,* Tokyo, Vol. 5, No. 2, Feb. 1950, pp. 3–70. DLC.

The lead article is concerned with children's literature and the succeeding articles treat of children's art, drama and other cultural expressions and experiences.

2578. Fukagawa, Tsuneki. *Dōtoku kyōiku to dokusho shidō.* Tokyo, Kōfū Shuppan-sha, 1961. 346p. 6p. DLC.

"Moral education and reading guidance." The means of using books and reading in the character development of children. Some case studies are given as examples.

2579. ———. [History of school libraries in 1965.] *Toshōkan zasshi,* Tokyo, Vol. 59, No. 12, Dec., 1965, pp. 508–510. DLC.

The revision of the school library law and how it affected school libraries; the emphasis is placed on reading guidance.

2580.   Fukagawa, Tsunenobu. *Development of school library in Japan and its present condition.* Tokyo, Ministry of Education, 1950. 43p. Mimeographed.

2581.   Fukuda, Kiyoto, *et al. Jidō bungaku gairon.* Tokyo, Maki Shoten, 1963. 440p.

"An outline of Japanese juvenile literature." The Meiji era was covered by Michio Namekawa, the Taishō era by Eiji Iwaya, the Shōwa era by Shin Torigoe, and the postwar Shōwa era by Teruo Jingū. The bibliography was compiled by Shin Torigoe.

2582.   Funaki, Shirō. *Kaitei gendai jidō bungakushi.* Rev. ed. Tokyo, Bunkyōdō Shuppan, 1961. 464p. (1952 ed. pub. by Shinchōsha.)

2583.   ———. *Ogawa Mimei dōwa kenkyū.* Tokyo Hōbunkan, 1954. 295p. ff. 7p. DLC.

"A study on the nursery rhymes and stories of Ogawa Mimei." Actually, this is as much on the ideas and persons which influenced his early thinking, and led to his writing for chldren.

2584.   Furukawa, Haruo. [Children's literature.] *Jidō bunka,* Tokyo, Vol. 1, No. 1, Sept. 1946, Unp. DLC.

This periodical, (Children's Culture), had many articles related to children's books and reading.

2585.   Furuta, Taruhi. *Jidō bungaku no shisō.* Tokyo, Maki Shoten, 1965. 205p. (Jidō bungaku kenkyū Series). DLC.

"Thoughts on children's literature." A defense of the tradition of Mimei Ogawa and Joji Tsubota, as part of the literary heritage of Japanese children, is followed by a summary of postwar and modern children's literature, comments on the problems of mass-communication media, and the popularity of war stories.

2586.   Furuya, Tsunatake. *Jidō bungaku no techō.* Tokyo, Ikuseisha, 1948.

"Memo-notes on juvenile literature."

2587.   *Gakkō toshōkan.* Zenkoku Gakkō Toshōkan Kyogikai; Tokyo-to, Bunkyo-ku, Suidō-chō 30. Monthly. Vol. 1 ff., 1950 ff. Annual subscription: 80 yen.

"School library," published by the National Council on School Libraries.

2588.   *Gakkō toshōkan sokuhōhan.* Zenkoku Gakkō Toshokan Kyogikai; Tokyo-to, Bunyko-ku, Suidō-chō 30. 3 times monthly (every ten days). Vol. 1 ff., 1954 ff. Annual subscription: 20 yen.

"School library newsletter," published by the National Council on School Libraries.

2589.   *Gakkō toshōkan tosho kyōiku.* Tokyo, Meguro Shoten. Monthly. Vol. 1, Oct. 1949—? DLC has sample copies.

A periodical devoted to problems of reading guidance and use of the school library. It was aimed at children and teachers, and included annotated book lists and book reviews.

2590.   *Gendai jidō bungaku jiten.* Tokyo, Hōbunkan, 1955. 452p. 60p. DLC.

"A dictionary of modern juvenile literature." Alphabetically arranged are terms used in the study and history of juvenile literature, authors' names, titles of well-known works, famous characters, critical studies, and surveys for each era for foreign literature as well as Japanese. There are some 612 entries written by 30 authorities, each signed. This is intended for libraries, and for children (to help them toward independent reading). Bibliography and index. The general editing was done by Tsunatake Furuya and others, under the supervisions of Mimei Ogawa and Yasunari Kawabata.

2591.   Hamanaka, Shigenobu. *Yōji to hon; dokusho shidō no jissai.* Tokyo, Saera (Sa.E.Ra) Shobō 1962. 254p.

"Infants and books; practice of reading guidance."

2592.   Harada, Naoshige. [Personal view on education through children's stories.] *Gakkō kyōiku,* Hiroshima, No. 389, Apr. 1950, pp. 21–25. DLC.

Experiences in working with children through storytelling, reading aloud and book discussions.

2593.   Hasegawa, Seiichi. *Nihon jidō bungaku jiten.* Tokyo, Kawade Shobō, 1954.

"An encyclopedia of Japanese juvenile literature."

2594.   Hatano, Kanji. *Jidō bunka.* Tokyo, Kokudosha, 1956. 322p. DLC. (Kokudosha Kyōiku Zensho, 4).

"The culture of children." Although this is a general study of the development and importance of cultural activities for children, Part 2, Chapters 1–6 (pp. 89–243) and Part 3, Chapters 1–2 (pp. 289–322) are on books and reading, magazines, children's theater, puppetry and other subjects related closely to literature.

2595.   ———. *Jidō shinri to jidō bungaku.* Tokyo, Kaneko Shobō, 1950. 307p.

"Child psychology and juvenile literature."

2596. Hazard, Paul. *Hon, kodomo, otona*. Tokyo, Kiinokuniya, 1957. 270p.

A translation into Japanese made by Genkurō Yazaki and Masao Yokoyama. For note see 814.

2597. Hisayama, Yasushi. *Dokusho no hanryo*. Rev. ed. Tokyo, Sōbunsha, 1958.

"The reading guidance companion."

2598. Horibuchi, Teruzō. *Dokusho no atode dokusho kiroku no tsukeka-ta*. Tokyo, Saera (Sa.E.Ra) Shobō, 1953.

2599. [How to use the school library.] *Kyōiku gijutsu, shō-6*, Tokyo, Vol. 4, No. 7, Oct., 1951, pp. 54–58. DLC.

This educational periodical was printed in nine different editions, one for each grade level. Each issue contained frequent references to children's books and libraries.

2600. Hürlimann, Bettina. "Momoko Ishii and her place in Japanese children's literature," *Bookbird*, Vienna, No. 3, 1966, pp. 15–18. DLC, IYL, NNY.

A brief biographical and historical account of the work of this important figure in the Japanese children's literature movement.

2601. Hyōgo-ken Toshōkan Kyokai. *Toshōkan to watakushitachi*. Tokyo, Bunkyō Shoin, 1950.

2602. Ishida, Sakuma. *Gakkō toshōkan no setsuei*. Tokyo, Fukumura Shoten, 1954. 284p. DLC.

"Establishment and management of the school library." The author writes from the experience of planning and organizing for a new school library. He describes in detail the eventual collection and program. An appendix lists the Japanese decimal classification system, and the school library law. Illustrated.

2603. Ishii, Momoko. "American children's books in Japan," *Horn book*, Boston, Vol. 25, July–Aug., 1949, pp. 259–264. DLC, NNY.

A moving tribute to the power of books is inherent in these letters sent to the editor of *Horn book* by a leading critic and author of Japanese children's books.

2604. ———. [Children's books in Japan.] *Library association record*, London, Vol. 66, No. 3, Mar., 1964, pp. 98–99. DLC, NNY.

"It is very interesting to watch how much our children enjoy hearing some foreign stories and how much less they enjoy our own stories, although, of course, this is a sad experience for us adults. Children do not mind, as long as they are good stories, whether they are home-produced or not." In this objective self-appraisal of Japan's children's books, a leading native writer and critic points out: ". . . it is difficult to find the objective criticism of children's books which comes from long observation of children's reaction to books and from extensive knowledge of children's books themselves."

2605. ———. *Kodomo no dokusho no michibiki-kata*. Tokyo, Kokudosho, 1960. 206p. (Kodomo no mondai, 6). DLC.

"How to guide children's reading," written for use by librarians and parents. Miss Ishii writes of the importance of book selection, from the time when the child is just beginning to be interested in books, through his school days. She further explores the interests of children in the various stages, writes of the effects of mass communication media, and points out means of training children in good reading habits. The final chapters are reminiscences of her visits with rural children, and her experiences in Tokyo. She concludes with a list of 80 favorite books, annotated with her personal comments.

2606. ———. *Kodomo to bungaku*. Tokyo, Chūō Kōronsha, 1960. DLC.

"Children and Literature." A critical study of Japanese juvenile literature, in which the author compares and contrasts it with the standards of Western children's literature, especially as evidenced in books of fantasy.

2607. Iwaya, Sazanami. *Dōwa no kokasekata*. Tokyo, Kenbunkan.

"How to tell children's stories."

2608. Izawa, Jun and Takeshi Morufushi. *Dokusho ni yoru dōtoku shidō*. Tokyo, Meiji Tosho, 1965. 183p. (Dōtoku shidō shirīzu, 4). DLC.

"Moral guidance through reading." The formation of humanistic, moral and literary values through the use of good children's books. Sample cases are cited.

2609. Japan. Monbushō. *Gakkō toshōkan no tebiki*. Tokyo, Shihan Gakkō Kyōkasho K.K., 1948. 126p. ff. 11p. DLC.

"School library guide." The first handbook edited and published by the Ministry of Education, this pointed out the significance and mission of the school library in the new education. Photographs and diagrams illustrate many points, and there is a bibliography.

2610. ———. *Shō-chūgakkō ni okeru gakkō to-shokan riyō no tebiki.* Tokyo, Tōyōkan Shuppansha, 1961. 229p. DLC.

"A guide to use of school libraries in middle and elementary schools," published officially by the Ministry of Education and guided by their standards.

2611. "The Japan center of books for young people," *Toshōkan zasshi,* Tokyo, Vol. 52, No. 12, Dec., 1958, p. 413. DLC.

The Japanese section of IBBY was inaugurated in October, 1958.

2612. Jidō Bungakusha Kyōkai. *Jidō bungaku nyūmon.* Tokyo, Maki Shoten. 1957. 378p. DLC.

"Introduction to juvenile literature." The basic qualities which distinguish it, and some of the forms in which it is most common: fairy tales, nursery rhymes, poetry, etc. This is aimed largely at the person interested in writing for children. There is a bibliography, and an annotated list of 25 magazines which review and write about children's literature, as well as those which contain children's literature.

2613. ———. *Kodomo no hon konohyakunenten.* Tokyo, Jidō Bungakusha Kyōkai, 1965. 73p. IYL.

"Children and books during the past 100 years." A selective list of the best titles, arranged first by era and then by age or subject or type of book. Each is annotated. There is also a section for translations, and an extensive bibliography. This is edited and published by the Japanese Juvenile Literary Writers Association.

2614. *Jidō bungei.* Nihin Jidō Bungeika Kyōkai; Tokyo-to, Chiyoda-ku, Kanda Mizaki-chō 2–28, Tōkō Biru. Monthly? Vol. 1 ff., 1956 ff. Annual subscription: 50 yen.

"Juvenile literature," published by the Japanese Juvenile Literary Arts Society.

2615. Jidō Bungeika Kyōkai. *Jidō bungaku.* 3 vols. Tokyo, Kadokawa Shoten, 1956.

The first volume is edited by Kiyota Fukuda; the second by Joji Tsubota.

2616. *Jidō bunka.* Tokyo, Jidō Bunka Kenkyūjo. Monthly. Vol. 1, Sept. 1946–?

A review of children's culture.

2617. *Jidōshi kyōiku.* Shōnen Shashin Shinbunsha; Osaka-shi, Abeno-ku, Nishitanabe-chō 1–78. Monthly. Vol. 1 ff., 19? ff. Annual subscription: 120 yen.

"Children's Poetry Education."

2618. [Juvenile literature.] *Jidō hyakka dai jiten,* Tokyo, Jidō Hyakka Dai Jiten Kankokai, Tamagawa Gakuen Shuppanbu, 1936. Vol. 23, Part 2, pp. 352–513. DLC.

In this volume of a leading children's encyclopedia, there is an extensive historical study on children's literature, by era and by type, with some information on universal children's literature, but more emphasis on Japanese. Examples of each are included. The section on nursery rhymes is especially complete. Further on in the volume, there is a separate section on children's drama.

2619. [Juvenile literature.] *Kyōiku to shakai,* Tokyo, Vol. 2, No. 9, Sept. 1947, pp. 8–27, 42–44. DLC.

Following a general article on the status of children's literature are discussions of drama and the *kamishibai* for children.

2620. Kagoshima Kenritsu Toshōkan. *Oyako nijippun dokusho kenkyu hōkokushū.* 2 vols. Kagoshima, 1962.

"A study report on a mother-child reading project."

2621. Kamei, Katsuichirō., et al. *Dokusho shidō kōza.* 10 vols. Tokyo, Maki Shoten, 1955. DLC.

"Lectures on reading guidance." Vols. 1–3: Principles, psychology, and plan of reading guidance. Vol. 4: Guidance for kindergarten through 2nd grade. Vol. 5: Guidance for grades 3 and 4. Vol. 6: Guidance for grades 5 and 6. Vol. 7: Guidance for children in the middle school. Vol. 8: School library and reading guidance. Vol. 9: Reading materials for children. Vol. 10: Curriculum and reading guidance.

2622. Kan, Tadamichi. "Kodomo no yomimono no rekishi." Ishiyama, Shūhei; *Kyōiku bunkashi taikei,* Vol. 5; Tokyo, Kaneko Shobo, 1954.

"History of children's reading materials."

2623. ———. *Nihon no jidō bungaku.* Tokyo, Otsuki Shoten, 1956. 327p.

"Japanese juvenile literature."

2624. Kanzaki, Kiyoshi. *Ai to chi no dokusho; atarashii bosei no tameni.* Tokyo, Tokuma Shoten, 1962. 383p.

"Reading for love and knowledge; a guide for new mothers."

2625. Kawazaki, D. [The birth of a children's story.] *Kyōiku to shakai,* Tokyo, Vol. 4, No. 1, Jan., 1949, pp. 49–51. DLC.

The author discusses how he creates stories for children.

2626. Kimura, Shōshū. *Meiji shōnen bunka shiwa.* Tokyo, Dōwa Shunjūsha, 1949. 378p. DLC.

"A history of juvenile culture in the Meiji era." This study treats of many subjects related to children and books such as drama, puppetry, libraries, songs, films, etc.

2627. —— *Shōnen bungakushi-meiji-hen.* 2 vols. Tokyo, Dōwa Shunjūsha, 1943, 1949. DLC has Vol. 1 of 1943 ed., 462p., and Vol. 2 of 1949 ed., 432p.

"A history of juvenile literature in the Meiji era." This covers the period of 1865–1912 when children's literature was in its infancy, but rapidly gaining in importance due to the new emphasis placed on child study. The 1949 edition is illustrated with black and white reproductions.

2628. Kishibe, Fukuo. *Dōwa no jissai to sono hihyō.* Tokyo, Heigo Shuppansha.

"The practice of storytelling and critical selection of stories." This includes translations from Sara Cone Bryant (3535), Julia D. Cowles (3633), and E. Porter St. John (4268).

2629. Kishida, Shōzō. *Taiken nijūnen shōgakkō ni okeru dokusho shidō.* Tokyo, Sōbunkan, 1949. 112p.

"20 years' experience of reading guidance in the elementary school."

2630. Kogawachi, Yoshiko. [Technical services for children.] *Toshōkan zasshi,* Tokyo, Vol. 59, No. 4, Apr., 1965, pp. 121–125. DLC.

How to approach children, and get the right book to the right child. The qualities of a good librarian and book selection and evaluation are also discussed.

2631. Kokubun, Ichitarō, *et al. Bungaku kyōiku kiso koza.* Tokyo, Meiji Toshō, 1957.

"Lectures on basic literary education." Included are sections by Tadamichi Kan, Hideo Seki, Taruhi Furuta and Shin Torigoe.

2632. ——. *Seikatsu kiroku.* Jidō bungaku. Tokyo, Miraisha, 1957.

"A life document. Juvenile literature."

2633. Kubota, Hiroshi and Sentaro Morikubo. *Kodomo to hon.* Tokyo, Seibundō Shinkōsha, 1955. 213p. (Kyōshitsu no techo series, 5.) DLC.

"Children and books." From the experiences of 80 persons who have worked with children these editors have compiled a series of short notes on reading guidance with all types of children. The closing portion includes 100 selections from foreign works for children. These editors also compiled *Gakkyū bunshū,* No. 11 in the same series, which is a collection of class compositions by Japanese children, based on their reading experiences.

2634. Kusano, Masana. *Nihon gakkō toshōkan shi gaisetsu.* Tokyo, Risōsha, 1955. 201p. DLC.

"A historical outline of the Japanese school library." Arranged chronologically, under the general periods of the aristocracy, the age of *samurai,* the era of the rise of the middle class, and contemporary times. Includes many statistical tables.

2635. Kyōiku Gijutsu Renmei. *Gakkō toshōkanhō ni yoru gakkō toshōkan no setsubi to unei.* Tokyo, Shōgakkan, 1954. 324p. DLC.

"The equipment and management of the school library, based on the school library law." Many short articles by leading school librarians cover all aspects of management and guidance. There is an annotated bibliography.

2636. Lohrer, Mary Alice. "Observations and impressions on school libraries in Japan," *School libraries,* Chicago, Vol. 10, No. 2, Jan., 1961, pp. 15–17, 33. DLC, NNY.

A school librarian from the U.S. records some of her experiences and impressions gained while on a teaching fellowship in Japan.

2637. Makarenko, A. S. *Jidō bungaku to jidō yomimono.* Tokyo. Shin Hyōronsha, 1955.

"Juvenile literature and children's reading materials," translated from the Russian (1956) by Junji Kitamura and others.

2638. Makimoto, Kusurō. *Puroretaria jidō bungaku no sho-mondai.* Tokyo, Sekaisha, 1930. 226p. DLC.

"Problems in proletarian juvenile literature." The merits and faults of traditional children's literature, particularly the fairy tale, and the ways in which modern proletarian writers can bring their works closer to reality.

2639. Mantarō, Joji. *Jidō bunka.* Tokyo, Nishimura Shoten, 1941.

"Children's culture."

2640. Matsumoto, Kenji. *Gakkō toshōkan.* Tokyo, Kaneko Shobō, 1948. 209p. (Kyōiku Gaku Zensh, No. 1.) DLC.

A brief history of the school library, and the problems it faces.

2641. Matsumura, Takeo. *Dōwa kyōiku shinron.* Tokyo, Baifūkan, 1929.
"New essays on fairy tales and education."

2642. ——. *Dōwa oyobi jidō no kenkyū.* Tokyo, Baifūkan, 1922.
"Fairy tales and children."

2643. ——. *Jidō kyōiku to jidō bungei.* Tokyo, Baifūkan, 1923.
"The education of children and children's literature."

2644. Mayer, Fanny Hagin. "The school library project at Naoetsu," *Contemporary Japan,* Tokyo, Vol. 19, Nos. 4–6, Apr.–June, 1950, pp. 227–233. NNY.

How a principal literally changed the reading habits of a whole community through persistence and good example in setting up a school library and making reading materials available to all.

2645. Melcher, Frederic G. "Japanese publications for children," *Top of the news,* Chicago, Vol. 4, Mar., 1948, pp. 14–15. DLC, NNY.

After his return from a visit to postwar Japan, this publisher had a number of pertinent comments on the state of children's books there. He found children to be reading chiefly periodicals.

2646. Miwa, Keiyū. *Gakkō toshōkan.* Tokyo, Iwasaki Shoten, 1952. 207p. ff. 19p. DLC.
The significance, nature and organization of school libraries, and the laws governing them in Japan.

2647. Miyazawa, Sanji. *Seinen dokusho no jissai.* Nagano, Shinyūsha, 1949.
"Practices of young people's reading."

2648. Mori, Ichirō. *Dokusho katsudō to gakushū shidō.* Tokyo, Shinsei Kyōiku Kenkyūkai, 1949.
"Reading activities and study guidance."

2649. Morikubo Sentarō. *Dokusho shidō 99 no sōdan.* Tokyo, Meiji Tosho, 1957. (Kyōshi no tameno sōdan sensho, 11).
"Consultations of 99 cases in reading guidance."

2650. Morishita, Iwao. [On the creative work of children's stories.] *Kyōiku kenkyū,* Tokyo, No. 19, Jan., 1948, pp. 29–33. DLC.
One of four articles on the subject of children's literature and reading. This monthly periodical which began in 1946 is called *The Study of Educa-*tion and frequently contained short articles of this nature.

2651. Muchaku, Seikyō. *Kodomo no hon 220-ssen.* Tokyo, Fukuinkan Shoten, 1964. 411p. DLC.
"A selection of 220 titles for children." Included are native works and translations. Arrangement is by age group, from preschool through 5th grade. Each entry is annotated, and gives a short passage from the text. A small reproduction from the illustrations of the book is also included for most of the titles.

2652. Murakami, Kan. *Katei narabi teigakunen dōwa hanrei.* Tokyo, Bunka Shobō, 1934. 544p. DLC.
"Examples of children's stories for family and elementary school use." An introductory chapter explains the use of stories in telling or reading aloud. The material is divided into lyrical or poetic stories for the very young child, and imaginative stories for the slightly older child.

2653. Murakami, Yuzuru. *Atarashii ohanashi no shikata to sono jitsurei.* Tokyo, Heibonsha.
"How to tell the stories, and examples."

2654. Murofushi, Takeshi. *Gakkō toshōkan shiryōron.* Tai 1, 2. Tokyo, Tamgawa Taigaku Tsūshin Kyōikubu, 1962.
"Essays on school library materials. Vols. 1, 2."

2655. Nagoya-shi Jidō Tosho Sentai. *Sentei jidō tosho mokuroku.* Nagoya, Sakae Toshokan, 19? ff. Yearly? DLC has Vol. 7, 1961–1962, 89p.
"Selected catalog of children's reading materials" edited by the Nagoya city children's literature selection committee.

2656. Namekawa, Michio. *Dokusho noto.* Tokyo, Maki Shoten, 196?.
"Reading notes."

2657. ——. *Dokusho shidō no jissen.* Tokyo, Maki Shoten, 1951, 282p.
"Practice of reading guidance."

2658. ——. *Gendai jidō bungaku jiten.* Tokyo, Shibundō, 1963, 218p. DLC.
"An encyclopedia of modern juvenile literature." The six parts of this book contain: 1) a geneology of juvenile literature study in Japan, translations of juvenile literature, juvenile literature in the European countries, and the geneology of proletarian juvenile literature; 2) essays on criticism; 3)

320

50 contemporary juvenile writers; 4) 100 selections from juvenile literature of the East and West; 5) writing, publishing and producing children's stories in books, theater, film; 6) discussion and conclusions.

2659. ———. *Jidō bungaku kenkyū bunken.* Tokyo, Shibundō, 1963.
"A bibliography of juvenile literature study."

2660. ———. *Jidō bungaku to dokusho shidō.* Tokyo, Maki Shoten, 1965. 194p. (Jidō bungaku kenkyū Series). DLC.
"Children's literature and reading guidance." The author opens with the importance of *Akai Tori* in the tradition of Japanese children's literature, and the clues it can provide to children's thinking. He then treats of the relationship between education and literature and some of the related problems of children's reading, such as comics.

2661. ———. *Kodomo manga no shidō—dokusho shidō.* Tokyo, Maki Shoten, 1959.
"How to guide children to comics—reading guidance."

2662. ———. *Kodomo no dokusho shidō.* Tokyo, Kokudosha, 1949 [1950]. 356p. DLC.
"Reading guidance for children." Theory and practice. On p. 64 is a list of organizations which recommend good books for children. Bibliography.

2663. ———. *Kodomo no dokusho dō michibiku-ka.* Tokyo, Maki Shoten, 1954. 262p. 4p. DLC.
"How to guide children's reading." The importance of reading, the best atmosphere and techniques to overcome children's resistance to reading, and the necessity of school libraries to assist in reading guidance.

2664. ———. *Manga to kodomo.* Tokyo, Maki Shoten, 1961. 240p.
"Comics and children."

2665. ———. *Seishōnen no dokusho shidō.* Tokyo, Kokudosha, 1950. 346p.
"Reading guidance for youth."

2666. ———. *Shōkokumin bungaku shiron.* Tokyo, Teikoku Kyōikukai Shuppanbu, 1942.
"A preliminary essay on children's literature."

2667. ———. *Toshōkan.* Tokyo, Maki Shoten, 1950. 347p. (Gakkō Toshōkan Bunko, No. 1.)
"The library—a reference book on the use of books and libraries for children."

2668. ———. *Watakushitachi no dokusho kurabu.* Tokyo, Kokumin Tosho, 1948. 120p.
"Our reading club."

2669. Nesbitt, Elizabeth. [Children's reading materials of today.] *Atarashii kyōiku to bunka,* Tokyo, Vol. 2, No. 10, Oct., 1948, pp. 18–21. DLC.
A translation of an article, whose source is not indicated.

2670. Nihon Dōwa Kyōkai. *Dōwashi.* Tokyo, Nihon Dōwa Shuppanbu, 1935.
"History of fairy tales" edited by the Japanese Fairy Tale Association.

2671. *Nihon jidō bungaku.* Jidō Bungakusha Kyōkai; Tokyo-to, Chiyoda-ku, Fujimi-chō 2–16, Nan-o Kaikan. Monthly, Vol. 1, 1955. Annual subscription: 120 yen.
"Japanese juvenile literature" published by the Juvenile Literary Writers' Association.

2672. Nihon Jidō Toshō Shuppan Kyōkai. *Yūryō jidō toshō sōgō mokuroku.* Tokyo, Nihon Jido. . . . , yearly? DLC has 1962 ed., 2 vols.
"General catalog of excellent children's books, edited and published by the Japanese Children's books, edited and published by the Japanese Children's Book Printers' Association." Vol. 1 contains material for elementary schools and Vol. 2 for middle schools.

2673. Nihon Shoseki Shuppan Kyōkai. *Nihon sōgō toshō mokuroku; jidōsho hen 1962.* Tokyo, Nihon Shoseki Shuppan Kyokai, 1961. 495p. DLC.
"Japanese general book catalog; children's literature section." Edited and published by the Japanese Book Publishers' Association. Contains 7,800 entries, which includes all books, comics, picture guides, encyclopedias and yearbooks available at the time. Entered alphabetically, under the general categories above, as well as age and subject categories. Each entry is given NDS classification number, and is briefly annotated. Prices are also included. Picture books are designated by P, comic books by C. Lists of the children's publishers, agents and dealers, societies and associations, dealing with children's books and reading, are found at the end, with current addresses. There are series and title indexes only.

2674. Nishihara, Keiichi. *Nihon jidō bunshōshi.* Tokyo, Tokai Shuppansha, 1952.
"A history of Japanese juvenile literature."

2675. Obara, Sunao. *Gakkō toshōkan gairon.* Tokyo, Ran Shobō.
"Outline of the school library."

2676. ———. *Gakkō toshōkan keiei no arikata.* 2nd ed. Ōsaka, Shinshindō, 1950. 157p. DLC.

"Managerial methods of school library." Chapters on technical processes as well as organization are given. An appendix includes the text of the Japanese library law, the standards for school libraries and the Nippon Decimal system.

2677. ———. *Gakkō toshōkan no sekkei.* Kyoto, Ran Shobō, 1955. 144p. DLC.

"Planning the school library." Many illustrations, photographs, designs, floor plans, etc., show the numerous methods of organizing and equipping the school library to suit the children's needs.

2678. Okamoto, Masaichi. *Seishōnen dokusho shidō.* Tokyo, Kōseikaku, 1943. 302p. DLC.

"Reading guidance for young people." Articles by many individuals covering all aspects of reading guidance.

2679. [On children's libraries.] *Toshōkan zasshi,* Tokyo, Vol. 58, No. 11, Oct., 1964, pp. 468–485. DLC.

This contains three articles: "My hope for children's libraries" by Momoko Ishii; "Present situations and problems in children's libraries" by Yoshiko Kogawachi; "Children's books" by Shigeo Watanabe; and an exchange of open letters between the directors of the city libraries in Yokosuga and Ōsaka on children's libraries.

2680. Ono, Noriaki. *Atarashii gakkō toshōkan-o tsukaraniwa.* Tokyo, Sōbunkan, 1949. 68p.

"To establish a new school library."

2681. Ozeki, Iwaji. *Jidō bungaku no riron to jissai.* Tokyo and Kyoto, Seki Shoin, 1949. 216p. DLC.

"The theory and practice of children's literature." The author characterizes the major trends in Japan, before and after the war, and points out the new directions which it is taking. There is also a chapter on the criticism of children's literature and one on arts related to children's literature.

2682. [Reading guidance.] *Kyōiku kaizō (Reformation of education),* Tokyo, No. 16, Sept.–Oct., 1948, pp. 2–50. DLC.

Several articles on the subject deal with reading guidance in the US as well as Japan.

2683. [Reading interests of elementary, middle and high school students.] *Kyōiku toshō nyūsu, (Education book news),* Tokyo, No. 4, Mar., 1950, pp. 7–9, DLC.

Each of the three levels is covered in a separate article followed by a list of new titles. This periodical had frequent articles on the school library as well.

2684. Sakamoto, Ichirō. *Dokusho no shinri.* Tokyo, Maki Shoten.

"Psychology of reading."

2685. ———. *Dokusho shidō—genri to hōhō.* Tokyo, Maki Shoten, 1951. 420p.

"Reading guidance—principles and methods."

2686. ———. *Dokusho shidō jiten.* Tokyo, Heibonsha, 1961–1962. 2 vols. Vol. 1, 469p. Vol. 2, 515p. DLC.

"An encyclopedia of reading guidance." Volume 1 contains general theory, methods of investigating children's reading interests, a list of organizations interested in work with children and books, and something about prize books. Volume 2 contains an article on the history and present situation of Japanese children's literature by Michio Namekawa, and other compositions on reading guidance, as well as illustrative selections.

2687. ———. *Dokusho shidō no tebiki.* Tokyo, Maki Shoten, 1955. 171p. 6p. DLC.

"A primer of reading guidance," its significance, the proper approach, and general selection principles. The diagnosis and correction of reading problems is treated briefly. Bibliographies.

2688. ——— and Michio Namekawa. *Dokusho sōdan.* Tokyo, Maki Shoten, 1952. 197p.

"Reading guidance."

2689. ———. *Manga to emonogatari—kodomo no dokusho to bunka.* Tokyo, Iwazaki Shoten, 1956.

2690. ———. *Shin dokusho-ron.* Tokyo, Kōdansha, 1959.

"New essays on reading."

2691. ———. *Shōgakusei no dokusho shidō kōza.* Tokyo, Iwazaki Shoten, 1958.

"Lecture series on reading guidance for elementary school children."

2692. ———. *Yomimono ni yoru seikaku keisei.* Tokyo, Maki Shoten, 1964. 178p. DLC.

"Character-formation through reading materials." This is one of several volumes, but the only one located. It classifies children's books according to aspects of character-building elements. The list of children's books is annotated.

2693. Satō, Tadayoshi. *Seishōnen no dokusho shisetsu.* Tokyo, Dai Nihon Shuppan Kabushiki Kaisha [1943]. 251p. DLC.

"Reading facilities for young people." The current situation in school libraries and libraries in factories for mobilized youth. The ideology of reading guidance is discussed in relation to Japan's political goals. Bibliography.

2694. [School libraries.] Special issue of: *Toshōkan zasshi,* Tokyo, Vol. 58, No. 2, Feb., 1964, pp. 48–63. DLC.

Articles included are: "The latest problems in the school libraries in Japan" by Jun Izawa, "Facing problems in the field" by Kisaburo Nakata; "What the public library can do for the school library" by Hiroaki Yamaoka and Saito Jutarō and "A new library in Hakuko High School, Tokyo" by S. Suzuki.

2695. [The school library has advanced up to this stage.] *Toshōkan zasshi,* Tokyo, Vol. 58, No. 2, Feb., 1964, pp. 50–53. DLC.

A case history of a particular elementary school library and how it has advanced in ten years.

2696. Sealoff, Georgia and Takeshi Murofushi. "Opportunities unlimited; Japan's school libraries," *School libraries,* Chicago, Vol. 7, Mar., 1958, pp. 20–23. DLC, NNY.

The history and development of Japanese school libraries with many statistics concerning the present status.

2697. Seikei Shōgakkō Dokusho Kenkyūkai. *Dokusho shidō no jissen.* Tokyo, Maki Shoten, 1951. 282p. DLC.

"The practice of reading guidance" edited by the reading study society of Seikei elementary school. Illustrated with photographs. Bibliography.

2698. Seki, Hideo. *Jidō bungakuron.* Tokyo, Shin Hyōronsha, 1955. 247p. DLC.

"Essays on juvenile literature." The nature, themes, and tendencies of past and present children's books. There are separate chapters on the leading writers of Japan, and on the fairy tales of Andersen, *Peter Pan, Alice in Wonderland* and *Robinson Crusoe.* The last section deals with selecting books for children, and storytelling.

2699. Shibata, Nobuo. *Jidō-shi kyōiku no hōhō.* Tokyo, Maki Shoten, 1964. 168p. DLC.

"Methods of children's poetry education." The importance of poetry in the life and education of the child, the use of poetry to stimulate the child's creative forces, and some examples of children's poetry.

2700. Shigekawa, Toshio. [Young adult services in the public library.] *Toshōkan zasshi,* Tokyo, Vol. 59, No. 4, Apr., 1965, pp. 126–129. DLC.

Young people must be taught that a library is not merely a utility, but a place for leisure and cultural enjoyment. Too many misuse it in Japan, by taking up space to do homework and studying for examinations—this is due to the extreme pressure put on them by the competitive system in Japanese secondary education.

2701. Sonobe, Saburō. *Nihon no kodomo no uta— rekishi to tenbō.* Tokyo, Iwanami shoten, 1962. 227p. (Iwanami Shinsho.)

"Japanese nursery rhymes—history and prospects."

2702. [Survey on *kamishibai* plays for children.] *Jidō shinri,* Tokyo, Vol. 4, No. 5, May, 1950, pp. 60–65. DLC.

A questionnaire survey on children's reactions to the *kamishibai,* the frequency of their attendance at street performances, what types they like, whether they have ever attempted making them on their own.

2703. [Survey on school children's reading material.] *Kyōiku,* Tokyo, Vol. 8, No. 2, Feb., 1940, pp. 71–78. DLC.

A survey undertaken among the children of Akita city to determine their reading interests. Results are given in statistical tables.

2704. Takayama, Tsuyoshi. *Kiki no jidō bungaku.* Tokyo, Mikamo Shobo, 1958. 235p.

"Juvenile literature at a crucial stage."

2705. Takenouchi, Inchirō. *Dōtoku shidō ni okeru yomimono no riyō.* Tokyo, Meiji Toshō Shuppan K.K., 1963. 197p. DLC.

"Uses of reading materials in moral guidance." The importance of selection for best results, the process of guidance, and some practical, illustrative cases.

2706. Takeshita, Naoyuki. *Gakkō toshōkan unei no jissai to dokusho shidō.* Tokyo, Nishiogi Shoten, 1954. 270p. DLC.

"Practice of school library management and reading guidance." Special emphasis is on teaching children the use of the library. There are chapters on the relationship between school and public libraries, on the school library in the U.S., and on the status of Japanese school libraries.

2707. Takeuchi, Zensaku. *Gakkō kōkyō toshōkan.* 2 vols. Tokyo, Tōkyōdō, 1950. Vol. 1, 250p. Vol. 2, 273p. DLC.

"School and public library" in reference to services for children. Vol. 1 covers building and equipment, organization and budgeting. Vol. 2 is largely on selection and processing of materials.

2708. Tenri Gakuen Gakkō Toshōkan Kenkyū kai. *Shōgakkō kara daigaku made toshōkan-ka no kenkyū.* Niwa (Nara Prefecture), Yōtokusha, 1950. 302p. DLC.

"A study on the subject of the school library, from elementary school through high school." A list of reference materials for each level is given. This was prepared by the School Library Research Club of Tenri Academy.

2709. Tōkai Chiku Gakkō Toshōkan Kenkyu. Taikai Jimukyoku, 6th. *Shūroku . . .* Nagoya, 1962. 76p.

"Proceedings of the 6th school library conference of the Tokai area."

2710. Tokyo. Gakugei Daigaku. Daiichi Shihan Fuzoku Shōgakko. *Shōgakko no toshōkan kyōiku.* Tokyo, Gakugei Toshō Shuppansha, 1949. 229p. DLC.

"Library education in the elementary school" prepared by the staff of the elementary school attached to the normal school at Tokyo Gakugei Daigaku (Fine Arts University). All aspects of library organization and management are treated briefly.

2711. Tokyo. Jido Kenkyūkai. *Jidō to yomimono.* Tokyo, Kaneko Shobō, 1952. 191p. (Jidō Mondai Shinshō, No. 21). DLC.

"Children and reading materials" edited by the Child Study Association of Japan. Sections are: "How to select books for children" by Ichirō Sakamoto; "The child who reads too much and the nonreading child" by Ryōichi Zukahara; "Bad reading materials" by Tadamichi Suga; "Collections of children's works" by Ichitarō Kokobun; and "School newspapers" by Shinji Ashitate.

2712. Torigoe, Shin. *Jidō bungaku gairon.* Tokyo, Maki Shoten.

"An introduction to juvenile literature."

2713. ———. *Jidō bungaku heno shōtai.* Tokyo, Kuroshio Shuppan, 1964. 208p. DLC.

"An invitation to juvenile literature." The nature, history and present situation and what there is in the future for writers of juvenile literature.

2714. ———. *Jidō bungaku nyūmon: Sekai meisaku no kodomotachi.* Tokyo, Kokudosha, 1962. 210p.

"An introduction to juvenile literature: Characters in classics."

2715. ———. *Jidō bungaku to bungaku kyōiku.* Tokyo, Maki shoten, 1965. 214p. (Jidō bungaku kenkyū series). DLC.

"Children's literature and teaching of literary values." The selection and evaluation of materials, mass communication effects on children's literature, and foreign folk and fairy tale literature for children are the three major topics from which the subject is approached.

2716. ———. *Nihon jidō bungaku annai.* Tokyo, Rironsha, 1963. 204p. DLC.

"Guide to Japanese juvenile literature." A chronological presentation by era, beginning with the late 19th century and continuing up to the present time. Foreign influences are discussed at length, as are children's magazines since they were the only media in which children's literature was available for the earliest period. The nursery-rhyme movement is of particular interest, for it paralleled and influenced that of Korea as well. The bibliography on pp. 190–204 provided many entries for the present work. This is the first volume of a projected set of three: the remaining two will deal with theory and history of world children's literature.

2717. Toshākōn Kyōiku Kenyūkai. *Dokusho kiroku no shidō.* Tokyo, Gakugei Toshō, 1956, 210 ff. 11 ff. 7p. (Tokusho Shidō Kenkyū Sōsho, 2). DLC.

"Guidance in taking reading notes." Teaching children to make notes on reading they do, both for study and recreational purposes.

2718. ———. *Toshōkan kyōiku-dokusho shidō no tebiki.* Tokyo, Gakugei Toshō, 1951. 383p. (Gakkō Toshōkan-gaku Sōsho, No. 2). DLC.

"Library education—a guide to reading guidance." Training children to use the library, and matching their reading needs with the curriculum.

2719. Tsubota, Jōji, *et al.* "*Akai Tori" daihyōsaku shū.* 3 vols. Tokyo, Komine Shoten, 1958.

"A collection of the representative work in *Akai Tori.*"

2720. Tsubota, Jōji. *Meisaku no kenkyū jiten.* Tokyo, Komine Shoten, 1960. 554p. DLC.

"Encyclopedia for the study of world masterpieces for children." More than 300 selections from children's books are here arranged by country. The largest number are Japanese, but England, France, Germany and Switzerland, U.S., and U.S.S.R., Scandinavia, southern Europe, and the myths of all the great religions are represented. Each is accompanied by one or more illustrations from the original, but greatly reduced. Children's books which have been made into movies are discussed separately.

2721. Tsutsui, Keisuke and Takashi Inui. *Kodomo ni yomasetai gojū no hon.* Tokyo, Sanichi Shobō 1963. 232p. DLC.
"Fifty recommended books for children." Actually, a digest of the contents of 50 foreign and native "classics" and some modern popular books. There is also one chapter on comics, another on a discussion about children's literature among five persons working in the field, and one chapter each on drama and photographic picture books.

2722. Uemura, Chōsaburō. *Gakkō toshōkan no uneihō.* Tokyo, Buntokusha, 1949. 205p. DLC.
"Managerial methods of the school library." An earlier version of the work in 2723.

2723. ———. *Setsubi to keiei no gijutsu gakkō toshōkan nyūmon.* Tokyo, Myogen Shobō, 1955. 244p. DLC.
"A primer of school library establishment and management." Includes a short bibliography.

2724. Uno, Kōji (Khoji). "Juvenile literature in Japan," *Contemporary Japan,* Tokyo, Vol. 9, No. 8, Aug., 1940, pp. 1025–1031. NNY, DLC.
The two major figures in the early stages of Japanese children's literature were Miekichi Suzuki and Mimei Ogawa. Both had been influenced by reading the works of Sazanami Iwaya, who was actually the first to write a book specifically for children (*Koganemaru,* 1891?). Suzuki was a northerner and his works show a characteristic sense of disillusionment; whereas Ogawa was a southerner and gave way more often to feelings of aspiration. They both published many of their works in *Akai Tori (Red Bird),* which Suzuki edited from 1918–1936. By 1928, children's literature was well established as a branch of writing.

2725. ———. "Nihon jidō bungaku shōshi," *Enpō no omoide.* Tokyo, Shōwa Shobō, 1941.
"A historical sketch of Japanese juvenile literature."

2726. Utsunomiya. Gakkō Toshōkan No Shiori Henshū Iinkai. *Gakkō toshōkan no shiori.* Utsono-

miya, Tochigi-ken Kyōiku Iinkai, 1950. 131p. ff. 31p.
"School library guide" edited by the Utsonomiya city commission on school libraries.

2727. Vining, Elizabeth G. "What the children read in Japan," *Top of the news,* Chicago, Vol. 7, Oct., 1950, pp. 3–7. DLC, NNY.
A woman who knew the Japanese intimately in the periods before and after the war here comments on the books Japanese children read, and the changes evident in their content when contrasted with the earlier period.

2728. Wada, Toshio. *Miyasawa Kenji no dōwa bungaku.* Tokyo, Nishiogi Shoten, 1950. 196p. DLC.
"The fairy tale literature of Miyasawa Kenji." Its qualities, how he came to write for children, and something of his life.

2729. Yanagida, Kunio. *Momotarō no tanjō.* Tokyo, Sanseido, 1933. 577p. ff. 20p. DLC.
"The birth of Momotaro" and other essays on fairy tales of Japan.

2730. Yashima, Sen. *Dokkai ryoku no bunseki to shidō.* Tokyo, Maki Shoten, 1963. 261p. DLC.
"Analysis of reading comprehension." Old and new methods of reading guidance are compared and the functions of reading are explored at length.

2731. Zenkoku Gakkō Toshōkan Kyogikai. *Gakkō toshōkan-gaku kōza.* 40 vols. Tokyo, Meiji Tosho Shuppan, 1953–?
"Lecture series on school library science."

2732. ———. *Gakkō toshōkan-ho no kaisetsu.* Tokyo, Meiji Tosho Shuppan, 19.
"Interpretation of the school library law."

2733. ———. *Gakkō toshōkan jissen sōsho.* 6 vols. Tokyo, Meiji Tosho Shuppan, 19? ff.
"School library practice series."

2734. ———. *Gakkō toshōkan kenmei hyōmoku-hyō.* 2 vols. Tokyo, Meiji Tosho Shuppan, 1954. 328p. DLC.
"A list of subject headings for school library use." Vol. 1 is for high schools and Vol. 2 is for middle schools.

2735. ———. *Gakkō toshōkan kijin-kaisetsu to unei.* Tokyo, Jiji Tsūshinsha, 1950. 286p. DLC.
"Standards of school libraries—interpretation and management." The interpretation of the terms used in expressing school library standards, effective means of implementing them and a comparison of standards in the U.S. and Japan.

2736. ———. *Gakkō toshōkan nenkan.* Tokyo, Dai Nihon Tosho K.K., 1956 ff. Annual? 1956—569p; 1957—524p.

"School library yearbook." The volume for 1956 covered developments from 1945–1955. There are numerous statistical tables and a very extensive bibliography of several hundred entries. Recommended lists of books for children are also mentioned.

2737. ———. *Gakkō toshōkan no setsubi to sekkai.* Tokyo, Meiji Tosho Shuppan, 1956. 174p. DLC.

"Planning and furniture of the school library." Many photographs illustrate this reference book on library equipment and furniture. Bibliography.

2738. ———. *Shichōkaku kyōiku to gakkō toshōkan.* Tokyo, Meiji Tosho Shuppan, 1953.

"Audio-visual education in the school library."

2739. ———. *Zukai gakkō toshōkan no jitsumu.* 5 vols. Tokyo, Zenkoku Gakkō . . . , 1962.

"The practice of school library work, illustrated" published and edited by the National School Library Association of Japan. Vol. 1 [Selection and processing of books] by Kiyoshi Serytani. Vol. 2 [Arrangement and circulation of books] by Tomohiko Sano. Vol. 3 [How to make a subject catalog] by Eiji Suzuki. Vol. 4 [Processing of non-book material] by Kiyomichi Kahi. Vol. 5 [Reading guidance] by Yatarō Matsuo.

2740. ———. Hitsu Doku Tosho Iinkai. *Nani-o dō yomaseruka.* 5 vols. Tokyo, Zenkoku Gakkō Toshokan Kyōgikai, 1964. DLC has Vol. 2, 302p.; Vol. 3, 308p.; Vol. 4, 342p.; Vol. 5, 348p.

"A digest of standard works for children." Each volume is for a different level, from the lower elementary grades to high school, considering the question of what and how each level should read.

2741. ———. Kihon Tosho Mokuroku Henshū Iinkai. *Gakkō toshōkan kihon toshō mokuroku.* Tokyo, Zenkoku Gakkō . . . 19?? ff. Annual?

"Basic book catalog for school libraries."

Korea

Korea has a recorded history of more than 2,000 years, but much of this time it was associated with the Chinese empire. It was known as the "hermit kingdom" until Japan forced China into allowing treaty relations with Korea in 1876. This was followed by similar treaties with the Western powers of the late 19th century. For about 30 years Korea absorbed the cultural impact of both East and West, so that the literature of this period represents more a testing-out of new ideas than a commitment to them. A number of translations of the Western classics were published, but a far greater influence stemmed from the Japanese literature. It was as though history had turned the tables, for it was Korean scholars who had introduced the first written form of the Japanese language (in Chinese characters) during the first century B.C.

No sooner did Korea get a taste of national identity, when she was annexed by Japan in 1910. A modern school system was introduced, but it could handle only about a fifth of Korean children and the education was intended as a means of "Japanizing" the child as much as it was to make him literate. This did not always turn out, however, for there was considerable nationalistic spirit kept alive by folk literature and other folk arts. There were also a few writers who deftly manipulated their Japanese education to fit Korean needs.

The first of these who wrote specifically for children was Pang Chong-hwan, affectionately known by his pseudonym, Sop 'a Sonsaeng. He felt very strongly that Korean children should be educated in their own language and by keen observation noticed that the elements of greatest appeal in the Japanese texts were the folk rhymes and songs. He took one of the most rhythmic Japanese songs, put very symbolic Korean words to it, and immediately had a smashing success. This he continued to do, with such successful imitations that children soon came to accept them as if they had always been around.

A young boy growing up then was Yun Sok-chung. He and his classmates were so taken with Sop 'a Sonsaeng's songs that they formed a boys' club for the express purpose of writing stories and songs in their native Korean. They published their efforts in a mimeographed magazine. Soon, the poems and rhymes of Yun Sok-chung were more popular than any. He was a typical example of the pupil outstripping the teacher, but he never forgot the debt he owed to Sop 'a Sonsaeng, whose work is now largely forgotten, while that of Mr. Yun lives on. Yun's rhymes are considered the first truly Korean literature for children, and a few have passed into the language as folk rhymes which every child learns by word of mouth.

Other writers who achieved a certain renown for their children's books were Kim So-un, Yi Won-su, Pang Ki-hwan, Kim Hyo-sop and Kang So-ch'on. The latter had a career which extended from the beginnings of children's literature, in the 1920's, up to his death in 1963. He was admired as one of the few writers who succeeded in getting a child-like vision into his stories.

The entire period has been one of political unrest for Korea, and when the agreements entered into by allies caused the division of the country after the end of World War II, it was quite natural that the educational system and the literature followed patterns set by the occupation forces. In the North, everything was modeled on the Russian scheme; in the South, it was directed to U.S. standards. Many of the educational and cultural reforms in both North and South were interrupted by the Korean War. At the present time there is extensive publishing of children's books and magazines in both Koreas, although North Korea probably produces more books per child, and they are of generally good quality. The South has the larger population, scattered in less industrialized areas. The books for children of the South are published mostly in Seoul, and while they are more varied than those of the North, there are quite a number which are of very poor quality.

Libraries for children are still in the formative stages, in both North and South. The tendency is to emphasize school libraries, since the educational systems are being expanded more quickly than the public libraries. The Korean Library Association has strong memberships among teacher-librarians, and it's bulletin contains articles describing the progress which is being made.

2742. An, Hong-mo. [Management of the model elementary school library in Kangnŏng School.] *Kyoyuk p'yongnon,* Seoul, No. 76, Feb., 1965, pp. 66–71. DLC.

Designated as a model library in 1963, this was to serve as an example for a large number of surrounding schools. Its collection, staff, management and services exemplify national standards.

2743.	[Articles on children's books and reading.] *Sae kyosil,* Seoul, Vol. 3, No. 5, May, 1958, pp. 8–21.

Includes: "How to solve the problem of the children's book shortage" by Yŏn-han Mun; "What books are to be recommended for children?" by Hyo-sŏn Ŏ; "Adventure stories which influence children" by So-ch'ŏn Kang; and an article on comic books. This is a leading educational periodical, printed in two editions, one for the lower and one for upper elementary grades.

2744.	[Articles on children's reading.] *Sae kyosil,* Seoul, Vol. 3, No. 5, May, 1958.

Includes: "Why do children read in such a place?"; "Recommended and not recommended books for children" by Wŏn-su Yi; and an article by Mun-gu Hong.

2745.	[Articles on school libraries and reading.] *Sae kyosil,* Seoul, Vol. 4, No. 11, Nov., 1959, pp. 8–30.

Includes: "Necessity for a classroom library" by T'ae-yul Kim; an article on the school library by Ch'ang-u Yi; "Recommendable books for children" by Yŏng-il Kim; and an article on reading guidance and book reports by Yan-su Pak.

2746.	Chang, Il-se. *Hakkyo tosŏgwan unyŏng chich'im.* Seoul, Sinsŏgak, 1964. 310p. APP. (1st ed., *Hakkyo tosŏgwan unyong po,* pub. by Hakkyo Toso Kanhaenghoe, 1961).

"School library management guide." A manual of instruction with many diagrams as illustrations. The author is a well-known school librarian.

2747.	———. "School libraries in Chun Nam provincial area," *KLA bulletin,* Seoul, Vol. 4, No. 7, Sept.–Oct., 1963, pp. 28–33. DLC.

The school libraries in this province are extremely active. Since the new government law allowed collecting small sums of money to use for the purchase of books, the teachers tried to put this into effect. However, even this proved to be too much of a hardship on most students so the author recommends that budgeting for books be done on a national basis.

2748.	Chang, Kwan-jin. "School library reference service," *KLA bulletin,* Seoul, Vol. 6, No. 4, May, 1965, pp. 13–17. DLC.

An effective approach to the school library reference service: analyzing the student motives, curriculum needs, and available materials; methods of research, keeping of records, and processing of materials. Results of a survey on reference questions made in a school library are in graph form.

2749.	Ch'angwŏn. Kyoyuk Yonguso. *Kunmin hak-*

kyo tosŏgwan unyŏng charyo. Seoul, Tongsŏng Munh-wasa, 1964. 345p.

"Materials on elementary school library management," published by the Educational Research Institute of Ch'angwŏn.

2750.	"Ch'ang-yŏng elementary school library," *KLA bulletin,* Seoul, Vol. 1, No. 4, June, 1960, pp. 12–13. DLC.

This library, opened in March, 1960 contains 2500 volumes, is staffed by a full time professional, and is housed in its own building. It serves the children after school and evenings as well as during the day. Illustrated with photographs.

2751.	[Children and reading—a survey.] *Pusan kyoyuk,* Pusan, No. 107, Oct., 1960, pp. 4–12.

2752.	[Children's books.] *Chosŏn tosŏ mongnok. Catalog of Korean books.* Pyongyang, Export and Import Company of North Korean Publications. 19? ff. Irregular. DLC has some issues.

An annotated catalog which lists children's books separately. Titles are usually given in Russian, English and Chinese, as well as in Korean.

2753.	Cho, Chae-hu. "Improvement of secondary education and the role of the school library." *KLA bulletin,* Seoul, Vol. 5, No. 2, Mar., 1963, pp. 2–5. DLC.

The new significance of the school library and its functions as foreseen under the reformation of the education act.

2754.	———. [A plan for school library development in terms of Pusan City.] *Kyoyuk p'yŏngnon,* Seoul, No. 75, Jan., 1965, pp. 92–93. DLC.

The present status of libraries in the city's schools, and recommendations for future development.

2755.	———. *Saeroun hakkŭp mungo ŭi unyŏng.* Pusan, Chinhaksa, 1965. 200p. APP.

"Management of the new class library." A translation of a Japanese handbook, not located in the original. This approaches school library work from the classroom collection theory.

2756.	Cho, Mun-jae. [Report on annual research in the library.] *Yŏngu yŏngbo,* Seoul?, No. 15, Oct., 1957, pp. 395–429.

2757.	Ch'oe, Kŭn-man. "Korean libraries in 1965. School libraries," *KLA bulletin,* Seoul, Vol. 6, No. 10, Dec., 1965, pp. 11–13. DLC.

A report on the increase in number of school libraries, on the teacher-librarian training seminars and workshops and the 4th national conference of school librarians. A few of the statistics given are: 1964—950 school libraries with more than 500 volumes; 1965—1422 school libraries with more than 500 volumes. Of this increase, 354 were elementary, 72 middle and 46 high school libraries. More than 400 teachers took the workshops or training courses offered by the various universities or the Korean Library Association.

2758.   ———. "Reality of school library—its establishment and operation—the case of Jaimoolpo High School," *KLA bulletin,* Seoul, Vol. 4, No. 3, Apr. 1963, pp. 7–14. DLC.

This high school library of 6,000 volumes has a fulltime program, and its librarian here describes the implementation of service.

2759.   ———. "School libraries," *KLA bulletin,* Seoul, Vol. 3, No. 8, Dec., 1962, pp. 10–14. DLC.

One of the results of the internal revolution in 1962 was that education and libraries suffered. At that time, out of 6,182 schools, only 292 had libraries, and ten of these could be considered good. The library law of 1959 brought more attention to the rural and small city areas, but the standards of a minimum of 300 volumes for each school still cannot be met. Also, too many schools were collecting volumes with no thought of quality in selection. The author felt that Korean libraries at this time were in the same condition as Japan's in 1949, and recommended formations of clearer, more applicable standards.

2760.   Ch'oe, Sin-yong. "On children's library," *KLA bulletin,* Seoul, Vol. 1, No. 4, June, 1960, pp. 8–11. DLC.

A librarian tells of her experiences in an elementary school attached to the College of Education of Ihwa Women's University. She particularly deplores the lack of children's books in Korean.

2761.   Ch'oe, T'ae-ho. [How to manage school libraries.] *Mun'gyo kongbo,* Seoul, No. 62, July, 1962, pp. 18–21. DLC.

The former director of the national library writes of the necessity for more and better school library management. This periodical is the official journal of the Ministry of Education and its issues contain other shorter articles on the school library and reading guidance.

2762.   Ch'oe, To-ch'ŏl. "Chŏn-ju high school library," *KLA bulletin,* Seoul, Vol. 6, No. 5, June, 1965, pp. 11–13. DLC.

A principal describes the large, attractive library built for his school in 1964. Before work was begun, the chairman of the library building committee made a trip to all the better school libraries of South Korea. It was built with funds collected from parents, businessmen, the Asia Foundation, and other local and national agencies. Students and the USIS donated some of the books. The library is staffed with a fulltime librarian, and is open the year round to the general public as well as students.

2763.   Chŏng, Un-hak. [Fundamental contents of teaching storytelling.] *Inmin kyoyuk,* Pyongyang, No. 4, 1965, pp. 20–22. DLC.

Written from a technical, educational point of view, this periodical is one of the official publications of the Ministry of Education in North Korea.

2764.   Ch'u, Sik. [Let's read without fail such books as the masterpieces of the world.] *Kajŏng kyoyuk,* Seoul, No. 38, Dec., 1961, pp. 48–51. DLC.

The author recommends that children read the universal classics, and gives examples of those which are available in Korean, such as *Pinocchio, Cuore, The Bluebird, Dog of Flanders, A Little Princess, Tom Sawyer* and the collections of Grimm and Andersen fairy tales.

2765.   [The creation of typical characters for children in the age of Ch'ollima], *Chosŏn munhak,* Pyongyang, No. 3, 1964, pp. 80–87. DLC.

There are many children's books today, but few which have in them characters who represent the ideals of *Ch'ollima* (the national socialist plan for the improvements of economic, social and cultural affairs). This writer believes children's books in North Korea should present stronger characters who symbolize national ideals.

2766.   Douglas, Mary Peacock. *Sasŏ kyosa haendbuk.* Seoul, Yŏnse Taehakkyo, Tosŏgwan Hakkwa, 1961. 195p.

A translation, by T'ae-yul Kim, of 3676, published by the Library Science Department of Yonsei University.

2767.   [The educational value of children's stories.] *Kyoyuk p'yŏngnon,* Seoul, No. 42, Apr., 1962, pp. 56–59. DLC.

The author (anonymous) has translated portions of Rudolf Meyer's *Die Weisheit der deutschen Volksmärchen* and added comments on the nature of fairy tales, their moral significance and their influence on children.

2768.   [General examination of school libraries.] *Sae kyoyuk,* Seoul, Vol. 17, No. 10, Oct., 1965, pp. 28–58, 128–131. DLC.

Among the ten articles in this symposium on the school library are: "The mission of the school library" by Yŏng-su Paek; "Library law enforcement and the problems involved" by Kyong-il Kim; and a statistical survey on the reading conditions, tendencies and interests of rural children by Ch'ang-hu Pak. A translation of one chapter from Lillian Smith (3383) was made by Yo-sŏp Kim and appears on pp. 128–131.

2769. Ha, Yŏng-T'ae. "Regional materials in the school library—its acquisition and processesing," *KLA bulletin,* Seoul, Vol. 5, No. 10, Dec. 1964, pp. 18–20. DLC.

The importance of acquiring regional and local materials to serve the needs of students.

2770. *Hakkyo tosŏgwan yŏngo.* "Research Society of School Library, Federation of Korean Education Associations, Seoul, Korea. Quarterly?. No. 1 ff. Oct., 1964 ff. DLC has some issues.

The title means school library studies, and in the first issue some of the best-known school librarians sum up the present status, and write of school library problems. The first chapter of *Standards for School Library Services* (3413) is given in Korean translation.

2771. Ham, Ch'ŏ-sik. "Ŏrini wa kŭrim ch'aek," *Poyuk tokpon,* Seoul, Saenghwal Kongnonsa, 1948; pp. 57–63.

"Children and picture books." In his: *Nursery Reader.*

2772. Han, Ŭng-su. "Hakkyo tosŏgwan," *Sich'ŏng gak kyoyuk,* Seoul, Hanguk Sich'ŏnggak Kyoyukhoe, 1953, pp. 253–259.

"School library." In his: *Audio-Visual Education.*

2773. *Hanguk adong munhak tokpon.* 10 Vols. Seoul, Ŭryu Munhwasa, 1962, DLC.

"Korean juvenile literary readers." Each of the volumes contains selections from traditional and modern literature, from nursery rhymes to short stories, drama poetry and short novels. Vols. 9 and 10 include only traditional Korean tales. Each volume is edited by a different author. All are attractive in format and illustrations, and are designed as anthologies for use by teachers and parents, as well as by children.

2774. Hanguk Adong Munhakhoe. *Hyŏndae hanguk adong munhak sŏnjip.* Seoul, Tongguk Munhwasa, 1955. 331p. DLC.

A collection of writings by the members of the Korean children's literature society. Poetry, short stories and fairy tales are among the types included. There is a biographical sketch of each author.

2775. Hanguk Tosŏgwan Hyŏphoe. *Hakkyo tosŏgwan ŭi sisŏl.* Seoul, Hanguk Tosŏgwan Hyŏphoe, 1965. 166p. APP. (Earlier ed. had title *Hakkyo tosŏgwan sŏlgye sisŏl*).

"Design of school libraries and their equipment," edited and published by the Korean Library Association. This actually consists of many photographs of existing school and children's libraries demonstrating their design and use.

2776. [Harmful comics and means of combatting them.] *Kyoyuk py'ongnŏn,* Seoul, No. 13, June, 1959, pp. 62–67.

2777. Hong, Nae. "Yong San middle and high school library," *KLA bulletin,* Seoul, Vol. 6, No. 9, Nov. 1965, pp. 20–22, 29. DLC.

From a small room in 1958, this library progressed to the entire third floor of the school for middle grades in 1961, and finally in March 1965 a new three-story library building was opened to serve both schools. It contains 8,000 vols., is served by two full-time librarians (with assistance from 36 student helpers), and is open evenings. However, it does not serve the general public.

2778. [How to read fairy tales effectively to children.] *Pusan kyoyuk,* Pusan, No. 88, Jan.–Feb., 1959, pp. 47–53.

2779. Hong, Mun-gu. [Children, reading and books.] *Sae kyoyuk,* Seoul, Vol. 7, No. 5, June, 1955, pp. 82–86.

2780. Inch'on Ch'ang Yŏng Kungmin Hakkyo. [Management of a class library.] *Sae kyoyuk,* Seoul, Vol. 7, No. 5, June, 1955, pp. 31–36.

2781. [Juvenile literature.] *Hanguk ch'ulp'an yŏngam. Books in print, Korea.* Seoul, Korean Publisher's Association, yearly. 1963 ff. DLC, NNY.

Since children's books are listed separately, it is possible to note how many and what types are available during each year. For 1964, approximately 500 titles were listed, in such general categories as picture books, fairy tales, biography, history, nonfiction.

2782. Kang, So-ch'ŏn. [The mother and children's literature.] *Kajŏng kyoyuk,* Seoul, No. 37, Nov., 1961, pp. 14–15. DLC.

A well-known writer for children gives advice to mothers on choosing books for children, and he encourages women to turn to writing for them, as they have in other countries. (He states that at present there are no women writers for children in Korea).

2783. Kim, Chŏng-ho. [Reading experiences.] *Ch'ulp'an munhwa, The Korean books journal*, Seoul, Vol. 2, No. 10, Feb.–Mar., 1966, pp. 28–29. DLC.

The director of the bureau for women's and children's needs in the Ministry of Social Affairs here reminisces about her childhood reading, and how it influenced her. She mentions many titles and remarks that she particularly enjoyed sad books!

2784. Kim, Ki-sang [Collection, arrangement and utilization of vertical file materials.] *Sae kyoyuk*, Seoul, No. 108, Oct., 1963, pp. 92–95. DLC.

Experience in setting up and using the vertical file in Yŏsu elementary school is analyzed by the teacher-librarian. On pp. 38–42 of this same issue, Chin-gil Kang writes of experience with audio-visual materials in the library.

2785. Kim, Kyŏng-il. "Equipment and administration of the school library," *KLA bulletin*, Seoul, July–Aug., 1958, pp. 27–32. DLC.

Although education in general has made great strides in Korea, school libraries have not kept up. This librarian characterizes the difficulties encountered in establishing his school library.

2786. ———. *Hakkyo tosŏgwan chojik kwa kwalli ŭi sil-che*. Seoul, Hyŏndae Kyoyuk Ch'ongso Ch'ulp'ansa, 1966. 278p. (Hyŏndae kyoyuk kisul kangjwa, 38). APP.

"Organization of the school library and practice of its management." A handbook written by a leading school librarian.

2787. ———. "How to conduct the research activities in the school library," *KLA bulletin*, Seoul, Vol. 4, No. 4, May, 1963, pp. 3–7. DLC.

The significance, objectives and methods of directing reference work with pupils.

2788. ———. "School libraries in 1960," *KLA bulletin*, Seoul, Vol. 1, No. 9, Dec., 1960, pp. 10–12. DLC.

A report on the organization of the school library organization, the publication of a handbook for the teacher-librarian, and general information about school libraries in Korea in 1960.

2789. ———. "School library staff manual," *KLA bulletin*, Seoul, Vol. 3, No. 1, Apr., 1962, pp. 1–4. DLC.

The structure and use of a staff manual with sample contents.

2790. ———. "Student assistant in the school library," *KLA bulletin*, Seoul, Vol. 4, No. 6, July–Aug., 1963, pp. 3–9. DLC.

How to manage a program of student assistants in the school library. The author believes they are important not for the help they offer but for the value it can have for them.

2791. ———. "A survey on the school library," *Bulletin of the Library Science Society*, Seoul, Vol. 1, No. 1, Oct., 1963, pp. 11–14. DLC.

In order to improve the school library, it is usually wise to make a survey on existing conditions, past experience, and present and future needs. This librarian here makes suggestions as to how to go about constructing such a survey, and how to implement its use.

2792. "Teacher-librarian as a profession," *KLA bulletin*, Seoul, Vol. 6, No. 10, Dec., 1965, pp. 16–20. DLC.

The definition of the position, its duties, and the problems of specialization. The author feels that the library law requiring a teacher librarian in each school does more harm than good since, in order to comply, a principal must often put a non-professional in charge.

2793. Kim, Po-rin. [Educational value of fairy tales for children.] *Kajŏng kyoyuk*, Seoul, No. 36, Feb., 1961, pp. 64–65. DLC.

The author writes that fairy tales can calm mental tension, give a feeling of intimate relationship, develop creative power, and bring out the humor in children.

2794. Kim, Se-ik. [Children and reading.] *Yŏwŏn*, Seoul, Vol. 10, No. 2, Feb., 1964, pp. 376–379. DLC.

An article aimed at mothers, encouraging them to prepare their children to be receptive to reading by reading aloud and by creating a harmonious reading environment in the family.

2795. Kim, So-un. *Chosŏn kujŏn minyojip*. Seoul, Yŏng Ch'ang Sŏgwan, 1950. 606p. DLC.

A definitive collection of Korean nursery rhymes, game songs, folk songs and children's sayings edited by a leading folklorist.

2796. Kim T'ae-yul. [School library.] *Sae kyoyuk*, Seoul, Vol. 11, No. 2, Feb., 1959, pp. 54–65, 78.

2797. Kim, Tŏg-yang. [School library management.] *Kyoyuk yŏngu*, Taegu, No. 22, Oct., 1954, pp. 29–36.

2798. Kim, Tŏk-pin. [Reading guidance in the school.] *Ch'ulp'an munhwa, The Korean books journal,* Seoul, Aug., 1965, pp. 16–17. DLC.

A librarian describes the active reading program in his middle and high school library. A Saturday book club, the pupils' own journal with their book reviews, and special programs to mark such events as book week, are only some of the activities carried out.

2799. Kim, Tong-ni. [Significance of the establishment of the Soch'ŏn juvenile literature prize.] *Sae kyoyuk,* Seoul, Vol. 17, No. 7, July, 1965, pp. 55–56. DLC.

Established in honor of the writer of children's books, Kang-Soch'ŏn, this prize was first awarded in May, 1965, to Yo-sŏp Kim. It is given by Pae Yŏng-Sa, publishers of the periodical *Adong munhak* (Children's literature).

2800. Kim, Tu-hong. *Hakkyo tosŏgwan ŭi pŏŏt'ik'ol p'ail.* Pusan, Samhyŏp Munhwasa, 1965. 37p. (Hanguk hakkyo tosŏgwan silnu siriijŭ, 8). APP.

"School library vertical file," published by the Korean Research Society of Library Education. This and the following entry are two of a series on Korean school library practice.

2801. ———. *Hakkyo tosŏgwan ŭi sŭt' aep maenyuŏl.* Pusan, Samhyop Munhwasa, 1965. 58p. (Hanguk hakkyo tosŏgwan silmu siriijŭ, 1). APP.

"School library staff manual"; illustrated with many instructional diagrams. See note in 2800.

2802. ———. "Korean libraries in 1964. School libraries," *KLA bulletin,* Seoul, Vol. 5, No. 10, Dec., 1964, pp. 9–12. DLC.

Contrary to previous years, in 1964 the school libraries emphasized teaching the use of the library to students and helping them to develop solutions themselves to library problems. Instruction began in the first grade, and grew more frequent with the older grades. A national survey of school libraries was also undertaken in 1964, and a journal for school librarians was established.

2803. ———. "Role of supervision for the school libraries," *KLA bulletin,* Seoul, Vol. 5, No. 1, Jan.–Feb., 1964, pp. 20–23. DLC.

A speech delivered at the 2nd nation-wide conference of school librarians on the establishment of the official job title of teacher librarian in the public service law.

2804. ———. [Selection of reading materials for children.] *Radio hakkyo,* Seoul?, No. 3, June, 1953, pp. 244–249.

2805. ———. [Three elements in the school library.] *KLA bulletin,* Seoul, Vol. 2, No. 2, Mar.–Apr., 1961, pp. 1–3. DLC.

A general statement as to the characteristics a good school library should have.

2806. Kim, Wan-gi. "Managing the school library in terms of national language study," *Sae kyoyuk,* Seoul, Vol. 15, No. 12, Dec., 1963, pp. 98–105. DLC.

The special ways in which the library can assist in developing better reading, writing and speaking in Korean children.

2807. Kim, Yŏng-dal and Sŏg-U Yi. [Establishing the children's library.] *Sae kyosil,* Seoul, Vol. 3, No. 7, July, 1958, pp. 88–99.

2808. Kim, Yong-ho. "Life and view of a teacher-librarian," *KLA bulletin,* Seoul, Vol. 2, No. 4, June, 1961, pp. 1–7. DLC.

A secondary school librarian tells of his reasons for going into the field, what it means to him, and some personal experiences it has brought him.

2809. Kim, Yong-t'aek. [For children who dislike reading.] *Sae kyosil,* Seoul, Vol. 4, No. 1, Jan., 1959, pp. 29–31.

2810. Ko, Hyŏn-sang, *et al. Kunmin hakkyo tosŏgwan kyoyuk.* Seoul, Munhwagak, 1964. 324p.

"Elementary school library education," co-edited by Chin-yong Kwak and Kyŏng-ch'ae An, and the above author.

2811. Ko, Im-su. [A review of *Kkotpongŏri (Buds of flowers),* the children's literature.] *Inmin kyoyuk,* Pyongyang, Nov., 1960, pp. 46–48. DLC.

A review of an illustrated magazine for kindergarten children, praising it for the socialistic, patriotic attitude which it develops.

2812. Ku, Chun-hoe. [Equipment of our class library and its use.] *Kyoyuk yŏngu,* Taegu, No. 22, Oct., 1954, pp. 37–38, 60.

2813. Kwŏn, Chae-Wŏn. [Practice of reading guidance.] *Kyoyuk yŏngu,* Taegu, No. 30, Nov., 1955, pp. 99–103.

2814. Kwŏn, O-il. [Survey on children's reading.] *Kyoyuk munje,* Inchon, Vol. 2, No. 12, Oct.–Dec., 1959, pp. 16–19.

2815. Kyoyuk Taehak Tosŏgwan Yŏnguhoe. *Hakkyo tosŏgwan.* Seoul, Kyohak Tosŏ Chusik Hoesa, 1964. 325p.

"Manual on school library" compiled by the Library Science Research Society, College of Education, Seoul University.

2816. Landis, E. B. "Rhymes of Korean children," *Journal of American folk-lore,* Boston, Vol. 11, July–Sept., 1898, pp. 203–209. DLC, NNY.

A selection of nursery rhymes, counting rhymes and other oral folklore of children, together with commentary on some of the characteristics of Korean nursery rhymes.

2817. [Lecture on juvenile literature and experiences of creative work.] *Ch'ŏngyŏn munhak,* Pyongyang, No. 9, Sept., 1965, pp. 52–65. DLC.

An introductory lecture by Bok-chin Yun, on nursery rhymes, is followed by the explanations of two writers, on how they came to write nursery rhymes and game songs. Mr. Yun depicts the stages at which children begin liking the various kinds of rhymes, and he uses many traditional ones as examples. He believes that this oral literature plays a most important role in the child's development, since it is liked most and used most during the formative years, when the child is most receptive to language.

2818. Lohrer, Mary Alice. "Teacher-librarians' education in America 1900–1944," *KLA bulletin,* Seoul, Vol. 5, No. 5, June, 1964, pp. 18–24; No. 6, July–Aug., 1964, pp. 18–25; No. 7, Sept., 1964, pp. 23–31. DLC.

This is a translation (by Kyŏng-il Kim) of the 4th chapter in Miss Lohrer's doctoral dissertation with conclusions to apply to the Korean situation.

2819. [Mr. Kang So-ch'ŏn—his humanity and his literature.] *Hyondae munhak,* Seoul, Vol. 9, No. 6, June, 1963, pp. 30–58. DLC.

Tributes to this beloved author and critic of children's books, written by his colleagues and friends shortly after his death. In reviewing the work of So-ch'on they reveal much of the history of the development of children's literature in Korea, from the early years of this century up to the present day.

2820. Mun, Ki-yŏng. "Mah-san school library," *KLA bulletin,* Seoul, Vol. 6, No. 7, Sept., 1965, pp. 15–17. DLC.

In an earlier article, in the *KLA Bulletin* for June, 1963, this librarian told of organizing the library in the Mah-san middle school. Here he relates the expanded service and activities which have developed. This library serves the general public as well, during the entire year, and even on Sundays.

2821. Na, Cha-yun. "Recorders in school libraries," *KLA bulletin,* Seoul, Vol. 1, No. 6, Sept. 1960, pp. 1–4. DLC.

The handling and use of all audio-visual materials in the school library.

2822. Nam-hae. Kungmin Hakkyo. [Problem and solution for school library management.] *Kyoyuk yŏngu, Pusan?,* Feb., 1959, pp. 82–85.

2823. *Orini.* Kyŏngsŏng (Seoul) Kaebyŏksa. No. 1, Mar., 1923–No. 8, Feb., 1931.

According to several historical reviews, this periodical was devoted to children's literature and its criticism. It was edited by Chŏng-hwan Pang.

2824. Pak, Hong-gŭn. [Review and recommendation of *Adong Munhak Yŏnganjip.*] *Yŏwŏn,* Seoul, Vol. 10, No. 11, Nov., 1964, pp. 286–287. DLC.

In reviewing this annual collection of the best children's literature, the author writes of the importance of parents' involvement in their children's reading. He stresses a knowledge and use of native literature.

2825. "Proceedings of the school library symposium," *KLA bulletin,* Seoul, Vol. 5, No. 3, Apr., 1964, pp. 13–32. DLC.

Includes "The educational role of school library" by T'ae Si Chŏng; "Teaching method improvement and shcool library" by Chong-ch'ŏl Kim; "School library as a learning center" by Pong-sun Yi; "Problems toward the school library development" by Kŭn-man Ch'oe. Their general conclusions are that the library is the most important part of the school; that the librarian must have special training to give service and guidance; standards must be set up and maintained; the collections must be selected on the basis of providing recreational reading as well as reference materials. A table of library standards in Japan and the U.S. is on p. 28. The qualifications and salaries for Korean school librarians are on p. 31.

2826. Pusan. Kyŏng-sang Nam-do. Kyoyuk yŏnguso. "Conference on the establishment of primary school pilot library," *KLA bulletin,* Seoul, Vol. 3, No. 8, Dec., 1962, pp. 26–28. DLC.

A conference of the county educational supervisors of south Kyŏngsang province to establish the Chinzu Chungan elementary school library as a model library, and to make plans to assure that it will continue to be excellent in quality so that it may be used as a training center.

2827. [Reading and environment.] *Kajŏng kyoyuk,* Seoul, Vol. 45, July–Aug., 1962, pp. 44–45. DLC.

Expressions of the feelings of a parent, a teacher and a child in relation to the meaning of books and reading.

2828. [Reading guidance and the school library.] *Sae kyoyuk,* Seoul, Vol. 11, No. 10, Oct., 1959, pp. 55–71.

Includes: "Reading guidance for the middle and high school student" by Kil-su Kang; "Reading guidance for pleasure and interest" by Bong-sun Yi; "Reading for young people" by Tong-ni Kim; "Reading tendencies of girl students" by Ik-se Kim; "School library" by Sin-yong Ch'oe.

2829. "The school libraries; a study of administration and prospects," *KLA bulletin,* Seoul, Vol. 5, No. 10, Dec., 1964, pp. 23–58. DLC.

The results of the survey mentioned in 2802. Each of the provinces is treated separately with tables indicating number and size of school libraries, staff, budgets, equipment, processing of materials, extent of catalogs, student assistants, hours of opening, types of access.

2830. "School library conference," *KLA bulletin,* Seoul, Vol. 5, No. 9, Nov., 1964, pp. 20–35. DLC.

After the reports of the committees follow speeches given by Tu-hong Kim, Yang Won Kwon, and Chon-hi Kim, on the occasion of the annual library conference. They were concerned with provincial library planning, reading guidance, and the qualifications of teacher-librarians, respectively.

2831. "School library conference," *KLA bulletin,* Seoul, Vol. 3, No. 4, July–Aug., 1962, pp. 66–69, pp. 98–101. DLC.

"The practice of school library management" by Kyŏng-il Kim; "Present problems in the school library" by Kyu-bŏm Yi; and a discussion among the librarians present concerning their specific problems.

2832. "The school library I have started," *KLA bulletin,* Seoul. 5, No. 6, July–Aug. 1964, pp. 26–30. DLC.

In an interview, two principals tell of the school libraries they set up in their high schools in Pusan, beginning from nothing after the war had left the city in ruins.

2833. Seoul. Ansan Elementary School. "Summary of research report," *KLA bulletin,* Seoul, Vol. 4, No. 5, June, 1963, pp. 8–12. DLC.

This school has a model library assigned by the special city authority. This report describes how the collection was acquired, and how the organization was set up.

2834. Son, Chin-t'ae. *Hanguk minjok sŏrhwa ŭi yŏngu.* Seoul, Ŭryu Munhwasa, 1954. 236p. DLC.

"Folk tales, myths, legends—a cultural historical study." Chinese, Japanese, Manchurian and other northern influences are pointed out. Some Korean versions of universal folk themes are included here.

2835. Sŏul Taehakkyo. Sabŏm Taekak. Kungmunkwa Yŏngusil. [Report on the reading of middle and high school students.] *Kyoyuk,* Vol. 9, Apr., 1959, pp. 77–114.

Survey undertaken by Seoul University College of Education, National Language Study Institute.

2836. "The stage of library service," *KLA bulletin,* Seoul, Vol. 5, No. 1, Jan.–Feb., 1964, pp. 24–53. DLC.

Reports by school librarians from seven provinces and Pusan city on their school library activities. There are a number of statistical tables comparing past and present situations.

2837. [Survey on reading tendencies of children], *Kyoyuk yŏngu,* Seoul, No. 18, Sept., 1961, pp. 93–105.

"Published by Ihwa Women's University."

2838. "The teacher-librarian workshop," *KLA bulletin,* Seoul, Vol. 5, No. 6, July–Aug., 1964, pp. 38–44. DLC.

Although Yonsei University has had a library science program since 1958, only 132 teacher librarians have completed the work. This is in contrast to the 5,564 elementary, and 1,575 secondary school librarian positions authorized by law. Therefore, the school library workshops will be opened in some of the other provinces, with teachers from Seoul. This issue also includes a translation of an article on the teacher-librarian by Mary Alice Lohrer.

2839. "Workshop for teacher-librarians in 1965," *KLA bulletin,* Seoul, Vol. 6, No. 6, July–Aug., 1965, pp. 26–28, 21. DLC.

The contents, purposes and methods of the workshop which granted official professional status to its participants.

2840. Yang, Pyŏng-T'aek. [A proposal for the school library movement.] *Kyoyuk munhwa,* Seoul, No. 26, Mar., 1955, pp. 68–73.

2841. Yi, Chun-gu. [Reading guidance for children.] *Sae kyosil,* Seoul, Vol. 6, No. 4, Apr., 1961, pp. 135–137; No. 9, Sept., 1961, pp. 111–115.

2842. Yi, Hoe-U. [Middle and high school students' reading.] *Sae kyoyuk,* Seoul, Vol. 7, No. 5, June, 1955, pp. 87–89.

2843. Yi, Kang-su. "Problems on children's book selection," *KLA bulletin,* Seoul, Vol. 6, No. 9, Nov., 1965, pp. 14–19. DLC.

The results of a study made in the Yŏsu East Elementary School on the reading interests of the children, the motives parents and teachers have in recommending books, and the difficulties librarians face in getting the right book to the right child. The librarian observed that the least popular books were: translations, books printed in the old, vertical form, books with small type and no illustration. He does not feel the list recommended by the ministry of education is valid, or useful, and has begun his own list, using standards based on experience.

2844. Yi, Kwan-il. [Reading guidance—in terms of Taegwang School.] *Ch'ulp'an munhwa,* Seoul, Vol. 2, No. 9, Jan., 1966, pp. 20–21. DLC.

In this school it is compulsory for students to read more than ten books. The author goes into activities and programs which are used to stimulate reading.

2845. Yi, Kyu-bŏm. "Study on school library materials," *KLA bulletin,* Seoul, Vol. 5, No. 4, May, 1964, pp. 14–23. DLC.

The problems of selecting materials for the school library: quantity, subject coverage, non-book materials, duplication, reviewing media, organization of selection committees. The processing and circulating of materials: cataloging, arrangement, control, repair, discarding.

2846. Yi, Kyu-sŏp. [A study on reading of rural school children.] *Sae kyoyuk,* Seoul, No. 107, Sept., 1963, pp. 94–99. DLC.

Results of a survey carried out among rural elementary school children to determine their reading habits and interests.

2847. Yi, Pong-nae. [On juvenile literature.] *Sin ch'ŏnji,* Seoul, Vol. 9, No. 7, July, 1954, pp. 58–64. DLC.

The history, characteristics and methodology of Korean children's literature. According to the author the geneology of this literary movement can be traced through the following writers: 1.) Chŏng-hwan Pang, 2.) So-un Kim, 3.) Sŏk-chung Yun, 4.) Wŏn-su Yi, 5.) So-ch'ŏn Kang, 6.) Ki-hwan Pang and 7.) Hyo-sŏp Kim. He states that its general characteristics were combinations of pessimism and sentimentality, dreaminess and naturalism. Often, it was

controlled by rank commercialists who forced the writing of pseudo-adventures. He contrasts the methods used by H. C. Andersen and those used by writers of Korean fairy tales and concludes that the latter confused their own environment with realism, which resulted in an undertone of unrelieved pessimism. In conclusion, he states his requirements for a good children's literature: it must be natural and logical; it must have a kind of romantic action capable of stimulating healthy fantasy and aesthetic experience; it must sometimes use symbolic elements; and it must represent sound morality.

2848. Yi, Pyŏng-su. "School library as well as A. V. center," *KLA bulletin,* Seoul, Vol. 4, No. 5, June, 1963, pp. 16–19. DLC.

The importance of coordinating the audio-visual program with the school library.

2849. Yi, Sang-sŏn and Ung-sŏn Hong. [Significance of choosing excellent books for children. Reading guidance.] *Mun'gyo wŏlbo,* No. 54, July, 1960, pp. 28–33. DLC.

To control the flood of comics and cheap literature, the Ministry of Education recently appointed a commission to review children's books. Those which pass with approval will be stamped with an appropriate sign by their publisher. Since this commission will have no real authority (due to the freedom of press law) the system will be tried out on a voluntary basis.

2850. Yi, Sin-bok. [Comics' influence on children's reading.] *Yŏwŏn,* Seoul, Vol. 4, No. 4, Apr., 1958, pp. 250–255. DLC.

A teacher in the elementary school attached to the college of education at Seoul University describes the survey on comic books made at that institution. The literary content, vocabulary and illustrations were analyzed.

2851. Yi, Sŏk-hyŏn. [On juvenile literature.] *Kyoyuk p'yŏngnon,* Seoul, No. 34, Aug., 1961, pp. 88–89. DLC.

This is part two of a series of articles of which only this could be located. This discusses the qualities of children's literature which bring it close to the child's intellectual and imaginative spirit.

2852. Yi, Wŏn-su. [A historical survey on juvenile literature.] *Hyŏndae munhak,* Seoul, Vol. 11, No. 4, April, 1965, pp. 81–85. DLC.

Children's literature during the twenty years since the liberation can be divided into three phases: 1945–1950—the reprinting of a few prewar books and some translations, and the first periodicals for children; 1950–1960—prose literature which was pragmatic, secular, and matching the sober, fearful state brought about by the war; 1960–to the present, a return to more literary, imaginative and poetic forms and themes.

2853. ———. [*Sonyŏn Segye* and the juvenile literary movement during the Korean war.] *Hyŏndae munhak*, Seoul, Vol. 11, No. 8, pp. 242–244. DLC.

During the Korean war, children's literature suffered from the confusion and corruption of the political and social environment. In 1952 the magazine *Sonyŏn Segye* was founded to counteract the influence of commercial enterprisers who were flooding the market with cheap paper books and comics.

2854. Yi, Yŏng-bok. [Reading guidance in Chŏngsin girls' middle and high school.] *Ch'ulp'an munhwa, The Korean books journal*, Seoul, Vol. 2, No. 10, Feb.–Mar., 1966, pp. 26–27. DLC.

A description of the very active reading club program in force at this school.

2855. Yim, Myŏng-ok. "Reading guidance in the school library," *KLA bulletin*, Seoul, Vol. 6, No. 10, Dec., 1965, pp. 28–31. DLC.

It is particularly important for the librarian to have a good knowledge of native literature, and the works which especially interest children. This means the ability to guide each child to specific books, rather than to general categories. Since there is very little in the way of Korean reference material on children's authors and their books, this librarian made her own file of 700 cards with information on many authors and their works.

2856. Yim, Ŭi-do, *et al.* [A study on some factors influencing children's reading of the Korean language.] *Sae kyoyuk*, Seoul, No. 107, Sept., 1963, pp. 90–93. DLC.

The results of a study as to how extensively the size of type, length of lines, and vertical or horizontal placement influences the reading choices and tendencies of children. Results are tabulated in statistics.

2857. Yu, Chal-sik. "Use of library in primary schools," *KLA bulletin*, Seoul, Vol. 6, No. 4, May, 1965, pp. 18–22. DLC.

How to teach use of the library to children in the elementary grades.

2858. Yu, Yŏng-hyŏn. [Administration of the school library.] *Sae kyoyuk*, Seoul, Vol. 11, No. 2, Feb., 1959, pp. 34–41.

2859. Yun, Sŏk-chung. [Forty years of nursery rhymes.] *Yŏwŏn*, Seoul, Vol. 10, No. 5, May, 1964, pp. 130–135. DLC.

This is the first part of a series, but the only one to be located. It is a reminiscence of a well-known writer concerning his early school years, when he was greatly influenced by the works of Sop'a Sŏnsaeng. As a young boy he organized a writer's club with his fellow pupils, and they published their own magazine. From this venture came several songs and rhymes which became national favorites, which brought the author fame and established him thenceforth as a writer for children.

2860. ———. [A pioneer of the juvenile literary movement—Sop'a Sŏnsaeng.] *Hyŏndae munhak*, Seoul, Vol. 9, No. 1, Jan., 1963, pp. 254–257. DLC.

Sop'a Sŏnsaeng was the pseudonym of Chŏng-hwan Pang, writer of children's books, critic, storyteller, and organizer of societies for the furthering of children's literature. He was particularly active in the 1920's, and this article discusses some of the results of this early work.

2861. ———. "The publication of comics," *Ch'ulp'an munhwa, The Korean books journal*, Seoul, Vol. 2, No. 9, Jan., 1966, p. 7. DLC.

This short article is included because of its description of the Hanguk Adong Manhwa Chayurhoe, a publishers' society recently formed for the self-control of comics and cheap literature with no standards.

336

Australia, New Zealand, Great Britain, Ireland, The West Indies, Canada, and The United States

These countries were not grouped together only because of their common use of English as a national language; further than this they share a historical and contemporary use of much of the same literature for children. The decision to place a given book or article describing this literature, under the bibliography of any one country, was often arbitrary. It is suggested that the reader search through all of the bibliographies in this section, before beginning any serious study of English-language literature for children or work with children and books in one of these areas.

2862.   Cannons, Henry George. "Work with children," *Bibliography of library economy . . . 1876–1920,* Chicago, ALA, 1927. Pp. 125–196. DLC, NNY.

The most important bibliography for the study of the history and early development of children's books and libraries, in the English speaking countries of the world. Almost 5,000 entries of periodical articles are arranged into more than 100 categories (e.g., public library work, planning children's rooms, book selection, illustration, exhibits, reading guidance, storytelling, school libraries, training of librarians, and many more). The entries are further arranged by date of appearance, with oldest entries coming first.

2863.   "Children's literature." Morsch, Lucile M. *Library literature 1921–1932.* Chicago, ALA, 1934. DLC, NNY.

This continued the bibliography begun in Cannons (2862). There are many entries under other subject headings as well, e.g., Children's library service, Children's reading, School libraries, Story hour and storytelling, Young people's literature, etc.

2864.   Crouch, Marcus. *Books about children's literature.* London, The Library Association, 1963. 31p. DLC.

A very inclusive bibliography "of interest to the student of children's books as a form of literature." Books on librarianship and the techniques of introducing books to children have been omitted. The main sections are on history, criticism and bibliog-

raphy, illustration, authorship, periodicals, and biographies of children's authors, both collective and individual. Each is briefly annotated.

2865.   Darrah, Jane. "The story of books for children," *Carnegie magazine,* Pittsburgh, Vol. 25, June, 1951, pp. 198–200. DLC, NNY.

A brief history of children's books, concentrating only on the highlights, but sufficient for the average reader to get an idea of some of the major trends.

2866.   Dohm, Janice. "Two and a half centuries of children's books: John Newbery, 1713–1767, and Frederic Melcher, 1879–1963," *Junior bookshelf,* Vol. 27, Oct., 1963, pp. 191–195. DLC, NNY.

A comparison of the contributions of these two kindred spirits, who both did so much to further the cause of good, lively books for children.

2867.   Lane, William C. *Catalogue of English and American chap-books and broadside ballads in Harvard College Library.* Cambridge, Mass., Harvard University, 1905. 171p. (Harvard University Library. Bibliographical contributions, 56). DLC, NNY.

A list of some 2,400 items, arranged by general subjects and types, and annotated in part. There are excellent indexes by title, subject, printer, publisher and bookseller.

2868.   Langley, A. K. B. "A children's librarian

abroad," *New Zealand libraries,* Wellington, Vol. 18, No. 6, July, 1955, pp. 129–135. DLC, NNY.

Impressions of a New Zealand children's librarian, gained while visiting libraries in England, the U.S. and Canada.

2869.   Meigs, Cornelia, *et al. A critical history of children's literature.* New York, Macmillan, 1953. 624p. DLC, IYL, NNY.

A definitive survey of the literature from its very beginnings, touching on all aspects and treating of the writers of the classics at greatest length. Foreign children's literature is treated only insofar as it influenced English and U.S. writing, or found itself a classic in the English translation (e.g. Selma Lagerlof's *Wonderful Adventures of Nils*). The four parts are: "Roots in the past, up to 1840" by Cornelia Meigs; "Widening horizons, 1840–1890" by Anne Eaton; "A rightful heritage, 1890–1920" by Elizabeth Nesbitt; "The golden age, 1920–1950" by Ruth Hill Viguers. In spite of its bibliographical shortcomings and inaccuracies (as pointed out by Earle F. Walbridge in the *Papers* of the Bibliographical Society of America, Vol. 48, 2nd Quarter, 1954), this is a laudable attempt at synthesizing a vast amount of material into an eminently readable account. There is an expanded and revised edition in preparation, which, it is to be hoped, will rectify the errors and bring the last section up-to-date. The bibliographies for each part also need considerable expansion. Index.

2870.   Neuberg, Victor E. *Chapbooks.* London, Vine Press, 1964. 88p. DLC.

"A bibliography of references to English and American chapbook literature of the 18th and 19th centuries." Index to authors, printers and publishers, and an index to subjects and authors of works recorded in the bibliography. Some reproductions.

2871.   Thomas, M. O. "Juvenile libraries, British and American," *Modern librarian,* Lahore, Vol. 4, No. 2, Jan., 1934, pp. 53–62. DLC.

The philosophy of service to children in libraries, as it developed in Great Britain and the U.S. from the late 19th century onward.

2872.   Weiss, Harry B. *A book about chapbooks, the people's literature of bygone times.* Trenton, N.J. [Ann Arbor, Michigan, Edwards], 1942. 149p. DLC, NNY.

A history of chapbooks in England, Scotland, the U.S. and some of the other European countries. They are treated by type, by subject, by printer, by author, and the like. There is a section on some of the best private and public collections, and a five page bibliography.

Australia

During the 19th century there were few books for children written and published in Australia, but there were more having Australian backgrounds which appeared in England. Both types suffered from a too heavy dose of the "exotic," presenting this newly settled country in rather untrue terms. Not until the 20th century were there less stereotyped stories, and not until after the Second World War was there a literature which was substantial and consistent, rather than a few intermittant titles.

Rosemary Wighton has written a brief history of the early didactic literature, but there is as yet no study on contemporary trends. There are, however, several book lists (2873, 2874, 2899) which indicate the scope and variety of the literature which does exist. There is also the annual children's book issue of the *Australian Book Review,* containing short articles on the history and criticism of Australian children's books, and some of their authors. More and more of these titles are being published in British and U.S. editions, and a fair number are also being translated into European languages. While Australian libraries and schools still import numerous titles from England and somewhat fewer from the U.S., it must be gratifying to note that there is now a flow of materials in both directions.

Much of the credit for the over-all interest in children's books is due to the Children's Book Councils. These are modeled on the U.S. original and exist in each of the states, with the exception of Western Australia. The first one was begun in New South Wales in 1945. At the present time, the headquarters rotates among the four states, but local activities are always carried out through the individual state councils. They promote the annual Children's Book Week, instigate studies on Australian children's book problems and in general work to keep children's literature as much in the public eye as is possible.

If one judges by statistics, children's libraries in Australia are widespread, contain generous stocks, and are widely used. However, one must look well beyond statistics to get a qualitative grasp of the situation, and in the case of Australia, the closer one looks, the less bright the picture seems. A book and some recent articles indicate that there is still much to be desired in the improvement of library work with children.

Ernest Roe concentrates on school libraries in his book, *Teachers, Librarians and Children*. His comments obviously stem from long experience in working with children. His main contention is that school libraries are not enhancing education as they should, but are rather working at cross purposes to it. There are a number of points on which the author is sure to meet disagreement, in Australia and in other countries, but the book is nevertheless one of the most stimulating to be written on the subject in recent years.

Another important contribution to library literature is the article by D. R. Hall, "Why Children's Libraries?" (2888). This librarian is also extremely critical of the type of service given in most children's libraries, blaming it partly on "the too-rapid growth of local libraries with a consequent lack of informed staff." But the basic reasons why children's libraries fail, the article goes on to say, are indifference, ignorance or lack of understanding of the real needs of children. "You will know that a real children's library exists only when a group of people realizes how important children are, how essential it is that children who are born unequal should be given equality of opportunity, and how books can be selected, organized and promoted to give this opportunity" (2888).

The Mary Matheson Children's Library movement began in New South Wales in the 1940's. It is discussed briefly in the Hall article, in very unfavorable terms, because the author felt that the movement substituted social therapy in place of genuine library aims. This movement did not spread to the other states to any great extent, but its practices are still prevalent in New South Wales. A library of this type is described in the article by Findlay, under New Zealand (2908).

On the whole, one can say that although in Australia children's books have had a very successful rise in importance, children's libraries have yet to come up to the same good standards.

2873. *Australian book review.* "Children's book and educational supplement." (Kensington Park), 1962 ff. Annual. DLC has 1962, 1963.

This annual supplement contains articles of history and criticism, reviews of the year's best children's books and other related material.

2874. *Australian children's books.* 2nd ed. Melbourne, Children's Book Council of Victoria, 1962. 32p. DLC.

"A firmly chauvinistic attempt to list what Australian authors, artists and publishers have achieved in this field" states the introduction to this annotated list arranged by fiction (for four age levels) and different areas of nonfiction. There is also a list of the "Books of the Year, 1946–1962." Index.

2875. Boniwell, Joyce. "Children's books: The mirror of their age," *Australian library journal,* Sydney, Vol. 10, Jan., 1961, pp. 8–12. DLC, NNY.

This critic writes of those aspects of children's books which indicate social mores and customs to the extent that it is possible to study the social history of a people through children's books.

2876. ———. "Children's libraries today and tomorrow, an account of Australian services and needs, August, 1961," *Australian library journal,* Sydney, Vol. 11, Jan., 1962, pp. 37–44. DLC, NNY.

Exactly what the title implies—an in-depth survey of the present and future status. The author is the children's librarian in the national library.

2877. ———. "Children's reading," *Australian library journal,* Sydney, Vol. 11, July, 1962, pp. 131–137. DLC, NNY.

Much of what children read or want to read depends upon the examples of the adults they meet and live with. Therefore, in order to inculcate good reading habits in children, the librarian or parent must first become a good reader himself.

2878. ———. "The Lady Clark Memorial Children's Library, Tasmania," *New Zealand libraries,* Wellington, Vol. 15, No. 8, Oct., 1952, pp. 171–176. DLC, NNY.

A history of library service to children on this island-state, with specific reference to the central Lady Clark Library.

2879. *Books for young people.* Adelaide, Libraries Board of South Australia. Part 1, 3rd ed., 1964, 90p. Part II, 2nd ed., 1963, 82p. DLC.

Part I is concerned with children up to 13 years, Part II with children from 13 to 17 years. Each of them is divided into fiction and nonfiction, with the latter further divided into general subject areas. The annotations are concise, and there are illustrations from the books scattered throughout these attractive lists. Indexes.

2880. *Books for young people; a guide to Christmas buying.* Adelaide, Libraries Board of South Australia. Annual, 1961 ff. DLC.

These shorter recommended lists are intended as a guide to purchasers of books for gifts.

2881. Buick, Barbara. "Australian school libraries," *Australian library journal,* Sydney, Vol. 13, No. 1, Mar., 1964, pp. 18–26. DLC.

The president of the Children's Libraries Section outlines the present status of school libraries in each of the six states of Australia, and makes recommendations for their improvement in the areas of financing, training of professional staff and relation to the national organization of librarians.

2882. ———. "Children's library services in South Australia," *Australian library journal,* Sydney, Vol. 14, No. 3, Sept., 1965, pp. 115–118. DLC.

Children's public library service in Australia began with the establishment of a department in the Public Library of South Australia in February, 1915. The author traces its development since then and stresses the influence of British thinking and practice in this field. This is only the first part of a series, but the others were not located.

2883. *Bulletin.* Children's Book Council of New South Wales. 3 times a year.

2884. Children's Book Council. *Judges' report on awards.* Bellerive, Tasmania, 1964. 9p. DLC.

Critical comments of the judges, concerning the recent award winners in the Book of the Year and Picture Book of the Year prizes given by the Council. Additional titles are commented on, if the judges felt they could be highly recommended. These reports are usually to be found in the children's book number of the *Australian Book Review* (see 2873).

2885. "Children's Book Week issue," *Australian book news,* Sydney, Vol. 1, Nov., 1946, pp. 169–205. DLC, NNY.

This carried a number of articles on Book Week, as well as on Australian writers for children and their works. This periodical also reviewed children's books.

2886. *Children's choice of books. Suggested books for girls and boys from 2–18.* Melbourne, Parents' National Educational Union, 1925. 47p.

2887. "Children's library guild of Australia," *Australian library journal,* Sydney, Vol. 11, July, 1962, p. 138. DLC, NNY.

Description of the founding of a new guild to stimulate publication of Australian children's books, and their plans to publish a series of children's books on Australia.

2888. Hall, D. R. "Why children's libraries?," *Australian library journal,* Sydney, Vol. 9, No. 3, July, 1960, pp. 111–117. DLC, NNY. Also in: *New Zealand libraries,* Wellington, Vol. 23, No. 11, Dec., 1960, pp. 277–285. DLC, NNY.

A speech given at the annual meeting of the Australian Library Association, in which this librarian excoriates the staff in many present-day libraries for children, claiming they are not worthy of being called librarians until they face up to the question: why children's libraries? He gives his answer in admirable terms, and outlines the forms which service should take.

2889. Ifould, W. H. "Australia: New South Wales," *School library review,* London, Vol. 2, No. 3, pp. 106–108. NNY.

The author refers to school libraries in New South Wales. Most of this work was done through "book boxes" or parcels.

2890. Kirby, Frank Gordon. *Libraries in secondary schools. A report on the libraries of secondary schools in Victoria with suggestions for a postwar plan for school libraries.* Melbourne, Melbourne University Press, 1945. 48p. DLC, NNY.

A pamphlet devoted principally to the mechanics of organization and administration.

2891. McCallum, Ann. "Writing for children: a seminar conducted by the Children's Book Council of Canberra, May 6, 1965," *New Zealand libraries,* Wellington, Vol. 28, Oct., 1965, pp. 225–228. DLC.

A report on this seminar which was held in order to stimulate more interest among Australians in writing for children.

2892. Matheson, M. "Children's leisure-time movement in Australia," *New era,* London, Vol. 19, No. 3, Mar., 1938, pp. 70–71. DLC.

A report on the extensive social program of the Children's Library and Crafts Club in Sydney.

2893. Miller, E. Morris. *School libraries and reading.* Melbourne, J. Kemp, 1912. 12p. NNY.

A very general outline of the principles of good school library service.

2894. Paltridge, Cynthia. "Australia," *Library service to children, 2.* Lund, Bibliotekstjänst, 1966, pp. 7–15. DLC, NNY.

This chapter in the IFLA publication gives the history and present status of library service to children in Australia.

2895. Roe, Ernest. *Teachers, librarians and children.* Melbourne, F. W. Cheshire Pty., 1965. 189p. DLC, IYL, NNY. Also: London, Crosby Lockwood, 1965, 189p. 25s.

A thought-provoking book in which the author claims that school libraries of the present are largely irrelevant in education, as they now operate. He gives some reasons as to why this is the situation and points out possible changes for the better.

2896. ———. Why do children read? *Australian library journal,* Sydney, Vol. 13, No. 1, Mar., 1964, pp. 3–14. DLC.

This educator observed and questioned intensively a group of children. He presents here the in-depth reasons which eight of them gave for their reading habits.

2897. Saxby, H. M. "Australian books for children 1841–1900," *Australian library journal,* Sydney, Vol. 11, July, 1962, pp. 125–130. DLC, NNY.

A history of children's books in the period, describing specific titles as well as general trends.

2898. "Training of school and children's librarians in Australia," *Australian library journal,* Sydney, Vol. 6, Jan., 1958, pp. 248–252. DLC, NNY.

An excellent summary on a state-by-state basis.

2899. Wallace, G. M. "School libraries, the true foundation . . ." Australian Library Conference, *Proceedings,* 1928, pp. 36–40.

2900. Wells, June. "A children's library in the Australian tropics," *Wilson library bulletin,* New York, Vol. 31, Oct., 1956, pp. 160–162. DLC, NNY.

A description of the public library in Queensland, and its services for children.

2901. Wighton, Rosemary. *Early Australian children's literature.* Melbourne, Lansdowne Press, 1963. 40p. (Australian Writers and Their Work). DLC.

The author includes "any children's book of the last century which presented some aspect of life in Australia, irrespective of the origin or habitat of the author," within the scope of her study. Most of them, in fact, were not published in Australia, and were very misleading in their presentation of Australian realities.

New Zealand

Here is a country with virtually no indigenous children's literature which has managed to get its children to be avid readers or at least heavy users of books. This has been achieved through the sound establishment of a national library service, with professional children's librarians to guide the development of services to the young. This has been accomplished in less than three decades.

Until 1942, the only children who had free and easy access to books were those who lived in the few large cities which maintained public library service. In 1938, the Country Library Service was inaugurated, and officials soon were aware of the need for children's books. It was not until 1941 that the Minister of Education could announce the beginning of service to schools, and at that only those in smaller towns (2921). This soon became very popular and there was more demand for wider coverage. There was, however, growing concern among the public librarians as to whether this was in the best interests of all children. In 1945, a committee of public and school children's librarians set out to determine the best way in which all children could get the widest possible use of books. Their general conclusion was that school libraries were the answer.

Later, some librarians were to regret this decision for the emphasis placed on school libraries caused the state to allot all funds to them, leaving none for the public libraries. Eventually this misunderstanding was worked out, so that at the present time one could say school and public libraries for children are considered equally important and both receive adequate support to maintain good libraries to suit the individual needs of each area.

The quality of service depends pretty much on the professional staff and in this respect, too, New Zealand has worked out a system which, while it never provides quite enough children's librarians, at least seems to keep the number of new librarians from falling too far behind the number of new library positions. Mrs. Catherine Bishop, in her editorial introducing a special issue of *New Zealand Libraries* on school libraries, could state: "Courses in children's literature are an established part of teacher training and teachers generally know much more about the wide range of books available for children than they did a few years ago" (2915).

Which are these books? In all fairness a slight modification to the opening sentence of this introduction is in order. There are perhaps half a dozen quality books by New Zealand writers, using the background of their own country. Some of them came about because of commissions by the New Zealand School Publications Branch of the Department of Education. These publications, inexpensive in format but very attractive, are an outstanding example of an official government policy related to the introduction of other cultures to children, through the means of children's books. Naturally, textbooks reflect more closely the life of the country, but in the process of getting these written, few writers were successful in producing stories which can qualify as first-rate literature. Another type of literature which is distinctly national is the oral or chanted tales of the Maori population. These children receive their education either in integrated schools, or, by choice, in schools centered entirely around the Maori culture with few white children in them. Not much of this literature has yet been put down in written form.

The largest proportion (perhaps 95%) of children's books are chosen from the current production of British and U.S. publishers. New Zealand has been surprisingly successful in integrating the use of both types, and they have come to realize that the extra expense involved does not matter when the book is truly well-done and received with delight by their children. This country, with its small population scattered over a wide area, and far removed from the publishing centers of the world, has yet succeeded in exposing its children to the best in books. It is not difficult to sense the infectious pleasure of one of its leading children's librarians and critics, Mrs. Dorothy White, when she writes: ". . . it may be stated that the most exciting event in children's librarianship in New Zealand during the past five years has been the coming of Colombo Plan students and UNESCO fellows to our shores. Children's librarians suddenly realized that after borrowing so much and for so long, their profession had something to offer 'for export?' " (2949).

2902. Bishop, C. A. C. "Children's Book Week 1952," *New Zealand libraries,* Wellington, Vol. 15, No. 9, Nov., 1952, pp. 193–197. DLC, NNY.

Before describing the current year's activities of Book Week, the author writes of its history from 1944 on.

2903. Buchanan, H. "Publicity for school libraries," *New Zealand libraries,* Wellington, Vol. 4, Jan., 1941, pp. 68–71. DLC, NNY.

2904. Burns, J. A. S. "School libraries and teacher-librarian training," *New Zealand libraries,* Wellington, Vol. 26, No. 6, July, 1963, pp. 169–179. DLC, NNY.

The bibliography contains some 86 items pertinent to the subject.

2905. *Children's books to buy.* School Library Service, Wellington. Monthly, July, 1958 ff. Mimeographed.

2906. Edmonds, M. J. "Children's book week," *Here and now,* Auckland, No. 53, Aug., 1956, pp. 21–23.

2907. Fazackerley, Joan. "Sir John McKenzie Memorial Children's Library," *New Zealand libraries,* Wellington, Vol. 22, No. 8, Oct., 1959, pp. 179–185. DLC, NNY.

How a children's library came to be built, organized, stocked and staffed by a group of volunteer women.

2908. Findlay, Aileen. "A children's library and something more," *New Zealand libraries,* Wellington, Vol. 9, July, 1946, pp. 89–92. DLC, NNY.

A children's librarian describes a movement in New South Wales in which books are only one part of the cultural media used through the library. There were music, theater, ballet, crafts, and many other programs available. She questions why such activities cannot be expanded in New Zealand as well.

2909. Gordon, L. G. "The correspondence school library," *New Zealand libraries,* Wellington, Vol. 16, No. 1, Jan.–Feb., 1953, pp. 7–14. DLC, NNY.

A description of a unique library which serviced children in remote rural and island areas, as well as homebound children.

2910. ———. "The school library in the commission's report," *New Zealand libraries,* Wellington, Vol. 25, No. 9, Oct., 1962, pp. 249–252. DLC, NNY.

A librarian comments on the governmental

Education Commission's report and its implications for school library service.

2911. Greig, Lynette. *Standards and aims for a post-primary school library.* Wellington, Library School, 1961. 22p. (N.Z. National Library Service. Library School. Studies in Administration, 4).

2912. Harvey, Kathleen. "School library service," *New Zealand libraries,* Wellington, Vol. 7, Aug., 1944, pp. 121–124. DLC, NNY.
This describes the terms of the service to schools set up by the County Library Service. It is followed by an article on the future of the post-primary school library by Elma Turner.

2913. Heeks, Peggy. *Eleven to fifteen: A basic book list of nonfiction for secondary school libraries.* 3rd ed. Wellington, School Library Association, 1963.

2914. Kazak, P. "School library; its function as a factor in education for a changing world," *National education,* Wellington, Vol. 26, Aug., 1944, pp. 226–228; Sept., 1944, pp. 257–260.

2915. "Library service in schools," *New Zealand libraries,* Wellington, Vol. 25, No. 7, Aug., 1962, pp. 171–207. DLC, NNY.
This entire issue is devoted to the problems of the school library and includes articles by H. C. D. Somerset on secondary school libraries, by H. J. R. Brown on post-primary school libraries, by Kathleen McCaul on the school library conference, and by C. R. Tibbles on libraries in education. There is an official statement of the New Zealand Library Association submitted to the Commission on Education, and a select bibliography on school libraries, pp. 203–204.

2916. "Library service to children," *New Zealand libraries,* Wellington, Vol. 16, July–Aug., 1953, pp. 130–133. DLC, NNY.
This report was by a committee similar in function to the one which prepared the report in 1945 (2936) which led to emphasis on school library development. It questioned whether the best of the possibilities had been chosen.

2917. McCaul, Kathleen. "New Zealand," *Top of the news,* Chicago, Vol. 7, Oct., 1950, pp. 20–21. DLC.
In this issue devoted to children's library work in many countries, this librarian describes the various methods and types of children's library work in New Zealand.

2918. ———. "Three years of discussion: School libraries 1960–62," *New Zealand libraries,* Wellington, Vol. 26, No. 5, June, 1963, pp. 142–145. DLC, NNY.
A review and bibliography covering the period mentioned.

2919. McDonald, J. D. "The adolescent and the public library," *New Zealand libraries,* Wellington, Vol. 9, Aug., 1946, pp. 110–114; Sept., 1946, pp. 129–133. DLC, NNY.
How to get the child reader to change over from school library use to public library use as a young adult.

2920. "Magic casements: Art in children's library," *New Zealand libraries,* Wellington, Vol. 6, No. 14, Oct., 1943, pp. 213–216. DLC, NNY.
A description of an unusual project attempting to teach children art appreciation through the use of picture books.

2921. Mason, H. G. R. "School library service," *New Zealand libraries,* Wellington, Vol. 5, Oct., 1941, pp. 65–67. DLC, NNY.
The Minister of Education makes a statement to the effect that school library service would be handled through the County Library Service, but only to towns under 10,000 in population. He outlines how the service will work.

2922. Milne, Mary. "The training of teacher-librarians," *New Zealand libraries,* Wellington, Vol. 20, No. 4, June, 1957, pp. 81–90. DLC, NNY.
A review of existing policies, and some recommendations for improvement.

2923. ———. "The work of a teacher librarian," *New Zealand libraries,* Wellington, Vol. 22, No. 1, Jan.–Feb., 1959, pp. 1–7. DLC.
The librarian of the Takapuna Grammar School describes her work in the school's library.

2924. Neal, Dorothy M. *Junior books: A recommended list for boys and girls.* Wellington, New Zealand Library Association, 1940. 95p. DLC. Mimeographed.
The first truly selective list made for the children's section of the New Zealand Library Association. The introduction gave some bases for selection, and the entries were annotated and arranged by decimal classification scheme.

2925. ———. "Matter of picture books," *New Zealand libraries,* Wellington, Vol. 1, No. 12, July, 1938, pp. 93–94. DLC, NNY.

This librarian stresses the importance of extending library service to very young children, since they are not likely to be able to afford buying beautiful picture books.

2926. ———. "Social studies and the children's librarian," *New Zealand libraries,* Wellington, Vol. 5, No. 10, May, 1942, pp. 205–212. DLC, NNY.

An introduction to the part of the course in children's librarianship which dealt with social studies.

2927. New Zealand. National Library Service. School Library Service. *Basic books for primary schools.* Wellington, National Library Service, 1961. 59p.

2928. ———. *Books about New Zealand; a list for use in schools.* 2nd ed. Wellington, National Library Service, 1964. 14p.

2929. ———. *Books to enjoy: Forms I and II. Standards 1 and 2.* 2nd ed. Wellington, National Library Service, 1964. 55p. and 35p.

2930. ———. *Books to enjoy, standards 3 and 4.* Wellington, National Library Service, 1956. 37p. DLC.

A list to help children in these grades to choose their books in various categories. No annotations.

2931. ———. *Fiction for post-primary schools.* 2nd ed. Wellington, National Library Service, 1960. 180p. DLC. (Mimeographed.)

A selective list of reading for teen-aged children, including classics and modern adult novels for older children. It is in author arrangement, annotated, and with a subject index of great detail.

2932. ———. *Junior fiction.* Wellington, National Library Service, 1950. DLC. Supplements: 1961 and 1963. DLC.

Selective lists of fiction for young children, arranged by author and with title and subject indexes. There are annotations and grade levels given.

2933. ———. *Manual for school libraries.* 2nd ed., rev. Wellington, National Library Service, 1964. 48p. 25p.

2934. ———. *Planning the school library.* New ed. Wellington, National Library Service, 1964. 52p.

2935. New Zealand Library Association. Children's and Young People's Section. *Reference books for the home.* Wellington, New Zealand Library Association, 1964. 11p.

2936. ———. Planning Committee, School and Children's Libraries. "Report to Council," *New Zealand libraries,* Wellington, Vol. 8, Dec., 1945, pp. 201–210. DLC, NNY

An important report which documents the findings of a committee which set out to explore the three types of library service to children New Zealand could attempt: 1. complete service from public libraries; 2. divided service, from both public and school libraries; 3. complete service from school libraries. The Committee recommended opting for the third type, and gives the reasons why.

2937. New Zealand Library School. *Training of librarians for post-primary school libraries.* Wellington, The School, 1963. 62p.

2938. Pryor, D. C. "Presidential address. School libraries," *New Zealand libraries,* Wellington, Vol. 20, No. 2, Mar.–Apr., 1958, pp. 17–30. DLC, NNY.

One half of the speech was devoted to the library association president's belief that service to children in New Zealand could be more effectively carried out through the schools.

2939. Purton, Barbara. "Public library services for children," *New Zealand libraries,* Wellington, Vol. 23, No. 9, Oct., 1960, pp. 233–240. DLC, NNY.

This experienced librarian outlines the aims of such service, and questions the use of extra or "extension" services and activities, which she feels can usually be done better by commercial or professional groups.

2940. Scott, Walter J. *Reading, film and radio tastes of high school boys and girls.* Wellington, New Zealand Council for Educational Research, 1947. 207p. DLC.

A survey of the out-of-school interests of 4000 post-primary (12–19 years) boys and girls in New Zealand. This elaborate study includes a sample questionnaire and a final chapter of conclusions and implications.

2941. "Standards for school libraries," *New Zealand libraries,* Wellington, Vol. 24, No. 2, Mar., 1961, pp. 37–40. DLC, NNY.

The terms submitted by the library association to the Commission on New Zealand Education. These are essentially the standards in operation today, with some modifications.

2942. Tibbles, C. "Service to children at the small public library," *Education,* Wellington, Vol. 13, No. 2, Mar., 1964, pp. 17–19. DLC.

2943. Tolley, C. W. "What our libraries are doing for children," *New Zealand parent and child,* Wellington, Vol. 4, No. 11, Nov., 1956, pp. 7–9.

2944. Verry, L. H. "Young New Zealand's book hunger," *New Zealand magazine,* Wellington, Vol. 24, No. 2, Mar.–Apr., 1945, pp. 19–21.

2945. "What shall I give him to read: A parent's notes," *New Zealand libraries,* Wellington, Vol. 8, Dec., 1945, pp. 214–218, DLC, NNY.

A parent questions as to how one can select books which are good, and at the same time genuinely enjoyed by children.

2946. White, Dorothy Neal. *About books for children.* Wellington, New Zealand Council for Educational Research in conjunction with New Zealand Library Association, 1946. 222p. IYL, DLC, NNY.

A sensitively written book on the values to look for in children's literature. Many of the specific titles mentioned are no longer available, but the general critical judgments are still very valid.

2947. ———. *Books before five.* Oxford University Press, in association with the New Zealand Council for Educational Research, 1954. 196p. DLC, NNY, IYL.

A diary of Mrs. White's own experience with her preschool child and her books. Her perceptive comments clearly indicate her years of previous experience as a leading children's librarian in New Zealand. It is interesting to compare this with Chukovsky (1877) since they both cover the same age span.

2948. ———. "Children's library service," *The Dunedin Public Library 1908–1958.* Wellington, A. H. and A. W. Reed, 1958, pp. 49–58. IYL.

Children's services began in this pioneer library in 1910. This commemorative publication recounts the development of these services decade by decade.

2949. ———. "New Zealand," *Library service to children.* Lund, Bibliotekstjänst, 1963, pp. 72–84. DLC, IYL, NNY.

This chapter in the IFLA publication deals with the history and present status of children's library work in this country.

2950. ———. "A 'Newbery' for New Zealand," *Horn book,* Boston, Vol. 22, Sept., 1946, pp. 339–343. DLC, NNY.

Beginning in 1945, the Esther Glen award is to be given to "the most distinguished contribution to New Zealand literature for children." This explains the terms of the award, and tells a little about the author for whom the award is named.

2951. ———. "Some 19th century books for 20th century children," *National education,* Wellington, Vol. 24, May, 1942, pp. 143–145.

2952. ———. "Some historical notes on New Zealand development to 1946," *New Zealand libraries,* Wellington, Vol. 24, No. 2, March, 1961, pp. 29–37. DLC, NNY.

The title refers to library service to children. The author writes of this early work with insight and charm, and points out the influences of U.S. and British systems. She also mentions that New Zealand is unique in that it continues to evaluate both the U.S. *and* British children's book production, selecting the best of both.

2953. Woodley, Myrtle. "All country districts should have children's libraries," *New Zealand journal of agriculture,* Vol. 97, No. 2, Aug., 1958, p. 176. DLC.

Describes the means whereby volunteers can run rural children's libraries, with the help of the National Library Service.

2954. Wylie, D. M. "Children's and school library service," *New Zealand libraries,* Wellington, Vol. 17, No. 9, Nov., 1953, pp. 201–206. DLC, NNY.

Comments on the reports of the 1945 and 1953 committees (2936 and 2916) which indicate dissatisfaction with the Schools Library System, in that it was not accomplishing what it set out to do.

England

The history of children's literature in English begins in whatever century of the Middle Ages one chooses to place the origins of the romances, epics and fables which were passed on through oral narration as well as through handwritten manuscripts. Darton begins his survey in roughly the 15th century, when the first printed fables of Caxton appeared (3053). But he also keeps referring back to the previous centuries which had produced the heroic deeds recounted in the King Arthur, Robin Hood and other cycles. Mrs. Meigs calls this the period of the "deepest roots," but gives it no specific dates (2869). These two sources, as well as the first chapters in Louise F. Field's book (3074) and portions of Mr. Muir's study (3180) all present this complex material in engaging terms, having far more appeal than their brief mention here can possibly suggest.

The realistic school of historians would probably set the date of 1744 as the actual beginning of children's book publishing in English, for that was the year John Newbery brought out *A Little Pretty Pocket Book,* first of many books for children to appear under his imprint. Darton himself considers this the best date of the commencement of a children's literature meant primarily to amuse and entertain, and only secondarily to instruct. He wrote: ". . . Before 1744, . . . children with imaginative minds still had to steal in order to satisfy their free desires. Nothing cheerfully original was offered to *them,* nor were there facilities for them to look for it. They somehow got what they liked. The moralist was still a heavy burden upon them—then and for a century and a half to come—and the practical openings for literary enjoyment were scant and usually illicit. Newbery made the facilities plain and adequate; it was his great service to children's literature; but he could hardly even scotch the moralist" (3053, p. 120).

There is very little one can add about John Newbery, to what has already been said in the biography by Charles Welsh (3278), and in any number of later articles and books. It is not that his life has been completely documented, for there still remains much mystery as to how much of his books he himself wrote, and who the other authors were. This will probably rest in mystery forever, for although Newbery kept careful accounts, it was the fashion of the day for the author to disguise himself when writing fictional matter of this type, and Newbery was ever the knowledgeable tradesman in knowing just how far to go. Perhaps it is surprising to learn that Newbery, in his own lifetime, published only some 20 children's books, but this was about 19 more than most of his predecessors and competitors. It was not uncommon for a person to "publish" a single book, and then turn to other interests. The Newbury name, however, remained in use as an imprint up to about 1800; thereafter the firm was in other hands, among them those of Charles Welsh, to whom we owe much of the historical data on Newbery.

One of the titles listed in Newbery's copyrights list for 1780 is *Mother Goose's Melody: or, Sonnets for the Cradle.* No surviving copy of an edition dated that early has been found, but a number of later editions, published by Newbery's stepson, survive in a handful of copies. These seem to be the first books which use the name "Mother Goose" in connection with these rhymes, in print. There are myriad articles and books on the history of Mother Goose rhymes, as well as on the manner in which they came to be connected with the character mentioned on the title page of Perrault's tales, *Ma Mere l'Oie*. All of them make fascinating reading. But far more compelling is the realization that these rhymes stayed intact through so many years of oral transmission. When they finally were put into print in the 18th century and openly given to children, they seem to have been "loved to pieces." Very few surviving copies of any edition of Mother Goose is in pristine condition. One wonders if perhaps it was an early collection of the rhymes which John Locke labeled "silly," in his essay *Some Thoughts Concerning Education* (1690). He wrote of the success one could have with Aesop's fables and Old Testament stories when teaching children to read, but "this sort of useful books amongst the number of silly ones that are of all sorts, have yet had the fate to be neglected" (3156).

John Locke's theories did have some influence on children's books throughout the 18th century. But as Darton so clearly points out, it was not so much that writers employed the theories of Locke, as rather a case of Locke knowing the long-established habits of the English beforehand. The educator who truly affected English children's books of the period was Jean Jacques Rousseau. His influence, and that of his compatriots Mme. de Genlis and Arnaud Berquin, was keenly felt after the publication of *Émile* in 1762. This domination lasted well into the 19th century in English children's books, due in no small measure to Thomas Day, Richard Lovell Edgeworth and his daughter Maria Edgeworth.

When Rousseau indicated that children should be allowed to speak and behave according to the dictates of Nature, he could hardly have imagined how this was to be interpreted by parents and educators in England. The two boy protagonists of Day's *Sandford and Merton* are anything but "natural," no matter what period they are viewed from. The same is true of the works of Maria Edgeworth, although she came closer to the truth, and was, besides, a much more gifted writer than Day. The truth of the matter is that Day, Maria Edgeworth and her father were responsible for repressing, rather than encouraging, much of the natural spirit in childhood. This spirit had found partial release in the fairy tales and chapbooks of a century earlier, but this trio of well-meaning educators succeeded in convincing several generations of parents and teachers that they must control the child's imagination by use of "benevolent reason." They expressed the hope that Dr. Johnson, who opposed them, would "not have power to restore the reign of fairies" (2976 p. 190).

To assign only this type of didactic writing to the influence of Rousseau is not quite just. Because of his extraordinary recommendation of *Robinson Crusoe* (as the only book to be given the child, and that after the age of 12) there was a spurt of interest in the Defoe book which then burst into a veritable flood of imitations. In all likelihood, *Robinson Crusoe* would have survived to this day even without the Rousseau endorsement. It is not so likely that Campe's version or that of Wyss would have appeared without the stimulation and inspiration generated by *Émile*.

Maria Edgeworth had an admirer in Sir Walter Scott. He tried to put some of her theories to work in his history of Scotland, which he worked on for many years and which finally was published in the years from 1828 to 1830. He intended this as a book for children (specifically, his grandson) and called it therefore *Tales of a Grandfather*. However, it was constantly interrupted by his work on the Waverley novels, which he did *not* intend for children, but which they so eagerly picked up because of the rousing stories and the romance. Scott can also be considered important in the history of children's literature for two other reasons: he was the direct inspiration for *Holiday House*, by Catherine Sinclair, and for much of the work of Charlotte Yonge.

Before turning to Miss Yonge and her contemporaries of the Victorian age, a word about Miss Sinclair's book, and about the ubiquitous *Peter Parley* is in order. When Scott commented to Miss Sinclair that there would be no "poets, wits or orators" in the coming generation, because the play of imagination was discouraged, that lady promptly set herself the task of writing a book which "would paint that species of noisy, frolicsome, mischievous children which is now almost extinct . . ." (Preface to *Holiday House*). She wished to show children who had "individuality of character and feeling," and this she did, to a far greater degree than anyone else in her day. R. L. Green finds this book, from the historical point of view, "one of the most important books in the history of children's literature, for it was written with the intention of changing the quality and kind of reading for young people, and it was so successful that not only did it achieve its purpose but it remained in print, and was read by children for precisely a hundred years" (3090, p. 60).

The original *Peter Parley* was the creation of the American writer, Samuel Griswold Goodrich. One must use the term "original" because bibliophiles have not yet completely separated the list of Peter Parley books into those written and published by Goodrich himself, and the many imitations in the U.S. and England. They were published in greatest numbers during the years from 1827 to 1860, and sold, according to Darton, well over seven million volumes (the originals alone). They looked much alike, except for the frequent changes in illustrators, and treated their subjects (travels, social studies, history, etc.) in much the same openly didactic manner.

With the hindsight we now have, it seems incredible that such a gifted person as Charlotte Yonge could criticize so accurately the faults in many of the children's books of her time, and not recognize these same faults in her own works. In the third part of her article for *MacMillan's Magazine* (3295), she takes to task a number of writers for their priggish class consciousness. Her final advice is admirable: "Bring children as soon as possible to stretch up to books above them, provided those books are noble and good. Do not give up such books on account of passages on which it would be inconvenient to be questioned on. If the child is in the habit of meeting things beyond comprehension it will pass such matters unheeded with the rest . . . The only things to put out of its way are those that *nobody* ought to read, certainly not its mother."

The books Charlotte Yonge wrote satisfied all of these qualities, and were in fact read as much by families as by children. For all of their liveliness of story and character, they are pervaded by a blindness to the social ills and realities around them. In this respect, Miss Yonge's books are very much a mirror of their time, for not even the power of Dickens' characters could quite bring the Victorians to act on social reforms reaching wide areas of the poorer classes. The novels of Charlotte Yonge and those of her successors, Mrs. Gatty, Mrs. Ewing and Mrs. Molesworth, make some of the most satisfying nostalgic reading, even for adults of today. There is such assurance in the rightness of their way of life, such security of family and close friends, that even with our knowledge that in all families it was not so, we become convinced of the invincible ignorance of these self-assured characters and identify with them in spite of historical objections.

Two more works stand out among the pre-*Alice* books for children and each is of a distinct type, new for the time. *Tom Brown's School-days*, by Thomas Hughes, appeared in 1857; *The Water-Babies*, by Charles Kingsley, in 1863. The two men were friends, and shared similiar religious and political beliefs, as well as a predilection for writing children's books.

To backtrack for just a moment, the genre of poetry had not been as neglected as this brief survey might so far suggest. In the 17th and 18th centuries, it more or less followed the hard moral line of prose literature for children, with Isaac Watts, Ann and Jane Taylor and others providing the young with simple lessons in easily memorized lines. William Blake's poetry was also used with children, but to a lesser extent, because there was something disturbing in it to the average reader. Even Mrs. Field, writing in 1891, found that he "might have written admirable verses for children, but the note of oddity and eccentricity recurs too often in most of those which he actually produced to allow them to be reckoned quite satisfactory" (3074, p. 309).

A lively contrast to both the Taylors and Blake was provided by William Roscoe's *The Butterfly's Ball*. It owed some of its success to the illustrations of Mulready, but more to the nonsense of Mother Goose, which it unconsciously mimicked. No wonder it was in turn literally imitated to death.

The poet who presages the work of Lewis Carroll and the other great writers of nonsense, is Edward Lear, whose first *Book of Nonsense* was published in 1846. Most of his other nonsense volumes appeared after 1870, however, so he can be considered more a contemporary of Lewis Carroll than a precursor.

In the mid-Victorian era the fairy tale began its slow comeback, aided by the translations of Grimm, Andersen, Asbjørnsen and Moe and others. Two original works belong to this channel of the stream of children's literature: '*The King of the Golden River,* written by John Ruskin, is a very successful imitation of the Grimms. Thackeray's *The Rose and the Ring* is almost a spoof of the traditional fairy tale.

It might seem, from the number of authors and titles cited above, that the 18th and early 19th century offered more to delight the child than is usually credited to this period. These names, however, represented only a small percentage in the flood of cheap and poorly-written books which were actually available. It was only when the last part of the century brought out greater numbers of quality books that the selection was worthy of that term.

This golden age begins, of course, with Lewis Carroll and is to last up to about 1910. (Because of its greater familiarity, this pseudonym for Charles Lutwidge Dodgson will be used throughout.) Lewis Carroll has been analyzed and biographed by so many persons and in so many languages that the few words allowable here can hardly add much. The one note which seems most in order in this work of international scope is Carroll's universality. The many translations of *Alice* run counter to all theories of the suitability or even feasibility of translation. Puns, double entendres, satires on well-known verses, indeed much of what would today be termed "too British" or "too local" if *Alice* were offered for translation, had not proven too impossible a task for the best translators. "That *Alice* has indeed appealed widely to the world's children is evidenced by the number of times that the story has been translated and the enthusiasm with which the translations—even those which do not seem especially skillful—have been received." (60, p. 7)

George MacDonald and Oscar Wilde seem perhaps an odd pair to be in the same company, but they were contemporaries in writing for children and their literary, allegorical fairy tales, although quite different in approach, reflect a kind of similar release from self. It is curious that MacDonald is always given considerable space in English histories of children's literature, but Oscar Wilde hardly any. It cannot be merely a question of MacDonald's superiority, nor his larger body of work. Percy Muir, who is the only British critic other than Green to mention Wilde, hints that it just might be because of Wilde's personal life that he is not considered suitable material for a discussion related to children's literature. For all of their berating of 18th and 19th-century hypocritical moralists, 20th century British critics have not themselves always taken an honest approach.

Like MacDonald and Wilde, Edith Nesbit owed the acceptance of her work to the climate created by Lewis Carroll. However, she was most directly inspired by Kenneth Grahame, through his poetic recollections of childhood, *The Golden Age* and *Dream Days*. With Grahame there is never any doubt that the child protagonist is the product of an adult's memories. When Edith Nesbit put to paper the events of her childhood, she did not so much recall or evoke them, as she reproduced or relived them. For the duration of the stories (most of them) she *is* the child she writes about.

The only other writer of this period who created children's novels with equally convincing characters and good plot construction was Frances Hodgson Burnett, who was British by birth and tradition, but a resident of the U.S. from her 16th year until her death. Her early stories, and in a sense all of her works, belong to the Victorian age. Neverthless, *A Little Princess* (in the final version of 1905) and *The Secret Garden* are outstanding for the naturalness of character in the children, making one quite forget the unlikelihood of the surroundings and events.

Running along almost simultaneously with the new trends in nonsense writing, literary fantasy and the family story or child novel, was a flow of adventure novels. Frederick Marryat, R. M. Ballantyne, Mark Twain, Robert Louis Stevenson and a host of lesser talents suddenly brought the romance out of the past and made it also a part of the present. The translations of Verne took it into the future.

By all rights, the illustrators from this same period (approximately 1865 to 1910) should receive equal or more space in this review. In addition, much credit should be given to George Cruikshank, whose illustrations for the first English Grimm collection and for other fairy tales, preceded the fine work of Walter Crane, Randolph Caldecott and Kate Greenaway. To this writer at least, it seems far more difficult to describe illustration through words, than vice versa. Consequently, the reader will be referred rather to the picture books themselves, for we are fortunate in having available examples of most of the great illustrators of this time: the *Alice's*, as pictured by Tenniel; the MacDonald books and others illustrated by Arthur Hughes; Grimm's tales adorned by Walter Crane's decorations and illustrations; Kate Greenaway's *Mother Goose* and *A Apple Pie;* and the superb and humorous interpretations of old English rhymes as drawn by Randolph Caldecott. These were the artists who created the picture book, and having come as they did, in a cluster, England depleted her resources. Only Leslie Brooke, and possibly E. H. Shepard and Edward Ardizzone, were to come near the perfection achieved in the illustrations of the "triumvirate."

The culmination of the golden age in writing took place in the 15 years from 1894 to 1908. The former date represents the publication of Kipling's *The Jungle Book*, and the latter date is that of the publication of *The Wind in the Willows,* by Kenneth Grahame. In between is the first Beatrix Potter, *The Tale of Peter Rabbit,* as well as a number of successors, more from Kipling, Edith Nesbit's books, and the J. M. Barrie play, *Peter Pan.* Each was so different from the other, yet all shared the common bond of fantasy. Combined with *Alice*, they were to give England a preeminent position in this type of writing, and as though this weren't enough, they were followed, in each succeeding decade, by at least two works having similar qualities, but by new writers. Hugh Lofting, John Masefield, A. A. Milne, P. L. Travers, J. R. R. Tolkien, Eric Linklater, Mary Norton, Rumer Godden, C. S. Lewis, Lucy M. Boston and Pauline Clarke have added immeasurably to the riches which English-reading children can delve into. There is no comparable body of literature in any other language or country.

In other types of books for children, the United Kingdom has not done as well in the 20th century. In the adventure novel, Arthur Ransome, with his *Swallows and Amazons* and sequels, has almost no rivals. Historical fiction found only two strong advocates, in Geoffrey Trease and Rosemary Sutcliff. Noel Streatfeild gave the career book a good start. But the picture book, the family story and the story centered around the everyday lives of ordinary children, and non-fiction—these were all sorely lacking, and those which did exist were poor in quality when contrasted with the fantasy fiction. This leads invariably to a comparison with the United States which had followed, or exchanged, British trends in children's book publishing up to around 1910.

The contrast is due in no small measure to the public library movement, and to the specifically different ways in which it developed in England, especially in regard to children's services. Despite the Public Libraries Act of 1861, there were very few libraries which grew into sizable collections. Still fewer had the funds to spend on children's books. W. C. B. Sayers wrote that there was still no trained children's librarian in England as of 1910. This is not to discount the efforts of such pioneers as John Ballinger at Cardiff, Wales, J. Potter Briscoe at Nottingham and James Duff Brown at Islington. These men did a tremendous volume of work with children, getting their training in the doing. Still, the great majority of public libraries, if they had any children's books at all, kept them behind locked doors or circulated them to boys and girls over 12. It was not until 1919, when a new Public Libraries Act lifted the old tax limitation, that local authorities could authorize spending as much as they saw fit for library service and the purchase of books. This is the real beginning of the children's library movement in England, and when one realizes that in the U.S. this same period was witnessing the peak of new children's book activity growing out of public library service to the young, it is not surprising to note the further differences that developed in the approach to children's books in England and the U.S.

There has not been the close cooperation between children's book editors and children's librarians, although this is now changing to a certain degree. Publicity events such as Children's Book Week have only recently been undertaken to any nation-wide extent. Children's book reviewing was begun by the *Junior Bookshelf* in 1936, 12 years after *The Horn Book*. Other outlets have been added to this, but many critics agree that there has never been reviewing considering the number of titles published annually.

Formal training for children's librarians was not available in the library schools until 1954, when the first special course was organized at North Western Polytechnic. Of course, much training had been done within general courses, and in special training in the children's libraries themselves. Nevertheless, part of the reason children's librarians had difficulty in getting adequate professional recognition and promotion was due to this lack of beginning training on which to build.

An Association of Children's Librarians, apart from the Library Association (LA) was formed by Eileen Colwell and other leading children's librarians. In 1947, the Youth Libraries Section of the LA took over the work of this Association. It remains the strongest group working in England to "collect and disseminate information relating to young people's literature, and use all the means in its power to raise the standard of book production and selection" (3047).

School libraries began to come to life in the 1930's just as they did in the U.S. In 1937 the School Library Association was founded, separately from the LA. It has worked to promote standards and to bring good library service to every school. More and more, cooperation between the Youth Libraries Group of the LA and the School Library Association is resulting in a multiple attack on the lack of trained children's librarians. When this problem can be solved, England will certainly be on the way to a solution of related problems in children's book criticism, selection and use.

2955.   Alder, Catherine E. M. *Social studies*. London, School Library Association, 1965, 36p.
"An annotated list of recent books on politics, sociology, economics, international relations and world affairs."

2956.   Ainger, Alfred. Children's books of a hundred years ago, *Lectures and essays,* Vol. 1, London, Macmillan, 1905, pp. 382–407. DLC. Also in: *The Hampstead annual,* London, 1902, pp. 24–44. DLC.
Canon Ainger defends the presence of a moral purpose in literature for children, especially when it is concealed by storytelling or poetry as effective as that in the works of Maria Edgeworth and Jane and Ann Taylor.

2957.   Albert, Edward. *What shall I read?* London, Collins, 1938. 231p. Originally issued as *Children's story of literature,* 1930.

2958.   Alexander, Mary. "School libraries: Their history, organization and management," *Library association record,* London, Vol. 24, Jan. 16, 1922, pp. 12–19. DLC, NNY.
A brief but thorough survey of development up to that time.

2959.   Allen, G. W. "To market, to market to buy a fat book," *Publishers' weekly,* New York, Vol. 131, Apr. 24, 1937, pp. 1759–1761. DLC, NNY.
A children's book editor records her impressions of some new children's books in England and some of the new children's libraries as well. She points out that the growing library market will probably soon have as great an importance in England as it does in the U.S., and that the individual children's book buyer will be a rarity.

2960.   Andreae, Gesiena. *The dawn of juvenile literature in England.* Amsterdam, H. J. Paris, 1925. 122p. DLC.
The evolution of the child's book through the centuries and the effect this development had on the whole concept of childhood in the 18th century. An excellent book with which to begin a detailed study of English children's literature.

2961.   "Are juvenile libraries desirable?" *Library world,* London, Vol. 11, June, 1909, pp. 477–479. DLC, IYL.
A debate giving first the affirmative and then the negative arguments, followed by discussion. The chief argument against them seemed to be that children were a nuisance to the library assistants!

2962.   "Are story hours justified?" *Library association record,* London, 4th series, Vol. 1, Sept., 1934, pp. vi–vii. DLC.
A summary of a paper given at the annual conference, together with a report on the discussion which followed. The question of the title was answered in the affirmative.

2963.   Ashton, John. *Chap-books of the eighteenth century with facsimiles, notes, and introduction.* London, Chatto and Windus, 1882. 486p. DLC.

Reproductions of the title pages of many representative chapbooks, with comments on some. There are additional reproductions of some of the more striking illustrations, and also quotes from the texts. A useful study of this type, presented in a scholarly manner.

2964.   Association of Assistant Masters in Secondary Schools. *Guide for school librarians.* Oxford, 1937.

2965.   "Association of children's librarians," *Junior bookshelf,* Birmingham, Vol. 2, July, 1938, pp. 187–190. DLC, NNY.
The history, growth and activities of the special association together with some suggestions for further improvement.

2966.   Aston Manor Public Library. *Catalogue of books for the young.* Aston Manor, 1899. 32p. NNY.
An early list of a public library collection, not annotated and arranged by author.

2967.   Avery, Gillian E. *Nineteenth century children. Heroes and heroines in English children's stories 1780–1900.* London, Hodder and Stoughton, 1965. 260p. DLC.
"The Child Improved," "The Child Amused," and "Adult Attitudes" are the titles of the three sections and each indicates the attitude prevalent in the successive periods. An enlightening study which could well be used by the social scientist as well as the bibliophile. There are biographical notes on the authors, and an index.

2968.   Axon, William E. A. "The juvenile library," *Library,* London, new ser., Vol. 2, Jan. 1, 1901, pp. 67–81. DLC, NNY.
The title refers to a periodical or series for children which began appearing in 1800. This is concerned with the literature in it, and some of the contributors who wrote for it.

2969.   Baker, Ernest A. "The children's department," *The public library.* London, O'Connor, 1924. pp. 63–74. DLC.
A contemporary description of the service facilities and book collections of the average children's library. The author stressed the need for wide improvement.

2970.   ———. "What the public libraries are doing for children," *World's work (and play),* London, Vol. 6, No. 33, Aug., 1905, pp. 244–247. DLC.
The history of this work in England since 1865, and the virtues which will result as it is spread into the schools.

2971.   Ballinger, John. "Children and public libraries," *British library year book (Greenwood's),* London, 1900, pp. 46–52. NNY.
This librarian contended that the great majority of children could not avail themselves of public library service. He outlines here a scheme for making lifetime readers out of all children.

2972.   ———. "Library work with children in Great Britain," *Library journal,* New York, Vol. 29, No. 12, Dec., 1904, pp. 46–49. DLC, NNY.
Landmarks in the history of this movement are pointed out, and some of the philosophy of service is explained.

2973.   ———. "School children in the public libraries," *Library association record,* London, Vol. 1, No. 1, Jan., 1899, pp. 64–72. DLC, NNY.
The sequel to the experiment with children's reading, recorded in the 1897 article in *The Library,* see 3319. A marked quickening of interest was the result, creating support for extended service.

2974.   ———. "Work with children; discussion at library association conference," *Library association record,* London, Vol. 19, Dec., 15, 1917, pp. 449–467. DLC, NNY.
One of the annual reports usually read at the LA conferences. This is followed by an interesting discussion and comments from a number of leading librarians present. These annual reports provide a consistent pattern in the trends of children's work in the United Kingdom.

2975.   Baring-Gould, Sabine. *A book of nursery songs and rhymes.* London, Methuen, 1895. 159p. NNY.
This comprehensive collection often serves as the basis for modern versions of the rhymes.

2976.   Barry, Florence V. *A century of children's books.* London, Methuen, 1922. 257p. DLC, NNY. (Also New York, Doran, 1923, 257p.).
A savory and scholarly survey of children's books from about 1700 to 1825, conveying with obvious enjoyment the flavor of the various periods and types. There is an appendix of footnotes, and a chronological list of books studied.

2977.   Bell, John, "L'édition enfantine en Grande-Bretagne," *Enfance,* Paris, No. 3, 1956, pp. 196–199. IYL. Also in English in: *British book news,* London, No. 186, Feb., 1956, pp. 77–81. DLC, NNY.
According to this observer, children's book publishing in Great Britain had a tendency to over-

produce, and was weak in the area of the well illustrated book.

2978. Belloc, Hilaire. "Children's books," *Living age*, Boston, Vol. 276, Jan., 18, 1913, pp. 186–189. DLC, NNY.

Reprint of an article from *The New Witness*. The author gives his own personal advice to writers interested in reaching the child audience.

2979. Berkeley, Mrs. "About books that amused and taught the children of olden days," *Reports and papers, associated architectural societies*, Lincoln, Vol. 27, Pt. 1, 1903, pp. 149–178. NNY.

A description of some early English books from the author's private collection which covered the years 1740–1830, and was especially rich in the works of authors who had come from Worcestershire or wrote about it.

2980. Bett, Henry. *Nursery rhymes and tales; their origin and history*. London, Methuen [1924]. 130p. DLC, NNY.

A discussion of nursery rhymes in folkloristic terms, comparing those of various countries to the English Mother Goose and other rhymes. Bibliography and index.

2981. Bland, David. "Children's books," *The illustration of books*. London, Faber and Faber, 1962, pp. 127–137. DLC, NNY.

An informative discussion of the principles and progress of children's book illustration from Bewick, Blake and Cruikshank to the present era.

2982. Blodget, T. C. "As it is in English school libraries," *Educational outlook*, Philadelphia, Vol. 8, Jan., 1934, pp. 65–72. DLC.

This U.S. librarian visited many private and public school libraries in England and here compares them with those of U.S. schools. She found her British counterparts to be far better informed on books and bibliography, and having higher standards of scholarship.

2983. Bloomfield, B. C. "School libraries in the 19th century," *Library association record*, London, Vol., 68, Jan., 1966, pp. 16–18. DLC, NNY.

A brief history.

2984. Bodger, Joan. *How the heather looks*. New York, Viking, 1965. 276p. $4.95. DLC, NNY.

A personal account of the visits an American family makes to the people and places they had read about in children's books centered in the British Isles.

2985. *Bodley Head monographs*. London, Bodley Head, 1960 ff. IYL, DLC, NNY.

This excellent series of biographies of children's writers is under the general editorship of Kathleen Lines. The following persons have been the subjects of individual volumes: J. M. Barrie, Lucy Boston, Lewis Carroll, Walter de la Mare, Mrs. Ewing, Eleanor Farjeon, Kenneth Grahame, Rudyard Kipling, Andrew Lang, C. S. Lewis, John Masefield, Mrs. Molesworth, E. Nesbit, Beatrix Potter, Arthur Ransome, Ruth Sawyer, Noel Streatfeild, Rosemary Sutcliff and Geoffrey Trease. Each has been written by a recognized expert in the field of children's literature.

2986. Böckheler, Lotte. *Das englische Kinderlied*. Leipzig, R. Noske, 1935. 114p. DLC.

A history of English nursery rhymes, written in German. This also includes other folk rhymes and game songs and chants. Bibliography.

2987. Bone, Woutrina A. *Children's stories and how to tell them*. London, Christophers, 1923. 193p. (Also: Harcourt, 1924). DLC, NNY.

The origins of folklore and storytelling, the techniques involved, and the significance of the art.

2988. *Books for children*. London, National Book League, Yearly 1956–1957 ff. DLC has 1956–1961.

An annual selection of approximately 100 titles, annotated and arranged in general categories.

2989. "Books for children," *Times literary supplement*, London, 1902 ff. DLC, NNY.

Although this weekly magazine did not begin to review children's books on a regular basis until some years after it started, there are occasional articles and reviews in the first volumes as well. Two children's book supplements are published each year, in the spring and fall. They may be purchased separately, and because they review a good percentage of the half-year's production, they offer an excellent overall view of new trends.

2990. "Books of fiction for children," *Quarterly review*, London, Vol. 122, Jan., 1867, pp. 29–46. DLC, NNY.

Reviews of *The Fairchild Family* by Mrs. Sherwood, *Norse Tales*, translated by Dasent, several volumes of Aesop, and of Andersen, *Parables from Nature* by Mrs. Gatty, and numerous other children's books of the time. In addition, there are interesting comments on fiction in general for children.

2991. *Books, the teacher and the child*. London, National Book League, 1961. 26p. IYL.

Compiled by the Association of Teachers in Colleges and Departments of Education, together with the National Book League, this is a list with comments designed to help teachers make the best use of books and to learn to apply sound principles of selection.

2992.   Braine, Sheila E. "Our ancestors' lesson-books," *Good words,* London, Vol. 40, June, 1899, pp. 403–405. NNY.

"The immediate forerunners of our modern school books were very scrappy affairs. Cathechisms, Outlines, and Abridgements were the order of the day . . . One little insignificant volume was made to do duty for six . . ."

2993.   Bridge, Mrs. Charles. *Catalogue of the circulating library of the Children's Book Club.* London, The Club, 1933. 141p. DLC.

2994.   Briggs, I. "Concerning the juvenile library," *Library assistant,* London, Vol. 6, No. 11, Aug., 1908, pp. 172–179. DLC.

This librarian believed the educational element should be paramount in the children's library. He considered discipline essential to reading.

2995.   Briscoe, J. Potter. "Libraries for the young," *Library chronicle,* London, Vol. 3, 1886, pp. 45–48. DLC.

This librarian was an early advocate of separate rooms and services for children in public libraries. He outlines here the standards he recommended.

2996.   Briscoe, W. A. "A recent development in library work amongst the young," *Library association record,* London, Vol. 11, June 15, 1909, pp. 264–267. DLC, NNY.

To counteract the influence of cheap and trashy books, schools were cooperating with the public libraries in issuing books through the classroom on a controlled basis.

2997.   *British children's books.* London, National Book League, 1963. 83p. DLC. (Revised frequently).

The catalog of an exhibition, arranged in four chronological sections: pre-1914, 1914–1939, 1940–1960, and 1961–1963. The principle of the selectors, according to the preface, was "to choose representative titles of British authors whose books have played a significant part in the reading of children . . ." This is only one of the many exhibitions sponsored by the National Book League, concerning children's books. Others listed in their *Guide to Touring Exhibitions* are: *The Commonwealth in Books* (large children's section) ; *Five to Seven; For the Youngest; Growing up with Books; Paperbacks for Young People; Reference Books for Infants; Science Books for Primary Schools; Science Books for Secondary Schools; School Library Books: Nonfiction.* Almost all have annotated catalogs, attractively and inexpensively produced.

2998.   Brown, James Duff. "Books for very young children," *Library world,* London, Vol. 9, Feb., 1907, pp. 282–288. DLC, NNY.

General characteristics of books for children under nine, and a list of recommended titles. This is followed (pp. 289–292) by a spirited article, "Children's departments in municipal libraries," by Mizpah Gilbert, asserting that the U.S. "cult of children's libraries" as "nurseries" is not suited to British taste. The author outlines what she feels are the true reasons for children's service.

2999.   ———. "Children's home libraries," *The small library.* New York, Dutton, 1907, pp. 11–27.

3000.   ———. "Library work with children," *Manual of library economy.* 3rd ed. London, Grafton, 1920, pp. 439–456. DLC.

An excellent summary of the types of children's work then in existence. Later editions were edited by W. C. Berwick Sayers. The emphasis here, in the 3rd edition, was largely on book selection.

3001.   Brown, Stephen James M. *Catholic juvenile literature.* London, Burns, Oates and Washbourne, 1935. 70p. (Catholic Bibliographical Series, No. 5). DLC.

A classified list of books designed to surround the Catholic child with desirable influences. The introduction points out the difficulty of finding high quality in books on religious subjects. There are two sections on Ireland, one listing Gaelic and the other English books.

3002.   Bruijn, Margreet. "Een kijkje en het jeugdleeszaalwerk in Engeland," *Bibliotheekleven,* Rotterdam, Jaargang 36, No. 4, Apr. 1951, pp. 108–113. DLC, NNY.

Impressions of visits made to children's libraries in and around London and Manchester. The author notes particularly the extension work and work with schools of these libraries.

3003.   Bunce, John Thackray. *Fairy tales: Their origin and meaning, with some account of dwellers in fairyland.* London, Macmillan, 1878. 205p. Also: New York, Appleton, 1879. 172p. DLC, NNY.

A straightforward presentation of the commonly held Aryan theory of the 19th century. In the process, Bunce retells a number of parallel stories and discusses a variety of fairy creatures found in different parts of the world.

3004. Burrell, Arthur. *A guide to storytelling*. London, Isaac Pitman and Sons, 1926. 336p. DLC.

A manual for teachers and parents. A historical review, the various kinds of stories, children's need for stories, and how to tell them are all part of the coverage. Index.

3005. Burt, Cyril. "Typography of children's books; a record of research in the U. K.," *Communication media and the school, Yearbook of education*, London, 1960, pp. 242–256. DLC, NNY.

A very detailed review of past research regarding readability of children's books, as judged by use of different type faces, leading, design, format, etc.

3006. Bushell, Warin Foster. *Teaching boys to read*. Birkenhead, Birkenhead Public Library, 1950. 20p.

3007. Butterworth, Charles C. "Early primers for the use of children," *Bibliographical Society of America. Papers*, New York, Vol. 43, Oct.–Dec., 1949, pp. 374–382. NNY.

Detailed descriptions of some early English primers and ABC books.

3008. Cammaerts, Émile. *The poetry of nonsense*. London, George Routledge & Sons, 1925. 86p. NNY.

The meaning of nonsense, its place in art and specifically in poetry, its special appeal to the child, and the English superiority in this genre. This was written in the belief that nonsense is only appreciated by the child, or by one who remembers childhood clearly.

3009. Cannons, Harry G. T. *Descriptive handbook of juvenile literature*. London, T. Bean, 1906. 336p. DLC.

Printed for the Finsbury Public Library, as a guide to their juvenile collection. Fiction and non-fiction were separate and there was a classification key and index to subjects.

3010. Carnegie United Kingdom Trust. *Books for club libraries: A selection of books suitable for boys' and girls' club libraries*. Edinburgh, Constable, 1926. 128p.

3011. ———. *Libraries in secondary schools. A report to the Carnegie United Kingdom Trust by the committee appointed to inquire into the provision of libraries in secondary schools in Great Britain and Northern Ireland*. Edinburgh, 1936. 85p.

3012. Carrington, Noel. "The children's picture book in England," *Wilson library bulletin*, New York, Vol. 22, No. 2, Oct., 1947, pp. 146–148. DLC, NNY.

An editor of the Puffin Books, juvenile department of Penguin, writes of the contemporary trends in picture books.

3013. Cass, Joan E. *Picture books for young children*. London, Nursery School Association, [1966]. 8p. (Pamphlets, No. 78). DLC.

The kinds of picture books to use with nursery school children, and why and how to use them. A short recommended list is appended.

3014. Chaundler, Christine. *The children's author; a writer's guide to the juvenile market*. London, I. Pitman and Sons, 1934. 111p. DLC.

Principally a discussion from the point of view of market demand.

3015. "Children yesterday and today," *Quarterly review*, London, Vol. 183, Apr., 1896, pp. 374–396. NNY.

Reviews of *Sanford and Merton, Evenings at Home* by John Aikin and Mrs. Barbauld, books by Mrs. Trimmer, Mrs. Sherwood and Maria Edgeworth, and a number of others. It offers dismal proof that in many quarters the didactic school still found more followers and admirers than *Alice*, which this critic felt did not have lasting appeal.

3016. *Children's book news*. "Children's Book Centre," 140 Kensington Church Street, London, W.8. Bimonthly. Vol. 1 ff., No. 1 ff., May, 1964 ff. Subscription: £1:1:0 in U.K. Foreign rates vary.

A new periodical, originally called *New books*, which attempts to review as many as possible of the children's books published yearly in the United Kingdom. Reviewers include librarians, teachers, parents and other specialists. Arranged by subject and indexed by title in each issue.

3017. "Children's books," *Paperbacks in print*. London, Whitaker & Sons, 1957 ff. Annual. DLC, NNY.

This subject index to paperback books in England has a separate section for children's books.

3018. "Children's books," *Quarterly review*, London, Vol. 74, No. 147, June, 1844, pp. 1–14. NNY, DLC. Also in French in: *Bibliothèque de Genève*, Tome 53, Sept., 1844, pp. 24–55. NNY.

A review of books by M. Edgeworth, Mrs. Marshall, J. White, Mrs. Sherwood and Mary Howitt, as well as several anonymous children's books. The comments provide revealing contemporary thought concerning this type of children's literature. See also the entry under the U.S., called "Books for children," by the same reviewer (3507).

3019. "Children's books," *Spectator*, London, 1920 ff.

From the 1920's on up to the time of the First World War, this periodical reviewed children's books with regularity, and in depth. In the 19th century there were only occasional columns of reviews, or articles.

3020. "Children's libraries." Entire issue of *Library world*, London, Vol. 60, No. 698-9, Aug.–Sept., 1958, pp. 17–40. DLC.

Three of the longer articles in this special issue are by: Nancy Dale, on training for youth library work in Great Britain; W. C. Berwick Sayers on children's libraries in general; Janet Hill on book selection for children.

3021. "Children's libraries movement," *Library association record*, London, Vol. 22, Dec. 15, 1920, p.395. DLC, NNY.

A report on the organizational meeting at which a movement for special children's libraries in London was to get under way. The first was to be housed in a building once occupied by Dickens. This was a project which seemingly foundered for lack of funds.

3022. "Children's literature," *London quarterly review*, London, Vol. 13, No. 26, Jan., 1860, pp. 469–500. NNY.

This reviewer has much to say on the imaginative power of children. Followed by reviews of Thackeray's *The Rose and the Ring,* Grimm and Andersen collections, a Charles Kingsley book, Ruskin's *The King of the Golden River,* Mrs. Howitt's *Children's Year* and others.

3023. "Children's literature," *Subject index to periodicals,* London, 1915–1953, annual; 1954 ff. quarterly. DLC, NNY. (Present title: *British humanities index*) (Not published 1923–1925).

In this index published by the Library Association, articles in periodicals from the U.K., the U.S. and to a lesser extent from the continent can be traced. Up to 1926, children's literature can be found in the section called "Education and child welfare." In the later years it is under the heading "Children's literature and reading" or "Children's books and reading."

3024. "Children's reading and writing." Special issues of: *Journal of education,* London, Aug., 1955, 1956, 1957. DLC.

For three years running the August issues of this journal were devoted to the subject of children's literature, approached from many angles, including that of children writing their own literature. The illustration of children's books is also discussed.

3025. Cholmeley, R. F. "Boys' libraries," *Library,* London, new series, Vol. 4, Jan. 27, 1903, pp. 11–21. DLC, NNY.

The author suggested the types of books which were suitable and good for a boy's library. The specific suggestions he makes are interesting from a historical point of view.

3026. Clark, Elizabeth. *Stories to tell: How to tell them.* London, University of London, 1917. 159p.

3027. Clay, Laurence. "Mental and moral pabulum for juveniles 1820 to 1870," *Manchester quarterly,* Vol. 33, 1914, pp. 61–85. NNY.

The one element common to the books of the period seemed to be their religious tone. The author selects excerpts from a number of them to comment upon and criticize.

3028. Coke, Desmond. "Penny dreadfuls," *Connoisseur,* London, Vol. 86, Nov., 1930, pp. 297–304. NNY.

A round dozen of illustrations from books with such heroes as Ned Nimble, Jack Harkaway, Ned Kelly and Dick Turpin. The author comments on the difficulty of locating bibliographic descriptions of this type of publication, because of the poor coverage they get in histories of literature. He gives some clues on how to go about tracing them.

3029. Colwell, Eileen H. "Children's libraries," *New era,* London, Vol. 22, Mar., 1941, pp. 62–64. NNY, DLC.

The author defines the type of library and the access to books which are the right of every child.

3030. ———. "The development of a school library system," *Library world,* London, Vol. 33, Mar., 1931, pp. 235–238. DLC, NNY.

A detailed description of this librarian's efforts to build up service to schools in Hendon. This system is considered one of the most effective in Great Britain, and it is largely due to this librarian that it has achieved its reputation for consistently good service.

3031. ———. "England," *Top of the news,* Chicago, Vol. 7, Oct., 1950, pp. 19–20. DLC.

In this special issue devoted to children's library work in many countries, this librarian of many years' experience presents in capsule form the methods this service takes in the libraries of Great Britain.

3032. ———. "Kate Greenaway Medal," *Library association record,* London, Vol. 57, Dec., 1955, pp. 481–482. DLC, NNY.

A discussion of the new medal which is to be given annually, from 1956 on, to the illustrator of an outstanding picture book published in England.

3033. ———. "Story hour—its aims and methods," *Library association record,* London, Vol. 2 (4th series), July, 1935, pp. 266–270. DLC.

The writer is a storyteller-librarian herself. The aims she stresses here are the awakening of appreciation for literature, and enjoyment of it. She believed that the best method was one of naturalness and careful selection. In her opinion, most stories needed some adaptation.

3034. ———. *A storyteller's choice.* London, Bodley Head, 1963. 225p. DLC, NNY.

A selection of stories to tell, together with suggestions for telling each story. Miss Colwell has made a second selection in a later book, published by the same press.

3035. ———. *To begin with . . . a guide to reading for the under fives.* London, Kenneth Mason, 1964. 24p. DLC.

"It is vitally important that a child's first introduction to books, and therefore to literature, should be a pleasurable one. This list is an attempt to offer some guidance to parents and others interested, as to some of the best books available at present for children who have not yet learnt to read." Miss Colwell is a leading children's librarian in England, and has worked on the selection of countless basic lists. This is one of the more recent.

3036. ———. "Your library," *Mine,* London, Vol. 2, Sept., 1935, pp. 183–188.

3037. "Conference of library and educational authorities, Birmingham, May 3, 1906," *Library association record,* London, Vol. 8, No. 6, June, 1906, pp. 265–277. DLC, NNY.

The members of the conference discussed and enacted a resolution on the importance of libraries for children in schools and public libraries.

3038. Cooper, A. B. "The nursery rhyme in art," *Royal magazine,* London, Vol. 31, Dec., 1913, pp. 105–112. NNY.

The author speculates as to why so few new rhymes catch on and remain part of children's oral literature as does Mother Goose. He also ventures to trace some of the historical origins of Mother Goose.

3039. Coutts, Henry T. "Work amongst children in the library," *Library assistant,* London, Vol. 5, Oct., 1905, pp. 34–38. DLC, NNY.

The rules and regulations to have in guiding this work, a description of the facilities necessary, and the importance of a good book collection.

3040. Crouch, Marcus S. "Children's classics: Some modern editions," *School librarian and school library review,* London, Vol. 8, Dec., 1956, pp. 172–177. DLC, NNY.

An annotated list, chosen for attentiveness to preserving the original text, and for quality of illustration.

3041. ———. *Treasure seekers and borrowers: Children's books in Britain 1900–1960.* London, Library Association, 1962. 160p. DLC, IYL, NNY.

Mr. Crouch believed E. Nesbit's *Treasure Seekers* to be a turning point in English children's literature. He approaches the developments chronologically. There is a reading list and an index.

3042. Cruse, Amy. *The Englishman and his books in the early nineteenth century.* London, Harrap, 1930. 301p. NNY.

This has numerous references to Mrs. Barbauld, Thomas Day, the Edgeworths, Aikin, and Scott, as well as many other didactic writers for children who practised in the pre-Victorian period. See also the author's study in 3043.

3043. ———. "A young Victorian's library," *The Victorians and their books.* London, Allen & Unwin, 1935, pp. 286–309. DLC, NNY.

This chapter records some of the comments of well-known Victorians, concerning the books they read in their childhood and youth.

3044. Cutforth, J. A. and S. H. Battersby. *Children and books.* Oxford, Basil Blackwell, 1962. 137p. DLC.

According to the author's preface, the purpose of this book is to point out the ways of using books in the primary school, in the very broadest of applications. Books for infant schools or kindergartens are given a separate chapter, as are reference materials. An appendix lists "sources of information and help."

3045. Dagenham Public Libraries. *One thousand*

books for boys and girls. 2nd ed. The libraries, 1957. 38p. DLC.

A thoroughly delightful list, illustrated with amusing and gay selections from some of the books. Intelligently categorized, with eye-catching headings. It was not possible to check the quality of all of the entries, but certainly from the point of view of format, this is a children's booklist to be emulated.

3046. Daish, A. N. "The comic and the schoolbook," *British printer,* London, Vol. 65, July–Aug., 1952, pp. 35–39. DLC, NNY.

"Comments on the typographical standard of contemporary publications for children and its relation to that of the school textbooks."

3047. Dale, N. A. "The United Kingdom," *Library service to children.* Lund, Bibliotekstjänst, 1963, pp. 109–116. DLC, IYL, NNY.

This chapter deals with the history and present status of library work with children in this country. The publication was produced under the auspices of IFLA.

3048. Dalglish, Doris N. "Some Victorian juvenile books," *Library review,* Glasgow, No. 113, Spring, 1955, pp. 28–32. DLC, NNY.

Critical and historical comments on a number of children's books from the Victorian era.

3049. Dallimore, Frank. "Object lessons to school children in the use of libraries," *Library association record,* London, Vol. 11, No. 2, Feb., 1909, pp. 49–68. DLC, NNY.

Teachers have no time to do the job of moral education that parents are neglecting, so books should be used to fill this need. The author outlines the qualities of the ideal children's librarian. Bibliography.

3050. Daniels, E. "Common sense and the children's library," *Library assistant,* London, Vol. 27, Mar., 1934, pp. 71–74. DLC, NNY.

This librarian felt that it was unnecessary for the children's librarian to have special training and study in child psychology. The most important part of children's library work is a good collection, a knowledge and appreciation of its contents, and a natural affinity for children on the part of the librarian.

3051. Darton, C. C. *A checklist of the C. C. Darton collection of children's books.* London, Extract from? book?, pp. 28–49. NNY.

Rather brief descriptions of 427 volumes in this collection, which was *not* that of Harvey Darton. The Darton family was involved in publishing in

England for many years. The books in this list were acquired by the family, and span the years from 1706–1877. They are arranged chronologically.

3052. Darton, F. J. Harvey. "Children's books," *The Cambridge history of English literature,* Vol. 11. London & New York, Putnam, 1914, pp. 418–420; 426–429. DLC, NNY.

This is only a brief survey of early children's literature, but it was important because of its appearance in this scholarly multi-volume work.

3053. ———. *Children's books in England: Five centuries of social life.* 2nd ed. Cambridge, Cambridge University Press, 1958. 367p. DLC, IYL, NNY.

"It is probably safe to say that Darton will never be supplanted" writes Kathleen Lines in her Preface to this 2nd edition. It was she who made the few corrections necessary to bring the 1932 original text up-to-date and accurate. Mr. Darton himself declared, in the first chapter, that his purpose was to view those who wrote children's books in their human aspect, and he defined children's books as "those produced ostensibly to give children spontaneous pleasure, and not primarily to teach them." This did not presuppose that he treated his subject lightly, for the result can undeniably be called scholarly. For each chapter there are book lists, and Miss Lines has given supplementary items, published since 1932, at the end. There is an excellent index.

3054. Davies, E. S. "School library," *Library association record,* London, Vol. 41, June, 1939, pp. 316–320. DLC, NNY.

A definition of the aims and standards of the school library.

3055. Davis, Joan A. and Helena E. S. Wood. *Books for school libraries.* London, National Froebel Foundation, 1950. 26p. DLC.

Listed by general subject areas, with headings arranged alphabetically. No annotations.

3056. Dearmer, Geoffrey. "Forgotten children's books," *Living age,* Boston, Vol. 324, No. 4200, Jan. 3, 1925, pp. 256–258. DLC, NNY.

This was reprinted from the *Saturday review,* London, Nov. 22, 1924. It is a tongue-in-cheek review of moralistic children's books.

3057. Delattre, F. "La littérature enfantine en Angleterre," *Revue pédagogique,* Paris, Tome 51, No. 8 (New series), Aug. 15, 1907, pp. 101–152. DLC.

A rather complete study of children's literature in England from the 18th through the 19th centuries. While the critic does not go into each author's work to a great extent, he does cover most of the trends. Certain U.S. works are also discussed, but only because they were also currently popular in England. This article had a definite influence on Paul Hazard.

3058. Dent, Robert K. "Children's books and their place in the reference library," *Library association record,* London, Vol. 1, No. 4, Apr., 1899, pp. 216–220. DLC, NNY.

Suggestions for amassing children's books to preserve them for posterity, rather than for "immediate and current issue to readers."

3059. Dexter, Walter. "Boys' periodicals of the 'nineties," *Chamber's journal,* London, Dec., 1943, pp. 641–644. DLC, NNY.

The author describes his unusual collection of first issues of some 200 magazines which appeared in the 5 year period, 1894–1898. He cites many of them by title and publisher and identifies them as to type of content.

3060. Dodd, Catherine I. "Some aspects of children's books," *National review,* London, No. 263, Jan., 1905, pp. 846–852. DLC, NNY.

A survey of the moralistic literature for children in the late 18th and early 19th centuries.

3061. Dodd, Catherine I. "Some old school-books," *National review,* London, Vol. 45, Aug., 1905, pp. 1006–1014. NNY.

The influence of Comenius and Pestalozzi on early children's books, and some examples of text from a number of them.

3062. Doyle, Brian. *Who's who of boys' writers and illustrators.* London, The Author, 1964. 99p.

3063. Draper, M. Christabel. "Country life in cautionary tales," *Country life,* London, Vol. 89, May 10, 1941, pp. 402–404. NNY.

Some examples of country life as pictured and described in children's books of the 19th century are given here, with reproductions of 5 illustrations and a fan calendar.

3064. Eckenstein, Lina. *Comparative studies in nursery rhymes.* London, Duckworth, 1911. 231p. DLC, NNY.

Comparisons of versions of familiar rhymes as chanted in the British Isles, parts of Europe and Scandinavia. This is, of course, much more limited than the Opies' work, but it was an auspicious beginning. There is a list of the foreign collections used, as well as an index of first lines.

3065. Edwards. *Early books for children.* Ashmore Green, Edwards, 1945.

A book dealer's catalog.

3066. Egoff, Sheila A. *Children's periodicals of the nineteenth century.* London, The Library Association, 1951. 55p. (Pamphlet No. 8). DLC, NNY.

A chronological listing of periodicals from approximately 1752–1900. A scholarly discussion of the more important titles indicates great breadth of knowledge on the part of the author, who is a prominent Canadian children's librarian, currently at work on a major study of the children's literature of that country. Bibliographies and an index.

3067. Ellis, A. *How to find out about children's literature.* London, Pergamon, 1966. 188p.

3068. Emery, J. W. "British libraries," *The library, the school and the child.* Toronto, Macmillan, 1917, pp. 174–190. DLC, NNY.

A brief history of British library service to children, taken city by city.

3069. *English children's books 1863–1900: An exhibition.* London, Times Bookshop, 1960.

3070. Eyre, Frank. *Twentieth century children's books.* London, Longmans, 1952. 72p. IYL, DLC.

Published for the British Council, this examines the main trends in children's books of this century, mentioning specific examples of authors, and reasons for their importance of distinction. Bibliography and index.

3071. Faraday, Joseph G. *Twelve years of children's books.* Birmingham, C. Combridge, Ltd., 1939. 156p. DLC.

"A selection of the best books for children published during the years 1926 to 1939." Each is annotated and the source of the recommendations is indicated. Author and title index.

3072. Farjeon, Eleanor. "Children's books," *Spectator,* London, Vol. 187, Dec. 7, 1951, p. 782. DLC, NNY.

"Miss Farjeon looks back to 1851." This well-known children's writer selects some of the books she would have liked for Christmas, from among the titles which came out in 1851. This is followed by the usual signed reviews which were customary at regular intervals in this periodical.

3073. Farr, Harry. "Library work with children." Congrès International des Archivistes et Bibliothécaires; *Actes;* Bruxelles, 1910, pp. 450–462. DLC.

The author, who was librarian in the Cardiff Public Libraries, presented this report to the public libraries section of the Congress. He spoke of the general philosophy of service to children, and compared Great Britain to the United States in the various stages of development.

3074. Field, Louise Frances. *The child and his book.* London, Wells W. Gardner, Darton, and Co., 1895. 358p. DLC, NNY.

"Some account of the history and progress of children's literature in England." The chapter titles indicate the periods and types covered: "Before the Norman Conquest," "From the Conquest to Caxton," "Manners makyth man," "ABC," "Fear of the Lord and of the broomstick." This work marks the starting point of historical studies of children's literature and its criticism.

3075. Fish, Helen Dean. "Book fare of English children," *Horn book,* Boston, Vol. 10, Mar., 1934, pp. 106–108. DLC, NNY.

The writer believed that there was a great disparity between the few outstanding classics for children and the majority of English books produced for children. She felt that there was very little experimentation or originality in most of them, and urged more exchange of books between the U.S. and England to stimulate new approaches to the children's book.

3076. Fisher, Emily C. *The study of literature as a mode of expressing life. Mother Goose—humor.* Boston, 1903. 80p. DLC.

An essay on Mother Goose as universal literature. Bibliography.

3077. Fisher, Margery. *Intent upon reading: A critical appraisal of modern fiction for children.* Leicester, England, Brockhampton Press, 1961. 331p. DLC, IYL, NNY. (U.S. edition, New York, F. Watts, 1962. $4.95).

"To a child who is intent upon reading, all books are children's books"—this quotation from E. V. Lucas provided Mrs. Fisher with her title, and her central theme. She ranges through the fiction of the past 30 years, including a number of adult titles in the sections for older children. The reading lists contain additional titles which she was not able to work into the text. There is an author, title, and illustrator index.

3078. Ford, Boris. *Young writers, young readers.* London, Hutchinson, 1960. 172p. IYL.

"An anthology of children's reading and writing." The writing and drawings by children, as well as the critical essays which follow, had originally appeared in *The Journal of Education.* The four essays on teaching children to write are by James Britton, Nancy Martin, William Walsh and E. W. and D. Hildick. The essays on individual authors of children's books and general criticism are by Janice Dohm, William Walsh, D. R. Barnes, Douglas Brown, and Rosemary Thompson. E. W. Hildick also has contributed an article on boys' weeklies, David Holbrook one on the comics and James Reeves on writing poetry for children. The annotated booklist was made by Janice Dohm.

3079. Forster, A. Makepiece. "Books and village children," *Library association record,* London, Vol. 12, No. 11, Nov., 1910, pp. 566–572. DLC, NNY.

A discussion centered around the organization and progress of a village library which was begun under the New Libraries Act.

3080. Forsyth, J. W. "Children's library; present and ?," *Junior bookshelf,* Birmingham, Vol. 2, May, 1938, pp. 125–128. DLC, NNY.

An article which caused considerable disagreement because it presented the case for children's library work in a somewhat unorthodox fashion. The author felt that cooperation with teachers and schools could be overdone and believed that the reason for the success of the public library lay precisely in its lack of compulsion on the child and his reading.

3081. Gagg, J. C. *Beginning the three R's.* London, Evans Brothers, 1959. 208p.

3082. ———. *Learning to learn, with a booklist of children's books for use in learning libraries.* London, E. J. Arnold, 1957. 165p.

3083. Gaskin, [Georgie E.] *Horn-book jingles.* London, Leaden Hall Press, 1896–97. 72p. NNY.

Although intended for children, this collection is useful for the student of early children's literature, since it gives such a wide variety of rhymes, verses, sayings, etc., taken from old horn books.

3084. Godfrey, Elizabeth. "Nursery lore," *English children in the olden time.* 2nd ed. London, Methuen, 1907, pp. 13–29. DPL.

About some of the nursery rhymes and tales popular with English children in past eras.

3085. Godley, Eveline Charlotte. "A century of

children's books," *National review,* London, May, 1906, pp. 437–449. NNY.

The author reviews the work of 19th-century writers, in particular that of Maria Edgeworth, Charlotte Yonge, and Catherine Sinclair.

3086.   Gomme, Alice B. *Children's singing games, with the tunes to which they are sung.* 2 vols. London, D. Nutt [1894]. 70p. each. DLC, NNY.

A scholarly survey of the games children have made up and passed along orally, together with the words and songs which go with them.

3087.   Great Britain. British Council. *Exposição de livros ingleses para crianças.* Lisboa, Livraria Portugal, 1943. 63p. DLC.

The catalog of an exhibition which took place in Lisbon, and which included books for parents about children, their reading and upbringing.

3088.   Great Britain. Department of Education and Science. *The use of books.* London, Her Majesty's Stationery Office, 1964.

3089.   Green, Percy. *History of nursery rhymes.* London, Greening, 1899. 196p. DLC.

3090.   Green, Roger Lancelyn. "The golden age of children's books." English Association, *Essays and Studies,* London, Vol. 15, (New series), 1962, pp. 59–73. DLC.

The author believed that while there were excellent books describing the growth and developments of writing for children over several centuries, none of them approached the subject similarly to the whole or part of adult literature. His attempt here was to write "at least the first draft of what might be developed by some expert into a chapter in a future history of English literature."

3091.   ———. *Tellers of tales.* London, Ward, 1965. 320p. DLC, IYL, NNY.

The earlier editions (1946, 1953, 1956) had the sub-title "An account of children's favourite authors from 1839 to the present day, their books and how they came to write them, together with an appendix and indexes giving the titles and dates of these books." This new edition has had some expansion and revision in all parts. There is a very useful list of authors and their works, with dates, followed by "a chronological list of famous children's books 1800–1964." There is also a fine index. Mr. Green writes with obvious delight on his subjects, and the critical judgements indicate a good sense of perspective.

3092.   Grimshaw, Ernest. *The teacher librarian.* Leeds, E. J. Arnold, 1952. 179p. DLC.

"It is the primary duty of the schools to train the children for the proper use of the public library" is the refrain which echoes throughout this manual of organization and management of the school library. Methods of training pupils are discussed in great detail. Bibliography and index.

3093.   Groom, Arthur. *Writing for children, a manual for writers of juvenile fiction.* London, A. and C. Black, 1929. 118p. DLC.

An early manual which was decidedly more commercial than literary in intent. The first general hint the author gave was to avoid long or difficult words. Of some historical interest.

3094.   *Growing point.* Ashton Manor, Northampton. 1962 ff. 9 issues a year. Vol. 1 ff. No. 1 ff. 1962 ff. Subscription: 21s yearly. DLC, IYL, NNY.

"Margery Fisher's regular review of books for the growing families of the English reading world, and for parents, librarians and other guardians." The editor reviews mostly books for children, but some of general interest are also included. There are occasional articles on authors, illustrators, exhibits, historical books, etc. Perceptive and consistent criticism is the hallmark of this review.

3095.   Gumuchian, Kirkor. "Forgotten children's flowers," *Print,* Woodstock, Vermont, Vol. 4, Winter 1945–46, pp. 3–10. NNY.

"If we can judge from the juvenile literature of the time, the appeal and significance of flowers must have played a necessary part in the social and educational life of children in England during the first half of the 19th century." There are a number of examples cited, with six reproductions.

3096.   Guppy, Henry. "French fiction and French juvenile literature for the public library," *Library association record,* London, Vol. 2, July, 1900, pp. 357–371. DLC, NNY.

The author is referring here to French books in English translation. His claim was that the works of Dumas (fils), Flaubert, Gautier, Feydeau, Goncourt, Huysman, Maupassant, Voltaire, Balzac, Daudet, Halevy, Malot and Zola were unsuitable for young people, with a few exceptions, such as *Sans Famille* by Malot and some of the short stories of Daudet.

3097.   Haas, Paula de. "Course on library work with young people," *De openbare bibliotheek,* 's-Gravenhage, Jaargang 1, No. 6, Nov., 1958, pp. 327–332. NNY.

The author-librarian was among the students taking part in a special course for foreign librarians. She describes the content and approach of each of the five subject areas covered.

3098. Halbert, J. F. "Libraries and children: A survey of modern practice," *Library association record,* London, Vol. 2, 3rd ser., Oct., 1932, pp. 305–308. DLC, NNY.

"Children's libraries in this country are not all Hendon's or yet Croydon's" wrote this critic, referring to two libraries which were and are known for first-rate service. She also gave some examples of the areas in which improvement could be undertaken, in the libraries which were not up to standards.

3099. Hall, Wendy. "Children's libraries cooperate with British schools," *Wilson library bulletin,* New York, Vol. 31, Feb., 1957, pp. 459–461. DLC, NNY.

Concerning the methods of public and school library cooperation in the U.K.

3100. Halliwell-Phillips, James O. *A catalog of chap-books, garlands, and popular histories.* London, Privately printed, 1849. 190p. DLC, NNY.

An annotated list of 241 chapbooks and other popular books, which formed the greater part of children's reading in the 17th century.

3101. ———. *The nursery rhymes of England, obtained principally from oral tradition.* London, Printed for the Percy Society by T. Richards, 1842. NNY.

It is from this collection that modern Mother Goose editions are usually drawn. There are extensive historical notes. The rhymes are separated into types or subject groups.

3102. Handley-Taylor, Geoffrey. *A selected bibliography of literature relating to nursery rhyme reform, to which is added an introductory note and statistical analysis.* 3rd ed. Manchester, True Aim, 1953. 8p. NNY.

A bibliography documenting the efforts of such writers as Mrs. Trimmer, Samuel Goodrich, Allen Abbott and others, who tried to change nursery rhymes so that they would express no harsh or "sadistic" tendencies.

3103. Hansard, Gillian. *Old books for the new young.* London, W. Heinemann, 1932. 123p. DLC.

An encouragement for brighter and bolder reading for children, followed by an annotated book list. The compiler was apparently herself a young girl.

3104. Hardie, Martin. "The Chiswick Press and children's books," *English coloured books.* London, Methuen, 1906. pp. 257–265. DLC, NNY.

This chapter deals with the works of the Chiswick Press, many of which were stories with appeal to children. They were noted for their hand-coloured illustrations. There are also chapters in this book on William Blake and G. Cruikshank, as well as a chapter on Crane, Greenaway and Caldecott and their designer-printer E. Evans.

3105. Harker, Lizzie Allen. "Some eighteenth-century children's books," *Longman's magazine,* London & New York, Vol. 38, Oct., 1901, pp. 548–557. NNY.

A description of some of the books published by Newbery and his successors, as well as other publishers of the time.

3106. Harrod, L. M. "Is the children's library a luxury?," *Library world,* London, Vol. 35, Jan., 1933, pp. 158–159. DLC, NNY.

This librarian disapproved strongly of the statement in the County Libraries Section Report of 1930, that children's libraries should be regarded as a luxury.

3107. ———. "Work with young people in London," *Library world,* London, Vol. 52, Dec., 1949, pp. 99–103. DLC, NNY.

This librarian believed that children's services had been the most neglected aspect of London libraries. Only a few boroughs provided sufficient funds for staff and books to give quality service.

3108. Harter, Evelyn and M. B. Glick. "Building the book beautiful," *Junior bookshelf,* Birmingham, Vol. 2, No. 4, July, 1938, pp. 175–182. DLC, NNY.

Some details of artists' methods of reproducing different kinds of pictures, and a general discussion on the size and quality of children's books.

3109. Hartland, Edwin Sidney. *The science of fairy tales.* 2nd ed. London, Methuen, 1925. 372p.

3110. Heeks, Peggy. *Books of reference for school libraries.* London, School Library Association, 1961. 42p. 7s. 6d.

"An annotated list based on the 4th edition of *A List of General Reference Books,* with some additional material on school subjects and children's leisure interests."

3111. Hildick, E. W. "Boys' weeklies since Orwell," *Journal of education,* London, Vol. 87, Sept., 1955, pp. 416–420. DLC, NNY.

The conclusion of an article begun in the August issue, pp. 369 ff. The author gives a critical-historical appraisal of the contents of boys' magazines of the past few decades.

3112.   Hindley, Charles. "A collection of juvenile books printed and published by James Catnach," *The history of the Catnach Press at Berwick-upon-Tweed, Alnwick and Newcastle-upon-Tyne, in Northumberland, and Seven Dials*. London, Charles Hindley, 1886, pp. 95–217. DLC.

The text and illustrations of a number of the children's books are reproduced.

3113.   Holbrook, David. "A service to love?," *Views,* London, No. 4, Spring 1964, pp. 33–39. DLC, NNY.

A chapter from the author's book *The Secret Place*. This contains thoughtful reflections on the consequences of the contents of seemingly harmless magazines for youth. Under the guise of advice, the author feels they engender a fierce spirit of acquisitiveness and bring about a completely false attitude toward love and sex.

3114.   Holmes, W. Kersley. "An editor on juvenile books," *Library review,* Glasgow, No. 99, Autumn 1951, pp. 158–161. DLC, NNY.

This editor contends that life in juvenile books should be romanticized, but not in a sloppy, sentimental or morbid fashion as it too often is.

3115.   Horsfall, Magdalene. "Children's books of a hundred years ago," *Treasures of darkness*. London, Skeffington and Son, 1938; pp. 41–72. DLC.

A lecture in which the author commented on the general characteristics of early 19th-century children's books, and pointed out specific examples which were extreme examples of didacticism, pietism and sentimentality.

3116.   Hunter, Kenneth. "The illustration of books . . . for children," *Artist,* London, Vol. 31, Apr., 1946, pp. 41–43. DLC, NNY.

This was Part 14 in a series. It is concerned with the technical problems of illustrating children's books.

3117.   Hutton, Raddice A. *Children's reading in home and school*. London, Partridge, 1926.

3118.   James, Philip. "Children's books: A retrospect," *Library association record,* London, Vol. 1, 4th Series, Oct., 1934, pp. 355–361. DLC, NNY.

At times appreciative, at times indignant, this presents a review of children's books to 1850.

The author closes by urging every library to build a noncirculating collection of historic and representative contemporary children's books. This is followed by an article on poetry for children, by Rose Fyleman.

3119.   ———. *Children's books of yesterday*. London, The Studio, Autumn 1933. 128p. DLC, NNY.

Illustrations selected from an exhibit of children's books held at the Victoria and Albert Museum in 1932. This provides an invaluable catalog of the representative work of all major and some minor illustrators. There is an alphabetical list of the artists and their works, arranged by book title and by author. Short bibliography.

3120.   Jast, Louis Stanley. *The child as reader*. London, Libraco, 1927. 60p. DLC.

A collection of essays which provide insight into the early public library work with children in England and the philosophy behind it.

3121.   ———. "Work with children," *Library association record,* London, Vol. 21, Mar., 1919, pp. 91–102. DLC, NNY.

A paper reporting some of the work done the previous year, followed by a general discussion as to the trends library work with children should begin to take.

3122.   Jenkinson, Augustus J. *What do boys and girls read?* 2nd rev. ed. London, Methuen, 1946. 286p. DLC.

"An investigation into reading habits, with some suggestions about the teaching of literature in secondary and senior schools." This subtitle serves as an adequate summary. There are numerous tables and an appendix with suggestions for further study.

3123.   Jones, Linda Harris. *A comparison of the works of Walter Crane, Randolph Caldecott, and Kate Greenaway, and their contribution to children's book illustration*. Chapel Hill, University of North Carolina, 1966. 57p. Thesis.

3124.   *The Junior bookshelf*. Marsh Hall, Thurstonland, Huddersfield. Bimonthly. Vol. 1 ff. No. 1 ff. 1936 ff. Subscription: 21s. DLC, IYL, NNY.

This is the children's book reviewing periodical with the longest history in England. It is devoted almost entirely to reviews, with usually one or two articles on some aspect of children's books and reading. Throughout the years it has maintained its reputation for reliable, critical judgement. There are also reviews of professional books, and of foreign children's books, but not in every issue. Annual index.

3125. "Juvenile library; being a collection of books particularly adapted to the amusement and instruction of young persons," *A catalogue of books, in all languages and classes of learning, for the year 1806.* London, Lackington, Allen & Co., pp. 131–139. NNY.

The entries numbered 3705 through 3946 in this bookseller's catalogue are children's books, chiefly of the didactic sort. Bibliographic information is not too complete.

3126. "Juvenile literature," *British quarterly review*, London, Vol. 47, Jan. 1, 1868, pp. 128–149. NNY.

"The combination of instruction and amusement is presumably the aim and object of every writer of children's books. How difficult it is to blend these two unsympathetic elements without becoming prosy and wearisome . . ."

3127. Kamm, Anthony and Boswell Taylor. *Books and the teacher.* London, University of London Press, 1966. 176p. IYL.

"How educational publishing affects teachers and librarians. A handbook on the choice, requisition and use of books." The reference section includes booklists, bibliographies, a list of publishers, sources of information on children's books and school libraries, and a glossary of printing and book trade terms.

3128. Kay (Pseud). "Illustrating children's books," *Artist*, London, Vol. 34, Sept., 1947–Feb., 1948. Six parts in six consecutive months. NNY.

In this series, a children's book illustrator tries to explain the special methods which can or should be used in making picture books and in illustrating children's books written by others. Each part is approximately three pages, and has illustrations by the artist.

3129. Kent County Council. Kent Education Committee. *Books and publications recommended for use with dull and backward children.* Springfield, Maidstone, John Haynes, Nov., 1964. 22p. DLC.

One of a series of lists published by the Kent County Council. This contains books especially written for this kind of child as well as general books which have proven to be especially valuable. Many are texts or series. Briefly annotated.

3130. Ker, John Bellenden. *An essay on the archeology of our popular phrases, and nursery rhymes.* 2nd ed. 2 vols. London, Longmans, 1835. pp. 243–290 in Vol. 1; pp. 289–304 in Vol. 2. DLC, NNY.

Chiefly a linguistic study but interesting for the comparisons of Mother Goose rhymes in high Saxon (English) and low Saxon (Dutch).

3131. Kernahan, John Coulson. *The reading girl.* London, Harrap, 1925. 249p.

3132. Klingerowa, Zofia. [English books for children and youth.] *Ruch pedagogiczny,* Warszawa, Vol. 31, No. 1, 1947–1948.

Paper given at the Polish Congress on Children's Literature (see 2114). In Polish.

3133. Knaufft, Ernest. "Picture books in color," *Review of reviews,* London, Vol. 46, Dec., 1912, pp. 759–765. DLC, NNY.

A discussion of the technical processes and the artistic effort which go into the production of a good picture book. The author cites a number of examples, from which a dozen or more pictures are reproduced in black and white.

3134. Lang, Andrew. *Essays in little.* 2nd ed. London, Henry and Co., 1891. 205p. DLC.

A number of these essays are concerned with such children's authors as Robert Louis Stevenson, Charles Kingsley, John Bunyan, Rudyard Kipling, etc.

3135. Law, Alice. "The cult of the child spirit in modern literature," *Royal Society of Literature, Transactions,* London, Ser. 2, Vol. 33, part iii, 1915, pp. 117–142. NNY.

"It can scarcely have escaped notice how many distinguished writers of our day have, in the plenitude of their powers and genius, broken off, as it were, from their more serious labours, and occupied themselves with the writing of *Fairy Tales* and stories for children." Before going further into the modern examples, the author surveys the "child spirit" as it appears in the history of literature.

3136. Lee, Elizabeth. "Reading for young people," *Parents' review,* London, Feb., 1917, pp. 89–103.

3137. Lee, W. R. "Early literature," *Manchester Literary Club, Papers,* Vol. 59, 1934, pp. 229–237. NNY.

Some ruminations on what boys read and why. The author concludes: "If you tell him a book is good he will avoid it like the plague. Tell him Shakespeare is not fit for him to read and he will get a copy somehow or other." He recommends letting boys go through the magazine or "series" stages if they seem so inclined, making sure that there is always other good material available for choosing when the fancy begins to wane.

3138. Lewis, Morris Michael. *Children's reading and illiteracy*. London, School Library Association, 1954. 8p.

An address given at a School Library Association meeting in December, 1953.

3139. Lewis, Naomi. *The best children's books of* ———. London, Hamilton, 1963 ff. Yearly. DLC has 1963, 1964.

An annual review, containing around 250–350 titles. Arrangement is by general age and subject groups and the annotations are short, critical paragraphs.

3140. Leyland, Eric. *Libraries in schools*. London, Oldbourne, 1962. 143p. DLC, IYL.

A manual on library organization and practice. There is a bibliography, list of selection aids, and an index.

3141. ———. *The public library and the adolescent*. London, Grafton and Co., 1937. 203p. DLC.

An early study in the field of what is now called young adult services. Some important points are made about the particular demands of the adolescent years. There is a long list of books suitable for this section of the library.

3142. London. Library Association. *Chosen for children; an account of the books which have been awarded the Library Association Carnegie Medal 1936–1957*. London, Library Association, 1957. 89p. DLC, IYL, NNY.

An informative compilation of biographical and anecdotal material about the Carnegie medal winners with short excerpts from their books and a sample of the illustrations.

3143. ———. County Libraries Section. *Books for the reluctant reader*. London, The Association, 1962.

3144. ———. County Libraries Section. *Readers' guide to children's books*. London, The Association, 1958 ff. DLC.

An annotated list, frequently revised. Other sections of the Association publish complementary lists.

3145. ———. London and Home Counties Branch. *Books for young people: Fourteen and up*. London, The Association, 1957. 85p. DLC.

An annotated list of fiction and nonfiction, with author and subject indexes. See the following two entries for matching lists.

3146. ———. North Midland Branch. *Books for young people: Eleven to thirteen plus*. 3rd ed. rev. London, Library Association, 1960. 239p. DLC.

An annotated and classified list, with author and subject indexes. Each of the Branches edits a different list for the various age groups.

3147. ———. North-Western Branch. *Books for young people: Under eleven*. Rev. ed. London, The Association, 1955. 103p. DLC.

An annotated list matching the two listed above.

3148. ———. Youth Libraries Section. *Children's books of this century; a first list of books covering the years 1899 to 1956 chosen for the library of children's literature now being formed at Chaucer House*. London, The Association, 1958. 36p. DLC.

A chronological and annotated list of the books included in this historical collection. Donors are indicated and there is an index.

3149. ———. Youth Libraries Section. *Public library service for children*. rev ed. London, Library Association, The Section, 1960. 11p.

3150. ———. Youth Libraries Section. *Survey of public library service for children, 1954*. London, Library Association, 1955. 7p. DLC.

A report on the status and aims of national service to children. This was the first overall survey on this subject in the United Kingdom. It pointed out that the local authorities were not providing satisfactory funds and support for adequate service. A supplement to the report made in 1958–1959 showed that not much progress had been made in the areas of trained staff and selective book collections.

3151. "Library service for children in country areas," *Librarian and book world*, London, Vol. 24, Dec., 1934, pp. 104. DLC.

Comments on the County Libraries Section report of 1930, which stated that children's libraries were luxuries.

3152. Linden, Ronald O. *Books and libraries: A guide for students*. London, Cassell, 1965. 308p.

3153. Lines, Kathleen M. *Four to fourteen: A library of books for children*. 2nd ed. Cambridge, Cambridge University Press, 1956. 351p. DLC, IYL, NNY.

This was published for the National Book League (1st ed., 1950). It has extensive, substantive annotations for each of the entries, arranged by age and subject groups. An appendix gives a bibliography and the list of Carnegie medal winners. Indexed and illustrated.

3154. ———. *The one hundred best books for children; a special Sunday Times survey*. London, Kemsley Newspapers Ltd., 1958. 16p. DLC.

A personal selection by an eminent critic, annotated and illustrated with reproductions from some of the books. *The Times* has, in its Literary Supplement, a special "Children's Books" issue which appears twice a year—in early summer and late fall. These supplements contain excellent lead articles of criticism, history or similar aspects, and there are lengthy reviews of a generous sampling of the half-year's output of children's books.

3155. Ling, Kenneth J. "The illustration of children's books," *Library assistant,* London, Apr., 1940, pp. 67–73. DLC, NNY.

This critic minced no words in stating that the general quality of children's book illustration in England was extremely poor.

3156. Locke, John. "Children's reading," *Some thoughts concerning education*. Cambridge, Cambridge University, 1895, pp. 129–136. DLC, NNY.

This is only one of many editions of this famous work which appeared in 1694, and was so influential in its effect on the education of children. Locke recommended the reading of Aesop and certain of the Old Testament stories. He proposed a type of block game which would teach the child to read while playing.

3157. Lockhead, Marion. "Social history in miniature: Domestic tales for children," *Quarterly review,* London, Vol. 291, Oct., 1953, pp. 516–530. DLC, NNY.

From *Sandford and Merton* to the stories of E. Nesbit, the author surveys examples of numerous cases in which the fiction of the 19th century can be said to reflect the social history of the time.

3158. London County Council. Education Department. *Schools and libraries; an account of the development of library activities in the London Education Service*. London, The Council, 1925. 8p.

3159. Lostalot, Alfred de. "Les livres en couleur publiés en Angleterre pour l'enfance," *Gazette des beaux-arts,* Paris, Tome 25, Jan., 1882, pp. 68–78. DLC, NNY.

A discussion of the work of Crane, Caldecott, Greenaway and other English illustrators of children's books with some reproductions in black and white.

3160. Low, Florence B. "The reading of the modern girl," *Nineteenth century,* London, Vol. 59, Feb., 1906, pp. 278–287. NNY.

". . . on the subject of girls' reading, it was suggested that new series of books, especially written for girls, were needed, and that the modern girl suffered from lack of suitable material on which to feed her mental hunger. The suggestion seems almost farcical considering our stock of noble English novels and stories . . ." Following this is a summary of the results of a reading inquiry which the author conducted among some school girls.

3161. Lucas, E. V. *Forgotten tales of long ago*. London, Wells-Gardner-Darton, 1906. 425p. DLC, NNY.

Examples of children's stories of the didactic type which appeared from 1785 to 1830.

3162. Lumby, J. H. "School libraries," *Librarian and book world,* Gravesend, Vol. 11, No. 1, Aug., 1921, pp. 4–11. DLC, NNY.

A hopeful discussion of the value of school libraries and the methods for getting them off to an effective start.

3163. McCracken, Elizabeth. "On fiction as an educator," *Blackwood's Edinburgh magazine,* Vol. 108, Oct., 1870, pp. 449–459. DLC, NNY.

Speculations on the childhood reading of some of the great writers and how it might have affected their work.

3164. MacCulloch, John Arnott. *The childhood of fiction*. London, John Murray, 1905. 509p. DLC, NNY.

"A study of folk tales and primitive thought." A scholarly work on the origins of folk-tale elements.

3165. MacCunn, Florence. "Children's storybooks," *Good words,* London, May, 1904, pp. 341–346. NNY.

A review of the works of Maria Edgeworth, Miss Martineau, Mrs. Sherwood, Charlotte Yonge, and Mrs. Ewing.

3166. MacDonald, Frederic W. "Of certain boys and their books," *In a nook with a book*. London, H. Marshall & Son, 1907, pp. 45–58. NNY.

The childhood reading of Wordsworth, Coleridge, Scott and other British writers is discussed.

3167. McDonald, Lilia Scott. *Babies' classics*. Illustrated by Arthur Hughes. London, Longmans, 1904. 79p.

3168. MacFall, Haldane. "English illustrators of juvenile books," *Good housekeeping,* Springfield, Mass., Vol. 51, No. 5, Nov., 1910, pp. 523–531. DLC, NNY.

A paean of praise for the works of Caldecott, Crane and the other illustrators who were making England pre-eminent in the field of children's book illustration. Illustrated with reproductions from some of the books.

3169. McGill, Hilda M. "Children's book illustrators of the twentieth century," *Manchester review,* Vol. 6, Summer 1953, pp. 432–436. DLC, NNY.

This critic believed that modern illustrators were not given their due but were always being compared unfavorably with the great illustrators of the 19th century. She found a number of current artists produced illustrations quite generally good in quality.

3170. MacNamara, Thomas J. "One hundred best books," *Library assistant,* London, Vol. 5, 1905, pp. 15–20. DLC, NNY.

A headmaster in a school selected the 100 books which he would have included in every school library.

3171. "Mags for muggers up," *Economist,* London, Vol. 209, Dec. 7, 1963, pp. 1033–1034. DLC, NNY.

A report on the publishing boom in "part books," sets and magazines for children in England. This is written from the point of view of the economic success of these ventures, not from a literary one. A number of statistics are given.

3172. Marsh, Gwen. "Children's literature," *Life and letters* . . . Middlesex, Vol. 47, Nov., 1945, pp. 73–81. NNY.

How the reading tastes of the modern child differ from those of the 19th-century child, and also how they are alike.

3173. Mellor, E. "Libraries in infant schools," *School librarian and school library review,* London, Vol. 7, July, 1955, pp. 303–306. DLC, NNY.

Some of the reasons why even kindergartens should have libraries and the types of materials which are suitable for use in them.

3174. Meynell, Alice. et al. "The illustration of children's books," *Imprint,* London, Vol. 6, Feb., 1913, pp. 95–104.

3175. Milne, A. A. *Reader's guide to children's books.* Published for National Book League by Cambridge University Press, 1948.

One of the predecessors of the current National Book League list (see 2997).

3176. Molesworth, [Mary Louisa]. "On the art of writing fiction for children," *On the art of writing fiction.* London, W. Gardner, Darton, [1894], pp. 84–98. DLC, NNY.

A successful writer for children in the Victorian Age here explains that she considers this not a lesser gift, but a "peculiar" one. Her advice to the beginning author is to study children and what they read voluntarily, as well as the books generally considered the "classics" of the field. Much of the advice given here is very similar to that found in today's handbooks on writing for children.

3177. ———. "Story-reading and story-writing," *Chamber's Edinburgh journal,* Vol. 87, Nov. 5, 1898, pp. 772–775. DLC, NNY.

After recollecting some of the books of her own childhood, this well-known author then proceeded to describe the qualities which she felt important in the writing of modern children's literature.

3178. Morris, Charles H. *The illustration of children's books.* London, The Library Association, 1957. 18p. (Library Association Pamphlet No. 16). DLC.

A brief history of this art in Britain, with hints as to how to judge the better illustrators. The processes for producing pictures are defined and there is a bibliography of books on illustrating.

3179. Morris, Joyce M. *Reading in the primary school.* London, Newnes Educational Pub. Co., for the National Foundation for Educational Research, 1959.

3180. Muir, Percival Horace. *English children's books 1600 to 1900.* London, B. T. Batsford, 1954. 256p. DLC, NNY, IYL. (U.S. edition published by Frederick Praeger).

An outstanding historical review, more selective than Darton, but with more material on the authors covered, and many reproductions in color and black and white. Because of his experience as a collector, Mr. Muir pays closer attention to bibliographic details and his work in this respect is more accurate and inclusive than Darton or the other general critical histories. Indexed.

3181. Muthesius-Trippenbach, Anna. "Das moderne Englische Bilderbuch," *Dekorative kunst,* München, Jahrgang 5, No. 8, May, 1902, pp. 300–320. NNY.

A review of the best picture books in contemporary England with 36 reproductions from them.

The author claimed England to be pre-eminent in this genre.

3182. National Book League. *Children's books of yesterday*. London, The League, 1946. 192p. DLC.

The catalog of an exhibition from the private collection of F. J. Bussell. It was unusually rich in odd or unique types of children's books, e.g., hieroglyphic books, moveable books, harlequinades, peepshow and puzzle books, chapbooks, John Newbery books, etc. Percy Muir prepared the catalogue and John Masefield wrote the foreword. Later, this collection was purchased by *Good Housekeeping* magazine, which prepared its own catalog for an exhibition in 1949 (27p., DLC).

3183. Nielsen-Svinning, E. "Fra engelske børnebiblioteker," *Bogens verden*, København, Ag. 16, Mar., 1934, pp. 81–83. DLC.

This Danish librarian spent some time visiting libraries in Croydon and Manchester. She records her impressions and compares work in England to that in Denmark.

3184. Northcroft, George J. H. *Writing for children*. London, A. and C. Black, 1935. 148p. DLC.

A competent, even perceptive, manual on writing for children with emphasis placed on a respect for the task. Although its purpose was to encourage the commercial writer, it reveals an understanding of children and does not downgrade their demands on the writer.

3185. O'Brien, Mrs. Dermod. "Pernicious habit of reading," *Parents' review*, London, Mar., 1927, pp. 151–157.

3186. O'Gara, Florence. "A group of English favorites," *Publishers' weekly*, New York, Vol. 116, Oct. 26, 1929, pp. 2055–2060. DLC, NNY.

Discussions of the work of Mrs. Ewing, Charlotte Yonge, George MacDonald and others.

3187. Ogle, John J. *The connection between the public library and the public elementary school*. London, Wyman, 1898. 37p.

3188. Olsen, Mary Jane. *Children's libraries in England*. Chicago, Chicago Teachers College, 1958. 62p. Thesis.

3189. *100 children's books of* ———. Stafford, Staffordshire County Library, yearly. 191 ff. DLC has 1963, 1964.

Annotated and arranged by age group.

3190. Opie, Iona and Peter. *The lore and language of schoolchildren*. Oxford, Clarendon Press, 1959. 417p. DLC, NNY.

One of the first scholarly studies of the oral folk lore of children in England and Ireland. The authors are well-known also for their study and compilation of the Mother Goose and other nursery rhymes. This book traces the rhymes, jokes, word rites, sayings, riddles, etc., as they are expressed orally by children in different parts of the country. Bibliography and indexes.

3191. ———. *The Oxford dictionary of nursery rhymes*. Oxford, Clarendon Press, 1951. 467p. DLC, NNY.

This impressive collection commands the respect of any student of nursery rhymes, be he folklorist, bibliophile or rank beginner. Arrangement is by loose alphabetical order according to first line or principal subject. Each rhyme is accompanied by extensive notes on known or probable origin. There is an index of notable figures associated with the invention, diffusion, or illustration of nursery rhymes. The introduction is notable for its delightful readability, while giving the historical framework of nursery rhyme development.

3192. Osborne, Edgar. "Children's books in the 19th century," *Junior bookshelf*, Kirkburton, Vol. 2, No. 2, Dec., 1937, pp. 62–67. DLC, IYL, NNY.

How and why the highly didactic, moral literature of the early 19th century was gradually ameliorated by the folk tale and the nonsense of Edward Lear and Lewis Carroll.

3193. ———. "Children's books to 1800," *Junior bookshelf*, Kirkburton, Vol. 4, No. 1, Oct., 1939, pp. 15–22. DLC, IYL, NNY.

A fine summary of books for children from the Middle Ages through the age of Perrault and Newbery. The gist of this article is the basis for many a history and critical study.

3194. ———. *From morality and instruction to Beatrix Potter: An exhibition of tales for children*. Eastbourne Corporation, 1949.

Catalog of an exhibition held just before the Osborne collection was to be sent to Toronto.

3195. Page, H. A. "Children and children's books," *Contemporary review*, London, Vol. 11, May, 1869, pp. 7–26. DLC, NNY.

Reviews of *Alice's Adventures* . . . , *The Rose and the Ring*, two volumes of Andersen, books by Jean Ingelow and Mrs. Ewing and others. The author precedes these with such remarks as: "The only humour which children can comprehend is the humour of the simple grotesque . . . Surprise is the soul of juvenile literature . . ."

3196.　Parrott, Phyllis. *Books for children.* London, National Book League, 1955. 26p. DLC.

A model, selected book list with one sentence annotations. This list is now revised annually by the National Book League (see 2997).

3197.　Parsons, Florence M. W. *Recommended gift books for children; a classified and graded catalogue, compiled . . . for the Parents' National Educational Union.* London, W. S. Crowell, 1906. 40p. DLC.

Thoughts on the difficulties of choosing gift books for comparatively unknown children written in an amusing manner.

3198.　Paul, Frances. "A collection of children's books illustrated by W. Crane, K. Greenaway and R. Caldecott," *Apollo,* London, Vol. 43, June, 1946, pp. 141–143. NNY.

A description of the collection owned by Guy Little together with a number of black and white reproductions from some of the books.

3199.　Pearson, Edwin. *Banbury chap-books and nursery toy book literature.* London, Arthur Reader, 1890. 116p. DLC.

Subtitled "Of the XVIII and early XIX centuries, with impressions from several hundred original wood-cut blocks." Reproduced are the works of such artists as: Bewick, Blake, Cruikshank, Craig, Lee, Austin and others.

3200.　Percival, Arthur. *Discovery with books: An adventure guide to the library.* London, Blond, 1965. 117p. ff. Pupil's ed., 39p.

This manual has both a teacher's and a pupil's edition.

3201.　Pickard, P. M. *I could a tale unfold; violence, horror and sensationalism in stories for children.* London, Tavistock Publications, 1961, 227p. Also: New York, Humanities Press, 1961, 227p. DLC, IYL, NNY.

A scholarly exploration of the problems mentioned in the title, but entirely from the psychologist's point of view.

3202.　Pickering, Pamela. "Nineteenth-century books in a twentieth-century nursery," *Parents' review,* London, Mar., 1951, pp. 79–82.

3203.　Piggott, O. and Frank Keyse. "Library serv-

ices to children in branch libraries and schools," *Assistant librarian,* London, Vol. 55, No. 10, Oct., 1962, pp. 183–192. DLC, NNY.

A heartening report on the results of the wider development of school libraries, with trained teacher-librarians in charge. It is interesting to contrast this with the later work by Roe (2895).

3204.　Pinches, Stella. *Library work with young people; an examination guidebook.* London, Clive Bingley, 1966. 70p. DLC.

"The purpose of this book is to provide a basic pattern for study of children's librarianship for formal examination purposes." The eight chapters cover history, school libraries, public libraries, buildings, staff, extension activities, special classes of readers, and children's reading. There is an index.

3205.　Pumphrey, G. H. *Children's comics; a guide for parents and teachers.* London, Epworth Press, 1955. DLC.

A school principal reports on his findings after many years of studying the subject.

3206.　Purton, Rowland W. *Surrounded by books; the library in the primary school.* London, Education Supply Association, 1962. 125p.

3207.　Quiller-Couch, Arthur. "Children's reading," *On the art of reading;* London, G. P. Putnam, 1920; pp. 39–76. DLC, NNY.

A wise and witty essay on the need for children to have free, imaginative reading, instead of didactic and purely educational matter. The central theme of the discourse is chosen from the preface of an old English edition of the Grimm fairy tales: "Much might be urged against that too rigid and philosophic exclusion of works of fancy and fiction from the libraries of children . . . Our imagination is surely as susceptible of improvement by exercise as our judgement or our memory."

3208.　Ralph, Richard George. *The library in education.* Rev. ed. London, Turnstile Press, 1960. 152p. DLC.

The aims and methods of school library work, selection of books and other materials and technical matters of organization and management. There is a selected, classified bibliography.

3209.　Ray, C. H. *Attitudes and adventures.* London, Library Association, 1965. 54p. 2s.6d. DLC.

A list "to assist those working with young people in the selection of titles which may provide the interest necessary to catch their attention and the stimulus to convince them of the relevance of reading to their own lives."

3210. Raymond, Ernest. "How to massacre innocents," *Parents' review*, London, Aug., 1931, pp. 495–508.

3211. Rayner, Claire. "Picture books for young children," *Design*, London, No. 180, Dec., 1963, pp. 29–37. DLC, NNY.

A mother writes of the "unsatisfactory" state of picture books for the very young. She expresses firm belief in the "here and now" theory, i.e. that children of this age need representational art on subjects out of their experience. For this reason, for example, she was against such books as the Brian Wildsmith *ABC*.

3212. Reeves, James. "Writing for children." Library Association. *Proceedings, papers and summaries of discussions at the Brighton conference*. London, The Association 1958, pp. 10–16. DLC.

A writer of poetry for children discusses here the special difficulties of this field, and its even more special satisfactions.

3213. Robinson, Maude. "Children's books [of the early 19th century,]" *Friends' quarterly examiner*, London, Vol. 70, Oct., 1934, pp. 360–369. NNY.

A historical survey of the children's books of the period, dealing more with general trends than with specific titles.

3214. Robinson, W. V. "Index of children's book illustrators," *YLG news*, London, Vol. 6, May, 1962, pp. 7–8. DLC.

3215. Rollington, Ralph. *A brief history of boys' journals, with interesting facts about the writers of boys' stories*. Leicester, England, H. Simpson, 1913. 111p. DLC.

A personal reminiscence, by the editor of several of the boys' journals of the late 19th century. An appendix gives dates and facts about many of the individual journals.

3216. Roose, Pauline W. "Children's books," *Book lore*, London, Vol. 5, Apr., 1887, pp. 131–135. NNY.

A brief history, somewhat sentimental in tone.

3217. Roscoe, William Caldwell. "Fictions for children," *Poems and essays*, Vol. 2. London, 1860, pp. 481–509.

3218. Ryder, John. *Artists of a certain line; a selection of illustrators for children's books*. London, Bodley Head, 1960. 125p. DLC.

An excellent introduction to the study of illustrated children's books. By placing contrasting illustrations of similar scenes or stories next to each other, the author demonstrates what one should begin looking for in the appraisal of pictures and their relation to the text. There are short biographies of the illustrators mentioned, all of whom are from Commonwealth countries or the European continent with the exception of Maurice Sendak. There is an index.

3219. Sackville-West, Victoria M. *Nursery rhymes*. London, Dropmore Press, 1947. 66p. DLC, NNY.

Essays concerning the qualities of nursery rhymes, and their eternal appeal to children.

3220. Salmon, Edward. *Juvenile literature as it is*. London, Henry J. Drane, 1888. 243p. NNY.

A survey of the contemporary types of children's books, magazines and other reading materials. Index.

3221. ———. "Literature for the little ones," *Nineteenth century*, Philadelphia, Vol. 22, No. 128, Oct., 1887, pp. 563–580. DLC, NNY.

A useful, contemporary review of some of the better editions of the classics and books which have since reached that stature. It epitomizes the critical approach to children's literature prevalent in the 1880's, placing the works of George MacDonald higher in the ranks than *Alice in Wonderland* for example.

3222. Saunders, W. L. *A guide to book lists and bibliographies for the use of school librarians*. 2nd ed. London, School Library Association, 1961. 40p. 5s.6d.

3223. Savage, Ernest A. "Boys' and girls' reading," *A librarian looks at readers*. 2nd ed. London, The Library Association, 1950, pp. 1–72. DLC.

"What they like," "Mental development through reading" and "The right books" are the chapter headings of this first section. The emphasis is on boys' reading, more than girls'.

3224. Sayers, W. C. Berwick. *Books for youth*. London, The Library Association, 1936. 364p. DLC. (Earlier editions called *Books to read*).

"A classified and annotated guide for young readers." The annotations indicate this is definitely for youth, not children. Author, title and subject indexes.

3225. ———. "Library work with children in Great Britain." International Congress of Libraries and Bibliography, 2nd. *Actas y trabajos, Vol. 3;* Madrid, Librería Julián Barbazán, 1936; pp. 271–274. DLC.

Beginning with 1917, the author traces the history of library service to children in England to 1935.

3226. ———. *A manual of children's libraries.* London, Allen and Unwin, 1932. 270p. DLC, NNY.

Mr. Sayers was a strong and early champion of the professional quality of library service which is due children as much as it is adults. He covered, in this useful manual, all aspects of the work, even to the librarian's health. There is a helpful chapter on reading guidance and extensive bibliographies at the end of each chapter. Index.

3227. Schatzki. "Alte kinderbücher," *Philobiblon,* Wien, Jg. 7, Heft 9, 1934, pp. 405–406. NNY.

Although written in German, this is a review of the special *Studio* number on children's book illustration (3119), and on the private collecting of children's books in England and the U.S.

3228. *The school book review.* Schoolmaster Publishing Company, London. Twice yearly. Vol. 1 ff. No. 1 ff. 1965? ff.

3229. *The school librarian and school library review.* School library Association, Gordon House, 29 Gordon Square, W.C. 1, London. 3 times a year. Vol. 1 ff. No. 1 ff. 1953 ff. Subscription: 2 guineas yearly. DLC, IYL, NNY.

An important periodical which contains articles on library and literature evaluation, signed book reviews, biographies of children's authors, a review of other periodical and book literature concerned with children's books and libraries, and countless bits and pieces of helpful information.

3230. "School libraries," *Journal of education,* London, Vol. 66, Jan., 1933. Vol. 68, May, 1934.

A monthly series of articles.

3231. "School libraries under the new English Education Act; a symposium," *Library review,* Glasgow, No. 81, Spring 1947, pp. 228–232. DLC, NNY.

A number of comments have been compiled here from leading educators and librarians concerning the effects this law would have on school libraries and their future development.

3232. *The school library.* London, Her Majesty's Stationery Office, 1952. 32p. (Ministry of Education Pamphlet No. 21). IYL.

The report of a survey undertaken by the Ministry of Education, together with a statement of aims as to what constitutes good school library service.

3233. School Library Association. *School libraries today.* 2nd ed. London, School Library Association, 1961. 54p. DLC.

The present status of school libraries, what standards they aim for, and how they are organized and run. The preface by C. H. C. Osborne surveys developments since 1945. Appendix 1 is a memorandum on training by C. A. Stott. Appendix 2 is a memorandum by C. H. C. Osborne on school and public library relations. Appendix 3 is a short bibliography.

3234. ———. Primary Schools Sub-Committee. *The library in the primary school.* 3rd imp. London, School Library Association, 1960. 100p. 7s6d.

A report first made in 1951, and complementing the one titled *School Libraries Today.* Both have prefaces by W. O. Lester Smith.

3235. ———. Primary Schools Sub-Committee. *Using books in the primary school.* London, School Library Association, 1962. 101p. 15s. DLC.

An outline of the principles which should govern the use of books in teaching, together with some examples of situations where these principles have been carried out. The editing was done by C. H. C. Osborne and there is a foreword by Boris Ford.

3236. *School library review and educational record.* Library Association, London (School Libraries Section). Monthly. Vol. 1, Mar., 1936—Vol. 6, Mar., 1953. DLC, NNY.

This was replaced by the periodical *School Librarian and School Library Review.*

3237. Sewell, Elizabeth. *The field of nonsense.* London, Chatto and Windus, 1952. 198p. DLC.

Chiefly a study of the work of Lear and Carroll, although the author does attempt to define "nonsense" in general rather philosophical terms. It is interesting to compare this with the work by Cammaerts (3008).

3238. Shute, Nerina. *Favourite books for boys and girls: A book guide for parents, teachers and children.* London, Jarrolds, 1955. 176p.

3239. Simsová, Mrs. S. "Books before two: Some observations on the reading of the very young," *Assistant librarian,* London, Vol. 55, Sept., 1962, pp. 168–170. DLC, NNY.

This librarian believes there are children

who express interest in books long before they are two years old. She points out how difficult it is to find information on the subject, and from her own experience with children tells of the types of books (not always children's books, strictly speaking) which very young children respond to.

3240. Sketchley, R. E. D. "Some children's book illustrators," *The library*, London, 2nd series, Vol. 3, No. 12, Oct., 1902, pp. 358–397. DLC, NNY.

This was Part 4 of a series on "English book illustration of today." The contemporary judgements of Crane, Brooke, Caldecott, Rackham, Batten, and others, make interesting reading. There is a bibliography arranged by illustrators.

3241. Smith, B. O. "Children's and reading-rooms," *Library assistant*, London, Vol. 26, Mar., 1933, pp. 52–55. DLC.

In the county libraries, children's rooms must be considered as luxuries, because the money could be spent more profitably elsewhere, wrote this librarian. The author felt that children's rooms were disproportionately costly in the light of their "returns."

3242. Smith, Janet Adam. *Children's illustrated books*. London, Collins, 1948. 50p. IYL, DLC.

Illustrations of English children's books, from the horn books, through Blake, to the present time. An informative and interesting analysis.

3243. Smith, R. D. H. "Report on children's reading," *Library association record*, London, Vol. 1, 4th ser., June, 1934, pp. 172–175. DLC, NNY.

This report was based on one prepared by the East Ham Education Commission. It gives numerous statistics.

3244. Sproston, Ruth. "I want to be a moron," *Library assistant*, London, Vol. 34, Oct., 1941, pp. 154–157. DLC, NNY.

There are two extremes of approach in the selection of children's books. Some libraries believe even cheap series fiction should be included in the collection, because the children like this kind of reading material. Others believe only the best classics and solid, instructive books should be purchased. The middle road, according to this librarian, offers the best possibilities for improving a children's library collection.

3245. Stebbing, Lionel. *How to write for children; the easiest way to break into print, a practical course in writing for boys and girls, with nearly 200 markets*. London, Stebbing Publications, 195?. 31p. DLC.

Written from a commercial point of view. Bibliography.

3246. Steel, Muriel. *Books you'll enjoy*. London, Grafton and Co., 1939. 103p. DLC.

"An annotated guide for readers of from twelve to eighteen years." Enthusiastic in its recommendations. Arranged alphabetically by author.

3247. Stern, C. M. "Bloods," *Library assistant*, London, Vol. 34, No. 9, Nov., 1941, pp. 160–165. DLC, NNY.

The appeal of sensational literature to youngsters remote from good libraries with a wide choice of books. Although the author is against their use, he finds new books to substitute for them, which combine good writing with the action and adventure these readers seem to want and need.

3248. Stevens, B. F., firm. *A list of new English books suitable for school district and other public libraries*. London, B. F. Stevens, 1881. 31p. DLC.

Although this was a commercial buying list, it has some items of historical interest. It is arranged by subject.

3249. Stevenson, Lilian. *A child's bookshelf*. London, Student Christian Movement, 1918. 149p. Supplement, 1920. 18p. DLC.

"Suggestions on children's reading, with an annotated list of books on heroism, service, patriotism, friendliness, joy and beauty."

3250. Stevenson, Robert Louis. "A penny plain and twopence coloured," *Memories and portraits*. New York, Scribner's, 1890, pp. 213–227. NNY.

Reminiscences about the stories which were part of *Skelt's Juvenile Drama* (later Park's, Webb's, Redington's, and Pollock's), and the part which they played in this author's young life. He had loved these thrilling tales as a child and still had a fondness for them as a grown-up.

3251. Stevenson, W. B. "What the judges are looking for: Carnegie Medal and Kate Greenaway Medal awards," *Bookseller*, London, May 23, 1964, pp. 1964–1966. DLC, NNY.

Some of the special points which distinguish the children's book deserving of these awards.

3252. Stone, Peter. "When children read from horn-books," *Country life*, London, Vol. 130, Oct. 19, 1961, pp. 941–943. NNY.

A brief history of the hornbook, together with reproductions from a number of them.

3253. Stott, Cecil A. *School libraries; a short manual*. 3rd ed. London, Cambridge University Press, 1965. DLC. (NNY has 1st ed., 1947 and 2nd ed. 1955, same pub.).

A succinct outline of the principles of administration and routine, finance and use of the school library. The appendix lists bibliographies for each chapter. Index.

3254. ———. "School library movement in England and Wales," *Library trends,* Chicago, Vol. 1, Jan., 1953, pp. 402–422. DLC, NNY.

For this special issue on the problems of the school library in the U.S., this librarian contributed an excellent survey and history of the history and development of the school library in the U.K. There is an extensive list of helpful references given.

3255. Sturt, Felicity. *Primary school library books.* 2nd ed. London, School Library Association, 1965. 106p. 10s 6d.

An annotated list compiled by the Primary Schools Book Panel and edited by Miss Sturt. The first edition was edited by C. H. C. Osborne.

3256. Sutton, H. M. A. "Children and modern literature," *National review,* London, Vol. 18, No. 106, Dec., 1891, pp. 507–519. NNY.

". . . children play a much more important part in the literature of the 19th century than they have ever played in literature before."

3257. Swinstead, M. "Some old-fashioned children's books," *Month,* London, Vol. 147, June, 1926, pp. 523–530. NNY.

A selection of texts from the didactic period of 1795–1827, together with comments on them.

3258. Thackeray, William Makepiece. "On some illustrated children's books," *Fraser's magazine,* London, Vol. 33, 1846, pp. 495–502. NNY.

Written under his pseudonym, Michael Angelo Titmarsh, this is an essay of observations on the generally poor quality of children's books, and a review of some specific children's books appearing during that season.

3259. Thirkell, Angela. "Mother Goose; a critical review of her collected works," *London mercury,* Vol. 26, May, 1932. pp. 62–69. NNY.

A delightful tongue-in-cheek essay, celebrating "that excellent but neglected authoress Mother Goose."

3260. Thomas, M. O. "Juvenile libraries, British and American," *Modern librarian,* Lahore, Vol. 4, Jan., 1934, pp. 53–62. DLC, NNY.

The author traces the beginnings and growth of children's work in England and the U.S. The three main characteristics of the children's library are: accommodation and furniture; reading materials; the children's librarian. A typical day's work is described.

3261. Toase, Charles A. "British multivolume encyclopedias for children: A critical survey," *Library association record,* London, Vol. 63, No. 10, Oct., 1961, pp. 338–344. DLC, NNY.

A review to aid librarians in purchasing and advising others on the purchase of such sets.

3262. Tolkien, J. R. R. *Tree and leaf.* London, Allen & Unwin, 1964. 92p. Also: Boston, Houghton, 1965. 112p. DLC, NNY.

The first part, which is an essay, "On fairy stories," contains perhaps the most definitive statement ever thought out on the subject of "faerie." The author distinguishes between fairy tales and fantasy, and specifically delimits the fairy world of much of the material usually placed there in the minds of average thinkers. Mr. Tolkien disagrees that fairy tales are the special or even favorite province of the young.

3263. Tollemache, Lionel A. *et al.* "Children and poetry," *Essays, mock-essays and character sketches.* London, W. Rice & Co., 1898, pp. 140–149. NNY.

"The time has happily gone by when Dr. Watts' hymns were regarded as the proper beginning of a child's poetical education." The author then suggests the poets and the methods he believes to be better in introducing poetry to children.

3264. Townsend, John Rowe. *Written for children; an outline of English children's literature.* London, Garnet Miller, 1965. 160p. DLC, IYL, NNY.

A very readable critical account of the prose written for children in England from the time of the first printers up to the present day, with the greatest emphasis on late 19th- and 20th-century works. In his preface the author states that he intended to cover the more important works at length, rather than merely give mention to a great number of works. He specifically excluded poetry, picture books, and fiction by foreign authors. An index and bibliography.

3265. Travers, Pamela L. *A radical innocence.* *New York times book review,* May 9, 1965, Part 2 pp. 1, 38. DLC, NNY.

Miss Travers compares her own childhood reading with that of present day children. In the Nov.

7, 1965 issue of the special Children's Book Supplement she discourses on villains in fiction for children. Both are delightful reading.

3266. Trease, Geoffrey. *Enjoying books*. Rev. ed. London, Phoenix House, 1963. 160p.

3267. ———. *Tales out of school;* 2nd ed. London, Heinemann, 1964. 181p. DLC, IYL, NNY.
"A personal survey of general tendencies as they are discoverable by a single critic." Mr. Trease writes with great charm of the tales he believes children will (and do) enjoy "out of school," when they are made available at the proper time. He is concerned here only with fiction. There is a bibliography and index.

3268. Tuer, Andrew W. *The history of the horn-book*. 2 vols. London, Leadenhall Press, 1896. Vol. 1, 179p. Vol. 2, 278p. DLC, NNY.
An exhaustive study covering all imaginable categories of this early type of children's book. There are numerous reproductions throughout the text and the volumes contain several facsimiles in pockets attached to the binding. There is a separate index to each volume.

3269. ———. *1,000 quaint cuts from books of other days including amusing illustrations from children's story books, fables, chapbooks . . .* London, Field & Tuer [1886]. 170p. DLC.
Reproductions of more than 1,000 woodcuts from the early 19th century. A large proportion are from books usually considered children's books. A few are reproduced from chapbooks.

3270. ———. *Pages and pictures from forgotten children's books*. London, Leadenhall Press, 1898–1899. 510p. DLC.
Representative pages and pictures from 111 books of the 18th and 19th century, with brief informative notes on the various styles of illustrations. This, and Mr. Tuer's other works, 3269 and 3271, provide an excellent means of experiencing the total flavor of these early books.

3271. ———. *Stories from old fashioned children's books*. London, Leadenhall Press, 1899–1900. 439p. DLC, NNY.
A delightful and interesting addition to the author's earlier collection (3271). There are some 250 selections reproduced here, all of which are English in origin, and most of which were in the author's private collection.

3272. Turner, E. S. *Boys will be boys*. Rev. ed. London, Michael Joseph, 1957. 277p. IYL. (DLC has 1948 edition, 269p.).
A reminiscence of the "penny dreadfuls" read avidly by boys of the late 19th and early 20th centuries, and some of the more recent means through which boys get their "thrills." This affectionate study clearly indicates the author's feeling of benevolence toward a group of books not usually included in more serious studies of children's literature.

3273. University of Bristol. Institute of Education. *A second survey of books for backward readers*. London, University of London Press, 1962.
Compiled by a subcommittee of the Bristol Teachers' Backwardness Research Group.

3274. Vale, George F. "Writing, reading and selection of children's books," *Library association record*, London, Vol. 41, No. 6, June, 1939, pp. 309–316. DLC, NNY.
A representative survey of good children's books, old and current, with pertinent comments on contents, quality and criticism. Only a few mentioned are still familiar.

3275. Victoria and Albert Museum. *Exhibition of illustrated books for children (Historical section)*. *Catalogue*. London, National Book Council, 1932. 55p. NNY.
The 676 items are arranged chronologically in the catalogue, and include not only books but hornbooks, battledores, drawings and engravings. The majority of items are from private collections, chiefly those of C. T. Owen, Guy Little, R. M. J. Knaster. The remainder are from the collection of the Museum. In the introduction, E. V. Lucas discusses the books in seven main categories.

3276. Waters, Alice. "Some old children's books," *Strand magazine*, London, Vol. 15, Jan., 1898, pp. 32–40. DLC, NNY.
The author describes some of the books to be found in the South Kensington Museum. Illustrated with many black and white cuts.

3277. Weisse, H. V. "Reading for the young," *Contemporary review*, London, Vol. 79, June, 1901, pp. 829–838. DLC, NNY.
The writer was in favor of limiting children in the amount of reading, and that to only reading of an instructive sort. Magazines and most novels were not recommended.

3278. Welsh, Charles. *A bookseller of the last century; being some account of the life of John Newbery, and of the books he published, with a notice of the later Newberys.* London, Griffith, Farran, Okeden and Welsh, 1885; New York, E. P. Dutton, 1885. 373p. DLC, NNY.

This biography has an appendix listing Newbery's publications from 1740–1800 in alphabetical and then chronological order.

3279. ———. "The children's books that have lived," *The library,* London, Vol. 1, No. 3, June 1, 1900, pp. 314–323. DLC, NNY.

A general history.

3280. ———. *On coloured books for children.* London, C. W. H. Wyman, 1887. 47p. DLC.

Another informative lecture by Mr. Welsh, reprinted with a list of the books in the exhibition. They are arranged chronologically, and include entries up to 1886.

3281. ———. *On some of the books for children of the last century.* London, Griffith, Farran, Okeden and Welsh, 1886. 108p. DLC.

A handsome, privately-printed, small book containing a lecture on the children's books published by John Newbery, together with a list of those books.

3282. ———. "Some notes on the history of books for children," *Newbery house magazine,* London, Vol. 3, Aug., 1890, pp. 221–226; Sept., 1890, pp. 336–343; Oct., 1890, pp. 458–471; Nov., 1890, pp. 599–613. DLC, NNY.

Chapters on the history of children's books, chiefly those in England from the introduction of printing to the early part of the 19th century.

3283. "What do they read? A symposium on the reading habits of schoolchildren today," *English,* London, Vol. 13, Summer 1960, pp. 55–58; Autumn 1960, pp. 99–101. NNY.

The first article surveys the reading interests of boys, and the second, those of girls. The authors are teachers or headmasters in British schools.

3284. White, Gleeson. "Children's books and their illustrators." Special No. of: *The international studio,* New York, Winter 1898, pp. 3–68. DLC, NNY.

A milestone in the study of children's book illustration. The text is critical and there are almost 100 black and white reproductions chosen to support the points made. The majority of illustrators covered are British, with a few from the U.S., France and Germany discussed as well.

3285. Whitehouse, William Hemming Sandys. *Medal winning children's books: The Newbery,*

Caldecott and Carnegie Medal awards; a catalogue. Cambridge, 1951. 31p.

3286. Wileman, Frances M. "The modern style of format in children's books," *Library world,* London, Vol. 39, No. 447, Oct., 1936, pp. 63–64; Nov., 1936, pp. 87–88. DLC, NNY.

A discussion of some of the aspects of children's book design which are or are not appealing to children. Many specific examples are cited.

3287. Williams, A. R. "The magazine reading of secondary school children," *British journal of educational psychology,* Birmingham, Vol. 21, Nov., 1951, pp. 186–198. DLC.

Report of an extensive survey made among adolescents.

3288. Wilson, Albert E. *Penny plain, twopence coloured; a history of the juvenile drama.* London, G. Harrap, 177p. DLC, NNY.

This history discusses the style of text and illustration of this type of publication. There are a number of extracts included and 83 illustrations are reproduced. Lists of titles and publishers are followed by a bibliography and an index. See also the entry under Robert Louis Stevenson (3250).

3289. Wilson, Barbara Ker. *Writing for children, an English author and editor's point of view.* New York, F. Watts, 1961. 128p. DLC.

A manual on writing for children with higher standards in mind than some of the more commercial handbooks. It is admittedly difficult to write about writing, and this author sometimes resorts to generalities.

3290. Wilson, J. Dover. *Poetry and the child.* London, English Association, 1916. 18p. (Pamphlet 34).

"Poet and child belong to the same species. Not instruction . . . but recreation is here the teacher's function."

3291. Wilson, John James. "Penny dreadfuls and penny bloods," *Connoisseur,* London, Vol. 89, Apr., 1932, pp. 226–233. DLC, NNY.

A review of a large number of titles which can be classified as this type of literature, with eight pictures reproduced in black and white.

3292. Woodthorpe, Gertrude. "The Fairchilds and others," *Cornhill magazine,* London, Vol. 151, Jan., 1935, pp. 42–54. DLC, NNY.

Studies on the work of Mary Sherwood, Ann Taylor and Mary Howitt.

3293.   Wrigley, M. J. "The film in its relation to the library: A neglected educational agency," *Library world*, London, Vol. 23, Mar., 1920, pp. 625–628. DLC, NNY.

"What a formidable force to be reckoned with would be the co-operation of these three main factors in education," wrote this librarian, referring to the school, the library and the cinema. His article is quite prophetic.

3294.   *YLG news*. Youth Libraries Group, Library Association, 7 Ridgmount Street, Store Street, London W.C. 1. Vol. 1 ff. 1958 ff. 3 issues yearly.

News of interest to the members of this section of the Library Association is presented in depth.

3295.   Yonge, Charlotte. "Children's literature of the last century," *Macmillan's magazine*, London, Vol. 20, No. 117, July, 1869, pp. 229–237; No. 118,

Aug., 1869, pp. 302–310; No. 119, Sept., 1869, pp. 448–456. DLC, NNY.

Part I, "Nursery books of the 18th century," is a reminiscent, yet discriminating, perusal of the nursery favorites of the 18th century. Part II, "Didactic fiction," is a perceptive critical review of the works of Maria Edgeworth, her imitators, and the Sunday school story writers. Part III is a discussion of "Class literature of the last 30 years." Very few specific titles are mentioned in this last part, and the generalizations are very dated. On the whole, the three-part article provides an unusual, almost contemporary, view of early children's literature in English.

3296.   ———. *What books to lend and what to give*. London, National Society's Depository, 1887. 126p. DLC.

In the interest of keeping children at home instead of playing "questionable games" out-of-doors in the dark, Miss Yonge made up this list to help with parish work. It is chiefly of historical interest as an example of book selection in the Victorian age.

Scotland, Ireland and Wales

3297.   Bellis, Hannah. *Lives of favourite authors*. Glasgow, Collins, 1940. 192p.

3298.   Butchart, R. "School libraries in Edinburgh," *Library association record*, London, Vol. 38, Aug., 1936, pp. 410–413. DLC, NNY.

The history and present status of these libraries.

3299.   Douglas, Alison M. "The Scottish contribution to children's literature." *Library review*, Glasgow, Vol. 20, Winter 1965, pp. 241–246. DLC, NNY. DLC also has as a reprint.

A summary of some of the works of writers who have come from Scotland or used it as their background for children's stories. The author also reviews the wealth of legendary material which comes from Scotland and is now considered part of the heritage of English literature.

3300.   Dunlop, D. C. "Children's leisure-reading interests." Scottish Council for Research in Education. *Studies in reading, II*. London, 1950, pp. 82–105. (Publication no. 34.) DLC.

A review of earlier surveys, as well as results of another made by the author in the public libraries of Glasgow. Bibliography.

3301.   Glasgow. Public Libraries. Woodside District Library. *Guide for young readers*. Glasgow, Committee on Libraries, 1921. 355p. DLC.

A guide to the children's collections by decimal classification with some annotations and an incomplete index.

3302.   Mason, B. S. "Some school libraries in Scotland," *School librarian and school library review*, London, Vol. 1, Dec., 1937, pp. 31–34. DLC, NNY.

An interesting history. The author points out that some of the best schools in the country were also the oldest; consequently their buildings were extremely cramped and out-of-date and they could not make room for adequate and separate libraries.

3303.   *150 years of Scottish children's books*. Mimeographed list prepared by the Youth Libraries Group for the Weekend School at St. Andrews, Sept., 1965. 7p. DLC.

This is a straight author list in two sections (historical and present-day) with no annotations. It was made as a supplement to a talk on children's books in Scotland given by Miss A. Douglas.

3304.   *The planning of school libraries in new buildings*. Lochgilphead (Argyll), School Library Association in Scotland, 1963. 8p.

3305. "School libraries: Kinds and results: A symposium," *Library review,* Coatbridge, No. 43, Autumn 1937, pp. 106–115. DLC.

Revealing of the state of school libraries at that time. No statistics, but an excellent general account.

3306. School Library Association of Scotland. *100 non-fiction books for a school library.* Edinburgh, The Association, 1954. 16p.

3307. Scouller, E. "Schools are to blame," *Library review,* Coatbridge, No. 35, Autumn 1935, pp. 106–112. DLC.

The author deplores the type of texts used for teaching literature and contends that they are the reasons children do not enjoy reading it.

3308. Spalding, Elsie Lilian. *Books through the child's eyes; the story of a children's library.* Edinburgh, Grant, 1960. 89p.

A description of the Agnes Hislop Memorial Children's Library, founded in 1946 and maintained in branches in private homes.

3309. *Studies in the school library.* Edinburgh, School Library Association in Scotland, 1960. 20p.

3310. Brown, Stephen J. "Irish fiction for boys," *Studies,* Dublin, Vol. 7, Dec., 1918, pp. 665–670; Vol. 8, Sept., 1919, pp. 469–472; Dec., 1919, pp. 658–663. NNY.

The author treats of Irish fiction in eight parts: School stories, home stories, adventure, hero tales, historical tales, humorous stories, fairy tales and miscellaneous. Each section has an annotated list of titles. In his concluding remarks, the compiler regrets the paucity of good Irish books for children, which he feels should form a small part of the reading of every Irish boy or girl.

3311. ———. "Libraries in national schools—why not?" *Irish library bulletin,* Dublin, Vol. 7, Apr., 1946, pp. 67–69. DLC, NNY.

The author summarizes the points made at the conference held at the Catholic University of America in June, 1944, and then asks why such ideas could not be put into practice in Ireland.

3312. Colum, Padraic. "Story-telling in Ireland," *Horn book,* Boston, Vol. 10, May, 1934, pp. 190–194. DLC, NNY.

A well-known storyteller and folklorist from Ireland reminisces here about the storytelling he experienced in his childhood. He also writes of the work of the Folklore Society of Ireland which is working to preserve this traditional art.

3313. Doherty, Alexander. "Ulster juvenile book service," *Irish library bulletin,* Dublin, Vol. 4, Jan.–Feb., 1943, p. 13. DLC, NNY.

The county library systems of Northern Ireland were "spending generously on books for boys and girls." A number of statistics are given here.

3314. "Dublin public libraries' committee's scheme to provide books for loan through the primary school," *An leabharlann,* Dublin, Vol. 1, 1905, pp. 152–156. NNY.

A report telling how the scheme was operating.

3315. Madden, P. J. "Children's books in Ireland," *An leabharlann,* Dublin, Vol. 13, Mar., 1955, pp. 33–44. DLC, NNY.

An excellent survey of English literature as it has touched the lives of Irish children and some of the special Irish literature for the young. The author mentioned that at the time there were no collections of Irish nursery rhymes in print, and not a single anthology of original poetry for children.

3316. Reddin, Kenneth. "Children's books in Ireland," *Irish library bulletin,* Dublin, Vol. 7, May, 1946, pp. 74–76. DLC, NNY.

This critic found Irish children's books to be very stereotyped and centered around stage-Irish characters rather than of real life people. He contended that this was what was most wanted in England and America and since most sales went there, writers played up to these desires.

3317. White, Peter. "The child in the library," *An leabharlann,* Dublin, Vol. 1, No. 2, June, 1905, pp. 100–108. DLC.

An emotional plea to bring model children's services to "the beginnings of the future Irish nation."

3318. Ballinger, John. "A municipal library and its public: Children," *The library,* London, (New series), Vol. 9, No. 34, Apr., 1908, pp. 173–185. DLC.

The further story of the Cardiff library and how it persuaded tax authorities of its value to children in the schools.

3319. ———. "The public libraries and the schools: An experiment," *The library,* London, Vol. 9, Nos. 102–107, June–Nov., 1897, pp. 239–250. DLC, NNY.

The librarian at Cardiff describes in detail a new program of cooperation with schools in which children visited the library in class groups. This was a pioneer effort in bringing new meaning to library service to children.

3320. Evans, H. Keith. "Libraries and the use of books in primary schools," *School librarian and school library review,* London, Vol. 13, July, 1965, pp. 141–148. DLC, NNY.
"Memorandum submitted to the Central Advisory Council for Education (Wales)." This includes some well-stated reasons for the necessity of central school libraries.

3321. Houghton, S. M. "Concerning school libraries in Wales," *School librarian and school library review,* London, Vol. 1, No. 4, Easter 1937, pp. 86–90. DLC, NNY.
Recommendations for the organization and development of school libraries in Wales.

3322. Owen, E. T. and J. Lloyd Jones. "Books children like best: An enquiry," *Welsh outlook,* Cardiff, Vol. 14, Dec., 1927, pp. 327–328; Vol. 15, Dec., 1928, pp. 367–368.

The West Indies

The Barbados, Windward Islands, Leeward Islands, Bermuda, Bahamas, British Honduras, British Guiana are the British colonies included in this group, together with the independent commonwealth nation of Trinidad and Tobago, treated separately below. Also placed here because of geographic proximity are: the Netherlands Antilles and Surinam (Dutch Guinea); the French islands of Martinique and Guadeloupe; and the U.S. Virgin Islands. The Commonwealth of Puerto Rico is to be found in the Latin American section.

According to Mr. Savage's report in 1934 (3328), there were only adequate children's libraries in: Hamilton Public Library, Bermuda; Public Library, Bridgetown, Barbados; and libraries on St. Thomas, St. John and St. Croix in the U.S. Virgin Islands, which were managed under one supervisory unit. Practically all of these had small subscription fees required for the privilege of library use. There were also a few good school libraries, mostly in private schools. Miss Baa indicates in her later study (3323) that some progress had been made, especially in Jamaica, Bermuda and the Bahamas. According to her, the Netherlands Antilles had the most modern, up-to-date libraries and trained staff.

There is practically no publishing at all on any of the islands, so that most books are imported from the U.S. and England. The Netherlands Antilles and Surinam use Dutch, so their books are imported from the Netherlands or Belgium. Martinique and Guadeloupe import theirs from France.

3323. Baa, Enid M. "Libraries of the Caribbean area, with a statement on the reasons why a West Indian library conference is necessary, and the comparative status of library services which exist among the islands today," Charlotte Amalie, St. Thomas, 1959. Unp. DLC.
This was a "plea for more improved library and information services in all islands, particularly in the French territories of the West Indies." In assessing the library services in each of the islands, the author makes frequent reference to school and children's libraries.

3324. Evans, P. C. C. "Libraries and nationhood,"

Library world, London, Vol. 63, June, 1962, pp. 323–328. DLC, NNY.

The effects which independence has had and will have on the Jamaica Library Service and the Schools Library Service.

3325.   Hartog, John. Libraries in the Netherlands Antilles," *Blatt,* St. Augustine, Trinidad, Vol. 1, No. 4, Dec., 1962, pp. 46–48. NNY.

This includes a description of the government library of the Department of Education, which has a children's collection, and the public library of St. Nicholas, Aruba, which also has a children's department.

3326.   Merriman, Stella E. "The Public Free Library in British Guiana," *Blatt,* St. Augustine, Trinidad, Vol. 1, No. 4, Dec., 1962, pp. 34–39. NNY.

This article includes descriptions of the children's and young people's departments of the public library, and mentions also the 11 small libraries operated on sugar estates, by the Sugar Producers Association.

3327.   "Operation St. Croix," *Wilson library bulletin,* New York, Vol. 36, Apr., 1962, pp. 674–676. DLC, NNY.

An American school collected books and funds for two school libraries in St. Croix. Some 18 students then raised the money for their fares, and together with their school librarian and some teachers, went to the island to assist in setting up the libraries.

3328.   Savage, Ernest A. *The libraries of Bermuda, the Bahamas, the British West Indies, British Guiana, British Honduras, Puerto Rico and the American Virgin Islands: A report to the Carnegie Corporation of New York.* London, Library Association, 1934. 102p. NNY.

A very specific survey of library service on each of the islands, with references to children's services and school libraries wherever there were any.

Trinidad and Tobago

For its size (less than 1,000,000 population) the nation of Trinidad and Tobago is one of the most racially and culturally variegated in the world. There are large populations of Negroes, East Indians (descendents of immigrants from India in the 1840's), Lebanese and Syrian, and smaller segments which are descendents of Chinese, British or European immigrants. While there is as yet no publishing of children's books locally, children's libraries have been in existence for a number of years. The chapter in the IFLA publication, *Library Service to Children, 2,* indicates that the Trinidad Public Library, which originally was a subscription library, now offers free services to children in the central library, branches, and travelling bookmobiles. All of the books are imported from the U.S. or England. The major difficulty is getting enough books with a West Indian background, or treating of history and geography of the islands. It is for this reason that UNICEF and UNESCO are cooperating on a government-subsidized project for the production of children's books.

3329.   Baker, Augusta B. "Trinidad's children and their library," *School library association of California, bulletin,* Los Angeles, Vol. 27, May, 1956, pp. 5–9. DLC, NNY.

This U.S. librarian visited the West Indies on a grant in order to study the folklore of the area. She reports here on the library service which children have available there.

3330.   "Trinidad and Tobago," *Library service to children, 2.* Lund, Bibliotekstjänst, 1966, pp. 68–76. DLC, NNY.

This publication was sponsored by IFLA (see 32). This chapter is concerned with the history and present status of library work with children in Trinidad and Tobago.

Canada

The number of entries in Canada's bibliography belies the true extent of activities in that country. Library service to children in public and school libraries has developed along the same lines as in the United States. There are professional organizations in each of the provinces as well as a national organization. Canadian membership in the American Library Association has also been very active, with general acceptance of the same standards. As is the case in the U.S., there are sections of Canada which cannot or do not maintain these standards as well as might be hoped. By the same token, there are libraries which provide outstanding service to children, and thus serve as models for the rest of the country. Certainly the leader in this respect is the Boys and Girls House of the Toronto Public Library, the central children's library of the system which has branches throughout the city.

In 1922, when the headquarters of the central library grew too small to accommodate all the services, a neighboring building was purchased and remodeled to suit children's library needs. This was the first library building on the continent, devoted entirely to children's work. Prior to that, of course, children's work had been carried out not only in the main library (since 1912) but also in most of the branches. In 1950–1951, an addition was built on to Boys and Girls House, into which the main children's room and the story hour room were moved. This left more space in the original building for the Osborne Collection of Early Children's Books, given to the library in 1949 by Edgar Osborne, in recognition of the outstanding work done with children and young people. This Collection is now housed in a new building suited to its particular needs.

Many newcomers to the field of children's literature are unaware of the fact that Lillian Smith's eloquent book, *The Unreluctant Years,* was the culmination of many years' work in directing Boys and Girls Services in the Toronto Public Library. Miss Smith was both the first Canadian and the first children's librarian to be a member of the Executive Board of the American Library Association. Her demonstrated understanding of children, and her impeccable taste in selecting for them the best books available, have been the inspiration for children's librarians throughout the English-speaking world. The Toronto Public Library has honored her by naming after her the historical collection of children's books published after 1910. This will complement the Osborne Collection, which ends at that date.

School libraries in Ontario province also had a vigorous and book-minded supporter in their early years. This was Egerton Ryerson, Chief Superintendent of Education from 1846 to 1876. Seemingly, Mr. Ryerson was a little too far ahead of his colleagues, for his scheme to make libraries a part of every community, through the schools, was short-lived. What he had succeeded in doing was in getting local communities interested in supporting their boards of education with funds to purchase books from a government depository, at a greatly reduced rate. Within 25 years, more than a million volumes had been distributed, no small figure when one considers the total population of the province at that time. The general consensus was that if the books had been more carefully selected so as to excite the interest in the young, and if there had been some skilled person put in charge of the collection, there would have been greater success and a chance of survival. However, by 1880 most of the collections had fallen into disuse or were locked up and forgotten about. When a new school library law was passed in 1903, educators had to begin all over again. The process has been slow and tedious, particularly in the primary schools. Only in the last decade has the central school library begun to receive proper attention.

In Toronto, the public library had served the schools through a system of book lending or through the establishment of branches in some of the schools. This has been replaced with a plan by the board of education to put librarians in all the schools, hopefully to be achieved within another three years. In other areas, public libraries still contract for some service to schools.

The greatest deficiencies in library service to children occur in the rural areas, where very few children have free and easy access to books. A few localities are served by a regional library system with mobile libraries; still others get book boxes from a central point. This does not satisfy the need many children have for guidance in reading, and it leaves little room for the wide choice in book selection which city youngsters enjoy.

For her English children's books, Canada has turned both to England and the U.S., but more extensively to the latter, because of proximity. This is in contrast to the other Commonwealth countries, which import far more from Britain than they do from the U.S. While the typically English handling of subject matter, language and point-of-view has not been a major difficulty, children in Canada take more readily to a U.S. book of similar quality. In recent years, there has been an increase in the number of books written and published by Canadians, often jointly with a British or U.S. firm, because the small edition needed for Canadian consumption is not economically feasible. The total number of these is still well under a hundred.

French books are published in small quantities also, but the majority are imported from France. There is even greater disparity in the tastes and language patterns of French and French-Canadian children, than is the case with English and English-Canadian children. Canadian French has retained much of the vocabulary which has long since disappeared in France, and it has acquired new words in forms quite different from those of France. As one librarian has pointed out, no sooner is the French-Canadian child beyond the ABC and picture book stage when he must learn to cope with reading a French completely different from his everyday speech. This often frustrates the child to the point of making him not want to read in French, at least not any books chosen for pleasure (3348).

There are many types of activities going on which are related to children and books. Young Canada's Book Week has been celebrated annually since 1948. It is sponsored by the Canadian Association of Children's Librarians. There are also prizes offered to the best Canadian children's books in English (since 1946) and in French (since 1950). These are awarded by the national Canadian Library Association and are usually announced in connection with Young Canada's Book Week. Most important, there is much public discussion of the importance of children's reading, and the necessity for good selection.

3331. d'Anjou, Joseph, *et al. Pour mieux choisir ce que nos jeunes liront.* Montreal, Bellarmin, 1957. 171p. DLC.

Essays on children's reading, selected from such periodicals as *Ma Paroisse, Collège et Famille, Relations,* etc. They are written mostly by librarians and educators and are from the Roman Catholic point of view.

3332. Bagshaw, Marguerite. "Canadian book awards," *Top of the news,* Chicago, Vol. 16, Dec., 1959, pp. 49–51. DLC, NNY.

The history of the Book of the Year Medal which the Canadian Library Association awards to the best children's book published in Canada or by a Canadian author. There is also a list of the winners from 1947 to 1959 for the English language, and those from 1952 to 1959 for the French language.

3333. Bélisle, Alvine. "Albums pour enfants," *Canadian library association bulletin,* Ottawa, Vol. 16, July, 1959, pp. 43–45. DLC, NNY.

An annotated list of picture books in French for children from 2 to 8 years of age.

3334. ———. "Choix de livres pour jeunes, 8 à 15 ans," *Canadian librarian,* Ottawa, Vol. 17, July, 1960, pp. 30–41. DLC, NNY.

An annotated list arranged by subject and age groups. All are books in French.

3335. ———. "Les écrivains canadiens racontent a nos jeunes," *Canadian library association bulletin,* Ottawa, Vol. 13, Aug., 1956, pp. 32–34. DLC, NNY.

"Canadian authors write for our youth." An account of some of the newer books which have come out in Canada written by Canadians.

3336. Boulizon, Guy. *Livres roses et séries noires. Guide psychologique et bibliographique de la littérature de jeunesse.* Montreal, Beauchemin, 1957. 188p.

3337. ——— et Jeanne. *Nos jeunes liront . . . 1,000 titres de livres.* Quebec, École des Parents de Québec, 1950. 40p. APP.

An annotated list of 1,000 books in French arranged by subject groups.

3338. Broadus, Edmund Kemper. *What shall our children read?* Edmonton, Jas. E. Richards, 1909. 15p. NNY.

A speech delivered at a Trustees' Convention. This is a perceptive criticism of the themes of death, violence and animal behavior as they appear in children's literature.

3339. Busterd, Irene. *What do they read; books for Canadian children.* Toronto, Canadian Library Association, 1954. (Occasional paper, No. 3). Reprint from: *Queens quarterly,* Kingston, Vol. 41, Autumn 1954, pp. 367–380. NNY.

"As most of our juvenile books were published primarily for the American market, our children come to assume that Canada is a 'poor relation,' living outside those walls of the United States within which things happen and exist as they do in Books." The situation was improving, however, and the author cites some of the books which helped to bring this about.

3340. Campbell, Henry C. "New ways with old books," *Library journal,* New York, Vol. 90, No. 20, Nov. 15, 1965, p. 5043. DLC, IYL, NNY.

Although brief, this account provides a quick survey of the results of the Toronto colloquium on children's book collecting.

3341. Canadian Library Association. School Library Association. *Basic book list for Canadian schools: Elementary division, grades 1–6.* Ottawa, The Association, [1965]. 69p.

3342. ———. Young People's Section. *Canadian books [for young people].* Ottawa, Canadian Library Association, 1955 ff. 22p. Annual. APP.

An annotated list of the previous year's outstanding books arranged by subject groups. Some French titles are included.

3343. Carter, Mary Duncan. . . . *Why chil-*

dren's libraries? Montreal, McGill University, 1928. 2p. (Publications, Series 7, Library, No. 15.) DLC.

The author urged the establishment of children's libraries in Montreal which was far behind Toronto and some of the other provinces in public library work with children.

3344. "Challenge of the new course of studies to the children's libraries," *Ontario library review,* Toronto, Vol. 22, Aug., 1938, pp. 209–211. DLC.

Because the Department of Education had adopted a new curriculum, children were pouring into the libraries and book supplies were not adequate to meet the demand.

3345. Chandler, Bramwell. "School libraries in the maritime provinces," *Ontario library review,* Toronto, Vol. 23, No. 3, Aug., 1939, pp. 296–298. DLC.

There are great difficulties in supplying these out-lying rural provinces with books. Each was attempting to cope in a different way: through central book distribution (Nova Scotia); through regional service (Prince Edward Island) and through re-examination of the whole question of school libraries (in New Brunswick).

3346. "Children's book illustration," *Canadian library association bulletin,* Ottawa, Vol. 11, Aug., 1954, pp. 9 ff. DLC, NNY.

"To show the progression of book illustration in the past 200 years pictures from various editions of "Puss in Boots" that are in the Osborne Collection of Children's Books . . . have been microfilmed . . . and are reproduced in this issue of the *Bulletin.*"

3347. "Children's librarians' section. School and intermediate libraries section," *Ontario library review,* Toronto, Vol. 23, No. 2, May, 1939; pp. 185–188, 195–200. DLC.

Reports given at the annual meeting of the Ontario Library Association. The first is on children's library work in Quebec by Donalda Putnam, the second contains two articles on school libraries, one by Elizabeth St. John for Ontario, and one by Joseph Brunet for Quebec. There is also a brief article by John W. Perks on libraries in the Protestant schools of Quebec.

3348. Clement, Beatrice. "Children's national literature in French Canada," *Top of the news,* Chicago, Vol. 17, No. 2, Dec., 1960, pp. 27–31. DLC, NNY.

There are sad gaps in French Canadian literature for children, except in ABC and nature books. Children's books from France do not answer the needs satisfactorily according to this writer.

3349. Desroches, Jean-Guy. "Les 'nursery rhymes,' Paul Hazard et les bibliothécares," *APLA bulletin,* Halifax, Vol. 28, Feb., 1964, pp. 2–5. NNY.

A French librarian comments on the fact that there still exist no collections of French nursery rhymes, equivalent to the English Mother Goose, and he cites passages from Paul Hazard to give reasons why.

3350. Ellison, Shirley E. *Library service to children in the rural areas of British Columbia.* Seattle, University of Washington, 1952. 72p. Thesis.

3351. Emery, J. W. *The library, the school and the child.* Toronto, Macmillan, 1917. 216p. DLC.

Historical and contemporary developments, with special reference to the work as carried on in Canada. This refers as much to public library work as it does to schools and gives specific statistics and dates for most of the children's libraries then in operation. It is also concerned with the philosophy of service, and in this reference, was very influential in Canadian library development.

3352. Farley, R. P. Paul-Emile. *Livres d'enfants.* Montreal, C. S. V., 1929.

3353. Francis de Sales, Sister. "Are libraries meeting the needs of our children?" *Canadian library association bulletin,* Ottawa, Vol. 6, Sept., 1949, pp. 30–35. In French, pp. 73–78. DLC, NNY.

The author writes that such a question is difficult to answer on a national level. The situation is different for each librarian and it is only when each one seriously asks himself this question that libraries will begin to meet children's needs.

3354. Fraser, Margaret. "School libraries in Ontario," *School libraries,* Chicago, Vol. 9, No. 4, May, 1960, pp. 19–20, 59. DLC, NNY.

A brief historical review and survey of the contemporary status.

3355. Gouin, Paul. "La littérature enfantine, école de patriotisme," *Relations,* Montreal, No. 162, June, 1954, p. 167.

Children should be taught patriotic ideals through their books: therefore, it is important to have more native literature than translations.

3356. Grenier, Hélène. "School libraries in the Province of Québec," *School libraries,* Chicago, Vol.

9, No. 4, May, 1960, pp. 17–18, 43. DLC, NNY.

Libraries in French schools in this province are divided into three types: those in rural schools, in city schools and in the "colleges classiques." The author describes their differences, which are more complex than in other parts of the country, due to the dual language and religion problems.

3357.   Holmes, Alfred. *Voluntary reading of Toronto public school pupils.* Toronto, University of Toronto, 1932. Thesis.

3358.   Johnston, Alethea. "Rx: 1 child, 1 book. Mix well," *Canadian library association bulletin,* Ottawa, Vol. 14, Aug., 1957, pp. 28–33. DLC, NNY.

A lively account of the physical as well as mental demands made on the children's librarian of the busy branch library.

3359.   Kassirer, Eve. *What's what for children; the original work of twenty-one Canadian authorities; a parent's handbook.* 3rd ed. Ottawa, Citizen's Committee on Children, 1959.

Includes a bibliography on children's books and libraries.

3360.   Lacasse, Arthur. "De l'influence du livre sur la formation de l'enfant," *Royal Society of Canada, Transactions,* Ottawa, Ser. 3, Vol. 33, Sec. 1, May, 1939, pp. 179–181. NNY.

On the influence of reading on the character formation of the child. From the Roman Catholic point of view.

3361.   Leacock, Stephen B. "What I read as a child." Sawyer, Harriet P. *The library and its contents.* New York, H. W. Wilson, 1925, pp. 143–144. DLC, NNY.

Reprinted from the *Toronto Public Library Bulletin,* July–Sept., 1920, p. 1 ff. The author writes: "I have no difficulty whatever in naming the books that I used to read as a child, inasmuch as I am reading them still." He goes on to cite a number of them by title.

3362.   Lewis, Rita C. "Library service to schools in Toronto," *Wilson library bulletin,* New York, Vol. 22, No. 2, Oct., 1947, pp. 141–143. DLC, NNY.

A program in which the public librarian served neighborhood schools by going to each one on set "library days," giving reading guidance to many classes of children.

3363.   Lines, Kathleen M. "Boys and girls book house, Toronto," *Junior bookshelf,* Kirkburton, Vol. 3, No. 1, Oct., 1938, pp. 5–11. DLC, IYL, NNY.

A warm and pleasant picture of the operation of this children's library described with pardonable pride.

3364.   "Littérature de jeunesse," *Lectures,* Montréal, 1956 ff. DLC, NNY.

Signed reviews of children's books published in France and in Canada, in French. This is of interest to librarian, parent and teacher.

3365.   Locke, G. H. "Library service to children in Canada," *ALA children's library yearbook,* No. 1, 1929, p. 64. DLC.

A short sketch of the early development of children's library service in Canada.

3366.   MacIver, Dolina. "School libraries in Western Canada," *School libraries,* Chicago, Vol. 9, No. 4, May, 1960, pp. 21–23. DLC, NNY.

The author reviews the patterns which prevail in the sparsely populated western provinces.

3367.   Marchand, Louise. "La littérature pour enfants au Canada français," *Canadian library association bulletin,* Ottawa, Vol. 11, Aug., 1954, pp. 21–24. DLC, NNY.

This is one article in an issue devoted to Young Canada's Book Week.

3368.   "The Marian Thompson collection and early children's literature," *British Columbia library quarterly,* Vancouver, Vol. 25, July, 1961, pp. 2–22. NNY.

A short description of this small collection owned by the Vancouver Public Library, followed by articles by Anna Smith (on some of the special treasures in the collection) and by Margaret Turnbull (on illustrations in these early books).

3369.   Massicotte, E. Z. "Formulettes, rimettes et devinettes du Canada," *Journal of American folklore,* Lancaster, Pa., Vol. 33, Oct.–Dec., 1920, pp. 299–320. DLC, NNY.

This compilation of Canadian children's folklore includes formulas, riddles, rhymes and game songs.

3370.   Millar, John. *Books: A guide to good reading.* Toronto, W. Briggs, 1897. 112p. DLC.

Intended as a means of insuring young persons with a love for literature. There are chapters on public libraries, reading circles, courses, and a list of books by grade level.

3371.   "New books for boys and girls," *Ontario library review,* Toronto, Vol. 1 ff. 1916 ff. DLC.

Under this or similar titles, a column of reviews of children's books has been prepared by the Boys and Girls House staff, since this quarterly began. There is a separate column of "Books for youth." In addition, there are frequent general articles on children's literature and libraries, school libraries, a series on authors for children, reports of the annual national and regional meetings, and many other features.

3372.   Potter, J. C. "Library work with children," *Ontario Library Association proceedings*, 1911, pp. 100–104. DLC.

3373.   Putnam, D. "Children's library work in Quebec," *Ontario library review,* Toronto, Vol. 23, May, 1939, pp. 185–188. DLC, NNY.

This paper, presented at a conference of the Ontario Library Association, gives the history and present status of children's libraries in the province of Quebec. Noted especially are the two children's library systems in Montreal, one serving the French speaking children and the other the English speaking children.

3374.   Reid, Dorothy M. "Where the legends live," *Canadian library,* Ottawa, Vol. 22, July, 1965, pp. 34–36. DLC, NNY.

This is only one article in an issue devoted to Young Canada's Book Week. Mrs. Reid was the winner of the Mme. Rollet Hébert Medal for the best book by a Canadian in the English language published in the preceding year. She describes here how she came to write her award-winning book, which was based on Indian legends. She also writes of the importance of this Indian heritage for Canada and the need for holding a part of it intact.

3375.   Robertson, Catherine C., *et al. Books for youth; a guide for teen-age readers.* 3rd ed. Toronto, Toronto Public Libraries, 1966. 1954p. APP. (1st ed., 1940).

An attractive list of about 1,450 titles arranged by type of literature and subject and carefully indexed.

3376.   Russell, David H. "Reading preferences of younger adolescents in Saskatchewan," *English journal,* Chicago, Vol. 30, Feb., 1941, pp. 131–136. DLC, NNY.

A report, together with statistics, gleaned from a regional survey. There is a short bibliography.

3377.   St. John, Judith. *The Osborne Collection of early children's books 1566–1910.* Toronto, Toronto Public Library, 1958. 561p. DLC, NNY.

A profusely illustrated catalog of some 3000 items in the collection, arranged by subjects and types (e.g. fables, "penny dreadfuls," etc.). The annotations are descriptive, rather than critical. Occasionally, contemporary comments on some of the historical items are quoted. The informative introduction by Edgar Osborne is written with charm and style. Appendix I is a chronological list of editions from 1566–1799, Appendix II is a list of engravers and illustrators and Appendix III is a list of publishers, booksellers and printers. The general index is of authors, titles, series, editors and translators. All of these combine to make a work of outstanding importance in the study of children's literature.

3378.   Saint-Pierre, J. M. "Les bibliothèques pour enfants," Quebec Library Association Conference, 1st. *Proceedings,* Part III. Quebec, 1945. pp. 8–12.

3379.   *School libraries.* Toronto, Canadian Education Association, 1958. 17p. (CEA Information Service, Report No. 90). Mimeographed. IYL.

Reports of a questionnaire concerning the status of school libraries in each of the provinces. Includes many statistical tables.

3380.   "The school library in modern education," *Canadian Library Association bulletin,* Ottawa, Vol. 4, 1947, DLC, NNY.

This entire issue was devoted to an exploration of the role of the school library. There are a number of short articles describing the status of school libraries in each of the provinces at that time.

3381.   Selby, Joan. "Landmarks in Canadian historical fiction for children," *Ontario library review,* Toronto, Vol. 45, May, 1961, pp. 91–96. DLC, NNY.

Some general comments about such fiction, and criticism of a number of specific titles.

3382.   Shklanka, O. *An evaluative study of Canadian biography materials available for use in the social studies programs of the secondary schools of British Columbia, Alberta, and Saskatchewan.* Seattle, University of Washington, 1956. 94p. Thesis.

3383.   Smith, Lillian H. *The unreluctant years. A critical approach to children's literature.* Chicago, ALA, 1953. 193p. $4.50. DLC, IYL, NNY.

This book is a graceful statement of the superb book selection behind the children's collections in Toronto Public Library where the author was for many years Head of Boys and Girls Room. It is a book to use with *The Critical History of Children's*

Literature, being less historical and more inspirational. It treats of all types of literature for children and is valuable for all persons doing book selection for children. Eminently readable, it is often quoted in more recent works on children's literature.

3384. Steward, Christina Duff. "Boys' and Girls' House, Toronto; an interne's-eye view," *Library association record,* London, Vol. 58, Jan., 1956, pp. 6–9. DLC, NNY.

One of the interne's working in this library gives her impressions of its work, its aims and its success in dealing with children and books.

3385. *Subscription reviews.* Toronto Public Library, Boys and Girls House, College & St. George Street, Toronto, Canada. Quarterly. Vol. 1 ff. 1964 ff. DLC.

A mimeographed set of reviews, compiled by the staff of Boys and Girls Division, indicate books accepted, rejected or "to be tried out." This is intended as a buying guide for Boys and Girls Division of the Toronto Public Library, but also goes out on a limited basis to other libraries in Canada.

3386. Tétreault, Ruth. "Cours de littérature enfantine aux normaliens du Nouveau Brunswick," *Canadian library association bulletin,* Ottawa, Vol. 14, June, 1958, pp. 270–271. DLC, NNY.

Preceding this is an account and outline in English of this course in children's literature, given to teachers in training in New Brunswick.

3387. Thomson, Jean. *Books for boys and girls.* 3rd ed. Toronto, Ryerson Press, 1954. 297p. DLC, IYL, NNY. Supplement: 1959, 116p. DLC, IYL, NNY.

An annotated, selective list, still useful because it includes so many standard favorites. There are lists of library aids and reference books, and the indexes to both volumes are author and title only.

3388. ———. "Highroads to children's reading in Canada." White, Carl M. *Bases of modern librarianship.* Oxford, London, etc., Pergamon Press, 1964, pp. 120–123. DLC, NNY.

A general but enthusiastic review of the ways in which young Canadians get their reading materials.

3389. Toronto Public Library. Boys and Girls House. *Books for boys and girls* Toronto, Toronto Public Library, 1962 ff. Annual. APP.

A yearly selection of outstanding books, briefly annotated and arranged by age and subject groups.

3390. Toupin, Laurette E. *La bibliothèque à l'école.* Montreal, Fides, 194?. 85p. DLC.

The educative, moral and social roles of the library in the school; the training of the librarian to carry out the roles; the selection and organization of materials.

3391. Toye, William. "Children's book publishing in Canada," *Canadian library association bulletin,* Ottawa, Vol. 16, July, 1959, pp. 11–14. DLC, NNY.

The author discusses some of the problems of publishing children's books in English in Canada. Although some of the difficulties lie in the fact that the field is dominated by the large U.S. and British publishers, he believes the crucial point is that there is simply a lack of good Canadian writers.

3392. Vansickle, P. M. "Canada," *Library service to children.* Lund, Bibliotekstjänst, 1963, pp. 11–16. DLC, NNY, IYL.

This chapter in the IFLA publication deals with school and public library services for children in Canada.

3393. Vries, Leonard de. *Flowers of delight.* New York, Pantheon, 1965. 232p. $8.95. DLC, IYL, NNY.

"Culled from the Osborne Collection of Early Children's Books. An agreeable garland of prose and poetry for the instruction and amusement of little masters and misses and their distinguished parents; embellished with some 700 elegant woodcuts and engravings on wood and copper of which upwards of 125 are neatly coloured; selected with the greatest care from books for juvenile minds 1765–1830." Although this was published in the United States and reproduces excerpts from books published largely in England, this is placed here in Canada to do honor to Mr. Osborne and to the Toronto Public Library for maintaining and making available the treasures of this remarkable collection.

3394. Webster, Catherine. "Some history of the development of literature for children," *Ontario library review,* Toronto, Vol. 14, No. 3, Feb., 1930, pp. 79–82; Vol. 15, No. 1, Aug., 1930, pp. 8–12. DLC.

Some of the earliest mentions of children in literature, the historic background of Aesop, Mother Goose, King Arthur, Robin Hood and Celtic heroes, and other diverse points about the early literature now associated most with children.

United States

Because so much of the history of U.S. children's literature up to the 20th century is also that of England, this survey will pass quickly over the 17th, 18th and 19th centuries, and turn to the trends of the 20th century which carried U.S. children's books off on another stream altogether. The Puritans had brought with them a number of children's books, and it was not long before U.S. imitations were being published. Then came the American contributions: the *New England Primer,* the books of Isaiah Thomas (often called the "American John Newbery"), Nathanial Hawthorne, Washington Irving, and James Fenimore Cooper, Samuel Goodrich's *Peter Parley* series and Jacob Abbott's *Rollo* series and his travel books, the *Elsie Dinsmore* series, the books of Mrs. A. D. T. Whitney, Susan Coolidge, Harriet Beecher Stowe, Louisa May Alcott, Horatio Alger, Frances Hodgson Burnett, Lucretia P. Hale, the *St. Nicholas* magazine, Mark Twain, and Mary Mapes Dodge. These are only a few of the names which have starring roles in the history of U.S. children's literature up to about 1890. Many of them would also continue to be associated with the next period of transition, through their later works, but in temperament and style they belong more to the 19th century.

The person who best exemplifies the change over from the Victorian age to the modern age is Howard Pyle. His stories and illustrations have themes and elements of style which deftly combine the traditional and the innovative. Much of his early work first appeared in *St. Nicholas* magazine. Not until 1883 did he begin to synthesize his writing and illustrating abilities, producing books which were nearly perfect examples of excellence and harmony in text and picture: *Merry Adventures of Robin Hood, Pepper and Salt, Twilight Land, the Wonder Clock, The Garden Behind the Moon,* the four volumes of the Arthurian Cycle, *Otto of the Silver Hand,* and *Men of Iron.* Starting with Pyle, the U.S. no longer had to rely entirely on British or European children's book illustrators for their chief inspiration.

The most important quality of the children's literature of this period was its broadening of interests. Previously the folk and fairy tale collections had been limited chiefly to those of the British Isles, the Grimm tales and those of Hans Christian Andersen. Andrew Lang's "colored" fairy books became as popular here as in England, and contained a wide variety of stories from many countries. More importantly, story collections based on the works of Asbjørnsen and Moe (Norway), Afanas'ev (Russia), Basile (Italy), Erben and Nemčova (Czechoslovakia), and the Panchatantra (India), began to be published in versions which have remained standard up to today.

Not only in folklore was the U.S. child's view expanded. More and more, the stories of children in other lands gained popularity. *The Wonderful Adventures of Nils* from Sweden, Dikken Zwilgmeyer's stories from Norway, Boutet de Monvel's pictures from France and many others less-known vied with the "Twins" series of Lucy Fitch

Perkins, the superior successors to Jacob Abbott's attempts at introducing children to the cultures of other countries.

Another trend which began in this period and which was to achieve such success in the next was the use of animal characters as central "heroes" of a story. These were not usually animals personifying humans, as in the charming *Old Mother West Wind* stories of Thornton Burgess. They were the strong, wild creatures of Jack London's imagination, of Olaf Baker's *Shasta of the Wolves,* of Alfred Ollivant's *Bob, Son of Battle,* of even the somewhat sentimentalized strength of Anna Sewell's *Black Beauty,* of Marshall Saunders' *Beautiful Joe* and of Ernest Thompson Seton's *Wild Animals I Have Known*. This latter name demands clarification, especially for the person not familiar with English names. Ernest Seton-Thompson was born in England and came to the United States under that name. Probably because he was constantly being referred to as Mr. Thompson in the United States, which is not accustomed to the hyphenated name, he changed his name to Ernest Thomson Seton, and wrote under that name.

The history of U.S. children's libraries cannot be separated from that of children's literature. The same 30 year period (1890–1920) which witnessed the throwing off of Victorian priggishness in children's books saw also the crucial first steps of the fledgeling movement in public library service to the young. There are arguments as to which public library had the first children's corner and the first children's room. The former claim is usually accorded the Pawtucket (Rhode Island) Library, whose librarian, Mrs. Minerva Saunders, set aside a corner for children's books in 1877 (Meigs, p. 417). The latter claim goes to either the Brookline (Massachusetts) Public Library or the New York Public Library, depending upon which authority one wishes to credit. The dates for these children's rooms are given as 1890 and 1888 respectively. Alice M. Jordan makes the claim that all three of the above libraries were superseded by the free juvenile library established in West Cambridge, Massachusetts, in 1835, from a bequest made by Dr. Ebenezer Learned (3950). It is useless to quibble about such claims for one could probably keep going back further and further, depending on one's definition of "children's library." What most do agree with is the importance of certain individuals who gave impetus to the work in the first years, and began to set standards which have not changed much to this day.

The first important book lists were made by John F. Sargent (4272), William M. Griswold (3819), George E. Hardy (3845) and Caroline M. Hewins. Of the four, Miss Hewins was perhaps the most influential. She was the librarian of the Hartford (Connecticut) Library Association, who in 1882 presented a report to the ALA conference in Cincinnati on what was being done by libraries "to encourage a love of good reading in boys and girls." Most of the librarians who had replied to her inquiry had indicated the initiation of some service to the young reader (3878). Years later, Miss Hewins conducted another private survey and by this time, 77 libraries reported they had special shelves for children's books, as well as finding lists and/or card catalogs (3877). Miss Hewins was not essentially statistically minded, as her delightful autobiographical reminiscence will prove (3875). Jennie Lindquist quotes one of Miss Hewins' sisters as saying: "To the time of her death she was ready for adventure any time, with children or grown-ups. She was interested in everything and everybody" (3875).

In just the few years between Miss Hewins' first contributions, and the end of the century, a half-dozen other names began appearing with regularity in the pages of professional journals and on speakers' lists of the library conferences. Mary Wright Plummer's was among the first. Although she was not a children's librarian, as a graduate of the first class of the first library school (Columbia College, 1888) she was well qualified in general library work. From 1890 to 1904, she was the librarian of the Pratt Institute Free Library, and directed the Institute of Library Science connected with the library. Later, she became head of the library school connected with the New York Public Library. She believed children's work to be of great importance to the total structure of libraries, and trained large numbers of librarians to appreciate this work.

One of Miss Plummer's students was Anne Carroll Moore who, as soon as she had graduated from Pratt in 1896, became the children's librarian in the Pratt Free Library. She too joined the staff of The New York Public Library, but in 1906, five years ahead of Miss Plummer. Miss Moore organized the children's department of the New York Public Library and stayed on as its supervisor until her retirement in 1941.

Two early graduates of the New York State Library School became pioneers in children's work. Frances Jenkins Olcott, graduate of 1896, headed the children's department of the Carnegie Library in Pittsburgh from 1898 to 1911, during which time she organized the famous training school for children's librarians at that Library. It was the beginning of an outstanding contribution to library education, continuing on up to today. Clara Whitehill Hunt, graduate of 1898, became head of children's services in the Newark Free Public Library that same year and left to take the same position with the Brooklyn Public Library in 1903.

Like Miss Plummer, Linda A. Eastman was not specifically a children's librarian. However, as an assistant in the Cleveland Public Library 1892–1894, and later its vice-director, she felt concerned for the special needs of child readers, whom she believed were getting scant attention. It was during Miss Eastman's tenure that the organization of the children's department in Cleveland, under Effie L. Power, took place. Miss Power then went on to St. Louis, and in 1904 Miss Caroline Burnite (later Mrs. Walker) took her position at Cleveland.

These are just some of the individuals who contributed to the quick spread of special library work with children. In a few years their ranks were joined by such others as Alice M. Jordan of Boston Public

Library, Alice Hazeltine of the Pittsburgh and St. Louis libraries and the Columbia University School of Library Service, Mary E. Dousman of the Milwaukee Library, Carrie Scott of Indianapolis, Mary E. S. Root of Providence, Anna Cogswell Tyler, of The New York Public Library, and Elva S. Smith of the Pittsburgh Library School. Still another decade or two added the names of Julia Carter, Louise Latimer, Helen Martin Rood, Lillian Smith, Jessie Gay Van Cleve, Mary Gould Davis and others.

Two other important events belong to this period, both occurring in the year 1919. They were: the establishment of a national children's book week, and the appointment of a "children's book editor" in the first juvenile book department of a major publishing house. There are great names in these areas as well, and it is important to consider them separately.

Franklin K. Mathiews, librarian for the Boy Scouts of America, had toured the U.S. before World War I and was appalled at the poor quality of books boys were reading. He approached Frederic G. Melcher (then Executive Secretary of the American Booksellers' Association) and the American Association of Book Publishers with the idea of a national "Book Week" which would stimulate a wider interest in reading and "bring together in common cause the many groups which had a deep interest in the reading of children—librarians, teachers, publishers, artists, authors, scout leaders, and the like" (4092). With characteristic enthusiasm, Mr. Melcher delved into the work of making concrete plans. By July, 1919, they were sufficiently developed for the Children's Libraries Section of ALA to give official support. Each year since then, the second week in November has been designated as Children's Book Week, and as such it has been the occasion for many book-related celebrations.

The first juvenile book department was created at Macmillan in 1919, and its first children's editor was Louise Seaman Bechtel. This was followed by May Massee's appointment to a similar position at Doubleday in 1923. Soon all of the publishing houses were creating special departments for juvenile books, and often the persons chosen to head them were former librarians who had had some years of experience in working with children and books.

All too often articles and books concerned with the history of children's literature in the U.S. tend to disregard the interplay of forces that were at work. Certain personalities are given more or less credit depending on the writer's individual feelings about them. What is rarely stated is that it took a developing children's library system *and* a publishing industry with a sense of purpose *and* a few good editors and critics to sift out the quality from the mass *and* a publicity program such as Children's Book Week to win the affections and interest of the general public—it took all of these to create a kind of ferment out of which came the rare vintage stock of the golden age of children's books in the U.S. Certainly some of the voices were a bit stronger, more effective; but it is doubtful whether even a clarion call can have much effect if there is no one to hear it and give it echo. This was the great good fortune of those critical voices: they had attentive listeners who could give back ideas in kind.

In *A Critical History of Children's Literature,* Ruth Hill Viguers writes of "the golden age" as the period from 1920–1950. Dora Smith gives this name to the years from 1925 to 1940. Since there was a distinct tapering off of good books during the war years, it seems more natural to end this period at about 1940. As to its title, there is very little dispute. The children's books which have survived from this period are still some of the most widely read among U.S. children. That they are not kept alive by the sentimental feelings of aunts, parents, or just grown-ups in general, can be witnessed in any busy modern children's library, where the latest books on all subjects are available. Over and over again the favorite choices of both child and librarian will be carrying a late 1920 or 1930 copyright.

One of the chief reasons this period should be calculated as beginning before 1925 is the appearance, in 1942, of the first issue of *The Horn Book Magazine.* This did not rise up out of the sidewalks of Boston, fully developed, like some goddess armed with words instead of swords. It was the fruit of long years of work by Bertha Mahony in the Bookshop for Boys and Girls, first sponsored by the Women's Educational and Industrial Union. Miss Mahony and her colleague, Elinor Whitney, had been compiling lists periodically, but there seemed to be a definite need for more frequent reviews, and an outlet for some of the things authors, artists, librarians and others had to say about their work. *The Horn Book* came into being at just the right moment and because it arrived so auspiciously, and has had such dedicated membership, it has survived to this day and is regarded as a necessary part of the life of anyone interested in children and books.

The Elementary English Review, under the editorship of C. C. Certain of Detroit came out with its first issue in the same year as *The Horn Book.* Now known as *Elementary English,* it is the official organ of the National Council of Teachers of English and is particularly helpful to the teaching profession.

The other event which makes the five years from 1921–1925 a part of the golden age is the establishment of the Newbery award in 1922, as "envisaged and motivated by Frederic Melcher" (Meigs, p. 431). At the ALA conference in 1921, Mr. Melcher had proposed that the Children's Librarians Section award a medal each year for the most distinguished book for children, written by a citizen or resident of the U.S., and published during the preceding year. The Section recognized the value of such an award, and immediately set into motion the plans for its selection. In 1922, the first Newbery Award was given to Hendrik Van Loon for his book *The Story of Mankind.* Each year since that time, a committee of 17 members selects the winner. Often there is much discussion among the general membership of the Children's Services Division, with some children's librarians taking the stand that most Newbery winners are too much what adults would like children to read, rather than what children themselves enjoy reading. There are an equal number who argue that this is one of the few instances where sheer quality has won out in the past. This is always a theme for a lively discussion, and denotes a high interest in this award, which it so justly deserves.

The books of the period can be divided into the two decades: 1920–1930, a time of new printing processes, experimentation in different types of books, and a further reaching out toward internationalism of themes; 1930–1940, the decade of the picture book, "here and now" stories, lively historical fiction, realistic family stories, excellent versions of the old folk tales and new fantasy, biography and science based on respect for subject and reader—in short, a wealth of good writing with wide appeal.

"The battle for the fairy tale," as Chukovsky called it, was waged in the U.S. as well. The two points of view are inherent in two works of the early 1920's. Lucy Sprague Mitchell's *Here and Now Story Book,* for children from two to seven, was published in 1921. It grew out of the author's conviction that young children enjoy most that which is familiar to them and understandable through sensory experience. She believed that fairy tales told to the young child excited and confused him, instead of helping him to come to terms with his world. Young children, she felt, first had to know the ordinary, before they could appreciate the preposterous. As if in direct answer to her challenge,, *Rootabaga Stories* by Carl Sandburg, appeared in 1922. Mr. Sandburg was already a poet of some renown, and in all probability did not know of Mrs. Mitchell. He only knew that the stories which were available for him to read to his children did not satisfy his or their needs—needs for the poetry of words, for an appreciation of the ridiculous and nonsensical side of life, for the unexpected and unpredictable.

The "battle" still goes on, but it is now largely one of tempered words. There are no longer the extremes of "all" fairy tales or "no" fairy tales to argue about, since the young child has such a wide variety of books at his disposal. The fact that both types, the "here and now" and the preposterous, have proven popular with so many two to seven year olds has given the middle road the winning factors. A decisive element was the arrival of the picture book on the scene—not the book of pictures or the story made palatable by colored plates, but the picture book in which text and illustrations were one cohesive force.

Crane, Caldecott, Greenaway and Brooke, as well as a number of European artists, had had an appreciative audience in this country as they did elsewhere. Their illustrative art was of the highest quality, and they were accorded the serious attention of first-rate designers and careful reproduction processes. Because of this they made the work of later illustrators much easier. But in spite of the fact that the texts they illustrated were most often classic folk rhymes or tales, and in spite of (or because of) their attention to detail in interpreting the text, the books remain essentially "picture" books i.e. the pictures are more important than the text. They sometimes say far more than the text! The new type of picture book which was developing in the U.S.

was one in which both artist and writer were at their best. One found it difficult to separate which part gave more enjoyment. Sometimes, it is true, one part had the edge over the other, but this only set off the rare perfection of the great ones.

It is not difficult to single out the first examples. *Clever Bill* by William Nicholson, written and illustrated in England, was published first in the U.S., in 1927. *Millions of Cats* by Wanda Gág was published in 1928. These were followed in the 1930's by Marjorie Flack's *Angus* books; *Ola* and others by Ingri and Edgar Parin d'Aulaire; *The Story of Ping* and *The Five Chinese Brothers*, illustrated by Kurt Wiese; *The Story of Ferdinand*, illustrated by Robert Lawson; *And To Think That I Saw It on Mulberry Street*, written and illustrated by Theodore Seuss Geisel who used the pseudonym of Dr. Seuss; *Andy and the Lion*, written and illustrated by James Daugherty; *Mei Li*, written and illustrated by Thomas Handforth; *Madeline*, written and illustrated by Ludwig Bemelmans; *Little Toot*, written and illustrated by Hardie Gramatky; *Mike Mulligan and His Steam Shovel*, written and illustrated by Virginia Lee Burton.

Two elements which were quite noticeable in the picture book also were in evidence in the older story book. A fair number of authors were talented in both writing and illustrating and a goodly number chose to use themes and backgrounds from the foreign lands they had grown up in. The U.S. had experienced wave upon wave of immigration in the late 19th and early 20th century, but never before had such a large number of artists and writers appeared. Perhaps they were among the numbers of early immigrants, but did not get the opportunity to express themselves in print and pictures. The new group which arrived in the period from 1920 to the present, has had a receptive audience right from the start. Their work has added immeasurable stature and diversity to the American children's book field.

England had always had the highest claim to first-rate fantasy, and such books as *Alice in Wonderland, The Wind in the Willows, Mary Poppins* and *The Hobbit* were as beloved in the U.S. as they were in most English-speaking nations. They were not replaced by the new type of humorous fantasy which slowly began to develop in the U.S.; they simply had to begin sharing the honors as favorites in the hearts of children. Robert Lawson, Robert McCloskey, William Pène du Bois, James Thurber, Richard and Florence Atwater were some of the writers who added new dimensions to the pleasure to be found in books of this kind.

The family story, laid in present or past times, in this country or another, grew out of the great popularity of such forerunners as *Little Women*. This genre seemed especially suited to women writers, and a number of them excelled at it. Often the stories were centered more closely around one of the children, but the family as a unit was firmly in control of the background. Eleanor Frances Lattimore, Elizabeth Coatsworth, Carolyn Haywood, Eleanor Estes, Elizabeth Enright,

Elizabeth Janet Gray, Kate Seredy, Hilda van Stockum, Carol Ryrie Brink, and above all, Laura Ingalls Wilder, were those who succeeded in bringing into their stories the sense of security which satisfies the child as few other feelings can. Some writers used this type of story to introduce the children of the working classes or of the minorities. Doris Gates, Lois Lenski, Florence Cranwell Means, Laura Armer and Grace Moon were the innovators in this area.

One could go on like this for history, biography, science, poetry collections, for so many types of books that the list of names would stretch out far longer than this book can accommodate. It is important to indicate that almost all of the works of the authors cited above are still available, 30 years later. In most cases they have never gone out of print. This is a unique situation which is not easily comprehended in foreign countries, indeed, not even in the U.S. To study the history of one's national literature is vitally necessary, yet there is a comparatively small percentage of this early literature which can be used with contemporary children. Add to this the classics of other countries, and chances are the number of titles is still well below 50. How then, can a teacher, librarian or parent learn enough to stimulate the child into reading under broad categories? This can only be done by wide reading of contemporary literature, and if these books do not stay in print longer than two or three years, a heavy burden is placed upon those who must sift through each year's output for the very best, to be recommended with special emphasis and care. In England and the U.S., a librarian or teacher can take a course in children's literature with the reasonable assurance that the majority of current books studied will still be available when the time comes to begin working with children. *This is not true of most countries.* The flood of new books published each year can be extremely bewildering, but if there are tested favorites to always turn back to, it is a tremendous assurance to both adult critic and child reader. It is likely that these books of the late 1920's, the 1930's and the early 1940's will produce more than the usual number of "classics" for a given era. It is also likely, however, that a number will die natural deaths (many already have). But a number of books from the late 1940's and 1950's have already taken their places and, having passed the 15-year mark, show all signs of living 30 years as well. It is this continuity of books which is the backbone of the U.S. children's book publishing industry, and an asset to every person working with children and books.

Before turning to the final period of children's book trends, it must be noted that there was additional impetus added to the children's book movement, by the formation, in 1945, of the Children's Book Council, the establishment, in 1936, of a Library Services Branch in the U.S. Office of Education, and by wider activities on the part of such organizations as the Children's Services Division of ALA, the Child Study Association, the National Council of Teachers of English, the National Education Association and the Association for Childhood Education International. These are the present names; in some cases they were called differently at that time.

Criticism of children's books during the period 1920–1940 reached heights it has not touched since. Serious literary periodicals such as *The Bookman* and the *Saturday Review of Literature,* as well as the literary Sunday supplements to the two leading newspapers, *The New York Times* and the now defunct *New York Herald Tribune,* had regular columns by such leading critics as Anne Carroll Moore, May Lamberton Becker, Anne Thaxter Eaton and Marion Canby.

During the war there were not many new writers appearing on the scene. A few great favorites appeared, but for the most part they were by established authors and illustrators. Themes of patriotism were prevalent, but most of these books were short lived and few of the contemporary critics mentioned them at any length. In general, children just kept on reading from the wonderful riches which had been given them in the preceding decade.

After the war, there was the same reaching out toward other lands which had been evident to a lesser degree after World War I. More artists and writers from all corners of the globe turned up at children's book editors' desks. If they did not come to the U.S., their work often did, for translations grew apace. Family stories centered around children who were quite ordinary, but the reality with which they came to life gave these books a strong appeal. Fantasy and poetry continued to have their special advocates and the picture book was available in a wider variety than ever. Two new trends began in the late 1940's and early 1950's: the nonfiction series and the rise of the children's book clubs. They both brought more readers into the ranks, especially among the boys.

Before turning to the trends which have developed in the last decade, it is necessary to return for a moment to children's libraries, but this time to libraries in schools. Public library work continued to increase in volume, causing shortage of staff and consequently decreasing the amount of extension work, such as storytelling, which could be carried out only with great expense of time. Essentially, however, the basic standards in public library service had been set at the turn of the century and have only been modified, reiterated, expanded or illuminated by the succeeding decades of work.

School libraries were another matter. There had been a few pioneers, but almost all were in the field of high school libraries. Primary schools, when they had any kind of book service at all, were more often than not considered part of the responsibilities of the public library, which in many cases loaned classroom collections or made some kind of extension arrangements. Not until the 1930's was there much attention given to the work of such librarians as Anne Thaxter Eaton, Phyllis Fenner, and Lucille Fargo. Early school library studies indicate a preoccupation with statistics which hardly indicate qualitative service at all. There was much argument about the relative merits of the classroom library and the central library. When the central library idea gradually did begin to win more advocates, there was still not a concise picture of its organization within the framework of the school, or of its functions. The idea of circulating books was practically unexplored. Another decade passed before sufficiently strong professional steps were taken to get school administrators to sit up and pay attention. In this the school library movement was aided by two things: the formulation of more definite professional standards and an increasing amount of federal monies being channeled into education.

Because their main concern was with books, public libraries succeeded more easily in getting book funds from local authorities. School libraries, on the other hand, were only one part of the total educational complex, and local authorities often found in them the easiest place to cut corners on budgets. Often, if there was an established public library in the locality, it was difficult to convince the board that another central library was needed in the school. Beginning in the 1930's, many educators reached the conclusion that only generous state and federal support could bring about an equalization of educational facilities in the country. Several bills were introduced in Congress in those years, but none ever reached the point of passing. The war intervened, and with the postwar years came a mild depression. Finally, in the late 1950's, plans and programs began to jell and the professional organizations turned all of their combined efforts toward effective federal legislation. The result has been, in the early 1960's, a spate of educational and library legislation unequalled in the history of Congress. The National Defense Education Act, the Elementary and Secondary Education Act, the Higher Education Act, the Library Services and Construction Act, as well as several others, all contributed directly to the status of children's public and school library work, and the books and materials used in that work.

Librarians got more training through special institutes, more specialists could be given time off for study on grants, libraries could be built or expanded, research into special problems could be funded and many new projects aimed at serving public not previously reached were initiated. Most important of all, books and materials could be purchased in much greater quantities.

In work with children, the school libraries benefitted more from the initial legislation than did public libraries. They had prepared themselves with standards (3413) and had sought out effective means of putting them to work. Leaders such as Mary Peacock Douglas, Ruth Ersted, Mary Gaver and Frances Henne supplemented this with many articles and books on the necessity of a professional approach to the problems. The Knapp School Library Project, funded on a private grant, could provide initial clues to future directions.

Many agencies and organizations foresaw the activity which would be generated by federal legislation, and by the momentum of the information explosion. They began to explore the possibilities of materials and services which would be of use in libraries. The H. W. Wilson Company and the R. R. Bowker Company had both expanded tremendously over the years their publication of guides, reference materials, catalog cards, and numerous aids to make simpler the technical tasks of organizing and maintaining libraries, book stores and the like. Now their ranks were joined by other companies offering similar or new services, for the need seemed almost limitless. Children's book lists on hundreds of subjects sprung up in answer to the demand for selection aid. For in spite of all these materials, no amount of money has solved the shortage in qualified professional staff.

It is this area which still needs the most careful scrutiny and possible reorganization. The present system of accredited graduate library schools in universities does not satisfy the demand. Much questioning must be done and the roles of professional and sub-professional must be re-examined. Technology cannot answer all needs. No amount of good books in beautiful libraries will significantly change the mass taste of children for reading, or raise their level of education if there is not some person to direct each child to the books he needs and wants at any given moment.

The effects of federal legislation are only beginning to be felt. That they are directly touching the children's book field is obvious. Millions of dollars spent each year for the purchase of children's books, in addition to the regular municipal and state budgets, is putting a demand on the publishers which they have never faced before. Some were caught short of stock and are still behind on the printing of popular titles. Many began to publish "to-order" nonfiction books designed to supplement the school curriculum. All age levels can now select science and social studies books, biographies, art and literature. The easy-to-read series is an accepted form of supplementary reader, sometimes even replacing the old stereotyped primers and textbooks of former years. Much argument has ensued on the part of librarians as to the value of such books but the general consensus is that they are here to stay and the thing to do is choose those which best satisfy the criteria of inventiveness, good illustration and imaginative use of the limited vocabulary. Two among the first books of this type have given pleasure to children for a decade already. They are *Little Bear* by Elsa Holmelund Minarek and *The Cat in the Hat* by Dr. Suess.

Two trends have slowly been gaining momentum without much direct initiative from the federal government. The first came about through a growing realization of authors, illustrators, editors and librarians that there was a lack of books centered around the minority groups, most particularly the Negro. Since 1938, Mrs. Augusta Baker had compiled the list *Books about Negro Life for Children,* and it expanded with each new edition. The new movement for civil rights forced publishers to consider more closely whether they were doing an injustice to a large segment of the population. The conditions attached to Federal aid, which required proof of compliance with the new integration law, made everyone doubly concerned about the need for more books depicting the history of the Negro in America, the accomplishments of this race, and the everyday lives of Negro children and families. Such books had long been available about the other minorities, with the exception of the American Indian, which has also suffered from the stereotyped image.

In attempting to make up for past mistakes, some publishers have gone to the other extreme of producing too high a proportion of made-to-order books about the Negro. With all the best will in the world, one cannot accept a number of these for their unrealistic depiction of the complex problems of the race issue. The most significant progress has been made in the books concerning history and the social studies, where at last the Negro is given his rightful place and part in the making of this country, with great and small contributions just like those of other races and nationalities.

The rise of paperback books for children had also begun some time ago. At first limited to school sales, these inexpensive books can now be found in more and more general stores as well. Many are reprints of children's favorites which have heretofore only been available in more expensive hard-cover editions. This trend may be the U.S. answer to a dilemma facing many countries: how to make books easily and cheaply available to children, and at the same time provide attractive, longer-lasting editions for libraries.

All of these developments make the field of children's books one of the most challenging in which to work in the United States today. There are still many problems of quality to be faced among all the quantity, but the means to bring good books in wide variety to all children seem closer than ever before.

3395. "ALA creates Batchelder Award for best foreign juvenile," *Library journal,* New York, Vol. 91, Oct., 15, 1966, pp. 5144–5145. DLC, NNY.

A description of the terms of a new award in U.S. children's book publishing to be given to the best translation of a foreign language original children's book published in the U.S. in the preceding year. The Award is to be selected by a special committee of the Children's Services Division, and is named in honor of the former executive secretary of that division.

3396. Abe, Meiko. "Children's books about Japan," *Top of the news,* Chicago, Vol. 14, May, 1958, pp. 45–49. DLC, NNY.

In evaluating the books about Japan which have appeared in the U.S., the author points out that the historical information was easier to check, and was usually accurate. It was the smaller things which were often incorrect and glaringly noticeable to the Japanese (e.g., the fold of the kimono for ceremonial occasions).

3397. Abbott, Lysla I. *Over the bookland trail.* Portland, Maine, Craigie Co., 1931. 63p. DLC.

"A reading list for boys and girls in senior and junior high schools." Arranged by author and by vocation (occupation), with a title index.

3398. Adams, Bess Porter. *About books and chil-dren; a historical survey of children's literature.* New York, Holt, 1953. 573p. IYL, DLC, NNY.

A textbook which covers briefly the history of books for children while emphasizing changing educational theories and the needs of children and youth. A critical discussion of all categories of books for children and young people is included and there is a long and carefully selected bibliography. Especially useful with teachers and parents.

3399. Adams, Charles Francis, Jr. "Fiction in public libraries and educational catalogues," *Library journal,* New York, Vol. 4, Nos. 9–10, Sept.–Oct., 1879, pp. 330–338. DLC. NNY.

The writer contends that social distinctions make a great difference in the choice of reading, and that libraries have not taken this into account when making up their school lists. Later in this issue is an article by T. W. Higginson disputing much of what Mr. Adams says. In defending fictional reading further, Higginson writes: "If we cannot make sense as interesting as nonsense, it is because we have not learned how to teach or write." See also entries 3462 and 3816.

3400. ———. "The public library and the public schools," *Library journal,* New York, Vol. 1, No. 12, Aug. 31, 1877, pp. 437–441. DLC, NNY.

A slightly shortened version of a talk given to the teachers of Quincy, Massachusetts, "on the use which could be made of the public library in connection with the school system in general." This was historically important in that it set the trend for early work with schools.

3401.   Adams, Edith E. *A guide to children's literature in the early elementary grades.* Rev. ed. Ann Arbor, G. Wahr, 1933. 157p. DLC.
"For training classes, kindergarten-primary teachers, and parents."

3402.   Adams, Mary E. *Study of regional library services for rural children in Vermont 1930–1950.* Philadelphia, Drexel Institute of Technology, 1952. 38p. Thesis.

3403.   Adams, Oscar Fay. *The dear old story tellers.* Boston, Lothrop, 1889. 209p. NNY.
Essays on Homer, the Arabian Nights, Aesop, Mother Goose, Perrault, the Grimm brothers, La Fontaine, Andersen, Defoe and others.

3404.   Adler, Felix. *Moral instruction of children.* New York, Appleton, 1893. 270p. (International education series, No. 21). NNY.
Mr. Adler was a noted social reformer and educator who began the Society for Ethical Culture. He believed that the best method of instructing children was through storytelling, and here explains how this can be done.

3405.   Alexander, E. C. *Budgetary practices of centralized school library agencies.* New York, Columbia University, 1947. 62p. Thesis.

3406.   Allen, Dorothy. *Status of children in stories of present day life for children.* Chicago, University of Chicago, 1953. 177p. Thesis.

3407.   Allen, Mary E. "Picture-books of olden days," *Cosmopolitan,* New York, Vol. 26, No. 3, Jan., 1899, pp. 337–344. NNY.
Illustrations and quotes from a number of early American picture-books, chiefly the travel series put out by Isaac Taylor.

3408.   Altstetter, M. F. "Early American magazines for children," *Peabody journal of education,* Nashville, Tenn., Vol. 19, No. 3, Nov., 1941, pp. 131–136. DLC.
A history, from the time of the *Children's Magazine* in 1789 to *The American Boy* in 1941.

3409.   Ambler, B. H. *A history of the children's department of the Free Library of Philadelphia 1898–1953.* Philadelphia, Drexel Institute of Technology, 1956. 60p. Thesis.

3410.   American Antiquarian Society. *Exhibit of American children's books printed before 1800.* Worcester, Mass., The Society, 1928. 14p. NNY.
A catalog of 120 titles arranged by types, but not annotated.

3411.   American Association for the U.N. *Read your way to world understanding.* New York, Scarecrow Press, 1963. 320p. $6.50. DLC, NNY.
An annotated list of U.S. children's books which can help the child to learn about other countries and cultures. Arranged by area and indexed.

3412.   American Association of School Librarians. *The school librarian and the partially seeing child.* New York, National Society for the Prevention of Blindness, 1966. Unp. APP.
A brochure which offers advice to the librarian on how to deal with partially-seeing children who wish to read.

3413.   ———. *Standards for school library services.* Chicago, ALA, 1960. 132p. DLC, NNY. *Discussion guide,* 16p. DLC, NNY.
These standards were formulated in consultation with every major educational and library organization involved in schools and/or libraries related to children and youth. Part 1 is "The school library as an educational force," Part 2 has "Planning and implementing school library programs," and Part 3 is "Resources for teaching and learning." One of the most important documents on school libraries in the U.S. Bibliography.

3414.   *American children's books, 1723–1939* (Catalog Six). Boston, E. Morrill and Son, 1941?. 99p. DLC.
A bookseller's catalog of possible interest to the researcher or collector. The items are not annotated, but bibliographical information is quite complete.

3415.   "American children's books around the world," *Publishers' weekly,* New York, Vol. 158, Oct., 28, 1950, pp. 1919–1923. DLC, NNY.
Comments on U.S. children's library contacts in a number of countries, in particular those of the U.S. Information Service libraries.

3416.   American Council on Education. Committee on Intergroup Education in Cooperating Schools. *Literature for human understanding.* Washington, The Council, 1948. 61p. $1.00. DLC, NNY.

One of the early lists which grouped children's books into categories useful for parents and teachers who wished to help children bridge the gap to understanding other cultural and social values.

3417. American Friends Service Committee and Anti-Defamation League of B'nai Brith. *Books for friendship*. Philadelphia, The American Friends Service Committee, 1962. 63p. $.50. DLC, NNY. Supplement: 1966, p. $00.15. DLC, NNY. (Earlier editions, published by the League were called *Books are bridges*).

The two sponsoring organizations have compiled this annotated list of children's books "introducing the children of all races and creeds to each other." The editors have sought advice from librarians, teachers and parents representing a cross section of ethnic, religious, national and regional backgrounds.

3418. American Institute of Child Life. *Young folks' directory; lists of the best books, toys, stories and pictures*. Philadelphia, The Institute, 1915. 193p. DLC.

An annotated list arranged by age and by subject.

3419. American Institute of Graphic Arts. *Children's books*. New York, The Institute, 1937–1941, 1941–1943, 1945–1950, 1920–1952, 1958–1960, 1961–1962, 1963–1964. DLC, NNY.

These catalogues were issued in connection with the exhibits which the AIGA organized, showing those books which they had selected as being superior in format, design, and illustration. Most of them have comments by the jury or essays on the general qualities of the books for each period. They make excellent guides for the beginner learning how to judge the artistry of the design and format, rather than the contents.

3420. American Library Association. *Books about the school library*. Chicago, ALA, 1932. 14p.

3421. ———. Children's Services Division. *Children's books of international interest*. Chicago, ALA, 1955 ff. Annual DLC.

This list was originally called *Children's Books Recommended for Translation Abroad*. It is compiled annually by the Sub-committee of the ALA International Relations Committtee. The first list was a retrospective one, covering the period from 1930–1954.

3422. ———. Children's Services Division. *"Good Reading" children's book list*. Akron, Ohio, Pilgrim Book Society, 1965. 10p. DLC.

A selective list prepared for the Jaycee (U.S. Junior Chamber of Commerce) program of "Good Reading" which sends the 400 books out on exhibit to any community desiring its use for book fairs, special reading campaigns, etc.

3423. ———. Children's Services Division. *Foreign children's books available in the United States*. Chicago, ALA, The Division, 1952. 32p. NNY.

Printed by The New York Public Library for ALA, this list was eventually replaced by the one annotated in 3426.

3424. ———. Children's Services Division. *Library/USA—Children's World, New York World's Fair, Information Center for the U.S. Pavilion, 1964–65*. New York, 1964, Unp. DLC, NNY.

A computer-produced list of 2,000 U.S. children's books chosen by a committee for use in the library at the Fair.

3425. ———. Children's Services Division. *Selected lists of children's books and recordings*. Washington, Office of Economic Opportunity, 1966. 48p. DLC, NNY.

Lists include: "Books for pre-school children," "Stories to tell," "Recordings for children," "Books for boys and girls in the city," "Books for boys and girls in rural America," "Books for boys and girls, 12 to 16 years of age, who need special encouragement to read," "Books for Spanish-speaking children."

3426. ———. Children's Services Division. Committee on Package Library of Foreign Children's Books. *Package library of foreign children's books available in the U.S.* Chicago, ALA, Annual. Free.

An annotated list of titles, mostly from Eastern and Western Europe. This is usually reprinted in *Top of the News*. Past selections are available in the catalog of the actual book dealer, The Package Library of Foreign Children's Books, 119 Fifth Avenue, New York, N.Y.

3427. ———. Public Library Association. Committee on Standards. Subcommittee on Standards for Children's Service. *Standards for children's services in public libraries*. Chicago, ALA, 1964. 24p. DLC, NNY.

The official standards adopted by ALA, which set forth the objectives of service and standards for administration, personnel, materials and physical facilities.

3428. ———. Section for Library Work with Children. *Easy reading books of the reader and primer type and readers for the first three grades; a selection for libraries and schools.* Chicago, ALA, 1933.

"Selected by the Committee on Readers and Primers."

3429. ———. Section for Library Work with Children. "Training of children's librarians," *Library quarterly,* Chicago, Vol. 5, Apr., 1935, pp. 164–188. DLC, NNY.

This is based on a report made by a special committee to the ALA Section. Questionnaires were sent out to children's librarians, administrators and library schools, asking for recommendations. The greatest lack was in training for good book selection.

3430. *And something more . . .* Chicago, ALA, American Association of School Librarians, 1964 (Charles Guggenheim Productions). 28 minutes, color.

A film documenting the effect which excellent school library service can have on the entire school—teachers, children and administration. The Knapp School Library Project financed the film, using one of its project schools as the background for the film.

3431. Anderson, E. J. *An analytical study of some reviewing media of children's books.* Chicago, University of Chicago, 1957. 93p. Thesis.

3432. Anderson, Floyd. *Comics, television and children.* Notre Dame, Indiana, Ave Maria Press, 1955. 23p. NNY.

A pamphlet issued for the guidance of parents. This is typical of a large number of such items, usually put out by a religious or civic organization. This one is Roman Catholic in point of view.

3433. Anderson, Marian Posey. *Books to grow on; helping the very young to explore their world and its people.* New York, American Jewish Committee, 1961. 40p. NNY.

An annotated list arranged according to general themes and subject categories. Most of the books are picture books.

3434. Andrews, Siri. *The Hewins lectures 1947–1962.* Boston, Horn Book, 1963, 375p. $10.00. DLC, IYL, NNY.

A compilation of the yearly lectures given at the Massachusetts Library Association meetings since 1947, with the exception of 1948. Siri Andrews edited the collection and wrote on "Criticism and reviewing of children's books" as an introduction. The essays are all concerned with New England books for children, by New England authors (Jacob Abbott, Eliza Orne White, Laura E. Richards, Lucretia P. Hale, Susan Coolidge, Kate Douglas Wiggin, Rachel Field, Mrs. A. D. T. Whitney and the like). The authors are, for the most part, well-known librarians of the New England area.

3435. Arbuthnot, May Hill. . . . *Anthology of children's literature.* Rev. ed. Chicago, Scott, Foresman & Co., 1961. 207, 418, 459p. $10.50. DLC, NNY.

Three books, previously published under the titles *Time for Poetry, Time for Fairy Tales,* and *Time for True Tales and Almost True* are bound together to form the *Arbuthnot Anthology of Children's Literature.* This is the second edition in one volume. It retains almost all the poetry and stories in the original edition and adds new and recent material as well as a new section on choral reading. This collection was planned to be used in the classroom, home or camp, but especially for college classes in children's literature to provide selections from children's books when the books themselves might not be readily available to the students. The author planned it to complement her text book in children's literature: *Children and Books.*

3436. ———. *Children and books.* 3rd ed. Chicago, Scott, Foresman & Co., 1964. 688p. $8.50. DLC, IYL, NNY.

A standard textbook in children's literature courses offered in schools of education where it is required reading for many students, this book has come to be used also in library school courses, particularly when directed to the training of school librarians. Useful also as an outline of children's literature from the earliest times to the present. The 1964 edition has substantial expansion in the sections on storytelling, reading aloud, and the mass media.

3437. ———. *Children's books too good to miss.* Rev. ed. Cleveland, Western Reserve University, 1963. 67p. $1.25. DLC, NNY.

This attractive paper bound bibliography is addressed primarily to parents. It is an annotated guide to some 250 books selected by Miss Arbuthnot and Harriet Long of Western Reserve University together with Margaret Mary Clark, Head of the Lewis Carroll Room of the Cleveland Public Library. The pamphlet is well printed with a middle section of illustrations from some of the titles. The index lists titles and prices.

3438. ———. "Today's child tomorrow," *Catholic library world,* Haverford, Pa., Vol. 36, Sept., 1964, pp. 18–22. DLC, NNY.

This speech was given upon the occasion of

the author's acceptance of the Regina Medal. In it this well-known critic and teacher expresses her concern for children of today, whom she feels are not always being well-prepared to face the complex world of tomorrow. She speaks of the role books have in this preparation.

3439. Armstrong, Helen T. and Ruth Ann Robinson. *Books on Africa for children.* Chicago, ALA, 1965, 3p.

A reprint from the June, 1965 issue of *Top of the News.* These are currently available books on Africa in general or on one of the African countries in particular.

3440. Arnold, Gertrude Weld. *A mother's list of books for children.* Chicago, A. C. McClurg, 1909. 270p. DLC.

A very personal selection, with comments on how to use books with children at various stages in their lives.

3441. Arnoldowa, M. "Biblioteki dziecięce w Stanach Zjednoczonych," *Bibliotekarz,* Warszawa, Rok 27, No. 9, 1960, pp. 265–271; Nr. 11–12, 1960, pp. 341–345. DLC, NNY.

"Children's libraries in the U.S." Their early history and development.

3442. Arnstein, Flora J. *Poetry in the elementary classroom.* New York, Appleton-Century-Crofts [1962]. 124p. DLC.

Methods of introducing poetry to children, and ways to bring children to express themselves imaginatively through poetry.

3443. Association for Childhood Education International. *Adventuring in literature for children.* Washington [1953]. (Bulletin No. 92 of the Association). DLC, NNY.

A guide for the teacher to use in introducing books to children in the classroom or outside it.

3444. ———. *A bibliography of books for children.* Washington, The Association, annual 1937–1948, biennial 1950 ff. (Bulletin No. 37 of the Association). $1.50. DLC, NNY.

An annotated and classified list, revised every two years, of children's books recommended by this organization. Age levels are given.

3445. ———. *Children's books for $1.25 or less.* Rev. ed. Washington, The Association, 1965. 35p. (Bulletin No. 36 of the Association). $.75. DLC, NNY.

This paperback pamphlet lists and briefly annotates nearly 300 inexpensive children's books. It is sent as part of membership service to International and Life members of The Association and to Association branches. This edition was compiled for the Association by a committee of children's librarians chaired by Siddie Joe Johnson, former Head of Dallas Public Library. It is arranged by subject and includes a title index and an index of publishers.

3446. Austin, Marjorie Anne. *Women and work in children's fiction.* Chicago, University of Chicago, 1965. 83p. Thesis.

3447. Ayres, Leonard Porter and Adele McKinnie. *The public library and the public schools.* Cleveland, Survey Committee of the Cleveland Foundation, 1916. 93p. (Cleveland Education Survey, No. 12). DLC.

An influential study on the interdependence of school and public libraries, in which the conclusions drawn were remarkably similar to those of many present-day studies.

3448. Bacon, George B. "The literature of our Sunday Schools," *Hours at home,* New York, Vol. 10, Feb., 1870, 293–300; Mar., 1870, pp. 450–459; Apr., 1870, pp. 558–567. DLC.

An unusual article in that it reflects an attitude contrary to the prevailing one of the time. The three parts deal with the excessive amounts of this didactic literature, the exaggerated piety of much of it, and methods of improving the religious book for children.

3449. Baker, Augusta. *Books about Negro life for children.* 5th ed. New York, The New York Public Library, 1965. 33p. DLC, NNY.

A list of books for children "that give an unbiased, accurate, well-rounded picture of Negro life in all parts of the world." Each entry is annotated, and arrangement is geographical and by subject areas.

3450. Baker, Franklin T. "A bibliography of children's readings." 2 parts. *Teachers college record,* New York, Vol. 9, Nos. 1 and 2, 1908. 65p. each. DLC, NNY.

An annotated list of children's books, arranged by subject and type. The introduction lists the purposes and criteria. Designed for use in schools.

3451. Baker, R. Ray. "What is the educational or moral value for boys and girls in reading books about the American Indian?" *Public libraries,* Chicago, Vol. 27, June, 1922, pp. 323–326. DLC, NNY.

The author protested against the unfair picture of the American Indian, which is usually shown in books about him, whether they originate in the U.S. or elsewhere.

3452. Ballard, F. V. *A survey of information about school libraries and related topics in professional periodicals*. Chicago, University of Chicago, 1947. 131p. Thesis.

3453. Bamman, Henry, *et al. Oral interpretation of children's literature*. Dubuque, Iowa, W. C. Brown, 1964. 119p. DLC.
Methods and techniques of introducing literature to children through reading aloud, poetry, choral speaking, creative dramatics and storytelling.

3454. Bank Street College of Education. *Books for children; a selected list*. Revised. New York, The College, 1965. 31p. NNY.
The criteria for the selections on this list are those of the College which is considered one of the progressive schools of education.

3455. Banta, Nola K. *An analytical study of the independent reading of junior high school pupils*. Chicago, University of Chicago, 1928. 111p. Thesis.

3456. Barakian, Harriet V. "Adolescent literature," *Education,* Vol. 43, Feb., 1923, pp. 373–380. DLC, NNY.
The necessity for reading guidance during the years of adolescence, together with a suggested list of books appealing to this age.

3457. Barchilon, Jacques and Henry Petit. *The authentic Mother Goose fairy tales and nursery rhymes*. Denvery, Alan Swallow, 1960. Various paging. DLC, NNY.
Included are facsimiles of: *Histories or Tales of Past Times . . . With Morals,* by M. Perrault. Translated into English. London, Printed for J. Pote and R. Montagu, 1729; *Mother Goose's Melody: or, Sonnets for the Cradle. . .* London, Printed for E. Power, 1791. The first is from the Houghton Library, Harvard University and the second is from the private collection of Elizabeth Ball, Muncie, Indiana. The introduction attempts to trace the oral tradition of the nursery rhymes, and their connection with Perrault's tales. Bibliography.

3458. Bart, Peter and Dorothy. "As told and sold by Disney," *New York times book review,* May 9, 1965, Part 2, pp. 2, 32–34. DLC, NNY.
". . . there is a considerable, though by no means unanimous, body of opinion that maintains that Disney books stand for an almost aggressive mediocrity." The authors describe some of the Disney books, and critically evaluate them in terms of literary and aesthetic value.

3459. Bartleson, E. *American historical fiction for children*. New York, Columbia University, 1946. 93p. Thesis.

3460. Batchelder, Mildred L. "Learning about children's books in translation," *ALA bulletin,* Chicago, Vol. 60, Jan., 1966, pp. 33–42. DLC, NNY.
The executive secretary of the Children's Services Division, ALA, writes of her travels abroad, in a study trip undertaken to determine some of the means and methods whereby U.S. children's books are translated in Europe and European children's books are translated in the U.S.

3461. Batchelor, Lillian L. *et al. Reading guidance for the gifted*. Los Angeles, Immaculate Heart College, School of Library Science, 1960. 145p. DLC.
The Proceedings of the 3rd Library Institute.

3462. Bean, M. A. "The evil of unlimited freedom in the use of juvenile fiction," *Library journal,* New York, Vol. 4, Nos. 9–10, Sept. Oct., 1879, pp. 341–343. DLC, NNY.
This librarian was against having too much fiction in the library. She deplored the policy of some libraries in allowing children to get as much as a book a day. See also entries 3399 and 3816.

3463. ———. "Report on the reading of the young," *Library journal,* New York, Vol. 8, Nos. 9–10, Sept.–Oct., 1883, pp. 217–227. DLC, NNY.
Given at the Buffalo conference of ALA. Miss Bean continues the report in the same fashion as Miss Hewins had begun, listing what the individual city libraries were doing for children.

3464. Beard, Patten. "Why banish the fairy tale?" *Libraries,* Chicago, Vol. 34, Nov., 1929, pp. 457–459. DLC, NNY.
The author contended that fairy tales were only permitted as long as they were folk lore, but that this left out a great amount of fairy tale literature. While the moral of the folk tale is often doubtful, he wrote, the moral of the fairy tale is a spiritual truth or an ethical one given in symbol.

3465. Bechtel, Louise Seaman. *Books in search of children*. New York, The New York Public Library, 1946. 47p. (R.R.Bowker Memorial Lectures, 10). DLC, NNY.

Mrs. Bechtel was one of the first children's book editors in the U.S. In this paper she examined the state of children's book publishing, 20 years after her initial work. She does this from the points of view of the authors, illustrators, publishers, libraries, booksellers, schools, and the general public. In summary, she gives her criteria for judging good children's books.

3466. ———. "Thinking about children's classics," *The packet, Heath's service bulletin,* Boston, Vol. 10, No. 2, Fall 1955, pp. 3–19. DLC, NNY.

This author and editor recommends introducing the great works of adult literature "in cut or simplified form, before they reach high school age." She attempts defining a children's classic. In general, these are opinions not held by the majority of the recognized authorities in children's literature.

3467. Beck, Warren. "Huckleberry Finn versus the cash boy," *Education,* Boston, Vol. 49, Sept., 1928, pp. 1–13. DLC.

The author contrasts the literary merit of the Alger books and other similar series, to the prose of Mark Twain.

3468. Becker, May Lamberton. *First adventures in reading.* New York, F. A. Stokes, 1936. 286p. DLC, NNY.

A series of essays subtitled "Introducing children to books," these were the result of Mrs. Becker's practical experience as a mother and a well-known critic. The book was meant as a guide for parents.

3469. ———. "First children's spring book festival," *Elementary english review,* Champlain, Illinois, Vol. 15, Mar., 1938 pp. 98–100. DLC, NNY.

Some reactions in the children's book world to the spring book festival, initiated and carried out each spring by the *N.Y. Herald Tribune,* through 1966. Due to the demise of this daily paper, it is not known whether these awards will continue.

3470. Beebe, Elinor Lee, *et al.* . . . *Books for the young child; a list annotated on the basis of a study of the child's interests conducted in the Albany Nursery School.* Albany, University of the State of New York Press, 1935. 20p. NNY.

An early list of books, chiefly picture books, having special appeal to the preschool child.

3471. Beggs, Berenice B. "Present-day books eclipse Alger thrillers," *English journal,* Chicago, Vol. 21, Nov., 1932, pp. 727–733. DLC, NNY.

The author contended that the boy of the 1930's could hardly have appreciated Henty and Alger because so much in real life was already far more exciting. There is a list of some "old and new books popular with boys."

3472. Belser, Danylu, *et al.* "The reading interests of boys," *Elementary english review,* Detroit, Vol. 3, Nov., 1926, pp. 292–296. DLC.

Some results of an inquiry conducted through the use of questionnaires and personal observation of choices made in the library.

3473. Bender, A. N. "Criteria for evaluating children's books," *Reading and the school library,* Chicago, Vol. 1, June, 1935, pp. 21–22. DLC.

The author suggests that librarians and teachers have proven more effective in improving the standards of children's books than have the publishers. The criteria to look for are: quality of experience and quality of expression; quality of presentation; quality of illustration and design.

3474. Bengtson, Phyllis J. *Bibliography of the beginnings of children's library work in the United States 1876–1901.* Pittsburgh, Carnegie Institute of Technology, 1954. 58p. Thesis.

3475. Bennett, Jessie W. *Developmental tasks of middle childhood as reflected in the fiction written for children in the intermediate grades during the ten-year period of 1940–1949.* Austin, University of Texas, 1952. 200p. Thesis.

3476. Benson, Isabel M. *The American Institute of Graphic Arts and an analysis of the juvenile books in its children's exhibits and the "50 Books" exhibits.* Cleveland, Western Reserve University, 1952. 81p. Thesis.

3477. Bentley, Martha C. "Children's paperbacks; a long hard look," *Library journal,* New York, Vol. 90, Jan., 15, 1965, pp. 309–311. DLC, NNY.

The challenge of putting paperback books to use in the children's library, their limitations, and a selective list of some of the current titles available in paperback.

3478. ———. "Operation Head Start materials collections: Preschool reading readiness program," *Library journal,* New York, Vol. 89, Nov., 15, 1964, pp. 4606–4607. DLC, NNY.

A description of the aims of this federal program, and the ways in which libraries can assist its leaders. A list of books and materials suitable for the preschool child is included. Operation Head Start is a nation-wide attempt to expose preschool children from low income, culturally deprived areas to language, music, art and other forms of creative expression.

3479.   Berresford, Ella. *A preliminary guide to books reflecting the interests of the pre-school and primary child.* Kent, Ohio, Kent State University, 1959. 99p. Thesis.

3480.   Berry, Erick and Herbert Best. *Writing for children.* Miami, Miami University Press, 1964. 202p. DLC, NNY.

This husband and wife writing team explain here some of the "tricks of the trade." They use many examples from well-known children's books to illustrate their points.

3481.   *Best books for children.* New York, R. R. Bowker. Revised annually. $3.00 ($10.00 for 5 yrs.). DLC, NNY.

This is a useful, annotated buying guide for parents, teachers and librarians which has been compiled annually in the offices of *Library Journal* since 1959. Editor now is Joan Sragow. It is arranged by age and subject and titles are coded to show the recommended lists from which they have been taken. 1966 edition lists 3700 titles including adult books for young people. Roughly one-fourth of listed titles are books of the current year.

3482.   Betzner, Jean and Annie Egerton Moore. *Everychild and books.* Indianapolis, Bobbs-Merrill, 1940. 174p. DLC.

How children react to children's books in the home, school and public library, together with some practical suggestions for parents and teachers and others working with children, on how to take advantage of this natural curiosity in children. The book lists and bibliography are very dated.

3483.   Beust, Nora Ernestine. *Books to help build international understanding.* Washington, U.S. Department of Health, Education and Welfare, Office of Education, 1954. 31p. Mimeographed. DLC.

Annotated and arranged by area of the world. Recordings are also given, in some instances.

3484.   ———., et al. *Graded list of books for children.* Chicago, ALA, 1930. 149p. DLC.

An annotated list of 1000 titles, prepared with the needs of the teacher in mind. Author, title and subject list. This was one of the first such lists compiled under the auspices of ALA. The earlier edition (1922) was compiled by the National Education Association and published by ALA.

3485.   ———., et al. *Growing with books; a read-*

ing guide. Rev. ed. Eau Claire, Wisconsin, Hale, 1942. 206p. DLC.

A guide intended for children to use themselves, or for teachers to use. This was frequently revised and was published by a large commercial prebinder of books for children.

3486.   ———. *School library administration; an annotated bibliography.* Washington, Office of Education, 1941. (Bulletin No. 7).

3487.   "A bibliography of Indian and pioneer stories for young folks," *United States Indian Affairs Office. Bulletin,* Washington, No. 13, 1931, pp. 1–37. DLC, NNY.

An annotated list which attempted to guide children into reading those books which did not present such stereotyped pictures of Indian characters as were often read and absorbed by children.

3488.   *Bibliography of juvenile holdings in the Library of Congress . . .* 36 vols. Washington, Catholic University, 1957–1965. (Typewritten manuscripts). DLC.

Undertaken by students in the graduate library school of the Catholic University, these bibliographies attempted to identify the holdings which the Library of Congress has in each of its classifications. They were compiled by the following persons: Luck Beck, Anne G. Blankinship, Daphne M. Brownell, J. E. Cole, Doris L. Danes, Margaret V. Danforth, M. V. Doyle, M. L. Engel, Clair Foley, M. Gyulahazi, G. C. Huckabee, Richard J. Ikena, G. Jenkins, D. King, Frances King, Adele J. Krug, Katherine A. Lam, H. H. McLay, Clara W. Marcoux, Kathleen Meier, R. G. Moses, Francis C. Murphy, Therese G. Nye, Doris H. Owen, Barbara A. Paine, Mary Louise Presson, Margaret B. Riordan, Mary L. Shaffer, Maria Huang Shih, Lillian Siegel, Grace L. Sim, J. H. Stiles, G. B. Tabler, Mel R. Uzdrowski, O.S.B., Mildred L. Zens, and L. C. Zugby.

3489.   Bishop Claire Huchet. *French children's books for English speaking children.* New York, The author, 1938. 31p. DLC.

Sixty French books suitable for the child with a beginner's knowledge of the language, annotated and with complete bibliographic information. One section represents the most beautiful and artistic books in French available for children.

3490.   ———. "Obstacle race," *Horn book,* Boston, Vol. 11, July–Aug., 1935, pp. 203–209. DLC, NNY.

A strongly-worded protest against the theories of Thorndike (4388), in regard to limiting the vocabularies of children's books. The author quotes parallel passages from some of the masterpieces of children's literature, in their original form and the version changed according to Thorndike methods. Her belief was that if the child could not manage the original, he should wait until later, or have it read aloud to him.

3491.   Bissell, Fannie S. "What the libraries are doing for the children," *Outlook,* New York, Vol. 70, Feb. 15, 1902, pp. 420–424. NNY.

A general survey, with the most attention given to the work of the New York city libraries and those of Pittsburgh and Hartford.

3492.   Blair, Virginia B. *Directed reading through the library for improving the social adjustment of older children.* Denton, Texas State College for Women, 1951. 58p. Thesis.

3493.   Blake, Eunice. "Children's book publishing." Grannis, Chandler B., *What happens in book publishing.* New York, Columbia University Press, 1957, pp. 299–306. DLC, NNY.

A well-known children's book editor describes the work of her department, its special relations with libraries and schools, and the reasons for the general increase in children's book publishing over the years.

3494.   Blanck, Jacob. *Peter Parley to Penrod.* New York, R. R. Bowker, 1956. 153p. DLC, IYL, NNY.

"A bibliographical description of the best-loved American juvenile books." A personal choice of "outstanding books which have withstood the years of change in reading tastes and are favorites still." Arranged chronologically from their appearance, 1827 to 1926, are the 113 titles which form the main position of the book. An additional 43 "border-line selections" follow. Each is described in fairly complete bibliographic terms. This was first printed in 1938.

3495.   Blank, Catherine M. *Critical analysis of the value of summer reading projects for children.* Pittsburgh, Carnegie Institute of Technology, 1952. 114p. Thesis.

3496.   Bogle, S. C. N. "Education of school librarians in America," *Modern librarian,* Lahore, Vol. 3, Jan., 1933, pp. 71–74. DLC.

A review of professional standards, and how they are effected by accredited library school teaching.

3497.   Bolton, Henry C. *The counting-out rhymes of children, their antiquity, origin and wide distribution.* New York, Appleton, 1888. 123p. DLC.

Although this covers many countries, the greater proportion are from the U.S. More than 800 are given in all. Index and bibliography.

3498.   Boney, Cecil DeWitt. *Study of library reading in the primary grades.* New York, Columbia University, Teachers' College, 1933. 70p. (Contributions to education, no. 578).

3499.   Bonner, Mary Graham. *A parent's guide to children's reading.* New York, Funk & Wagnall's, 1926. 161p. DLC.

Personal recommendations of good books which the author says should never be given to children as "must" reading. "No one should be ordered to like what in itself is likable," she writes. There are author and title indexes to the books mentioned in her text.

3500.   [Book selection issues]. *Library journal,* New York, Vol. 86, Dec. 15, 1961. DLC, NNY.

In the children's library section of this issue are articles by Elizabeth Gross, Virginia Haviland, Marian C. Young, Mary Peters, and Dorothy Broderick all dealing with the problems of book selection for children's and school libraries.

3501.   "Books—children's reading," *New York times index,* Vol. 1 ff. 1913 ff. DLC, NNY.

This index to a leading U.S. newspaper is invaluable in tracing facts relating to children's books and libraries, as well as the numerous articles in the special supplements which appear twice yearly and which are not indexed elsewhere. In the early years, these references are listed under "Literature."

3502.   "Books and reading; the list of one hundred books," *St. Nicholas,* New York, Vol. 27, Mar., 1900, pp. 444–446. DLC, NNY.

This was one of many lists compiled for the pages of this outstanding children's periodical. It resulted from a competition in which children were asked to name their favorite books.

3503.   "Books for boys and girls," *Book week,* New York, Vol. 1, 1924 ff. Weekly. DLC. NNY.

This literary supplement was formerly titled the *New York Herald Tribune Books.* It now appears in many Sunday newspapers throughout the country. Anne Carroll Moore first began to review for it in 1924 under the "Three Owls" column (see 4122). Later reviewers were May Lamberton Becker and Louise Seaman Bechtel. At present the editing is done by Margaret Sherwood Libby. There are two special issues each year devoted entirely to children's books, one during Book Week in November and the other in spring, when the Spring Festival Book Awards are announced.

3504. "Books for children," *Childhood education,* Washington, 1924 ff. Monthly.

This educational periodical maintains a regular review column for children's books. Each year the editor of the column is selected from among outstanding librarians and educators who are knowledgeable in the field of children's books.

3505. "Books for children," *Parents magazine,* New York, 1929 ff. DLC. NNY.

Throughout almost the entire period this magazine has been issued, there have been reviews of children's books included in a regular column. Such distinguished reviewers as Alice Dalgliesh and Anne Thaxter Eaton were among those who contributed for longer periods.

3506. "Books for children," *Library journal,* New York, Vol. 14, No. 11, Nov., 1889, pp. 443–445. DLC, NNY.

A newspaper in St. Louis offered a set of Irving's works to the boy or girl who submitted the best list of ten books for the young. This report lists the 50 titles most frequently cited among the replies. The first three were *Little Lord Fauntleroy, Robinson Crusoe* and *Little Women.*

3507. "Books for children," *Quarterly review,* London, Vol. 71, No. 141, Dec., 1842, pp. 30–46. DLC, NNY. Also in French in: *Bibliothèque de Genève,* Tome 43, Feb., 1843, pp. 263 ff. NNY.

In commenting upon the general children's literature of the day, this reviewer wrote: ". . . it may be justly questioned whether in banishing the world of fiction and advancing one of reality in its place, we have not sometimes dismissed a protector, and introduced an enemy. The more we aim at reality in the precepts and models we offer to children, the more delicate and difficult does our task become . . . any error in what you give forth as truth is immeasurably more pernicious than all the extravagances which a child knows to be fiction." These comments are followed by reviews of books by T. H. Gallaudet, two *Peter Parley* books, three by Jacob Abbott, and others.

3508. *Books for children 1965–1966.* Chicago, ALA, 1966. 128p. $2.00.

Some 770 titles have been selected from the reviews of *The Booklist,* and are here annotated and classified and indexed. This type of list will be issued to keep up the larger list, *Books for Children 1960–1965.*

3509. *Books for children 1960–1965.* Chicago, ALA, 1966. 447p. $10.00. DLC, IYL, NNY.

Some 3,000 reviews of children's books selected from the issues of the *Booklist,* official reviewing periodical of ALA. They were selected by Helen E. Kinsey and her staff. Arrangement is by a modified Dewey system and subject headings are given. There is a complete index.

3510. *Books for young readers.* Detroit, Vol. 1, No. 1, 1961–Vol. 3, No. 3, 1963. NNY.

This short-lived periodical, issued by the Educational Press Association of America, contained reviews of books of interest to the young.

3511. Bowerman, George Franklin. *A chief librarian looks at work with children.* Pittsburgh, Carnegie Institute Press, 1930. 22p. DLC. Also in his: *Censorship and the public library, with other papers.* New York, H. W. Wilson, 1931, pp. 175 ff. DLC, NNY.

In this commencement address, a librarian surveys the importance of children's library work, its history and its future.

3512. Bowker, R. R. "Some children's librarians," *Library journal,* New York, Vol. 46, Oct. 1, 1921, pp. 787–790. DLC, NNY.

The backgrounds and work of five pioneers in the field: Anne Carroll Moore, Clara W. Hunt, Alice M. Jordan, Effie L. Power and Mary E. S. Root. There are photo portraits of the last four reproduced in the article.

3513. Bowman, Charles L. *1250 best books for boys and girls, recommended for public and school libraries, with ALA or other reliable annotations.* New York, The Union Library Association, 1916. 59p. DLC, NNY.

A book jobber's catalog, interesting for its annotations. Picture books and books in series are given separately.

3514. Boylan, Lucile and Robert Sattler. *A catalog of paperback for grades 7–12.* New York, Scarecrow Press, 1963. 209p. $5.00. DLC.

An annotated list of over 1,000 titles arranged by Dewey decimal system and indicating reading levels. All are paper back books currently available.

3515. Boynton, Henry Walcott. "For the young,"

Journalism and literature. Boston, Houghton, 1904, pp. 103–120. NNY.

The writer claims that children were written down to in much of the literature of his day.

3516. Boys' Clubs of America. *Junior book awards.* New York, The organization, 1957 ff. DLC.

A yearly selection based on book reports submitted by boys in clubs throughout the U.S. Since there is no established criteria set up for the final choices, the award books are often uneven and undistinguished.

3517. Bramlette, Selma G. *Responsibilities of the school librarian in the guidance program.* Denton, Texas State College for Women, 1950. 65p. Thesis.

3518. Brent, Eleanor. "Understanding customers' needs; the key to selling children's books creatively," *Publishers' weekly,* New York, Vol. 152, Oct. 25, 1947, pp. 2079–2083. DLC, NNY.

One of the lectures given to a group of booksellers, under the auspices of the Women's National Book Association. This still contains many sound ideas, although a few of the specific titles are no longer available.

3519. Brett, W. H. "Books for youth," *Library journal,* New York, Vol. 10, No. 6, June, 1885, pp. 127–128. DLC, NNY.

A reprint from the newspaper, *The Cleveland Plain Dealer,* in which the author recommends the establishment of children's libraries in that city.

3520. Brewton, John E. and Sara W. *Index to children's poetry.* New York, H. W. Wilson, 1942. 966p. $12.00. DLC, NNY. Supplements: 1st, 1957, 405p. $8.00; 2nd, 1965, 453p. $10.00. DLC, NNY.

A title, author, subject and first line index to children's poetry in the English language, available in current collections.

3521. Brinsmade, E. M. *Children's books on Alaska: An annotated list.* Fairbanks, Alaska, Adler's Book Shop, 1956.

3522. Broderick, Dorothy. "Introducing elementary school children to the classics," *Instructor,* Danville, Vol. 73, Nov., 1963, pp. 50–52. DLC, NNY.

This critic stresses the importance of the classics, but recommends that they not be forced on children because the result is often a dislike for this type of reading. She offers suggestions to teachers on introducing these books in the classroom.

3523. ———. *An introduction to children's work in public libraries.* New York, H. W. Wilson, 1965. 176p. DLC, NNY.

This practical tool is based on wide experience in training new children's librarians, both in library schools and in special workshops. The author teaches at the Western Reserve University Library School in Cleveland. This covers the philosophy, book selection criteria, library programs and general administration.

3524. ———. *The opportunities that books offer.* New York, Children's Book Council, 1960. 12p. DLC, NNY.

A bibliography prepared in connection with the 1960 White House Conference on Children and Youth. The books and articles pertain to: Character development and the acquisition of values through books; books aid the physically, mentally, and emotionally handicapped; intergroup relations; toward a life of creativity; youth against the community.

3525. ———. "A study in conflicting values," *Library journal,* New York, Vol. 91, May 15, 1966, pp. 2557–2564. DLC, NNY.

"What are the characteristics of the books which cause otherwise gentle ladies to remove their white gloves and come out swinging?" This well-known librarian is a frequent contributor of articles and reviews of children's books. They often bring up for discussion the more sensitive and controversial issues of work with children. This article centers on the evaluation of "provocative" children's books, i.e. those which deal with subjects hitherto not considered suitable for children and/or those on which critics have held sharply differing views.

3526. Brooks, Matha H. "Sunday School libraries," *Library journal,* New York, Vol. 4, Nos. 9–10, Sept.–Oct., 1879, pp. 338–341. DLC, NNY.

A description of the work of the Ladies Committee on Sunday School Books, which made annual selective lists for such schools, and for home use.

3527. Brown, Clarke L. "The influence of war stories on children," *Public libraries,* Chicago, Vol. 20, Oct., 1915, pp. 354–356. DLC, NNY.

A perceptive essay on the negative and positive aspects of war stories. On the negative side the author writes persuasively of the false ideals and the wrong perspective of history which war stories bestow. On the positive side she writes: ". . . it is because they reveal human ideals—valour at its best, fortitude at its best, resistance at its best, sorrow at its deepest, mercy at its finest, and remembrance at its truist . . . no one loves loyalty, fidelity, or patriotism, even when spelled with ever so large capitals but children do love the people who have stood for these things . . ."

3528.   Brown, Corinne. *Suggested readings for a course in children's literature*. n. p. Dannervike Printing Co., 1918.

3529.   Brown, George I. "Criteria used by editors in selecting manuscripts of children's books," *Elementary english,* Chicago, Vol. 40, Nov., 1963, pp. 719–723. DLC.

The author collected data from some 46 members of the Children's Book Council and here reports on the results.

3530.   Brown, H. W. *A study of methods and practices in supplying library service to public elementary schools in the United States*. Camden, N.J., The author, 1941. Thesis.

3531.   Brown, Sister M. L. *Bio-bibliography of modern Catholic authors of children's and young people's books*. Washington, Catholic University of America, 1961. 122p. Thesis.

3532.   Brown, Walter L. "The classroom library," *Child welfare,* Philadelphia, Vol. 24, Nov., 1929, pp. 127–129. Also in: *Wilson bulletin,* New York, Vol. 5, Sept., 1930, pp. 47–50. DLC, NNY.

This describes a type of library service which had become fairly common by 1930—the loan of small collections from the public library children's room to the individual classrooms of neighboring schools. Following this is a description, by N. H. Price, of an experiment in which schools actually took over use of the children's library during the morning hours. The entire issue is devoted to school library problems.

3533.   Browne, William Hand. "Harlequin and hurly-burly," *Sewanee review,* New York, Vol. 18, Jan., 1910, pp. 23–31. DLC, NNY.

3534.   Bruce, H. Addington. "The fairy-tale and your child," *Good housekeeping,* New York, Vol. 61, Sept., 1915, pp. 325–331. DLC, NNY.

The author conjures up the dangers which lurk in the over-use of the frightening and violent fairy tale, but he also points out the harm which can result in withholding them entirely from the life of the child.

3535.   Bryant, Sara Cone. *How to tell stories to children*. Boston, Houghton Mifflin, 1905. 260p. DLC, NNY.

This early handbook on the art of storytelling is still useful for its practical advice on techniques for the beginner. Especially helpful is the section on telling stories to very young children. There is also a selection of stories to tell.

3536.   *Bulletin of the center for children's books.* University of Chicago, Graduate Library School, 5750 Ellis Avenue, Chicago, Illinois 60637. Monthly except Aug., Vol. 1 ff., No. 1 ff., Dec., 1947 ff. Annual subscription: $4.50. DLC, NNY.

Reviews of current children's books, written by the staff of the Center for Children's Books. The recommendations are very specific, and grade levels are included. Periodically, there are reviews of books in the following categories: bibliographies, reading for parents, reading for teachers, reading for librarians. The annual index appears in the July–August issue.

3537.   Bunt, Cyril G. E. "B is for book," *Antiques,* New York, Vol. 41, Feb., 1942, pp. 126–129. DLC, NNY.

Some facts about ABC books, hornbooks, battledores, reading boards and hieroglyphic books, and their value as collectors' items. There are about 20 reproductions in black and white.

3538.   Burbank, L. V. *A survey of children's book clubs for the elementary school*. Washington, Catholic University of America, 1956. 176p. Thesis.

3539.   Burger, I. Victor, *et al. Bringing children and books together*. New York, Library Club of America, 1956, 133p. DLC, NNY.

"Assisted by Theresa A. Cohen and Paul Bisgaier." A report on an intensive planned program of library and book-related events, undertaken in selected New York City schools in 1955–1956. There are many photographs illustrating the activities in which the children participated.

3540.   Burnite, Caroline. "The beginnings of a literature for children," *Library journal,* New York, Vol. 31, No. 8, Aug., 1906, pp. 107–112. DLC, NNY.

A short, scholarly survey presented at the ALA conference in 1906. Bibliography.

3541.   ——. "Instruction in work with children in library schools and summer schools," *ALA bulletin,* Chicago, Vol. 3, Sept., 1909, pp. 420–427. DLC, NNY.

". . . In my opinion work for children can not be given in a general library school course as a special subject, but as a necessary part of the general training . . . finally, that more specialized schools for this particular work are needed."

3542. ———. "The standard of selection of children's books. The beginnings of a literature for children." Sawyer, Harriet Price, *The library and its contents*. New York, H. W. Wilson, 1925, pp. 111–134 ff. DLC, NNY.

These two articles, reprinted from *Library Journal,* are only the first of seven in the section called "Book selection; Children's literature." Others are: Theresa H. Elmendorf, "Good literature and little children"; Stephen B. Leacock, "What I read as a child"; Anne Carroll Moore, "Making your own library"; Harriet A. Wood, "Sets for children"; and Clara W. Hunt, "Picture books for children."

3543. Burress, Lee A. "Censorship is capricious," *Top of the news,* Chicago, Vol. 20, May, 1964, pp. 281–287. DLC, NNY.

The author writes of the problems of censorship, stating that deference to it usually produces apathy. In a study made among certain libraries, the primary reason given for censorship was "immorality." Quotes from *The Student's Right to Read* are given to support the view that more curiosity is aroused by invoking censorship than would be the case if books were quietly allowed to remain on the open shelves.

3544. Burt, Mary E. *Literary landmarks; a guide to good reading for young people* . . . Boston, Houghton, [1892]. 174p. DLC, NNY.

A handbook containing texts of introduction to the classics, science and geographic reading, history and biography, and utilitarian literature. There is also a list of 700 books recommended for reading for grades one through eight.

3545. Burton, Richard. "Literature for children," *Literary likings.* Boston, Copeland & Day, 1898, pp. 363–384. NNY. Also in: *North American review,* Boston, Vol. 167, 1898, pp. 278–286. NNY.

The author believes children should be given the classics in their entirety, rather than in watered-down versions. He lists those he especially recommends.

3546. Bussey, J. C. *Study of the reading interests of a selected group of elementary school children at the John M. Tutt Elementary School, Augusta, Georgia.* Atlanta, Atlanta University, 1961. 64p. (Thesis).

3547. Butler, George E. *State certification requirements for librarians working with children and young people in schools and public libraries.* Chicago, University of Chicago, 1953. 159p. Thesis.

3548. Butler, Helen L. "Wartime changes in the school library," *ALA bulletin,* Chicago, Vol. 37, Apr., 1943, pp. 116–120; May, 1943, pp. 159–162. DLC, NNY.

Based on a study made through field visits, questionnaire reports from 225 school libraries and discussions with many children's librarians.

3549. Butterworth, Elsie Walker. "A legacy for children; a collection of children's books," *Antiques,* New York, Vol. 54, Sept., 1948, pp. 178–179. DLC, NNY.

Some facts about the Rosenbach collection (see 4260) together with four reproductions from books which are part of it.

3550. "Buying children's books; a symposium," *Library journal,* New York, Vol. 64, Jan. 1, 1939–June 1, 1939. Monthly for six issues. DLC, NNY.

The selection and purchase procedures of some large and small libraries, and one library school. Contributors to the series were Siri Andrews, Gladys English, M. C. Young, D. L. Wood, R. E. Lawrence, L. T. Place, and D. Dawson.

3551. *Caldecott Medal books.* Chicago, ALA, Annual, 6p.

This brochure is revised annually to include the new winners. It includes the entire list of past winners.

3552. *Calendar.* Children's Book Council, 175 Fifth Avenue, New York, New York 10010. Quarterly. Vol. 1 ff. 1943 ff. $1.00 per year. DLC, IYL, NNY on current basis only.

The official publication of this organization of trade publishers of children's books. It contains sections on book-oriented events, prizes and awards, television and radio programs related to children and books, materials and publications available, and numerous tid-bits of news concerning the world of children's books.

3553. California Library Association. Children's and Young People's Section. *Illustrations for children: The Gladys English Collection.* Los Angeles, Ward Ritchie, 1963. 42p. (Keepsake Series, 5). DLC.

This collection of more than 125 original pieces of art which was used to illustrate children's books is named in honor of the former Supervisor of Children's Work in the Los Angeles Public Library. It is housed and maintained by the California State Library. This brochure contains an annotated list of all the items, reproductions of eight of them, and articles on illustration by Ruth Robbins and Marion Horton.

3554. Caller, Mary Alice. *Literary guide for home*

and school. New York, Merrill, 1892. 205p. NNY.

A guide for girls, very sentimental in tone, but interesting for its selected lists and chronological tables of historical reading.

3555.   Carpenter, Charles. *History of American school-books.* Philadelphia, University of Pennsylvania Press, [1963]. 322p. DLC, NNY.

Although this deals almost exclusively with books used in schools as texts, there is some mention of other types of reading for children. There is a long bibliography which includes many early dealers' catalogs, studies on hornbooks, etc.

3556.   Carpenter, Frances. "Visualizing foreign countries for the American child," *Publishers' weekly,* New York, Vol. 110, July 31, 1926, pp. 317–320. DLC, NNY.

"Vicarious travel is rarely successful in real life and almost never in books written for children." The author then describes some of the techniques which have been used and which have proven successful.

3557.   Carrier, Esther J. "Fiction for young people," *Fiction in public libraries 1876–1900.* New York, Scarecrow Press, 1965, pp. 179–233. DLC, NNY.

The historical place of juvenile fiction in public libraries is explored here, from almost complete non-acceptance in the early days to gradual complete acceptance. This documents very well the varying points of view in regard to the selection of quality fiction for children.

3558.   Carter, Julia F. *et al. Subject and title index to short stories for children.* Chicago, ALA, 1955. 344p. $5.00.

An index to some 5,000 stories arranged under more than 2,000 subjects. Most are in currently available collections.

3559.   Carton, Lonnie Caming. *The use of original developmental literature as a projective and therapeutic technique in late childhood.* Ann Arbor, University of Michigan, 1957. 98p. Dissertation DLC has on microfilm.

3560.   Cather, Katherine Dunlop. *Educating by storytelling.* New York, World Book Co., 1918. 396p. DLC. (British edition published in London by Harrap, 1919). DLC.

"Showing the value of story-telling as an educational tool for the use of all workers with children." Story lists by grade, a discussion of their use, and a good bibliography are given.

3561.   Cathon, Laura E. *Stories to tell to children.* Pittsburgh, Carnegie Library, 1960. 114p. $2.00.

This is the 7th edition of one of the outstanding lists of stories for children. It is based on the actual use of stories in the programs of the Carnegie Library, and is arranged by general age groups as well as by holidays and other special occasions.

3562.   Cazamian, M. L. "Bibliothèques enfantines. États-Unis," *Archives et bibliothèques,* Paris, No. 2, 1936, pp. 137–144. DLC.

This French librarian reports on the school and public libraries for children which he toured while on a visit to the U.S.

3563.   Cecil, Henry L. and Willard A. Heaps. *School library service in the United States; an interpretative survey.* New York, H. W. Wilson, 1940. 334p. DLC, NNY.

For its time, an important survey on the state of school library service in rural and some more urban areas. Historical aspects, administrative details, and federal and state involvement are among the points discussed. There are numerous sample contracts, programs, statistical tables, etc. Indexed.

3564.   Cernich, Louise. *Latin America: A selected list of juvenile fiction and folklore.* Washington, Catholic University, 1965. 42p. Thesis.

3565.   Certain, C. C. *et al.* "Elementary school library standards." Chicago, ALA, 1925. Unp.

These standards were set up by a Joint Committee of the National Education Association, Division of Elementary School Principals and the ALA.

3566.   Chamberlain, A. H. "Increasing the efficiency of the library as an educational factor," *ALA bulletin,* Chicago, Vol. 5, No. 4, July, 1911, pp. 154–163. DLC, NNY.

The importance of model children's libraries in normal schools and all schools, as well as in public libraries. This article urged authorities to study and analyze new approaches for more efficiency and service.

3567.   Chamberlayne, Ellen F. *et al. Pupil's permanent reading record.* Philadelphia, John C. Winston, 1928. 31p. DLC.

3568.   Chambers, Beatrice. *Children's work al fresco.* New York, Pratt Institute Library School, 1952. 35p. Thesis.

3569.   Chandler, Jenny Young. "The Children's Museum Library of Brooklyn," *The public library bulletin,* Boston, Vol. 2, No. 1, Jan., 1902, pp. 11–17. DLC.

This children's library was opened to specifically provide books on the natural sciences and history for the young visitors to the museum. The author includes a short list of some favorites. Illustrated with photographs of the library.

3570.   Chapman, John Jay. "Children's books," *ALA bulletin,* Chicago, Vol. 10, No. 3, May, 1916, pp. 122–125. DLC, NNY.

An admirable address, delivered at one of the general sessions of the annual conference in Asbury Park: The entire speech is quotable, but only a few excerpts can be given here: "It is strange how seldom the chief end of education is mentioned. That end is happiness. Our theorists talk of fitting men for life—whereas it is life itself that is at stake . . . Education is the antidote to environment, it is the spiritual life of the world, which men cannot find for themselves—no not though they be great geniuses—unless its language has been furnished to them in their early years . . . The task of the educator is to bring the young and the great together. Now, curiously the greatest works are just the ones which the young understand. It is only the great things that are both spontaneous and profound, and whose meaning leaps out fiercely enough to attract the child . . ."

3571.   Chase, Judith Wragg. *Books to build world friendship: Europe.* Dobbs Ferry, N.Y., Oceana Publications, 1964. 76p. DLC.

"An annotated bibliography of children's books from preschool to 8th grade." 296 books from 28 countries are described. All are fiction, folk lore or stories based on actual experiences. Additional sources of materials are given and there are author and illustrator indexes.

3572.   Chase, Mary Ellen. *Recipe for a magic childhood.* New York, Macmillan, 1953. 22p. NNY.

"There is no substitute for books in the life of the child" writes the author, in this memorable essay which first appeared in the *Ladies Home Journal,* May, 1951.

3573.   Chase, Virginia. "Trends in children's books," *Carnegie magazine,* Pittsburgh, Vol. 22, Oct., 1948, pp. 90–92. DLC, NNY.

The 1940's, in contrast to the 1930's, seemed mainly a period of rank commercialism according to this critic.

3574.   ———. *World war and children's books; a study of a selected group of books published 1902–1930.* New York, Columbia University, 1938. 164p. (Thesis.)

3575.   Chester, Eliza. "How shall we read? What shall we read? *Chats with girls on self-culture.* New York, Dodd, 1891, pp. 95–113. NNY.

Two chapters in this guide book for girls. Typical of the author's attitude is this statement: "There are half a dozen fresh, sweet story-writers girls are always the better for reading—Mrs. Mulock-Craik, Mrs. Whitney, Miss Thackeray (sic), Miss Yonge, Miss Alcott, Black."

3576.   Chicago. Library of International Relations. *On the shelves of the story cove; an international library for children, Century of Progress, Summer 1934.* Chicago, 1934, 51p. DLC.

A list of books, arranged by country and ethnic group, which appeared in the library exhibit. There are no annotations, but there is an author index.

3577.   Child Study Association of America. *Children's books of the year.* New York, The Association, Annual. DLC and NNY have recent copies.

Selected for parents and those working with children. "Along with literary values, reader appeal, integrity of plot and authenticity of information, the Committee considers as well the possible emotional and intellectual impact on a young reader." Also included is a list of the award-winning books honored by this association since 1943.

3578.   ———. *The children's bookshelf: A parent's guide to good books for boys and girls.* New York, Bantam Books, 1965. 194p. $00.95. DLC, IYL, NNY.

A helpful collection of essays on a variety of subjects, all written by experts in their field, and aimed at assisting the parent in guiding the reading of his children. There is also a selected list of recommended titles, together with an extensive bibliography of further reading. This is a mine of practical information, and has been an invaluable aid to librarians in reaching the home audience.

3579.   Children's Book Council. *Children's books, awards and prizes.* New York, Children's Book Council, 1960–1961 ff. Annual. DLC, NNY.

An annual booklet, listing the history and terms of awards and prizes for children's books, either in writing, illustrating or design. This is limited to U.S. awards, wth the exception of the Hans Christian Andersen Medal, the Canadan Book of the Year Medals, and the Carnegie and Greenaway Medals of England.

3580.   ———. *Aids to choosing books for children.* New York, The Council, 1967. 8p. $00.15.

One of the most valuable tools in tracing quickly and easily the selection lists available in the U.S., on various subject and grade areas, as well as in general. The addresses of each organization publishing the aids are given, as are the prices. The annotations are brief but pointed.

3581. "Children's book illustration through the ages," *Print,* New York, Vol. 18, Mar.–Apr., 1964, pp. 24–29. NNY.

In reviewing the Pitz book (see 4214), the critic passes over the highlights in the history of children's book illustration, from Caxton's *Aesop* to Marcia Brown. Some 22 illustrations are reproduced.

3582. "Children's book needs in a changing society," *Publishers' weekly,* New York, Vol. 190, July 25, 1966, pp. 35–38. DLC, NNY.

A conference at Tarrytown, New York brought together juvenile editors, reading specialists, librarians, and educators to discuss the problem of children and books in a changing world. The conference speeches are excerpted here in brief.

3583. "Children's book week; A.L.A. Resolution," *ALA bulletin,* Chicago. Vol. 13, No. 3, July, 1919, p. 388. DLC, NNY.

The official record of the resolution made by the Children's Librarians Section, indicating support of the idea for a children's book week as proposed by the American Booksellers Association. See also 3584.

3584. "Children's book week—a national movement," *ALA bulletin,* Chicago. Vol. 15, No. 4, July, 1921, p. 172. DLC, NNY.

A report on the meeting at the annual conference, which was devoted to the new book week celebrations, as viewed by three persons: Frederic G. Melcher, Clara W. Hunt, and Bertha E. Mahoney.

3585. "Children's Book Week Issue," *Wilson library bulletin,* 1919 ff. DLC, NNY.

At first, the November issue contained articles related to Book Week, but later this was changed to the October issue, so that notices of activities could reach libraries well before the actual Week. Often, there were suggestions as to how Book Week could be celebrated.

3586. *Children's books.* Washington, D.C., Library of Congress, 1964 ff. Annual.

An annual selective list usually limited to about 200 titles, arranged by subject and annotated.

3587. "Children's books," *Booklist and subscription books bulletin,* Chicago, Vol. 1 ff. Jan., 1905 ff.

This semi-monthly review of the books is published by the American Library Association. The current output of children's books is reviewed by regular and special advisory staff. Indications are given as to the suitability of purchase by all libraries, only by large libraries, or by special libraries. Each book reviewed is also classified and given subject headings. There is also a section reviewing books of interest to young adults. Reference works are reviewed in the *Subscription Books Bulletin Section.*

3588. "Children's books and the Library of Congress," *Horn book,* Boston, Vol. 38, No. 3, June, 1962, p. 239. DLC, IYL, NNY.

An editorial prodding the Congressional committee into some move to organize the children's book collection in the Library of Congress.

3589. *Children's books in the United States.* Chicago, American Library Association, 1929. 32p. DLC, IYL, NNY.

"Prepared for the World Federation of Education Associations in conference at Geneva July 25–Aug. 3, 1929, by the Committee on Library Work with Children, ALA." An annotated booklist of some 200 titles, preceded by an article "Children's books and the American public library," by Anne Carroll Moore.

3590. "Children's books of the year," *North American review,* Boston, Vol. 102, No. 210, 1866, pp. 236–249. DLC, NNY.

Reviews of some editions of Mother Goose, a *Little Prudy* book, and books by Oliver Optic, Kingston, Jane Andrews, Sophie May and others.

3591. *Children's books suggested as holiday gifts.* New York, The New York Public Library, 1920. Annual in November. IYL, DLC, current lists only; NNY, complete set.

Selected from the year's production, arranged into general types of books and subjects, and annotated. In honor of the 50th anniversary of the central building, and the opening of the first holiday exhibit in the Central Children's Room, a retrospective list was prepared in 1960, to include some titles from 1910–1960.

3592. "Children's books with fangs," *Free world,* New York, Vol. 10, Dec., 1945, pp. 14–16. DLC, NNY.

"For the future security of his children, every parent, through the International Education Organization must urge elimination of biased books from schools everywhere if he would have his child live in a world of unbiased people." Although he cites specific examples from Japan, Russia, Italy and Germany, the author (anonymous) states that each country has such books available for children, and that the U.S. is no exception.

3593. *Children's catalog; a catalog of 3310 selected books for public and school libraries.* 10th ed. New York, H. W. Wilson, 1961. 915p. Supplements. DLC, NNY. 11th ed. in preparation, 1967. $17.00. (1st ed., 1909.)

This selected and annotated catalog was the basic tool used by libraries for many years. It is now usually used in conjunction with other selection aids. Inclusions are made on the basis of reports from a selected group of school and public libraries. The entries are arranged by the decimal classification system, with fiction arranged by author. Index. An indispensable tool.

3594. "The children's department," *A survey of libraries in the United States, conducted by the American Library Association.* Chicago, ALA, 1927. Vol. 3, pp. 3–103. DLC, NNY.

A summary of the results of a major survey, covering points from "Registration," to "Personal work with children," to "Work with schools," etc. Of some historical interest.

3595. "Children's librarians' section," *ALA bulletin,* Chicago, Vol. 1, No. 4, July, 1907, pp. 288–293. DLC, NNY.

This conference was chiefly devoted to methods to be used by libraries working with schools to encourage the use of "real literature."

3596. "Children's Library Association," *Library journal,* New York, Vol. 14, No. 3, Mar., 1889, pp. 90–91. DLC, NNY.

At this point, the children's library begun by Mrs. Hanaway moved out of the George Bruce Library. However, it was noted that "the work has proved so interesting that it is not improbable that, should the trustees of the Free Circulating Library have new opportunities in the way of branch buildings, they may plan for a children's room with a separate access."

3597. "Children's Library Association," *Library notes,* Boston, Vol. 1, No. 4, Mar., 1887, pp. 261–266. DLC, NNY.

The history and constitution of the children's library founded by Mrs. Hanaway in New York.

3598. "The children's library in New York, and its constitution," *Library journal,* New York, Vol. 12, No. 6, June, 1887, pp. 224–225. DLC, NNY.

This gives the formal constitution of this early children's library considered by many to be the first in the U.S.

3599. *Children's library yearbook.* American Library Association, Section on Library Work with Children, Chicago. No. 1, 1929–No. 4, 1932. Annual. DLC, NNY.

Only four numbers of this yearbook appeared, but each contains valuable information on the progress of library work with children during that time, as well as many articles on children's book publishing, book week, etc. For a similar type of yearbook covering school libraries of the same period, see *School Library Yearbook.*

3600. "Children's literature," *Bibliographic index,* New York, H. W. Wilson Co., Vol. 1, 1937–1942; Vol. 2, 1943–1946; Vol. 3, 1947–1950; Vol. 4, 1951–1955; Vol. 5, 1956–1959; Vol. 6, 1960–1962; thereafter, annual compilations. DLC, NNY.

These volumes bring together the quarterly (now semi-annual) issues of the *Index.* Under the above title, there is perhaps the most complete listing of children's book lists printed in the U.S., including those in book and pamphlet form, as well as those in periodical articles.

3601. *Children's reading list on arts and artists.* Boston, Boston Book Co., 1900. 14p. (Bulletin of Bibliography Pamphlets, 8.) NNY.

Arranged by subjects and including parts of books as well as complete ones, on all of the arts.

3602. Childs, Mary C. "Book Week and the Children's Book Council," *Elementary english,* Vol. 40, Apr., 1963, pp. 461–463. DLC.

The executive secretary of the Children's Book Council explains the work and publicity which are behind the spread of Children's Book Week.

3603. Chubb, Percival. "The child as a literary personage," *Kindergarten review,* Springfield, Mass., Vol. 20, No. 1, Sept., 1909, p. 6. DLC.

Oral literature, particularly nursery rhymes, is needed in great quantity by the young child, to train the ear and the imaginative powers of the mind.

3604. ———. "The value and place of fairy stories in the education of children," *National education association, addresses and proceedings,* 44th Annual Conference, 1905, pp. 871–879. DLC.

An intelligently stated rebuttal of the arguments of the anti-fairy tale adherents.

3605. Cianciolo, Patricia Jean. "Children's literature can affect coping behavior," *Personnel and guidance journal,* Washington, Vol. 43, May, 1965, pp. 897–903. DLC, NNY.

"Books can provide a source of psychological relief from the various pressures and concerns that stem from the things that happen to children . . . Books that are used for therapeutic purposes should exemplify good literature and should be used in a manner that is based on sound educational and psychological principles." Following the text is a list of 80 titles of chlidren's books dealing with special problems, and a bibliography of further reading on the therapeutic use of books.

3606. Claremont Reading Conference. *Yearbook.* Claremont, California, Claremont Colleges, 1937 ff. Annual.

Each year this conference concentrates on some theme related to reading, most often that of children and young people. To cite some examples, the themes of the past five conferences were: "Beyond literacy," 1966; "On becoming a reader," 1965; "Reading and emerging cultural values," 1964; "Readers for the twenty-first century," 1963; "Reading is the process of making discriminative responses," 1962.

3607. Clark, C. H. and Latimer, Louise P. "The taxpayer and reading for young people," *Library journal,* New York, Vol. 59, Jan. 1, 1934, pp. 9–15. DLC, NNY.

The supervisor of work with schools and the director of work with children from the Washington, D.C. Public Library contend that the trend to have a library in each school was not wise and economical because public libraries were already meeting the demand for books quite adequately. They felt the trend would result in makeshift libraries giving poor service; that the public library would be hampered in its work; that cultural reading would be sacrificed to school problems. See entry 3725.

3608. Cleary, Florence Damon. *Blueprints for better reading; school programs for promoting skill and interest in reading.* New York, H. W. Wilson, 1957. 216p. DLC.

3609. ———. "Why children read," *Wilson bulletin,* New York, Vol. 14, Oct., 1939, pp. 119–126. DLC, NNY.

Results of an extensive reading interest survey undertaken in Detroit. The major conclusion was that children pretty much read what materials are put in their sight, particularly in the home.

3610. Cleveland Public Library. Children's Department. *Children's books for holiday giving and year 'round reading.* Cleveland, The Library, Annual.

An annotated list arranged by general age levels.

3611. Cody, Sarah Isabella. *A study of the summer reading club as a recreational reading guidance method with children.* Cleveland, Western Reserve University, 1958. 172p. Thesis.

3612. Coggins, Herbert L. "More red blood in Mother Goose," *North American review,* New York, Vol. 233, May, 1932, pp. 465–470. DLC, NNY.

"The real danger of the nursery censor is not only the possible spoilage from a literary standpoint, but also that he might prevent the filling in and rounding out of our reading to conform to the important ideals of life that have been overlooked."

3613. Colburn, Evangeline. *Books and reading for pupils of the intermediate grades.* Chicago, University of Chicago, 1942. 167p. (Laboratory Schools Publication No. 10). DLC.

Developmental reading and the enrichment of classroom teaching, approached through the use of the school library. The annotated list is dated, but the general suggestions are still valid.

3614. ———. *A library for the intermediate grades.* Chicago, University of Chicago Press, 1930. 150p. (Publications of the Laboratory Schools, No. 1). DLC.

Based on the voluntary reading choices of children using the library in the University of Chicago School. The titles are arranged in subject groups appealing to the young reader, and are annotated.

3615. Colby, J. Rose. *Literature and life in school.* Boston, Houghton, 1906, 229p. DLC, NNY.

"A plea for the presence of literature in school, from the first day to the last."

3616. Colby, Jean Poindexter. *The children's book field.* New York, Pellegrini and Cudahy, 1952. 246p. IYL, DLC, NNY.

An earlier version of the work listed below.

3617. ———. *Writing, illustrating and editing children's books.* New York, Hastings House, 1966. 320p. $6.95. DLC.

A practical manual, discussing not so much the actual writing of children's books, as the editing, revising, designing, illustrating, printing and binding of them.

3618. Cole, Doris M. *et al. The reading of children.* Syracuse, New York, Syracuse University, School of Library Science, 1964. 48p. (Frontiers of Librarianship, 7). DLC.

The report of the 7th annual symposium on children's reading, sponsored by the Library School. The three major papers were by Ruth Hill Viguers, Paul A. Witty, and Sara Krentzman Srygley.

3619. Cole, Maud D. "Children's rare book treasures," *AB bookman's yearbook 1956.* Newark, Antiquarian Bookman, 1956, pp. 28–30. NNY, DLC.

A talk given by a librarian to a group of children concerning some early types of children's reading materials, and some of the specific books from the rare children's book collections of the New York Public Library. She also gives directions for making a hornbook.

3620. Coleman, A. *Publicity methods to be used in the elementary school library.* Kent, Ohio, Kent State University, 1955, 125p. Thesis.

3621. "Collections of rare children's books," *Library journal,* New York, Vol. 63, Jan. 1, 1938, pp. 20–21; Feb. 1, 1938, pp. 105–107; Mar. 1, 1938, pp. 192–193; Apr. 1, 1938, pp. 360–362; May 1, 1938, pp. 452–453; June 1, 1938, pp. 536–537. DLC, NNY.

A symposium which covered the major private and public collections of early and rare children's books. The first concerns the Library of Congress, the second the H. E. Huntington Library, the third Wilbur Macey Stone's collection, the fourth the Carnegie Library of Pittsburgh, the fifth the C. M. Hewins' collection at Hartford, and the sixth the New York Public Library.

3622. Conkling, Grace Hazard. *Imagination and children's reading.* 2nd ed. Northampton, Mass., Hampshire Bookshop, 1922. 31p. DLC.

An inspirational discussion of the best imaginative books available for children.

3623. Connor, Mary Ann. *A quantitative analysis of science material in five editions of the Children's Catalog.* Cleveland, Western Reserve University, 1958. 66p. Thesis.

3624. Conover, Mary. "What can the library best do for children," *Public libraries,* Chicago, Vol. 4, July, 1899, pp. 317–320. DLC, NNY.

The author answers her question by relating the history of work with children in the Detroit Public Library.

3625. Cook, Elizabeth M. *Across the drawbridge and into the castle (in which a plan for a summer reading program in East Aurora is unfolded.)* Geneseo, N.Y., State University Teachers College, 1958. 88p. Thesis.

3626. Copeland, Frances V. *Children's literature as it reflects life in the Near East.* Seattle, University of Washington, 1954. 60p. Thesis.

3627. Cory, Patricia B. *School library services for deaf children.* Washington, Volta Bureau, 1960. 142p. (Lexington School for the Deaf, Education Series Book 2). DLC, NNY.

Some of the special techniques of working with deaf children and books are discussed here. The author suggests specific books which have proved successful in this work, and mentions many additional sources of ideas.

3628. Council of Chief State School Officers. *A consolidated, classified and annotated list of recommended books on science, mathematics and foreign languages which may be purchased by elementary and secondary schools with funds made available by the National Defense Education Act.* Hillside, N.J., Baker & Taylor, 1963. 82p. DLC.

A list compiled by the Council with the advice and assistance of the National Science Foundation, the U.S. Office of Education and other educational organizations.

3629. ———. *Responsibilities of state departments of education for school library services: A policy statement.* Washington, The Council, 1961, 21p.

3630. Countryman, G. A. "The school libraries of the United States." International Congress of Libraries and Bibliography, 2nd; *Actas y trabajos, Vol. 3;* Madrid, Librería de Julián Barbazán, 1936; pp. 226–236. DLC.

A review of school library development in the U.S. presented to the Congress (in English).

3631. Cowing, Agnes. "What shall we read now?" 5th ed. rev. New York, H. W. Wilson, 1926. 4 vols. Unp.

Based on the original list compiled at the Pratt Institute children's library. This is arranged according to age groups with some brief annotations.

3632. Cowing, Herbert L. "The intermediate collection for young people in the public library," *Library journal,* New York, Vol. 37, Apr., 1912, pp. 189–192. DLC, NNY.

One of the earliest references to young adult work in public libraries as distinctly separate from children's and adult.

3633. Cowles, Julia D. *The art of story-telling.* Chicago, A. C. McClurg, 1914. 269p. DLC.

Storytelling in the home, school, religious education class and vacation camp—why and how to tell them, and a list of selected stories to tell. Bibliography.

3634. [Craik, Dinah Maria Mulock]. "Want something to read," *Studies from life.* Leipzig, Bernhard Tauchnitz, 1961, pp. 67–86.

After reminiscences concerning her childhood reading, the author concludes: "I do think that with children brought up in a virtuous, decorous home . . . the best plan is to exclude entirely all glaring coarseness and immoralities . . . for the tone of a book has far more influence than its language."

3635. Cropper, Mary Bess. *Syllabus for teaching history of children's literature with papers on certain highlights in both England and America.* Ann Arbor, University of Michigan, 1950. 120p. Thesis.

3636. Crosby, Muriel. *Reading ladders for human relations.* Washington, American Council on Education, 1963. 242p. DLC, NNY. (Earlier editions edited by M. B. Heaton and H. B. Lewis).

A list of books which help children develop sensitivity in human relationships, and an awareness of varying value patterns. Annotated with many cross references, and a publisher, author, title index.

3637. Crothers, Samuel McChord. *Miss Muffet's Christmas party.* Boston, Houghton, 1902. NNY has reprint of an earlier copy from the private collection of George Arents.

Through the use of a story describing an imaginary party, the author introduces the titles and characters of books for children. The effect is somewhat labored.

3638. Cruzat, Gwendolyn S. *Study of the relationship between books selected by children who patronize the Negro branches of the Atlanta Public Library and their television interests.* Atlanta, Atlanta University, 1954. 52p. Thesis.

3639. Culbertson, Marjorie. *McGuffy readers and their influence on modern education and readers.* Kent, Ohio, Kent State University, 1959. 103p. Thesis.

3640. Cummins, Alice C. *Mother Goose.* New York, Pratt Institute Library School, 1952. 38p. Thesis.

"A study of one hundred editions of Mother Goose."

3641. Cundiff, Ruby E. *101 plus magazines for schools.* 4th ed. Nashville, Tennessee, Tennessee Book Co., 1964. 24p. DLC.

An alphabetical and annotated list of magazines for children in elementary and secondary grades.

3642. —— and Barbara Webb. *Story-telling for you.* Yellow Springs, Ohio, Antioch Press, 1957. 103p. DLC.

Details on selection, preparation and performance together with four sample stories and commentary on specific pitfalls to watch for in presentation. Selected bibliography.

3643. Currier, D. L. "Services to youth in United States Information Libraries abroad," *Top of the news,* Chicago, Vol. 7, Oct., 1950, pp. 23–28. DLC, NNY.

The types of book collections and the activities related to children's books which are available in a number of these libraries. Most of the children's services in USIS libraries have now been discontinued.

3644. Curry, Charles Madison and E. E. Clippinger. *Children's literature.* Chicago, Rand McNally, 1927. 693p. DLC, NNY.

"A textbook of sources for teachers and teacher training classes." This first appeared in 1920, and was for many years the standard text. Bibliography, book list and index.

3645. Curtis, John Gould. "Saving the infant class from hell," *Scribner's magazine,* New York, Vol. 86, No. 5, Nov., 1929, pp. 564–570. DLC, NNY.

A humorous essay on the Sunday-school literature prevalent in the 19th century giving some examples of the threats and consequences which would befall children who misbehaved.

3646. Cushing, Helen Grant. *Children's song index; an index to more than 22,000 songs in 189 collections comprising 222 volumes.* New York, H. W. Wilson, 1936. 798p. DLC, NNY.

This is included for the numerous accompaniments listed for Mother Goose and nursery rhymes, and for well-known children's poems.

3647. Dalgliesh, Alice. "Books for young people," *Saturday review,* New York, 1952. DLC, NNY.

Known previously as the *Saturday Review of Literature* this periodical has included reviews of children's books quite regularly in all of its long career. Miss Dalgliesh has been the reviewer now for a number of years, and usually prefaces her column with well thought out comments about the general qualities of the books of the particular season she is reviewing. The column appears about four times each year.

3648. ———. *First experiences with literature.* New York, Scribner's, 1932. 162p. DLC, NNY.

A skimming over of the picture books, poetry, stories and fairy tales with children enjoy, and some methods of using this literature with children.

3649. Dalphin, Marcia. *Light the candles!* Boston, Horn Book, 1960. 22p. $1.00.

This was first compiled in 1942. This edition was revised by Anne Thaxter Eaton. It is a classified and annotated list of materials to use during the Christmas season.

3650. Dana, John Cotton. "Children's reading: What some of the teachers say." *Library journal,* New York, Vol. 22, No. 4, Apr., 1897, pp. 187–190. DLC, NNY.

One of the lead articles in the annual "School number." This discusses the results of a questionnaire Mr. Dana had submitted to Denver school teachers, regarding the free reading of children in their schools. It is followed by an araticle on school libraries.

3651. ———, et al. "The school department," *Modern American library economy . . . , Vol. 1.* Woodstock, Vermont, The Elm Tree Press, 1910, pp. 283–560. DLC, NNY.

This is Part V of a very lengthy treatise published originally in the form of pamphlets. Its five sections treat of: the "school department" room (in reality the children's room of the public library); a course of study in the use of the library for normal school pupils by Marjary L. Gilson; the picture collection; school libraries by Grace Thompson and Mr. Dana; and a course of study on literature for children by Julia S. Harron, Corinne Bacon and Mr. Dana. All examples are drawn from the work carried out by the Newark, N.J. Public Library.

3652. Darling, Richard L. "Book reviews ninety years ago," *Library journal,* New York, Vol. 86, May, 1961, pp. 1942–1944. DLC, NNY.

An article based on the research in the author's doctoral dissertation (see 3653). The general conclusion was: "Reviewing of children's books today may be more systematic but it is basically no better than it was in the post-Civil War era."

3653. ———. *The reviewing of children's books 1865–1881.* Ann Arbor, Michigan, University of Michigan, 1960. 548p. DLC has on microfilm.

A doctoral dissertation concerning the extent and quality of children's book reviewing in the U.S., chiefly in the following periodicals: *Atlantic Monthly, Harper's Monthly, Literary World, Nation, North American Review, Putnam's Magazine,* and *Scribner's Magazine.* See also the matching thesis by Dorothy Erazmus (3710). Mr. Darling's dissertation was published by the R. R. Bowker Company in 1968 under the title of *The Rise of Children's Book Reviewing in America 1865–1881.*

3654. Davidson, Gustav. *First editions in American juvenilia and problems in their identification.* Chicago, Normandie House, 1939. 29p. DLC.

An attempt at outlining a set of standards to be used in determining the genuineness of a first edition.

3655. Davidson, S. G. *et al. Model library of books for deaf children.* Philadelphia, American Association to Promote Teaching of Speech to the Deaf, 19 ? . 18p.

3656. Davis, Louise, *et al.* "Book reviewers' summit conference; the big four speak," *Library journal,* New York, Vol. 88, May 15, 1963, pp. 2067–2080. DLC, NNY.

Papers presented at a conference of the New York Library Association. Participants were Zena Bailey, representing the *Bulletin of the Center for Children's Books;* Ruth Hill Viguers of *The Horn Book Magazine;* Helen Kinsey of the *Booklist* (ALA), and Louise Davis of *School Library Journal.* Each discussed the policies, procedures and problems of children's book reviewing in relation to her own publication, and in general.

3657. Davis, Mary Gould. "The children's room in the American public library." International Congress of Libraries and Bibliography, 2nd; *Actas y trabajos, Vol. 3;* Madrid, Librería de Julián Barbazán, 1936; pp. 248–253. DLC.

In her report to the Congress concerning work with children in the American public library, Miss Davis stressed the unique philosophy of service which it acted on: the free distribution of reading materials which had been selected because they were good literature and because they pleased, with no ulterior motives of teaching, moralizing or preaching.

3658. Dawson, Mildred A. *Children, books and reading.* Newark, N.J., International Reading Association, 1964. 150p. $2.50. NNY.

A collection of speeches and papers most related in part with the teaching of good reading habits. There are bibliographies for most of the chapters.

3659. —— and Louise Pfeiffer. *A treasury of books for the primary grades.* San Francisco, Howard Chandler, 1959. 32p.

3660. De Cordova, Frances M. *Elementary library; its value as a resourceful aid to teaching.* Denton, Texas State College for Women, 1951. 85p. Thesis.

3661. Deason, Hilary J. *The AAAS science book list for children.* Washington, D.C., American Association for the Advancement of Science, 1963. 224p. $1.50. (Paper).

This list is revised every few years and comprises the latest accurate children's books on the subjects related to science and mathematics. It is arranged by Dewey decimal system, and annotated.

3662. Delany, Jack J. *The school librarian; human relations problems.* Hamden, Conn., Shoe String Press, 1961. 183p. DLC, NNY.

A manual designed to give practical advice on solving the problems which can develop in human relationships in the school library setting. There are references given for each chapter.

3663. Depew, Ollie. *Children's literature by grades and types.* Boston, Ginn, 1938. 706p. DLC, NNY.

A history and anthology designed to serve as a textbook in college or university courses on children's literature. Examples are given for each grade and type.

3664. Detroit Public Library. *John S. Newberry gift collection of Kate Greenaway presented to the library.* Detroit, Friends of the Detroit Public Library, 1959. 24p.

3665. Devereaux, Sister M. Cecil. "Children's literature; an annotated bibliography of books and periodical articles about children's literature and reading," *ALA Children's library yearbook,* Chicago, No. 4, 1932, pp. 125–68. DLC, NNY.

A very fine annotated bibliography, divided into six parts: General works, History, Study and Teaching, Poetry, Writing for Children, Illustrating for Children. This last named is particularly useful in locating works about individual illustrators. There is a subject index to the whole bibilography which breaks down into more specific subdivisions.

3666. DiMuccio, Sister M. R. *The relationship between elementary school children's choices and their parents' choices in children's leisure reading.* Los Angeles, Immaculate Heart College, 1960. (Thesis).

3667. Dinkel, Robert M. "The influence of nursery literature on child development," *Sociology and social research,* Los Angeles, Vol. 31, Mar., 1947, pp. 285–290. NNY.

This educator was against fantasy and fairy tales for the young child. He suggests methods of writing stories which "can assist in the socialization of the child."

3668. Dixon, Dorothy G. *Individual patterns in reading development.* Chicago, University of Chicago, University of Chicago, 1953. 193p. Thesis.

3669. Dober, V. D. *An analysis of the social life and customs of the Southern Appalachians as reflected in selected children's books.* Washington, Catholic University of America, 1957. 80p. Thesis.

3670. Dobler, Lavinia G. *The Dobler world directory of youth periodicals.* New York, Schulte Pub. Co., 1966. $3.00. DLC, NNY.

An annotated list of more than 400 periodicals arranged into two groups: those published in the U.S. and those published in other countries in English and foreign languages. Information includes age levels, interest, scope, editor, publishers, price. There is also a title index and a fine introductory chapter by Muriel Fuller, on youth magazines in the U.S.

3671. Dodson, Marguerite A. *An appraisal of biographies for children published between 1935 and 1951.* Pittsburgh, Carnegie Institute of Technology, 1952. 36p. Thesis.

3672. Dohlen, Elizabeth von. *A study and comparison of the biographies in four series of books for children.* Chapel Hill, University of North Carolina, 1954. 93p. Thesis.

3673. Dougherty, Joanna Foster. *The lively art of picture books.* Weston, Conn., Weston Woods Studio, 1964. 57 minutes, color.

This film was commissioned by the Children's Services Division of ALA, and produced by Morton Schindel. Miss Dougherty wrote the script and directed. The film is an attempt to present to the lay audience a concept of the picture book as an artistic expression. The works of many artists are shown and discussed in brief, and those of four illustrators are shown in greater detail: these are Ezra Jack Keats, Barbara Cooney, Robert McCloskey and Maurice Sendak. The latter three are shown expressing their personal reasons for working in this field, and the ways in which they set out to illustrate children's books. *The Snowy Day* by Mr. Keats and *Time of Wonder* by Mr. McCloskey, both picture books which have won the Caldecott award, are shown in full, with the text given by a narrator. This is done by a technique perfected by Mr. Schindel, called iconographic, which he used in putting dozens of favorite U.S. picture books on to films.

3674. Douglas, Alice W. *Religious books for Protestant children; an annotated, selected bibliography.* Cleveland, Western Reserve University, 1954. 116p. Thesis.

3675. Douglas, Mary Teresa Peacock. *School libraries for today and tomorrow.* Chicago, ALA, 1945. 43p. (Planning for libraries, 3). DLC, NNY.

A statement on the functions and standards of school libraries which served as a guide for postwar planning. The Committee formulating the standards was composed of many important figures in the school library movement in the U.S.

3676. ———. *The teacher-librarian's handbook,* 2nd ed. Chicago, ALA, 1949. 166p. IYL, DLC.

First published in 1941, this became one of the most widely used handbooks on working with children and books in the school. While its main purpose is practical, it also contains a chapter on the philosophy behind this work. This has been translated into many langauges. Some of the editions are noted in 362, 2543, 2571, 2766. The author has also written a more up-to-date, general work on school libraries, for UNESCO (see 10).

3677. Duff, Annis. *Bequest of wings; a family's pleasure with books.* New York, Viking, 1944. 204p. DLC, IYL, NNY.

A readable book by a literate parent which tells how books, poetry, music and pictures can be made an effective accompaniment to everyday living. The author is presently Children's Editor of Viking Press. The book is really the record of her personal experience with her own children.

3678. ———. "Literary heritage of childhood," *Wilson library bulletin,* New York, Vol. 33, Apr., 1959, pp. 563–570. DLC, NNY.

This well-known editor and commentator on children and their reading here discusses what makes a children's book great, and the importance of introducing this great literature to the child in the home beginning with nursery rhymes.

3679. ———. *Longer flight; a family grows up with books.* New York, Viking, 1955. 269p. DLC, IYL, NNY.

Mrs. Duff carries on the personal record of her family's reading, told first in *Bequest of Wings.* She describes "the continuation of happy companionship in exploring the delights of reading and its allied pleasures—the theatre, museums, the exchange of ideas, the satisfactin of growing into knowledge and understanding of the world and its people." The appendix gives citation of all books discussed.

3680. Dunn, Fannie Wyche. *Interest factors in primary reading material.* New York, Teachers College, Columbia University, 1921. 70p. (Contributions to Education, No. 113).

Experimentation and report on an educational study of childen's reading with charts and graphs.

3681. Dutton, E. P. "A primer for baby bibliophiles; with sundry remarks on Chap-books, Hornbooks and other matters of interest to young and old." New York, Dutton, 1915. Unp. NNY.

A small pamphlet describing the joys and possibilities in collecting old books of this type.

3682. Eakin, M. L. *Censorship in public high school libraries.* New York, Columbia University, 1948. 102p. Thesis.

3683. Eakin, Mary K. *Good books for children published 1948–1961.* Rev. and enl. Chicago, University of Chicago Press, 1962. 362p. $6.50, paper covers, $1.95. DLC, NNY.

Approximately 100 titles per year were chosen from among the reviews of the *Bulletin of the Center for Children's Books* (see 3536). The introduction discusses the criteria for selection and the methods of analyzing books for children.

3684. ———. *The reading of books from publishers' reprints series by children in the elementary grades.* Chicago, University of Chicago, 1954. 116p. Thesis.

3685. ———. *Subject index to books for intermediate grades.* 3rd ed., Chicago, ALA, 1963. 308p. $7.50.

A list of 1800 books for grades 4 through 6, arranged by subjects and annotated. Index.

3686. ——— and Eleanor Merritt. *Subject index to books for primary grades.* 2nd ed. Chicago, ALA, 1961. 167p. $4.50. DLC, NNY.

Text and trade books are indexed in this standard tool for school libraries. Arrangement is alphabetical and is preceded by a list of the books indexed. Poetry and folk tales are not included since they are well indexed in other tools.

3687. Earle, Alice Morse. *Child-life in colonial days.* New York, Macmillan, 1899. 418p. DLC, NNY.

There are a number of chapters pertaining to early children's books in the U.S.: Hornbook and primer, pp. 117–132; School-books, pp. 133–149; Diaries and commonplace books, pp. 163–175; Religious books, pp. 248–263; Story and picture books, pp. 264–304. Each is illustrated with many black and white reproductions.

3688. Easterbook, Elizabeth M. *Critical analysis of the sources of information about children's books published during the years 1861–1865, including a list of the books for children published during these years.* Chicago, University of Chicago, 1952. 176p. Thesis.

3689. Eastman, Linda A. *The child, the school and the library.* New York, Reprinted from the *Library journal,* 1896. 22p. NNY.

This is an account of attempts at coordinating school and public library service, mostly in the Cleveland area. The author was a leading children's librarian of the time and was influential in furthering the cause of good children's libraries.

3690. ———. "The children's room and the children's librarian." *Public libraries,* Chicago, Vol. 3, Dec., 1898, pp. 417–420. DLC, NNY.

The physical space of the children's library is considered here at length as well as the qualities of the good children's librarian.

3691. ———. "Methods of work for children: The Cleveland Library League," *Library journal,* New York, Vol. 22, No. 11, Nov., 1897, pp. 686–687. DLC, NNY.

One of the early attempts at making the public library more appealing to children.

3692. Eaton, Anne Thaxter. *Reading with children.* New York, Viking, 1940. 354p. DLC, IYL, NNY.

This is a lively and graceful statement of the child's right to read books of high standards. It is also a testament to the fact that he does read them. The author was long a school librarian of note (Lincoln School, Teacher's College, Columbia University) and an anthologist and lecturer of distinction. An invaluable book for the new librarian but indispensable also to those who teach children's literature.

3693. ———. *School library service.* Chicago, ALA, 1923. 44p.

3694. ———. *Treasure for the taking.* Rev. ed. New York, Viking, 1957. 322p. $4.00. DLC, IYL, NNY.

Designed as a supplement to the author's *Reading with Children,* this is the 2nd edition of an excellent list by the former librarian of The Lincoln School, New York City, who was for many years on the faculty of St. John's University in Brooklyn. She is an anthologist of note whose book annotations are sparkling and informed. Though revised in 1957, most of the titles listed are still currently in print. The books are grouped by subject for the use of parents who may expect to find them in children's libraries. Publisher and date is given for each title but not price.

3695. Eaton, Jeanette. "Pleasures and perplexities of writing authentic biography for the young," *ALA bulletin,* Chicago, Vol. 27, Dec. 15, 1933, pp. 777–782. DLC, NNY.

A paper read at the annual conference of the School Libraries Section, ALA. The author is a noted writer of children's books, especially biographies.

3696. Eddins, Doris Kerns. *A critical evaluation of a selected list of children's literature.* East Lansing, Michigan State University, 1956, DLC has on microfilm.

3697. Edmonds, Mary D. "Literature and children," *North American review,* Vol. 244, No. 1, Autumn 1937, pp. 148–61. DLC, NNY.

"My plea is for more literature and less of what is, in form at least, the book written to project a thesis." This author felt keenly the lack of oral literature with its deep and personal effect.

3698. "Education market for books other than textbooks," *Publishers' weekly,* New York, Vol. 177, May 23, 1960, pp. 10–17. DLC, NNY.

A report on a panel discussion of the American Book Publishers Council regarding wider and wider use of trade books in situations usually covered by textbooks. A number of statistics are quoted to illustrate this trend, now even more pronounced.

3699. Edwards, Louise Betts. "The literary cult of the child," *Critic,* New York, Vol. 39, 1901, pp. 166–170. DLC, NNY.

3700. "The effective secondary-school library," *National Association of Secondary School Principals, Bulletin,* Vol. 43, No. 250, Nov., 1959, pp. 1–190. (Entire issue). DLC, NNY.

The articles written by some of the best-known experts in the field, cover every aspect of junior and senior school library work: physical design and layout, relations with the teachers and students, programs, personnel, administration, selection of materials, etc.

3701.   *Elementary english.* National Council of Teachers of English, 508 S. Sixth St., Champaign, Illinois, 61822. Monthly Oct. through May. 1924. Subscription: $5.00 a year DLC, NNY.

This professional journal is related more to the teaching of reading, but it contains many fine articles on the history and criticism of children's literature. Children's books are reviewed on a regular basis in each issue. Actually, from the period 1924–1947 it was known as *Elementary English Review* and was edited by C. C. Certain of Detroit, having no official connection with NCTE.

3702.   "The elementary school library," *ALA bulletin,* Chicago, Vol. 56, No. 2, Feb., 1962, pp. 99–126. DLC, NNY, IYL.

This issue devoted space to six articles on the problems, trends and organization of the school library. Mary V. Gaver's article, "Research on elementary school libraries," includes information on more than fifty research projects then in process throughout the country.

3703.   Ellinger, B. D. "Literature for Head Start classes," *Elementary english,* Chicago, Vol. 43, May, 1966, pp. 453–459. DLC.

An article describing the types of books suitable for use with this federal program of education for preschool children. An annotated list of books is included.

3704.   Ellsworth, Ralph Eugene. *The school library.* New York, Center for Applied Research in Education, 1965. 116p. (The library in education). $3.95. DLC.

The author is "concerned primarily with the secondary school, although much of what he recommends is applicable to the elementary school." This is a series of specific recommendation rather than a study of the status quo.

3705.   Elmendorf, Mrs. T. H. "Great literature and the little children." Sawyer, Harriet P. *The library and its contents.* New York, H. W. Wilson, 1925, pp. 135–140.

Truly great literature has no age limits, states this critic. She recommended more reading aloud and storytelling in the home. This article first appeared in the *Chautauquan.*

3706.   Emerson, Laura S. *Storytelling, the art and the purpose.* Grand Rapids, Mich., Zonder-Van Publishing House, 1959. 181p.

3707.   Emery, J. W. "School libraries in the United States," *The library, the school and the child.* Toronto, Macmillan, 1917, pp. 97–116. DLC, NNY.

This chapter as well as one on classroom libraries and another on public services for children are devoted to the historical developments in the U.S., as compared with Canada.

3708.   Emery, Raymond C. and Margaret B. Houshower. *High interest—easy reading for junior and senior high school reluctant readers.* Champaign, Illinois, National Council of Teachers of English, 1966. 40p. $1.00.

A pamphlet describing the reading interests of this type of reader, and a list of suggested books according to interest level and reading difficulty.

3709.   Emery, Susan L. "Children's books in the public library," *Donahoe's magazine,* Boston, Vol. 44, Dec., 1900, pp. 532–540. NNY.

A rather sanctimonious article questioning why there were so many children's books by Protestant and other religious writers in the public library, and so few by Catholic writers.

3710.   Erazmus, Dorothy. *The reviewing of children's books 1882–1890.* Ann Arbor, Mich., University of Michigan, 1956. 174p. Thesis.

3711.   Ersted, Ruth and Mildred L. Batchelder. "Education for library service to children and youth." Berelson, Bernard. *Education for librarianship.* Chicago, ALA, 1949, pp. 150–169. DLC, NNY.

Miss Ersted presented the title paper at the Library Conference, University of Chicago Graduate Library School, August, 1948, and Miss Batchelder reported on the discussion following the presentation. The gist of the report was that there was not enough being done in special training and that the literature on the subject was woefully inadequate.

3712.   Esenwein, Joseph B. and Marietta Stockard. *Children's stories and how to tell them.* Springfield, Mass., Home Correspondence School, (1917). 352p. DLC.

Just what the title suggests. The major portion, pp. 127–327, is a list of stories by categories, types, subjects, etc. There is an index.

3713.   Estes, Mayme. *Book reviewing adequacy of certain periodicals for the selector of children's books.* Denton, Texas State College for Women, 1951. 61p. Thesis.

3714. Evans, Ernestine. "Trends in children's books," *New republic,* New York, Vol. 48, Nov. 10, 1926, pp. 336–339. DLC, NNY.

". . . in the field of children's books, inhabited by teachers, librarians and publishers, parents and children, there is an air of excitement and a lively exchange of ideas that makes one wish Ruskin were alive." The author then characterizes some of the trends most evident in the contemporary children's books.

3715. Evans, Margaret. "Printing of children's books," *Horn book,* Boston, Vol. 11, No. 4, July–Aug., 1935, pp. 214–222. DLC, IYL, NNY.

Although many children's books are lavishly illustrated and printed on expensive paper, very few are notable for their quality of design and format. This critic points out the pioneer work done by Helen Gentry of Holiday House, and urges children's librarians, parents and teachers to be more observant of the overall looks, rather than be taken in by the deluxe.

3716. *Explore the world with books.* New York, World Affairs Center for the U.S., 1957. 26p. IYL, NNY.

A catalog of an exhibit of more than 800 children's books. It was sponsored by the Children's Book Council and the World Affairs Center.

3717. Fadiman, Clifton. "Children's reading," *Party of one.* Cleveland, World, 1955, pp. 369–420. NNY.

This section contains five witty essays on Mother Goose, Edward Lear, Lewis Carroll, and on children's books in general, as well as an autobiographical "portrait of the author as a young reader."

3718. Faegre, Marion E. and Nora Beust. *For the children's bookshelf.* Washington, Government Printing Office, 1949. 41p. (U.S. Children's Bureau, Publication No. 304). DLC.

A selective book list, annotated and arranged by age and subject groups. This was intended for family use.

3719. Fairchild, Edwin Milton and Emma Louise Adams. "Methods of children's library work as determined by the needs of children. 2 parts," *Library journal,* New York, Vol. 22, No. 10, Oct., 1897, pp. 19–27; pp. 28–31. DLC, NNY.

Two papers read at the Philadelphia conference. Mr. Fairchild's is very important in that it describes very specifically the aims of the children's library. Many of these aims were those eventually chosen as important by the profession. He also advocated separate children's neighborhood libraries which would be administered within the framework of the public library system. An interesting discussion of the paper is recorded on pp. 156–158.

3720. Fairchild, Salome Cutler. "What American libraries are doing for children and young people," *Library association record,* London, Vol. 5, No. 11, Nov., 1903, pp. 541–51. DLC, NNY.

An informal history of the beginnings of children's library work in the U.S. This is one of the best contemporary accounts of the pioneer work of such libraries as the Pittsburgh, Pratt (Brooklyn), Brookline (Massachusetts), New York, and others. The author mentions the unusual rotating "home libraries" for children, which were placed in selected homes in Pittsburgh for the children of the neighborhood to share.

3721. Famin, M. M. "Bibliothèques enfantines aux États-Unis," *Revue du livre,* Paris, Ire année, No. 2, Dec., 1933, pp. 43–46. DLC.

A French librarian writes of the early development of children's libraries in the U.S.

3722. *Fanfare . . . 1961–1965.* Boston, Horn Book, 1966. 4p.

A list of books selected from the reviews of the *Horn Book* for the period.

3723. Fannin, Gwendolyn Marie. *The history, growth and development of the story hour in The New York Public Library.* Atlanta, Atlanta University, 1958. 47p. Thesis.

3724. Fargo, Lucile F. *Activity book for school libraries.* Chicago, ALA. No. 1, 1938, 208p. No. 2, 1945, 239p. $2.50 each. DLC, IYL, NNY.

Suggestions for library projects for children and young adults.

3725. —— and H. S. Carpenter. "Economy or efficiency? Let the taxpayer decide," *Library journal,* New York, Vol. 59, Feb. 1, 1934, pp. 100–105. DLC, NNY.

A spirited reply to the article by Clark and Latimer (3607). This defends the central school library as a necessity in the new educational program. Instead of competing with the public library, it will create greater numbers of library users. The service rendered to schools by public libraries is not the same thing as service organized as an intrinsic part of the school curriculum.

3726. ——. *The library in the school.* 4th ed. Chicago, ALA, 1947. 405p. $4.00. IYL, DLC, NNY.

A textbook for the use of those preparing for librarianship in the secondary school. Each chapter has a bibliography and there is an index. Many sections must be up-dated by the use of supplementary material, but the basic philosophy remains the same.

3727. ———. *Preparation for school library work.* New York, Columbia University Press, 1936. 190p. (Studies in Library Service, 3). NNY.

The functions of the school library, standards and certification, professional migration and professional background, changing patterns in library education, and similar areas related to the training of school librarians.

3728. ———. *Program for elementary school library service.* Chicago, ALA, 1930. 218p.

3729. ———. *The superintendent makes a discovery. The answer to the rural school reading program.* Chicago, ALA, 1931. 32p. NNY.

Through the technique of an imaginary conversation between a school superintendent and officials of a county library system, the librarian explains how this system works in bettering rural library service. This is somewhat condescending in tone.

3730. Farmer, A. N. "What should be stressed in the Indian's character in the pioneer stories written for children?" *Public libraries,* Chicago, Vol. 27, Nov., 1922, pp. 521–525. DLC, NNY.

A discussion of the unfair one-sidedness in the portrayal of the American Indian, who is so often depicted as brutal, when in reality it was the European settlers who provoked this cruelty.

3731. Farnham, Myrtle. "German propaganda in children's library books," *Public libraries,* Chicago, Vol. 24, Jan., 1919, pp. 14–17. DLC, NNY.

This librarian contended that there were a great number of children's books in the U.S. which had been written and published as outright propaganda for the theory of German superiority. She cites a number of textual examples.

3732. *Father and son library; a practical home plan of all round development for the boy, prepared under supervision of the editorial board of the Father and Son League.* New York, The University Society, 1921. Various pagings. NNY.

Suggested book lists for father on raising boys, and for sons, on virtually every subject that might interest them. Practical but highly moralistic in tone.

3733. "Favorite books of my childhood," *Outlook,* Vol. 78, Dec. 3, 1904, pp. 833–837. DLC, NNY.

Henry Van Dyke, Alice Hegan Rice and Thomas Wentworth Higginson contributed short vignettes on their childhood reading.

3734. Faxon, Frederick Winthrop. *"Ephemeral bibelots." A bibliography of the modern chapbooks.* Boston, Boston Book Co., 1903. 26p. (Bulletin of Bibliography Pamphlets, No. 11). DLC, NNY.

A list of 229 "chapbooks, ephemerals, bibelots, Brownie magazines, Fadazines, magazettes, freak magazines which owe their origin probably to the success of the *Chap Book,* a little semi-monthly magazine which was born in Cambridge on May 15, 1894 . . ."

3735. Fay, Lucy Ella and Anne T. Eaton. *Instruction in the use of books and libraries.* Boston, Faxon, 1928. 465p. DLC, NNY.

More than any other handbook, this was used by teachers and school librarians to introduce children to the use of books and libraries. It is a model of interesting and practical style. There is a chapter on the history of children's literature and a bibliography of suggested readings.

3736. Feldman, Edith A. *Exhibit planning for children's rooms.* New York, Pratt Institute Library School, 1952. 61p. Thesis.

3737. Fenner, Phyllis Reid. *Our library.* New York, John Day, 1942. 174p. DLC, NNY.

Experiences in an elementary school library written in a chatty, informal style.

3738. ———. *The proof of the pudding: What children read.* New York, Day, 1957. 246p. DLC, IYL, NNY.

A skilled school librarian (now retired) who is also a prolific anthologist herein addresses parents and teachers about the books children read. The writing is breezy and the organization of the material is from the child to the book rather than according to the class of books discussed. The book is essentially a statement that children do read and a demonstration of what they read. A lively and informed book with full author and title index.

3739. ———. *Something shared: Children and books.* New York, Day, 1595. 234p. DLC, IYL, NNY.

Miss Fenner, whose experience with children and books is extensive and happy, has here collected a variety of essays, reminiscences, poetry, stories and cartoons that have to do with children and their reading. The book is in many short sections, each one preceded by quotations and an introduction by Miss Fenner.

3740. Fenwick, Sara I. *The education of librarians working with children in public libraries.* Chicago, University of Chicago, 1951. 191p. Thesis.

3741. ———. *New definitions of school-library service. Papers presented before the 24th Annual Conference of the Graduate Library School of the University of Chicago.* Chicago, University of Chicago, Graduate Library School, 1960. 90p. IYL, DLC, NNY. Also in: *Library quarterly,* Chicago, Vol. 30, No. 1, Jan., 1960, pp. 1–90. DLC, NNY.

The growth of school libraries reflects the spectacular growth of knowledge and of the school population. The papers of this conference set out to explore some of the implications of this growth. Titles of those directly related to school libraries were: "School and public library relationships" by Sara Innis Fenwick; "Elementary school libraries today" by Jean E. Lowrie; "Implications of the new educational goals for school libraries on the secondary level" by Margaret Hayes Grazier; "The role of the federal government in school library development" by Mary Helen Mahar; "Toward excellence in school library programs" by Frances Henne.

3742. Ferguson, E. A. *Reading and social activities of selected sixth and eighth grade children.* New York, Columbia University, 1948. 83p. Thesis.

3743. Ferris, Helen. *Writing books for boys and girls.* Garden City, New York, Doubleday, The Junior Literary Guild, 1952. 320p. IYL, DLC, NNY.

This has the subtitle "A young wings anthology of essays by 216 authors who tell how they came to write their special kind of books for young readers." It is of some interest since it contains biographical sketches of authors not included in other indexes.

3744. "Fiction in libraries and the reading of children," *Library journal,* New York, Vol. 4, Nos. 9–10, Sept.–Oct., 1879, pp. 319–367. DLC, NNY.

A set of articles, mostly by librarians, which depict better than any other contemporary source the early struggle between the two factions prevalent at the time. One side believed in free reading including light fiction; the other wished to limit the amount of fiction given to the young. For the individual points of view, see the entries under Charles Francis Adams, Jr.; Robert C. Metcalf; M. A. Bean; Martha H. Brooks; Kate Gannett Wells; S. S. Green; and T. W. Higginson.

3745. Field, Carolyn W. "Library service to children." Coplan, Kate M. and Edwin Castagna. *The library reaches out.* Dobbs Ferry, N.Y., Oceana, 1965, pp. 105–134. DLC.

The head of children's library services in the Free Library of Philadelphia here describes the qualities of good library service to children, and points out some effective means of broadening the usual aims of this service.

3746. Field, Rachel. "Reading and writing," *ALA bulletin,* Chicago, Vol. 33, Oct. 1, 1939, pp. 677–680. DLC, NNY.

An address given by this well-known author at the annual ALA conference. She pleaded for less "measuring and labeling" of children in their reading. This also contains reminiscences of her own childhood reading which was heavy and not controlled by anyone.

3747. Field, Walter Taylor. *A guide to literature for children.* Boston, Ginn, 1928. 287p. DLC, NNY. Earlier version called *Fingerposts to children's reading;* Chicago, McClurg, 1907, 1911, 1918; 275p. DLC.

A standard and much quoted work during the first 30 years of this century. In addition to a recommended booklist (updated in each edition), this contained practical advice on the teaching and evaluation of children's literature, information and criticism of illustrators and a chapter on Mother Goose.

3748. ———. "The illustrating of children's books," *Dial,* Chicago, Vol. 35, Dec. 16, 1903, pp. 457–460. DLC, NNY.

When hearing the complaints of critics about the poor state of current children's books, this author said he had only to go to his shelves and look at an example of his grandmother's reading to be reassured that children's books had improved a great deal. He did, however, take issue with the illustrations of Crane, Pyle, Charles Robinson and others, commending them for their artistry but condemning them for lack of appeal to children.

3749. Fischer, L. J. *Emotional needs of children as a basis for reading guidance.* Kent, Ohio, Kent State University, 1956. 74p. Thesis.

3750. Fitch, Viola K. *What becomes of children's librarians?* New York, Columbia University, 1950. 101p. Thesis.

3751. Fitzgerald, William A. *The family book shelf.* Patterson, N.J., St. Anthony Guild, 1954. 40p. DLC.

A graded and annotated list for home purchase and family reading selected from the Roman Catholic point of view. This is used in connection with a large book club and is revised periodically.

3752. Flandorf, Vera S. "Recent books to help children adjust to a hospital situation," *Top of the news,* Chicago, Vol. 14, Mar., 1958, pp. 35–38. DLC, NNY.

An annotated list of 50 titles which can be read to the child or given him to read to reassure him and settle his fears of going to the hospital.

3753. Fletcher, William I. "Public libraries and the young." U.S. Bureau of Education. *Public libraries in the United States of America; their history, condition and management.* Washington, The Bureau, 1876, pp. 412–418. DLC, NNY.

This important survey contains the first official recognition of the importance of work with children. It was recommended that there be no age restriction in allowing access to the library. The selection of juvenile books was discussed at length. The author's views on series books, as being unsuitable for inclusion in public libraries, is worthy of note: ". . . they give false views of life, making it consist, if it be worth living, of a series of adventures, hairbreadth escapes; encounters with tyrannical schoolmasters and unnatural parents; sea voyages in which the green hand commands a ship and defeats a mutiny out of sheer smartness; rides on runaway locomotives; strokes of good luck; and a persistent turning up of things just when they are wanted,—all of which is calculated in the long run to lead away the young imagination and impart discontent with the common lot of an uneventful life."

3754. "The flow of children's books from country to country," *Top of the news,* Chicago, Vol. 18, No. 2, Dec., 1961, pp. 7–14. DLC, IYL, NNY.

Abridgements of three speeches given at the Cleveland conference of ALA. They are by Virginia Haviland, Margaret McElderry and Datus C. Smith, and are concerned with U.S. books which appear in translations, as well as foreign books and how they get translated in the U.S.

3755. Foley, Patrick Kevin. *Catalogue of an extraordinary collection of children's books of olden times.* Boston, C. F. Libbie, 1925. 8p. NNY.

An antiquarian bookseller's catalog comprising 168 items.

3756. Folmsbee, Beulah. *A little history of the horn-book.* Boston, *Horn book,* 1942. 57p. $2.50. DLC, IYL, NNY.

A charming little collector's item which in format as well as in content gives one a notion of "the horn book" and its use as a lesson aid for school children of England and America from the 15th to 18th centuries.

3757. "For it was indeed he." *Fortune,* New York, Vol. 9, No. 4, Apr., 1934, pp. 86–89, 193–194, 204, 206, 208–209. DLC, NNY.

"The publishers (principally three), the authors (one in particular) and the profits (fabulous) of literature for adolescents." A lengthy article on the big business which is behind the cheap, popular series novel for the young, and how, why and by whom they were written. A revealing article on children's books which rarely get covered in the histories because they are rarely considered literature.

3758. Forbes, Edith Emerson. *Favourites of a nursery of seventy years ago, and some others of later date.* Boston, Houghton Mifflin, 1916. 620p. DLC.

3759. Forbes, Mildred P. *Good citizenship through storytelling.* New York, Macmillan, 1923. 255p. NNY.

"A textbook for teachers, social workers and homemakers." Quite didactic in approach.

3760. Forbush, W. B. "Studies of boys' tastes in reading," *Work with boys,* Fall River, Mass., Vol. 7, Nov., 1907, pp. 246–274.

3761. Ford, Paul L. *The New-England Primer; a history of its origin and development.* New York, Dodd, Mead, 1897. 354p. DLC, NNY.

Mr. Ford was a noted bibliophile who was an expert on the subject of early primers. He gives here a scholarly history of this famous U.S. primer, its British forerunners, its numerous editions and imitations. There is a facsimile reprint of the 1727 edition of the *New England Primer* included in the study.

3762. "Forecast of children's books," *Publishers' weekly,* New York, Vol. 1 ff. Jan., 1872 ff. Weekly. DLC, NNY.

Under various headings, new children's books have been previewed from the first years of this journal of the book trade industry. The reviews are not so much critical as they are annunciatory. The Spring Children's Book Number (in February) announces new titles to be published in that season. The Fall Children's Book Number (in July) does the same for the autumn season.

3763. "Foreign translations," *Library journal,*

New York, Vol. 64, No. 16, Sept., 15, 1939, pp. 692–697. DLC, NNY.

A short bibliography of some U.S. children's books which have been translated into other languages. It is followed by a list of U.S. children's books which have a foreign setting. These are arranged by country. Of historical interest only since the majority are out of print.

3764. Foster, W. E. "The relation of the libraries to the school system," *Library journal,* New York, Vol. 5, No. 4, Apr., 1880, pp. 99–104. DLC, NNY.

One of the earliest articles documenting the manner in which public libraries began working with the public schools. Class visits to the library are mentioned, as well as special lists compiled for teachers and pupils. In the Nov.–Dec. issue of this volume, 1880, appears an article on the same subject, by Mellen Chamberlain, pp. 299–302.

3765. Frank, Josette. *Your child's reading today.* Rev. ed. New York, Doubleday, 1960. 391p. $3.95. DLC, IYL, NNY.

The Consultant on Children's Books, Radio and Television for The Child Study Association brings up to date her practical guide which states the basic philosophy of the Association. It is a philosophy of moderation, of acceptance of the practical aspects of children's reading. While aiming for high standards in writing and illustration, the psychology of the child is always taken into account in selecting children's books. Graded and annotated booklists are included. The table of contents leads to the textual material and there is an author and title index to the books discussed and listed.

3766. Freeman, G. La Verne and Ruth Sunderlin Freeman. *The child and his picture book; a discussion of the preferences of the nursery child.* Chicago, Northwestern University Press, 1933. 102p. DLC.

An educational study complete with diagnostic chart for analyzing illustrations and a rating scale for picture books. The list of leading picture book illustrators includes some whose work has not continued to be important.

3767. Freeman, Ruth S. *Yesterday's school books.* Watkins Glen, N.Y., Century House, 1960. 128p. DLC.

A historical survey including information on some general children's books as well as text books.

3768. Freund, Roberta Bishop. *Open the book.* 2nd ed. New York, Scarecrow Press, 1966. 180p. DLC.

Suggested goals of the school library program, and the types of activities best suited to carrying them out, e.g., book talks, storytelling, oral reading, book reports, films, etc. There is also a chapter on coordinating the school library with community resources. The author writes from experience with the Newark Public Schools. Selected bibliography.

3769. Friesen, Ruby E. *Survey of articles on the school library published in library and educational periodicals.* Denver, University of Denver, 1949. 66p. Thesis.

3770. Fryatt, Norma R. *A Horn Book sampler on children's books and reading, selected from 25 years of the Horn Book Magazine, 1924–1948.* Boston, Horn Book, 1959. 261p. DLC, IYL, NNY.

An excellent selection on a wide variety of subjects, and often by the best-known experts in the field.

3771. Fuller, M. N. *The public library and the pre-school child.* Washington, Catholic University of America, 1963. 31p. Thesis.

3772. Fuller, Muriel. *More junior authors.* New York, H. W. Wilson, 1963. 235p. DLC, NNY.

A supplement to the Kunitz and Haycraft book listing all new and important juvenile authors with their biographies and portraits.

3773. "Furious children and the library," *Top of the news,* Chicago, Vol. 16, Mar., 1960, pp. 12–15; May, 1960, pp. 24–30; Vol. 17, Oct., 1960, pp. 48–63. DLC, NNY.

This three part article contains numerous short articles by the persons involved in an experiment conducted at the National Institutes of Health centered around a group of children who were uncontrollable, impulsive and incorrigible to an excessive degree. Chiefly, this describes the special therapeutic work with books which the various staff members undertook.

3774. Furness, Edna Lee. "Pupils, pedagogues and prose," *Education,* Indianapolis, Vol. 84, Mar., 1964, pp. 402–410. DLC, NNY.

This is only one article in an issue concerned with children's reading chiefly from the teaching point of view. The author here classifies the types of prose writing for children, and suggests procedures of introducing them into the classroom.

3775. "The future of library work with children," *Library journal,* New York, Vol. 61, No. 19, Nov. 1, 1936–Vol. 62, No. 7, April 1, 1937. DLC, NNY.

A symposium which includes ten papers, by the following: Louise P. Latimer, Carrie E. Scott, Clarence E. Sherman, Alice J. Hazeltine, Siri M. Andrews, Effie L. Power, Lillian H. Smith, Gladys English, Agatha L. Shea and Letha M. Davidson. All were concerned with the quality and extent of future library work with children.

3776. Gaines, M. C. "Narrative illustration, the story of the comics," *Print,* New Haven, Conn., Vol. 3, No. 2, Summer 1942, pp. 25–38; No. 3, Autumn 1942, pp. 19–24. DLC, NNY.

It is only fair to point out that this is the view on comic books which is opposite to that of most educators, librarians and literary and art critics. The author attempts a capsule history of the comics—from prehistoric cave paintings to 19th-century picture sheets to 20th-century strips. The second article is a detailed description of the production of a comic magazine.

3777. Galbraith, R. B. *Course for the storyteller.* New York, H. W. Wilson, 1943. 15p.

3778. ———. *The evaluation and teaching of school library functions.* New York, Columbia University, 1947. 99p. Thesis.

3779. Galloway, Louise. *An analytical study of the extent and nature of the reviewing of juvenile books in eight journals and newspapers with special regard to their usefulness as selection aids for school libraries.* New York, Columbia University, Teachers College, 1965, 138p. (Dissertation.)

3780. Gannett, Lewis. "Why do they hate the classics?" Marshall, John D. *Of, by and for librarians.* Hamden, Conn., Shoestring Press, 1960, pp. 74–77. DLC.

3781. Gans, Roma. *Reading is fun; developing children's reading interests.* New York, Columbia University, Teachers College, 1949. 51p. DLC.

Some methods for teachers to use in encouraging children to read more for their own pleasure.

3782. Gardiner, Jewel. *Administering library service in the elementary school.* 2nd ed. Chicago, ALA, 1954. 160p. DLC, NNY.

This standard work is still in print, and although it has some practical advice still of use to the librarian working with children, it is rather out of date in most of its approaches.

3783. Gardner, Emelyn E. and Eloise Ramsey. *A handbook of children's literature.* New York, Scott, 1927. 354p. DLC, NNY.

An outline and anthology of children's literature, used for many years as a primary source in the teaching of children's literature. Index and bibliographies.

3784. Garnett, Wilma Leslie. *Children's choices in prose.* Ames, State University of Iowa, 1924. 119p. Thesis. Summary in: *Elementary english review,* Detroit, Vol. 1, June, 1924, pp. 133–137. DLC.

A reading interest survey based on stories read aloud to intermediate grade children.

3785. Garwin, E. J. *Analysis of the treatment of the American Indian in juvenile fiction.* Chicago, University of Chicago, 1961. 104p. (Thesis.)

3786. Gates, Arthur I., *et al.* "Studies of children's interests in reading," *Elementary school journal,* Chicago, Vol. 31, No. 9, Sept., 1930–June, 1931, pp. 656–670. DLC.

An educational study based on 16 separate investigations. The influence of "sets" or series is discussed at length, with an examination of the reasons why children seem to like reading such repetitious books.

3787. Gates, Doris. *Helping children discover books.* Chicago, Science Research Associates. 1956. 48p. DLC.

A competently written booklet answering many questions and providing helpful suggestions to the parent or teacher who has no professional librarian at hand. Includes a list of recommended books.

3788. ———. "A lengthened shadow and Along the road to Kansas," *Kansas State Teachers College of Emporia, Bulletin of information,* Vol. 34, Dec., 1954. Unp. NNY.

This is a reprint of speeches made in connection with Miss Gates' acceptance of the William Allen White Children's Book Award given each year since 1952 to a book chosen by Kansas children, from a preselected list. Miss Gates tells of her own childhood reading, and how she came to be a writer of children's books. Each year the speeches of the winners are reprinted in the *Bulletin,* so that this represents only one of them.

3789. Gaver, Mary Virginia. *Effectiveness of centralized library service in elementary schools.* 2nd ed. New Brunswick, N.J., Rutgers University Press, 1963. 268p. DLC.

An account of the measures and methods used to test whether the central library is more effective than classroom collections. The results are in tabular and graph form with many textual comments and conclusions.

3790. ———, et al. *Elementary school library collection*. Rev. ed., Newark, N.J., Bro-Dart Foundation, 1966. 1108p. $20.00.

A list of more than 5,500 titles of books and audio-visual materials, arranged by decimal classification scheme and indexed by subject, author and title. This was intended as a basic guide for schools not having sufficient professional personnel time to evaluate the materials themselves. It has received both acclaim and criticism in the professional press, for its policies of selection.

3791. ———. *Every child needs a school library*. Chicago, ALA, 1948. 15p. DLC, NNY.

A pamphlet stating why every child needs a school library, what constitutes a good program, and how to get one.

3792. General Society of Mechanics and Tradesmen. Free Library. *Special catalogue of . . . prose fiction and juvenile literature*. New York, The Society, 1874. 99p. NNY.

A list of the books which were available on free loan to the apprentices. Not annotated.

3793. Gessleman, Daisy B. *Reading activities of third grade children from television homes*. Salt Lake City, University of Utah, 1951. Thesis.

3794. Gibbons, Emma. *Books for children*. Buffalo, Privately printed, 1910. 34p. DLC.

An early list of books for children, arranged by subject and meant for the parent.

3795. Gill, Gertrude. "Teacher education in children's literature," *Education*, Indianapolis, Vol. 81, Apr., 1961, pp. 460–466. DLC, NNY.

This educator believed that all teachers should be provided with a wide background in children's literature. She writes from experience in a state teacher training college.

3796. Gillette, Jean E. and Veva E. Gillette. *Elementary school library: Suggested principles and practices*. Chicago, Chicago Teachers College, 1958. 100p. Thesis.

3797. Gilman, Stella Scott. "The choice and use of books by children." *Mothers in council*. New York, Harper, 1885, pp. 62–75. NNY.

A discussion which resulted from a group

of mothers who met for the purpose of sharing and debating mutual problems of child-rearing. They showed themselves to be very much a part of the age which believed in the didactic over the pleasurable.

3798. Gilmore, E. C. *A survey of library services to Puerto Rican children, with recommendations for the public library at Bridgeport, Connecticut*. New York, Pratt Institute Library School, 1955. 48p. Thesis.

3799. Girolama, Sister Mary. *CLA booklist*. Haverford, Penn., Catholic Library Association, 1967. 68p. $1.50.

This is an annually revised list, annotated and graded from kindergarten to 8th grade.

3800. Gleason, Caroline F. "A word on picture books, good and bad," *Public libraries*, Chicago, Vol. 11, Apr., 1906, pp. 171–178. DLC, NNY.

Some examples of picture books this critic believed to be good, and others which were not so good.

3801. Glenn, Lily D. *A study of the animal and its role in the modern fairy tale*. Seattle, University of Washington, 1954. 118p. Thesis.

3802. Godden, Rumer. "Words make the book," *Ladies' home journal*, Philadelphia, Vol. 81, Jan., 1964, pp. 32, 36. DLC, NNY.

This well-known writer comments on the limited vocabulary books which she feels eventually do far more to hamper the child's education than the little good they might do in encouraging him to read more easily. She also discusses the problem of books in series and the misleading advertising of some sets of books.

3803. Goldhor, Herbert and John A. McCrossan. "An exploratory study of the effect of a public library summer reading club on reading skills," *Library quarterly*, Chicago, Vol. 36, Jan., 1966, pp. 14–24. DLC, NNY.

The authors first discuss previous research on the subject and then go into the details of their study, conducted among children in Evansville, Ind., "to test the hypothesis that children who join a public library summer reading club will receive significantly higher scores on a test of reading skill administered in the fall than children who do not join."

3804. Gordon, L. M. *Development of science literature for children, 1909–1944*. New York, Columbia University, 1948. 93p. Thesis.

3805. Gorman, Edith M. *A teaching guide for school library administration.* Nashville, Tennessee, George Peabody College for Teachers, 1956. 117p. Thesis.

3806. Graham, Gladys M. *Today's books for children and tomorrow's world.* Washington, D.C., American Association of University Women, 1950. 22p.

3807. Grambs, Jean D. *The development of lifetime reading habits.* New York, R. R. Bowker, 1954. 23p. (Printed for the National Book Committee). DLC, NNY.

A report of a conference called by the Committee on Reading Development, New York, June, 1954. This presents the methods and ideas suggested by the participants which can be used to develop the reading habit in children and youth.

3808. Grant, Margaret E. *Classics read and enjoyed by junior high school boys and girls.* New York, Columbia University, 1951. 40p. Thesis.

3809. Gray, Alice E. *Development of magazines for young people in the twentieth century.* Cleveland, Western Reserve University, 1950. 49p. Thesis.

3810. Gray, L. G. *A study of fiction books for children and young people on Indian life and customs published 1894–1950.* Atlanta, Georgia, Atlanta University, 1954. 87p. Thesis.

3811. Gray, William S. *Promoting personal and social development through reading.* Chicago, University of Chicago, 1948. 236p. (Proceedings of the Annual Conference on Reading, 1947. Supplementary Educational Monographs, No. 64.) DLC.

A series of papers providing an exhaustive discussion on children's personal and social needs, and how they can satisfy them through reading. There are bibliographies scattered throughout the papers.

3812. "A greater and better Children's Book Week; a nationwide report," *Publishers' weekly,* New York, Vol. 100, No. 27, Dec. 31, 1921, pp. 2048–2053. DLC, NNY.

A city by city report on some of the activities taking place during this special week.

3813. Green, Hattie Cora. *What shall I read?* Gulfport, Miss., Gulfport Printing Co., 1924. 53p. DLC.

3814. Green, Jenny Lind. *Reading for fun.* Boston, Richard G. Badger, 1925. 206p. DLC.

The author writes of books children would enjoy concerning each of the main subjects they study in school. There is a graded list of books for boys and girls, arranged according to reading interest and difficulty, and according to subject.

3815. Green, Samuel S. "Report on libraries and schools," *Library journal,* New York, Vol. 8, Nos. 9–10, Sept.–Oct., 1883, pp. 229–233. DLC, NNY.

This was given at the Buffalo conference of ALA. It indicated that the public libraries were giving help to teachers and schools chiefly in locating information and supplementary reading.

3816. ———. "Sensational fiction in public libraries," *Library journal,* New York, Vol. 4, Nos. 9–10, Sept.–Oct., 1879, pp. 344–354. DLC, NNY.

This librarian deplored the practice of putting fiction by such authors as Oliver Optic, Horatio Alger and Ouida in libraries for the young. He felt that the fables of Aesop, the works of Maria Edgeworth, and other didactic books of this type were far more valuable in their effect on youth. Following this is a short article by James Freeman Clark recommending that public libraries not destroy the taste for fiction in the young, but that they work to elevate it.

3817. Greene, Ellin, *et al. Stories: A list of stories to tell and to read aloud.* New York, The New York Public Library, 1965. 78p. $1.00.

This is the latest edition (the 6th) of a list which began wth Mary Gould Davis in 1927. It is an annotated, title list, with index of authors and titles of collections. There is a section classifying the stories according to holidays and country of origin.

3818. Grey, Rowland. "America and the girls' book," *Englishwoman,* London, Vol. 45, Mar., 1920, pp. 199–205. DLC, NNY.

The author speculates as to why girls' stories became so popular in the U.S., and why they found so much better writers than had the English girls' stories. According to this critic, there were no "modern" equivalents to the Misses Fielding, Yonge and Ewing.

3819. Griswold, William M. *A descriptive list of books for the young.* Cambridge, Mass., The Author, 1895. 175p. DLC.

A collection of reviews and critical annotations from various periodicals and other sources. Although there are a number of inaccuracies, this is of possible historical interest.

3820. Gross, Elizabeth H. *Children's services in public libraries: Organization and administration.* Chicago, ALA, 1963. 124p. $3.00. DLC, NNY.

A fairly recent report on present conditions in public libraries for children, and aspirations for the future with specific reference as to how organization and administration are serving these ideals and how they can improve them. The basic statistics and comments were the result of a questionnaire sent to libraries in 1957–58. This was the first comprehensive study since the appearance of the Lucas and Power books (4037 and 4226).

3821. Gross, Sarah Chokla and H. H. Watts. "Torments of translation," *School library journal,* New York, Vol. 8, No. 2, Oct., 1961, pp. 97–100. DLC, NNY.

The authors point out many of the difficulties involved in translating, even in "translating" from Anglicisms to Americanisms.

3822. *Growing up with books.* New York, R. R. Bowker Co., 1964. 36p. APP.

An annotated list of "250 books which every child should have a chance to enjoy" prepared by the staff of *School Library Journal.* It is frequently revised.

3823. *Growing up with science books.* New York, R. R. Bowker Co., 1963. 33p. APP.

A companion to the above list, listing over 200 science books chosen by the staff of *School Library Journal* in cooperation with Julius Schwartz. The preface and introductory notes are by Herman Schneider, a leading writer of science books for children. This is annotated and arranged by age and subject.

3824. Guilfoile, Elizabeth. *Books for beginning readers.* Champaign, Ill., National Council of Teachers of English, 1962. 73p. DLC.

A list with broad interest range and suitable for many age levels. The annotations are rather detailed.

3825. Gumuchian, Kirkor. "From piety to entertainment in children's books," *American scholar,* Camden, N.J., Vol. 10, No. 3, 1941, pp. 337–350. NNY.

A general survey of the didactic period in U.S. and British children's literature.

3826. Günzberg, H. C. "The subnormal boy and his reading interests," *Library quarterly,* Chicago, Vol. 18, Oct., 1948, pp. 264–274. DLC, NNY.

Some observations based on work with a group of boys who were intellectually or emotionally behind the levels of their average peers.

3827. Gunterman, Bertha L. "Publishing children's books," Wilson, L. R., *Practice of book selection.* Chicago, University of Chicago, 1940, pp. 209–225. DLC.

An editor of children's books discusses how a publisher selects the manuscripts, and tries to maintain a set of standards while satisfying commercial needs.

3828. Guthrie, Anna Lorraine. *Library work 1905–1911.* Minneapolis, H. W. Wilson, 1912. 409p. DLC, NNY.

Five sections of this bibliography of articles culled from library literature are helpful to the student of early children's reading and libraries: Children's department, pp. 80–88; Children's reading, pp. 88–102; Libraries and schools, pp. 221–237; School libraries, pp. 344–354; Storytelling, of pp. 380–384. Each is annotated at length.

3829. Guy, Altoise C. *A study of Mexican life and customs as portrayed in juvenile fiction published 1936–1949.* Atlanta, Atlanta University, 1952. 83p. Thesis.

3830. Gwynne, Sister Grace Margaret. *Comparative analysis of the cultural content of a selected list of children's books about Japan by Japanese and non-Japanese authors.* Washington, Catholic University of America, 1965. 179p. Thesis.

3831. Gymer, Rosina. "Personal work with children," *Public libraries,* Chicago, Vol. 11, Apr., 1906, pp. 191–193. DLC, NNY.

The special demands of work with boys, with girls, and with little children.

3832. Haight, Rachel Webb. "Fairy tales: An index," *Bulletin of bibliography,* Boston, Vol. 7, pp. 3–5, pp. 32–36, pp. 59–64, pp. 88–92, pp.110–112, pp. 135–138, pp. 165–167; Vol. 8, 1913, pp. 15–16, pp. 42–46, pp. 74–76, pp. 105–107. DLC, NNY.

A title and catch-word index to folk and fairy tales in collections of the time. Most were U.S. but some were British.

3833. Hall, Elvajean. *Books to build on.* 2nd ed. New York, R. R. Bowker, 1957. 79p. DLC, NNY.

Articles reprinted from *Junior Libraries* (now *School Library Journal*), together with three selective lists for the elementary, junior and senior high school levels.

3834. ———. "Got anything new on Russia?"

Library journal, New York, Vol. 90, No. 20, Nov. 15, 1965, pp. 5041–5042. DLC, NNY.

A list of recent nonfiction books.

3835.   Hall, G. Stanley. "Children's reading: As a factor in their education," *Library journal,* New York, Vol. 33, No. 4, Apr., 1908, pp. 123–128. DLC, NNY.

"The sad fact remains that children can develop . . . a passion for reading things on or below their own level that they ought to learn in the more vital ways of experience and conversation. Printing gives no added value to commonplaces, and the reading habit should not dignify platitudes . . . neither in the school nor the home should the book compete with the oral story . . . There is still a far too wide difference between reactions of children to spontaneous reading and to that prescribed for them by adults."

3836.   Halsey, Rosalie V. *Bibliography of early children's books, printed in America before 1840.* Princeton, 1911. On hand written cards in 3 metal files. DLC.

These are the notes on which the author based her work given in 3837. The first two files contain a chronological list of children's books from 1647–1840, and the third file is an index. Much of the material was not included in the final book form. The bibliographic care with which the cards were made makes this an invaluable source for the study of early U.S. children's literature.

3837.   ———. *Forgotten books of the American nursery.* Boston, Charles E. Goodspeed and Co., 1911. 244p. DLC, NNY.

A historical survey covering the period of 1647–1840, touching upon many authors and publishers, and replete with interesting and appropriate quotations from U.S. and British critics. A very readable and important landmark in the history of children's literature. The author's careful and scholarly approach is evident in the cardfile of her research materials in 3836.

3838.   Haman, Albert C. and Mary K. Eakin. *Library materials for elementary science.* Cedar Falls, State College of Iowa, 1964, 68p. (Instructional Materials Bulletin, 9). DLC.

A list of 700 titles in the areas of science, for children in grades 1 through 8.

3839.   Hammitt, Frances E. *School library legislation in Indiana, Illinois, and Wisconsin; a historical survey.* Chicago, University of Chicago, 1948. 266p. Dissertation.

3840.   Hammond, Lamont M. "Reading for children," *Nation,* New York, Vol. 83, Dec. 27, 1906, pp. 551–552. DLC, NNY.

Most of what was being published for children was "rubbish," according to this critic. He did not agree with teachers of the time who felt that the new public library movement was detracting from the studies of the children.

3841.   Hanaway, Emily S. "The children's library in New York," *Library journal,* New York, Vol. 12, No. 5, May, 1887, pp. 185–186. DLC, NNY.

This private library was originally based on subscriptions, but children could come in and read for free. Eventually, they could also take books without a fee. It was founded by the author, a school teacher, and made many moves because it kept growing out of its quarters. It is considered by many to be the first circulating children's library in the U.S.

3842.   Hanna, Geneva R. and Mariana K. McAllister. *Books, young people and reading guidance.* New York, Harper, 1960. 219p. $3.95. DLC, NNY.

Reading guidance for students in the junior and senior high school. Suggested readings for each chapter, and an alphabetical list of the books recommended in the text. Index.

3843.   Hanzow, H. M. *The didactic period in children's literature in America as represented by two writers: Samuel G. Goodrich and Jacob Abbott.* Cleveland, Western Reserve University, 1950. 80p. Thesis.

3844.   Hardendorff, Jeanne B. *Stories to tell.* 5th ed. Baltimore, Maryland, Enoch Pratt Free Library, 1965. 83p. $1.50. DLC.

This is one of the standard lists in the field, based on the stories told in the programs of this very active library. It is classified and annotated.

3845.   Hardy, George E. *Five hundred books for the young.* New York, Scribner's, 1892. 94p. NNY.

An annotated list which grew out of the author's experiences in building a classroom library that was appealing to the children and yet contained books of quality. Indexed.

3846.   Harrington, Mildred Priscilla. *The Southwest in children's books.* Baton Rouge, Louisiana, Louisiana State University Press, 1952. 124p. NNY.

A discussion and list of books having themes or locales in Arizona, Arkansas, Louisiana, New Mexico, Oklahoma and Texas.

3847.   Hauck, Carolyn Marie. *A selective anno-*

tated *bibliography of music and related material for the young child.* Cleveland, Western Reserve University, 1958. 61p. Thesis.

3848.   Havens, Ruth Mack and Ruth Andrus. "Desirable literature for children of kindergarten age," *Pedagogical seminary and journal of genetic psychology,* Worcester, Mass., Vol. 36, Sept., 1929, pp. 390–414. DLC, NNY.

A very elaborate study of the home reading patterns of a select group of kindergarten children, and of their ability to recall and retell stories they were told in the kindergarten.

3849.   Haviland, Virginia. "Serving those who serve children; a national reference library of children's books," *Quarterly journal of the Library of Congress,* Washington, Vol. 22, No. 4, Oct., 1965, pp. 311–316. DLC, NNY.

The head of the Children's Book Section tells of its beginnings, its present status and its purpose. She also describes the juvenile holdings in the general sections, in the old and rare book division, and in the foreign language areas. Illustrated with reproductions from U.S. and foreign children's books and manuscripts.

3850.   ———. Travelogue storybook of the nineteenth century. Boston, *Horn book,* 1950. 70p. DLC, NNY.

This fascinating account of an almost forgotten era in publishing gives a refreshing glimpse into a past which foreshadowed contemporary internationalism in children's books. The paper on which this was based was read in 1949 as the second of the Hewins lectures (see 3434).

3851.   Hawthorne, Julian. "Books for children," *Confessions and criticisms.* Boston, Ticknor, 1887, pp. 100–127. NNY. Also in: *North American review,* Boston, Vol. 138, pp. 383 ff.

This writer believed that the old classics were best for children, but that it should be left to the children to decide what they wish to read for they have a sure instinct for what is good.

3852.   Hazard, Paul. *Books, children & men.* 4th ed. Boston, Horn Book, 1960. 176p. $5.00; paper, $3.00. DLC, IYL, NNY. (1st ed., 1944 in DLC and NNY).

Translated into English by Marguerite Mitchell. For note see 814.

3853.   Hazeltine, Alice Isabel. *How to become a children's librarian.* St. Louis, St. Louis Library School, Public Library, 1927. 23p. DLC.

"With illustrations from St. Louis and the St. Louis Public Library." This pamphlet designed as a recruiting device, gives much of the feeling for children's work which was part of Alice Hazeltine's philosophy. The qualities necessary to be a good children's librarian are discussed at length.

3854.   ———. *Library work with children.* New York, H. W. Wilson, 1917. 396p. (Classics of American librarianship). DLC, NNY.

Essays, speeches and articles which had previously appeared in professional and general periodicals. Every major voice in the field is given expression here, and a goodly number of the minor ones as well.

3855.   ———. *Syllabus for the study of reading interests of children.* New York, Columbia University, School of Library Service, 1941. 101p. DLC, NNY.

One of the early course outlines developed by this well-known children's librarian who trained so many of those working in U.S. children's libraries.

3856.   ———. "What is a children's librarian?" *Public libraries,* Chicago, Vol. 26, Nov., 1921, pp. 513–519. DLC, NNY.

Many of the points in this inspiring definition of the children's librarian are still as valid today as they were when wrtten. The chief concern of the author here is that the good children's librarian not consider herself an isolated person, but one whose "vision of library work with children as an integral part of library work as a whole and as an educational movement is clear and compelling."

3857.   Hazeltine, Mary Emogene. "The children's room in the public library," *Chatauquan,* Springfield, Ohio, Vol. 39, June, 1904, pp. 369–374. DLC, NNY.

A very good contemporary description of the new children's libraries and their work. Illustrated with photographs. In this issue is also an article by H. L. Elmendorf on "Great literature for little children," pp. 380–384, concerning the importance of reading aloud and storytelling in the home.

3858.   Heaps, Willard A. *Book selection for secondary school libraries.* New York, H. W. Wilson Co., 1942. 335p. DLC, NNY.

This was for many years the standard work on the subject and still has many practical suggestions although much is very out of date.

3859.   Heard, Mrs. Eugene B. "The free traveling library: An aid to education and a factor in the national life." National Education Association. *Pro-*

ceedings and addresses. Washington, 1900, pp. 648–655. DLC.

The work of the free traveling library among rural children. This is one of the earlier articles on bookmobiles.

3860.   Heck, C. M. *A bio-bibliography of winners of the Caldecott Award, 1938–1955.* Washington, Catholic University of America, 1957. 225p. Thesis.

3861.   Heffernan, Helen and Vivian E. Todd. "Introducing children to literature," *The kindergarten teacher,* Boston, Heath, 1960, pp. 230–257. DLC.

A concentrated discussion covering stories and storytelling, poetry, and means of encouraging a love of books. Bibliography and book list.

3862.   Heller, Frieda M. *I can read it myself!* Columbus, Ohio State University, 1966. 46p. $1.25.

An annotated list of books for beginning readers arranged by reading levels.

3863.   ——— and Lou L. LaBrant. *The librarian and the teacher of English.* Chicago, ALA, 1938. 84p. DLC, IYL.

One of a series of bulletins on the place of the library in the school curriculum. This gives specific examples as to how to bring together children and books, by the teacher or by the librarian.

3864.   Henne, Frances, *et al. A planning guide for the high school library program.* Chicago, ALA, 1951. 140p. DLC, IYL, NNY.

Lists, sample charts and forms pertinent to the planning and evaluating of a school library. This is somewhat dated, but the outline of procedures could be used as a starting point. Bibliography.

3865.   ———. *Preconditional factors affecting the reading of young people.* Chicago, University of Chicago, 1949. 414p. Dissertation.

3866.   ——— and Frances Lander Spain. "The school and the public library," *Annals of the American Academy of Political and Social Science,* Philadelphia, Vol. 302, Nov., 1955, pp. 52–59. DLC, NNY.

The purpose of this paper was "to indicate the kinds of existing relationships that schools have with public libraries and . . . to note the types of cooperation and coordination that are desirable."

3867.   ———. "Special discussion of service for children and young people." Asheim, Lester. *A forum on the Public Library Inquiry.* New York, Columbia University Press, 1950, pp. 236–241. DLC, NNY.

In commenting on the Public Library Inquiry, Dr. Henne remarks that its greatest defect as a study, insofar as children's library service is concerned, is the lack of attention this service received.

3868.   ———, *et al. Youth, communication and libraries.* Chicago, ALA, 1949. 233p. DLC, IYL, NNY.

Papers presented at the first institute to be held at the University of Chicago Graduate Library School on the subject of children's and youth libraries. They are presented here in three parts: Youth and the communication of ideas; Materials of communication for youth; and Libraries for youth as agencies of communication. Virtually all the important figures in the field took part in this venture.

3869.   Henrotin, Ellen M. "Children's literature," *National magazine,* Boston, Vol. 7, No. 4, Jan., 1898, pp. 373–375. NNY.

"Modern literature is full of riches for the child. There never was a period when so many great men and women are writing for children." The author then goes on to mention specific names and titles.

3870.   Herzberg, Max John. *The world of books; a guide to reading for young people . . .* Boston, The Palmer Co., 1922. 64p. DLC.

A list for supplementary reading, together with elaborate instructions for writing book reports.

3871.   Hewes, Frances V. *Study of the origin and development of the modern imaginative story in England and America.* Pittsburgh, Carnegie Institute of Technology, 1949. 53p. Thesis.

3872.   Hewins, Carolyn M. *Books for boys and girls.* 1st ed., 1897, 31p.; 2nd ed., 1904, 56p.; 3rd ed., 1915, 112p. Boston, ALA Publishing Board, DLC, NNY.

This important list by a leading children's librarian and critic, expanded not only in number of titles annotated, but also in its introductory remarks of criticism. A very influential list and certainly one of the reasons for the high standards of selection set up by many U.S. children's libraries.

3873.   ———. *Books for the young.* New York, Leypoldt; Boston, Press of Rockwell & Churchill, 1882. 94p. DLC, NNY.

The first extensive, yet selective, list of children's books compiled by any U.S. librarian. This is arranged by general types, e.g., fiction, poetry, folklore, etc. It is interesting to note how similar in approach our modern lists are to this one.

3874. ———. "Books that children like." 2nd International Congress of Librarians. *Proceedings*. 1897, pp. 111–117.

3875. Hewins, Carolyn M. and Jennie D. Lindquist. *Carolyn M. Hewins: Her books, containing a mid-century child and her books,* and *Caroline M. Hewins and books for children* by Jennie D. Lindquist. Boston, Horn Book, 1954. 107p. DLC, IYL, NNY.

This is a wonderful picture of a pioneer in children's library work, and even for the librarian of today it proves to be an inspiration to read and ponder.

3876. ———. "The history of children's books," *Atlantic monthly,* Boston and New York, Vol. 61, No. 363, Jan., 1888, pp. 112–126. DLC, NNY.

An important survey of the early didactic works for children, from *Puer ad Mensam* in 1430 and *The Babees Book,* 1475, up to the 1850's. Only books of England and the U.S. are considered. This is written with the author's characteristic verve and style and ends on a note of dismay which has echoed up to the present day: "With fairy-tales and hero-legends re-written and simplified for children, with history told in story-form, there is only one danger,—that young readers will be satisfied with abridgments, and know nothing in later years of great originals."

3877. ———. "Reading of the young." U.S. Office of Education. *Report of the Commissioner, Vol. 1, Part 2, 1892–93.* Washington, Government Printing Office, 1895. pp. 944–949. DLC.

An important article which surveyed the history of library work with children beginning with the Fletcher report in 1876 (see 3753), and ending with the comments of more than 150 libraries concerning their current work with young people. There is also a short bibliography.

3878. ———. "Yearly report on boys' and girls' reading," *Library journal,* New York, Vol. 7, Nos. 7–8, July–Aug., 1882, pp. 182–190. DLC, NNY.

The first of a series of reports documenting the expansion of library service to the young in U.S. public libraries. Miss Hewins' report was based on answers she received from 25 libraries. For the later reports see 3463, 3929 and 4272. This was given at the Cincinnati conference.

3879. Hill, George Birkbeck. "Writing down to children," *Writers and readers.* New York, G. P. Putnam, 1892, pp. 186 ff. NNY.

The author quotes Scott and Johnson, among others, in citing reasons for not giving children simplified reading materials.

3880. Hill, Ruth A. and Elsa de Bondeli. *Children's books from foreign languages; English translations from published and unpublished sources.* New York, H. W. Wilson, 1937. 148p. DLC, NNY.

A valuable source book, listing some 900 titles from 39 countries, with original foreign titles and publisher given, whenever known. Quite a number are not translations in that they were written directly in English from oral sources. The list is most complete in the area of folklore. There is a name index.

3881. Hislop, Codman. "The Americanization of Mother Goose." *Colophon,* New York, New ser., Vol. 3, Summer 1938, pp. 435–440. DLC, NNY.

A description of the known editions which had appeared in the U.S. prior to 1860. The author's earlier article in Vol. 1, No. 2, Autumn 1925, pp. 167–182, "The old woman who lived in a book," discussed the issue of the identity of Mother Goose, particularly as related to the Mrs. Vergoose of Boston who was so frequently referred to by some scholars.

3882. Hölscher, E. "Amerikanische kinderbücher," *Gebrauchsgraphik,* Berlin, Vol. 17, July, 1940, pp. 2–12. DLC, NNY.

Numerous illustrations and a commentary in English and German. The author mistakenly credits some British artists (e.g., Ardizzone) as being from the U.S., because he used the American version of their books. His conclusion: "Those books which the illustrators themselves have written are far and away the best on the list."

3883. Hogan, Marita and Margaret Yeschko. "Latin American countries in children's literature," *Elementary english review,* Detroit, Vol. 15, Oct., 1938, pp. 225–232; Nov., 1938, pp. 270–274. DLC. Revised and enlarged in Vol. 17, Oct., 1940, pp. 230–234; Nov., 1940, pp. 276–284. DLC.

An annotated list of U.S. children's books which have themes, backgrounds or characters from one or another of the Latin American countries. Although most of the books are no longer available, this is interesting for comparison of current materials. There are more than 135 titles in all.

3884. Hogarth, Grace Allen. "Transatlantic editing," *Horn book,* Boston, Vol. 41, No. 5, Oct., 1965, pp. 520–523. DLC, IYL, NNY.

"Editors on both sides of the Atlantic are apt to say: 'American children would never understand this' or 'Whatever will English children make of those peculiar clothes?' What we tend to overlook is the obvious truth that children everywhere are keenly interested in, and ready to learn about, other children; and the odder, the better."

3885. Hohman, Leslie B. *As the twig is bent*. New York, Macmillan, 1940. 291p. DLC, NNY.

A handbook on child-rearing which has several chapters on reading, comics, fairy tales and similar subjects.

3886. Hollowell, Lillian. *A book of children's literature*. 3rd ed. New York, Holt, Rinehart, 1966. 580p. $8.50. DLC, NNY.

An anthology intended mostly for parents, but which is also of some use to teachers, librarians and students of children's literature. There are extensive bibliographies and appendices which cover historical material, award books, biographical sketches, etc.

3887. Homze, Alma. "Interpersonal relations in children's literature, 1920–1960," *Elementary english*, Champaign, Vol. 43, Jan., 1966, pp. 26–28, 52. DLC.

"The specific objectives of the investigation were to identify behaviors, backgrounds, and themes of the books and discern changes in those contents from the 1920–1940 period to the 1945–1960 period." After examining 780 realistic story books, the author came to the conclusion that there was an increasing emphasis on themes of problems and adjustments of individual child characters, and there was a decreasing number of family life stories.

3888. Hooker, Brian. "Fairy tales," *Forum*, New York, Vol. 40, No. 4, Oct., 1908, pp. 375–84. DLC, NNY.

An excellent article distinguishing fairy tales from ghostly or supernatural tales, from science fiction, and from the talking beast or animal fable. Tolkein's more recent essay (3262) substantiates this definition of "fairy" or "fantasy" and bears comparison with this earlier study.

3889. ———. "Narrative and the fairy tale," *Bookman*, New York, Vol. 33, No. 4, June, 1911, pp. 389–393; No. 5, July, 1911, pp. 501–505. DLC, NNY.

The perfection of the simplicity of fairy tales is discussed as the model for narrative prose in this excellent article.

3890. Hopkins, Frederick M. "Early American juveniles," *Publishers' weekly*, New York, Vol. 116, Nov. 16, 1929, pp. 2395–2398. DLC, NNY.

In describing five exhibitions of old children's books held recently, the author noted the growing interest in this type of book collecting.

3891. Horn, Thomas D. and Dorothy W. Ebert.

Books for the partially sighted child. Champaign, Illinois, National Council of Teachers of English, 1967. 80p. $1.00.

An annotated list giving type size and other factors affecting the partially sighted child.

3892. *Horn book magazine*. Horn Book, Inc., 585 Boylston St., Boston, Massachusetts 02116. 6 times a year. Vol. 1, No. 1, 1924 ff. Annual subscription: $5.00. DLC, IYL, NNY.

One of the earliest periodicals to be devoted exclusively to the criticism of children's books. The format has not changed much since the first issue, and in the entire history of its publication, there have been only three editors: Bertha E. Mahony Miller, Jennie D. Lindquist and Ruth Hill Viguers. For a short period in the early 1940's, Beulah Folmsbee, the managing editor, is also listed as the chief editor. These are not the only distinguished names connected with the periodical, however; virtually all of the luminaries of the past 50 years of criticism have voiced their opinions in reviews or articles. The *Horn Book* also contains a regular column of children's contributions. Its policy is to review only recommended books. Illustrations taken from the books are frequently reproduced. For special occasions and anniversaries, entire issues are devoted to a single subject, e.g., Marie Shedlock, Anne Carroll Moore, etc. All in all, this is an indispensable tool in the study of the history of children's literature.

3893. Horovitz, Carolyn: "Dimensions in time; a critical view of historical fiction for children," *Horn book*, Boston, Vol. 38, No. 3, June, 1962, pp. 255–267. DLC, IYL, NNY.

Some of the factors to be aware of in judging this type of book for children.

3894. Horseman, Jean M. *Analytical study of four reviewing media of children's books for the year 1962*. Washington, Catholic University of America, 1964. 75p. Thesis.

3895. Hosking Nancy K. and Spencer G. Show. "I'll tell you a story." 2 parts. Stefferud, Alfred. *The wonderful world of books*. Boston, Houghton, 1953, pp. 63–70. DLC, NNY.

In this collection of essays on the joys and merits of reading, two storytellers relate some of their experiences in introducing literature to children through the medium of storytelling. They give hints on technique for the beginner, and recommend further reading.

3896. Hosmer, Herbert Henry. *A brief history of toy books, exemplified in a series of characters with figures to dress and undress, 1810–1830.* South Lancaster, Mass., John Greene Chandler Museum, 1954. 16p. DLC.

Short comments for the collector and photographs of a variety of examples make up the greatest part of this pamphlet on the toy books of the 19th century. Bibliography.

3897.   "House Committee studies treatment of minorities in text and library books," *Publishers' weekly,* New York, Vol. 190, Sept. 19, 1966, pp. 34–40. DLC, NNY.

An indictment of the text and trade book publishers for failing to provide books which reflect the role of minority groups in the history and current social and cultural make-up of the U.S. The response of the publishers is also presented.

3898.   Hoyt, Helen P. "Books in a Hawaiian childhood, circa 1900," *Horn book,* Boston, Vol. 38, Aug., 1962, pp. 356–362. DLC, NNY.

Reminiscences of some of the U.S. and English books read by her mother, Chinese stories told by her nurse, and a Japanese primer from which she was taught to read by a Japanese gardener.

3899.   Hubbard, James M. "Are public libraries public blessings?" *North American review,* New York, Vol. 149, Sept., 1889, pp. 339–346. DLC, NNY.

"The libraries are in no true sense of the words educators of the people. They are the haunt, in every place, of a few scholars and persons of leisure, but their chief work is to furnish amusement for the young." This critic of public library service to children felt that they should be entitled only to books of an instructive nature.

3900.   Huber, Miriam Blanton, *et al. Children's interests in poetry.* Chicago, Rand McNally, 1927. 233p. DLC.

A report on an educational experiment in the uses of poetry with children.

3901.   Huchet, Claire. "La littérature enfantine aux États-Unis," *Enfance,* Paris, No. 3, 1956, pp. 191–195. IYL.

The former French librarian of L'Heure Joyeuse comments on the excellent quality of U.S. children's books, particularly in format, design, paper and illustration. She notes some of the nation-wide activities which have promoted children's books into the consciousness of the entire nation.

3902.   Huck, Charlotte, and Doris A. Young. *Children's literature in the elementary school.* New York,

Holt, Rinehart and Winston, 1961. 522p. DLC, IYL, NNY.

This is a textbook prepared to give basic information on children's literature to prospective teachers. The text is chatty in style and sparked with anecdotes. Emphasis is on the use of literature in the total curriculum. It is a popular book with teachers and school librarians. The appendix lists children's book awards in the U.S. and abroad and gives basic information on book selection aids in books, pamphlets, periodicals and newspapers. Included are a subject index and an author, illustrator and title index.

3903.   Hughes, Helen Sard. "Literature for children: A protest." *English journal,* Chicago, Vol. 2, Oct., 1913, pp. 494–499. DLC, NNY.

The author objects to a course outlined in an earlier issue, in which it was suggested that normal school students be taught children's literature. This teacher believed that such students first needed to be taught what good literature was, and needed contact with the classics of adult literature before they could successfully learn to evaluate those for children.

3904.   Hunley, Maxwell. *Tales of past times; old and rare juveniles, toy books, first editions . . .* Beverly Hills, Calif., Maxwell Hunley, 1941. 48p. DLC.

A bookseller's catalogue, listing 363 items with fairly complete bibliographic descriptions.

3905.   Hunt, Clara Mitchell. "Opening a children's room," *The public library bulletin,* Boston, Vol. 1, No. 3, Sept., 1901, pp. 109–112. DLC.

An address given at the 23rd annual meeting of ALA. The author believes that the children's room should be planned with as much care and foresight as any other division receives. "The same dignity, the same freedom, the same courteous attention," should prevail there as is the case in the adult sections.

3906.   Hunt, Clara Whitehall, *et al. The bookshelf for boys and girls.* New York, Bocoher, 1927. 48p.

3907.   ———. *Library work with children.* Chicago, ALA, 1924. (Manual of library economy, 29). DLC, NNY.

The planning and furnishing of the children's room, methods of influencing children's reading, and a system of administration for the children's library.

3908.   ———. *What shall we read to the children?* Boston and New York, Houghton, 1915. 156p. DLC, NNY.

A book still useful for its spirit of adventure in the approach to books as experiences which broaden the child's vision and satisfy his eagerness to know.

3909. Huddleston, B. B. *A study of centralized school library service.* Washington, Catholic University of America, 1956. Thesis.

3910. Hunt, Mate G. *Values resource guide; annotated for the elementary school teacher.* Washington, American Association of Colleges for Teacher Education, 1958. 108p.

3911. Hurley, Richard J. "The creative school librarian," *Library journal,* New York, Vol. 60, Jan. 15, 1935, pp. 52–57. DLC, NNY.
"To achieve results we must have a scientific hypothesis based upon all the factors in our work —the school, child, home and community; the past, present and future; the age, race, sex, mental age, individual difference and character pattern. All of this is to be interpreted in terms of progressive education. To an even greater extent than the teacher, should the librarian know the cultural background of the school, have an understanding of contemporary trends in psychology, philosophy of life, curriculum making, self education and use of leisure."

3912. ———. *Your library; how to organize an elementary school library.* Washington, Catholic University of America Press, 1956.

3913. Hutchinson, C. G. *A study of family life in selected children's books.* Chapel Hill, University of North Carolina, 1963. 53p. Thesis.

3914. Huus, Helen. *Children's books to enrich the social studies.* Rev. ed. Washington, National Council for the Social Studies, National Education Association, 1966. 196p. (Bulletin No. 32). $2.50. DLC, NNY.
A booklist arranged into categories as "Our world," "Times past," "People today," "The world's work," and "Living together." Each book is annotated at length. Author and title index.

3915. "Imagination and the child." Special issue of: *Wilson bulletin for libraries,* New York, Vol. 40, Dec., 1965, pp. 332–358. DLC, NNY.
A most attractive issue which contained the following articles: "Wells of fancy, 1865–1965" by Donnarae MacCann; "Creative dramatics . . ." by Carolyn W. Field; "The aliveness of Peter Rabbit" by Maurice Sendak; "A children's theater . . ." by Madalynne Schoenfeld; and "The ethos of the teller of tales" by Arthur T. Allen.

3916. "In praise of nursery lore," *Unpopular review,* New York, Vol. 6, Oct.–Dec., 1916, pp. 338–347. NNY.
"If you want your child to love Homer, do not withhold Mother Goose. Even a modern psychologist ought to be able to detect the intimate relationships which subsist between the literature of the nursery and the glory that was Greece." This essay is a championing of the value of nursery rhymes and fairy tales in the life of every child.

3917. Independent Schools Education Board. *Boys' own list of favorite books.* Milton, Mass., The Board, 1940. 59p. DLC.
An annotated list of books recommended for purchase in these schools. The list was designed for use by the boys themselves.

3918. ———. *Girls' own list of favorite books.* Milton, Mass., The Board, 1940. 51p. DLC.
An annotated list of books recommended for purchase by these schools. The list was designed to be used by the girls themselves.

3919. Institute on the Elementary School Library. *Proceedings.* Washington, Catholic University of America, 1944. 203p.

3920. "Interesting children in owning books," *Public libraries,* Chicago, Vol. 16, Apr., 1911, pp. 149–151. DLC, NNY.
How a library program set out to encourage children to begin purchasing their own books.

3921. Inyart, B. G. *A study of the problems, policies and procedures in selecting children's books in six major public libraries.* Washington, Catholic University of America, 1953. 117p. Thesis.

3922. Izard, Anne. "Behind the doors with the Newbery-Caldecott Committee," *Top of the news,* Chicago, Vol. 22, No. 2, Jan., 1966, pp. 160–163. DLC, NNY.
A good description of the method used for choosing the winners of the Newbery and Caldecott Medals.

3923. ———. "New books for children," *Grade teacher,* Darien, Conn., 1923 ff. Monthly.
This librarian has been the children's book reviewer for a number of years for this educational periodical, which has included similar review sections ever since it first began its publication.

3924. Jackson, E. P. *The effects of reading fiction*

upon attitudes toward the Negro race. New York, Columbia University, 1942. 55p. Thesis.

3925. Jackson, Francine L. *Study of juvenile fiction published 1940–1949, on Chinese life and customs.* Atlanta, Atlanta University, 1951. 109p. Thesis.

3926. Jacobs, Mrs. I. *An analysis of the "Outstanding Educational Books" lists, 1924–1953.* Washington, Catholic University of America, 1956. 169p. Thesis.

3927. Jacobs, Leland B., *et al. Using literature with young children.* New York, Columbia University, Teachers College, 1965. 63p. DLC, NNY.

A collection of 12 articles related to the special problems of using books with very young children. Storytelling, reading aloud, choral speaking and dramatization are only some of the techniques discussed. The author is a professor of children's literature at Teachers College.

3928. Jacobson, Helja. "Biblioteksarbete bland och ungdom i Nordamerikas Förenta Stater," *Biblioteksbladet,* Stockholm, Årgång 23, No. 1, 1938, pp. 10–17. Also in: *Bibliotheekleven,* Rotterdam, Jaargang 23, No. 10, Oct., 1938, pp. 197–204. DLC, NNY.

A Swedish librarian reports on her impressions of children's library work in the U.S. Text of the original in Swedish, in the second article mentioned, Dutch.

3929. James, Hannah P. "Yearly report on the reading of the young," *Library journal,* New York, Vol. 10, Nos. 9–10, Sept., 1885, pp. 278–291. DLC, NNY.

A survey of what children were reading as reflected in the 75 questionnaires which were returned to Miss James by libraries from around the country.

3930. James, Louise, "Books for the gifted child." Strang, Ruth May. *Helping your gifted child.* New York, Dutton, 1960. 270p. DLC, NNY.

An annotated list arranged by grade level, and followed by suggested book lists for parents, and a list of references used in compiling the bibliography.

3931. Janacek, Blanche. *An analysis of the literature on the education and preparation of librarians who work with youth.* Chicago, University of Chicago, Graduate Library School, 1946. Typewritten report.

3932. ———. *Comparison of the use made of the public library and the school library by elementary*

school students. Chicago, University of Chicago, 1949. 160p. Thesis.

3933. Jenks, Tudor. "At the book-fair in Yuletide," *Independent,* New York, Vol. 52, Dec. 13, 1900, pp. 2991–2994. DLC, NNY.

An amusing article conveying a sense of dismay at the number and poor quality of the books published for children each year.

3934. ———. "The modern child as a reader," *Book buyer,* New York, Vol. 23, No. 1, Aug., 1901, pp. 17–19. NNY.

"Modern children have so much else to do that they do not read as we used to read. They are embarrassed by riches. Books are cheap, abundant, and little valued . . . the taste for reading is blunted by the trash that tempts and disappoints young readers. Finding so many books dull, they conclude that none is worth the trouble of reading . . . Children who still 'love reading' are old fashioned."

3935. ———. "Reference books for boys and girls," *St. Nicholas,* New York, Vol. 25, No. 5, Mar., 1898, pp. 405–408. DLC, NNY.

A review of those reference books which children can enjoy using in checking facts related to some interest, or simply to explore the world of knowledge.

3936. Jeter, M. H. *Presentation of the Negro in children's books published between 1951–1960.* Atlanta, Atlanta University, 1962. 115p. Thesis.

3937. Jewett, Arno. *Improving reading in the junior high school.* Washington, D.C., Superintendent of Documents, 1957. (Department of Health, Education and Welfare, Conference on Improving Reading, 1956. Bulletin No. 10). DLC.

A report of a conference which dealt mostly with techniques of reading, but which also included many possible approaches to stimulating youth toward better choices in reading.

3938. Johnson, B. Lamar. "The school library." National Society for the Study of Education. *36th yearbook.* Bloomington, Ill., 1937. Part 1, pp. 255–274. DLC.

The school library can succeed only to the extent that it contributes to the educational program of the school as a whole.

3939. Johnson, Clifton. *Old time schools and school books.* New York, P. Smith, 1935, 381p. DLC.

A fascinating study of early American schools with emphasis on Massachusetts where much of the first experimentation took place. Although many references are to textbooks, there is a great deal said about reading in general. This is profusely illustrated with contemporary prints, engravings, etc., and covers approximately the period from 1640–1850.

3940.   Johnson, Crompton T. . . . *A book-collector's primer, being a selection of early American children's books offered for sale by Crompton T. Johnson from his stock of rare books at 84 Trumbull Street, Hartford, Conn.* . . . Windham, Conn., Hawthorn House, 1934. 7 ll. NNY.

The 26 items are designated by the alphabet instead of numbers and include both early U.S. originals as well as some modeled on the Newbery's and other British publications.

3941.   Johnson, Dorothy Turner. *Suggestion of methods to be used in integrating stories and their music.* Cleveland, Western Reserve University, 1958. 70p. Thesis.

3942.   Johnson, Edna. *et al. An anthology of children's literature.* 3rd rev. ed. Boston, Houghton, 1959. $12.00. DLC, NNY, IYL.

One of the more complete anthologies intended for the teachers and students of children's literature. There are very good introductory remarks to each of the chapters to aid in the personal evaluation of children's literature. An appendix includes the history of children's literature, storytelling, examples of the work of children's book illustrators, biographical sketches of writers of children's books, graded reading lists and lists of award books. Co-editors were Evelyn Sickels and Frances Clarke Sayers.

3943.   Johnson, Marjorie. "Children's books in English with Spanish or Spanish-American background," *Hispania,* Stanford University, Vol. 24, May, 1941, pp. 202–204. NNY.

A list of fifty books, not annotated.

3944.   Johnson, Sister Marie Inez. *The development of separate service for young people in public libraries in the United States, and its implications for library schools.* Baltimore, Enoch Pratt, 1940. 43p. DLC. (Mimeographed reproduction of a thesis, Columbia University, New York, 1940).

This is a compilation of the results of a detailed survey which was sent to a large number of libraries throughout the United States asking for information concerning their special services to the young adult reader.

3945.   Johrden, Judith A. *Bibliotherapy for children: A selective, annotated bibliography, 1950–1962.*

Washington, Catholic University of America, 1964. 34p. Thesis.

3946.   Joint Committee of the National Education Association and the American Library Association. *Choosing and buying books for school libraries.* Chicago, ALA, 1941.

Prepared by O. H. McPherson.

3947.   Joint Committee of the American Association of Teachers Colleges and the American Library Association. *How shall we educate teachers and librarians for library service in the schools?* New York, Columbia University Press, 1936. 74p. DLC, NNY.

Some joint recommendations on the qualifications necessary to have good quality school library service.

3948.   Jones, William Alfred. "Books for children," *Essays upon authors and books.* New York, Stanford and Swords, 1849, pp. 230–296. NNY.

A short but excellent essay in which the author writes that the majority of books for children at that time were puerile, not juvenile. He recommended a return to the fairy tales and romances of a hundred years ago.

3949.   Jordan, Alice M. *Books for boys and girls, in the Public Library of the city of Boston.* 2nd ed. rev. Boston, The Library Trustees, 1913. 110p. DLC.

An author, title, subject catalog, not annotated, of the entire collection of children's books in the Library at that time.

3950.   ———"A chapter in children's libraries," *Library journal,* New York, Vol. 38, Jan., 1913, pp. 20–21. DLC, NNY.

An article describing the history of the Ebenezer Learned juvenile library in West Cambridge, Massachusetts (later Arlington), which this librarian contended was the very first public children's library in the U.S.

3951.   ———. *Children's classics.* Boston, Horn Book, 1960. 16p. $00.75. DLC, NNY.

An enthusiastic and loving appreciation of some of the classics with a few thoughts as to why they have lasted. The revised and expanded list of recommended editions was compiled by Helen Masten.

3952.   ———. "Early children's books," *More books, Bulletin of the Boston Public Library,* Boston, Vol. 15, No. 5, Apr., 1940, pp. 185–191. DLC, NNY.

The purchase of 50 early children's books (by the Boston Public Library) gives rise to a discussion and speculation on the general nature of 19th-century children's books.

3953. ———. *From Rollo to Tom Sawyer and other papers.* Boston, *Horn book,* 1948. 160p. $3.75. DLC, NNY.

A series of charming essays on some 19th-century writers of books for children which show the relation between books for children and the social history of their period. The second chapter which gives its title to the book was the first Caroline M. Hewins lecture at Swampscott, Massachusetts. It presents a survey of the reading of New England children during the 1870's. The author was Supervisor of Work with Children at the Boston Public Library and lecturer on Children's Literature at Simmons College.

3954. Jordan, Arthur Melville. *Children's interest in reading.* Chapel Hill, University of North Carolina, 1926. 103p. DLC.

The author suggests observation of children at their reading in libraries as the best way to make a survey of reading preferences. He believed that questionnaires given to children brought unreliable results, since the answers children give rely on fleeting, day-to-day likes and dislikes.

3955. Julitta, Sister Mary. *A list of books for retarded readers.* Champaign, Illinois, National Council of Teachers of English, 1961. 8p. $00.20.

A reprint of an article in *Elementary english,* Feb., 1961. This is a classified and annotated list for the first three levels of reading.

3956. *Junior high school library catalog.* New York, H. W. Wilson, 1965. 768p. $20.00 NNY, DLC.

This is a companion volume to the *Children's catalog* (3593) classifying more than 3000 books of interest to this age level.

3957. Junior Literary Guild. *To enrich young life, 10 years with the Junior Literary Guild in the schools of our country.* Garden City, New York, Junior Literary Guild, 1939. 144p. DLC, IYL, NNY.

How one of the major commercial book clubs for children in the U.S. maintains its operations.

3958. "Juvenile and young adult books," *Paperbound books in print,* New York, Vol. 1 ff., 1955 ff. DLC. NNY.

This monthly and annual compilation has a separate section for the children's books currently available in paperback format. It is published by the R. R. Bowker Company which is compiling a separate

catalog for the hardbound trade children's books in print.

3959. Kahn, D. K. *An analysis of the treatment of minority groups in children's literature.* Chicago, University of Chicago, 1955. 78p. Thesis.

3960. Kapp, Isa. "Books for Jewish children; the limits of the didactic approach," *Commentary,* New York, Vol. 8, Dec., 1949, pp. 547–553. DLC, NNY.

A provocative evaluation of some of the U.S. books which treat of the Jewish religion, its holidays, practices, etc., as reflected in Jewish family life in the U.S. The author concludes: "The ability to confound simple ideologies is the test of a really good book." There are some replies to the article in the Feb., 1950 issue, pp. 189–191.

3961. Kaul, R. *An analysis of cultural content of a selected list of children's books on India.* Washington, Catholic University, 1960. 111p. Thesis.

3962. Kealy, Sister Mary E. *An empirical study of children's interests in spiritual reading.* Washington, Catholic University, 1930. 107p. NNY.

Children's ideals, beliefs and interests in religious reading, interpreted through their reactions to a selected set of books. Includes a graded list of spiritual reading. Bibliography and index.

3963. Kennedy, H. T. *Suggestive list of children's books for a small library.* Madison, Wisconsin, Free Library Commission, 1910. 102p.

3964. Kennerly, Sarah Law. *Confederate juvenile imprints.* Ann Arbor, Mich., University Microfilms, c. 1958. 485p. Thesis. DLC on microfilm.

Subtitled "Children's books and periodicals published in the Confederate States of America 1861–1865." Part I is a survey and Part II a bibliography of 6 periodicals and 150 books, 70 per cent of which were textbooks. This would prove equally valuable and fascinating to the historian of the Civil War period. There is an exhaustive bibliography.

3965. Kenney, William F. "How the Boston Public Library attends to the child readers and cooperates with the public schools." Congrès International des Archivistes et Bibliothécaires; *Actes;* Bruxelles, 1910, pp. 546–554. DLC.

A report presented by the director of the Library to the public library section of the Congress. He stressed the free aspects of services to children, and the ways in which the public schools have cooperated in introducing the public library to the child.

444

3966.   Kennon, Mary Frances and Leila A. Doyle. *Planning school library development.* Chicago, ALA, 1962. 89p. DLC, NNY.

"A report of the School Library Development Project, AASL, Feb. 1, 1961–July 31, 1962." This was a project funded by a grant from Council on Library Resources, which: "Provided leadership training for representatives from fifty states; allocated grant funds for twenty-one special projects in school library development, prepared and distributed a wide variety of printed and audio-visual materials; and gave consultant service to state and local groups in conferences, correspondence, and visits to the areas."

3967.   Kenworthy, Leonard Stout. *Introducing children to the world in elementary and junior high schools.* New York, Harper, 1956. 268p. $4.95. DLC, NNY.

Books, audio-visual materials, projects and trips which can help to broaden the horizons of children, and make them more aware of the world's cultures and peoples. The emphasis is decidedly on books. There are bibliographies and sources of information and materials. Indexed. Mr. Kenworthy is the compiler of several World Affairs Guides, published by Teachers' College, Columbia University aimed at teachers in elementary and secondary schools, to show how books can be used to bring about better international understanding.

3968.   ———. *Studying the world: Selected resources.* New York, Columbia University, Teachers College, 1965. 83p. $1.50.

One of several guides listing books, films, pamphlets, periodicals and other materials available on the major geographical areas of the world. The others are: *Studying Africa in Elementary and Secondary Schools,* 1965, 60p. $1.50; *Studying the Middle East . . . ,* 1965, 57p., $1.50; *Studying South America . . . ,* 1965, 54p., $1.50.

3969.   Kerlan, Irvin. "Collecting children's books," *Private library,* Middlesex, Vol. 5, Jan., 1964, pp. 1–4. DLC, NNY.

A well-known collector tells of how he came to acquire this interest, some of the joys it affords him, and something about his personal collection.

3970.   ———. *Newbery and Caldecott awards. A bibliography of first editions.* Minneapolis, University of Minnesota Press, 1949. 51p. DLC.

Of interest to the collector who needs concrete and specific signs to look for in first editions. Arranged chronologically.

3971.   Kern, Carl Benton. *Selected books for boys.* New York, Y.M.C.A. Press, 1907. 44p.

3972.   Keyes, Angela Mary. *Stories and storytelling.* New York, Appleton, 1911. 286p.

3973.   Kiefer, Monica. *American children through their books 1700–1835.* Philadelphia, University of Pennsylvania, 1948. 248p. $5.00. DLC, IYL, NNY.

This book reveals fresh and authentic material on many phases of child life in America through an analysis of the books they read. The writing is lively and interesting. Dorothy Canfield Fisher has written the introduction.

3974.   Kiely, Mary Frances. *Traffic lights; safe crossways into modern children's literature from the Catholic point of view.* New York, Pro Parvulis Book Club, 1941. 110p. DLC.

Exactly what the subtitle implies. Numerous selection guides and lists are suggested and there is an index.

3975.   King, Charles Manton. *Selected home readings for boys.* Cleveland, Ohio, E. Schulte, 1914. 51p. DLC.

A forward-looking list intended for use by boys at the University school in Cleveland based on the principles of selection approved by the National Council of Teachers of English. This makes interesting material for comparison with similar lists of today.

3976.   King, William A. *The elementary school library.* New York, Scribner's, 1929. 224p.

3977.   Kingman, Lee. *Newbery and Caldecott Medal books, 1956–1965.* Boston, Horn Book, 1965. 300p. DLC, IYL, NNY.

This brings further up to date the two earlier books of the same type (see 4099 and 4100). In addition to the usual acceptance speech, biography and excerpt, there are three fine evaluative articles: "Twenty medal books: in perspective" by Elizabeth H. Gross; "Picture books today" by Norma R. Fryatt; "Only the best" by Carolyn Horowitz. There is also an appendix listing runners-up for Newbery and Caldecott awards for all the years when such honors were given.

3978.   Kircher, Clara J. *Behavior patterns in children's books: A bibliography.* Washington, Catholic University Press, 1966. 132p. $3.75 ($1.95 paper cover). DLC, NNY.

This list is a replacement for *Character Formation Through Books,* 1952, although it has more titles and includes only children's books for preschool through grade nine, and does not include adult books as did the earlier edition. Arrangement of the 507 titles is by general situations, e.g., "Making friends," "Fitting in at school," "The new baby," etc. There is an extensive bibliography on the effects of reading on behavior and there is a behavior index as well as author and title indexes.

3979.　Kite, T. *Juvenile catalog for 1829*. Philadelphia, T. Kite, Bookseller, 1829. 12p. DLC.

3980.　Klemin, Diana. *The art of art for children's books: A contemporary survey*. New York, Clarkson N. Potter, 1966. 128p. $6.95. DLC, NNY.

The work of 63 contemporary illustrators of children's books is discussed in personal, informal terms, based on sound artistic judgement. For each artist, there is a black and white reproduction of a page from a recent book. There are also reproductions in color for eight of the artists. The author is an art director in a large publishing house. There is a short bibliography and an index.

3981.　Knox, Rose B. "The South in books for children," *Wilson bulletin*, New York, Vol. 9, No. 5, Jan., 1935, pp. 246–252. DLC, NNY.

An annotated list of children's books divided by historical periods and arranged chronologically.

3982.　Kodjhanoff, S. G. *The history of children's books*. Chicago, University of Chicago, 1911. Thesis.

3983.　Korff, Alice G. "Children's books, 1944–1945," *American magazine of art*, New York, Vol. 38, May, 1945, pp. 191–194. DLC, NNY.

A selected list of 20 titles chosen for excellence in illustration, format and text.

3984.　Kramer, Sister M. Immaculata. "Children's interests in magazines and newspapers," *Catholic educational review*, Washington, Vol. 39, May, 1941, pp. 284–290; June, 1941, pp. 348–358. NNY.

Comments and criticisms on a wide selection of reading interest surveys with a condensation and comparison of their conclusions.

3985.　Kready, Laura Fry. *A study of fairy tales*. Boston, Houghton, 1910. 313p. DLC, NNY.

The value of fairy tales, how to select them for telling, and how to tell them. The author also goes into the history and classes of folk and fairy literature and its sources. An appendix reprints some hard-to-find tales. Index.

3986.　Krieg, L. L. *Suggested method of analyzing children's fiction reading*. Chicago, University of Chicago, 1943. 83p. Thesis.

3987.　Kroeger, Alice B. "Children's reading," *Guide to the study and use of reference books*. 3rd ed. Chicago, ALA, 1917, pp. 189–191. DLC, NNY.

Annotated list of selection aids, useful for possible historical comparison.

3988.　Krutch, Joseph Wood. "Should we bring literature to children, or children to literature?" Marshall, John David. *Books, libraries, librarians*. Hamden, Conn., Shoestring Press, 1955, pp. 108–113. DLC, NNY.

Literature should stay right where it is, argues this writer, and children should be brought to it. He was against vocabulary control, attempts at categorizing children's reading tastes, and the over-use of books and other media for "information and propaganda" as opposed to true "education."

3989.　Krzywda, Sister M. M. *A study of "Why Johnny Can't Read" and its criticisms*. Cleveland, Western Reserve University, 1961. 172p. Thesis.

3990.　Kunitz, Stanley J. and Howard Haycraft. *The junior book of authors*. 2nd ed., rev. New York, H. W. Wilson, 1951. 309p. DLC, IYL, NNY.

Sketches of 289 individual authors, chosen by specialists and librarians. Many of them are autobiographical, and almost all are accompanied by a portrait. Most of the subjects are Americans, but some British writers are included. See also *More Junior Authors* (3772).

3991.　LaBrant, Lou Le Vanche and Frieda M. Heller. *An evaluation of free reading in grades seven to twelve inclusive in the Ohio State University School*. Columbus, Ohio, State University, 1939. 158p. (Contributions to Education, 4). DLC.

A reading interest study centered around the preteen-age group. The results are very elaborately tabulated and analyzed.

3992.　Ladies Commission on Sunday-School Books. *Books for children; a list selected from the annual catalogues of 1866–85; with descriptive notes*. Boston, American Unitarian Association, 1886. 48p.

3993.　Ladley, Winifred C. *et al*. "Current trends in public library service to children," *Library trends*, Chicago, Vol. 12, July, 1963, pp. 1–118. DLC, NNY.

Following an excellent historical summary of children's library services in the U.S., by Frances C. Sayers, there are articles on virtually all aspects of current work with children in public libraries. The authors include Virginia Haviland, Peggy Sullivan, Maxine LaBounty, Spencer Shaw, Jeanne Hardendorff, Hilda K. Limper, Bernice Bruner, Ruth Warncke and Elizabeth Burr.

3994. Landreth, Catherine and Willa Schmidt. *Book list for nursery school children*. Berkeley, University of California, Institute of Child Welfare, 1950. 15p. DLC.

A list which is selective, but not annotated. Arrangement is by subject or type of book, such as "Concept" books, "Sensory experiences," etc.

3995. Landry, K. B. "Bibliography of books written by children of the twentieth century," *More books, Bulletin of the Boston Public Library*, Boston, Vol. 12, April, 1937, pp. 149–157. DLC, NNY.

Although not all of the items can be considered children's books, they all were written by young persons under 17 years of age. Very few of the names would be recognized today. The appendix lists some contemporary critical references.

3996. Lanigan, Edith. "The child in the library," *Atlantic monthly*, Vol. 87, Jan., 1901, pp. 122–125. DLC, NNY.

What happens when the child is confronted with the privileges of the free public library for the first time. Somewhat sentimental in tone, but probably a close approximation of the impact of the library on many children.

3997. Larrick, Nancy. *A parent's guide to children's reading*. Garden City, New York, Doubleday, 1964. 312p. $2.95. Also: New York, Pocket Books, Inc., 1964. 258p. $00.50. DLC, IYL, NNY.

A popularly written manual for parents, giving sensible advice in terms understandable to and appreciated by them. Many books are recommended in the course of each chapter. Index.

3998. ———. *A teacher's guide to children's books*. Columbus, Ohio, C. E. Merrill Books, 1960. 316p. Also abridged edition 1963, 238p. DLC, NNY.

A curriculum-oriented handbook designed to inspire teachers toward a wider use of books with their pupils. The abridged edition leaves out the list of favorite books of boys and girls. Index.

3999. ———. *Your child and his reading; how parents can help*. New York, 1959. 28p. (Public Affairs Pamphlet, No. 278). DLC, NNY.

A pamphlet on reading guidance, based on the author's *A Parent's Guide to Children's Reading*.

4000. Lathrop, Edith A. *County library service to rural schools*. Washington, U.S. Government Printing Office, 1930. 53p. (Office of Education Bulletin, No. 20). DLC.

4001. Latimer, Louise Payson. *Illustrators; a finding list*. Boston, Faxon, 1927. 26p. DLC. Also in: *Bulletin of bibliography*, Boston, Vol. 13, Nos. 2, 3, 4, 5, Jan., 1927–Apr., 1928. DLC, NNY.

A very useful early list, arranging the illustrators alphabetically, and giving all of their known work which appeared in books.

4002. ———. *The organization and philosophy of the children's department of one public library*. (Washington, D.C. Public Library). Boston, Faxon, 1935. 41p. (Useful Reference Series, No. 55). DLC, IYL, NNY.

A remarkably comprehensive view of the work done by a children's department with examples of some of the handling of problems that can arise.

4003. ———. "They who get slapped," *Library journal*, New York, Vol. 49, July, 1924, pp. 623–626. DLC, NNY.

A well-known children's librarian speculates on the reasons behind the stereotype of the "old-maid" lady librarian. She expresses the belief that some of the stereotype is grounded in fact, and that more children's librarians must have the courage of their convictions and reject the mediocre regardless of what image this might project. She concludes: "We are cultivating commonness as if it were a virtue."

4004. Lawler, C. C. *Analysis and evaluation of the Newbery Award books*. Kent, Ohio, Kent State University, 1962. 44p. Thesis.

4005. Lawrence, Isabel. *Classified reading; books for the school, the library, and the home*. St. Cloud, Minn., the author, 1898. 423p. DLC.

Intended mainly for the teacher to improve her general knowledge as well as to point out ways of using books with children.

4006. Lazar, May. *Guiding the growth of reading interests*. New York, Bureau of Reference Research and Statistics, 1945. (Education Research Bulletin, 8).

4007. ———. *Reading interests, activities and opportunities of bright, average and dull children*. New York, Columbia University Teacher's College, 1937. (Contributions to Education, No. 707). DLC.

An investigation which went into the school facilities, home backgrounds, reading interests and activities of 4,300 children. Only general conclusions could be drawn from the results, which lead to more questions. An appendix includes tables and statistics. Bibliography.

4008.   Leacock, Stephen B. "Mother Goose step for children," *Forum*, New York, Vol. 79, Mar., 1928, pp. 365–369. DLC, NNY.

Concerning the expurgating of violence, horror, blood, giants, witches, ogres, etc., from fairy tales, which this critic and humorist found to be totally unnecessary. "Don't worry about the apparent terror and bloodshed in children's books . . . There is none there. It only represents the way in which little children, from generation to generation, learn in ways as painless as can be followed the stern environment of life and death."

4009.   Leary, B. E. and Dora V. Smith. *Growing with books: A reading guide*. Eau Claire, Wisconsin, Hale, 1952. DLC.

A revised edition of the earlier list by Nora Beust.

4010.   Leavitt, Marianne G. M. *Effect of school library facilities on fifth and sixth grade reading habits*. Philadelphia, Drexel Institute of Technology, 1954. 66p. Thesis.

4011.   Ledlow, Elaine A. *Reading interests in the second and third McGuffey readers*. Denton, Texas State College for Women, 1951. 101p. Thesis.

4012.   Lee, Gerald Stanley. *The child and the book*. New York, Putnam, 1907. 161p. DLC.

Essays on children, books and reading, which first appeared in the author's *The Lost Art of Reading*. They are humorous and full of tongue-in-cheek wit, but also contains many glittering generalities.

4013.   Lefevre, A. L. "Library service to children in the United States." International Congress of Libraries and Documentation Centres, 4th, Brussels; *Reports and Communications*, Vol. 2A; La Haye, Martinus Nijhoff, 1955; pp. 264–269. DLC.

A very general summing-up of the various services offered in school and public libraries.

4014.   Legler, Henry E. "Library work with children," *ALA bulletin*, Chicago, Vol. 5, 1911, pp. 240–246. DLC, NNY.

A paper read at the Pasadena conference. This was a passionate plea for putting more effort behind the work being done with children. It is followed here by papers by Gertrude Andrus on work

with children in the summer playgrounds, and by Harriet A. Wood on work with schools.

4015.   ———. "Library work with children: a synoptical criticism," *ALA bulletin*, Chicago, Vol. 10, July, 1916, pp. 205–208, 411–421. DLC, NNY.

Some of the conclusions were that children spent too many hours in reading, that their reading was fragmentary, that there were too many books being written for children, that the classics were being neglected or shamefully abridged, and that librarians purchased too many titles of second-rate books, rather than adding copies of the best books.

4016.   Leland, Claude G., *et al*. *The library and the school*. New York and London, Harper, 1910. 87p. DLC.

Reading activities for children in many areas of the U.S., as reported by teachers and school superintendents. Didactic, but of possible historical interest.

4017.   Lemley, Dawson E. *Development and evaluation of administrative policies and practices in public school library service as evidenced in city school surveys, 1907–1947*. Pittsburgh, University of Pittsburgh, 195? Dissertation.

4018.   Leonard, Sterling Andrus. *Essential principles of teaching reading and literature, in the intermediate grades and the high school*. Philadelphia, Lippincott, 1922. 460p. DLC.

What the teacher's own literary equipment should consist of, and how to use it effectively with children and young people. Bibliography and graded book lists.

4019.   Levi, Doris Jean. *Participation of three public libraries in leisure-time activities for youth in the field of fine arts*. Atlanta, Atlanta University, 1951. 58p. Thesis.

4020.   Lewis, Claudia. *Writing for young children*. New York, Simon and Schuster, 1954. 115p. DLC, NNY.

In this book of technique the author recommends using actual conversation among children as the take-off point on how to begin writing for the very young child. She cites many appropriate examples.

4021.   Leypoldt, Augusta H. and George Iles. *List of books for girls and women and their clubs*. Boston, Library Bureau, 1895. Pt. 1, 161p. NNY, DLC. Pt. 2, 153p. DLC.

An annotated list arranged under 25 general subject headings. Periodicals are listed separately. Part 1 is fiction and Part 2 is biography, history, travel literature (poetry, essays and criticism) and folklore.

4022.   "Libraries in secondary schools; a new look." Entire issue of: *Bulletin of the National Association of Secondary School Principals,* Washington, Vol. 50, No. 306, Jan., 1966, pp. 1–106. DLC, NNY.

These 16 articles provide some of the more current views expressed in print. The authors, all leaders in the area of school libraries and educations, are: Homer O. Elseroad, Gene L. Schwilk, Virginia McJenkin, Margaret Hayes Grazier, Sara Krentzman Srygley, Georgia Cole, Richard L. Darling, J. Lloyd Trump, Milbray J. Jones, Myrl Ricking, Jean E. Lowrie, Eleanor E. Ehlers, Frances Henne, Peggy Sullivan, Cora Paul Bomar and Margaret E. Nicholsen.

4023.   Lind, Katherine Niles. "The social psychology of children's reading," *American journal of sociology,* Chicago, Vol. 41, Jan., 1936, pp. 454–469. DLC, NNY.

The author compiled 44 documents from life histories of individual persons concerning the effects of their childhood reading. This is written from the point of view of reading as a social experience rather than a literary one.

4024.   Linscott, Robert Newton. *A guide to good reading.* Boston, Houghton Mifflin, 1912. 128p. DLC.

Practical directions for the use of *The Children's Hour* in the home. This was a kind of encyclopedia and collection of children's literature of many types, in a multi-volume set. This handbook gave suggested further reading on the subject of each volume, as well as biographical notes on the authors whose works appeared in the set. Index.

4025.   Lipkis, Rita. "Notes on: Growing up with books; a parents' course in children's literature," *Adult leadership,* Washington, Vol. 14, Feb., 1966, pp. 262–264, 275. NNY.

This unusual course was sponsored by the adult-education branch of the Los Angeles City Schools. The author was the teacher and she outlines here in brief the points which were covered.

4026.   Logasa, Hannah. *Book selection in education for children and young adults.* Boston, F. W. Faxon, 1965. 266p. (Useful reference series, No. 93.) DLC.

A revision of the author's earlier work, *Book Selection Handbook for Elementary and Secondary Schools.* This is arranged according to the subject areas of the curriculum, treating of the special problems of selection in each area and listing special aids and lists when available.

4027.   Loh, J. T. *A story hour program to introduce to children representative American composers; a combination of music and stories illustrating types of musical compositions in various historical periods.* Seattle, University of Washington, 1955. 75p. Thesis.

4028.   Lohrer, Alice, *et al.,* "Current trends in school libraries," *Library trends,* Chicago, Vol. 1, No. 3, Jan., 1953, pp. 259–422. DLC, NNY.

This special issue concerned all aspects of school library history, development, and current problems. Contributors were Frances Henne, Mildred Batchelder, Alice LeFevre, Hazelle M. Anderson, Viola James, Mary P. Douglas, Ruth Ersted, M. L. Nickel, F. F. Morton, Margaret Hayes and Alice N. Fedder. While much of the background material is still valid, a number of the articles are quite dated in their approach.

4029.   Long, Harriet G. *Rich the treasure. Public library service to children.* Chicago, ALA, 1953. 78p. $2.00. IYL, DLC, NNY.

The history, ramifications and present state of library work with children, and a rich catalogue of reasons to provide inspiration for the future.

4030.   ———. *Wider horizons in library service to boys and girls.* Geneseo, N.Y., State University College, 1962. 17p. (Mary C. Richardson lecture, No. 5.) DLC.

An inspiring call for an awareness of the burgeoning knowledge of child development and behavior patterns. There is a bibliography of books and articles mentioned.

4031.   Lovell, M. M. *Negro stories for children, a subjective criticism.* Berkeley, University of California, 1937. 40p. Thesis.

4032.   Lovett, R. M. "A boy's reading fifty years ago," *New republic,* New York, Vol. 48, Nov. 10, 1926, pp. 334–336. DLC, NNY.

An amusing "confession" as to the author's often poor taste in his boyhood reading. He even resorted to the series of girls' stories. However, his main point is that because he was also given much that was good to read, the dime novels and other pulp literature soon lost his interest.

4033.   Lowe, Orton. *Literature for children.* New York, Macmillan, 1914. 298p. DLC, NNY.

A history and criticism intended as a guide to the study of children's literature. Bibliography and index.

4034. Lowrey, Rosewell G. "What one child read, and why," *Peabody journal of education*, Nashville, Tenn., Vol. 5, Jan., 1928, pp. 246–250. NNY.

Recalling what he had read in his youth, the author attempts to analyze why he had so liked the cheap series books with stock characters and implausible action. He concludes that such reading is not detrimental, provided that care is taken to ensure a wide choice of materials when the time is ripe for the youngster to change.

4035. Lowrie, Jean E. *Elementary school libraries*. New York, Scarecrow Press, 1961. 235p. $5.00. DLC.

A current handbook of organization and practice, with bibliographies and recommended book lists. The author has also included copies of letters from various authorities on the subject of school libraries.

4036. ———. *Elementary school libraries; a study of the program in ten school systems in the areas of curriculum enrichment and reading guidance . . .* Cleveland, Western Reserve, 1959. 305p. Dissertation.

4037. Lucas, Mary R. *The organization and administration of library service to children*. Chicago, ALA, 1941. 107p. DLC, NNY.

Written as a master's thesis for the University of Chicago, this carries emphasis on organization and form rather than on actual discussion of service and its results. Extensive use of tables and charts.

4038. ———. "Our friendly enemy?" *Library journal*, New York, Vol. 66, Oct. 1, 1941, pp. 824–827. DLC, NNY.

Results of an interesting experiment in Baltimore libraries, using huge Superman posters in prominent displays in the children's rooms. There was a marked increase in circulation during the display period, especially among the 8–11 year-olds. The comics themselves were not given out, however. One of the conclusions was that there are simply not enough strong action books to give to this age to satisfy their demand for adventurous reading.

4039. Lumpkin, M. C. *An analysis of the content of a selected number of children's magazines*. Atlanta, Atlanta University, 1955. 104p. Thesis.

4040. Lutheran Church (Missouri Synod). Young People's Literature Board. *Notable books for Christian children*. St. Louis, Concordia, 1960. 52p. Supplements: 1961, 23p.

An annotated list, arranged by subject.

4041. Lynn, Ida M. *Cleanliness stories for children*. New York, Cleanliness Institute, 1931. 31p. NNY.

An annotated list typical of a large number which were put out by organizations having little to do with children's books.

4042. Mabie, Hamilton Wright. *Fairy tales every child should know*. New York, Doubleday, 1905. DLC.

This collection was important in that it counteracted much of the influence of those educators who were opposed to fairy tales. The preface by Mr. Mabie is a well-thought-out defense for the inclusion of fairy tale literature in the life of every child. The preface is not in some of the later editions of the book.

4043. McAree, J. "A select bibliography of paperback books on Africa for secondary school use," *Social studies*, Philadelphia, Vol. 57, Dec., 1966, pp. 304–307. DLC, NNY.

4044. MacClintock, Porter Lander. *Literature in the elementary school*. Chicago, University of Chicago Press, 1907. 305p. NNY.

A handbook exploring the types of books suitable for use in the elementary school with lists of the basic books to be used in each year. The author was a follower of the educator, John Dewey. Much of this appeared in articles in the *Elementary School Teacher*.

4045. McCracken, Elizabeth. "What children like to read," *Outlook*, New York, Vol. 78, Dec. 3, 1904, pp. 827–832. NNY.

The author points out how difficult and misleading it is to say what children like—each age has its particular enthusiasms and few children seem to be in the same age at the same time.

4046. McCrady, Louisa Lane. "The child and imaginative life," *Atlantic monthly*, Boston, Vol. 100, No. 4, Oct., 1907, pp. 480–488. DLC, NNY.

The writer believed that only the child who could be brought to imagine things from other points of view than his own would eventually grow up to become a mature person with natural sympathy for the human condition.

4047. McCrea, Mary Helen, *et al. Significance of the school library; an aid for speakers and writers*. Chicago, ALA, 1937. 40p. DLC.

Short and long quotations of varying excitement and literary merit on aspects of the school library.

4048. MacCunn, Florence. "A plea for precocious children," *Living age,* Boston, Vol. 213, No. 2759, May 22, 1897, pp. 543–548. NNY.

The author wishes that precocious children were not looked upon as some dreaded disease or as the personal accomplishment of the parents. She feels they should be given as much leeway and encouragement in breadth of reading matter as they seem able and willing to absorb.

4049. McElderry, Margaret K. "A few men and women; an editor's thoughts on children's book publishing," *The New York Public Library bulletin,* New York, Vol. 65, Oct., 1961, pp. 505–516. DLC, IYL, NNY.

A leading children's book editor speaks about this exciting and challening work. This was given as one of the Anne Carroll Moore Spring Lectures.

4050. McFadden, Dorothy L. *How to run a book fair.* New York, Children's Book Council, 1962. 35p. $1.25. DLC, NNY.

Practical suggestions to individuals or groups as to how to organize and manage a book fair in a school, church or other institution.

4051. McGee, N. S. *Developing a book selection program for a junior high school.* Los Angeles, University of Southern California, 1957. 76p. Thesis.

4052. McGreal, Mary Madeline. *Integration of the school library with classroom activities; an experiment in coopertion between the librarian and teachers of English.* Seattle, University of Washington, 1952. 43p. Thesis.

4053. McGuire, Alice Brooks. *Developmental values in children's literature.* Chicago, Department of Photoduplication, University of Chicago Library, 1958. 209p. DLC has microfilm.

An attempt to verify the presence of deeper purpose beyond that of giving pleasure, in four children's books. Comparisons are made of the authors' stated purposes, the opinions of students in children's literature and the appraisals made by a group of children.

4054. Mack, E. B. *The school library's contribution to the total educational program of the school: A content analysis of selected periodicals in the field of education.* Ann Arbor, University of Michigan, 1957. 378p. Dissertation.

4055. Mackassy, Louise. *Vocational approach to children's librarianship.* Kent, Ohio, Kent State University, 1954. 59p. Thesis.

4056. McLaughlin, O. L. *A study of three teaching materials centers.* Washington, Catholic University of America, 1956. 158p. Thesis.

4057. McLoughlin Brothers. *One hundred years of children's books.* Springfield, Mass., McLoughlin Brothers, 1928. 40p. NNY.

The history of a publishing house which specialized in trick books, shaped books and inexpensive series. With many colored illustrations.

4058. McMurry, Charles. *A special method in the reading of complete English classics in the grades of the common schools.* New York, Macmillan, 1903. 254p. NNY.

Chiefly pedagogical in approach, this is nevertheless of interest for its strong backing of keeping the classics intact and getting children to read up to them rather than watering them down.

4059. McPheeters, A. L. *The scarcity of children's librarians in public libraries.* Atlanta, Georgia, The author, 1961. 47p. Thesis.

4060. McPherson, O. H. "School library objectives; a program and a prophecy," *New York libraries,* Albany, Vol. 14, May, 1935, pp. 193–196. NNY.

A reply to an earlier article by Henry S. Canby excoriating the schools for not producing readers. This librarian contended that the school could not produce readers until taxpayers and school boards saw fit to appropriate enough money to purchase books for the school libraries.

4061. Macy, John Albert. *A child's guide to reading.* New York, The Baker and Taylor Co., 1909. 273p. DLC.

The guide refers to those adult books which older children will also enjoy. Much of what this critic wrote could be read today with equal profit.

4062. Mahar, Mary Helen. *Activities and services of the school library as related to modern concepts of its educational function.* New York, Columbia University, 1950. 30p. Thesis.

4063. ———. *Partners in school library progress: Administrators and librarians.* Kent, Ohio, Kent State University, 1960. 8p. (Aspects of librarianship, No. 24.)

4064. ———. *The school library as a materials center: Educational needs of librarians and teachers in its administration and use.* Washington, Office of Education, 1963. 84p. DLC.

Proceedings of a conference sponsored by the Office of Education in May, 1962. Participants whose papers are reprinted here were: J. A. Boula, Mary V. Gaver, Frances Henne, L. H. Janke, Jean E. Lowrie, Virginia McJenkin, and E. T. Schofield. This was extremely influential in turning the trend of school libraries toward this form of materials center.

4065. ———. *School library programs in the NDEA Title III program.* Washington, Office of Education, 1965. 15p.

4066. ———. *State Department of Education responsibilities for school libraries.* Washington, Office of Education, 1960. 42p.

4067. Mahoney, Sally M. and Liselotte Z. Stokes. "A school library program for the blind," *Wilson library bulletin,* New York, Vol. 40, No. 9, May, 1966, pp. 829–831. DLC, NNY.

A description (with photographs) of an unusual school library, which served children with normal sight as well as partially sighted and blind children. A Braille card catalog was developed with the assistance of the blind children.

4068. Mahoney, Bertha E. and Elinor Whitney. *Contemporary illustrators of children's books.* Boston, Bookshop for Boys and Girls, 1930. 135p. DLC, NNY.

Here are short biographies of illustrators working at the time of this publication, which also includes a bibliography of their works. Most of the pieces are autobiographical. This is a large, flat book with text printed in double columns on each page and illustrated in color and in black and white with attractive drawings from the artists' books. A partial bibliography is appended for each of some twenty illustrators from whom the editors were unable to get biographies.

4069. ———. *Five years of children's books,* supplement to *Realms of gold.* Garden City, New York, Doubleday, 1936. 599p. DLC, NNY.

This is still useful because of the annotated booklists along with *Realms of gold* to which it is a supplement.

4070. Mahony, Bertha E. *et al. Illustrators of children's books: 1744–1945.* Boston, Horn Book, 1947. 527p. $10.00. DLC, IYL, NNY.

This invaluable and beautiful book recreates the whole spectrum of children's book illustration from the earliest days. The contributors are distinguished people in the book world. They are Anne Thaxten Eaton, Jacqueline Overton, Bertha E. Mahony, Robert Lawson, Maria Cimino, Helen Gentry, Philip Hofer, Hellmut Lehmann-Haupt, May Massee, Lynd Ward and Louise Payson Latimer. The book is divided into four parts: I. History and Development, including ten articles dealing with different periods; II. Biographies of Living Illustrators; III. Bibliographies, including A Century and a Half of Illustration, A Bibliography of Illustrators and their works, and A Bibliography of Authors. The appendix gives sources, notes and references, a list of artists represented by illustrations and an Index to Part I.

4071. ———, and Elinor Whitney. *Realms of gold in children's books.* Garden City, New York, Doubleday, 1929. 796p. DLC, NNY.

This is the 5th edition of "Books for Boys and Girls—a Suggestive Purchase List" previously published by The Bookshop for Boys and Girls, Women's Educational and Industrial Union, Boston, Massachusetts. It came out of the work done in that unparalleled shop and still has its place in historical collections and library school collections.

4072. Maloff, Saul. "Teaching Johnny to cop out," *Commonweal,* New York, Vol. 82, May 28, 1965, pp. 321–323. DLC, NNY.

". . . sensibilities are shaped by what we feed them while they are still malleable; and arguing from that [I] suggest a spirit trained up on the aesthetic of compromise and the cop-out cannot later be expected to stand too much reality." The critic explores this trend of "evading the issue," which he feels is all too prevalent in contemporary children's books.

4073. Manthorne, Jane. *The whole world in your hands.* Washington, D.C., National 4-H Club Foundation, 1962. 4p. $00.10.

An annotated list of children's books arranged by geographical area.

4074. Marantz, Kenneth. *A bibliography of children's art literature.* Washington, D.C., National Education Association, 1965. 24p. $00.45.

A classified and annotated list of 165 books on art and its related fields.

4075. Markey, Lois R. *Books are vacations!* Boston, Horn Book, 1956. 32p. DLC.

An annotated list meant to be used by children in guiding them to good reading for their vacation and free time.

4076.   Martignoni, Margaret E. *Family reading and storytelling*. New York, Grolier Society, 1954. 21p.

4077.   ———. *Qualifications and performance of children's librarians in public libraries of the United States*. New York, Columbia University, 1951. 73p. Thesis.

4078.   Martin, Helen. *Children's librarianship as a profession*. Cleveland, Western Reserve University, School of Library Service, 1928.

4079.   ———. "Children's preferences in book illustration," *Western Reserve University bulletin*, Cleveland, Vol. 34 (New Series), No. 10, July 15, 1931. 58p. DLC.

"The aim of this study is to present in popular form the method of procedure followed and to summarize the results secured." It is interesting to note that most of the books used in this survey are still in print, often with the same original illustrations.

4080.   ———. "Nationalism in children's literature," *Library quarterly*, Chicago, Vol. 6. No. 4, Oct., 1936, pp. 405–418. DLC, NNY.

A careful study of a representative group of children's books from 17 countries, correlating the nationalistic factors present to conditions of national crisis in the country concerned. The U.S. had the highest nationalism score.

4081.   Martin, Laura K. *Magazines for school libraries*. Rev. ed. New York, H. W. Wilson, 1950. 196p. DLC.

A technical aid to help in selection, purchase and use of magazines with students. The list of periodicals and their indices are out-of-date, but the general criteria are still usable.

4082.   Marvin, Dwight E. *Historic child rhymes; a monograph on the origin and growth of the rhymes that children use and love*. Norwell, Mass., Ross Bookmakers, 1930. 266p. DLC.

A history of well-known U.S. and English rhymes. Bibliography and index.

4083.   Mary Paula, Sister. "The treatment of death in children's literature," *Catholic library world*, Haverford, Pa., Vol. 32, Jan., 1961, pp. 226–230. DLC, NNY.

The author examines some of the current children's books which treat of death, or in which a death is a central part of the action. Her analyses are made from the Christian point of view.

4084.   Mason, Eleanor B. *Contribution for the Junior Literary Guild books to the school library's reading program*. New York, Columbia University, 1949. 157p. Thesis.

4085.   Massee, May. "Twenty years of children's books," *Publishers' weekly*, New York, Vol. 134, No. 9, Sect. 2, Aug. 27, 1938, pp. 673–679. DLC, NNY.

An illustrated article reviewing this editor's contribution to the progress of children's literature. Most of the books referred to are still in print and being read.

4086.   Masterton, Elizabeth G. *Evaluation of the school library in the reading program of the school*. Chicago, University of Chicago, 1953. 47p. Thesis.

4087.   Mathes, Miriam Snow. *et al. A basic book collection for elementary grades*. 7th ed. Chicago, ALA, 1960. 144p. $2.00.

An annotated list of some 1,000 books and magazines arranged by decimal classification and with author, title and subject index.

4088.   Mathiews, Franklin K. "The influence of the Boy Scout movement in directing the reading of boys," *ALA bulletin*, Chicago, Vol. 8, Jan., 1914, pp. 223–228. DLC, NNY.

The author reports here on some of his observations made during a tour of the U.S., for the purpose of evaluating boys' reading.

4089.   Matthews, Caroline. "The growing tendency to over-emphasize the children's side," *Library journal*, New York, Vol. 33, Apr., 1908, pp. 135–138. DLC, NNY.

In the rural South, children's libraries and school libraries often overlap on their work to the detriment of service to adults, especially those barely literate, who could be helped so much.

4090.   Matthews, Harriet L. "Children's magazines," *Bulletin of bibliography*, Boston, Vol. 1, Apr., 1899, pp. 133–136. NNY.

An annotated list and critical comments on a number of children's magazines giving date of first issue and other useful data.

4091.   Mattill, Barbara A. *An international youth library in the United States*. Typewritten manuscript. IYL.

A rather idealistic proposal for the establishment of such a library in connection with one of the international organizations, or with an existing library system.

4092. Melcher, Frederic G. "Thirty years of children's books," *ALA children's library yearbook,* Chicago, No. 1, 1929, pp. 5–10. DLC, NNY.

The stimulation to book publishing which resulted from the growth of children's library work.

4093. ————. "What's ahead for children's books?" *ALA bulletin,* Chicago, Vol. 34, Aug., 1940, pp. 189–191. DLC, NNY.

A review of trends of the past 20 years and some ideas for the future. Mr. Melcher commented on the domination of the field by women, which he felt was one of the reasons for the lack of "red-blooded boys' books."

4094. Mennig, Mary Elizabeth. *Analysis of children's books published in 1951, available in one community.* Cleveland, Western Reserve, 1952. 81p. Thesis.

4095. Metcalf, Robert C. "Reading in the public schools," *Library journal,* New York, Vol. 4, Nos. 9–10, Sept.–Oct., 1879, pp. 343–345. DLC, NNY.

One of several articles on this subject in this issue. Others are by W. E. Foster, Wm. P. Atkinson, and Mellen Chamberlain. They all deal with the extent of responsibility public libraries have in providing service to teachers and pupils in the schools.

4096. Methodist Church (U.S.) Publishing House. *Chronological outline of church school story papers in America.* Nashville, Methodist Publishing House, Editorial Division, 1943. 23p. Mimeograph. NNY.

"Outline developed in cooperation with 26 denominational publishers of church school story papers." The period covered is from 1823 to 1941 and the information given includes title, sponsoring church or organization, year of first and last issues, place of publication and other pertinent remarks. An invaluable source for the person interested in this sidelight of U.S. children's literature.

4097. Metzner, Seymour. *American history in juvenile books.* New York, H. W. Wilson, 1966. 329p. $7.00.

A chronological list of children's books on U.S. history, graded and annotated.

4098. Meyer, Anne A. "Children's books about the Middle East," *Horn book,* Boston, Vol. 40, No. 3, June, 1964, pp. 308–314. DLC, NNY.

A list of 62 books divided into general subject categories and annotated.

4099. Miller, Bertha Mahony and Elinor Whitney Field. *Caldecott Medal books: 1938–1957.* Boston, Horn Book, 1957. 329p. (Horn Book Papers, Vol. 2). $10.00. DLC, IYL, NNY.

"With the Artists' Acceptance Papers and Related Material chiefly from the Horn Book Magazine." This companion volume to *Newbery Medal Books, 1922–1955* includes a survey of the Caldecott award-winning books as well as an introductory paper on Randolph Caldecott and a critical analysis of picture books by Esther Averill.

4100. ————. *Newbery Medal books: 1922–1955.* Boston, Horn Book, 1955. 458p. (Horn Book Papers, Vol. 1). $10.00. DLC, IYL, NNY.

This handsome book celebrates 33 years of Newbery awards. A review, a biographical note, the acceptance paper, an excerpt from the winning book, and in most cases, a facsimile paper are given for each winner. Where papers were incomplete, new ones were commissioned. For instance, Anne Carroll Moore wrote a biographical note on Hendrik van Loon.

4101. Miller, E. *Books and reading in homes for children in Los Angeles.* Los Angeles, University of Southern California, 1956. 38p. Thesis.

4102. Miller, Eleanor Olmstead. *A study of the preschool child's picture and story books by the battery of tests method.* Madison, University of Wisconsin, 1928. Thesis. Also in: *Journal of applied psychology,* Athens, Ohio, Vol. 13, No. 6, Dec., 1929, pp. 592–599. DLC, NNY.

This educator had applied a complicated system of "evaluation" for picture books, according to their physical sizes, design, number of pages, etc. This is perhaps typical of the kind of study which can result when the direct use of books with children is forgotten or overlooked in favor of a "modern" educational technique.

4103. Miller, Mrs. John A. *List of books for the earliest reading, prepared by Faith Latimer* (pseud.). New York, Ward and Drummond, 1887. 24p. DLC.

A publisher's list, arranged by general age groups and subjects, and briefly annotated. Of some historical interest.

4104. Miller, Marilyn M. *Application of audio-*

visual aids in the library pre-school storyhour. Kent, Ohio, Kent State University, 1954. 65p. Thesis.

4105. Miller, Olive (Beaupré). *Right reading for children. What is it? Where to find it? How to use it?* Chicago, The Book House for Children, 1921. 16p. DLC.

A plea for good literature for children, delivered as an address to a woman's club. The author describes at the end her editing plans for the *My Book House* series.

4106. Mills, Forrest Laird. "Trends in juvenile and young adult use and services." Chicago University. Graduate Library School. *The medium-sized public library: Its status and future.* Chicago, University of Chicago Press, 1963, pp. 58–69.

4107. Milton, Jennie Low. *Courses in children's literature in colleges and universities in the U.S.* Ann Arbor, Michigan, Edwards Bros., 1946. 271p. (Doctoral Thesis, Columbia University, Teachers' College, 1945). DLC.

A survey of courses offered in some 261 institutions with a view toward standardizing the teaching of children's literature.

4108. Mitcham, Merlin Lee. *Southwest folklore for junior high school libraries with special reference to the folklore of Texas.* Denton, Texas State College for Women, 1953. 64p. Thesis.

4109. Mitchell, Donald Grant. *About old story tellers: Of how and when they lived, and what stories they told.* New York, Scribner's, 1877. 237p. NNY.

Chapters on the history of books and printing and on such writers as Goldsmith, Swift, Maria Edgeworth, Bernardin de St. Pierre, the Grimms, Scott, Defoe, John Bunyan.

4110. Mitchell, Lucy Sprague. *Here and now story book.* New York, E. P. Dutton, 1921. 356p. DLC, NNY.

The introduction, pp. 1–72, is very important for the influence which this school of educators had on writing for very young children and the use of fairy tales with them. The theory behind it can be summed up in this quotation: "Children do not find the unusual piquant until they are firmly acquainted with the usual; they do not find the preposterous humorous until they have intimate knowledge of ordinary behavior . . . Too often we mistake excitement for genuine interest and give children stimulus instead of food. The fairy story, the circus, novelty hunting, delight the sophisticated adult; they excite and confuse the child. Red Riding-Hood and circus Indians excite the little child; Cinderella confuses him. Not one clarifies any relationship which will further his efforts to order the world. Nonsense recognized and enjoyed as such is more than legitimate . . . But nonsense which is confused with reality is vicious,— the more so because its insinuations are subtle. So far as their content is concerned, it is chiefly as a protest against this confusing presentation of unreality, this substitution of excitement for legitimate interest, that these stories have been written."

4111. Mohammed el-Hagrasy, S. *The teacher's role in library service: An investigation and its devices.* New Brunswick, N.J., Rutgers University, 1961. 267p. Dissertation.

4112. Monahan, Marietta. *A comparison of student reading in elementary schools with and without general libraries.* Chicago, University of Chicago, 1956. 63p. Thesis.

4113. Moody, E. L. *Establishment of good public relations between a school library and its community.* Los Angeles, University of Southern California, 1956. 34p. Thesis.

4114. Moore, Anne Carroll. *Creation and criticism of children's books.* Chicago, ALA, 1934. 8p. NNY.

Reprint of a paper read at the meeting of the Section for Library Work with Children, at the Montreal convention in 1934. This pays tribute to H. E. Scudder, Mary Mapes Dodge, John F. Sargent, Caroline M. Hewins and others who were influential in the development and criticism of 19th-century children's literature.

4115. ———. *List of books recommended for a children's library.* n.p., Iowa Library Commission, 1903. 22p. DLC, NNY.

This was one of the earliest works which Miss Moore was commissioned to compile. It reflects her concern for the highest standards in children's books.

4116. ———. *My roads to childhood. Views and reviews of children's books.* Boston, Horn Book, 1961. 399p. $2.00. DLC, IYL, NNY.

This contains the critical essays and reviews issued originally in book form in *Roads to Childhood* (1920), and *New Roads to Childhood* (1926), revised and expanded under the title *My Roads to Childhood* (1939). For this edition, Frances Clarke Sayers wrote an introduction, pointing out the timelessness of Miss Moore's literary criticism.

4117. ———. "Recoiling from reading; a consideration of the Thorndike library," *Library journal,* New York, Vol. 60, May 15, 1935, pp. 419–422. DLC, NNY.

Miss Moore was greatly disturbed by Professor Thorndike's experiments in vocabulary control. She believed that a deep love and knowledge of literature could not be instilled in children "by word changing or reconstruction of sentence at the cost of beauty, humor, the sound of words and the sense of their inner meaning."

4118. ———. "The reviewing of children's books," *The bookman,* New York, Vol. 61, May, 1925, pp. 325–331. DLC, NNY.

This represents the culmination of many of Miss Moore's views on the criticism of children's books. She divides them into the two classes of "creative, belonging to the very essence of literature, timeless and ageless in . . . appeal," and "informative, belonging to the social period for which the books are written." Miss Moore also laments the lack of teaching of children's literature in colleges and universities.

4119. ———. *Seven stories high—the child's own library.* Chicago, Compton, 1940 ff. Frequently revised. (Reprint from *Compton's pictured encyclopedia*).

This important list has now been replaced by Mrs. Sayers' *A Bounty of Books* (4278).

4120. ———. "Special training for children's librarians," *Library journal,* New York, Vol. 23, No. 8, Aug., 1898, pp. 80–82. Also in *Public libraries,* Chicago, Vol. 4, No. 3, Mar., 1899, pp. 99–102. DLC, NNY.

"Every kind of specialized work presupposes on the part of those who undertake it personal fitness, general training in the general work of which the special work forms a part, and special training in the special duties to be undertaken." Miss Moore then expands each of these three areas with reference to the children's librarian.

4121. ———. "Story hour at Pratt Institute Free Library," *Library journal,* New York, Vol. 30, No. 4, Apr., 1905, pp. 204–211. DLC, NNY.

A long, excellent article on this pioneering effort in story-telling giving much of the mood and purpose that has continued to animate story-telling to this day.

4122. ———. *The three owls.* Book 1, New York, Macmillan Co., 1925. 376p. Book 2, New York, Coward-McCann, 1928. 440p. Book 3, New York, Coward-McCann, 1931. 462p. DLC, IYL, NNY.

The first is subtitled "A book about chil-

dren's books; their authors, artists and critics" and the second and third have as a subtitle "Contemporary criticism of children's books." These phrases describe the contents of all three volumes outwardly, but do not begin to indicate the scope of the criticisms nor their influence. The reviews were the work of Miss Moore herself as well as of many of the leading writers, critics, librarians and editors of the day. Most of them appeared originally in *Books.* For consistent, sustained criticism of a major portion of the children's books produced, this period has never been equalled before or since.

4123. ———. "Touchstones for children's libraries," *Bookman,* New York, Vol. 63, No. 5, July, 1926, pp. 579–586. DLC, NNY.

A reminiscence of some of the persons and places which provided Miss Moore and others with the "touchstones" by which they could judge the quality of their efforts.

4124. ———. "Viewing and reviewing books for children," *Bookman,* New York, Vol. 50, No. 1, Sept., 1919, pp. 29–37. DLC, NNY.

"From the days of Peter Parley we have been taking 'peeps,' 'glimpses,' 'zigzag journeys,' and 'excursions' to various countries at an educational jog-trot." No wonder, wrote this critic and librarian, that our children never really get to know what other children's lives are like around the world. She felt that the reviewer should be particularly careful with the foreign-background book.

4125. ——— and Bertha Mahony Miller. *Writing and criticism; a book for Margery Bianco.* Boston, Horn Book, 1951. 93p. DLC, NNY.

Essays on writing books for children, and on criticism of these books. Although this is done in the framework of a commentary on Margery Bianco's work, the values apply to much of children's literature.

4126. Moore, Annie Egerton. *Literature old and new for children; materials for a college course.* Boston, Houghton, 1934. 446p. DLC, NNY.

An early outline for a course in children's literature, together with examples of each type of children's literature. Bibliographies and an index.

4127. Moore, Jean McCoy. *A study of the communications behavior of a selected group of children at a home for dependent children.* Atlanta, Atlanta University, 1960. 113p. Thesis.

4128. Moore, Vardine. *Pre-school story hour.* New York, Scarecrow Press, 1966, 123p. DLC.

Practices and procedures, the roles of child, storyteller, parent, suggested programs and materials and a book list are part of the many points included in this handbook. Bibliographies for each chapter.

4129. Moreland, George B. "What young people want to read about," *Library quarterly*, Chicago, Vol. 10, Oct., 1940, pp. 469–493. DLC, NNY.

A very extensive reading interest survey undertaken among a group of adolescents. There are many charts and graphs illustrating the results.

4130. Morin, Louise E. *Study of juvenile historical fiction concerned with the Colonial Period in United States history.* Pittsburgh, Carnegie Institute of Technology, 1952. 71p. Thesis.

4131. Morris, Effie L. *A mid-century survey of the presentation of the American Negro in the literature for children published in the United States between 1900 and 1950.* Cleveland, Western Reserve University, 1956. 124p. Thesis.

4132. ———. "Serving the handicapped child," *Wilson library bulletin*, New York, Vol. 38, Oct., 1963, pp. 165–169. DLC, NNY.

This librarian helped to establish the first separate children's library for the blind in one of the branches of the New York Public Library. She discusses here the history of library service to blind children on the national level, established by an act of Congress in 1952. Many of the children's books available in Braille or on talking books are mentioned specifically by title.

4133. Morse, James Herbert. "The training of boys: books," *Harper's bazaar*, New York, Vol. 34, No. 11, Mar. 16, 1901, pp. 728–731. DLC, NNY.

Advice to parents on how to guide boys in their reading, without forbidding them certain types, which will only lead them more surely to want exactly those to read.

4134. Moses, Montrose J. *Children's books and reading.* New ed. New York, Kennerley, 1924. 272p. DLC.

"A right action, a large human, melodramatic deed, are more healthy for boys and girls than all the reasons that are given for them." This characterizes Mr. Moses' forthright approach to the history of children's reading. An appendix gives lists of books for children on all subjects. This first appeared in 1907.

4135. ———. "The children's library and the

home, *Outlook*, New York, Vol. 87, No. 4, Sept. 28, 1907, pp. 177–185. DLC, NNY.

The complicated responsibility of the public library in relation to home reading is dealt with in this early article which is still pertinent, particularly in its emphasis on quality. Illustrated with photos of some pioneer children's rooms and a few of the reading club "shacks" in the industrial areas of Pittsburgh.

4136. ———. "Convalescent children's literature," *The North American review*, Boston, Vol. 221, Mar., 1925, pp. 528–539. DLC, NNY.

A plea for high standards in children's literature, together with a review of some old favorites.

4137. Mott, Carolyn and Leo B. Baisden. *The children's book on how to use books and libraries.* Rev. ed. New York, Scribner, 1961. 207p. $2.96, DLC, IYL, NNY.

A good example of a manual for use by children.

4138. Mott, Frank Luther. "For childhood and youth; The fertile vineyard; For the young in heart; Children's books again," *Golden multitudes; the story of best sellers in the United States.* New York, Macmillan, 1947. pp. 26–34; 97–103; 155–165; 224–225. DLC, NNY.

These four chapters cover four eras of the popular reading taste of America's youth.

4139. Moulton, Charles Wells. [Authors of children's classics.] *The library of literary criticism of English and American authors.* 7 vols. Buffalo, New York, Moulton Pub. Co., 1902. DLC, NNY.

Although the extracts are sometimes taken out of context, this is helpful in tracing contemporary reviews of the works by leading British and U.S. authors which have now come to be regarded as children's classics. The majority of works covered are general literature. The volumes are arranged chronologically, and within each the authors are arranged alphabetically.

4140. Moulton, Priscilla L. "Books on modern life in other countries," *Top of the news*, Chicago, Vol. 17, No. 1, Oct., 1960, pp. 12–24. DLC, NNY.

A list of 98 titles was selected from reliable sources and read; only 24 were recommended as being accurate. All had publication dates of 1950 or later.

4141. Mumford, Edward Warloch. *Juvenile readers as an asset.* Philadelphia, Penn Publishing Co., 1912. 5p. DLC. (DLC also has a modified version called *Choosing books for boys and girls,* same pub., 1912, 14p.).

A paper read before the American Booksellers' Association May 15, 1912, reprinted in pamphlet form. The problems of the bookseller, how to find good books and encourage parents to buy them, the ways of cooperating with libraries and other agencies are some of the points discussed.

4142.   Munro, Eleanor C. "Children's book illustration," *Art news,* New York, Vol. 53, Dec., 1954, pp. 41–48. DLC, NNY.

A survey of current trends with thirty reproductions in black and white.

4143.   Munson, Amelia. *An ample field; books and young people.* Chicago, ALA, 1950. 122p. $3.00. DLC, IYL, NNY.

The challenge, resources and techniques of work with young people. This was a milestone in the history of library work with the teen-age and had far-reaching influence in changing the patterns of this service.

4144.   Musichuk, Olga. *Place and role of the pre-school story hour in the public library.* Pittsburgh, Carnegie Institute of Technology, 1952. 93p. Thesis.

4145.   Myers, Gary Cleveland and Clarence Wesley Summer. *Books and babies.* Chicago, McClurg, 1938. 116p. DLC.

A chatty report on the "Mothers' Rooms" in the libraries of Youngstown, Ohio. This is some of the earliest documented work with pre-school children in the library. Bibliography and book list are very dated.

4146.   Myron, P. E. H. *A comparison of the grade placement given to selected books of children's fiction evaluated in the "Bulletin of the Center for Children's Books," the "Booklist," and "Library Journal."* Chapel Hill, University of North Carolina, 1955. 70p. Thesis.

4147.   National Aerospace Education Council. *Aeronautics and space bibliography for the elementary grades.* Washington, U.S. Government Printing Office, 1963. 33p. DLC.

"Prepared for the National Aeronautics and Space Administration" (NASA).

4148.   National Association of Independent Schools. *Current books, junior booklist.* Boston, The Association. Annual $1.00.

An annotated list arranged by age groups.

4149.   National Conference of Christians and

Jews. *Books for brotherhood.* New York, The Conference, 1966. 14p.

This list is revised annually and is free in single copy orders. It is a list of children's books which demonstrate the brotherhood of man.

4150.   National Congress of Parents and Teachers and Children's Services Division, ALA. *Let's read together: Books for family enjoyment.* Chicago, ALA, 1964. 91p. $1.50.

An annotated list of 750 titles arranged by subject interest and age groups.

4151.   National Council of Teachers of English. *Books for you.* New York, Washington Square Press, 1964. $.90. DLC, NNY.

This annotated list of books for young adults was compiled by Richard Alm.

4152.   ———. *Report of the Committee upon Home Reading.* Chicago, The Council, 1913. 16p. DLC.

A list of books for home reading intended for use by teachers. Arranged by broad subject areas.

4153.   ———. Elementary School Booklist Committee. *Adventuring with books.* Rev. ed. Champaign, Ill., The Council, 1966. 256p. DLC, NNY. Also available in paper: New American Library, 1966. 256p. $00.65.

This classified list of over 1,000 titles was compiled by Elizabeth Guilfoile and Jeannette Veatch. Publisher's index and index of titles, authors and illustrators.

4154.   National Education Association. Department of Elementary School Principals. "Elementary school libraries," *NEA yearbook,* 12th. Washington, National Education Association, 1933, pp. 1–518. DLC.

This extensive study had 10 chapters on: modern education and the library, status of school libraries, organization and administration, planning, relations with public libraries, the library and the classroom, the school librarian, rural and state practices, supervision, and research studies on reading interests. Each had several articles by different persons in the field, and for each there is a bibliography.

4155.   ——— and American Association of School Librarians. *The paperback goes to school.* New York, Bureau of Independent Publishers and Distributors, 1964–1965. 130p. DLC.

A list of 3,500 paperback titles arranged by subject, author and title. This is not a selective list, but rather indicates the wide assortment available.

4156. National Recreation and Park Association. *For the story teller.* Washington, D.C., The Association, 1961. 32p. $00.85.

A short guide to storytelling techniques and a list of stories to tell.

4157. ———. *A guide to books on recreation.* Washington, D.C., The Association, 1966. 31p. $00.25.

An annotated and classified list of more than 600 books on all types of recreation.

4158. National Union of Christian Schools. *Good reading.* Grand Rapids, Mich., The Union, 1963. 100p. DLC.

A list of recommended books by grade and subject areas.

4159. Naumburg, Elsa H. *Books for the young readers.* New York, Child Study Association of America, 1926. 80p. DLC.

"A list of over 500 selected books for boys and girls from seven to twelve." Annotated and arranged by general subjects. Index of titles only.

4160. Nesbitt, Elizabeth. "Library service to children," *Library trends,* Chicago, Vol. 3, Oct., 1954, pp. 118–128. DLC, NNY.

This was one article in an issue devoted to "Service to Readers." Miss Nesbitt gives an excellent brief survey of children's services and then characterizes the current trends.

4161. ———. "The shortening of the road," *Library journal,* New York, Vol. 63, Nov. 1, 1938, pp. 834–835. DLC, NNY.

A paper read at the yearly conference which states beautifully and succinctly the philosophy of children's library service which Miss Nesbitt was developing in her teaching at the Carnegie Library School, Pittsburgh.

4162. New York (City). Board of Education. Bureau of Libraries. *Catalogue of books for public school libraries in the city of New York.* New York, Bureau of Libraries, 1904. 202p. NNY.

This early catalog was used by the H. W. Wilson Company in its first compilation of the *Children's Catalog.* It is divided into graded class lists, and a reference library for teachers, arranged by subjects.

4163. ———. Mayor's Committee for the Selection of Suitable Books for Children in the Courts. *An invitation to read, the use of the book in child guidance.* 2nd ed. New York, Municipal Reference Library, 1941. 90p. NNY.

This annotated list arranged by age levels was a pioneer in the special area of social rehabilitation through reading guidance.

4164. ———. Pierpont Morgan Library. *Children's literature; books and manuscripts.* New York, Pierpont Morgan Library, 1954. Unp. DLC.

The catalog of an exhibit from the collections of the library. It is arranged in 4 groups: "Education," "Fables and fairy tales," "Poetry and nursery rhymes," and "The moral tale to Mickey Mouse." Each is carefully described and annotated. Among the important early works shown was a copy of the first Bible known to be made for children. Reference bibliography and index.

4165. New York Library Association. *Children's booklist for small public libraries.* Rev. ed. Albany, N.Y. State Library, 1964. 98p. NNY.

An annotated list of about 750 titles arranged by subject and graded for preschool to grade nine.

4166. ———. *Once upon a time.* Albany, New York Library Association, 1964. 16p. $00.50.

Suggestions for all types of storytelling programs, together with a list of sources.

4167. *Newbery Medal books.* Chicago, ALA, annual. 6p.

This brochure is revised annually to include the current year's winners. The complete list of past winners is also given.

4168. Newell, William W. *Games and songs of American children.* New York, Harper, 1883. 242p. DLC, NNY.

A historical study which serves as the basis for most of the later research on the subject. The various types and themes of games and songs are explored, and many are compared to those of other countries. Bibliography.

4169. Newman, Anna B. "Children as authors," *Wilson bulletin,* New York, Vol. 11, No. 7, Mar., 1937, pp. 476–477. DLC, NNY.

An annotated list of some 28 books which the compiler believed to qualify as written by a juvenile author.

4170. "Newspapers and children's books," *Top of the news,* Chicago, Vol. 15, May, 1959, pp. 7–12. DLC, NNY.

A symposium which attempted to explore the

reasons why parents are so ill-informed on the selection of good children's books for home purchase. The papers are by Helen Sattley, John M. Harrison, Lucille W. Raley and Mary E. Ledlie. The blame, most of them felt, lay in the poor reviewing of children's books and newspapers which reach the average home.

4171. Newton, Alfred Edward. "The books of my boyhood," *Ladies home journal,* New York, Vol. 44, Nov., 1927, pp. 22–23, 114–119. DLC, NNY.

A personal reminiscence about such books as *Sandford and Merton,* the Rollo Books, *Swiss Family Robinson* and many others. Illustrated with black and white cuts.

4172. Newton, Mary G. *Books for deaf children; a graded annotated bibliography.* Washington, Alexander Graham Bell Association for the Deaf, 1962. 173p. DLC, NNY.

This list was based on Mrs. Newton's experiences in working with deaf children at the Detroit Day School for the Deaf.

4173. Nolen, Eleanor W. "The national library builds a children's book collection," *Horn book,* Boston, Vol. 14, July, 1938, pp. 246–248. DLC, NNY.

A description of the collection of children's books being developed for the Library of Congress by Valta Parma. This refers only to those in the Rare Book Collection.

4174. Norvell, George W. *The reading interests of young people.* Boston, Heath, 1950. 262p. DLC.

"Three factors inherent in children influence their reading: intelligence, age, and sex." This is a classic example of the over-simplification which can result when manipulating the inexhaustible number of combinations available in a large statistical study. This was conducted among 50,000 high school students in New York state. Data tables, author and title index and an appendix giving a report on an experimental free reading project.

4175. ———. *What boys and girls like to read.* Morristown, New Jersey, Silver Burdett, 1958. 306p. DLC.

An exhaustive study of children's reading interests in the elementary school with most data provided in tabular form. Chapter summaries might be useful as indicators for selection and direction of reading. Author and title index is separate from general index.

4176. *Notable children's books 1940–1959.* Chicago, ALA, 1966. 48p. $1.50. NNY, DLC.

A reappraisal of 20 years of the notable book lists compiled by the Children's Services Division.

4177. *Notable children's books of* ———. Chicago, ALA, Annual. 4p.

This selection is made each year by a committee of the Children's Services Division. It is annotated and available free on request (single copy).

4178. Nowlin, Clifford Hiram. *The storyteller and his pack.* Springfield, Mass., Milton Bradley Co., 1929. 408p. DLC.

A storytelling textbook, reviewing the history, development of technique, etc. There are examples, questions and exercises for each chapter.

4179. Nunnally, Nancy. *Guide to children's magazines, newspapers, reference books.* Washington, D.C., Association for Childhood Education International, 1966. 8p. $00.10.

An annotated list of this kind of material arranged by type.

4180. O'Brien, Mae. *Children's reactions to radio adaptations of juvenile books.* New York, King's Crown Press, 1950. 146p. DLC, NNY.

A doctoral thesis at Columbia University, this study presents the results garnered from 5 years' work among a group of 10 year old children. The author found the children to be discriminating in taste and articulate in discussing the stories they had heard.

4181. O'Donnell, Athalene L. *International library service for children.* Cleveland, Western Reserve University, 1949. 64p. Thesis.

4182. O'Hanlon, M. C. *A bibliography of American Catholic juvenile literature 1850–1890.* Washington, Catholic University, 1961. 186p. Thesis.

4183. Ojemann, Ralph Henry. *The child and his reading.* Iowa City, University of Iowa Press [1941]. 12p. (Publications, new series, No. 1224, Dec., 1941). DLC.

A little of the history of children's books, some of the critical principles developed for the selection of books for children, and methods of introducing books to children in home and school.

4184. Olcott, Frances Jenkins. "American children have the literature of the world," *Publishers weekly,* New York, Vol. 104, No. 20, Nov. 17, 1923, pp. 1651–1654. DLC, NNY.

Some of the translations of foreign books, only a few of which are still in print and read.

4185. ———. "The children's free library and city education," *The American city,* New York, Vol. 8, No. 3, Mar., 1913, pp. 257–264. DLC, NNY.

"The ideal public library is the people's university, offering education free for all, and founding its work on the thorough training of the children." In this periodical devoted to city planning, the author stressed the importance of quality, rather than quantity, and deplored the attitudes of many city boards which would not appropriate further funds unless circulation statistics increased each year.

4186. ———. *The children's reading.* Boston, Houghton, 1927. 427p. DLC, NNY.

First published in 1912, this soon made its place in almost every children's library. The author dealt with good and bad reading, ways of guiding children in their reading, and observing their interests. An appendix listed the state and provincial library commissions in existence at that time. There is also a recommended book list. Index.

4187. ———. "Home libraries for poor children," *Chautauquan,* Springfield, Ohio, Vol. 39, No. 4, June, 1904, pp. 374–380. DLC, NNY.

A detailed description of the purposes and operation of the home libraries of Pittsburgh, most of which served immigrant families. Preceding this (pp. 369–374) is "The children's room in the public library" by Mary Emogene Hazeltine.

4188. ———. *Library work with children.* Chicago, ALA Publishing Board, 1914. 34p. DLC, NNY.

This is a reprint from the *Manual of Library Economy.* It was a guide to use in setting up a children's library. Bibliography.

4189. ———. "The public library; a social force in Pittsburgh," *Survey,* New York, Vol. 23, Mar. 5, 1910, pp. 849–861. DLC, NNY.

A very detailed report on the social service aspects of this library's work with children. This contains much historical data and statistics, as well as a number of photographs.

4190. ———. "Rational library work with children and the preparation for it," *Library journal,* New York, Vol. 30, No. 9, Sept., 1905, pp. 71–75. DLC, NNY.

This paper, read at the annual ALA conference in 1905, delineated the characteristics of the good children's librarian and suggested a training program which was then put into use at the Carnegie Library School. In an inspiring passage, Miss Olcott also illustrated how the particular physical and cul-

tural circumstances of an area or community can control the development of its library program.

4191. Olson, Barbara V. *Aids for librarians in elementary schools.* Champaign, Ill., National Council of Teachers of English, 1963. 7p. (Reprint from *Elementary english,* May, 1961).

General booklists, selection tools, indexes, sources of audio-visual materials, bibliographies, and other helpful material on children's books are listed here.

4192. Ørvig, Mary. "Den separata biblioteksservicen för tonårsgruppen vid större amerikanska folkbibliotek," *Biblioteksproblem.* Stockholm, Natur och Kultur, 1959. pp. 74–113. BTJ.

"Separate library services to teenagers in American public libraries." This Swedish librarian and observer comments on her visits to major and minor library systems and she outlines the service given in seven large cities. There is a four-page list of references, mostly in English.

4193. Owen, Helen H. "Photographic picture books," *Publisher's weekly,* New York, Vol. 120, Oct. 24, 1931, pp. 1923–1925. DLC, NNY.

Concerning the vogue of using photographs to illustrate picture books for children. A number of specific examples are shown. This is only one article in an interesting book week issue.

4194. Packer, K. H. S. *Early American school books; a bibliography based on the Boston booksellers' catalogue of 1804.* Ann Arbor, University of Michigan, Department of Library Science, 1954. (Studies, No. 1).

4195. Parker, Elinor M. and Natalie Norton. *Reading is fun; a guide to children's literature.* New York, Scribner, 1948. 52p. DLC.

This list was compiled for commercial use in a bookstore. It is arranged by general subject and age groups, and there is a short bibliography of further reading for parents and teachers.

4196. Parsons, Frank. "What to give to children," *The world's best books.* 3rd ed. Boston, Little, Brown, 1893, pp. 97–127. NNY.

The general principles by which to choose books for children, and some annotated lists of books for various levels and interests.

4197. Partridge, Emelyn Newcomb and George E. *Story telling in school and home.* New York, Sturgis & Walton Co., 1912. 323p. DLC.

"A study in educational aesthetics." Includes a bibliography.

4198. Pearson, Edmund Lester. "Wizards and enchanters. With, ho! such bugs and goblins," *Books in black and red*. New York, Macmillan, 1923, pp. 53–66, 129–138. DLC.

The first essay is an appreciation of the *St. Nicholas* magazine and the second is on the dime novel. Both make delightful reading.

4199. Peck, Harry Thurston. "The new child and its picture books," *The personal equation*. New York, Harper, 1898, pp. 193–210. NNY.

A very amusing essay on the effect "Educationists" have had on children's books.

4200. Peele, David Arnold. *Lollipops or dynamite —shall we censor the comics?* Cleveland, Western Reserve University, 1951. 46p. Thesis.

4201. Peltola, Bette J. "A study of children's book choices," *Elementary english*, Champaign, Vol. 40, Nov., 1963, pp. 690–695. DLC.

Children of the very early grades were given sets of picture books from the AIGA list for 1958–1960 (see 3419) and books not on that list, but on other recommended lists. The purpose was to test for children's choices as governed by illustrations. In the majority of cases, the non-AIGA list books were first choices.

4202. Penney, Ida Woodrow, *et al. Teaching children's literature,* New York, Globe Book Co., 1934. 46p. DLC.

An early manual for teachers, with suggested "book quiz" questions and other similar activities.

4203. Penniman, James Hosmer. *Children and their books.* Syracuse, C. W. Bardeen, 1921. 45p. DLC.

A slim volume giving a short, thoughtful discussion of children's reading and what can be done to improve it.

4204. Perdue, Helen. *Importance of the folk tale for children; including a bibliography of editions for an elementary school library.* Cleveland, Western Reserve University, 1953. 44p. Thesis.

4205. Perrine, Sister M. A. *Christian social principles in children's literature: A bibliography.* Washington, Catholic University of America, 1953. 42p. Thesis.

4206. Petty, M. J. *The need for certain out-of-print children's books in children's rooms of the larger public libraries of the United States.* New York, Columbia University, 1947. 50p. Thesis.

4207. Pfau, Eleanor. *Children's literature published in the United States during the year 1848.* Chicago, University of Chicago, 1951. 115p. Thesis.

4208. Philadelphia Free Library. *Children's books; reference and research collections of the Free Library of Philadelphia.* Philadelphia, The Library, 1962. 16p. APP.

A brochure describing the library's special collections of children's books, among them the Rosenbach (see 4260), the Elisabeth Ball collection of horn books, The American Sunday-School Union collection, collections centered on the work of Kate Greenaway, Beatrix Potter, Arthur Rackham, A. B. Frost, Howard Pyle, as well as a general one on illustrators, and many other smaller collections.

4209. Phillips, Grace Louise. "The books read by children of the ghetto," *World's work,* New York, Vol. 6, May, 1903, pp. 3475–3477. NNY.

Some of the generalizations which the author makes based on her observations while working with these children were that there were a large number who read seriously so as to prepare themselves for a better education, that there was a fondness for mournful stories, and that often the books in the family were read aloud by the children to the parents, rather than vice versa.

4210. Pierce, Helen Louise. *Annotated bibliography of books by and about Negroes for a six year high school library.* Cleveland, Western Reserve University, 1953. 53p. Thesis.

4211. Pittsburgh. Carnegie Library. *Catalog of books for the use of the first eight grades . . .* Pittsburgh, The Library, 1907. 331p. DLC.

Essentially contains the same books as in the list in 4212, but here the books have been arranged into subject patterns and grade levels as they might have been followed in the curriculum.

4212. ———. *Catalogue of books in the children's department.* Pittsburgh, The Library, 1909. 604p. DLC.

This library was one of the first to promote a selective children's book policy. This early list of the complete holdings at the time is very illuminating in showing what types of books were or were not included.

4213. ———. *Illustrated editions of children's books.* Pittsburgh, Carnegie Library, 1915. 20p. DLC, NNY.

An annotated list of children's books to provide adults with a selection of the more beautifully produced editions of the classics and modern children's stories. The compiler was Elva S. Smith.

4214. Pitz, Henry C. *Illustrating children's books: History, technique, production.* New York, Watson-Guptill, 1963. 207p. $9.75. DLC, IYL, NNY.

Although some portions of this book cover the same historical and modern illustrators as the two volume *Illustrators of Children's Books* (4070 and 4417), this is useful as supplementary material because of its detailing of techniques. It is intended more as an inspirational aid to the would-be illustrator of children's books. Many reproductions, and an index.

4215. Plummer, Mary Wright. "The work for children in free libraries," *Library journal,* New York, Vol. 22, No. 11, Nov., 1897, pp. 679–686. DLC, NNY.

A survey on the work of 15 of the earliest children's libraries, most of which did not provide for circulation of books. There is also a thoughtful discussion of the type of books to put on the children's shelves, and the kind of person to put in charge of the work.

4216. Poray, Aniela. "The foreign child and the book," *Library journal,* New York, Vol. 40, No. 4, April, 1915, pp. 233–239. DLC, NNY.

How one librarian coped with the special needs of children from different ethnic backgrounds. More than any article on this subject, covering the first decades of this century, this indicates the necessity of intercultural understanding and suiting books to the individual child.

4217. Portteus, Elnora M. *Awards in the field of children's books.* Kent, Ohio, Kent State University, Department of Library Science, 1959. 43p. (Aspects of librarianship, No. 21). DLC.

4218. Poucher, Florence Holbrook. *The boy and the books.* Evanston, Illinois, Kimball Press, 1909. 28p. DLC.

A mother's account of the books read to and by her son. A very personal selection of possible historical interest.

4219. Powell, Sophy H. *The children's library; a dynamic factor in education.* New York, H. W. Wilson Co., 1917. 460p. DLC, NNY.

Written from the conviction that children's libraries should exist not only to provide a means of entertainment, but also to become deeply involved in the educative process. There is a bibliography for each chapter and an index.

4220. ———. "The children's room plus the attic," *Library journal,* New York, Vol. 45, Oct. 15, 1920, pp. 833–835. DLC, NNY.

Some of the plans which were developed for the first children's book week, suggestions for programs to carry out, and a reproduction of the poster and other publicity material.

4221. Power, Effie L. *Bag o' tales; a source book for story-tellers.* New York, Dutton, 1951. 340p. (1st ed., Dutton, 1934).

4222. ——— "A century of progress in library work with children," *Library journal,* New York, Vol. 58, Oct. 15, 1933, pp. 822–825. DLC, NNY.

This pioneer librarian here reviews the history of library work with children and the areas in which it has made the most progress.

4223. ———. *Children's books for general reading.* Chicago, ALA, 1929. 16p. DLC.

The compiler was a leading children's librarian. This list was intended as a basic introduction to the field as well as a first-purchase list.

4224. ———. *First selection of 500 children's books for a library.* Lansing, Michigan State Library, 19?. 72p. DLC.

4225. ———, et al. *Lists of stories and programs for story hours.* New York, H. W. Wilson, 1915. 110p. DLC, NNY.

This list was compiled from the experiences of the staff of the St. Louis Public Library. It is arranged according to materials used with various age groups on special occasions and in general.

4226. ———. *Work with children in public libraries.* Chicago, ALA, 1943. 195p. DLC, IYL, NNY.

An earlier version (1930) was titled *Library Service for Children.* Here, the emphasis has been shifted from a lengthy discourse on book selection (in the earlier book) to a comprehensive discussion of organization and administration. This was a very influential book, as evidenced by its frequent appearance in bibliographies, not only in the U.S. but in many other countries.

4227. Prentice, M. H. and E. L. Power. *Children's library.* Cleveland, Cleveland Public Library, 1904. 78p. DLC.

A booklist for grades one through eight, compiled by two outstanding librarians of the time.

4228. Purdy, Betsy A. *Special children's libraries.*

New York, Pratt Institute Library School, 1952. 50p. Thesis.

4229. Quigley, May G. "Can we use war stories to train children for peace?" *Public libraries,* Chicago, Vol. 20, Nov., 1915, pp. 402–404.

The author's general conclusion was "No," but she polled a number of librarians and not all agreed with her. One wrote: ". . . it is difficult to teach a child the contradictory truths we all must learn, except by some sort of adjustment. A young person must be partisan; it is a part of youth."

4230. Quinnam, Barbara. *Fables, from incunabula to modern picture books.* Washington, Library of Congress, 1966. 85p. DLC, IYL, NNY.

An attractive catalog of an exhibit, covering historical items, source materials, and editions of fables for children. Illustrated with many reproductions from rare and unusual editions. Each entry is annotated, and there are introductory biographies on such fabulists as Aesop, La Fontaine and Krylov.

4231. ———. *Rachel Field collection of old children's books in the District of Columbia Public Library: A catalogue.* Washington, Catholic University of America, 1962. 100p. Thesis. DPL.

An annotated list of 271 items given by the Rachel Field estate to the illustrator's collection in this library which served as the basis for *Illustrators of Children's Books* (see 4070). Included in this list of additions is a large number of chapbooks, broadsides and other early children's literature.

4232. Quivers, Evelyn S. *Study of the school library experiences of a selected group of college freshmen.* Atlanta, Atlanta University, 1952. 64p. Thesis.

4233. Ragsdale, Winifred. *Children's services in a small public library.* Chicago, ALA, 1962. 12p. DLC, NNY.

A pamphlet which outlines the standards and aims of these services.

4234. Ramsey, Eloise. *Folklore for children and young people.* Philadelphia, American Folklore Society, 1952. 110p. DLC, NNY.

A guide to lead teachers and librarians to that folklore which is authentic and true to its origins. The compiler felt that too many collections being used in schools were unworthy of the name folklore. A list of recommended folk tale collections is included.

4235. Rankin, Marie. *Children's interests in library books of fiction.* New York, Columbia Uni-

versity Teacher's College, 1944. 146p. (Contributions to Education, No. 906).

A detailed study, conducted among boys and girls 12–14 years of age in the public libraries of New York.

4236. Rawlinson, Eleanor. *Introduction to literature for children.* Rev. ed. New York, Norton, 1937. 499p. DLC.

An extensive collection of excerpts from the traditional and "sophisticated" (original) literature for children with excellent bibliographies of sources at the end of each subsection. This was designed for use by teacher or librarian and the last 20 pages have information on teaching literature to children with useful indexes of various types.

4237. *Reading and the school library.* Chicago, Follett, Vol. 1, Oct., 1934–Vol. 4, May-June, 1937. NNY.

This short-lived periodical offered articles on children's reading, extensive book lists on a wide variety of subjects, and practical suggestions for making the school library an effective center in the school.

4238. "Reading for children," *Outlook,* New York, Vol. 69, Dec. 7, 1901, pp. 866–868. NNY.

An editorial explaining why this periodical takes such an interest in children's books and reading. This is followed by a series of short articles by well-known critics chiefly on the "classics" for children.

4239. "Reading rooms for children," *Public libraries,* Chicago, Vol. 2, No. 4, April, 1897, pp. 125–131. DLC.

Short reports by children's librarians in the libraries of Boston, Cambridge and Brookline, Massachusetts; Brooklyn and Buffalo, New York; Cleveland and Circleville, Ohio; Detroit and Kalamazoo, Michigan; and Pittsburgh, Pennsylvania. Each gave details on service and physical arrangement of the library.

4240. Reedy, William Marion. *A golden book* and *The literature of childhood.* Cedar Rapids, Iowa, The Torch Press, 1910. 53p. NNY.

While the first essay is concerned with Walter Pater, the second has to do with the child in literature and with literature for children. Both are exceedingly overstated.

4241. Rees, F. *Audio materials in the work with children in public libraries.* New York, Columbia University, 1948. 100p. Thesis.

4242. Reighard, Katherine Ferrand. "Books and

a boy," *Outlook,* New York, Vol. 65, May 19, 1900, pp. 178–180. NNY.

A mother records the reading phases of her son observed from the time he could read to adolescence.

4243.   Repplier, Agnes. "The children's poets," *Essays in idleness.* Boston, Houghton, 1893, pp. 33–64. DLC, NNY.

An essay which suggests some of the reasons children prefer romantic, adult poetry rather than that which is especially written for them.

4244.   ———. "What children read," *Books and men;* Boston, and New York, Houghton, 1888, pp. 64–93. DLC, NNY.

A well-known essayist's views on what children *want* to read, and what they *are given* to read. She believed in exposing children early to the great literature which stirs the imagination. This is only one of several pungent essays which this author wrote on the subject. Others are "Battle of the babies," in *Essays in Miniature,* 1892, and "Little pharisees in fiction," in *Varia,* 1897.

4245.   Rhodes, Clayton E. *Problems in selecting materials for a small school library.* Cleveland, Western Reserve University, 1959. 67p. Thesis.

4246.   Richards, Laura E. *What shall the children read?* New York, Appleton-Century, 1939. 62p. DLC.

The four chapter headings "A—Apple pie," "Nursery lore," "Song and story," and "The vision splendid" indicate the pleasure and delight in children's books Laura Richards still maintained as a great-grandmother. Her advice is still quotable: "Guard yourself somewhat from the immediate trend of thought . . . Just now, the emphasis of psychology is all on the negatives, on fears, inhibitions, frustrations, what not. The child must not grow up ignorant of the rocks, no! but still more important is it for him to know the perennial beacons, showing the fairways that lead between them: beacons of commonsense, duty, courage, and all bright lights of heroic example."

4247.   Richardson, Dorothy. "Phoebe and Mrs. Smith hold forth upon music and literature," *The long day.* New York, Century Co., 1905, pp. 75–91. NNY.

In this book, subtitled "the story of a New York working girl as told by herself," the writer records impressions of her working class colleagues on the books they read and enjoyed. Interesting as a social case history more than for its literary content.

4248.   *The right book for the right child.* 3rd ed. New York, John Day, 1942. 285p. DLC, IYL, NNY.

This graded buying list was selected by a committee of the American Library Association and graded by the research department of the Winnetka Public Schools according to their formula first used by Washburne and Vogel (see 4429). The first edition appeared in 1933. Contrary to the *Winnetka Graded List,* these selections were made entirely by librarians based on careful and extensive observation of children and their reading choices.

4249.   Robertson, G. E. *The role of the librarian in the reading guidance program of the elementary school.* Denton, Texas State College for Women, 1954. 60p. Thesis.

4250.   Robinson, Evelyn Rose. *Readings about children's literature.* New York, David McKay, 1966. 431p. DLC, IYL, NNY.

More than 60 excerpts from books, magazines, journals and newspapers arranged into several categories: the child and his reading, evaluation and selection of children's books, history and trends, illustration, the young child and his books, traditional and modern imaginative tales, fiction, nonfiction. The list of contributors contains the most respected names in the fields of education and library work with children.

4251.   Robinson, Mabel Louise. *A course in juvenile story writing and in the study of juvenile literature.* New York, Columbia University, 1923. 57p. DLC, NNY.

An outline using the author's *Juvenile story writing* as a textbook. This was intended as a course for home study.

4252.   ———. *Writing for young people.* New York, T. Nelson [1950]. 256p. DLC.

A revised version of *Juvenile story writing* (Dutton, 1922). This detailed discussion of literary devices and demands is the distillation of years of teaching the subject at Columbia University.

4253.   Roller, Bert. "Early American writers for children," *Elementary english review,* Detroit, Vol. 8, Nov., 1931, pp. 213–217, 224; Dec., 1931, pp. 241–242; Vol. 9, Nov., 1932, pp. 233–244; Vol. 10, May, 1933, pp. 119–120. DLC.

A series of sketches of the lives and works of the early didactic writers for children in the colonial era.

4254.   Rollins, Charlemae. *The magic world of*

books. Chicago, Science Research Associates, 1954. 40p. (Junior Life Adjustment Booklet). DLC.

An introduction to reading guidance.

4255. ———. *We build together; a reader's guide to Negro life and literature for elementary and high school use.* Chicago, N.C.T.E., 1948. 71p. DLC.

Criteria for evaluating text and illustrations in books on Negro life for children together with a list of books. Author, title index. A revised edition (not seen) is available.

4256. Roos, Jean Carolyn. *By way of introduction; a booklist for young people, compiled by a joint committee of the ALA and the National Education Association.* Chicago, ALA, 1938. 130p. DLC, NNY.

This replaced *Recreational Reading for Young People,* published in 1931. Both were among the first efforts to recognize the special reading interests and needs of the young adult.

4257. ———. *Patterns in reading.* 2nd ed. Chicago, ALA, 1961. 172p. $2.00. DLC, NNY. (IYL has 1st ed., 1954, 138p.).

An annotated list of 1,600 titles for young adults and adults who work with them, based on observation in Cleveland branch libraries and school libraries. Index.

4258. Root, Mary E. S. "An American past in children's work," *Library journal,* New York, Vol. 71, No. 8, April 15, 1946, pp. 547–551; No. 18, Oct. 15, 1946, pp. 1422–1424. DLC, NNY.

A pioneer among children's librarians reminisces about her work in Providence, Rhode Island from 1900 on. She casts interesting sidelights on the problems and joys of these early years.

4259. Rosenbach, Abraham S. W. "American children's books," *Books and bidders.* Boston, Little, Brown, 1927. pp. 179–209. DLC, NNY.

This chapter records the experiences of this noted collector in his search for the unusual and beautiful examples of early American children's books. Some of the finds which accorded him real pleasure are reproduced here. See also his catalogue in 4260.

4260. ———. *Early American children's books.* Portland, Maine, Southworth Press, 1933. 354p. DLC, NNY. (A catalog of an exhibition from this collection was printed at the New York Public Library, 1927, 15p. DLC, NNY). IYL has 1966 reprint made in New York by Kraus Reprint Corporation.

This is the catalog of the private collection formerly owned by Mr. Rosenbach, one of the leading collectors of American juvenilia. In his introduction (xxv–lix) he states how he came to inherit the beginnings of the collection and decided to continue developing it. He also writes about many of the individual treasures he managed to find. The catalog is arranged chronologically with entries from 1682 through 1836. There are more than 50 plates reproducing title pages or illustrations. There is an author-title index, an index of printers and publishers by state, and an alphabetical index of printers, publishers and booksellers.

4261. Rosenberg, Helene. *An evaluation of juvenile periodicals for library, school, and home use.* New York, Pratt Institute Library School, 1954. 54p. Thesis.

4262. Ross, Eulalie Steinmetz. "The United States," *Library service to children.* Lund, Bibliotekstjänst, 1963, pp. 117–124. DLC, IYL, NNY.

This chapter deals with the history and present status of library work with children in this country. The publication was produced under the auspices of IFLA.

4263. Rossoff, Martin. *The library in high school teaching.* 2nd ed. New York, H. W. Wilson, 1961. 166p. $3.00. DLC, NNY.

Sample problems and situations are set up and then solved in this useful handbook based on experience in a Brooklyn school. Individualized reading guidance, programs, instruction in the use of libraries, library use by teachers and building the collection are only some of the points covered.

4264. Rue, M. Eloise. *Subject index to books for intermediate grades.* Chicago, ALA, 1940, 495p. DLC.

The first edition of an index now compiled by M. K. Eakin.

4265. Rufsvold, Margaret I. *Audio-visual school library service; a handbook for librarians.* Chicago, ALA, 1949. 116p. $2.75. DLC.

A comprehensive, general survey which can still be used as a basic study of this rapidly expanding field. The chapter bibliographies and the 15 page appendix of sources of material and equipment are very much out-of-date. Index.

4266. ———. "School library handbooks, manuals, and booklists issued by state and local departments of education and state library agencies, 1936–37," *Wilson bulletin,* New York, Vol. 12, Mar., 1938, pp. 464–465. DLC, NNY.

The growing list of these materials indicates the rapid rise in importance which school libraries began to take in the 1930's.

4267. Saal, June E. *Picture books.* New York, Pratt Institute Library School, 1952. Thesis.

4268. St. John, Edward Porter. *Stories and storytelling.* Boston, Pilgrim Press, 1910. 100p. DLC.

Subtitled "in moral and religious education," this has, nevertheless, very sound values quite apart from moralizing, and practical advice which is suitable for any situation.

4269. Saintsbury, George. *National rhymes of the nursery.* New York, F. A. Stokes, [1902]. 334p. NNY.

An anthology which was meant more as a source book than for direct use by children. The author's introduction is interesting in that it recommended approaching children's rhymes not from the folkloristic view, but from the child's point of view, accepting each rhyme for the pleasure it could give and nothing more.

4270. Sanders, Minerva A. "Report on reading for the young," *Library journal,* New York, Vol. 15, Dec., 1890, pp. 58–64. DLC, NNY.

One of the first such reports culled from questionnaires which this librarian had sent out to all of the large libraries throughout the country. This was presented at the annual conference of the American Library Association.

4271. Sargent, John F., *et al. Reading for the young; a classified and annotated catalog.* Boston, Library Bureau, 1896. 225p. DLC.

An early U.S. booklist, briefly annotated and arranged by subject and age groups. This was a very comprehensive list, more inclusive than selective. This edition combined the 1890 list with the 1891–1895 supplement. Author and subject indexes.

4272. Sargent, Mary. "Reading for the young," *Library journal,* New York, Vol. 14, Nos. 5–6, May–June, 1889, pp. 226–236. DLC, NNY.

In this report given at the St. Louis conference, the author briefly surveys the work with children carried out in 49 libraries throughout the country.

4273. Sattley, Helen R. "Children come first," *Library journal,* New York, Vol. 77, Apr. 15, 1952, pp. 670–674. DLC, NNY.

This leading children's librarian says that the frictions between school and public libraries could be lessened if both sides learned how to guide their relationships so that the children themselves would come first rather than the libraries.

4274. Sauer, Julia. "Library services to children in a world at war," *Pan-American Child Congress, 8th, Washington, 1942.* Washington, Department of State, [1948], pp. 417–425. (Publication 2847, Conference Series 100). DLC.

In time of war, children need a sense of security more than ever, and there are books which can do much to sustain them. However, the librarian should watch out that the melodramatic and the propagandistic do not overwhelm the story for this can lead to false and superficial judgment.

4275. Sawyer, K. H. *The importance of reading guidance for the child gifted in science.* Cleveland, Western Reserve University, 1956. 79p. Thesis.

4276. Sawyer, Ruth. *How to tell a story.* Chicago, Encyclopedia Britannica Educational Corp., 1965. DLC, NNY.

This small pamphlet is a reprint from *Compton's Pictured Encyclopedia.* It gives practical suggestions and a list of sources.

4277. ———. *The way of the storyteller.* Rev. ed. New York, Viking, 1962. 360p. $4.00. DLC, IYL, NNY. (Also available in paper covers: Compass C176, $1.65).

A distinguished storyteller tells how she developed her art in this interesting book which is a must for storytellers to read. Included also are 11 stories from her repertory of tales from world folklore, a reading list, a story list and an index. The stories are: "Wee Meg Barnileg and the fairies," "The magic box," "Señora, will you snip? Señora will you sew?," "The peddler of Ballaghadereen," "Where one is fed a hundred can dine," "A matter of brogues," "The juggler of Notre Dame," "The deserted mine," "The bird who spoke three times," "The legend of Saint Elizabeth," and "The princess and the vagabone."

4278. Sayers, Frances Clarke. *A bounty of books.* Chicago, Encyclopedia Britannica Educational Corporation, 1965. 19p. IYL, DLC, NNY.

This reprint from *Compton's Pictured Encyclopedia* is of the article and list of books which replaces the earlier one by Anne Carroll Moore (see 4100). It is intended as a stimulant to the child and parent to select good books for home reading and purchase.

4279. ———. *Children's books in the Library of*

Congress. Washington, D.C., 1952. 57p. Mimeographed. IYL, DLC.

"A report based on a study made at the request of the Librarian of Congress and a Joint Committee of the American Association of University Women and the Association for Childhood Education International, April 1–June 30, 1952." Mrs. Sayers here outlines the findings of the committee and their recommendations for the founding of a children's book section, now a reality (see 3849).

4280. ———, *et al.* Institute on Library Work with Children. *Proceedings.* Berkeley, University of California, School of Librarianship, 1939. 177p. DLC.

Some of the participants whose papers are printed here were: S. B. Mitchell, Howard Pease, May Massee, Karl Kup, Conrad Buff, L. J. Lewis, René d'Harnoncourt, Mildred Batchelder, Frederic Melcher, Elizabeth Nesbitt, Ella Young, N. Unger, M. V. Girdner, and Ruth A. Hill.

4281. ———. *Summoned by books.* New York, Viking, 1965. 173p. $4.00. DLC, IYL, NNY.

It is difficult to describe the verve and eloquence of style evident in Mrs. Sayers' speeches and essays here compiled by Marjeanne Jensen Blinn. They express a philosophy of reading which has universal meaning. Although they are arranged under such topics as "On being a librarian," "The telling of tales" and "The writing of tales," each essay is filled with a spirit of total commitment to the power of printed and oral literature.

4282. ———. "Walt Disney accused," *Horn book,* Boston, Vol. 35, Dec., 1965, pp. 602–611. DLC, NNY.

An eminent librarian, author and lecturer in children's literature here disputes an educator who had praised the work of Disney. She explains that while Disney was in many ways a genius, he had very little regard for the innate qualities of children's classics and the great folk stories which he adapted to the cartoon. Mrs. Sayers deplored the distortion and destruction of the imaginative qualities of many of the stories Disney translated into film.

4283. Schatz, Esther. *et al. Exploring independent reading in the primary grades.* Columbus, Ohio State University, 1960. 70p.

4284. Schatzki, Walter. *Children's books, old and rare. Catalogue No. 1.* New York, Walter Schatzki, 1941. 46p. DPL.

An annotated dealer's catalog of 200 old children's books, from many countries and in many languages but with the majority in English and German. Pages are reproduced from some of them. Index. This is *not* a catalog of the collection Mr. Schatzki sold to the New York Public Library.

4285. Scherwitzky, Marjorie. "Children's literature about foreign countries," *Wilson library bulletin,* New York, Vol. 32, No. 2, Oct., 1957, pp. 142–148. DLC, NNY.

An annotated list by country of U.S. books about other lands. They were from the period of 1946–1957 and were chosen as being helpful in bringing children to better international understanding of other cultures.

4286. Schiffler, Marie C. *Critical analysis of juvenile periodicals 1940–1950.* Cleveland, Western Reserve University, 1951. 106p. Thesis.

4287. "School and public library relationships," *ALA bulletin,* Chicago, Vol. 53, Feb., 1959, pp. 111–134. DLC, NNY.

Following the title article by Mary Gaver are a number of other articles on the subject stated in the title. There is a bibliography prepared by Eleanor Ahlers on p. 134.

4288. *School libraries.* American Association of School Librarians, 50 East Huron St. Chicago, Illinois 60611. Quarterly, Vol. 1 ff., 1952 ff. Subscription: membership only. DLC, IYL, NNY.

The official publication of the Association containing articles on all aspects of school library work on children's literature, and related areas. Professional books are reviewed, but not children's books.

4289. "School libraries section," *Wilson bulletin,* New York, Vol. 6, No. 3, Nov., 1931—present.

Under this title, and under the title "School and children's libraries" this section has been a part of this library periodical since the above date. In addition, numerous other articles on children's literature and libraries have appeared with regularity. Frequently the October issue centered around children's book week.

4290. "The school library," *The public library monthly,* Boston, Vol. 1, No. 6, Jan., 1904, pp. 83–86. DLC.

Three short articles on the school library, as an adjunct to the secondary school, and as serviced by the public library.

4291. *School library journal.* R. R. Bowker Company, 1180 Avenue of the Americas, New York, New York 10036. Monthly, Sept.–May. Vol. 1 ff. No. 1 ff.,

1954 ff. Annual subscription: $5.00. DLC, IYL, NNY. (Also available as part of *Library journal*).

A commercial publication, containing articles on children's library work (both public and school), on children's literature, and on related matters. There are also signed reviews of current children's books. This periodical reviews the greatest percentage of the annual production of children's books.

4292. "School number," *Library journal,* New York, Vol. 28, No. 4, Apr., 1903, pp. 155–171. DLC, NNY.

Contrary to its title, this issue dealt with public library work as well as work with children in schools. Some of the articles are: "The work of the children's librarian" by Anne Carroll Moore; "Maintaining order in the children's room" by Clara W. Hunt; "Action upon bad books" by Electra C. Doren; "Work with children in the Madison, N.J. public library" by Mary M. Miller; "The public library and the public museum (Children's Museum of Brooklyn)" by Richard E. Call.

4293. *School library yearbook.* American Library Association, Committee on School Libraries, Chicago. No. 1, 1927–No. 5, 1932. DLC, NNY.

This yearbook contained articles on all aspects of school library work, a report on progress made each year, lists of professional reading, some school library statistics, and other related information.

4294. Schwartz, Delmore. "Masterpieces as cartoons," *Partisan review,* New York, Vol. 19, July, 1952, pp. 461–471. DLC, NNY.

A well-known poet comments on the versions of the classics as they are published in comic book form, discussing three of them at length. His conclusion is that such mass "cultural" media are here to stay and that the only way to counteract their influence is for educators who truly care about great literature to know both the original and the mass version very well, so that he can present an intelligent argument for reading the original.

4295. Scoggin, Margaret C. "Do young people want books?" *Wilson bulletin,* New York, Vol. 11, No. 1, Sept., 1936, pp. 17–20, 24. DLC, NNY.

This librarian, who was to become a pioneer in defining the special qualities of library work with the teen-aged or young adult group, writes of her experience with this type of reader in New York.

4296. Scott, Edna Lyman. *Storytelling: What to tell and how to tell it.* New ed. Chicago, McClurg, 1923. 252p. DLC.

A useful manual with clear instructions and a list of books for the storyteller.

4297. Charles Scribner's Sons. *First editions of juvenile fiction, 1814–1924.* New York, Scribner Book Store, 1936. 37p. NNY.

Because this publishing house brought out so many of the early classics for children and a large number of outstanding U.S. writers as well, this is important as a finding list of first editions.

4298. Scudder, Horace E. *Childhood in literature and art.* Boston, Houghton, 1895. 253p. DLC, NNY.

In his introduction the author sets out his purpose: "There is a correlation between childhood in literature and a literature for children, but it will best be understood when one has considered the meaning of the appearance and disappearance of the child in different epochs of literature and art." The author then sets out to review these epochs. Index.

4299. Seaman, F. *Museum services in school libraries.* New York, Columbia University, 1943. 81p. Thesis.

4300. Seaman, Louise H. "Children's books and the depression," *Wilson bulletin,* New York, Vol. 7, Mar., 1933, pp. 413–417. DLC, NNY.

Miss Seaman was the first children's book editor in charge of a special children's section of a major book publisher. She writes here of the drastic effects which the depression had had on many of the newly formed children's book sections; because of greatly reduced sales, they were forced to dissolve or once again be absorbed in the general editorial staff. She writes of the importance children's libraries have in giving intelligent support of the industry.

4301. "Section on library work with children," *ALA bulletin,* Chicago, Vol. 7, No. 1, Jan., 1913, pp. 275–295. DLC, NNY.

Some of the addresses given at the annual conference are reprinted here, among them, "Values in library work with children" by Clara W. Hunt and Caroline Burnite; "Volume of children's work in the United States" (statistics) by Dr. Bostwick; "Possibilities of the rural school library" by Martha Wilson; and articles by Maude McLelland and Jesse B. Davis on the high school library.

4302. "Section on library work with children," *ALA bulletin,* Chicago, Vol. 8, No. 2, Mar., 1914, pp. 215–228, 238–243. DLC, NNY.

At the annual congress Miss Laura Thompson reported on the work of the Federal Children's Bureau; Miss Mary Ely, head of children's work in the Dayton, Ohio, public library, spoke on the problem of the cheap, series books which get purchased by the thousands for home use, and which children are disappointed at not finding in the library; Mr. F. K. Mathiews, librarian of the Boy Scouts of America, told of the influence which this organization was beginning to have in directing the reading of boys. In a later section on professional training, Miss Anne Carroll Moore expanded her earlier outline (4120) of the special training needed for the work of the children's librarian.

4303. Sell, Violet, *et al. Subject index to poetry for children and young people.* Chicago, ALA, 1957. 592p. $9.00.

Slightly different from Brewton in approach, this is not nearly as comprehensive. It indexes some 150 recent collections according to subjects useful in school curriculums.

4304. Shang, Chung I. *A method of selecting foreign stories for the American elementary schools: Applied to the evaluation of stories translated by the author from the Chinese folk literature.* New York, Columbia University Teachers' College, 1929. 46p. (Contributions to Education, No. 398). DLC.

The author describes his painstaking efforts to select and translate stories which would be meaningful and enjoyable to the U.S. child, while remaining true to the Chinese original. Much of the difficulty came from the fact that he had no experience in the reading intereset or tastes of children and had to rely on others for these vital matters. This demonstrates quite graphically the underlying reasons for the failure of many translations to catch hold of the nonnative reader. The first chapter is an excellent brief review of the classics of Chinese literature which have become in many cases the classics for Chinese children.

4305. Shanklin, Lucille. *A tour of the United States in children's books, 1933–1936.* Chicago, Follett, 1936. 4p. DLC.

A list of 129 books arranged by states. Many of the selections were of mediocre quality, but the basic idea was a useful one.

4306. ———. "Two trends in books for children," *Reading and the school library,* Chicago, Vol. 2, Nov.–Dec., 1935, pp. 11–16. DLC, NNY.

"There are two trends in writing for children which are producing results interesting enough to merit attention and analysis: first, readable books of information; second, stories centering about vocations for boys and girls."

4307. Shea, A. L. *Publications read by school children who use the public library.* Chicago, University of Chicago, 1938. 74p. Thesis.

4308. Shedlock, Marie L. *The art of the storyteller.* 3rd ed. New York, Dover, 1951. 290p. $1.75. (Paper covers). DLC, NNY, IYL.

Anne Carroll Moore considered this the best book on the subject of storytelling and this judgment still holds true. Miss Shedlock was an Englishwoman whose storytelling in the early part of the 20th century influenced the development of storytelling programs in public libraries in the United States. It is still the most practical guide to the art and it includes also an admirable selection of stories to tell. A new list of stories was compiled by Eulalie Steinmentz Ross for this edition.

4309. Sheehan, E. M. *Reviewing of books of juvenile fiction in certain serial publications.* New York, Columbia University, 1945. 66p. Thesis.

4310. Sheeler, H. *Analysis of the cultural content of a selected list of children's books on China.* Washington, Catholic University, 1953. Thesis.

4311. Shores, Louis. "School library service," *Library journal,* New York, Vol. 64, Apr. 1, 1939, pp. 265–266. DLC, NNY.

This expands the ideas expressed in an article which appeared in Vol. 61, Feb. 1, 1936, p. 112 and Feb. 15, 1936, p. 156. The author felt that organization and bibliography were lesser functions of the school librarian, secondary to that of instruction in the use of libraries. He believed that teacher training colleges should not become concerned with education of teacher-librarians, but should concentrate on educating teachers and principals in intelligent acceptance and use of their school library.

4312. Sieving, Hilmar A. *Le centre de livres pour enfants de l'Université de Chicago.* Paris, UNESCO, 1961. 11p. Also in English in: *UNESCO. Education abstracts,* Paris, Vol. 12, No. 9, Nov., 1960, pp. 1–11. DLC.

A description of the work of the Center for Children's Books at the University of Chicago, followed by an annotated bibliography of selected professional books about children's literature.

4313. Skarzynska, Janina. [Literature for children and youth in the United States,] *Ruch pedagogiczny,* Warszawa, Vol. 31, No. 1, 1947–1948.

Paper given at the Polish Congress on Children's Literature (see 2114). In Polish.

4314. Sloane, William. *Children's books in England and America in the seventeenth century.* New York, Columbia University, 1955. 251p. DLC, IYL, NNY.

A scholarly book of interest to the student of old books which also gives a readable view of the life and condition of children of the period through their books. Includes many invaluable bibliographical notes to books which are not to be found in other histories of children's literature. Appended is, in facsimile, the first printed catalog of books for children of the 17th century.

4315. Smit, D. "Opleidingschool voor kinderbibliotheek-bibliothekaressen," *De boekzaal,* Zwolle, Jaargang 6, 1912, pp. 192–195. NNY.

Describes the program of the Carnegie library school (Pittsburgh).

4316. Smith, Arline Parker. *A study of reading achievement and personal and social adjustment of eighth grade youth.* Chapel Hill, University of North Carolina, 1960. 64p. Thesis.

4317. Smith, Dolores Ann. *Study of quarters and equipment for children's library science.* Kent, Ohio, Kent State University, 1951. 65p. Thesis.

4318. Smith, Dora V. *Fifty years of children's books 1910–1960: Trends, backgrounds, influences.* Champaign, Illinois, National Council of Teachers of English, 1963. 149p. $2.95. DLC, IYL, NNY.

A good survey of the field showing all the influences at work since 1910—people, newspapers, publishing houses, library schools, organizations and movements coming out of the social conditions of the times. Appended are good bibliographic notes to the text; a list of significant children's books; a list of books about children's books; helpful lists of children's books; listings of Books of the Year; bibliographical sources for old books and a brief directory of publishers. The author is a Minneapolis school librarian closely associated for many years with the National Council of Teachers of English and with its organ, *Elementary English.*

4319. ———. "Lists of books for retarded readers," *English journal,* Chicago, Vol. 29, Apr., 1940, pp. 318–323. DLC.

A bibliography of lists, annotated and with fairly complete information. There are also titles of some children's books which were specifically written or adapted for the pupil with a low reading ability. This library educator was an early advocate of the controlled vocabulary book for certain types of readers.

4320. Smith, Dorothy Elizabeth. *Reading list on the four freedoms and the Atlantic Charter.* Chicago, National Council of Teachers of English, 1943. 30p. DLC.

Books on all aspects of the basic freedoms of speech and religion, and the freedom from want and fear. Index.

4321. Smith, Elva Sophronia. *The history of children's literature.* Chicago, ALA, 1937. 244p. DLC, IYL, NNY.

A general bibliography followed by period outlines and bibliographies. This is restricted to the English language material available at the time, with a few exceptions in German and French. It is particularly valuable for the materials on individual authors and illustrators, and for the related background material for each of the historical periods. There is a chronological list of children's books in England and America, 1659–1900, and an author and title index. This is still an invaluable historical tool.

4322. Smith, Franklin Orion. "Pupils' voluntary reading," *The pedagogical seminary,* Worcester, Mass., Vol. 14, No. 2, June, 1907, pp. 208–222. DLC.

The reading interests of grammar and high school students as recorded during the period of a year.

4323. Smith, Irene. *A history of the Newbery and Caldecott Medals.* New York, Viking, 1957. 146p. $3.00. DLC, IYL, NNY.

This readable book gives the historical background of the Caldecott and Newbery awards and discusses the books themselves giving the author's opinion about the popularity and value of certain books based on consultation with some libraries not identified. The appendix lists the winners and runners-up of both medals from the earliest awards to the date of this book's publication. One of the most useful sections is Chapter 1 which relates the careers of three bookmen, Frederic Melcher, John Newbery and Randolph Caldecott. The author was long Supervisor of Work with Children at the Brooklyn Public Library.

4324. Smith, Jean Gardiner. "Latin America: Books for young readers," *The booklist,* Chicago, Vol. 37, No. 14, 1941, pp. 369–380. DLC, NNY.

Books in English about the Latin American countries, with a few titles in Spanish from South America. Listed by subject and by country.

4325. Smith, Jerome I. "New York children's books, prior to 1900," *Bulletin of the Museum of the City of New York,* Feb., 1938, pp. 31–34. NNY.

A history of some of the early children's book publishers with four illustrative reproductions from their work.

4326. Smith, Katherine Louise. "The provision for children in public libraries," *Review of reviews*, New York, Vol. 22, July, 1900, pp. 48–55. NNY.

A thorough review of the work being done in the major library systems throughout the U.S., illustrated with photographs.

4327. Smith, Lillian H. "The library's responsibility to the child," Danton, E. V. M. *Library of tomorrow*. Chicago, ALA, 1939, pp. 124–143. DLC, NNY.

In delineating the library's responsibility to the future child, Miss Smith quotes from Quiller-Couch: "If we limit the children of the next generation to what we admire ourselves we pauperize their minds."

4328. ———. *The unreluctant years. A critical approach to children's literature*. Chicago, ALA, 1953. 193p. $4.50. DLC, IYL, NNY.

For annotation see 3383.

4329. Smith, Nora Archibald. "Tell me a story," *The children of the future*. Boston, Houghton, 1898, pp. 191–213. NNY.

The author attempts to define the secret power which the narrated story has on the child's imaginative development. She was strongly in favor of folk and fairy tales as the best material for storytelling.

4330. ———. "Training the imagination," *Outlook*, New York, Vol. 64, Feb. 24, 1900, pp. 459–461. DLC, NNY.

The writer suggests that imagination can best be nurtured through books, but only if they are offered in sufficient quality, quantity and variety.

4331. Smith, Robinson. "Winnowing world literature for children," *Publishers' weekly*, New York, Vol. 104, Oct. 20, 1923, pp. 1371–1374. DLC, NNY.

A description of a plan to publish some 200 works from world literature in an inexpensive series for children. The list of the 200 works is given in entirety. This book week issue has a number of other articles related to children's books and reading.

4332. Smith, Susan T. "Outside reading for the children's librarian," *Public libraries*, Chicago, Vol. 30, Nov., 1925, pp. 467–470. DLC, NNY.

In this paper read at the Seattle conference, the author goes into the broad types of reading which every children's librarian should cover: biographical and autobiographical recollections of childhood, educational and professional journals, books recording the experiences of other children's librarians, folklore, general literature, etc.

4333. "Some old-fashioned children's books," *Living age*, Boston, Vol. 261, No. 3389, June 19, 1909, pp. 754–760. NNY.

Examples from the prose of early, didactic children's books.

4334. Soneda, Mary Shizuye. *Hawaiian Islands; books and films for children and young people 1930–1953*. Seattle, University of Washington, 1954. 51p. Thesis.

4335. Spache, George D. *Good reading for poor readers*. Champaign, Ill., Garrard Publishing Co., 1964. 203p. $3.00. DLC, NNY.

This is the 3rd edition of a handbook which answers questions of those who are interested in reluctant readers. The viewpoint of the articles and bibliographies is that of a professional educator but one who appears to have direct experience with children and books. Useful primarily with teachers but parents, publishers and writers go to the book for explanations of educational terms and attitudes. Includes the Spache Readability Formula and a list of adapted classics.

4336. ———. *Sources of good books for poor readers*. Newark, N.J., International Reading Association, 1966. 8p. $00.40.

A list of some 70 sources.

4337. Spain, Frances Lander. *Contents of the basket and other papers on children's books and reading*. New York, The New York Public Library, 1960. 83p. DLC, NNY.

Reprints of papers delivered either as Anne Carroll Moore lectures or during the November Book Week celebrations. They are by: Taro Yashima, Annis Duff, William Pene du Bois, Elizabeth Gray Vining, Elizabeth Enright, Ruth Sawyer, Amelia Munson, Harry Behn, and Elizabeth Nesbitt.

4338. ———. "A mid-century look at children's books." Simmons College. School of Library Science. *Books and publishing*, Vol. 2. Boston, The School, 1955, pp. 41–55. NNY.

A restrospective view of some of the trends which have shaped children's books and others which are beginning to appear.

4339. ———. *Reading without boundaries, essays presented to Anne Carroll Moore on the occasion of the fiftieth anniversary of the inauguration of library service to children at The New York Public Library*. New York, The New York Public Library, 1956. 104p. DLC, IYL, NNY.

Papers in celebration of library work with

children (as influenced by Miss Moore who developed it at The New York Public Library) by authors, illustrators, editors, designers, librarians and critics. Contributors are Harry Miller Lydenberg, Mary Strang, Helen Adams Masten, Frances Clarke Sayers, James Daugherty, Alice Dalgliesh, Margaret B. Evans, May Massee, Maria Cimino, Anne Thaxter Eaton, Ruth Sawyer, Alice M. Jordan, Elizabeth Nesbitt, John Mackenzie Cory, Frederic G. Melcher, Elizabeth Harriet Weeks. Mrs. Spain was, at the time of publication, Coordinator of Children's Services for The New York Public Library. Included is a bibliography of publications by Miss Moore.

4340.   Spaulding, W. E. "How America will read tomorrow: Look to the school," *Publishers' weekly,* New York, Vol. 178, No. 24, Dec. 12, 1960, pp. 16–23. DLC, NNY.

This 20th annual Bowker lecture was a penetrating commentary on the scope of new educational procedures and what their eventual effect might be on the use of books.

4341.   Spengler, Margaret V., *et al. A basic book collection for junior high schools.* 3rd ed. Chicago, ALA, 1960. 144p. $2.00.

An annotated list of about 1,000 books and periodicals, arranged by decimal classification and with an author, title and subject index.

4342.   Stafford, Mae D. H. *Survey of the annual library reports from a selected number of public school systems.* Atlanta, Atlanta University, 1960. 68p. Thesis.

4343.   Stallman, Esther. "Books about children's literature," *Peabody journal of education,* Nashville, Tenn., Vol. 19, No. 3, Nov., 1941, pp. 124–130. DLC.

A bibliography covering history and criticism, booklists, reading guidance and related areas.

4344.   Stanley, Harriet Howard. *550 children's books.* Chicago, ALA Publishing Board, 1910. 24p. DLC.

An early purchase list for public libraries, not annotated.

4345.   Starbuck, Edwin D., *et al. A guide to literature for character training.* New York, Macmillan, 1928. 389p. DLC.

Children's literature explored from a sociological point of view. This, and a succeeding volume *A Guide to Books for Character* (New York, Macmillan, 1930), both contained lists of books to be used in building certain attitudes and moral character in children and young people.

4346.   Starrett, Vincent. *All about Mother Goose.* n.p., Appelicon Press, 1930. 40p. DLC.

An essay which speculates on the identity of Mother Goose but comes to no conclusions.

4347.   Stearns, Lutie E. *The child and the small library.* Madison, Wisconsin Free Library Commission, 1898. 9p. DLC.

The services which the small library can offer to the child, and the advantages of personal contact with children which is only possible in the small library.

4348.   ———. "Educational force of children's reading," *Public libraries,* Chicago, Vol. 2, No. 1, Jan., 1897, pp. 6–7. DLC, NNY.

"In the attempt . . . to remove every possible stumbling block, modern compilers of reading books have gone to the opposite extreme and there is now the tendency to make all this too easy . . ." There are a number of articles besides this one concerning the reading of children. There is also one on the relationship of schools to the public library.

4349.   ———. "The problem of the girl," *Library journal,* New York, Vol. 31, Aug., 1906, pp. 103–106. DLC, NNY.

A speech delivered at one of the annual library conferences. The author pointed out the need for some further guidance and supervision of girls who went from the children's room to the adult room at age 14, yet in few libraries did they get any attention at all. She also recommended that librarians use their influence in getting teachers not to "teach" literature to the young, but to enjoy it with them.

4350.   Steinbach, Frances Marie. *An analysis of moral leanings in the John Newbery books.* Boulder, University of Colorado Libraries, 1944. DLC has on microfilm.

An effort to determine whether 15 specific winners of the Newbery Award helped to contribute to the moral growth of their child readers.

4351.   Steinmetz, Eulalie M. "Storytelling versus recordings," *Horn book,* Boston, Vol. 24, May–June, 1948, pp. 163–172. DLC, NNY.

This well-known storyteller pleads for staying with traditional methods of telling stories to groups of children rather than playing them recordings of stories.

4352.   Stewart, James D. "Cult of the child and common sense," *Library association record,* London, Vol. 10, No. 6, June, 1908, pp. 281–288. DLC, NNY.

An article on children's library work in the U.S., which this person felt was characterized by misdirected missionary zeal that comes from an over-supply of "the almighty dollar." Of interest because it shows the opposition of certain factions in the early days of children's services.

4353.   Stone, C. H. "Difficulties encountered by trained school librarians as a basis for the revision of the professional curriculum," *Library quarterly*, Chicago, Vol. 3, Jan., 1933, pp. 66–86. DLC, NNY.

A summary and interpretation of the report of the Committee on Professional Training of School Librarians. The general conclusion was that the training in organization and techniques was quite adequate, but the lack of study of the place of the library in the total school organization caused greatest misunderstanding.

4354.   Stone, Wilbur Macey. "Children's books of long ago," *Saturday review of literature*, New York, Vol. 5, Mar. 9, 1929, pp. 762–763. DLC, NNY.

This is the first in a series of three articles. It is concerned with chapbooks and broadsides. The second is called "Flowery and gilt," and is in the Mar. 23, 1929 issue, pp. 810–812. It is concerned with books of the period 1750–1830. The third is on the Victorian era, and is called "Pinafores and pantalettes," in the Apr. 6, 1929 issue, pp. 864–865. Some illustrations are reproduced.

4355.   ———. "Emasculated juveniles," *American book collector*, Metuchen, N.J., Vol. 5, Mar., 1934, pp. 77–80. NNY.

This collector of children's books deplored the current tendencies to take out all violence from fairy tales and other children's literature.

4356.   ———. *Four centuries of children's books from the collection of W. M. Stone.* Newark, The Public Library, 1928. 32p. DLC.

The catalog of an exhibit shown Sept.–Oct., 1928, arranged alphabetically within the categories used in the display.

4357.   Strang, Ruth May, *et al. Gateways to readable books, an annotated graded list of books in many fields, for adolescents who find reading difficult.* 4th ed. New York, H. W. Wilson, 1966. 245p. $5.00. DLC, NNY.

A comprehensive list including textbooks and workbooks, books in series, periodicals, simple dictionaries, etc. There is a bibliography as well as author and title indexes. Arrangement of the more than 1,000 titles is by general subject areas.

4358.   Strauss, Beverly V. *Survey to determine whether high school students using five branches of the Brooklyn Public Library have a preference between the public library and the school.* New York, Pratt Institute Library School, 1952. 38p. Thesis.

4359.   Stuber, A. R. *United States regional fiction as an aid to developing intercultural understanding.* Seattle, University of Washington, 1960. 48p. Thesis.

4360.   *Subject index to children's magazines.* Meribah Hazen, 301 Palomino Lane, Madison, Wisconsin. Vol. 1, 1949 ff. Monthly except June and July. Subscription: $7.50 per year.

An index to current U.S. magazines for children, or of interest to children.

4361.   Sullivan, Helen Blair and Lorraine E. Tolman. *High interest—low vocabulary reading materials.* Boston, Boston University, Journal of Education, 1964. 132p. $1.00.

A list of more than 1,000 books for the elementary grades arranged by subject and vocabulary level.

4362.   Sullivan, Peggy A. "School library service." Coplan, Kate M. and Edwin Castagna. *The library reaches out.* Dobbs Ferry, Oceana, 1965, pp. 241–265. DLC, NNY.

The director of the Knapp School Library Project describes here some of the new trends in school library service.

4363.   Summers, Sister M. Rosa. *A critical analysis of three series of children's books.* Washington, Catholic University, 1965. 96p. Thesis.

4364.   Sumner, C. W. *Birthright of babyhood.* Chicago, A. Whitman, 1940. 100p. DLC.

The story of the Mothers' Room at the Youngstown, Ohio Public Library, and suggestions to give to parents on beginning the use of books with very young children.

4365.   Switzer, C. F. *et al.* "Love stories for children," *Public libraries*, Chicago, Vol. 22, Feb., 1918, pp. 49–56. DLC, NNY.

Some of the questions asked in this symposium were: Should love stories be in public libraries? If so, what kind? To whom do they appeal, boys or girls or both?

4366.   Syler, Mary E. *Record collection in a children's library.* Kent, Ohio, Kent State University, 1952. 73p. Thesis.

4367. "Symposium on juvenile reading." *Saturday review of literature,* New York, Vol. 6, No. 17, Nov. 16, 1929, pp. 398–399. DLC, NNY.

Children's book editors, librarians, authors and other experts give their brief opinions on the state of children's reading.

4368. Szkudlarek, Marie Ellen. *Historical development of work with children in the Toledo Public Library.* Cleveland, Western Reserve University, 1954. 44p. Thesis.

4369. Tackitt, Hope. *Organization and administration of school library clubs.* Denton, Texas State College for Women, 1952. 85p. Thesis.

4370. Taggard, Genevieve. "Children really like poetry," *New republic,* New York, Vol. 52, Nov. 16, 1927, pp. 353–355. DLC, NNY.

Why children like poetry, and some of the kinds of poetry they like. The author has another article on the same subject in the Nov. 10, 1926 issue. This periodical had a fairly regular coverage of children's books, with reviews by such outstanding reviewers as Padraic Colum, Katherine Anne Porter, Marcia Dalphin, Babette Deutsch, Lewis Mumford, Jacqueline Overton and many others.

4371. Tanner, N. L. *A selected list of American ballads adapted from English and Scottish ballads of the eighteenth century useful for children's story hour programs.* Kent, Ohio, Kent State University, 1960. 97p. Thesis.

4372. Tappaan, Beth. *Children's books around the year; a handbook of practical suggestions for teachers, librarians, and booksellers.* New York, Children's Book Council, 1945. 128p. DLC.

Suggested programs centered around books for every possible occasion and involving large or small groups.

4373. Targ, William. *Bibliophile in the nursery; a bookman's treasury of collectors' lore on old and rare children's books.* Cleveland, World Pub. Co., 1957. 503p. $12.50. DLC, IYL, NNY.

A collector of old children's books here presents a spirited apology for his avocation and gathers together some excerpts from books which treat of the subject of old books for children—a chapter from Hazard's *Books, Children and Men,* an abridgment of the first 35 pages of the 1891 publication of Mrs. E. M. Field, *The Child and his Book,* a chapter from Marchette Chute's *Geoffrey Chaucer of England* in which are discussed the books of a fourteenth-century schoolboy. The book includes a selection from the cat-alogue of the Pierpont Morgan Library Exhibit (see 4164) and a series of random papers from the books of the Opies, Monica Kiefer, Vincent Starrett, and others.

4374. Tassin, Algernon. "Books for children," *Cambridge history of American literature,* Vol. 2. New York, Macmillan, 1918, pp. 396–409. DLC, NNY.

A short but perceptive survey of American children's literature from the 17th century to approximately 1885.

4375. Taylor, James L., *et al. Library facilities for elementary and secondary schools.* Washington, Office of Education, 1965. 44p. DLC.

A description of buildings and floor plans which have proven sound in the developing of school library service, together with a current bibliography of books and articles on the building and equipping of school libraries.

4376. Taylor, Mark. "Television is ruining our folk tales," *Library journal,* Vol. 84, Dec. 15, 1959, pp. 3882–3884. DLC, NNY.

The author contends that the distortion of the folk tales as they are being presented on television is going to destroy a tradition which has survived for centuries. He believed that oral tradition had suffered much less in its transition into the printed word than it is now undergoing in the newer visual medium.

4377. "Ten years—$500,000," *Publishers' weekly,* New York, Vol. 116, No. 20, Nov. 16, 1929, pp. 2410–2412. DLC, NNY.

The history of the promotion of Book Week with special reference to Children's Book Week.

4378. Terman, Lewis Madison and Margaret Lima. *Children's reading, a guide for parents and teachers.* 2nd ed. New York, Appleton, 1931. 422p. DLC, NNY.

One of the earliest guides with a clear discussion of current reading interests among children. The annotated lists are by subjects and grades, and are now out-of-date, but of some possible sociological or historical interest.

4379. Thomas, Della. *Books for enrichment.* Stillwater, Oklahoma State University Library, 1966. 52p. $1.00.

A list of books on the language arts including a section on literatures of other countries, for grades 1–12.

4380. Thomas, Frances. *The extent to which*

World War II entered the field of children's literature during the period 1939 to 1950. Cleveland, Western Reserve University, 1951. 87p. Thesis.

4381.   Thomas, Katherine E. *The real personages of Mother Goose.* Boston, Lothrop, 1930. 352p. DLC, NNY.

An attempt to connect the names and events of Mother Goose rhymes with those of real persons and happenings from past history. While this makes fascinating reading, many authorities question the scholarly accuracy of the identifications. The list of 305 reference works is very helpful for the student of nursery rhymes.

4382.   Thomas, Marjorie. "Some in velvet gowns," *Peabody journal of education,* Nashville, Tenn., Vol. 7, Nov., 1929, pp. 139–146. DLC, NNY.

A critical discussion of the early Newbery Medal-winning books from the standpoint of content and format.

4383.   Thomas, Timmie D. *Reading guidance through the school library.* Denver, University of Denver, 1949. 66p. Thesis.

4384.   Thompson, Hugh Miller. "The unhappy children," *Copy; essays from an editor's drawer.* Hartford, Conn., The Church Press: M. H. Mallory, 1872, pp. 268–273. NNY.

A strong but effective essay against the "enormous production of so-called 'children's' books which are sent forth in countless bales, hourly, to stuff the little intellectual stomachs of the unsuspecting innocents, give them incurable spiritual dyspepsia, and addle their poor brains for their whole lives." The author was referring to the many series books, the weeklies, dime novels, Sunday school stories and similar types.

4385.   Thompson, Laura A. "The Federal Children's Bureau," *ALA bulletin,* Chicago, Vol. 8, Jan., 1914, pp. 215–218. DLC, NNY.

In this speech delivered at the annual library conference, the author explained the functions of the newly established Children's Bureau, especially as they were related to books and libraries.

4386.   Thompson, Maxine E. *Poetry for memorization from kindergarten through sixth grade.* Kent, Ohio, Kent State University, 1960. 107p. Thesis.

4387.   Thomsen, Gudrun Thorne. "The practical results of storytelling in Chicago's park reading rooms," *ALA bulletin,* Chicago, Vol. 3, Sept., 1909, pp. 408–410. DLC, NNY.

A detailed description of the procedure followed in setting up these special story hours and some of the results. One of the most visible results was that the reading rooms were soon to be made circulating.

4388.   Thorndike, E. L. "Vocabularies of juvenile books," *Library quarterly,* Chicago, Vol. 5, No. 2, April, 1935, pp. 151–63. DLC, NNY.

One of the first and strongest of the educators' appeals for the limitation of vocabularies in children's books. This idea was challenged by numerous critics and librarians, and the controversy continues to this day.

4389.   Thorndike, Robert L. *A comparative study of children's reading interests, based on a fictitious annotated titles questionnaire.* New York, Columbia University, Teachers College, 1941. 48p. NNY.

This study was conducted using the unusual method of a checklist of nonexistent titles which the student was supposed to check off as to whether he would or would not like to read.

4390.   Thorning, R. J. *The publication of children's books in the United States, 1863–1864.* Chicago, University of Chicago, 1955. 272p. Thesis.

4391.   Thrasher, Frederick M. "The comics and delinquency: Cause or scapegoat," *Journal of educational sociology,* New York, Vol. 23, No. 4, Dec., 1949, pp. 195–205. DLC.

A refutation of Frederic Wertham's contention that comics are a leading cause of juvenile delinquency.

4392.   Thyng, Mrs. F. B. *They all like to read; reading attitudes and patterns of eleven- and twelve-year-olds.* New York, Association for Arts in Childhood, 1943. 24p. (Bulletin no. 7.)

Bound with: Jacob W. Wrightstone, "An evaluation of adolescent reading interests."

4393.   Tomlinson, Everett. "Reading for boys and girls," *Atlantic monthly,* Boston, Vol. 86, Dec., 1900, pp. 693–699. DLC, NNY.

An excellent summary of the reasons how and why children's literature developed as a special type, distinct from the "classics," or from general literature read by adults.

4394.   Tomlinson, Josie C. *Analysis of the social life and customs of Mexico as reflected in selected children's fiction books published 1950–1959.* Chapel Hill, University of North Carolina, 1964. 127p. Thesis.

4395. Tooze, Ruth. *Storytelling.* Englewood Cliffs, N.J., Prentice-Hall, 1959. 268p. DLC.

The heritage of storytelling, the teller and the telling, some stories and poems to use with children, and a subject bibliography of sources of story material are the three sections of this work.

4396. ———. *Your children want to read; a guide for teachers and parents.* Englewood Cliffs, N.J., Prentice-Hall, 1957. 222p. IYL, DLC, NNY.

A discussion of the reading needs of children, with recommended lists of books.

4397. *Top of the news.* Children's Services Division and Young Adult Services Division, American Library Association, 50 East Huron Street, Chicago, Illinois 60611. Quarterly. Vol. 1 ff., No. 1 ff., 1942 ff. Annual subscription: free to members and $1.25 to non-members. DLC, IYL, NNY.

The official bulletin of the two divisions of ALA which are concerned specifically with children's and young adult libraries. It contains general articles on library work, history and criticism of children's literature, booklists, official and non-official announcements, and articles on subjects related to children and books.

4398. "The training of children's librarians," *Library quarterly,* Chicago, Vol. 5, Apr., 1935, pp. 164–188. DLC, NNY.

An article based on an extensive survey and report undertaken by a special committee of ALA. This contains a number of graphs and statistical tables and presents a few of the general conclusions.

4399. *Translated children's books.* Locust Valley, New York, Storybooks International, 1963. 43p. Supplement, 3p. DLC, IYL, NNY.

A catalog purporting to list all children's books translated into English from a foreign language and currently available from publishers in the U.S. They are listed alphabetically according to original language. The compilation was the work of Edelgaard van Heydekampf Bruehl. Author and title index.

4400. Traxler, Arthur E. "Research in reading in the U.S.," *Journal of educational research,* Madison, Wis., Vol. 42, No. 7, Mar., 1949, pp. 481–499. DLC.

Some of the 19th-century educators, and more from the 20th century are represented in this survey, of borderline interest since it deals largely with the techniques of reading.

4401. Treasure-Trove School and Family Library. *Books for young people* . . . Part 1. New York, E. L. Kellogg & Co., 1887. 20p. NNY.

This "Library" was a preselected set of some 500 volumes suitable for use in home or school. It was selected by a large bookselling organization.

4402. Trinkner, Charles L. *Better libraries make better schools.* Hamden, Connecticut, Shoe String Press, 1962. 335p. DLC, NNY.

Reprints of articles appearing in many journals on the many aspects of school library work.

4403. True, John Preston. "Juvenile literature (so called)," *Atlantic monthly,* Boston, Vol. 92, Nov., 1903, pp. 690–692. NNY, DLC.

"During the last season a Boston daily gave in each case a prodigious amount of space to the reviews of some historical novels . . . although apparently finding little in them really to commend . . . It remarked of a juvenile book . . . that it was much better written than the average boy's book, and more interesting to adults than nine tenths of the historical novels of the year. And how much space did the reviewer devote to this literary discovery? Just one inch."

4404. Tucker, Joanna. *Publicity manual for the children's department of a public library.* Pittsburgh, Carnegie Institute of Technology, 1951. 64p. Thesis.

4405. Turner, Pearl. *Critical analysis of picture books by American author-illustrators.* Denton, Texas State College for Women, 1951. 65p. Thesis.

4406. Twomey, John E. *The anti-comic book crusade.* Chicago, University of Chicago, 1955. 56p. Thesis. NNY has on film.

A study of the reasons for this crusade, some of the groups taking part, and the methods used.

4407. Tyler, Anna Cogswell. "Library reading clubs for boys and girls," *Library journal,* New York, Vol. 37, Oct., 1912, pp. 547–550. DLC, NNY.

The storytelling specialist of the New York Public Library here describes some of the clubs formed in the branch libraries and the programs they followed.

4408. U.S. Indian Affairs Office. Education Division. *Suggested books for Indian schools.* 9th ed. Washington, The Office, 1959. 130p. NNY.

An annotated list of children's books, arranged by subjects and indexed. The compilers noted that there was very little material written from the Indian point of view.

4409. U.S. Library of Congress. Division for the

Blind. "Books for younger readers," *Books on magnetic tape,* Washington, The Division, 1962, pp. 73–76. DLC, NNY.

Similar in format to the other two lists put out by this division listing Braille and Talking Books.

4410. ———. *Catalog of Braille books for juvenile readers, 1953–1962.* Washington, The Library, 1963. 174p. DLC, NNY.

A catalog intended for use by partially seeing children, or by adults working with blind children. The type is very large. Arrangement is by broad subject areas, and the entries are annotated. This is kept up-to-date by annual supplements. All books are available free to children considered legally blind.

4411. ———. *Catalog of talking books for juvenile readers.* Washington, The Library, 1961. 118p. DLC, NNY.

An annotated list arranged by subjects and presented in format similar to the above list.

4412. U.S. Office of Education. Educational Materials Center. *Reports.* Washington, D.C. 1961 ff. Irregular.

Lists of trade and textbook materials for children in elementary and secondary schools. Inclusion is on the basis of favorable reviews in at least one recognized journal or other media. Each list is devoted to one major area of the world, or a subject involving the world, e.g., The United Nations.

4413. Van Liew, Charles C. "The duty of the normal school toward the problem of school literature." National Education Association, *Proceedings,* 1894, pp. 833–840. DLC.

Developing the use of good literature demands better cultural training of normal school students. Therefore, model children's libraries are essential.

4414. Vaughan, Delores K. *The role of the elementary school library in the compensatory education programs.* Chicago, University of Chicago, 1965. 67p. Thesis.

4415. Vautier, Gerda. *A child's bouquet of yesterday.* New York, American Studio Books, 1946. 56p. DLC.

Excerpts of texts and accompanying illustrations are reproduced from a number of 18th and 19th-century children's books.

4416. Veatch, Jeannette. *How to teach reading*

with children's books. New York, Columbia University, Teachers College, 1964. 28p. DLC.

An amusing pamphlet done in semi-cartoon style, demonstrating how a teacher can use trade books (as opposed to regular textbooks) in teaching and stimulating an interest in reading. The author is also noted for her textbook *Reading in the Elementary School,* Ronald Press, 1966, which attempts to apply some of the principles of teaching reading which had been explored and advocated by Sylvia Ashton-Warner.

4417. Viguers, Ruth Hill, *et al. Illustrators of children's books, 1946–56.* Boston, Horn Book, 1958. 299p. $20.00. DLC, IYL, NNY.

This supplement to *Illustrators of Children's Books 1744–1945* includes the biographies of 500 illustrators (of many nationalities) whose work has appeared in U.S. picture books. Chapter I, "Distinction in picture books," is by Marcia Brown; Chapter II, "The book artist: ideas and techniques," is by Lynd Ward; and chapter III, "The European picture book," is by Fritz Eichenberg. The closing bibliographies of the illustrators were prepared by Marcia Dolphin. This has some representative reproductions of the illustrators mentioned in the first three chapters, but it is not as profusely illustrated as the first volume.

4418. ———. *Margin for surprise; about books, children and librarians.* Boston, Little, Brown, 1964. 175p. $4.50. DLC, IYL, NNY.

The editor of *Horn Book Magazine* has delivered many speeches and written many articles on the subject of children's literature. This collection is a sampling from the best of them, dealing with criticism, storytelling, publishing trends, and the challenge of children's librarianship, among other things. Frances Clarke Sayers characterized it as "work rooted in knowledge of children's books, respect for the minds and imaginative scope of children, and recognition of the living attributes of literature."

4419. Vostrovsky, Clara. "A study of children's reading tastes," *The pedagogical seminary,* Worcester, Mass., Vol. 6, No. 4, Dec., 1899, pp. 523–535. DLC.

An early survey conducted in Stockton, California. Some of the conclusions: more girls than boys preferred fiction; more authors girls read have lasted than boys' favorites.

4420. Wagner, Joseph and Robert W. Smith. *Teacher's guide to storytelling.* Dubuque, Iowa, W. C. Brown, 1958. 145p.

4421. Wagoner, Lovisa C. *An unimportant resi-*

due; or books that did not live. n.p. [1937. 12p.]. DLC.

Some examples of the moral tales of the 19th century, and reasons for their disappearance.

4422. Walker, Clare C. "Children's book center on Guam," *Top of the news,* Chicago, Vol. 21, June, 1965, pp. 352–353. DLC, NNY.

The Education Committee of the Guam Women's Club stimulated local interest by bringing in the Jaycees exhibit of children's books selected by a committee of the Children's Services Division of ALA (see 3422). The author also describes other activities related to books which were begun by the Club.

4423. Walker, Margaret L. *Types of juvenile patrons of two branches of the Atlanta Public Library.* Atlanta, Atlanta University, 1952. 67p. Thesis.

4424. Walraven, Margaret Kessler and Alfred L. Hall-Quest. *Library guidance for teachers.* New York, Wiley, 1941. 308p. DLC.

A textbook on library science for the secondary school teacher-librarian. Extensive, detailed and still useful, when supplemented with additional materials of more recent years.

4425. ———. *Teaching through the elementary school library.* New York, H. W. Wilson, 1948. 183p. DLC.

Designed for use as a text in teacher training programs. Although the bibliographies and standards are out of date, the general principles of using books with children are still very applicable. Index.

4426. Walter, Henriette R. "Reading interests and habits of girls," *Girl life in America: A study of background.* New York, 1927. pp. 117–137.

4427. Ward, Martha E. and Dorothy A. Marquardt. *Authors of books for young people.* New York and London, The Scarecrow Press, 1964. 285p. $6.00. DLC, NNY.

Brief biographies of 1030 authors, with symbols to indicate where additional information can be located about some of them. All are authors whose works are available in the English language and the greatest number are from the U.S.

4428. Washburn, J. *A study of the transitional stage of "free reading" patterns of boys and girls, ages from ten to thirteen.* Denton, Texas State College for Women, 1954. 45p. Thesis.

4429. Washburne, Carleton and Mabel Vogel.

Winnetka graded book list. Chicago, ALA, 1926. 286p. DLC, NNY. Also appeared as: *What children like to read.* Chicago, Rand McNally, 1926. 286p. DLC, NNY.

"Results of a statistical investigation as to the books enjoyed by children of various ages and measured degrees of reading ability." This definitive study is perhaps the most influential reading-interest study produced in the U.S. Its impact was felt in many other countries as well, and a number of books were translated on the strength of their appearance in the highly recommended ranks. The arrangement is first by grade and then by age. Children's comments are included in the grade listings. There is a subject and author index.

4430. Watson, Katherine W. "Boyhood favorites of famous men," *Library journal,* New York, Vol. 56, Apr. 15, 1931, pp. 356–358, 373. DLC, NNY.

The author quizzed some well-known Americans about their favorite books in their boyhood. She reports here on the results. Robinson Crusoe was at the top of the list.

4431. ———. *Once upon a time.* New York, H. W. Wilson, 1942. 263p. DLC, NNY.

A collection of children's stories retold for radio broadcasting, together with some techniques on how to tell stories through this medium. Sources are indicated, and material about some of the authors is also included.

4432. ———. *Tales for telling.* New York, H. W. Wilson, 1950. 267p. $4.00.

A classified list of stories including time indications.

4433. Watt, Homer A. and Karl J. Holzknecht. *Children's books of long ago; a garland of pages and pictures.* New York, Dryden Press, 1942. 32p. DLC.

Illustrations from the tiny books for children popular in the 19th century chosen for their charm and reproduced (together with appropriate verses or passages) for the reminiscent adult.

4434. Way, O. R. "Books for children," *The instructor,* Dansville, New York, 1891 ff. Monthly.

O. R. Way is the current reviewer of children's books in this periodical, which has consistently had review columns since its inception. Other recent reviewers of note were Christine Gilbert, Leland Jacobs, and Phyllis Fenner.

4435. Wead, Katherine Howes and May G. Quigley. *A list of series and sequels for juvenile readers.* Boston, F. Faxon, 1923. 63p. DLC.

A guide to locating the titles and the order of the many series and sequels popular with children in the early part of the century. The main body is alphabetically arranged by author, and there is a list of series by name.

4436. Weekes, Blanche E. *The influence of meaning on children's choices of poetry.* New York, Columbia University, 1929. 51p. (Contributions to Education Series No. 354, N.Y. Teachers College, Bureau of Publications). DLC.

A rather uninspired study of the use and enjoyment of poetry for children written from a teacher's point of view. Short bibliography.

4437. ———. *Literature and the child.* New York, Silver, Burdett, 1935. 456p. DLC.

A textbook designed for the guidance of elementary school teachers with projects and suggestions at the end of each chapter. Includes a list of books and some reference materials, all of which are outdated. Index.

4438. Weight, Glenn S. *Study of the contributions of selected prominent American authors to St. Nicholas magazine.* Pittsburgh, Carnegie Institute of Technology, 1951. 87p. Thesis.

4439. Weiss, Harry Bischoff. *American chapbooks.* Trenton, New Jersey, Privately printed, 1938. 31p. DLC, NNY.

A brief history of the chapbook in the U.S., together with a list of those produced from 1713 to 1860.

4440. ———. *American chapbooks, 1722–1842.* New York, The New York Public Library, 1945. 19p. DLC, NNY. Reprint from: *Bulletin of the New York Public Library,* Vol. 49, July–Aug., 1945, pp. 491–498, 587–596. DLC, NNY.

This is a revised version of the author's earlier history (see 4439) of chapbooks and broadsides in the U.S. The author quotes from a number of them. There is a "preliminary checklist" of more than 200 titles.

4441. ———. "Metamorphoses and harlequinades," *American book collector,* Metuchen, Vol. 2, Aug.–Sept., 1932, pp. 100–118. NNY.

"A metamorphosis may be described as a manifold paper, which in its various combinations produces new pictures. Or it may be described as a narrow sheet of paper, printed on both sides and folded . . . three times so as to produce four sheets, each sheet having on its upper and lower edges a folding flap or half sheet, both of which meet in the middle and form an additional page." A harlequinade is essentially a metamorphosis in which the subject is the exploits of Harlequin; however, the term has now come to mean virtually any type of metamorphosis, and it is so used in the Gumuchian catalog. The author cites a number of specific examples from England and the U.S., as well as a few from France. There are reproductions in black and white of 12 examples.

4442. ———. *Penny decalcomanias and other transfer-picture lithographs for the amusement of children.* Trenton, New Jersey, Privately printed, 1935. 11p. NNY.

Although these novelties can hardly be classed as children's literature, this interesting study is included here for the bibliophile interested in children's picture stories of the most unlikely sort.

4443. ———. *The printers and publishers of children's books in New York City 1698–1830.* New York, The New York Public Library, 1948. 21p. NNY, DLC.

This survey of early children's book publishing contains lists of the books issued by the publishers, and comments on some of the individual titles. There is a reference list of sources.

4444. Welch, D'Alté A. "A bibliography of American children's books printed prior to 1821," *American Antiquarian Society, Proceedings,* Worcester, Massachusetts, Vol. 73, Part 1, Apr., 1963, pp. 121–324; Part 2, Oct., 1963, pp. 465–596; Vol. 74, Part 2, Oct., 1964, pp. 262–387.

A monumental project, undertaken with great bibliographic care as well as evident enthusiasm. The entries through H are printed here, alphabetically by author (or title, when author unknown) and complete in description. Libraries owning copies are indicated, and those titles listed in the National Union Card Catalog are so indicated. Private collections are also coded, since these contain many of the rarest items. There is an excellent summary of private and institutional collections of early American juveniles, at the beginning of the first part of the bibliography. There is also a very complete list of works consulted, and a brief chronological history of American children's books up to 1821. It is to be hoped that this valuable beginning to a U.S. national bibliography of children's books can soon be printed in entirety.

4445. Wellman, Hiller C. "What public libraries are doing for children," *Atlantic monthly,* Boston, Vol. 90, 1902, pp. 402–409. DLC, NNY.

A brief history and a description of the type of guidance offered to children in the public libraries of the time.

4446. Wells, A. R. C. *A study of selected juvenile fiction about Norwegian life and customs published 1933–1953.* Atlanta, Atlanta University, 1956. 87p. Thesis.

4447. Wells, Carolyn. "Writers of juvenile fiction," *Bookman,* New York, Vol. 14, Dec., 1901, pp. 348–355. NNY.
A general history of the chief purveyors of fiction for children in the 18th and 19th centuries. Illustrated.

4448. Wells, Kate Gannett. "The responsibility of parents in the selection of reading for the young," *Library journal,* New York, Vol. 4, Nos. 9–10, Sept.–Oct., 1879, pp. 325–330. DLC, NNY.
This librarian felt that libraries could not watch out carefully enough that children did not read too much fiction, and recommended that parents be made aware of the danger in over-reading.

4449. Welsh, Charles. "Early history of children's books in New England," *New England magazine,* Boston, Vol. 20, No. 2, April, 1899, pp. 147–160. DLC, NNY.
A lengthy, detailed critique of the didactic books published in the early years of colonialism.

4450. ———. *The right reading for children in the school, the home and the library.* Boston, Heath, 1905. 82p. DLC.
An interesting compilation of quotations from authorities on reading, in the three categories indicated in the title. Followng this are graded, annotated lists of children's books.

4451. ———. "The right reading for very young children," *Dial,* New York, Vol. 31, Dec. 1, 1901, pp. 427–429. DLC, NNY.
Young children need lively action and a choice of styles in their reading, as well as attractive and artistic illustrations.

4452. Wendel, C. E. *An analysis of questions asked by children in public libraries.* Chicago, University of Chicago, 1946. 92p. Thesis.

4453. Westervelt, G. *What juvenile books should form the nucleus of the collection in the libraries in the schools of practice of the New York state normal schools?* New York, Columbia University, 1939. 187p. Thesis.

4454. "What is a children's literature? a symposium," *Elementary english,* Champaign, Vol. 41, May, 1964, pp. 467–499. DLC.
This issue presented a joint attempt to define children's literature, to assess its value in the school life of the child and to point to some methods of using literature in the elementary classroom. There is also an article on children's book illustration. Chief contributors were Virginia M. Reid, Charlotte S. Huck, Leone Garvey, Patricia J. Ciancolo, and William A. Jenkins.

4455. Wheeler, H. E. "The psychological case against the fairy tale," *Elementary school journal,* Chicago, Vol. 29, June, 1929, pp. 754–755. DLC, NNY.
This educator cites the words of Dr. Harry Overstreet and Dr. Alfred Adler in attempting to prove that the fairy tale is harmful.

4456. Wheeler, J. L. "Thoughts on the preparation of school librarians," *Library journal,* New York, Vol. 60, Mar. 15, 1935, pp. 242–245. DLC, NNY.
A paper read before the meeting of the Association of American Library Schools in Chicago, Dec., 1934. Mr. Wheeler wrote: "My plea is that the schools represented in this association make a break with the past; that their courses of study in school librarianship be definitely tied to the idea that the school librarian is a part of the school and not a transfer from the public library field into the schoolhouse."

4457. White, Pura Belpré. "Bilingual story hour program," *Library journal,* New York, Vol. 89, Sept. 15, 1964, pp. 3379–3381. DLC, NNY.
The Spanish storytelling specialist of the New York Public Library describes her experiences in the schools, libraries, and parks of New York, telling stories to mixed groups of Puerto Rican and other American children.

4458. White, R. M. *The school-housed public library: A survey.* Chicago, ALA, 1963. 62p.

4459. White House Conference on Children's Reading. *A study of voluntary reading of boys and girls in the U.S. Report of the Sub-committee on Reading.* New York, Century, 1932. 90p. DLC.
Prepared under the chairmanship of Carl H. Milam, this report gives specific details on reading as related to movies, racial differences, publishing, libraries, etc. There is a selective bibliography arranged by category.

4460. Whitenack, Carolyn I. "The historical development of the elementary school library," *Illinois libraries,* Springfield, Vol. 38, June, 1956, pp. 143–149. DLC, NNY.

A very clear survey and history of the elementary school library from the 19th century to the present. There is a very good list of additional references.

4461. Whitney, Phyllis. *Writing juvenile fiction.* Rev. ed. Boston, The Writer, 1960. 213p. $3.50. DLC, NNY.

This author is best known for her girls' stories and mystery stories. She is an experienced teacher of writing as well, and this book reflects much of the materials she has used successfully in her courses.

4462. Wickham, Joseph Francis. "When the world was young," *Catholic world,* New York, Vol. 95, No. 567, June, 1912, pp. 376–385. DLC, NNY.

An essay on the qualities which children's books of the previous centuries had.

4463. Widdemer, Margaret. "A bibliography of books and articles relating to children's reading," *Bulletin of bibliography,* Boston, Vol. 6, No. 8, July, 1911, pp. 240–243; No. 9, Oct., 1911, pp. 270–273; No. 10, Jan., 1912, pp. 301–303; Vol. 7, No. 1, April, 1912, pp. 9–13. DLC, NNY.

An important early bibliography which listed books and articles related to children's reading in general, the history of children's literature, children's reading in the home, the relationship of the school with the library, the guidance of children's reading, girls' reading, boys' reading, sensational reading, Sunday School books, the story hour and fairy tales, illustrators and illustrating, writers' early reading, writing for children, children's reading in France and Germany, reports and statistics and booklists. Each entry is briefly annotated.

4464. Wiggin, Kate D. and Norah Smith. *The story hour.* Boston, Houghton, 1899. 185p. DLC, NNY.

Practical suggestions on how to tell stories to children, and some stories to tell.

4465. Wiggin, Kate Douglas. "What shall children read?" *Children's rights.* Boston, Houghton, 1892, pp. 69–89. NNY.

A brief history of early children's literature, contrasting it to that of the turn of the century. This is followed by advice on what qualities to look for in choosing books for children.

4466. Willard, Charles B. *Your reading.* Champaign, Illinois, National Council of Teachers of English, 1966. 222p. $00.75.

An annotated list for grades seven through nine.

4467. Williams, Gweneira M. and Jane S. Wilson. "Why not? Give them what they want!" *Publishers' weekly,* New York, Vol. 141, No. 6, Apr., 18, 1942, pp. 1490–1496. DLC, NNY.

In defense of comics and cheap, series books which give children the thrills, action, conflict, humor and pathos which these authors believe children are looking for and need. They sum up with fulsome praise of Disney.

4468. Williams, Mary Floyd and Bertha M. Brown. *Reading list for children's librarians.* Albany, New York State Library, 1901. (Bulletin 62, Report 84, Bibliography No. 27.) DLC.

Made for use by those librarians lacking pedagogical training as well as general knowledge about child psychology, sociology, library administration, etc. Author, subject and title index.

4469. Williams, M. J. "Library work in a children's hospital," *ALA hospital and institution book guide,* Chicago, Vol. 1, Jan., 1959, pp. 79–85. DLC.

A description of the methods and demands of this special work.

4470. Willis, D. M. G. *Public libraries' utilization of television as a part of the program activities of a department of service to children.* Philadelphia, Drexel Institute of Technology, 1955. 39p. Thesis.

4471. Wilson, D. B. *A survey and evaluation of books written for children by Negro authors.* Cleveland, Western Reserve University, 1956. 34p. Thesis.

4472. Wilson, Ellen. "The books we got for Christmas," *American heritage,* New York, Vol. 8, No. 1, Dec., 1956, pp. 26–37. DLC, NNY.

A reminiscence about the early editions of the classics, often especially illustrated and bound to make a special appeal as a gift. There are reproductions in color from a number of them, e.g., *Hans Brinker, Tom Sawyer, The Peterkin Papers, Little Women,* etc. In this same issue is a two-page article on the rebus, with an early sample, reproduced in color, pp. 44–45.

4473. Wilson, Martha and Althea M. Currin. *School library maagement.* 6th ed. New York, H. W. Wilson Co., 1939. 169p. DLC, NNY. (1st ed., New York, H. W. Wilson Co., 1919. 126p. DLC).

An early handbook on school library administration and practice.

4474. Wilson, Martha, *et al. Selected articles on school library experience*. 2nd series. New York, H. W. Wilson, 1932. 328p.

4475. Winn, R. E. *World War II fiction for children; an annotated bibliography of stories with European background*. New York, Pratt Institute Library School, 1955. 45p. Thesis.

4476. Winnick, Pauline. "A time for self-renewal," *Library journal*, New York, Vol. 91, Jan. 15, 1966, pp. 317–353. DLC, NNY.

Miss Winnick was guest editor of this issue which dealt with the federal anti-poverty programs, and the role of libraries in them.

4477. Winslow, Jessica R. L. *Study of Japanese life and customs as portrayed in selected juvenile fiction published from 1912–1954*. Atlanta, Atlanta University, 1955. 116p. Thesis.

4478. Winterburn, Florence Hull. "The child's taste in fiction," *New England magazine*, Boston, Vol. 27, Nov., 1902, pp. 325–330. NNY.

An extremely perceptive article arguing that the spate of reading interest studies generated by the new public library movement had little value in the final judging of children's tastes. The author suggests some ways of guiding children's reading without imposing on them the inflexible values of the adult.

4479. Winterich, John Tracy. *The first R; an address delivered at the opening of the exhibition of children's literature, November 18, 1954*. New York, Pierpont Morgan Library, 1955. 19p. DLC.

This speech provided glimpses into the early reading of some great men and placed children's literature in the mainstream of all literature.

4480. Witmer, Eleanor M. "School library studies and research," *Library quarterly*, Chicago, Vol. 6, Oct., 1936, pp. 382–404. DLC, NNY.

A suggested list of areas where further study and research is needed together with a bibliography of some 200 items describing existing surveys and studies already completed.

4481. Witty, Paul. "Some observations from studies of the comics," *Association for Arts in Childhood, Bulletin*, New York, No. 6, 1942, pp. 1–6. DLC.

4482. Wofford, Azile. *Book selection for school libraries*. New York, H. W. Wilson, 1962. 318p. $5.00. DLC, NNY.

A standard work in the field often used as a textbook for courses in school library work. There are helpful suggestions in selecting materials as well as for coping with such special problems as series books, comics, and censorship. The appendix includes a reading list and further selection aids.

4483. ———. *The school library at work: Acquisition, organization, use and maintenance of materials in the school library*. New York, Wilson, 1959. $3.50. 256p. DLC, IYL, NNY.

The title indicates very clearly the scope of this work, still widely used as a textbook and guide. The appendix lists aids for selection of materials, manuals on teaching the use of the library, a glossary of terms, and a directory of publishers and suppliers. Index.

4484. Wolfe, Ann G. "About 100 books . . . a gateway to better inter-group understanding." 5th ed. New York, American Jewish Committee, 1965. Unp. DLC, NNY.

This list is revised approximately every two years. Its purpose is to point out books which "foster constructive social attitudes," with emphasis on honest portrayal of people and problems.

4485. Wolfenstein, Martha. *The impact of a children's story on mothers and children*. Washington, Society for Research in Child Development, National Research Council, 1947. 54p. (Monographs, Vol. 11, No. 1, Series No. 42). NNY.

A fascinating account, more related to psychology than literature, of an experiment with mothers who read aloud to their children a story concerning a new baby. This is included for its unusual approach to categorizing the responses of the mothers as well as those of the children.

4486. Wollner, Mary H. B. *Children's voluntary reading as an expression of individuality*. New York, Columbia University, Teachers College, 1949. Thesis.

4487. Wong, May Seong. *Story telling in the Brooklyn Public Library*. New York, Pratt Institute Library School, 1952. 42p. Thesis.

4488. Wood, Harriet, A. "Sets for children," *Public libraries*, Chicago, Vol. 18, Apr., 1913, pp. 138–141. DLC, NNY.

The author investigated the purchasing of sets and series by children's libraries and solicited the opinions of a number of children's librarians on some specific examples. She reports here on her findings.

4489. Woodfield, H. J. B. "Children's books in

America," *Library assistant,* London, Vol. 35, Dec., 1942, pp. 154–160. DLC, NNY.

The author comments on the high standards of U.S. children's books and suggests some of the reasons why these standards exist.

4490. "Work with children; a symposium," *Public libraries,* Chicago, Vol. 11, Apr., 1906, pp. 193–202. DLC, NNY.

A survey of the work being done in many of the larger cities of the U.S.

4491. *Workshop in school library problems.* University of Nevada, June 13–24, 1955. Reno, University of Nevada, 1955. 123p. DLC.

The contents reflect the problems encountered in serving the dispersed, thin population of this state.

4492. *The world of children's books.* New York, Children's Book Council, 1952. 128p. DLC, IYL, NNY.

A collection of critical, appreciative and practical essays pertinent to the world of children's books, from the points of view of bookseller, librarian, author, publisher, teacher, parent, critic. Appendix has a list of good booklists, a bibliography of histories, Book Week slogans and posters from 1919, organizations which cooperated with the Children's Book Council, and other lists related to exhibits and publishing.

4493. Wurzburg, Dorothy Adele. *East, west, north and south in children's books.* Boston, F. W. Faxon, 1939. 158p. DLC.

"An annotated regional bibliography for use in grade and junior high schools." The books are listed by country and for the U.S. by state or region. Now outdated but useful in comparing with later lists.

4494. Young, Nancy A. *Study of biographies published in the United States for younger children; 1940–1949.* Cleveland, Western Reserve University, 1951. 32p. Thesis.

4495. *Young readers review.* L. R. Stolzer, Box 137, Wall Street Station, New York, New York 10005. Monthly, Sept.–June. Vol. 1 ff. 1964 ff. Annual subscription: $5.00. DLC, NNY.

Lengthy reviews of current children's books intended both for the child reader and the adult person buying children's books. There is a column reviewing well-known children's books of the past.

4496. Yungmeyer, Elinor. *Magazine reading by elementary school pupils.* Chicago, University of Chicago, 1954. 187p. Thesis.

Index

490

492

493

Gebt uns Bücher gebt uns Flügel, 1214
Gedanken zum Jugendbuch, 1520
Gedike, Friedrich, 2100, 2112
Gefaell, María Luisa, 542
Gefahren moderner Jugendlektüre, 1282
Gegen den Missbrauch des Vaterländischen in Jugendschriften, 1406
Gegen den Strom, 1192
Gehain, Adhemar, 253
Geist, Hans Friedrich, 12
Gelderblom, Gertrud, 1216, 1217
Genčiova, M. Holešovská-; *see* Holešovská-Genčiova, M.
Gendai jidō bungaku jiten, 2590
Gendai jidō bungaku jiten, 2658
Genestet, Petrus Augustus de, 982
Gengivet efter den første undgave 1866, 1597
Gentry, Helen, 3715, 4070
Gerber, Dieter, 1377
Gerd, A. IA, *with* V. M. Garshin, 1903
Gerena, Carmen, 427
Gerhard, Annie C., 1005
Gerhard, J. W., 983, 984, 985
Gerhardt, Mia I., 986
Gérin, Elisabeth, 791, 792, 793
Gerlović, Alenka, 2220
Gesammlete Schulschriften, 1215
Gesamteuropäisches Studienwerk, 1218
Geschichte der deutschen Jugendliteratur, 1295
Geschichte der deutschen Jugendliteratur, 1333
Geschichte der Luxemburger Jugendliteratur, 1062
Geschichte des deutschen Jugendbuches, 1193
Geschichte des deutschen Jugendschrifttums, 1358
Geschiedenis des leeszaalbeweging in Nederland, 998
Geschlechtliche im Unterricht und in der Jugendlektüre, 1296
Gesichtspunkte und praktische Ratschläge für die Anlegung von Schülerbibliotheken, 1199
Gespräche mit Lesern in der Kinderbibliothek, (Berlin), 1219
Gessleman, Daisy B., 3793
Gestaltete sachbuch und seine probleme, 1220
Gestern, heute, morgen, 1077
Giacobbé, Olindo, 657
Giaever, Hanna, 1634, 1637
Gibbons, Emma, 3794
Gibon, Marcel, *with* S. Mayence 853
Giehrl, Hans Eberhard, 1221
Gierke, 1222
Gieseler, Hanns, 1223
Giessen, H. W. van der, 987
Gilbert, Christine, 4434
Gilbert, Mizpah, 2998
Gill, Gertrude, 3795
Gillette, Jean E. and Veva E., 3796
Gil'man, M., 1904
Gilman, Stella Scott, 3797
Gilmore, E. C., 3798
Gilson, Marjary L., 3651
Giménez, Eduocio S., 134

Giorgi, G., 658
Giorgi, Olga Mazzei de; *see* Mazzei de Giorgi, Olga
Girdner, M. V., 4280
Girl life in America, 4426
Girls' own list of favorite books, 3918
Girl's stories; *see* Reading interests —girls
Girolama, Sister Mary, 3799
Gitée, Aug, 911
Glaister, Geoffrey, 2455
Glaser, Martha, 1224
Glaubsrecht, O., 1175
Gleason, Caroline F., 3800
Gleave, Betty M., 2546
Glen, Esther, 2950
Glenn, Lily D., 3801
Glick, M. B., 3108
Gobetti, A. Marchesini, 1905
Godart, M., 794
Godden, Rumer, 3802
Godfrey, Elizabeth, 3084
Godinez, Ada, 307
Godley, Eveline Charlotte, 3085
Göbels, Hubert, 1225
Goehring, Ludwig, 1226
Goerlitz, Theo Ludwig, 1086
Goerth, Albrecht, 1227
Goethe, 171, 2218
Goetz, Delia, 86, *with* B. Nolan 381
Götze, O., 1228, 1229
Goicochea, Caridad Fernández; *see* Fernández Goicochea, Caridad
Golden book and the literature of childhood, 4240
Golden multitudes; the story of best sellers in the United States, 4138
Goldhor, Herbert, *with* J. A. McCrossan 3803
Gollmitz, Renate, 13
Gomes, Giselda G., 200
Gómez, Beatriz Parra de, 350
Gómez, Ermilo Abreu; *see* Abreu Gómez, Ermilo
Gómez, Gabriel Anzola; *see* Anzola Gómez, Gabriel
Gómez Vilá, María de los Angeles, 308
Gomme, Alice B., 3086
Goncourt, 3096
Gonsáles Ramírez, Mario Gilberto, 344, 345
Gonzalvo Mainar, Gonzalo, 543
Good books for children published 1948–1961, 3683
Good citizenship through storytelling, 3759
Good reading, 4158
"Good reading" children's book list, 3422
Good reading for poor readers, 4335
Goodrich, Samuel, 3102
Gordon, L. G., 2909, 2910
Gordon, L. M., 3804
Goretti, Maria, 659
Goriszowski, Włodzimierez, 2059
Gorki, Maxim, 1230, 1842, 1874, 1906, 1919, 1957, 1988, 2148, 2218, 2225, 2537
Gorkina, A., 1907
Gorman, Edith M., 3805

Gorodkina, L., 1908
Gosudarstvenny i pedagogicheskii institut imeni A.I. Gertsena, 1946
Gottgetreu, Erich, 2247
Gottschalk, Rudolf, 1231
Gouin, Paul, 3355
Gould, F. J., 2399
Gould, Sabine Baring-; *see* Baring-Gould, Sabine
Goyau, L. Felix-Faure; *see* Felix-Faure-Goyau, L.
Graded list of books for children, 3484
Graebsch, Irene Dyhrenfurth-; *see* Dyhrenfurth-Graebsch, Irene
Grafika w książkach naszej księgarni, 2123
Graham, Gladys Murphy, 1909, 3806
Grahame, Kenneth, 2985
Grambs, Jean D., 3807
Grandin, Nicole, 795
Grandjeat, J., 847
Grannis, Chandler B., 3493
Grant, Margaret E., 3808
Grantha Panjee, 2463
Gratiot-Alphendéry, Hélène, 844
Graucob, Karl, 1232
Gray, Alice E., 3809
Gray, L. G., 3810
Gray, Patricia, 2286
Gray, William S., 3811
Graziani-Camillucci, I., 660
Grazier, Margaret Hayes, 3741
Grechishnikova, A. D., 1910, 1911
Green, Hattie Cora, 3813
Green, Jenny Lind, 3814
Green, Percy, 3089
Green, Roger Lancelyn, 3090, 3091
Green, S. S., 3744, 3815, 3816
Greenaway, K., 1460, 3104, 3159, 4208
Greene, Ellin, 3817
Greig, Lynette, 2911
Grenier, Hélène, 3356
Greve, H. E., 998
Grey, Rowland, 3818
Grieder, Elmer M., 2233
Griffin, Ella, 2294
Grimalt, Manuel, 544
Grimm Brothers, 173, 1333, 1386, 2010, 2125, 2218, 2764, 3022
Grimmelshausen, H. J. C. von, 1448
Grimshaw, Ernest, 3092
Griswold, William M., 3819
Groffi, Y. M. Vanhaegendoren-; *see* Vanhaegendoren-Groffi, Y. M.
Grolier, G. and E. de, 796
Groniowska, Barbara, 2120, *with* M. Gutry, 2060
Groom, Arthur, 3093
Grosglikowa, Barbara 2061, *with* Maria Gutry, 2063
Gross, Elizabeth, 3500, 3820, 3977
Gross, Julius, 1234
Gross, Sarah Chokla, *with* H. H. Watts 3821
Grossi, L., 661
Grossmacht der Jugend- und Volksliteratur, 1085
Grossman, S., 1912
Grotowska, Helena, 662
Growing point, 3094
Growing up with books, 3822

Growing up with science books, 3823
Growing with books; a reading guide, 3485
Growing with books: A reading guide, 4009
Grube, A. W., 1175
Grundriss der Geschichte deutscher Jugendlitteratur, 1209
Grundriss der Pedagogik, 1291
Gruny, Marguerite, 797, 799, 800, 801, 802, 803, 804, 805, 806, 847, with M. Leriche 798
Gruzewska, K., 2120
Guadalupe, Delia E. Riet v de, 450
Guardia, Angel, 366
Guaspari, Maria Bartolozzi, 715
Günnell, J. G., 1235
Günther, Victor, 1236
Guérard, François, 847
Guerrero, Amor C., 2515
Guerrero, Lilia A., 2508
Guevara, Dario C., 335, 336, 337, 338
Guglielmelli, Amedeo, 663
Guia del maestro, 116
Guida all'esame scritto . . . , 659
Guida di letture giovanili per le biblioteche scholastiche e popolari, 633
Guide de la littérature enfantine, 878
Guide for school librarians, 2964
Guide for school libraries, 2505
Guide for young readers, 3301
Guide to book lists and bibliographies for the use of school librarians, 3222
Guide to books for character, 4345
Guide to books on recreation, 4157
Guide to children's literature in the early elementary grades, 3401
Guide to children's magazines, newspapers, reference books, 4179
Guide to good reading, 4024
Guide to literature for character training, 4345
Guide to literature for children, 3747
Guide to storytelling, 3004
Guide to the study and use of reference books, 3987
Guiding the growth of reading interests, 4006
Guidotti, Enrichetta Monaci-; see Monaci-Guidotti, Enrichetta
Guilfoile, Elizabeth, 3824, 4153
Guillien, G., 807
Guillot, René, 22, 847
Gul'binskiĭ, Ignatiĭ Vladislavovich, 1913
Gumuchian, Kirkor, 3095, 3825
Gumuchian, MM. et Cie, 808
Gunnemo, Bertil, 1694
Gunterman, Bertha L., 3827
Gunzberg, H. C., 3826
Gunzel, Marianne, with H. Schneider 1237
Guppy, Henry, 3096
Gupta, Rādhākrṣṇa, 2400
Gurusamy, John R., with L. Y. Chin 2482
Gustafsson, Axel, 1695
Gute Jugendbuch, 1238
Gute Jugendbuch, 1431

Gute Jugendbuch, 1487
Gute Jugendbücher aus Deutschland, Österreich und der Schweiz, 1088
Guth, Paul, 848
Guthrie, Anna Lorraine, 3828
Gutman, Nahrem, 2249
Gutry, Maria, 1567, 2062, 2065, 2066, 2067, 2075, 2114, 2120, with B. Groniowska, 2060, with B. Grosglikowa, 2063, with A. Łasiewicka, 2064
Guy, Altoise C., 3829
Gwynne, Sister Grace Margaret, 3830
Gyermek és az irodalom, 1830
Gyermek és ifjúsági könyvtárak, 1824
Gyermekkönyvtáraink helyzete, 1825
Gymer, Rosina, 3831
Gyulahazi, M., 3488

Ha, Yŏng T'ae, 2769
Haas, Paula de, 3097, with L. J. de Vries 988
Hachette, Louis, 809
Haenel, Charlotte, 1240
Hāfiz, Muḥammad 'Alī, 2272
Hafner, Gustav, with H. Weber 1089
Hagemann, Sonia, 1634
Hagliden, Sten, 1780
Hagrasy, S. Mohammed el-; see Mohammed el-Hagrasy, S.
Haight, Rachel Webb, 3832
Hakkyo tosŏgwan, 2815
Hakkyo tosŏgwan chojik kwa kwalli ŭi sil-che, 2786
Hakkyo tosŏgwan ŭi pŏŏt 'ik 'ol p'ail, 2800
Hakkyo tosŏgwan ŭi sisŏl, 2775
Hakkyo tosŏgwan ŭi sŭt'aep maenyuŏl, 2801
Hakkyo tosŏgwan unyŏng chich 'im, 2746
Hakkyo tosŏgwan yongo, 2770
Halas, John, 2189
Halbert, J. F., 3098
Halbey, Hans Adolf, 14
Hale, Lucretia P., 3434
Halevy, 3096
Hall, D. R., 2888
Hall, Elvajean, 3833, 3834
Hall, G. Stanley, 3835
Hall, Wendy, 3099
Halliwell-Phillips, James O., 3100, 3101
Hall-Quest, Alfred L., with M. K. Walraven, 4424, 4425
Hallqvist, Britt G., 1697
Halphen-Istel, Claire, 810, 811, 812
Halsberghe, C., 912
Halsey, Rosalie V., 3836, 3837
Ham, Ch'ŏ-sik, 2771
Hamada, Hirosuke, 2576
Haman, Albert C., with M. K. Eakin 3838
Hamanaka, Shigenobu, 2591
Hamann, Chr., 1241
Hamidah, Mrs., 2472
Hammar, Stina, 1527
Hammitt, Frances E., 3839
Hammond, Lamont M., 3840
Hampe, J. Chr., 1267
Han, Ŭng-su, 2772

Hanaway, Emily S., 3597, 3841
Handbok in Norsk barnebibliotekarbeide, 1628
Handbook for elementary school librarians, 2510
Handbook for the improvement of textbooks and teaching materials as aids to international understanding, 15
Handbook of children's literature, 3783
Handbuch der Jugendarbeit, 1210
Handbuch der Jugendpflege in Hessen, 1349
Handbuch des Deutschunterrichts, 1147
Handbuch deutscher Prosa, 1436
Handelingen, 943
Handelman, Pearl, 428
Handicapped children; see Blind children, Deaf children
Handley-Taylor, Geoffrey, 3102
Hanguk Adong Manhwa Chayurhoe, 2861
Hanguk adong munhak tokpon, 2773
Hanguk Adong Munhakhoe, 2774
Hanguk ch'ulp'an yŏngam, 2781
Hanguk minjok sŏrhwa ŭi yŏngu, 2834
Hanguk Tosŏgwan Hyŏphoe, 2775
Hani, Setsuko, 2565
Hanif, Akhtar, 2456
Hanifah, Nj. Hafai Abu; see Abu Hanifah, Nj. Hafai
Hanna, Geneva R., with M. K. McAllister 3842
Hansard, Gillian, 3103
Hansen, E. Werring-; see Werring-Hansen, E.
Hansen, Knud, 1568
Hansen, N. Juel-; see Juel-Hansen, N.
Hansen, Rasmus, 1569
Hanzow, H. M., 3843
Harada, Naoshige, 2592
Hardendorff, Jeanne, 3844, 3993
Hardie, Martin, 3104
Hardy, George E., 3845
Harker, Lizzie Allen, 3105
Harlequinades; see Novelties
Harnoncourt, Rene d'; see D'Harnoncourt, Rene
Harper, A. E., 2401
Harrington, Mildred Priscilla, 3846
Harrison, John M., 4170
Harrod, L. M., 3106, 3107
Harron, Julia S., 3651
Harter, Evelyn, 3108
Hartland, Edwin Sidney, 3109
Hartmann, O., 1272
Hartog, John, 3325
Hartung, Hermann, with G. Paulsen 1242
Harussi, Emanuel, 2249
Harvey, Kathleen, 2912
Hasegawa, Seiichi, 2593
Hassler, Harriot E., 664
Haste, Hans, 1698
Hatano, Kanji, 2594, 2595
Hauck, Carolyn Marie, 3847
Hauff, Wilhelm, 2010

Insha, Ibne, 2360, 2457
Insley, N. J., 2295
Institut Metodov Vneshkol'noĭ Raboty, 1962
Institute on Library Work with Children, 4280
Institute on the Elementary School Library, 3919
Instituto Interamericano del Niño, (Montevideo), 94, 95
Instituto Nacional del Libro Espanol, 549, 550, 551
Instituto "San Jose de Calasanz," 573
Instruction in the use of books and libraries, 3735
Integration of the school library with classroom activities; an experiment in cooperation between the librarian and teachers of English, 4052
Intent upon reading: a critical appraisal of modern fiction for children, 3077
Inter-American Bibliographical and Library Association, 99, 195
Interest factors in primary reading material, 3680
Interguglielmo, Martha Scala de; *see* Scala de Interguglielmo, Martha
International Board on Books for Young People, 6, 7, 20, 21, 22, 23, 24, 25, 26, 44, 157, 225, 399, 556, 577, 2611
International Bureau of Education, (Geneva), 27, 28, 29, 51
International Children's Day, 1454
International Congress of Libraries and Bibliography, 2nd, 48, 61, 590, 797, 935, 1339, 3630, 3657
International Congress of Libraries and Documentation Centres, 487, 4013
International Congress on Children's Books, 604
International Congress on Press, Cinema and Radio for the Young, 30
International Federation of Library Associations, 31, 32, 33, 34
International Federation of University Women, 53
International friendship through children's books, 18
International Institute of Intellectual Cooperation, 53, 62
International library service for children, 4181
International Understanding: 646, 1084, 1273, 1731, 1777, 1948, 3411, 3416, 3417, 3421, 3483, 3571, 3636, 3806, 3914, 3967, 4073, 4074, 4149, 4150, 4359, 4360, 4379, 4380, 4484, 4485
International understanding through books for children and young people, 24
International understanding through children's books, 25
International Youth Library, 35, 36, 37, 38, 39, 44, 49
International youth library in the United States, 4091

Internationale Kinderbuchausstellung, 1956/1957, 4
Internationale Tagung für das Jugendbuch, 40
Introducción a las bibliotecas infantiles y escolares, 72
Introducing children to the world in elementary and junior high schools, 3967
Introduction to children's work in public libraries, 3523
Introduction to literature for children, 4236
Inui, Takashi, *with* K. Tsutsui, 2721
Invitation to read; the use of the book in child guidance, 4163
Invloed van de lectuur in de jaren der karakter-vorming, 1000
Inwijding in de Literatur Bronnenopgave, 941
Inyart, B. G., 3921
Ipolitov, S., 1918
Irodalmi érdeklödés o gyermekkorban, 1831
Irshad Ali, Syed, 2458
Irwin, J., 2411
Ishida, Sakuma, 2602
Ishii, Momoko, 2565, 2576, 2603, 2604, 2605, 2606, 2679
Isidro, Antonio, 2509
Iskolai könyvtárak szervezése es kezelése, 1815
Islam Riazul; *see* Riazul Islam
Israel Library Association, 2248
Istel, Claire Halphen-; *see* Halphen-Istel, Claire
Isoriîa russkoĭ detskoi literatury, 1861
Isubota, Joji, 2576
Ivanová-Šalingová, Mária, 2155
Ivich, Aleksandr, 1919
Iwaya, Sazanami, 2576, 2581, 2607, 2724
Iz decje književnosti, 2208
Izard, Anne, 3922, 3923
Izawa, Jun, *with* Morufushi, 2608, 2694
Izbor knjiga za decu, 2216
Izglitibas Ministrija, (Latvia), 1944
Izhevskaîa, M. A., 1263, 1920
Izquierdo Ríos, Francisco, 413, 414

Jackson, E. P., 3924
Jackson, Francine L., 3925
Jacobs, Leland B., 3927, 4434
Jacobs, Mrs. I., 3926
Jacobson, Helja, 1706, 1707, 1708, 1709, 3928, *with* A. Landergren, 1710, *with* A. Sandberg, 1768
Jacomé, G. Alfredo, 339
Jacucci, Giuseppe, 668
Jadin, Marcel, *with* L. Empain, 909
Järnesjö, Eva, *with* M. Ørvig, 1711
Jagannadhan, S., 2405
Jalkotzky, Alois, 1094
James, Hannah P., 3929
James, Louise, 3930
James, Philip, 3118, 3119
James, Viola, 4028
Jamieson, Nigel J., 1921
Jan, Isabelle, 818, 819
Janacek, Blanche, 3931, 3932

Jancovic, M., 2217
Janke, L. H., 4064
Januszewska, Hanna, 2086, 2114
Jaquetti, Palmira, 669
Jaramillo Arango, Rafael, 272
Jast, L. Stanley, 3120, 3121
Jena, Ruth Michaelis-; *see* Michaelis-Jena, Ruth
Jenkins, G., 3488
Jenkins, William A., 4454
Jenkinson, Augustus J., 3122
Jenks, Tudor, 3933, 3934, 3935
Jensen, E. Allerslev, 1574
Jeppensen, Poul, 1575
Jeter, M. H., 3936
Jeugd en lectuur, 976
Jeugdbibliotheckwerk, 924
Jeugdboek en school, 1040
Jeugdboek in de loop der eeuwen, 1037
Jeugdboeken lezen en kiezen, 966
Jeugdboekengids, 916
Jeune génération et la littérature, 11
Jeunes devant la littérature, 817
Jeungdboekenlijst, 939
Jew in Children's Books, The: 743, 1318, 3897, 3959, 3960, 4149, 4209
Jewett, Arno, 3937
Jidō bungaku, 2615
Jidō bungaku gairon, 2581
Jidō bungaku gairon, 2712
Jidō bungaku heno shōtai, 2713
Jidō bungaku kenkyū bunken, 2659
Jidō bungaku no riron to jissai, 2681
Jidō bungaku no shisō, 2585
Jidō bungaku no techō, 2586
Jidō bungaku nyūmon, 2612, 2613
Jidō bungaku nyūmon: sekai meisaku no kodomotachi, 2714
Jidō bungaku to bungaku kyōiku, 2715
Jidō bungaku to dokusho shidō, 2660
Jidō bungaku to jidō yomimono, 2637
Jidō bungakuron, 2698
Jidō Bungakusha Kyōkai, 2612
Jidō Bungei, 2614
Jidō Bungeika Kyōkai, 2615
Jidō bunka, 2616
Jidō bunka, 2639
Jidō bunka (Kokudosha Kyōiku Zensho), 2594
Jidō hyakka dai jiten, 2618
Jidō Kenkyukai, 2711
Jidō kyōiku to jidō bungei, 2643
Jidō shinri to jidō bungaku, 2595
Jidō to yomimono, 2711
Jidōshi kyōiku, 2617
Jidō-shi kyōiku no hōbō, 2699
Jiménez, Oscar Rojas; *see* Rojas Jiménez, Oscar
Jiménez-Placer, Javier; *see* Lasso de la Vega y Jiménez-Placer, Javier
Jingū, Teruo, 2581
Job, M. M., 2406
Johannesson, Fritz, 1264
Johansson, J. Viktor, 1753
John S. Newberry gift collection of Kate Greenaway presented to the library, 3664
Johnson, B. Lamar, 3938
Johnson, Clifton, 3939
Johnson, Crompton T., 3940
Johnson, Dorothy Turner, 3941

512

513

Koester, Hermann L., 1295, 1296, 1333
Középiskolasaink és irodalom, 1820
Közneveles, 1819
Kogawachi, Yoshiko, 2630, 2679
Kokubun, Ichitarō, 2563, 2631, 2632, 2711
Kol, Nellie van, 1009
Kolhatkar, V. P., 2409
Kolta, Ferec, 1817, 1818
Kommunebiblioteker, (København), 1578, 1579
Kommunes Bibliotekar, (København), 1579, 1580
Kommunes Børnebibliotekar Faelles bogsamlingens klassesaet, (Frederiksberg), 1566
Kommunisticheskoe vospitanie i sovremennaia literatura dlia detei i iunoshestva, 1885
Knigi—detiam, 1883
Knigi o shkole i detiakh, 1884
Kon, Lidiia Feliksovna, 1931, 1932, 1933
Koninklijk Instituut voor de Tropen, 1010
Kontoret for Kunst og Kulturarbeid, 1640
Kopeckij, Platon V., 1935
Korczewska, A., 2094
Korff, Alice G., 3983
Korff, W., 1297
Korn, Illse, 1298
Korovenko, A., 1936
Koszutska, Wanda, 2054
Kotzde, W., *with* J. Scholz, 1388
Kováč, Bohuš, 2151
Kozubowski, Feliks, 2077
Kracek, R., *with* K. Berdnikova, 1865
Krack, Hans-Günther, 1299
Kraft, Josef, 1102
Kragh-Muller, C. C., 1545, 1573, 1582
Krajowa Konferencja Bibliotekarska, 2049
Kramer, Sister M. Immaculata, 3984
Krasovskaia, N., 1937
Kratkii ocherk istorii iakutskoi detskoi literatury, 1915
Kraus, Hadassa, 2251
Kraut, Dora, 1500
Krautstengl, Ferdinand, *with* K. Moissl, 1109
Kready, Laura Fry, 3985
Krebser, H., 1501
Kriebitsch, 1175
Krieg, L. L., 3986
Kristensen, Niels K., 1583, 1584
Kristna ungdomen och litteraturen, 1764
Kritischer Führer durch die Jugendliteratur, 1110
Krivoshapkin, Il'ia Grigor'evich, 1938
Kroeger, Alice B., 3987
Krohn, Helmi, 1802
Krohn, Pietro, 1597
Królinski, Kazimierz, 2078, 2079
Kropatsch, Otwald, 1103
Krsmanović, Marija, *with* O. Zečević, 2218
Krüger, Anna, 1300, 1301
Krug, Adele J., 3488
Krupskaia, N. K., 1843

Krutch, Joseph Wood, 3988
Kruglov, Aleksandr Vasil'evich, 1939
Krupskaia, Nadezhda Konstantinovna, 1940, 1941, 1942, 2218
Kruyt, J., 1012
Krytyczny katalog ksiaxek dla dzieci i młodzieży, 2057
Krezmínska, Wanda, 2080
Krzywda, Sister M. M., 3965
Ksiazka i literatura na poziomie szkoły podstawowej, 2047
Ksiazka w szkole, 2081
Ksiazka w życiu młoziezy współczesnej, 2106
Ksiazka zakazana, jako przedmiot zainteresowania młodziezy w okresie dojrzewania, 2082
Ksiazki, dzieci i dorośli, 2068
Ku, Chun-hoe, 2812
Kubota, Hiroshi, *with* S. Morikubo, 2633
Kuchta, Jan, 2082
Kudalkar, Janardan S., 2410
Kuder, Manfred, 1302
Kühner, C., 1303
Künneman, Horst, 1304, 1305
Kuhn, H., 1435
Kułagowska, Zofia, 2083
Kuliczkowska, Krystyna, 2084, 2086, 2087, *with* I. Słońska, 2085
Kunczewska, Ludmila, 2088
Kungmin Hakkyo, 2822
Kunitz, Stanley J. and H. Haycraft, 3990
Kunmin hakkyo tosŏgwan kyoyuk, 2810
Kunmin hakkyo tosŏgwan unyŏng charyo, 2749
Kunst des Erzählens, 1403
Kunst durch Kunst zu erziehen, 42
Kunst im Leben des Kindes, 1405
Kunst in het leesboek voor het eerste schooljaar, 983
Kunst van het vertellen, 977
Kunst van vertellen, 1011
Kunstman, J. L., 1530
Kunze, Horst, 4, 1306, 2227
Kunzfeld, Alois, 1104
Kup, Karl, 43, 4280
Kupriianova, Kseniia N., 1943
Kurze Geschichte der Erziehung und des Unterrichts, 1285
Kurse Übersicht der Entwicklung der deutschen Jugendliteratur, 1522
Kusano, Masana, 2634
Kvaløy, Anders, 1641
Kwŏn, Chae-Wŏn, 2813
Kwŏn, O-il, 2814
Kwon, Yang Won, 2830
Kylberg, Anna Maria, 1720
Kyle, Anne Dempster, 670
Kyōiku benkashi taikei, 2622
Kyōiku Gijutsu Renmei, 2635
Kyŏng-sang Nam-do, 2826
Kyoyuk Taehak Tosogwan Yŏnguhoe, 2815
Kyoyuk Yonguso, 2749

Labor cultural de la biblioteca infantil de Chile, 264

LaBounty, Maxine, 3993
LaBrant, Lou, *with* F. Heller, 3863, 3991
Lacasse, Authur, 3360
Lades, H., 1159
Ladies Commission on Sunday-School Books, 3992
Ladley, Winifred C., 3993
Laerebog i biblioteksteknik og dansk biblioteksvaesen, 1565
Laererne og Samfundet, 1584
Laerobog i biblioteksteknik, 1547
Läsa lätt, 1739
Läsning för barn?, 1698
Läsning för ungt folk, 1716
Laesning og opalesning, 1596
Laesningens Glaede, 1599
Lagerlof, Selma, 173, 822, 2125, 2869
Lagerstedt, Sven, 1780
Lagos, Aida Moreno; *see* Moreno Lagos, Aida
LaGye, J. Nyns; *see* Nyns LaGye, J.
Lahy-Hollebecque, Marie, 822, 823
Laible, Hilda, *with* W. Lussnigg, 1107
Lakits, Pál, 1820
Lalitji, Kavi, 2420
Lam, Katherine A., 3488
Laminario en las bibliotecas juveniles, 314
Lan, Sun Mei-; *see* Mei-lan, Sun
Landergren, Anna, 1772, *with* H. Jacobson, 1710
Landis, E. B., 2816
Landreth, Catherine, *with* Schmidt, 3994
Landry, K. B., 3995
Landwehr, John, 1012
Lane, William C., 2867
Lang, Andrew, 2985, 3134
Lang, Paul, 1307
Lange, K., 1308
Lange, Marianne, 1309
Langfeldt, Johannes, 1310, 1311, 1312, 1313, 1721, *with* F. Schriewer 1391
Langley, A. K. B., 2868
Langosch, Karl, 1409
Langthaler, Johann, 1105
Lanigan, Edith, 3996
Lara, Juana Manrique de; *see* Manrique de Lara, Juana
Lareen, Joakim, 1585
Larese, Dino, 1502
Larrick, Nancy, 3997, 3998, 3999
Larrinaga, Albana, 452, 453
Larson, Lorentz, 1722, 1724, 1725, 1726, 1727, 1728, 1729, 1730, 1731, *with* M. Ørvig 1723
Łasiewicka, A., 2114, *with* M. Gutry 2064
Lasso de la Vega y Jiménez-Placer, Javier, 140, 552, 553
Lastemme Kirjat, 1789
Lasten ja nuorten kirjoja, 1796
Lasten ja nuorten kirjojen valioluettelo, 1797
Låt oss läsa högt, 1732
Lathrop, Edith A., 4000

517

Meeting of Experts on Book Production and Distribution in Asia, 2362
Mehta, Shrimati Hansaben, 2420
Meier, Kathleen, 3488
Meigs, Cornelia, 2869
Meiji shōnen bunka shiwa, 2626
Mei-lan, Sun, 2552
Meilink, J. Bos-; *see* Bos-Meilink, J.
Meireles, Cecília, 220, 221
Meisaku no kenkyū jiten, 2720
Melcher, Frederic G., 2645, 3584, 4092, 4093, 4280, 4323
Melegari, Vezio, 684, 685, 715
Melendez, Audry Mancebo; *see* Mancebo Melendez, Audry
Melhus, A. C., 1531
Melin, Gabriel, 855
Mellor, E., 3173
Melo, Carlos F., 146
Memoria. La enseñanza especial en America, 463
Memories and portraits, 3250
Méndez, Elsa, 457
Mendiolea, Gabriel Ferrer de; *see* Ferrer de Mendiolea, Gabriel
Mendióroz, Hugo Enrique, 147
Meneses Rodríguez, Mercedes, 313, 314, 315
Mennekens, J., 926
Mennig, Mary Elizabeth, 4094
Menzel, Wolfgang, 1332
Mercelis, Johan, 927, 1018
Merget, A., 1333
Merriman, Stella E., 3326
Merritt, Eleanor, 3686
Mescha, Ruth Terrasa; *see* Terrasa Mescha, Ruth
Mese, 1823
Meservey, Sabra, 2235
Metcalf, Robert C., 3744, 4095
Method of selecting foreign stories for the American elementary schools: Applied to the evaluation of stories translated by the author from the Chinese folk literature, 2553, 4304
Methodist Church, 4096
Metzger, Juliane, 1334
Metzker, Otto, 1220
Metzner, Seymour, 4097
Meulen, A. J. Moerkercken van der; *see* Moerkercken van der Meulen, A. J.
Meyer, Anne A., 4098
Meyer, Hans Georg, 1335
Meyer, Olga, 1509
Meyer-Markau, Wilhelm, 1336
Meynell, Alice, 3174
Mezhdunarodnaĭa kniga, Moscow, 1960
Michaelis-Jena, Ruth, 1510
Michalska, W., 2093
Michel, A., 928
Michelet, J., 856
Michels, W., 1159
Michieli, Armando, 686, 687, 688
Mid-century survey of the presentation of the American Negro in the literature for children published

in the United States between 1900 and 1950, 4131
Middelbare school en bibliotheek, 1043
Mieres de Rivas, Margarita; *see* Rivas, Margarita Mieres de
Migneaux, Marie, 857
Mignosi, P., 689
Mikucka, Aniela, 2094
Mil obras para los jóvenes, 583
Milam, Carl H., 4459
Milarić, Vlatko, 2211
Milasavljevic, S., 2224
Millar, John, 3370
Miller, Bertha E. Mahony, 3892, *with* E. Field, 4077 *and* 4078
Miller, E., 4101
Miller, E. Morris, 2893
Miller, Eleanor Olmstead, 4102
Miller, Mrs. John A., 4103
Miller, Marilyn M., 4104
Miller, Mary M., 4292
Miller, Olive (Beaupré), 4105
Miller, Paul G. *with* J. Padin, 429
Millî Egitim Vekâleti, 2241, 2242
Mills, Forrest Laird, 4106
Milne, A. A., 2125, 3175
Milne, Mary, 2922, 2923
Milton, Jennie Low, 4107
Min väg till barnboken, 1776
Ministerio de Educación Publica (Lima), 415
Ministerio de Educacion Publica Servicio Cooperativo Peruano-Norteamericano de Educación, 415
Ministerio de Instruccion Publica, (Honduras), 351
Ministerium für Volksbildung and Zentralinstitut für Bibliothekswesen, 1337
Ministerstvo Narodnogo Prosveshcheniĭa, 1979, 1980, 1981
Ministerstwo Kultury i Sztuki, 2095
Ministerul Culturii, (Bucureşti), 1835
Ministry of Education (India), 2404
Ministry of Education (Malaysia), 2488
Minke, Fromut, 1338
Minssen, Lucília, 222
Minter, M., 416
Miscellaneous papers on children's libraries, 198
Misrad ha-ḥinukh veha-tarbut, 2249, 2250
Miss Muffet's Christmas party, 3637
Mission sociale et intellectuelle des bibliothèques populaires, 53, 62
Mistral, Gabriela, 48, 97, 123, 148, 165, 172, 571
Mitä nuoret lukevat, 1799
Mitcham, Merlin Lee, 4108
Mitchell, Donald Grant, 4109
Mitchell, Lucy Sprague, 1701, 1900, 4110
Mitchell, Marguerite, 3852
Mitchell, S. B., 4280
Mitchison, Naomi, 1916
Mitra, Khagendranath, 2415
Mittheilungen über Jugendschriften an Eltern und Lehrer, nebst ge-

legentlichen Bemerkungen über Volksschriften, 1259
Miwa, Keiyū, 2646
Miyasawa kenji no dōwa bungaku, 2728
Miyazawa, Sanji, 2647
Mode des contes de fées, 882
Model library of books for deaf children, 3655
Modern American library economy . . . Vol. I, 3651
Moderna letteratura per l'infanzia e la giovinezza, 732
Moderne Formen der Jugendbildung, 1493
Moderne Kinderbuch-Illustration, 49
Moderne letterkunde en christelijke opvoeding, 960
Moderní česká literatura pro děti, 2193
Moe, Jörgen, 1638
Möhlenbrock, Sigurd, 1746
Moerkercken van der Meulen, A. J., 33, 1019, 1020, 1021, 1022, 1023, 1024
Mohammed el-Hagrasy, S. 4111
Mohanraj V. M., 2416
Moi upechatleniĭa, 1961
Moissl, Konrad, *with* F. Krautstengl, 1109
Moje dete i knjiga, 2221, 2222
Molesworth, Mary Louisa, 2985, 3176, 3177
Moll, Lizzie, 1747
Mollerup, Helga, 1532, 1586, 1587, 1588, 1590, *with* G. Franck, 1565, *with* J. Pederson, 1589
Momen, Abdul, 2461
Momotarō no tanjō, 2729
Monaci-Guidotti, Enrichetta, *with* M. Valeri, 59, *with* G. Fanciulli, 649
Monahan, Marietta, 4112
Monbushō, 2609, 2610
Monsanto, Luis Humberto, 326
Montagu, R., 3457
Montalvo, Herculano Angel Torres; *see* Torres Montalvo, Herculano Angel
Montègut, Émile, 858
Montemayor, Teodoro, 2510
Montenegro, Ernesto, 149
Montesanti, María de Lourdes M., 223
Montessori, 135, 174
Montilla, Francisca, 572, 573
Moody, E. L., 4113
Mooij-Gaastra, L., 1025
Moor, Emmy, 1511
Moore, Anne Carroll, 50, 859, 929, 3503, 3512, 3542, 3589, 4114, 4115, 4116, 4117, 4118, 4119, 4120, 4121, 4122, 4123, 4124, 4292, 4302, 4308, *with* B. M. Miller, 4125
Moore, Annie Egerton, 4126, *with* J. Betzner, 3482
Moore, Jean McCoy, 4127
Moore, Vardine, 4128
Mora, Morichu de la, 574
Mora, Vicente Moreno; *see* Moreno Mora, Vicente

526

531

535